GUARDIANS
OF THE GALAXY
ROAD TO ANNIHILATION

GUARDIANS OF THE GALAXY

ROAD TO ANNIHILATION

Tom Lyle, Peter David, Jim Starlin & Dan Slott
WRITERS

Tom Lyle, Ron Lim, James Fry, ChrisCross, Jim Starlin & Juan Bobillo with Frank Strom
PENCILERS

Robert Jones, Walden Wong, Anibal Rodriguez, Al Milgrom & Marcelo Sosa with Mark McKenna, Nelson, Scurry, Livesay & Harry Candelario
INKERS

Tom Smith, Steve Oliff, Christie Scheele, Heroic Age & Avalon Studios' Dave Kemp
COLORISTS

Jack Morelli, Dave Sharpe and Richard Starkings & Comicraft's Wes Abbott, Emerson Miranda, Saida Temofonte & Albert Deschesne
LETTERERS

Lysa Kraiger, Gregg Schigiel, Frank Dunkerly, Marc Sumerak, Andy Schmidt, Nicole Wiley & Molly Lazer
ASSISTANT EDITORS

Mark Bernardo & Tom Brevoort
EDITORS

Jorge Lucas, Scott Kolins & June Chung
FRONT COVER ARTISTS

Jim Starlin, Al Milgrom, Christie Scheele & Heroic Age
BACK COVER ARTISTS

COLLECTION EDITOR: Mark D. Beazley
ASSOCIATE MANAGING EDITOR: Kateri Woody
ASSOCIATE EDITOR: Sarah Brunstad
ASSOCIATE MANAGER, DIGITAL ASSETS: Joseph Hochstein
SENIOR EDITOR, SPECIAL PROJECTS: Jennifer Grünwald
VP PRODUCTION & SPECIAL PROJECTS: Jeff Youngquist
RESEARCH & LAYOUT: Jeph York
PRODUCTION: Ryan Devall
BOOK DESIGNER: Adam Del Re
SVP PRINT, SALES & MARKETING: David Gabriel
EDITOR IN CHIEF: Axel Alonso
CHIEF CREATIVE OFFICER: Joe Quesada
PUBLISHER: Dan Buckley
EXECUTIVE PRODUCER: Alan Fine

GUARDIANS OF THE GALAXY: ROAD TO ANNIHILATION VOL. 1. Contains material originally published in magazine form as WARLOCK #1-4, CAPTAIN MARVEL #4-6 and #15-16, INFINITY ABYSS #1-6, and SHE-HULK #7-8. First printing 2017. ISBN# 978-1-302-90441-8. Published by MARVEL WORLDWIDE, INC., a subsidiary of MARVEL ENTERTAINMENT, LLC. OFFICE OF PUBLICATION: 135 West 50th Street, New York, NY 10020.

Printed in the U.S.A. ALAN FINE, President, Marvel Entertainment; DAN BUCKLEY, President, TV, Publishing & Brand Management; JOE QUESADA, Chief Creative Officer; TOM BREVOORT, SVP of Publishing; DAVID BOGART, SVP of Business Affairs & Operations, Publishing & Partnership; C.B. CEBULSKI, VP of Brand Management & Development, Asia; DAVID GABRIEL, SVP of Sales & Marketing, Publishing; JEFF YOUNGQUIST, VP of Production & Special Projects; DAN CARR, Executive Director of Publishing Technology; ALEX MORALES, Director of Publishing Operations; SUSAN CRESPI, Production Manager; STAN LEE, Chairman Emeritus. For information regarding advertising in Marvel Comics or on Marvel.com, please contact Vit DeBellis, Integrated Sales Manager, at vdebellis@marvel.com. For Marvel subscription inquiries, please call 888-511-5480. **Manufactured between 11/18/2016 and 12/26/2016 by QUAD/GRAPHICS WASECA, WASECA, MN, USA.**

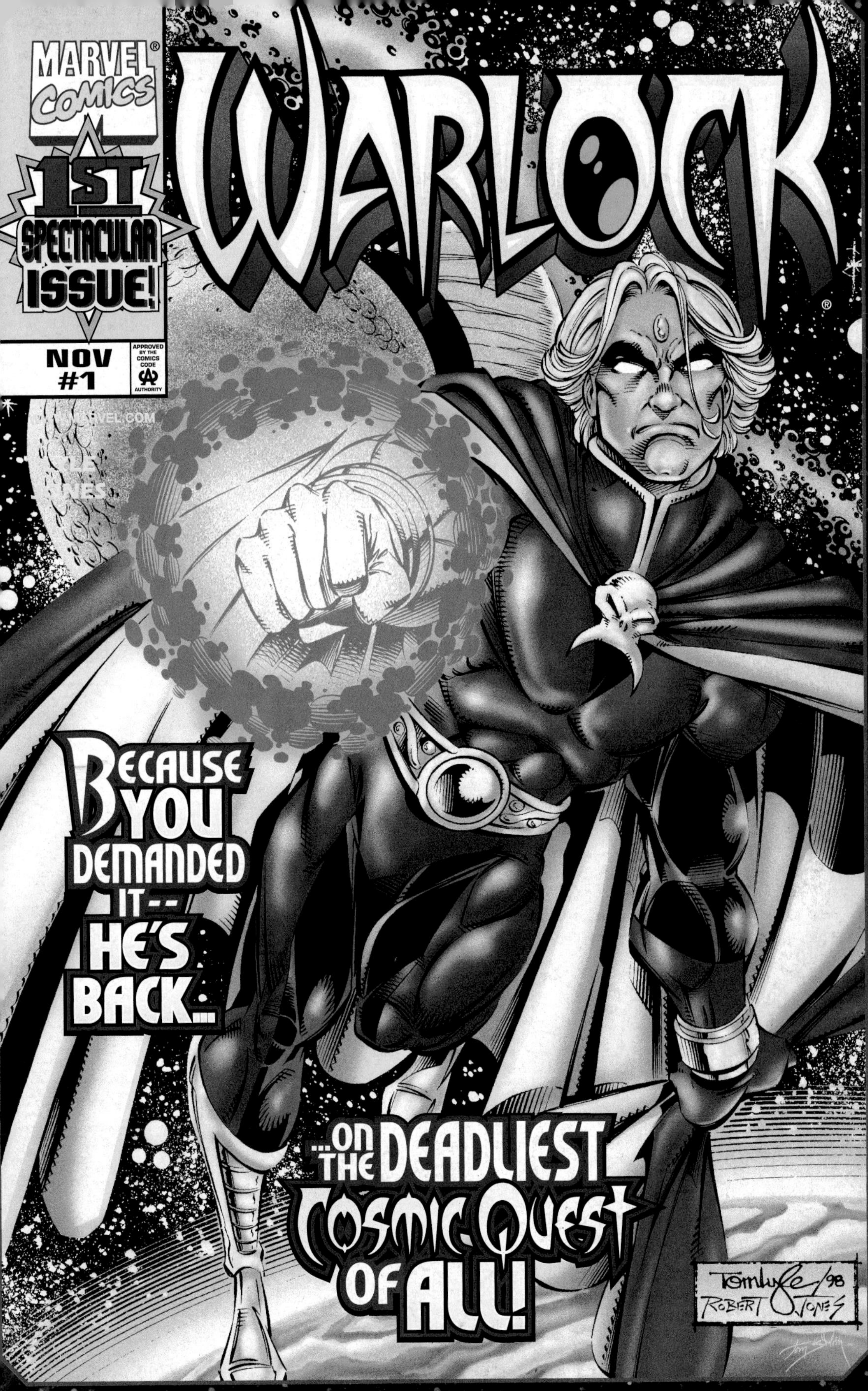
MARVEL® COMICS
WARLOCK®
1ST SPECTACULAR ISSUE!
NOV #1
APPROVED BY THE COMICS CODE AUTHORITY
BECAUSE YOU DEMANDED IT-- HE'S BACK...
...ON THE DEADLIEST COSMIC QUEST OF ALL!
Tom Lyle '98
ROBERT JONES

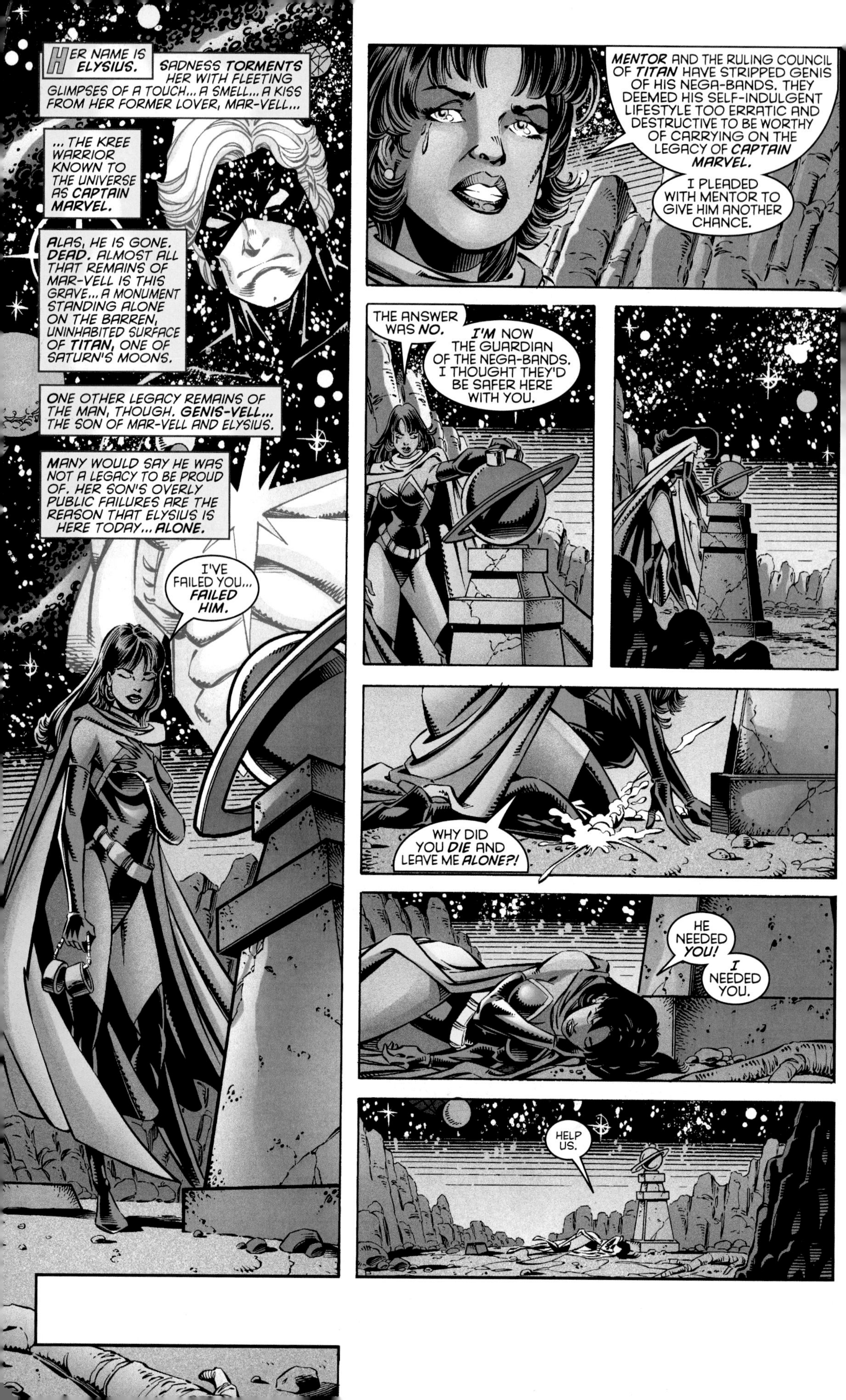
HER NAME IS ELYSIUS.
SADNESS TORMENTS HER WITH FLEETING GLIMPSES OF A TOUCH... A SMELL... A KISS FROM HER FORMER LOVER, MAR-VELL...
...THE KREE WARRIOR KNOWN TO THE UNIVERSE AS CAPTAIN MARVEL.
ALAS, HE IS GONE. DEAD. ALMOST ALL THAT REMAINS OF MAR-VELL IS THIS GRAVE... A MONUMENT STANDING ALONE ON THE BARREN, UNINHABITED SURFACE OF TITAN, ONE OF SATURN'S MOONS.
ONE OTHER LEGACY REMAINS OF THE MAN, THOUGH. GENIS-VELL... THE SON OF MAR-VELL AND ELYSIUS.
MANY WOULD SAY HE WAS NOT A LEGACY TO BE PROUD OF. HER SON'S OVERLY PUBLIC FAILURES ARE THE REASON THAT ELYSIUS IS HERE TODAY... ALONE.
I'VE FAILED YOU... FAILED HIM.
MENTOR AND THE RULING COUNCIL OF TITAN HAVE STRIPPED GENIS OF HIS NEGA-BANDS. THEY DEEMED HIS SELF-INDULGENT LIFESTYLE TOO ERRATIC AND DESTRUCTIVE TO BE WORTHY OF CARRYING ON THE LEGACY OF CAPTAIN MARVEL.
I PLEADED WITH MENTOR TO GIVE HIM ANOTHER CHANCE.
THE ANSWER WAS NO.
I'M NOW THE GUARDIAN OF THE NEGA-BANDS. I THOUGHT THEY'D BE SAFER HERE WITH YOU.
WHY DID YOU DIE AND LEAVE ME ALONE?!
HE NEEDED YOU!
I NEEDED YOU.
HELP US.

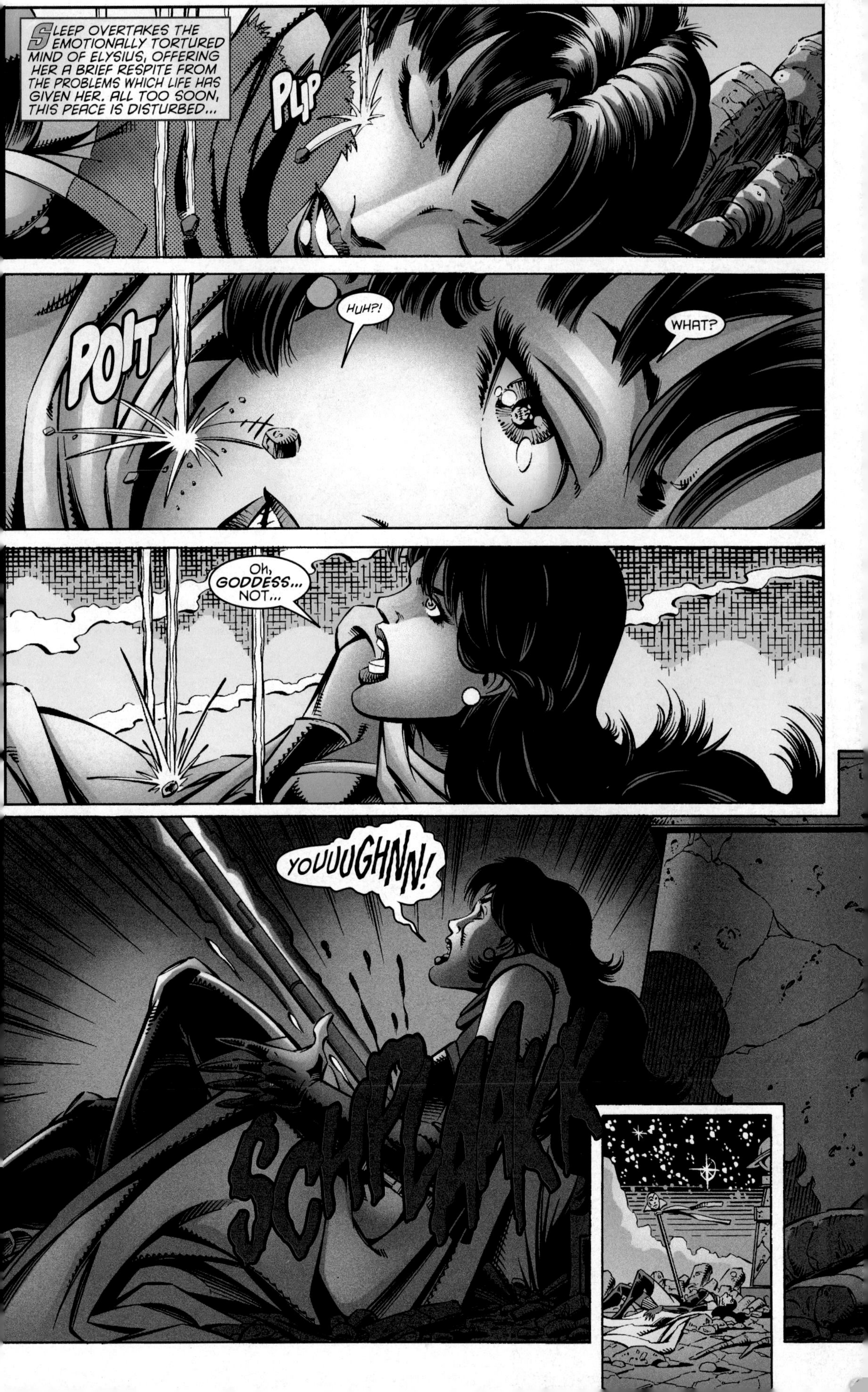
SLEEP OVERTAKES THE EMOTIONALLY TORTURED MIND OF ELYSIUS, OFFERING HER A BRIEF RESPITE FROM THE PROBLEMS WHICH LIFE HAS GIVEN HER. ALL TOO SOON, THIS PEACE IS DISTURBED...
PLIP
POIT
HUH?!
WHAT?
Oh, GODDESS... NOT...
YOUUUGHNN!
SCHRAKK

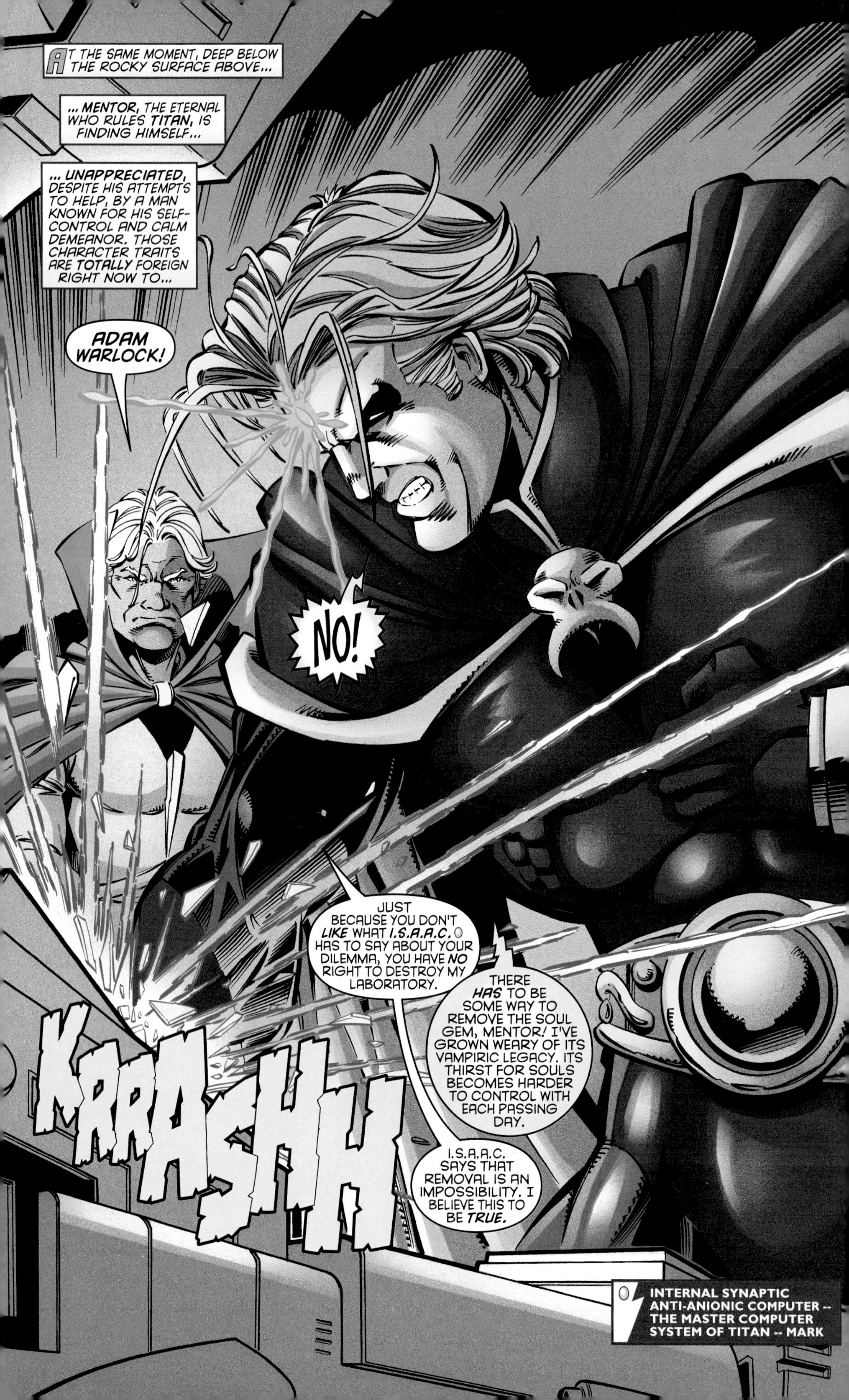
AT THE SAME MOMENT, DEEP BELOW THE ROCKY SURFACE ABOVE...
... MENTOR, THE ETERNAL WHO RULES TITAN, IS FINDING HIMSELF...
... UNAPPRECIATED, DESPITE HIS ATTEMPTS TO HELP, BY A MAN KNOWN FOR HIS SELF-CONTROL AND CALM DEMEANOR. THOSE CHARACTER TRAITS ARE TOTALLY FOREIGN RIGHT NOW TO...
ADAM WARLOCK!
NO!
KRRASHH
JUST BECAUSE YOU DON'T LIKE WHAT I.S.A.A.C. HAS TO SAY ABOUT YOUR DILEMMA, YOU HAVE NO RIGHT TO DESTROY MY LABORATORY.
THERE HAS TO BE SOME WAY TO REMOVE THE SOUL GEM, MENTOR! I'VE GROWN WEARY OF ITS VAMPIRIC LEGACY. ITS THIRST FOR SOULS BECOMES HARDER TO CONTROL WITH EACH PASSING DAY.
I.S.A.A.C. SAYS THAT REMOVAL IS AN IMPOSSIBILITY. I BELIEVE THIS TO BE TRUE.
INTERNAL SYNAPTIC ANTI-ANIONIC COMPUTER -- THE MASTER COMPUTER SYSTEM OF TITAN -- MARK

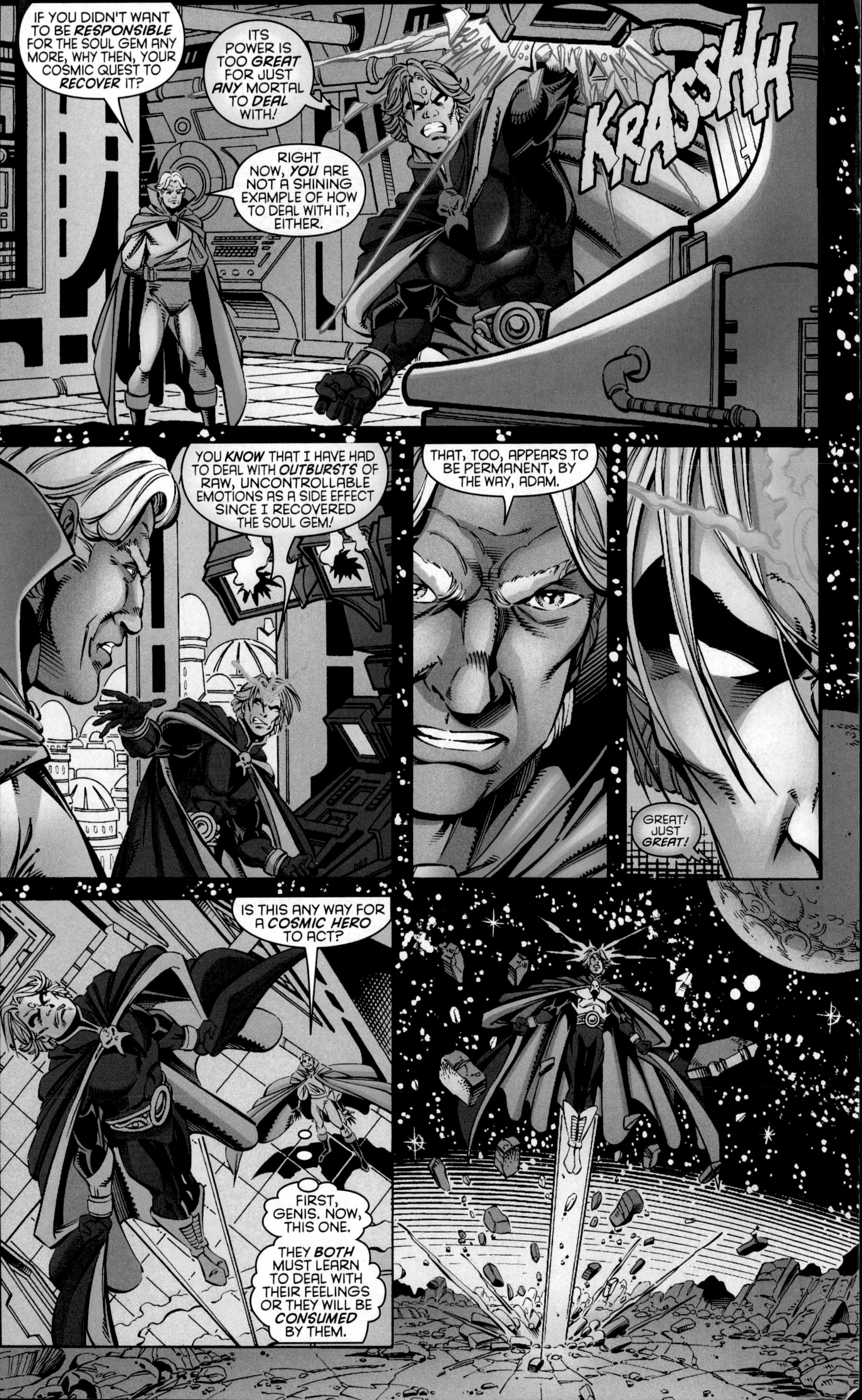
IF YOU DIDN'T WANT TO BE RESPONSIBLE FOR THE SOUL GEM ANY MORE, WHY THEN, YOUR COSMIC QUEST TO RECOVER IT?
ITS POWER IS TOO GREAT FOR JUST ANY MORTAL TO DEAL WITH!
KRASSHH
RIGHT NOW, YOU ARE NOT A SHINING EXAMPLE OF HOW TO DEAL WITH IT, EITHER.
YOU KNOW THAT I HAVE HAD TO DEAL WITH OUTBURSTS OF RAW, UNCONTROLLABLE EMOTIONS AS A SIDE EFFECT SINCE I RECOVERED THE SOUL GEM!
THAT, TOO, APPEARS TO BE PERMANENT, BY THE WAY, ADAM.
GREAT! JUST GREAT!
IS THIS ANY WAY FOR A COSMIC HERO TO ACT?
FIRST, GENIS. NOW, THIS ONE.
THEY BOTH MUST LEARN TO DEAL WITH THEIR FEELINGS OR THEY WILL BE CONSUMED BY THEM.

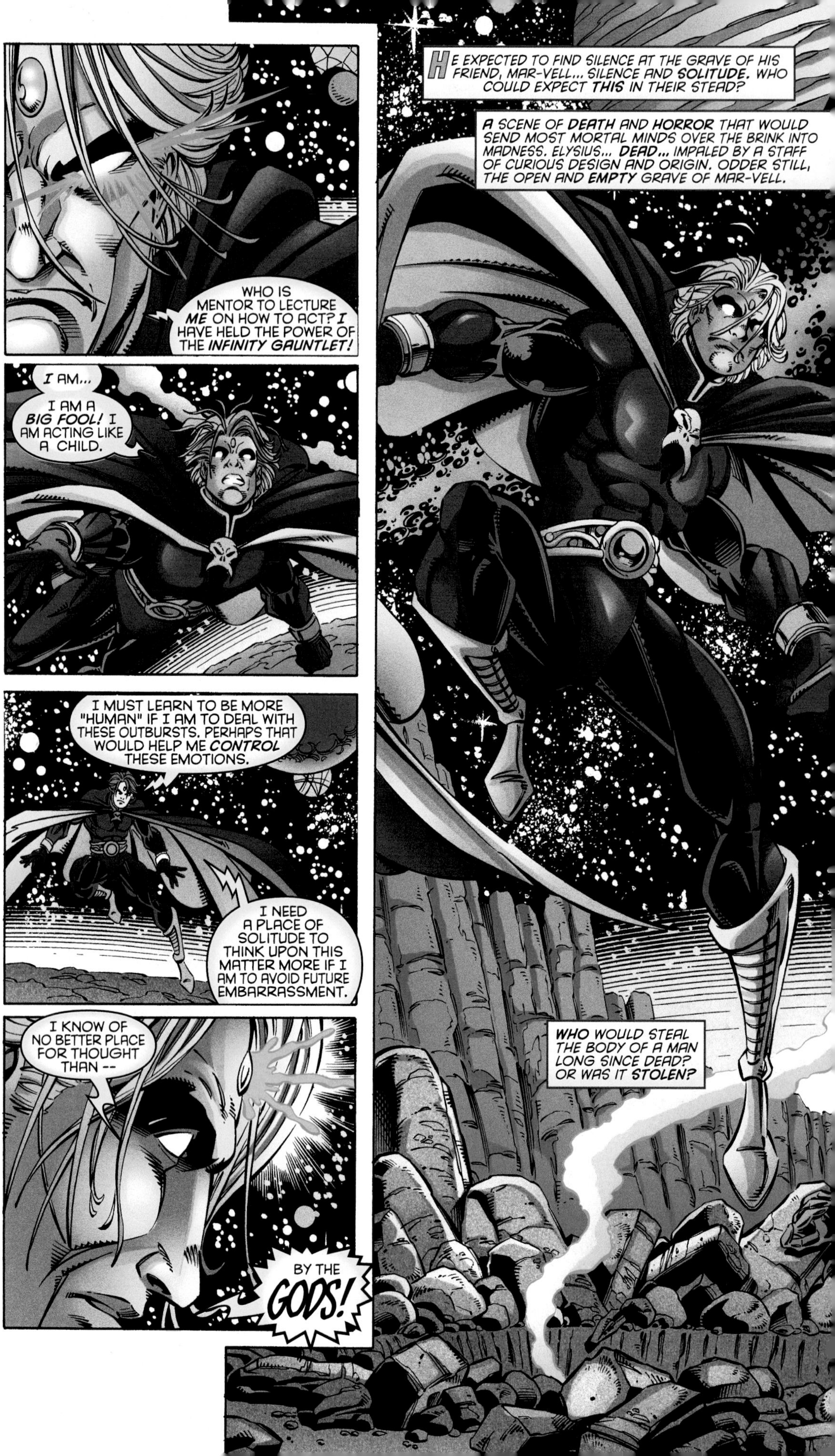

HE EXPECTED TO FIND SILENCE AT THE GRAVE OF HIS FRIEND, MAR-VELL... SILENCE AND SOLITUDE. WHO COULD EXPECT THIS IN THEIR STEAD?
A SCENE OF DEATH AND HORROR THAT WOULD SEND MOST MORTAL MINDS OVER THE BRINK INTO MADNESS. ELYSIUS... DEAD... IMPALED BY A STAFF OF CURIOUS DESIGN AND ORIGIN. ODDER STILL, THE OPEN AND EMPTY GRAVE OF MAR-VELL.
WHO IS MENTOR TO LECTURE ME ON HOW TO ACT? I HAVE HELD THE POWER OF THE INFINITY GAUNTLET!
I AM...
I AM A BIG FOOL! I AM ACTING LIKE A CHILD.
I MUST LEARN TO BE MORE "HUMAN" IF I AM TO DEAL WITH THESE OUTBURSTS. PERHAPS THAT WOULD HELP ME CONTROL THESE EMOTIONS.
I NEED A PLACE OF SOLITUDE TO THINK UPON THIS MATTER MORE IF I AM TO AVOID FUTURE EMBARRASSMENT.
I KNOW OF NO BETTER PLACE FOR THOUGHT THAN --
BY THE GODS!
WHO WOULD STEAL THE BODY OF A MAN LONG SINCE DEAD? OR WAS IT STOLEN?

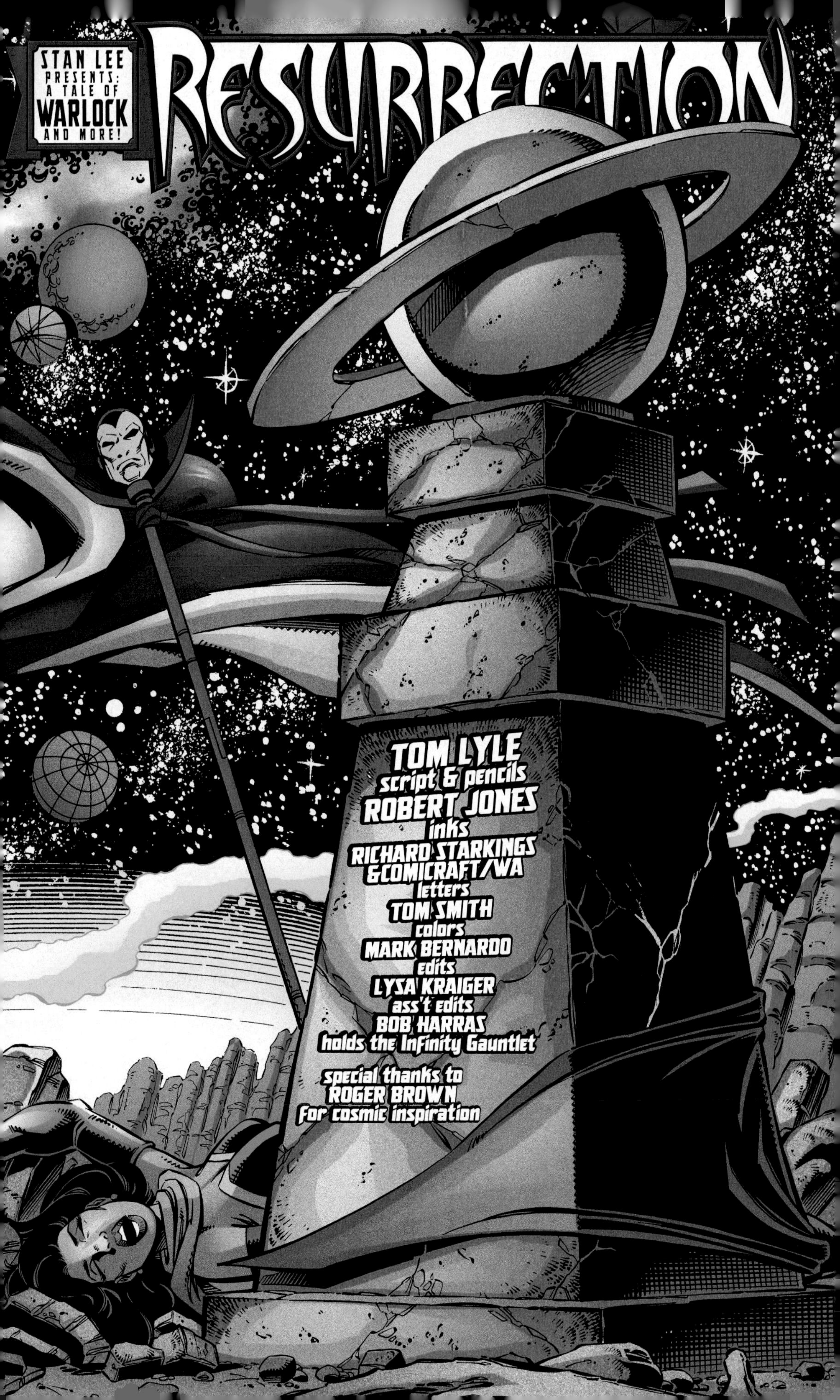
STAN LEE PRESENTS: A TALE OF WARLOCK AND MORE!
RESURRECTION
TOM LYLE script & pencils
ROBERT JONES inks
RICHARD STARKINGS &COMICRAFT/WA letters
TOM SMITH colors
MARK BERNARDO edits
LYSA KRAIGER ass't edits
BOB HARRAS holds the Infinity Gauntlet
special thanks to ROGER BROWN for cosmic inspiration

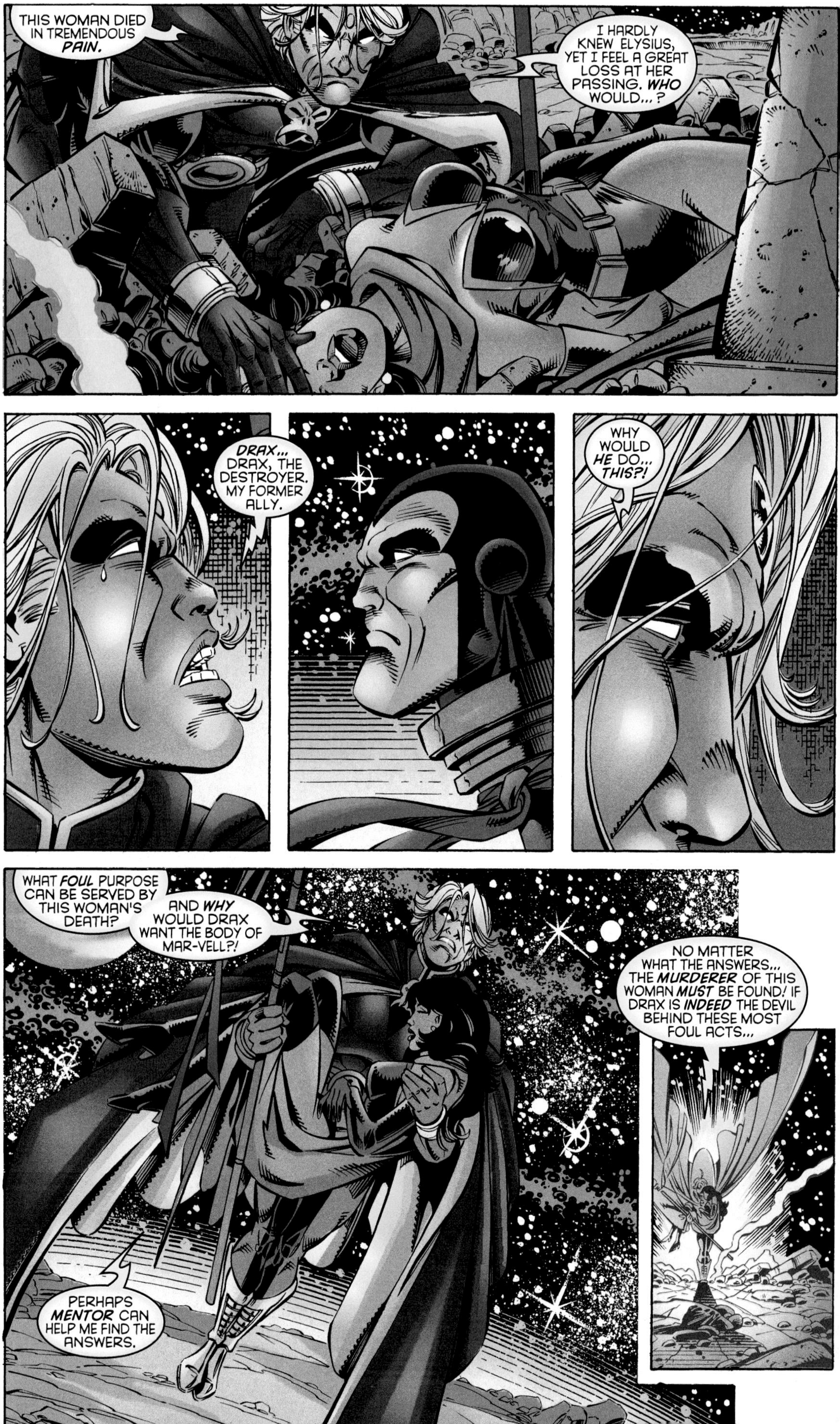
THIS WOMAN DIED IN TREMENDOUS PAIN.
I HARDLY KNEW ELYSIUS, YET I FEEL A GREAT LOSS AT HER PASSING. WHO WOULD...?
DRAX... DRAX, THE DESTROYER. MY FORMER ALLY.
WHY WOULD HE DO... THIS?!
WHAT FOUL PURPOSE CAN BE SERVED BY THIS WOMAN'S DEATH?
AND WHY WOULD DRAX WANT THE BODY OF MAR-VELL?!
PERHAPS MENTOR CAN HELP ME FIND THE ANSWERS.
NO MATTER WHAT THE ANSWERS... THE MURDERER OF THIS WOMAN MUST BE FOUND! IF DRAX IS INDEED THE DEVIL BEHIND THESE MOST FOUL ACTS...

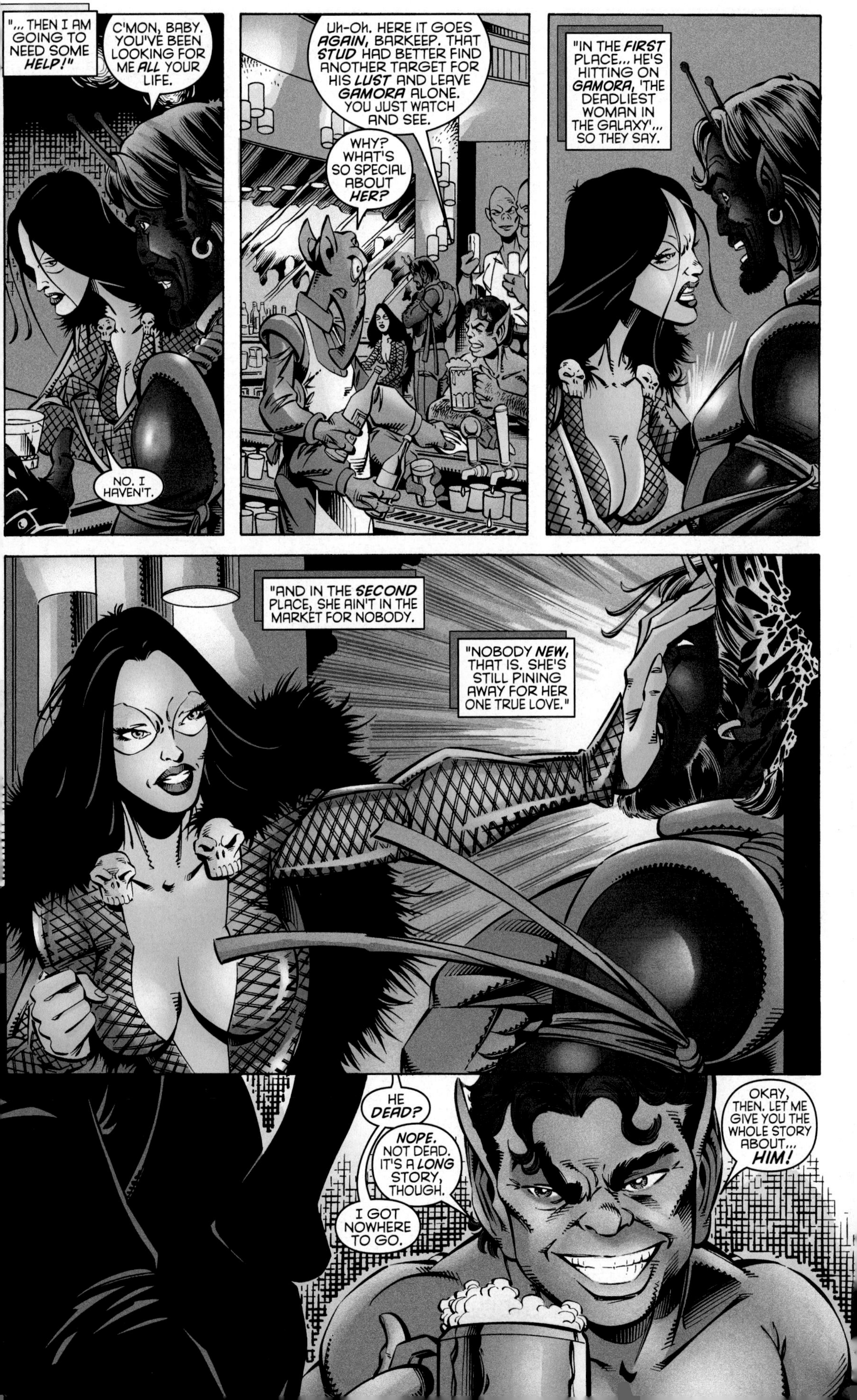
"... THEN I AM GOING TO NEED SOME HELP!"
C'MON, BABY. YOU'VE BEEN LOOKING FOR ME ALL YOUR LIFE.
NO. I HAVEN'T.
Uh-Oh. HERE IT GOES AGAIN, BARKEEP. THAT STUD HAD BETTER FIND ANOTHER TARGET FOR HIS LUST AND LEAVE GAMORA ALONE. YOU JUST WATCH AND SEE.
WHY? WHAT'S SO SPECIAL ABOUT HER?
"IN THE FIRST PLACE... HE'S HITTING ON GAMORA, 'THE DEADLIEST WOMAN IN THE GALAXY'... SO THEY SAY.
"AND IN THE SECOND PLACE, SHE AIN'T IN THE MARKET FOR NOBODY.
"NOBODY NEW, THAT IS. SHE'S STILL PINING AWAY FOR HER ONE TRUE LOVE."
HE DEAD?
NOPE. NOT DEAD. IT'S A LONG STORY, THOUGH.
I GOT NOWHERE TO GO.
OKAY, THEN. LET ME GIVE YOU THE WHOLE STORY ABOUT... HIM!

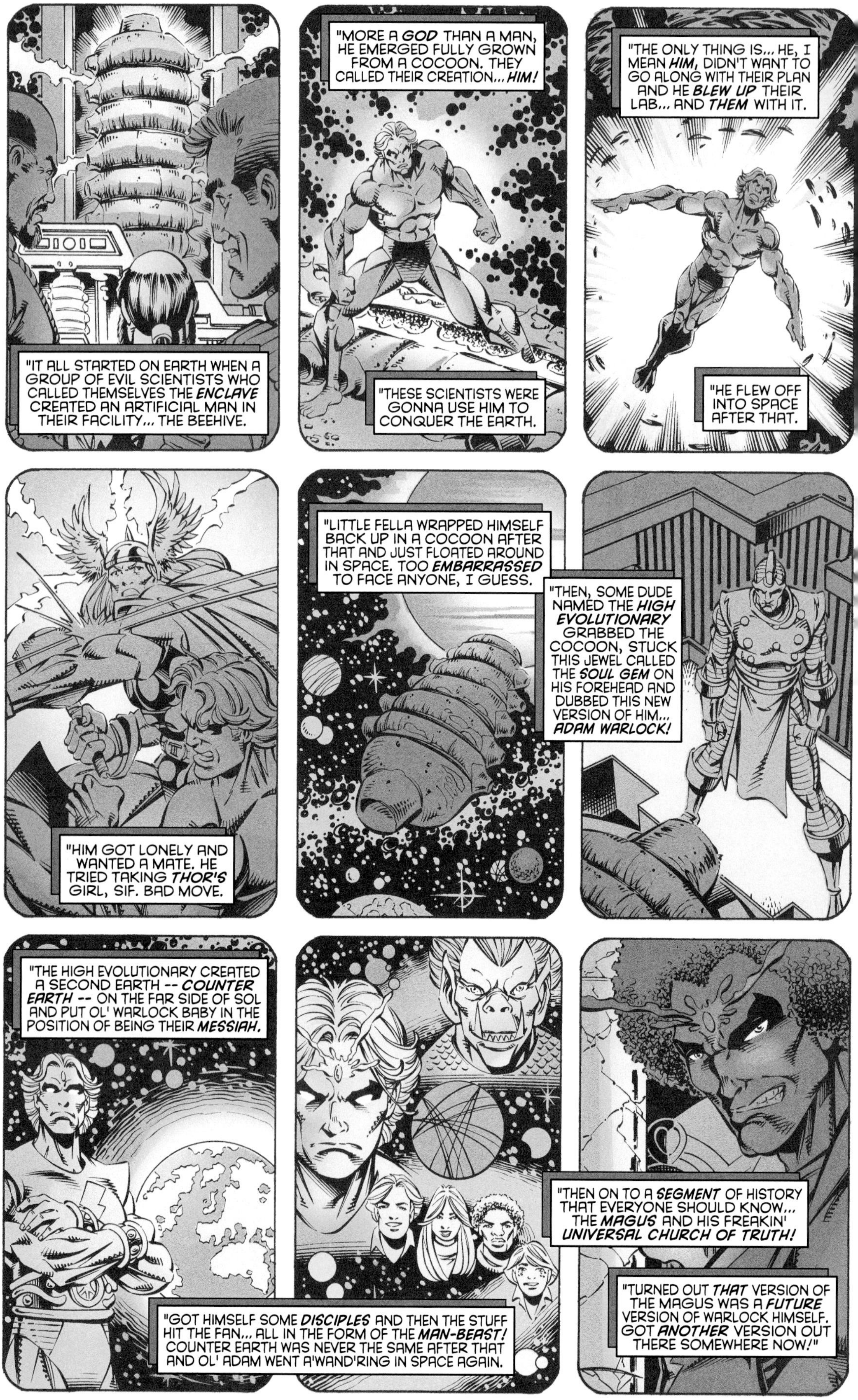
"IT ALL STARTED ON EARTH WHEN A GROUP OF EVIL SCIENTISTS WHO CALLED THEMSELVES THE ENCLAVE CREATED AN ARTIFICIAL MAN IN THEIR FACILITY... THE BEEHIVE.
"MORE A GOD THAN A MAN, HE EMERGED FULLY GROWN FROM A COCOON. THEY CALLED THEIR CREATION... HIM!
"THESE SCIENTISTS WERE GONNA USE HIM TO CONQUER THE EARTH.
"THE ONLY THING IS... HE, I MEAN HIM, DIDN'T WANT TO GO ALONG WITH THEIR PLAN AND HE BLEW UP THEIR LAB... AND THEM WITH IT.
"HE FLEW OFF INTO SPACE AFTER THAT.
"HIM GOT LONELY AND WANTED A MATE. HE TRIED TAKING THOR'S GIRL, SIF. BAD MOVE.
"LITTLE FELLA WRAPPED HIMSELF BACK UP IN A COCOON AFTER THAT AND JUST FLOATED AROUND IN SPACE. TOO EMBARRASSED TO FACE ANYONE, I GUESS.
"THEN, SOME DUDE NAMED THE HIGH EVOLUTIONARY GRABBED THE COCOON, STUCK THIS JEWEL CALLED THE SOUL GEM ON HIS FOREHEAD AND DUBBED THIS NEW VERSION OF HIM... ADAM WARLOCK!
"THE HIGH EVOLUTIONARY CREATED A SECOND EARTH -- COUNTER EARTH -- ON THE FAR SIDE OF SOL AND PUT OL' WARLOCK BABY IN THE POSITION OF BEING THEIR MESSIAH.
"GOT HIMSELF SOME DISCIPLES AND THEN THE STUFF HIT THE FAN... ALL IN THE FORM OF THE MAN-BEAST! COUNTER EARTH WAS NEVER THE SAME AFTER THAT AND OL' ADAM WENT A'WAND'RING IN SPACE AGAIN.
"THEN ON TO A SEGMENT OF HISTORY THAT EVERYONE SHOULD KNOW... THE MAGUS AND HIS FREAKIN' UNIVERSAL CHURCH OF TRUTH!
"TURNED OUT THAT VERSION OF THE MAGUS WAS A FUTURE VERSION OF WARLOCK HIMSELF. GOT ANOTHER VERSION OUT THERE SOMEWHERE NOW!"

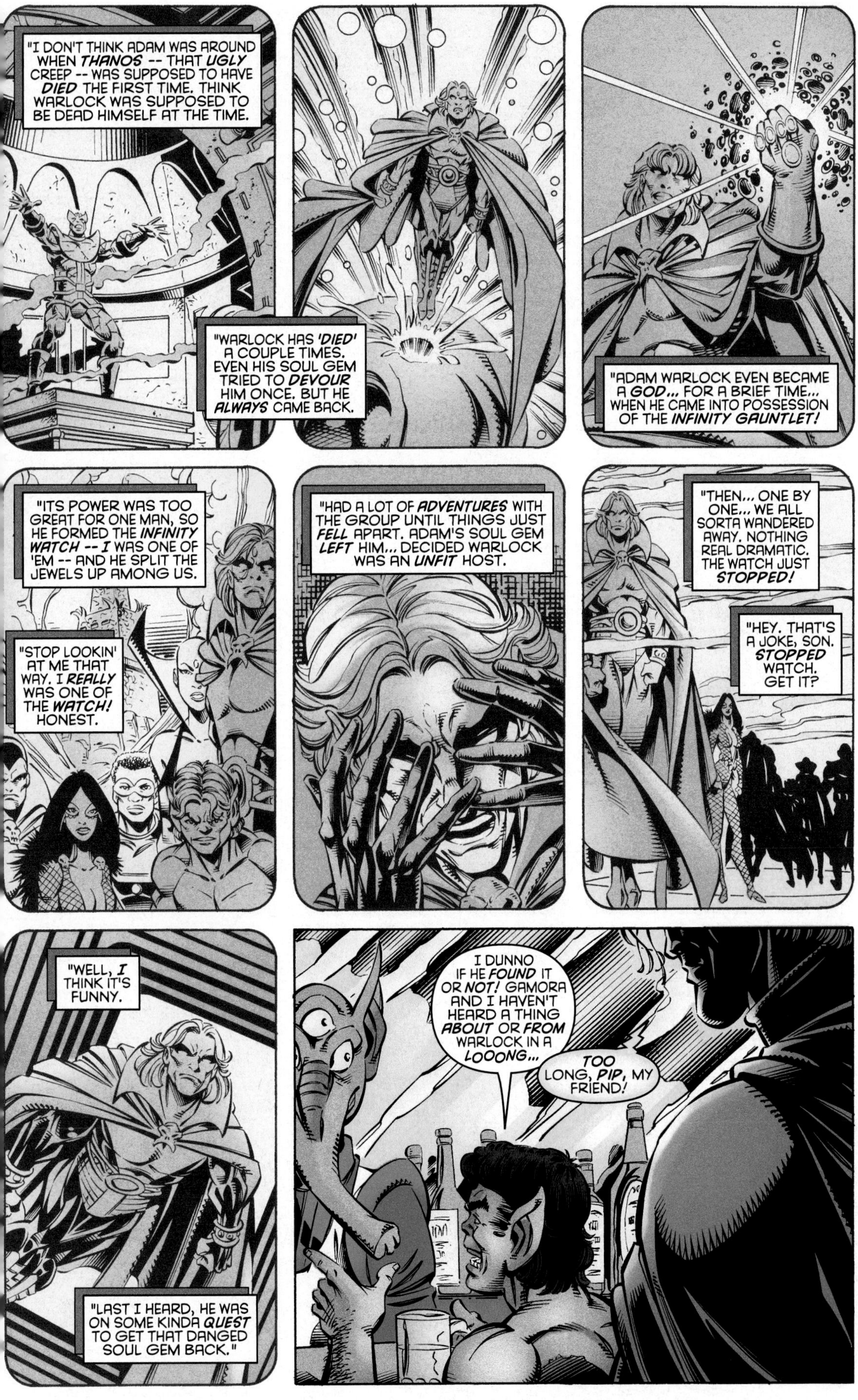
"I DON'T THINK ADAM WAS AROUND WHEN THANOS -- THAT UGLY CREEP -- WAS SUPPOSED TO HAVE DIED THE FIRST TIME. THINK WARLOCK WAS SUPPOSED TO BE DEAD HIMSELF AT THE TIME.
"WARLOCK HAS 'DIED' A COUPLE TIMES. EVEN HIS SOUL GEM TRIED TO DEVOUR HIM ONCE. BUT HE ALWAYS CAME BACK.
"ADAM WARLOCK EVEN BECAME A GOD... FOR A BRIEF TIME... WHEN HE CAME INTO POSSESSION OF THE INFINITY GAUNTLET!
"ITS POWER WAS TOO GREAT FOR ONE MAN, SO HE FORMED THE INFINITY WATCH -- I WAS ONE OF 'EM -- AND HE SPLIT THE JEWELS UP AMONG US.
"STOP LOOKIN' AT ME THAT WAY. I REALLY WAS ONE OF THE WATCH! HONEST.
"HAD A LOT OF ADVENTURES WITH THE GROUP UNTIL THINGS JUST FELL APART. ADAM'S SOUL GEM LEFT HIM... DECIDED WARLOCK WAS AN UNFIT HOST.
"THEN... ONE BY ONE... WE ALL SORTA WANDERED AWAY. NOTHING REAL DRAMATIC. THE WATCH JUST STOPPED!
"HEY. THAT'S A JOKE, SON. STOPPED WATCH. GET IT?
"WELL, I THINK IT'S FUNNY.
"LAST I HEARD, HE WAS ON SOME KINDA QUEST TO GET THAT DANGED SOUL GEM BACK."
I DUNNO IF HE FOUND IT OR NOT! GAMORA AND I HAVEN'T HEARD A THING ABOUT OR FROM WARLOCK IN A LOOONG...
TOO LONG, PIP, MY FRIEND!

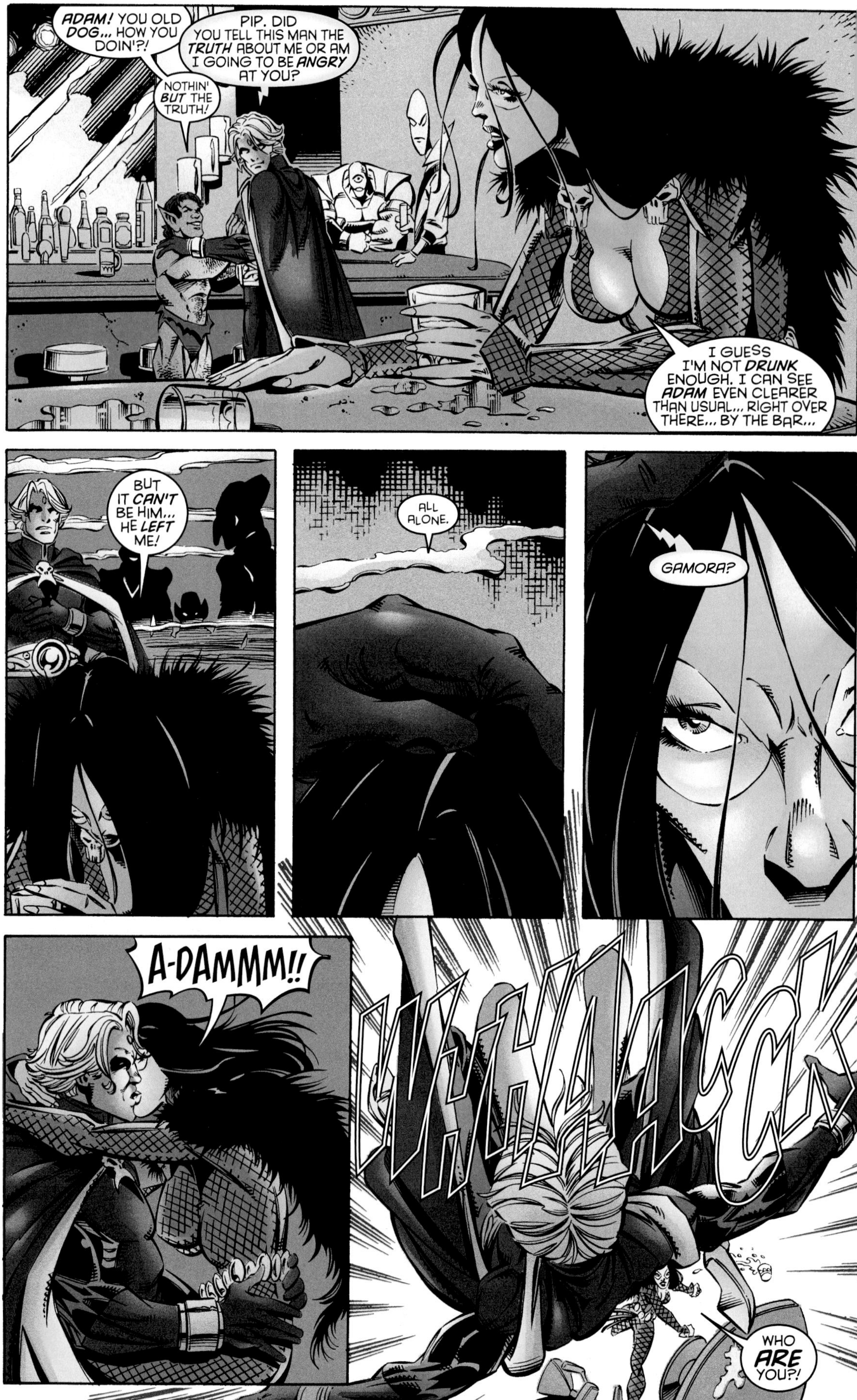
ADAM! YOU OLD DOG... HOW YOU DOIN'?!
PIP. DID YOU TELL THIS MAN THE TRUTH ABOUT ME OR AM I GOING TO BE ANGRY AT YOU?
NOTHIN' BUT THE TRUTH!
I GUESS I'M NOT DRUNK ENOUGH. I CAN SEE ADAM EVEN CLEARER THAN USUAL... RIGHT OVER THERE... BY THE BAR...
BUT IT CAN'T BE HIM... HE LEFT ME!
ALL ALONE.
GAMORA?
A-DAMMM!!
WHHAACCK
WHO ARE YOU?!

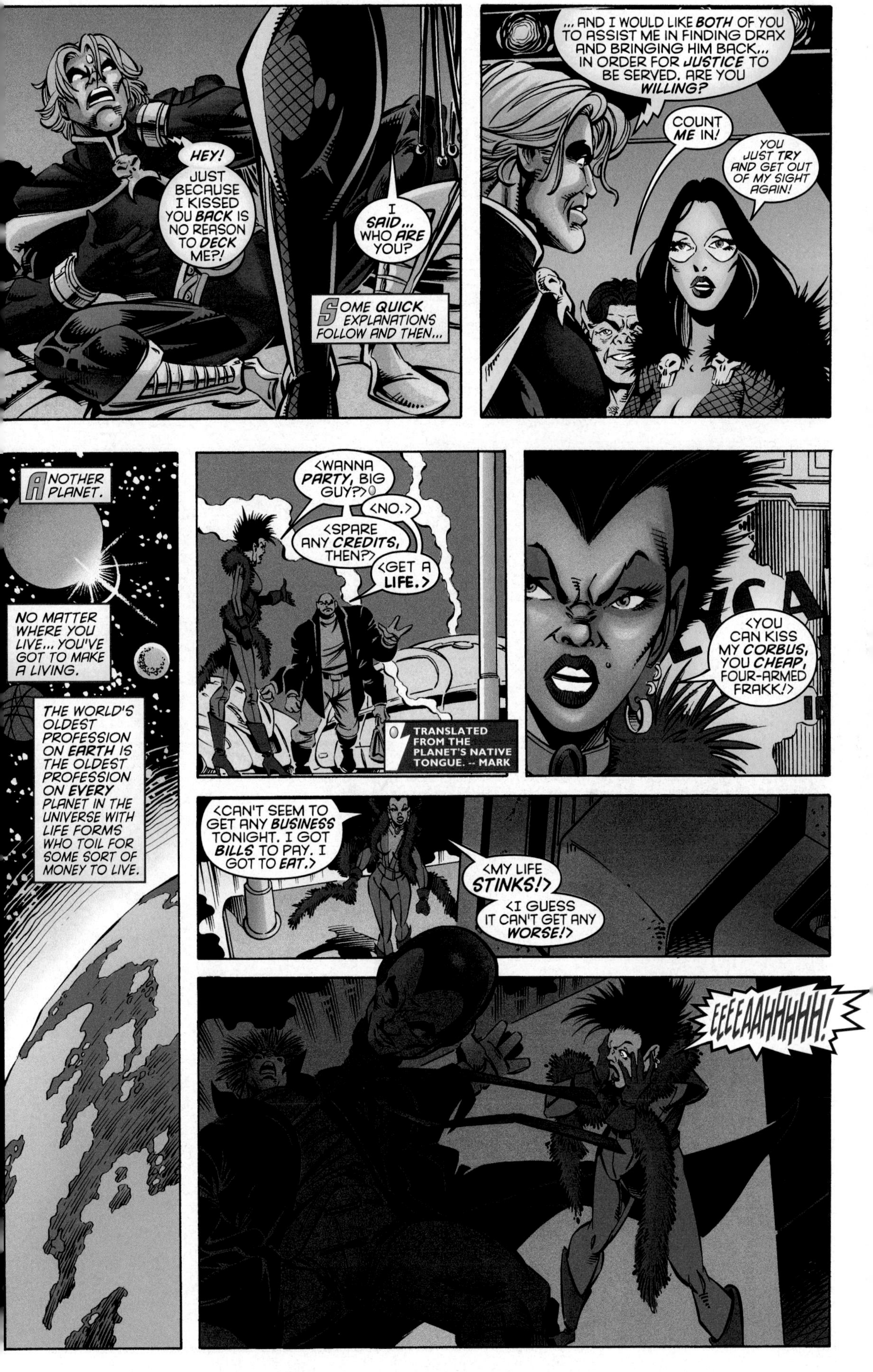
HEY! JUST BECAUSE I KISSED YOU BACK IS NO REASON TO DECK ME?!
I SAID... WHO ARE YOU?
SOME QUICK EXPLANATIONS FOLLOW AND THEN...
...AND I WOULD LIKE BOTH OF YOU TO ASSIST ME IN FINDING DRAX AND BRINGING HIM BACK... IN ORDER FOR JUSTICE TO BE SERVED. ARE YOU WILLING?
COUNT ME IN!
YOU JUST TRY AND GET OUT OF MY SIGHT AGAIN!
ANOTHER PLANET.
NO MATTER WHERE YOU LIVE... YOU'VE GOT TO MAKE A LIVING.
THE WORLD'S OLDEST PROFESSION ON EARTH IS THE OLDEST PROFESSION ON EVERY PLANET IN THE UNIVERSE WITH LIFE FORMS WHO TOIL FOR SOME SORT OF MONEY TO LIVE.
<WANNA PARTY, BIG GUY?>
<NO.>
<SPARE ANY CREDITS, THEN?>
<GET A LIFE.>
TRANSLATED FROM THE PLANET'S NATIVE TONGUE. -- MARK
<YOU CAN KISS MY CORBUS, YOU CHEAP, FOUR-ARMED FRAKK!>
<CAN'T SEEM TO GET ANY BUSINESS TONIGHT. I GOT BILLS TO PAY. I GOT TO EAT.>
<MY LIFE STINKS!>
<I GUESS IT CAN'T GET ANY WORSE!>
EEEEAAHHHHH!

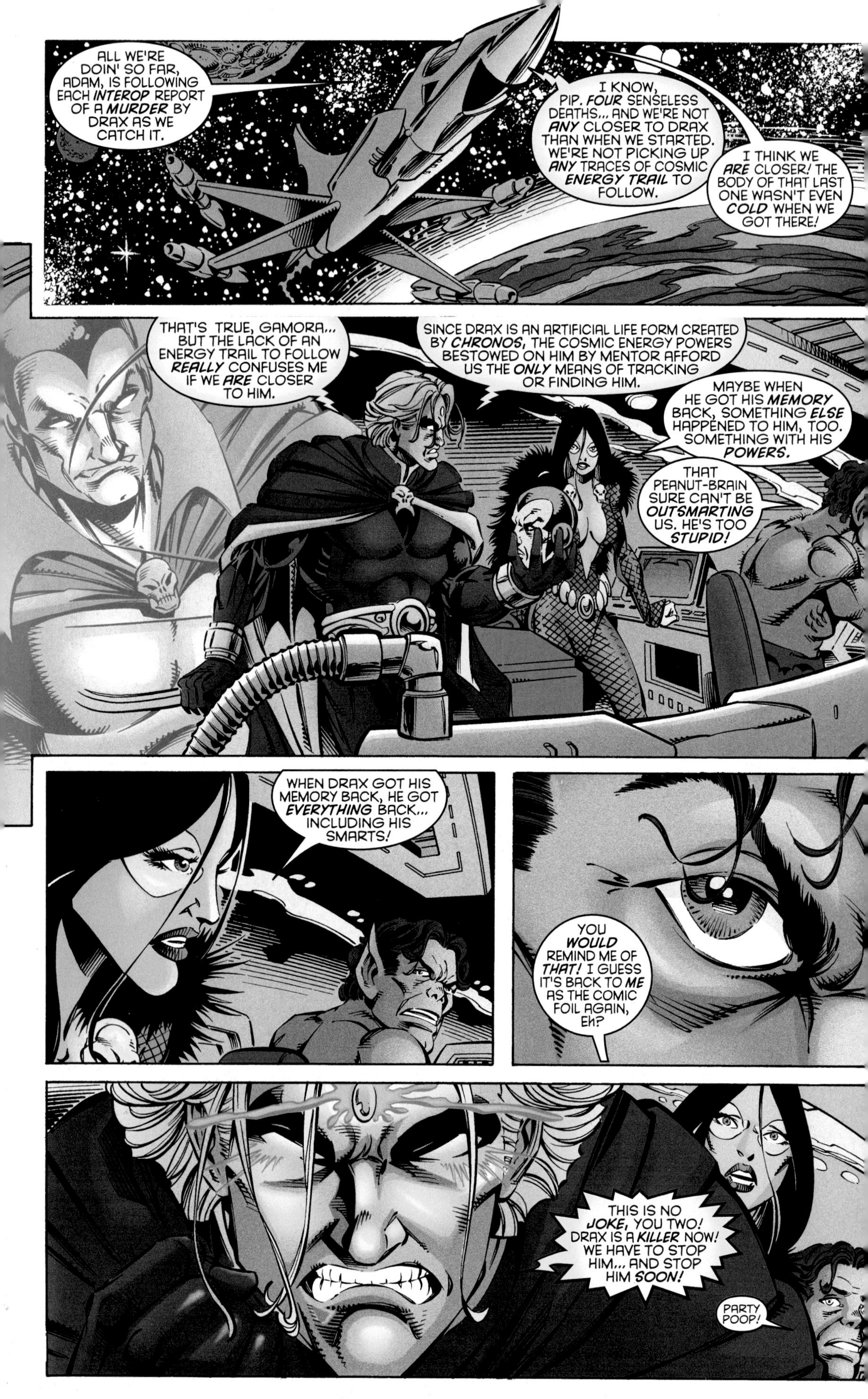

ALL WE'RE DOIN' SO FAR, ADAM, IS FOLLOWING EACH INTEROP REPORT OF A MURDER BY DRAX AS WE CATCH IT.
I KNOW, PIP. FOUR SENSELESS DEATHS... AND WE'RE NOT ANY CLOSER TO DRAX THAN WHEN WE STARTED. WE'RE NOT PICKING UP ANY TRACES OF COSMIC ENERGY TRAIL TO FOLLOW.
I THINK WE ARE CLOSER! THE BODY OF THAT LAST ONE WASN'T EVEN COLD WHEN WE GOT THERE!
THAT'S TRUE, GAMORA... BUT THE LACK OF AN ENERGY TRAIL TO FOLLOW REALLY CONFUSES ME IF WE ARE CLOSER TO HIM.
SINCE DRAX IS AN ARTIFICIAL LIFE FORM CREATED BY CHRONOS, THE COSMIC ENERGY POWERS BESTOWED ON HIM BY MENTOR AFFORD US THE ONLY MEANS OF TRACKING OR FINDING HIM.
MAYBE WHEN HE GOT HIS MEMORY BACK, SOMETHING ELSE HAPPENED TO HIM, TOO. SOMETHING WITH HIS POWERS.
THAT PEANUT-BRAIN SURE CAN'T BE OUTSMARTING US. HE'S TOO STUPID!
WHEN DRAX GOT HIS MEMORY BACK, HE GOT EVERYTHING BACK... INCLUDING HIS SMARTS!
YOU WOULD REMIND ME OF THAT! I GUESS IT'S BACK TO ME AS THE COMIC FOIL AGAIN, EH?
THIS IS NO JOKE, YOU TWO! DRAX IS A KILLER NOW! WE HAVE TO STOP HIM... AND STOP HIM SOON!
PARTY POOP!

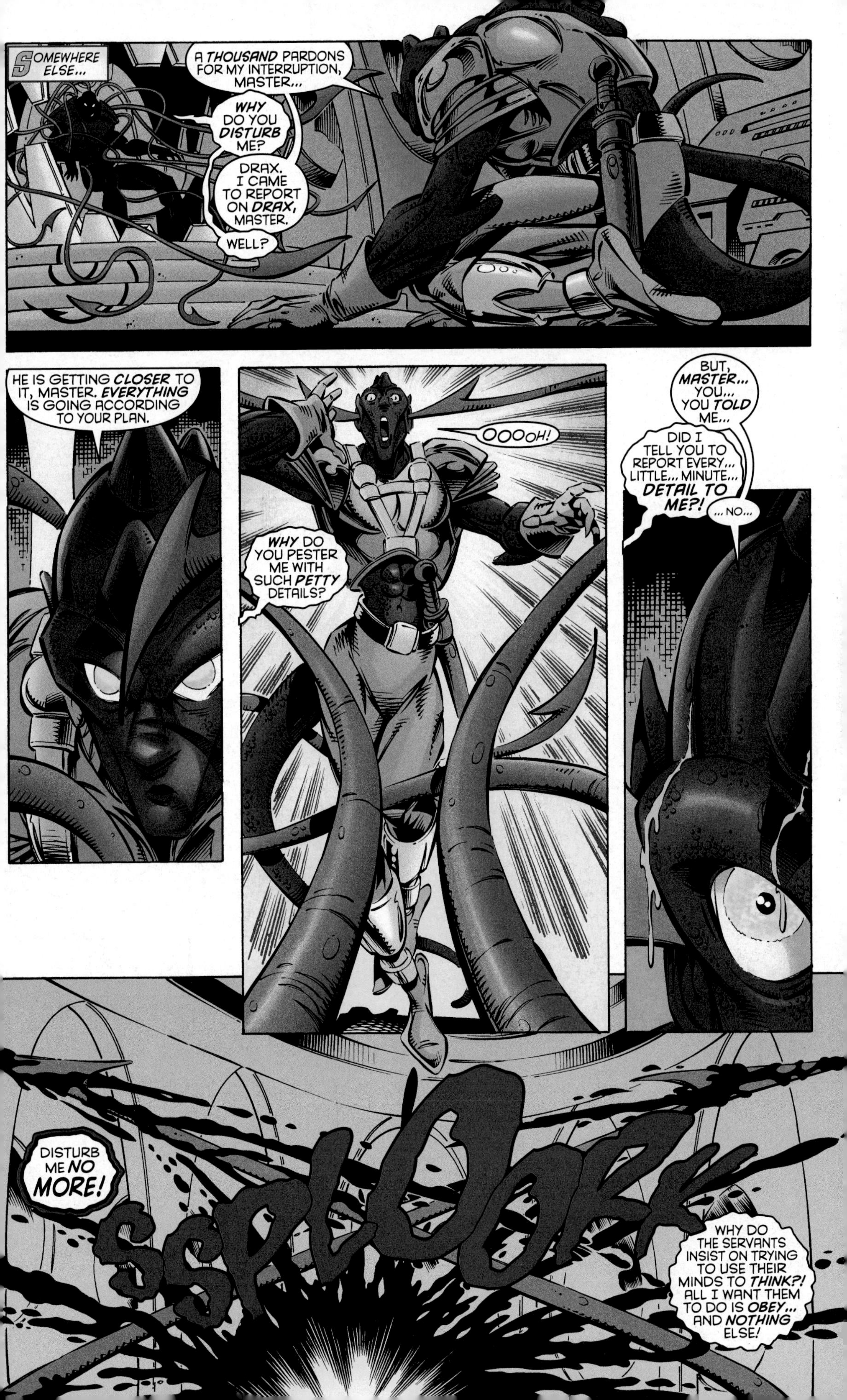
SOMEWHERE ELSE...
A THOUSAND PARDONS FOR MY INTERRUPTION, MASTER...
WHY DO YOU DISTURB ME?
DRAX. I CAME TO REPORT ON DRAX, MASTER.
WELL?
HE IS GETTING CLOSER TO IT, MASTER. EVERYTHING IS GOING ACCORDING TO YOUR PLAN.
OOOOH!
WHY DO YOU PESTER ME WITH SUCH PETTY DETAILS?
BUT, MASTER... YOU... YOU TOLD ME...
DID I TELL YOU TO REPORT EVERY... LITTLE... MINUTE... DETAIL TO ME?!
...NO...
DISTURB ME NO MORE!
SSPLOOKK
WHY DO THE SERVANTS INSIST ON TRYING TO USE THEIR MINDS TO THINK?! ALL I WANT THEM TO DO IS OBEY... AND NOTHING ELSE!

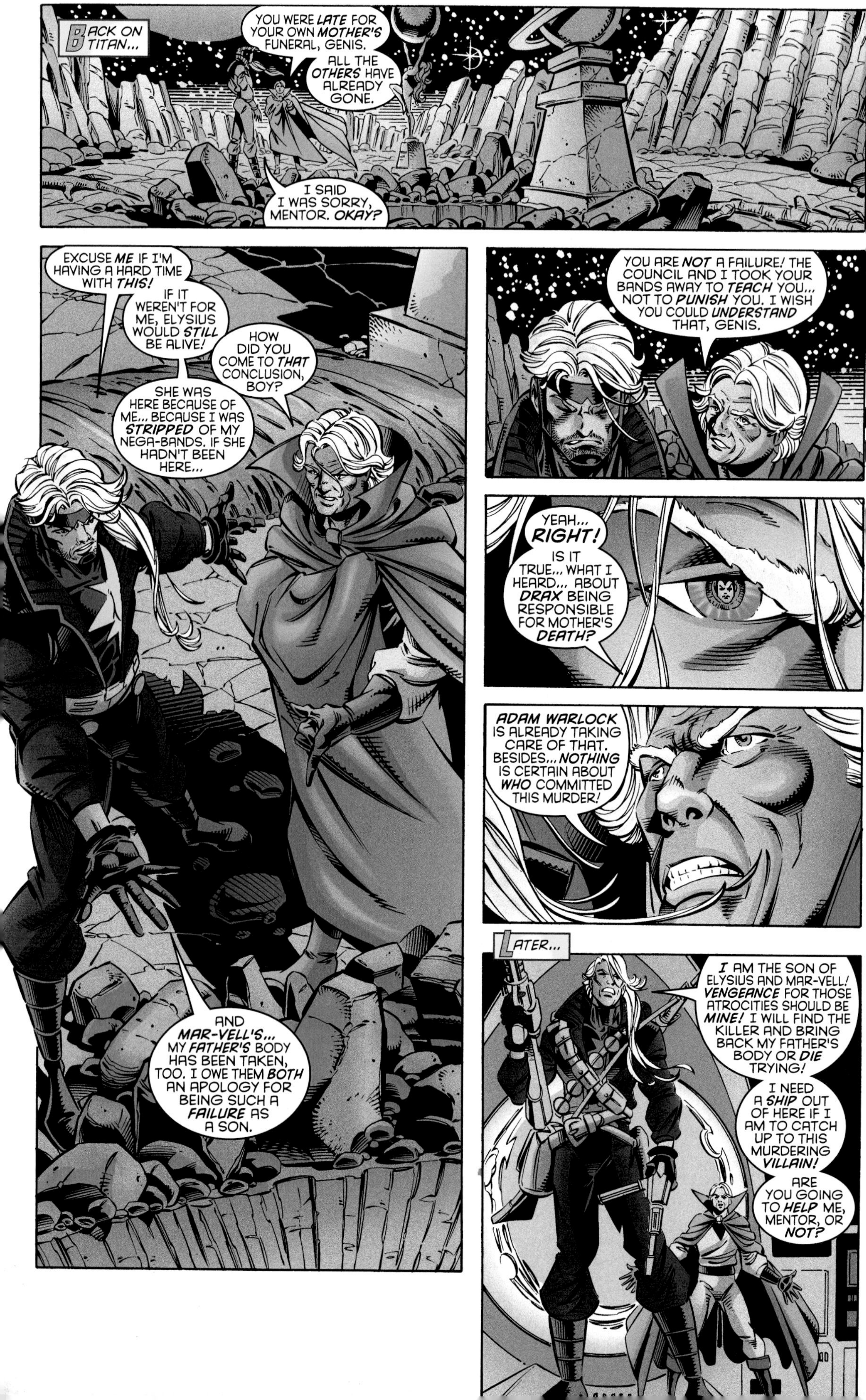

BACK ON TITAN...
YOU WERE LATE FOR YOUR OWN MOTHER'S FUNERAL, GENIS.
ALL THE OTHERS HAVE ALREADY GONE.
I SAID I WAS SORRY, MENTOR. OKAY?
EXCUSE ME IF I'M HAVING A HARD TIME WITH THIS!
IF IT WEREN'T FOR ME, ELYSIUS WOULD STILL BE ALIVE!
HOW DID YOU COME TO THAT CONCLUSION, BOY?
SHE WAS HERE BECAUSE OF ME... BECAUSE I WAS STRIPPED OF MY NEGA-BANDS. IF SHE HADN'T BEEN HERE...
AND MAR-VELL'S... MY FATHER'S BODY HAS BEEN TAKEN, TOO. I OWE THEM BOTH AN APOLOGY FOR BEING SUCH A FAILURE AS A SON.
YOU ARE NOT A FAILURE! THE COUNCIL AND I TOOK YOUR BANDS AWAY TO TEACH YOU... NOT TO PUNISH YOU. I WISH YOU COULD UNDERSTAND THAT, GENIS.
YEAH... RIGHT!
IS IT TRUE... WHAT I HEARD... ABOUT DRAX BEING RESPONSIBLE FOR MOTHER'S DEATH?
ADAM WARLOCK IS ALREADY TAKING CARE OF THAT. BESIDES... NOTHING IS CERTAIN ABOUT WHO COMMITTED THIS MURDER!
LATER...
I AM THE SON OF ELYSIUS AND MAR-VELL! VENGEANCE FOR THOSE ATROCITIES SHOULD BE MINE! I WILL FIND THE KILLER AND BRING BACK MY FATHER'S BODY OR DIE TRYING!
I NEED A SHIP OUT OF HERE IF I AM TO CATCH UP TO THIS MURDERING VILLAIN!
ARE YOU GOING TO HELP ME, MENTOR, OR NOT?

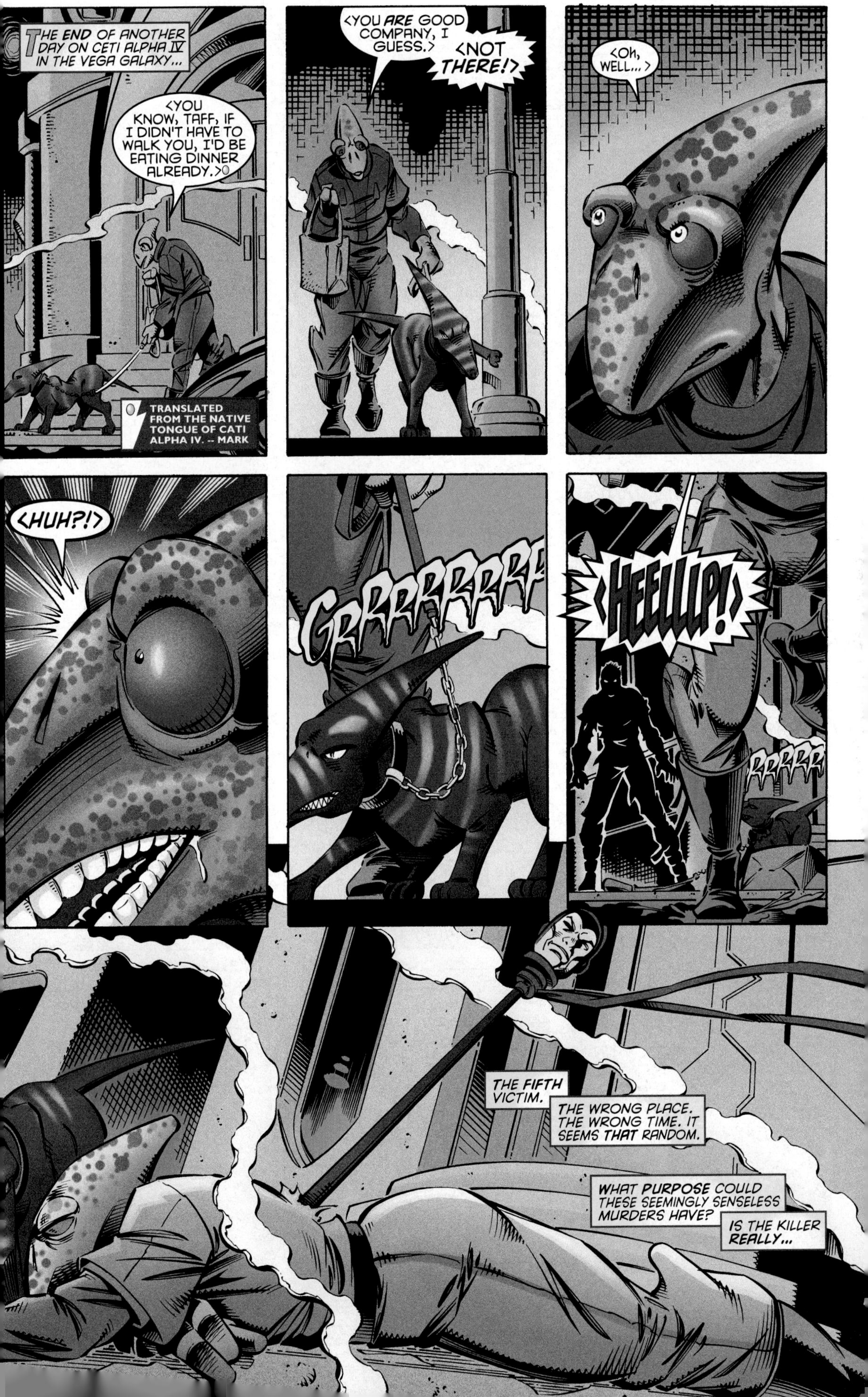
THE END OF ANOTHER DAY ON CETI ALPHA IV IN THE VEGA GALAXY...
<YOU KNOW, TAFF, IF I DIDN'T HAVE TO WALK YOU, I'D BE EATING DINNER ALREADY.>
TRANSLATED FROM THE NATIVE TONGUE OF CATI ALPHA IV. -- MARK
<YOU ARE GOOD COMPANY, I GUESS.>
<NOT THERE!>
<Oh, WELL...>
<HUH?!>
GRRRRRRRRR
<HEELLLP!>
RRRRR
THE FIFTH VICTIM.
THE WRONG PLACE. THE WRONG TIME. IT SEEMS THAT RANDOM.
WHAT PURPOSE COULD THESE SEEMINGLY SENSELESS MURDERS HAVE?
IS THE KILLER REALLY...

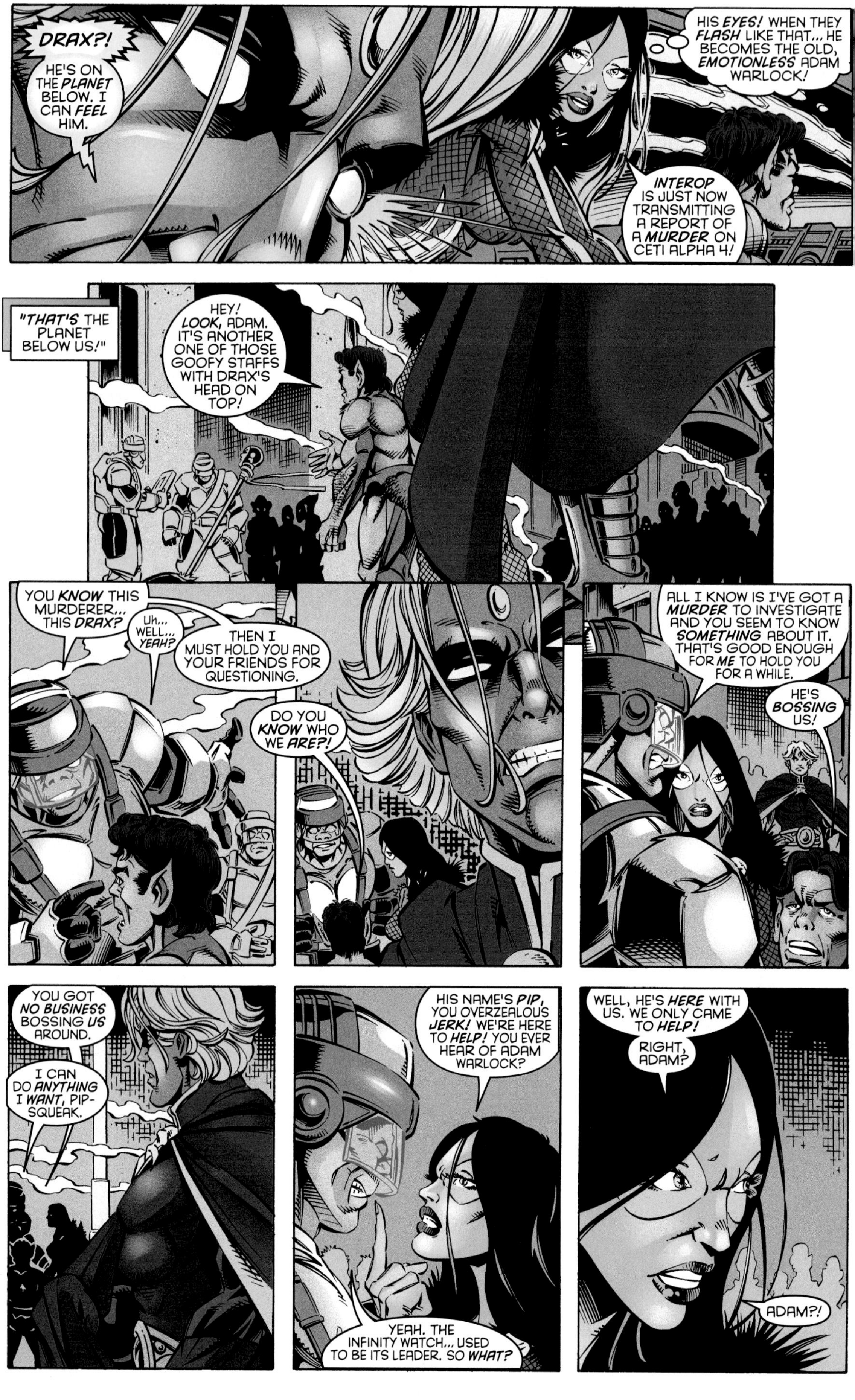
DRAX?!
HE'S ON THE PLANET BELOW. I CAN FEEL HIM.
HIS EYES! WHEN THEY FLASH LIKE THAT... HE BECOMES THE OLD, EMOTIONLESS ADAM WARLOCK!
INTEROP IS JUST NOW TRANSMITTING A REPORT OF A MURDER ON CETI ALPHA 4!
"THAT'S THE PLANET BELOW US!"
HEY! LOOK, ADAM. IT'S ANOTHER ONE OF THOSE GOOFY STAFFS WITH DRAX'S HEAD ON TOP!
YOU KNOW THIS MURDERER... THIS DRAX?
UH... WELL... YEAH?
THEN I MUST HOLD YOU AND YOUR FRIENDS FOR QUESTIONING.
DO YOU KNOW WHO WE ARE?!
ALL I KNOW IS I'VE GOT A MURDER TO INVESTIGATE AND YOU SEEM TO KNOW SOMETHING ABOUT IT. THAT'S GOOD ENOUGH FOR ME TO HOLD YOU FOR A WHILE.
HE'S BOSSING US!
YOU GOT NO BUSINESS BOSSING US AROUND.
I CAN DO ANYTHING I WANT, PIP-SQUEAK.
HIS NAME'S PIP, YOU OVERZEALOUS JERK! WE'RE HERE TO HELP! YOU EVER HEAR OF ADAM WARLOCK?
YEAH. THE INFINITY WATCH... USED TO BE ITS LEADER. SO WHAT?
WELL, HE'S HERE WITH US. WE ONLY CAME TO HELP!
RIGHT, ADAM?
ADAM?!

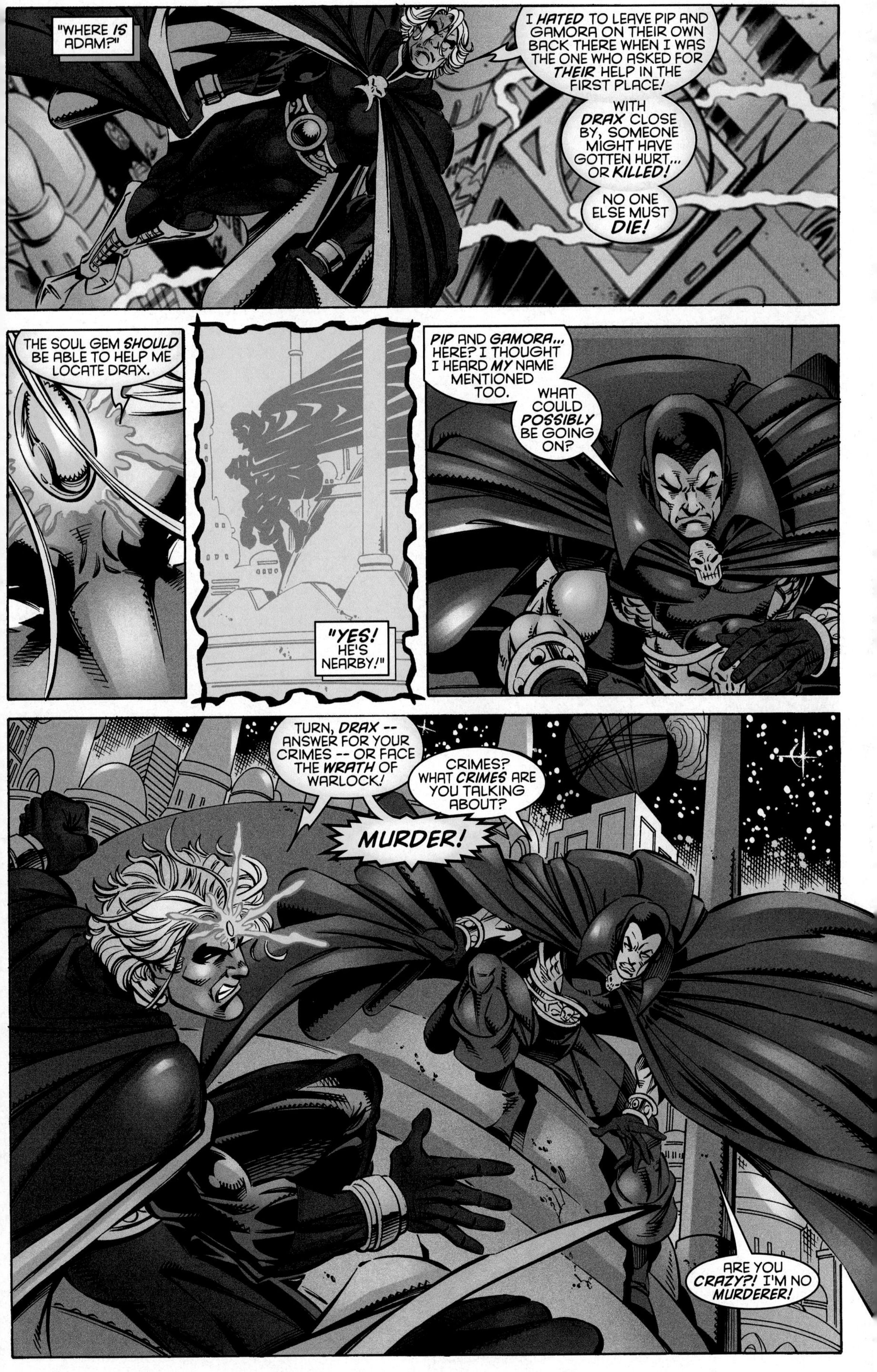
"WHERE IS ADAM?"
I HATED TO LEAVE PIP AND GAMORA ON THEIR OWN BACK THERE WHEN I WAS THE ONE WHO ASKED FOR THEIR HELP IN THE FIRST PLACE!
WITH DRAX CLOSE BY, SOMEONE MIGHT HAVE GOTTEN HURT... OR KILLED!
NO ONE ELSE MUST DIE!
THE SOUL GEM SHOULD BE ABLE TO HELP ME LOCATE DRAX.
"YES! HE'S NEARBY!"
PIP AND GAMORA... HERE? I THOUGHT I HEARD MY NAME MENTIONED TOO.
WHAT COULD POSSIBLY BE GOING ON?
TURN, DRAX -- ANSWER FOR YOUR CRIMES -- OR FACE THE WRATH OF WARLOCK!
CRIMES? WHAT CRIMES ARE YOU TALKING ABOUT?
MURDER!
ARE YOU CRAZY?! I'M NO MURDERER!

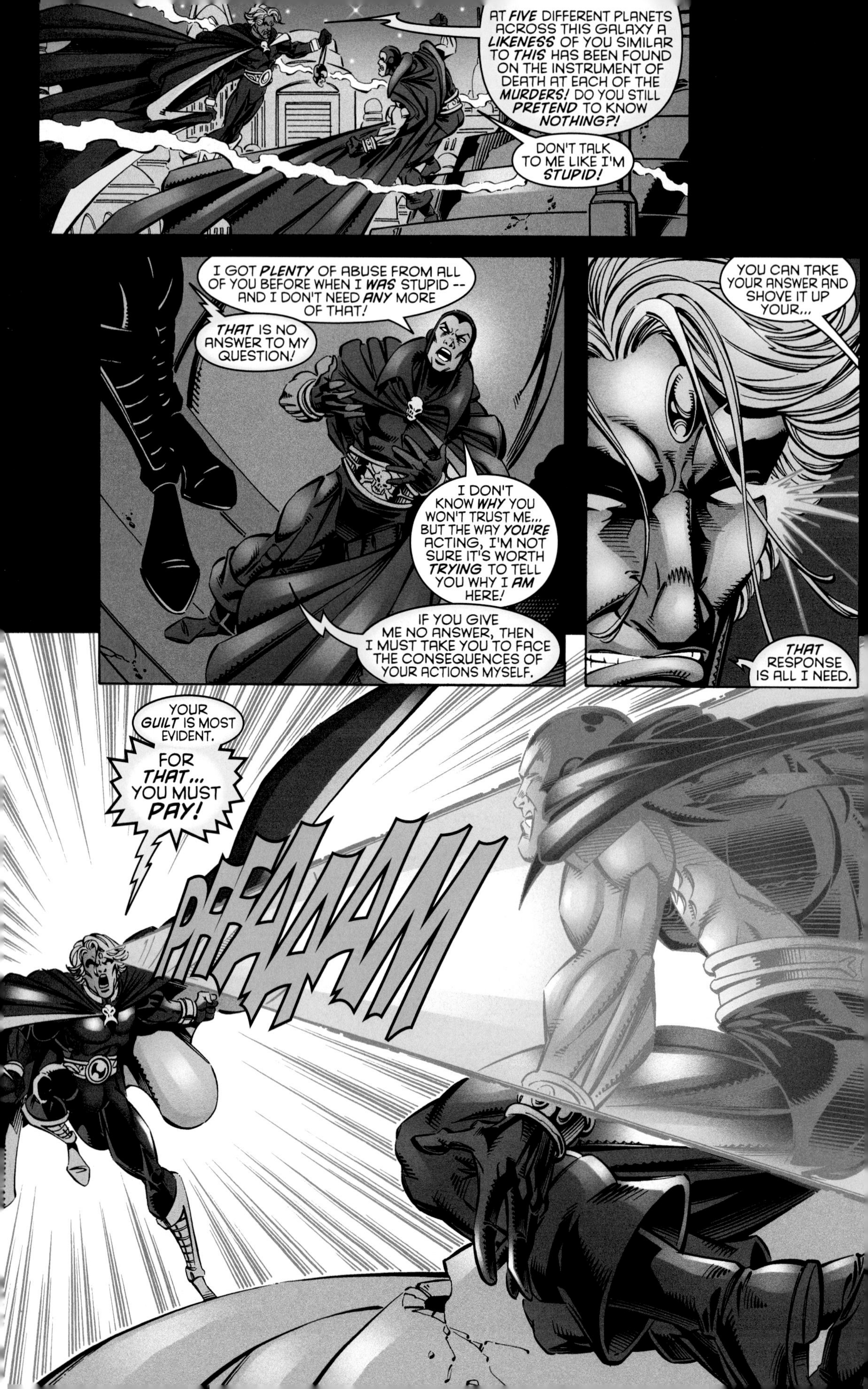
AT FIVE DIFFERENT PLANETS ACROSS THIS GALAXY A LIKENESS OF YOU SIMILAR TO THIS HAS BEEN FOUND ON THE INSTRUMENT OF DEATH AT EACH OF THE MURDERS! DO YOU STILL PRETEND TO KNOW NOTHING?!
DON'T TALK TO ME LIKE I'M STUPID!
I GOT PLENTY OF ABUSE FROM ALL OF YOU BEFORE WHEN I WAS STUPID -- AND I DON'T NEED ANY MORE OF THAT!
THAT IS NO ANSWER TO MY QUESTION!
I DON'T KNOW WHY YOU WON'T TRUST ME... BUT THE WAY YOU'RE ACTING, I'M NOT SURE IT'S WORTH TRYING TO TELL YOU WHY I AM HERE!
IF YOU GIVE ME NO ANSWER, THEN I MUST TAKE YOU TO FACE THE CONSEQUENCES OF YOUR ACTIONS MYSELF.
YOU CAN TAKE YOUR ANSWER AND SHOVE IT UP YOUR...
THAT RESPONSE IS ALL I NEED.
YOUR GUILT IS MOST EVIDENT.
FOR THAT... YOU MUST PAY!
PRRAAAAM

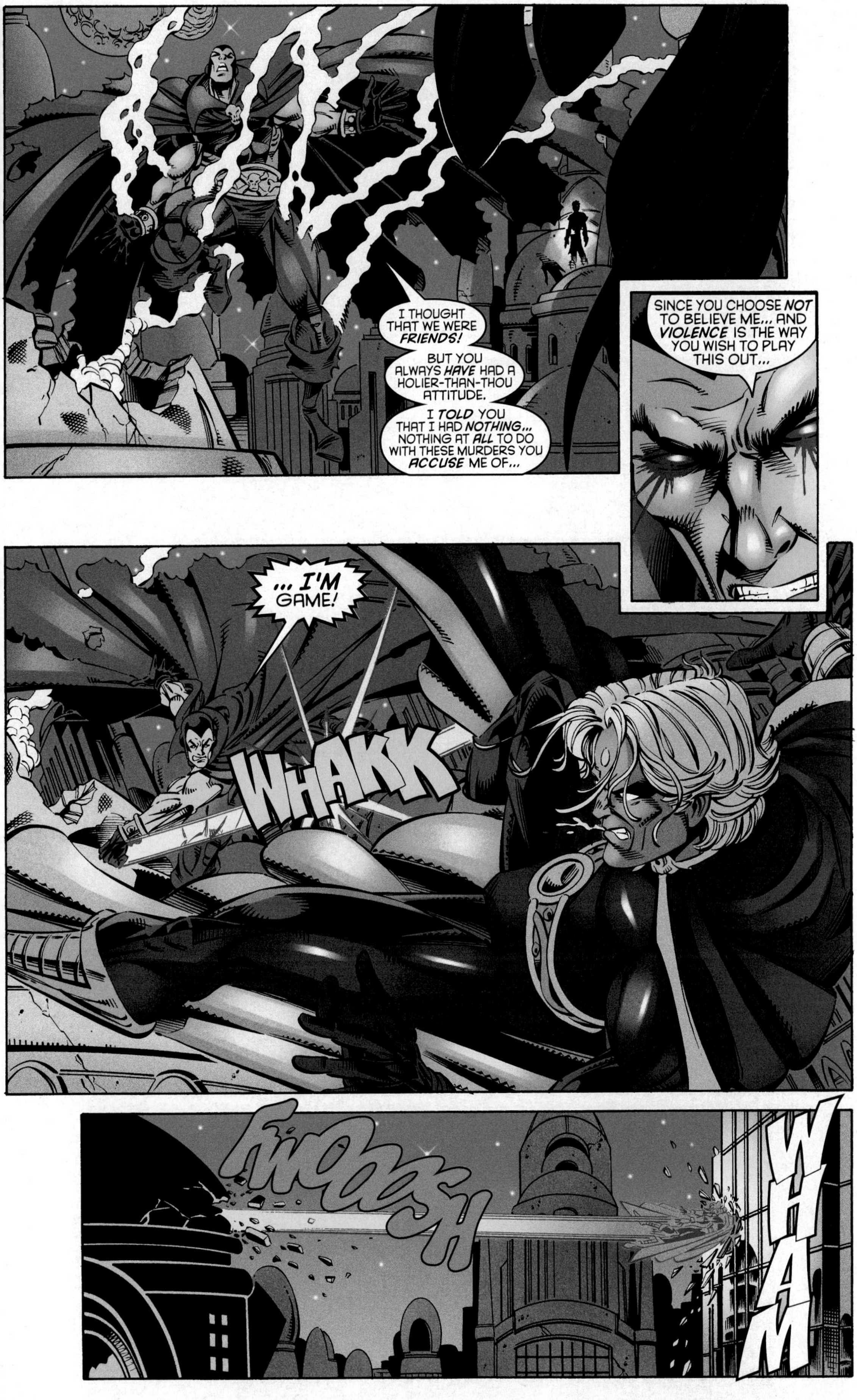

I THOUGHT THAT WE WERE FRIENDS!
BUT YOU ALWAYS HAVE HAD A HOLIER-THAN-THOU ATTITUDE.
I TOLD YOU THAT I HAD NOTHING... NOTHING AT ALL TO DO WITH THESE MURDERS YOU ACCUSE ME OF...
SINCE YOU CHOOSE NOT TO BELIEVE ME... AND VIOLENCE IS THE WAY YOU WISH TO PLAY THIS OUT...
...I'M GAME!
WHAKK
FWOOSH
WHAM

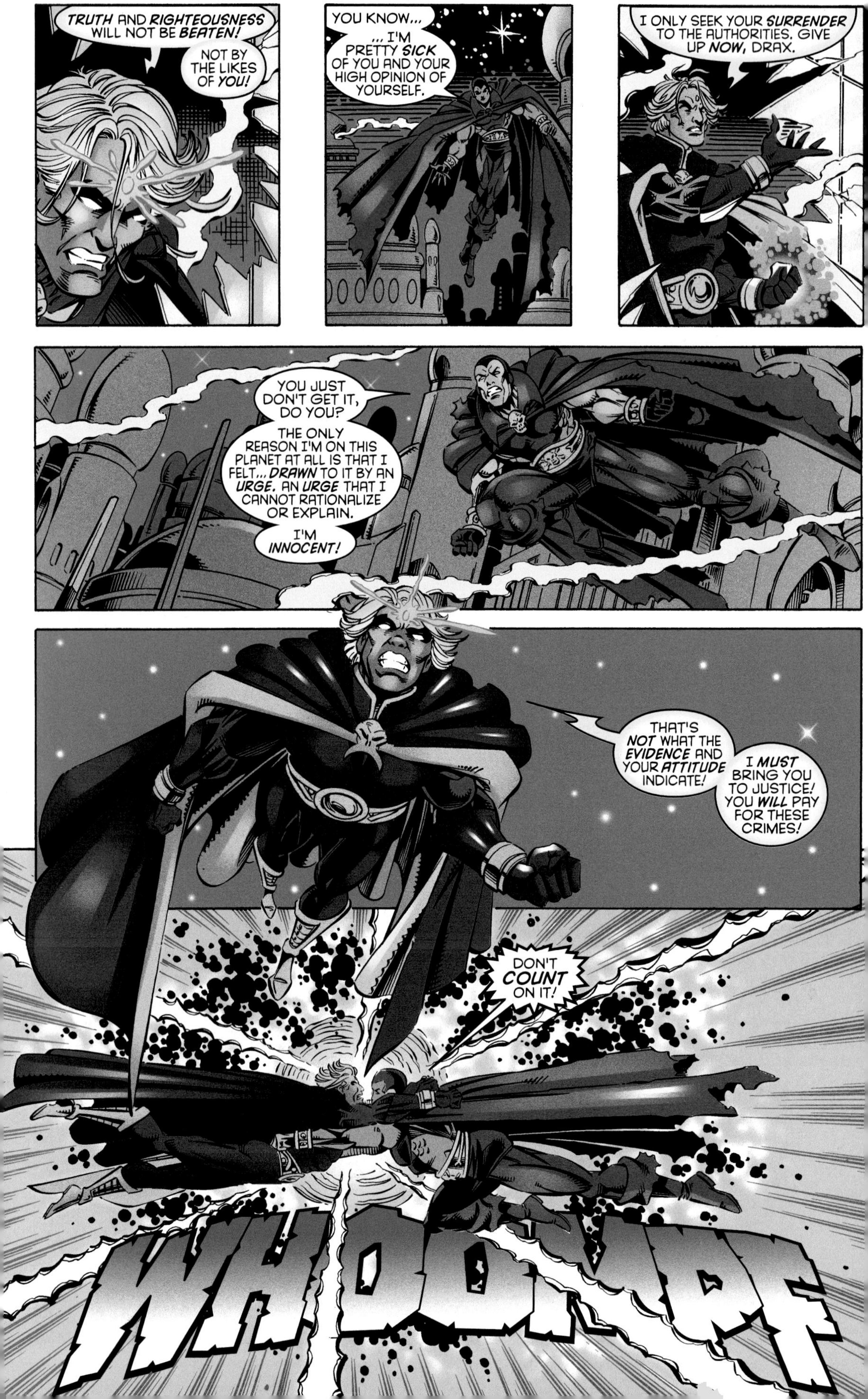
TRUTH AND RIGHTEOUSNESS WILL NOT BE BEATEN!
NOT BY THE LIKES OF YOU!
YOU KNOW...
...I'M PRETTY SICK OF YOU AND YOUR HIGH OPINION OF YOURSELF.
I ONLY SEEK YOUR SURRENDER TO THE AUTHORITIES. GIVE UP NOW, DRAX.
YOU JUST DON'T GET IT, DO YOU?
THE ONLY REASON I'M ON THIS PLANET AT ALL IS THAT I FELT... DRAWN TO IT BY AN URGE. AN URGE THAT I CANNOT RATIONALIZE OR EXPLAIN.
I'M INNOCENT!
THAT'S NOT WHAT THE EVIDENCE AND YOUR ATTITUDE INDICATE!
I MUST BRING YOU TO JUSTICE! YOU WILL PAY FOR THESE CRIMES!
DON'T COUNT ON IT!
WHOOMF

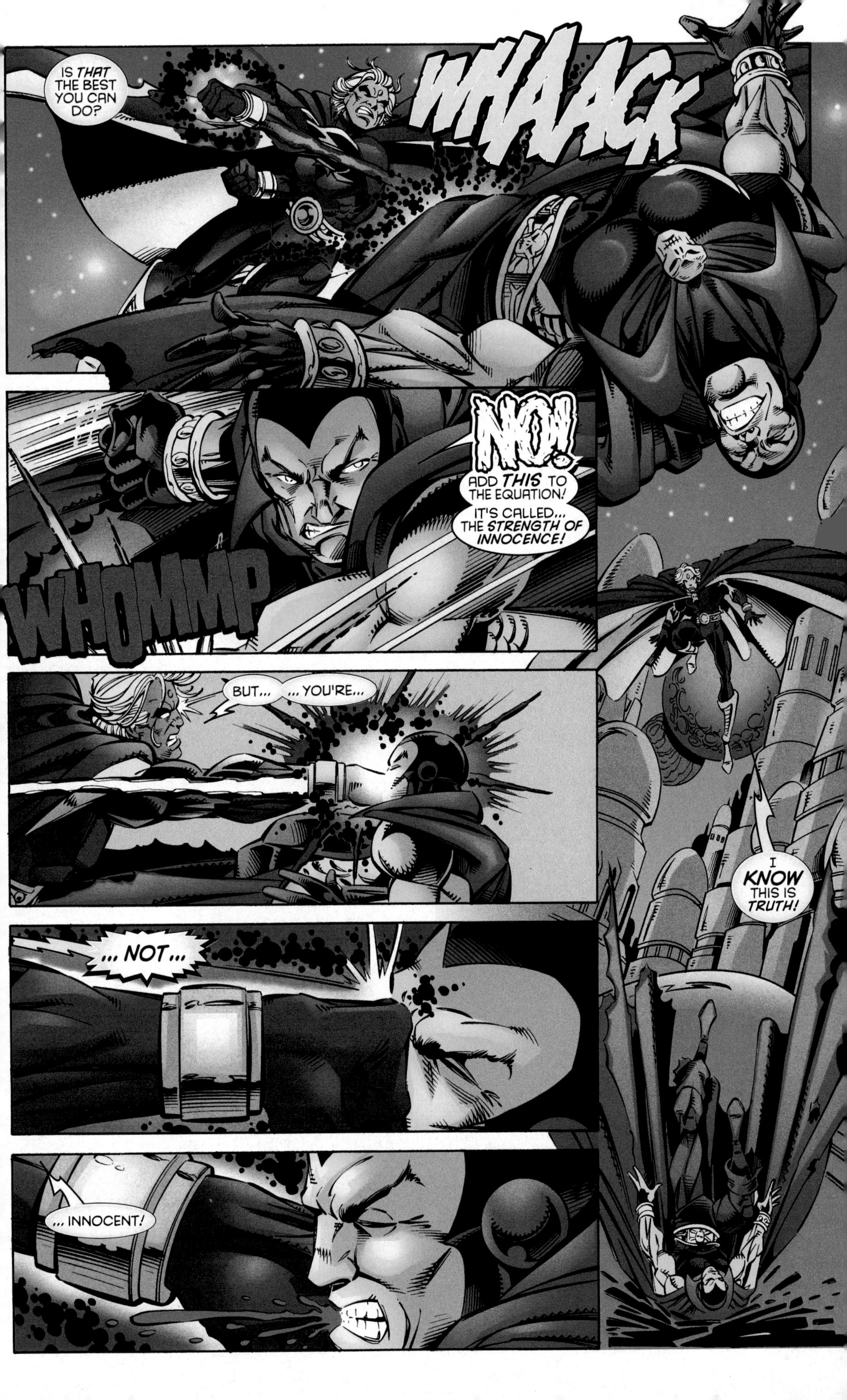
IS THAT THE BEST YOU CAN DO?
WHAAACK
NO!
ADD THIS TO THE EQUATION!
IT'S CALLED... THE STRENGTH OF INNOCENCE!
WHOMMP
BUT...
...YOU'RE...
...NOT...
...INNOCENT!
I KNOW THIS IS TRUTH!

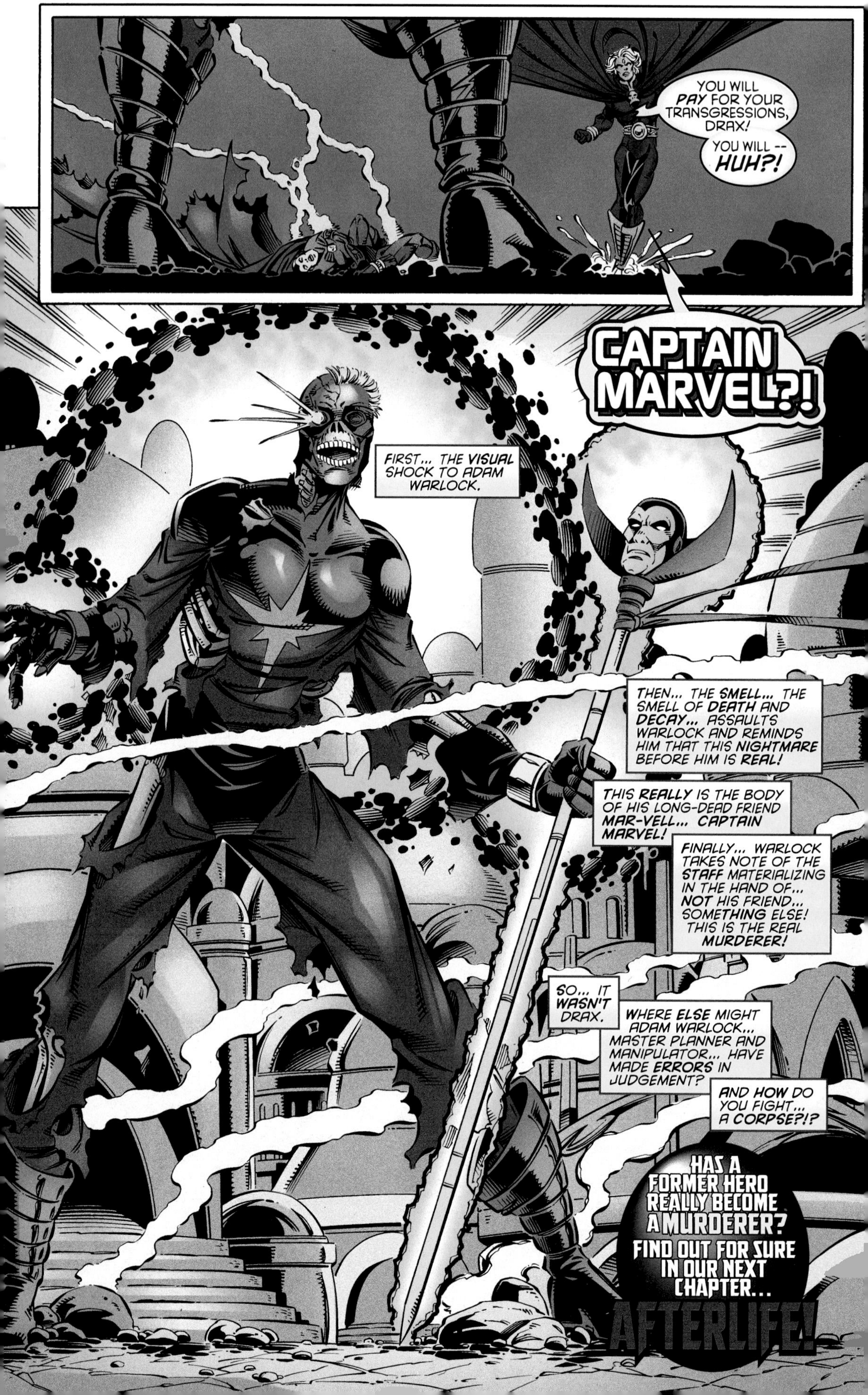

YOU WILL PAY FOR YOUR TRANSGRESSIONS, DRAX!
YOU WILL -- HUH?!
CAPTAIN MARVEL?!
FIRST... THE VISUAL SHOCK TO ADAM WARLOCK.
THEN... THE SMELL... THE SMELL OF DEATH AND DECAY... ASSAULTS WARLOCK AND REMINDS HIM THAT THIS NIGHTMARE BEFORE HIM IS REAL!
THIS REALLY IS THE BODY OF HIS LONG-DEAD FRIEND MAR-VELL... CAPTAIN MARVEL!
FINALLY... WARLOCK TAKES NOTE OF THE STAFF MATERIALIZING IN THE HAND OF... NOT HIS FRIEND... SOMETHING ELSE! THIS IS THE REAL MURDERER!
SO... IT WASN'T DRAX.
WHERE ELSE MIGHT ADAM WARLOCK... MASTER PLANNER AND MANIPULATOR... HAVE MADE ERRORS IN JUDGEMENT?
AND HOW DO YOU FIGHT... A CORPSE?!?
HAS A FORMER HERO REALLY BECOME A MURDERER?
FIND OUT FOR SURE IN OUR NEXT CHAPTER...
AFTERLIFE!

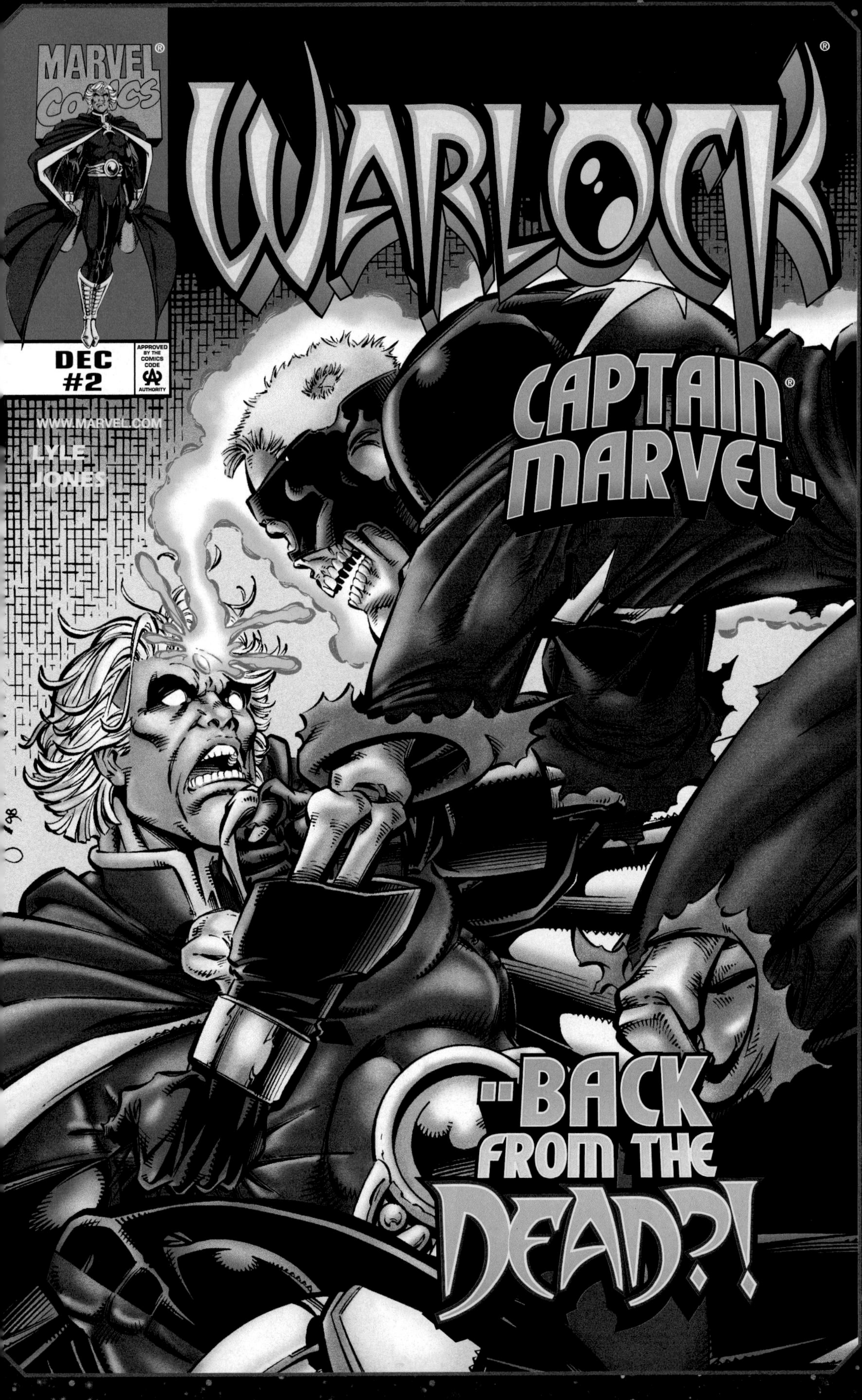
MARVEL COMICS
WARLOCK
DEC #2
APPROVED BY THE COMICS CODE AUTHORITY
WWW.MARVEL.COM
LYLE
JONES
CAPTAIN MARVEL..
..BACK FROM THE DEAD?!

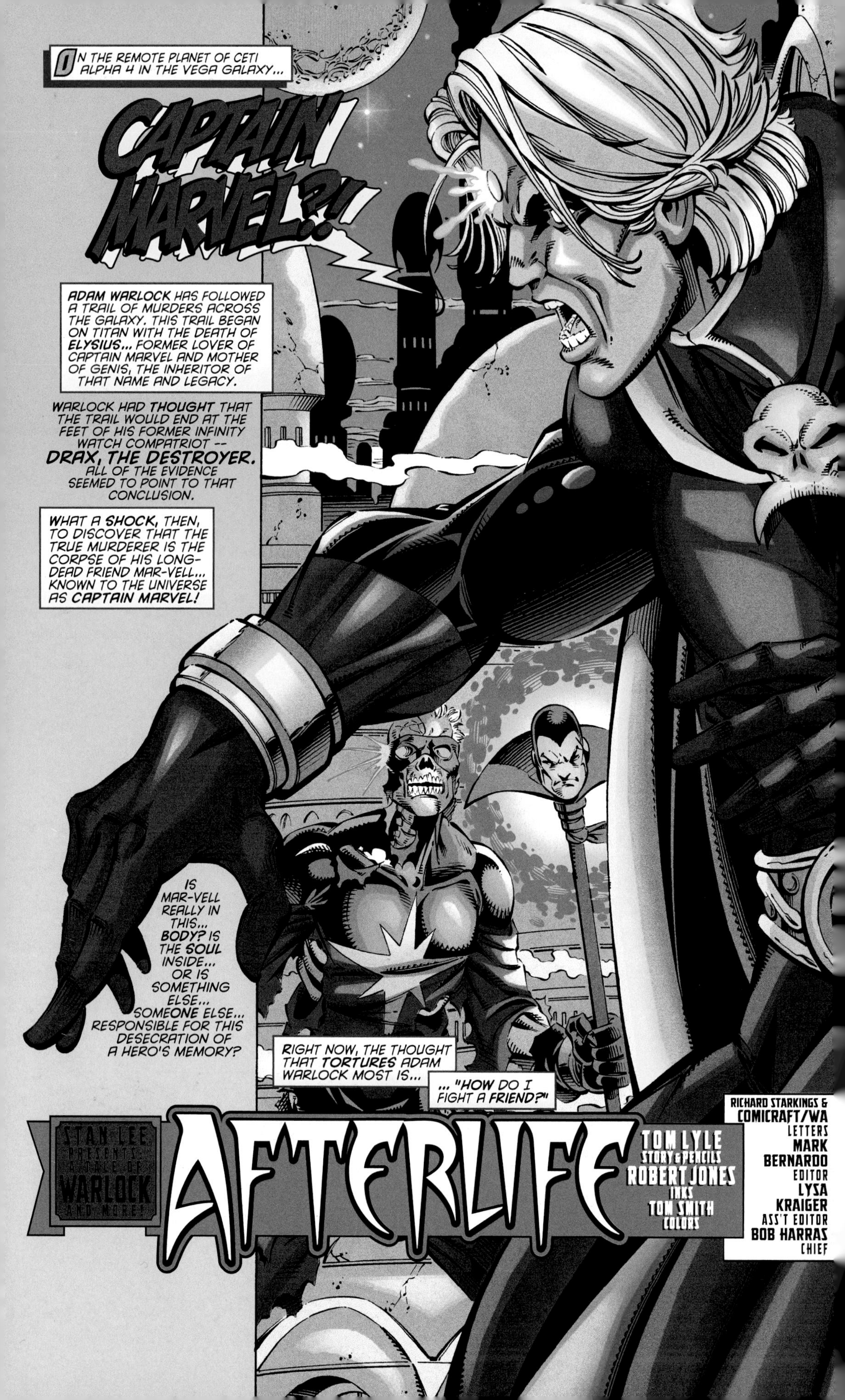
ON THE REMOTE PLANET OF CETI ALPHA 4 IN THE VEGA GALAXY...
CAPTAIN MARVEL?!
ADAM WARLOCK HAS FOLLOWED A TRAIL OF MURDERS ACROSS THE GALAXY. THIS TRAIL BEGAN ON TITAN WITH THE DEATH OF ELYSIUS... FORMER LOVER OF CAPTAIN MARVEL AND MOTHER OF GENIS, THE INHERITOR OF THAT NAME AND LEGACY.
WARLOCK HAD THOUGHT THAT THE TRAIL WOULD END AT THE FEET OF HIS FORMER INFINITY WATCH COMPATRIOT -- DRAX, THE DESTROYER. ALL OF THE EVIDENCE SEEMED TO POINT TO THAT CONCLUSION.
WHAT A SHOCK, THEN, TO DISCOVER THAT THE TRUE MURDERER IS THE CORPSE OF HIS LONG-DEAD FRIEND MAR-VELL... KNOWN TO THE UNIVERSE AS CAPTAIN MARVEL!
IS MAR-VELL REALLY IN THIS... BODY? IS THE SOUL INSIDE... OR IS SOMETHING ELSE... SOMEONE ELSE... RESPONSIBLE FOR THIS DESECRATION OF A HERO'S MEMORY?
RIGHT NOW, THE THOUGHT THAT TORTURES ADAM WARLOCK MOST IS...
..."HOW DO I FIGHT A FRIEND?"
STAN LEE PRESENTS: A TALE OF WARLOCK AND MORE!
AFTERLIFE
TOM LYLE STORY & PENCILS
ROBERT JONES INKS
TOM SMITH COLORS
RICHARD STARKINGS & COMICRAFT/WA LETTERS
MARK BERNARDO EDITOR
LYSA KRAIGER ASS'T EDITOR
BOB HARRAS CHIEF

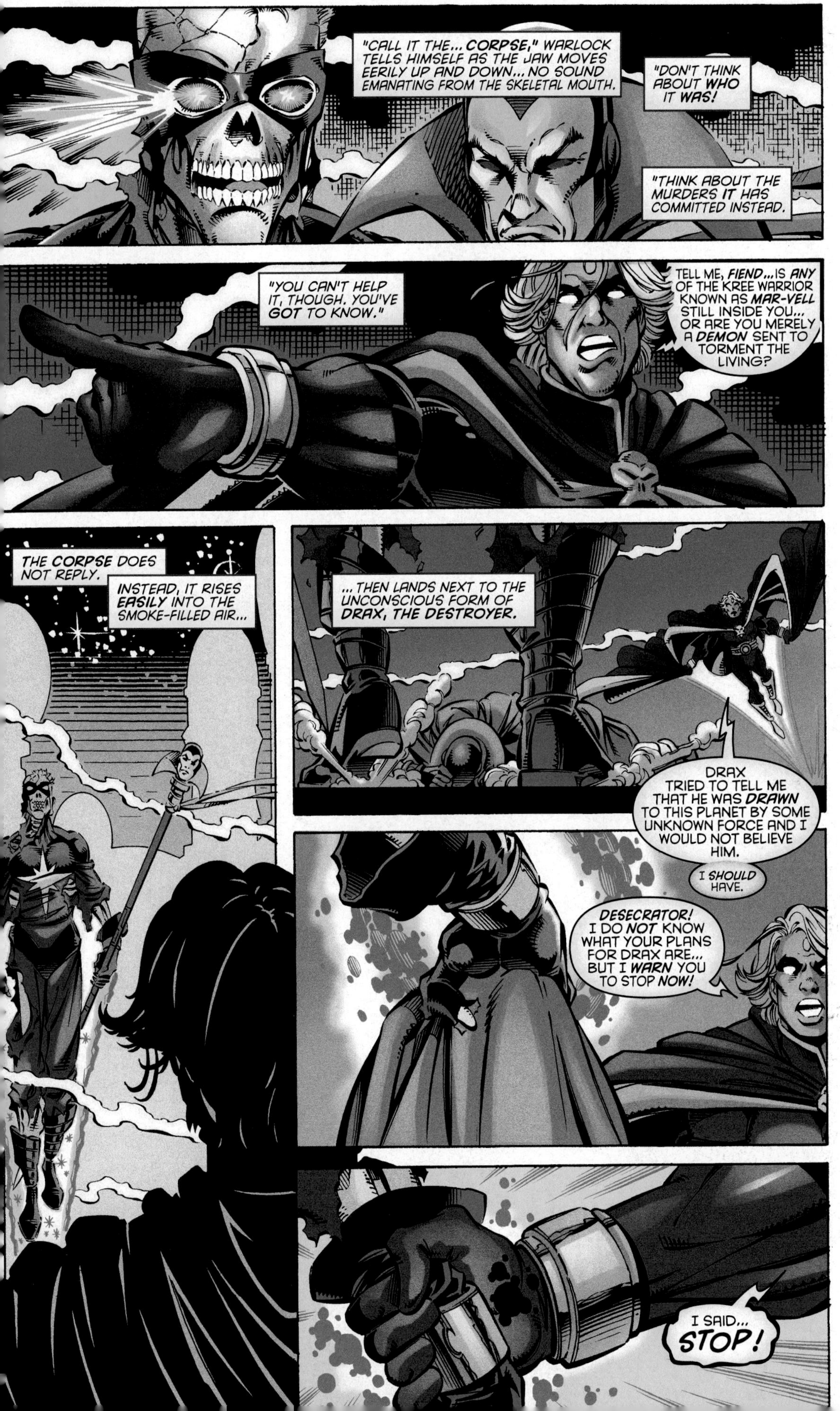
"CALL IT THE... CORPSE," WARLOCK TELLS HIMSELF AS THE JAW MOVES EERILY UP AND DOWN... NO SOUND EMANATING FROM THE SKELETAL MOUTH.
"DON'T THINK ABOUT WHO IT WAS!
"THINK ABOUT THE MURDERS IT HAS COMMITTED INSTEAD.
"YOU CAN'T HELP IT, THOUGH. YOU'VE GOT TO KNOW."
TELL ME, FIEND... IS ANY OF THE KREE WARRIOR KNOWN AS MAR-VELL STILL INSIDE YOU... OR ARE YOU MERELY A DEMON SENT TO TORMENT THE LIVING?
THE CORPSE DOES NOT REPLY.
INSTEAD, IT RISES EASILY INTO THE SMOKE-FILLED AIR...
...THEN LANDS NEXT TO THE UNCONSCIOUS FORM OF DRAX, THE DESTROYER.
DRAX TRIED TO TELL ME THAT HE WAS DRAWN TO THIS PLANET BY SOME UNKNOWN FORCE AND I WOULD NOT BELIEVE HIM.
I SHOULD HAVE.
DESECRATOR! I DO NOT KNOW WHAT YOUR PLANS FOR DRAX ARE... BUT I WARN YOU TO STOP NOW!
I SAID... STOP!

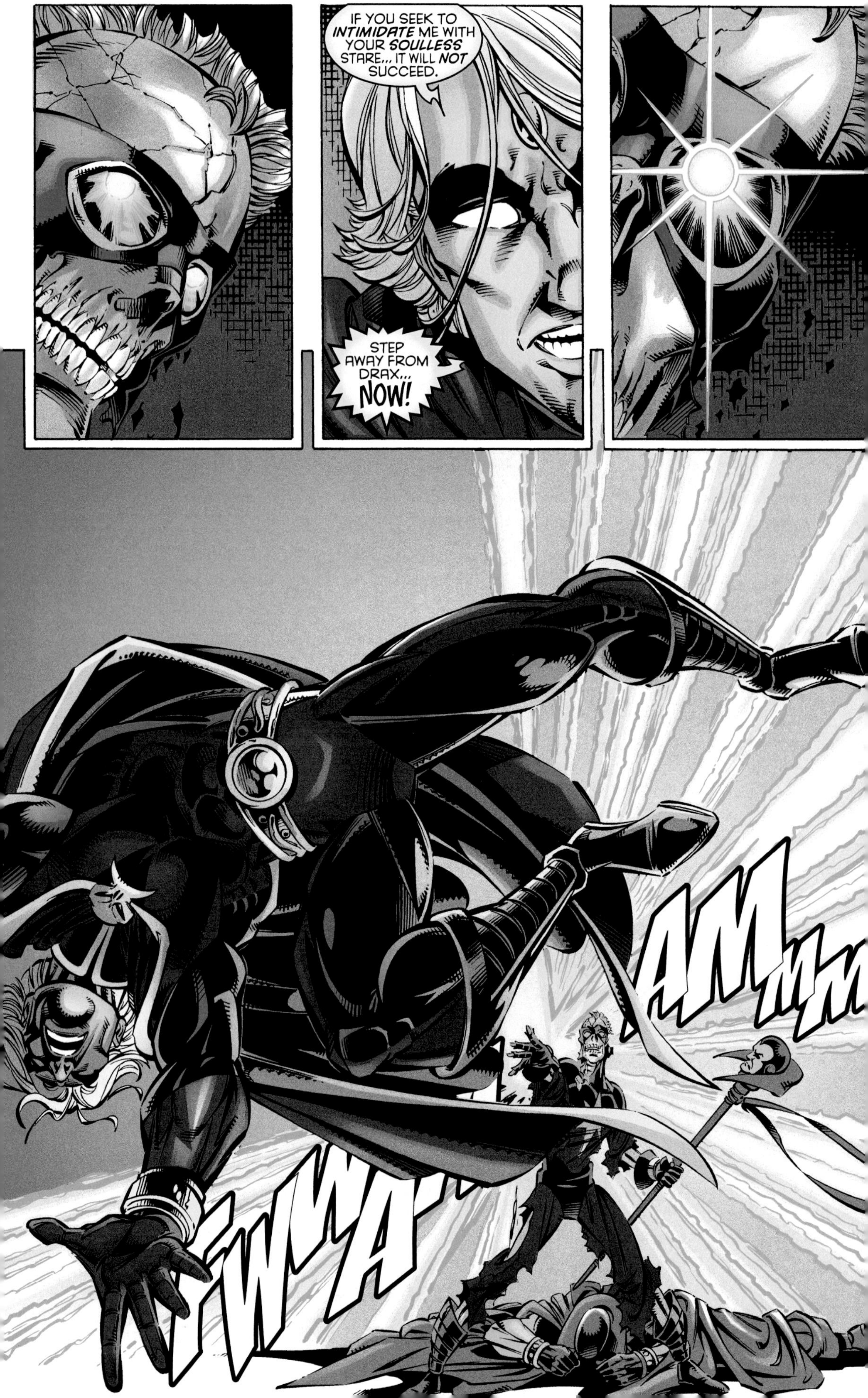
IF YOU SEEK TO INTIMIDATE ME WITH YOUR SOULLESS STARE... IT WILL NOT SUCCEED.
STEP AWAY FROM DRAX... NOW!
AMMM
FWMA

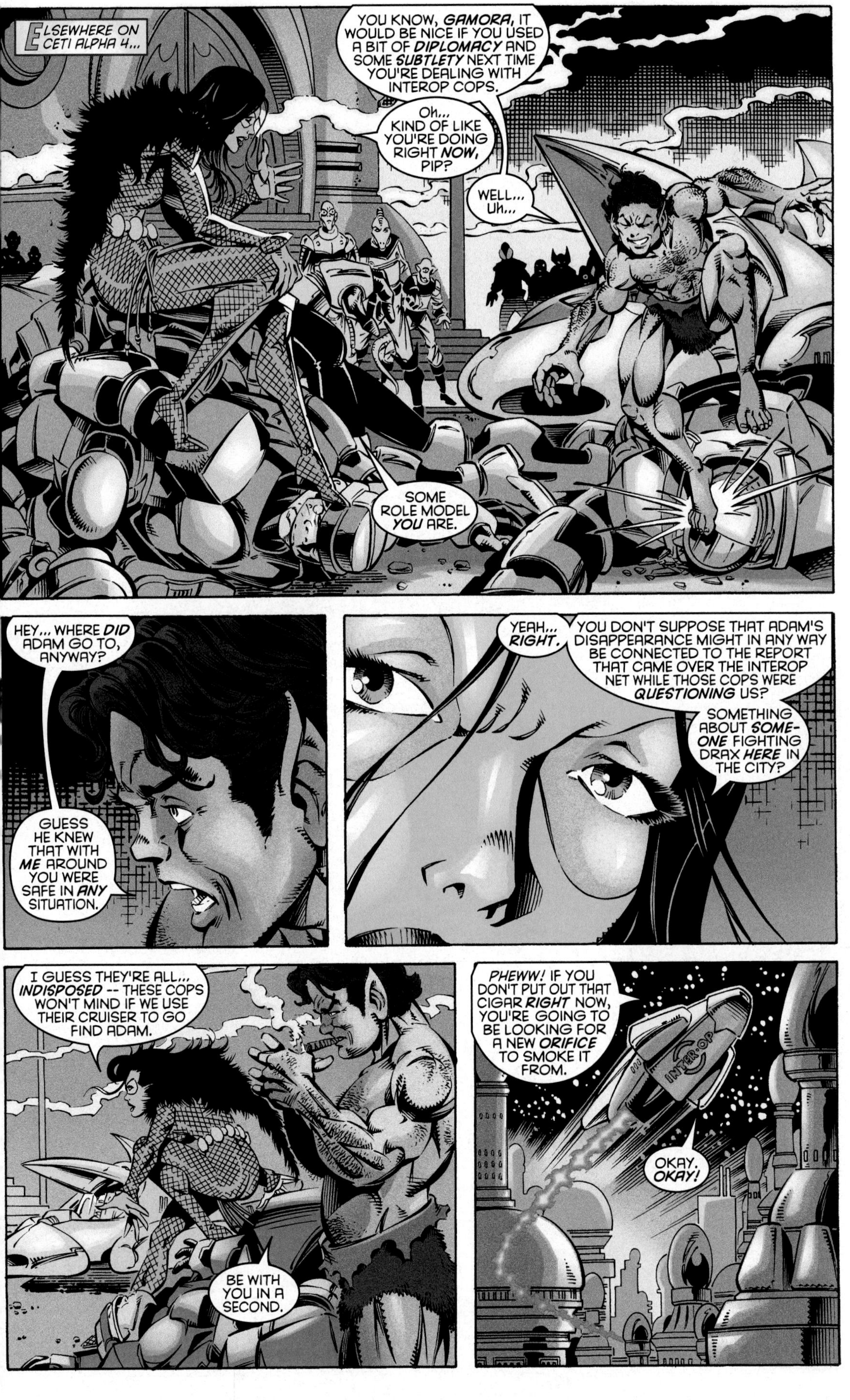
ELSEWHERE ON CETI ALPHA 4...
YOU KNOW, GAMORA, IT WOULD BE NICE IF YOU USED A BIT OF DIPLOMACY AND SOME SUBTLETY NEXT TIME YOU'RE DEALING WITH INTEROP COPS.
Oh... KIND OF LIKE YOU'RE DOING RIGHT NOW, PIP?
WELL... Uh...
SOME ROLE MODEL YOU ARE.
HEY... WHERE DID ADAM GO TO, ANYWAY?
GUESS HE KNEW THAT WITH ME AROUND YOU WERE SAFE IN ANY SITUATION.
YEAH... RIGHT.
YOU DON'T SUPPOSE THAT ADAM'S DISAPPEARANCE MIGHT IN ANY WAY BE CONNECTED TO THE REPORT THAT CAME OVER THE INTEROP NET WHILE THOSE COPS WERE QUESTIONING US?
SOMETHING ABOUT SOME-ONE FIGHTING DRAX HERE IN THE CITY?
I GUESS THEY'RE ALL... INDISPOSED -- THESE COPS WON'T MIND IF WE USE THEIR CRUISER TO GO FIND ADAM.
BE WITH YOU IN A SECOND.
PHEWW! IF YOU DON'T PUT OUT THAT CIGAR RIGHT NOW, YOU'RE GOING TO BE LOOKING FOR A NEW ORIFICE TO SMOKE IT FROM.
INTER-OP
OKAY. OKAY!

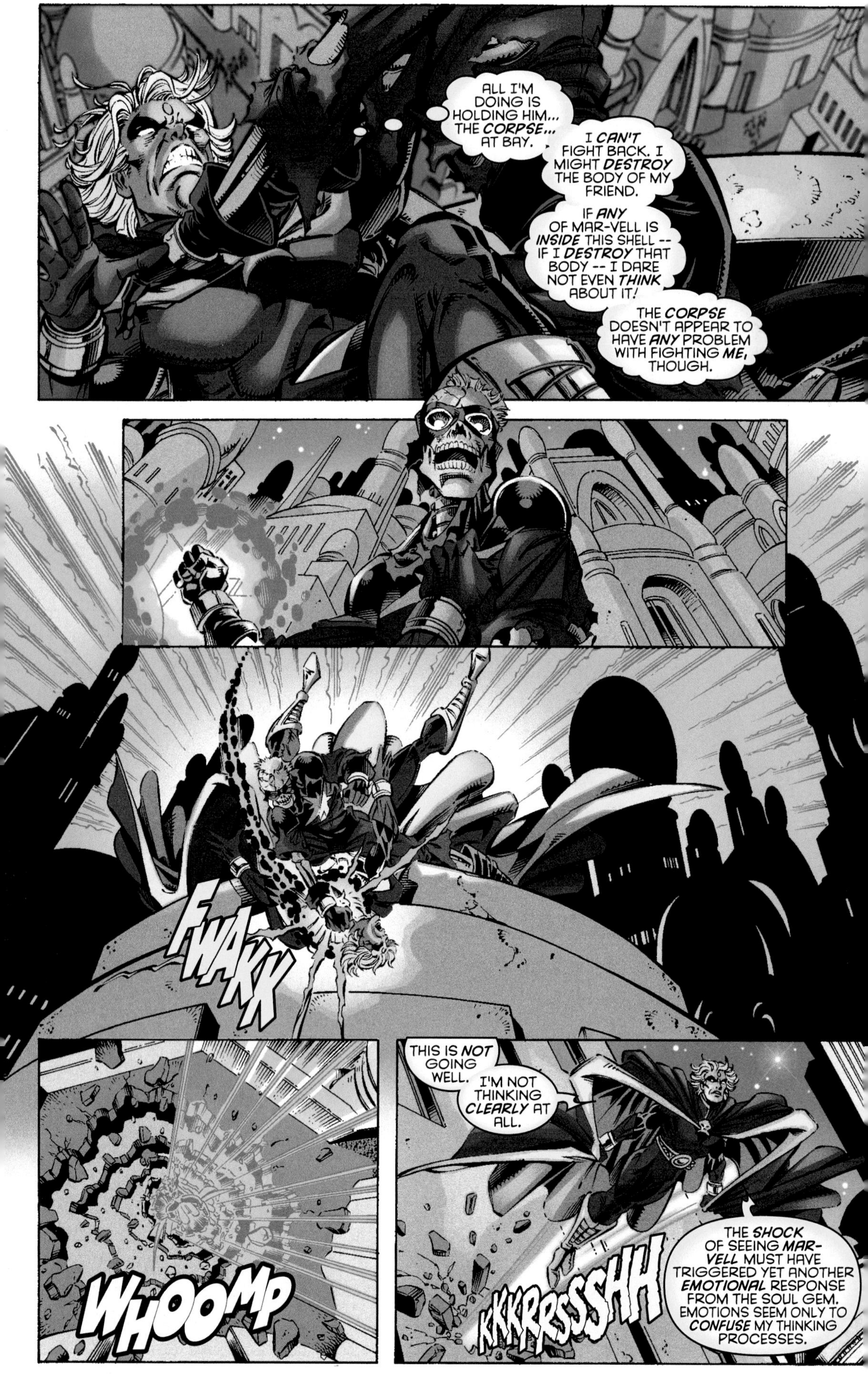
ALL I'M DOING IS HOLDING HIM... THE CORPSE... AT BAY.
I CAN'T FIGHT BACK. I MIGHT DESTROY THE BODY OF MY FRIEND.
IF ANY OF MAR-VELL IS INSIDE THIS SHELL -- IF I DESTROY THAT BODY -- I DARE NOT EVEN THINK ABOUT IT!
THE CORPSE DOESN'T APPEAR TO HAVE ANY PROBLEM WITH FIGHTING ME, THOUGH.
FWAKK
WHOOOMP
THIS IS NOT GOING WELL.
I'M NOT THINKING CLEARLY AT ALL.
KKKRRSSSHH
THE SHOCK OF SEEING MAR-VELL MUST HAVE TRIGGERED YET ANOTHER EMOTIONAL RESPONSE FROM THE SOUL GEM. EMOTIONS SEEM ONLY TO CONFUSE MY THINKING PROCESSES.

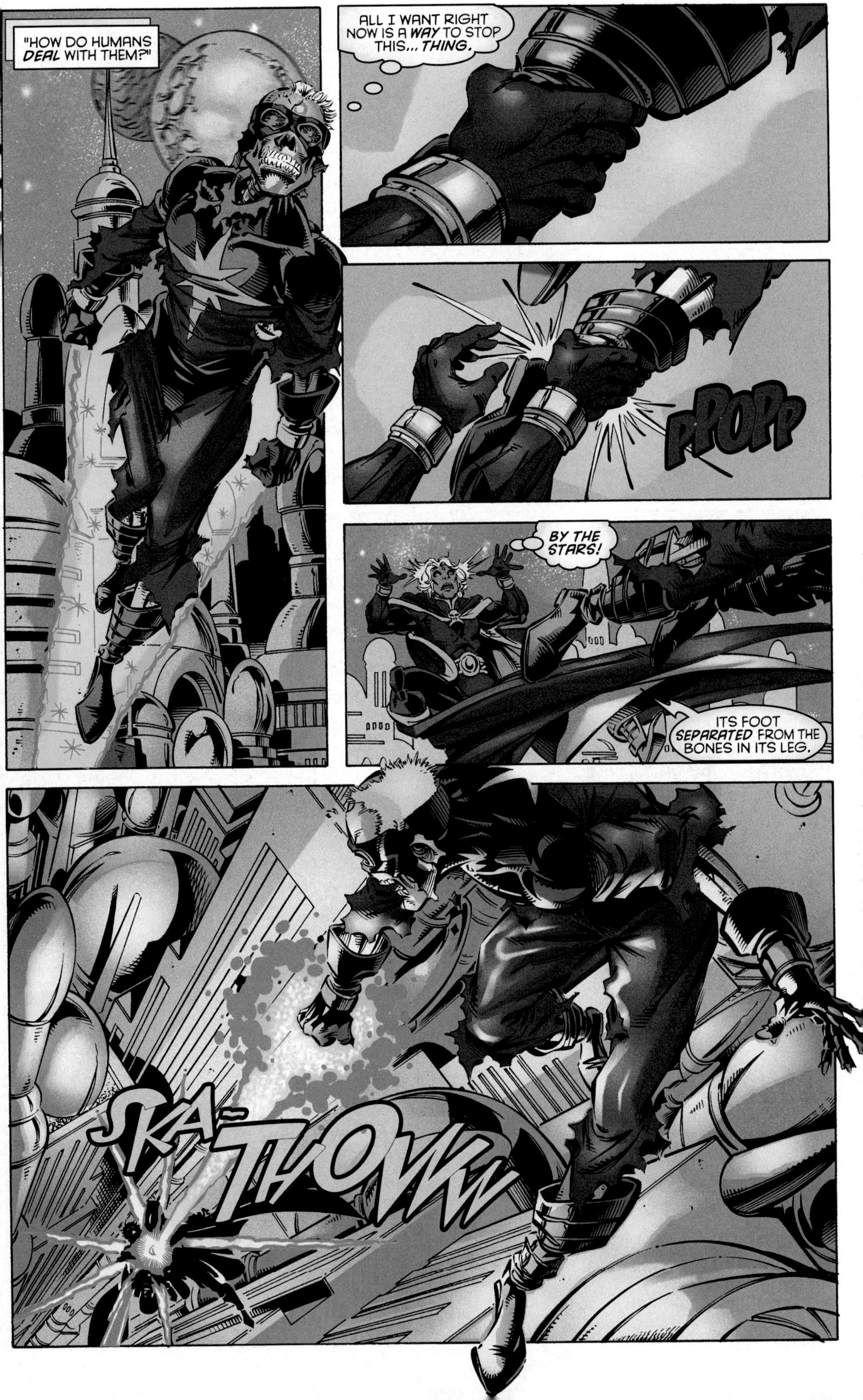
"HOW DO HUMANS DEAL WITH THEM?"
ALL I WANT RIGHT NOW IS A WAY TO STOP THIS... THING.
PPOPP
BY THE STARS!
ITS FOOT SEPARATED FROM THE BONES IN ITS LEG.
SKA-THOWW

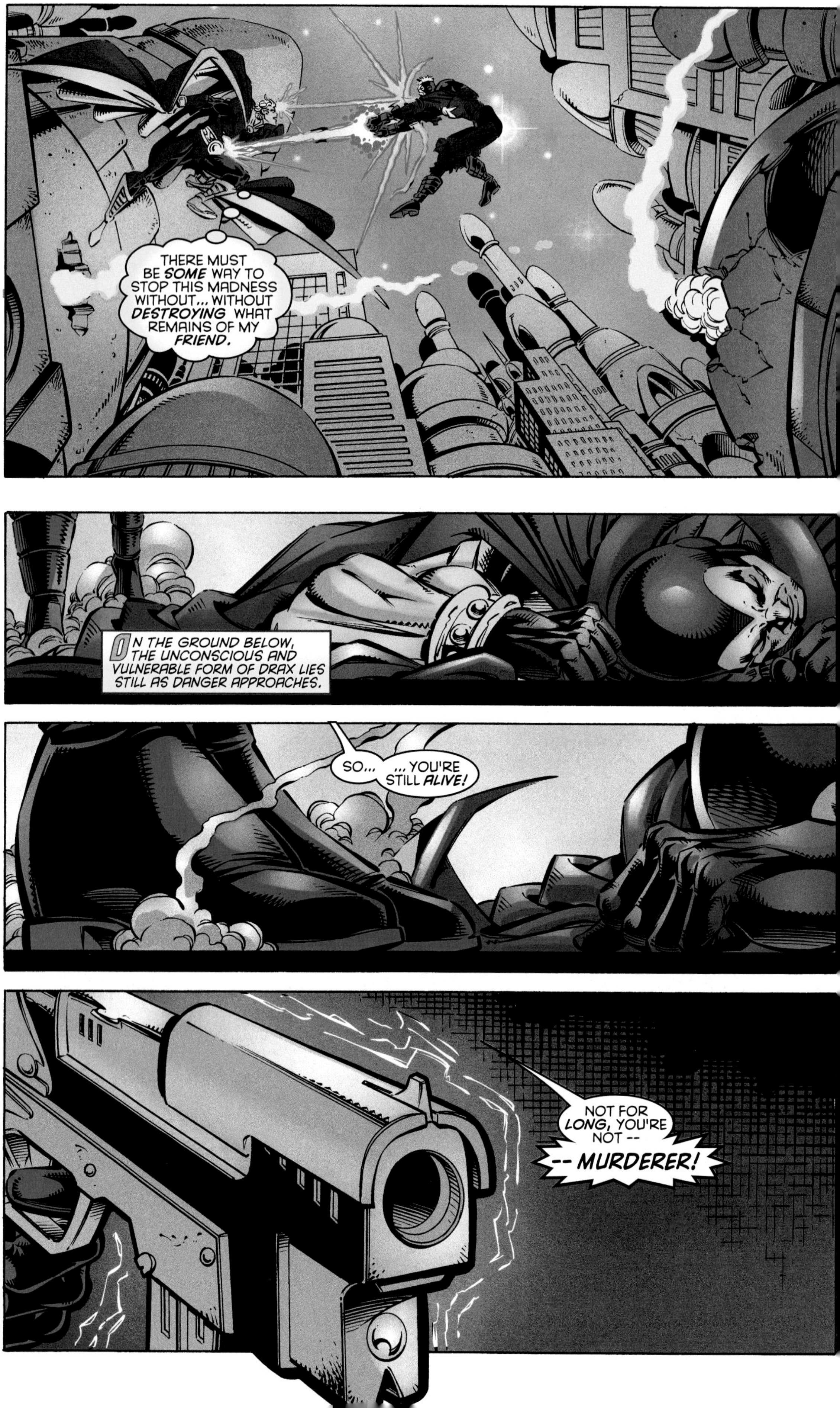
THERE MUST BE SOME WAY TO STOP THIS MADNESS WITHOUT... WITHOUT DESTROYING WHAT REMAINS OF MY FRIEND.
ON THE GROUND BELOW, THE UNCONSCIOUS AND VULNERABLE FORM OF DRAX LIES STILL AS DANGER APPROACHES.
SO...
...YOU'RE STILL ALIVE!
NOT FOR LONG, YOU'RE NOT --
-- MURDERER!

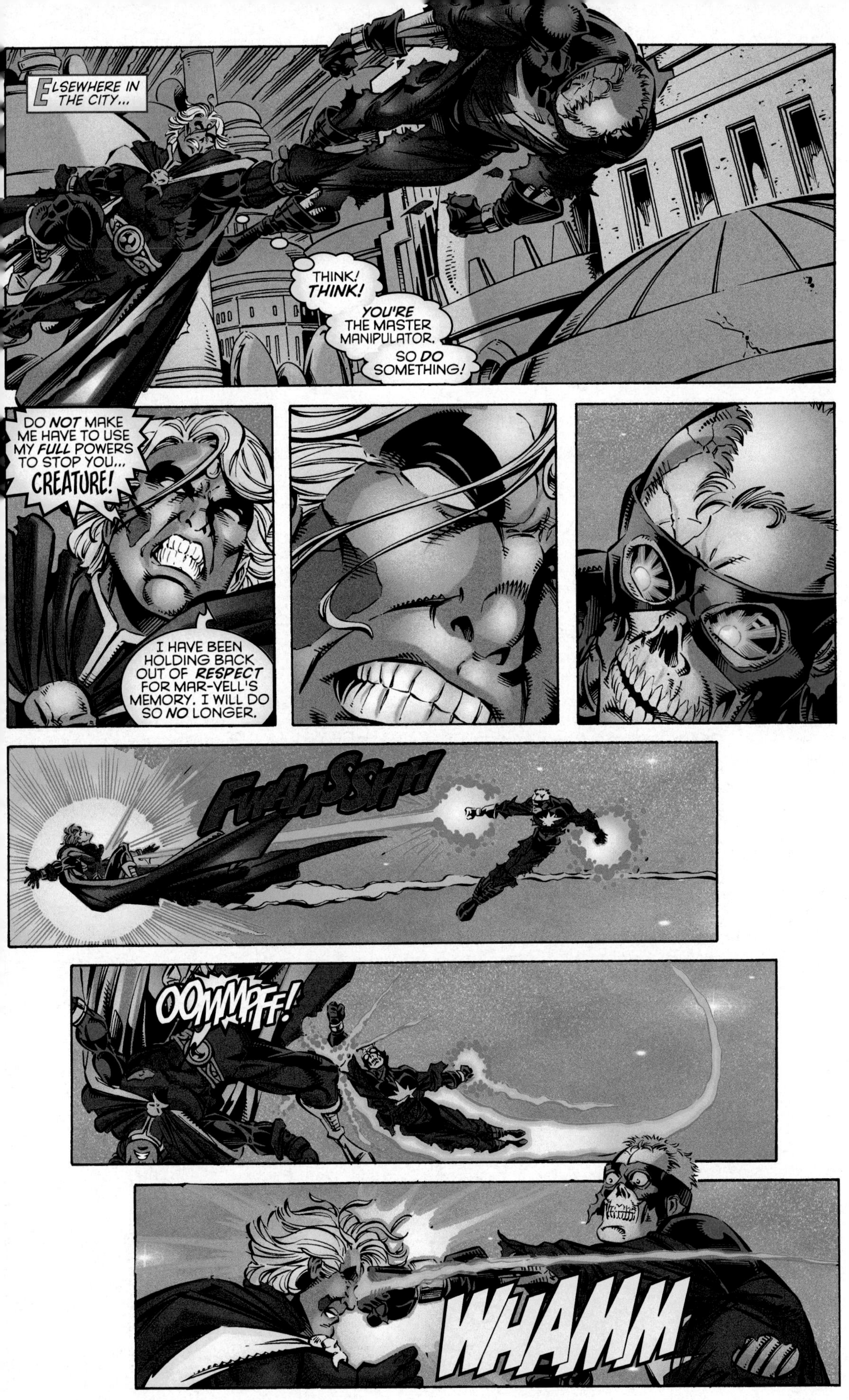
ELSEWHERE IN THE CITY...
THINK! THINK!
YOU'RE THE MASTER MANIPULATOR.
SO DO SOMETHING!
DO NOT MAKE ME HAVE TO USE MY FULL POWERS TO STOP YOU... CREATURE!
I HAVE BEEN HOLDING BACK OUT OF RESPECT FOR MAR-VELL'S MEMORY. I WILL DO SO NO LONGER.
FWAASSHH
OOMMPFF!
WHAMM

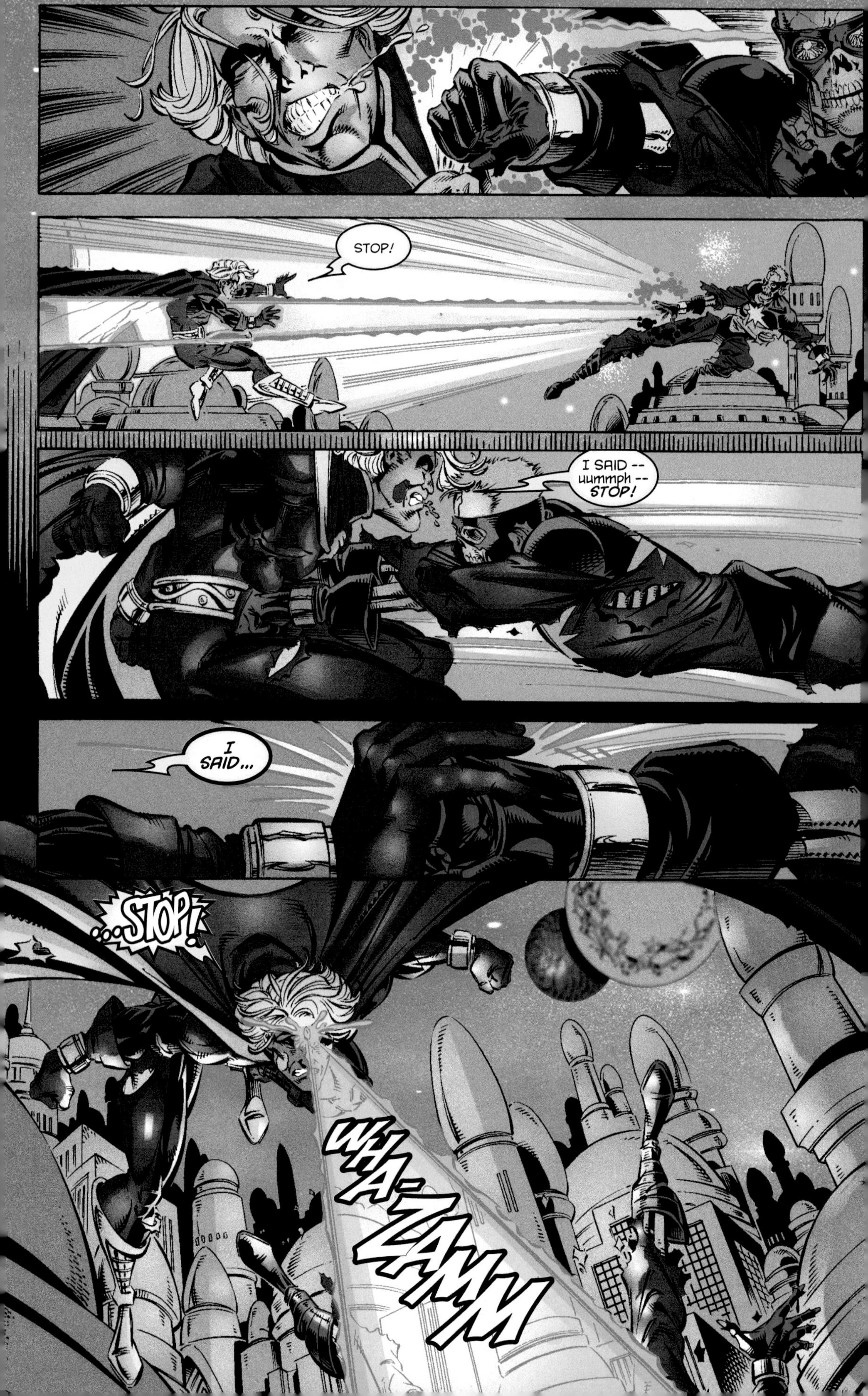
STOP!
I SAID -- uummph -- STOP!
I SAID...
...STOP!
WHA-ZAMM

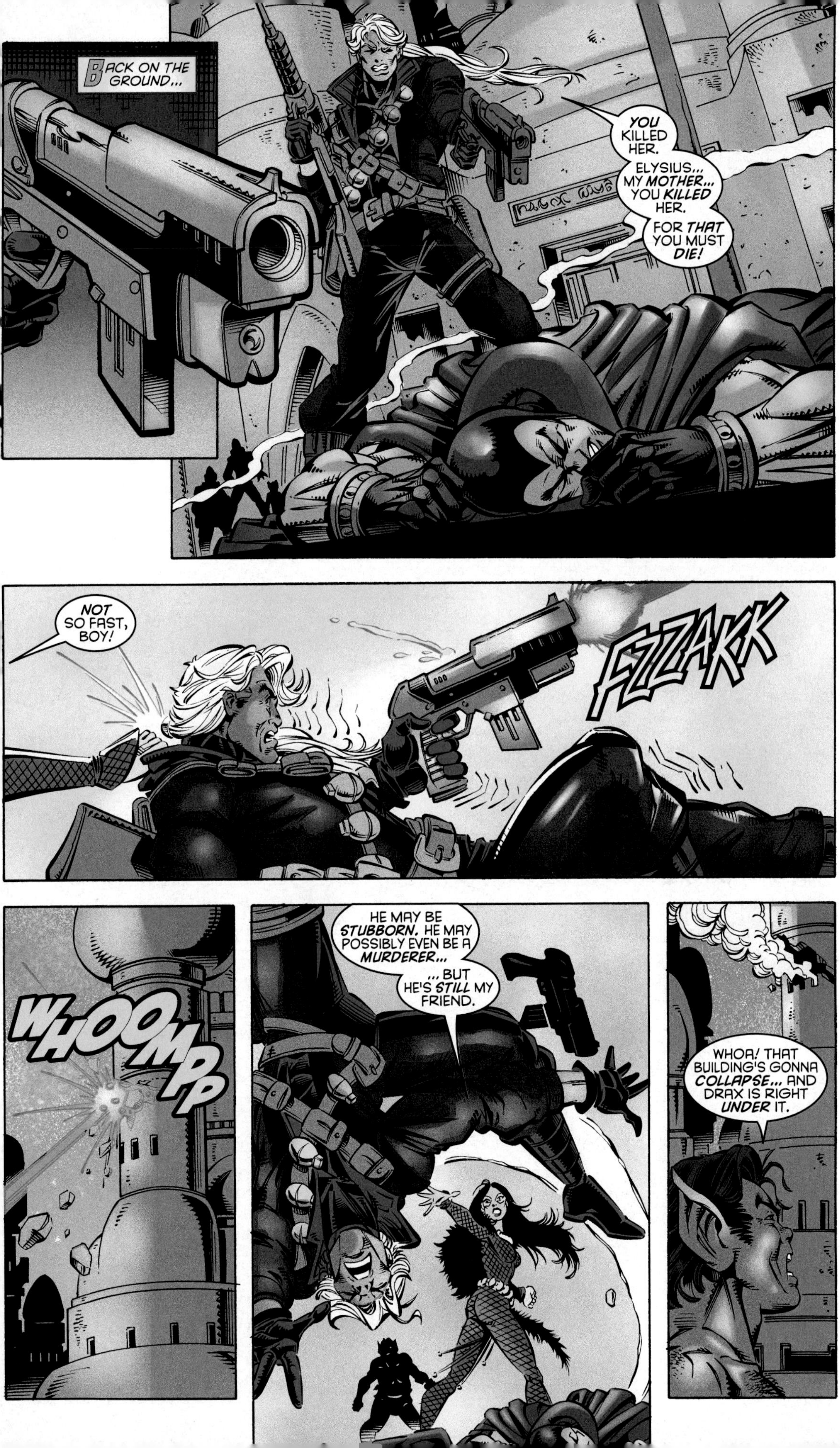
BACK ON THE GROUND...
YOU KILLED HER.
ELYSIUS... MY MOTHER... YOU KILLED HER.
FOR THAT YOU MUST DIE!
NOT SO FAST, BOY!
FZZAKK
WHOOMPP
HE MAY BE STUBBORN. HE MAY POSSIBLY EVEN BE A MURDERER...
... BUT HE'S STILL MY FRIEND.
WHOA! THAT BUILDING'S GONNA COLLAPSE... AND DRAX IS RIGHT UNDER IT.

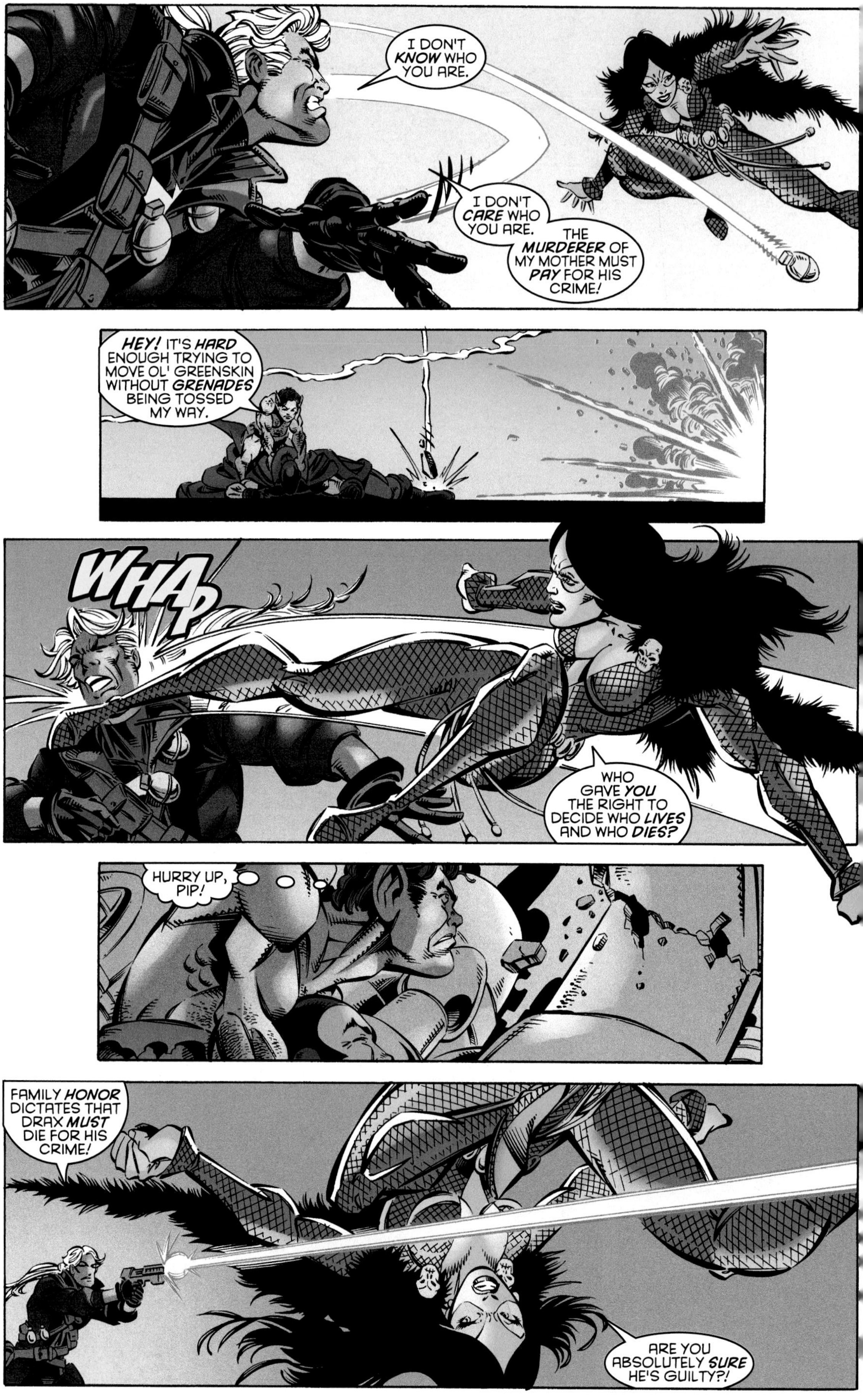

I DON'T KNOW WHO YOU ARE.
I DON'T CARE WHO YOU ARE.
THE MURDERER OF MY MOTHER MUST PAY FOR HIS CRIME!
HEY! IT'S HARD ENOUGH TRYING TO MOVE OL' GREENSKIN WITHOUT GRENADES BEING TOSSED MY WAY.
WHAP
WHO GAVE YOU THE RIGHT TO DECIDE WHO LIVES AND WHO DIES?
HURRY UP, PIP!
FAMILY HONOR DICTATES THAT DRAX MUST DIE FOR HIS CRIME!
ARE YOU ABSOLUTELY SURE HE'S GUILTY?!

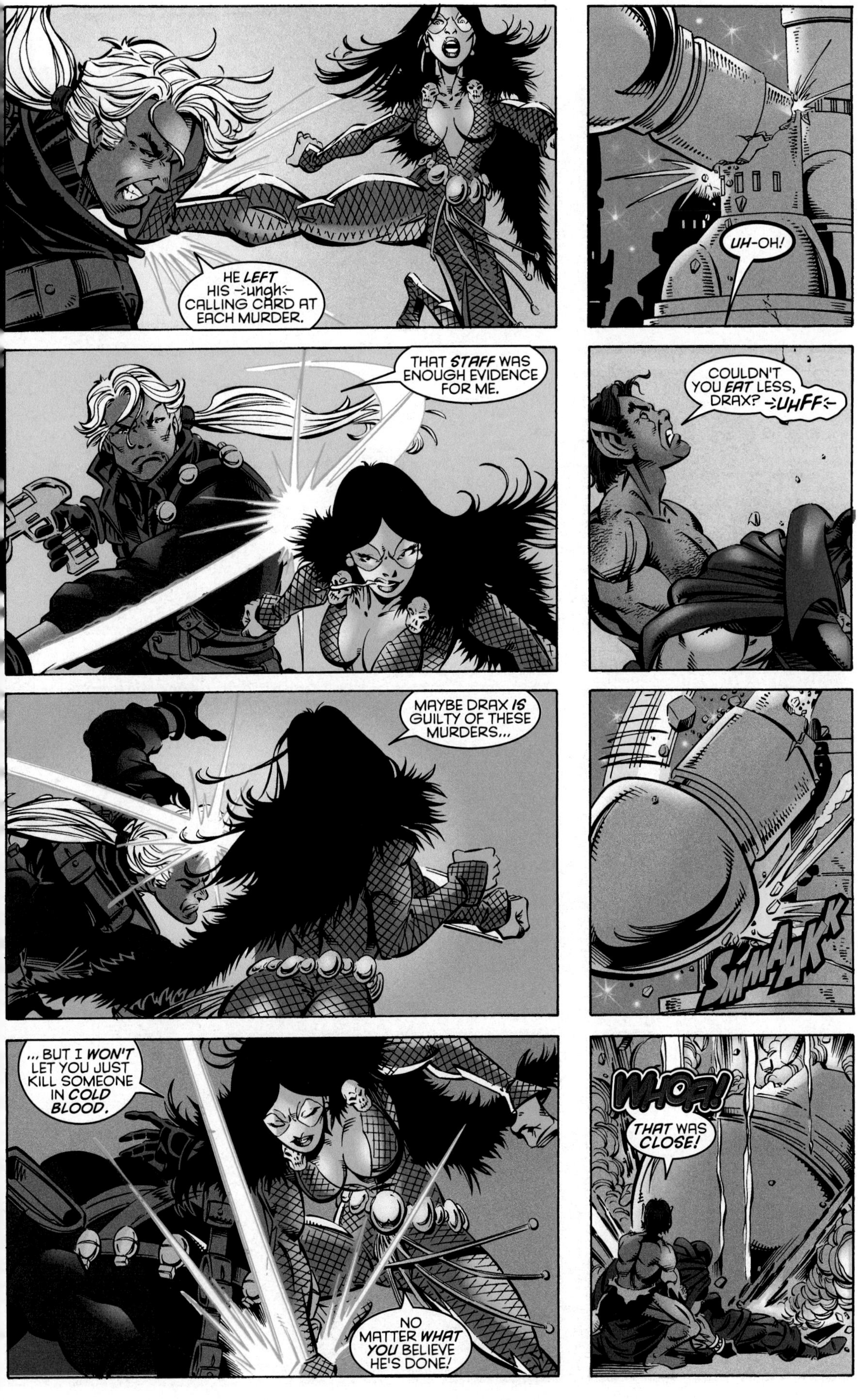
HE LEFT HIS -ungh- CALLING CARD AT EACH MURDER.
UH-OH!
THAT STAFF WAS ENOUGH EVIDENCE FOR ME.
COULDN'T YOU EAT LESS, DRAX? -UHFF-
MAYBE DRAX IS GUILTY OF THESE MURDERS...
SMMAAKK
...BUT I WON'T LET YOU JUST KILL SOMEONE IN COLD BLOOD.
NO MATTER WHAT YOU BELIEVE HE'S DONE!
WHOA!
THAT WAS CLOSE!

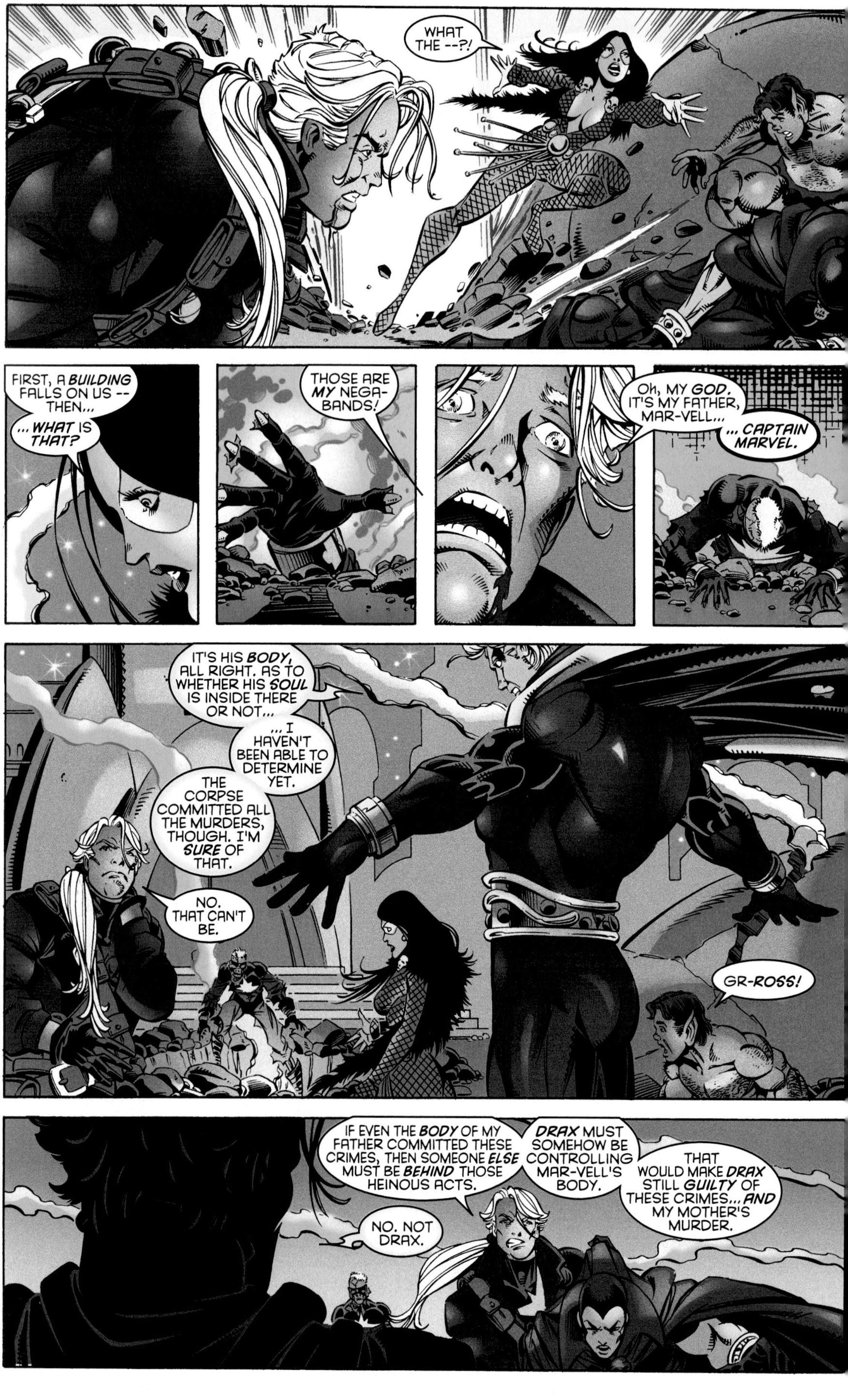
WHAT THE --?!
FIRST, A BUILDING FALLS ON US -- THEN...
...WHAT IS THAT?
THOSE ARE MY NEGA-BANDS!
Oh, MY GOD. IT'S MY FATHER, MAR-VELL...
...CAPTAIN MARVEL.
IT'S HIS BODY, ALL RIGHT. AS TO WHETHER HIS SOUL IS INSIDE THERE OR NOT...
...I HAVEN'T BEEN ABLE TO DETERMINE YET.
THE CORPSE COMMITTED ALL THE MURDERS, THOUGH. I'M SURE OF THAT.
NO. THAT CAN'T BE.
GR-ROSS!
IF EVEN THE BODY OF MY FATHER COMMITTED THESE CRIMES, THEN SOMEONE ELSE MUST BE BEHIND THOSE HEINOUS ACTS.
DRAX MUST SOMEHOW BE CONTROLLING MAR-VELL'S BODY.
THAT WOULD MAKE DRAX STILL GUILTY OF THESE CRIMES... AND MY MOTHER'S MURDER.
NO. NOT DRAX.

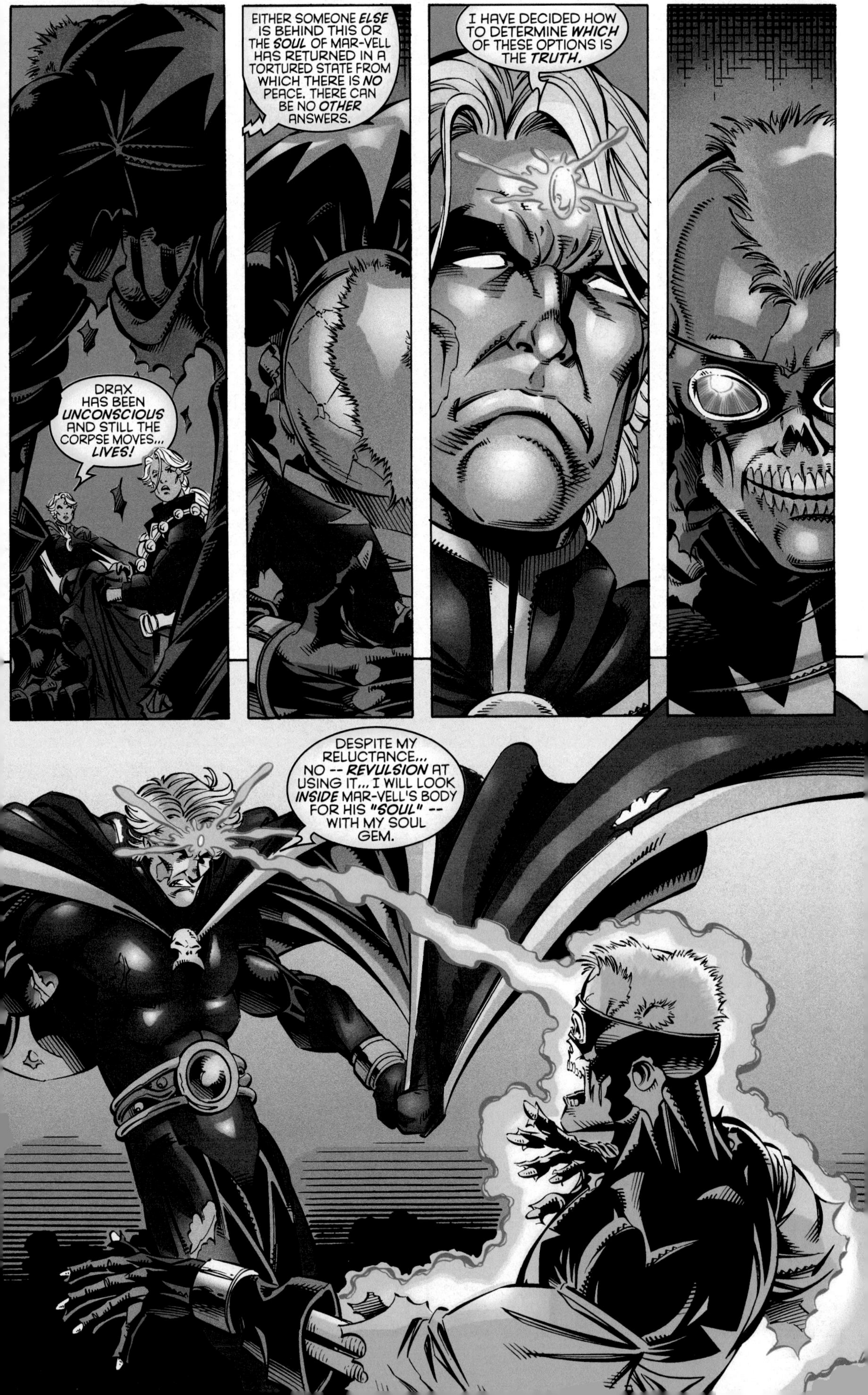
DRAX HAS BEEN UNCONSCIOUS AND STILL THE CORPSE MOVES... LIVES!
EITHER SOMEONE ELSE IS BEHIND THIS OR THE SOUL OF MAR-VELL HAS RETURNED IN A TORTURED STATE FROM WHICH THERE IS NO PEACE. THERE CAN BE NO OTHER ANSWERS.
I HAVE DECIDED HOW TO DETERMINE WHICH OF THESE OPTIONS IS THE TRUTH.
DESPITE MY RELUCTANCE... NO -- REVULSION AT USING IT... I WILL LOOK INSIDE MAR-VELL'S BODY FOR HIS "SOUL" -- WITH MY SOUL GEM.

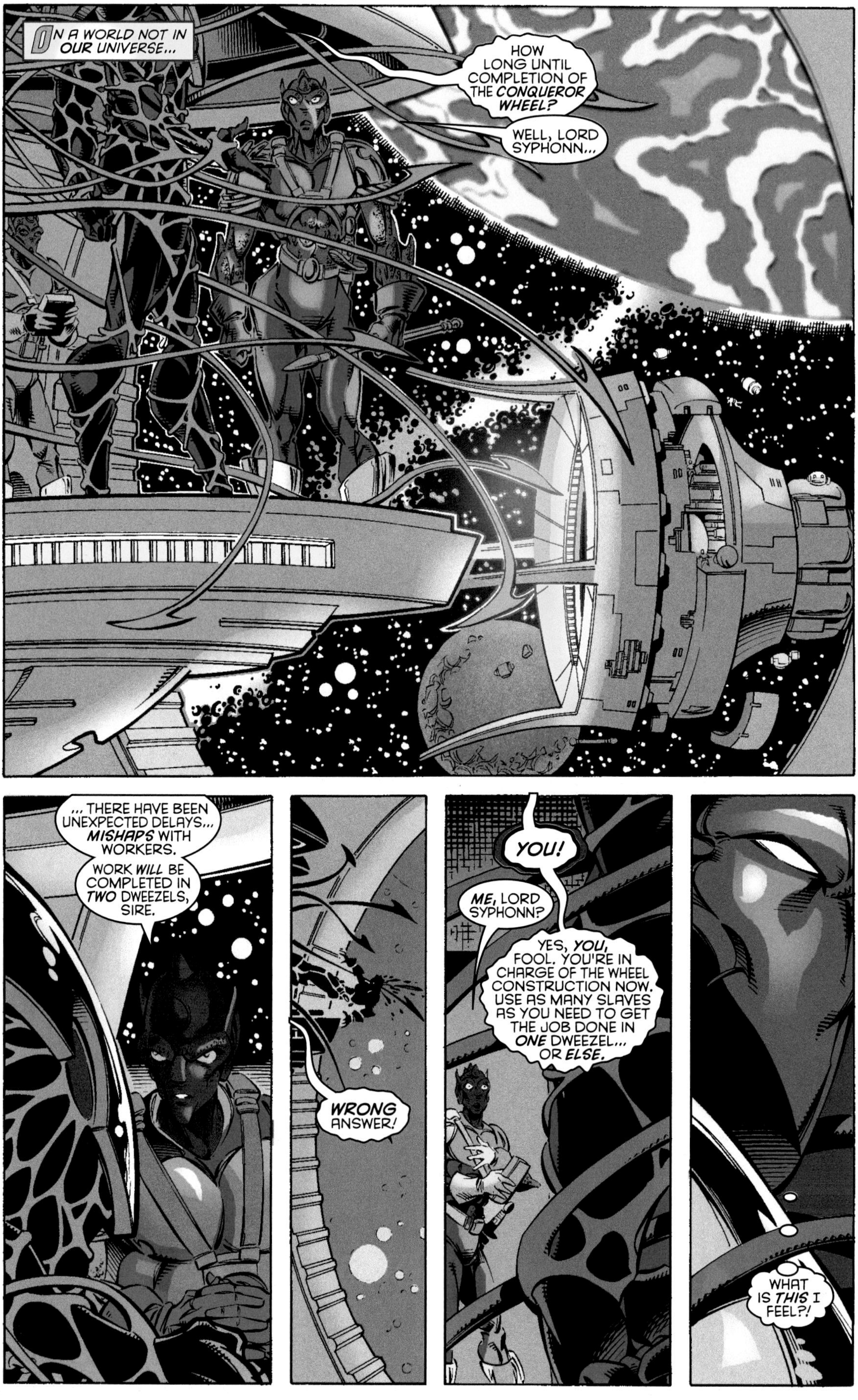
ON A WORLD NOT IN OUR UNIVERSE...
HOW LONG UNTIL COMPLETION OF THE CONQUEROR WHEEL?
WELL, LORD SYPHONN...
...THERE HAVE BEEN UNEXPECTED DELAYS... MISHAPS WITH WORKERS.
WORK WILL BE COMPLETED IN TWO DWEEZELS, SIRE.
WRONG ANSWER!
YOU!
ME, LORD SYPHONN?
YES, YOU, FOOL. YOU'RE IN CHARGE OF THE WHEEL CONSTRUCTION NOW. USE AS MANY SLAVES AS YOU NEED TO GET THE JOB DONE IN ONE DWEEZEL... OR ELSE.
WHAT IS THIS I FEEL?!

"SOMEONE *REACHES* OUT TO ME THROUGH ONE OF MY POWER PORTALS."

MAR-VELL... IS *NOT* HERE. HIS SOUL HAS DEPARTED *LONG* AGO.

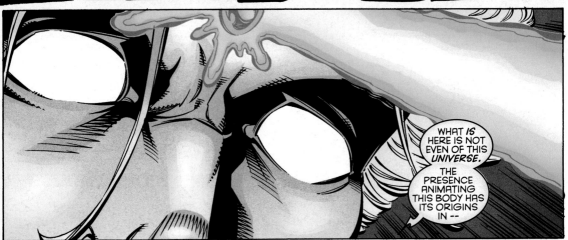

WHO *DARES* TO...?!

WHAT *IS* HERE IS NOT EVEN OF THIS *UNIVERSE.*

THE PRESENCE ANIMATING THIS BODY HAS ITS ORIGINS IN --

"-- THE *NEGATIVE ZONE!*"

KNOW THEN THE *WRATH* OF --

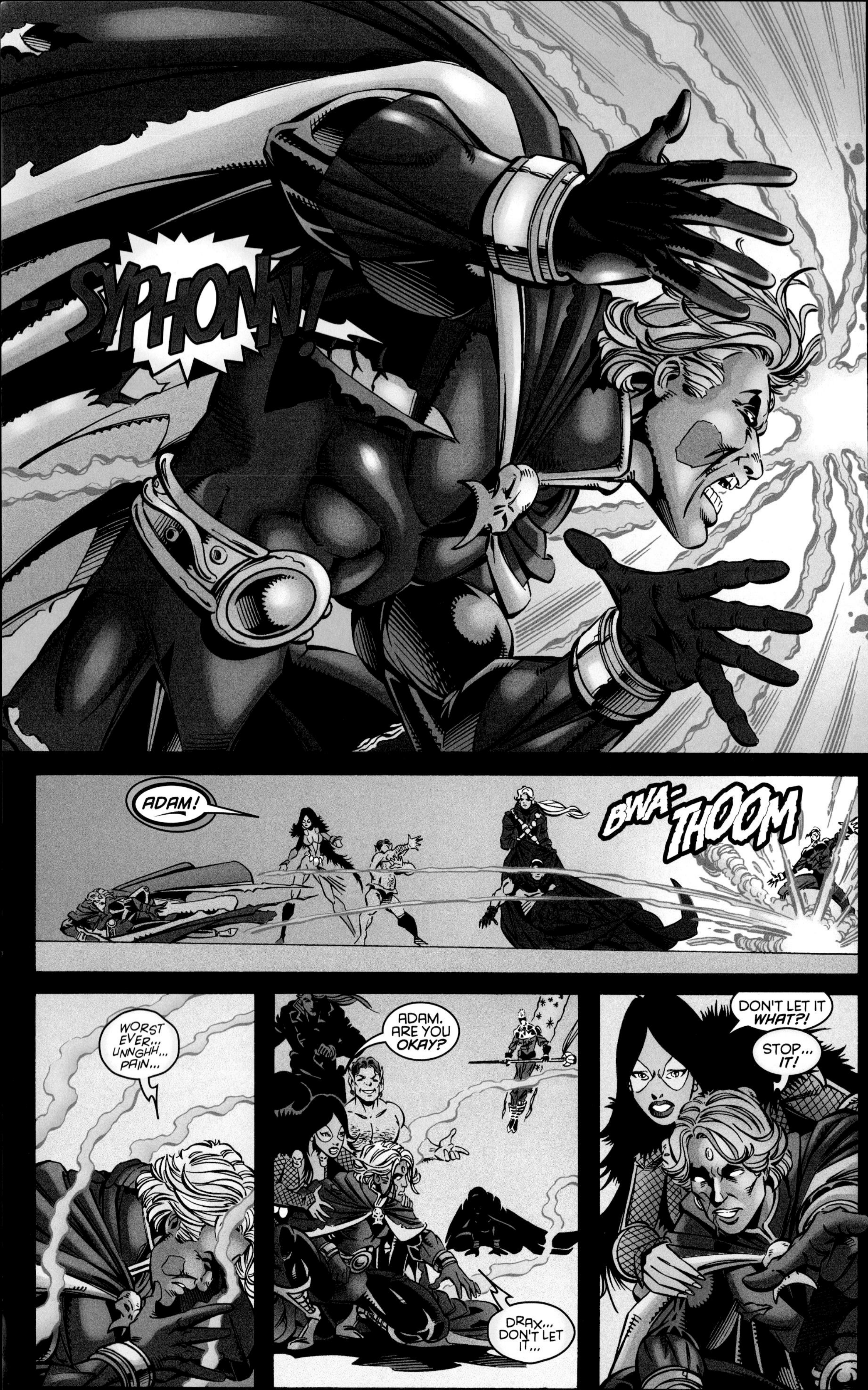
SYPHONN!
ADAM!
BWA-THOOM
WORST EVER... UNNGHH... PAIN...
ADAM. ARE YOU OKAY?
DRAX... DON'T LET IT...
DON'T LET IT WHAT?!
STOP... IT!

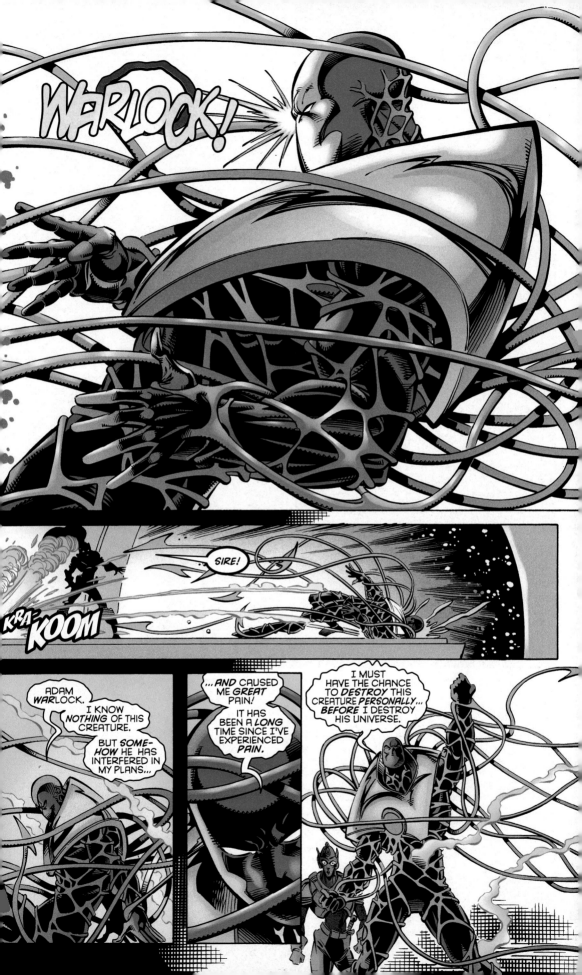

WARLOCK!

KRA KOOM

SIRE!

ADAM WARLOCK. I KNOW *NOTHING* OF THIS CREATURE.

BUT *SOMEHOW* HE HAS INTERFERED IN MY PLANS...

...AND CAUSED ME *GREAT* PAIN!

IT HAS BEEN A *LONG* TIME SINCE I'VE EXPERIENCED *PAIN.*

I MUST HAVE THE CHANCE TO *DESTROY* THIS CREATURE *PERSONALLY*... *BEFORE* I DESTROY HIS UNIVERSE.

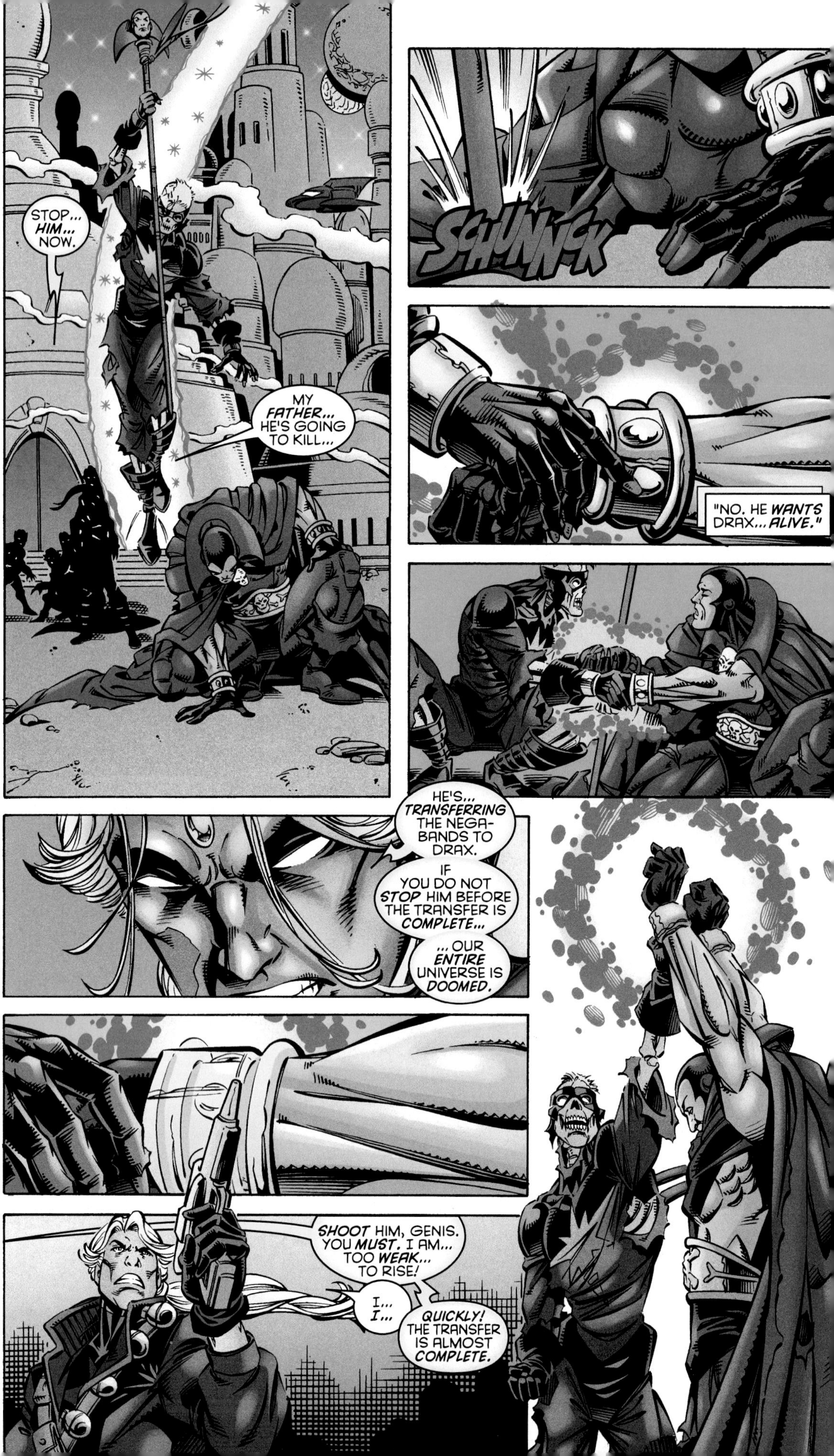
STOP... HIM... NOW.
MY FATHER... HE'S GOING TO KILL...
SCHUNNCK
"NO. HE WANTS DRAX... ALIVE."
HE'S... TRANSFERRING THE NEGA-BANDS TO DRAX.
IF YOU DO NOT STOP HIM BEFORE THE TRANSFER IS COMPLETE...
...OUR ENTIRE UNIVERSE IS DOOMED.
SHOOT HIM, GENIS. YOU MUST. I AM... TOO WEAK... TO RISE!
I... I...
QUICKLY! THE TRANSFER IS ALMOST COMPLETE.

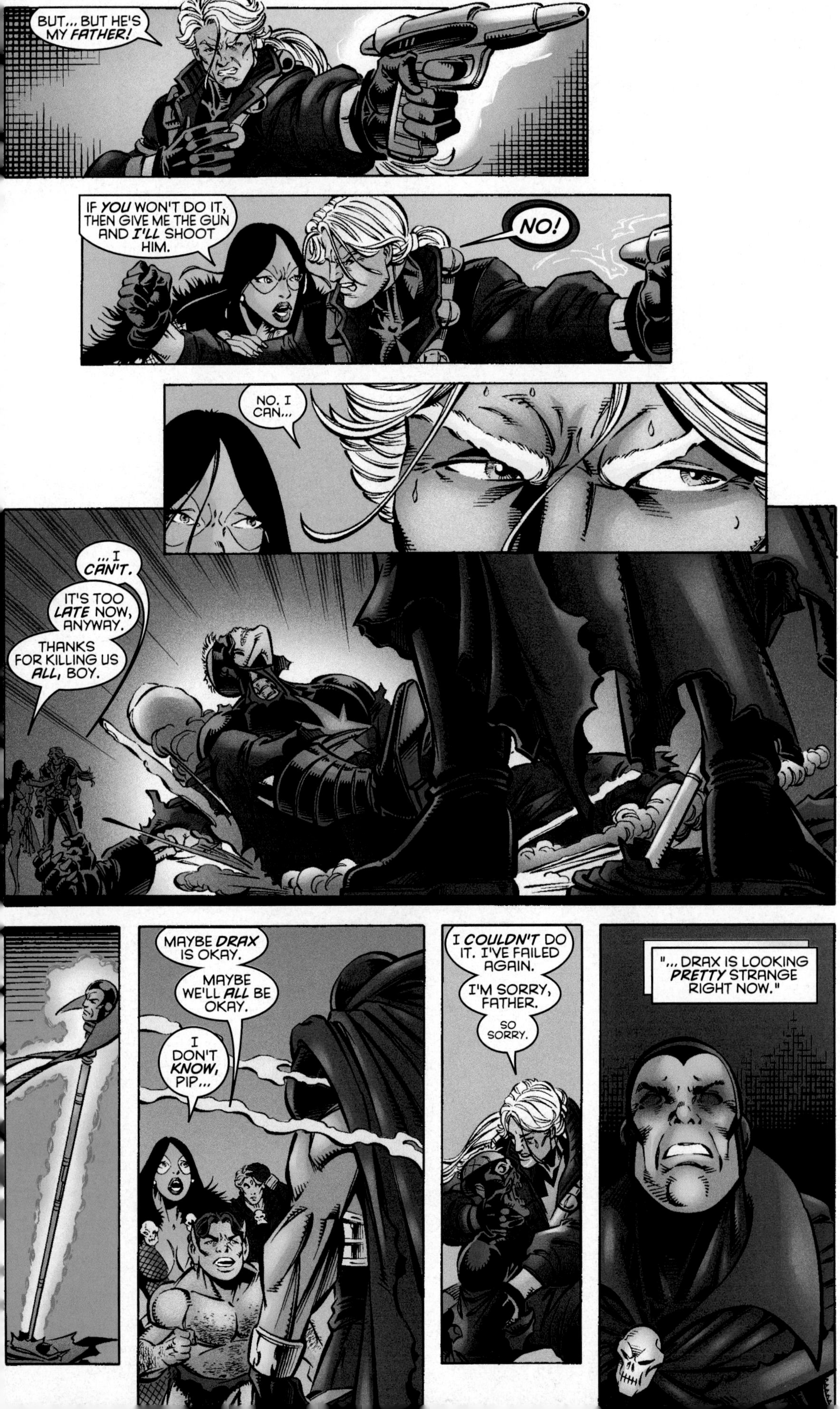
BUT... BUT HE'S MY FATHER!
IF YOU WON'T DO IT, THEN GIVE ME THE GUN AND I'LL SHOOT HIM.
NO!
NO. I CAN...
...I CAN'T.
IT'S TOO LATE NOW, ANYWAY.
THANKS FOR KILLING US ALL, BOY.
MAYBE DRAX IS OKAY.
MAYBE WE'LL ALL BE OKAY.
I DON'T KNOW, PIP...
I COULDN'T DO IT. I'VE FAILED AGAIN.
I'M SORRY, FATHER.
SO SORRY.
"...DRAX IS LOOKING PRETTY STRANGE RIGHT NOW."

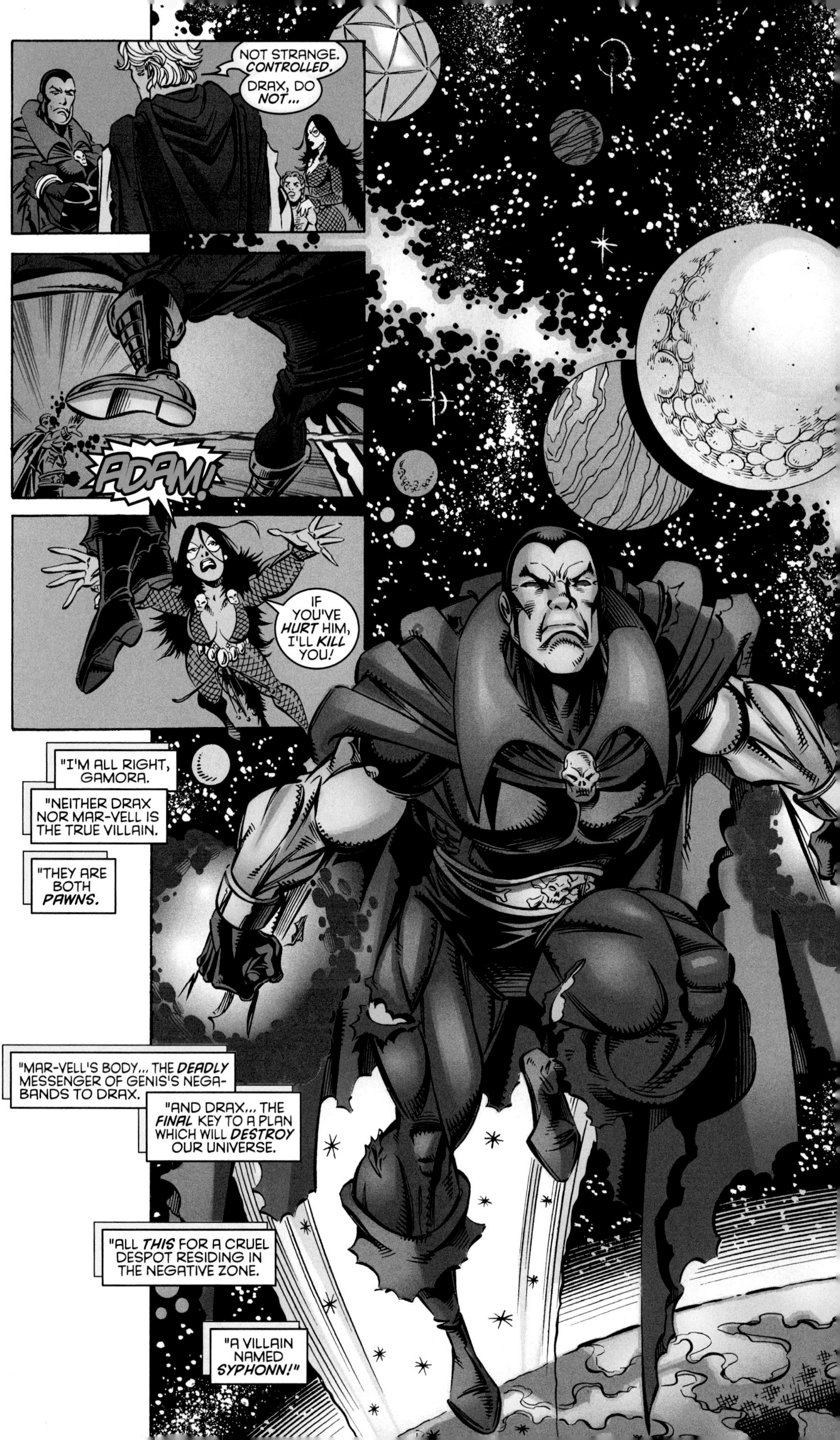
NOT STRANGE. CONTROLLED.
DRAX, DO NOT...
ADAM!
IF YOU'VE HURT HIM, I'LL KILL YOU!
"I'M ALL RIGHT, GAMORA.
"NEITHER DRAX NOR MAR-VELL IS THE TRUE VILLAIN.
"THEY ARE BOTH PAWNS.
"MAR-VELL'S BODY... THE DEADLY MESSENGER OF GENIS'S NEGA-BANDS TO DRAX.
"AND DRAX... THE FINAL KEY TO A PLAN WHICH WILL DESTROY OUR UNIVERSE.
"ALL THIS FOR A CRUEL DESPOT RESIDING IN THE NEGATIVE ZONE.
"A VILLAIN NAMED SYPHONN!"

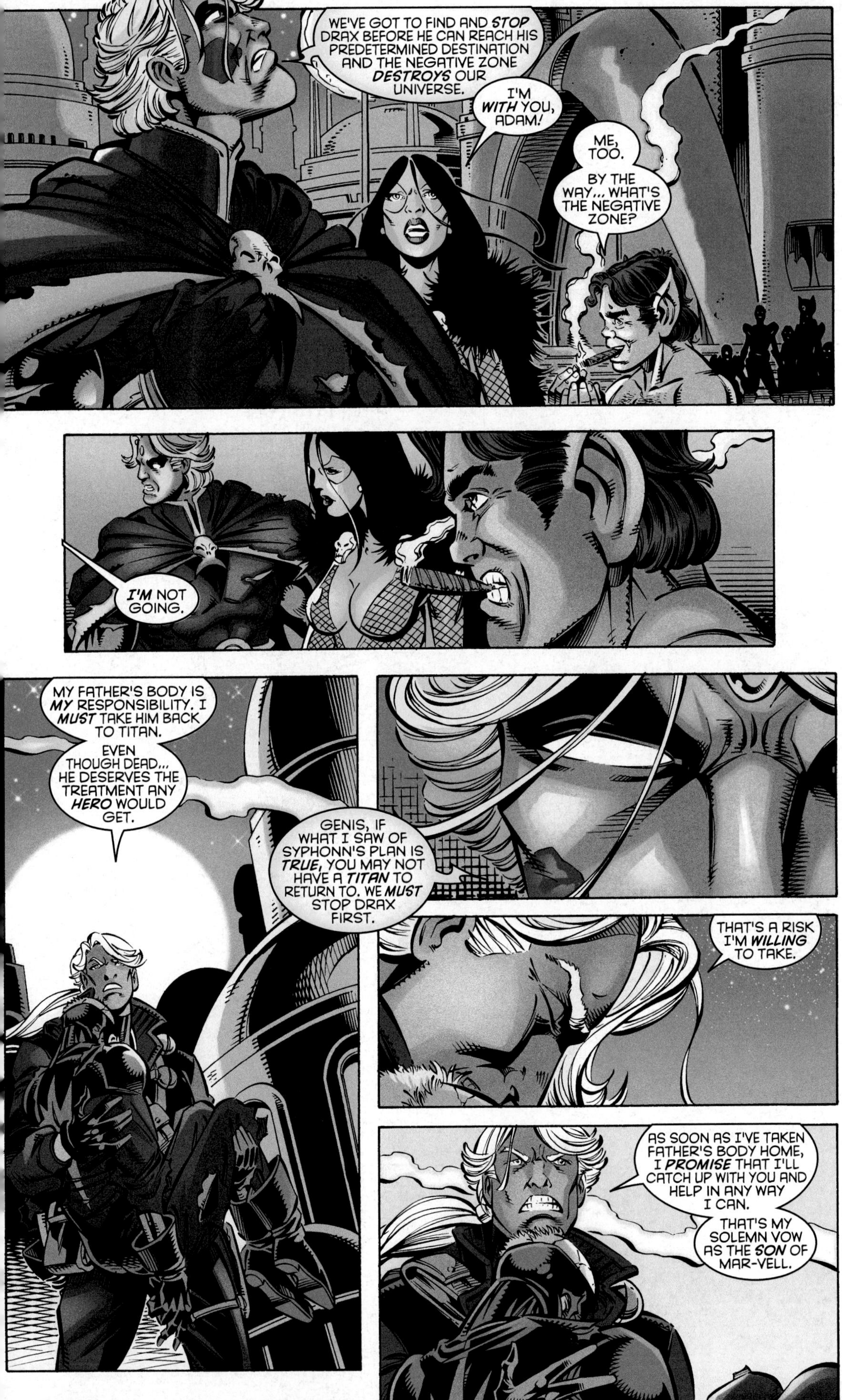

WE'VE GOT TO FIND AND STOP DRAX BEFORE HE CAN REACH HIS PREDETERMINED DESTINATION AND THE NEGATIVE ZONE DESTROYS OUR UNIVERSE.
I'M WITH YOU, ADAM!
ME, TOO.
BY THE WAY... WHAT'S THE NEGATIVE ZONE?
I'M NOT GOING.
MY FATHER'S BODY IS MY RESPONSIBILITY. I MUST TAKE HIM BACK TO TITAN.
EVEN THOUGH DEAD... HE DESERVES THE TREATMENT ANY HERO WOULD GET.
GENIS, IF WHAT I SAW OF SYPHONN'S PLAN IS TRUE, YOU MAY NOT HAVE A TITAN TO RETURN TO. WE MUST STOP DRAX FIRST.
THAT'S A RISK I'M WILLING TO TAKE.
AS SOON AS I'VE TAKEN FATHER'S BODY HOME, I PROMISE THAT I'LL CATCH UP WITH YOU AND HELP IN ANY WAY I CAN.
THAT'S MY SOLEMN VOW AS THE SON OF MAR-VELL.

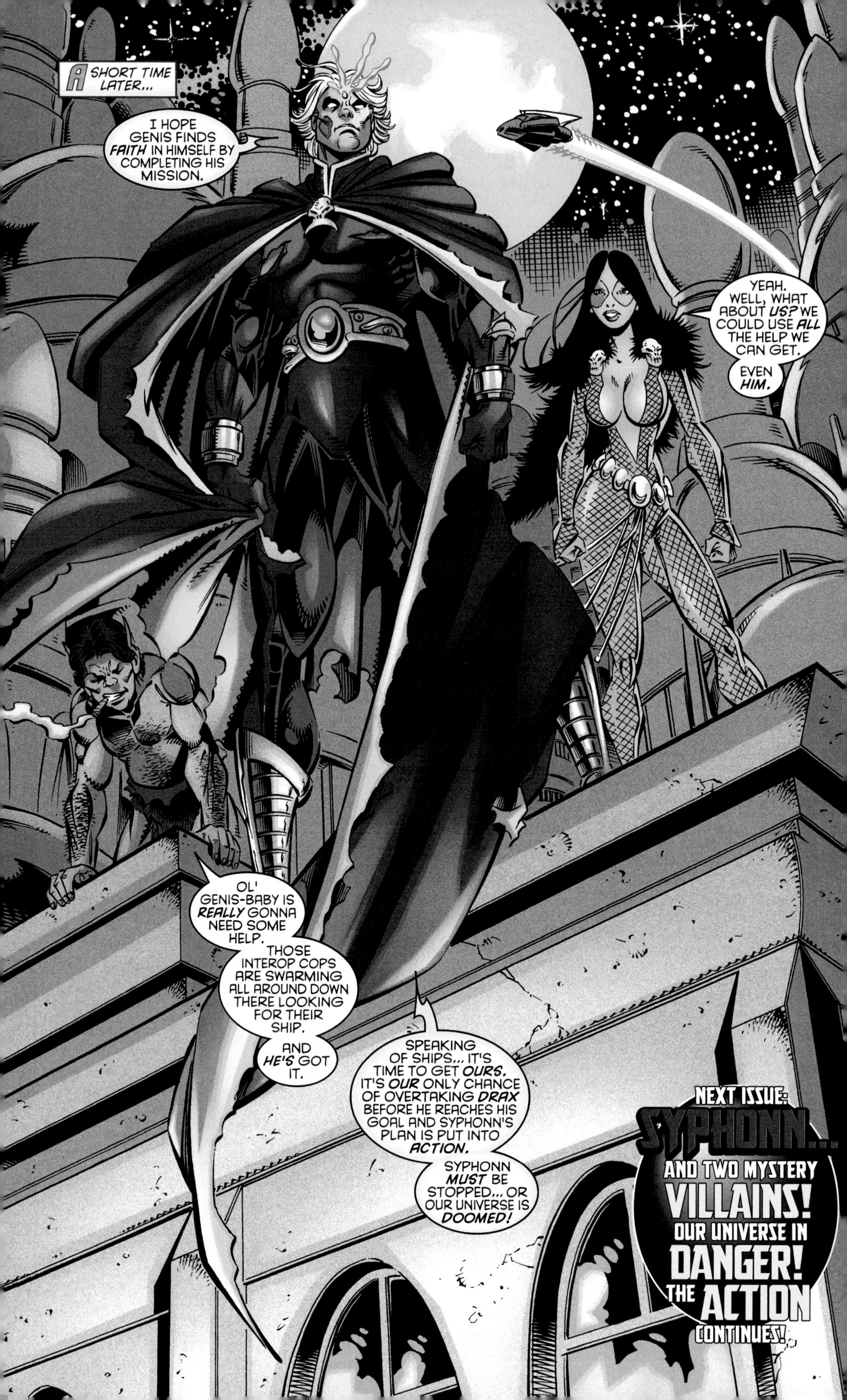
A SHORT TIME LATER...
I HOPE GENIS FINDS FAITH IN HIMSELF BY COMPLETING HIS MISSION.
YEAH. WELL, WHAT ABOUT US? WE COULD USE ALL THE HELP WE CAN GET.
EVEN HIM.
OL' GENIS-BABY IS REALLY GONNA NEED SOME HELP.
THOSE INTEROP COPS ARE SWARMING ALL AROUND DOWN THERE LOOKING FOR THEIR SHIP.
AND HE'S GOT IT.
SPEAKING OF SHIPS... IT'S TIME TO GET OURS. IT'S OUR ONLY CHANCE OF OVERTAKING DRAX BEFORE HE REACHES HIS GOAL AND SYPHONN'S PLAN IS PUT INTO ACTION.
SYPHONN MUST BE STOPPED... OR OUR UNIVERSE IS DOOMED!
NEXT ISSUE: SYPHONN... AND TWO MYSTERY VILLAINS! OUR UNIVERSE IN DANGER! THE ACTION CONTINUES!

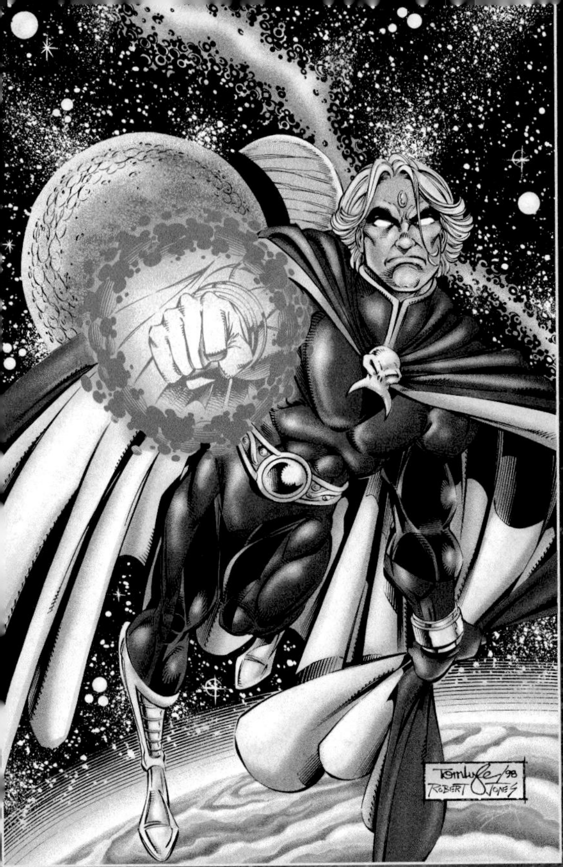
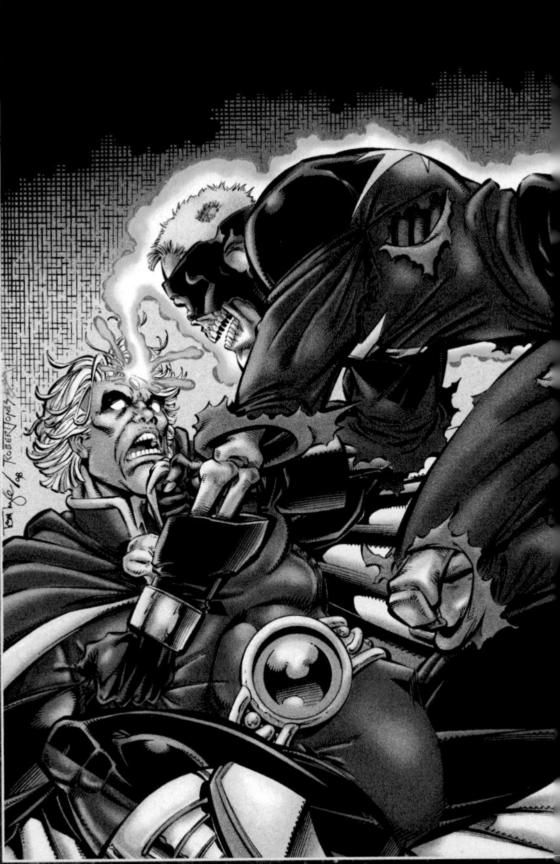
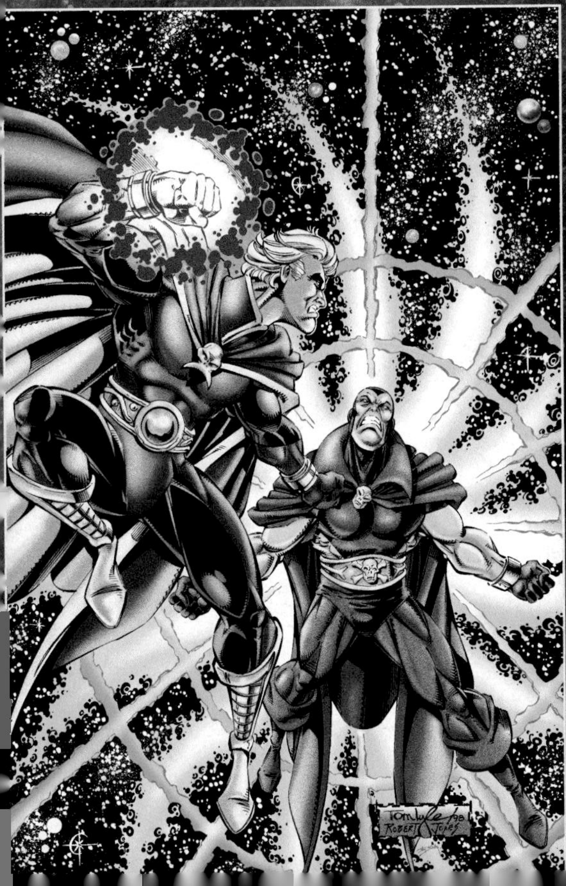
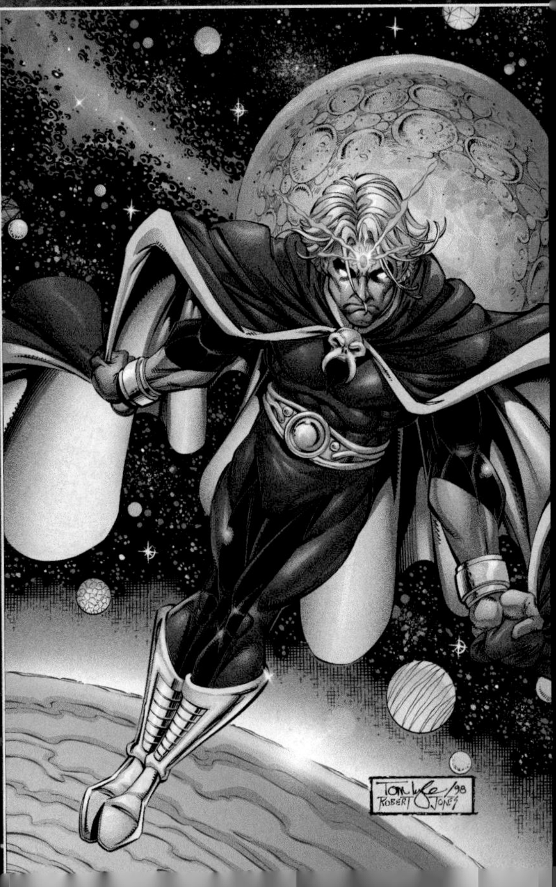

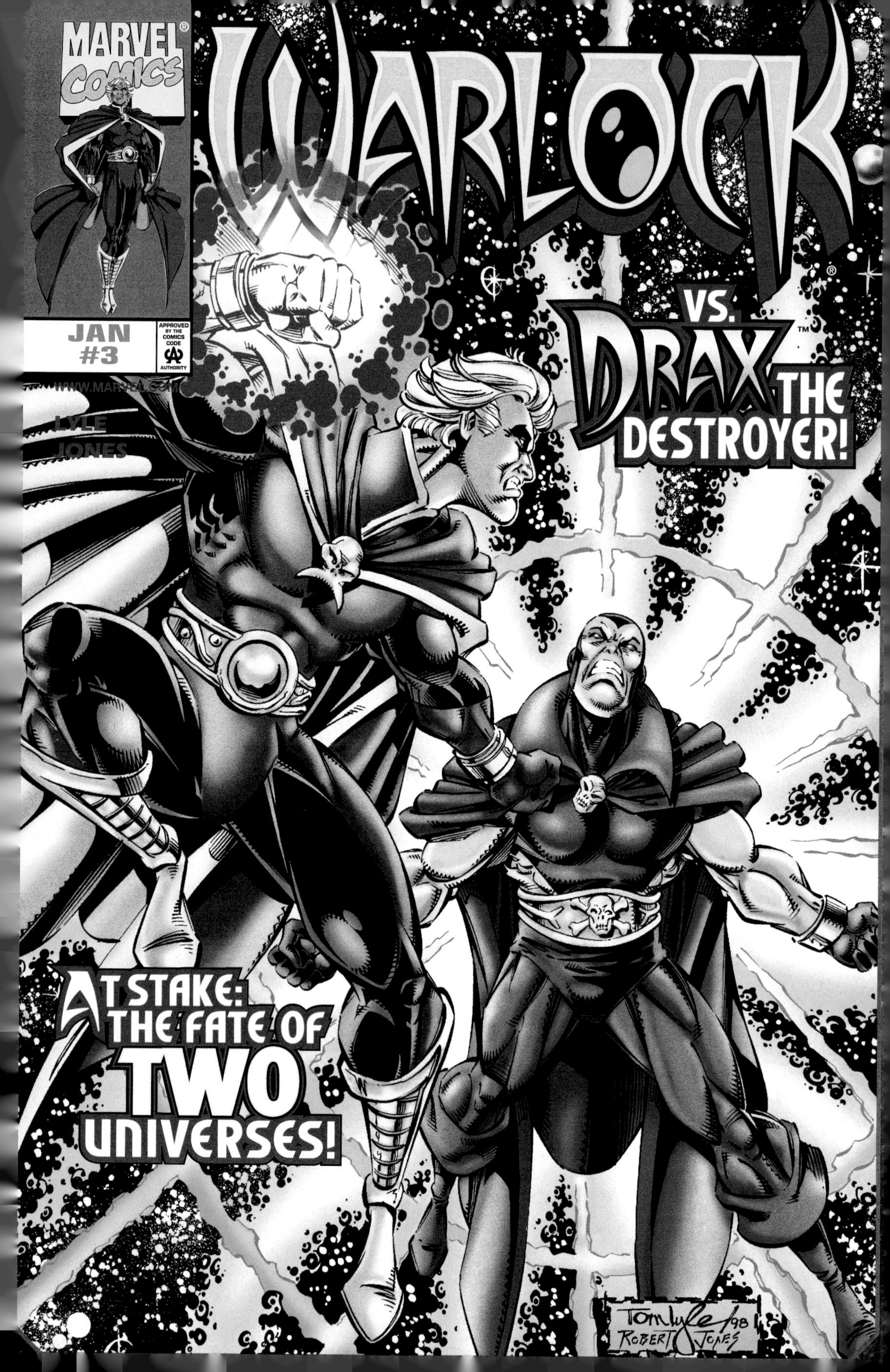

MARVEL® COMICS
JAN #3
APPROVED BY THE COMICS CODE AUTHORITY
WWW.MARVEL.COM
LYLE
JONES
WARLOCK®
VS. DRAX™ THE DESTROYER!
AT STAKE: THE FATE OF TWO UNIVERSES!
Tom Lyle '98
ROBERT JONES

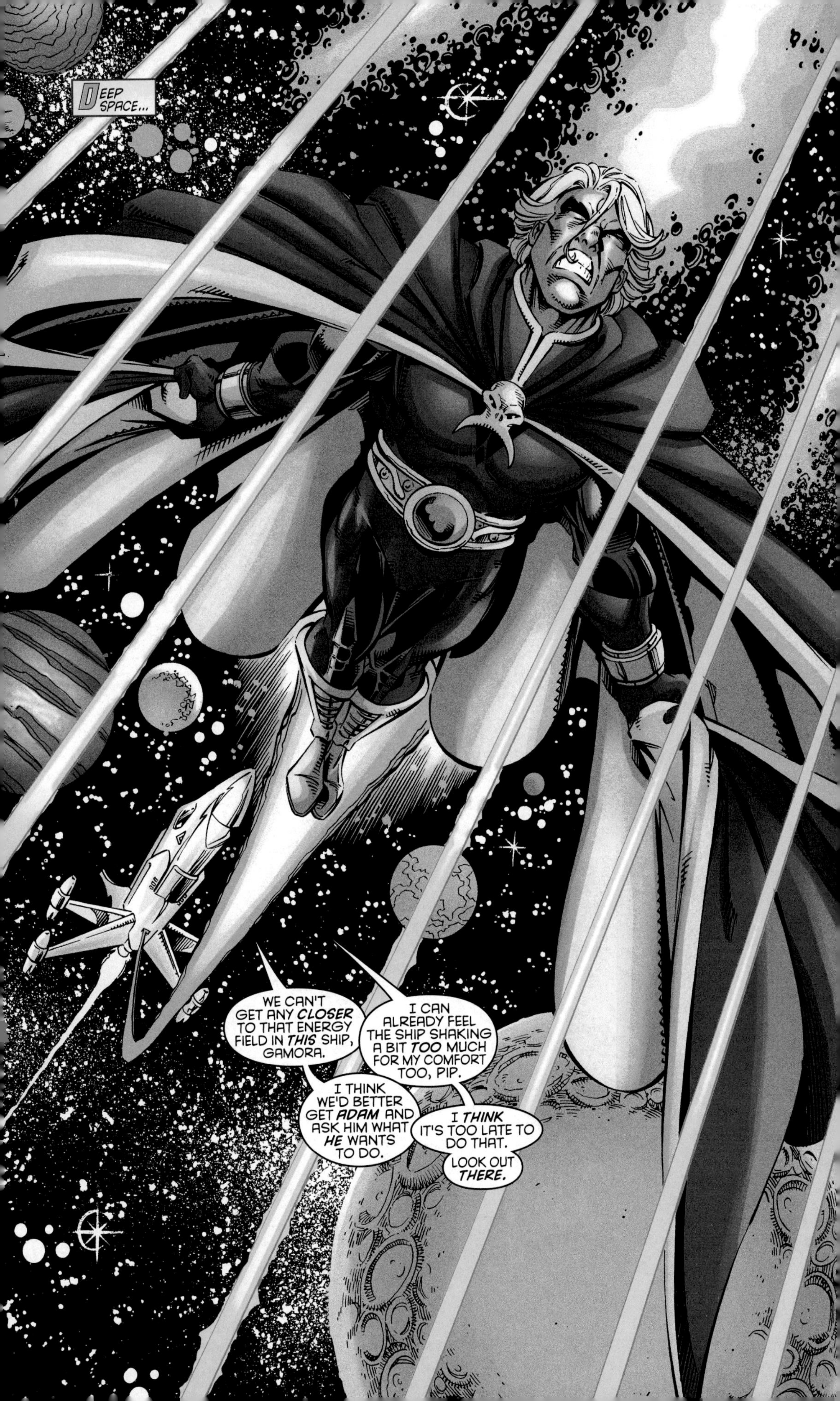
DEEP SPACE...
WE CAN'T GET ANY CLOSER TO THAT ENERGY FIELD IN THIS SHIP, GAMORA.
I CAN ALREADY FEEL THE SHIP SHAKING A BIT TOO MUCH FOR MY COMFORT TOO, PIP.
I THINK WE'D BETTER GET ADAM AND ASK HIM WHAT HE WANTS TO DO.
I THINK IT'S TOO LATE TO DO THAT.
LOOK OUT THERE.

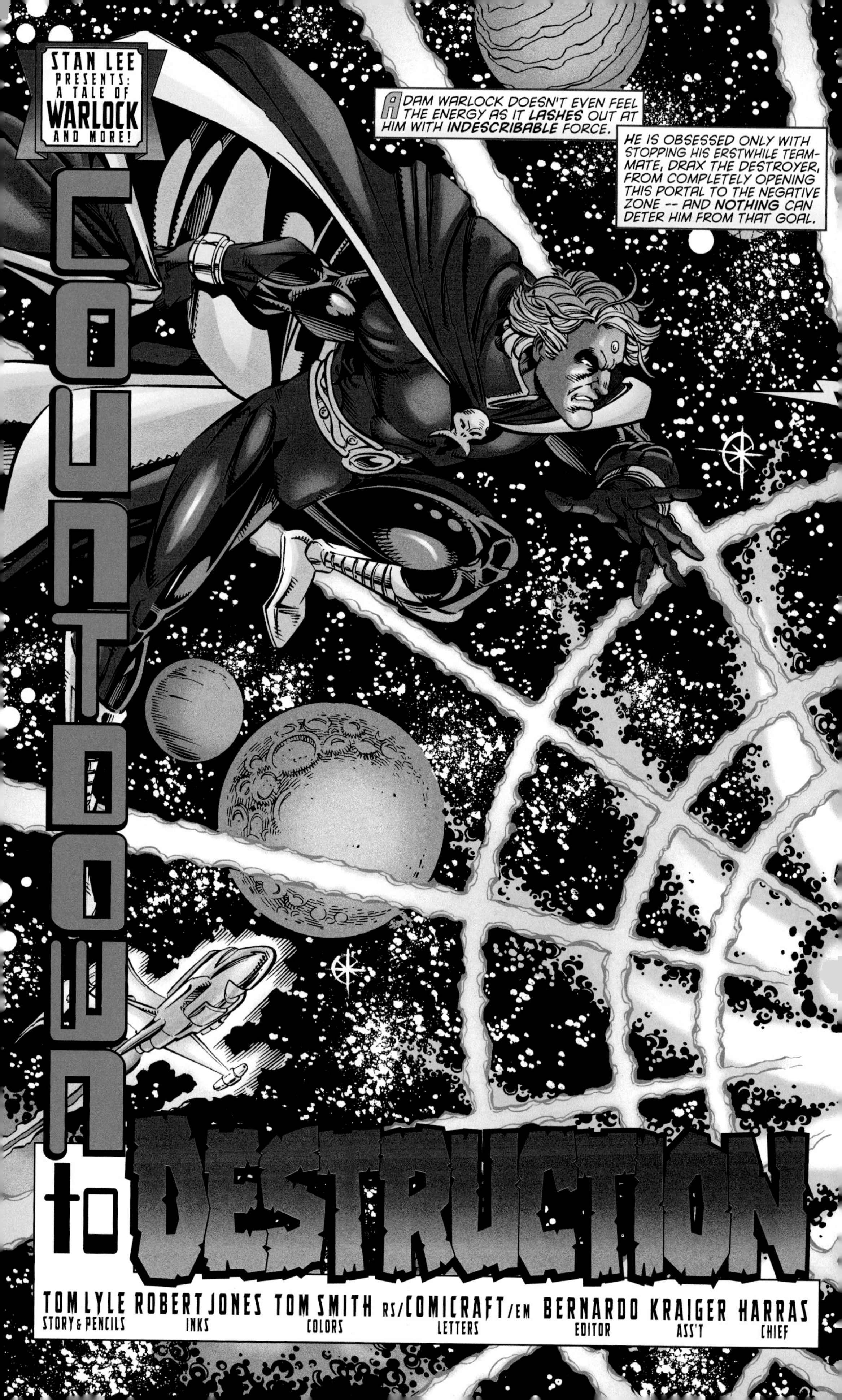
STAN LEE PRESENTS: A TALE OF WARLOCK AND MORE!
ADAM WARLOCK DOESN'T EVEN FEEL THE ENERGY AS IT LASHES OUT AT HIM WITH INDESCRIBABLE FORCE.
HE IS OBSESSED ONLY WITH STOPPING HIS ERSTWHILE TEAMMATE, DRAX THE DESTROYER, FROM COMPLETELY OPENING THIS PORTAL TO THE NEGATIVE ZONE -- AND NOTHING CAN DETER HIM FROM THAT GOAL.
COUNTDOWN to DESTRUCTION
TOM LYLE STORY & PENCILS
ROBERT JONES INKS
TOM SMITH COLORS
RS/COMICRAFT/EM LETTERS
BERNARDO EDITOR
KRAIGER ASS'T
HARRAS CHIEF

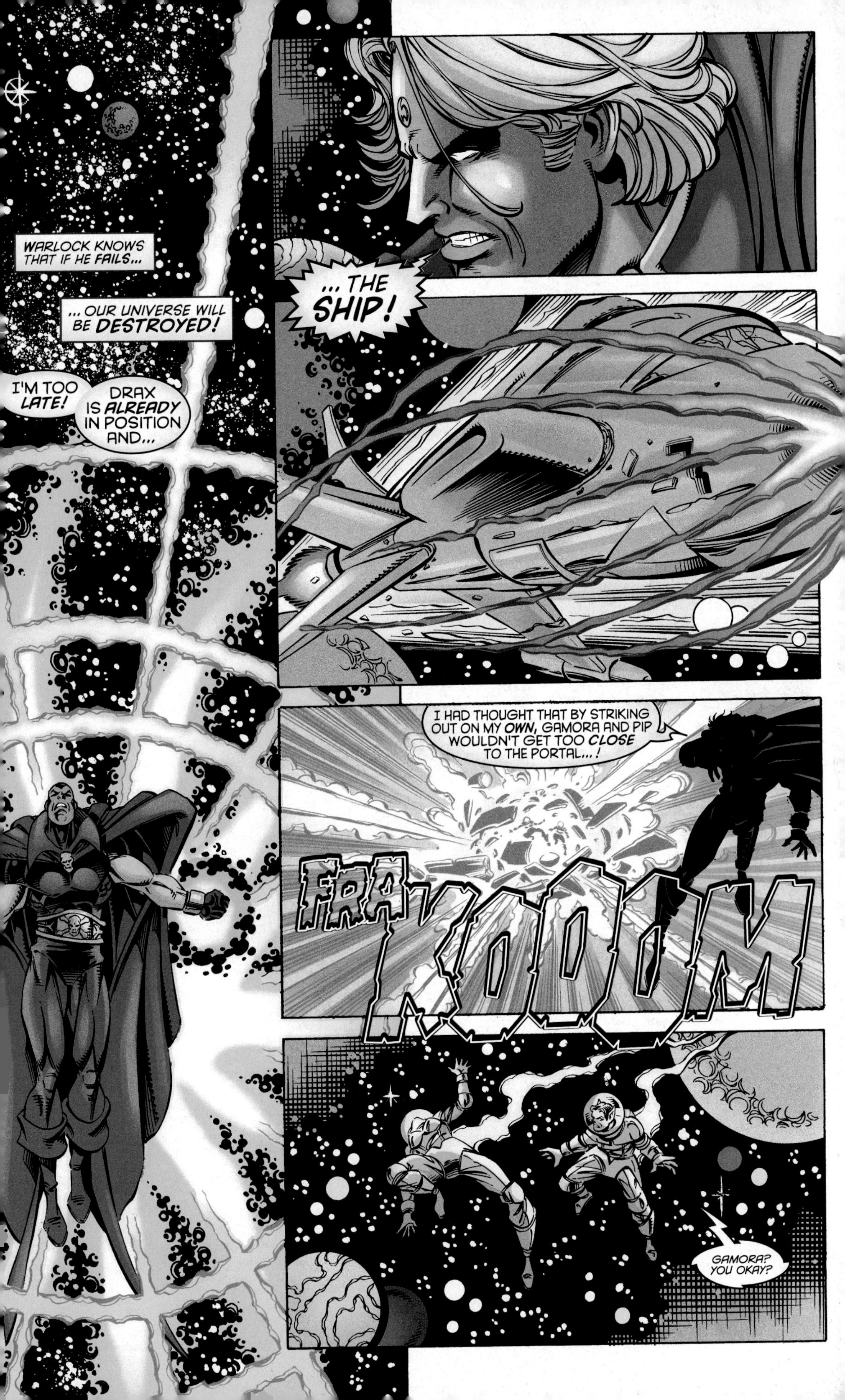
WARLOCK KNOWS THAT IF HE FAILS...
...OUR UNIVERSE WILL BE DESTROYED!
I'M TOO LATE!
DRAX IS ALREADY IN POSITION AND...
...THE SHIP!
I HAD THOUGHT THAT BY STRIKING OUT ON MY OWN, GAMORA AND PIP WOULDN'T GET TOO CLOSE TO THE PORTAL...!
FRAKOOOOM
GAMORA? YOU OKAY?

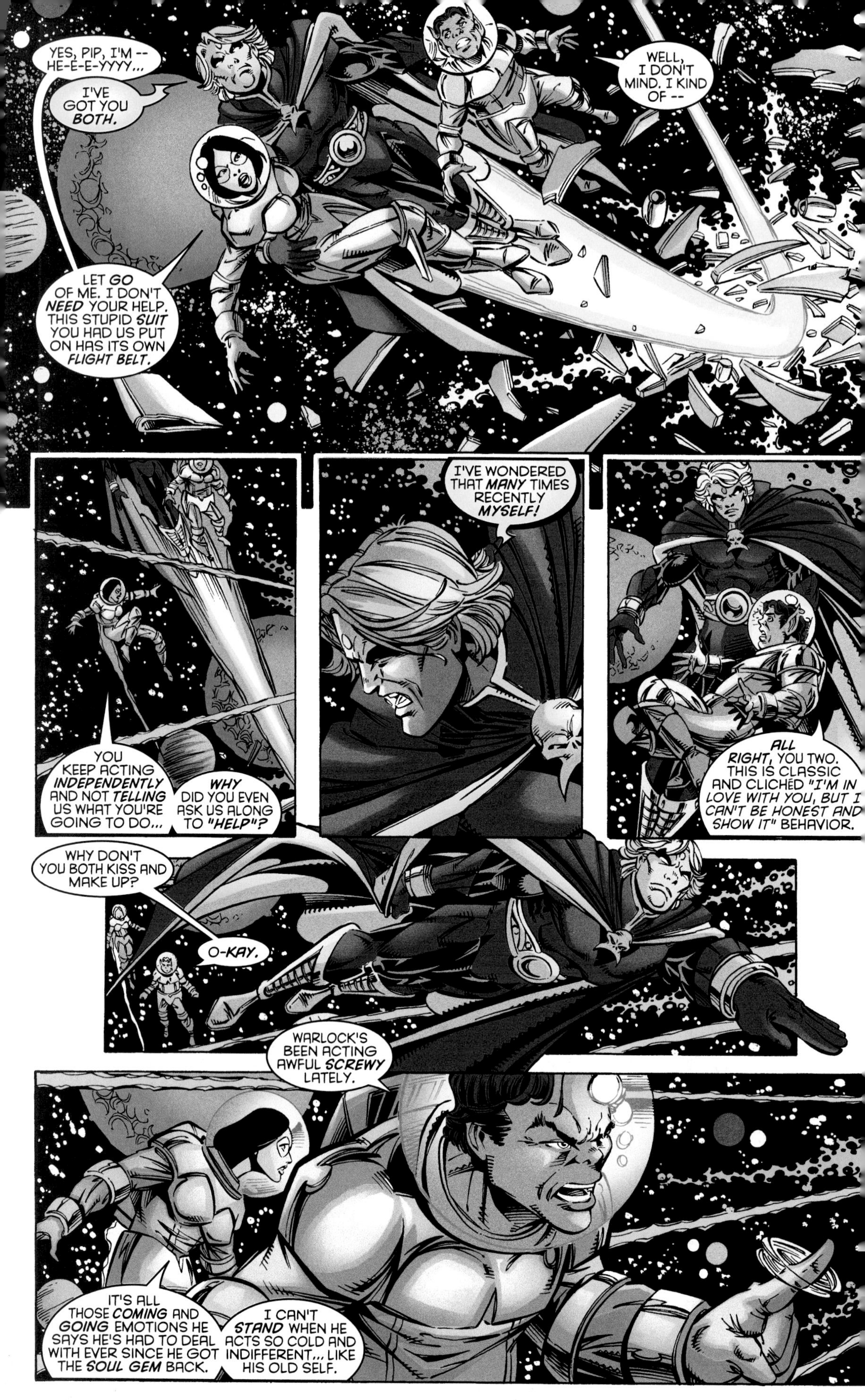
YES, PIP, I'M -- HE-E-E-YYYY...
I'VE GOT YOU BOTH.
WELL, I DON'T MIND. I KIND OF --
LET GO OF ME. I DON'T NEED YOUR HELP. THIS STUPID SUIT YOU HAD US PUT ON HAS ITS OWN FLIGHT BELT.
YOU KEEP ACTING INDEPENDENTLY AND NOT TELLING US WHAT YOU'RE GOING TO DO...
WHY DID YOU EVEN ASK US ALONG TO "HELP"?
I'VE WONDERED THAT MANY TIMES RECENTLY MYSELF!
ALL RIGHT, YOU TWO. THIS IS CLASSIC AND CLICHÉD "I'M IN LOVE WITH YOU, BUT I CAN'T BE HONEST AND SHOW IT" BEHAVIOR.
WHY DON'T YOU BOTH KISS AND MAKE UP?
O-KAY.
WARLOCK'S BEEN ACTING AWFUL SCREWY LATELY.
IT'S ALL THOSE COMING AND GOING EMOTIONS HE SAYS HE'S HAD TO DEAL WITH EVER SINCE HE GOT THE SOUL GEM BACK.
I CAN'T STAND WHEN HE ACTS SO COLD AND INDIFFERENT... LIKE HIS OLD SELF.

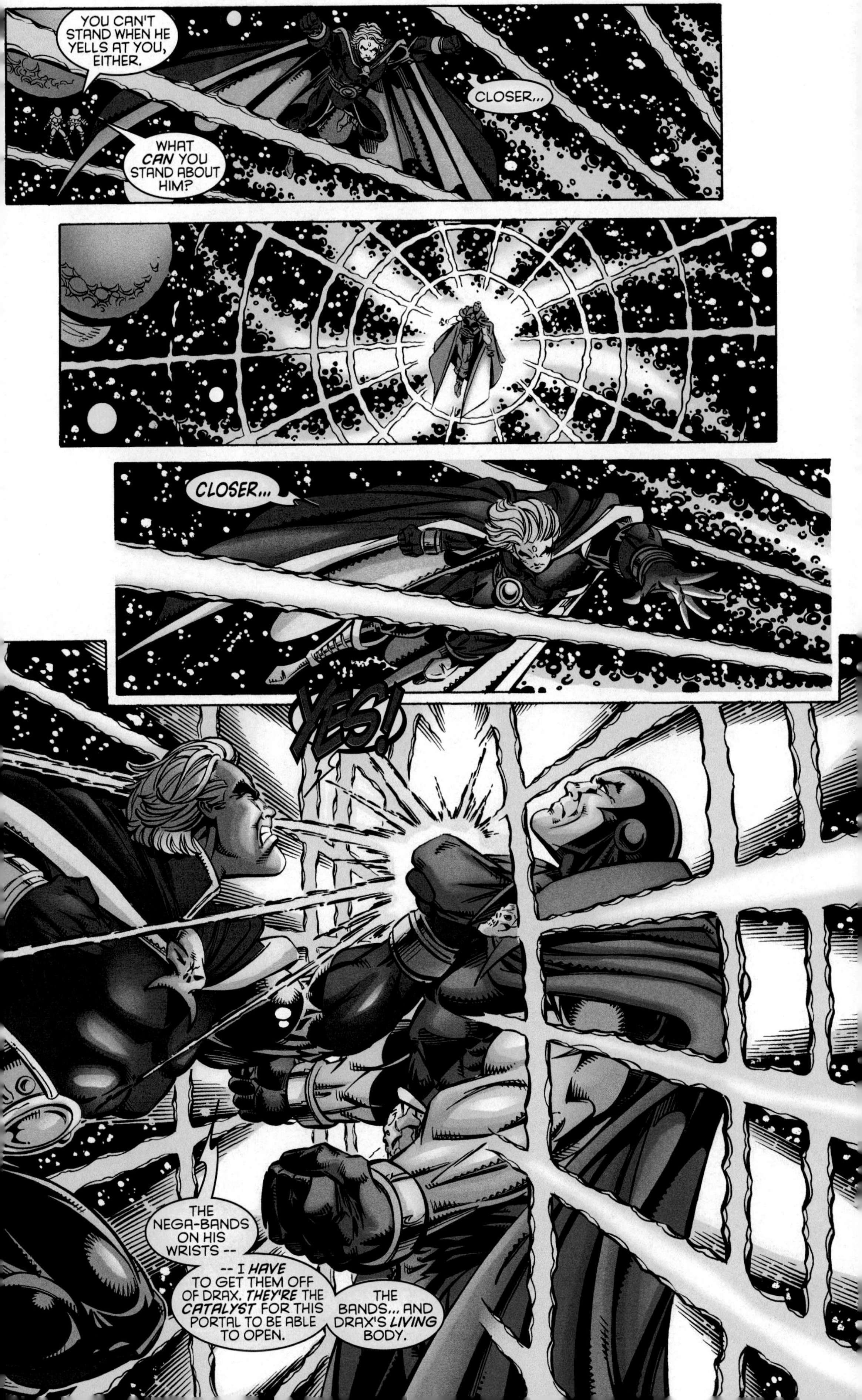

YOU CAN'T STAND WHEN HE YELLS AT YOU, EITHER.
WHAT CAN YOU STAND ABOUT HIM?
CLOSER...
CLOSER...
YES!
THE NEGA-BANDS ON HIS WRISTS --
-- I HAVE TO GET THEM OFF OF DRAX. THEY'RE THE CATALYST FOR THIS PORTAL TO BE ABLE TO OPEN.
THE BANDS... AND DRAX'S LIVING BODY.

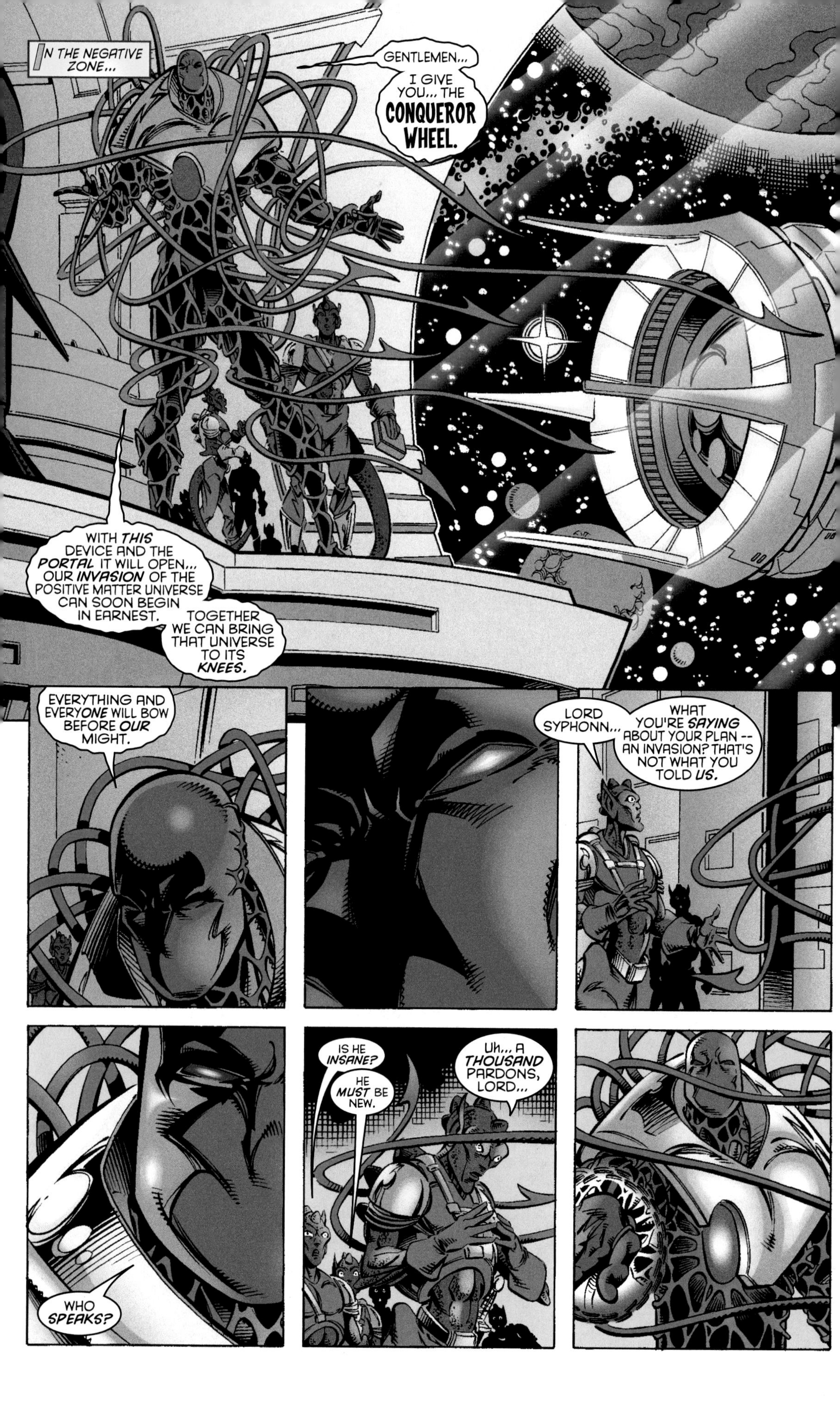
IN THE NEGATIVE ZONE...
GENTLEMEN...
I GIVE YOU... THE CONQUEROR WHEEL.
WITH THIS DEVICE AND THE PORTAL IT WILL OPEN... OUR INVASION OF THE POSITIVE MATTER UNIVERSE CAN SOON BEGIN IN EARNEST.
TOGETHER WE CAN BRING THAT UNIVERSE TO ITS KNEES.
EVERYTHING AND EVERYONE WILL BOW BEFORE OUR MIGHT.
LORD SYPHONN...
WHAT YOU'RE SAYING ABOUT YOUR PLAN -- AN INVASION? THAT'S NOT WHAT YOU TOLD US.
WHO SPEAKS?
IS HE INSANE?
HE MUST BE NEW.
Uh... A THOUSAND PARDONS, LORD...

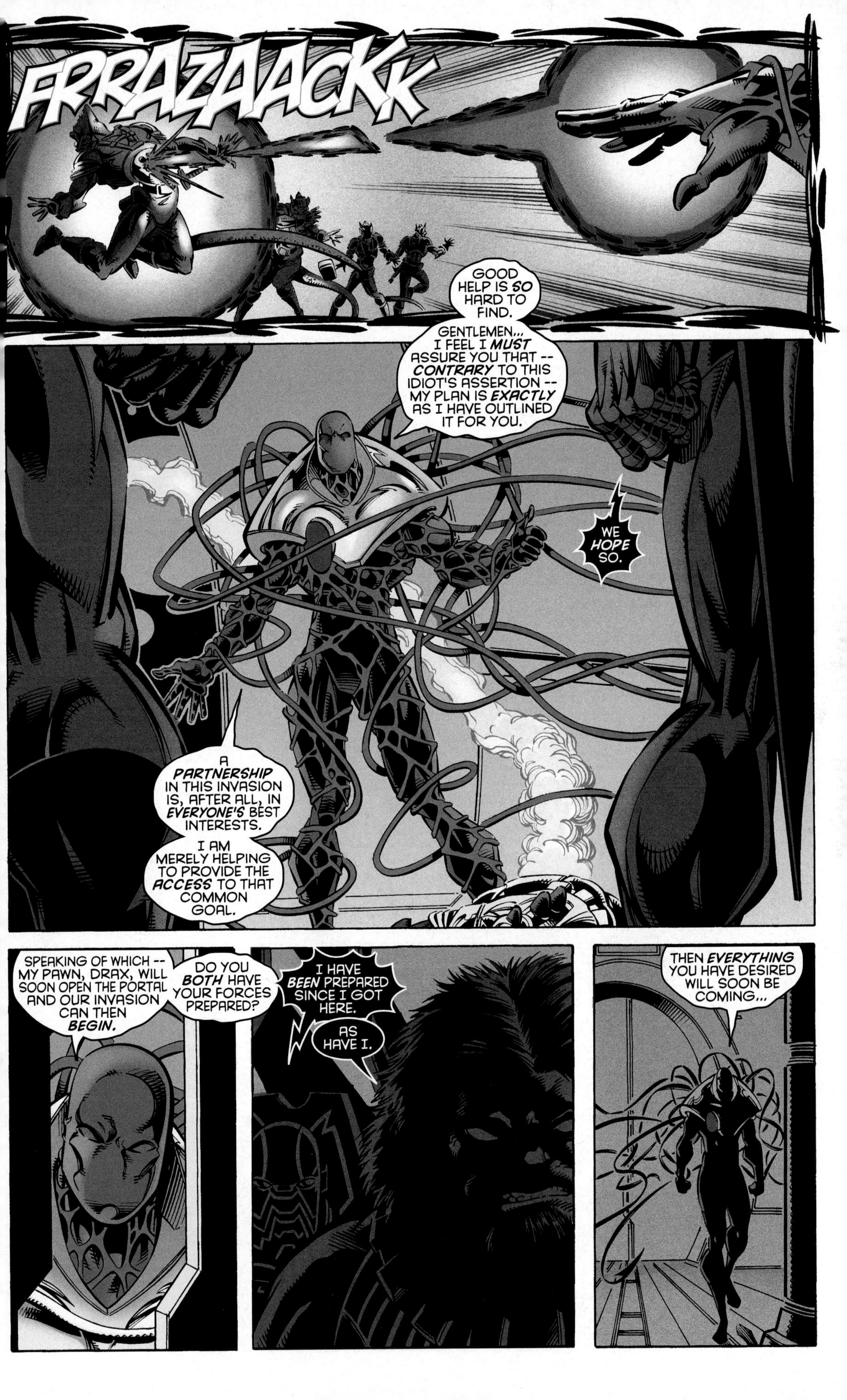
FRRAZAACKK
GOOD HELP IS SO HARD TO FIND.
GENTLEMEN... I FEEL I MUST ASSURE YOU THAT -- CONTRARY TO THIS IDIOT'S ASSERTION -- MY PLAN IS EXACTLY AS I HAVE OUTLINED IT FOR YOU.
WE HOPE SO.
A PARTNERSHIP IN THIS INVASION IS, AFTER ALL, IN EVERYONE'S BEST INTERESTS.
I AM MERELY HELPING TO PROVIDE THE ACCESS TO THAT COMMON GOAL.
SPEAKING OF WHICH -- MY PAWN, DRAX, WILL SOON OPEN THE PORTAL AND OUR INVASION CAN THEN BEGIN.
DO YOU BOTH HAVE YOUR FORCES PREPARED?
I HAVE BEEN PREPARED SINCE I GOT HERE.
AS HAVE I.
THEN EVERYTHING YOU HAVE DESIRED WILL SOON BE COMING...

...TO **ME!**

THOSE FOOLS ARE SO **EASY** TO MANIPULATE.

HOW DID THEY **EVER** BECOME RULERS?

LITTLE DO THEY REALIZE THAT THE **CONQUEROR WHEEL** IS **TRULY** AN ENERGY **FUNNEL...**

...THAT THE **ENERGY** RELEASED IN THE DESTRUCTION OF THE POSITIVE UNIVERSE WILL BE **HARNESSED -- USED** TO TRANSFORM ME INTO A **GOD!**

HAVING THOSE TWO FOOLS **CLOSE** AT HAND ONLY MAKES IT EASIER FOR ME TO **DESTROY** THEM -- **AFTER** I AM TRANSFORMED.

I **MUST** POSSESS **WARLOCK'S SOUL GEM** AS WELL.

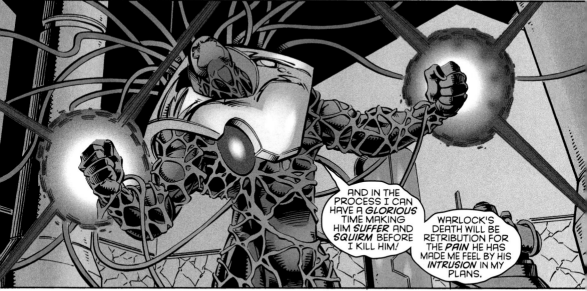

AND IN THE PROCESS I CAN HAVE A **GLORIOUS** TIME MAKING HIM **SUFFER** AND **SQUIRM** BEFORE I KILL HIM!

WARLOCK'S DEATH WILL BE RETRIBUTION FOR THE **PAIN** HE HAS MADE ME FEEL BY HIS **INTRUSION** IN MY PLANS.

BACK ON TITAN...

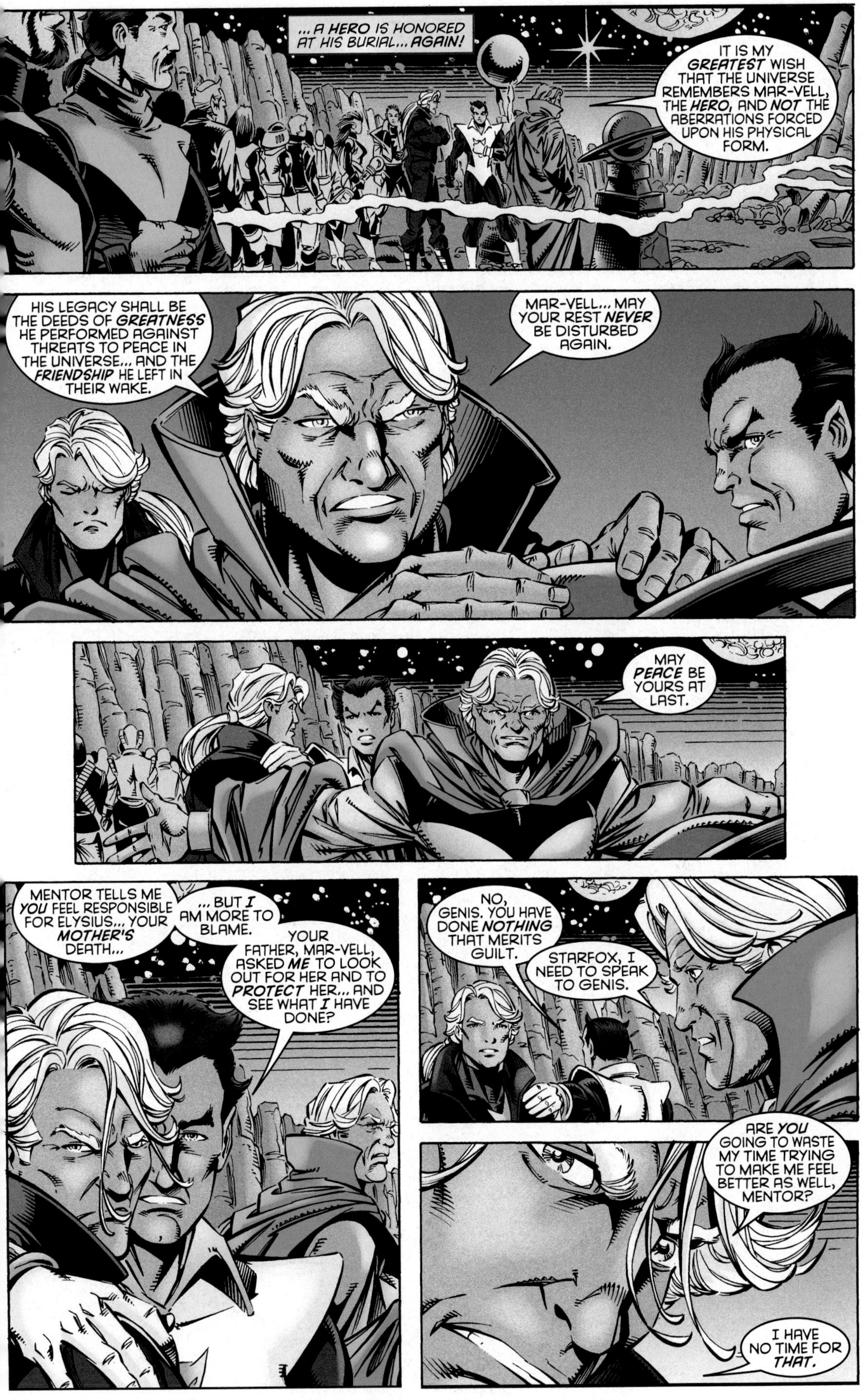

...A HERO IS HONORED AT HIS BURIAL... AGAIN!
IT IS MY GREATEST WISH THAT THE UNIVERSE REMEMBERS MAR-VELL, THE HERO, AND NOT THE ABERRATIONS FORCED UPON HIS PHYSICAL FORM.
HIS LEGACY SHALL BE THE DEEDS OF GREATNESS HE PERFORMED AGAINST THREATS TO PEACE IN THE UNIVERSE... AND THE FRIENDSHIP HE LEFT IN THEIR WAKE.
MAR-VELL... MAY YOUR REST NEVER BE DISTURBED AGAIN.
MAY PEACE BE YOURS AT LAST.
MENTOR TELLS ME YOU FEEL RESPONSIBLE FOR ELYSIUS... YOUR MOTHER'S DEATH...
...BUT I AM MORE TO BLAME.
YOUR FATHER, MAR-VELL, ASKED ME TO LOOK OUT FOR HER AND TO PROTECT HER... AND SEE WHAT I HAVE DONE?
NO, GENIS. YOU HAVE DONE NOTHING THAT MERITS GUILT.
STARFOX, I NEED TO SPEAK TO GENIS.
ARE YOU GOING TO WASTE MY TIME TRYING TO MAKE ME FEEL BETTER AS WELL, MENTOR?
I HAVE NO TIME FOR THAT.

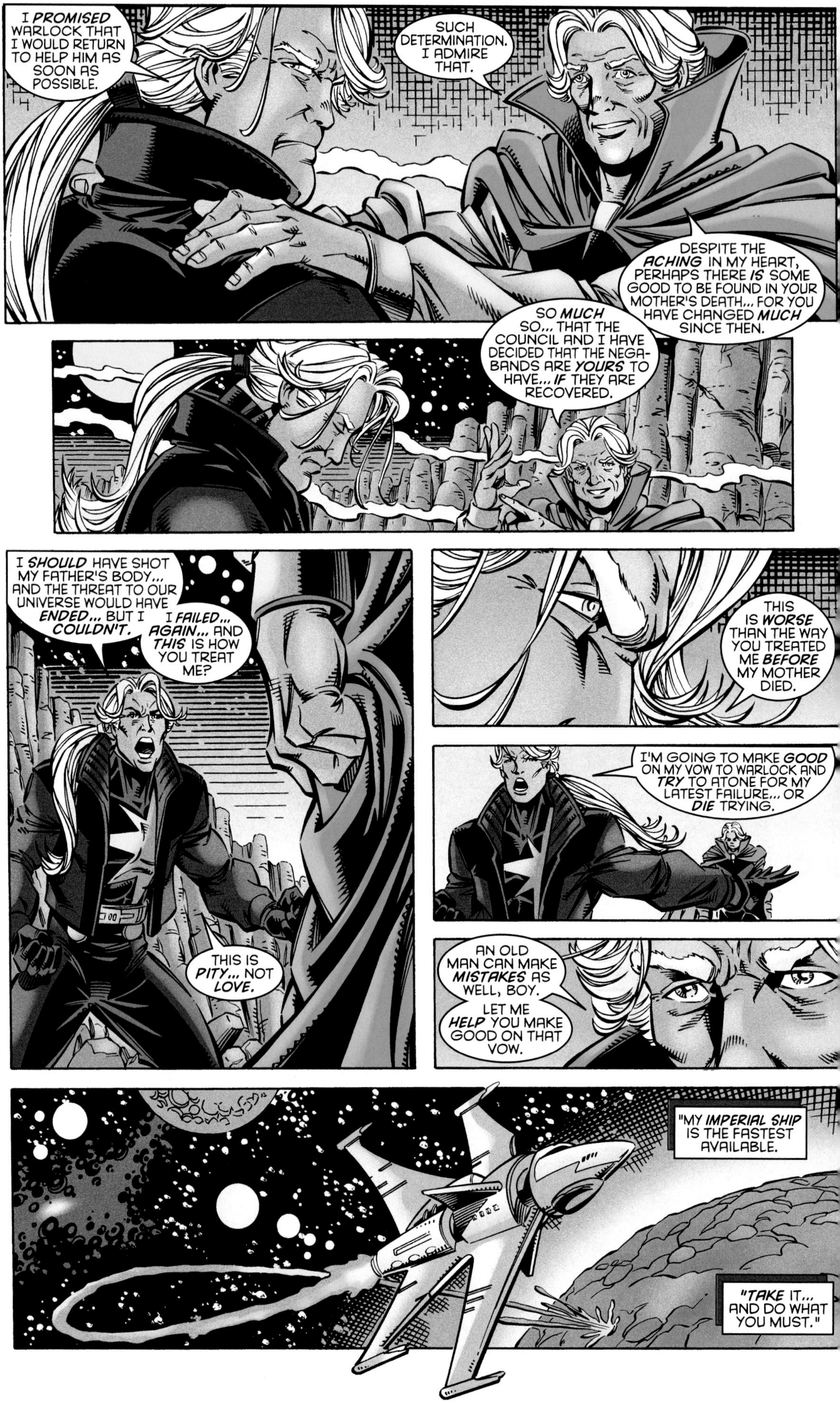

I PROMISED WARLOCK THAT I WOULD RETURN TO HELP HIM AS SOON AS POSSIBLE.
SUCH DETERMINATION. I ADMIRE THAT.
DESPITE THE ACHING IN MY HEART, PERHAPS THERE IS SOME GOOD TO BE FOUND IN YOUR MOTHER'S DEATH... FOR YOU HAVE CHANGED MUCH SINCE THEN.
SO MUCH SO... THAT THE COUNCIL AND I HAVE DECIDED THAT THE NEGA-BANDS ARE YOURS TO HAVE... IF THEY ARE RECOVERED.
I SHOULD HAVE SHOT MY FATHER'S BODY... AND THE THREAT TO OUR UNIVERSE WOULD HAVE ENDED... BUT I COULDN'T.
I FAILED... AGAIN... AND THIS IS HOW YOU TREAT ME?
THIS IS PITY... NOT LOVE.
THIS IS WORSE THAN THE WAY YOU TREATED ME BEFORE MY MOTHER DIED.
I'M GOING TO MAKE GOOD ON MY VOW TO WARLOCK AND TRY TO ATONE FOR MY LATEST FAILURE... OR DIE TRYING.
AN OLD MAN CAN MAKE MISTAKES AS WELL, BOY.
LET ME HELP YOU MAKE GOOD ON THAT VOW.
"MY IMPERIAL SHIP IS THE FASTEST AVAILABLE.
"TAKE IT... AND DO WHAT YOU MUST."

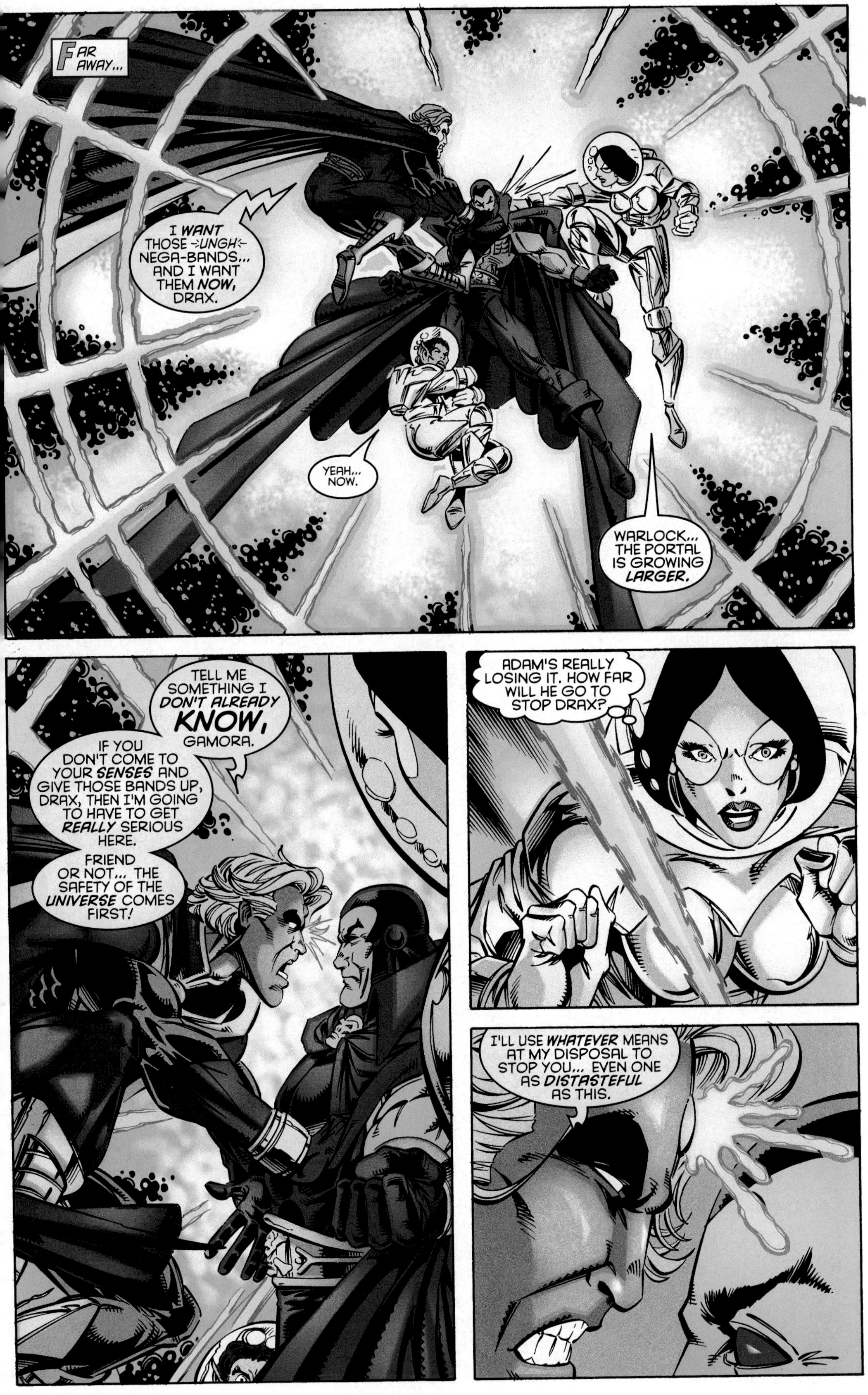
FAR AWAY...
I WANT THOSE -UNGH- NEGA-BANDS... AND I WANT THEM NOW, DRAX.
YEAH... NOW.
WARLOCK... THE PORTAL IS GROWING LARGER.
TELL ME SOMETHING I DON'T ALREADY KNOW, GAMORA.
IF YOU DON'T COME TO YOUR SENSES AND GIVE THOSE BANDS UP, DRAX, THEN I'M GOING TO HAVE TO GET REALLY SERIOUS HERE.
FRIEND OR NOT... THE SAFETY OF THE UNIVERSE COMES FIRST!
ADAM'S REALLY LOSING IT. HOW FAR WILL HE GO TO STOP DRAX?
I'LL USE WHATEVER MEANS AT MY DISPOSAL TO STOP YOU... EVEN ONE AS DISTASTEFUL AS THIS.

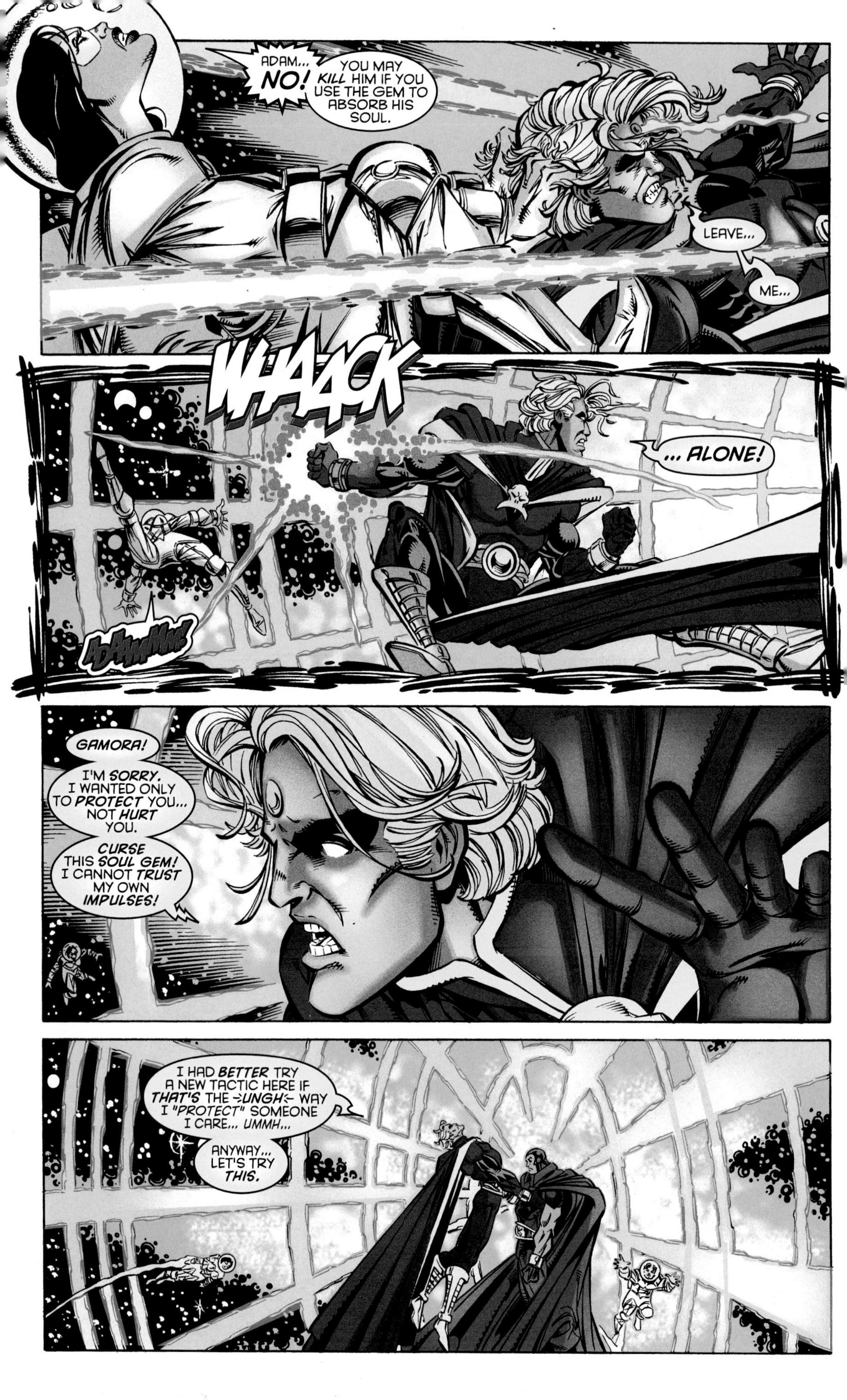
ADAM... NO!
YOU MAY KILL HIM IF YOU USE THE GEM TO ABSORB HIS SOUL.
LEAVE...
ME...
WHAACK
...ALONE!
ADAMMM!
GAMORA!
I'M SORRY. I WANTED ONLY TO PROTECT YOU... NOT HURT YOU.
CURSE THIS SOUL GEM! I CANNOT TRUST MY OWN IMPULSES!
I HAD BETTER TRY A NEW TACTIC HERE IF THAT'S THE -UNGH- WAY I "PROTECT" SOMEONE I CARE... UMMH...
ANYWAY... LET'S TRY THIS.

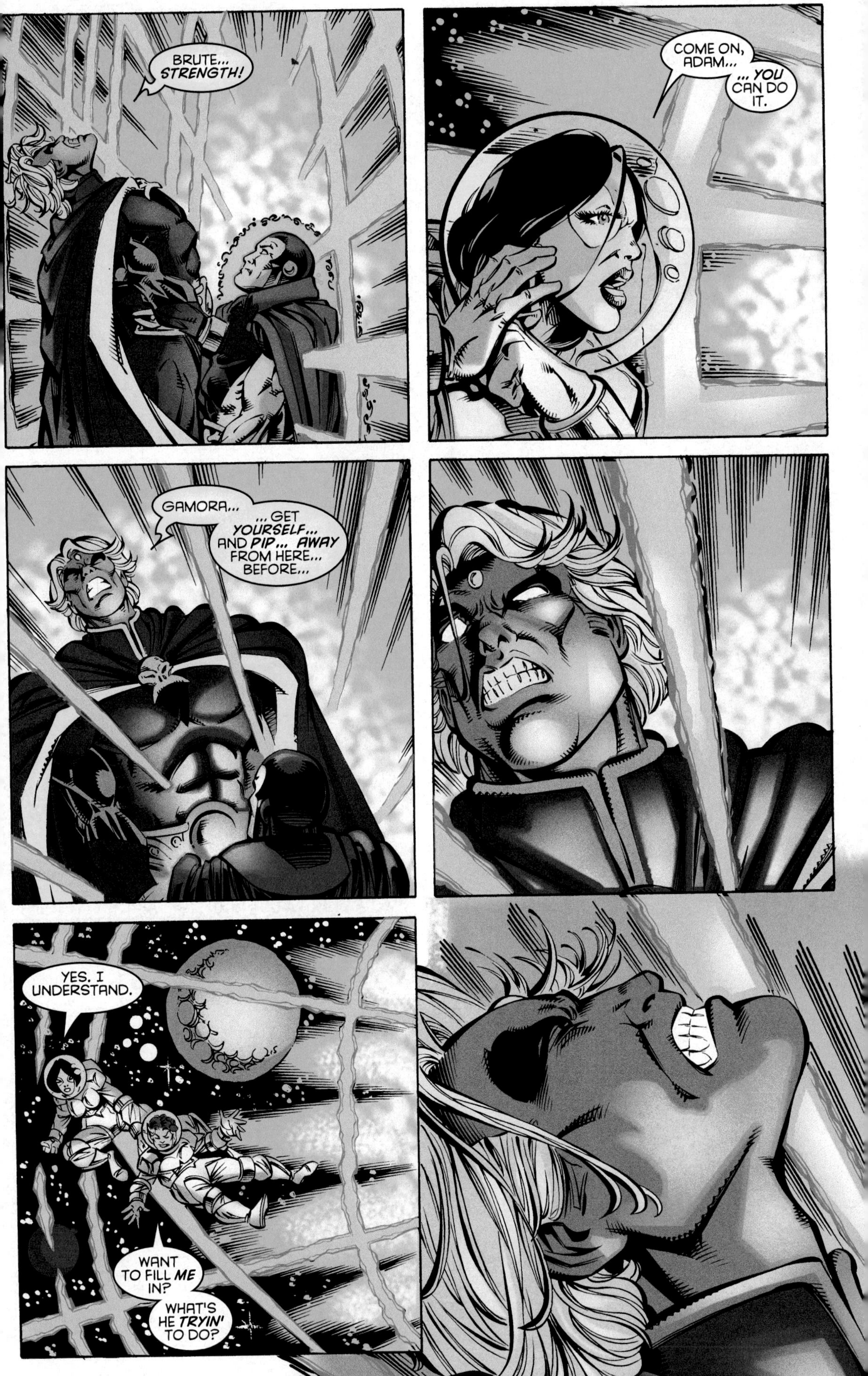

BRUTE... STRENGTH!
COME ON, ADAM...
...YOU CAN DO IT.
GAMORA...
...GET YOURSELF... AND PIP... AWAY FROM HERE... BEFORE...
YES. I UNDERSTAND.
WANT TO FILL ME IN?
WHAT'S HE TRYIN' TO DO?

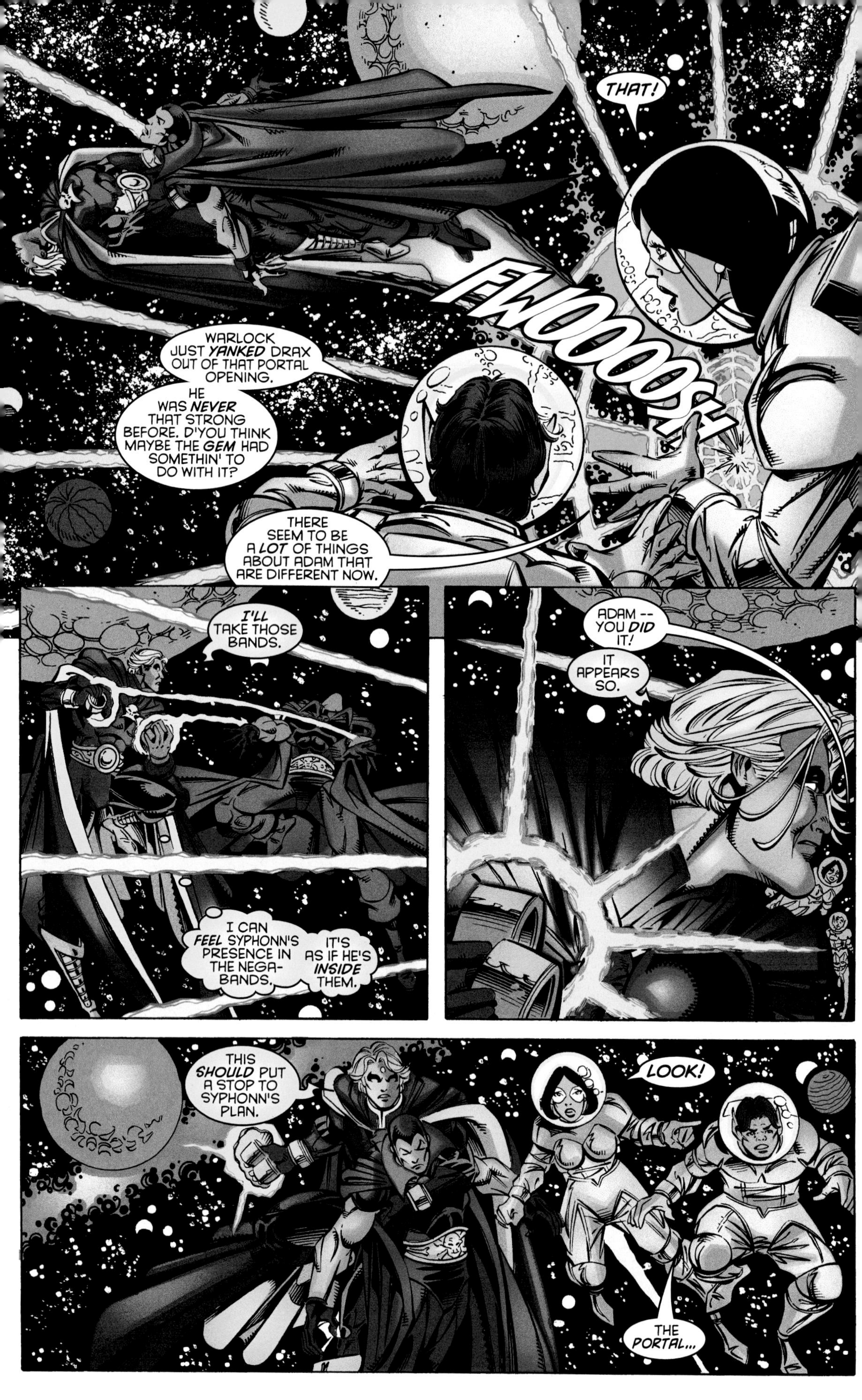
THAT!
FWOOOOSH
WARLOCK JUST YANKED DRAX OUT OF THAT PORTAL OPENING.
HE WAS NEVER THAT STRONG BEFORE. D'YOU THINK MAYBE THE GEM HAD SOMETHIN' TO DO WITH IT?
THERE SEEM TO BE A LOT OF THINGS ABOUT ADAM THAT ARE DIFFERENT NOW.
I'LL TAKE THOSE BANDS.
I CAN FEEL SYPHONN'S PRESENCE IN THE NEGA-BANDS.
IT'S AS IF HE'S INSIDE THEM.
ADAM -- YOU DID IT!
IT APPEARS SO.
THIS SHOULD PUT A STOP TO SYPHONN'S PLAN.
LOOK!
THE PORTAL...

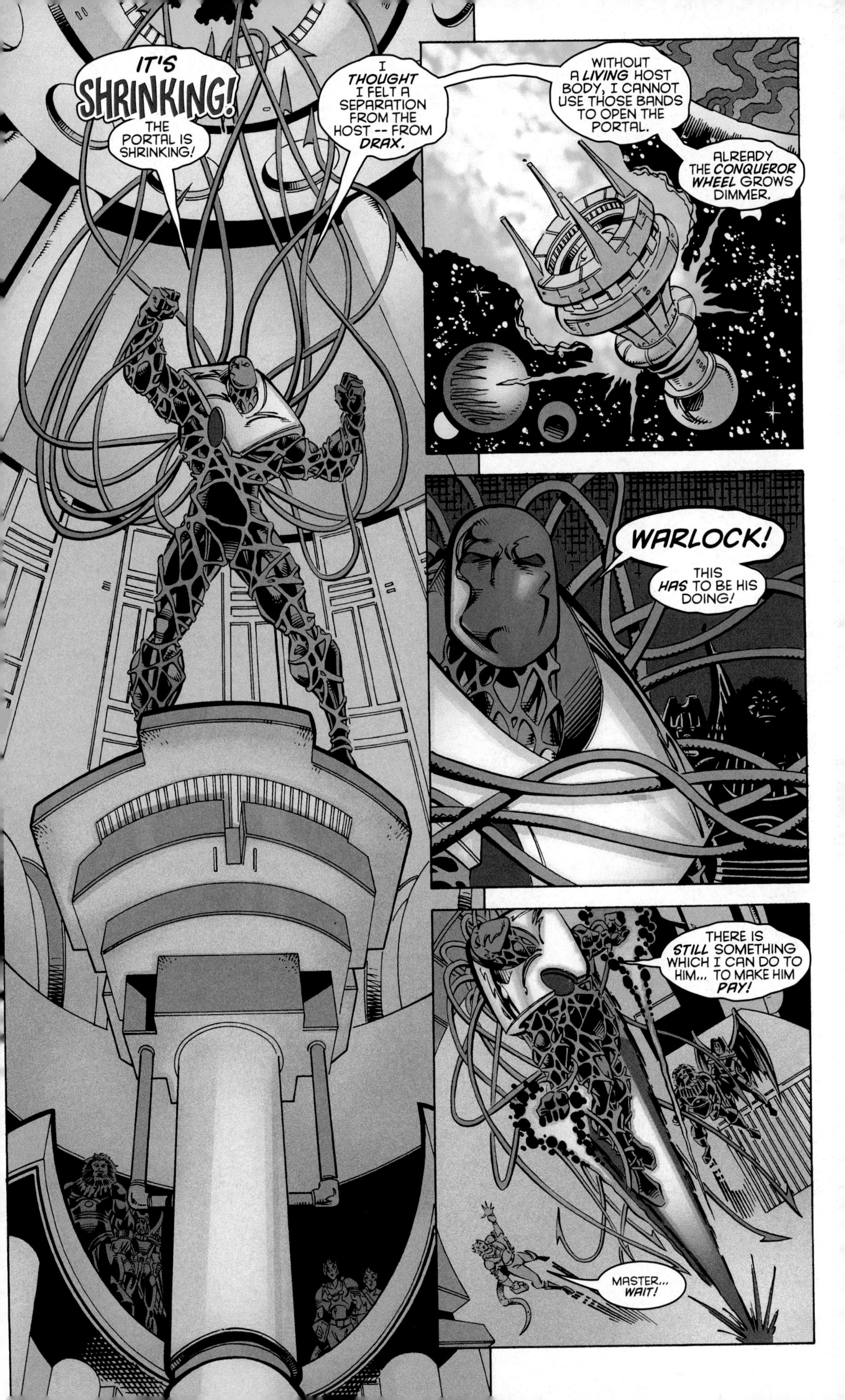
IT'S SHRINKING! THE PORTAL IS SHRINKING!
I THOUGHT I FELT A SEPARATION FROM THE HOST -- FROM DRAX.
WITHOUT A LIVING HOST BODY, I CANNOT USE THOSE BANDS TO OPEN THE PORTAL.
ALREADY THE CONQUEROR WHEEL GROWS DIMMER.
WARLOCK!
THIS HAS TO BE HIS DOING!
THERE IS STILL SOMETHING WHICH I CAN DO TO HIM... TO MAKE HIM PAY!
MASTER... WAIT!

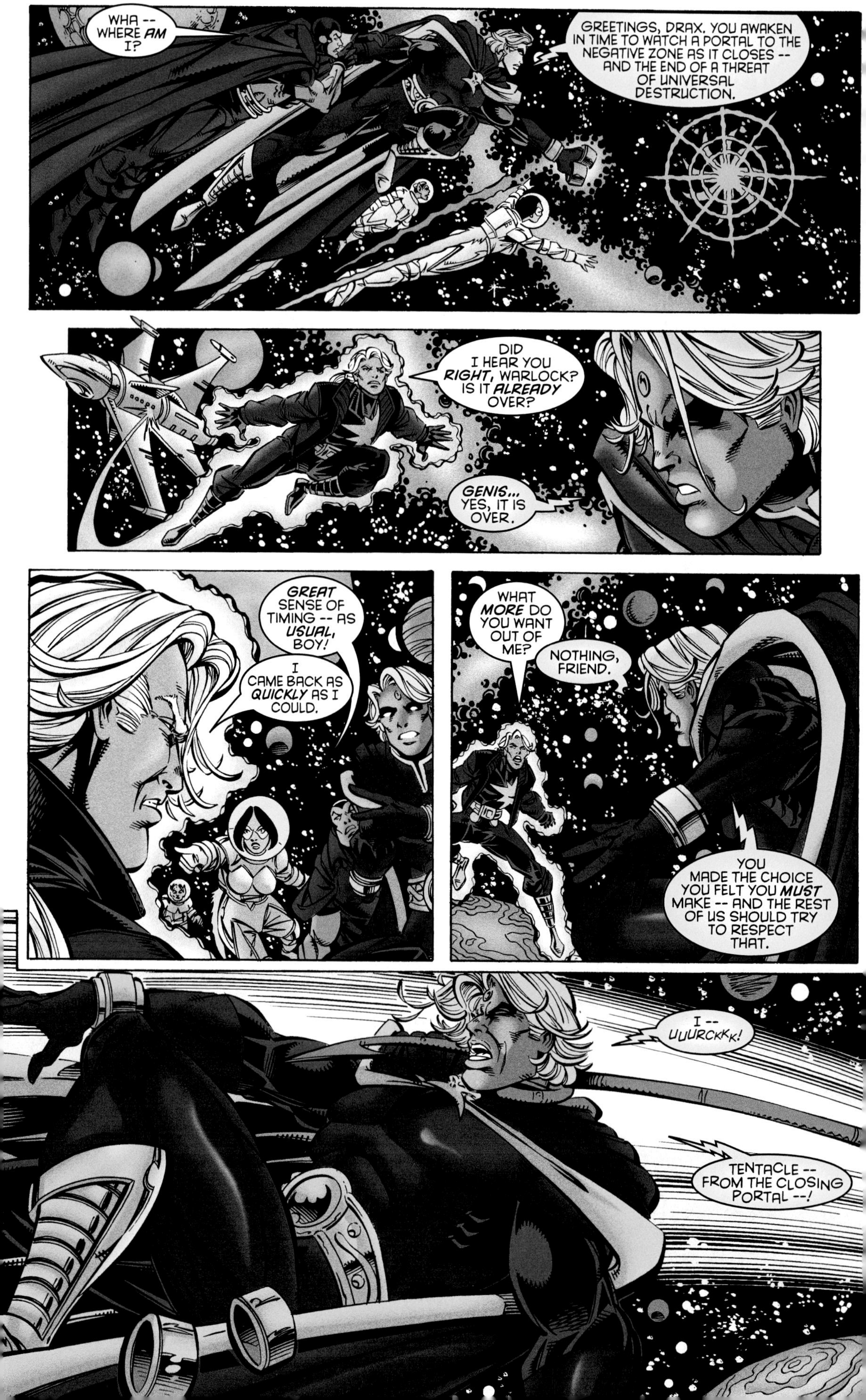
WHA -- WHERE *AM* I?
GREETINGS, DRAX. YOU AWAKEN IN TIME TO WATCH A PORTAL TO THE NEGATIVE ZONE AS IT CLOSES -- AND THE END OF A THREAT OF UNIVERSAL DESTRUCTION.
DID I HEAR YOU *RIGHT,* WARLOCK? IS IT *ALREADY* OVER?
GENIS... YES, IT IS OVER.
GREAT SENSE OF TIMING -- AS *USUAL,* BOY!
I CAME BACK AS *QUICKLY* AS I COULD.
WHAT *MORE* DO YOU WANT OUT OF ME?
NOTHING, FRIEND.
YOU MADE THE CHOICE YOU FELT YOU *MUST* MAKE -- AND THE REST OF US SHOULD TRY TO RESPECT THAT.
I -- UUURCKKK!
TENTACLE -- FROM THE CLOSING PORTAL --!

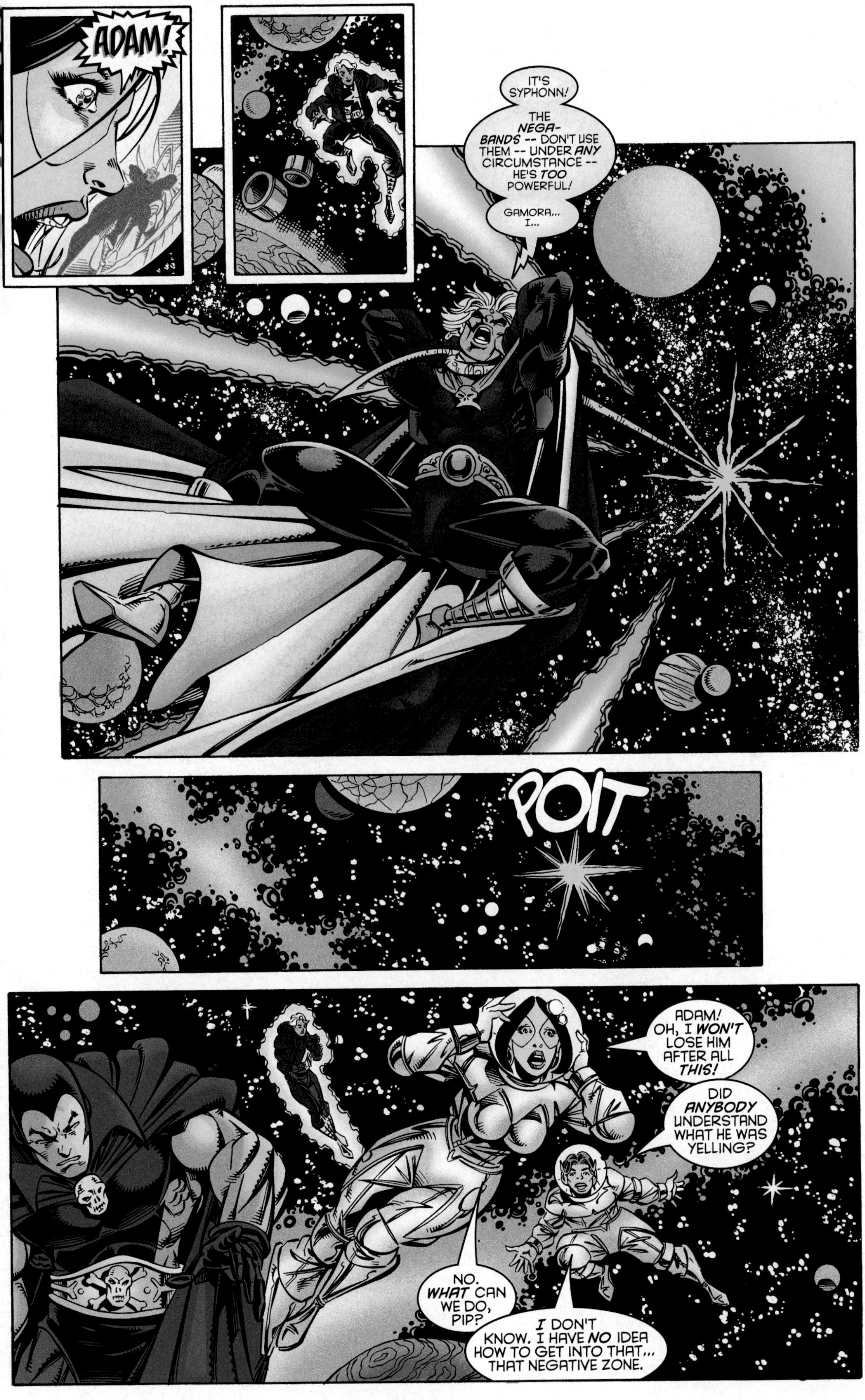
ADAM!
IT'S SYPHONN!
THE NEGA-BANDS -- DON'T USE THEM -- UNDER ANY CIRCUMSTANCE -- HE'S TOO POWERFUL!
GAMORA... I...
POIT
ADAM! OH, I WON'T LOSE HIM AFTER ALL THIS!
DID ANYBODY UNDERSTAND WHAT HE WAS YELLING?
NO. WHAT CAN WE DO, PIP?
I DON'T KNOW. I HAVE NO IDEA HOW TO GET INTO THAT... THAT NEGATIVE ZONE.

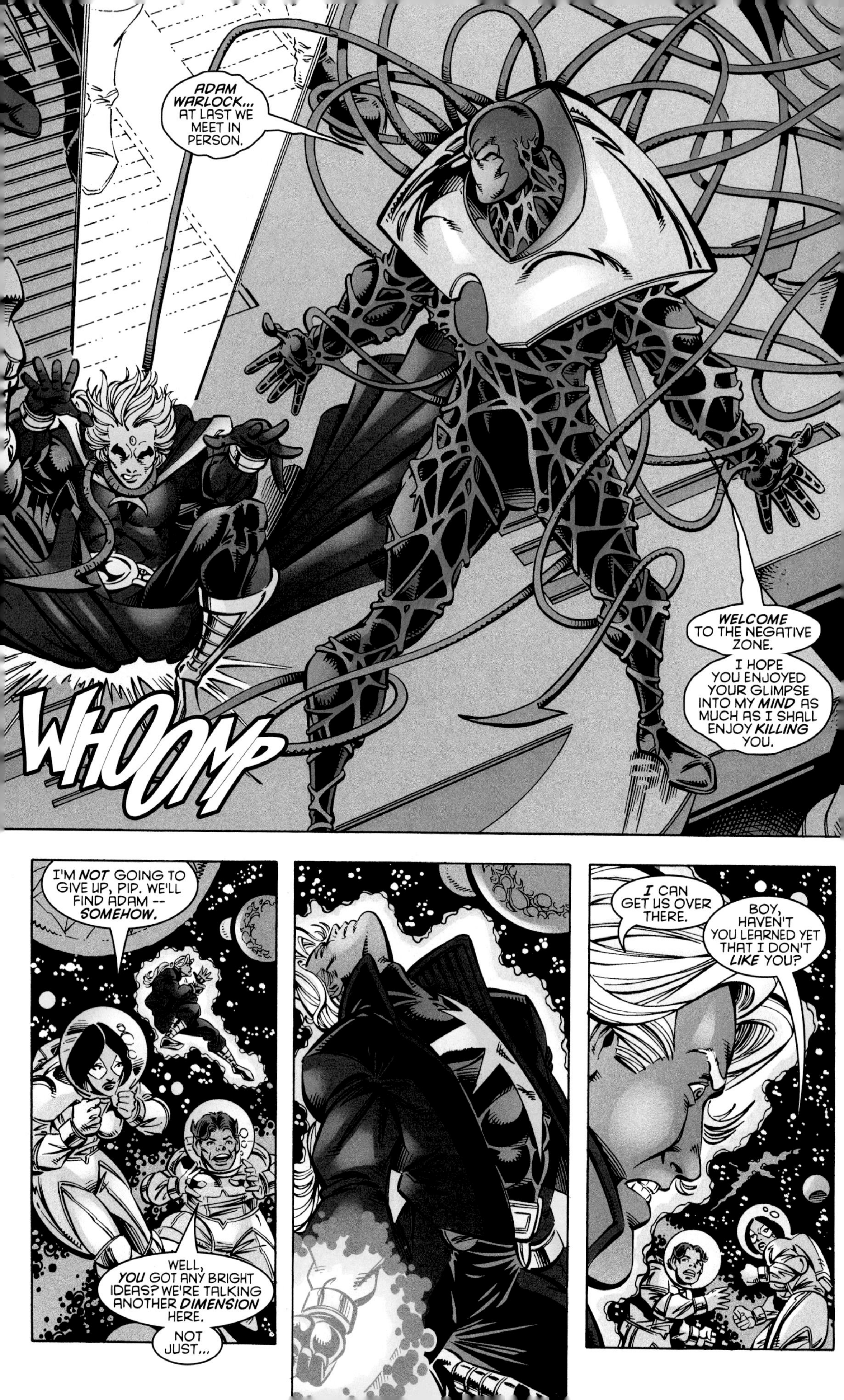
ADAM WARLOCK... AT LAST WE MEET IN PERSON.
WELCOME TO THE NEGATIVE ZONE.
I HOPE YOU ENJOYED YOUR GLIMPSE INTO MY MIND AS MUCH AS I SHALL ENJOY KILLING YOU.
WHOOMP
I'M NOT GOING TO GIVE UP, PIP. WE'LL FIND ADAM -- SOMEHOW.
WELL, YOU GOT ANY BRIGHT IDEAS? WE'RE TALKING ANOTHER DIMENSION HERE.
NOT JUST...
I CAN GET US OVER THERE.
BOY, HAVEN'T YOU LEARNED YET THAT I DON'T LIKE YOU?

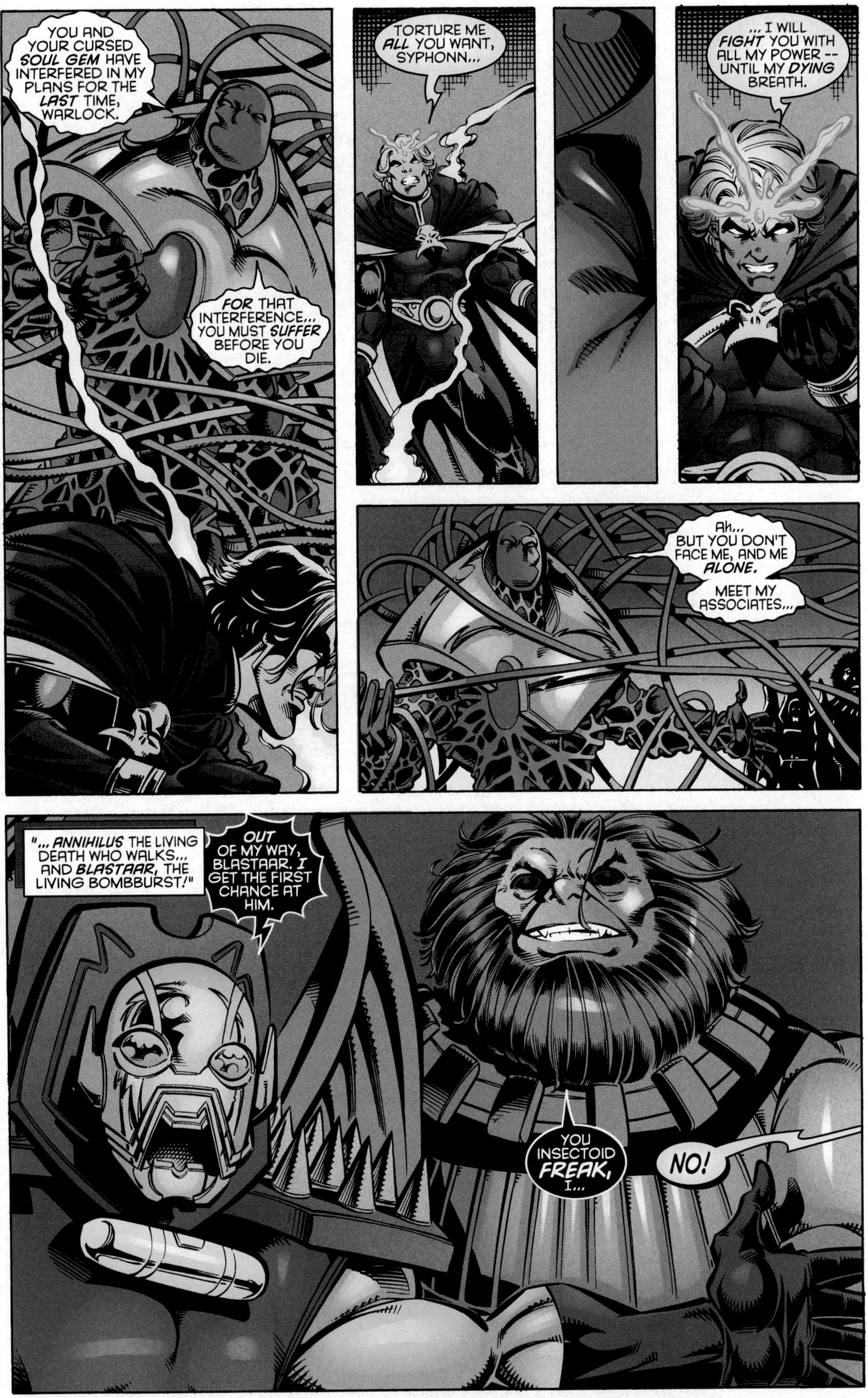

YOU AND YOUR CURSED SOUL GEM HAVE INTERFERED IN MY PLANS FOR THE LAST TIME, WARLOCK.
FOR THAT INTERFERENCE... YOU MUST SUFFER BEFORE YOU DIE.
TORTURE ME ALL YOU WANT, SYPHONN...
... I WILL FIGHT YOU WITH ALL MY POWER -- UNTIL MY DYING BREATH.
Ah... BUT YOU DON'T FACE ME, AND ME ALONE.
MEET MY ASSOCIATES...
"... ANNIHILUS THE LIVING DEATH WHO WALKS... AND BLASTAAR, THE LIVING BOMBBURST!"
OUT OF MY WAY, BLASTAAR. I GET THE FIRST CHANCE AT HIM.
YOU INSECTOID FREAK, I...
NO!

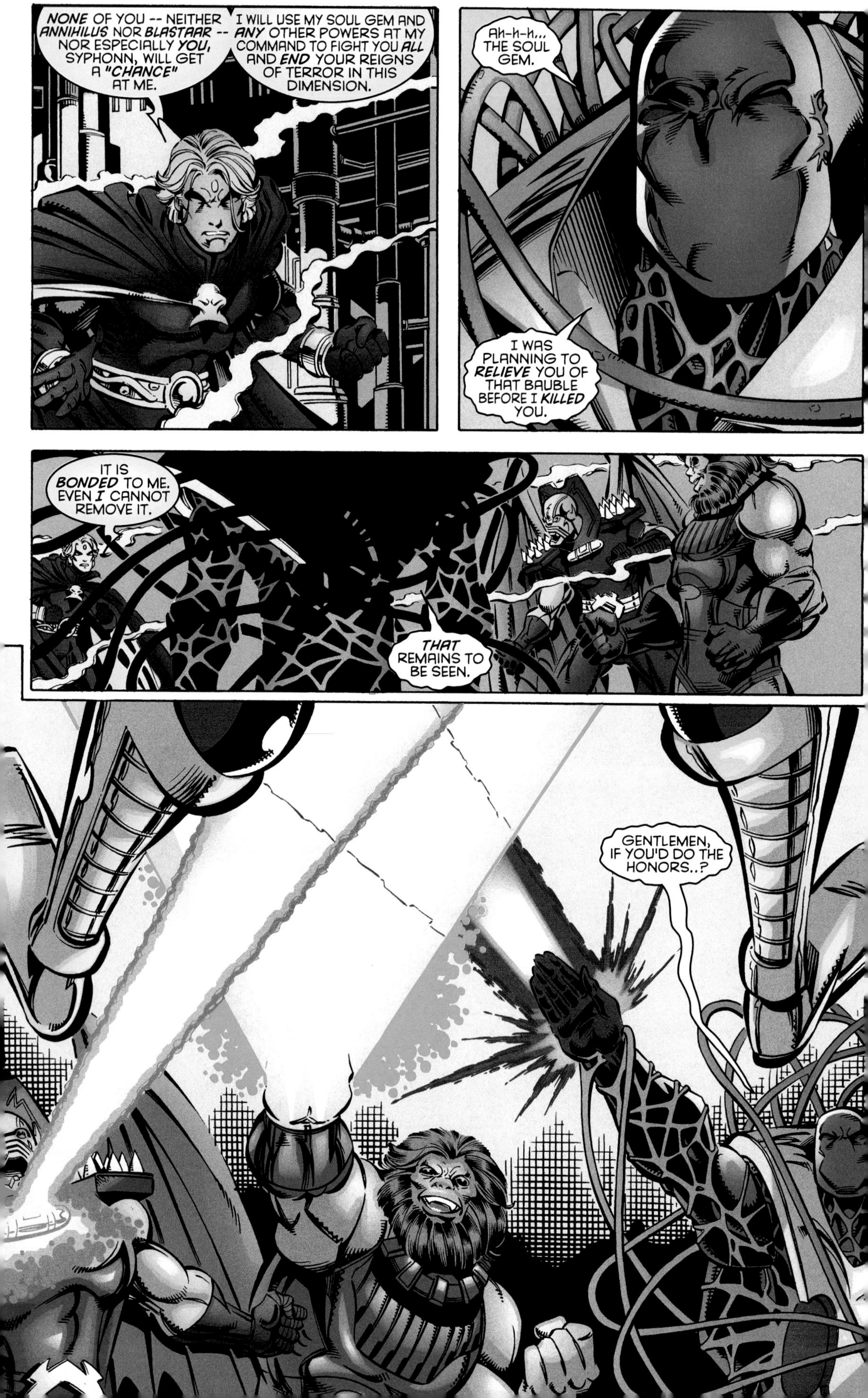
NONE OF YOU -- NEITHER ANNIHILUS NOR BLASTAAR -- NOR ESPECIALLY YOU, SYPHONN, WILL GET A "CHANCE" AT ME.
I WILL USE MY SOUL GEM AND ANY OTHER POWERS AT MY COMMAND TO FIGHT YOU ALL AND END YOUR REIGNS OF TERROR IN THIS DIMENSION.
Ah-h-h... THE SOUL GEM.
I WAS PLANNING TO RELIEVE YOU OF THAT BAUBLE BEFORE I KILLED YOU.
IT IS BONDED TO ME. EVEN I CANNOT REMOVE IT.
THAT REMAINS TO BE SEEN.
GENTLEMEN, IF YOU'D DO THE HONORS..?

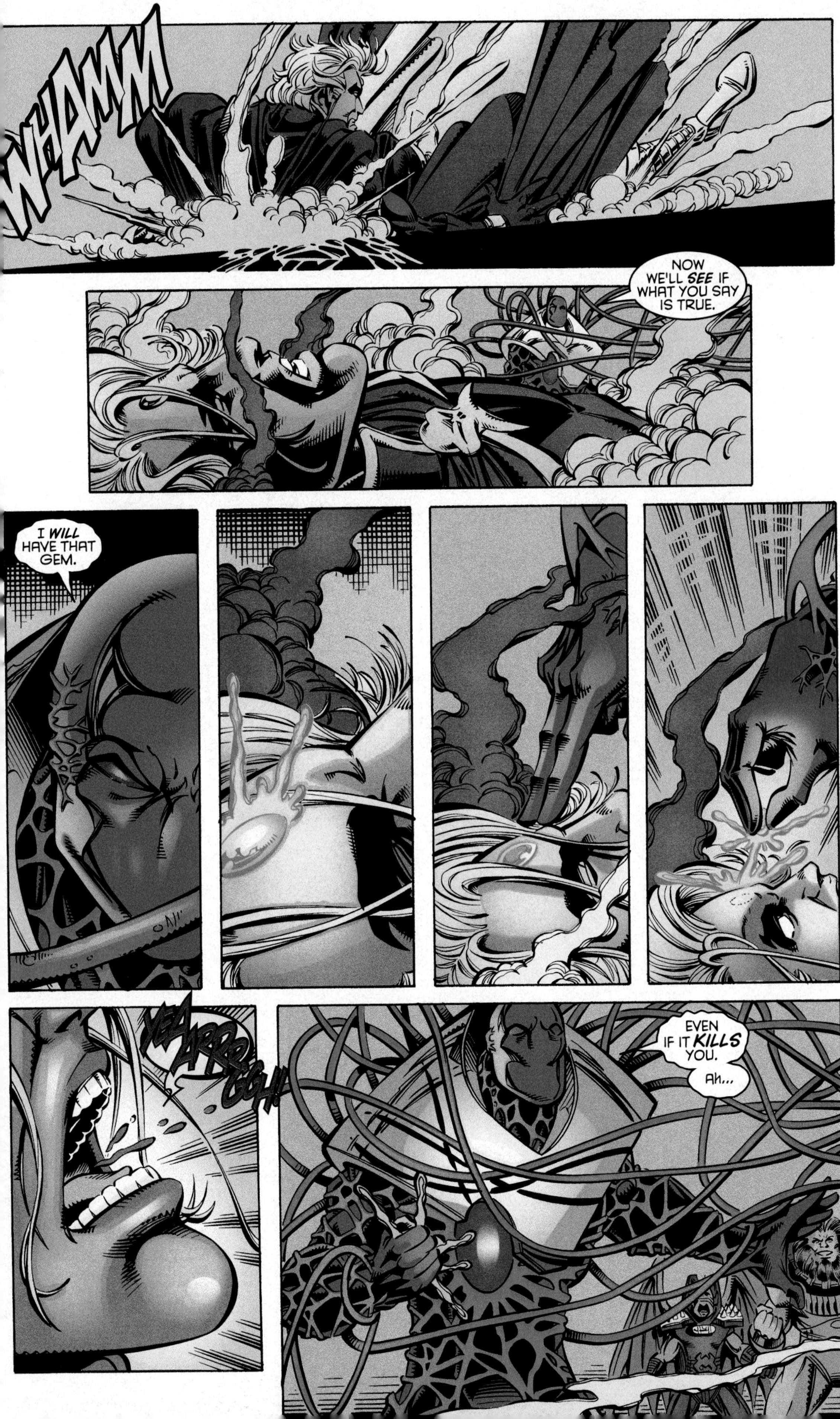
WHAMM
NOW WE'LL SEE IF WHAT YOU SAY IS TRUE.
I WILL HAVE THAT GEM.
YEAARRGGH!
EVEN IF IT KILLS YOU.
Ah...

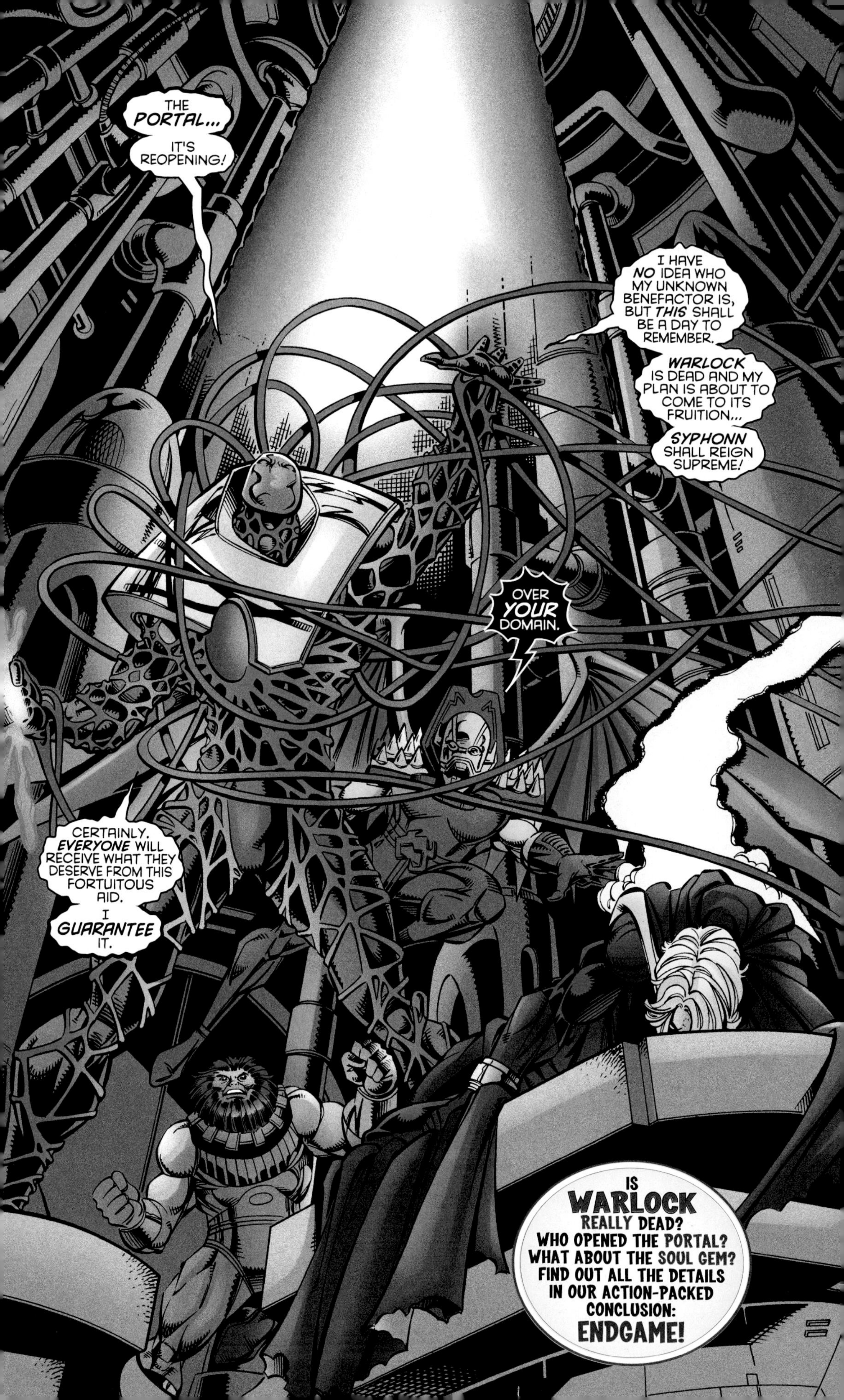
THE PORTAL... IT'S REOPENING!
I HAVE NO IDEA WHO MY UNKNOWN BENEFACTOR IS, BUT THIS SHALL BE A DAY TO REMEMBER.
WARLOCK IS DEAD AND MY PLAN IS ABOUT TO COME TO ITS FRUITION...
SYPHONN SHALL REIGN SUPREME!
OVER YOUR DOMAIN.
CERTAINLY. EVERYONE WILL RECEIVE WHAT THEY DESERVE FROM THIS FORTUITOUS AID.
I GUARANTEE IT.
IS WARLOCK REALLY DEAD? WHO OPENED THE PORTAL? WHAT ABOUT THE SOUL GEM? FIND OUT ALL THE DETAILS IN OUR ACTION-PACKED CONCLUSION: ENDGAME!

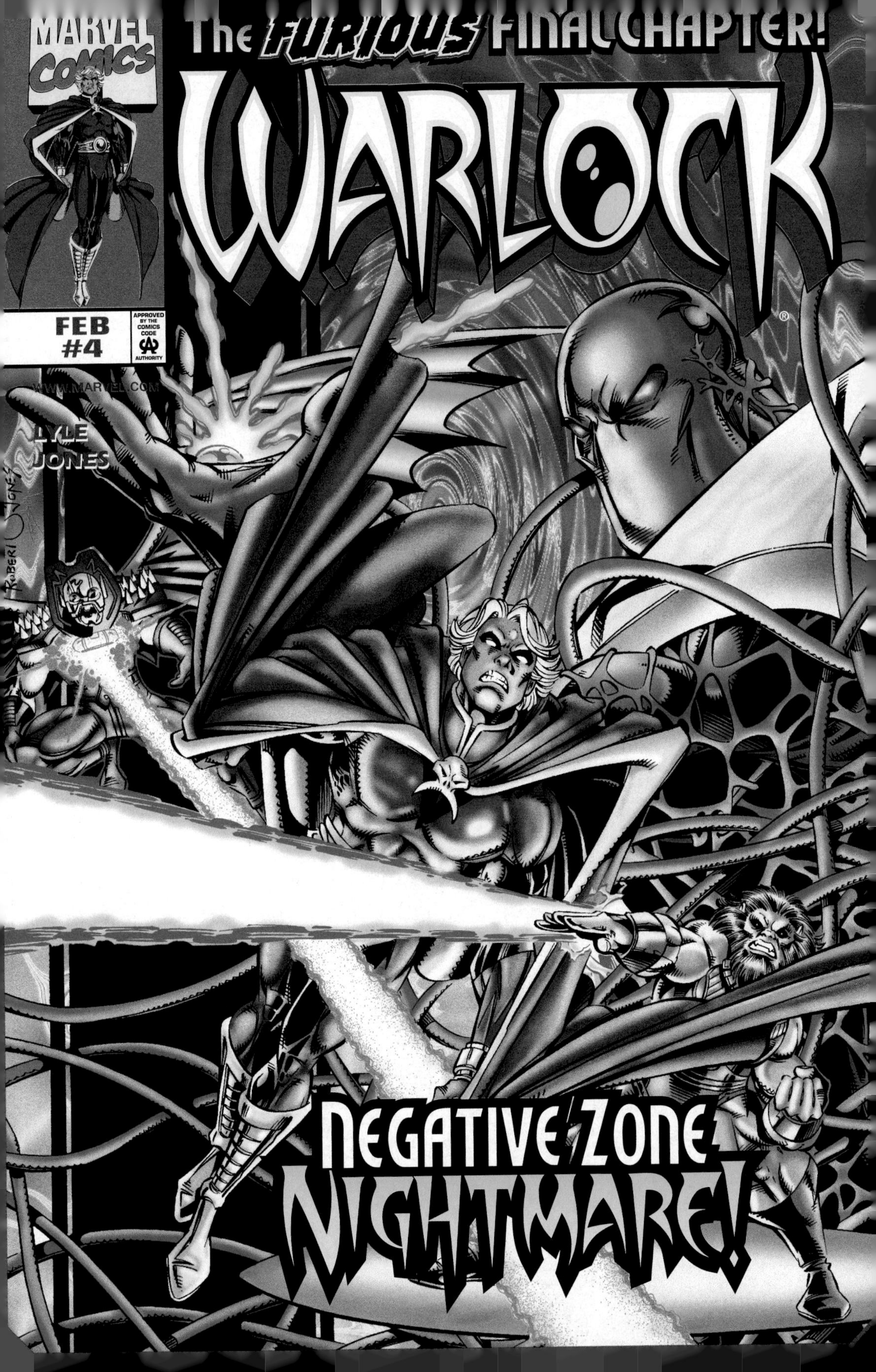
MARVEL COMICS
The FURIOUS FINAL CHAPTER!
WARLOCK
FEB
#4
APPROVED BY THE COMICS CODE AUTHORITY
WWW.MARVEL.COM
LYLE
JONES
NEGATIVE ZONE
NIGHTMARE!

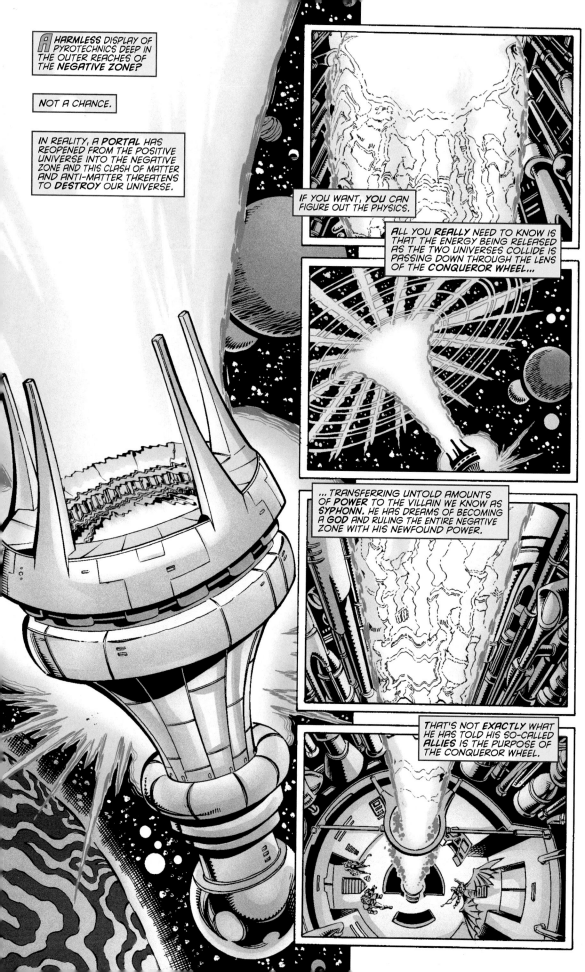

A HARMLESS DISPLAY OF PYROTECHNICS DEEP IN THE OUTER REACHES OF THE **NEGATIVE ZONE**?

NOT A CHANCE.

IN REALITY, A **PORTAL** HAS REOPENED FROM THE POSITIVE UNIVERSE INTO THE NEGATIVE ZONE AND THIS CLASH OF MATTER AND ANTI-MATTER THREATENS TO **DESTROY** OUR UNIVERSE.

IF YOU WANT, **YOU** CAN FIGURE OUT THE PHYSICS.

ALL YOU **REALLY** NEED TO KNOW IS THAT THE ENERGY BEING RELEASED AS THE TWO UNIVERSES COLLIDE IS PASSING DOWN THROUGH THE LENS OF THE **CONQUEROR WHEEL**...

...TRANSFERRING UNTOLD AMOUNTS OF **POWER** TO THE VILLAIN WE KNOW AS SYPHONN. HE HAS DREAMS OF BECOMING A **GOD** AND RULING THE ENTIRE NEGATIVE ZONE WITH HIS NEWFOUND POWER.

THAT'S NOT **EXACTLY** WHAT HE HAS TOLD HIS SO-CALLED **ALLIES** IS THE PURPOSE OF THE CONQUEROR WHEEL.

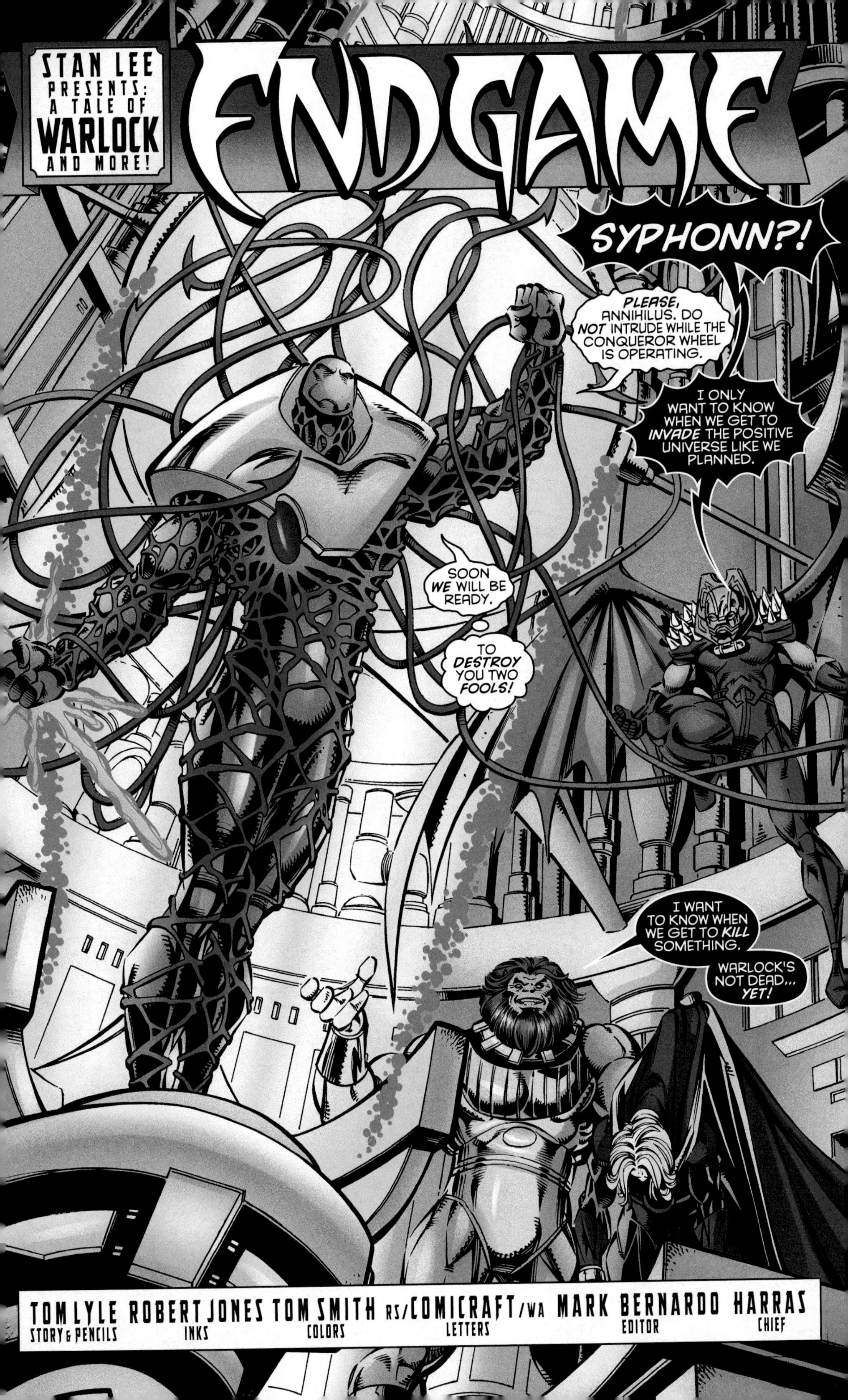
STAN LEE PRESENTS: A TALE OF WARLOCK AND MORE!
ENDGAME
SYPHONN?!
PLEASE, ANNIHILUS. DO NOT INTRUDE WHILE THE CONQUEROR WHEEL IS OPERATING.
I ONLY WANT TO KNOW WHEN WE GET TO INVADE THE POSITIVE UNIVERSE LIKE WE PLANNED.
SOON WE WILL BE READY.
TO DESTROY YOU TWO FOOLS!
I WANT TO KNOW WHEN WE GET TO KILL SOMETHING.
WARLOCK'S NOT DEAD... YET!
TOM LYLE STORY & PENCILS
ROBERT JONES INKS
TOM SMITH COLORS
RS/COMICRAFT/WA LETTERS
MARK BERNARDO EDITOR
HARRAS CHIEF

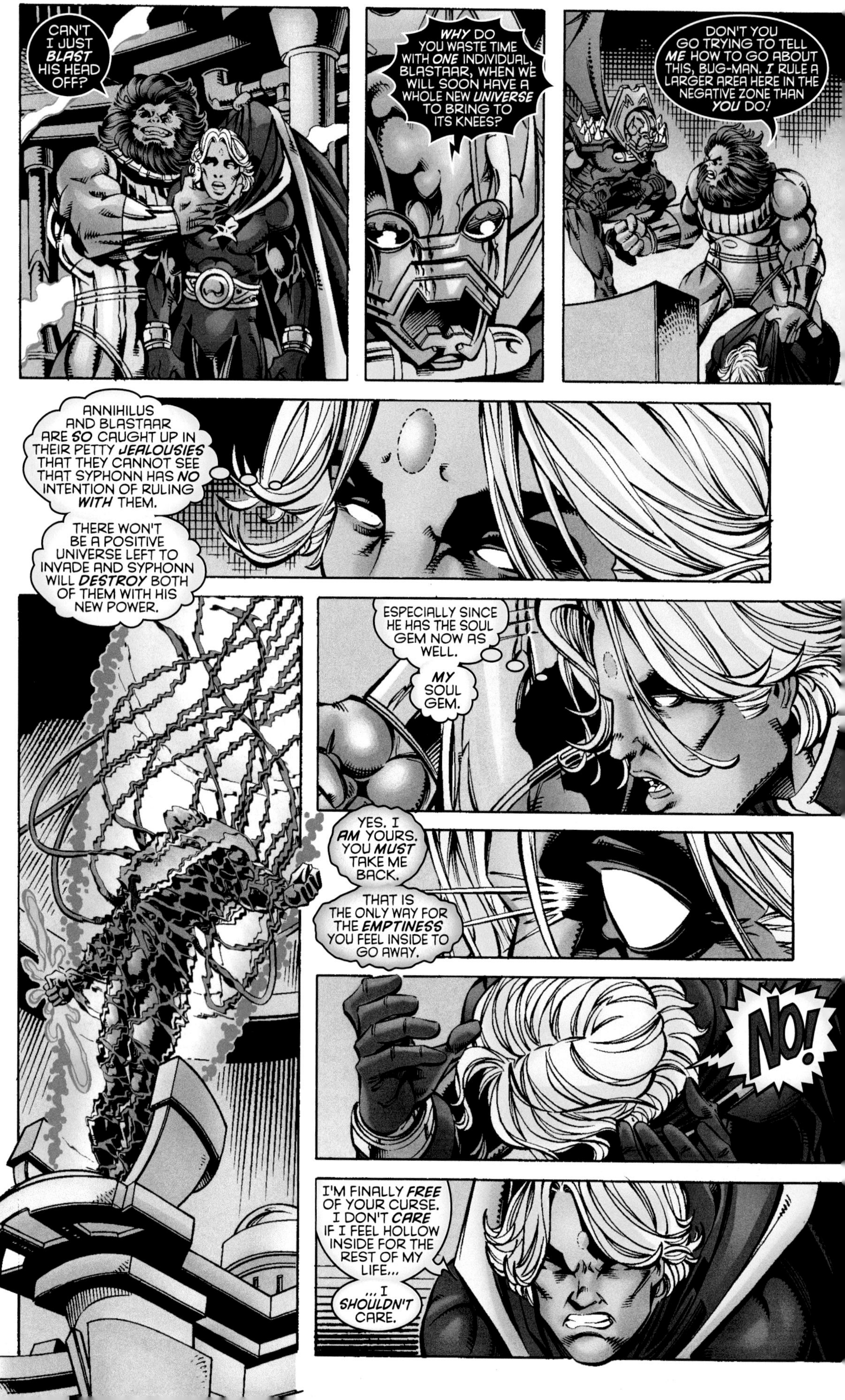
CAN'T I JUST BLAST HIS HEAD OFF?
WHY DO YOU WASTE TIME WITH ONE INDIVIDUAL, BLASTAAR, WHEN WE WILL SOON HAVE A WHOLE NEW UNIVERSE TO BRING TO ITS KNEES?
DON'T YOU GO TRYING TO TELL ME HOW TO GO ABOUT THIS, BUG-MAN. I RULE A LARGER AREA HERE IN THE NEGATIVE ZONE THAN YOU DO!
ANNIHILUS AND BLASTAAR ARE SO CAUGHT UP IN THEIR PETTY JEALOUSIES THAT THEY CANNOT SEE THAT SYPHONN HAS NO INTENTION OF RULING WITH THEM.
THERE WON'T BE A POSITIVE UNIVERSE LEFT TO INVADE AND SYPHONN WILL DESTROY BOTH OF THEM WITH HIS NEW POWER.
ESPECIALLY SINCE HE HAS THE SOUL GEM NOW AS WELL.
MY SOUL GEM.
YES. I AM YOURS. YOU MUST TAKE ME BACK.
THAT IS THE ONLY WAY FOR THE EMPTINESS YOU FEEL INSIDE TO GO AWAY.
NO!
I'M FINALLY FREE OF YOUR CURSE. I DON'T CARE IF I FEEL HOLLOW INSIDE FOR THE REST OF MY LIFE...
...I SHOULDN'T CARE.

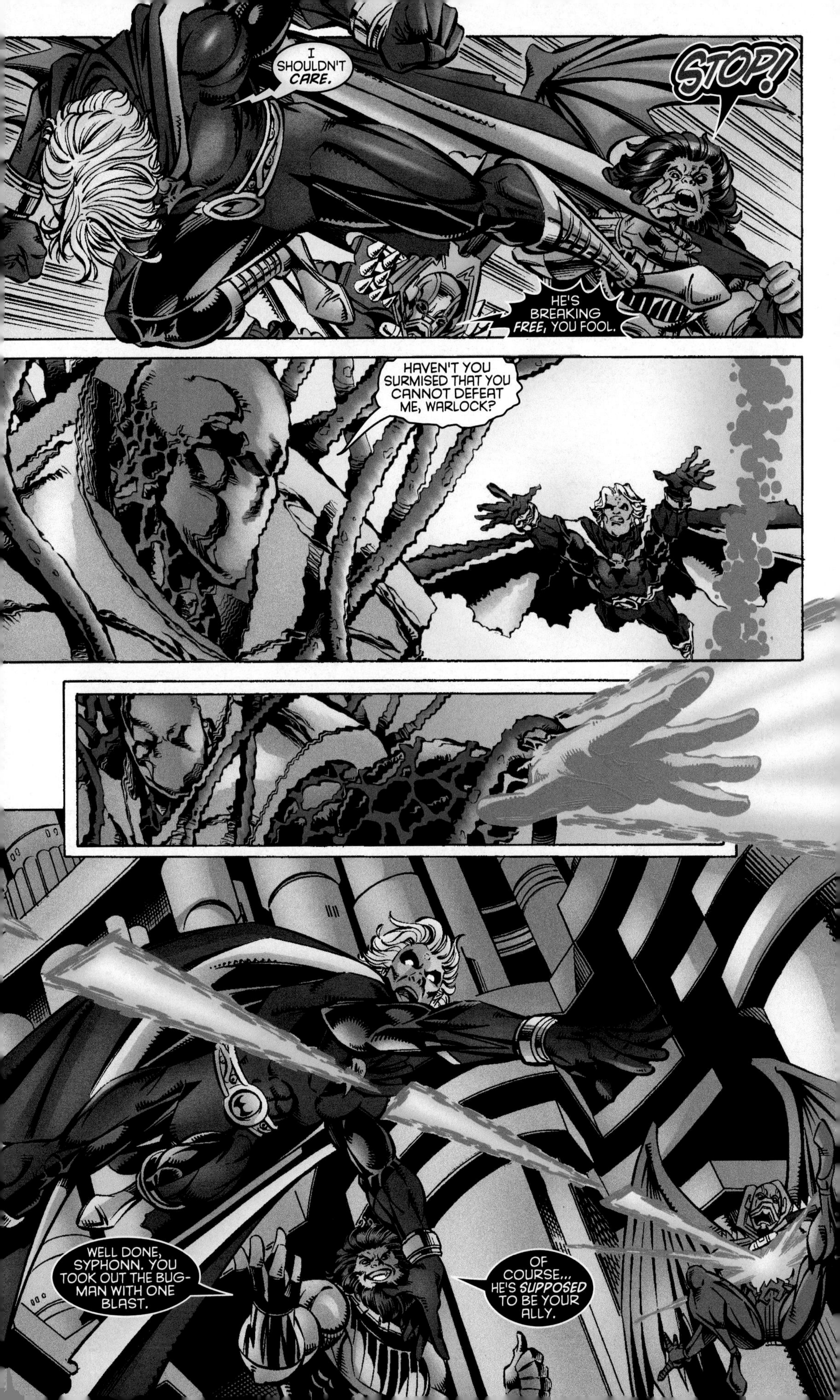
I SHOULDN'T CARE.
STOP!
HE'S BREAKING FREE, YOU FOOL.
HAVEN'T YOU SURMISED THAT YOU CANNOT DEFEAT ME, WARLOCK?
WELL DONE, SYPHONN. YOU TOOK OUT THE BUG-MAN WITH ONE BLAST.
OF COURSE... HE'S SUPPOSED TO BE YOUR ALLY.

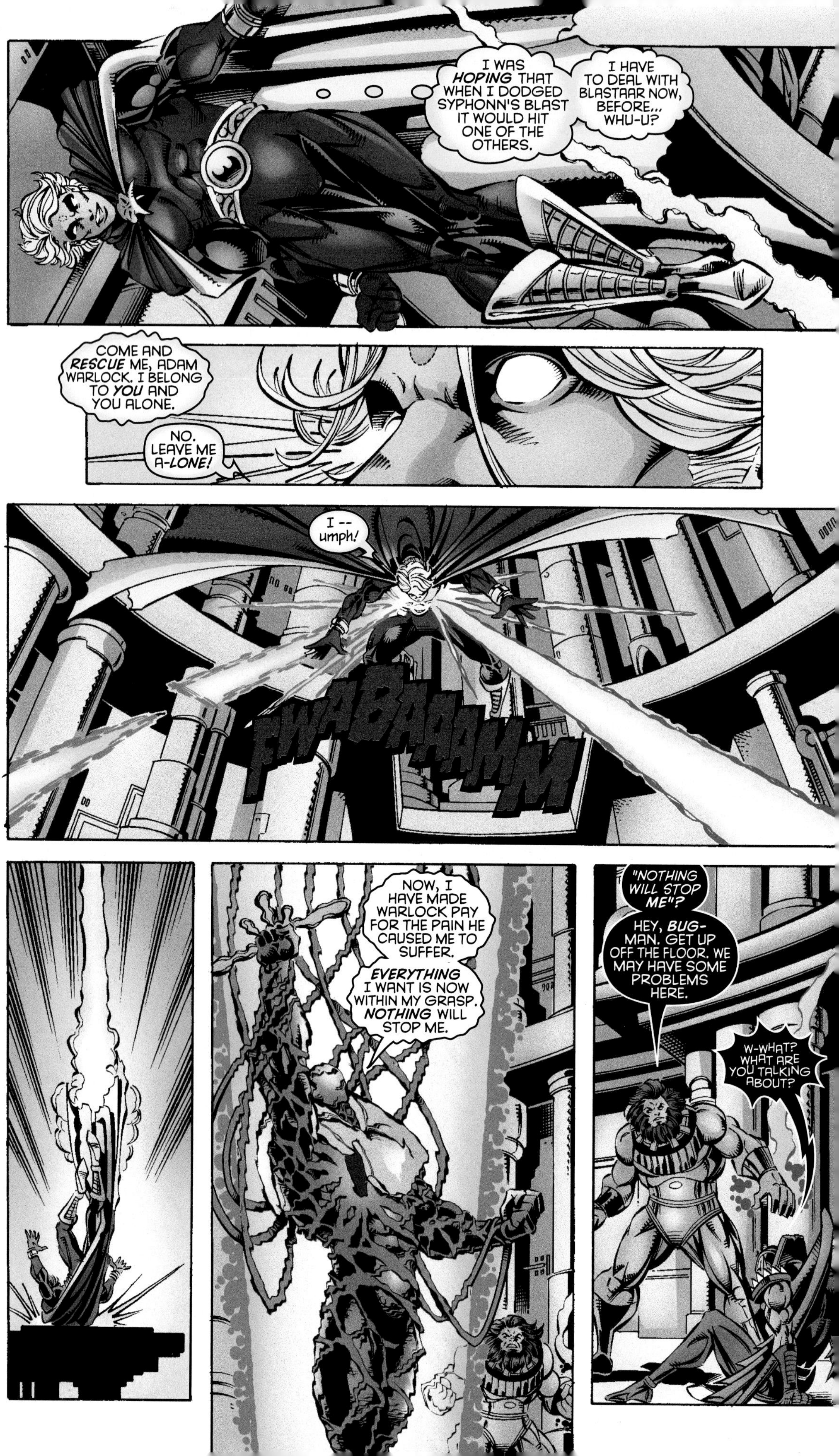
I WAS *HOPING* THAT WHEN I DODGED SYPHONN'S BLAST IT WOULD HIT ONE OF THE OTHERS.
I HAVE TO DEAL WITH BLASTAAR NOW, BEFORE... WHU-U?
COME AND *RESCUE* ME, ADAM WARLOCK. I BELONG TO *YOU* AND YOU ALONE.
NO. LEAVE ME A-*LONE!*
I -- umph!
FWABAAAAMMM
NOW, I HAVE MADE WARLOCK PAY FOR THE PAIN HE CAUSED ME TO SUFFER.
EVERYTHING I WANT IS NOW WITHIN MY GRASP. *NOTHING* WILL STOP ME.
"NOTHING WILL STOP *ME*"?
HEY, *BUG*-MAN. GET UP OFF THE FLOOR. WE MAY HAVE SOME PROBLEMS HERE.
W-WHAT? WHAT ARE YOU TALKING ABOUT?

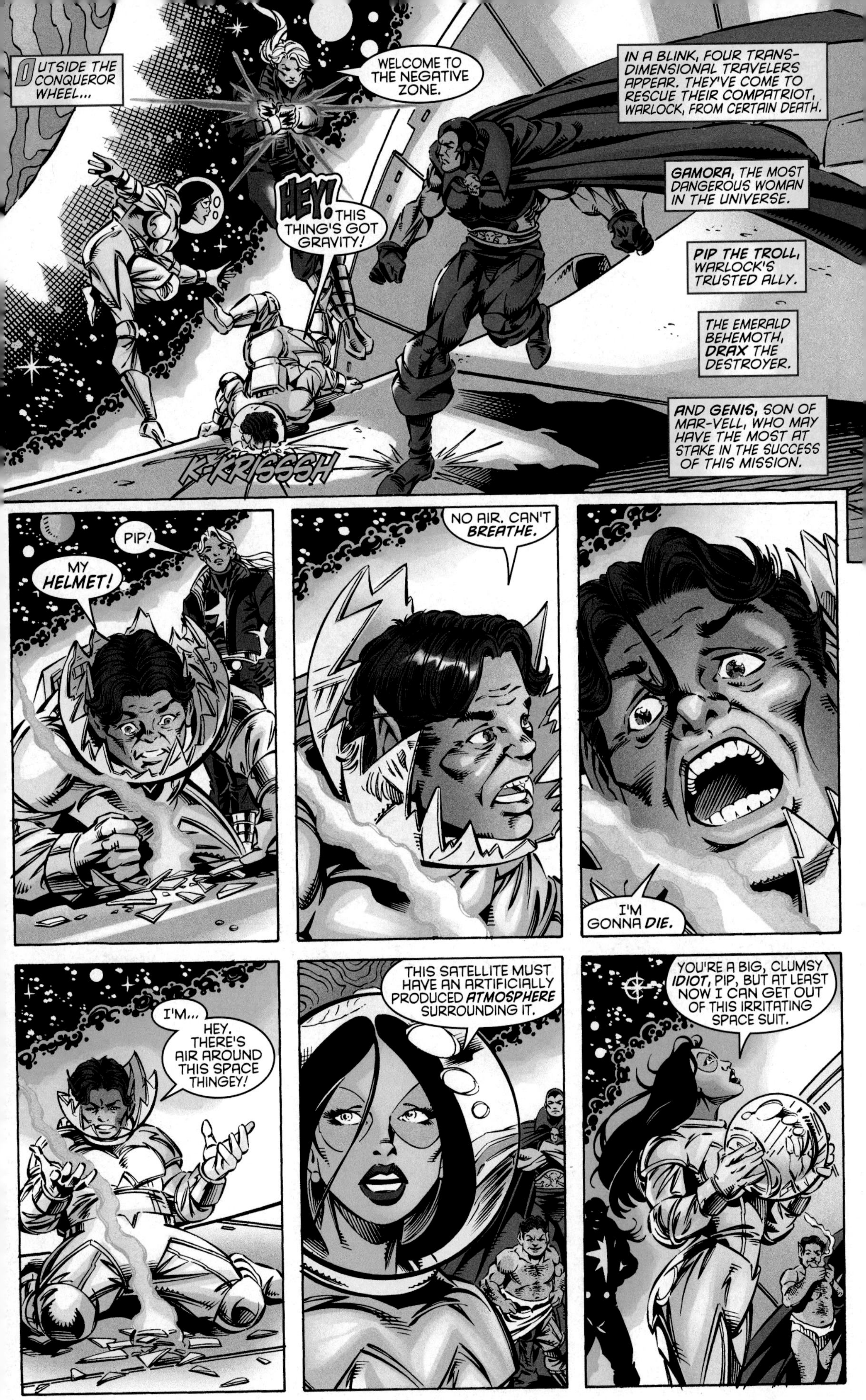
OUTSIDE THE CONQUEROR WHEEL...
WELCOME TO THE NEGATIVE ZONE.
IN A BLINK, FOUR TRANS-DIMENSIONAL TRAVELERS APPEAR. THEY'VE COME TO RESCUE THEIR COMPATRIOT, WARLOCK, FROM CERTAIN DEATH.
GAMORA, THE MOST DANGEROUS WOMAN IN THE UNIVERSE.
HEY! THIS THING'S GOT GRAVITY!
PIP THE TROLL, WARLOCK'S TRUSTED ALLY.
THE EMERALD BEHEMOTH, DRAX THE DESTROYER.
AND GENIS, SON OF MAR-VELL, WHO MAY HAVE THE MOST AT STAKE IN THE SUCCESS OF THIS MISSION.
K-KRISSSH
PIP!
MY HELMET!
NO AIR. CAN'T BREATHE.
I'M GONNA DIE.
I'M... HEY. THERE'S AIR AROUND THIS SPACE THINGEY!
THIS SATELLITE MUST HAVE AN ARTIFICIALLY PRODUCED ATMOSPHERE SURROUNDING IT.
YOU'RE A BIG, CLUMSY IDIOT, PIP, BUT AT LEAST NOW I CAN GET OUT OF THIS IRRITATING SPACE SUIT.

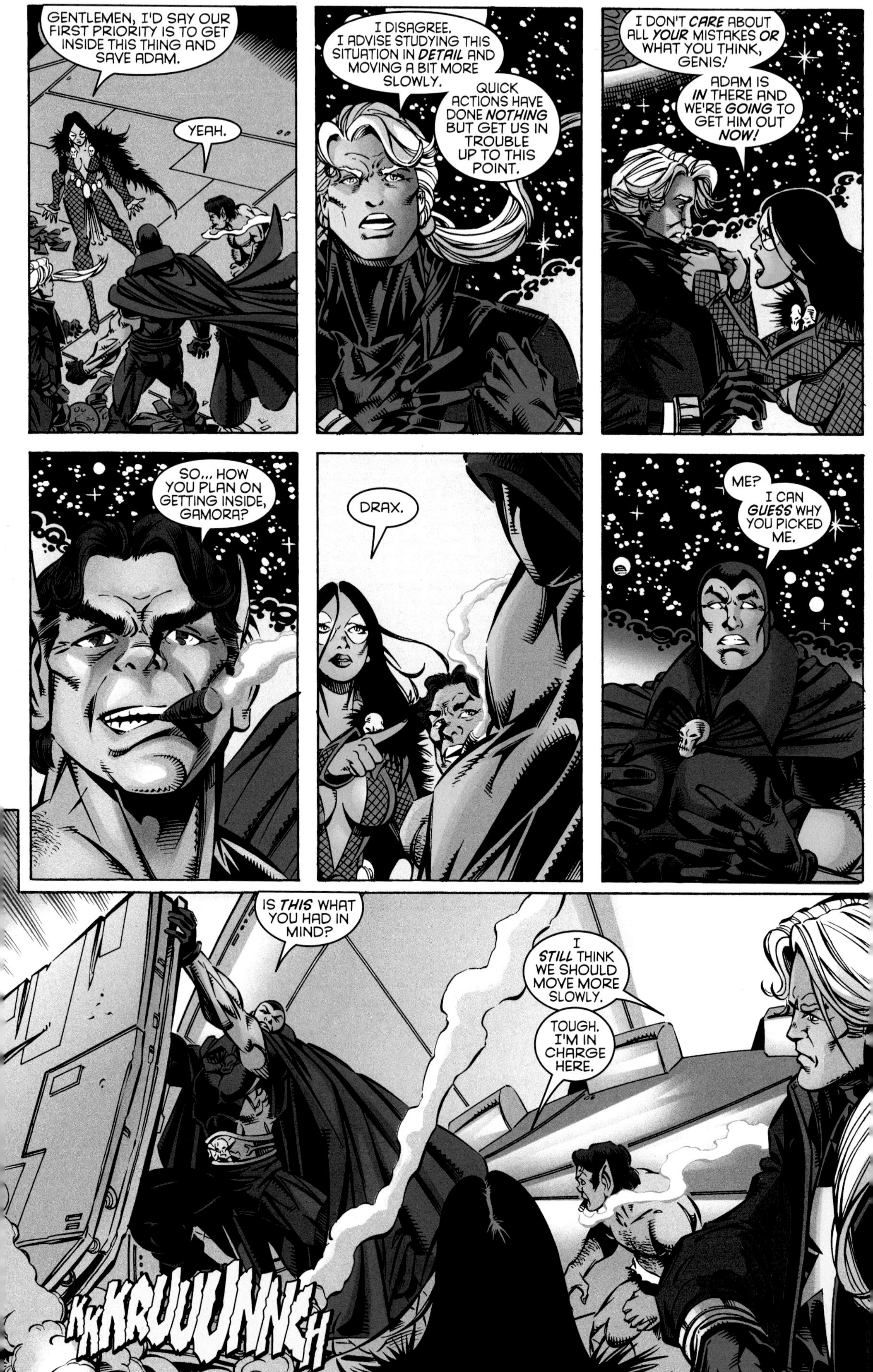
GENTLEMEN, I'D SAY OUR FIRST PRIORITY IS TO GET INSIDE THIS THING AND SAVE ADAM.
YEAH.
I DISAGREE. I ADVISE STUDYING THIS SITUATION IN DETAIL AND MOVING A BIT MORE SLOWLY.
QUICK ACTIONS HAVE DONE NOTHING BUT GET US IN TROUBLE UP TO THIS POINT.
I DON'T CARE ABOUT ALL YOUR MISTAKES OR WHAT YOU THINK, GENIS!
ADAM IS IN THERE AND WE'RE GOING TO GET HIM OUT NOW!
SO... HOW YOU PLAN ON GETTING INSIDE, GAMORA?
DRAX.
ME? I CAN GUESS WHY YOU PICKED ME.
IS THIS WHAT YOU HAD IN MIND?
I STILL THINK WE SHOULD MOVE MORE SLOWLY.
TOUGH. I'M IN CHARGE HERE.
KKKRUUUNNCH

I DON'T CARE *WHAT* YOU THINK YOU HEARD, BLASTAAR. SYPHONN IS OUR *PARTNER*.

YOU SHOULD *LISTEN* TO BLASTAAR, ANNIHILUS.

I'VE SEEN *INSIDE* SYPHONN'S MIND. AS SOON AS THIS ENERGY TRANSFER IS COMPLETE, HE'S GOING TO KILL YOU *BOTH*.

ENERGY TRANSFER? *WHAT* ENERGY TRANSFER?

YOU'RE WATCHING IT RIGHT NOW.

DON'T *LISTEN* TO HIM, BLASTAAR. HE'S JUST TRYING TO GET US TO TURN *AGAINST* EACH OTHER.

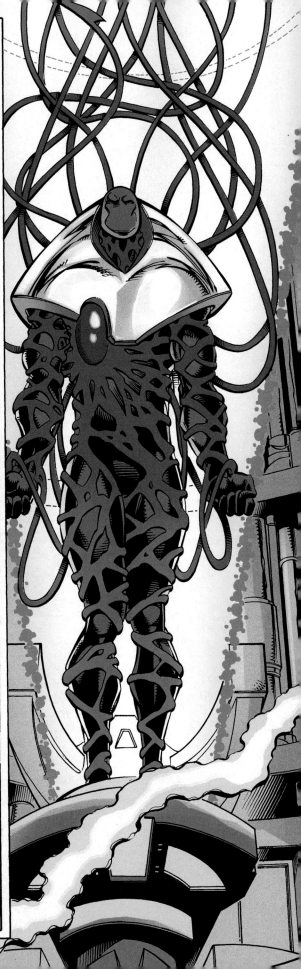

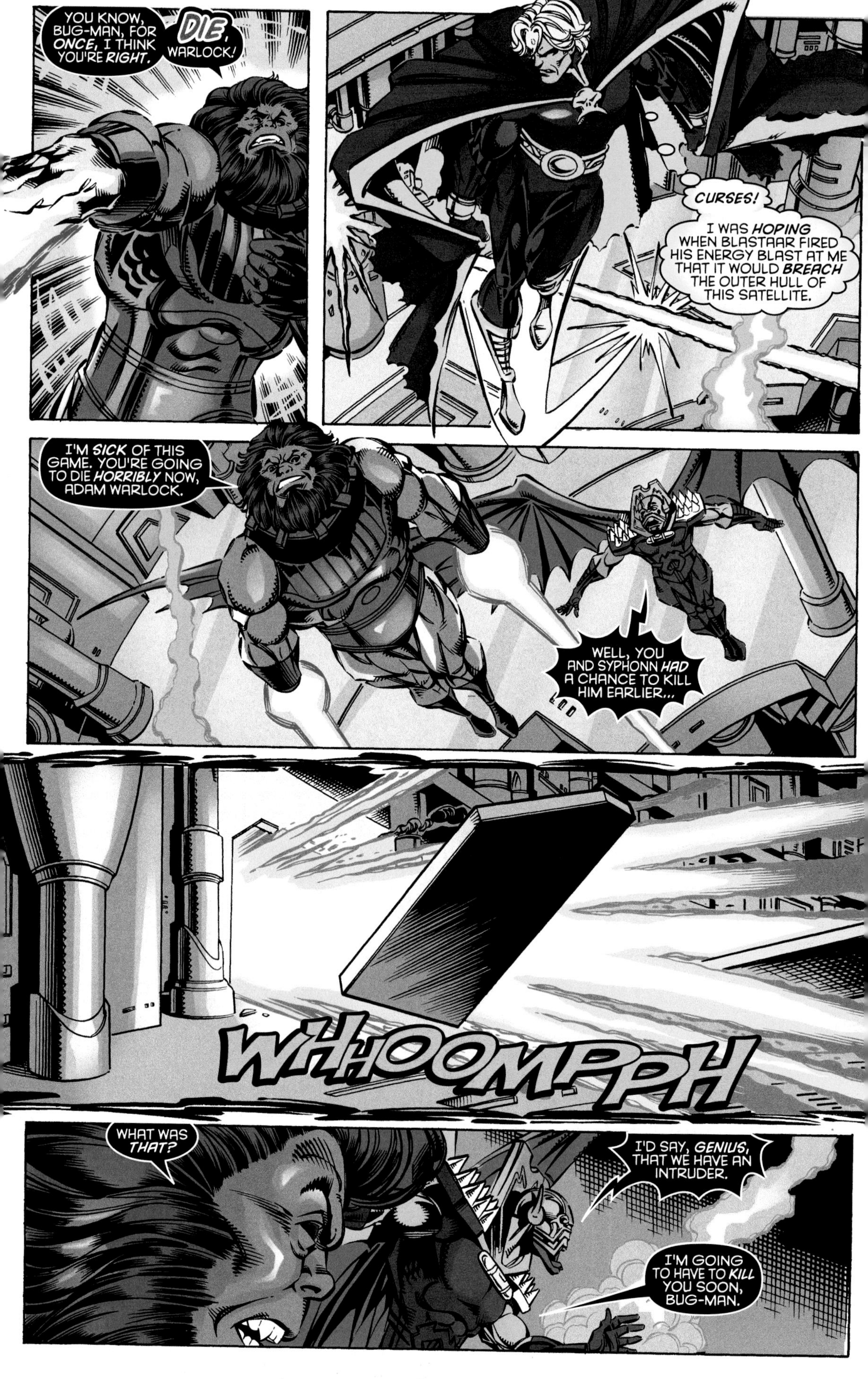
YOU KNOW, BUG-MAN, FOR ONCE, I THINK YOU'RE RIGHT.
DIE, WARLOCK!
CURSES!
I WAS HOPING WHEN BLASTAAR FIRED HIS ENERGY BLAST AT ME THAT IT WOULD BREACH THE OUTER HULL OF THIS SATELLITE.
I'M SICK OF THIS GAME. YOU'RE GOING TO DIE HORRIBLY NOW, ADAM WARLOCK.
WELL, YOU AND SYPHONN HAD A CHANCE TO KILL HIM EARLIER...
WHHOOMPPH
WHAT WAS THAT?
I'D SAY, GENIUS, THAT WE HAVE AN INTRUDER.
I'M GOING TO HAVE TO KILL YOU SOON, BUG-MAN.

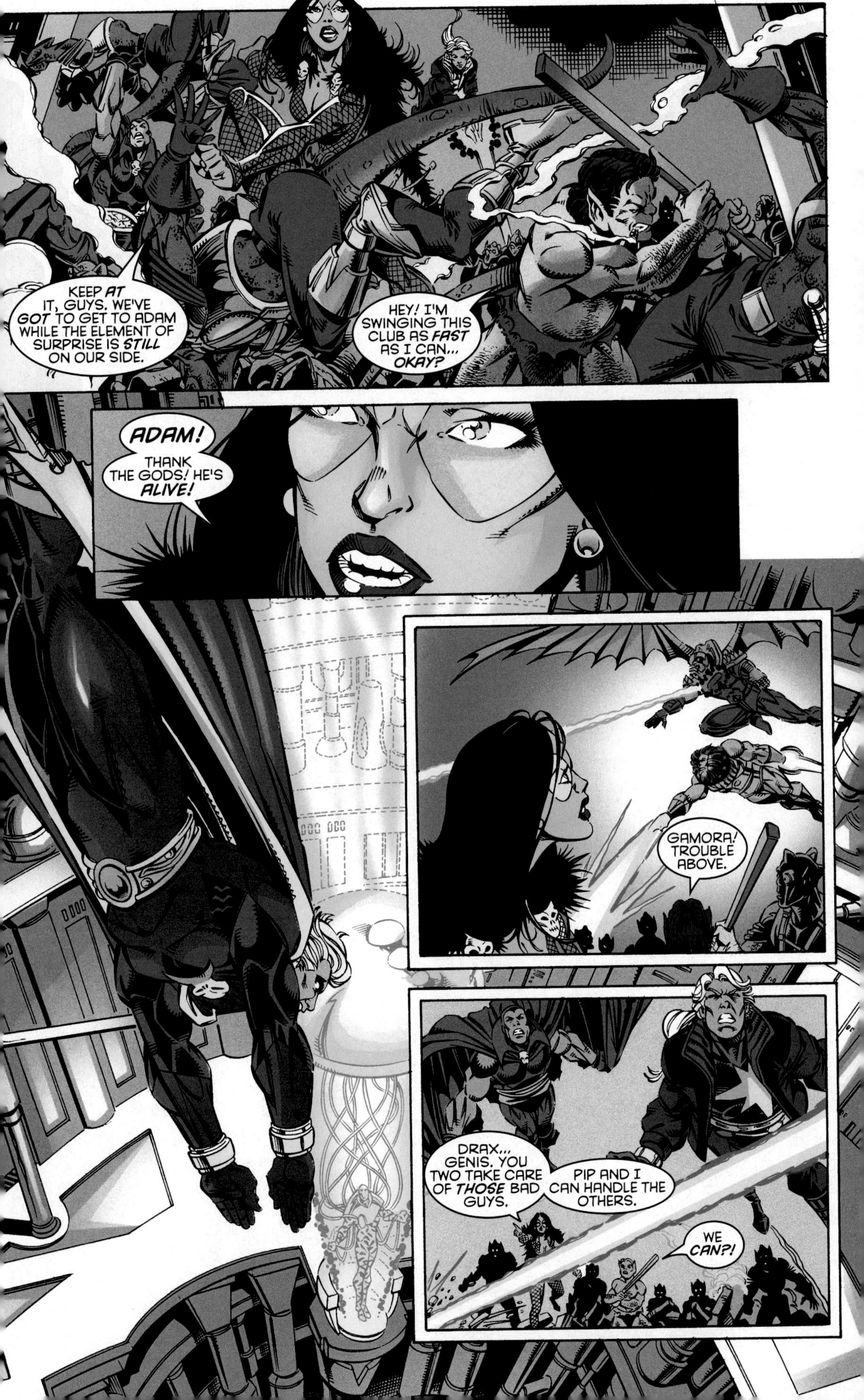
KEEP *AT* IT, GUYS. WE'VE *GOT* TO GET TO ADAM WHILE THE ELEMENT OF SURPRISE IS *STILL* ON OUR SIDE.
HEY! I'M SWINGING THIS CLUB AS *FAST* AS I CAN... *OKAY?*
ADAM!
THANK THE GODS! HE'S *ALIVE!*
GAMORA! TROUBLE ABOVE.
DRAX... GENIS. YOU TWO TAKE CARE OF *THOSE* BAD GUYS.
PIP AND I CAN HANDLE THE OTHERS.
WE *CAN?!*

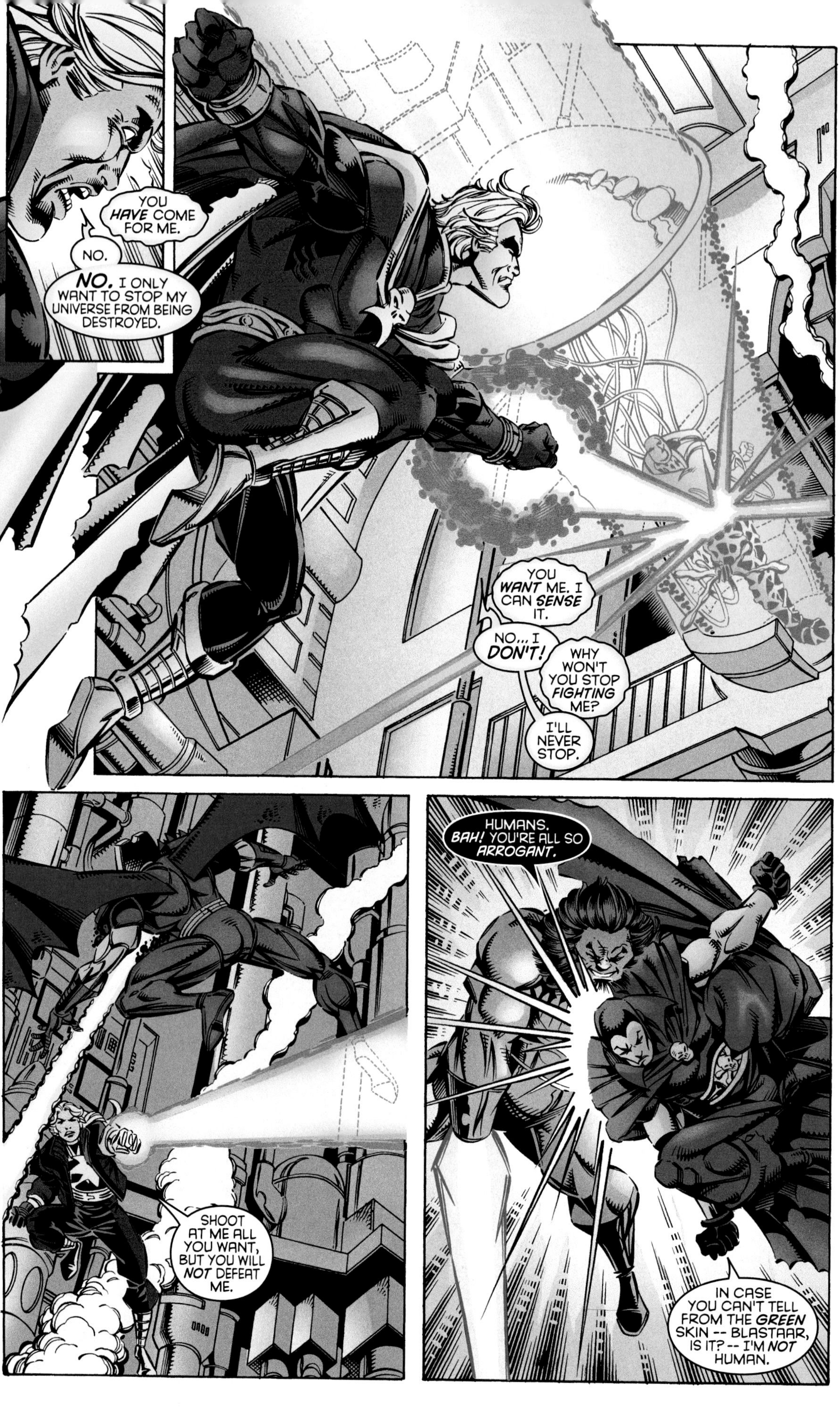
YOU HAVE COME FOR ME.
NO.
NO. I ONLY WANT TO STOP MY UNIVERSE FROM BEING DESTROYED.
YOU WANT ME. I CAN SENSE IT.
NO... I DON'T!
WHY WON'T YOU STOP FIGHTING ME?
I'LL NEVER STOP.
SHOOT AT ME ALL YOU WANT, BUT YOU WILL NOT DEFEAT ME.
HUMANS. BAH! YOU'RE ALL SO ARROGANT.
IN CASE YOU CAN'T TELL FROM THE GREEN SKIN -- BLASTAAR, IS IT? -- I'M NOT HUMAN.

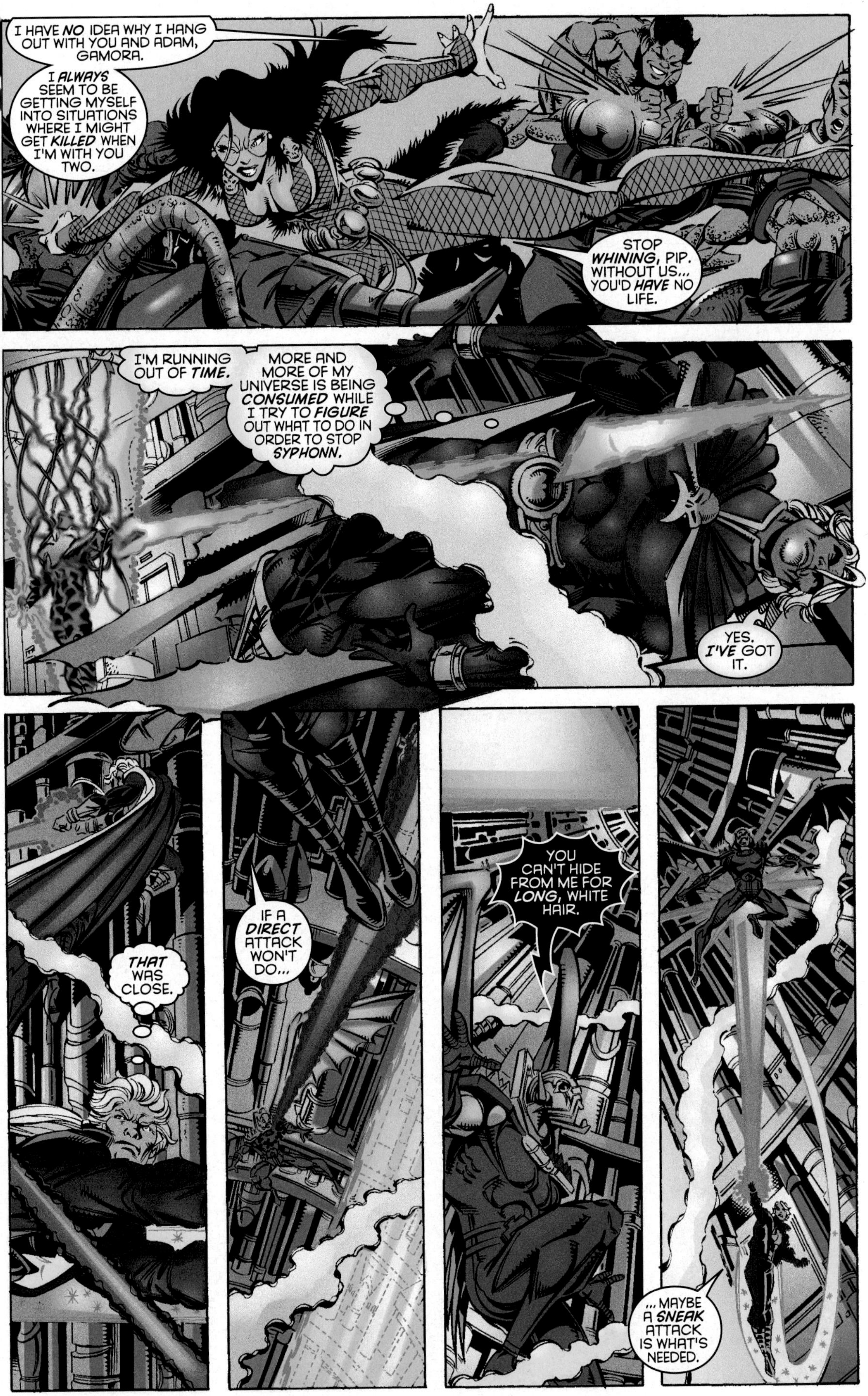
I HAVE NO IDEA WHY I HANG OUT WITH YOU AND ADAM, GAMORA.
I ALWAYS SEEM TO BE GETTING MYSELF INTO SITUATIONS WHERE I MIGHT GET KILLED WHEN I'M WITH YOU TWO.
STOP WHINING, PIP. WITHOUT US... YOU'D HAVE NO LIFE.
I'M RUNNING OUT OF TIME.
MORE AND MORE OF MY UNIVERSE IS BEING CONSUMED WHILE I TRY TO FIGURE OUT WHAT TO DO IN ORDER TO STOP SYPHONN.
YES. I'VE GOT IT.
THAT WAS CLOSE.
IF A DIRECT ATTACK WON'T DO...
YOU CAN'T HIDE FROM ME FOR LONG, WHITE HAIR.
...MAYBE A SNEAK ATTACK IS WHAT'S NEEDED.

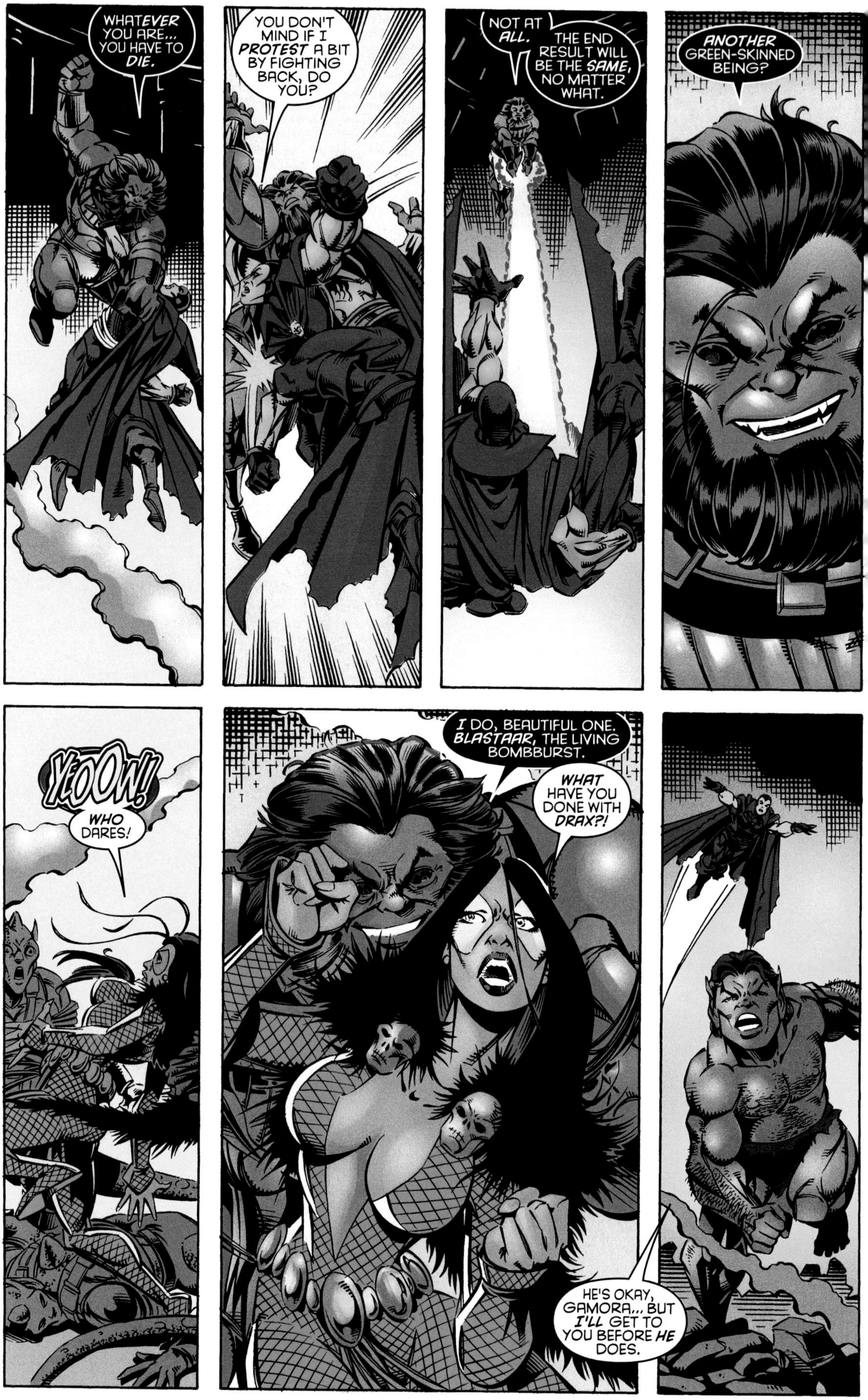
WHATEVER YOU ARE... YOU HAVE TO DIE.
YOU DON'T MIND IF I PROTEST A BIT BY FIGHTING BACK, DO YOU?
NOT AT ALL.
THE END RESULT WILL BE THE SAME, NO MATTER WHAT.
ANOTHER GREEN-SKINNED BEING?
YEOOW!
WHO DARES!
I DO, BEAUTIFUL ONE. BLASTAAR, THE LIVING BOMBBURST.
WHAT HAVE YOU DONE WITH DRAX?!
HE'S OKAY, GAMORA... BUT I'LL GET TO YOU BEFORE HE DOES.

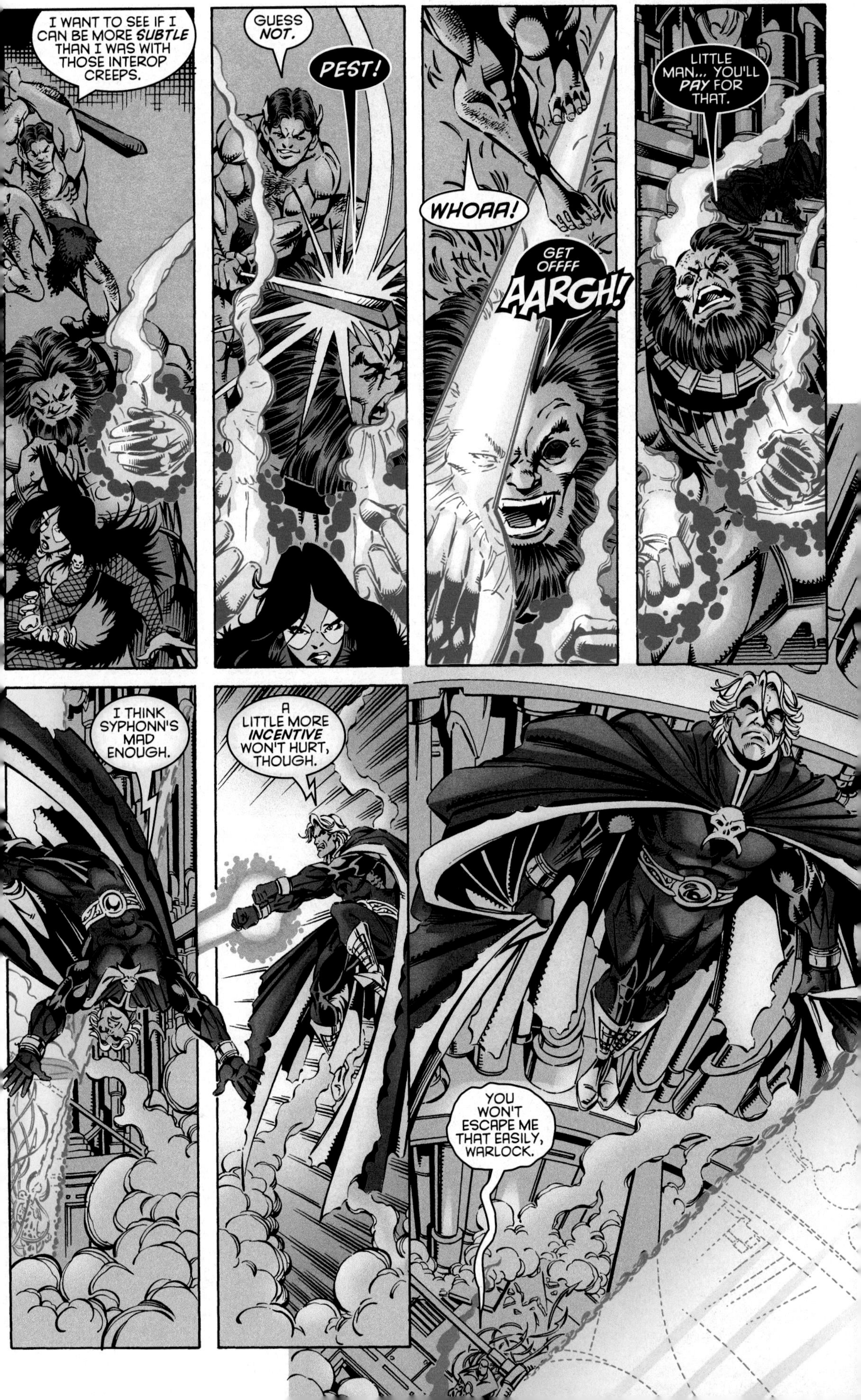
I WANT TO SEE IF I CAN BE MORE SUBTLE THAN I WAS WITH THOSE INTEROP CREEPS.
GUESS NOT.
PEST!
WHOAA!
GET OFFFF
AARGH!
LITTLE MAN... YOU'LL PAY FOR THAT.
I THINK SYPHONN'S MAD ENOUGH.
A LITTLE MORE INCENTIVE WON'T HURT, THOUGH.
YOU WON'T ESCAPE ME THAT EASILY, WARLOCK.

YES. *HE'S* MAD ENOUGH.

NOW... LET'S HOPE *HIS* BLAST DOES THE JOB.

THAT'S *ONE* STEP DOWN... *UNGH*... AND *ONE* TO GO.

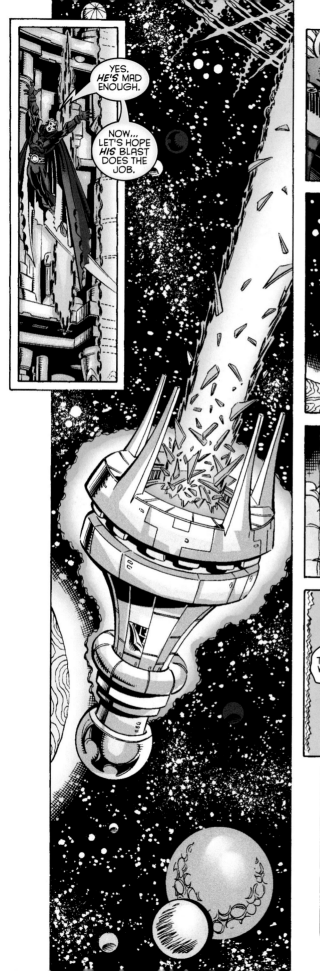

NOOOO!

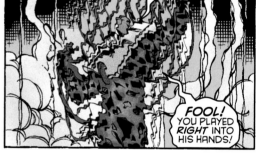

FOOL! YOU PLAYED *RIGHT* INTO HIS HANDS!

NOW THE PORTAL WILL *CLOSE* AGAIN.

"AND IT'S *MY* FAULT."

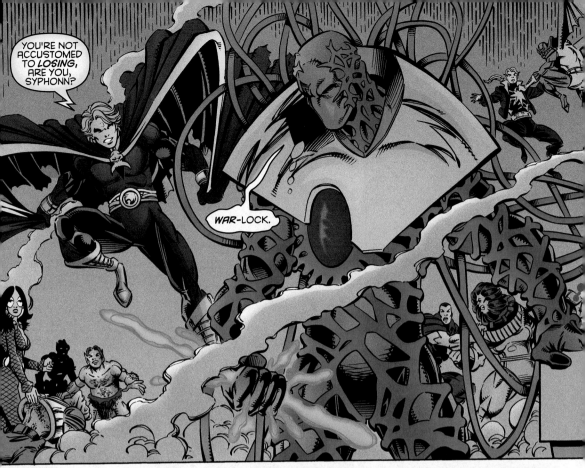

YOU'RE NOT ACCUSTOMED TO *LOSING*, ARE YOU, SYPHONN?

WAR-LOCK.

YOU MIGHT *STILL* BE ABLE TO CLAIM VICTORY FOR YOURSELF.

AND HOW IS *THAT*?

YOU *STILL* HAVE MY SOUL GEM. WHY DON'T YOU *USE* IT?

ADAM... HAVE YOU *LOST* YOUR MIND?!

WOW. *REALLY.* ARE YOU *NUTS*?

YOU *MUST* HAVE AN ULTERIOR MOTIVE FOR ENCOURAGING ME TO USE THIS GEM.

NONETHELESS, PERHAPS IT'S *NOT* A BAD IDEA AFTER ALL.

NOT A BAD IDEA AT *ALL*.

ESPECIALLY IF I CAN MAKE YOU *PAY* FOR YOUR INTERFERENCE BY STEALING *YOUR* SOUL WITH YOUR *OWN* GEM.

WHY DO YOU SMILE AT ME SO?

NO. *WAIT!*

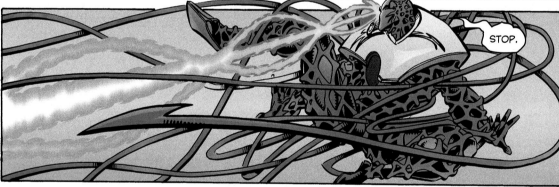

STOP.

THE GEM IS ATTACKING *ME!*

I AM *SYPHONNN!* I WILL NOT LOSE!

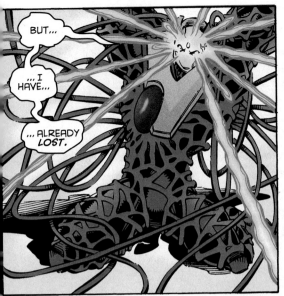

BUT...

...I HAVE...

...ALREADY LOST.

I WILL *NOT*... GIVE YOU THE... *SATISFACTION* OF HAVING MY... *SOUL*... AS WELL.

I HAVE USED THE POWER PORTALS I ESTABLISHED IN YOUR UNIVERSE TO SUSTAIN MYSELF WITH LIMITED POWER FOR YEARS.

VICTORY WILL ULTIMATELY BE MINE WHEN I TRANSMIT MY ENTITY INTO ONE OF THOSE POWER PORTALS.

FROM THERE, THE DESTRUCTION OF YOUR *HOME* WORLD, ADAM WARLOCK, WILL BE MY SWEET *REVENGE* FOR THIS IGNOMINIOUS DEFEAT.

EARTH WILL FALL BEFORE THE POWER OF...

...SYPHONNNNNNN.

POIT

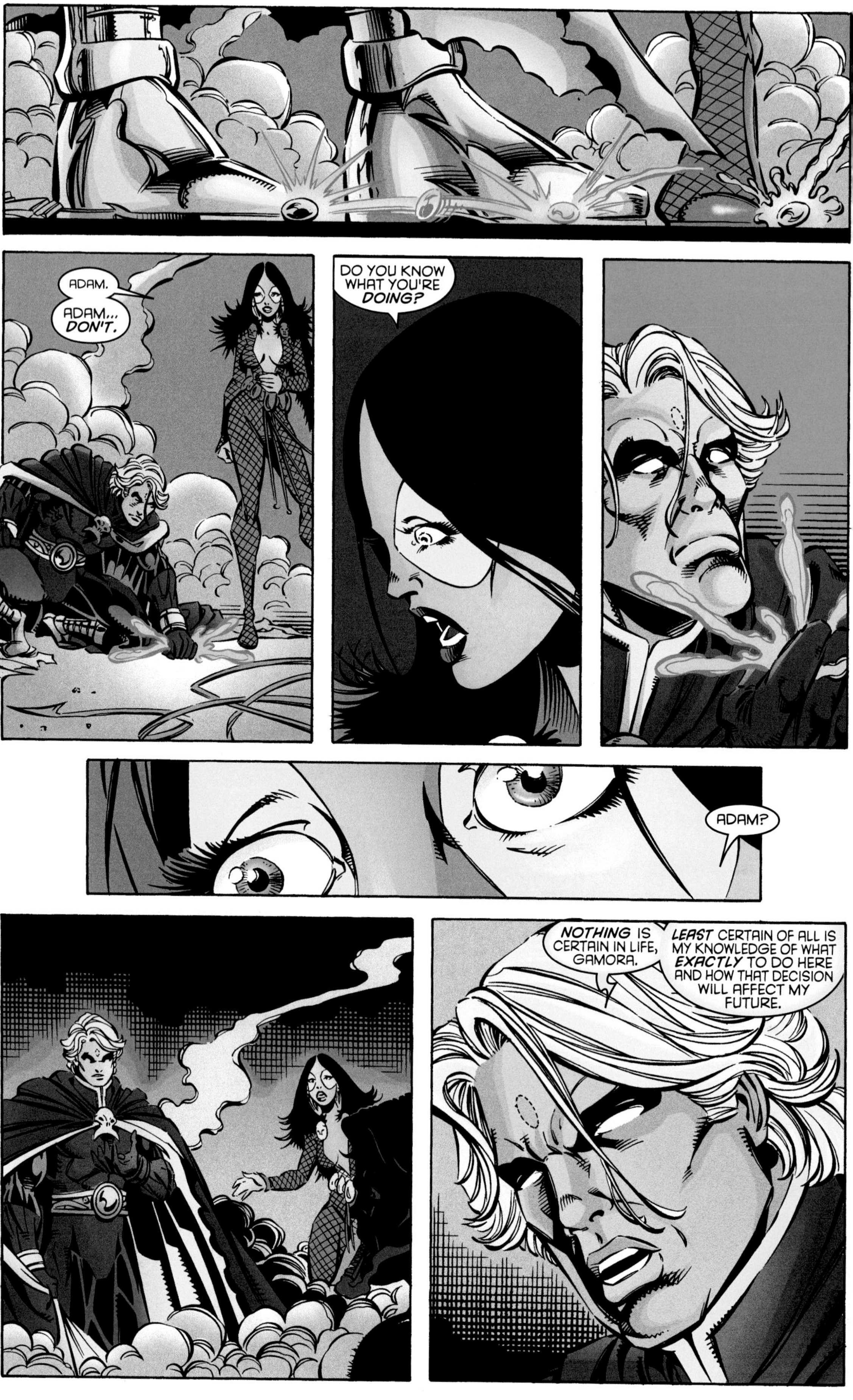
ADAM.
ADAM... DON'T.
DO YOU KNOW WHAT YOU'RE DOING?
ADAM?
NOTHING IS CERTAIN IN LIFE, GAMORA.
LEAST CERTAIN OF ALL IS MY KNOWLEDGE OF WHAT EXACTLY TO DO HERE AND HOW THAT DECISION WILL AFFECT MY FUTURE.

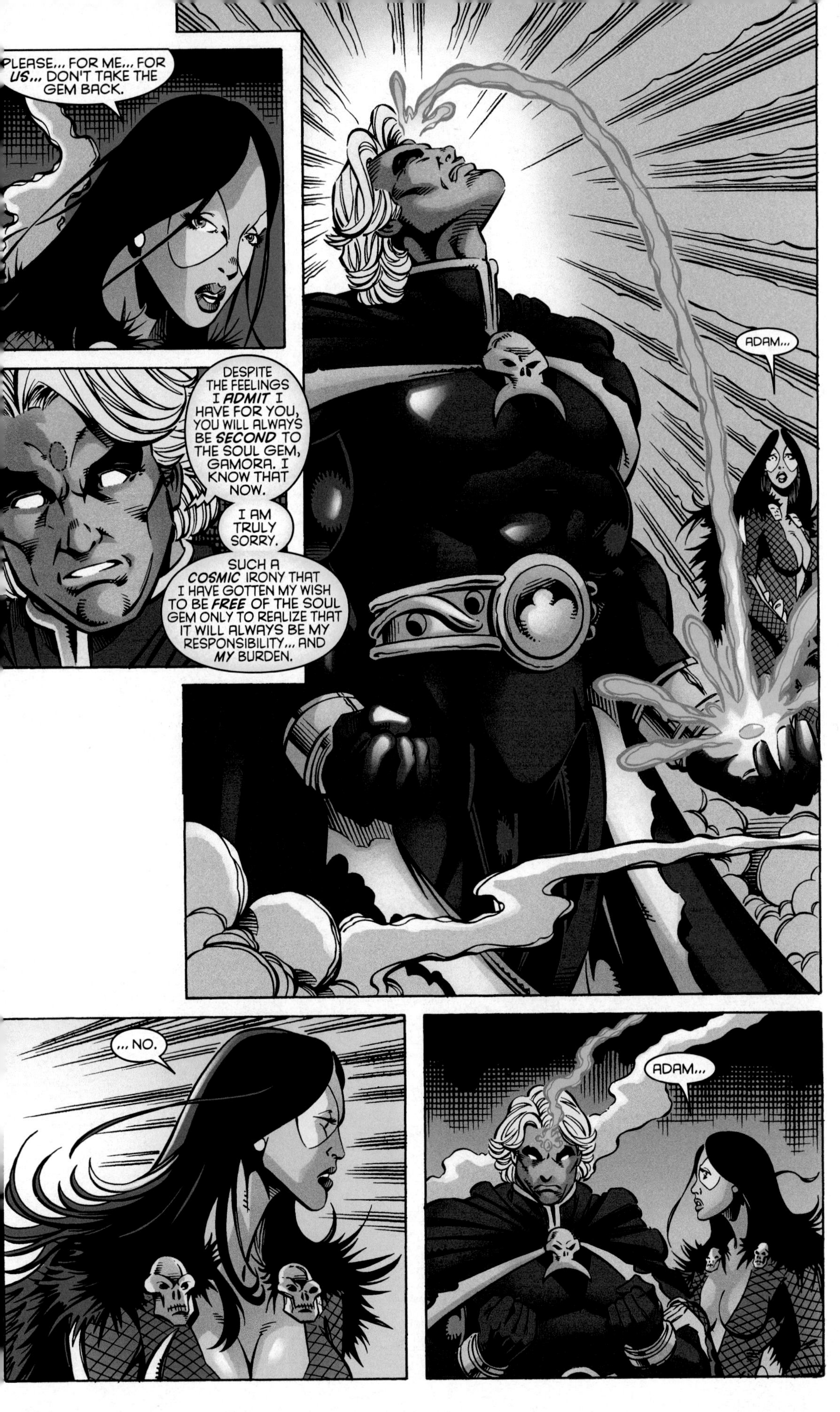
PLEASE... FOR ME... FOR US... DON'T TAKE THE GEM BACK.
ADAM...
DESPITE THE FEELINGS I ADMIT I HAVE FOR YOU, YOU WILL ALWAYS BE SECOND TO THE SOUL GEM, GAMORA. I KNOW THAT NOW.
I AM TRULY SORRY.
SUCH A COSMIC IRONY THAT I HAVE GOTTEN MY WISH TO BE FREE OF THE SOUL GEM ONLY TO REALIZE THAT IT WILL ALWAYS BE MY RESPONSIBILITY... AND MY BURDEN.
...NO.
ADAM...

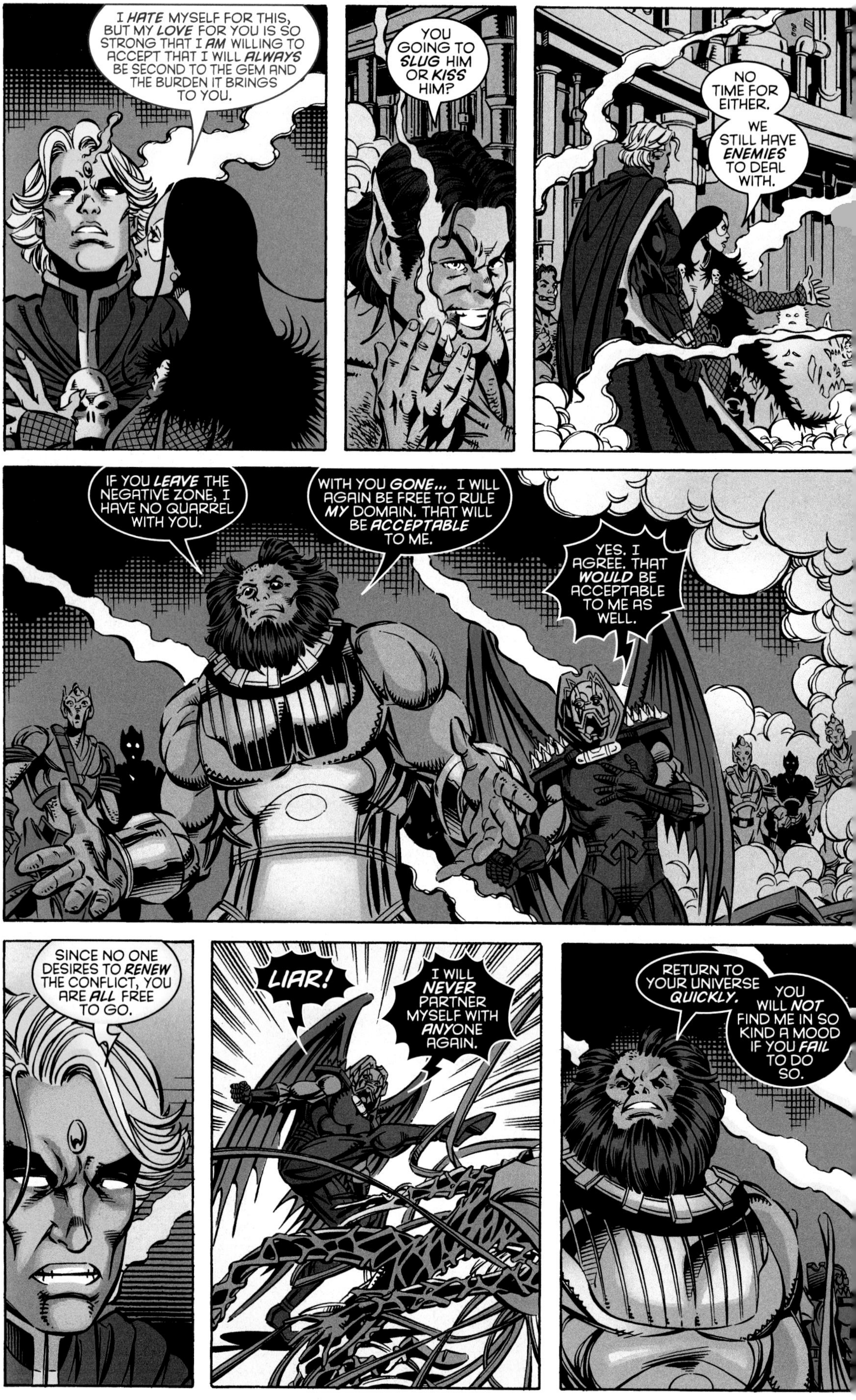
I HATE MYSELF FOR THIS, BUT MY LOVE FOR YOU IS SO STRONG THAT I AM WILLING TO ACCEPT THAT I WILL ALWAYS BE SECOND TO THE GEM AND THE BURDEN IT BRINGS TO YOU.
YOU GOING TO SLUG HIM OR KISS HIM?
NO TIME FOR EITHER.
WE STILL HAVE ENEMIES TO DEAL WITH.
IF YOU LEAVE THE NEGATIVE ZONE, I HAVE NO QUARREL WITH YOU.
WITH YOU GONE... I WILL AGAIN BE FREE TO RULE MY DOMAIN. THAT WILL BE ACCEPTABLE TO ME.
YES. I AGREE. THAT WOULD BE ACCEPTABLE TO ME AS WELL.
SINCE NO ONE DESIRES TO RENEW THE CONFLICT, YOU ARE ALL FREE TO GO.
LIAR!
I WILL NEVER PARTNER MYSELF WITH ANYONE AGAIN.
RETURN TO YOUR UNIVERSE QUICKLY.
YOU WILL NOT FIND ME IN SO KIND A MOOD IF YOU FAIL TO DO SO.

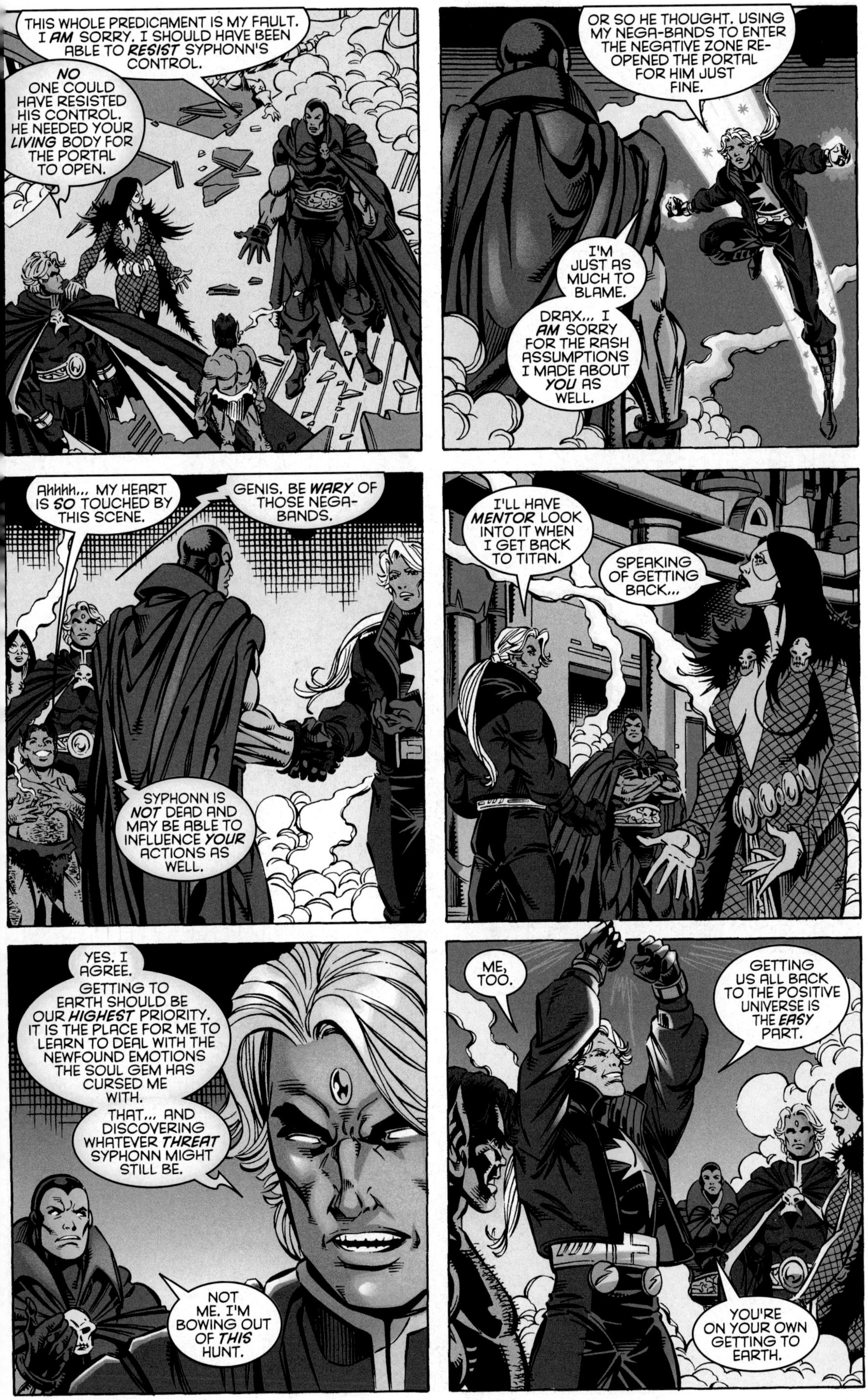
THIS WHOLE PREDICAMENT IS MY FAULT. I AM SORRY. I SHOULD HAVE BEEN ABLE TO RESIST SYPHONN'S CONTROL.
NO ONE COULD HAVE RESISTED HIS CONTROL. HE NEEDED YOUR LIVING BODY FOR THE PORTAL TO OPEN.
OR SO HE THOUGHT. USING MY NEGA-BANDS TO ENTER THE NEGATIVE ZONE RE-OPENED THE PORTAL FOR HIM JUST FINE.
I'M JUST AS MUCH TO BLAME.
DRAX... I AM SORRY FOR THE RASH ASSUMPTIONS I MADE ABOUT YOU AS WELL.
AHHHH... MY HEART IS SO TOUCHED BY THIS SCENE.
GENIS. BE WARY OF THOSE NEGA-BANDS.
SYPHONN IS NOT DEAD AND MAY BE ABLE TO INFLUENCE YOUR ACTIONS AS WELL.
I'LL HAVE MENTOR LOOK INTO IT WHEN I GET BACK TO TITAN.
SPEAKING OF GETTING BACK...
YES. I AGREE.
GETTING TO EARTH SHOULD BE OUR HIGHEST PRIORITY. IT IS THE PLACE FOR ME TO LEARN TO DEAL WITH THE NEWFOUND EMOTIONS THE SOUL GEM HAS CURSED ME WITH.
THAT... AND DISCOVERING WHATEVER THREAT SYPHONN MIGHT STILL BE.
NOT ME. I'M BOWING OUT OF THIS HUNT.
ME, TOO.
GETTING US ALL BACK TO THE POSITIVE UNIVERSE IS THE EASY PART.
YOU'RE ON YOUR OWN GETTING TO EARTH.

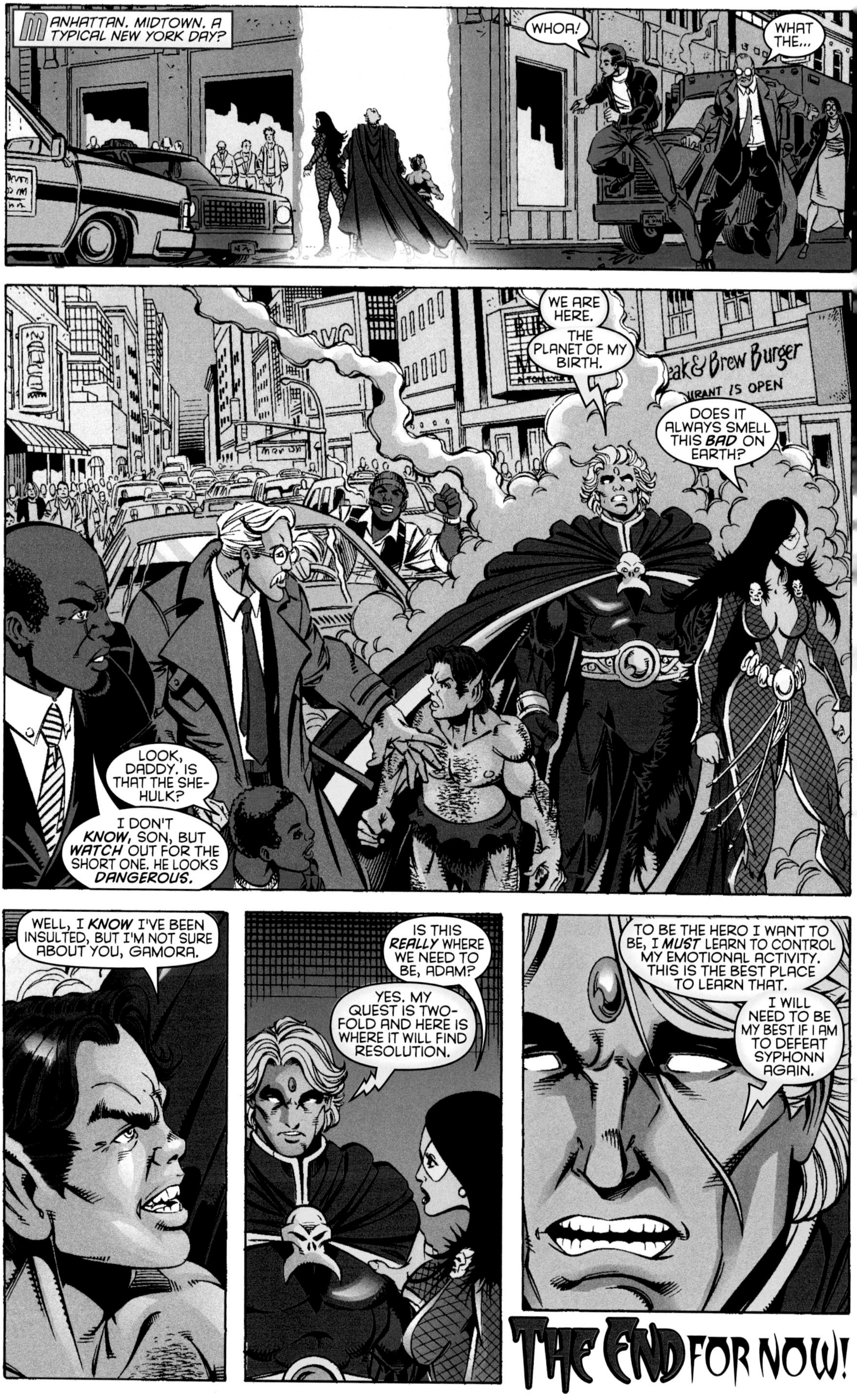
MANHATTAN. MIDTOWN. A TYPICAL NEW YORK DAY?
WHOA!
WHAT THE...
WE ARE HERE.
THE PLANET OF MY BIRTH.
DOES IT ALWAYS SMELL THIS BAD ON EARTH?
LOOK, DADDY. IS THAT THE SHE-HULK?
I DON'T KNOW, SON, BUT WATCH OUT FOR THE SHORT ONE. HE LOOKS DANGEROUS.
WELL, I KNOW I'VE BEEN INSULTED, BUT I'M NOT SURE ABOUT YOU, GAMORA.
IS THIS REALLY WHERE WE NEED TO BE, ADAM?
YES. MY QUEST IS TWO-FOLD AND HERE IS WHERE IT WILL FIND RESOLUTION.
TO BE THE HERO I WANT TO BE, I MUST LEARN TO CONTROL MY EMOTIONAL ACTIVITY. THIS IS THE BEST PLACE TO LEARN THAT.
I WILL NEED TO BE MY BEST IF I AM TO DEFEAT SYPHONN AGAIN.
THE END FOR NOW!

Excerpt from *CAPTAIN MARVEL #3*

Writer: Peter David • Penciler: ChrisCross • Inker: Anibal Rodriguez • Colorist: Steve Oliff
Letterer: Richard Starkings & Comicraft's Wes Abbott • Assistant Editor: Gregg Schigiel • Editor: Tom Brevoort

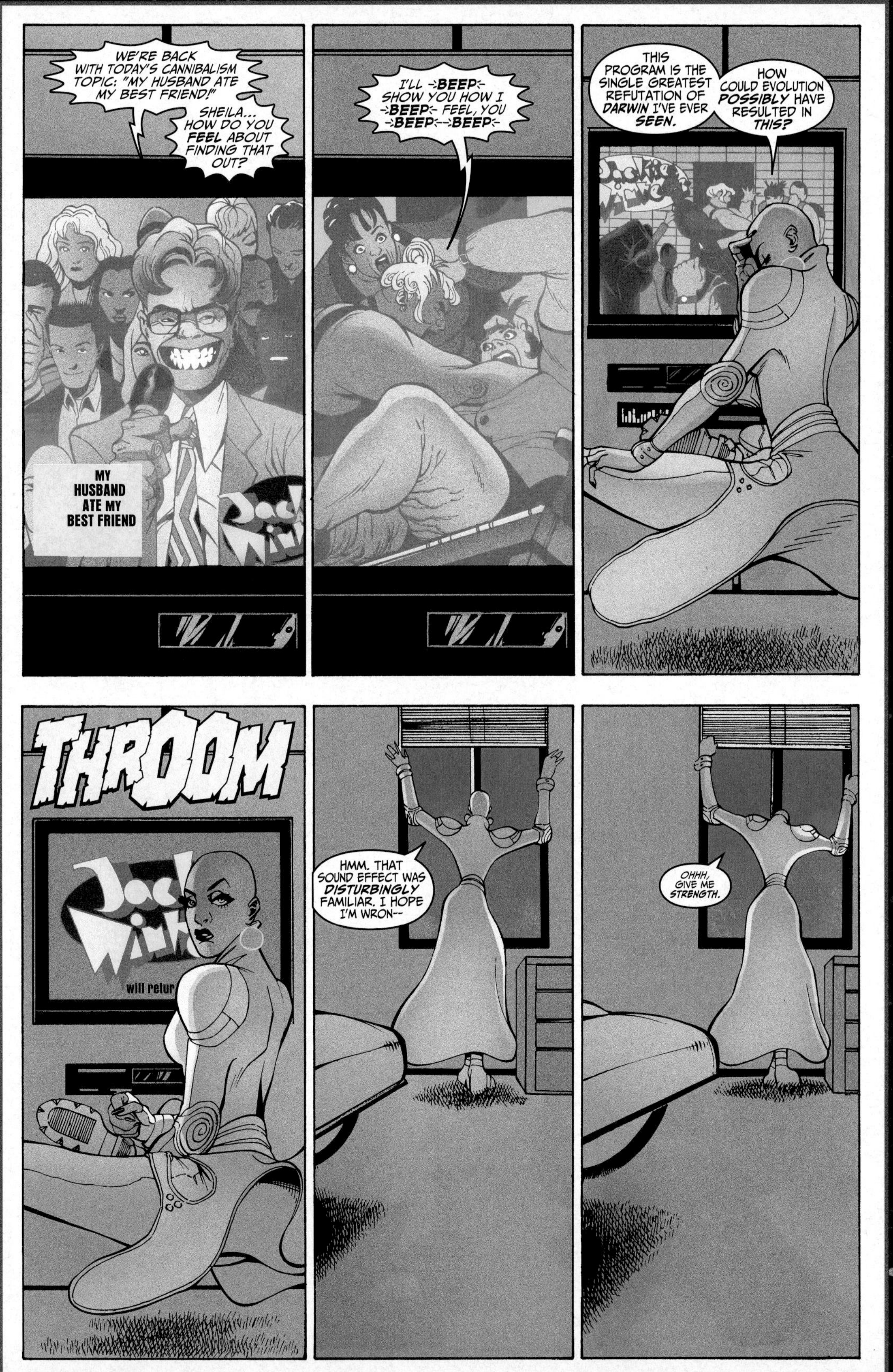

WE'RE BACK WITH TODAY'S CANNIBALISM TOPIC: "MY HUSBAND ATE MY BEST FRIEND!"
SHEILA... HOW DO YOU FEEL ABOUT FINDING THAT OUT?
MY HUSBAND ATE MY BEST FRIEND
I'LL -BEEP- SHOW YOU HOW I -BEEP- FEEL, YOU -BEEP--BEEP-
THIS PROGRAM IS THE SINGLE GREATEST REFUTATION OF DARWIN I'VE EVER SEEN.
HOW COULD EVOLUTION POSSIBLY HAVE RESULTED IN THIS?
THROOM
will retur
HMM. THAT SOUND EFFECT WAS DISTURBINGLY FAMILIAR. I HOPE I'M WRON--
OHHH, GIVE ME STRENGTH.

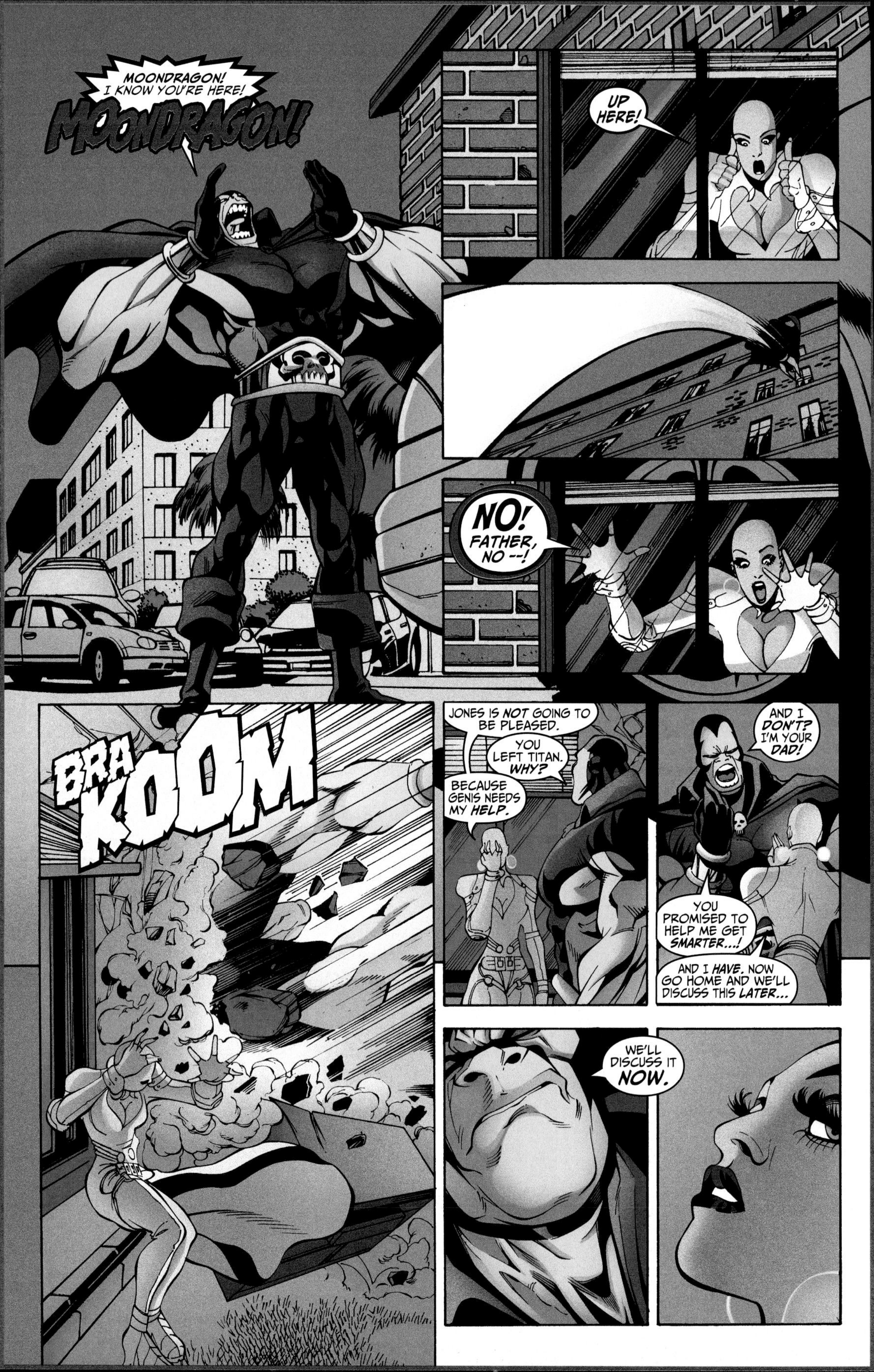
MOONDRAGON! I KNOW YOU'RE HERE!
MOONDRAGON!
UP HERE!
NO! FATHER, NO --!
BRA KOOM
JONES IS NOT GOING TO BE PLEASED.
YOU LEFT TITAN. WHY?
BECAUSE GENIS NEEDS MY HELP.
AND I DON'T? I'M YOUR DAD!
YOU PROMISED TO HELP ME GET SMARTER...!
AND I HAVE. NOW GO HOME AND WE'LL DISCUSS THIS LATER...
WE'LL DISCUSS IT NOW.

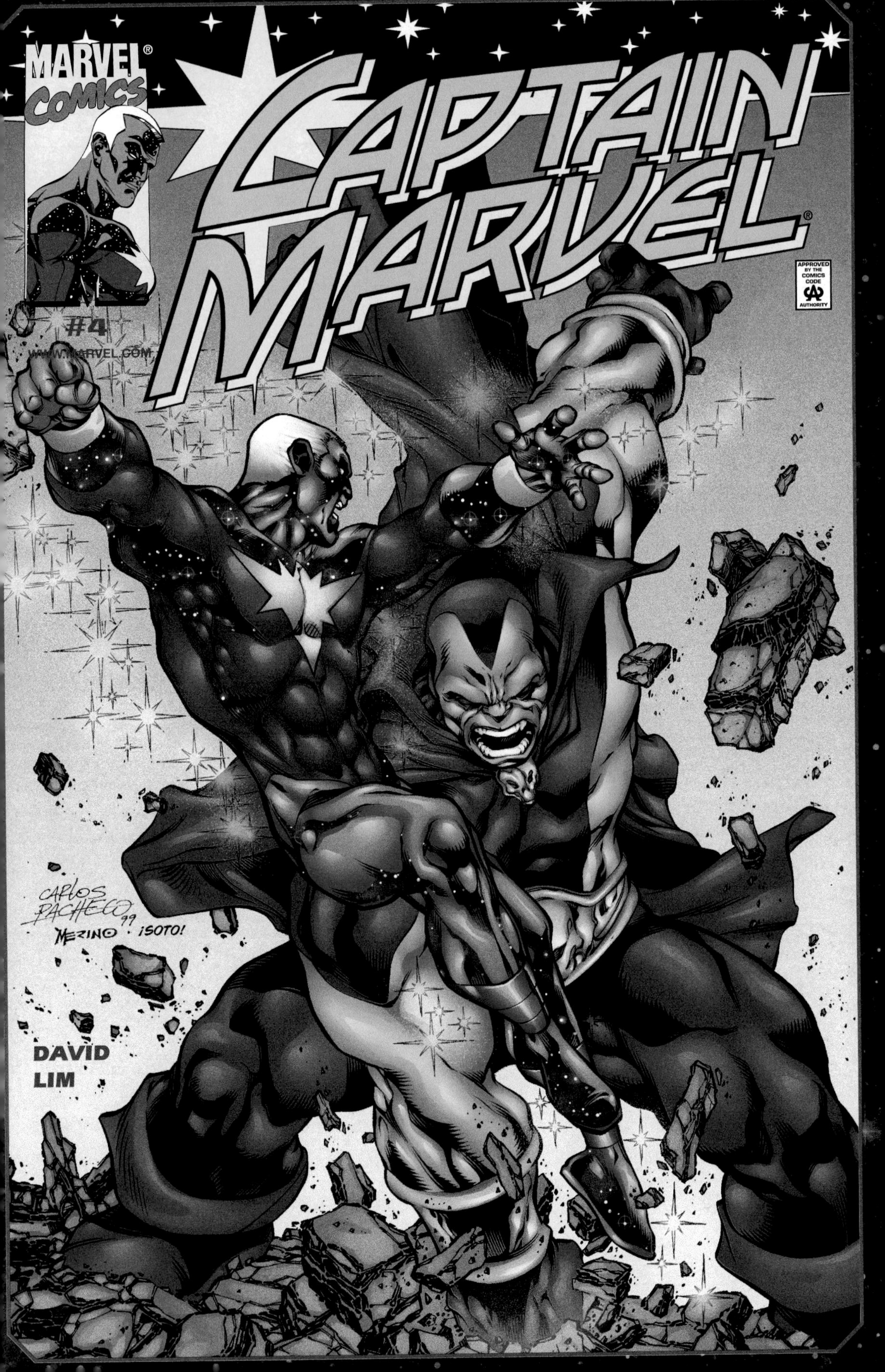
MARVEL COMICS
CAPTAIN MARVEL
APPROVED BY THE COMICS CODE AUTHORITY
#4
WWW.MARVEL.COM
CARLOS PACHECO 99
MERINO ¡SOTO!
DAVID
LIM

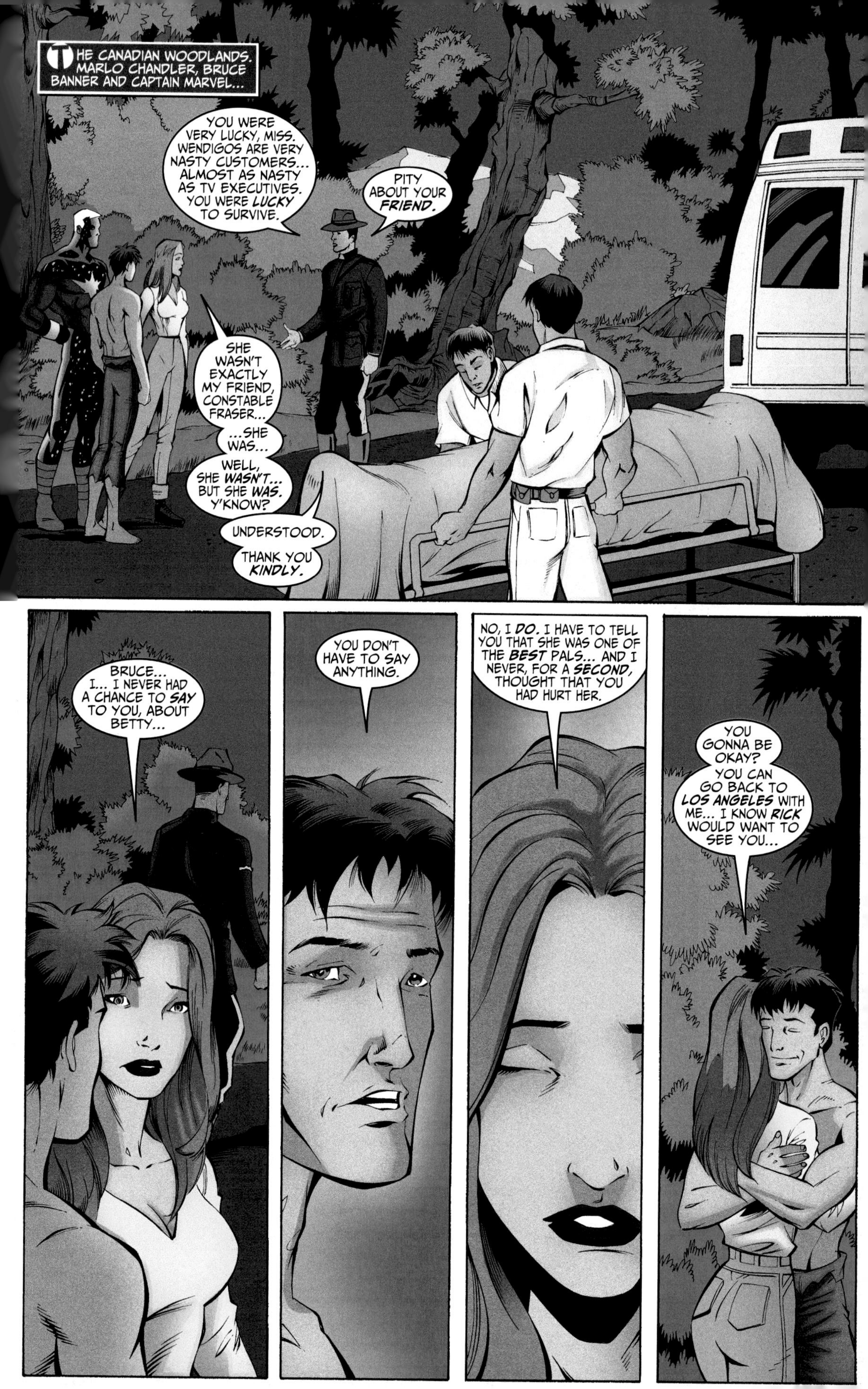
THE CANADIAN WOODLANDS. MARLO CHANDLER, BRUCE BANNER AND CAPTAIN MARVEL...
YOU WERE VERY LUCKY, MISS. WENDIGOS ARE VERY NASTY CUSTOMERS... ALMOST AS NASTY AS TV EXECUTIVES. YOU WERE LUCKY TO SURVIVE.
PITY ABOUT YOUR FRIEND.
SHE WASN'T EXACTLY MY FRIEND, CONSTABLE FRASER...
...SHE WAS...
WELL, SHE WASN'T... BUT SHE WAS. Y'KNOW?
UNDERSTOOD.
THANK YOU KINDLY.
BRUCE... I... I NEVER HAD A CHANCE TO SAY TO YOU, ABOUT BETTY...
YOU DON'T HAVE TO SAY ANYTHING.
NO, I DO. I HAVE TO TELL YOU THAT SHE WAS ONE OF THE BEST PALS... AND I NEVER, FOR A SECOND, THOUGHT THAT YOU HAD HURT HER.
YOU GONNA BE OKAY? YOU CAN GO BACK TO LOS ANGELES WITH ME... I KNOW RICK WOULD WANT TO SEE YOU...

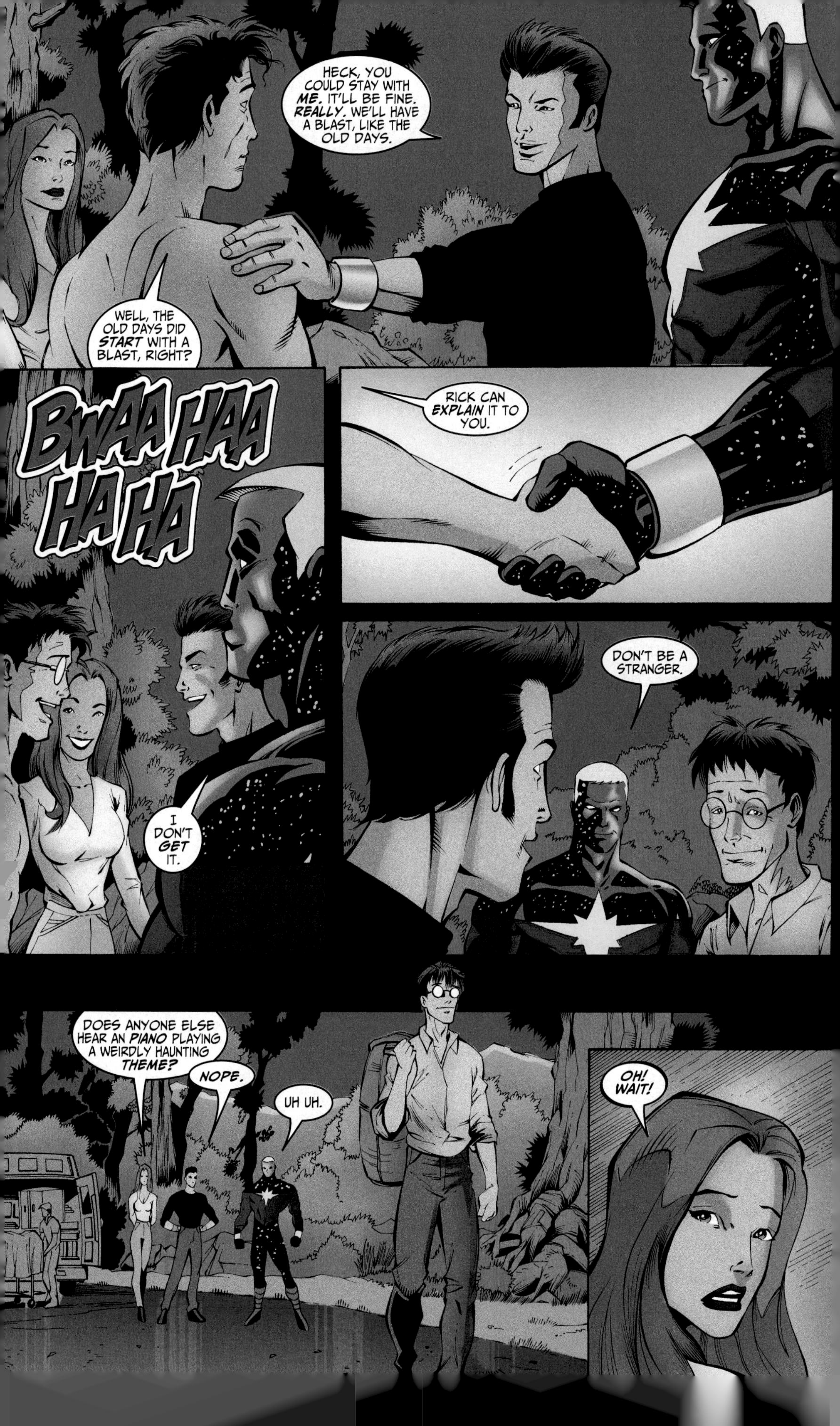
HECK, YOU COULD STAY WITH ME. IT'LL BE FINE. REALLY. WE'LL HAVE A BLAST, LIKE THE OLD DAYS.
WELL, THE OLD DAYS DID START WITH A BLAST, RIGHT?
BWAA HAA HA HA
I DON'T GET IT.
RICK CAN EXPLAIN IT TO YOU.
DON'T BE A STRANGER.
DOES ANYONE ELSE HEAR AN PIANO PLAYING A WEIRDLY HAUNTING THEME?
NOPE.
UH UH.
OH! WAIT!

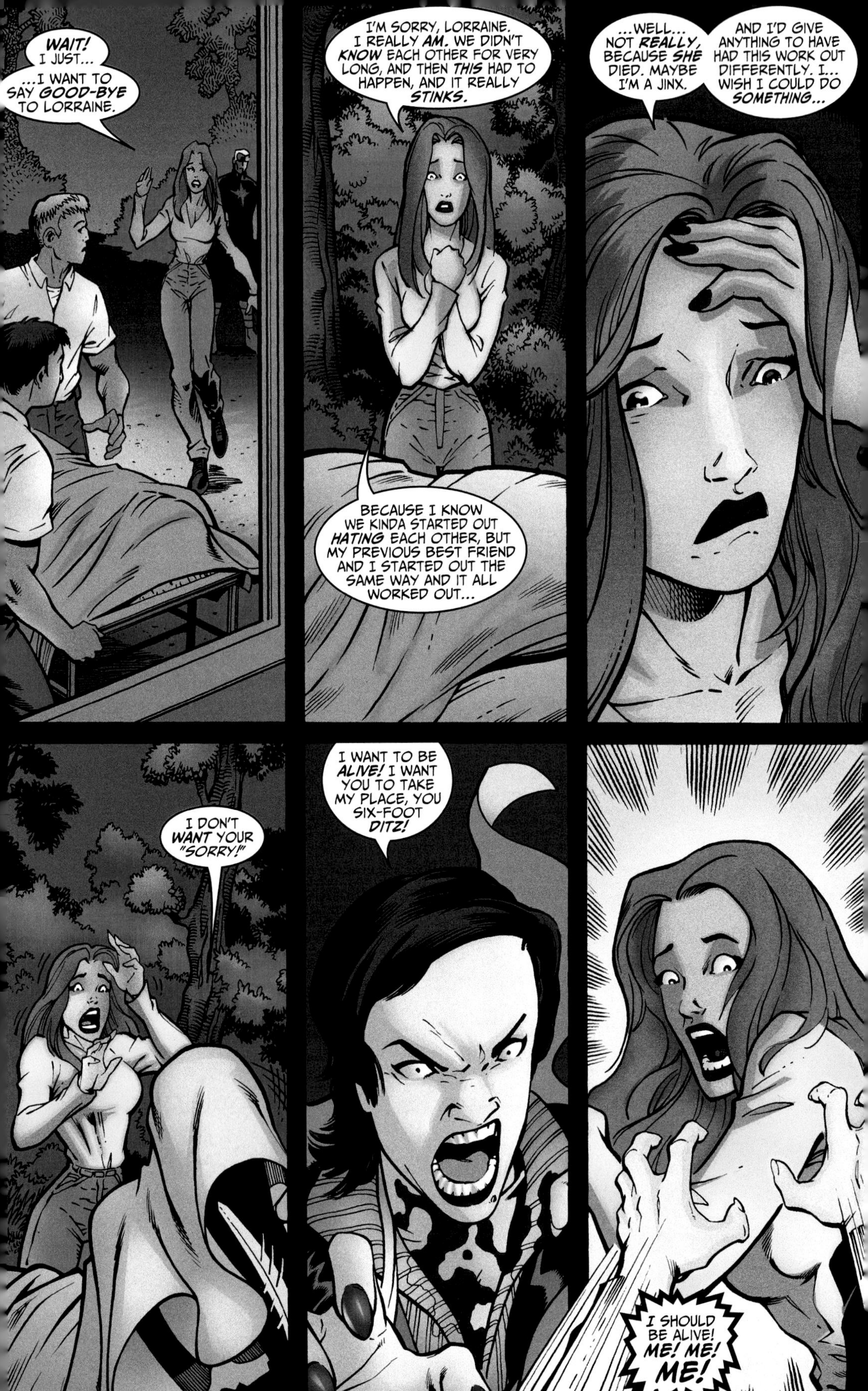
WAIT! I JUST...
...I WANT TO SAY GOOD-BYE TO LORRAINE.
I'M SORRY, LORRAINE. I REALLY AM. WE DIDN'T KNOW EACH OTHER FOR VERY LONG, AND THEN THIS HAD TO HAPPEN, AND IT REALLY STINKS.
BECAUSE I KNOW WE KINDA STARTED OUT HATING EACH OTHER, BUT MY PREVIOUS BEST FRIEND AND I STARTED OUT THE SAME WAY AND IT ALL WORKED OUT...
...WELL... NOT REALLY, BECAUSE SHE DIED. MAYBE I'M A JINX.
AND I'D GIVE ANYTHING TO HAVE HAD THIS WORK OUT DIFFERENTLY. I... WISH I COULD DO SOMETHING...
I DON'T WANT YOUR "SORRY!"
I WANT TO BE ALIVE! I WANT YOU TO TAKE MY PLACE, YOU SIX-FOOT DITZ!
I SHOULD BE ALIVE! ME! ME! ME!

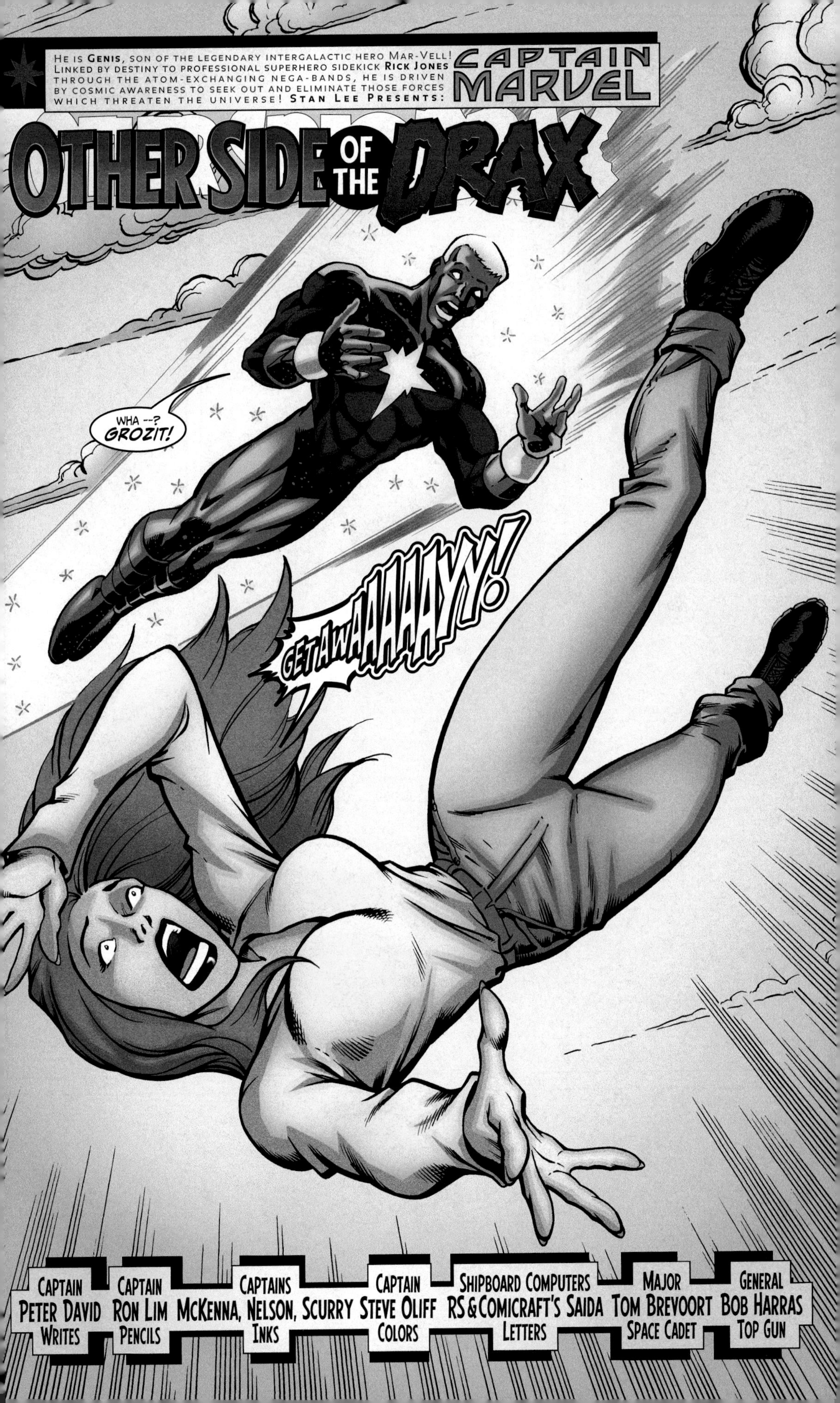
He is Genis, son of the legendary intergalactic hero Mar-Vell! Linked by destiny to professional superhero sidekick Rick Jones through the atom-exchanging nega-bands, he is driven by cosmic awareness to seek out and eliminate those forces which threaten the universe! Stan Lee Presents:
Captain Marvel
Other Side of the Drax
WHA --? GROZIT!
GET AWAAAAAYY!
Captain Peter David Writes
Captain Ron Lim Pencils
Captains McKenna, Nelson, Scurry Inks
Captain Steve Oliff Colors
Shipboard Computers RS & Comicraft's Saida Letters
Major Tom Brevoort Space Cadet
General Bob Harras Top Gun

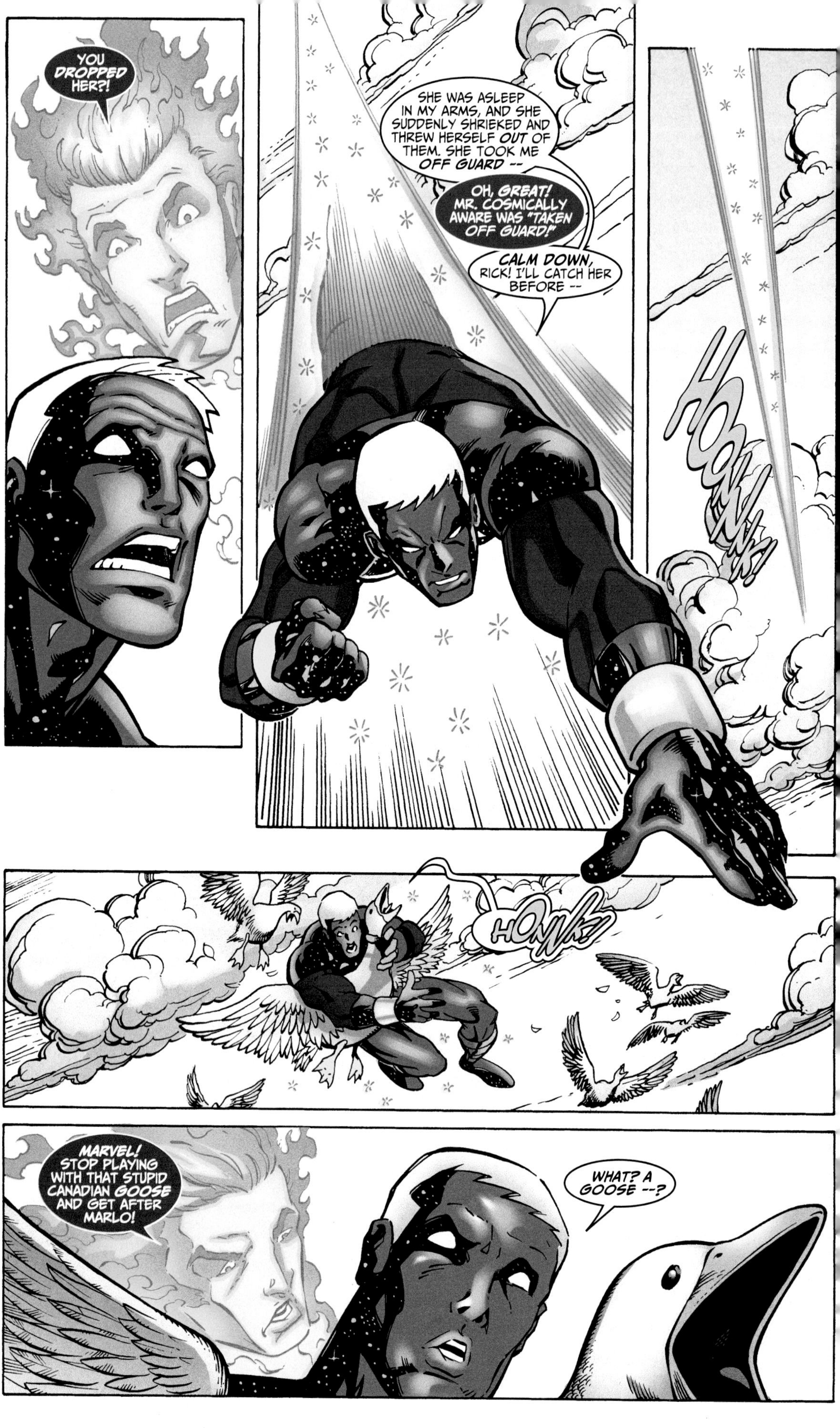
YOU DROPPED HER?!
SHE WAS ASLEEP IN MY ARMS, AND SHE SUDDENLY SHRIEKED AND THREW HERSELF OUT OF THEM. SHE TOOK ME OFF GUARD --
OH, GREAT! MR. COSMICALLY AWARE WAS "TAKEN OFF GUARD!"
CALM DOWN, RICK! I'LL CATCH HER BEFORE --
HOONNK!
HONNK!
MARVEL! STOP PLAYING WITH THAT STUPID CANADIAN GOOSE AND GET AFTER MARLO!
WHAT? A GOOSE --?

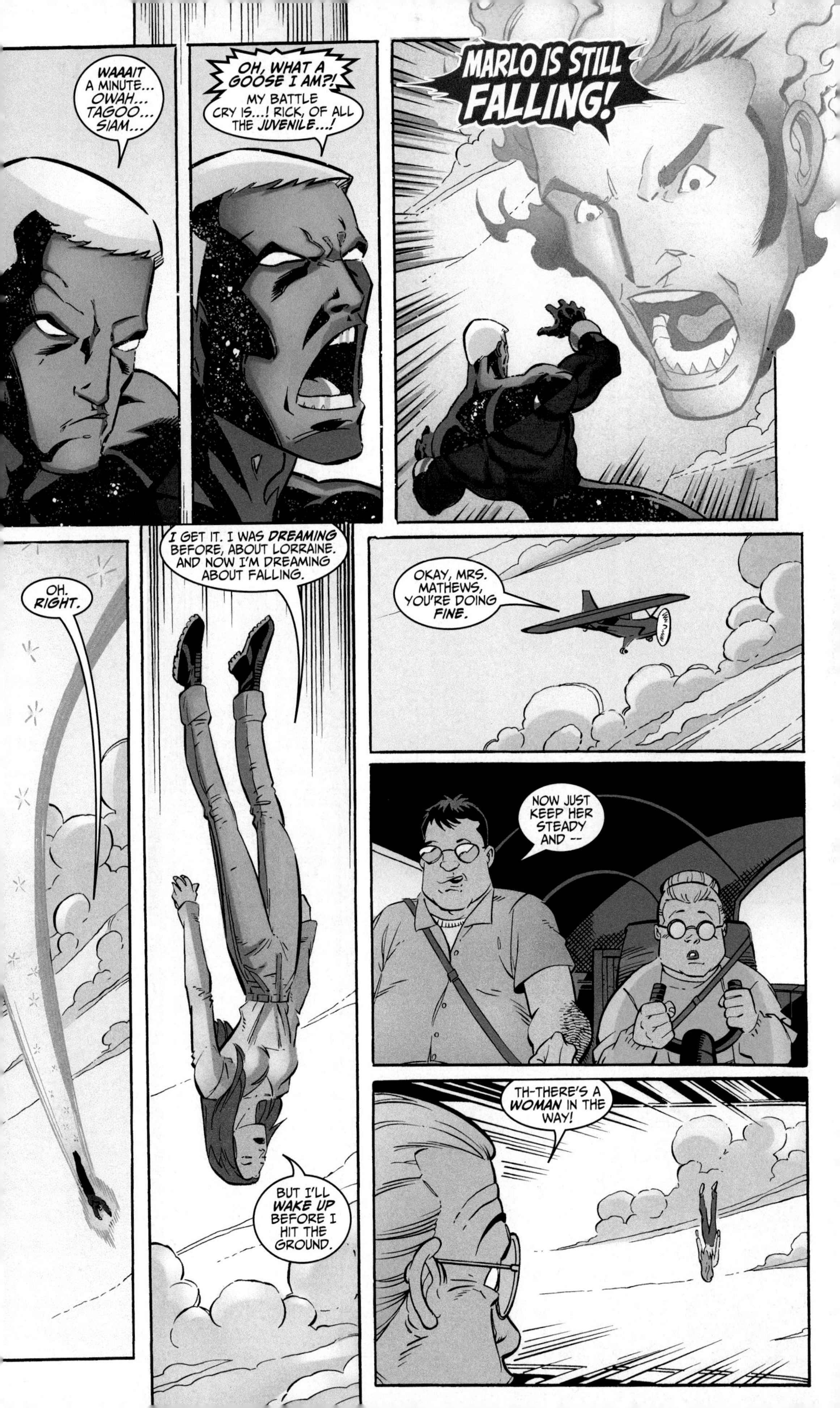
WAAAIT A MINUTE... OWAH... TAGOO... SIAM...
OH, WHAT A GOOSE I AM?!
MY BATTLE CRY IS...! RICK, OF ALL THE JUVENILE...!
MARLO IS STILL FALLING!
OH. RIGHT.
I GET IT. I WAS DREAMING BEFORE, ABOUT LORRAINE. AND NOW I'M DREAMING ABOUT FALLING.
BUT I'LL WAKE UP BEFORE I HIT THE GROUND.
OKAY, MRS. MATHEWS, YOU'RE DOING FINE.
NOW JUST KEEP HER STEADY AND --
TH-THERE'S A WOMAN IN THE WAY!

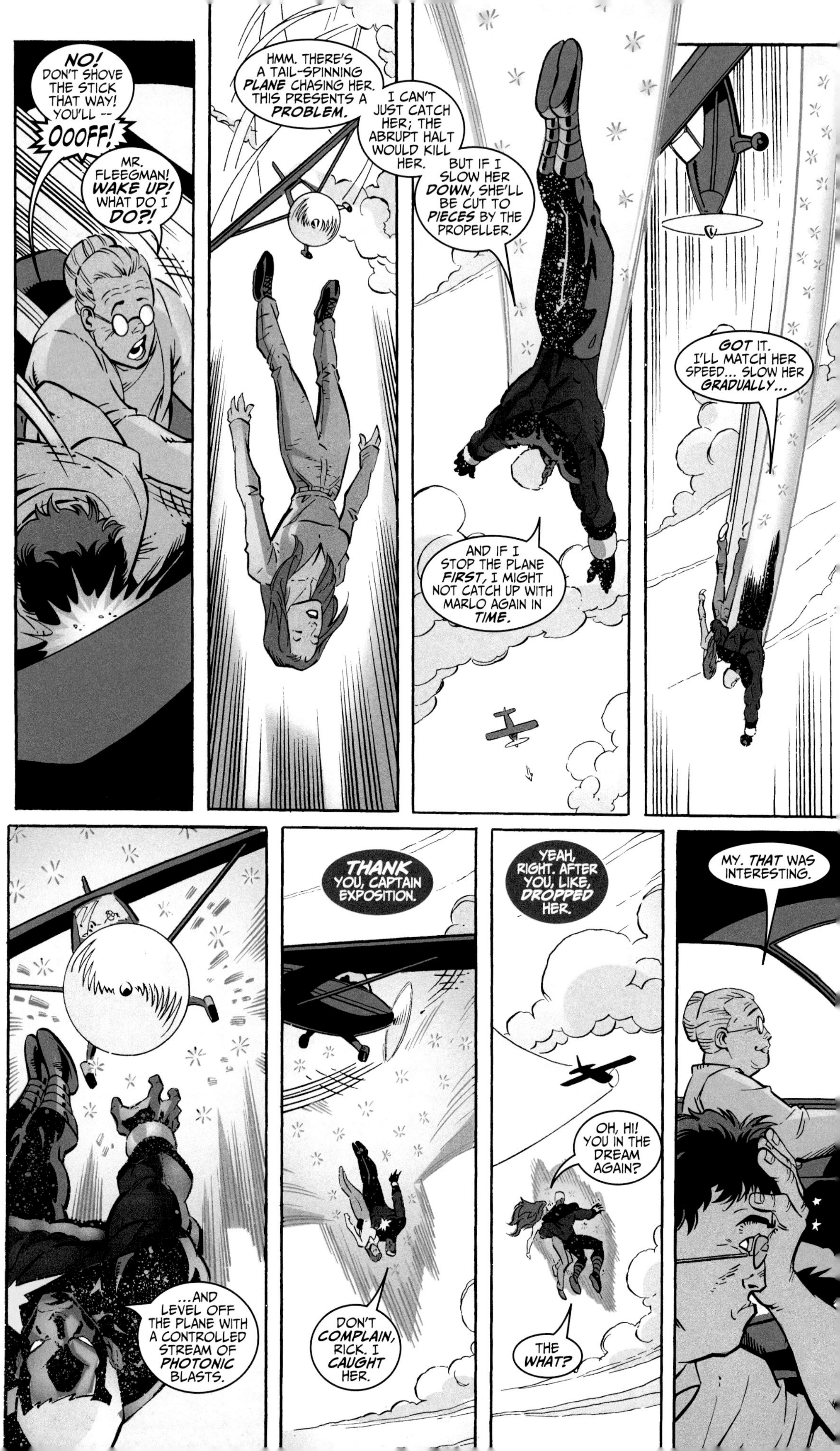
NO! DON'T SHOVE THE STICK THAT WAY! YOU'LL --
OOOFF!
MR. FLEEGMAN! WAKE UP! WHAT DO I DO?!
HMM. THERE'S A TAIL-SPINNING PLANE CHASING HER. THIS PRESENTS A PROBLEM.
I CAN'T JUST CATCH HER; THE ABRUPT HALT WOULD KILL HER.
BUT IF I SLOW HER DOWN, SHE'LL BE CUT TO PIECES BY THE PROPELLER.
AND IF I STOP THE PLANE FIRST, I MIGHT NOT CATCH UP WITH MARLO AGAIN IN TIME.
GOT IT. I'LL MATCH HER SPEED... SLOW HER GRADUALLY...
...AND LEVEL OFF THE PLANE WITH A CONTROLLED STREAM OF PHOTONIC BLASTS.
THANK YOU, CAPTAIN EXPOSITION.
DON'T COMPLAIN, RICK. I CAUGHT HER.
YEAH, RIGHT. AFTER YOU, LIKE, DROPPED HER.
OH, HI! YOU IN THE DREAM AGAIN?
THE WHAT?
MY. THAT WAS INTERESTING.

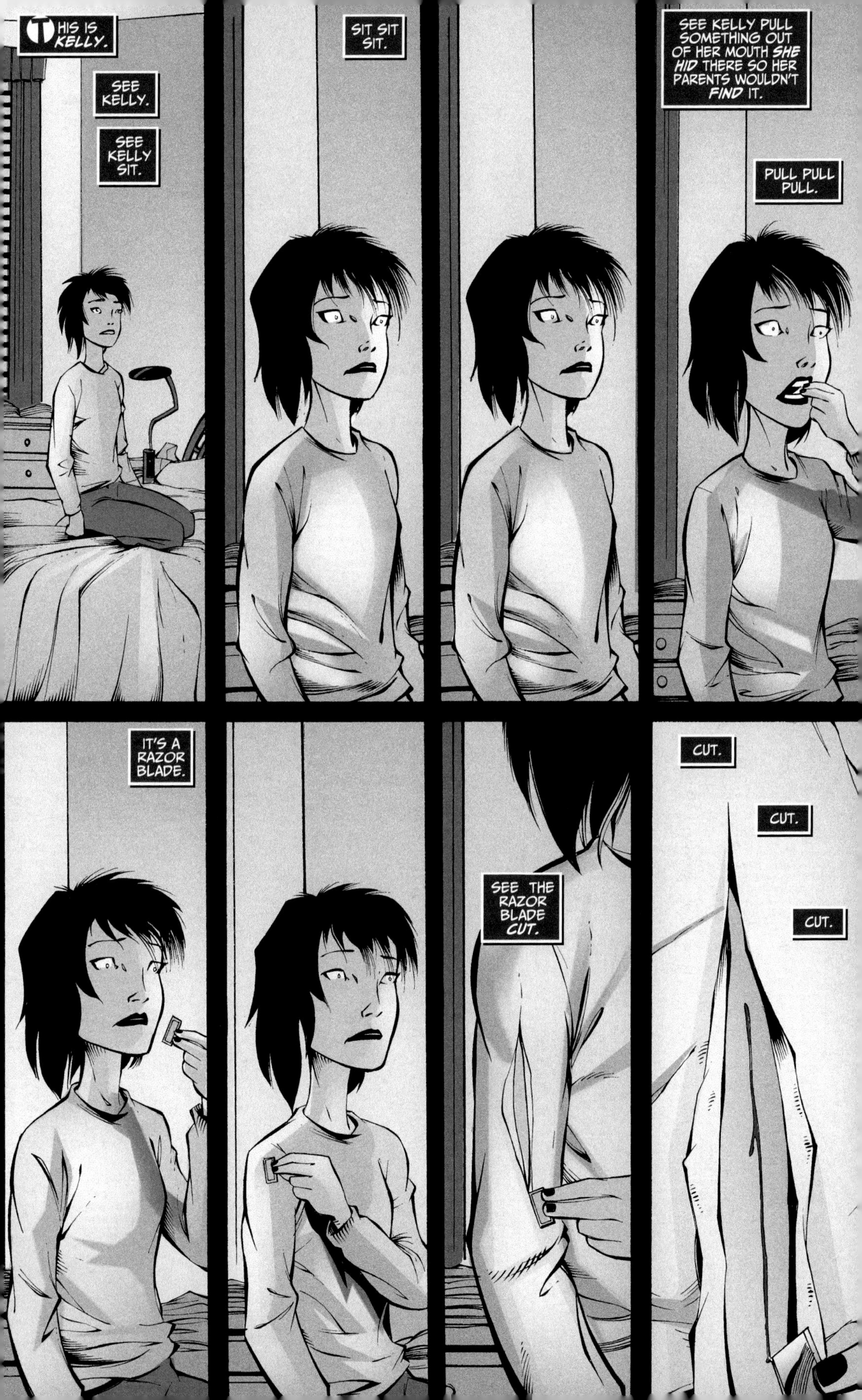
THIS IS KELLY.
SEE KELLY.
SEE KELLY SIT.
SIT SIT SIT.
SEE KELLY PULL SOMETHING OUT OF HER MOUTH SHE HID THERE SO HER PARENTS WOULDN'T FIND IT.
PULL PULL PULL.
IT'S A RAZOR BLADE.
SEE THE RAZOR BLADE CUT.
CUT.
CUT.
CUT.

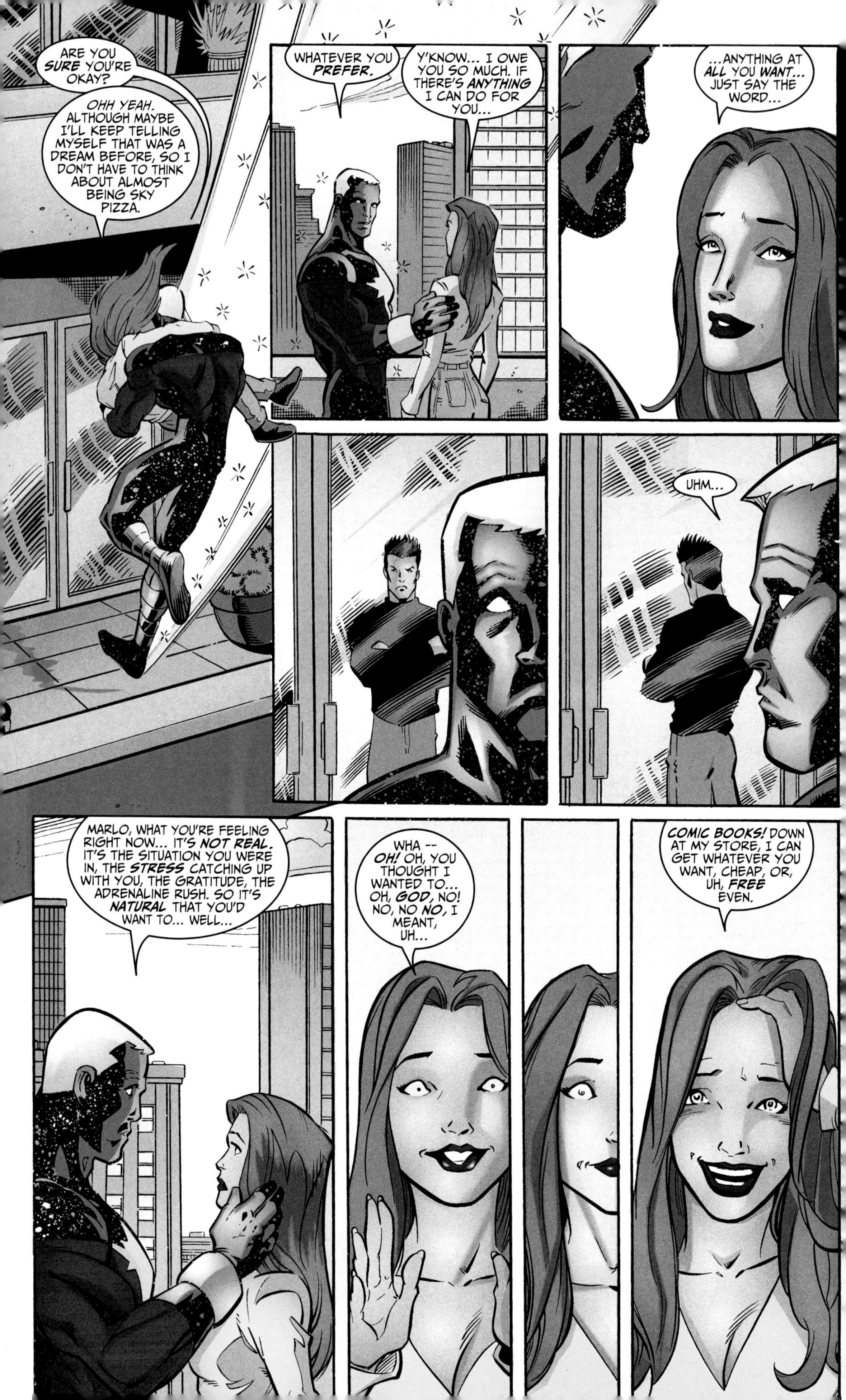
ARE YOU SURE YOU'RE OKAY?
OHH YEAH. ALTHOUGH MAYBE I'LL KEEP TELLING MYSELF THAT WAS A DREAM BEFORE, SO I DON'T HAVE TO THINK ABOUT ALMOST BEING SKY PIZZA.
WHATEVER YOU PREFER.
Y'KNOW... I OWE YOU SO MUCH. IF THERE'S ANYTHING I CAN DO FOR YOU...
...ANYTHING AT ALL YOU WANT... JUST SAY THE WORD...
UHM...
MARLO, WHAT YOU'RE FEELING RIGHT NOW... IT'S NOT REAL. IT'S THE SITUATION YOU WERE IN, THE STRESS CATCHING UP WITH YOU, THE GRATITUDE, THE ADRENALINE RUSH. SO IT'S NATURAL THAT YOU'D WANT TO... WELL...
WHA -- OH! OH, YOU THOUGHT I WANTED TO... OH, GOD, NO! NO, NO NO, I MEANT, UH...
COMIC BOOKS! DOWN AT MY STORE, I CAN GET WHATEVER YOU WANT, CHEAP, OR, UH, FREE EVEN.

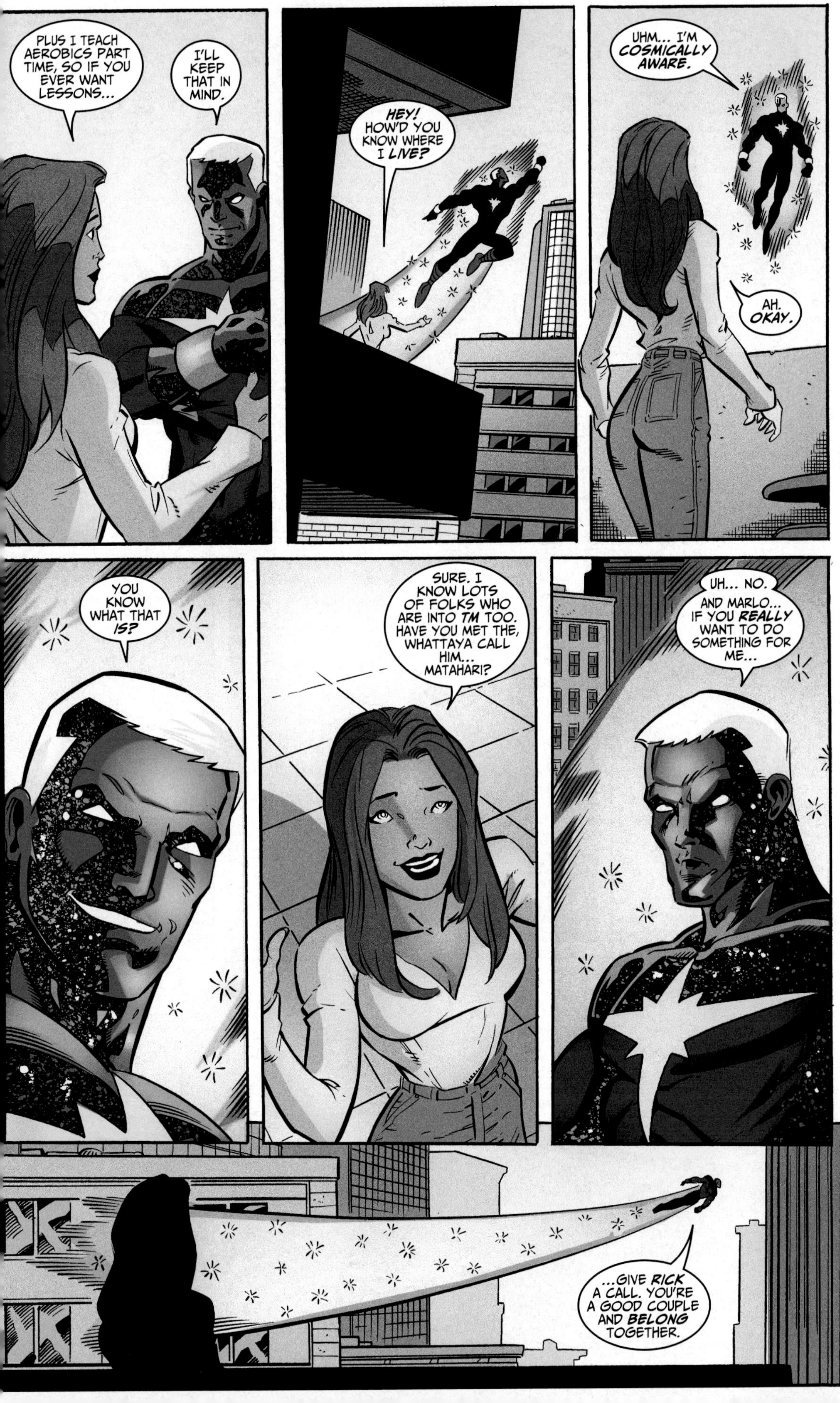
PLUS I TEACH AEROBICS PART TIME, SO IF YOU EVER WANT LESSONS...
I'LL KEEP THAT IN MIND.
HEY! HOW'D YOU KNOW WHERE I LIVE?
UHM... I'M COSMICALLY AWARE.
AH. OKAY.
YOU KNOW WHAT THAT IS?
SURE. I KNOW LOTS OF FOLKS WHO ARE INTO TM TOO. HAVE YOU MET THE, WHATTAYA CALL HIM... MATAHARI?
UH... NO.
AND MARLO... IF YOU REALLY WANT TO DO SOMETHING FOR ME...
...GIVE RICK A CALL. YOU'RE A GOOD COUPLE AND BELONG TOGETHER.

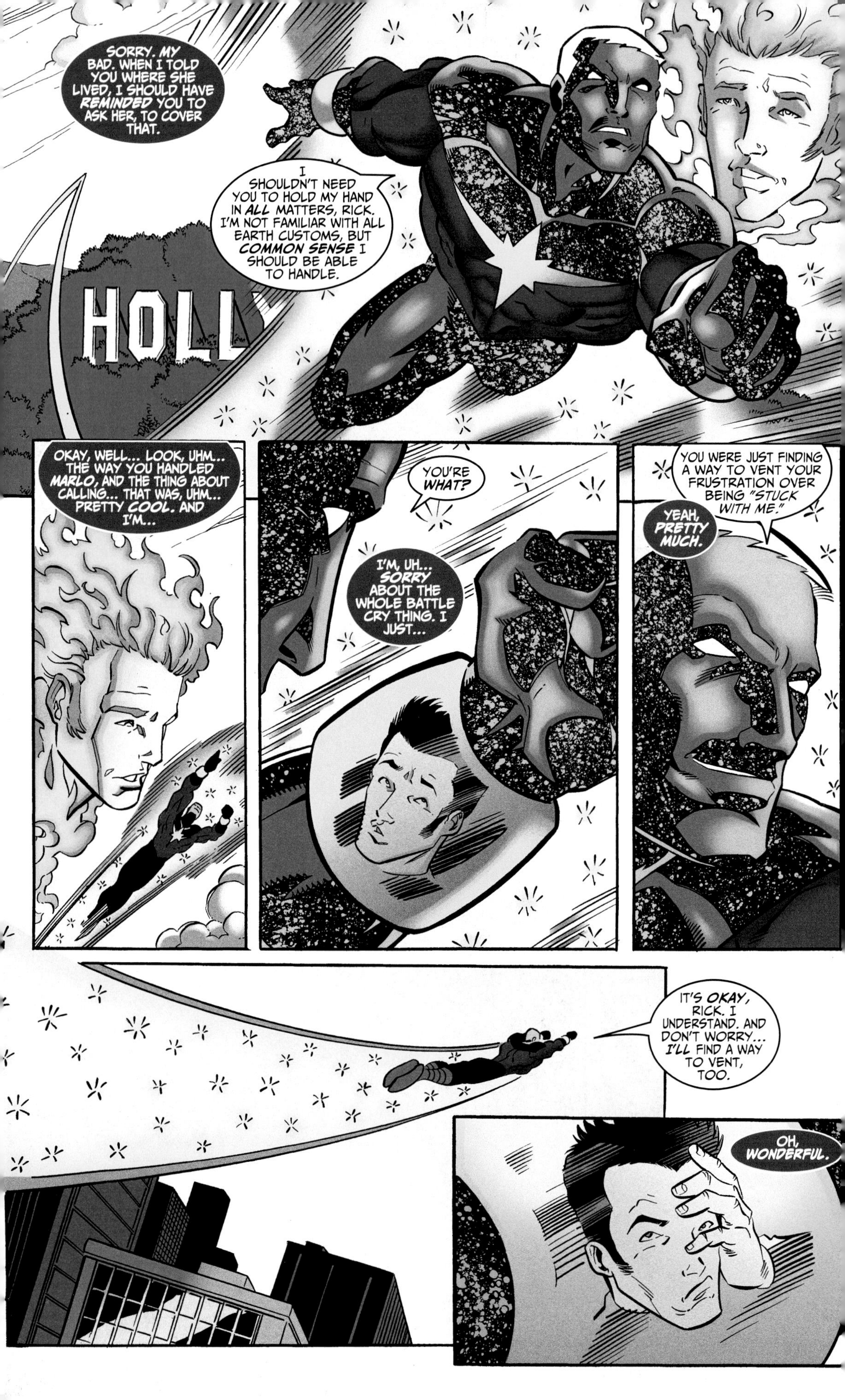
SORRY. MY BAD. WHEN I TOLD YOU WHERE SHE LIVED, I SHOULD HAVE REMINDED YOU TO ASK HER, TO COVER THAT.
I SHOULDN'T NEED YOU TO HOLD MY HAND IN ALL MATTERS, RICK. I'M NOT FAMILIAR WITH ALL EARTH CUSTOMS, BUT COMMON SENSE I SHOULD BE ABLE TO HANDLE.
HOLL
OKAY, WELL... LOOK, UHM... THE WAY YOU HANDLED MARLO, AND THE THING ABOUT CALLING... THAT WAS, UHM... PRETTY COOL. AND I'M...
YOU'RE WHAT?
I'M, UH... SORRY ABOUT THE WHOLE BATTLE CRY THING. I JUST...
YOU WERE JUST FINDING A WAY TO VENT YOUR FRUSTRATION OVER BEING "STUCK WITH ME."
YEAH, PRETTY MUCH.
IT'S OKAY, RICK. I UNDERSTAND. AND DON'T WORRY... I'LL FIND A WAY TO VENT, TOO.
OH, WONDERFUL.

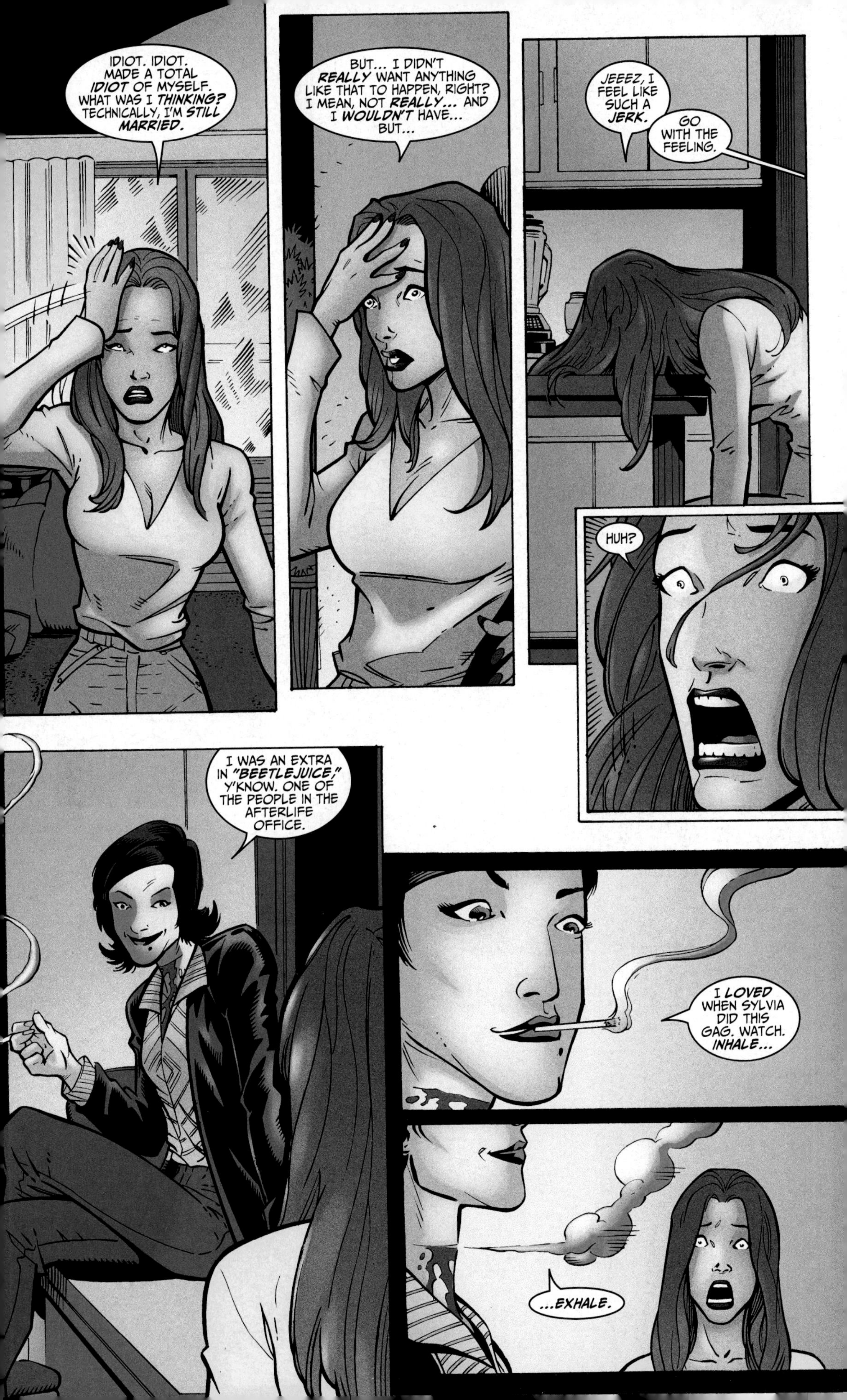
IDIOT. IDIOT. MADE A TOTAL IDIOT OF MYSELF. WHAT WAS I THINKING? TECHNICALLY, I'M STILL MARRIED.
BUT... I DIDN'T REALLY WANT ANYTHING LIKE THAT TO HAPPEN, RIGHT? I MEAN, NOT REALLY... AND I WOULDN'T HAVE... BUT...
JEEEZ, I FEEL LIKE SUCH A JERK.
GO WITH THE FEELING.
HUH?
I WAS AN EXTRA IN "BEETLEJUICE," Y'KNOW. ONE OF THE PEOPLE IN THE AFTERLIFE OFFICE.
I LOVED WHEN SYLVIA DID THIS GAG. WATCH. INHALE...
...EXHALE.

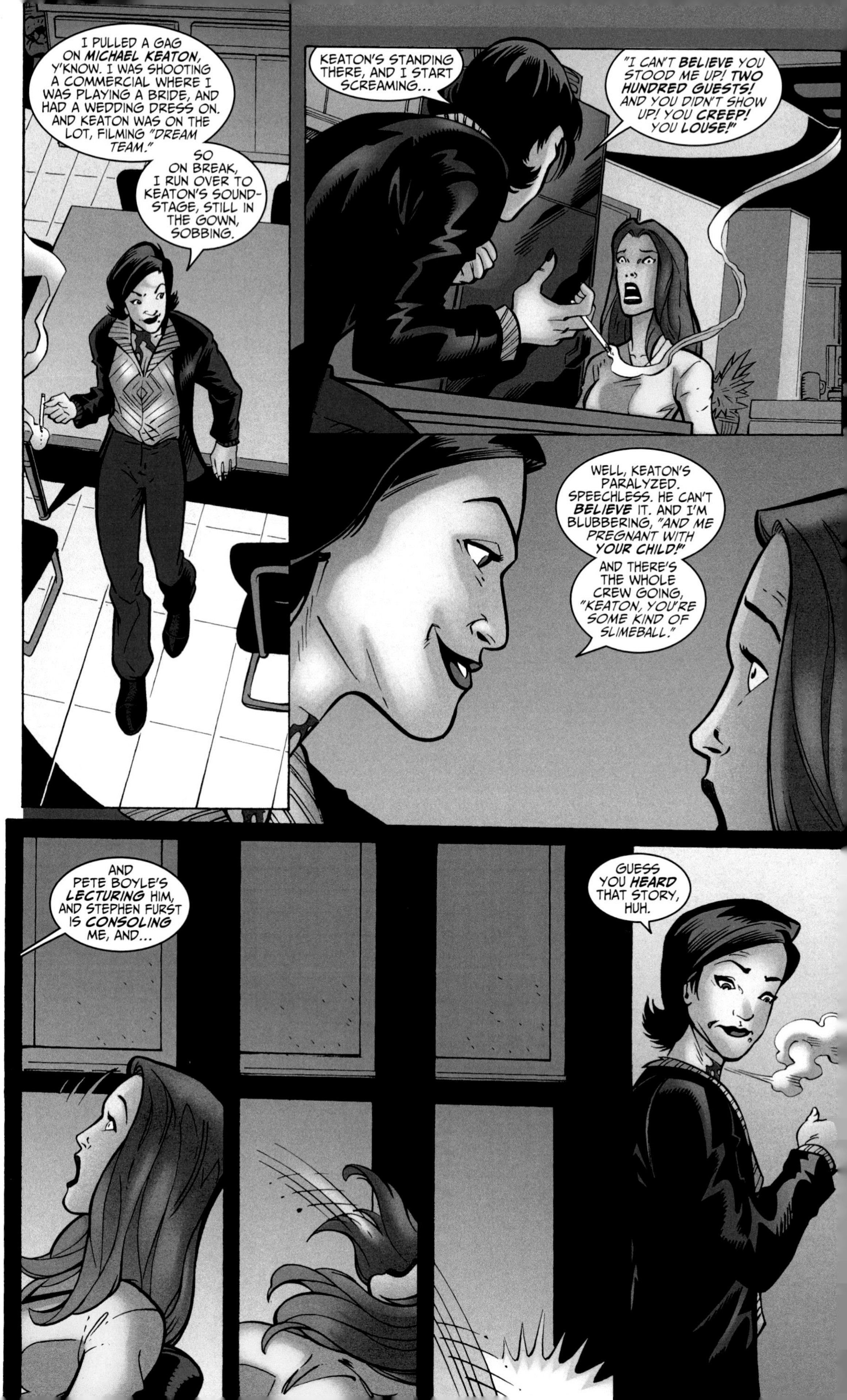
I PULLED A GAG ON MICHAEL KEATON, Y'KNOW. I WAS SHOOTING A COMMERCIAL WHERE I WAS PLAYING A BRIDE, AND HAD A WEDDING DRESS ON. AND KEATON WAS ON THE LOT, FILMING "DREAM TEAM."
SO ON BREAK, I RUN OVER TO KEATON'S SOUND-STAGE, STILL IN THE GOWN, SOBBING.
KEATON'S STANDING THERE, AND I START SCREAMING...
"I CAN'T BELIEVE YOU STOOD ME UP! TWO HUNDRED GUESTS! AND YOU DIDN'T SHOW UP! YOU CREEP! YOU LOUSE!"
WELL, KEATON'S PARALYZED. SPEECHLESS. HE CAN'T BELIEVE IT. AND I'M BLUBBERING, "AND ME PREGNANT WITH YOUR CHILD!"
AND THERE'S THE WHOLE CREW GOING, "KEATON, YOU'RE SOME KIND OF SLIMEBALL."
AND PETE BOYLE'S LECTURING HIM, AND STEPHEN FURST IS CONSOLING ME, AND...
GUESS YOU HEARD THAT STORY, HUH.

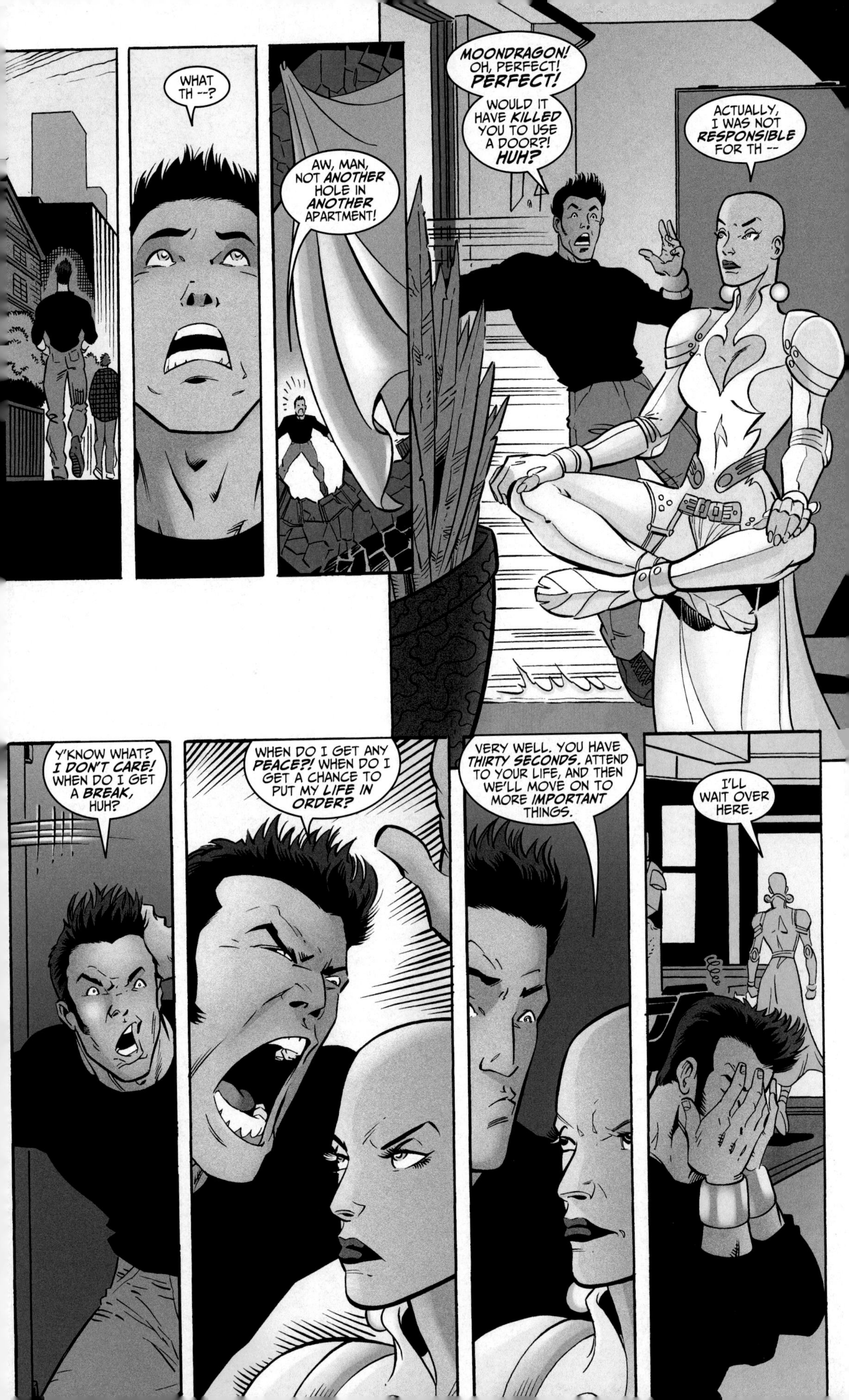
WHAT TH --?
AW, MAN, NOT ANOTHER HOLE IN ANOTHER APARTMENT!
MOONDRAGON! OH, PERFECT! PERFECT!
WOULD IT HAVE KILLED YOU TO USE A DOOR?! HUH?
ACTUALLY, I WAS NOT RESPONSIBLE FOR TH --
Y'KNOW WHAT? I DON'T CARE! WHEN DO I GET A BREAK, HUH?
WHEN DO I GET ANY PEACE?! WHEN DO I GET A CHANCE TO PUT MY LIFE IN ORDER?
VERY WELL. YOU HAVE THIRTY SECONDS. ATTEND TO YOUR LIFE, AND THEN WE'LL MOVE ON TO MORE IMPORTANT THINGS.
I'LL WAIT OVER HERE.

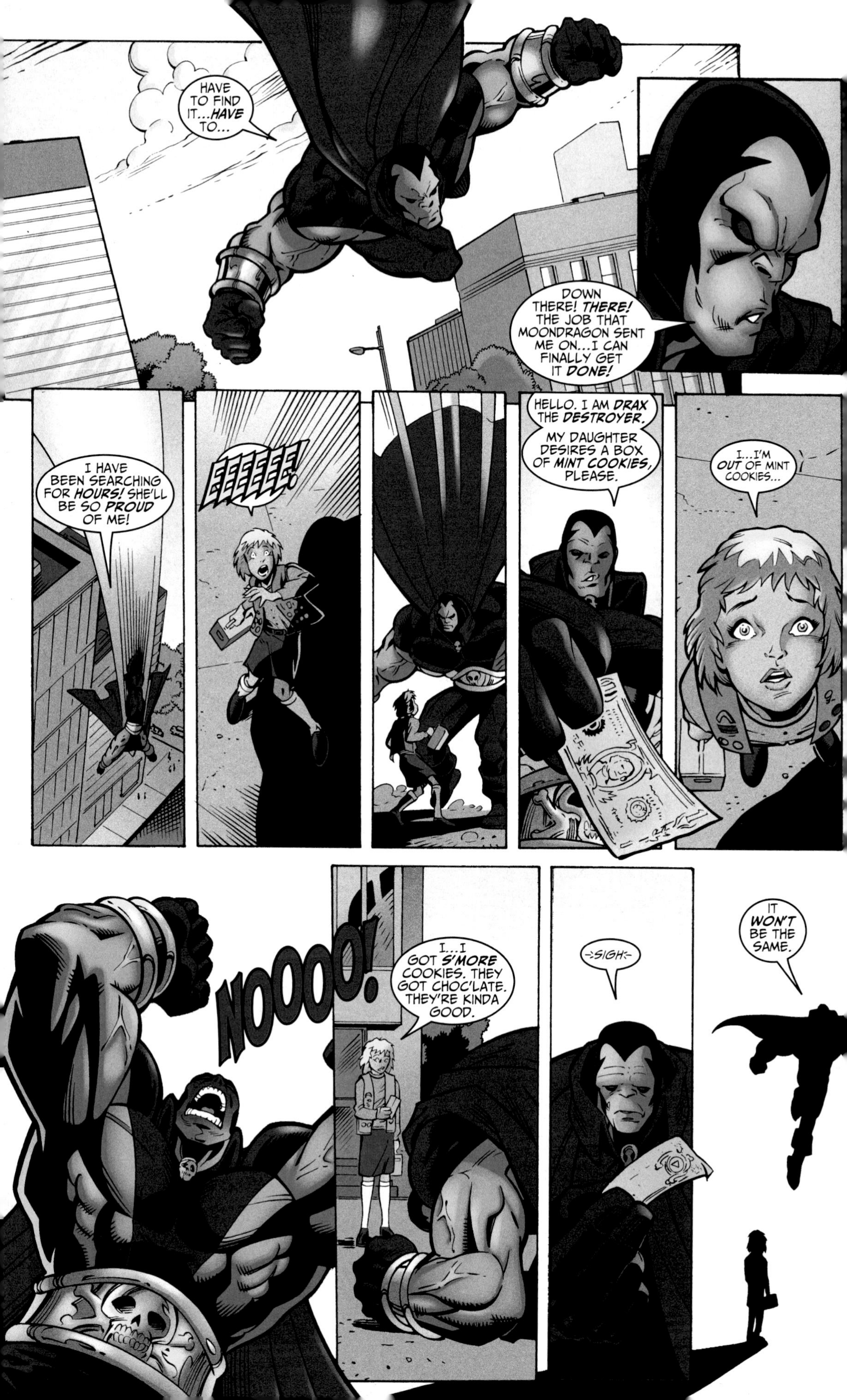
HAVE TO FIND IT...HAVE TO...
DOWN THERE! THERE! THE JOB THAT MOONDRAGON SENT ME ON...I CAN FINALLY GET IT DONE!
I HAVE BEEN SEARCHING FOR HOURS! SHE'LL BE SO PROUD OF ME!
EEEEEE!
HELLO. I AM DRAX THE DESTROYER.
MY DAUGHTER DESIRES A BOX OF MINT COOKIES, PLEASE.
I...I'M OUT OF MINT COOKIES...
NOOOO!
I...I GOT S'MORE COOKIES. THEY GOT CHOC'LATE. THEY'RE KINDA GOOD.
-SIGH-
IT WON'T BE THE SAME.

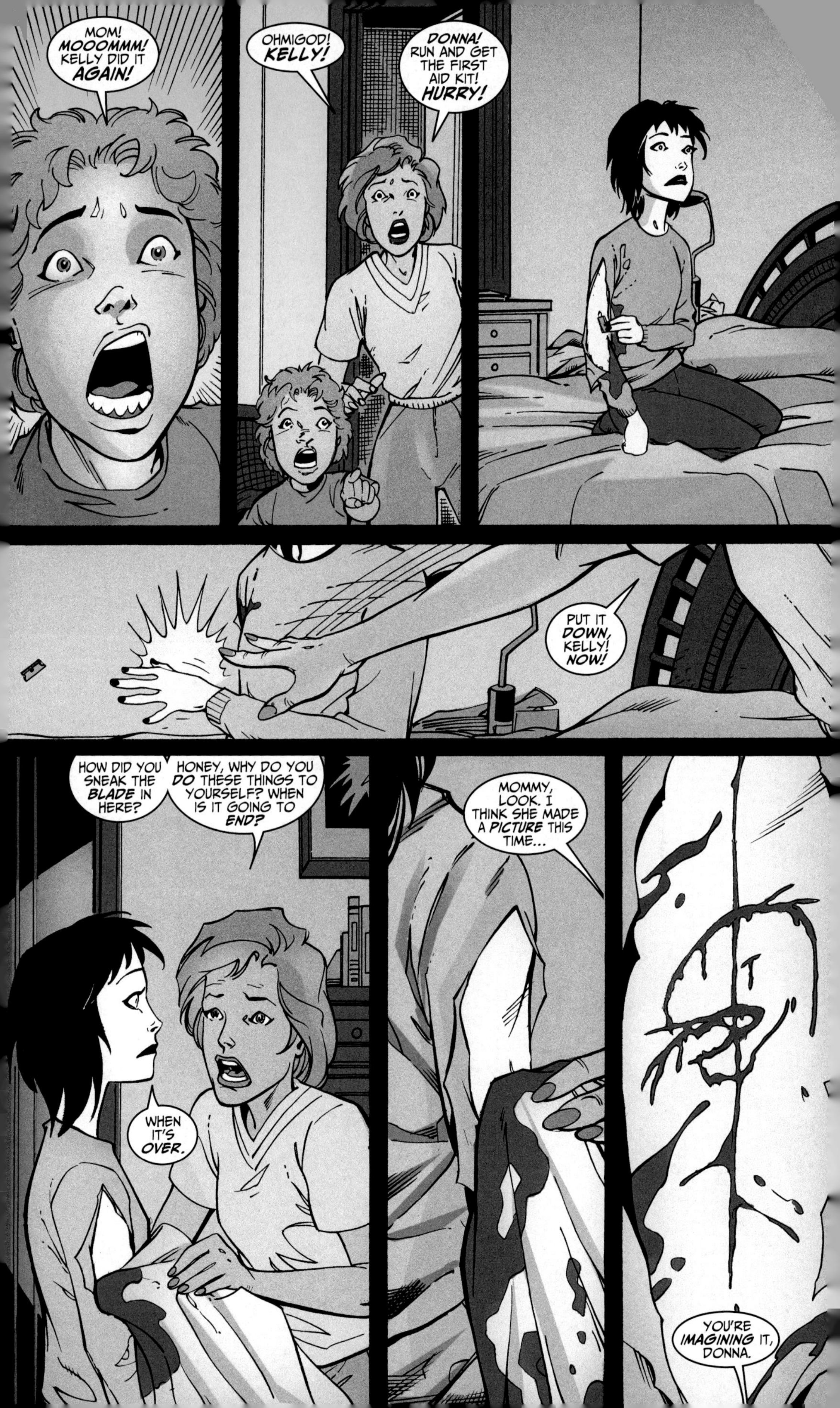

MOM! MOOOMMM! KELLY DID IT AGAIN!
OHMIGOD! KELLY!
DONNA! RUN AND GET THE FIRST AID KIT! HURRY!
PUT IT DOWN, KELLY! NOW!
HOW DID YOU SNEAK THE BLADE IN HERE?
HONEY, WHY DO YOU DO THESE THINGS TO YOURSELF? WHEN IS IT GOING TO END?
WHEN IT'S OVER.
MOMMY, LOOK. I THINK SHE MADE A PICTURE THIS TIME...
YOU'RE IMAGINING IT, DONNA.

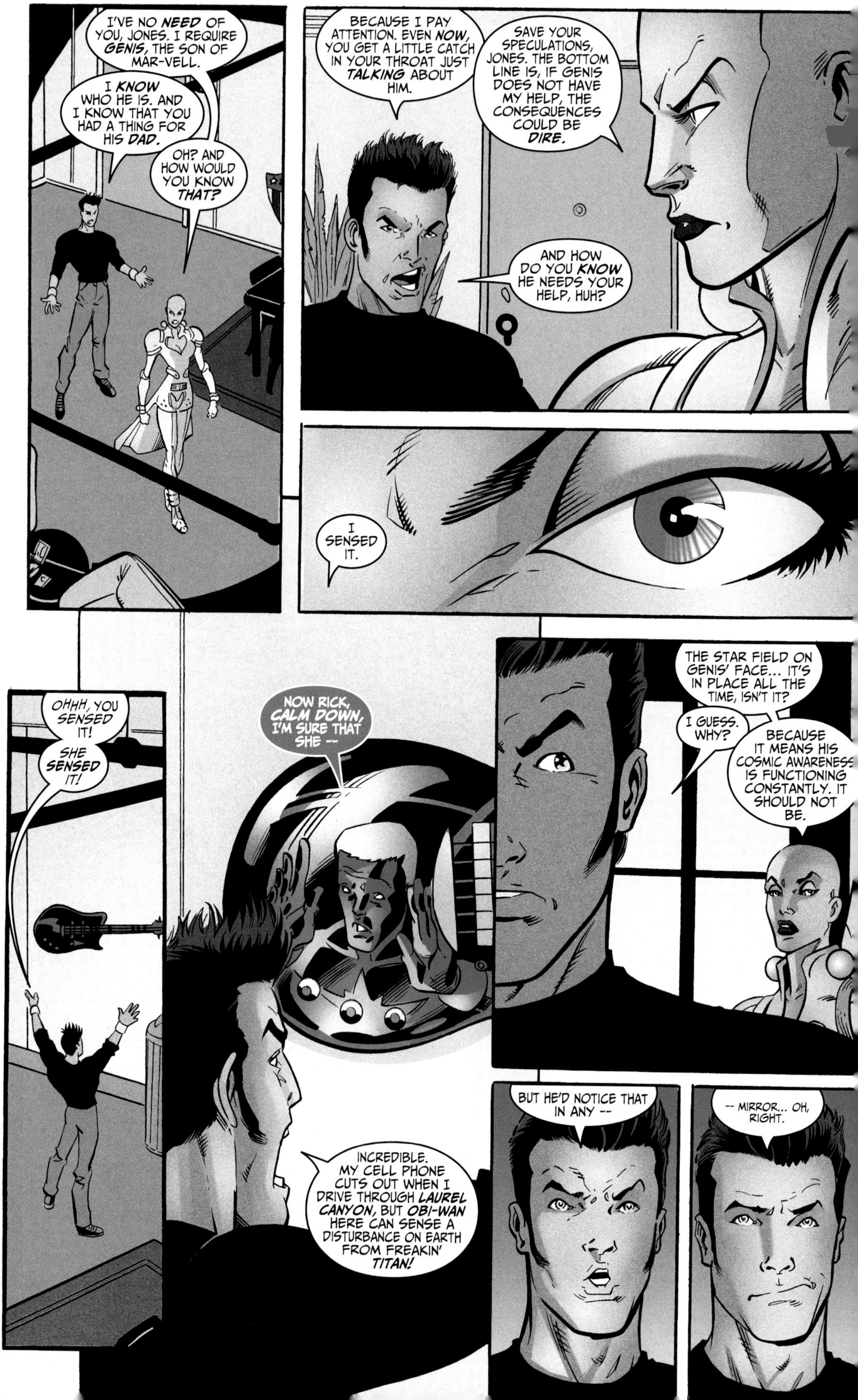

I'VE NO NEED OF YOU, JONES. I REQUIRE GENIS, THE SON OF MAR-VELL.
I KNOW WHO HE IS. AND I KNOW THAT YOU HAD A THING FOR HIS DAD.
OH? AND HOW WOULD YOU KNOW THAT?
BECAUSE I PAY ATTENTION. EVEN NOW, YOU GET A LITTLE CATCH IN YOUR THROAT JUST TALKING ABOUT HIM.
SAVE YOUR SPECULATIONS, JONES. THE BOTTOM LINE IS, IF GENIS DOES NOT HAVE MY HELP, THE CONSEQUENCES COULD BE DIRE.
AND HOW DO YOU KNOW HE NEEDS YOUR HELP, HUH?
I SENSED IT.
OHHH, YOU SENSED IT!
SHE SENSED IT!
NOW RICK, CALM DOWN, I'M SURE THAT SHE --
INCREDIBLE. MY CELL PHONE CUTS OUT WHEN I DRIVE THROUGH LAUREL CANYON, BUT OBI-WAN HERE CAN SENSE A DISTURBANCE ON EARTH FROM FREAKIN' TITAN!
THE STAR FIELD ON GENIS' FACE... IT'S IN PLACE ALL THE TIME, ISN'T IT?
I GUESS. WHY?
BECAUSE IT MEANS HIS COSMIC AWARENESS IS FUNCTIONING CONSTANTLY. IT SHOULD NOT BE.
BUT HE'D NOTICE THAT IN ANY --
-- MIRROR... OH, RIGHT.

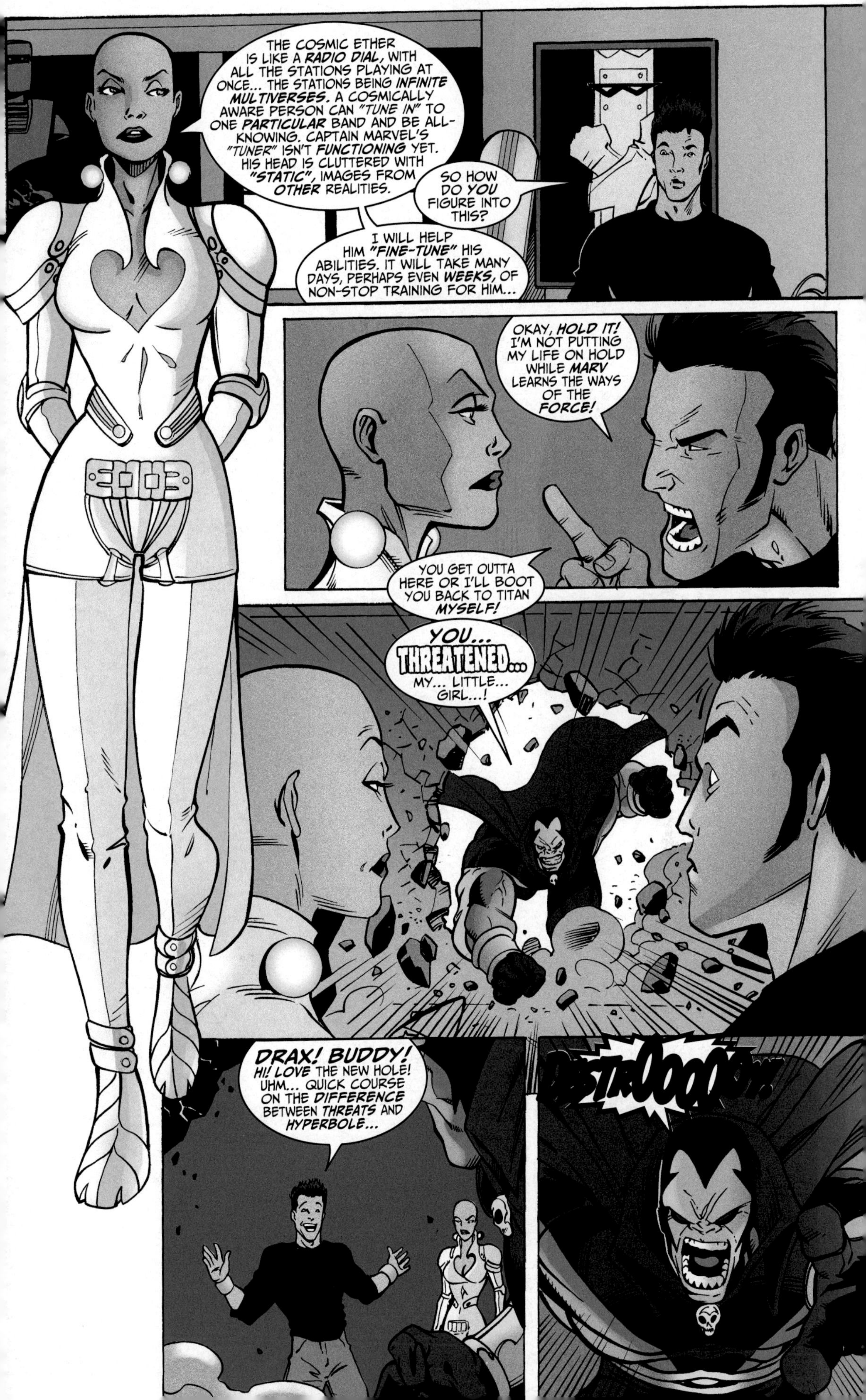
THE COSMIC ETHER IS LIKE A RADIO DIAL, WITH ALL THE STATIONS PLAYING AT ONCE... THE STATIONS BEING INFINITE MULTIVERSES. A COSMICALLY AWARE PERSON CAN "TUNE IN" TO ONE PARTICULAR BAND AND BE ALL-KNOWING. CAPTAIN MARVEL'S "TUNER" ISN'T FUNCTIONING YET. HIS HEAD IS CLUTTERED WITH "STATIC", IMAGES FROM OTHER REALITIES.
SO HOW DO YOU FIGURE INTO THIS?
I WILL HELP HIM "FINE-TUNE" HIS ABILITIES. IT WILL TAKE MANY DAYS, PERHAPS EVEN WEEKS, OF NON-STOP TRAINING FOR HIM...
OKAY, HOLD IT! I'M NOT PUTTING MY LIFE ON HOLD WHILE MARV LEARNS THE WAYS OF THE FORCE!
YOU GET OUTTA HERE OR I'LL BOOT YOU BACK TO TITAN MYSELF!
YOU... THREATENED... MY... LITTLE... GIRL...!
DRAX! BUDDY! HI! LOVE THE NEW HOLE! UHM... QUICK COURSE ON THE DIFFERENCE BETWEEN THREATS AND HYPERBOLE...
DESTROOOOOY!

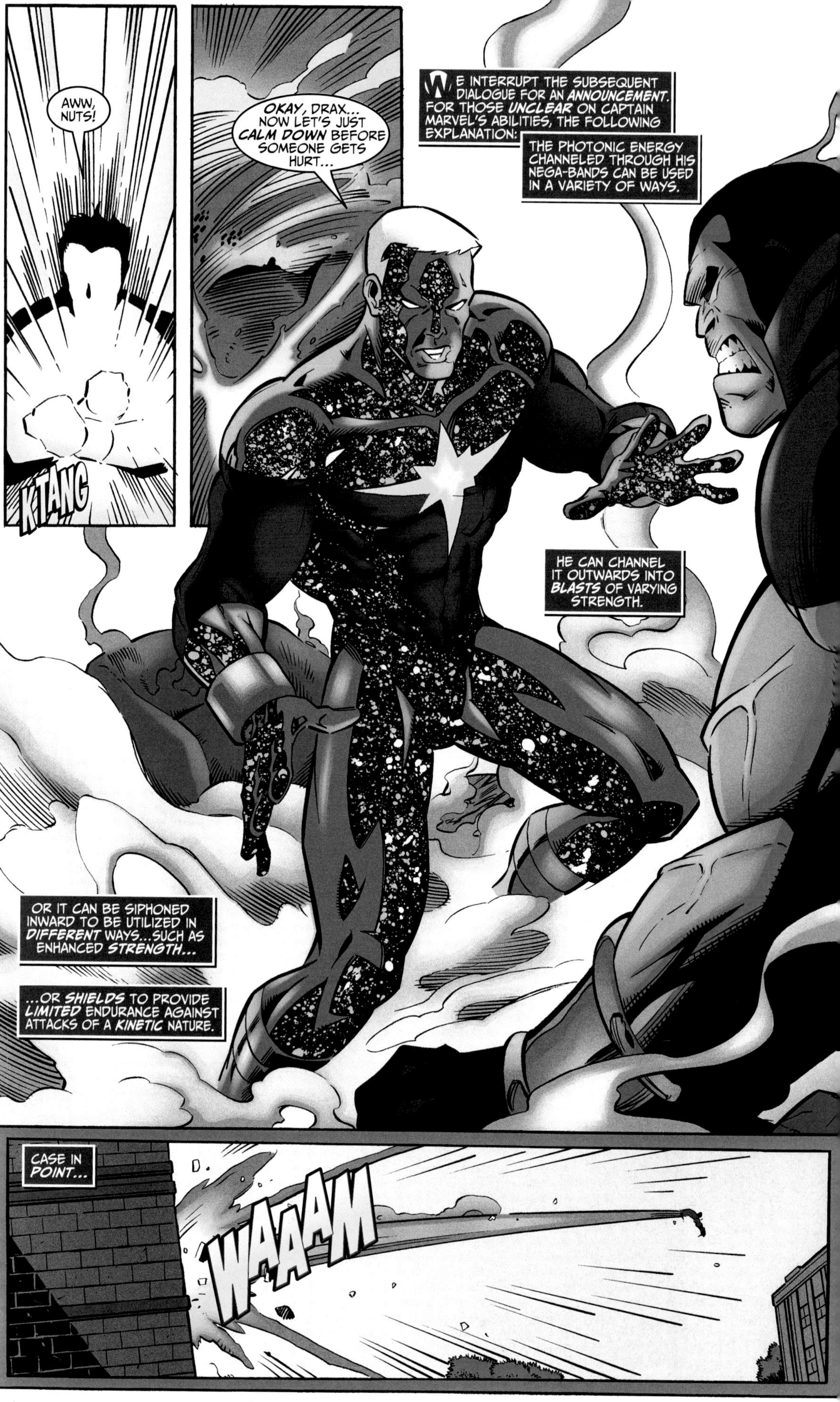
AWW, NUTS!
K-TANG
OKAY, DRAX... NOW LET'S JUST CALM DOWN BEFORE SOMEONE GETS HURT...
WE INTERRUPT THE SUBSEQUENT DIALOGUE FOR AN ANNOUNCEMENT. FOR THOSE UNCLEAR ON CAPTAIN MARVEL'S ABILITIES, THE FOLLOWING EXPLANATION:
THE PHOTONIC ENERGY CHANNELED THROUGH HIS NEGA-BANDS CAN BE USED IN A VARIETY OF WAYS.
HE CAN CHANNEL IT OUTWARDS INTO BLASTS OF VARYING STRENGTH.
OR IT CAN BE SIPHONED INWARD TO BE UTILIZED IN DIFFERENT WAYS...SUCH AS ENHANCED STRENGTH...
...OR SHIELDS TO PROVIDE LIMITED ENDURANCE AGAINST ATTACKS OF A KINETIC NATURE.
CASE IN POINT...
WAAAM

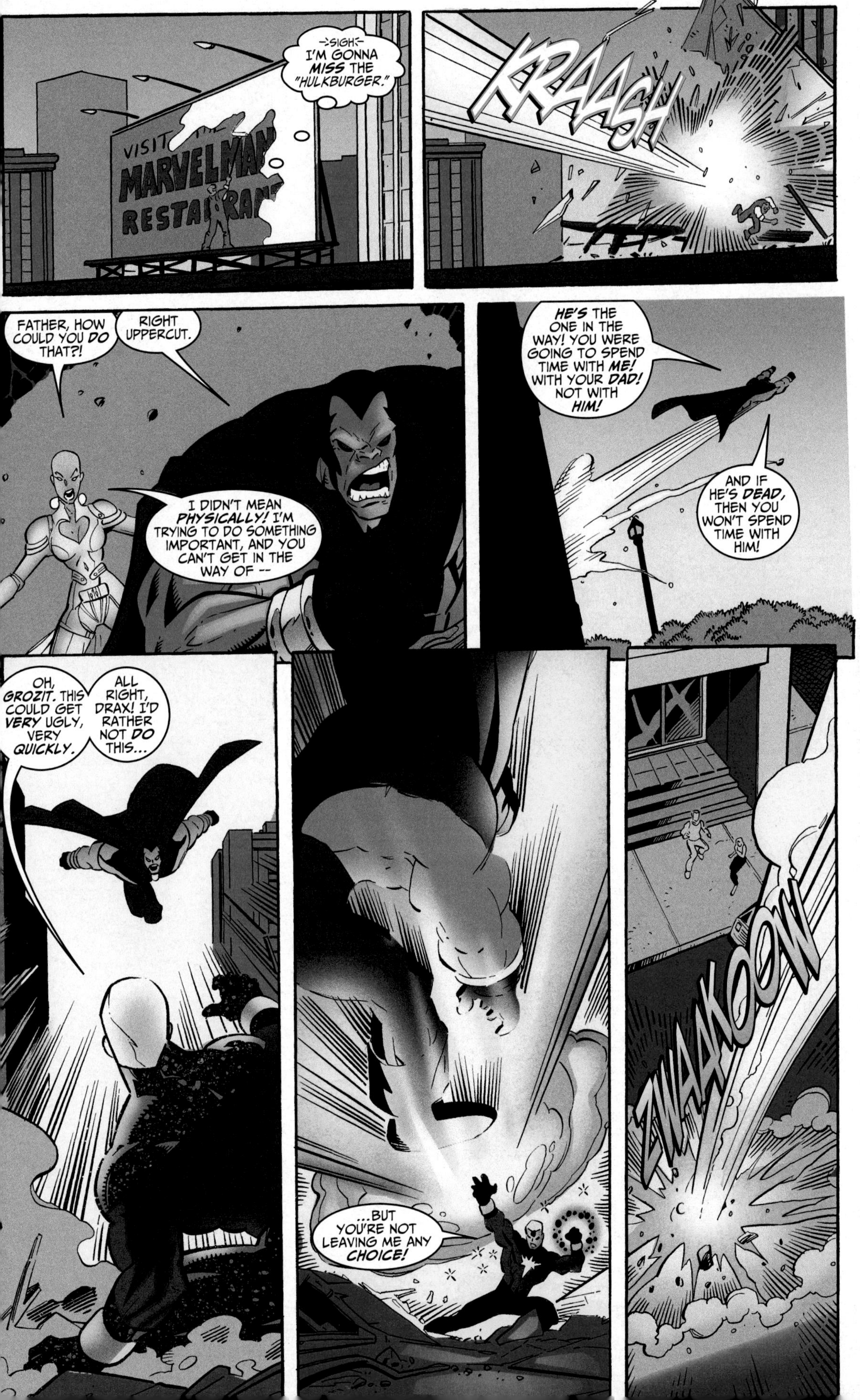

VISIT MARVELMAN RESTA RAN
-SIGH- I'M GONNA MISS THE "HULKBURGER."
KRAASH
FATHER, HOW COULD YOU DO THAT?!
RIGHT UPPERCUT.
I DIDN'T MEAN PHYSICALLY! I'M TRYING TO DO SOMETHING IMPORTANT, AND YOU CAN'T GET IN THE WAY OF --
HE'S THE ONE IN THE WAY! YOU WERE GOING TO SPEND TIME WITH ME! WITH YOUR DAD! NOT WITH HIM!
AND IF HE'S DEAD, THEN YOU WON'T SPEND TIME WITH HIM!
OH, GROZIT. THIS COULD GET VERY UGLY, VERY QUICKLY.
ALL RIGHT, DRAX! I'D RATHER NOT DO THIS...
...BUT YOU'RE NOT LEAVING ME ANY CHOICE!
ZWAAKOOW

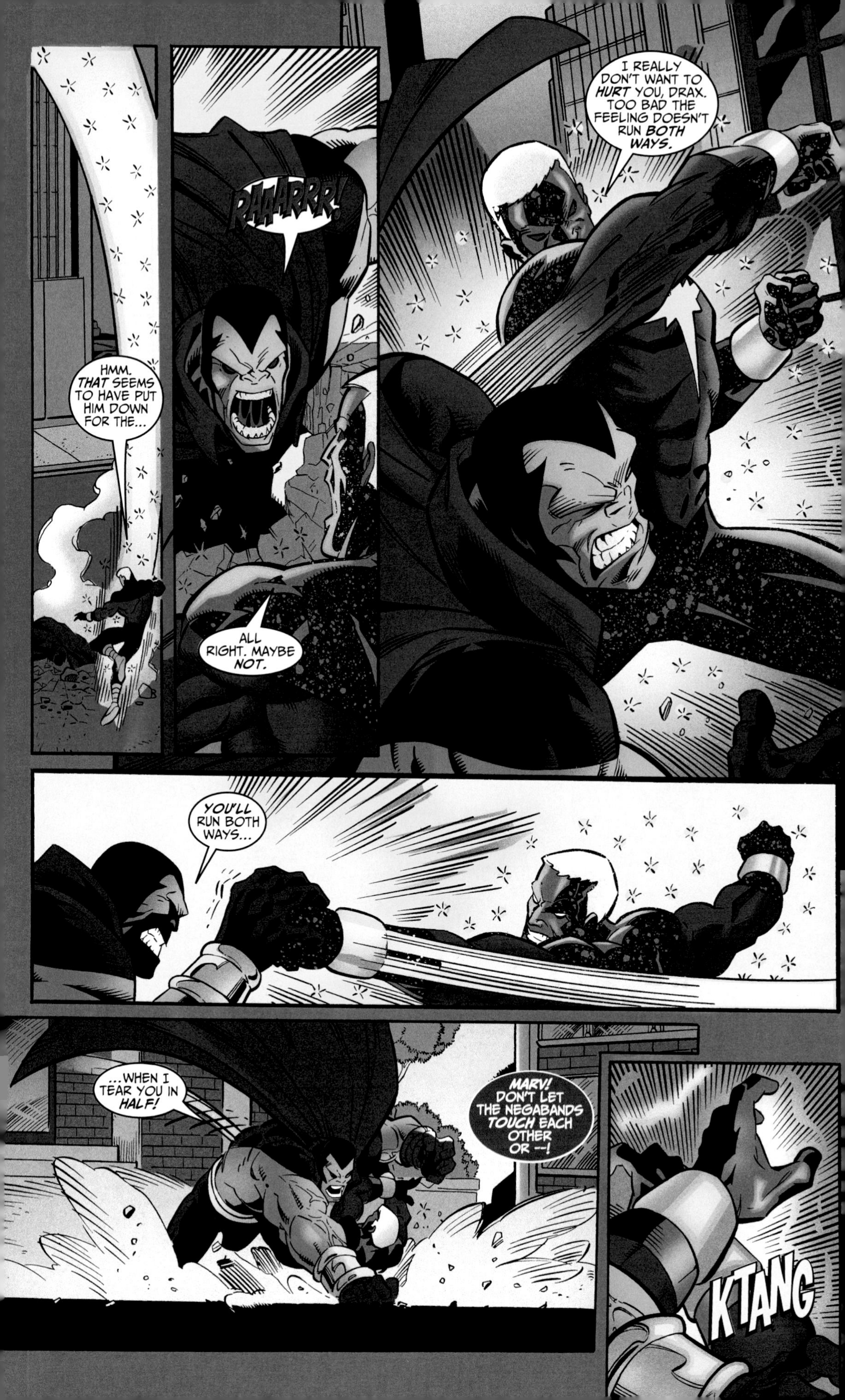
HMM. THAT SEEMS TO HAVE PUT HIM DOWN FOR THE...
RAAARRR!
ALL RIGHT. MAYBE NOT.
I REALLY DON'T WANT TO HURT YOU, DRAX. TOO BAD THE FEELING DOESN'T RUN BOTH WAYS.
YOU'LL RUN BOTH WAYS...
...WHEN I TEAR YOU IN HALF!
MARV! DON'T LET THE NEGABANDS TOUCH EACH OTHER OR --!
KTANG

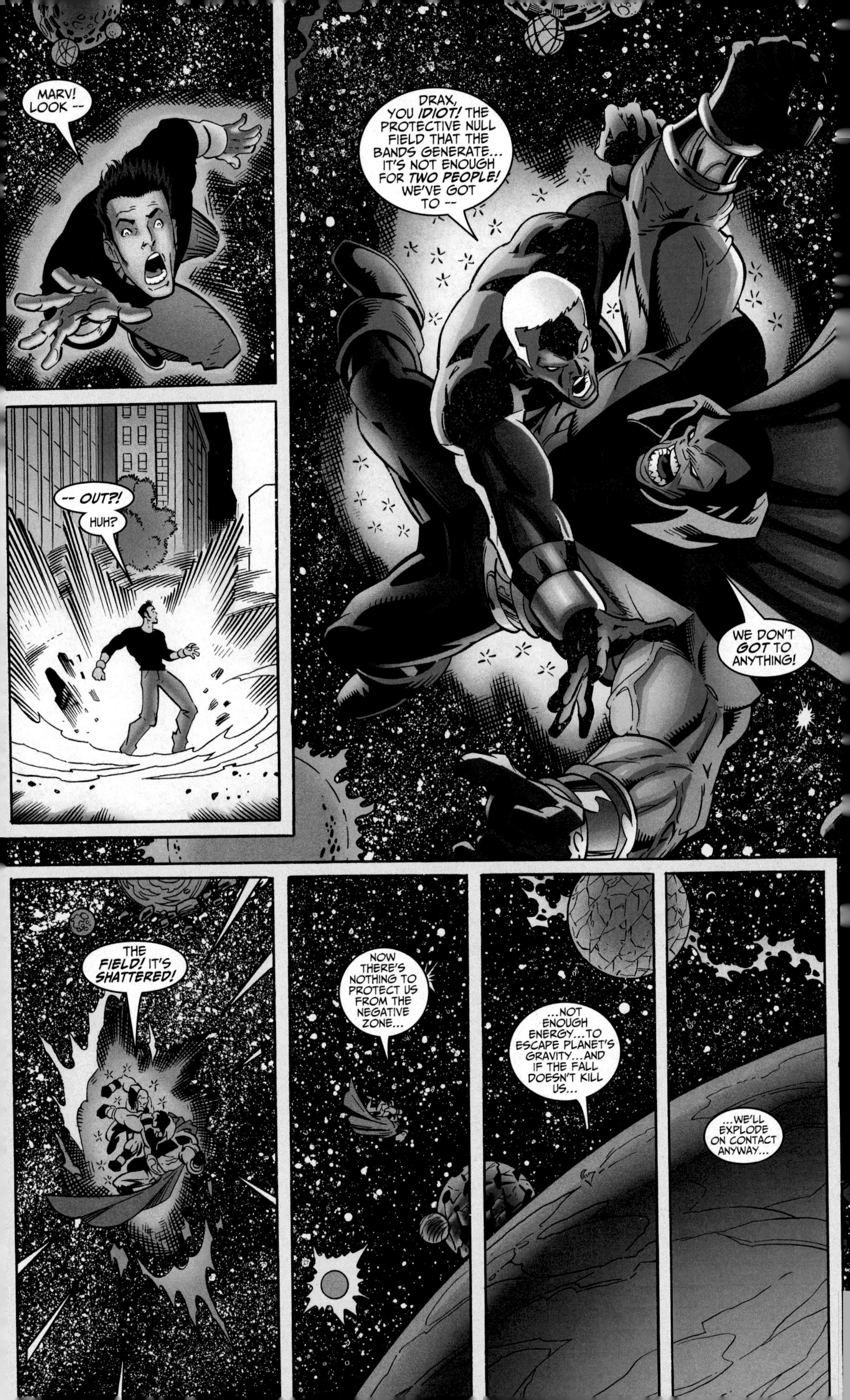
MARV! LOOK --
DRAX, YOU IDIOT! THE PROTECTIVE NULL FIELD THAT THE BANDS GENERATE... IT'S NOT ENOUGH FOR TWO PEOPLE! WE'VE GOT TO --
WE DON'T GOT TO ANYTHING!
-- OUT?!
HUH?
THE FIELD! IT'S SHATTERED!
NOW THERE'S NOTHING TO PROTECT US FROM THE NEGATIVE ZONE...
...NOT ENOUGH ENERGY...TO ESCAPE PLANET'S GRAVITY...AND IF THE FALL DOESN'T KILL US...
...WE'LL EXPLODE ON CONTACT ANYWAY...

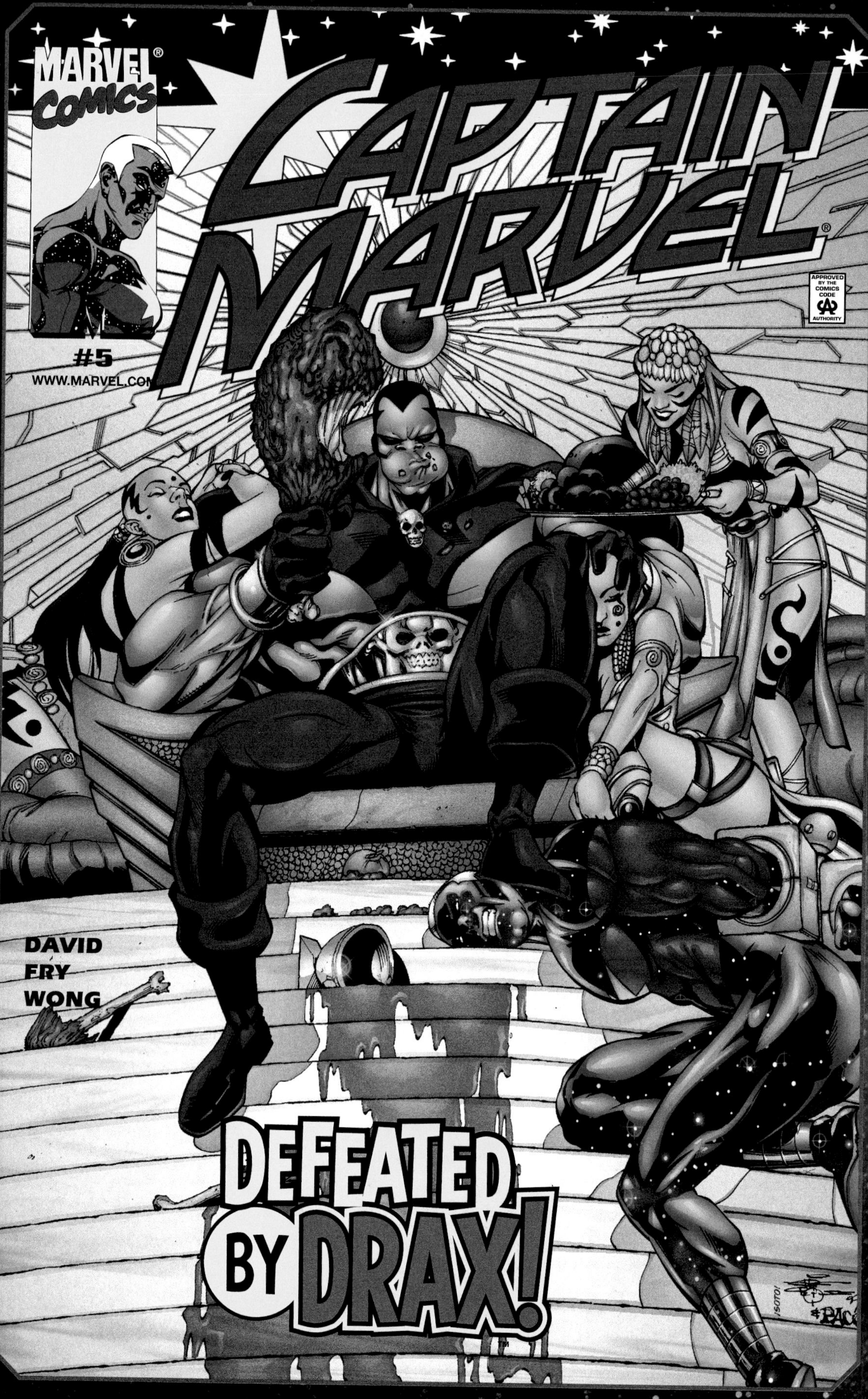

MARVEL COMICS
CAPTAIN MARVEL
APPROVED BY THE COMICS CODE AUTHORITY
#5
WWW.MARVEL.COM
DAVID
FRY
WONG
DEFEATED BY DRAX!

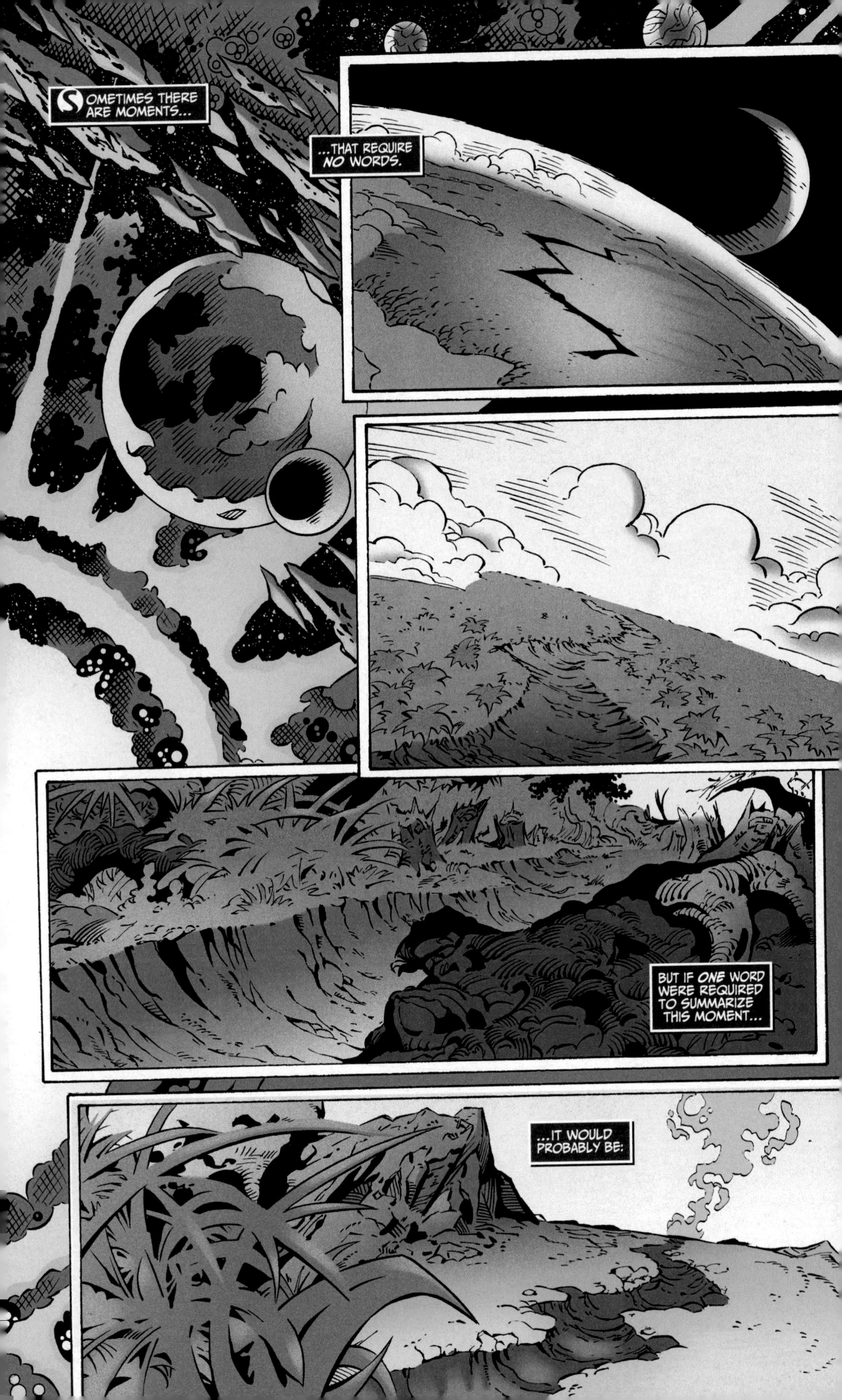
SOMETIMES THERE ARE MOMENTS...
...THAT REQUIRE NO WORDS.
BUT IF ONE WORD WERE REQUIRED TO SUMMARIZE THIS MOMENT...
...IT WOULD PROBABLY BE:

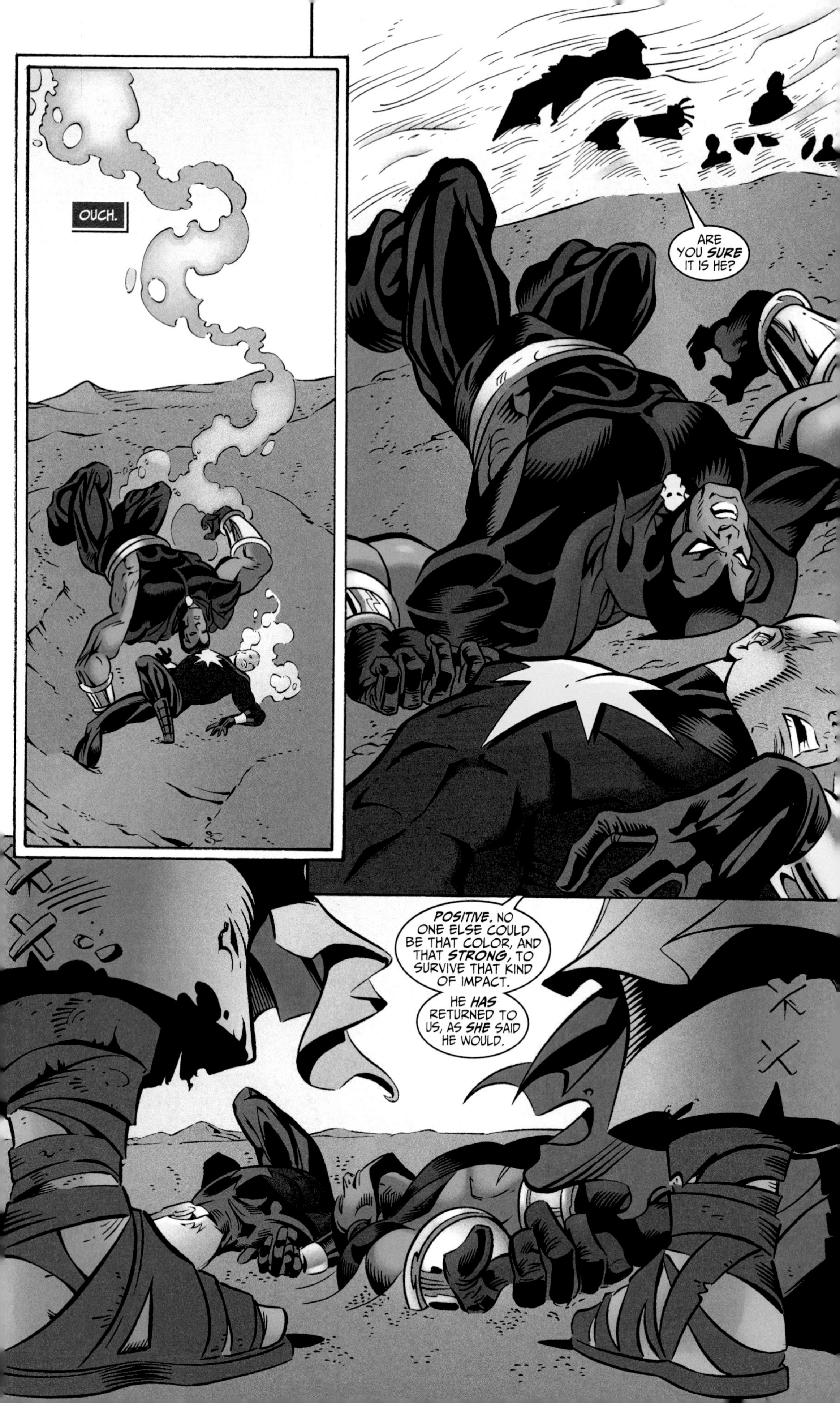

OUCH.
ARE YOU SURE IT IS HE?
POSITIVE. NO ONE ELSE COULD BE THAT COLOR, AND THAT STRONG, TO SURVIVE THAT KIND OF IMPACT.
HE HAS RETURNED TO US, AS SHE SAID HE WOULD.

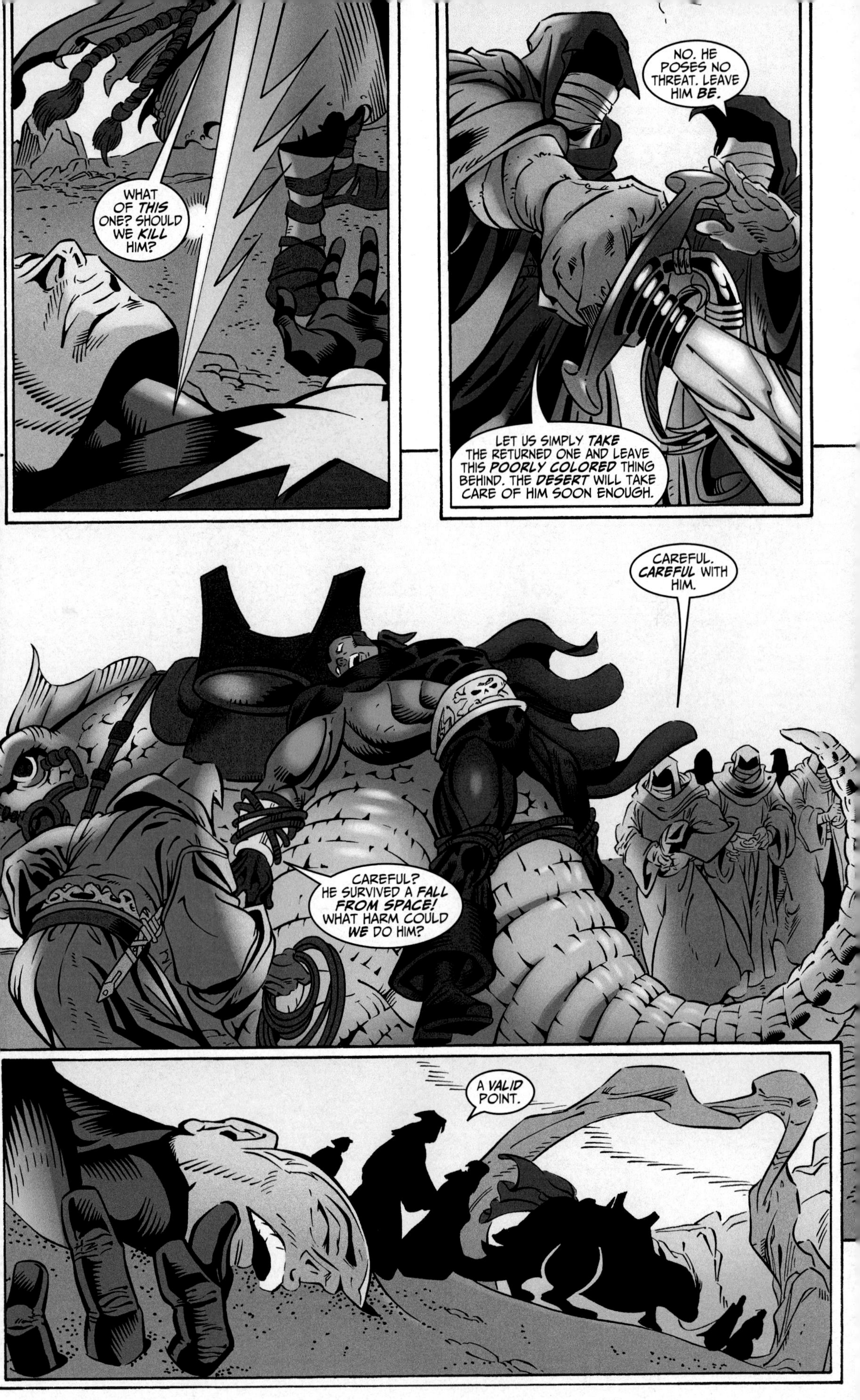

WHAT OF THIS ONE? SHOULD WE KILL HIM?
NO. HE POSES NO THREAT. LEAVE HIM BE.
LET US SIMPLY TAKE THE RETURNED ONE AND LEAVE THIS POORLY COLORED THING BEHIND. THE DESERT WILL TAKE CARE OF HIM SOON ENOUGH.
CAREFUL. CAREFUL WITH HIM.
CAREFUL? HE SURVIVED A FALL FROM SPACE! WHAT HARM COULD WE DO HIM?
A VALID POINT.

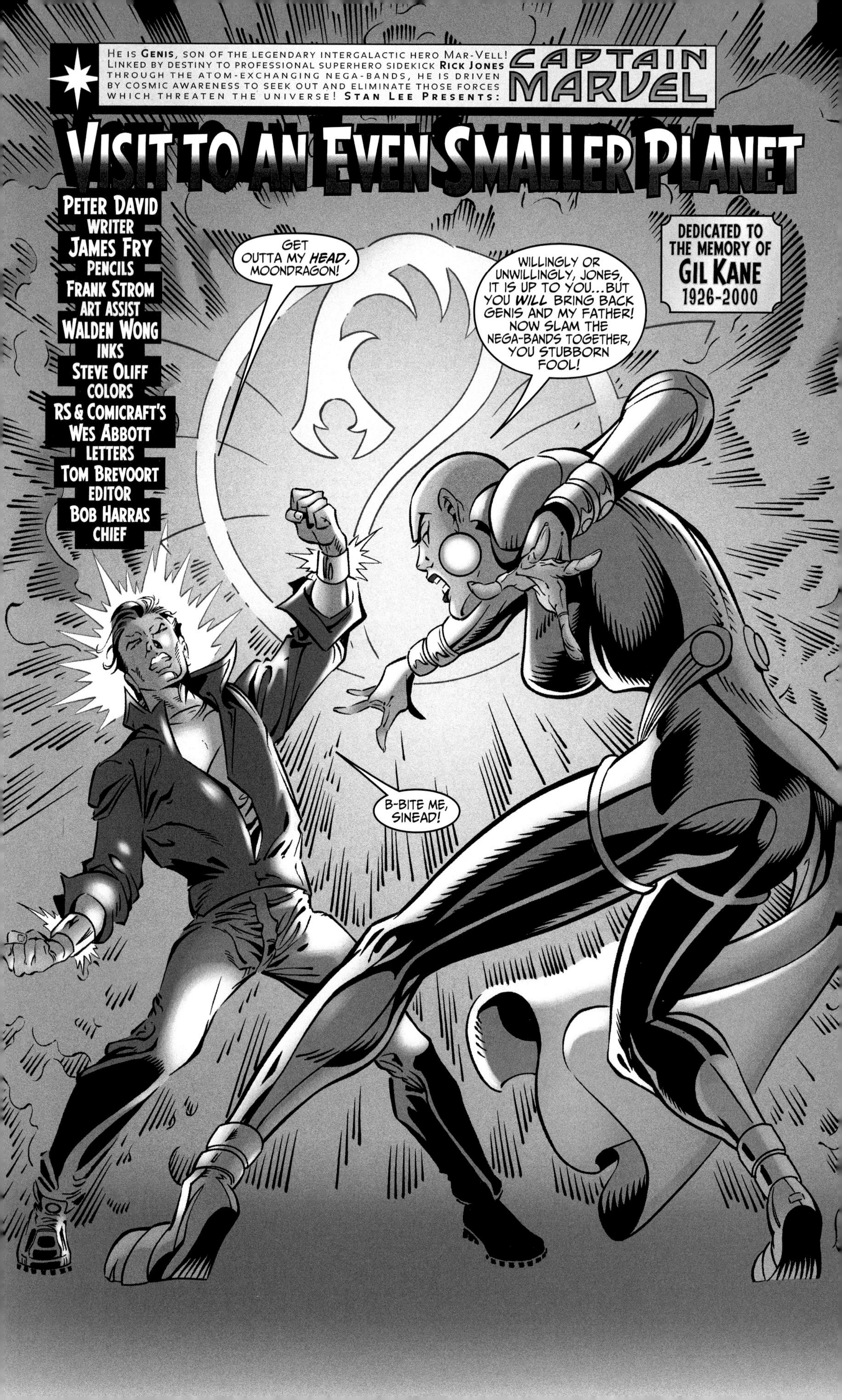

He is Genis, son of the legendary intergalactic hero Mar-Vell! Linked by destiny to professional superhero sidekick Rick Jones through the atom-exchanging nega-bands, he is driven by cosmic awareness to seek out and eliminate those forces which threaten the universe! Stan Lee Presents:
CAPTAIN MARVEL
VISIT TO AN EVEN SMALLER PLANET
PETER DAVID WRITER
JAMES FRY PENCILS
FRANK STROM ART ASSIST
WALDEN WONG INKS
STEVE OLIFF COLORS
RS & COMICRAFT'S WES ABBOTT LETTERS
TOM BREVOORT EDITOR
BOB HARRAS CHIEF
DEDICATED TO THE MEMORY OF GIL KANE 1926-2000
GET OUTTA MY HEAD, MOONDRAGON!
WILLINGLY OR UNWILLINGLY, JONES, IT IS UP TO YOU...BUT YOU WILL BRING BACK GENIS AND MY FATHER! NOW SLAM THE NEGA-BANDS TOGETHER, YOU STUBBORN FOOL!
B-BITE ME, SINEAD!

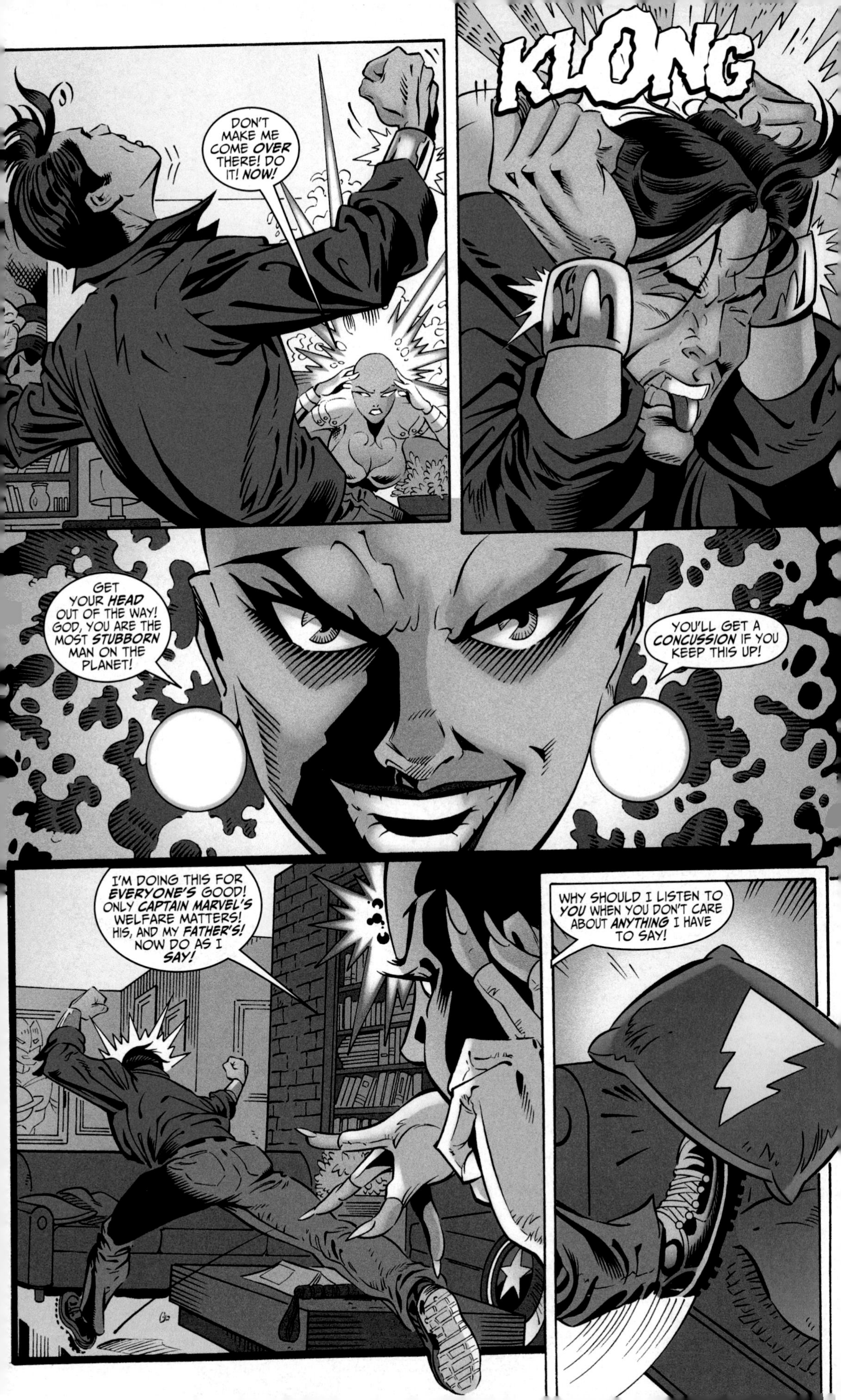
DON'T MAKE ME COME OVER THERE! DO IT! NOW!
KLONG
GET YOUR HEAD OUT OF THE WAY! GOD, YOU ARE THE MOST STUBBORN MAN ON THE PLANET!
YOU'LL GET A CONCUSSION IF YOU KEEP THIS UP!
I'M DOING THIS FOR EVERYONE'S GOOD! ONLY CAPTAIN MARVEL'S WELFARE MATTERS! HIS, AND MY FATHER'S! NOW DO AS I SAY!
WHY SHOULD I LISTEN TO YOU WHEN YOU DON'T CARE ABOUT ANYTHING I HAVE TO SAY!

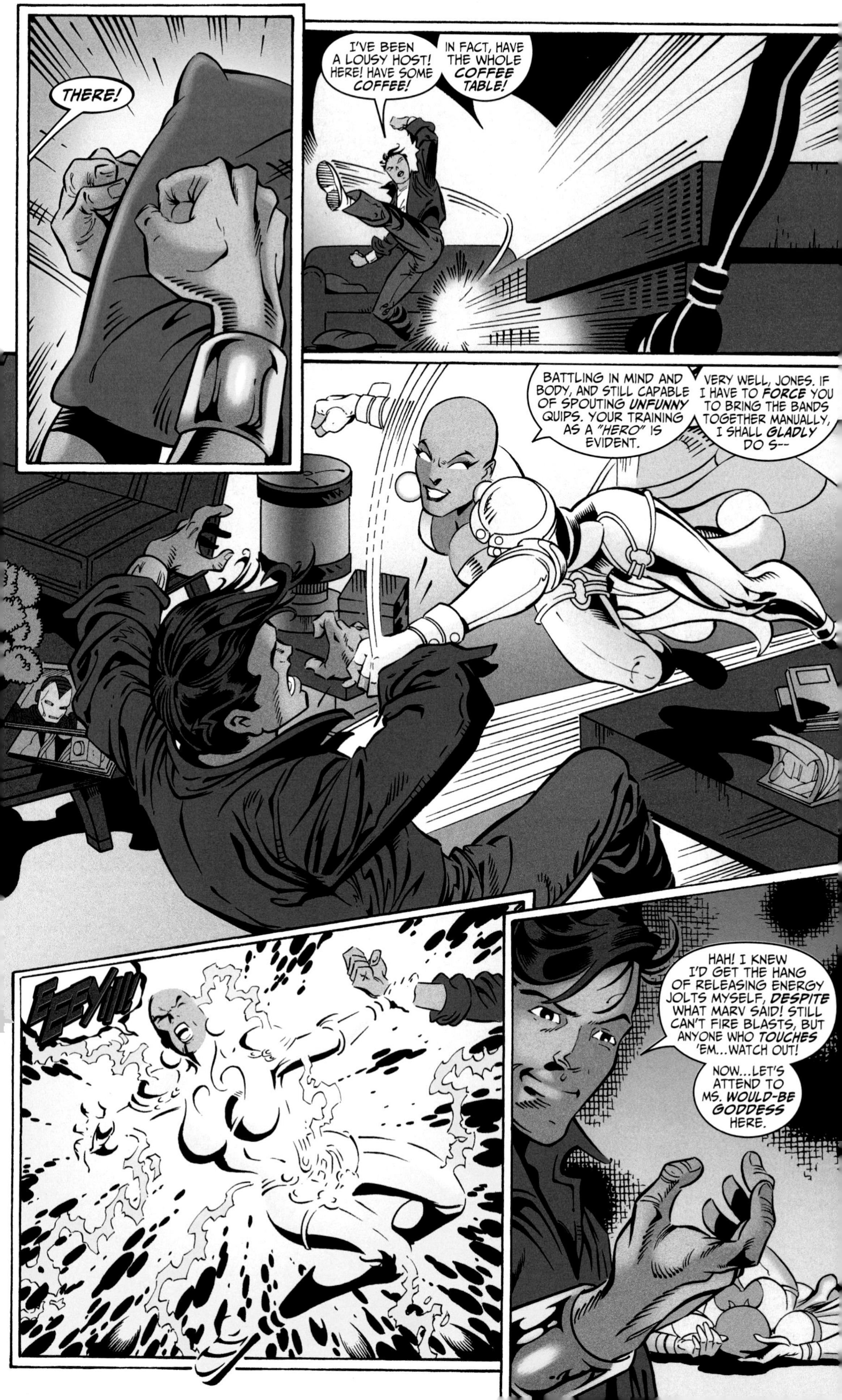
THERE!
I'VE BEEN A LOUSY HOST! HERE! HAVE SOME COFFEE!
IN FACT, HAVE THE WHOLE COFFEE TABLE!
BATTLING IN MIND AND BODY, AND STILL CAPABLE OF SPOUTING UNFUNNY QUIPS. YOUR TRAINING AS A "HERO" IS EVIDENT.
VERY WELL, JONES. IF I HAVE TO FORCE YOU TO BRING THE BANDS TOGETHER MANUALLY, I SHALL GLADLY DO S--
EEEYII!
HAH! I KNEW I'D GET THE HANG OF RELEASING ENERGY JOLTS MYSELF, DESPITE WHAT MARV SAID! STILL CAN'T FIRE BLASTS, BUT ANYONE WHO TOUCHES 'EM...WATCH OUT!
NOW...LET'S ATTEND TO MS. WOULD-BE GODDESS HERE.

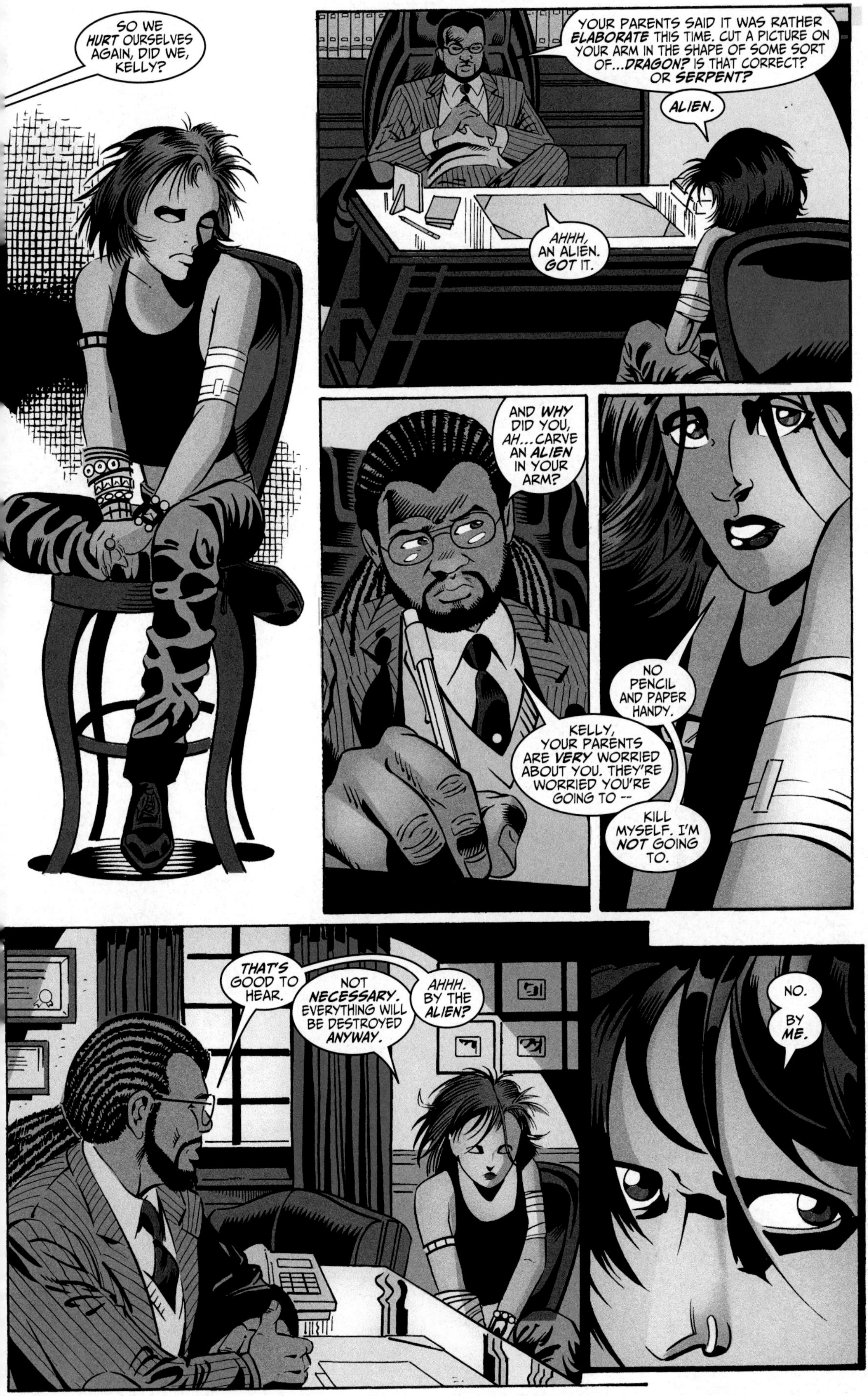
SO WE HURT OURSELVES AGAIN, DID WE, KELLY?
YOUR PARENTS SAID IT WAS RATHER ELABORATE THIS TIME. CUT A PICTURE ON YOUR ARM IN THE SHAPE OF SOME SORT OF...DRAGON? IS THAT CORRECT? OR SERPENT?
ALIEN.
AHHH, AN ALIEN. GOT IT.
AND WHY DID YOU, AH...CARVE AN ALIEN IN YOUR ARM?
NO PENCIL AND PAPER HANDY.
KELLY, YOUR PARENTS ARE VERY WORRIED ABOUT YOU. THEY'RE WORRIED YOU'RE GOING TO --
KILL MYSELF. I'M NOT GOING TO.
THAT'S GOOD TO HEAR.
NOT NECESSARY. EVERYTHING WILL BE DESTROYED ANYWAY.
AHHH. BY THE ALIEN?
NO.
BY ME.

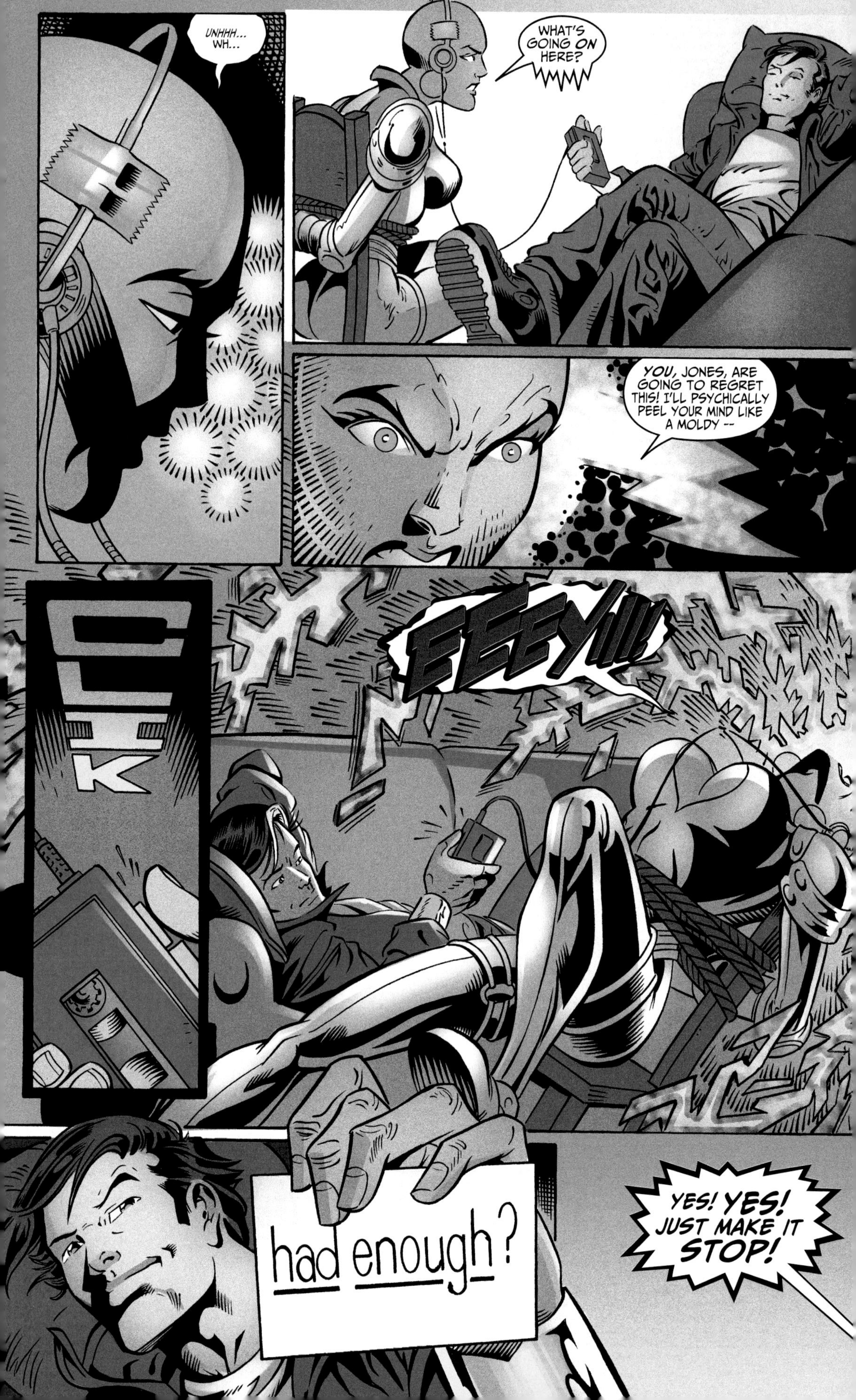
UNHHH... WH...
WHAT'S GOING ON HERE?
YOU, JONES, ARE GOING TO REGRET THIS! I'LL PSYCHICALLY PEEL YOUR MIND LIKE A MOLDY --
CLIK
EEEY!!!!
had enough?
YES! YES! JUST MAKE IT STOP!

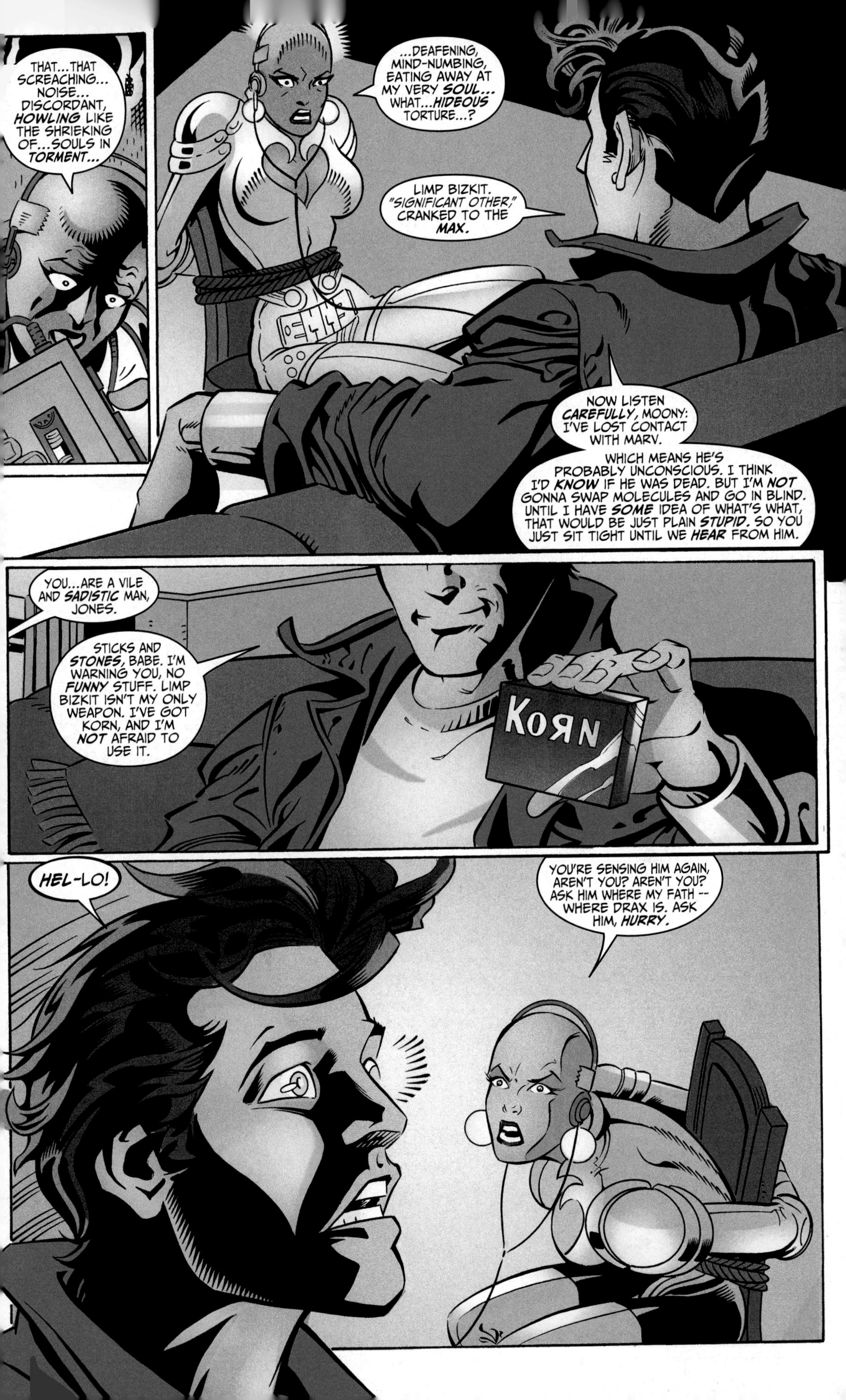

THAT...THAT SCREACHING... NOISE... DISCORDANT, HOWLING LIKE THE SHRIEKING OF...SOULS IN TORMENT...
...DEAFENING, MIND-NUMBING, EATING AWAY AT MY VERY SOUL... WHAT...HIDEOUS TORTURE...?
LIMP BIZKIT. "SIGNIFICANT OTHER," CRANKED TO THE MAX.
NOW LISTEN CAREFULLY, MOONY: I'VE LOST CONTACT WITH MARV.
WHICH MEANS HE'S PROBABLY UNCONSCIOUS. I THINK I'D KNOW IF HE WAS DEAD. BUT I'M NOT GONNA SWAP MOLECULES AND GO IN BLIND. UNTIL I HAVE SOME IDEA OF WHAT'S WHAT, THAT WOULD BE JUST PLAIN STUPID. SO YOU JUST SIT TIGHT UNTIL WE HEAR FROM HIM.
YOU...ARE A VILE AND SADISTIC MAN, JONES.
STICKS AND STONES, BABE. I'M WARNING YOU, NO FUNNY STUFF. LIMP BIZKIT ISN'T MY ONLY WEAPON. I'VE GOT KORN, AND I'M NOT AFRAID TO USE IT.
KORN
HEL-LO!
YOU'RE SENSING HIM AGAIN, AREN'T YOU? AREN'T YOU? ASK HIM WHERE MY FATH -- WHERE DRAX IS. ASK HIM, HURRY.

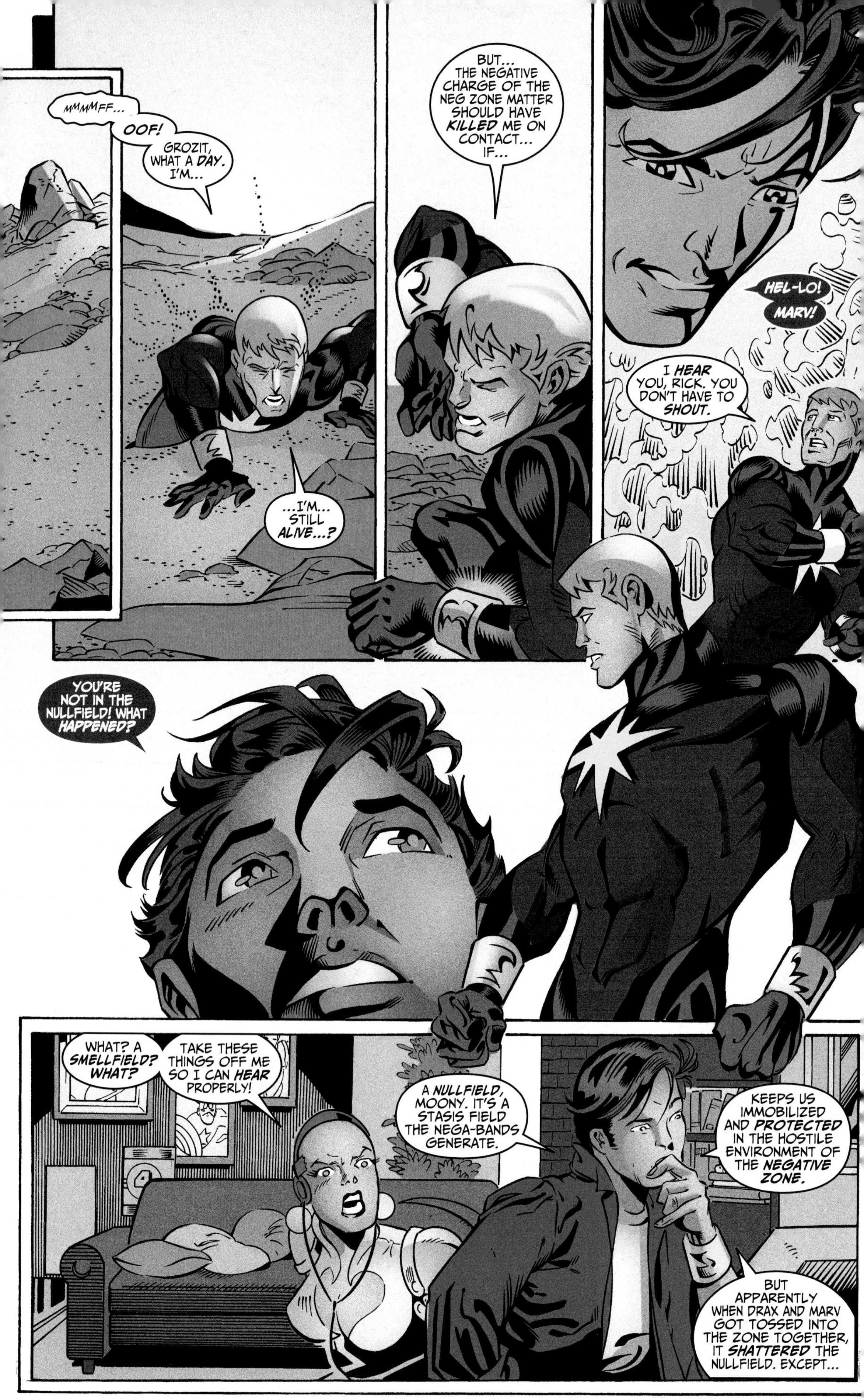

MMMMFF...
OOF!
GROZIT, WHAT A DAY. I'M...
...I'M... STILL ALIVE...?
BUT... THE NEGATIVE CHARGE OF THE NEG ZONE MATTER SHOULD HAVE KILLED ME ON CONTACT... IF...
HEL-LO! MARV!
I HEAR YOU, RICK. YOU DON'T HAVE TO SHOUT.
YOU'RE NOT IN THE NULLFIELD! WHAT HAPPENED?
WHAT? A SMELLFIELD? WHAT?
TAKE THESE THINGS OFF ME SO I CAN HEAR PROPERLY!
A NULLFIELD, MOONY. IT'S A STASIS FIELD THE NEGA-BANDS GENERATE.
KEEPS US IMMOBILIZED AND PROTECTED IN THE HOSTILE ENVIRONMENT OF THE NEGATIVE ZONE.
BUT APPARENTLY WHEN DRAX AND MARV GOT TOSSED INTO THE ZONE TOGETHER, IT SHATTERED THE NULLFIELD. EXCEPT...

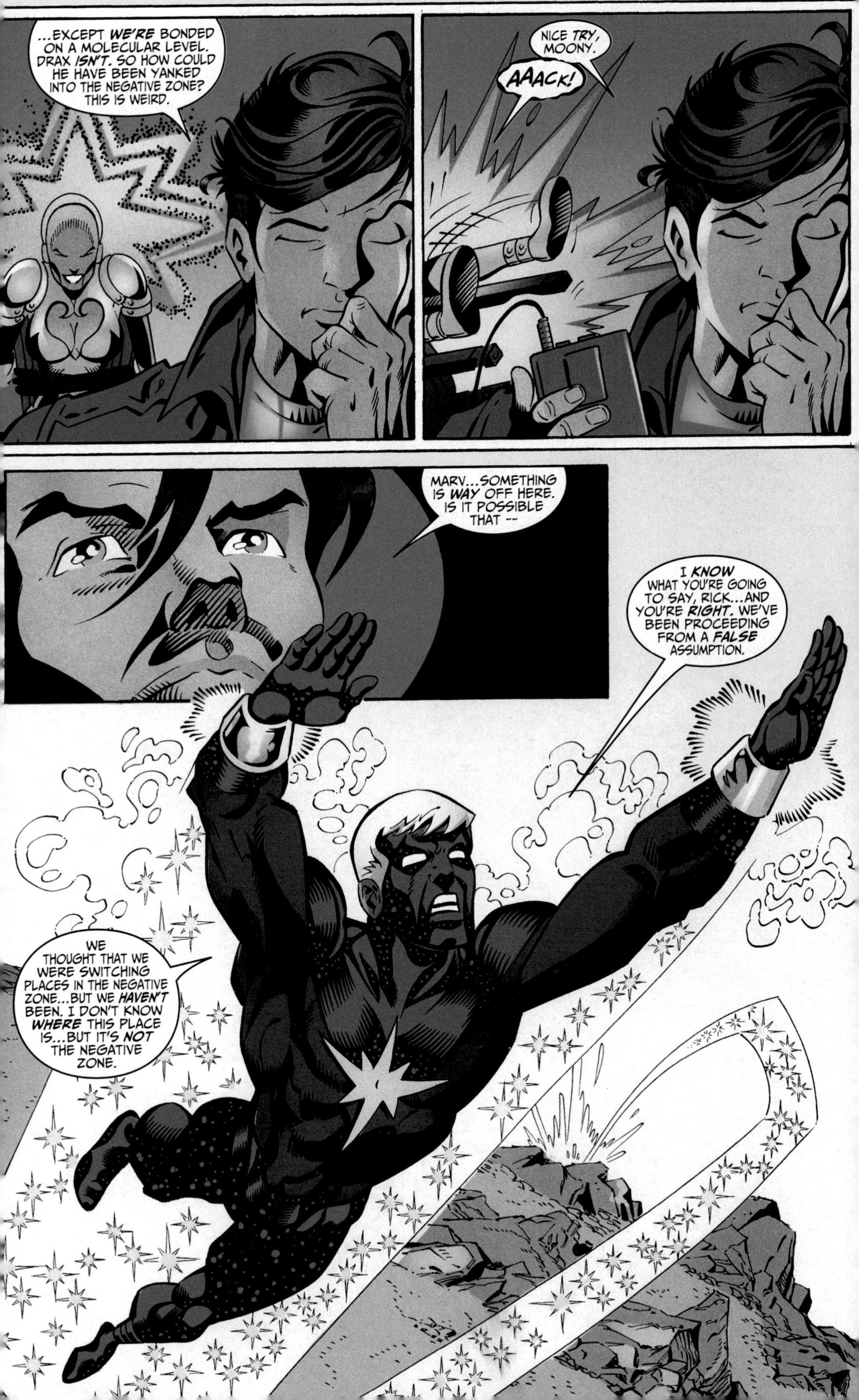
...EXCEPT WE'RE BONDED ON A MOLECULAR LEVEL. DRAX ISN'T. SO HOW COULD HE HAVE BEEN YANKED INTO THE NEGATIVE ZONE? THIS IS WEIRD.
NICE TRY, MOONY.
AAACK!
MARV...SOMETHING IS WAY OFF HERE. IS IT POSSIBLE THAT --
I KNOW WHAT YOU'RE GOING TO SAY, RICK...AND YOU'RE RIGHT. WE'VE BEEN PROCEEDING FROM A FALSE ASSUMPTION.
WE THOUGHT THAT WE WERE SWITCHING PLACES IN THE NEGATIVE ZONE...BUT WE HAVEN'T BEEN. I DON'T KNOW WHERE THIS PLACE IS...BUT IT'S NOT THE NEGATIVE ZONE.

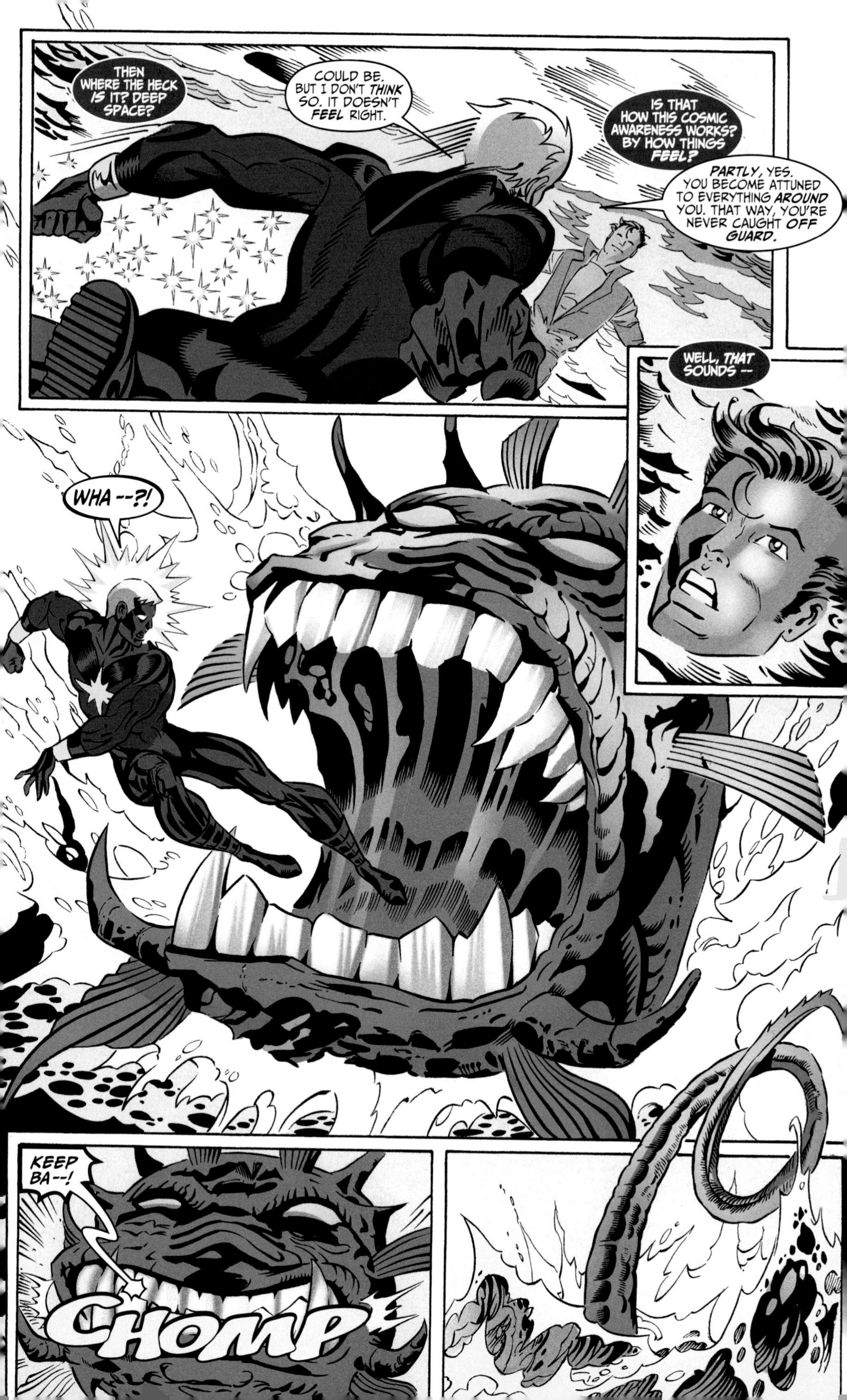
THEN WHERE THE HECK IS IT? DEEP SPACE?
COULD BE. BUT I DON'T THINK SO. IT DOESN'T FEEL RIGHT.
IS THAT HOW THIS COSMIC AWARENESS WORKS? BY HOW THINGS FEEL?
PARTLY, YES. YOU BECOME ATTUNED TO EVERYTHING AROUND YOU. THAT WAY, YOU'RE NEVER CAUGHT OFF GUARD.
WELL, THAT SOUNDS --
WHA --?!
KEEP BA--!
CHOMP

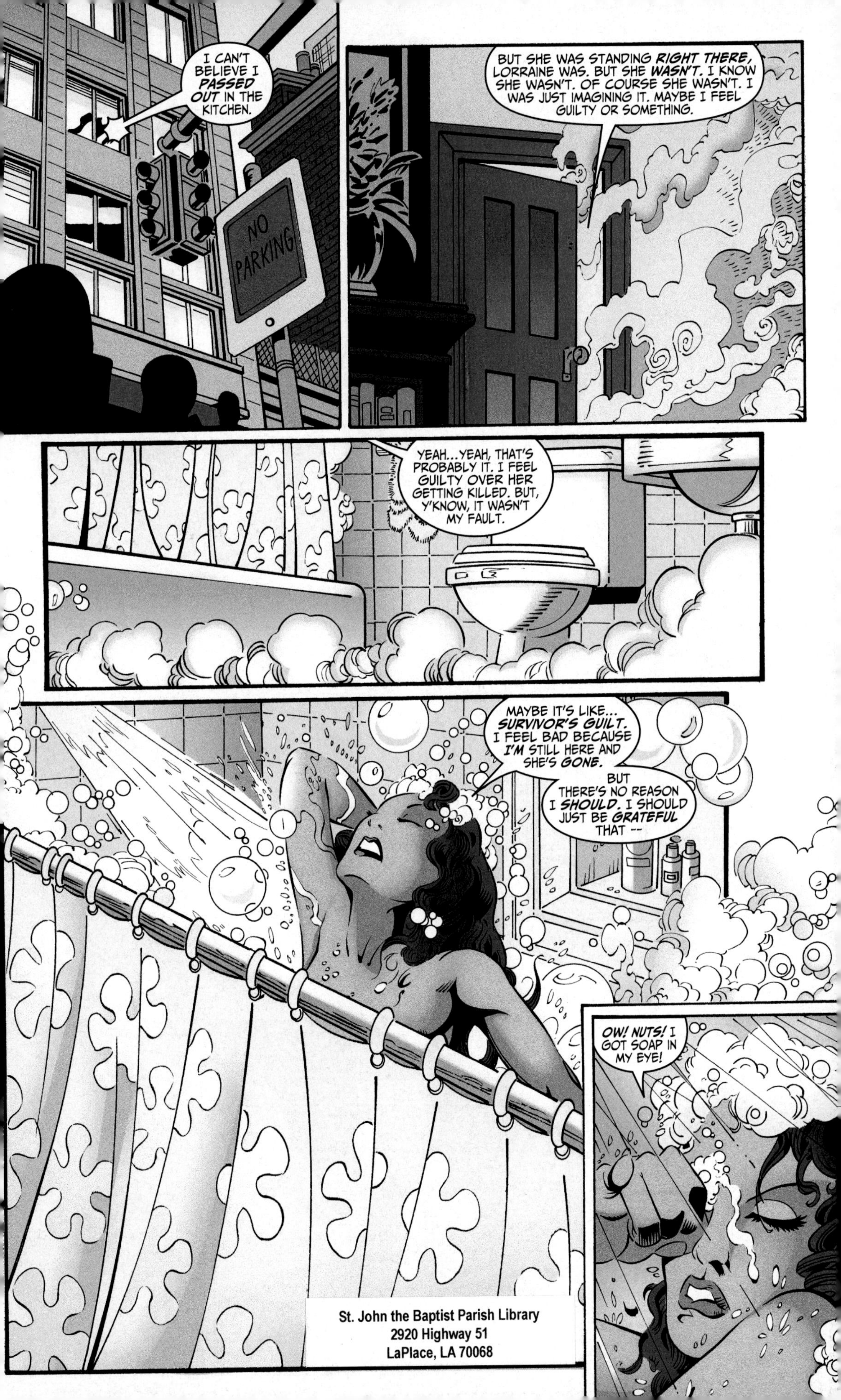
I CAN'T BELIEVE I PASSED OUT IN THE KITCHEN.
NO PARKING
BUT SHE WAS STANDING RIGHT THERE, LORRAINE WAS. BUT SHE WASN'T. I KNOW SHE WASN'T. OF COURSE SHE WASN'T. I WAS JUST IMAGINING IT. MAYBE I FEEL GUILTY OR SOMETHING.
YEAH...YEAH, THAT'S PROBABLY IT. I FEEL GUILTY OVER HER GETTING KILLED. BUT, Y'KNOW, IT WASN'T MY FAULT.
MAYBE IT'S LIKE... SURVIVOR'S GUILT. I FEEL BAD BECAUSE I'M STILL HERE AND SHE'S GONE.
BUT THERE'S NO REASON I SHOULD. I SHOULD JUST BE GRATEFUL THAT --
OW! NUTS! I GOT SOAP IN MY EYE!

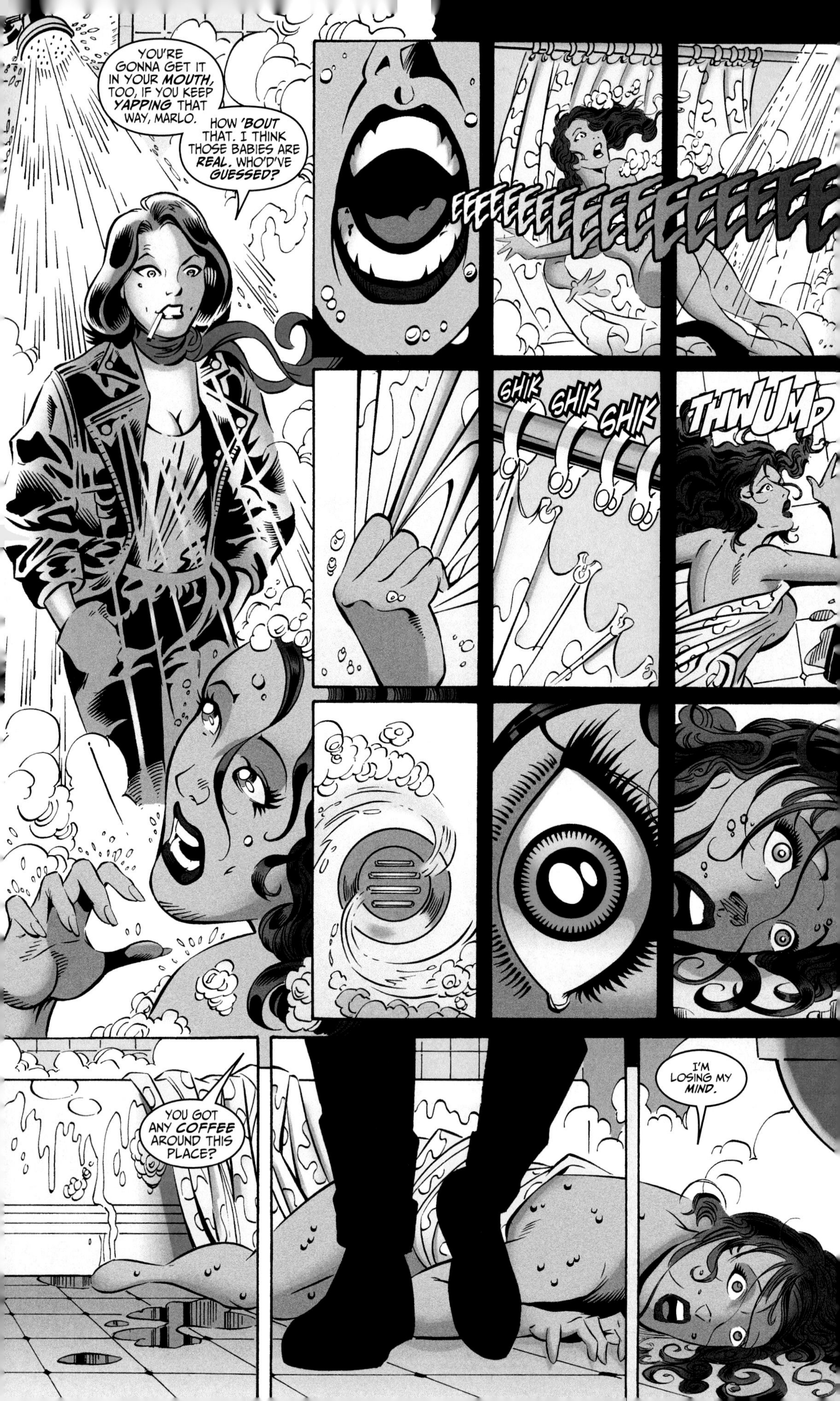

YOU'RE GONNA GET IT IN YOUR MOUTH, TOO, IF YOU KEEP YAPPING THAT WAY, MARLO.
HOW 'BOUT THAT. I THINK THOSE BABIES ARE REAL. WHO'D'VE GUESSED?
EEEEEEEEEEEEEEEEEEE
SHIK SHIK SHIK
THWUMP
YOU GOT ANY COFFEE AROUND THIS PLACE?
I'M LOSING MY MIND.

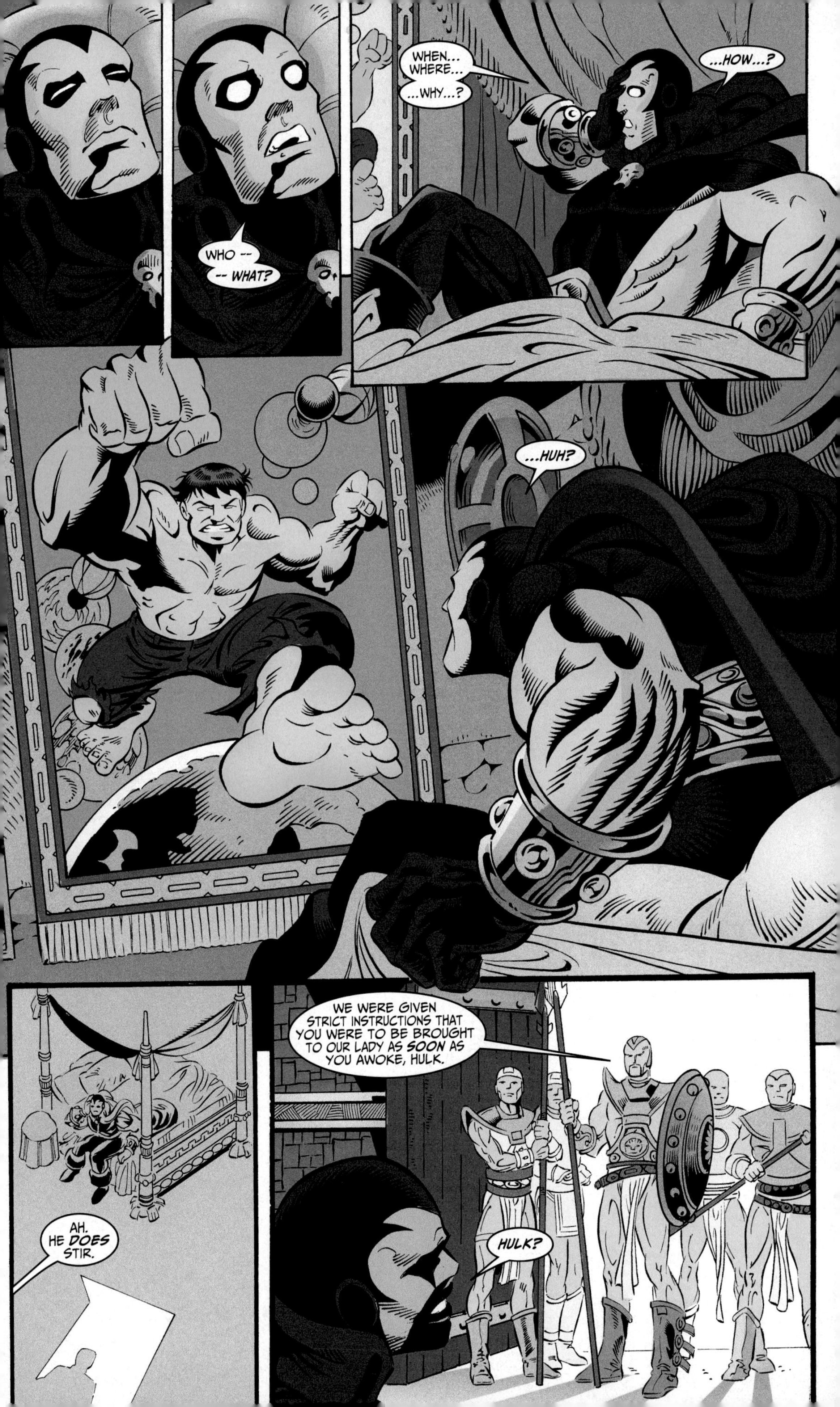
WHO --
-- WHAT?
WHEN... WHERE... ...WHY...?
...HOW...?
...HUH?
AH. HE DOES STIR.
WE WERE GIVEN STRICT INSTRUCTIONS THAT YOU WERE TO BE BROUGHT TO OUR LADY AS SOON AS YOU AWOKE, HULK.
HULK?

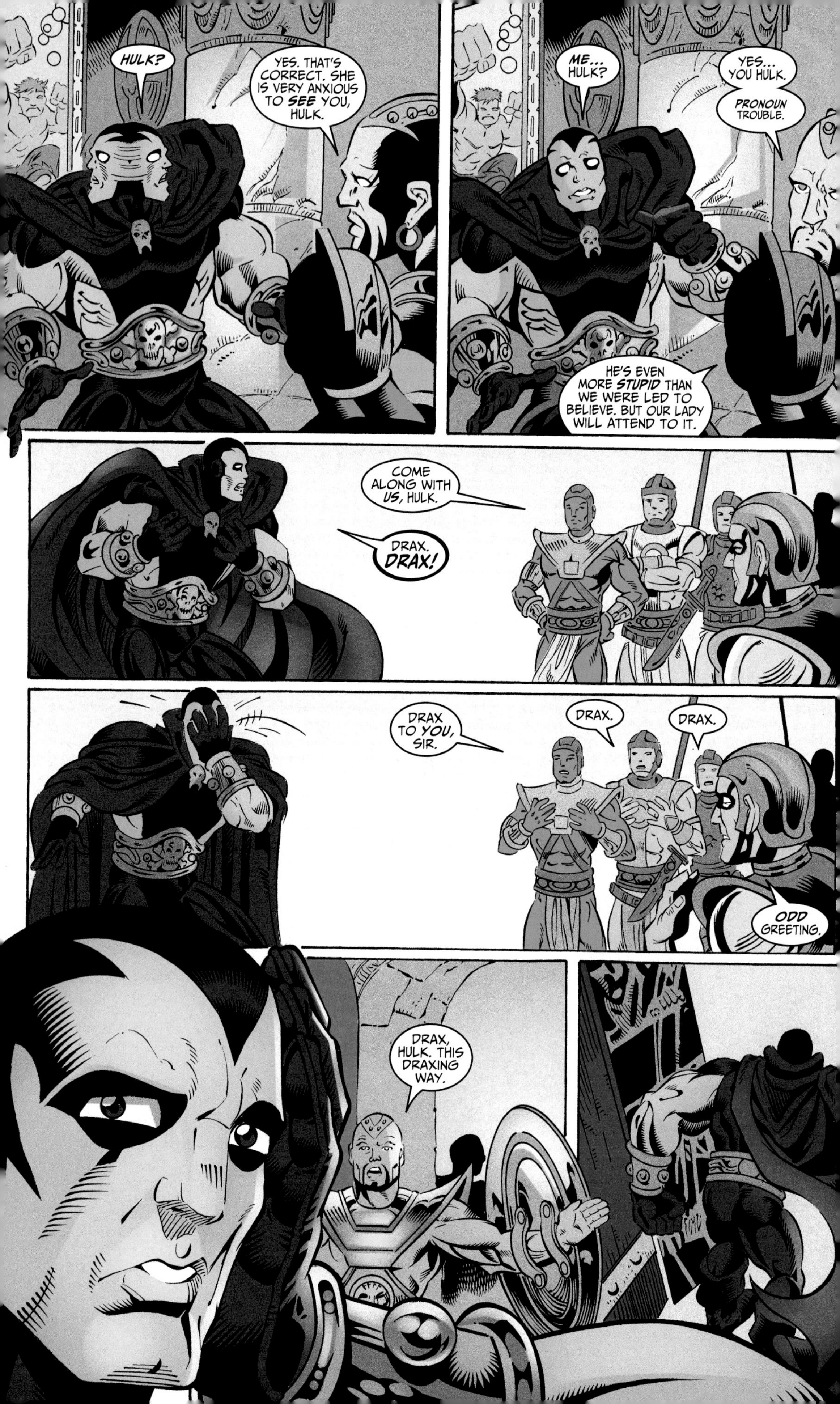
HULK?
YES. THAT'S CORRECT. SHE IS VERY ANXIOUS TO SEE YOU, HULK.
ME... HULK?
YES... YOU HULK.
PRONOUN TROUBLE.
HE'S EVEN MORE STUPID THAN WE WERE LED TO BELIEVE. BUT OUR LADY WILL ATTEND TO IT.
COME ALONG WITH US, HULK.
DRAX. DRAX!
DRAX TO YOU, SIR.
DRAX.
DRAX.
ODD GREETING.
DRAX, HULK. THIS DRAXING WAY.

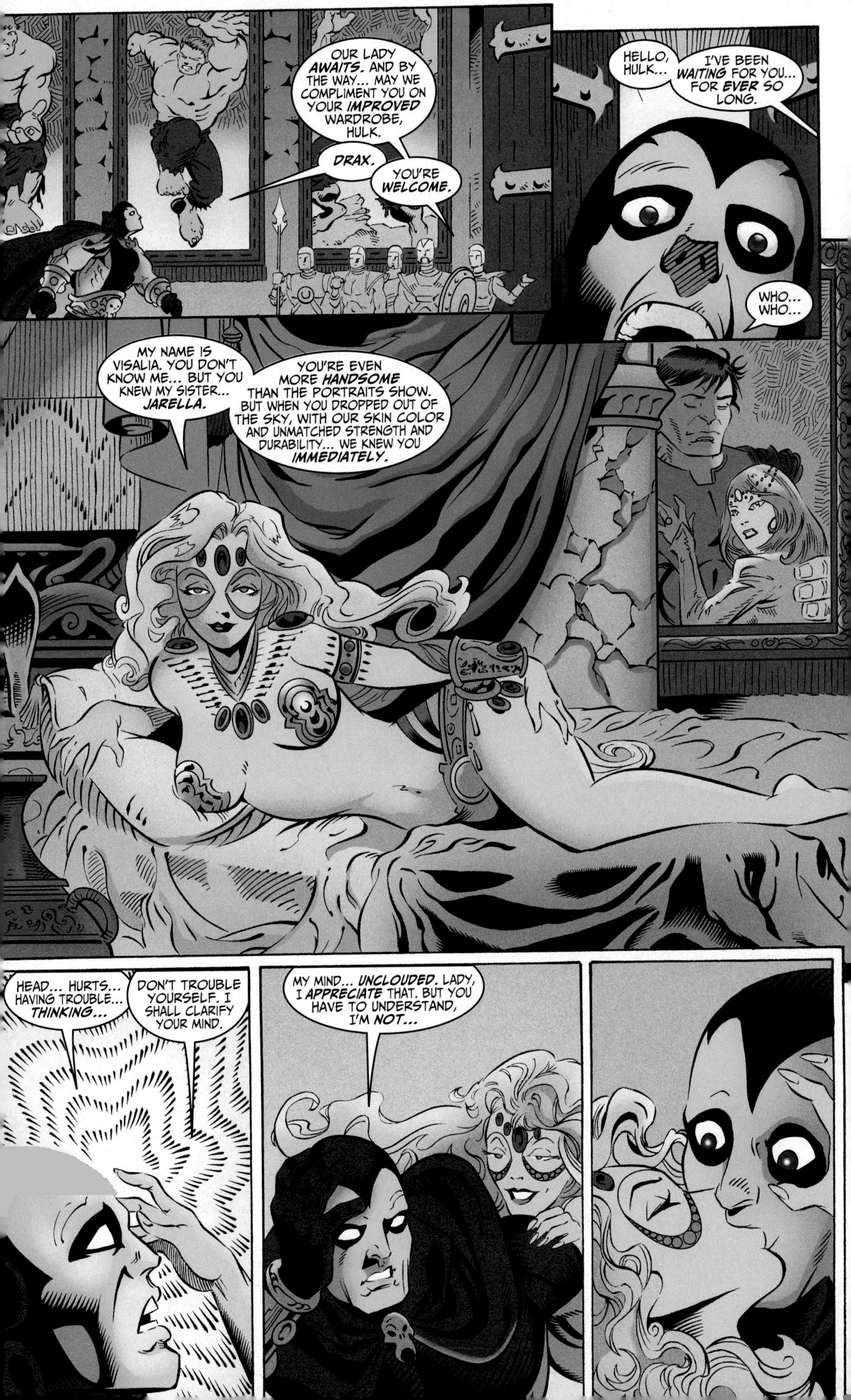
OUR LADY *AWAITS.* AND BY THE WAY... MAY WE COMPLIMENT YOU ON YOUR *IMPROVED* WARDROBE, HULK.
DRAX.
YOU'RE *WELCOME.*
HELLO, HULK...
I'VE BEEN *WAITING* FOR YOU... FOR *EVER* SO LONG.
WHO... WHO...
MY NAME IS VISALIA. YOU DON'T KNOW ME... BUT YOU KNEW MY SISTER... *JARELLA.*
YOU'RE EVEN MORE *HANDSOME* THAN THE PORTRAITS SHOW. BUT WHEN YOU DROPPED OUT OF THE SKY, WITH OUR SKIN COLOR AND UNMATCHED STRENGTH AND DURABILITY... WE KNEW YOU *IMMEDIATELY.*
HEAD... HURTS... HAVING TROUBLE... *THINKING...*
DON'T TROUBLE YOURSELF. I SHALL CLARIFY YOUR MIND.
MY MIND... *UNCLOUDED.* LADY, I *APPRECIATE* THAT. BUT YOU HAVE TO UNDERSTAND, I'M *NOT...*

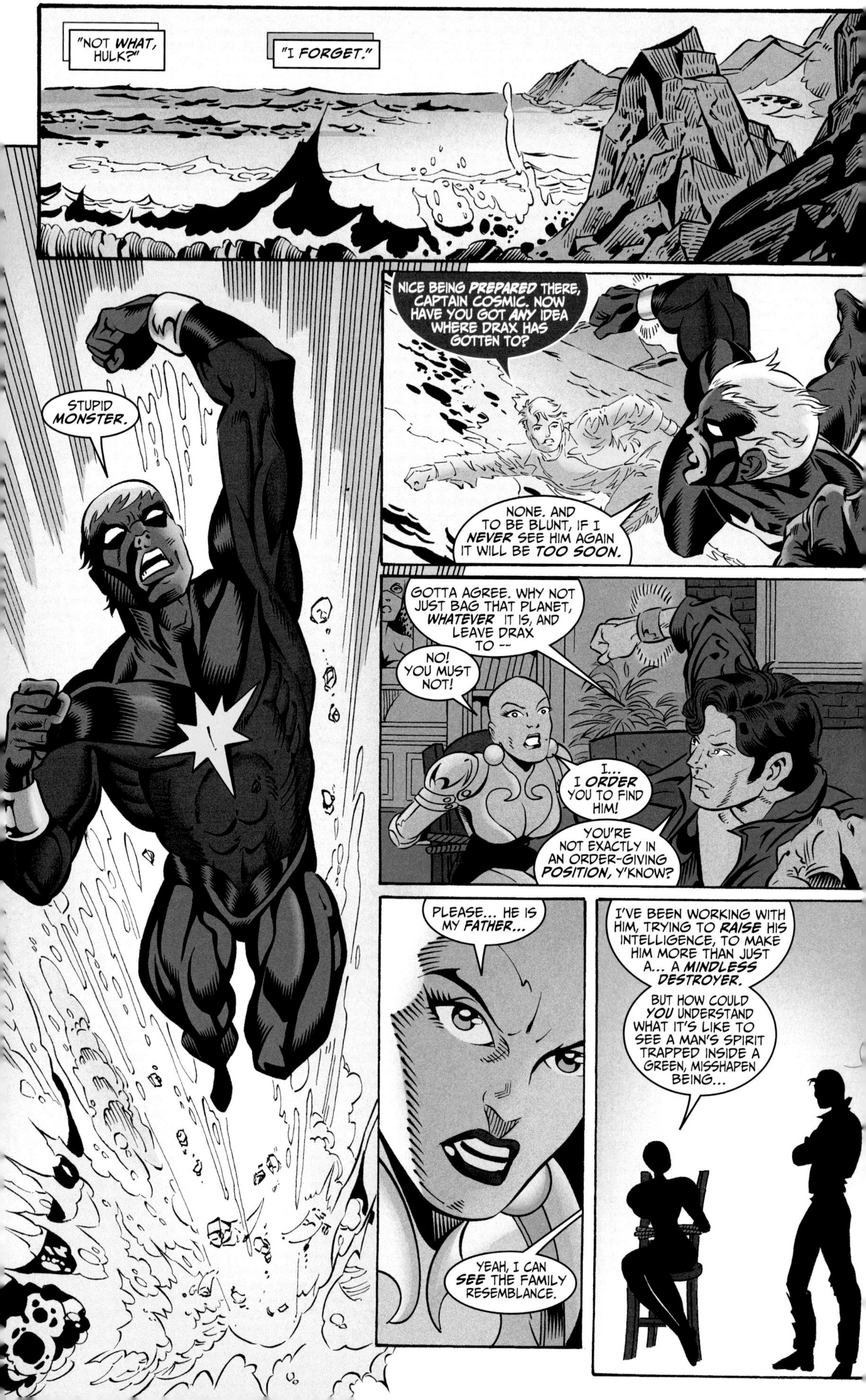
"NOT WHAT, HULK?"
"I FORGET."
STUPID MONSTER.
NICE BEING PREPARED THERE, CAPTAIN COSMIC. NOW HAVE YOU GOT ANY IDEA WHERE DRAX HAS GOTTEN TO?
NONE. AND TO BE BLUNT, IF I NEVER SEE HIM AGAIN IT WILL BE TOO SOON.
GOTTA AGREE. WHY NOT JUST BAG THAT PLANET, WHATEVER IT IS, AND LEAVE DRAX TO --
NO! YOU MUST NOT!
I... I ORDER YOU TO FIND HIM!
YOU'RE NOT EXACTLY IN AN ORDER-GIVING POSITION, Y'KNOW?
PLEASE... HE IS MY FATHER...
YEAH, I CAN SEE THE FAMILY RESEMBLANCE.
I'VE BEEN WORKING WITH HIM, TRYING TO RAISE HIS INTELLIGENCE, TO MAKE HIM MORE THAN JUST A... A MINDLESS DESTROYER.
BUT HOW COULD YOU UNDERSTAND WHAT IT'S LIKE TO SEE A MAN'S SPIRIT TRAPPED INSIDE A GREEN, MISSHAPEN BEING...

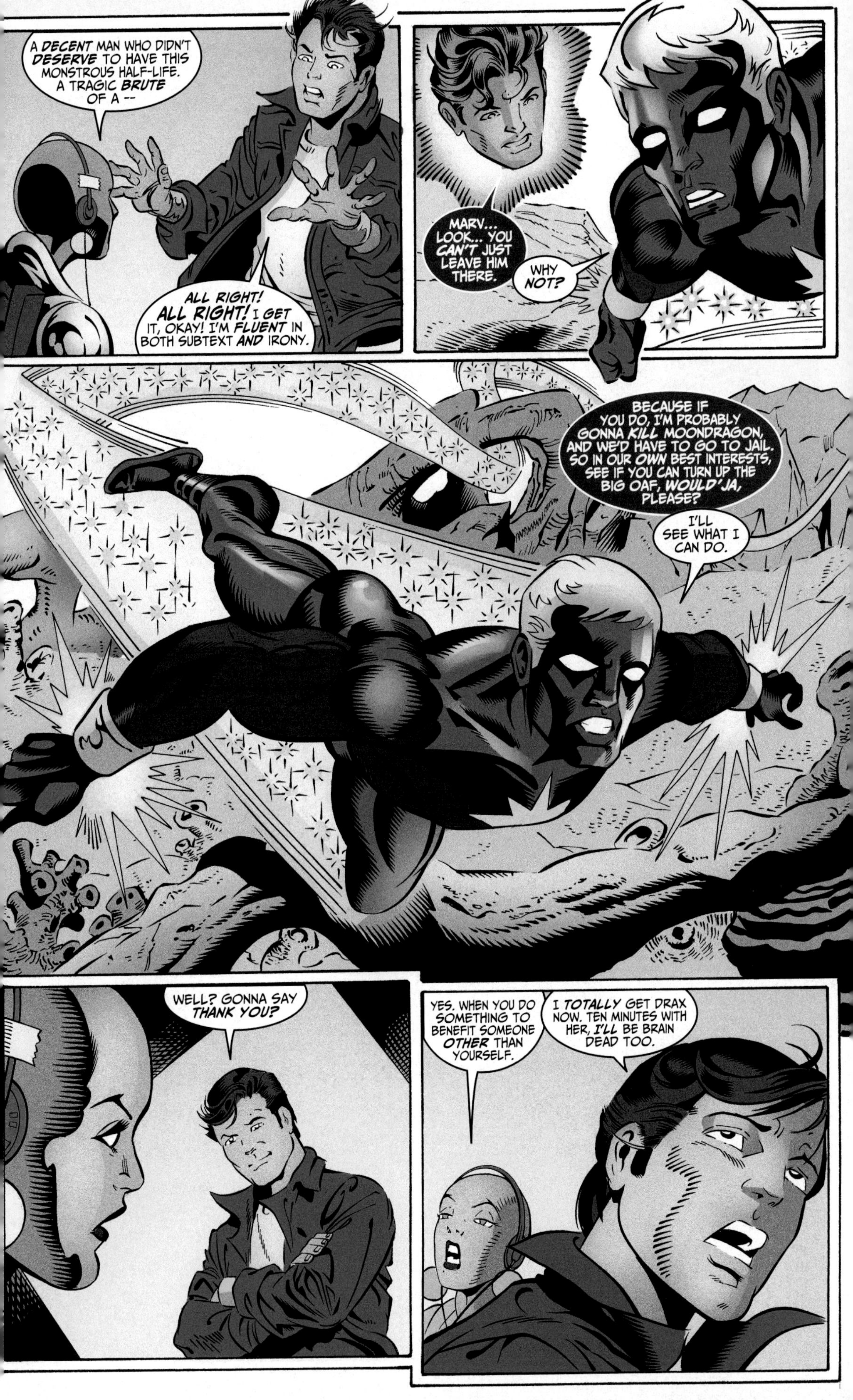
A DECENT MAN WHO DIDN'T DESERVE TO HAVE THIS MONSTROUS HALF-LIFE. A TRAGIC BRUTE OF A --
ALL RIGHT! ALL RIGHT! I GET IT, OKAY! I'M FLUENT IN BOTH SUBTEXT AND IRONY.
MARV... LOOK... YOU CAN'T JUST LEAVE HIM THERE.
WHY NOT?
BECAUSE IF YOU DO, I'M PROBABLY GONNA KILL MOONDRAGON, AND WE'D HAVE TO GO TO JAIL. SO IN OUR OWN BEST INTERESTS, SEE IF YOU CAN TURN UP THE BIG OAF, WOULD'JA, PLEASE?
I'LL SEE WHAT I CAN DO.
WELL? GONNA SAY THANK YOU?
YES. WHEN YOU DO SOMETHING TO BENEFIT SOMEONE OTHER THAN YOURSELF.
I TOTALLY GET DRAX NOW. TEN MINUTES WITH HER, I'LL BE BRAIN DEAD TOO.

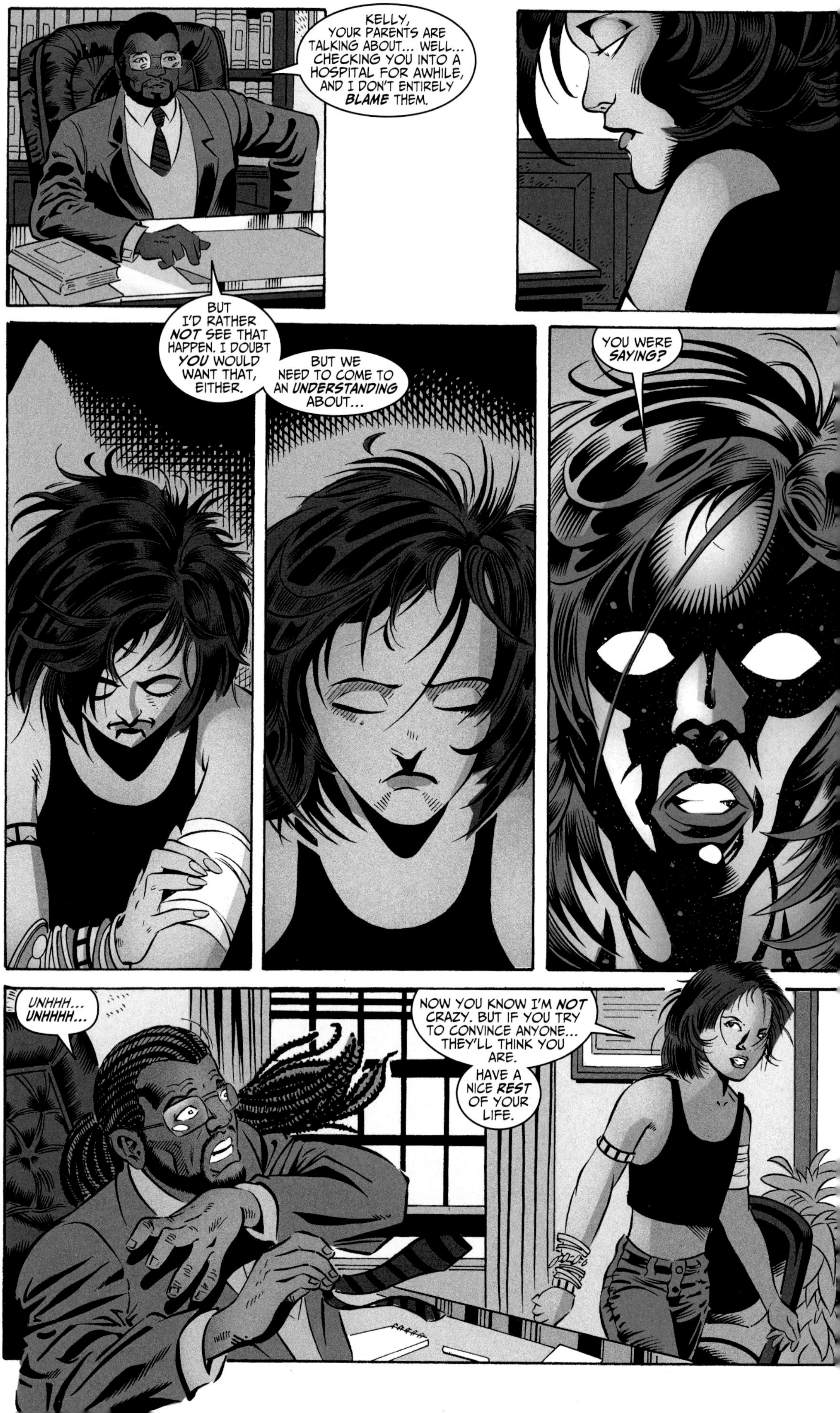

KELLY, YOUR PARENTS ARE TALKING ABOUT... WELL... CHECKING YOU INTO A HOSPITAL FOR AWHILE, AND I DON'T ENTIRELY BLAME THEM.
BUT I'D RATHER NOT SEE THAT HAPPEN. I DOUBT YOU WOULD WANT THAT, EITHER.
BUT WE NEED TO COME TO AN UNDERSTANDING ABOUT...
YOU WERE SAYING?
UNHHH... UNHHHH...
NOW YOU KNOW I'M NOT CRAZY. BUT IF YOU TRY TO CONVINCE ANYONE... THEY'LL THINK YOU ARE.
HAVE A NICE REST OF YOUR LIFE.

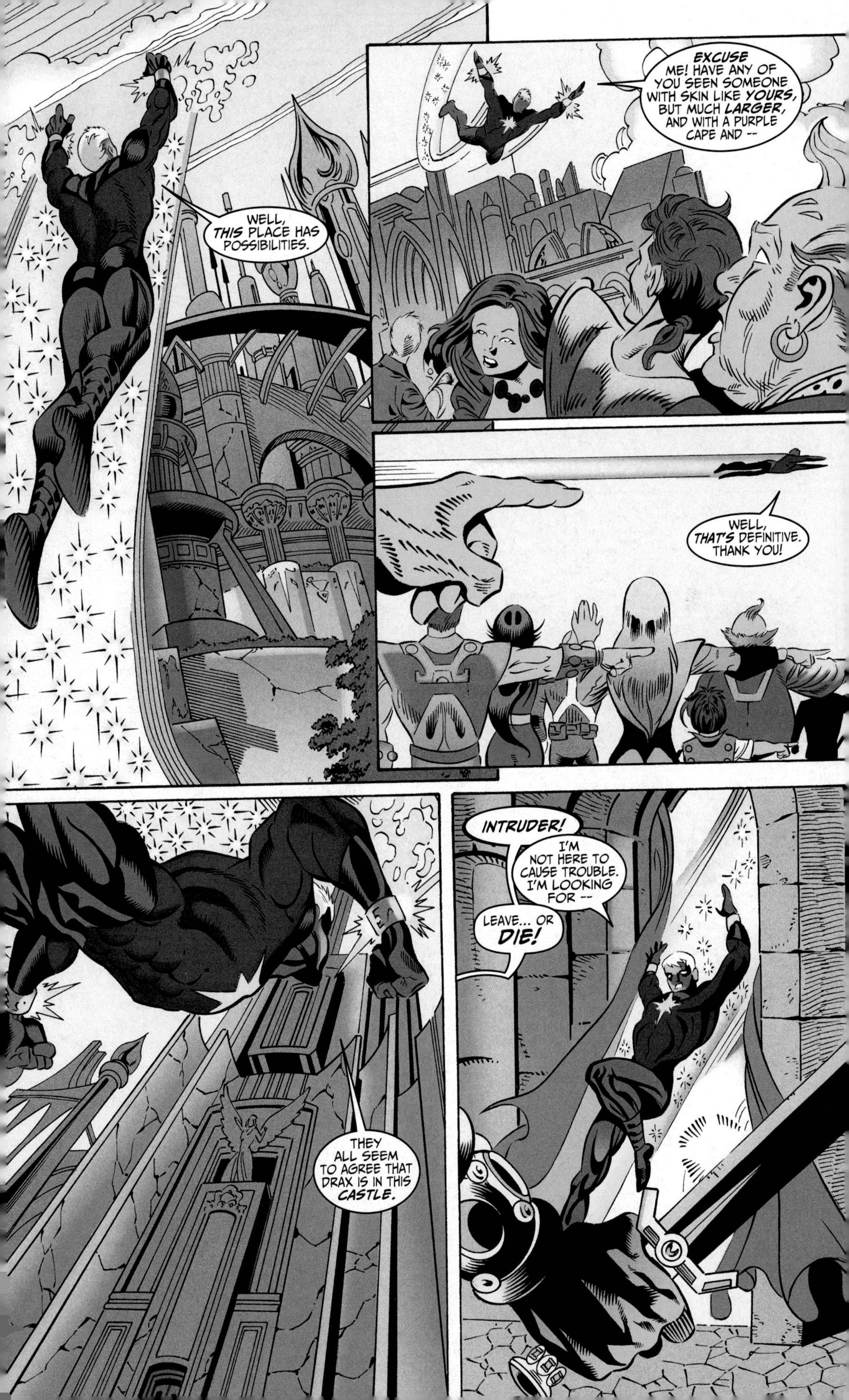
WELL, THIS PLACE HAS POSSIBILITIES.
EXCUSE ME! HAVE ANY OF YOU SEEN SOMEONE WITH SKIN LIKE YOURS, BUT MUCH LARGER, AND WITH A PURPLE CAPE AND --
WELL, THAT'S DEFINITIVE. THANK YOU!
THEY ALL SEEM TO AGREE THAT DRAX IS IN THIS CASTLE.
INTRUDER!
I'M NOT HERE TO CAUSE TROUBLE. I'M LOOKING FOR --
LEAVE... OR DIE!

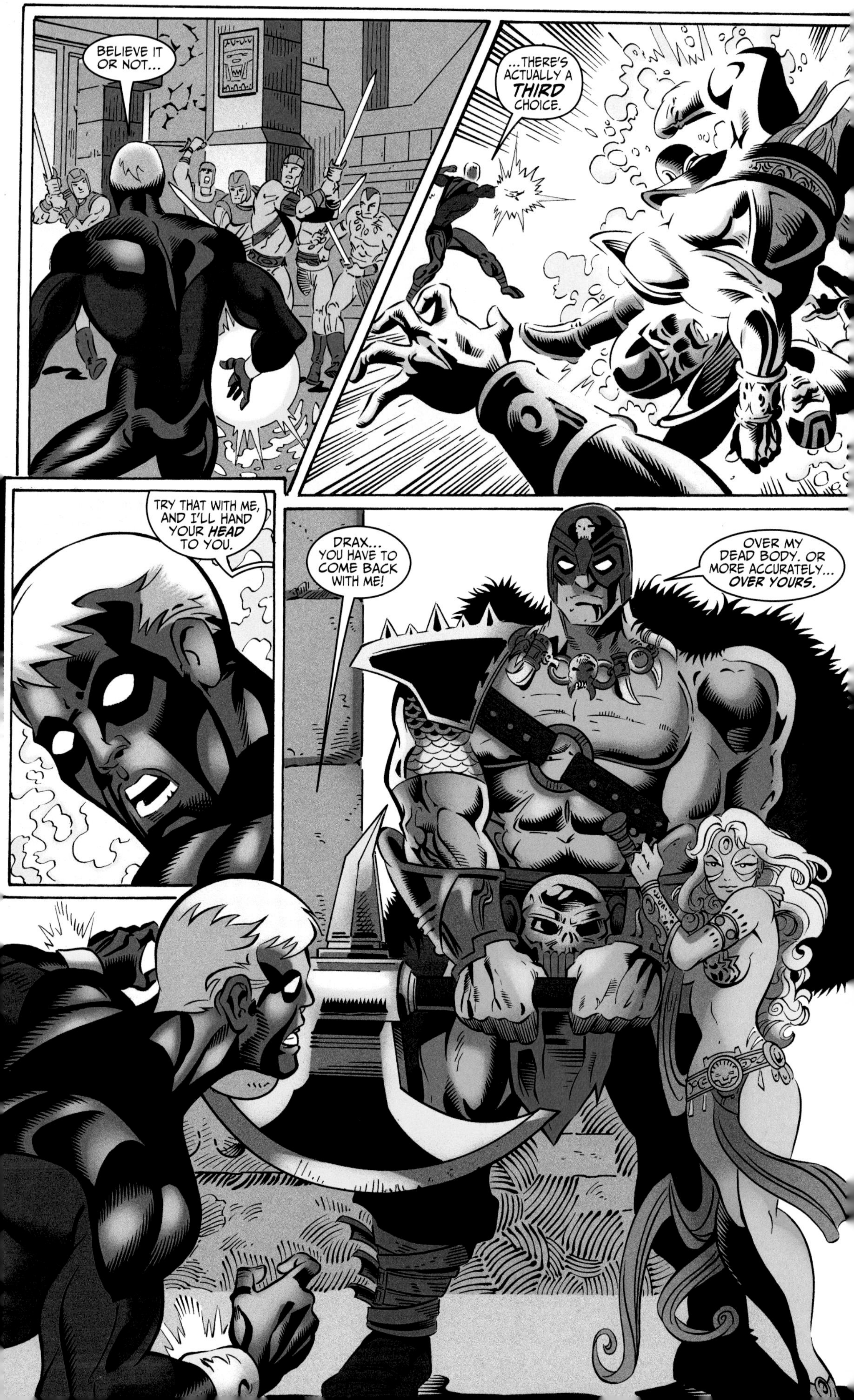
BELIEVE IT OR NOT...
...THERE'S ACTUALLY A THIRD CHOICE.
TRY THAT WITH ME, AND I'LL HAND YOUR HEAD TO YOU.
DRAX... YOU HAVE TO COME BACK WITH ME!
OVER MY DEAD BODY. OR MORE ACCURATELY... OVER YOURS.

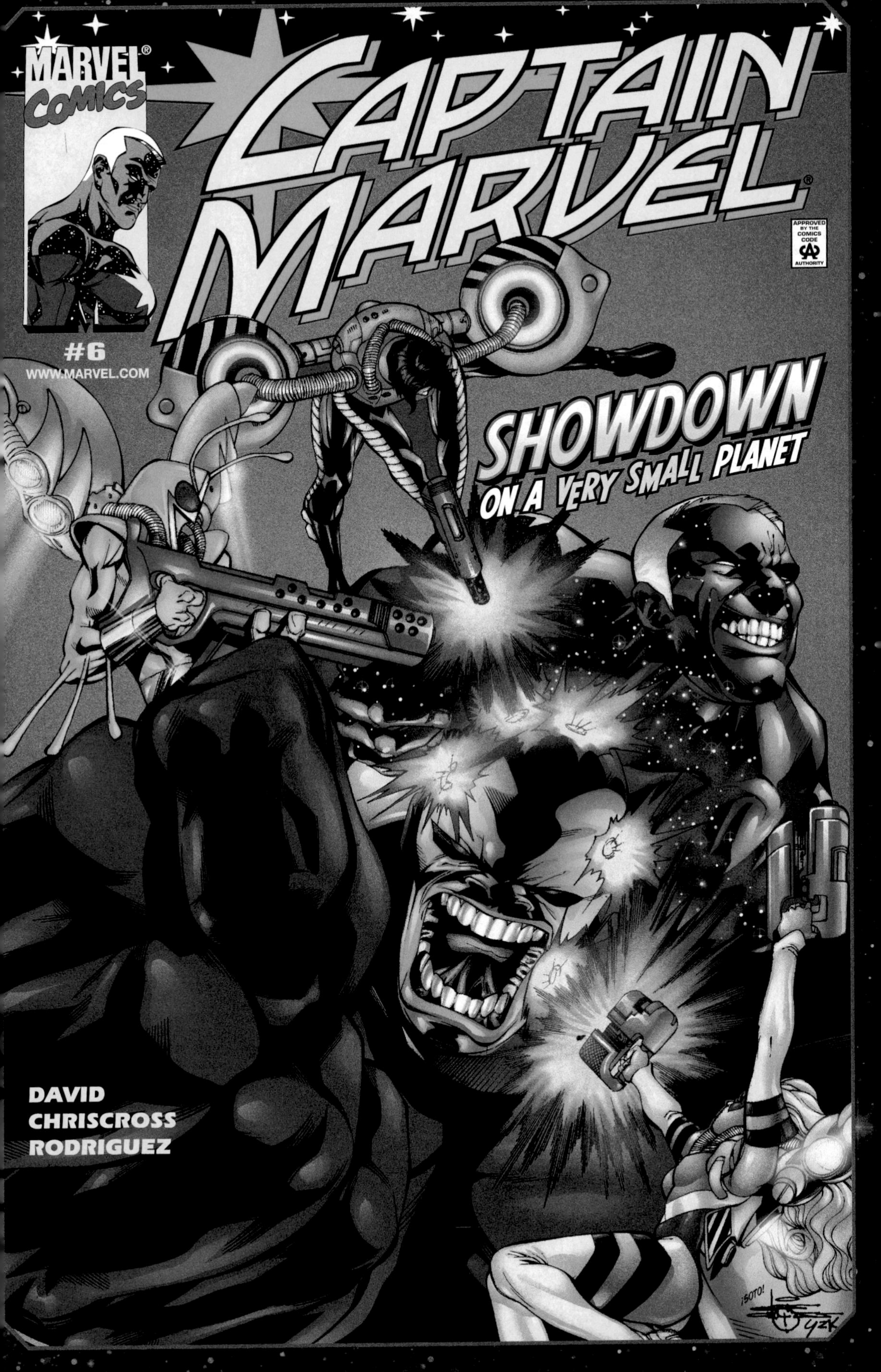
MARVEL® COMICS
CAPTAIN MARVEL®
#6
WWW.MARVEL.COM
APPROVED BY THE COMICS CODE AUTHORITY
SHOWDOWN ON A VERY SMALL PLANET
DAVID
CHRISCROSS
RODRIGUEZ

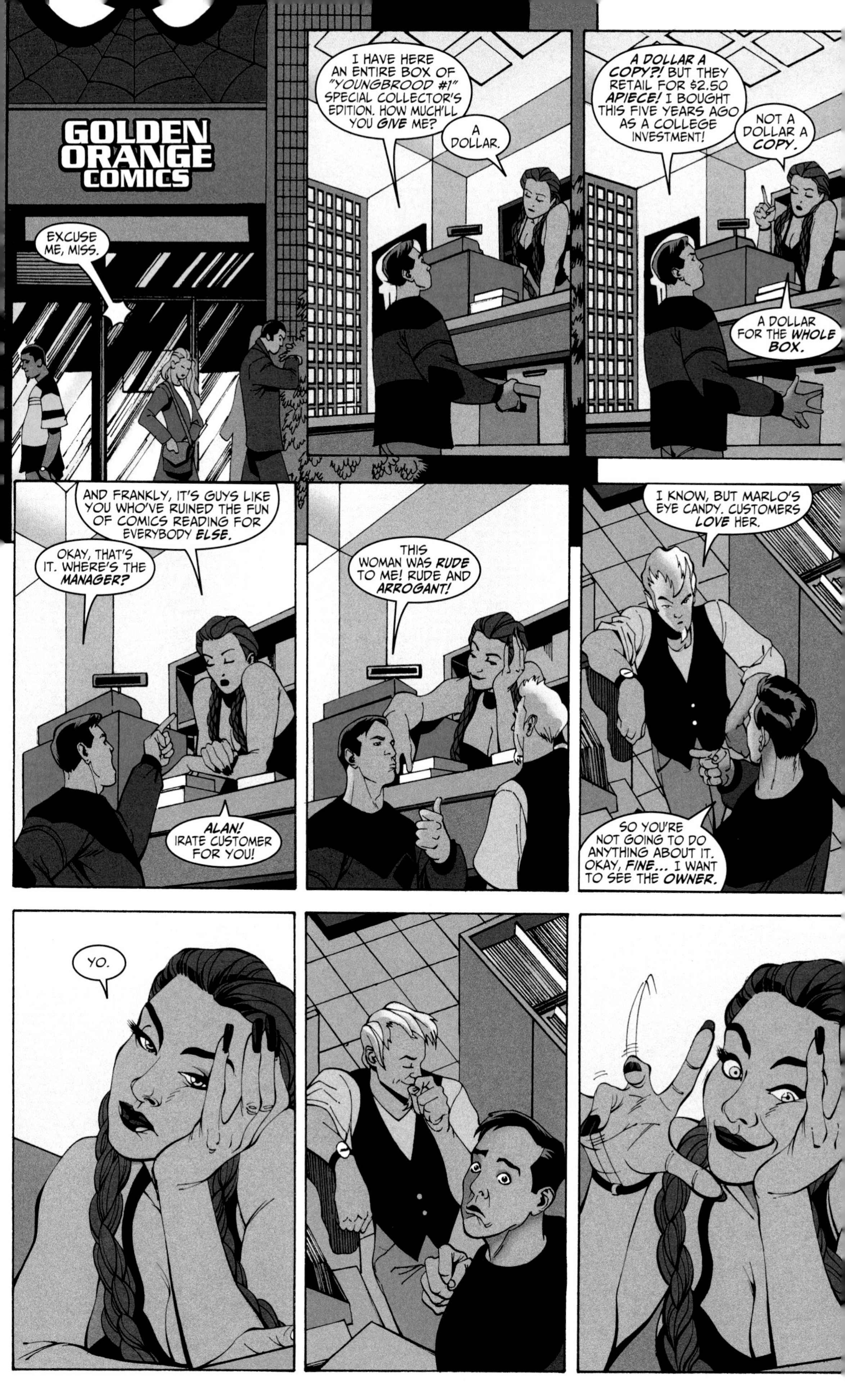
GOLDEN ORANGE COMICS
EXCUSE ME, MISS.
I HAVE HERE AN ENTIRE BOX OF "YOUNGBROOD #1" SPECIAL COLLECTOR'S EDITION. HOW MUCH'LL YOU GIVE ME?
A DOLLAR.
A DOLLAR A COPY?! BUT THEY RETAIL FOR $2.50 APIECE! I BOUGHT THIS FIVE YEARS AGO AS A COLLEGE INVESTMENT!
NOT A DOLLAR A COPY.
A DOLLAR FOR THE WHOLE BOX.
AND FRANKLY, IT'S GUYS LIKE YOU WHO'VE RUINED THE FUN OF COMICS READING FOR EVERYBODY ELSE.
OKAY, THAT'S IT. WHERE'S THE MANAGER?
ALAN! IRATE CUSTOMER FOR YOU!
THIS WOMAN WAS RUDE TO ME! RUDE AND ARROGANT!
I KNOW, BUT MARLO'S EYE CANDY. CUSTOMERS LOVE HER.
SO YOU'RE NOT GOING TO DO ANYTHING ABOUT IT. OKAY, FINE... I WANT TO SEE THE OWNER.
YO.

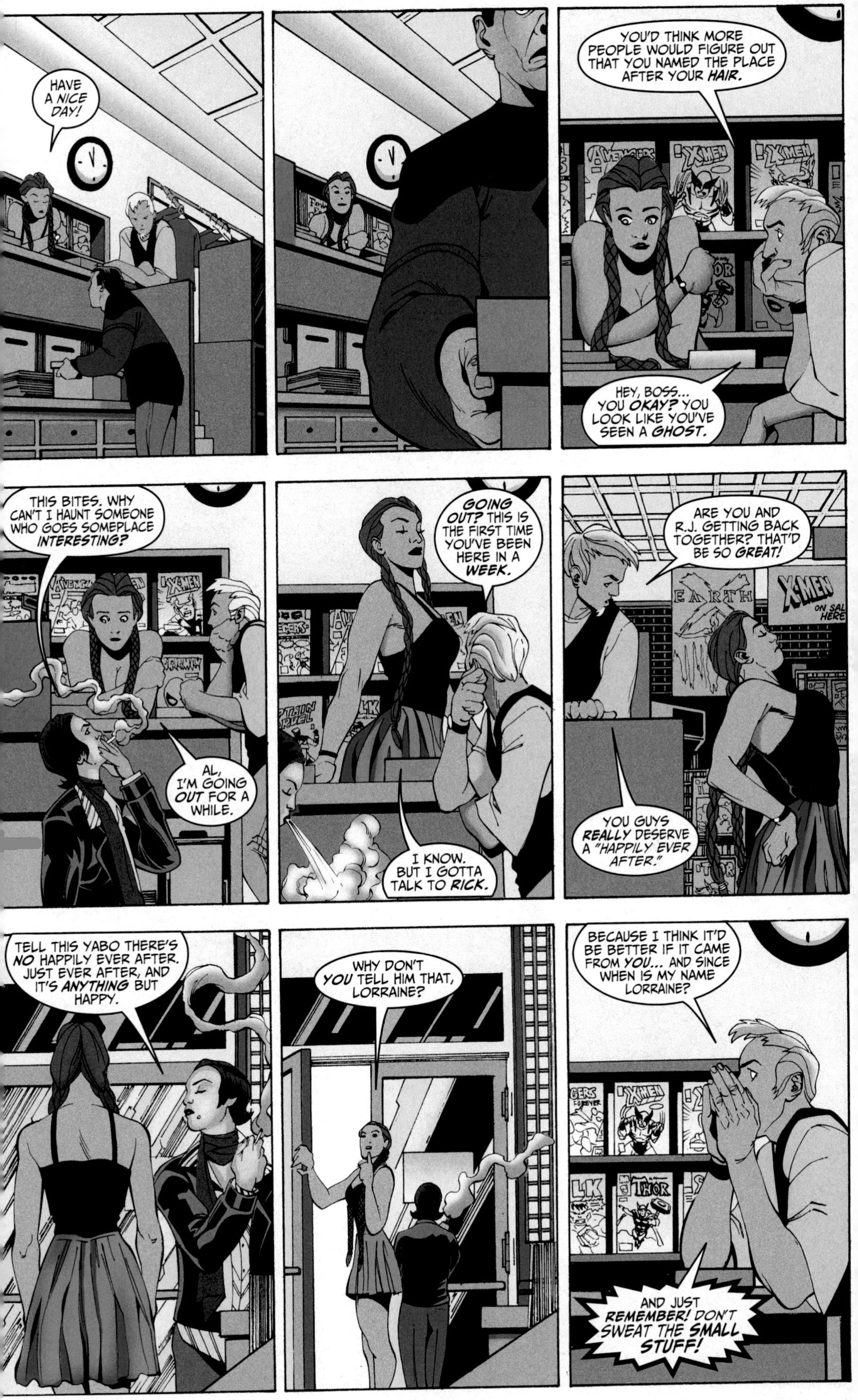
HAVE A NICE DAY!
YOU'D THINK MORE PEOPLE WOULD FIGURE OUT THAT YOU NAMED THE PLACE AFTER YOUR HAIR.
HEY, BOSS... YOU OKAY? YOU LOOK LIKE YOU'VE SEEN A GHOST.
THIS BITES. WHY CAN'T I HAUNT SOMEONE WHO GOES SOMEPLACE INTERESTING?
AL, I'M GOING OUT FOR A WHILE.
GOING OUT? THIS IS THE FIRST TIME YOU'VE BEEN HERE IN A WEEK.
I KNOW. BUT I GOTTA TALK TO RICK.
ARE YOU AND R.J. GETTING BACK TOGETHER? THAT'D BE SO GREAT!
YOU GUYS REALLY DESERVE A "HAPPILY EVER AFTER."
TELL THIS YABO THERE'S NO HAPPILY EVER AFTER. JUST EVER AFTER, AND IT'S ANYTHING BUT HAPPY.
WHY DON'T YOU TELL HIM THAT, LORRAINE?
BECAUSE I THINK IT'D BE BETTER IF IT CAME FROM YOU... AND SINCE WHEN IS MY NAME LORRAINE?
AND JUST REMEMBER! DON'T SWEAT THE SMALL STUFF!

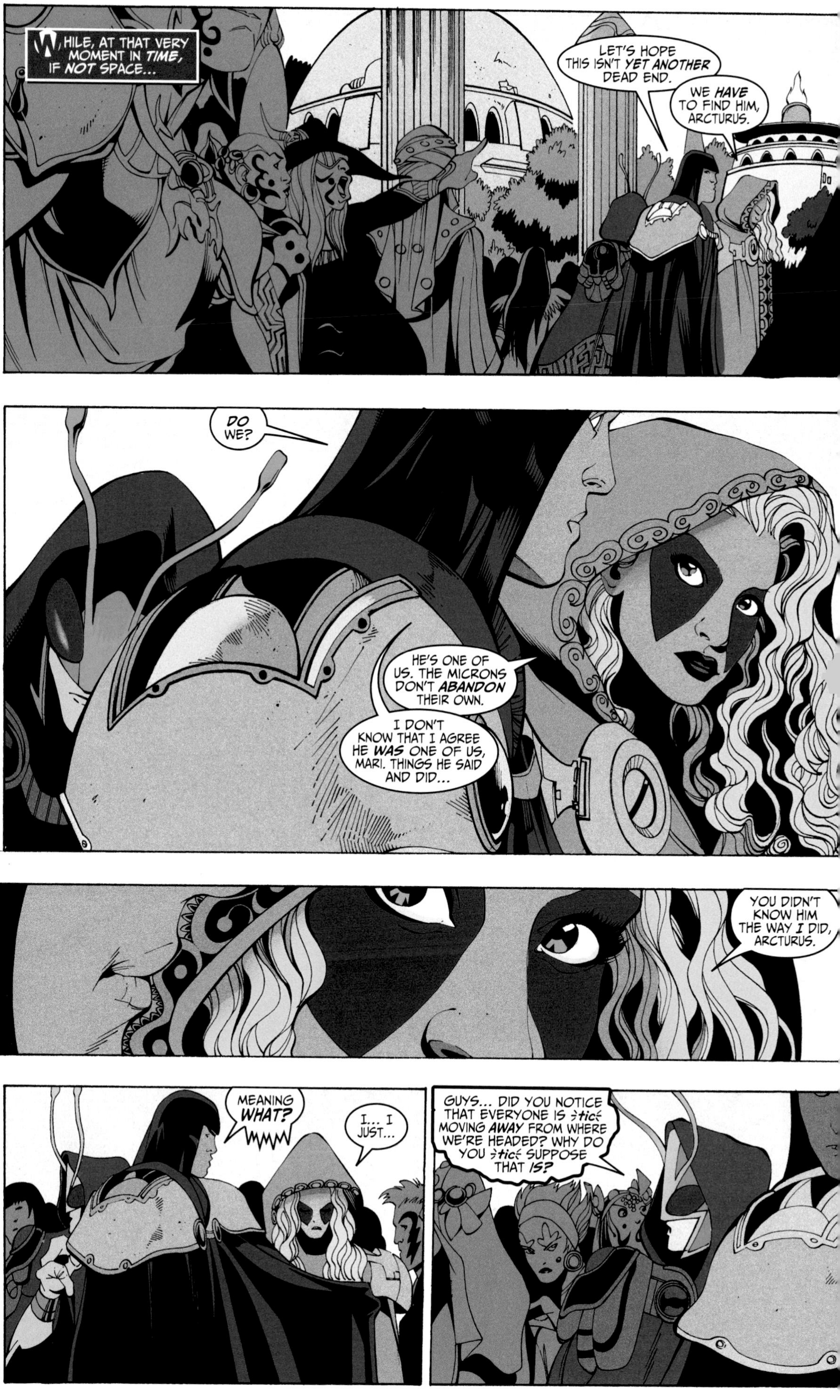

WHILE, AT THAT VERY MOMENT IN *TIME*, IF *NOT* SPACE...
LET'S HOPE THIS ISN'T *YET ANOTHER* DEAD END.
WE *HAVE* TO FIND HIM, ARCTURUS.
DO WE?
HE'S ONE OF US. THE MICRONS DON'T *ABANDON* THEIR OWN.
I DON'T KNOW THAT I AGREE HE *WAS* ONE OF US, MARI. THINGS HE SAID AND DID...
YOU DIDN'T KNOW HIM THE WAY *I* DID, ARCTURUS.
MEANING *WHAT?*
I... I JUST...
GUYS... DID YOU NOTICE THAT EVERYONE IS *tic* MOVING *AWAY* FROM WHERE WE'RE HEADED? WHY DO YOU *tic* SUPPOSE THAT *IS?*

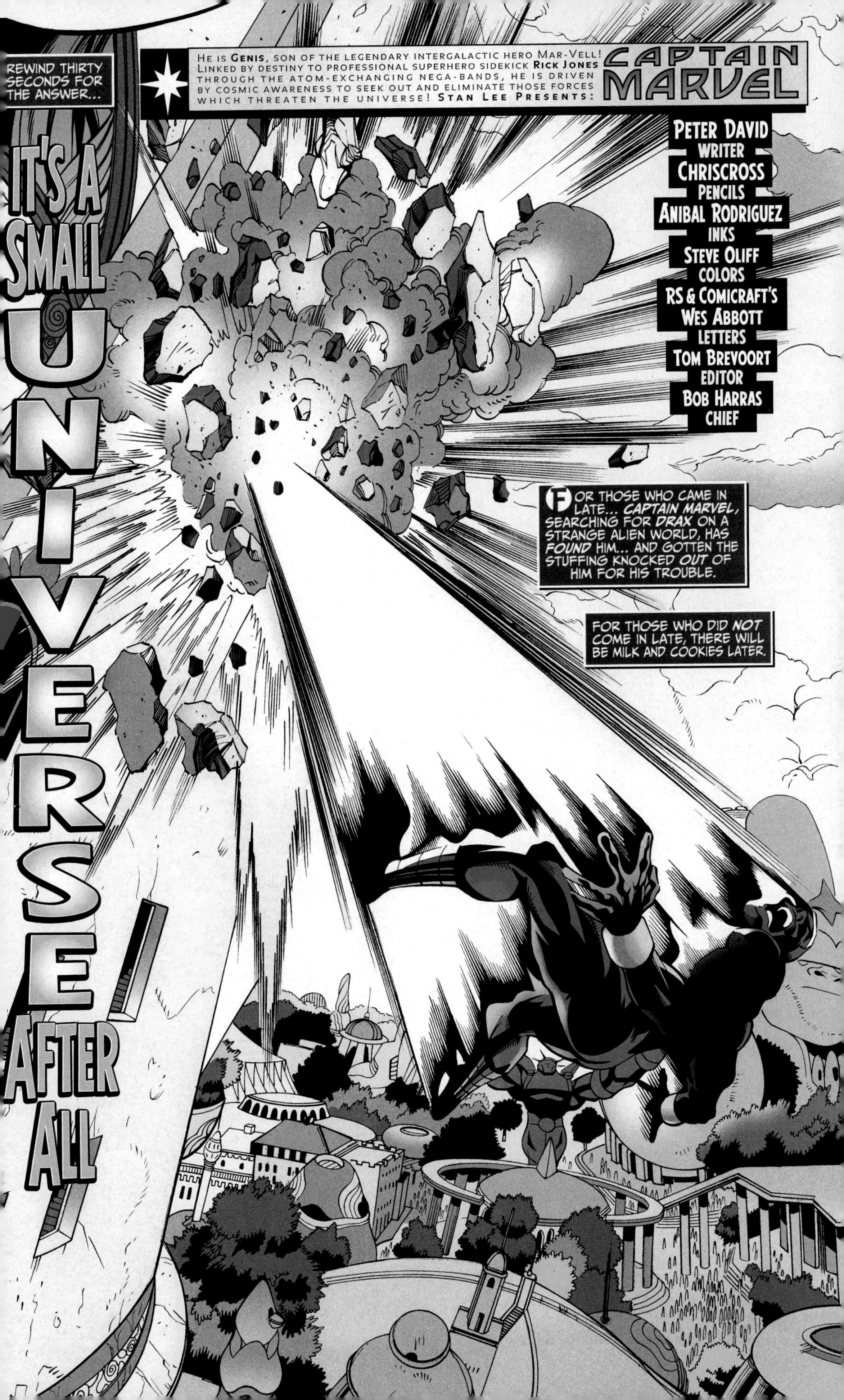
REWIND THIRTY SECONDS FOR THE ANSWER...
HE IS GENIS, SON OF THE LEGENDARY INTERGALACTIC HERO MAR-VELL! LINKED BY DESTINY TO PROFESSIONAL SUPERHERO SIDEKICK RICK JONES THROUGH THE ATOM-EXCHANGING NEGA-BANDS, HE IS DRIVEN BY COSMIC AWARENESS TO SEEK OUT AND ELIMINATE THOSE FORCES WHICH THREATEN THE UNIVERSE! STAN LEE PRESENTS:
CAPTAIN MARVEL
IT'S A SMALL UNIVERSE AFTER ALL
PETER DAVID WRITER
CHRISCROSS PENCILS
ANIBAL RODRIGUEZ INKS
STEVE OLIFF COLORS
RS & COMICRAFT'S WES ABBOTT LETTERS
TOM BREVOORT EDITOR
BOB HARRAS CHIEF
FOR THOSE WHO CAME IN LATE... CAPTAIN MARVEL, SEARCHING FOR DRAX ON A STRANGE ALIEN WORLD, HAS FOUND HIM... AND GOTTEN THE STUFFING KNOCKED OUT OF HIM FOR HIS TROUBLE.
FOR THOSE WHO DID NOT COME IN LATE, THERE WILL BE MILK AND COOKIES LATER.

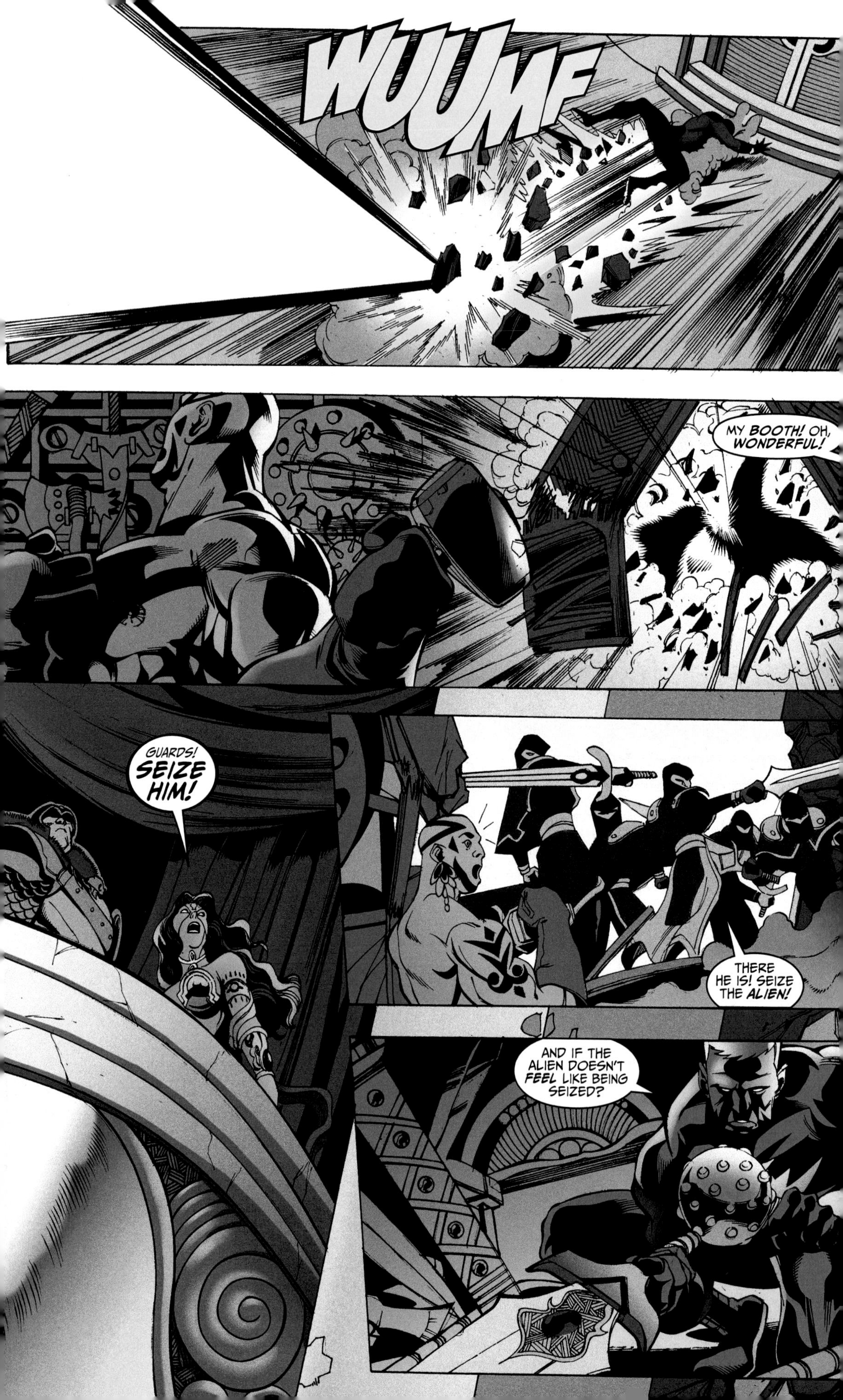
WUUMF
MY BOOTH! OH, WONDERFUL!
GUARDS! SEIZE HIM!
THERE HE IS! SEIZE THE ALIEN!
AND IF THE ALIEN DOESN'T FEEL LIKE BEING SEIZED?

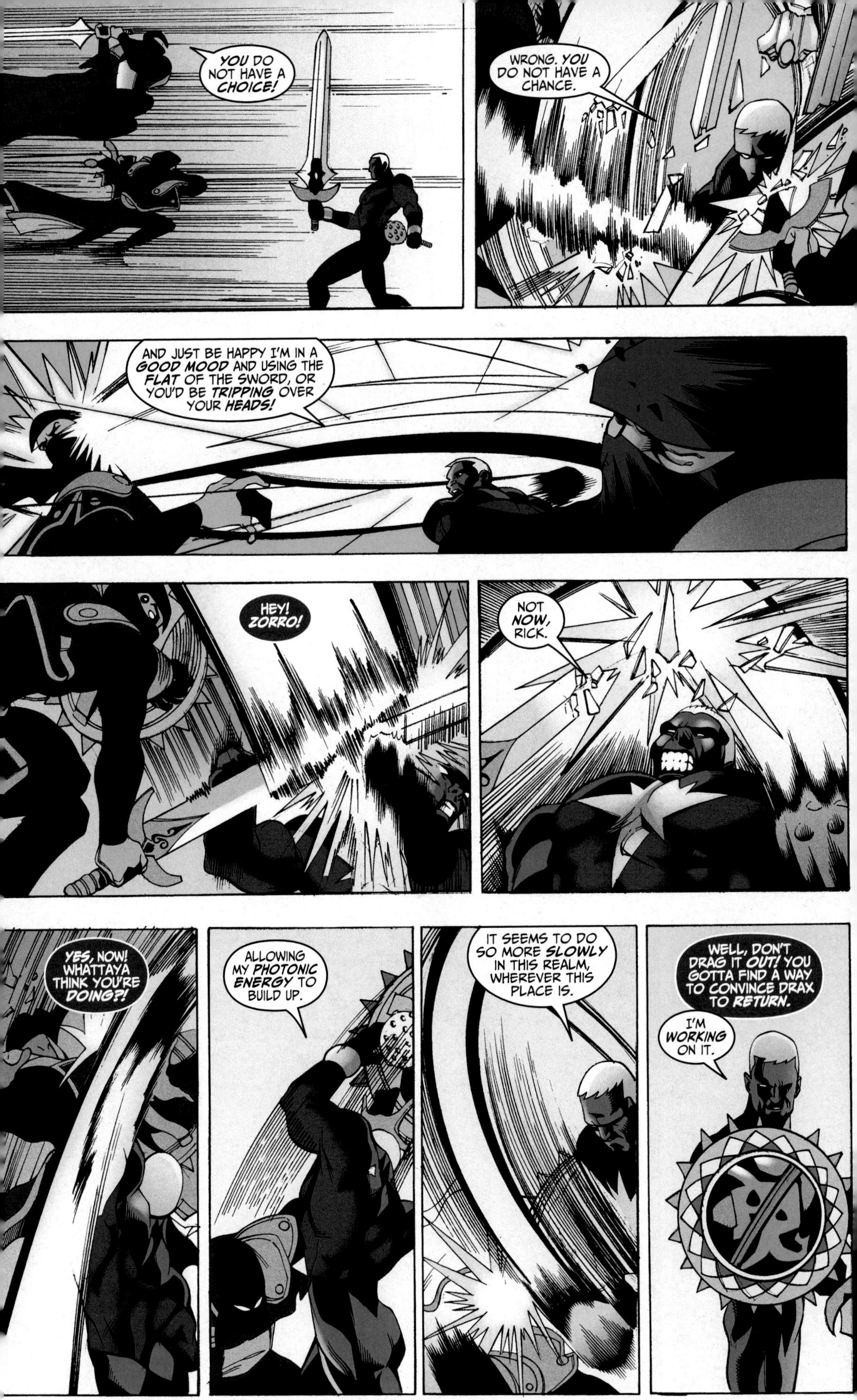
YOU DO NOT HAVE A CHOICE!
WRONG. YOU DO NOT HAVE A CHANCE.
AND JUST BE HAPPY I'M IN A GOOD MOOD AND USING THE FLAT OF THE SWORD, OR YOU'D BE TRIPPING OVER YOUR HEADS!
HEY! ZORRO!
NOT NOW, RICK.
YES, NOW! WHATTAYA THINK YOU'RE DOING?!
ALLOWING MY PHOTONIC ENERGY TO BUILD UP.
IT SEEMS TO DO SO MORE SLOWLY IN THIS REALM, WHEREVER THIS PLACE IS.
WELL, DON'T DRAG IT OUT! YOU GOTTA FIND A WAY TO CONVINCE DRAX TO RETURN.
I'M WORKING ON IT.

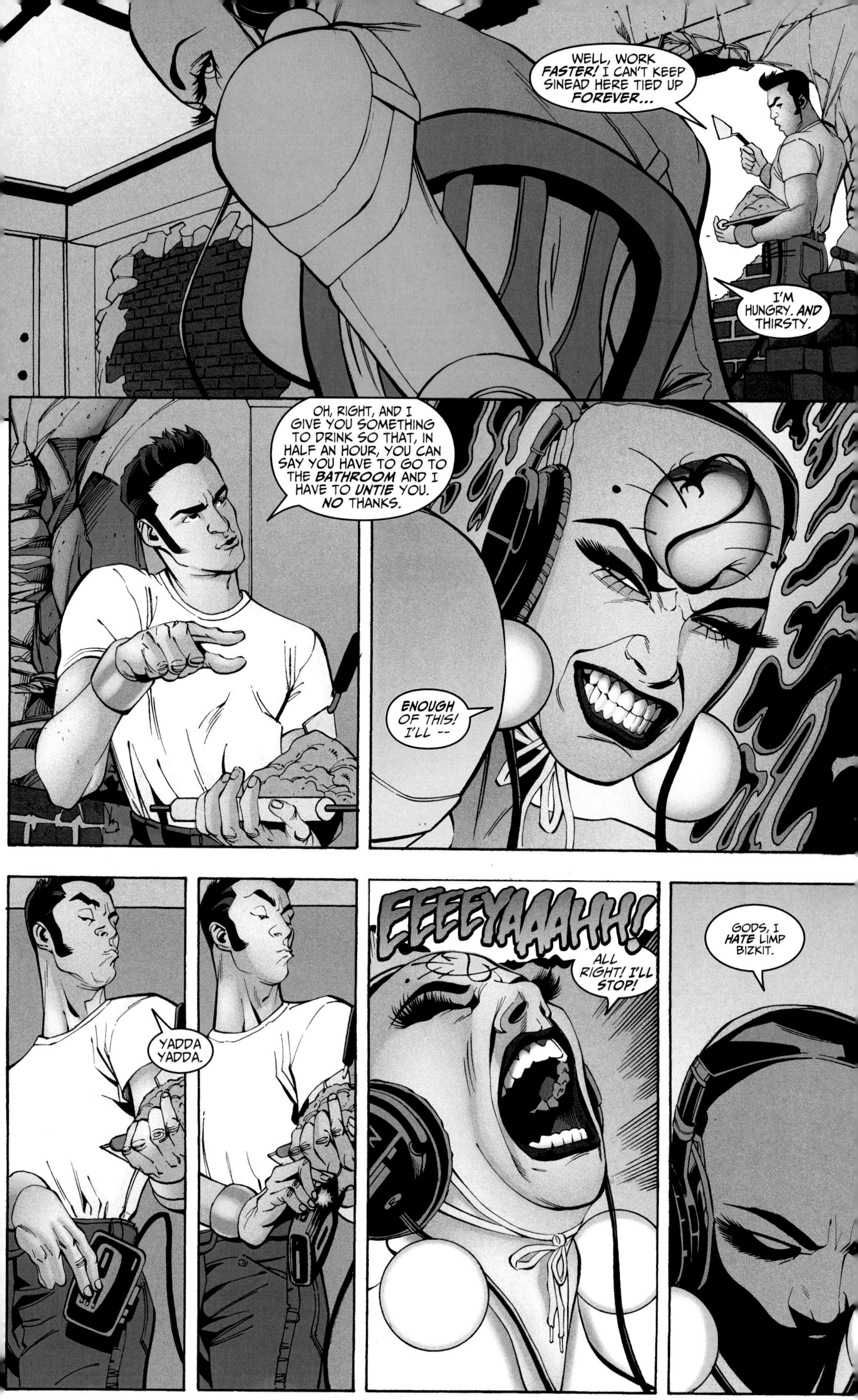

WELL, WORK FASTER! I CAN'T KEEP SINEAD HERE TIED UP FOREVER...
I'M HUNGRY. AND THIRSTY.
OH, RIGHT, AND I GIVE YOU SOMETHING TO DRINK SO THAT, IN HALF AN HOUR, YOU CAN SAY YOU HAVE TO GO TO THE BATHROOM AND I HAVE TO UNTIE YOU. NO THANKS.
ENOUGH OF THIS! I'LL --
YADDA YADDA.
EEEEYAAAHH!
ALL RIGHT! I'LL STOP!
GODS, I HATE LIMP BIZKIT.

YOU THINK I'M *ENJOYING* THIS? HUH?

YOU THINK THIS IS *FUN* FOR ME?

YES. I THINK YOU ARE FILLED WITH *RAGE* OVER YOUR SITUATION. AND YOU'RE TAKING ALL THAT ANGER OUT ON *ME*.

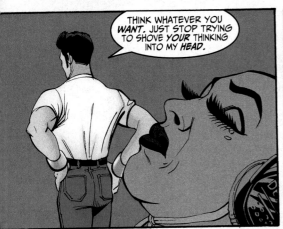

THINK WHATEVER YOU *WANT*. JUST STOP TRYING TO SHOVE *YOUR* THINKING INTO MY *HEAD*.

JONES...

RICHARD...

I'M WORRIED ABOUT MY FATHER. MY FATHER *AND* GENIS, THEY...

MOONDRAGON... ARE YOU *CRYING*?

NO.

LOOK... MOONDRAGON... I...

KNOK KNOK

RICK? IT'S *MARLO*.

...AM *DEAD*.

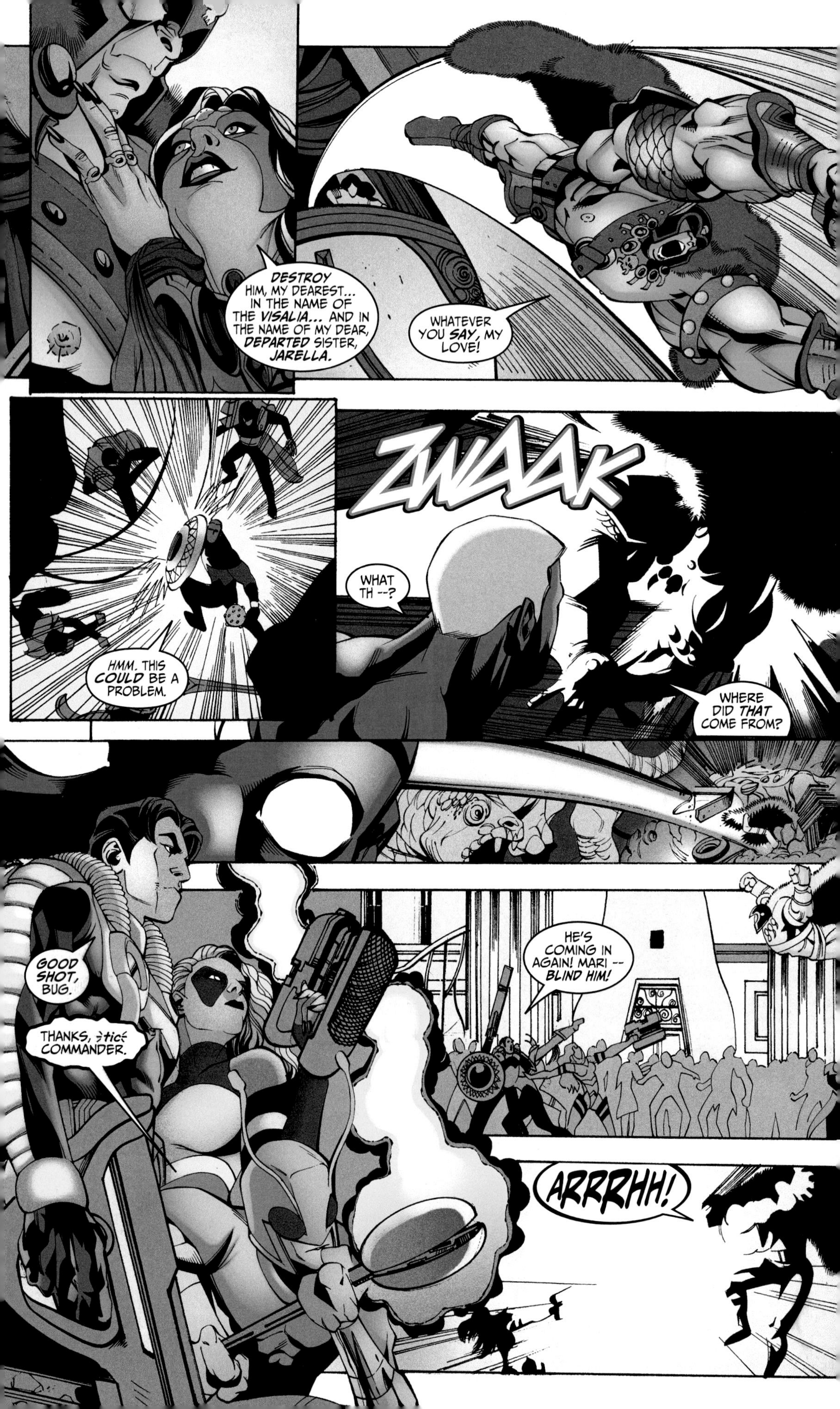

DESTROY HIM, MY DEAREST... IN THE NAME OF THE VISALIA... AND IN THE NAME OF MY DEAR, DEPARTED SISTER, JARELLA.
WHATEVER YOU SAY, MY LOVE!
HMM. THIS COULD BE A PROBLEM.
ZWAAK
WHAT TH --?
WHERE DID THAT COME FROM?
GOOD SHOT, BUG.
THANKS, *tic* COMMANDER.
HE'S COMING IN AGAIN! MARI -- BLIND HIM!
ARRRHH!

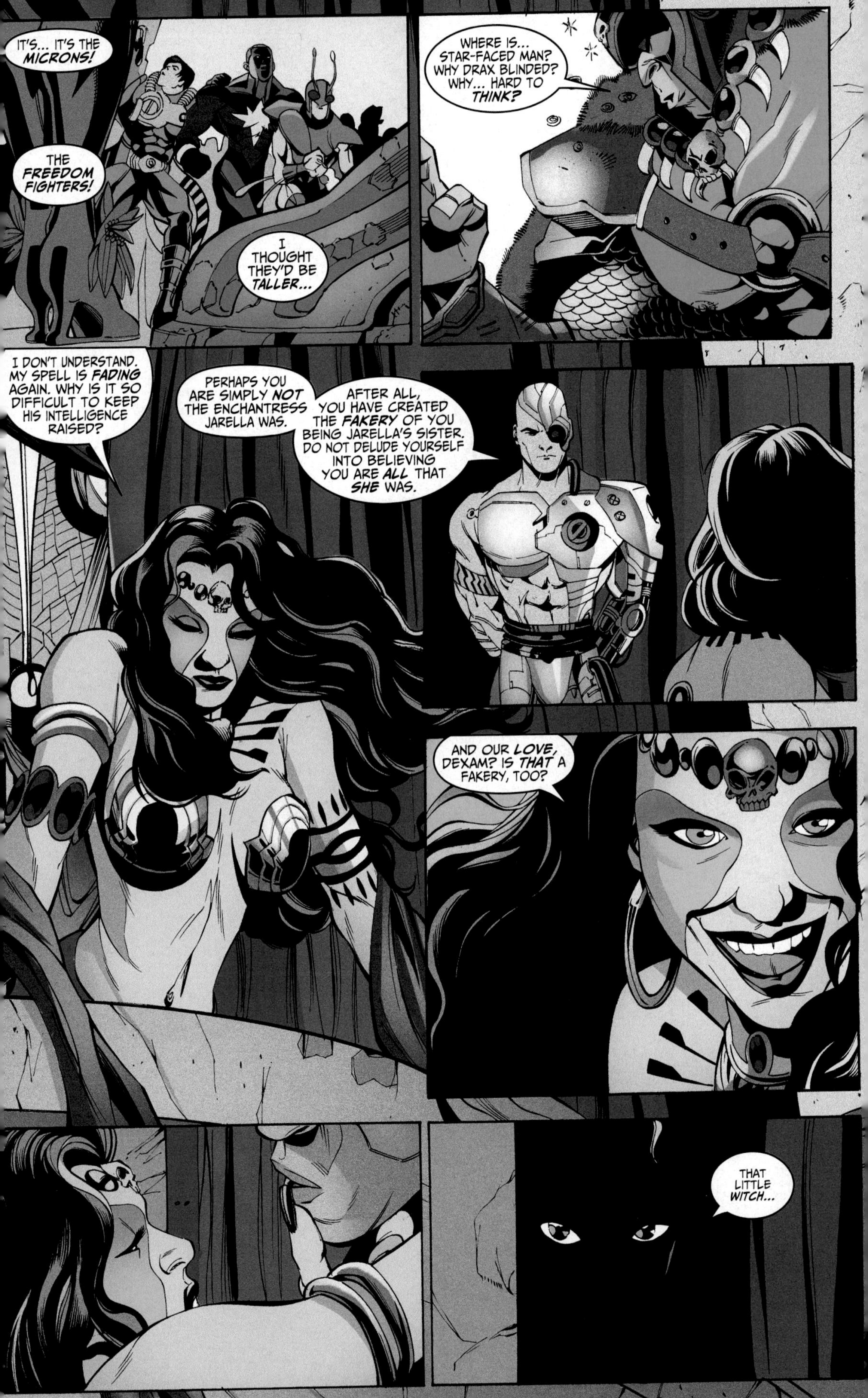
IT'S... IT'S THE MICRONS!
THE FREEDOM FIGHTERS!
I THOUGHT THEY'D BE TALLER...
WHERE IS... STAR-FACED MAN? WHY DRAX BLINDED? WHY... HARD TO THINK?
I DON'T UNDERSTAND. MY SPELL IS FADING AGAIN. WHY IS IT SO DIFFICULT TO KEEP HIS INTELLIGENCE RAISED?
PERHAPS YOU ARE SIMPLY NOT THE ENCHANTRESS JARELLA WAS.
AFTER ALL, YOU HAVE CREATED THE FAKERY OF YOU BEING JARELLA'S SISTER. DO NOT DELUDE YOURSELF INTO BELIEVING YOU ARE ALL THAT SHE WAS.
AND OUR LOVE, DEXAM? IS THAT A FAKERY, TOO?
THAT LITTLE WITCH...

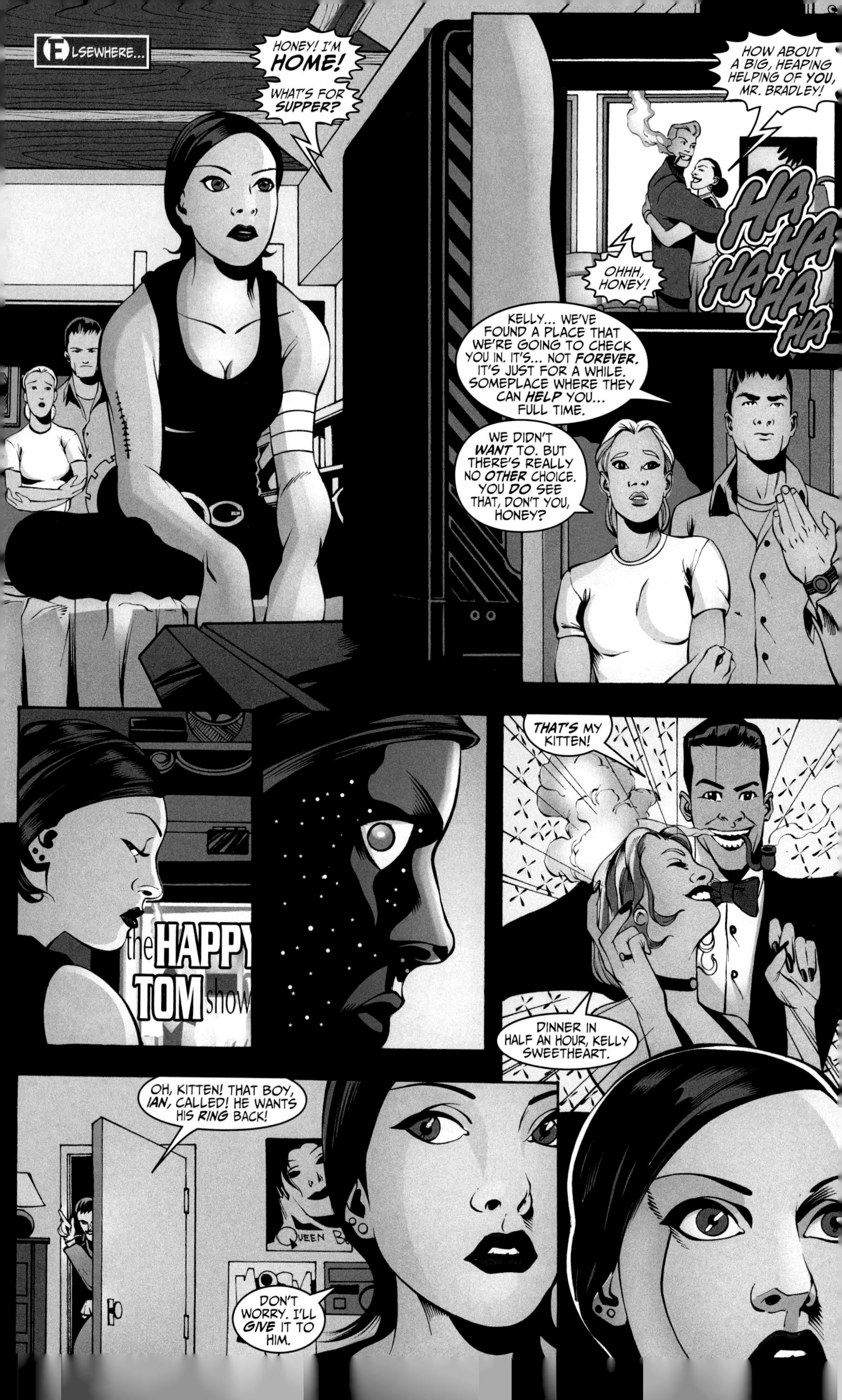
ELSEWHERE...
HONEY! I'M HOME!
WHAT'S FOR SUPPER?
HOW ABOUT A BIG, HEAPING HELPING OF YOU, MR. BRADLEY!
OHHH, HONEY!
HA HA HA HA HA
KELLY... WE'VE FOUND A PLACE THAT WE'RE GOING TO CHECK YOU IN. IT'S... NOT FOREVER. IT'S JUST FOR A WHILE. SOMEPLACE WHERE THEY CAN HELP YOU... FULL TIME.
WE DIDN'T WANT TO. BUT THERE'S REALLY NO OTHER CHOICE. YOU DO SEE THAT, DON'T YOU, HONEY?
the HAPPY TOM show
THAT'S MY KITTEN!
DINNER IN HALF AN HOUR, KELLY SWEETHEART.
OH, KITTEN! THAT BOY, IAN, CALLED! HE WANTS HIS RING BACK!
QUEEN B
DON'T WORRY. I'LL GIVE IT TO HIM.

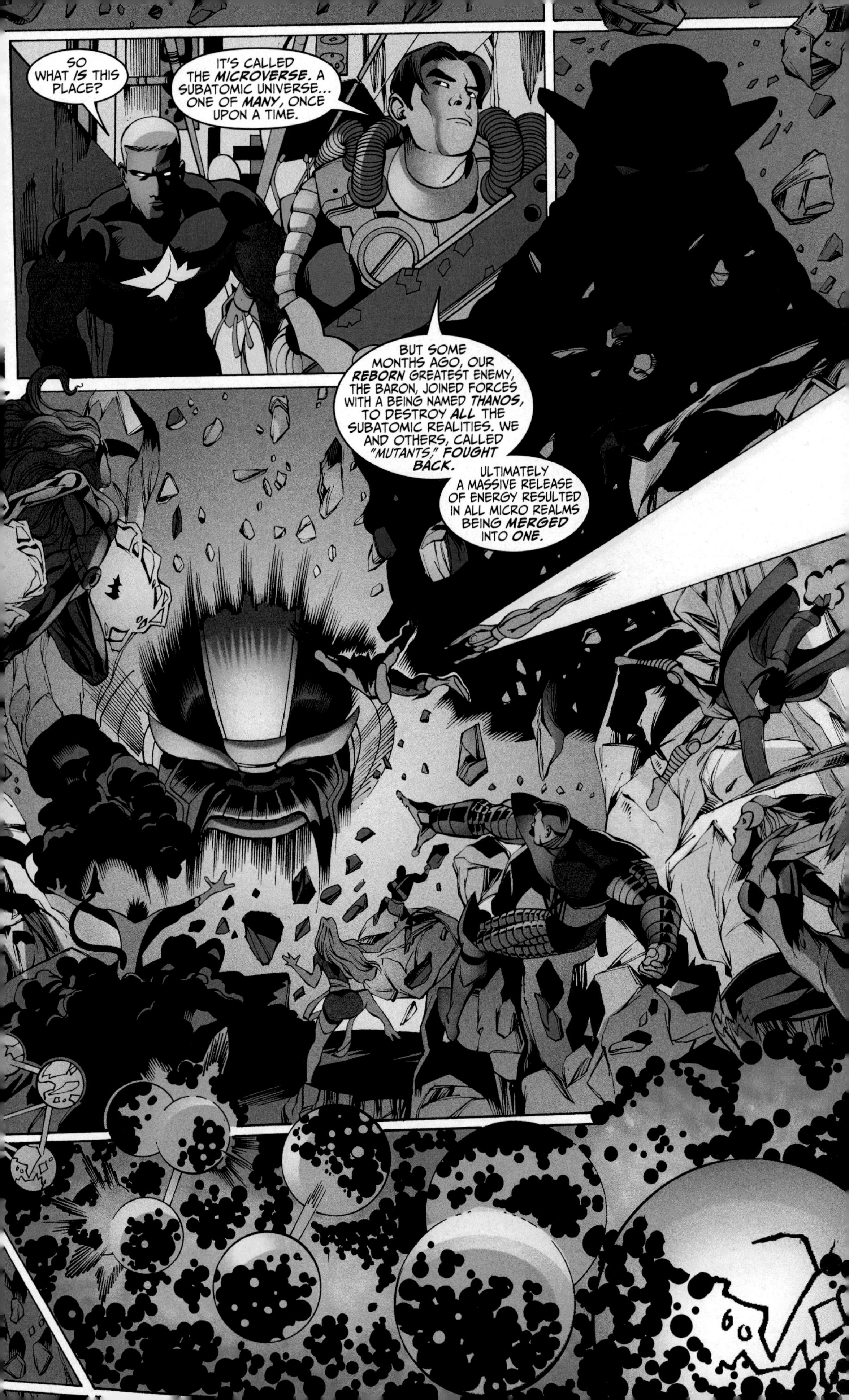
SO WHAT *IS* THIS PLACE?
IT'S CALLED THE *MICROVERSE*. A SUBATOMIC UNIVERSE... ONE OF *MANY*, ONCE UPON A TIME.
BUT SOME MONTHS AGO, OUR *REBORN* GREATEST ENEMY, THE BARON, JOINED FORCES WITH A BEING NAMED *THANOS*, TO DESTROY *ALL* THE SUBATOMIC REALITIES. WE AND OTHERS, CALLED "MUTANTS," *FOUGHT BACK*.
ULTIMATELY A MASSIVE RELEASE OF ENERGY RESULTED IN ALL MICRO REALMS BEING *MERGED* INTO *ONE*.

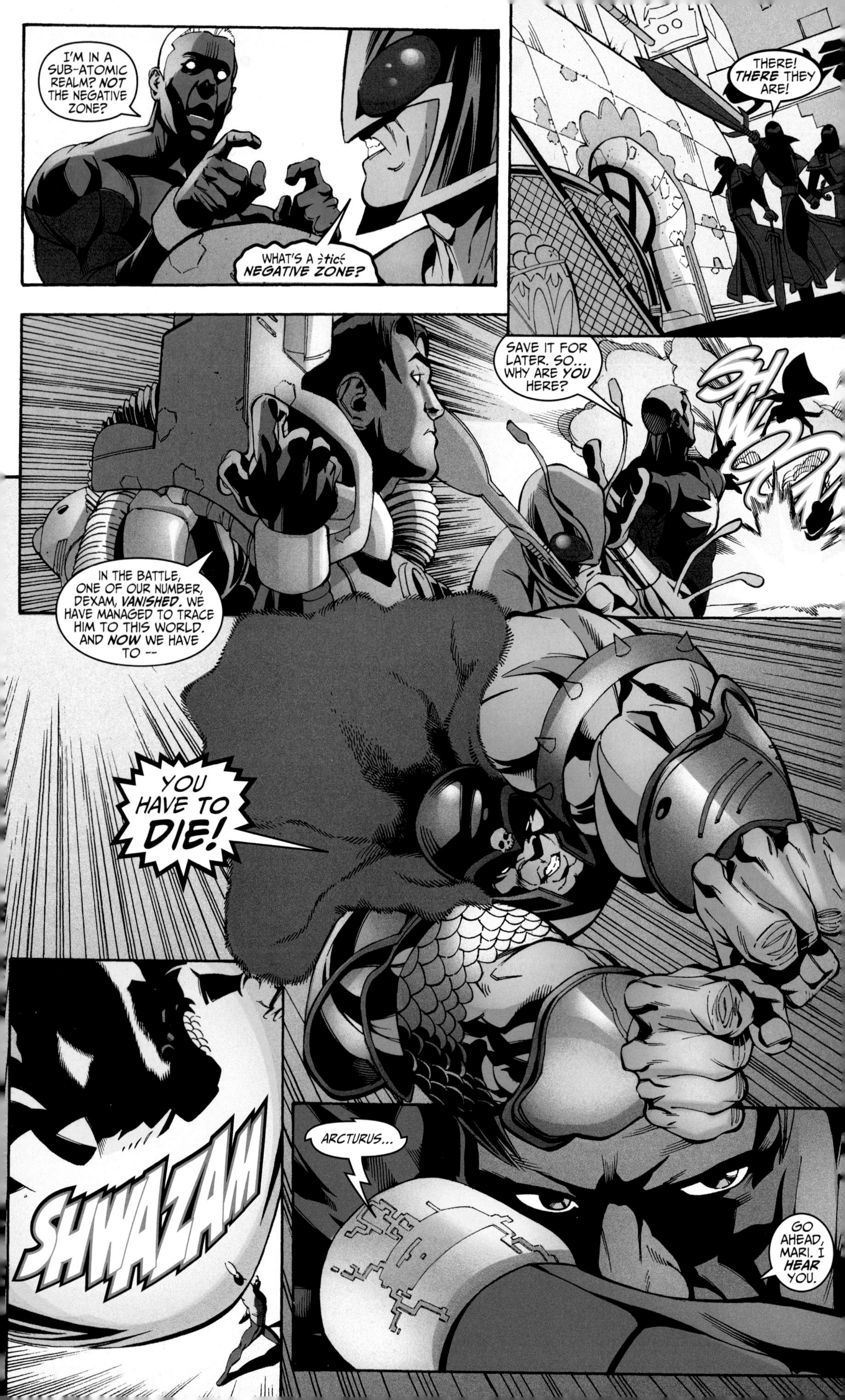
I'M IN A SUB-ATOMIC REALM? NOT THE NEGATIVE ZONE?
WHAT'S A ✱tic✱ NEGATIVE ZONE?
THERE! THERE THEY ARE!
SAVE IT FOR LATER. SO... WHY ARE YOU HERE?
IN THE BATTLE, ONE OF OUR NUMBER, DEXAM, VANISHED. WE HAVE MANAGED TO TRACE HIM TO THIS WORLD. AND NOW WE HAVE TO --
YOU HAVE TO DIE!
SHWAZAM
ARCTURUS...
GO AHEAD, MARI. I HEAR YOU.

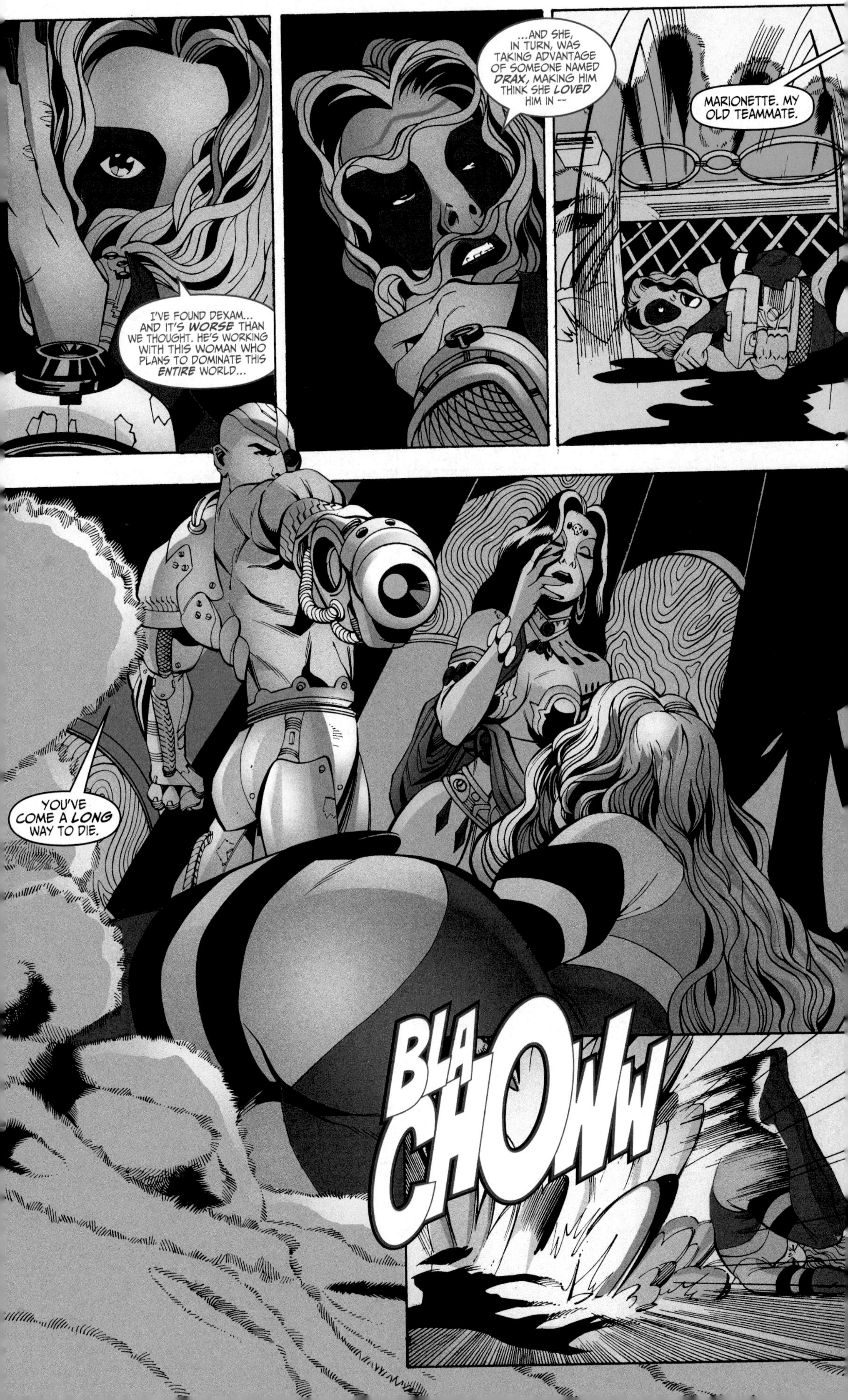

I'VE FOUND DEXAM... AND IT'S WORSE THAN WE THOUGHT. HE'S WORKING WITH THIS WOMAN WHO PLANS TO DOMINATE THIS ENTIRE WORLD...
...AND SHE, IN TURN, WAS TAKING ADVANTAGE OF SOMEONE NAMED DRAX, MAKING HIM THINK SHE LOVED HIM IN --
MARIONETTE. MY OLD TEAMMATE.
YOU'VE COME A LONG WAY TO DIE.
BLA CHOWW

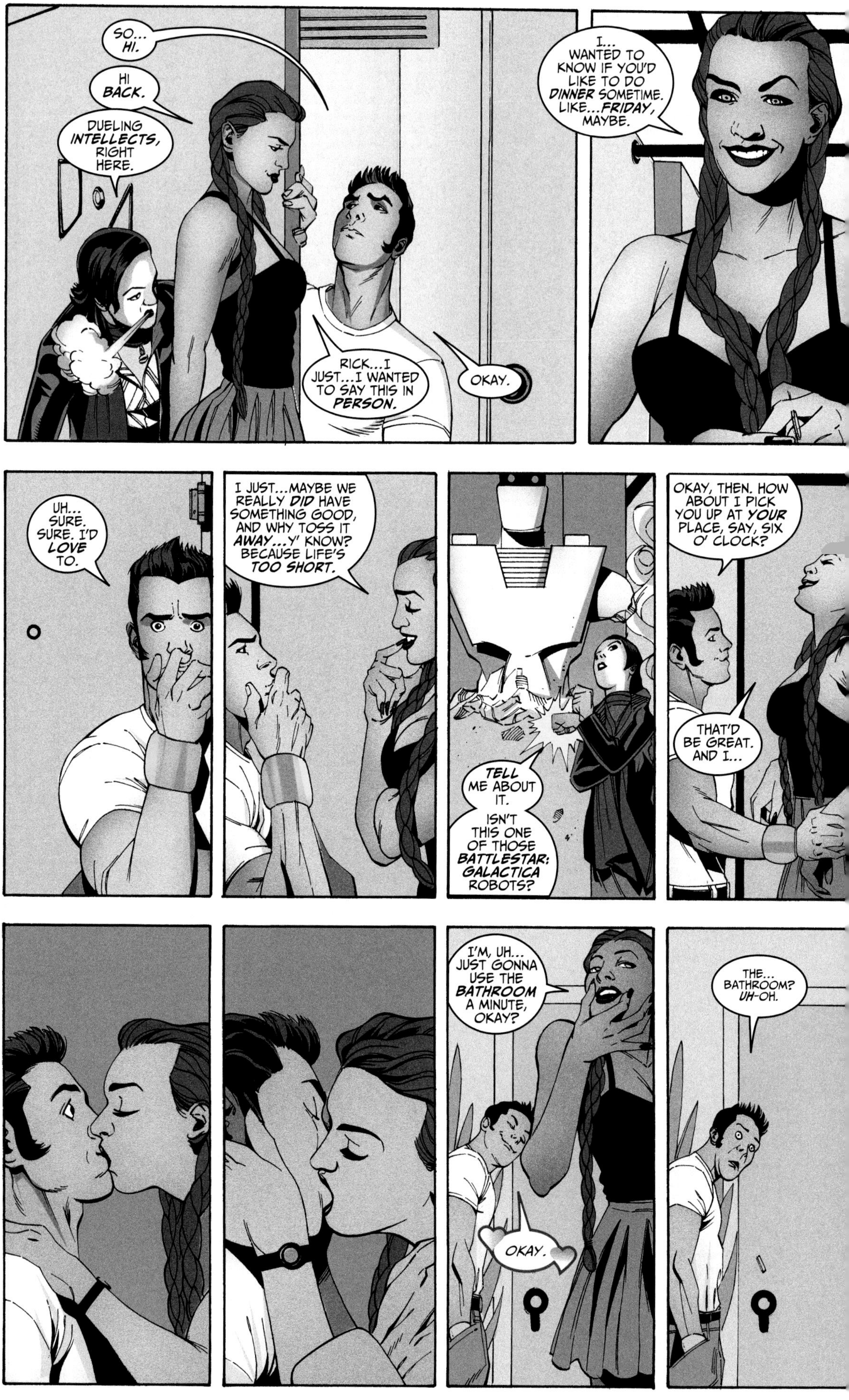
SO... HI.
HI BACK.
DUELING INTELLECTS, RIGHT HERE.
RICK...I JUST...I WANTED TO SAY THIS IN PERSON.
OKAY.
I... WANTED TO KNOW IF YOU'D LIKE TO DO DINNER SOMETIME. LIKE...FRIDAY, MAYBE.
UH... SURE. SURE. I'D LOVE TO.
I JUST...MAYBE WE REALLY DID HAVE SOMETHING GOOD, AND WHY TOSS IT AWAY...Y' KNOW? BECAUSE LIFE'S TOO SHORT.
TELL ME ABOUT IT.
ISN'T THIS ONE OF THOSE BATTLESTAR: GALACTICA ROBOTS?
OKAY, THEN. HOW ABOUT I PICK YOU UP AT YOUR PLACE, SAY, SIX O' CLOCK?
THAT'D BE GREAT. AND I...
I'M, UH... JUST GONNA USE THE BATHROOM A MINUTE, OKAY?
OKAY.
THE... BATHROOM? UH-OH.

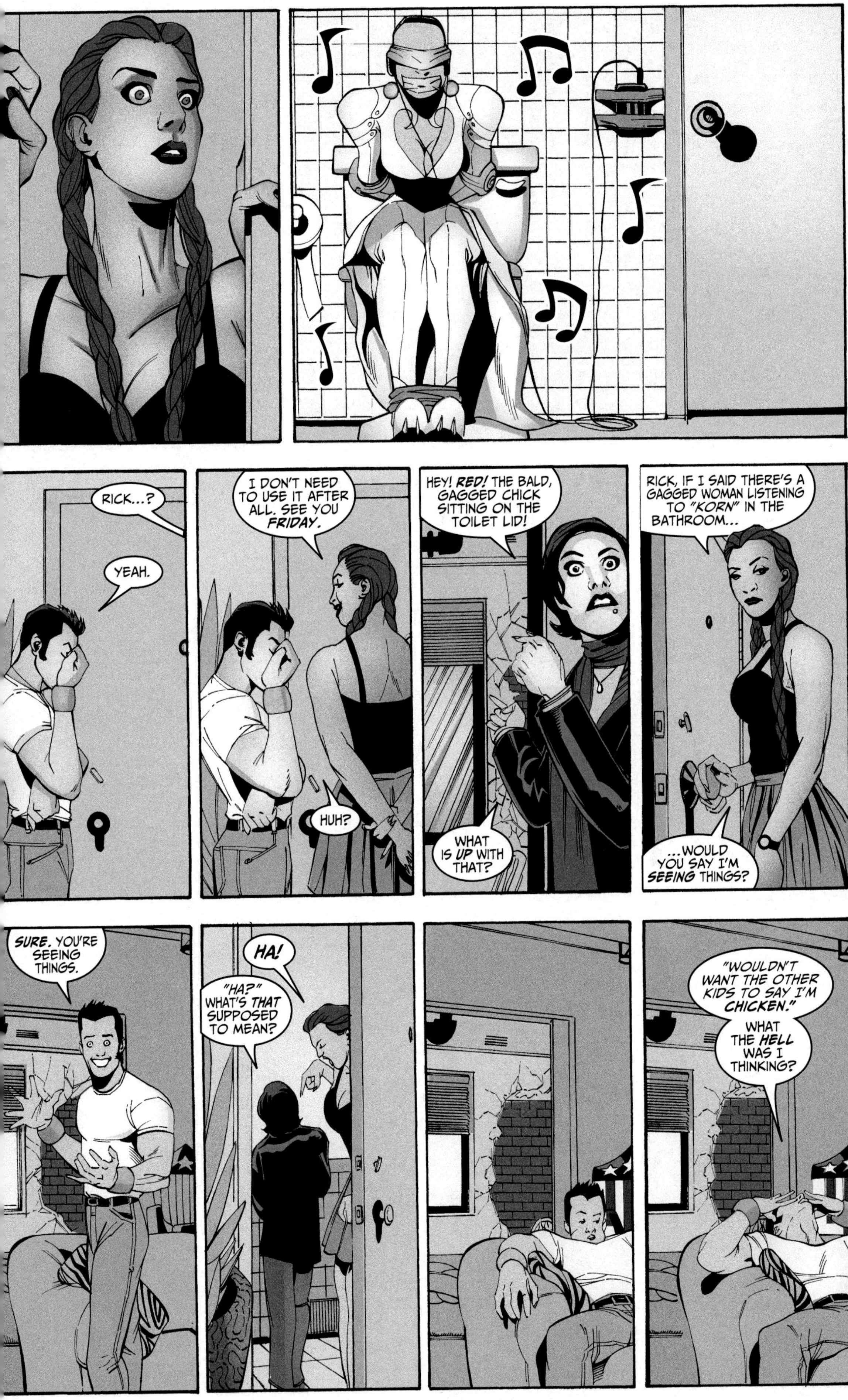
RICK...?
YEAH.
I DON'T NEED TO USE IT AFTER ALL. SEE YOU FRIDAY.
HUH?
HEY! RED! THE BALD, GAGGED CHICK SITTING ON THE TOILET LID!
WHAT IS UP WITH THAT?
RICK, IF I SAID THERE'S A GAGGED WOMAN LISTENING TO "KORN" IN THE BATHROOM...
...WOULD YOU SAY I'M SEEING THINGS?
SURE. YOU'RE SEEING THINGS.
HA!
"HA?" WHAT'S THAT SUPPOSED TO MEAN?
"WOULDN'T WANT THE OTHER KIDS TO SAY I'M CHICKEN."
WHAT THE HELL WAS I THINKING?

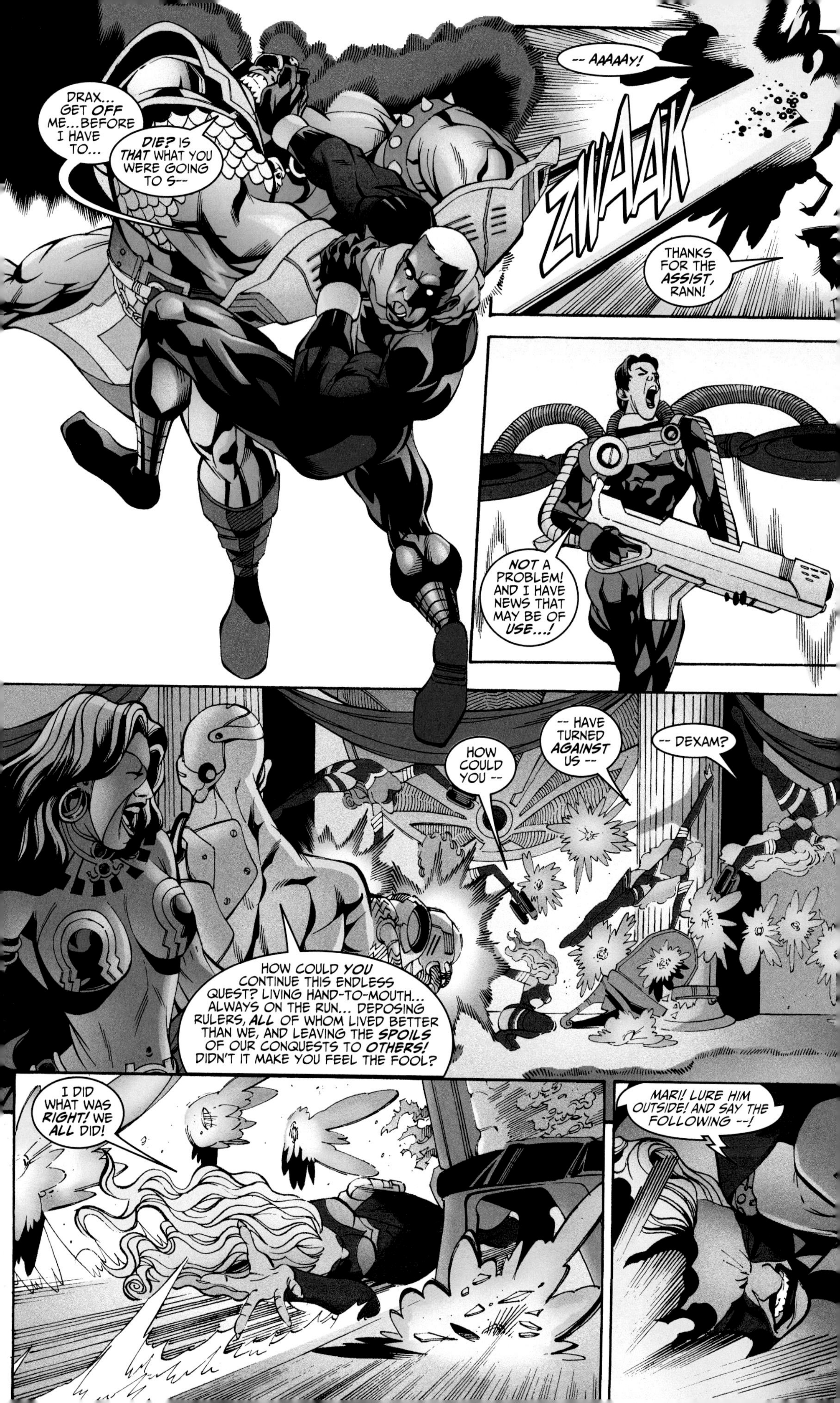

-- AAAAAY!
DRAX... GET OFF ME...BEFORE I HAVE TO...
DIE? IS THAT WHAT YOU WERE GOING TO S--
ZWAAK
THANKS FOR THE ASSIST, RANN!
NOT A PROBLEM! AND I HAVE NEWS THAT MAY BE OF USE...!
HOW COULD YOU --
-- HAVE TURNED AGAINST US --
-- DEXAM?
HOW COULD YOU CONTINUE THIS ENDLESS QUEST? LIVING HAND-TO-MOUTH... ALWAYS ON THE RUN... DEPOSING RULERS, ALL OF WHOM LIVED BETTER THAN WE, AND LEAVING THE SPOILS OF OUR CONQUESTS TO OTHERS! DIDN'T IT MAKE YOU FEEL THE FOOL?
I DID WHAT WAS RIGHT! WE ALL DID!
MARI! LURE HIM OUTSIDE! AND SAY THE FOLLOWING --!

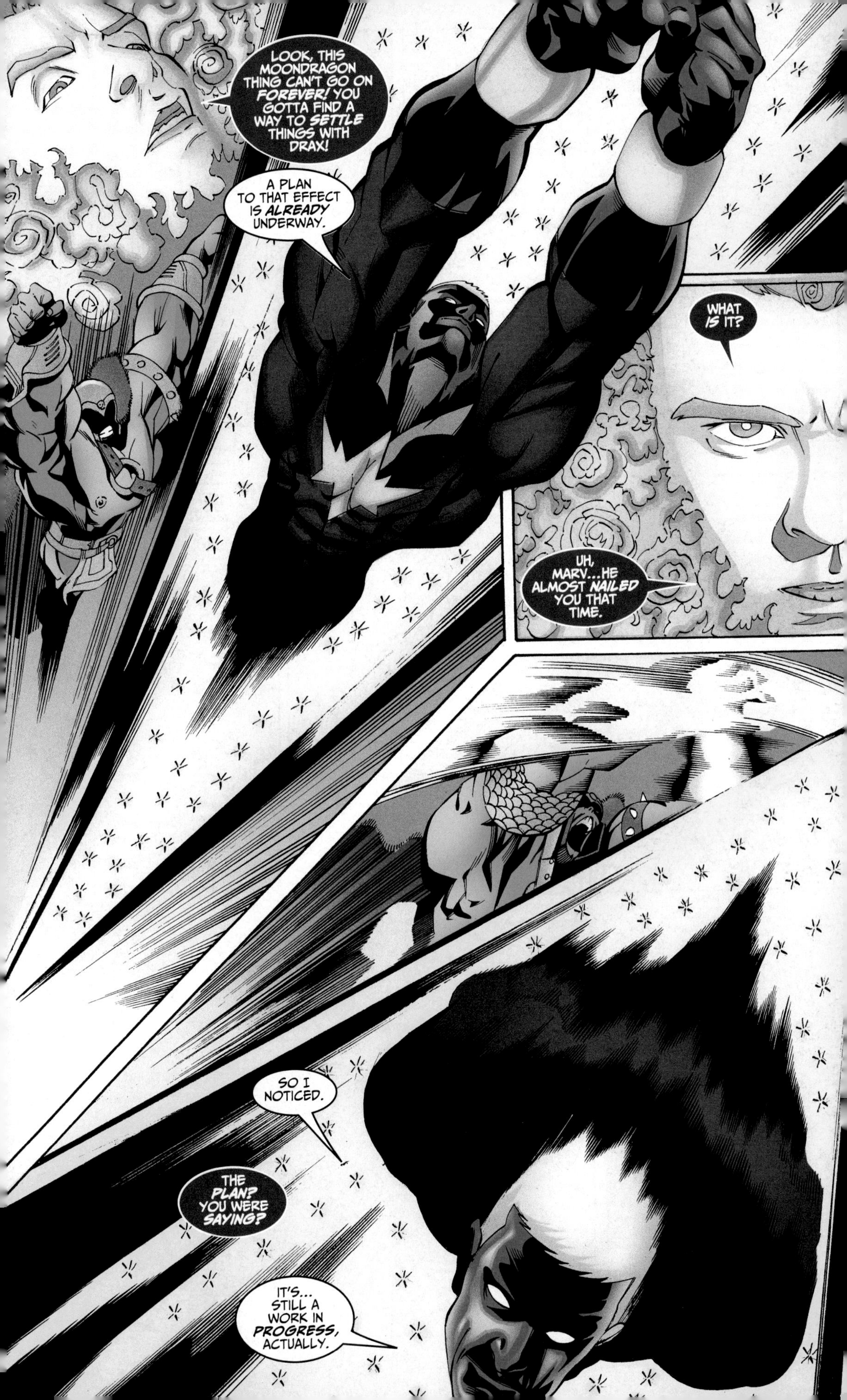
LOOK, THIS MOONDRAGON THING CAN'T GO ON FOREVER! YOU GOTTA FIND A WAY TO SETTLE THINGS WITH DRAX!
A PLAN TO THAT EFFECT IS ALREADY UNDERWAY.
WHAT IS IT?
UH, MARV...HE ALMOST NAILED YOU THAT TIME.
SO I NOTICED.
THE PLAN? YOU WERE SAYING?
IT'S... STILL A WORK IN PROGRESS, ACTUALLY.

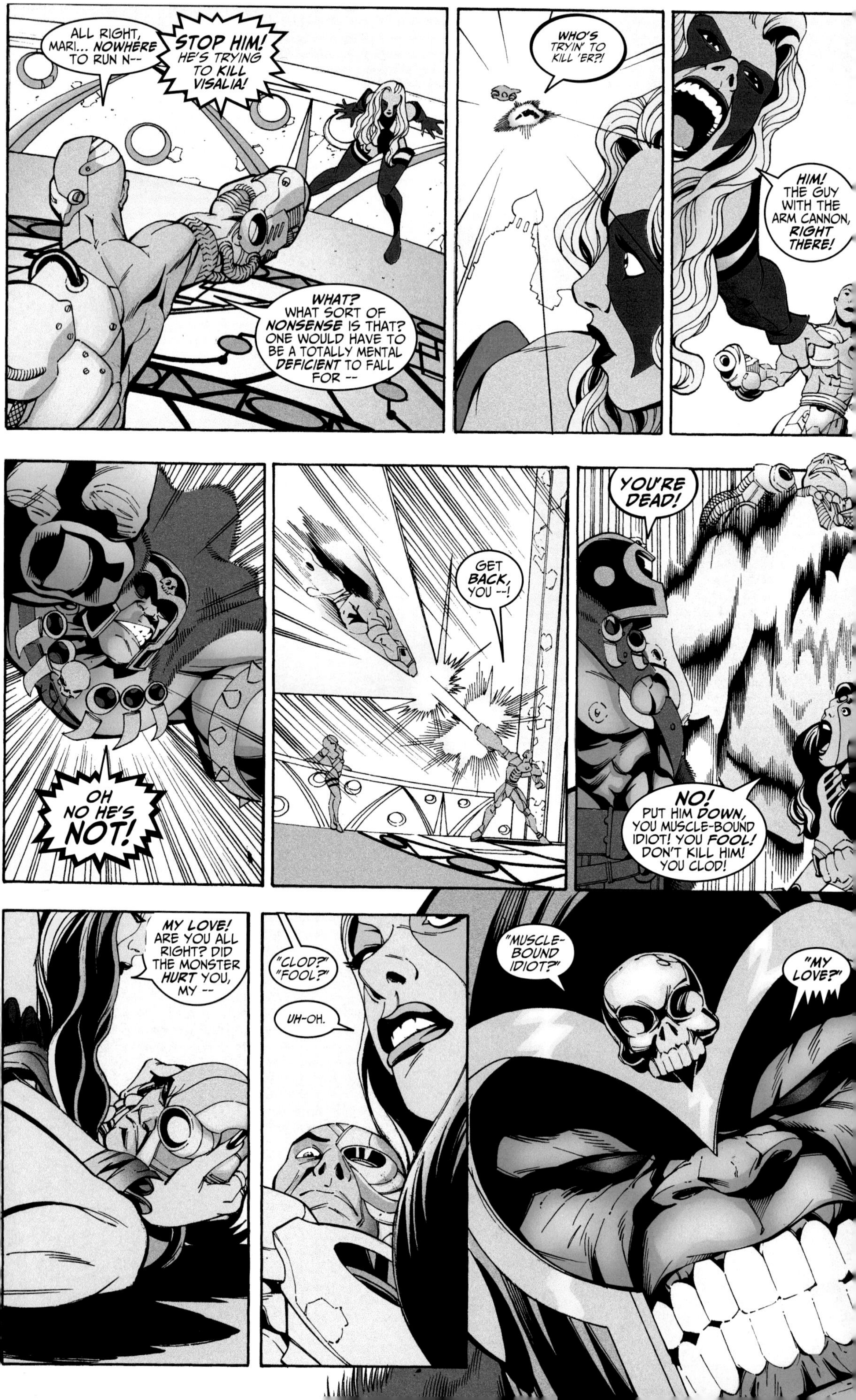
ALL RIGHT, MARI... NOWHERE TO RUN N--
STOP HIM! HE'S TRYING TO KILL VISALIA!
WHAT? WHAT SORT OF NONSENSE IS THAT? ONE WOULD HAVE TO BE A TOTALLY MENTAL DEFICIENT TO FALL FOR --
WHO'S TRYIN' TO KILL 'ER?!
HIM! THE GUY WITH THE ARM CANNON, RIGHT THERE!
OH NO HE'S NOT!
GET BACK, YOU --!
YOU'RE DEAD!
NO! PUT HIM DOWN, YOU MUSCLE-BOUND IDIOT! YOU FOOL! DON'T KILL HIM! YOU CLOD!
MY LOVE! ARE YOU ALL RIGHT? DID THE MONSTER HURT YOU, MY --
"CLOD?" "FOOL?"
UH-OH.
"MUSCLE-BOUND IDIOT?"
"MY LOVE?"

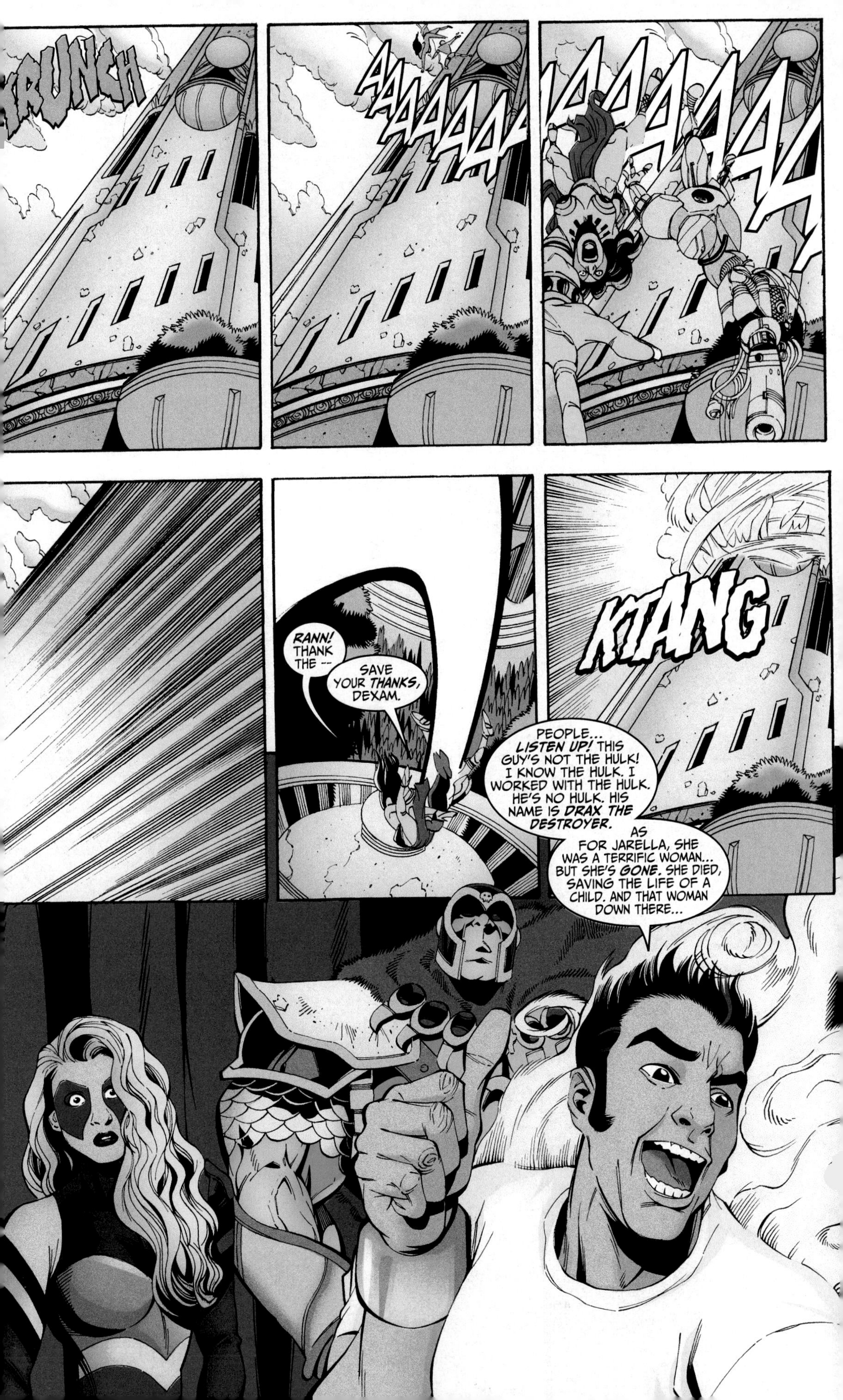
KRUNCH
AAAAAAAAAAAAAAAAAAA
RANN! THANK THE --
SAVE YOUR THANKS, DEXAM.
KTANG
PEOPLE... LISTEN UP! THIS GUY'S NOT THE HULK! I KNOW THE HULK. I WORKED WITH THE HULK. HE'S NO HULK. HIS NAME IS DRAX THE DESTROYER.
AS FOR JARELLA, SHE WAS A TERRIFIC WOMAN... BUT SHE'S GONE. SHE DIED, SAVING THE LIFE OF A CHILD. AND THAT WOMAN DOWN THERE...

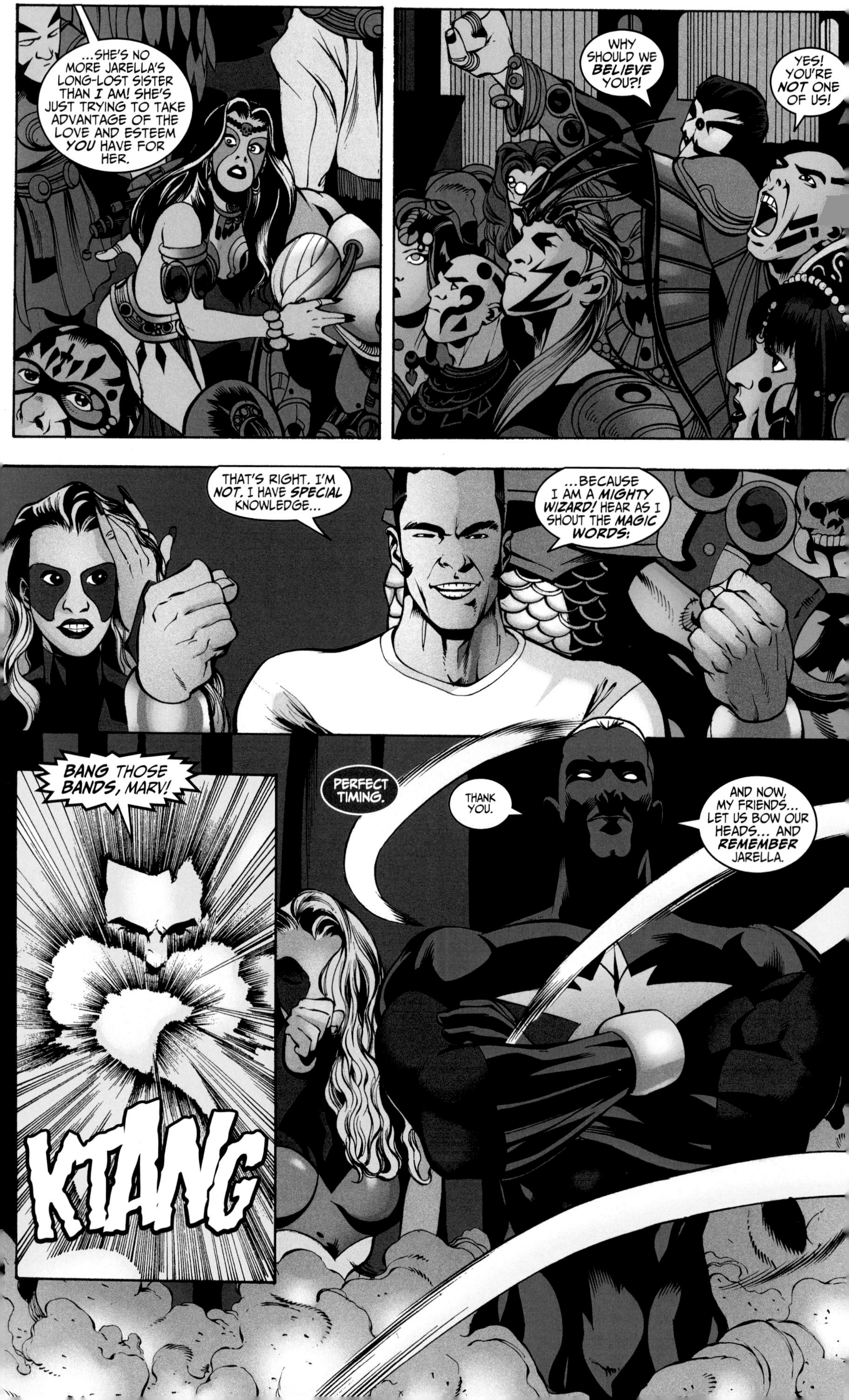
...SHE'S NO MORE JARELLA'S LONG-LOST SISTER THAN I AM! SHE'S JUST TRYING TO TAKE ADVANTAGE OF THE LOVE AND ESTEEM YOU HAVE FOR HER.
WHY SHOULD WE BELIEVE YOU?!
YES! YOU'RE NOT ONE OF US!
THAT'S RIGHT. I'M NOT. I HAVE SPECIAL KNOWLEDGE...
...BECAUSE I AM A MIGHTY WIZARD! HEAR AS I SHOUT THE MAGIC WORDS:
BANG THOSE BANDS, MARV!
KTANG
PERFECT TIMING.
THANK YOU.
AND NOW, MY FRIENDS... LET US BOW OUR HEADS... AND REMEMBER JARELLA.

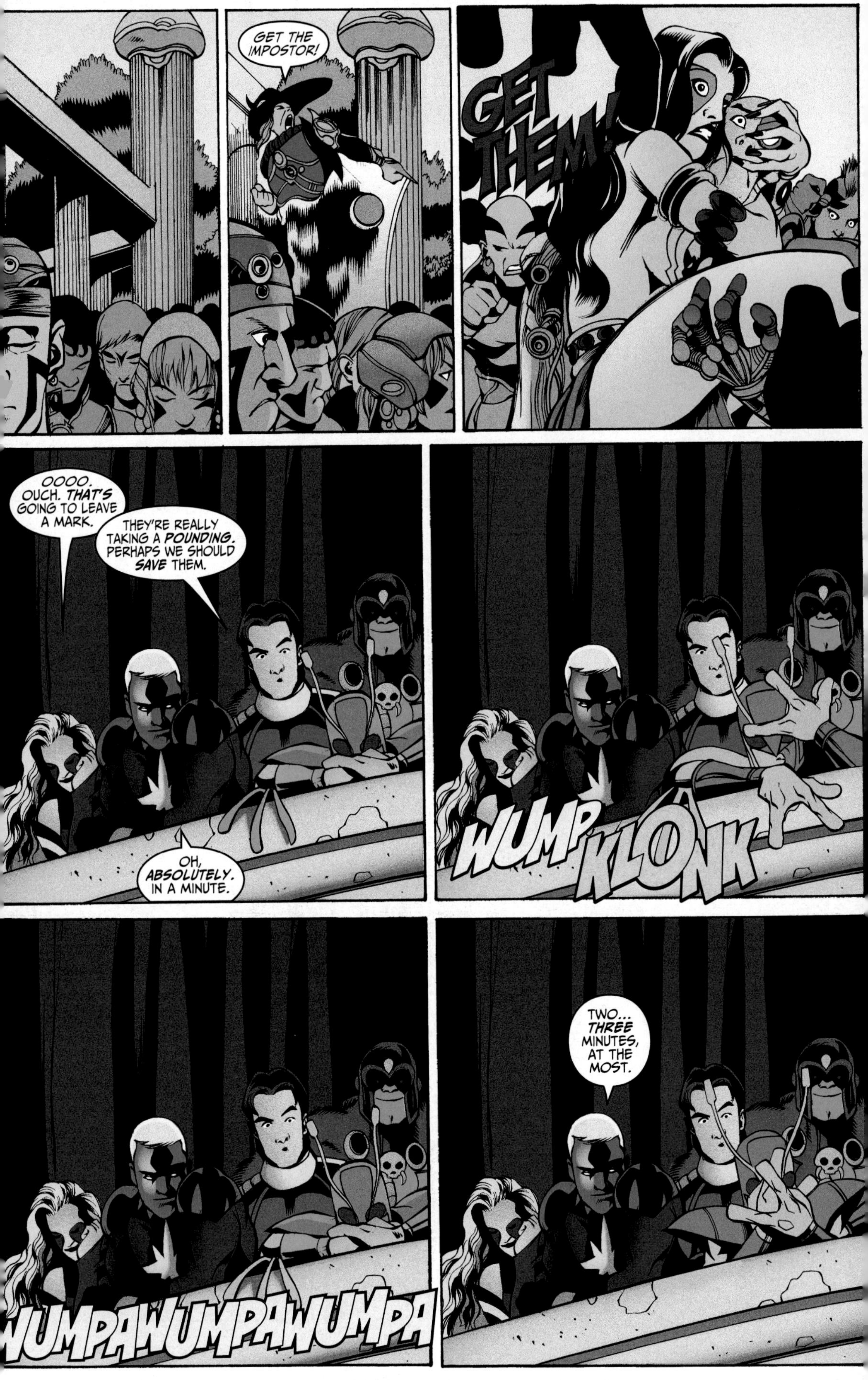
GET THE IMPOSTOR!
GET THEM!
OOOO. OUCH. THAT'S GOING TO LEAVE A MARK.
THEY'RE REALLY TAKING A POUNDING. PERHAPS WE SHOULD SAVE THEM.
OH, ABSOLUTELY. IN A MINUTE.
WUMP
KLONK
WUMPAWUMPAWUMPA
TWO... THREE MINUTES, AT THE MOST.

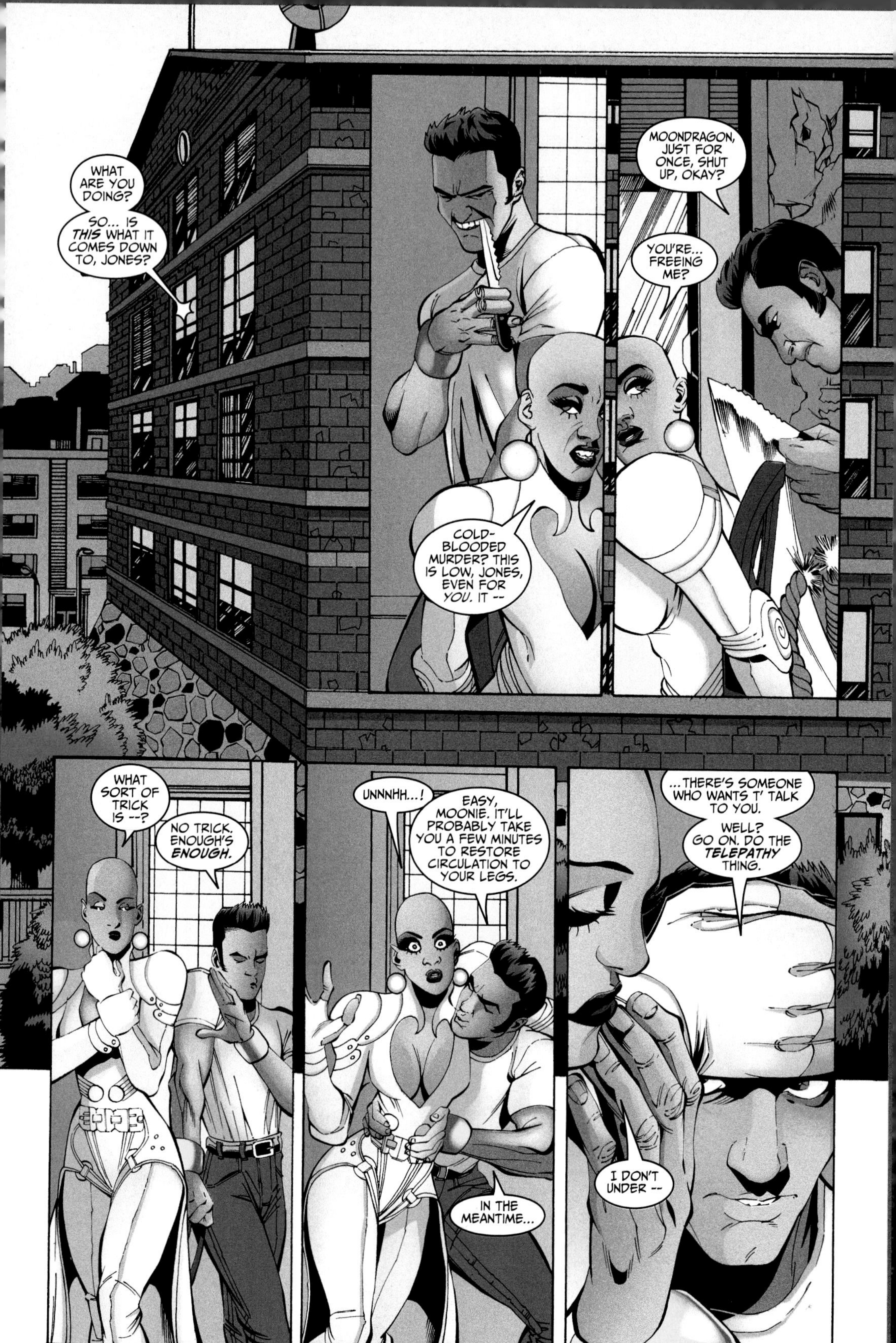
WHAT ARE YOU DOING?
SO... IS THIS WHAT IT COMES DOWN TO, JONES?
COLD-BLOODED MURDER? THIS IS LOW, JONES, EVEN FOR YOU. IT --
MOONDRAGON, JUST FOR ONCE, SHUT UP, OKAY?
YOU'RE... FREEING ME?
WHAT SORT OF TRICK IS --?
NO TRICK. ENOUGH'S ENOUGH.
UNNNHH...!
EASY, MOONIE. IT'LL PROBABLY TAKE YOU A FEW MINUTES TO RESTORE CIRCULATION TO YOUR LEGS.
IN THE MEANTIME...
...THERE'S SOMEONE WHO WANTS T' TALK TO YOU.
WELL? GO ON. DO THE TELEPATHY THING.
I DON'T UNDER --

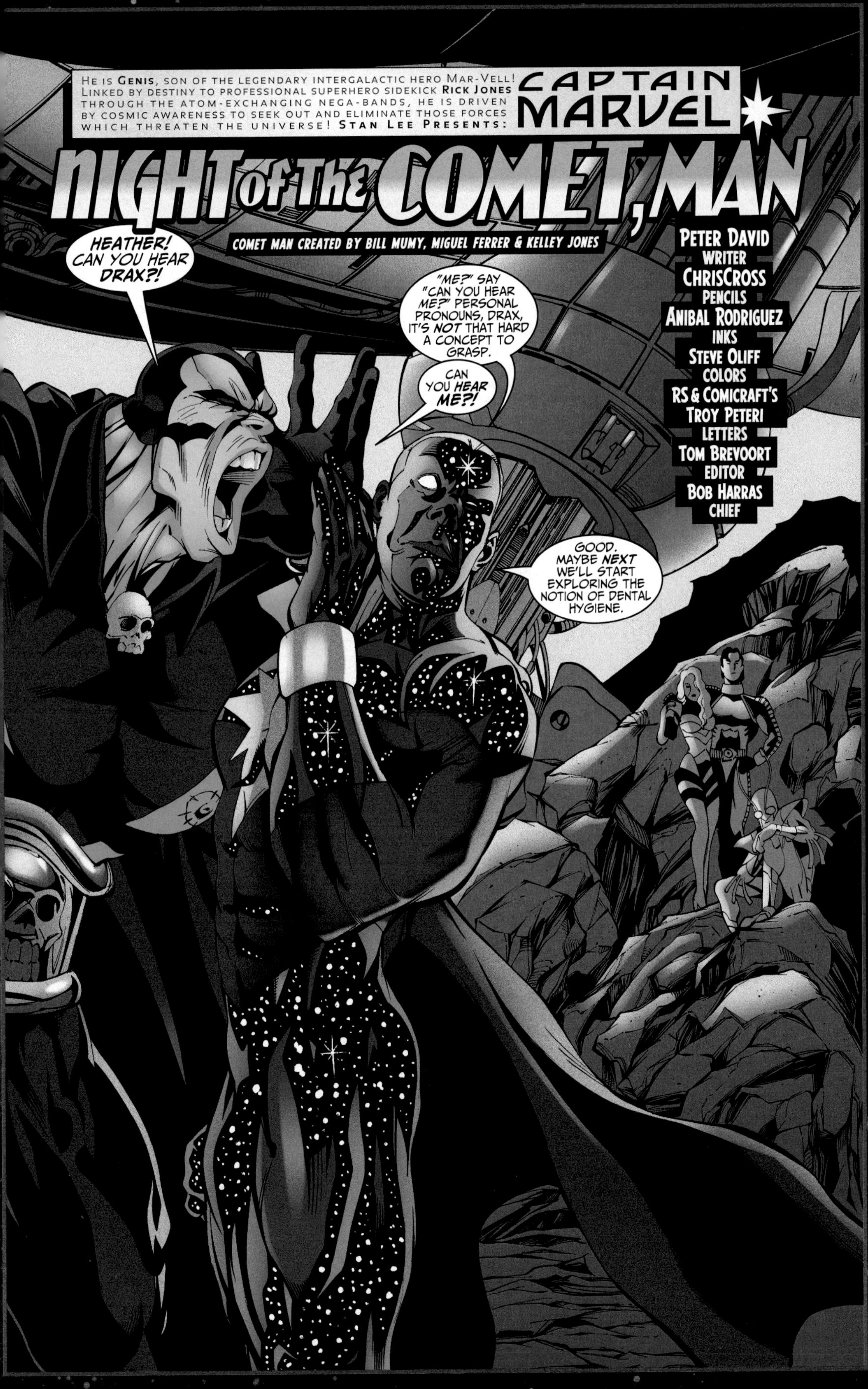

He is Genis, son of the legendary intergalactic hero Mar-Vell! Linked by destiny to professional superhero sidekick Rick Jones through the atom-exchanging nega-bands, he is driven by cosmic awareness to seek out and eliminate those forces which threaten the universe! Stan Lee Presents:
CAPTAIN MARVEL
NIGHT of the COMET, MAN
COMET MAN CREATED BY BILL MUMY, MIGUEL FERRER & KELLEY JONES
HEATHER! CAN YOU HEAR DRAX?!
"ME?" SAY "CAN YOU HEAR ME?" PERSONAL PRONOUNS, DRAX, IT'S NOT THAT HARD A CONCEPT TO GRASP.
CAN YOU HEAR ME?!
PETER DAVID WRITER
CHRISCROSS PENCILS
ANIBAL RODRIGUEZ INKS
STEVE OLIFF COLORS
RS & COMICRAFT'S TROY PETERI LETTERS
TOM BREVOORT EDITOR
BOB HARRAS CHIEF
GOOD. MAYBE NEXT WE'LL START EXPLORING THE NOTION OF DENTAL HYGIENE.

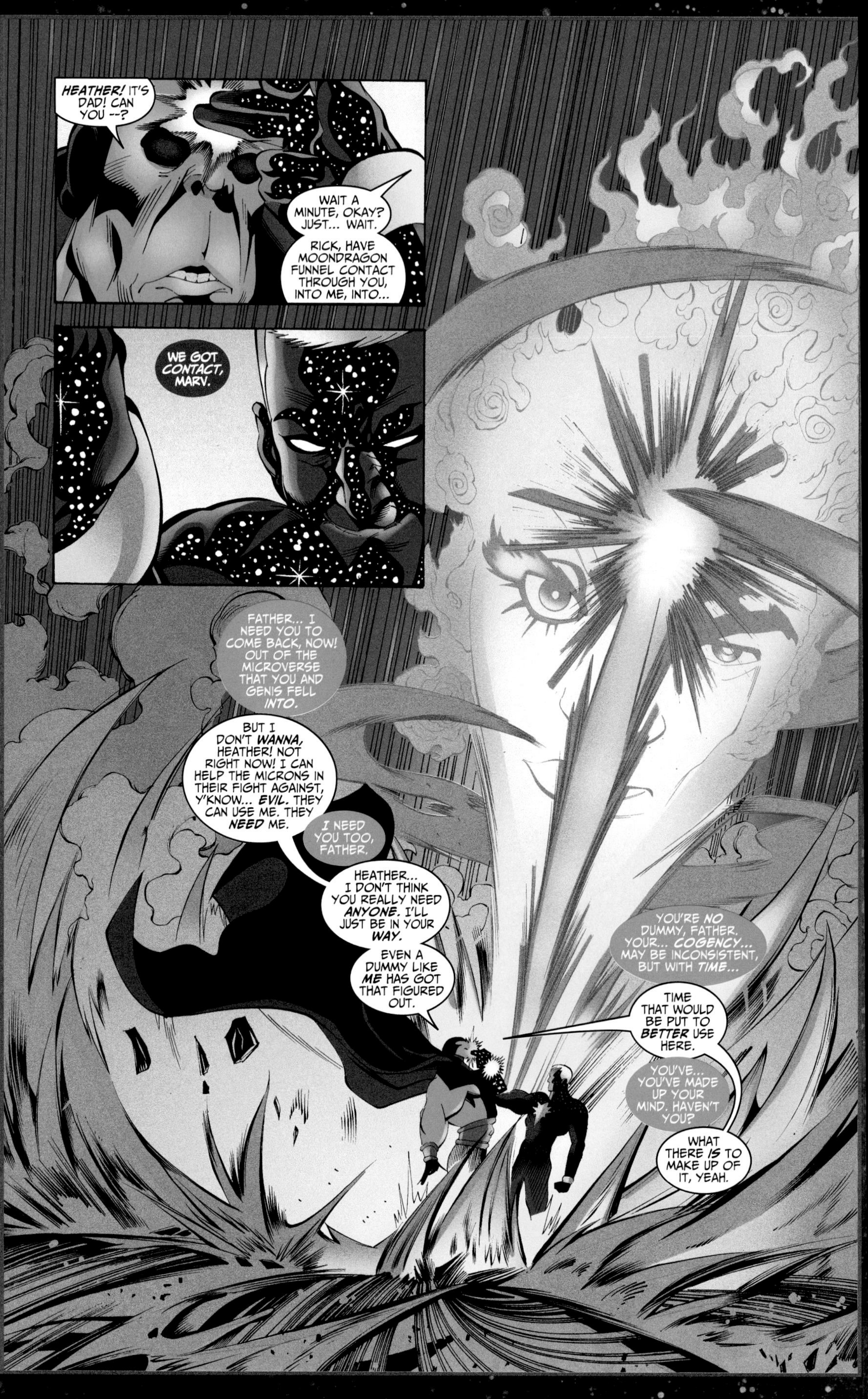
HEATHER! IT'S DAD! CAN YOU --?
WAIT A MINUTE, OKAY? JUST... WAIT.
RICK, HAVE MOONDRAGON FUNNEL CONTACT THROUGH YOU, INTO ME, INTO...
WE GOT CONTACT, MARV.
FATHER... I NEED YOU TO COME BACK, NOW! OUT OF THE MICROVERSE THAT YOU AND GENIS FELL INTO.
BUT I DON'T WANNA, HEATHER! NOT RIGHT NOW! I CAN HELP THE MICRONS IN THEIR FIGHT AGAINST, Y'KNOW... EVIL. THEY CAN USE ME. THEY NEED ME.
I NEED YOU TOO, FATHER.
HEATHER... I DON'T THINK YOU REALLY NEED ANYONE. I'LL JUST BE IN YOUR WAY.
EVEN A DUMMY LIKE ME HAS GOT THAT FIGURED OUT.
YOU'RE NO DUMMY, FATHER. YOUR... COGENCY... MAY BE INCONSISTENT, BUT WITH TIME...
TIME THAT WOULD BE PUT TO BETTER USE HERE.
YOU'VE... YOU'VE MADE UP YOUR MIND. HAVEN'T YOU?
WHAT THERE IS TO MAKE UP OF IT, YEAH.

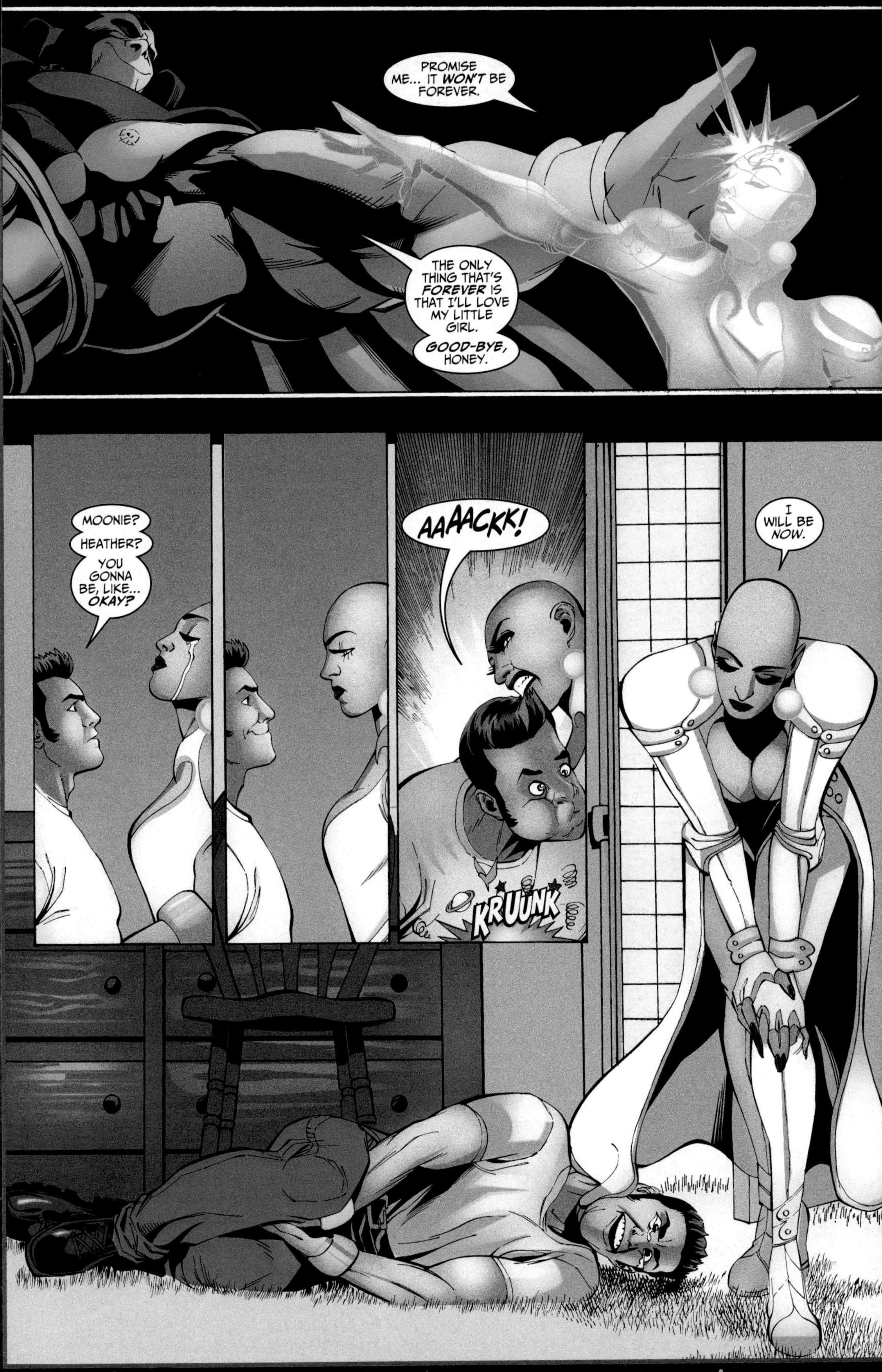
PROMISE ME... IT WON'T BE FOREVER.
THE ONLY THING THAT'S FOREVER IS THAT I'LL LOVE MY LITTLE GIRL.
GOOD-BYE, HONEY.
MOONIE?
HEATHER?
YOU GONNA BE, LIKE... OKAY?
AAAACKK!
KRUUNK
I WILL BE NOW.

Excerpt from *CAPTAIN MARVEL #12*

Writer: Peter David • Penciler: ChrisCross • Inker: Anibal Rodriguez • Colorist: Steve Oliff
Letterer: Richard Starkings & Comicraft's Wes Abbott • Assistant Editor: Marc Sumerak • Editor: Tom Brevoort

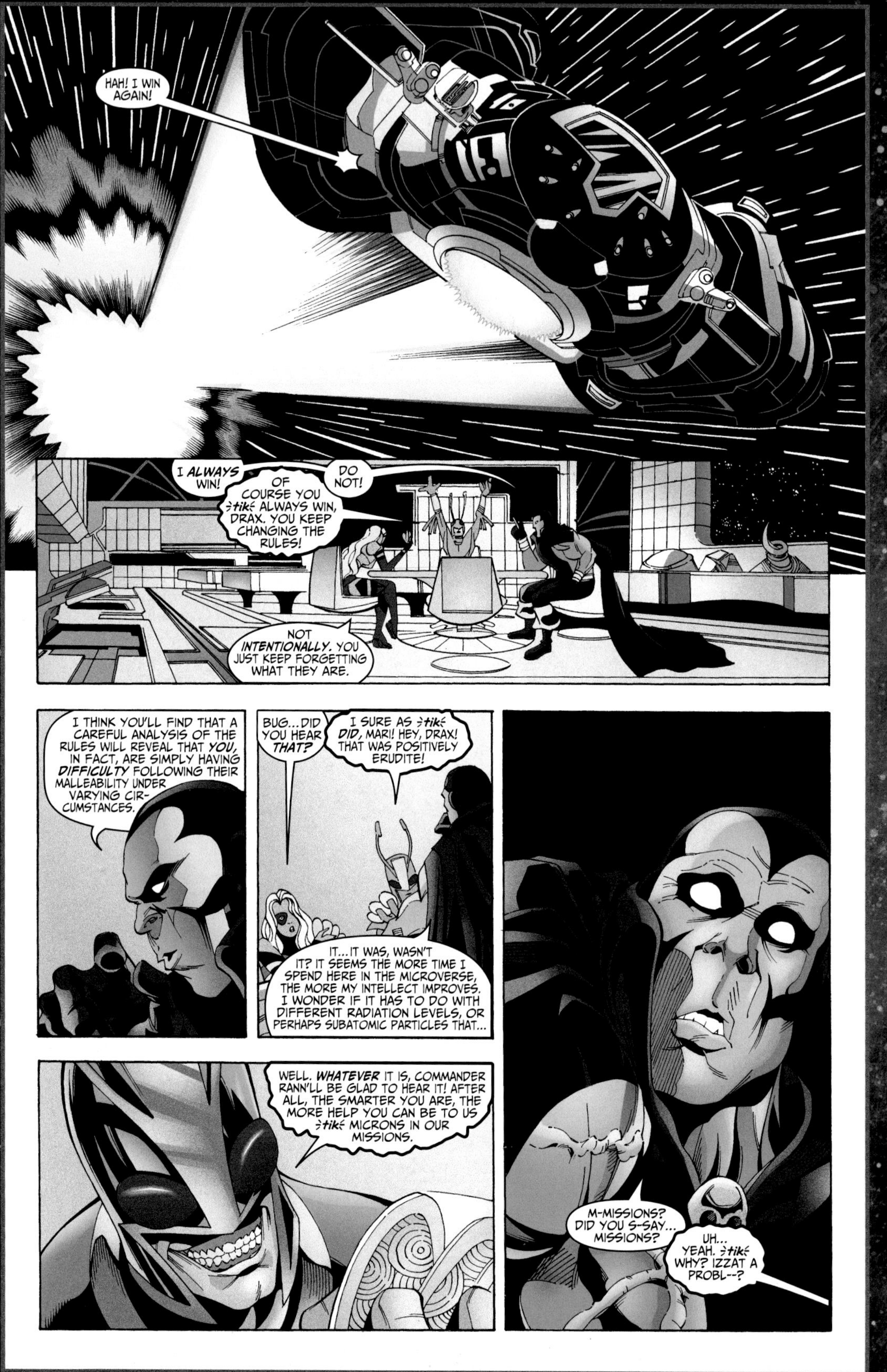

HAH! I WIN AGAIN!
I ALWAYS WIN!
DO NOT!
OF COURSE YOU ≠tik≠ ALWAYS WIN, DRAX. YOU KEEP CHANGING THE RULES!
NOT INTENTIONALLY. YOU JUST KEEP FORGETTING WHAT THEY ARE.
I THINK YOU'LL FIND THAT A CAREFUL ANALYSIS OF THE RULES WILL REVEAL THAT YOU, IN FACT, ARE SIMPLY HAVING DIFFICULTY FOLLOWING THEIR MALLEABILITY UNDER VARYING CIR-CUMSTANCES.
BUG...DID YOU HEAR THAT?
I SURE AS ≠tik≠ DID, MARI! HEY, DRAX! THAT WAS POSITIVELY ERUDITE!
IT...IT WAS, WASN'T IT? IT SEEMS THE MORE TIME I SPEND HERE IN THE MICROVERSE, THE MORE MY INTELLECT IMPROVES. I WONDER IF IT HAS TO DO WITH DIFFERENT RADIATION LEVELS, OR PERHAPS SUBATOMIC PARTICLES THAT...
WELL. WHATEVER IT IS, COMMANDER RANN'LL BE GLAD TO HEAR IT! AFTER ALL, THE SMARTER YOU ARE, THE MORE HELP YOU CAN BE TO US ≠tik≠ MICRONS IN OUR MISSIONS.
M-MISSIONS? DID YOU S-SAY... MISSIONS?
UH... YEAH. ≠tik≠ WHY? IZZAT A PROBL--?

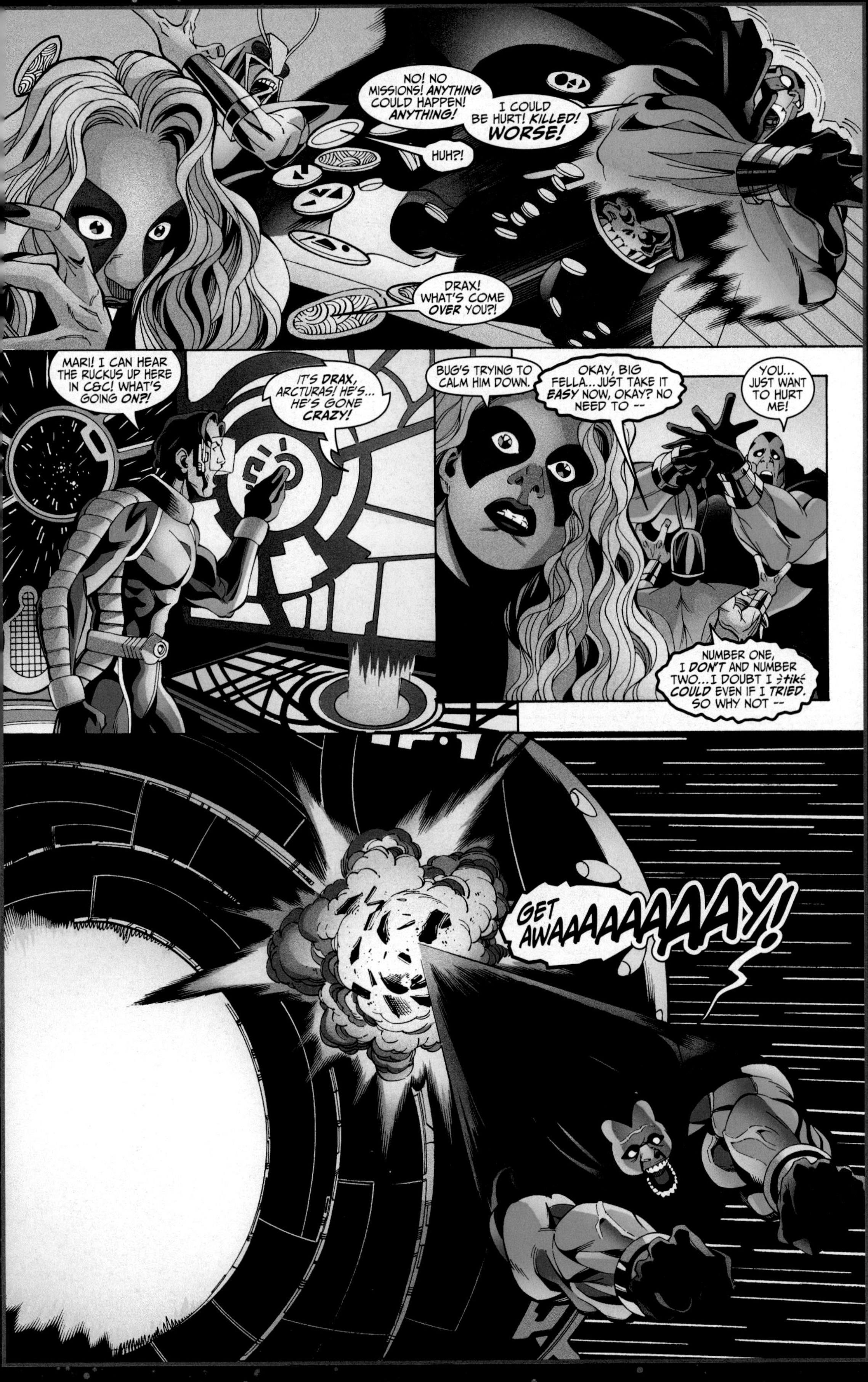
NO! NO MISSIONS! ANYTHING COULD HAPPEN! ANYTHING!
I COULD BE HURT! KILLED! WORSE!
HUH?!
DRAX! WHAT'S COME OVER YOU?!
MARI! I CAN HEAR THE RUCKUS UP HERE IN C&C! WHAT'S GOING ON?!
IT'S DRAX, ARCTURAS! HE'S... HE'S GONE CRAZY!
BUG'S TRYING TO CALM HIM DOWN.
OKAY, BIG FELLA... JUST TAKE IT EASY NOW, OKAY? NO NEED TO --
YOU... JUST WANT TO HURT ME!
NUMBER ONE, I DON'T AND NUMBER TWO... I DOUBT I COULD EVEN IF I TRIED. SO WHY NOT --
tik
GET AWAAAAAAAAY!

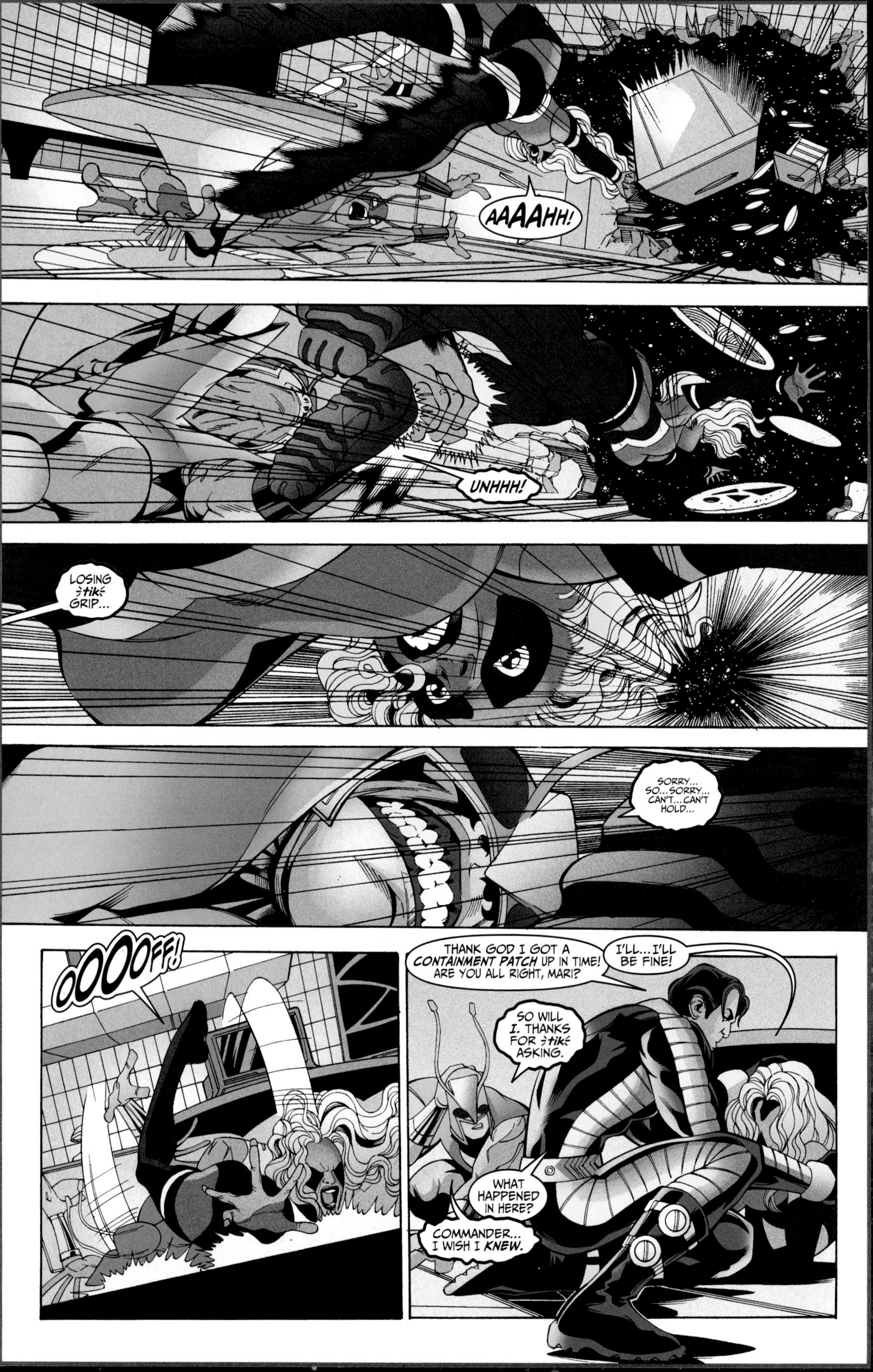
AAAAHH!
UNHHH!
LOSING ~tik~ GRIP...
SORRY... SO...SORRY... CAN'T...CAN'T HOLD...
OOOOFF!
THANK GOD I GOT A CONTAINMENT PATCH UP IN TIME! ARE YOU ALL RIGHT, MARI?
I'LL...I'LL BE FINE!
SO WILL I. THANKS FOR ~tik~ ASKING.
WHAT HAPPENED IN HERE?
COMMANDER... I WISH I KNEW.

Excerpt from *CAPTAIN MARVEL #13*

Writer: Peter David • Penciler: ChrisCross • Inker: Anibal Rodriguez • Colorist: Steve Oliff
Letterer: Richard Starkings & Comicraft's Saida Temofonte • Assistant Editor: Marc Sumerak • Editor: Tom Brevoort

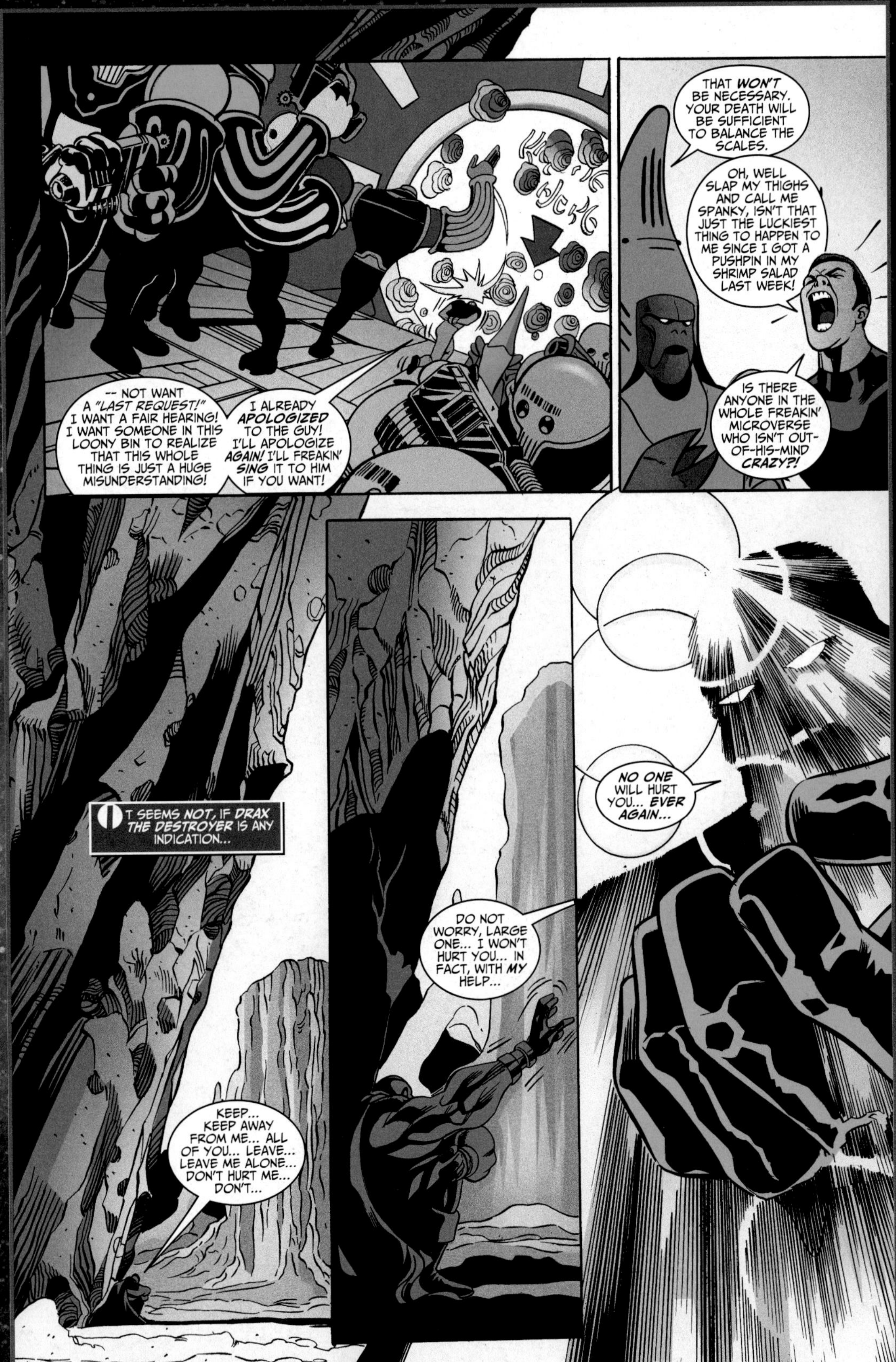

-- NOT WANT A "LAST REQUEST!" I WANT A FAIR HEARING! I WANT SOMEONE IN THIS LOONY BIN TO REALIZE THAT THIS WHOLE THING IS JUST A HUGE MISUNDERSTANDING!
I ALREADY APOLOGIZED TO THE GUY! I'LL APOLOGIZE AGAIN! I'LL FREAKIN' SING IT TO HIM IF YOU WANT!
THAT WON'T BE NECESSARY. YOUR DEATH WILL BE SUFFICIENT TO BALANCE THE SCALES.
OH, WELL SLAP MY THIGHS AND CALL ME SPANKY, ISN'T THAT JUST THE LUCKIEST THING TO HAPPEN TO ME SINCE I GOT A PUSHPIN IN MY SHRIMP SALAD LAST WEEK!
IS THERE ANYONE IN THE WHOLE FREAKIN' MICROVERSE WHO ISN'T OUT-OF-HIS-MIND CRAZY?!
IT SEEMS NOT, IF DRAX THE DESTROYER IS ANY INDICATION...
KEEP... KEEP AWAY FROM ME... ALL OF YOU... LEAVE... LEAVE ME ALONE... DON'T HURT ME... DON'T...
DO NOT WORRY, LARGE ONE... I WON'T HURT YOU... IN FACT, WITH MY HELP...
NO ONE WILL HURT YOU... EVER AGAIN...

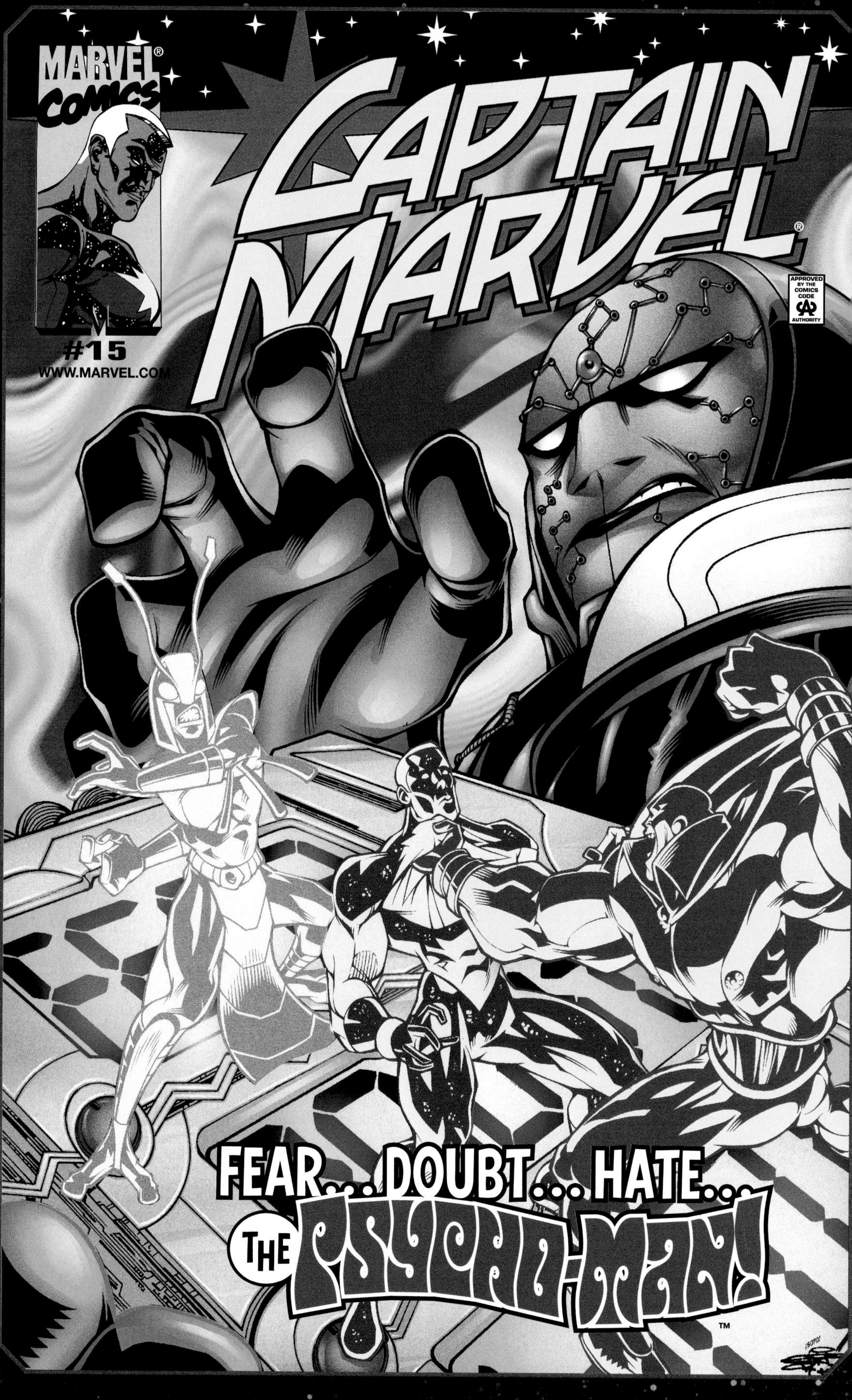

MARVEL®
COMICS
CAPTAIN MARVEL®
APPROVED BY THE COMICS CODE AUTHORITY
#15
WWW.MARVEL.COM
FEAR... DOUBT... HATE...
THE PSYCHO-MAN!
™

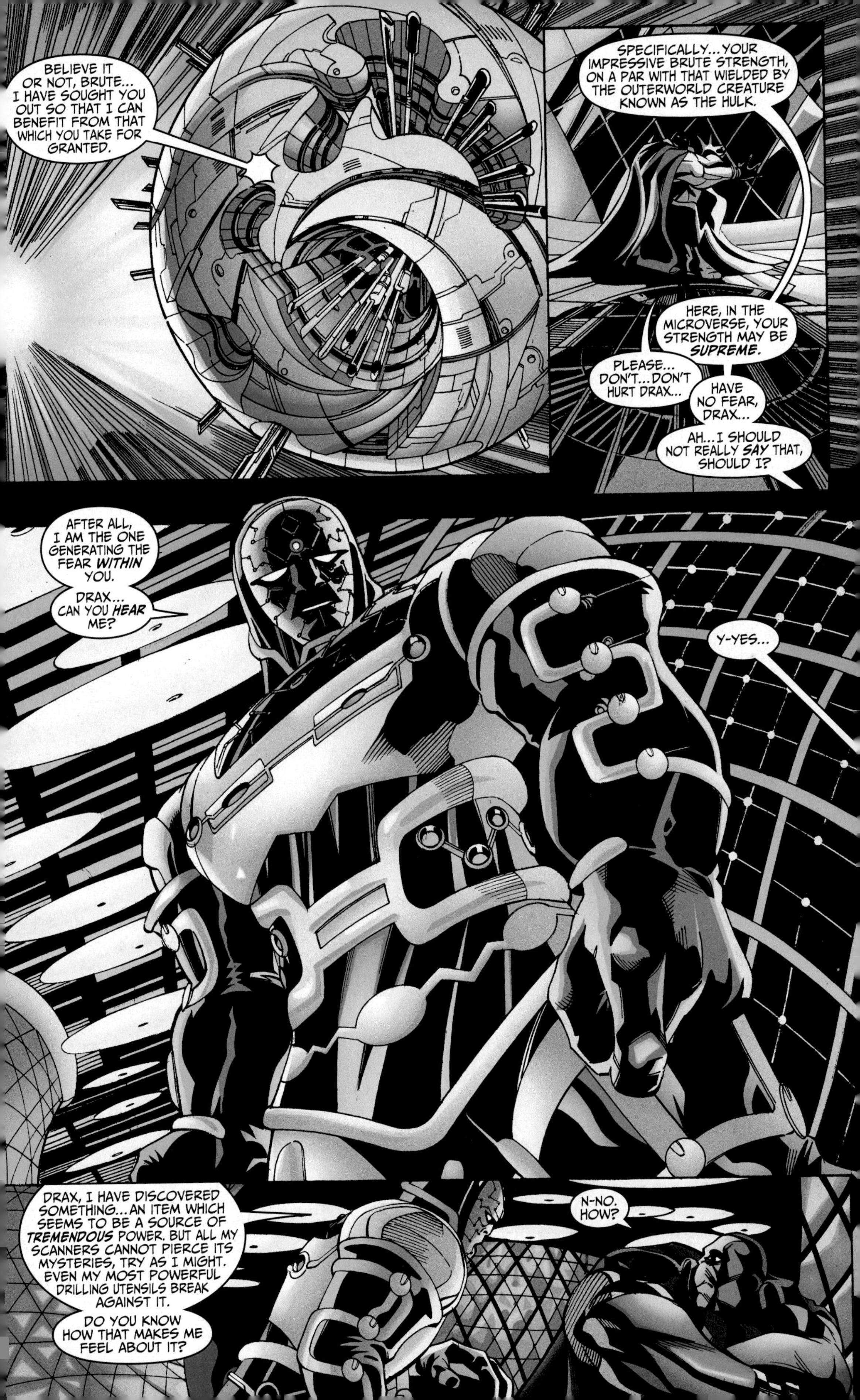
BELIEVE IT OR NOT, BRUTE... I HAVE SOUGHT YOU OUT SO THAT I CAN BENEFIT FROM THAT WHICH YOU TAKE FOR GRANTED.
SPECIFICALLY... YOUR IMPRESSIVE BRUTE STRENGTH, ON A PAR WITH THAT WIELDED BY THE OUTERWORLD CREATURE KNOWN AS THE HULK.
HERE, IN THE MICROVERSE, YOUR STRENGTH MAY BE SUPREME.
PLEASE... DON'T... DON'T HURT DRAX...
HAVE NO FEAR, DRAX...
AH... I SHOULD NOT REALLY SAY THAT, SHOULD I?
AFTER ALL, I AM THE ONE GENERATING THE FEAR WITHIN YOU.
DRAX... CAN YOU HEAR ME?
Y-YES...
DRAX, I HAVE DISCOVERED SOMETHING... AN ITEM WHICH SEEMS TO BE A SOURCE OF TREMENDOUS POWER. BUT ALL MY SCANNERS CANNOT PIERCE ITS MYSTERIES, TRY AS I MIGHT. EVEN MY MOST POWERFUL DRILLING UTENSILS BREAK AGAINST IT.
DO YOU KNOW HOW THAT MAKES ME FEEL ABOUT IT?
N-NO. HOW?

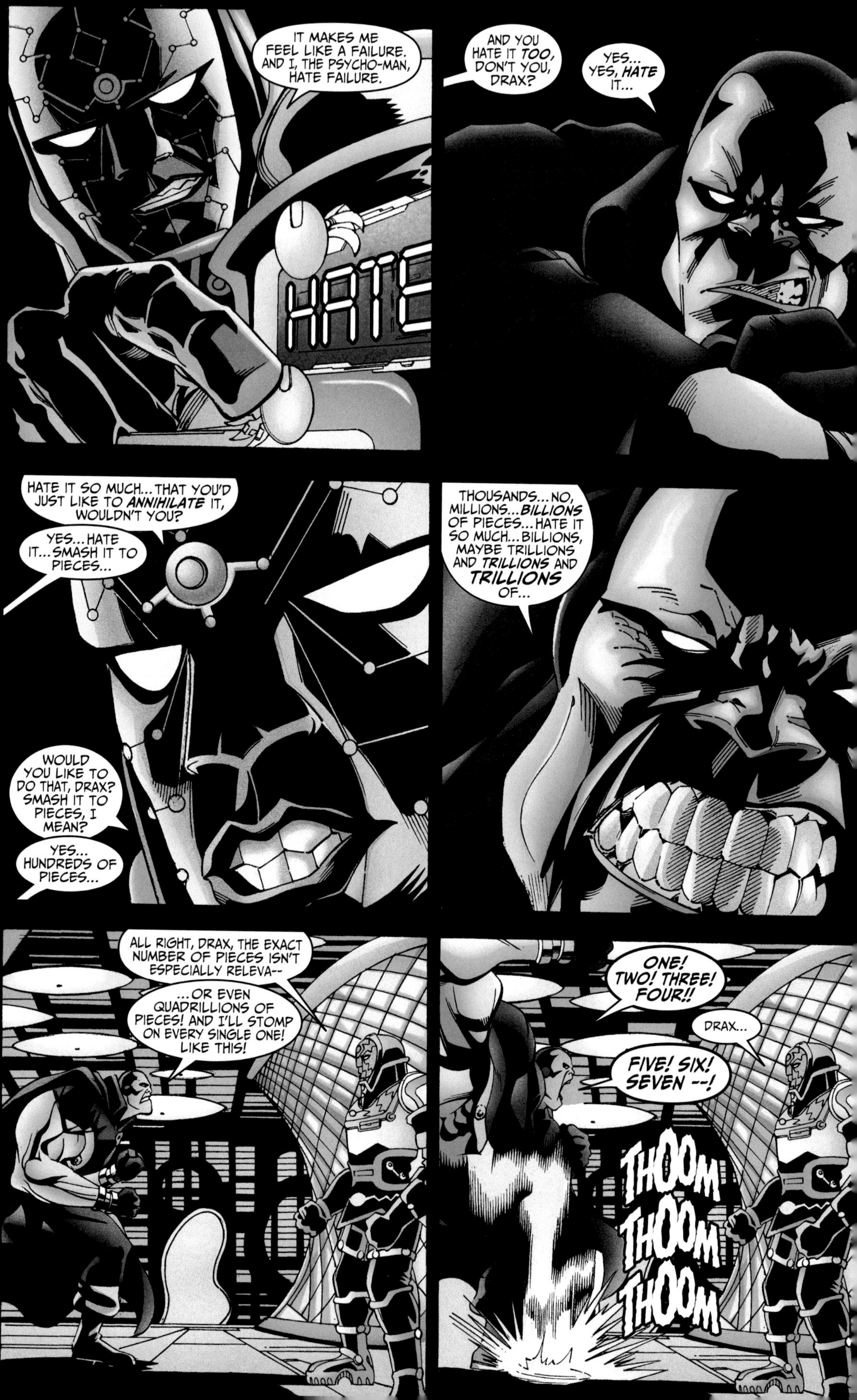
IT MAKES ME FEEL LIKE A FAILURE. AND I, THE PSYCHO-MAN, HATE FAILURE.
HATE
AND YOU HATE IT TOO, DON'T YOU, DRAX?
YES... YES, HATE IT...
HATE IT SO MUCH...THAT YOU'D JUST LIKE TO ANNIHILATE IT, WOULDN'T YOU?
YES...HATE IT...SMASH IT TO PIECES...
WOULD YOU LIKE TO DO THAT, DRAX? SMASH IT TO PIECES, I MEAN?
YES... HUNDREDS OF PIECES...
THOUSANDS...NO, MILLIONS...BILLIONS OF PIECES...HATE IT SO MUCH...BILLIONS, MAYBE TRILLIONS AND TRILLIONS AND TRILLIONS OF...
ALL RIGHT, DRAX, THE EXACT NUMBER OF PIECES ISN'T ESPECIALLY RELEVA--
...OR EVEN QUADRILLIONS OF PIECES! AND I'LL STOMP ON EVERY SINGLE ONE! LIKE THIS!
ONE! TWO! THREE! FOUR!!
DRAX...
FIVE! SIX! SEVEN --!
THOOM THOOM THOOM

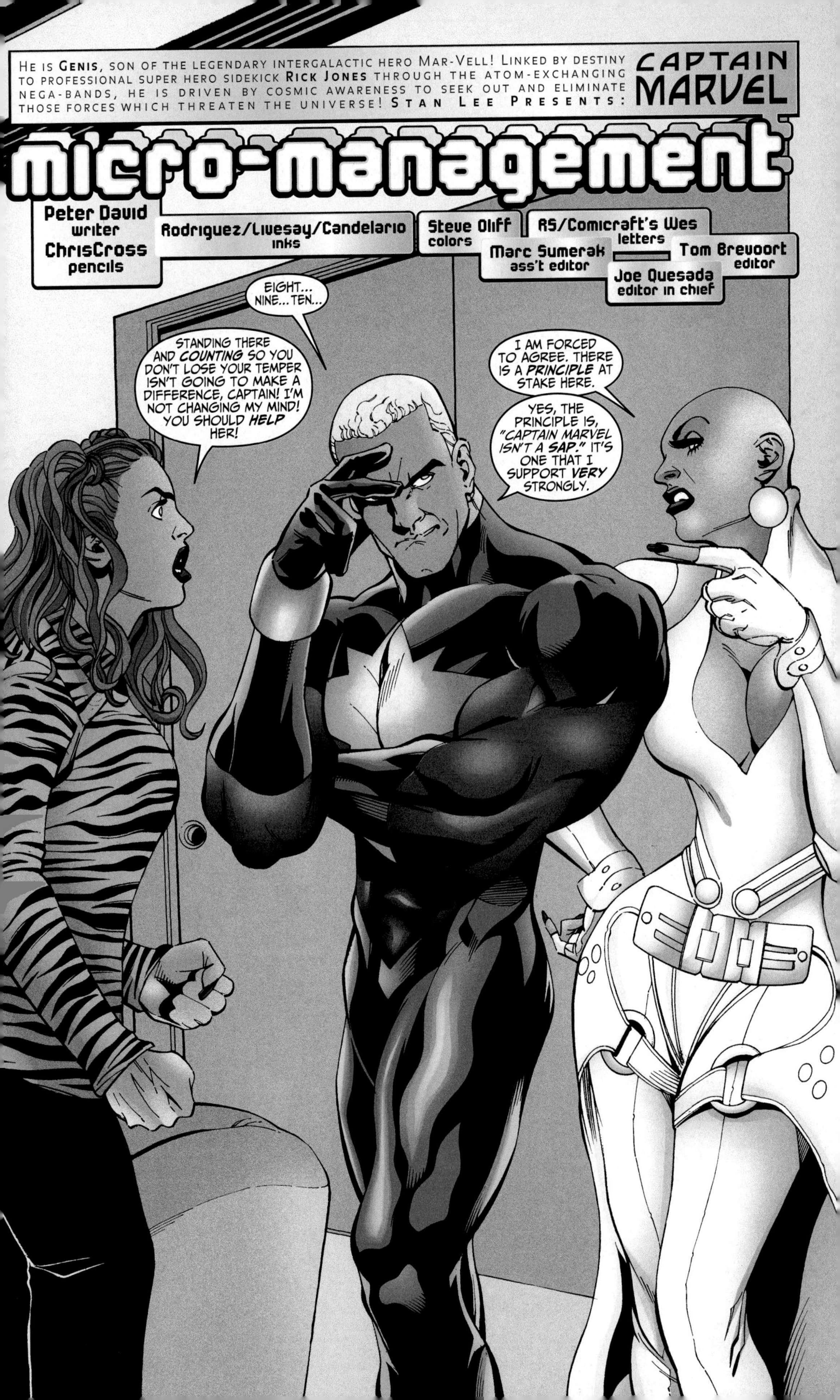

He is Genis, son of the legendary intergalactic hero Mar-Vell! Linked by destiny to professional super hero sidekick Rick Jones through the atom-exchanging nega-bands, he is driven by cosmic awareness to seek out and eliminate those forces which threaten the universe! Stan Lee Presents:
CAPTAIN MARVEL
micro-management
Peter David writer
ChrisCross pencils
Rodriguez/Livesay/Candelario inks
Steve Oliff colors
RS/Comicraft's Wes letters
Marc Sumerak ass't editor
Tom Brevoort editor
Joe Quesada editor in chief
EIGHT... NINE... TEN...
STANDING THERE AND COUNTING SO YOU DON'T LOSE YOUR TEMPER ISN'T GOING TO MAKE A DIFFERENCE, CAPTAIN! I'M NOT CHANGING MY MIND! YOU SHOULD HELP HER!
I AM FORCED TO AGREE. THERE IS A PRINCIPLE AT STAKE HERE.
YES, THE PRINCIPLE IS, "CAPTAIN MARVEL ISN'T A SAP." IT'S ONE THAT I SUPPORT VERY STRONGLY.

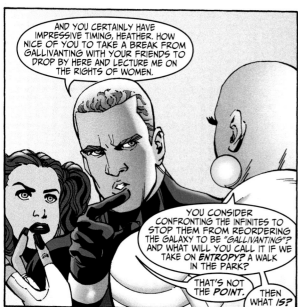

AND YOU CERTAINLY HAVE IMPRESSIVE TIMING, HEATHER. HOW NICE OF YOU TO TAKE A BREAK FROM GALLIVANTING WITH YOUR FRIENDS TO DROP BY HERE AND LECTURE ME ON THE RIGHTS OF WOMEN.

YOU CONSIDER CONFRONTING THE INFINITES TO STOP THEM FROM REORDERING THE GALAXY TO BE "GALLIVANTING"? AND WHAT WILL YOU CALL IT IF WE TAKE ON *ENTROPY?* A WALK IN THE PARK?

THAT'S NOT THE *POINT.*

THEN WHAT *IS?*

THE POINT IS THAT I DON'T APPRECIATE YOU AND MARLO GANGING UP ON ME, TRYING TO PRESSURE ME INTO BEING --

A HERO?

A *SAP!* JUST AS I SAID.

YOU WANT ME TO GO FLYING OFF TO THE KREE HOMEWORLD IN ORDER TO HELP UNA-ROGG. TO SAVE HER FROM BEING *"PSYCHICALLY MUTILATED"* OR SOMESUCH.

TOTALLY OVERLOOKING THE FACT THAT SHE'S THE DAUGHTER OF MY FATHER'S GREATEST ENEMY... THAT SHE TRIED TO *KILL* ME... AND THAT IF I WAS IN TROUBLE, SHE WOULDN'T RAISE A FINGER TO HELP ME.

HEROISM, GENIS, ISN'T ABOUT QUID PRO QUO. IT'S ABOUT STANDING UP FOR AN IDEAL.

KREE WOMEN ARE BEING SUBJECTED TO PAINFUL PROCEDURES THAT DEPRIVE THEM OF THEIR ABILITY TO GIVE AND RECEIVE PLEASURE BECAUSE THE MEN FEEL THREATENED BY SUCH ABILITIES. THEY WANT TO CONTROL THEM.

IT'S NOT *RIGHT.* HEROES ARE SUPPOSED TO FIGHT FOR WHAT'S RIGHT --!

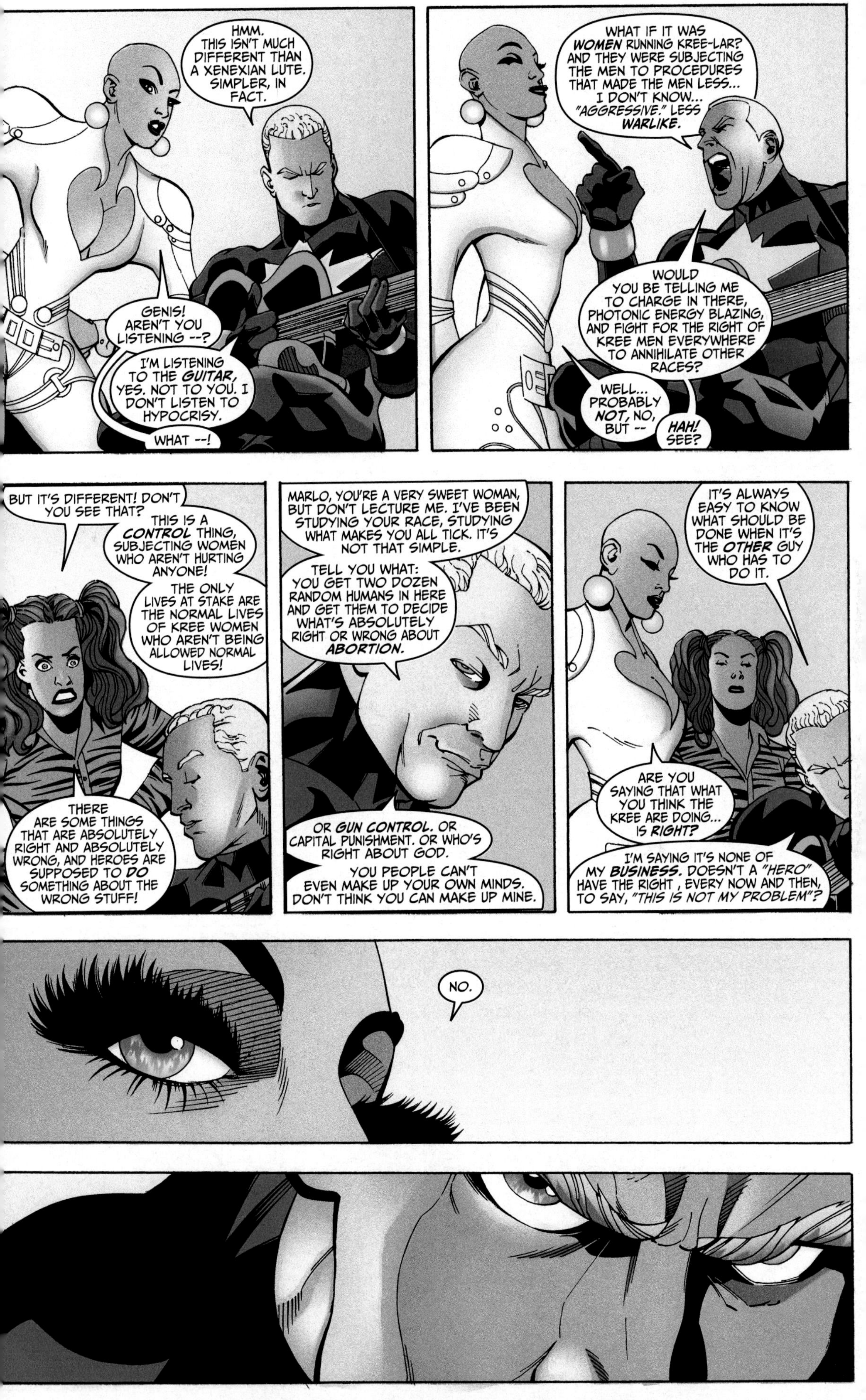
HMM. THIS ISN'T MUCH DIFFERENT THAN A XENEXIAN LUTE. SIMPLER, IN FACT.
GENIS! AREN'T YOU LISTENING --?
I'M LISTENING TO THE GUITAR, YES. NOT TO YOU. I DON'T LISTEN TO HYPOCRISY.
WHAT --!
WHAT IF IT WAS WOMEN RUNNING KREE-LAR? AND THEY WERE SUBJECTING THE MEN TO PROCEDURES THAT MADE THE MEN LESS... I DON'T KNOW... "AGGRESSIVE." LESS WARLIKE.
WOULD YOU BE TELLING ME TO CHARGE IN THERE, PHOTONIC ENERGY BLAZING, AND FIGHT FOR THE RIGHT OF KREE MEN EVERYWHERE TO ANNIHILATE OTHER RACES?
WELL... PROBABLY NOT, NO, BUT --
HAH! SEE?
BUT IT'S DIFFERENT! DON'T YOU SEE THAT?
THIS IS A CONTROL THING, SUBJECTING WOMEN WHO AREN'T HURTING ANYONE!
THE ONLY LIVES AT STAKE ARE THE NORMAL LIVES OF KREE WOMEN WHO AREN'T BEING ALLOWED NORMAL LIVES!
THERE ARE SOME THINGS THAT ARE ABSOLUTELY RIGHT AND ABSOLUTELY WRONG, AND HEROES ARE SUPPOSED TO DO SOMETHING ABOUT THE WRONG STUFF!
MARLO, YOU'RE A VERY SWEET WOMAN, BUT DON'T LECTURE ME. I'VE BEEN STUDYING YOUR RACE, STUDYING WHAT MAKES YOU ALL TICK. IT'S NOT THAT SIMPLE.
TELL YOU WHAT: YOU GET TWO DOZEN RANDOM HUMANS IN HERE AND GET THEM TO DECIDE WHAT'S ABSOLUTELY RIGHT OR WRONG ABOUT ABORTION.
OR GUN CONTROL. OR CAPITAL PUNISHMENT. OR WHO'S RIGHT ABOUT GOD.
YOU PEOPLE CAN'T EVEN MAKE UP YOUR OWN MINDS. DON'T THINK YOU CAN MAKE UP MINE.
IT'S ALWAYS EASY TO KNOW WHAT SHOULD BE DONE WHEN IT'S THE OTHER GUY WHO HAS TO DO IT.
ARE YOU SAYING THAT WHAT YOU THINK THE KREE ARE DOING... IS RIGHT?
I'M SAYING IT'S NONE OF MY BUSINESS. DOESN'T A "HERO" HAVE THE RIGHT , EVERY NOW AND THEN, TO SAY, "THIS IS NOT MY PROBLEM"?
NO.

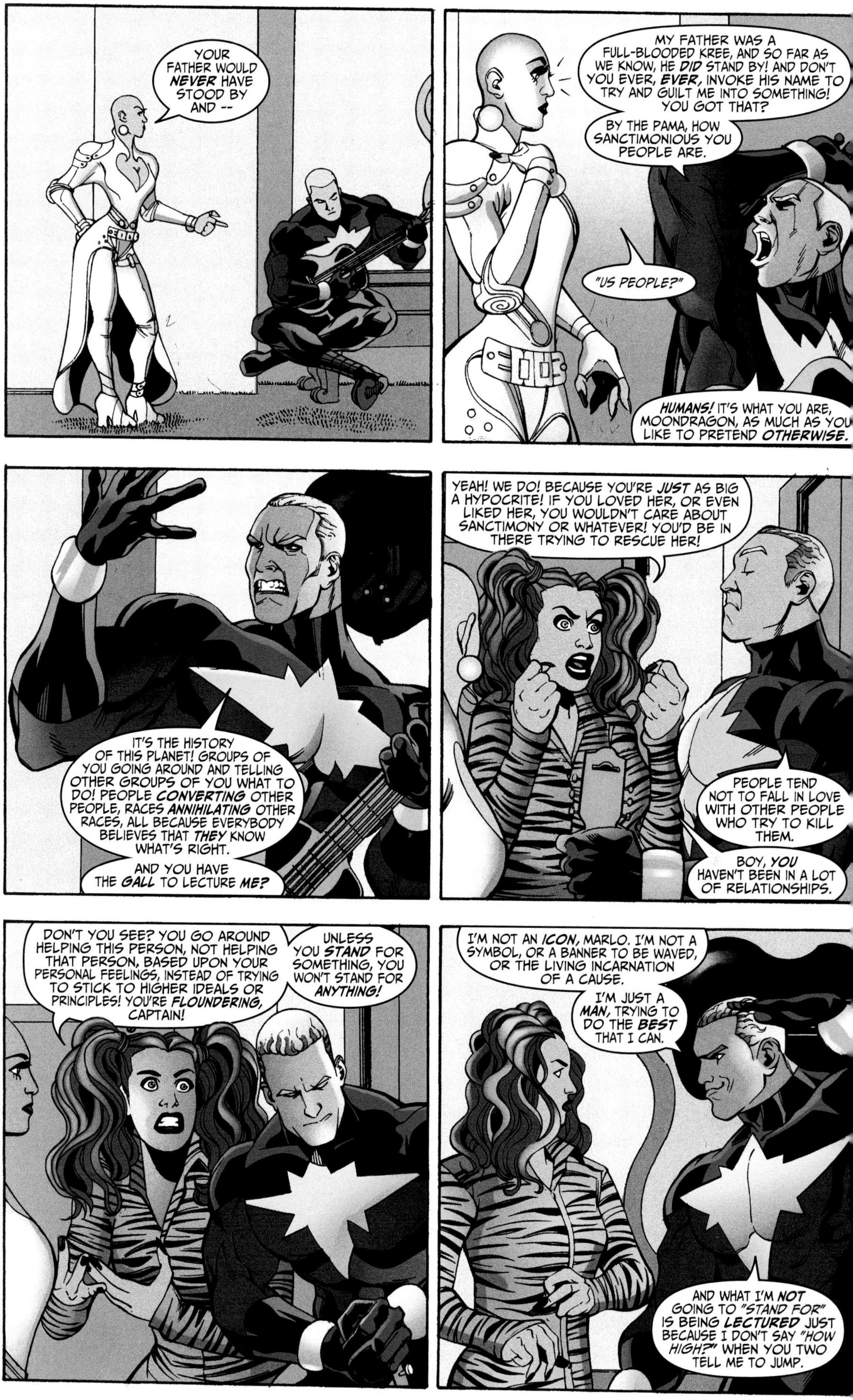

YOUR FATHER WOULD NEVER HAVE STOOD BY AND --
MY FATHER WAS A FULL-BLOODED KREE, AND SO FAR AS WE KNOW, HE DID STAND BY! AND DON'T YOU EVER, EVER, INVOKE HIS NAME TO TRY AND GUILT ME INTO SOMETHING! YOU GOT THAT?
BY THE PAMA, HOW SANCTIMONIOUS YOU PEOPLE ARE.
"US PEOPLE?"
HUMANS! IT'S WHAT YOU ARE, MOONDRAGON, AS MUCH AS YOU LIKE TO PRETEND OTHERWISE.
IT'S THE HISTORY OF THIS PLANET! GROUPS OF YOU GOING AROUND AND TELLING OTHER GROUPS OF YOU WHAT TO DO! PEOPLE CONVERTING OTHER PEOPLE, RACES ANNIHILATING OTHER RACES, ALL BECAUSE EVERYBODY BELIEVES THAT THEY KNOW WHAT'S RIGHT.
AND YOU HAVE THE GALL TO LECTURE ME?
YEAH! WE DO! BECAUSE YOU'RE JUST AS BIG A HYPOCRITE! IF YOU LOVED HER, OR EVEN LIKED HER, YOU WOULDN'T CARE ABOUT SANCTIMONY OR WHATEVER! YOU'D BE IN THERE TRYING TO RESCUE HER!
PEOPLE TEND NOT TO FALL IN LOVE WITH OTHER PEOPLE WHO TRY TO KILL THEM.
BOY, YOU HAVEN'T BEEN IN A LOT OF RELATIONSHIPS.
DON'T YOU SEE? YOU GO AROUND HELPING THIS PERSON, NOT HELPING THAT PERSON, BASED UPON YOUR PERSONAL FEELINGS, INSTEAD OF TRYING TO STICK TO HIGHER IDEALS OR PRINCIPLES! YOU'RE FLOUNDERING, CAPTAIN!
UNLESS YOU STAND FOR SOMETHING, YOU WON'T STAND FOR ANYTHING!
I'M NOT AN ICON, MARLO. I'M NOT A SYMBOL, OR A BANNER TO BE WAVED, OR THE LIVING INCARNATION OF A CAUSE.
I'M JUST A MAN, TRYING TO DO THE BEST THAT I CAN.
AND WHAT I'M NOT GOING TO "STAND FOR" IS BEING LECTURED JUST BECAUSE I DON'T SAY "HOW HIGH?" WHEN YOU TWO TELL ME TO JUMP.

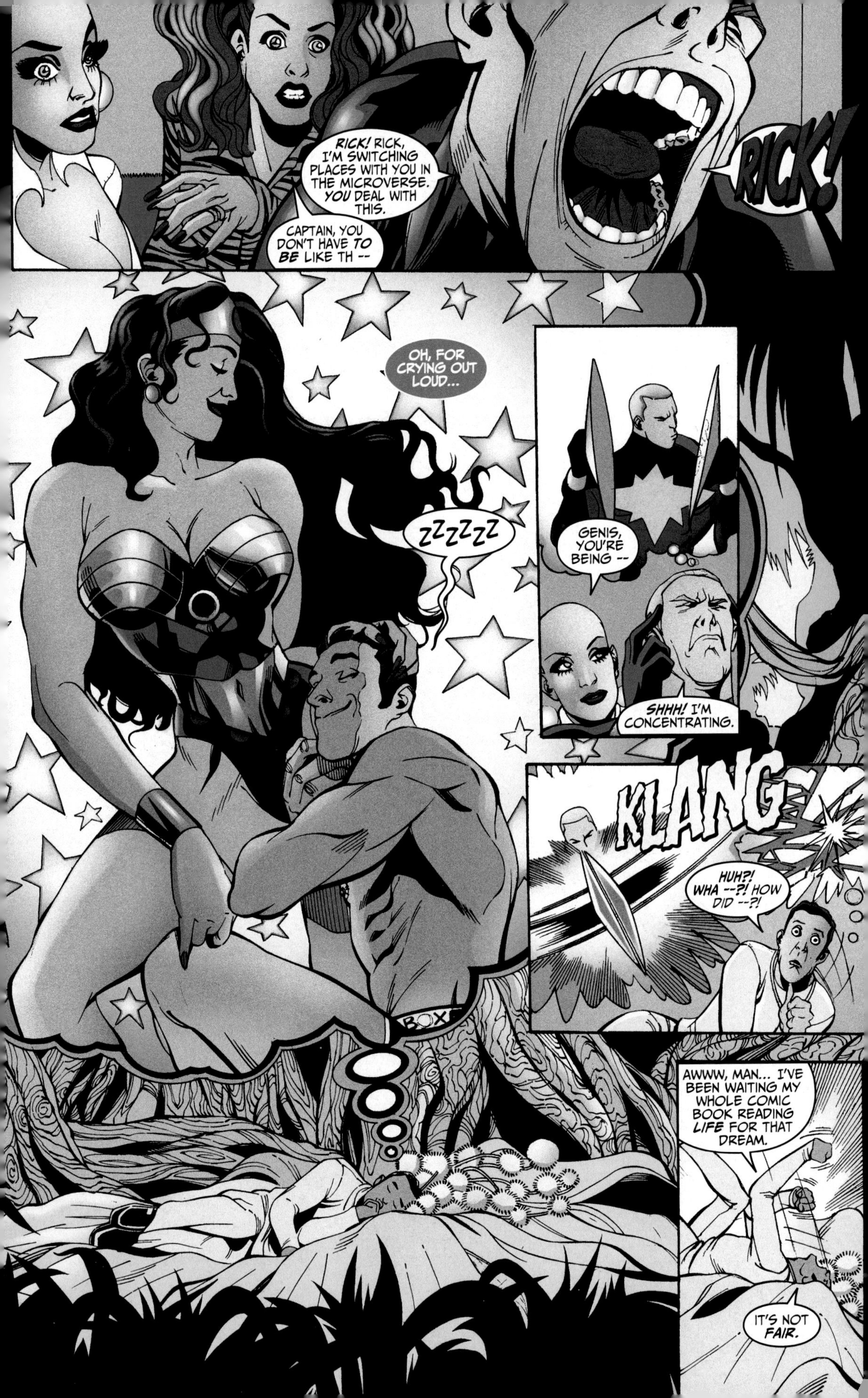
RICK! RICK, I'M SWITCHING PLACES WITH YOU IN THE MICROVERSE. YOU DEAL WITH THIS.
CAPTAIN, YOU DON'T HAVE TO BE LIKE TH --
RICK!
OH, FOR CRYING OUT LOUD...
ZZZZZZ
GENIS, YOU'RE BEING --
SHHH! I'M CONCENTRATING.
KLANG
HUH?! WHA --?! HOW DID --?!
AWWW, MAN... I'VE BEEN WAITING MY WHOLE COMIC BOOK READING LIFE FOR THAT DREAM.
IT'S NOT FAIR.

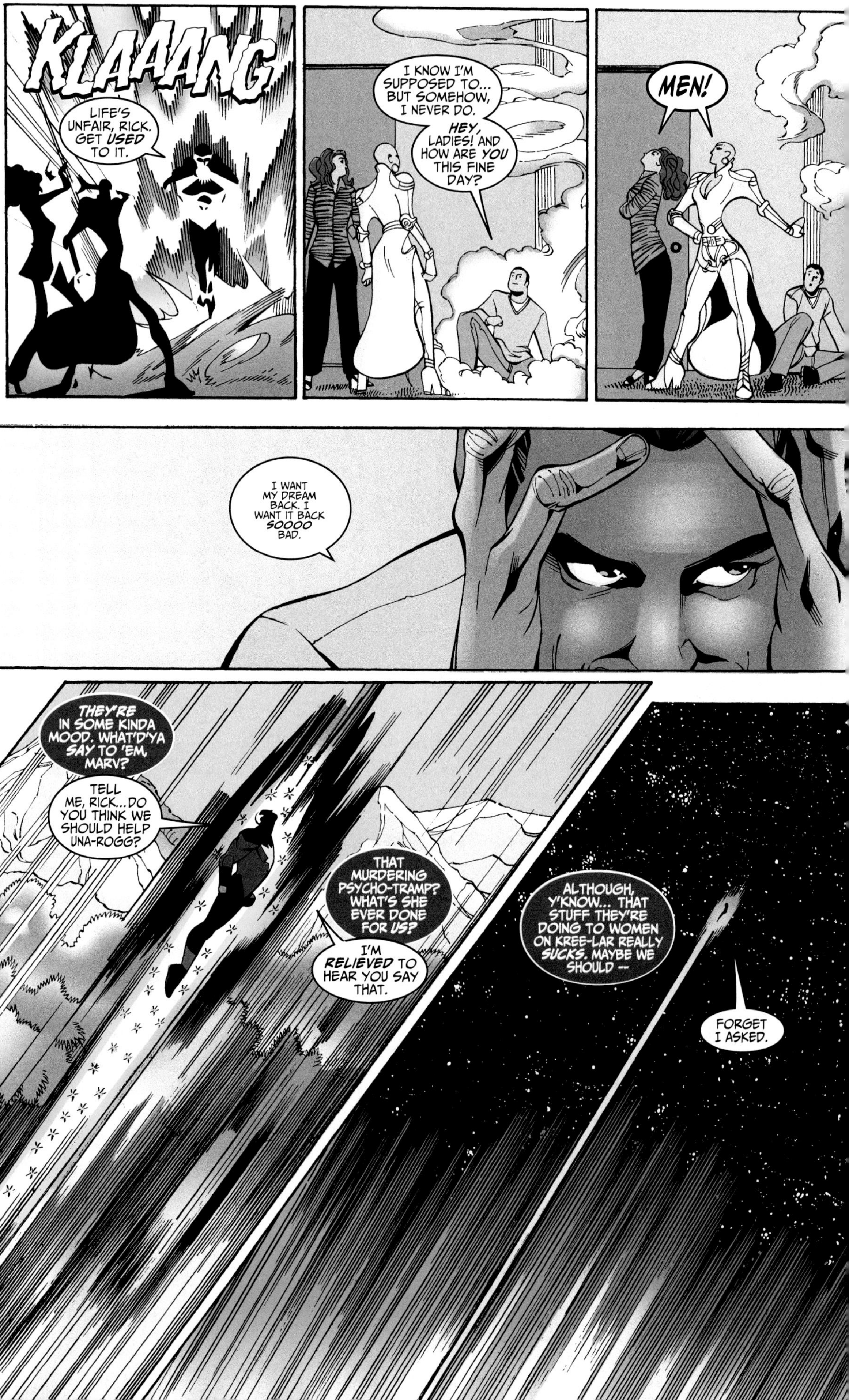
KLAAANG
LIFE'S UNFAIR, RICK. GET USED TO IT.
I KNOW I'M SUPPOSED TO... BUT SOMEHOW, I NEVER DO.
HEY, LADIES! AND HOW ARE YOU THIS FINE DAY?
MEN!
I WANT MY DREAM BACK. I WANT IT BACK SOOOO BAD.
THEY'RE IN SOME KINDA MOOD. WHAT'D'YA SAY TO 'EM, MARV?
TELL ME, RICK...DO YOU THINK WE SHOULD HELP UNA-ROGG?
THAT MURDERING PSYCHO-TRAMP? WHAT'S SHE EVER DONE FOR US?
I'M RELIEVED TO HEAR YOU SAY THAT.
ALTHOUGH, Y'KNOW... THAT STUFF THEY'RE DOING TO WOMEN ON KREE-LAR REALLY SUCKS. MAYBE WE SHOULD --
FORGET I ASKED.

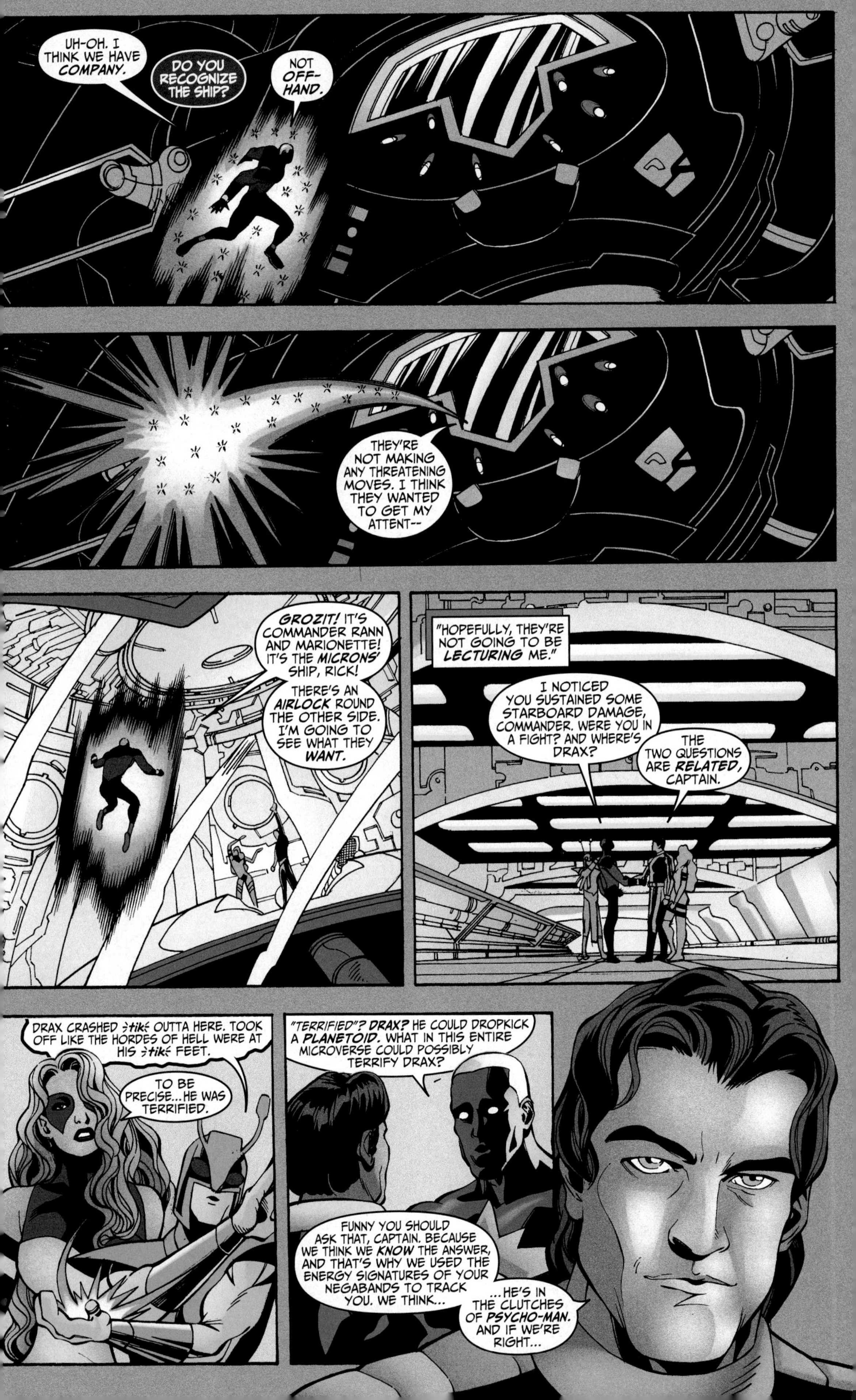
UH-OH. I THINK WE HAVE COMPANY.
DO YOU RECOGNIZE THE SHIP?
NOT OFF-HAND.
THEY'RE NOT MAKING ANY THREATENING MOVES. I THINK THEY WANTED TO GET MY ATTENT--
GROZIT! IT'S COMMANDER RANN AND MARIONETTE! IT'S THE MICRONS' SHIP, RICK!
THERE'S AN AIRLOCK ROUND THE OTHER SIDE. I'M GOING TO SEE WHAT THEY WANT.
"HOPEFULLY, THEY'RE NOT GOING TO BE LECTURING ME."
I NOTICED YOU SUSTAINED SOME STARBOARD DAMAGE, COMMANDER. WERE YOU IN A FIGHT? AND WHERE'S DRAX?
THE TWO QUESTIONS ARE RELATED, CAPTAIN.
DRAX CRASHED ⋟tik⋞ OUTTA HERE. TOOK OFF LIKE THE HORDES OF HELL WERE AT HIS ⋟tik⋞ FEET.
TO BE PRECISE...HE WAS TERRIFIED.
"TERRIFIED"? DRAX? HE COULD DROPKICK A PLANETOID. WHAT IN THIS ENTIRE MICROVERSE COULD POSSIBLY TERRIFY DRAX?
FUNNY YOU SHOULD ASK THAT, CAPTAIN. BECAUSE WE THINK WE KNOW THE ANSWER, AND THAT'S WHY WE USED THE ENERGY SIGNATURES OF YOUR NEGABANDS TO TRACK YOU. WE THINK...
...HE'S IN THE CLUTCHES OF PSYCHO-MAN. AND IF WE'RE RIGHT...

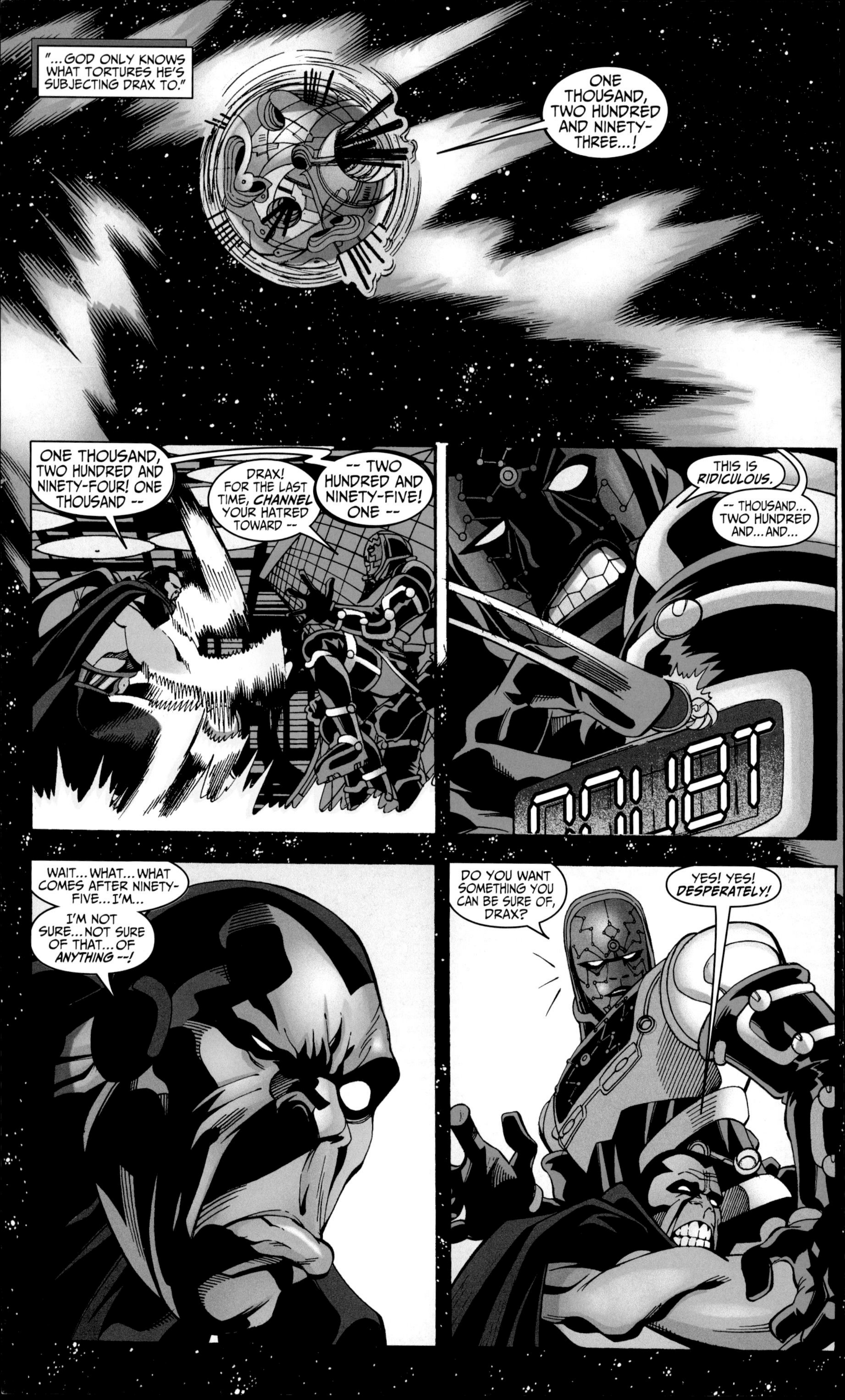

"...GOD ONLY KNOWS WHAT TORTURES HE'S SUBJECTING DRAX TO."
ONE THOUSAND, TWO HUNDRED AND NINETY-THREE...!
ONE THOUSAND, TWO HUNDRED AND NINETY-FOUR! ONE THOUSAND --
DRAX! FOR THE LAST TIME, CHANNEL YOUR HATRED TOWARD --
-- TWO HUNDRED AND NINETY-FIVE! ONE --
THIS IS RIDICULOUS.
-- THOUSAND... TWO HUNDRED AND...AND...
WAIT...WHAT...WHAT COMES AFTER NINETY-FIVE...I'M...
I'M NOT SURE...NOT SURE OF THAT...OF ANYTHING --!
DO YOU WANT SOMETHING YOU CAN BE SURE OF, DRAX?
YES! YES! DESPERATELY!

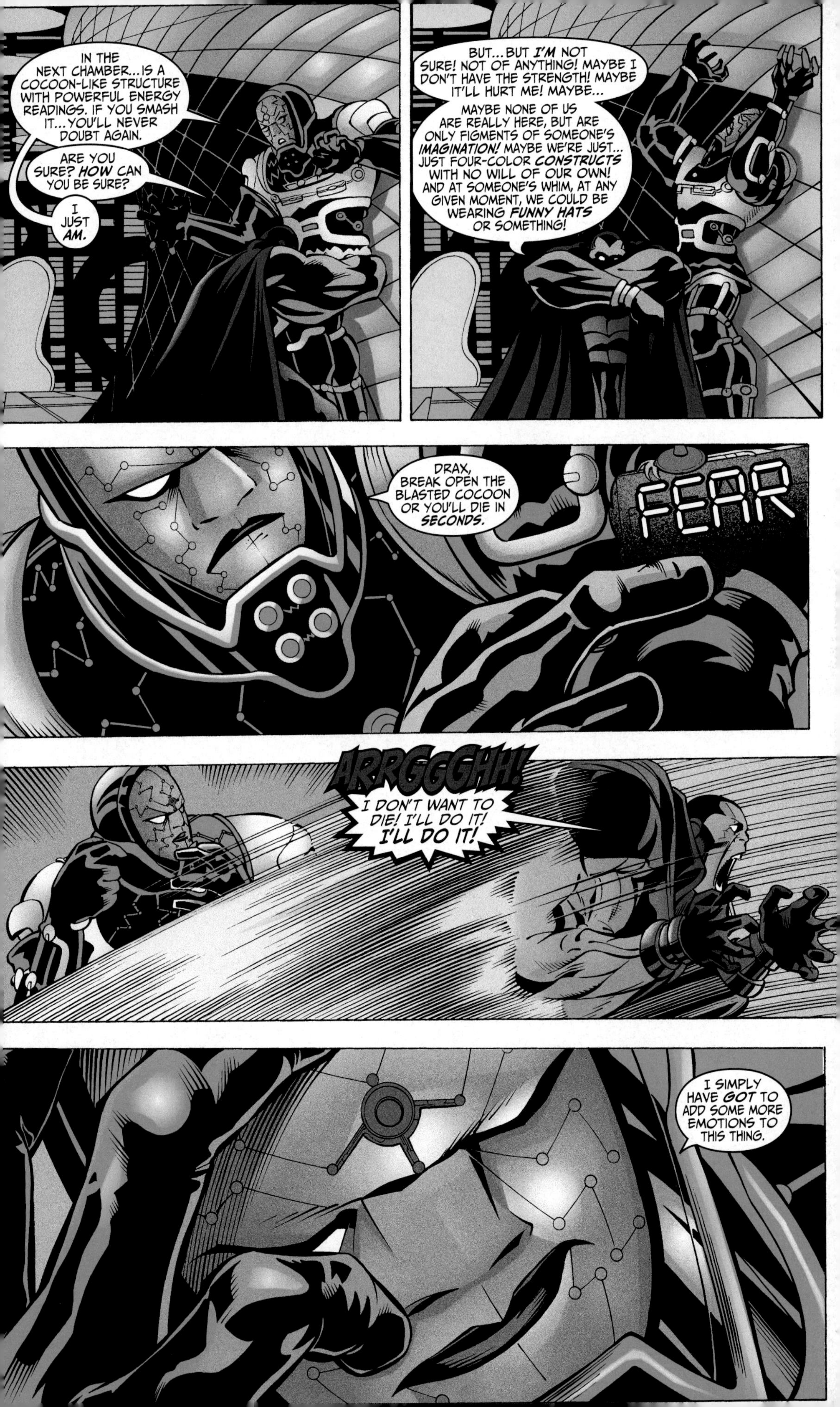

IN THE NEXT CHAMBER...IS A COCOON-LIKE STRUCTURE WITH POWERFUL ENERGY READINGS. IF YOU SMASH IT...YOU'LL NEVER DOUBT AGAIN.
ARE YOU SURE? *HOW* CAN YOU BE SURE?
I JUST *AM.*
BUT...BUT *I'M* NOT SURE! NOT OF ANYTHING! MAYBE I DON'T HAVE THE STRENGTH! MAYBE IT'LL HURT ME! MAYBE...
MAYBE NONE OF US ARE REALLY HERE, BUT ARE ONLY FIGMENTS OF SOMEONE'S *IMAGINATION!* MAYBE WE'RE JUST... JUST FOUR-COLOR *CONSTRUCTS* WITH NO WILL OF OUR OWN! AND AT SOMEONE'S WHIM, AT ANY GIVEN MOMENT, WE COULD BE WEARING *FUNNY HATS* OR SOMETHING!
DRAX, BREAK OPEN THE BLASTED COCOON OR YOU'LL DIE IN *SECONDS.*
FEAR
ARRGGGHH!
I DON'T WANT TO DIE! I'LL DO IT! *I'LL DO IT!*
I SIMPLY HAVE *GOT* TO ADD SOME MORE EMOTIONS TO THIS THING.

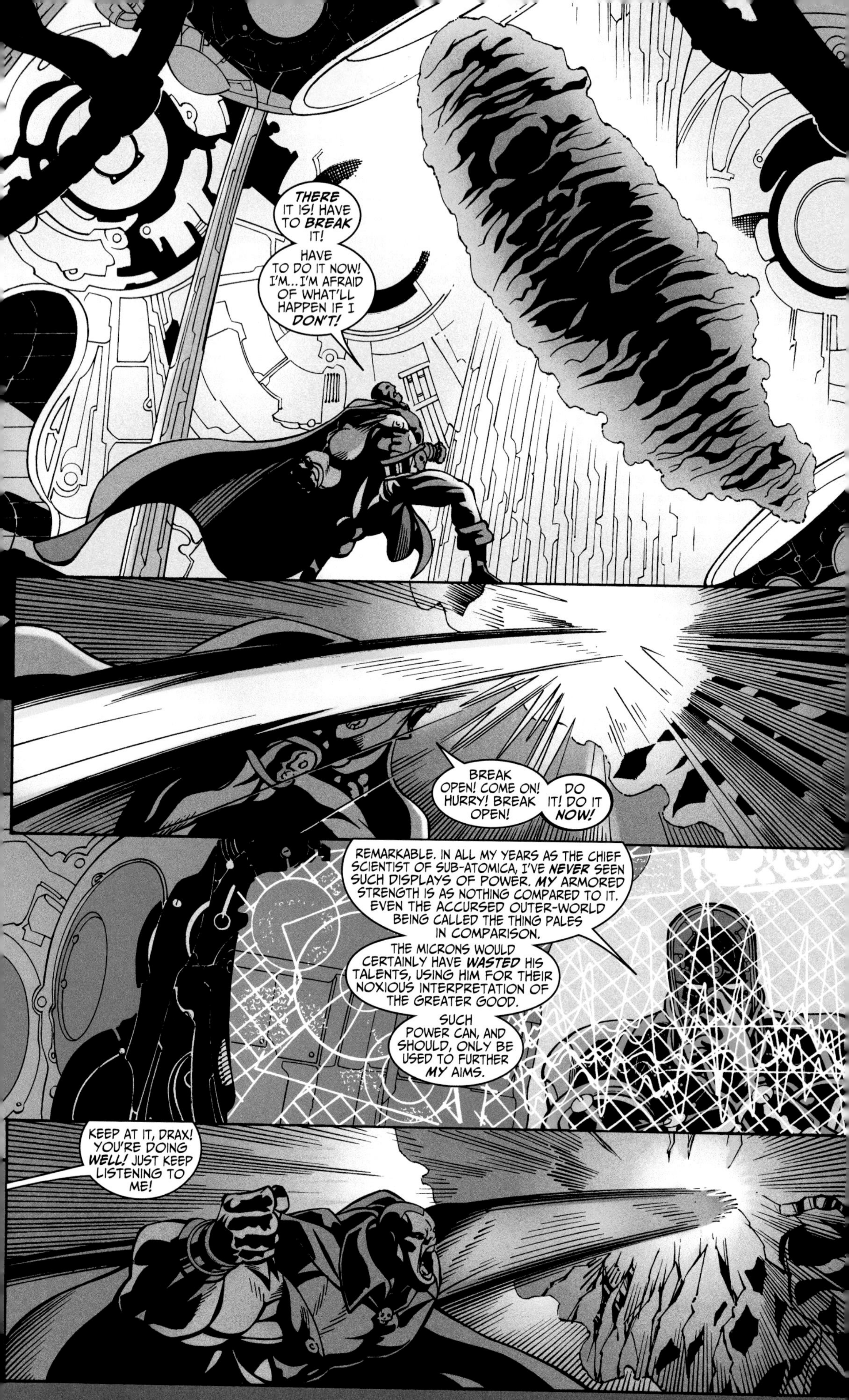
THERE IT IS! HAVE TO BREAK IT!
HAVE TO DO IT NOW! I'M...I'M AFRAID OF WHAT'LL HAPPEN IF I DON'T!
BREAK OPEN! COME ON! HURRY! BREAK OPEN!
DO IT! DO IT NOW!
REMARKABLE. IN ALL MY YEARS AS THE CHIEF SCIENTIST OF SUB-ATOMICA, I'VE NEVER SEEN SUCH DISPLAYS OF POWER. MY ARMORED STRENGTH IS AS NOTHING COMPARED TO IT. EVEN THE ACCURSED OUTER-WORLD BEING CALLED THE THING PALES IN COMPARISON.
THE MICRONS WOULD CERTAINLY HAVE WASTED HIS TALENTS, USING HIM FOR THEIR NOXIOUS INTERPRETATION OF THE GREATER GOOD.
SUCH POWER CAN, AND SHOULD, ONLY BE USED TO FURTHER MY AIMS.
KEEP AT IT, DRAX! YOU'RE DOING WELL! JUST KEEP LISTENING TO ME!

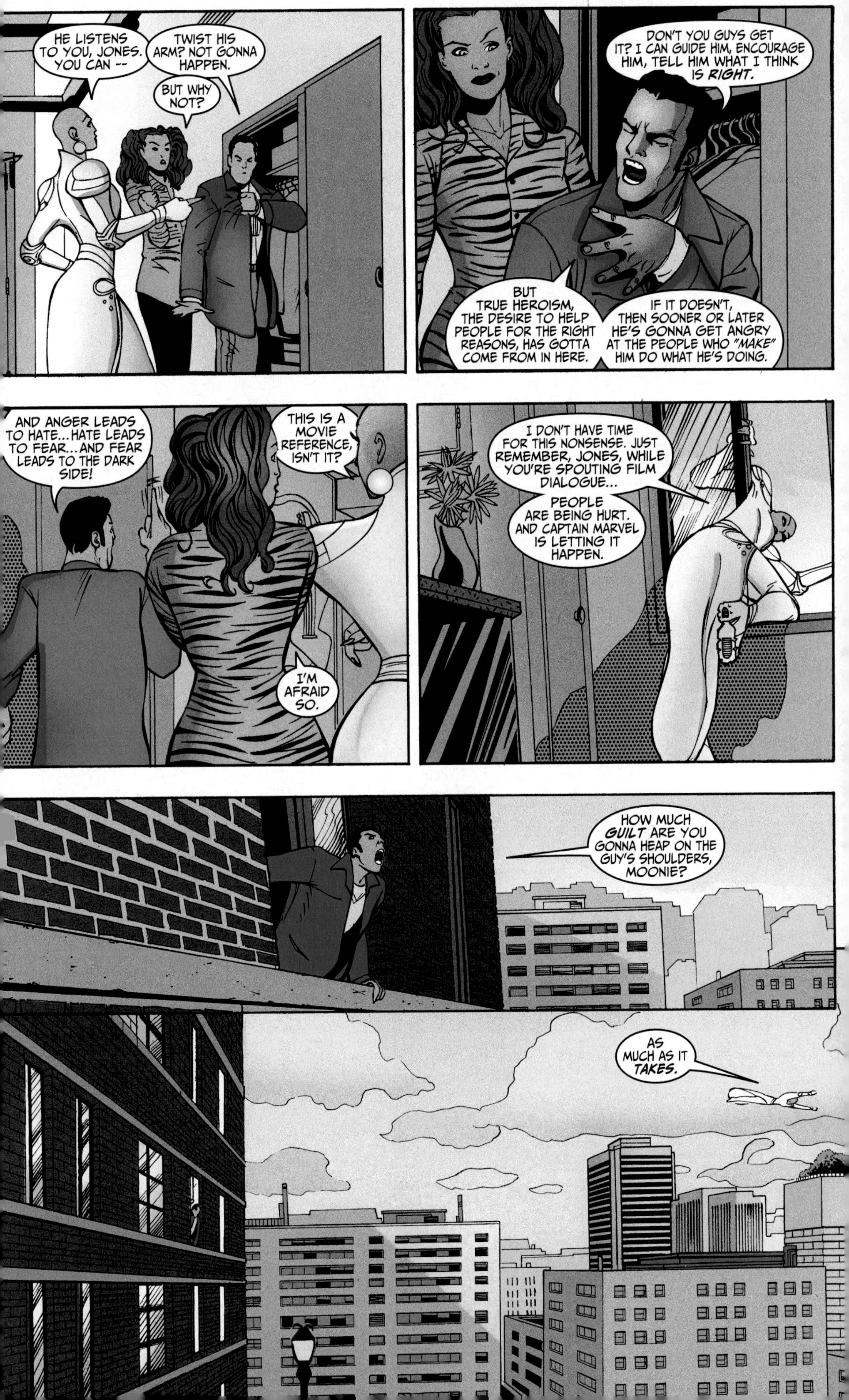
HE LISTENS TO YOU, JONES. YOU CAN --
TWIST HIS ARM? NOT GONNA HAPPEN.
BUT WHY NOT?
DON'T YOU GUYS GET IT? I CAN GUIDE HIM, ENCOURAGE HIM, TELL HIM WHAT I THINK IS *RIGHT.*
BUT TRUE HEROISM, THE DESIRE TO HELP PEOPLE FOR THE RIGHT REASONS, HAS GOTTA COME FROM IN HERE.
IF IT DOESN'T, THEN SOONER OR LATER HE'S GONNA GET ANGRY AT THE PEOPLE WHO "MAKE" HIM DO WHAT HE'S DOING.
AND ANGER LEADS TO HATE...HATE LEADS TO FEAR...AND FEAR LEADS TO THE DARK SIDE!
THIS IS A MOVIE REFERENCE, ISN'T IT?
I'M AFRAID SO.
I DON'T HAVE TIME FOR THIS NONSENSE. JUST REMEMBER, JONES, WHILE YOU'RE SPOUTING FILM DIALOGUE...
PEOPLE ARE BEING HURT. AND CAPTAIN MARVEL IS LETTING IT HAPPEN.
HOW MUCH *GUILT* ARE YOU GONNA HEAP ON THE GUY'S SHOULDERS, MOONIE?
AS MUCH AS IT *TAKES.*

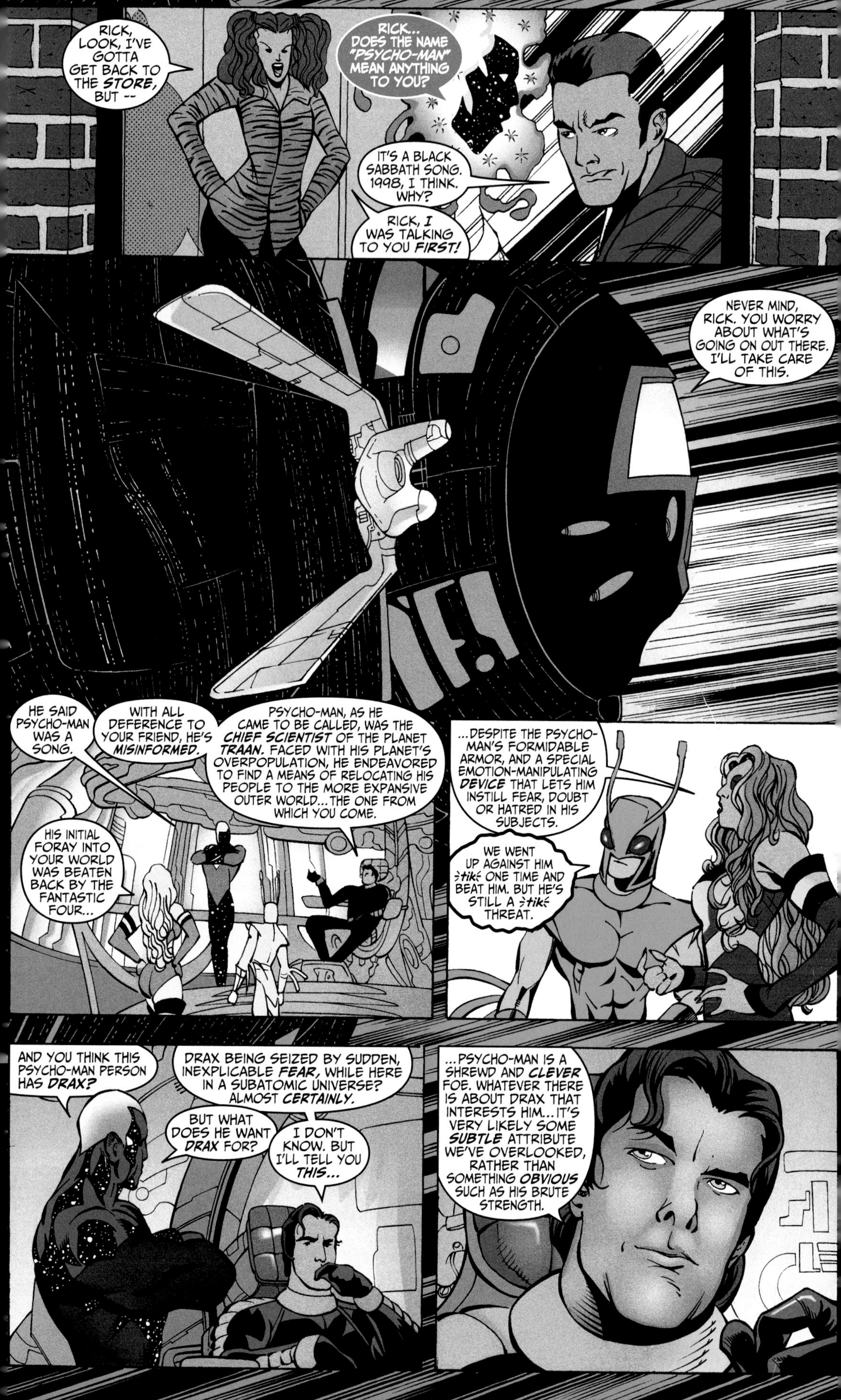
RICK, LOOK, I'VE GOTTA GET BACK TO THE STORE, BUT --
RICK... DOES THE NAME "PSYCHO-MAN" MEAN ANYTHING TO YOU?
IT'S A BLACK SABBATH SONG. 1998, I THINK. WHY?
RICK, I WAS TALKING TO YOU FIRST!
NEVER MIND, RICK. YOU WORRY ABOUT WHAT'S GOING ON OUT THERE. I'LL TAKE CARE OF THIS.
HE SAID PSYCHO-MAN WAS A SONG.
WITH ALL DEFERENCE TO YOUR FRIEND, HE'S MISINFORMED.
PSYCHO-MAN, AS HE CAME TO BE CALLED, WAS THE CHIEF SCIENTIST OF THE PLANET TRAAN. FACED WITH HIS PLANET'S OVERPOPULATION, HE ENDEAVORED TO FIND A MEANS OF RELOCATING HIS PEOPLE TO THE MORE EXPANSIVE OUTER WORLD... THE ONE FROM WHICH YOU COME.
HIS INITIAL FORAY INTO YOUR WORLD WAS BEATEN BACK BY THE FANTASTIC FOUR...
...DESPITE THE PSYCHO-MAN'S FORMIDABLE ARMOR, AND A SPECIAL EMOTION-MANIPULATING DEVICE THAT LETS HIM INSTILL FEAR, DOUBT OR HATRED IN HIS SUBJECTS.
WE WENT UP AGAINST HIM *tik* ONE TIME AND BEAT HIM. BUT HE'S STILL A *tik* THREAT.
AND YOU THINK THIS PSYCHO-MAN PERSON HAS DRAX?
DRAX BEING SEIZED BY SUDDEN, INEXPLICABLE FEAR, WHILE HERE IN A SUBATOMIC UNIVERSE? ALMOST CERTAINLY.
BUT WHAT DOES HE WANT DRAX FOR?
I DON'T KNOW. BUT I'LL TELL YOU THIS...
...PSYCHO-MAN IS A SHREWD AND CLEVER FOE. WHATEVER THERE IS ABOUT DRAX THAT INTERESTS HIM... IT'S VERY LIKELY SOME SUBTLE ATTRIBUTE WE'VE OVERLOOKED, RATHER THAN SOMETHING OBVIOUS SUCH AS HIS BRUTE STRENGTH.

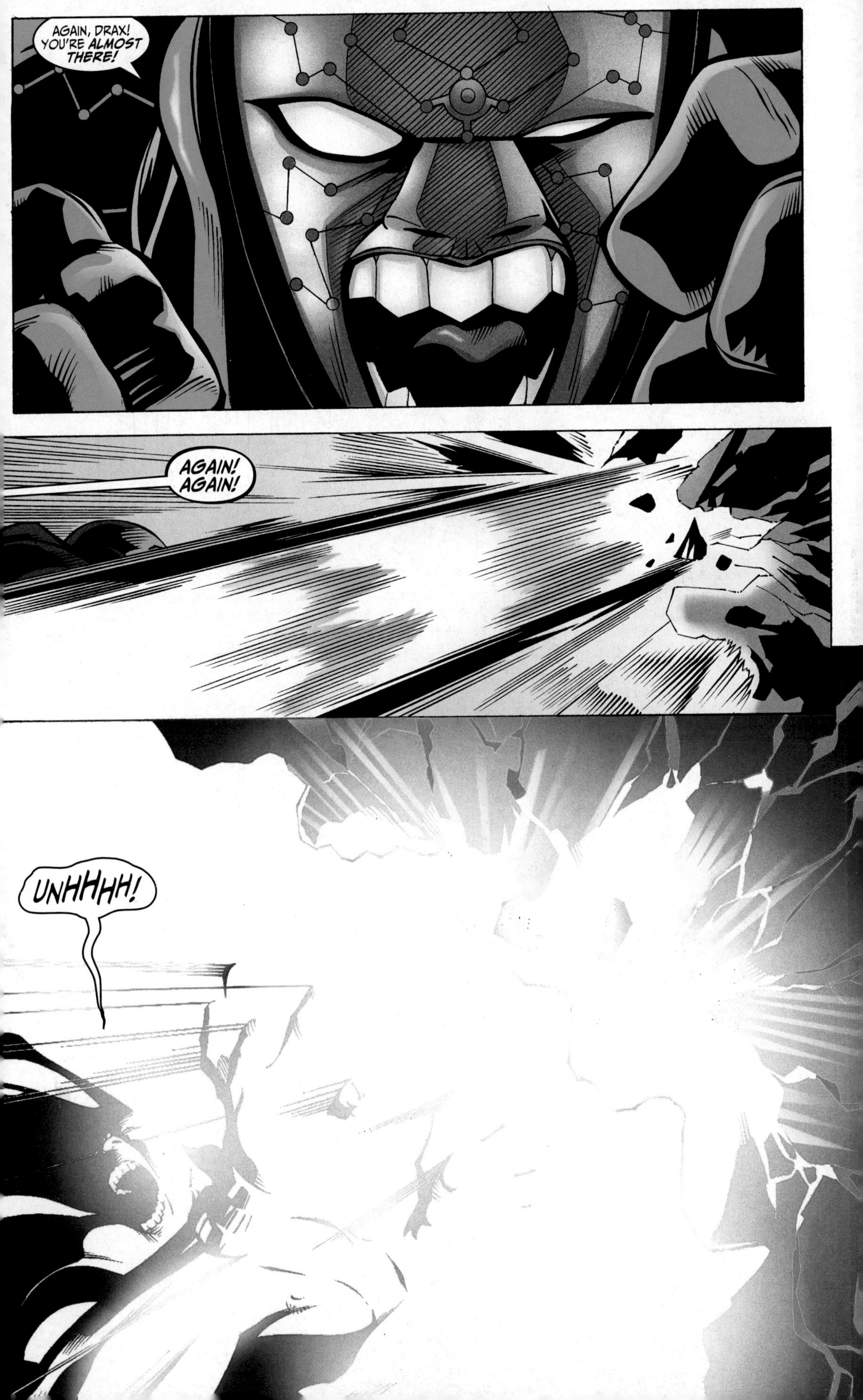
AGAIN, DRAX! YOU'RE ALMOST THERE!
AGAIN! AGAIN!
UNHHHH!

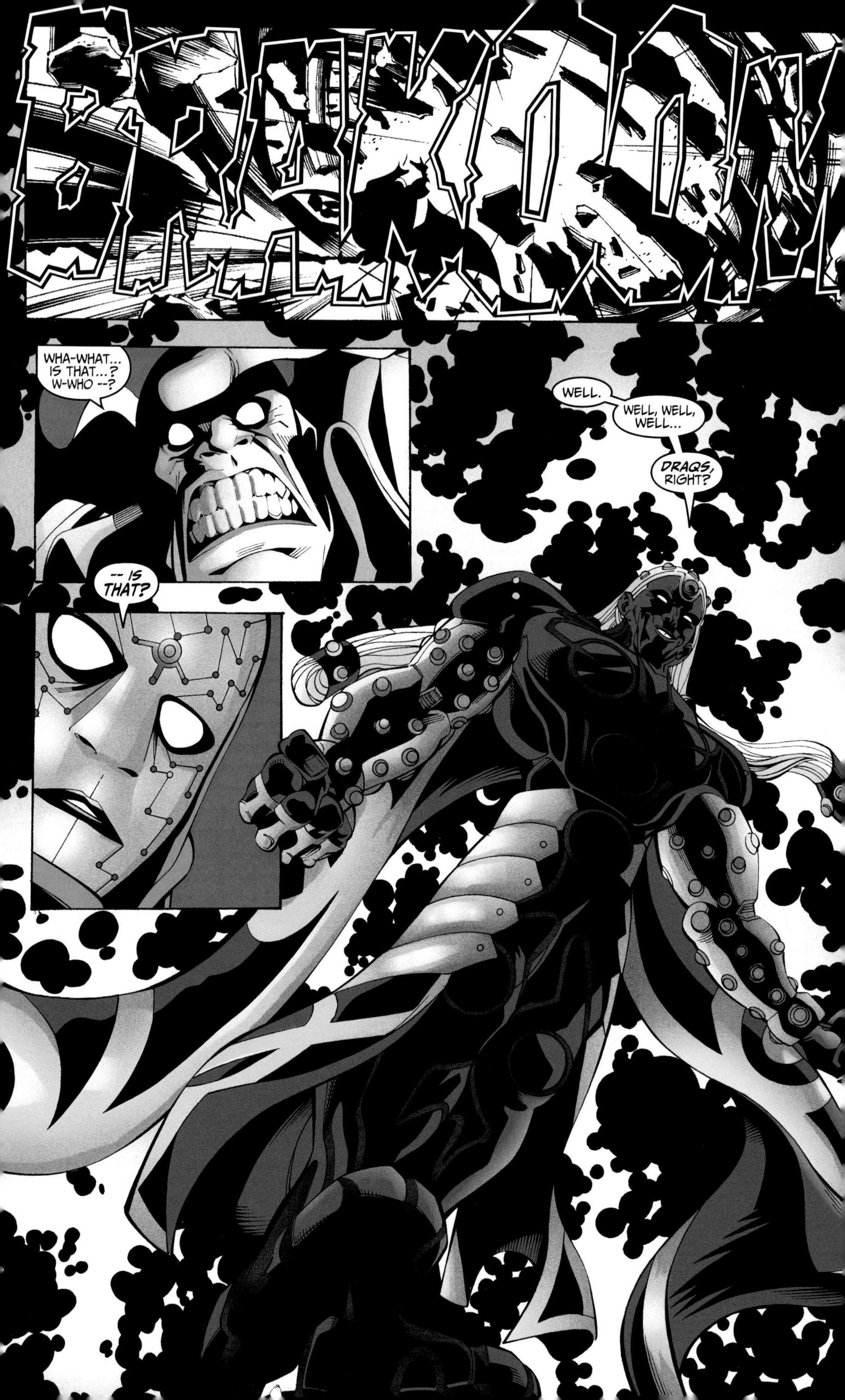
WHA-WHAT... IS THAT...? W-WHO --?
WELL.
WELL, WELL, WELL...
DRAQS, RIGHT?
-- IS THAT?

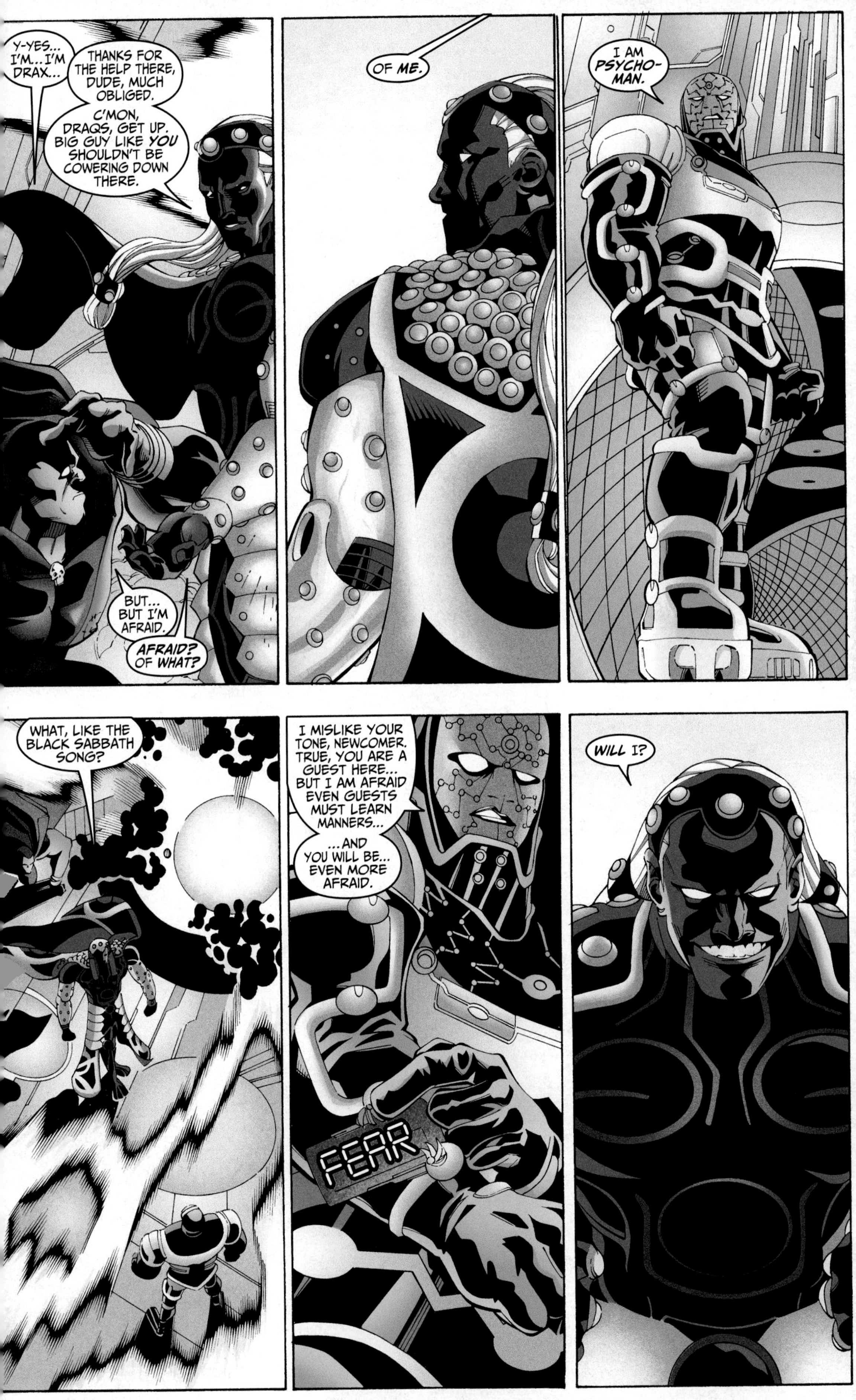
Y-YES... I'M...I'M DRAX...
THANKS FOR THE HELP THERE, DUDE, MUCH OBLIGED.
C'MON, DRAQS, GET UP. BIG GUY LIKE YOU SHOULDN'T BE COWERING DOWN THERE.
BUT... BUT I'M AFRAID.
AFRAID? OF WHAT?
OF ME.
I AM PSYCHO-MAN.
WHAT, LIKE THE BLACK SABBATH SONG?
I MISLIKE YOUR TONE, NEWCOMER. TRUE, YOU ARE A GUEST HERE... BUT I AM AFRAID EVEN GUESTS MUST LEARN MANNERS...
...AND YOU WILL BE... EVEN MORE AFRAID.
FEAR
WILL I?

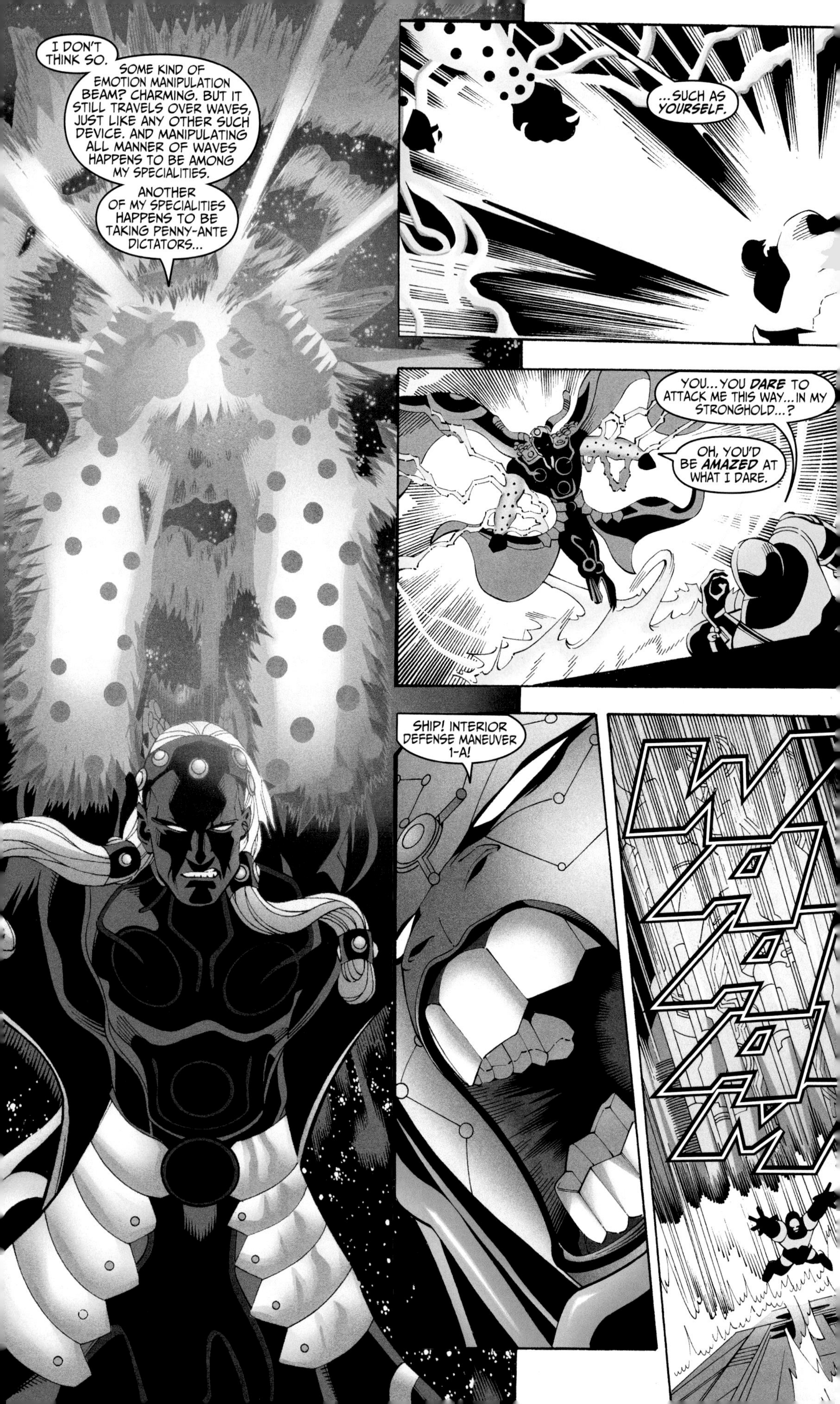

I DON'T THINK SO.
SOME KIND OF EMOTION MANIPULATION BEAM? CHARMING. BUT IT STILL TRAVELS OVER WAVES, JUST LIKE ANY OTHER SUCH DEVICE. AND MANIPULATING ALL MANNER OF WAVES HAPPENS TO BE AMONG MY SPECIALITIES.
ANOTHER OF MY SPECIALITIES HAPPENS TO BE TAKING PENNY-ANTE DICTATORS...
...SUCH AS YOURSELF.
YOU...YOU DARE TO ATTACK ME THIS WAY...IN MY STRONGHOLD...?
OH, YOU'D BE AMAZED AT WHAT I DARE.
SHIP! INTERIOR DEFENSE MANEUVER 1-A!
WHAM

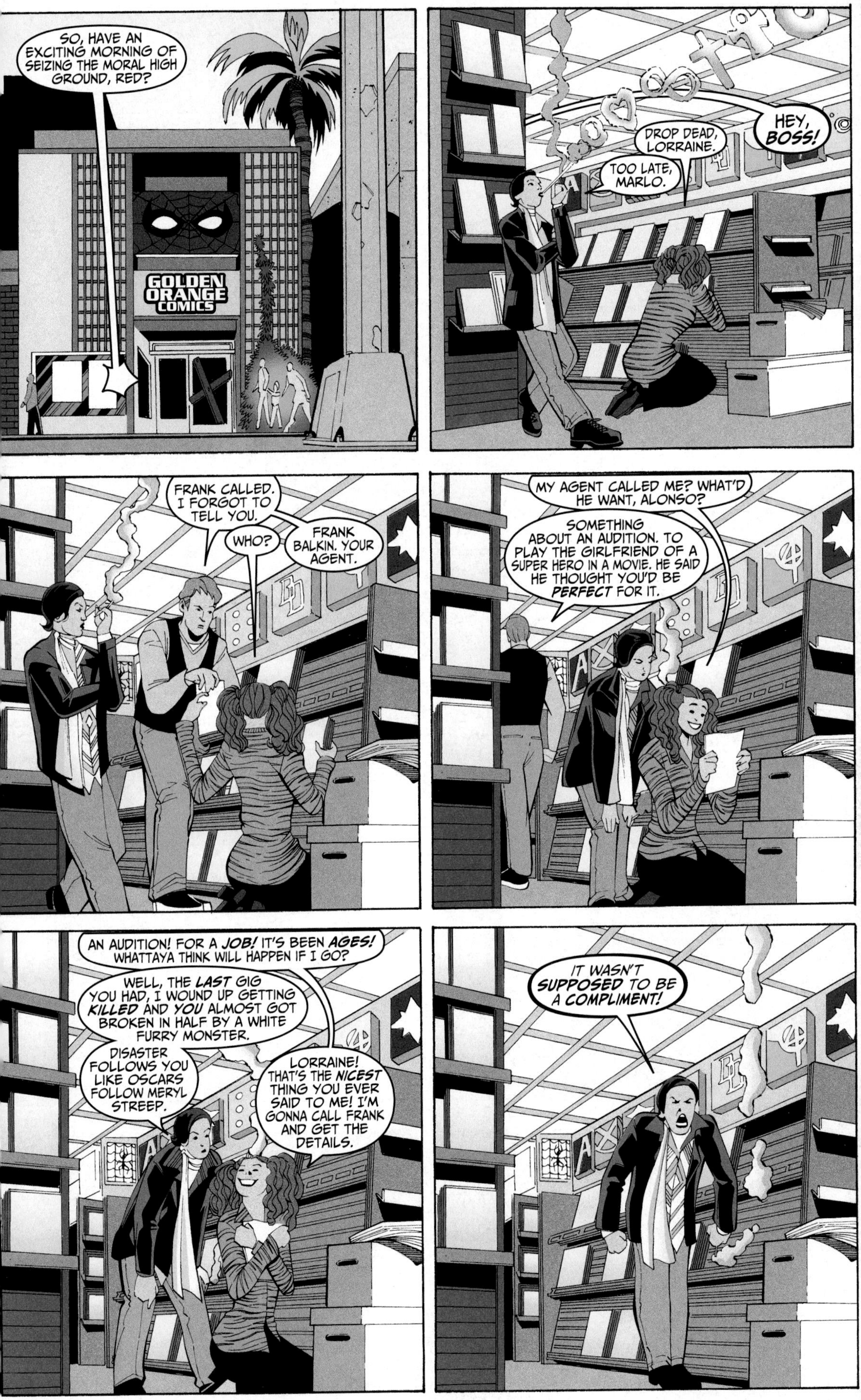
SO, HAVE AN EXCITING MORNING OF SEIZING THE MORAL HIGH GROUND, RED?
GOLDEN ORANGE COMICS
HEY, BOSS!
DROP DEAD, LORRAINE.
TOO LATE, MARLO.
FRANK CALLED. I FORGOT TO TELL YOU.
WHO?
FRANK BALKIN. YOUR AGENT.
MY AGENT CALLED ME? WHAT'D HE WANT, ALONSO?
SOMETHING ABOUT AN AUDITION. TO PLAY THE GIRLFRIEND OF A SUPER HERO IN A MOVIE. HE SAID HE THOUGHT YOU'D BE PERFECT FOR IT.
AN AUDITION! FOR A JOB! IT'S BEEN AGES! WHATTAYA THINK WILL HAPPEN IF I GO?
WELL, THE LAST GIG YOU HAD, I WOUND UP GETTING KILLED AND YOU ALMOST GOT BROKEN IN HALF BY A WHITE FURRY MONSTER.
DISASTER FOLLOWS YOU LIKE OSCARS FOLLOW MERYL STREEP.
LORRAINE! THAT'S THE NICEST THING YOU EVER SAID TO ME! I'M GONNA CALL FRANK AND GET THE DETAILS.
IT WASN'T SUPPOSED TO BE A COMPLIMENT!

MY COMPLIMENTS, FOOL. YOU ACTUALLY HAD ME WORRIED FOR A MOMENT OR TWO THERE. HERE, IN MY STRONGHOLD, YOU GAVE ME CAUSE FOR CONCERN.

I WOULD HAVE LIKED TO LEARN *MORE* OF YOU.

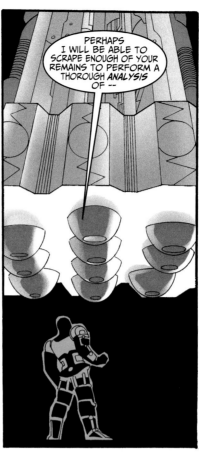

PERHAPS I WILL BE ABLE TO SCRAPE ENOUGH OF YOUR REMAINS TO PERFORM A THOROUGH *ANALYSIS* OF --

EH?

ARRGGGHHHHH!!!

MAKE THE *SLIGHTEST* ATTEMPT ALONG THOSE LINES AGAIN, AND I'LL CRUSH YOU IN YOUR SHELL LIKE AN EGG. DO WE *UNDERSTAND* EACH OTHER?

YOU *DARE* TO --!

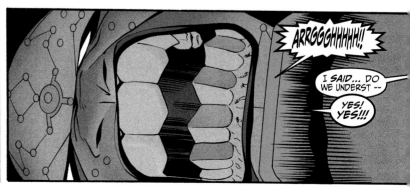

ARRGGGHHHHH!!

I *SAID*... DO WE UNDERST --

YES! YES!!!

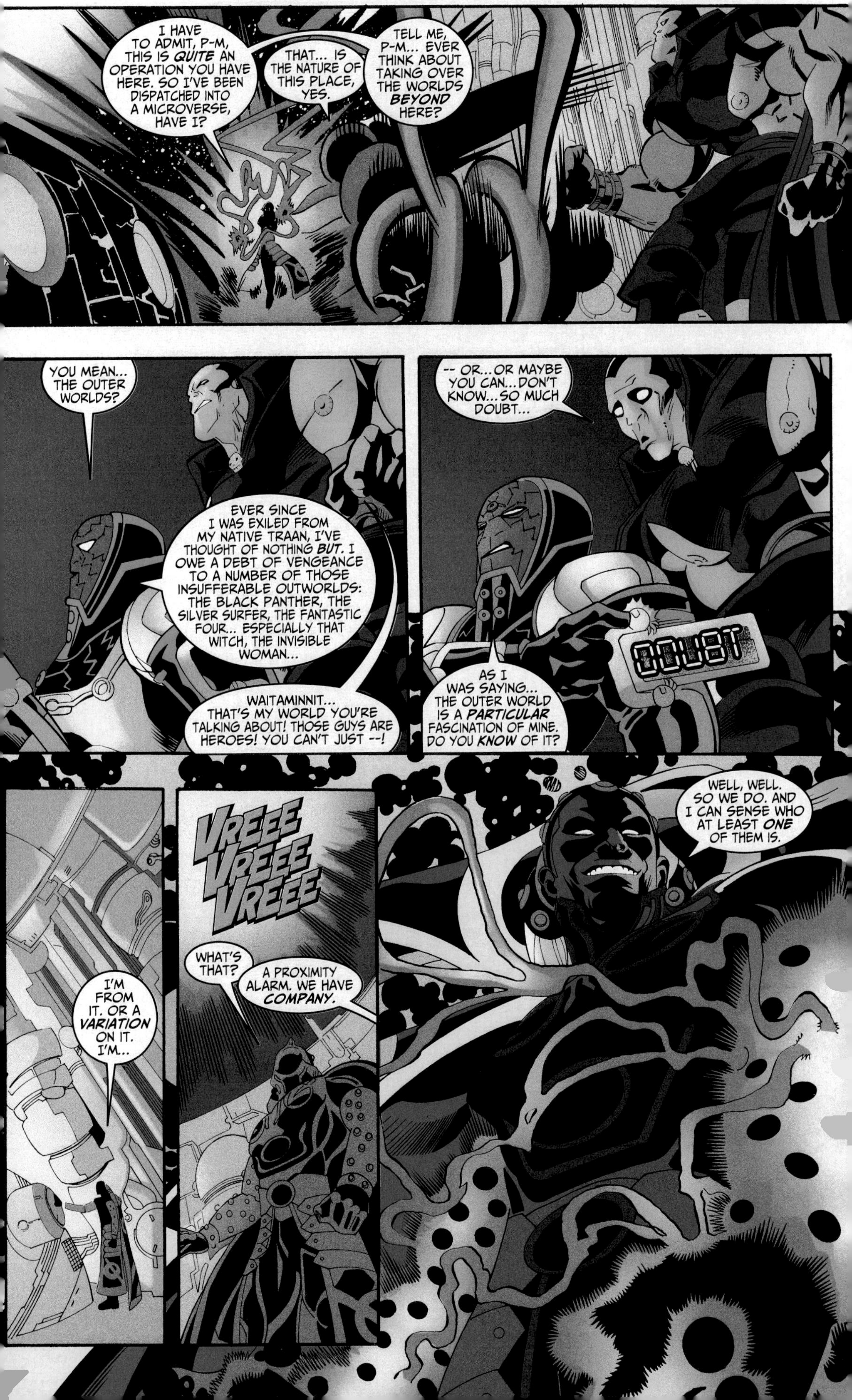
I HAVE TO ADMIT, P-M, THIS IS QUITE AN OPERATION YOU HAVE HERE. SO I'VE BEEN DISPATCHED INTO A MICROVERSE, HAVE I?
THAT... IS THE NATURE OF THIS PLACE, YES.
TELL ME, P-M... EVER THINK ABOUT TAKING OVER THE WORLDS BEYOND HERE?
YOU MEAN... THE OUTER WORLDS?
EVER SINCE I WAS EXILED FROM MY NATIVE TRAAN, I'VE THOUGHT OF NOTHING BUT. I OWE A DEBT OF VENGEANCE TO A NUMBER OF THOSE INSUFFERABLE OUTWORLDS: THE BLACK PANTHER, THE SILVER SURFER, THE FANTASTIC FOUR... ESPECIALLY THAT WITCH, THE INVISIBLE WOMAN...
WAITAMINNIT... THAT'S MY WORLD YOU'RE TALKING ABOUT! THOSE GUYS ARE HEROES! YOU CAN'T JUST --!
-- OR...OR MAYBE YOU CAN...DON'T KNOW...SO MUCH DOUBT...
DOUBT
AS I WAS SAYING... THE OUTER WORLD IS A PARTICULAR FASCINATION OF MINE. DO YOU KNOW OF IT?
I'M FROM IT. OR A VARIATION ON IT. I'M...
VREEE VREEE VREEE
WHAT'S THAT?
A PROXIMITY ALARM. WE HAVE COMPANY.
WELL, WELL. SO WE DO. AND I CAN SENSE WHO AT LEAST ONE OF THEM IS.

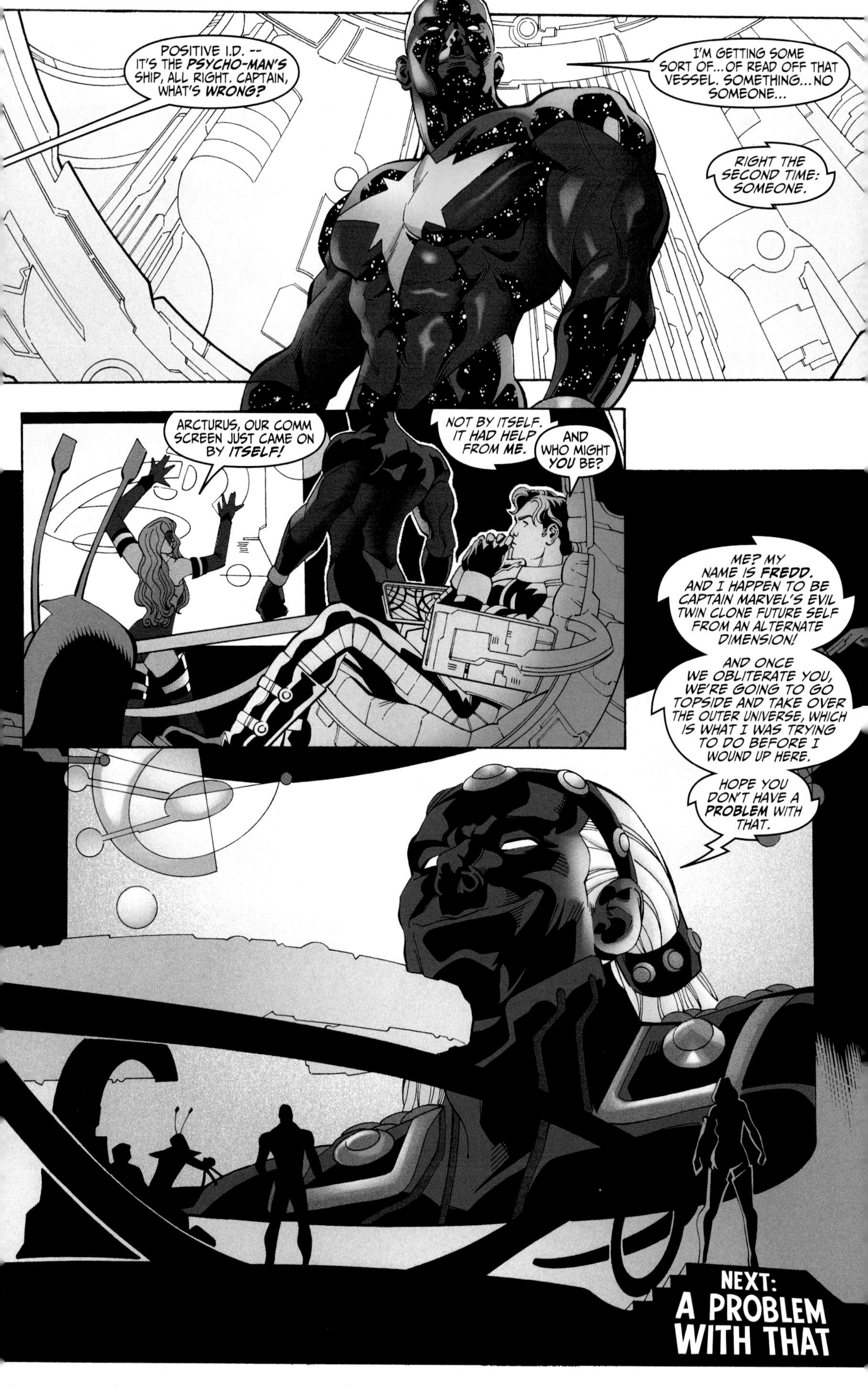
POSITIVE I.D. -- IT'S THE PSYCHO-MAN'S SHIP, ALL RIGHT. CAPTAIN, WHAT'S WRONG?
I'M GETTING SOME SORT OF...OF READ OFF THAT VESSEL. SOMETHING...NO SOMEONE...
RIGHT THE SECOND TIME: SOMEONE.
ARCTURUS, OUR COMM SCREEN JUST CAME ON BY ITSELF!
NOT BY ITSELF. IT HAD HELP FROM ME.
AND WHO MIGHT YOU BE?
ME? MY NAME IS FREDD. AND I HAPPEN TO BE CAPTAIN MARVEL'S EVIL TWIN CLONE FUTURE SELF FROM AN ALTERNATE DIMENSION!
AND ONCE WE OBLITERATE YOU, WE'RE GOING TO GO TOPSIDE AND TAKE OVER THE OUTER UNIVERSE, WHICH IS WHAT I WAS TRYING TO DO BEFORE I WOUND UP HERE.
HOPE YOU DON'T HAVE A PROBLEM WITH THAT.
NEXT: A PROBLEM WITH THAT

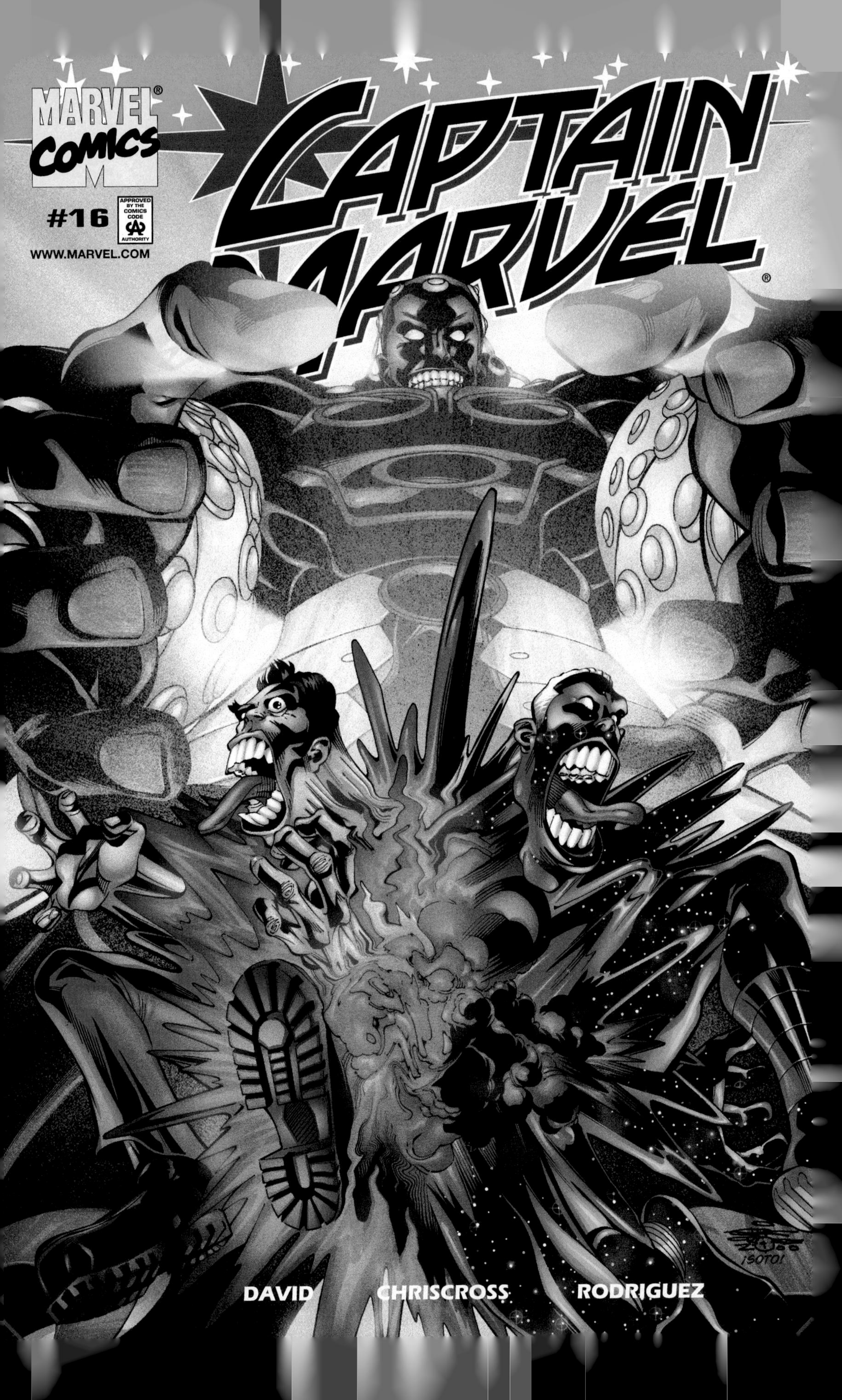

MARVEL COMICS
CAPTAIN MARVEL
#16
APPROVED BY THE COMICS CODE AUTHORITY
WWW.MARVEL.COM
DAVID
CHRISCROSS
RODRIGUEZ

LOS ANGELES. THE SKIES ABOVE THE COMIC BOOK CASTLE COMICS SHOP.

THAT IS THE PLACE. THE PLACE WHERE MY *OPPONENT* IS HIDING.

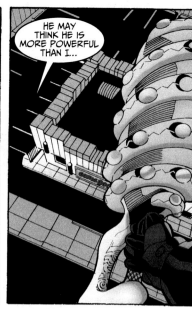

HE MAY THINK HE IS MORE POWERFUL THAN I...

...BUT HE WILL NOT BE THE FIRST OPPONENT OF MINE TO BE DISABUSED OF *THAT* NOTION!

OHHH, THERE WILL BE A *RECKONING* THIS DAY!

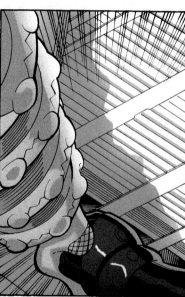

KRAAASH

WIZARD! *FACE ME!* FACE THE ONE YOU HAVE SO USED AND ABUSED! FOR I'VE FINALLY TRACED MY PROBLEMS TO THEIR SOURCE: NAMELY, YOU!

YOU MEDDLED WITH MY VERY *MIND!* TRANSFORMED ALL MY THOUGHTS OF HEROISM INTO *VILLAINY!* TURNED ME AGAINST THE *WORLD!*

AND NOW... NOW SHALL COME --

...A RECKONING?

OH, F --

FWOOF

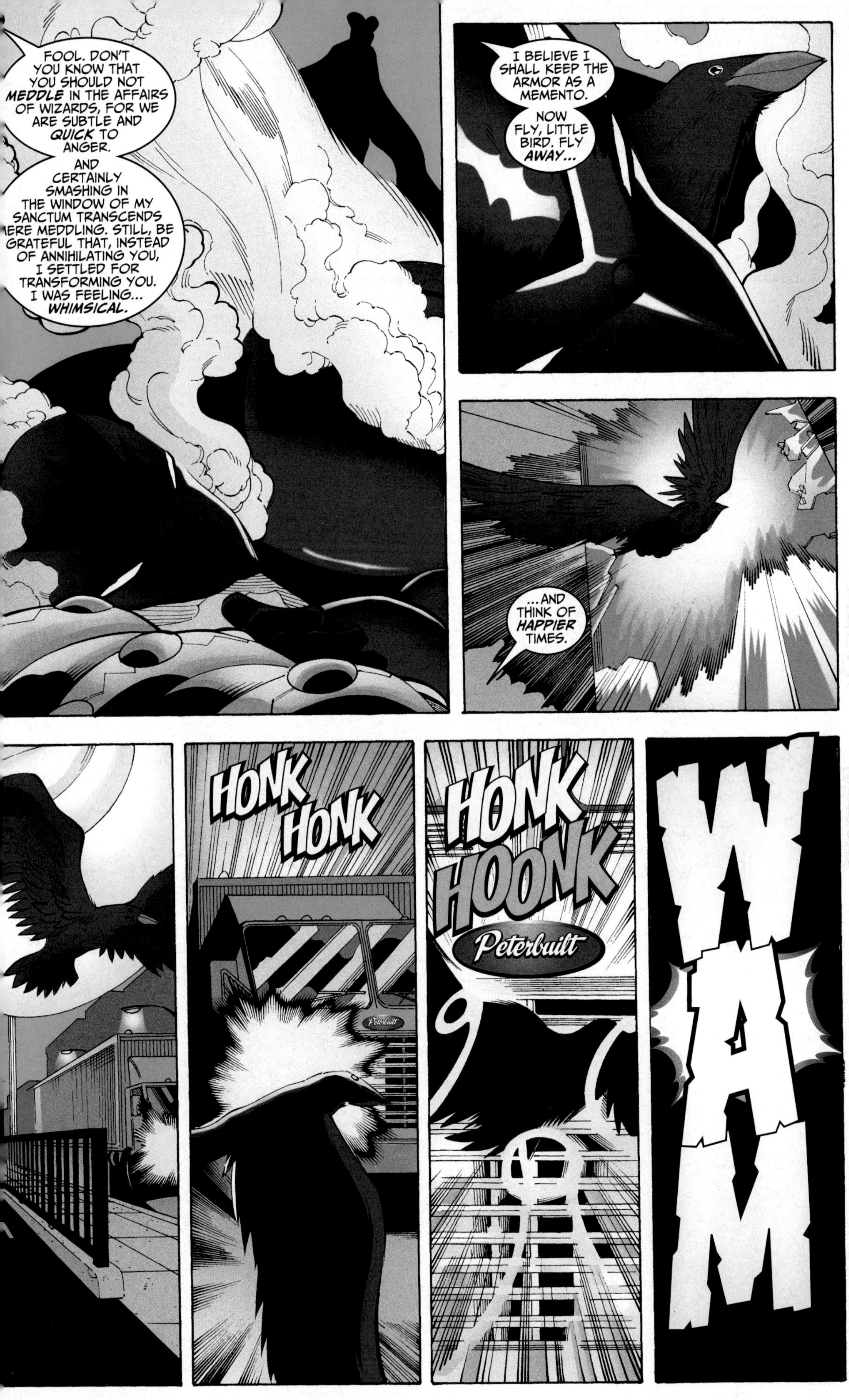
FOOL. DON'T YOU KNOW THAT YOU SHOULD NOT MEDDLE IN THE AFFAIRS OF WIZARDS, FOR WE ARE SUBTLE AND QUICK TO ANGER.
AND CERTAINLY SMASHING IN THE WINDOW OF MY SANCTUM TRANSCENDS MERE MEDDLING. STILL, BE GRATEFUL THAT, INSTEAD OF ANNIHILATING YOU, I SETTLED FOR TRANSFORMING YOU. I WAS FEELING... WHIMSICAL.
I BELIEVE I SHALL KEEP THE ARMOR AS A MEMENTO.
NOW FLY, LITTLE BIRD. FLY AWAY...
...AND THINK OF HAPPIER TIMES.
HONK HONK
HONK HOONK
Peterbuilt
WAM

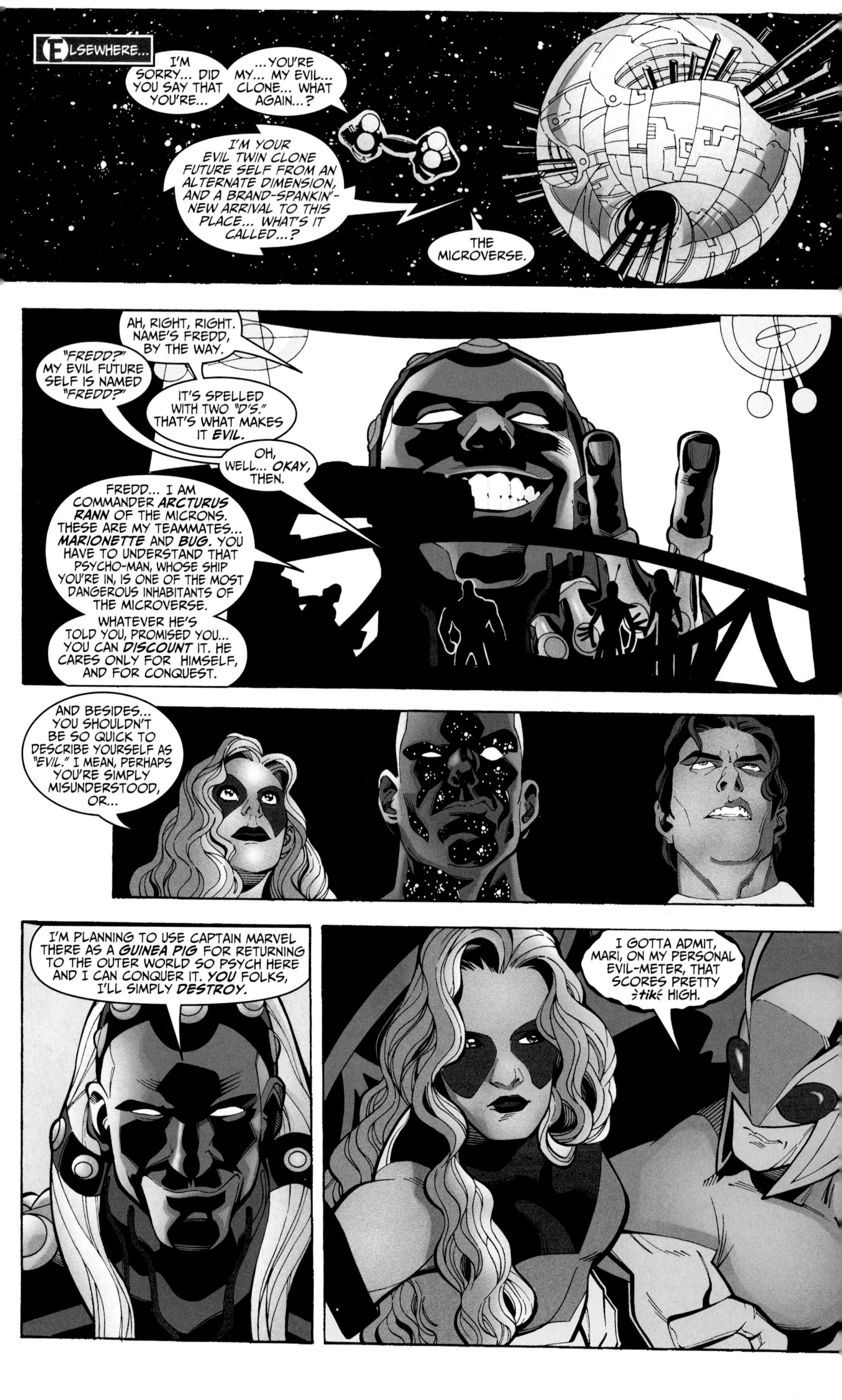
ELSEWHERE...
I'M SORRY... DID YOU SAY THAT YOU'RE...
...YOU'RE MY... MY EVIL... CLONE... WHAT AGAIN...?
I'M YOUR EVIL TWIN CLONE FUTURE SELF FROM AN ALTERNATE DIMENSION, AND A BRAND-SPANKIN'-NEW ARRIVAL TO THIS PLACE... WHAT'S IT CALLED...?
THE MICROVERSE.
AH, RIGHT, RIGHT. NAME'S FREDD, BY THE WAY.
"FREDD?" MY EVIL FUTURE SELF IS NAMED "FREDD?"
IT'S SPELLED WITH TWO "D'S." THAT'S WHAT MAKES IT EVIL.
OH, WELL... OKAY, THEN.
FREDD... I AM COMMANDER ARCTURUS RANN OF THE MICRONS. THESE ARE MY TEAMMATES... MARIONETTE AND BUG. YOU HAVE TO UNDERSTAND THAT PSYCHO-MAN, WHOSE SHIP YOU'RE IN, IS ONE OF THE MOST DANGEROUS INHABITANTS OF THE MICROVERSE.
WHATEVER HE'S TOLD YOU, PROMISED YOU... YOU CAN DISCOUNT IT. HE CARES ONLY FOR HIMSELF, AND FOR CONQUEST.
AND BESIDES... YOU SHOULDN'T BE SO QUICK TO DESCRIBE YOURSELF AS "EVIL." I MEAN, PERHAPS YOU'RE SIMPLY MISUNDERSTOOD, OR...
I'M PLANNING TO USE CAPTAIN MARVEL THERE AS A GUINEA PIG FOR RETURNING TO THE OUTER WORLD SO PSYCH HERE AND I CAN CONQUER IT. YOU FOLKS, I'LL SIMPLY DESTROY.
I GOTTA ADMIT, MARI, ON MY PERSONAL EVIL-METER, THAT SCORES PRETTY ≥tik≤ HIGH.

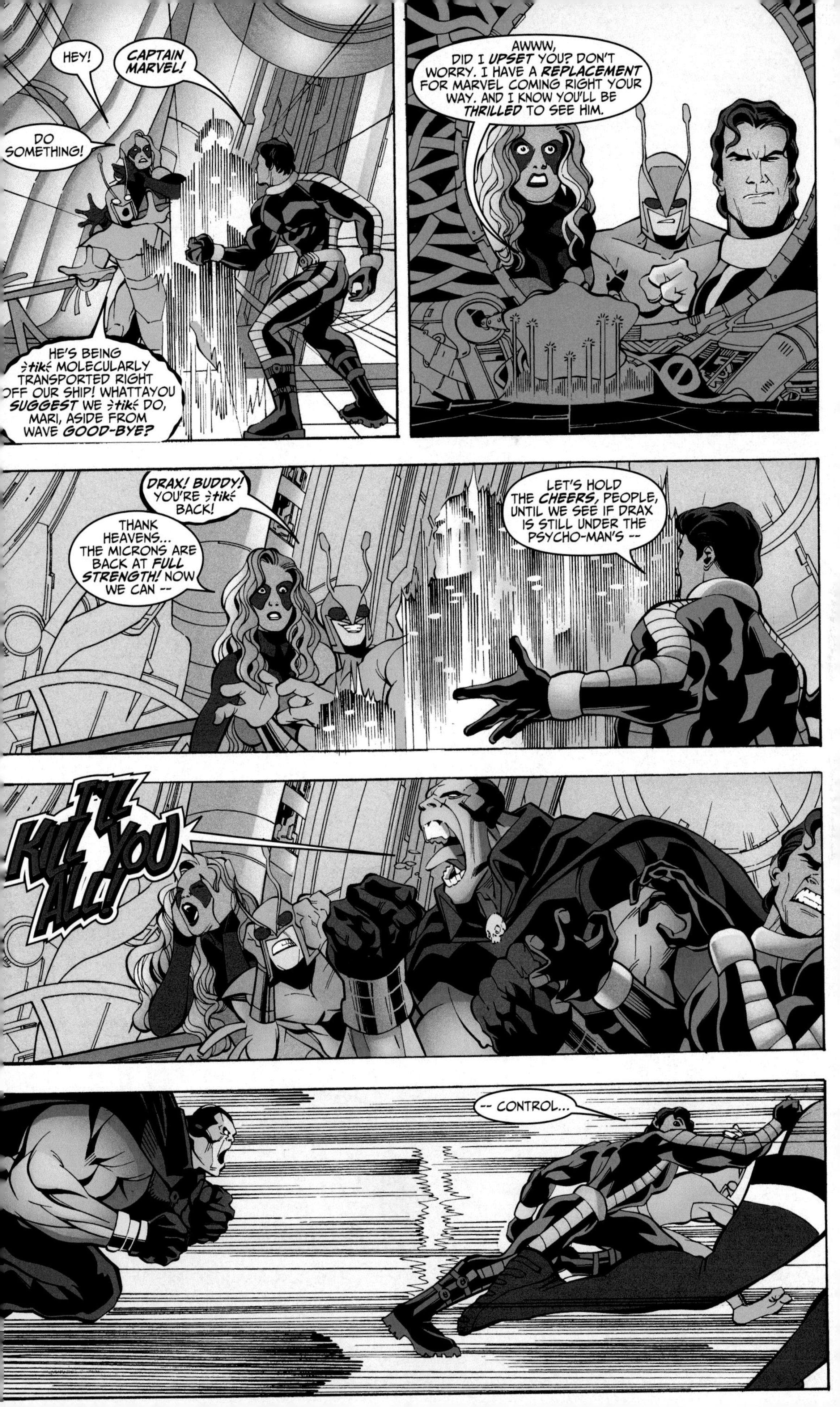
HEY!
CAPTAIN MARVEL!
DO SOMETHING!
HE'S BEING ⸗tik⸗ MOLECULARLY TRANSPORTED RIGHT OFF OUR SHIP! WHATTAYOU SUGGEST WE ⸗tik⸗ DO, MARI, ASIDE FROM WAVE GOOD-BYE?
AWWW, DID I UPSET YOU? DON'T WORRY. I HAVE A REPLACEMENT FOR MARVEL COMING RIGHT YOUR WAY. AND I KNOW YOU'LL BE THRILLED TO SEE HIM.
DRAX! BUDDY! YOU'RE ⸗tik⸗ BACK!
THANK HEAVENS... THE MICRONS ARE BACK AT FULL STRENGTH! NOW WE CAN --
LET'S HOLD THE CHEERS, PEOPLE, UNTIL WE SEE IF DRAX IS STILL UNDER THE PSYCHO-MAN'S --
I'LL KILL YOU ALL!
-- CONTROL...

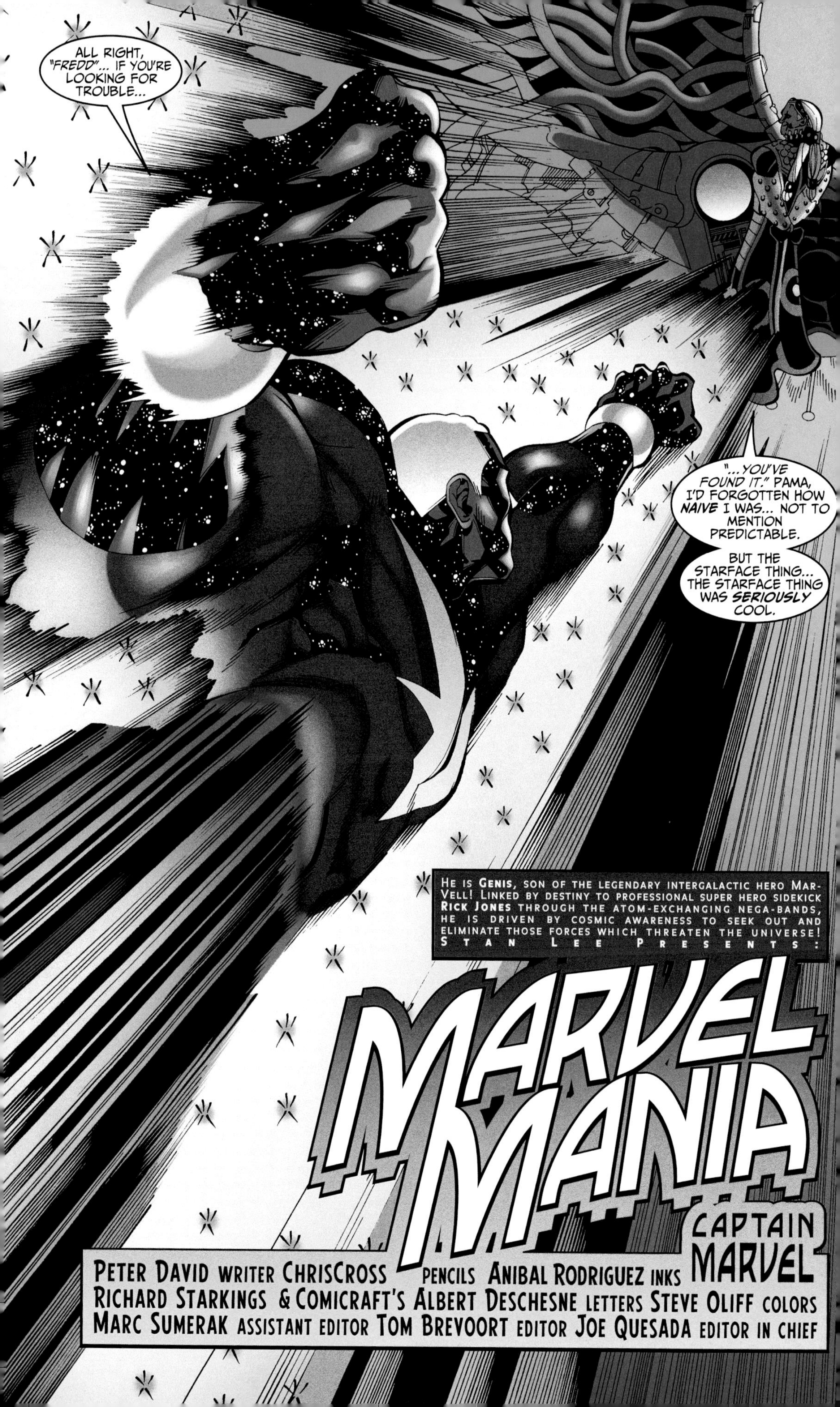

ALL RIGHT, "FREDD"... IF YOU'RE LOOKING FOR TROUBLE...
"...YOU'VE FOUND IT." PAMA, I'D FORGOTTEN HOW NAIVE I WAS... NOT TO MENTION PREDICTABLE.
BUT THE STARFACE THING... THE STARFACE THING WAS SERIOUSLY COOL.
HE IS GENIS, SON OF THE LEGENDARY INTERGALACTIC HERO MAR-VELL! LINKED BY DESTINY TO PROFESSIONAL SUPER HERO SIDEKICK RICK JONES THROUGH THE ATOM-EXCHANGING NEGA-BANDS, HE IS DRIVEN BY COSMIC AWARENESS TO SEEK OUT AND ELIMINATE THOSE FORCES WHICH THREATEN THE UNIVERSE! STAN LEE PRESENTS:
MARVEL MANIA
CAPTAIN MARVEL
PETER DAVID WRITER CHRISCROSS PENCILS ANIBAL RODRIGUEZ INKS
RICHARD STARKINGS & COMICRAFT'S ALBERT DESCHESNE LETTERS STEVE OLIFF COLORS
MARC SUMERAK ASSISTANT EDITOR TOM BREVOORT EDITOR JOE QUESADA EDITOR IN CHIEF

FREDD... HAVE YOU NEED OF HELP?

YOU MEAN FROM YOUR EMOTION-CONTROLLING THING? NAH, NO PROBLEM...

SEE, MARV HERE IS COSMICALLY AWARE, WHICH USUALLY HELPS HIM SUBCONSCIOUSLY ANTICIPATE AN OPPONENT'S NEXT MOVE. BUT HE CAN'T GET A READ ON ME BECAUSE I'M HIM...

...WELL, A VARIATION ON HIM. SO ALL HE'S GETTING IS A BOUNCEBACK, LIKE LOOKING IN A MIRROR.

AND WHILE HE GETS THAT SORTED OUT...

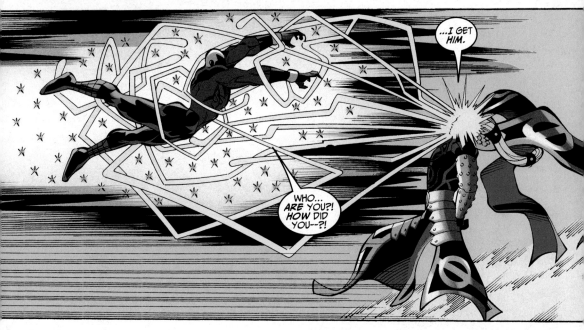

...I GET HIM.

WHO... ARE YOU?! HOW DID YOU--?!

BEAT YOU IN UNDER FIVE SECONDS? KID... YOU'RE TALKING TO SOMEONE WHO CAME CLOSE TO BEATING THE FORCES OF THE AVENGERS AND THE FANTASTIC FOUR COMBINED...

WELL... MY FUTURISTIC, ALTERNATE WORLD VERSION OF THEM, AT ANY RATE.

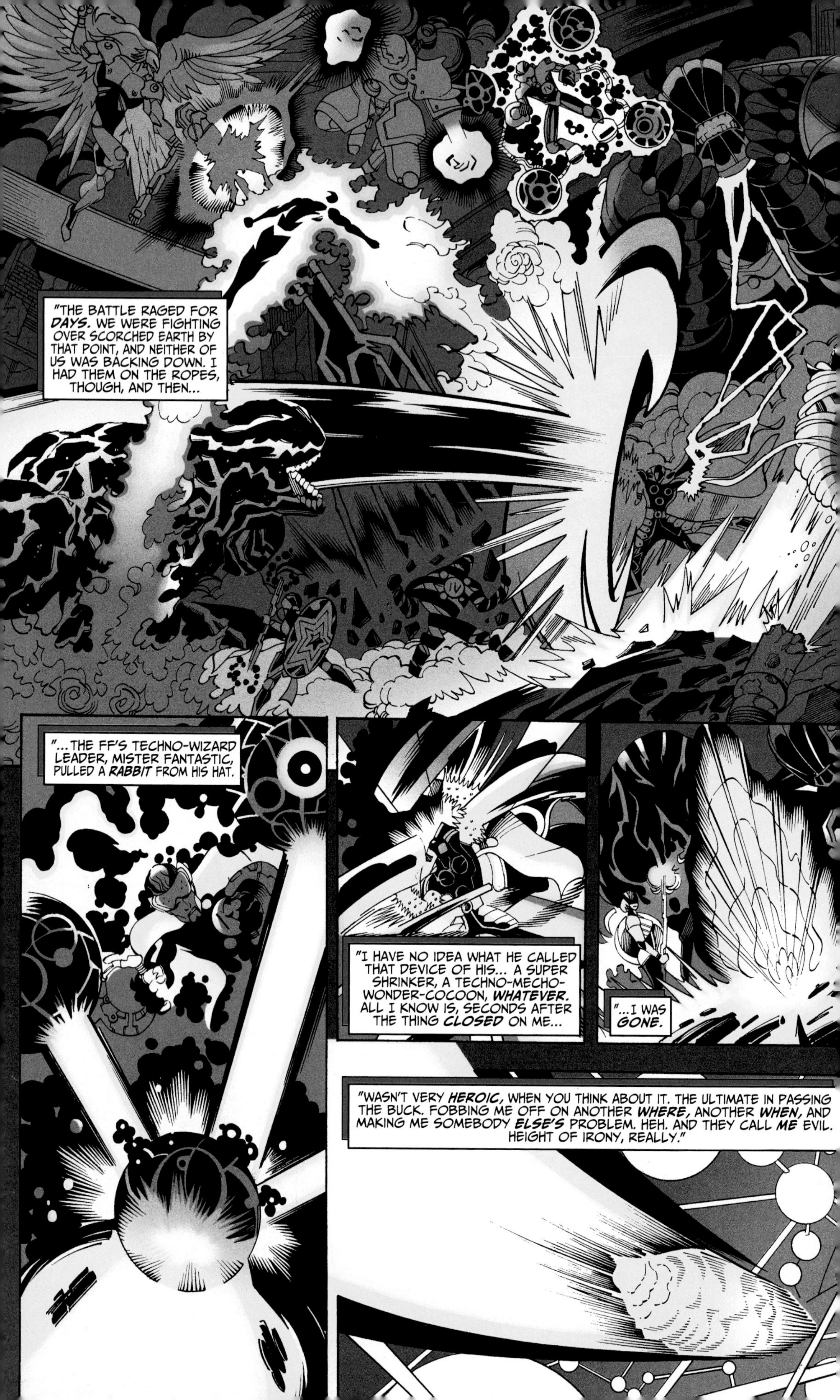
"THE BATTLE RAGED FOR DAYS. WE WERE FIGHTING OVER SCORCHED EARTH BY THAT POINT, AND NEITHER OF US WAS BACKING DOWN. I HAD THEM ON THE ROPES, THOUGH, AND THEN...
"...THE FF'S TECHNO-WIZARD LEADER, MISTER FANTASTIC, PULLED A RABBIT FROM HIS HAT.
"I HAVE NO IDEA WHAT HE CALLED THAT DEVICE OF HIS... A SUPER SHRINKER, A TECHNO-MECHO-WONDER-COCOON, WHATEVER. ALL I KNOW IS, SECONDS AFTER THE THING CLOSED ON ME...
"...I WAS GONE.
"WASN'T VERY HEROIC, WHEN YOU THINK ABOUT IT. THE ULTIMATE IN PASSING THE BUCK. FOBBING ME OFF ON ANOTHER WHERE, ANOTHER WHEN, AND MAKING ME SOMEBODY ELSE'S PROBLEM. HEH. AND THEY CALL ME EVIL. HEIGHT OF IRONY, REALLY."

SO... HERE'S WHERE WE STAND. PSYCH-BOY THERE SAYS HE HAS A SIZE-RAY THAT'LL RESTORE ME TO FULL-SIZE. PROBLEM IS, HE'S NEVER USED IT ON ANYONE CLOSE TO MY PHYSIOLOGY. THAT'S WHERE *YOU* COME IN.

WE *TEST* IT ON YOU. IF IT WORKS, THEN WE USE IT ON *ME*. PRETTY SIMPLE, REALLY.

I...I DON'T UNDERSTAND... HOW'RE YOU... HOLDING ME IMMOBILE... HOW...?

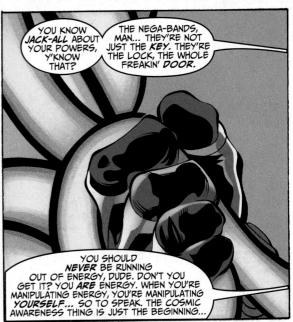

YOU KNOW *JACK-ALL* ABOUT YOUR POWERS, Y'KNOW THAT?

THE NEGA-BANDS, MAN... THEY'RE NOT JUST THE *KEY*. THEY'RE THE LOCK, THE WHOLE FREAKIN' *DOOR*.

YOU SHOULD *NEVER* BE RUNNING OUT OF ENERGY, DUDE. DON'T YOU GET IT? YOU *ARE* ENERGY. WHEN YOU'RE MANIPULATING ENERGY, YOU'RE MANIPULATING *YOURSELF*... SO TO SPEAK. THE COSMIC AWARENESS THING IS JUST THE BEGINNING...

I SWEAR TO YOU, DUDE, WHEN YOU GET IN TOUCH WITH YOUR COSMIC SIDE, WHEN YOU TAP INTO EVERYTHING YOU CAN DO, YOU'LL BE...

YOU?

EXACTLY! AIN'T IT *GREAT!*

OOOOFF!

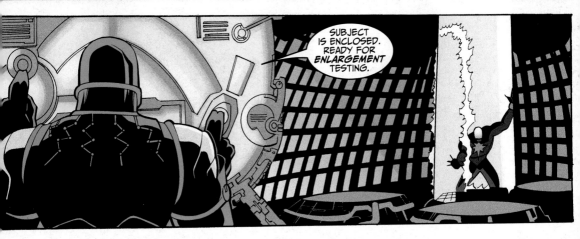

SUBJECT IS ENCLOSED. READY FOR *ENLARGEMENT* TESTING.

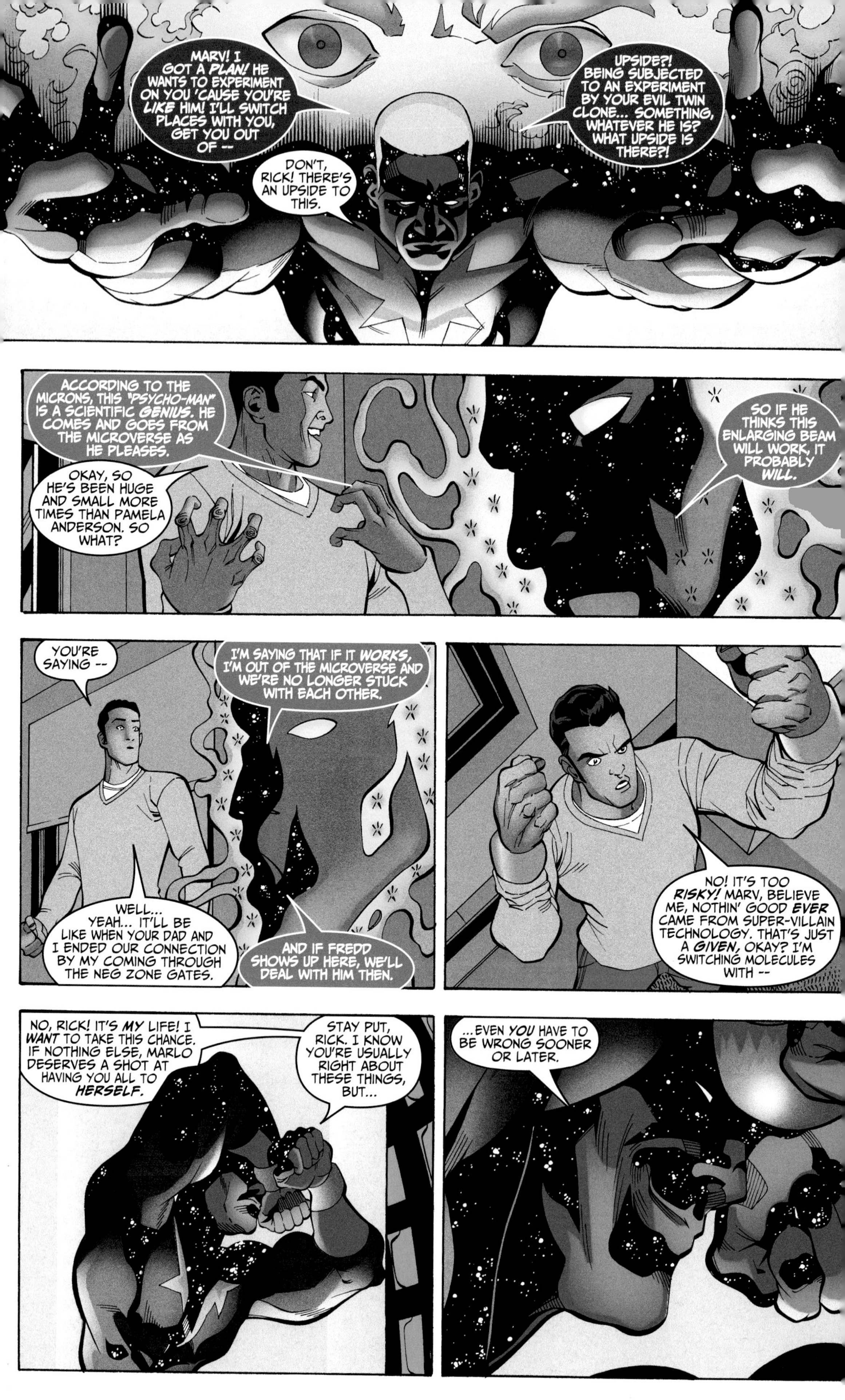
MARV! I GOT A *PLAN!* HE WANTS TO EXPERIMENT ON YOU 'CAUSE YOU'RE *LIKE* HIM! I'LL SWITCH PLACES WITH YOU, GET YOU OUT OF --
DON'T, RICK! THERE'S AN UPSIDE TO THIS.
UPSIDE?! BEING SUBJECTED TO AN EXPERIMENT BY YOUR EVIL TWIN CLONE... SOMETHING, WHATEVER HE IS? WHAT UPSIDE IS THERE?!
ACCORDING TO THE MICRONS, THIS "PSYCHO-MAN" IS A SCIENTIFIC *GENIUS.* HE COMES AND GOES FROM THE MICROVERSE AS HE PLEASES.
OKAY, SO HE'S BEEN HUGE AND SMALL MORE TIMES THAN PAMELA ANDERSON. SO WHAT?
SO IF HE THINKS THIS ENLARGING BEAM WILL WORK, IT PROBABLY *WILL.*
YOU'RE SAYING --
I'M SAYING THAT IF IT *WORKS,* I'M OUT OF THE MICROVERSE AND WE'RE NO LONGER STUCK WITH EACH OTHER.
WELL... YEAH... IT'LL BE LIKE WHEN YOUR DAD AND I ENDED OUR CONNECTION BY MY COMING THROUGH THE NEG ZONE GATES.
AND IF FREDD SHOWS UP HERE, WE'LL DEAL WITH HIM THEN.
NO! IT'S TOO *RISKY!* MARV, BELIEVE ME, NOTHIN' GOOD *EVER* CAME FROM SUPER-VILLAIN TECHNOLOGY. THAT'S JUST A *GIVEN,* OKAY? I'M SWITCHING MOLECULES WITH --
NO, RICK! IT'S *MY* LIFE! I *WANT* TO TAKE THIS CHANCE. IF NOTHING ELSE, MARLO DESERVES A SHOT AT HAVING YOU ALL TO *HERSELF.*
STAY PUT, RICK. I KNOW YOU'RE USUALLY RIGHT ABOUT THESE THINGS, BUT...
...EVEN *YOU* HAVE TO BE WRONG SOONER OR LATER.

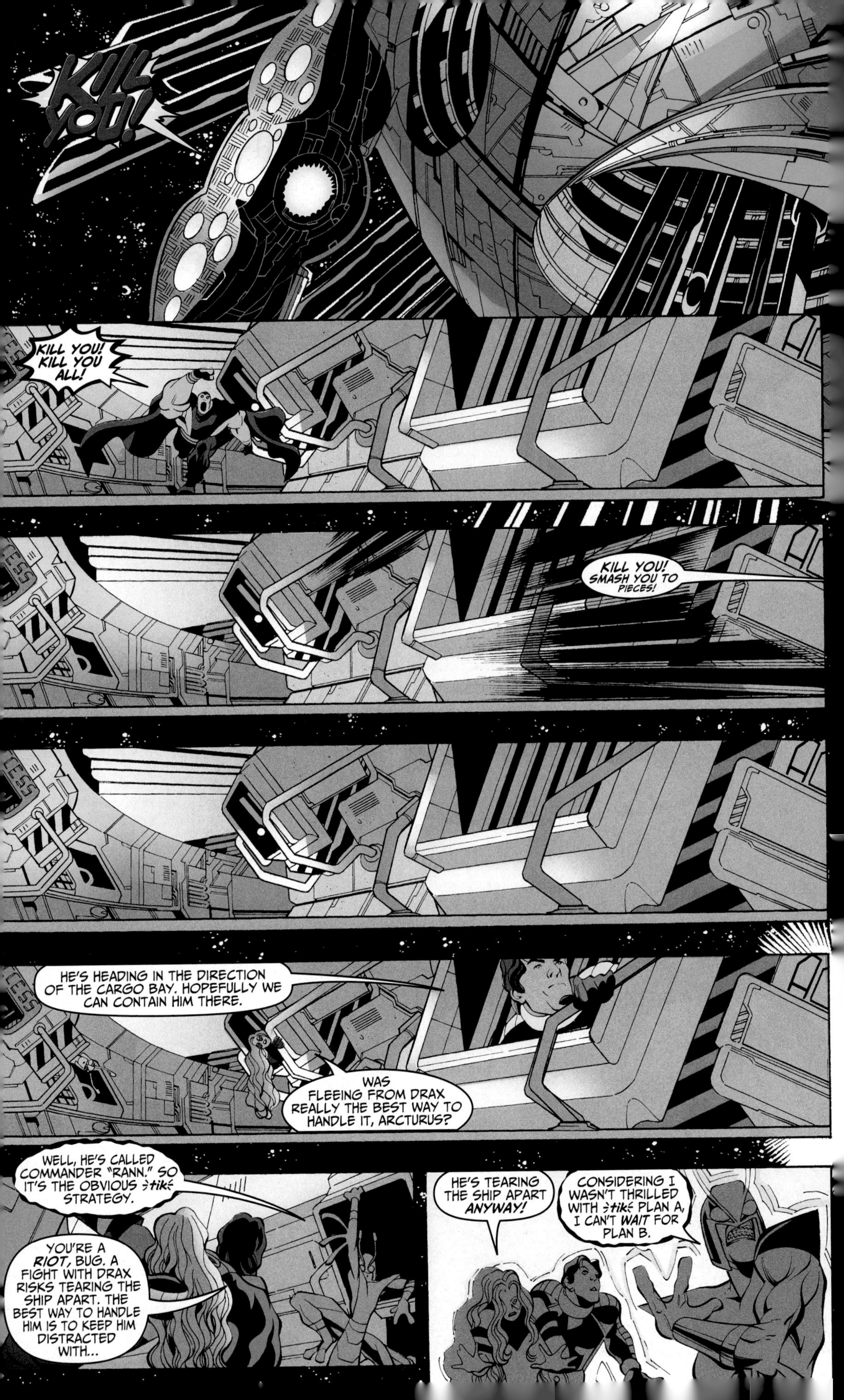
KILL YOU!
KILL YOU! KILL YOU ALL!
KILL YOU! SMASH YOU TO PIECES!
HE'S HEADING IN THE DIRECTION OF THE CARGO BAY. HOPEFULLY WE CAN CONTAIN HIM THERE.
WAS FLEEING FROM DRAX REALLY THE BEST WAY TO HANDLE IT, ARCTURUS?
WELL, HE'S CALLED COMMANDER "RANN." SO IT'S THE OBVIOUS tik STRATEGY.
YOU'RE A RIOT, BUG. A FIGHT WITH DRAX RISKS TEARING THE SHIP APART. THE BEST WAY TO HANDLE HIM IS TO KEEP HIM DISTRACTED WITH...
HE'S TEARING THE SHIP APART ANYWAY!
CONSIDERING I WASN'T THRILLED WITH tik PLAN A, I CAN'T WAIT FOR PLAN B.

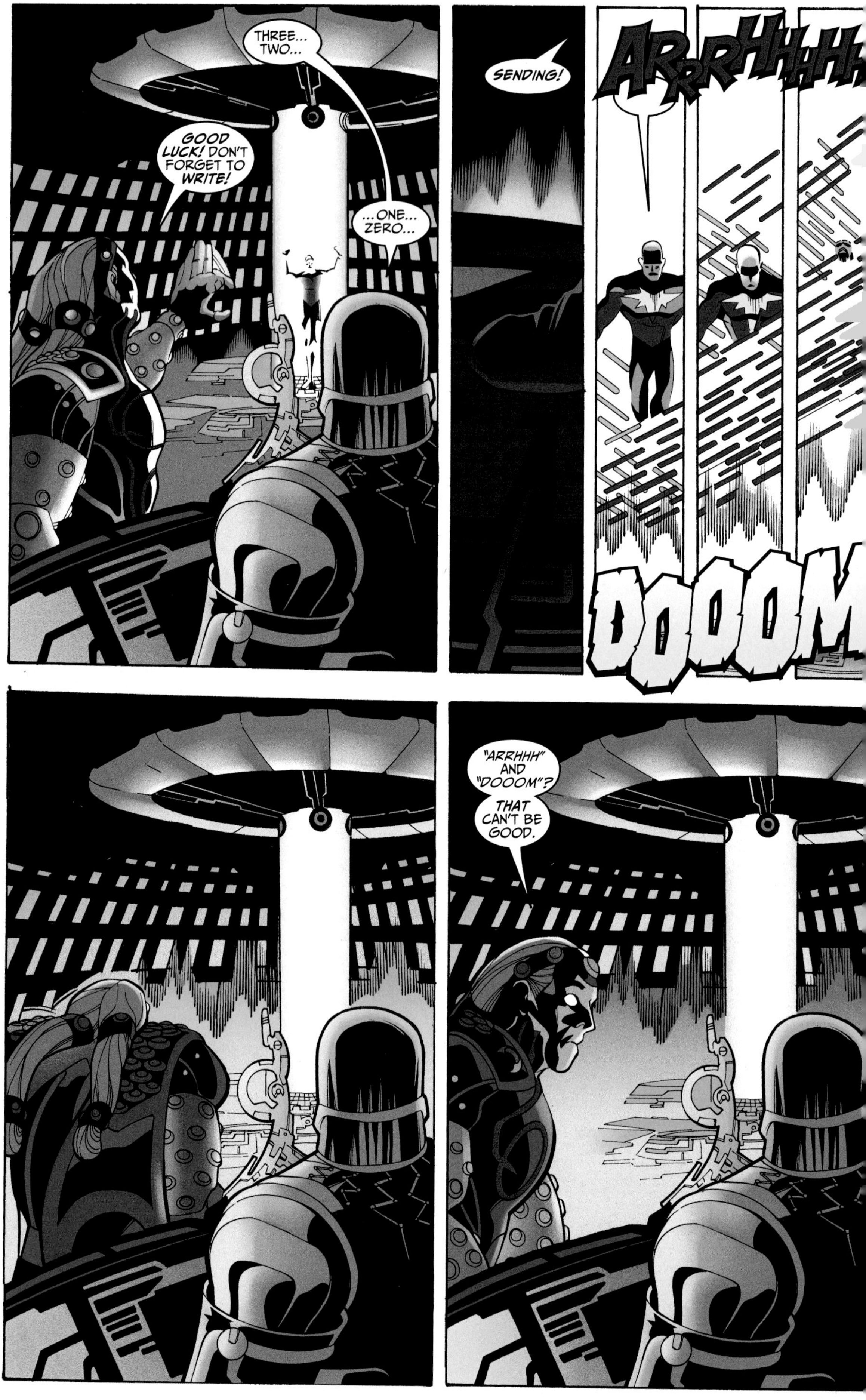
THREE... TWO...
GOOD LUCK! DON'T FORGET TO WRITE!
...ONE... ZERO...
SENDING!
ARRRHHHHH
DOOOM
"ARRHHH" AND "DOOOM"? THAT CAN'T BE GOOD.

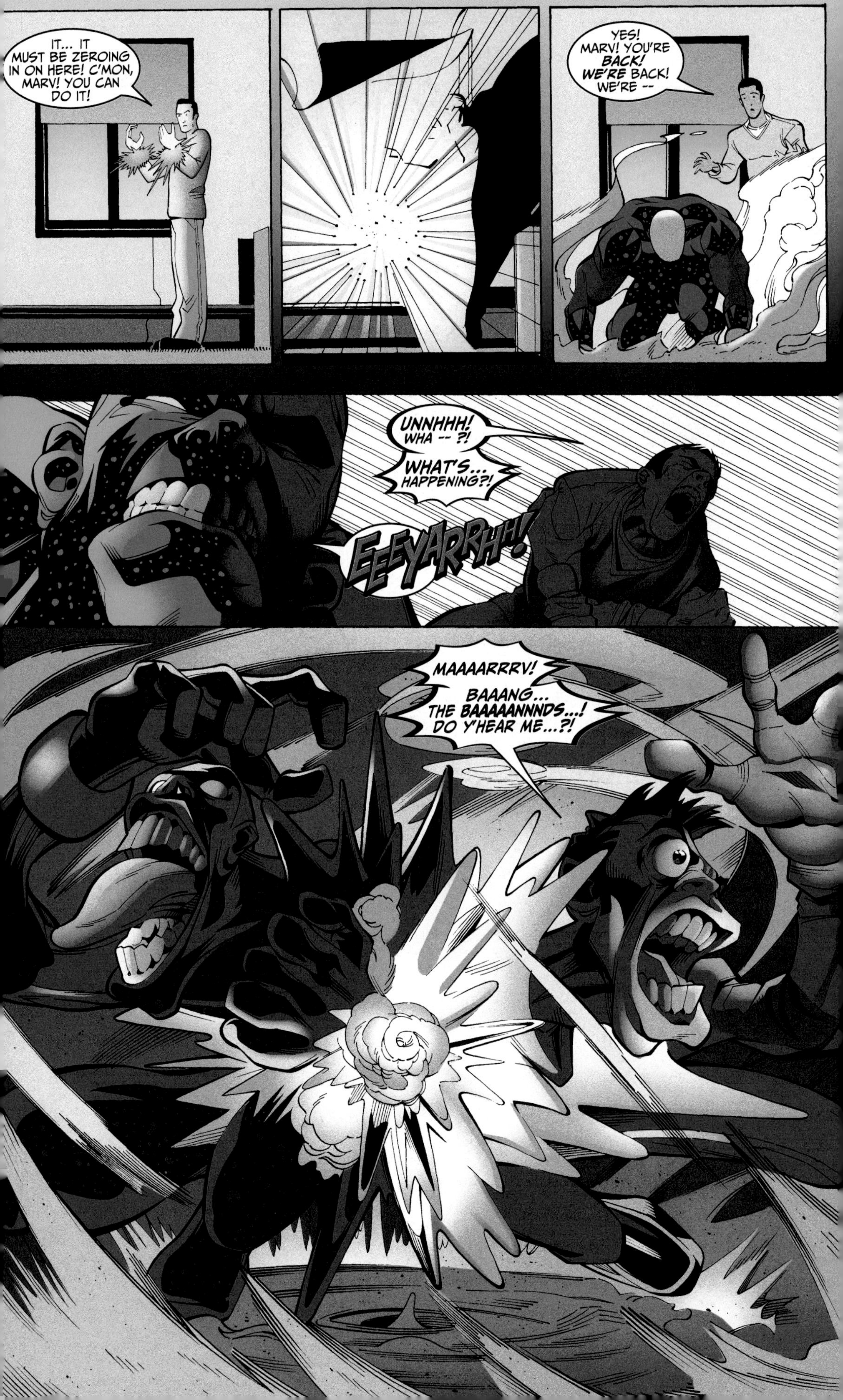

IT... IT MUST BE ZEROING IN ON HERE! C'MON, MARV! YOU CAN DO IT!
YES! MARV! YOU'RE BACK! WE'RE BACK! WE'RE --
UNNHHH! WHA -- ?!
WHAT'S... HAPPENING?!
EEEYARRHH!
MAAAARRRV!
BAAANG... THE BAAAAANNNDS...! DO Y'HEAR ME...?!

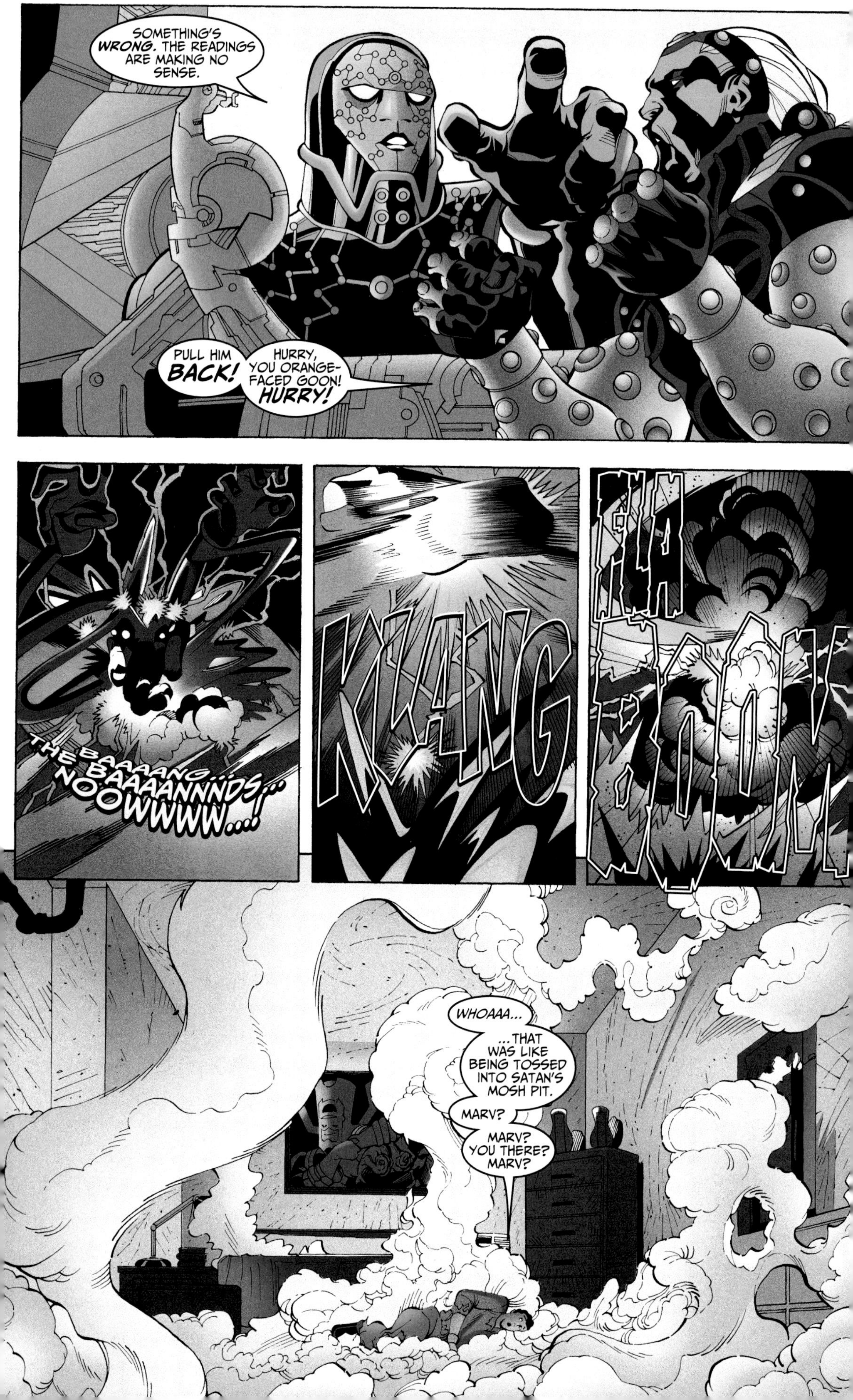

SOMETHING'S WRONG. THE READINGS ARE MAKING NO SENSE.
PULL HIM BACK!
HURRY, YOU ORANGE-FACED GOON! HURRY!
THE BAAAANG... THE BAAAANNNDS... NOOWWWW...!
KLANG
BOOM
WHOAAA...
...THAT WAS LIKE BEING TOSSED INTO SATAN'S MOSH PIT.
MARV?
MARV? YOU THERE? MARV?

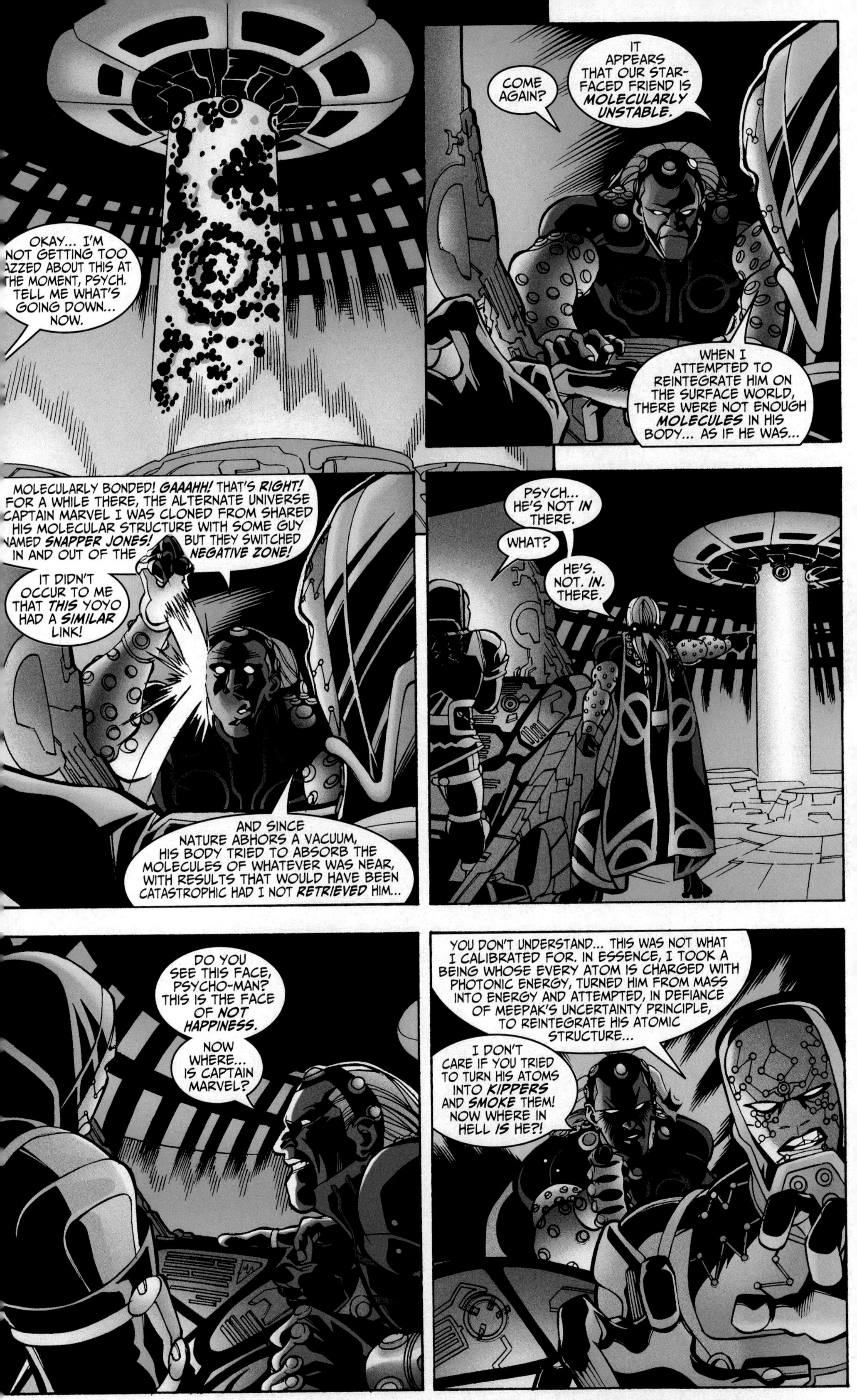
OKAY... I'M NOT GETTING TOO AZZED ABOUT THIS AT THE MOMENT, PSYCH. TELL ME WHAT'S GOING DOWN... NOW.
COME AGAIN?
IT APPEARS THAT OUR STAR-FACED FRIEND IS MOLECULARLY UNSTABLE.
WHEN I ATTEMPTED TO REINTEGRATE HIM ON THE SURFACE WORLD, THERE WERE NOT ENOUGH MOLECULES IN HIS BODY... AS IF HE WAS...
MOLECULARLY BONDED! GAAAHH! THAT'S RIGHT! FOR A WHILE THERE, THE ALTERNATE UNIVERSE CAPTAIN MARVEL I WAS CLONED FROM SHARED HIS MOLECULAR STRUCTURE WITH SOME GUY NAMED SNAPPER JONES! BUT THEY SWITCHED IN AND OUT OF THE NEGATIVE ZONE!
IT DIDN'T OCCUR TO ME THAT THIS YOYO HAD A SIMILAR LINK!
AND SINCE NATURE ABHORS A VACUUM, HIS BODY TRIED TO ABSORB THE MOLECULES OF WHATEVER WAS NEAR, WITH RESULTS THAT WOULD HAVE BEEN CATASTROPHIC HAD I NOT RETRIEVED HIM...
PSYCH... HE'S NOT IN THERE.
WHAT?
HE'S. NOT. IN. THERE.
DO YOU SEE THIS FACE, PSYCHO-MAN? THIS IS THE FACE OF NOT HAPPINESS.
NOW WHERE... IS CAPTAIN MARVEL?
YOU DON'T UNDERSTAND... THIS WAS NOT WHAT I CALIBRATED FOR. IN ESSENCE, I TOOK A BEING WHOSE EVERY ATOM IS CHARGED WITH PHOTONIC ENERGY, TURNED HIM FROM MASS INTO ENERGY AND ATTEMPTED, IN DEFIANCE OF MEEPAK'S UNCERTAINTY PRINCIPLE, TO REINTEGRATE HIS ATOMIC STRUCTURE...
I DON'T CARE IF YOU TRIED TO TURN HIS ATOMS INTO KIPPERS AND SMOKE THEM! NOW WHERE IN HELL IS HE?!

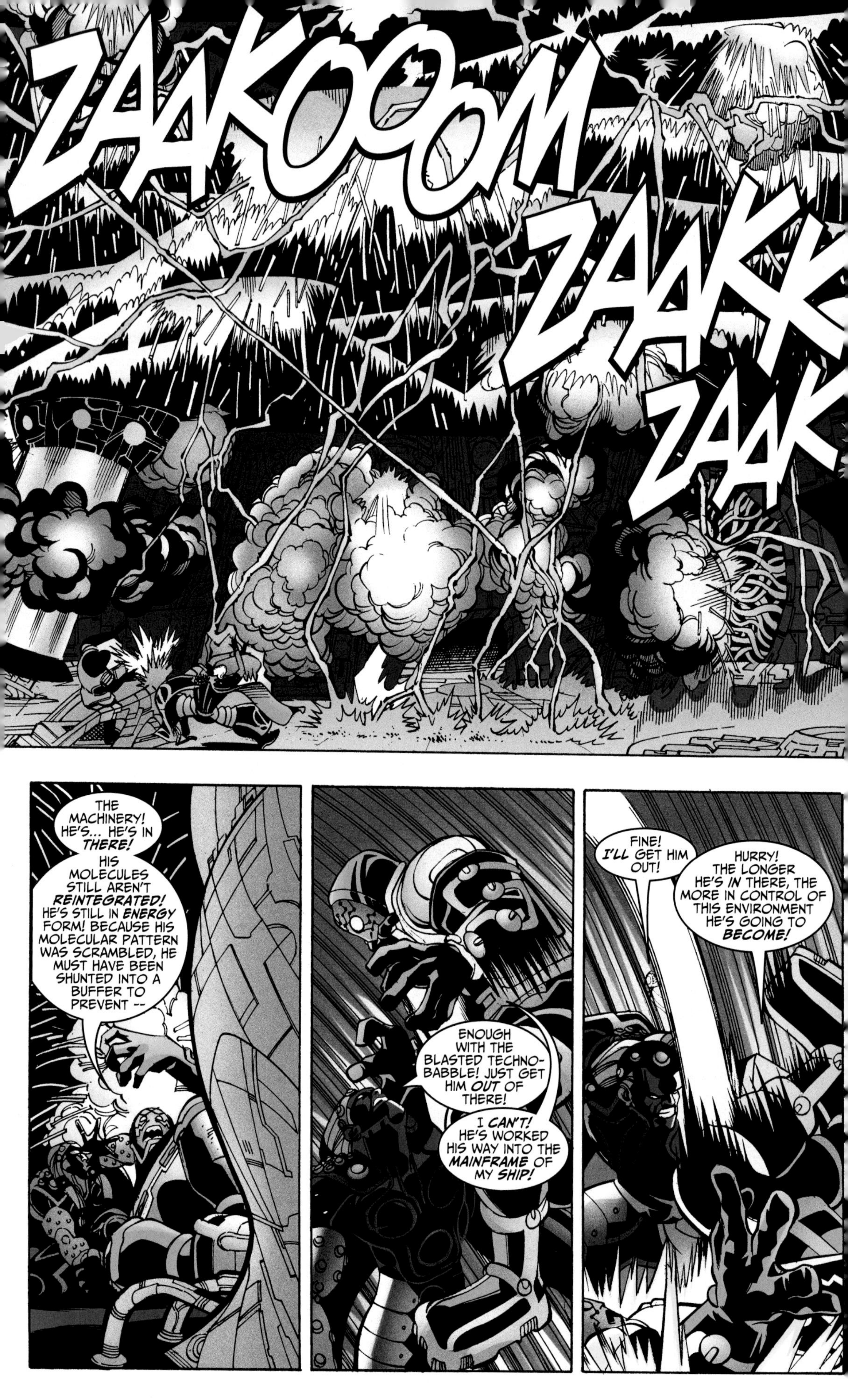

ZAKOOOM
ZAAKK
ZAAK
THE MACHINERY! HE'S... HE'S IN THERE!
HIS MOLECULES STILL AREN'T REINTEGRATED! HE'S STILL IN ENERGY FORM! BECAUSE HIS MOLECULAR PATTERN WAS SCRAMBLED, HE MUST HAVE BEEN SHUNTED INTO A BUFFER TO PREVENT --
ENOUGH WITH THE BLASTED TECHNO-BABBLE! JUST GET HIM OUT OF THERE!
I CAN'T! HE'S WORKED HIS WAY INTO THE MAINFRAME OF MY SHIP!
FINE! I'LL GET HIM OUT!
HURRY! THE LONGER HE'S IN THERE, THE MORE IN CONTROL OF THIS ENVIRONMENT HE'S GOING TO BECOME!

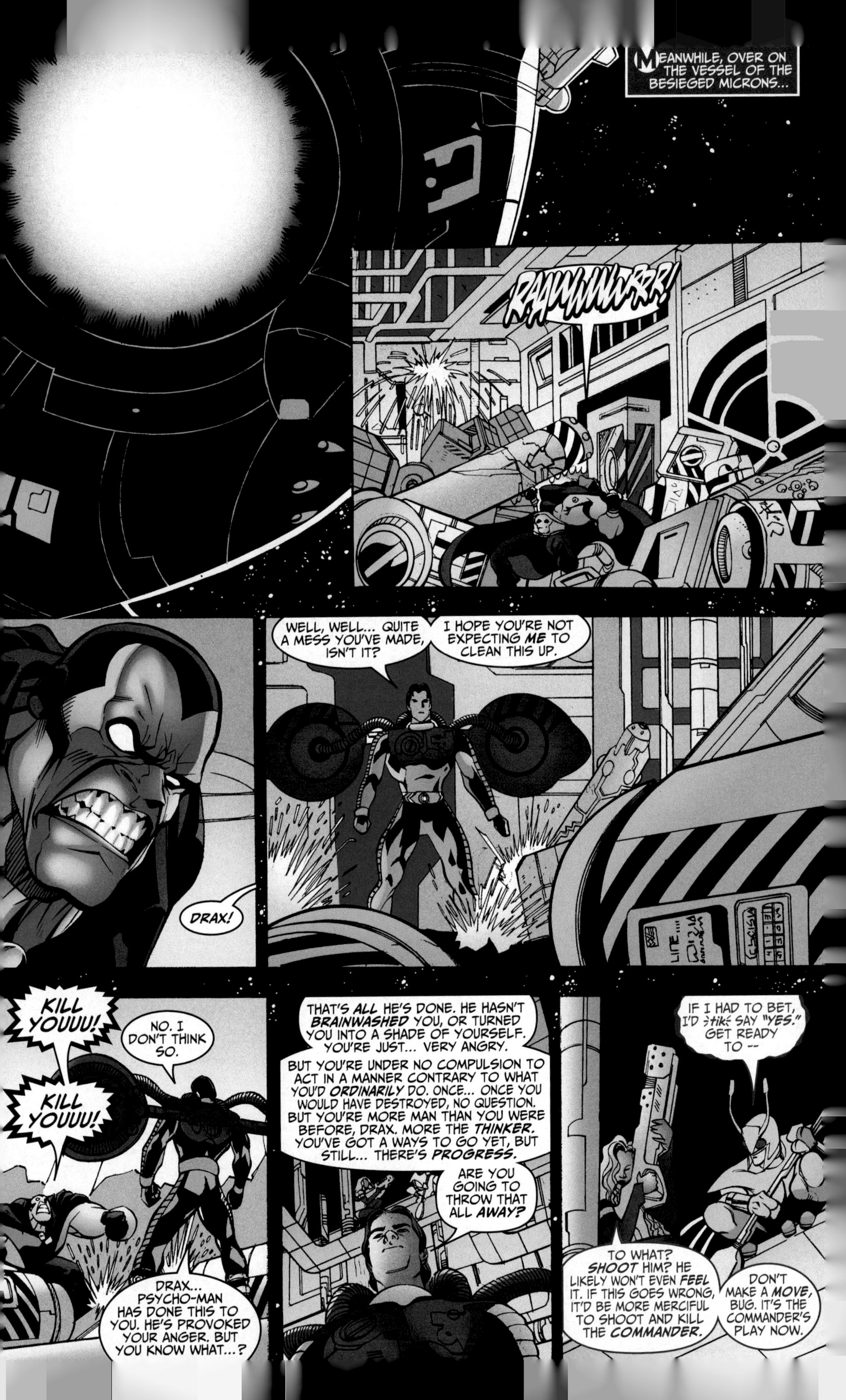

MEANWHILE, OVER ON THE VESSEL OF THE BESIEGED MICRONS...
RAAWWWRRR!
DRAX!
WELL, WELL... QUITE A MESS YOU'VE MADE, ISN'T IT?
I HOPE YOU'RE NOT EXPECTING ME TO CLEAN THIS UP.
KILL YOUUU!
NO. I DON'T THINK SO.
KILL YOUUU!
DRAX... PSYCHO-MAN HAS DONE THIS TO YOU. HE'S PROVOKED YOUR ANGER. BUT YOU KNOW WHAT...?
THAT'S ALL HE'S DONE. HE HASN'T BRAINWASHED YOU, OR TURNED YOU INTO A SHADE OF YOURSELF. YOU'RE JUST... VERY ANGRY.
BUT YOU'RE UNDER NO COMPULSION TO ACT IN A MANNER CONTRARY TO WHAT YOU'D ORDINARILY DO. ONCE... ONCE YOU WOULD HAVE DESTROYED, NO QUESTION. BUT YOU'RE MORE MAN THAN YOU WERE BEFORE, DRAX. MORE THE THINKER. YOU'VE GOT A WAYS TO GO YET, BUT STILL... THERE'S PROGRESS.
ARE YOU GOING TO THROW THAT ALL AWAY?
IF I HAD TO BET, I'D ≠tik≠ SAY "YES." GET READY TO --
TO WHAT? SHOOT HIM? HE LIKELY WON'T EVEN FEEL IT. IF THIS GOES WRONG, IT'D BE MORE MERCIFUL TO SHOOT AND KILL THE COMMANDER.
DON'T MAKE A MOVE, BUG. IT'S THE COMMANDER'S PLAY NOW.

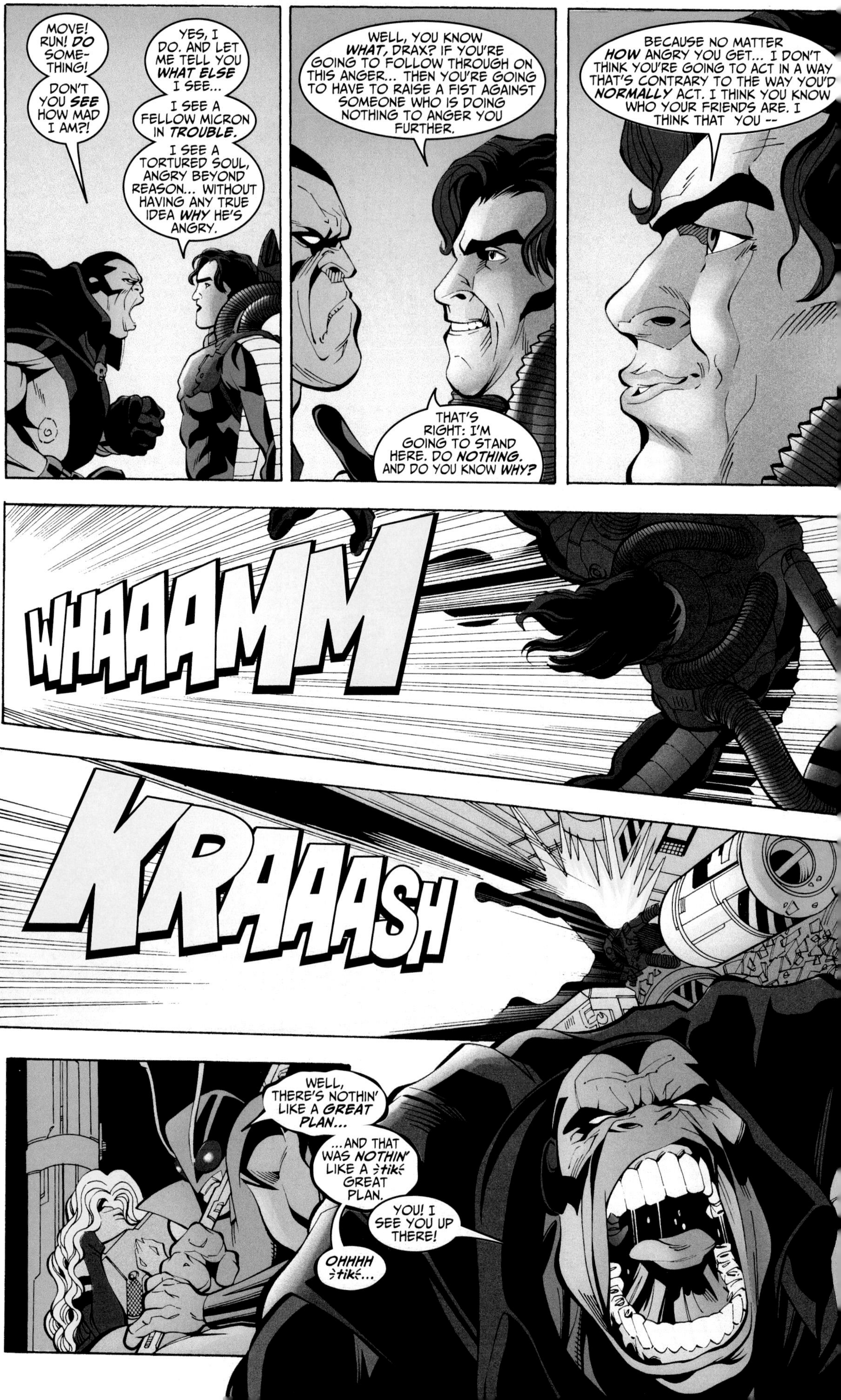
MOVE! RUN! DO SOME-THING!
DON'T YOU SEE HOW MAD I AM?!
YES, I DO. AND LET ME TELL YOU WHAT ELSE I SEE...
I SEE A FELLOW MICRON IN TROUBLE.
I SEE A TORTURED SOUL, ANGRY BEYOND REASON... WITHOUT HAVING ANY TRUE IDEA WHY HE'S ANGRY.
WELL, YOU KNOW WHAT, DRAX? IF YOU'RE GOING TO FOLLOW THROUGH ON THIS ANGER... THEN YOU'RE GOING TO HAVE TO RAISE A FIST AGAINST SOMEONE WHO IS DOING NOTHING TO ANGER YOU FURTHER.
THAT'S RIGHT: I'M GOING TO STAND HERE. DO NOTHING. AND DO YOU KNOW WHY?
BECAUSE NO MATTER HOW ANGRY YOU GET... I DON'T THINK YOU'RE GOING TO ACT IN A WAY THAT'S CONTRARY TO THE WAY YOU'D NORMALLY ACT. I THINK YOU KNOW WHO YOUR FRIENDS ARE. I THINK THAT YOU --
WHAAAMM
KRAAASH
WELL, THERE'S NOTHIN' LIKE A GREAT PLAN...
...AND THAT WAS NOTHIN' LIKE A ⇉tik⇇ GREAT PLAN.
YOU! I SEE YOU UP THERE!
OHHHH ⇉tik⇇...

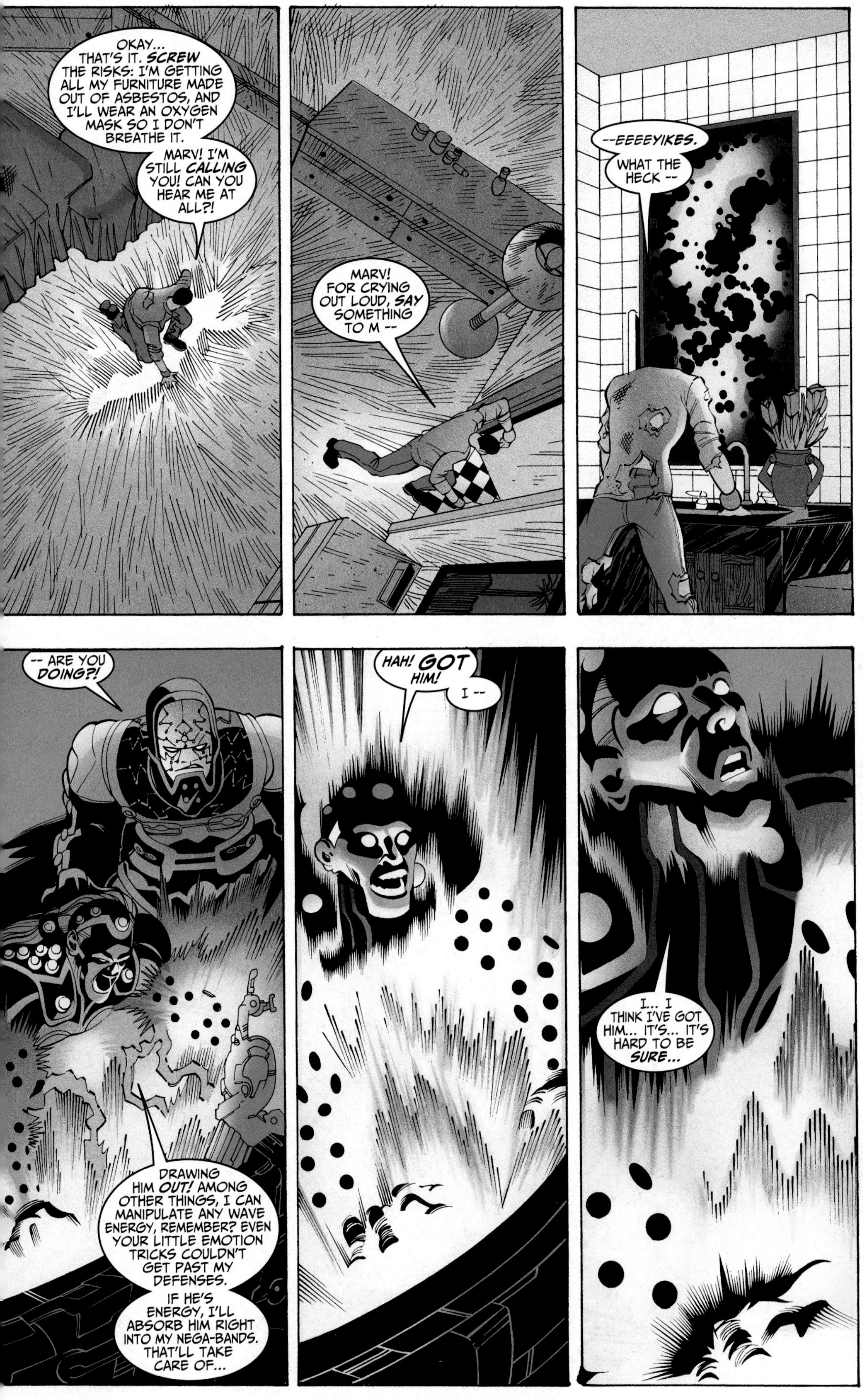
OKAY... THAT'S IT. SCREW THE RISKS: I'M GETTING ALL MY FURNITURE MADE OUT OF ASBESTOS, AND I'LL WEAR AN OXYGEN MASK SO I DON'T BREATHE IT.
MARV! I'M STILL CALLING YOU! CAN YOU HEAR ME AT ALL?!
MARV! FOR CRYING OUT LOUD, SAY SOMETHING TO M --
--EEEEYIKES.
WHAT THE HECK --
-- ARE YOU DOING?!
DRAWING HIM OUT! AMONG OTHER THINGS, I CAN MANIPULATE ANY WAVE ENERGY, REMEMBER? EVEN YOUR LITTLE EMOTION TRICKS COULDN'T GET PAST MY DEFENSES.
IF HE'S ENERGY, I'LL ABSORB HIM RIGHT INTO MY NEGA-BANDS. THAT'LL TAKE CARE OF...
HAH! GOT HIM!
I --
I... I THINK I'VE GOT HIM... IT'S... IT'S HARD TO BE SURE...

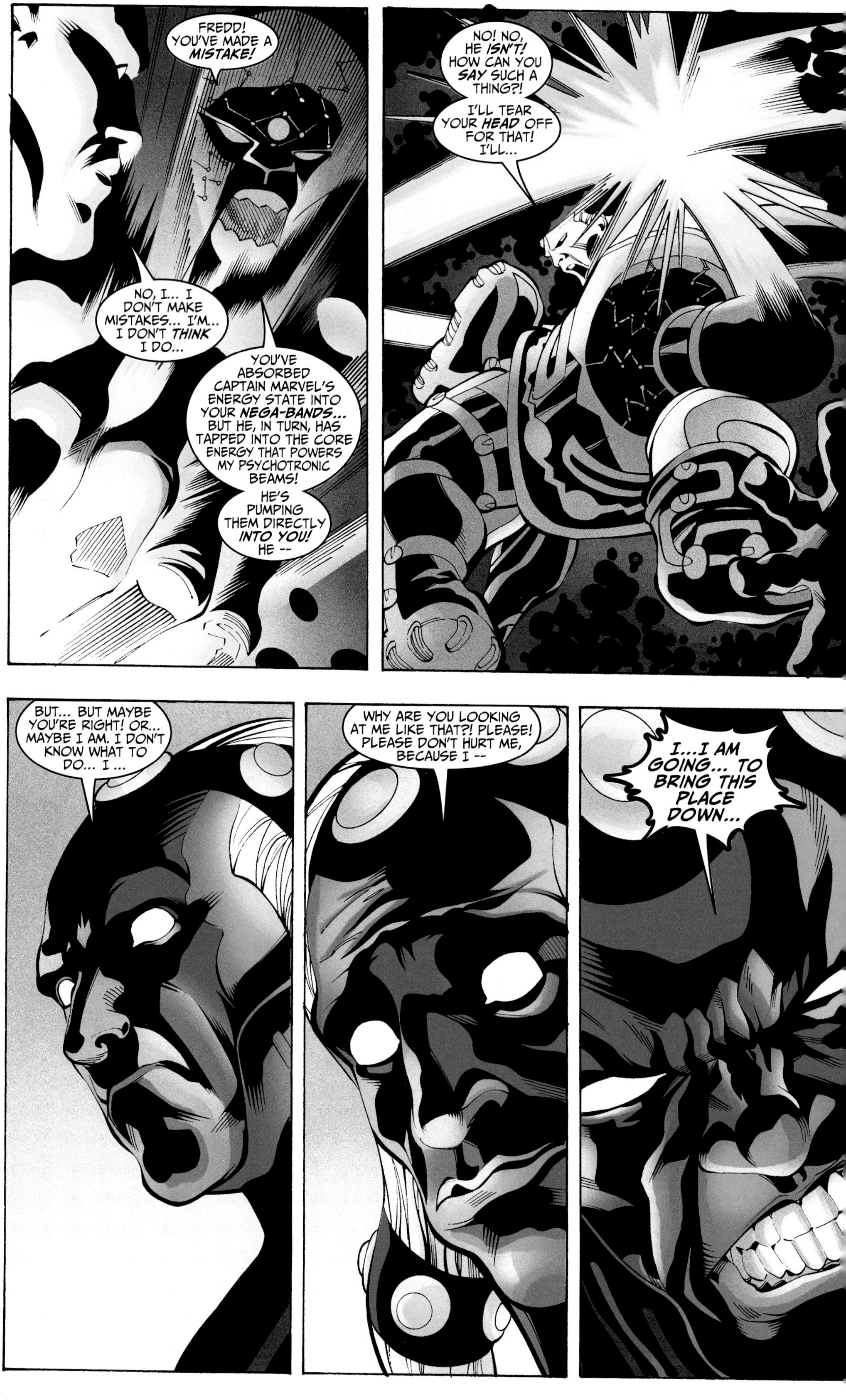
FREDD! YOU'VE MADE A MISTAKE!
NO, I... I DON'T MAKE MISTAKES... I'M... I DON'T THINK I DO...
YOU'VE ABSORBED CAPTAIN MARVEL'S ENERGY STATE INTO YOUR NEGA-BANDS... BUT HE, IN TURN, HAS TAPPED INTO THE CORE ENERGY THAT POWERS MY PSYCHOTRONIC BEAMS!
HE'S PUMPING THEM DIRECTLY INTO YOU! HE --
NO! NO, HE ISN'T! HOW CAN YOU SAY SUCH A THING?!
I'LL TEAR YOUR HEAD OFF FOR THAT! I'LL...
BUT... BUT MAYBE YOU'RE RIGHT! OR... MAYBE I AM. I DON'T KNOW WHAT TO DO... I ...
WHY ARE YOU LOOKING AT ME LIKE THAT?! PLEASE! PLEASE DON'T HURT ME, BECAUSE I --
I...I AM GOING... TO BRING THIS PLACE DOWN...

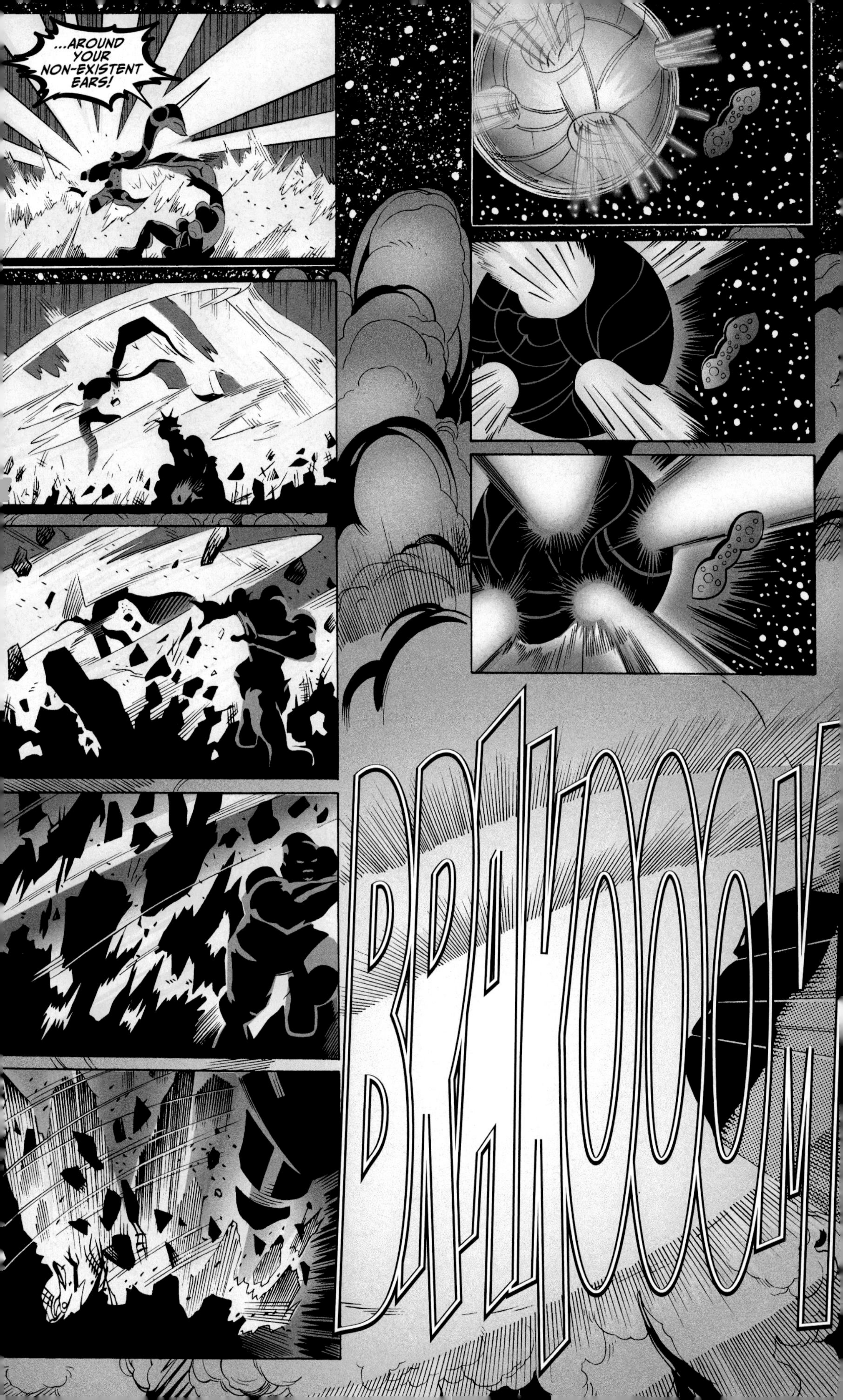
...AROUND YOUR NON-EXISTENT EARS!
BRAHOOOOM

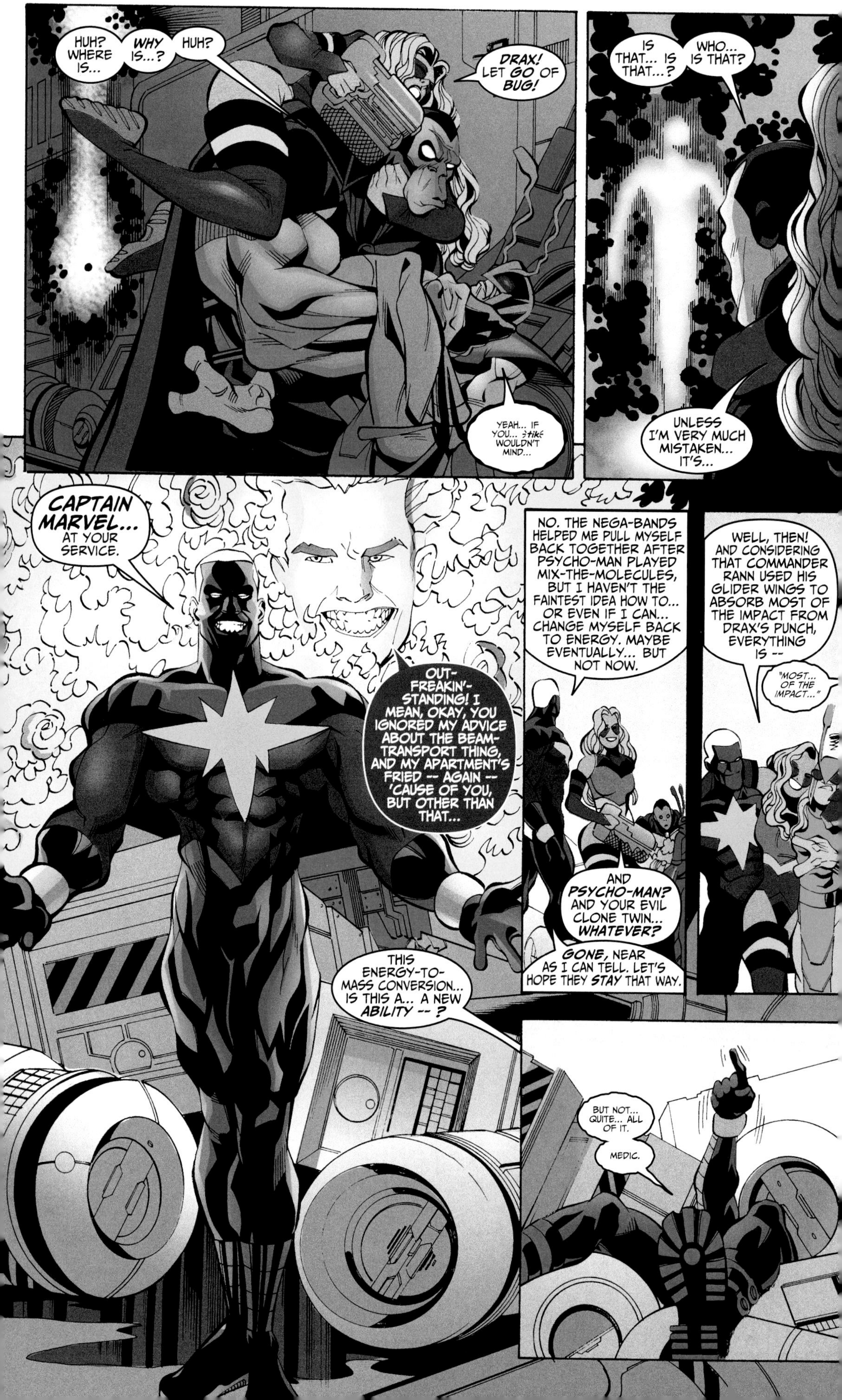

HUH? WHERE IS...
WHY IS...?
HUH?
DRAX! LET GO OF BUG!
YEAH... IF YOU... *tik* WOULDN'T MIND...
IS THAT... IS THAT...?
WHO... IS THAT?
UNLESS I'M VERY MUCH MISTAKEN... IT'S...
CAPTAIN MARVEL... AT YOUR SERVICE.
OUT-FREAKIN'-STANDING! I MEAN, OKAY, YOU IGNORED MY ADVICE ABOUT THE BEAM-TRANSPORT THING, AND MY APARTMENT'S FRIED -- AGAIN -- 'CAUSE OF YOU, BUT OTHER THAN THAT...
THIS ENERGY-TO-MASS CONVERSION... IS THIS A... A NEW ABILITY -- ?
NO. THE NEGA-BANDS HELPED ME PULL MYSELF BACK TOGETHER AFTER PSYCHO-MAN PLAYED MIX-THE-MOLECULES, BUT I HAVEN'T THE FAINTEST IDEA HOW TO... OR EVEN IF I CAN... CHANGE MYSELF BACK TO ENERGY. MAYBE EVENTUALLY... BUT NOT NOW.
AND PSYCHO-MAN? AND YOUR EVIL CLONE TWIN... WHATEVER?
GONE, NEAR AS I CAN TELL. LET'S HOPE THEY STAY THAT WAY.
WELL, THEN! AND CONSIDERING THAT COMMANDER RANN USED HIS GLIDER WINGS TO ABSORB MOST OF THE IMPACT FROM DRAX'S PUNCH, EVERYTHING IS --
"MOST... OF THE IMPACT..."
BUT NOT... QUITE... ALL OF IT.
MEDIC.

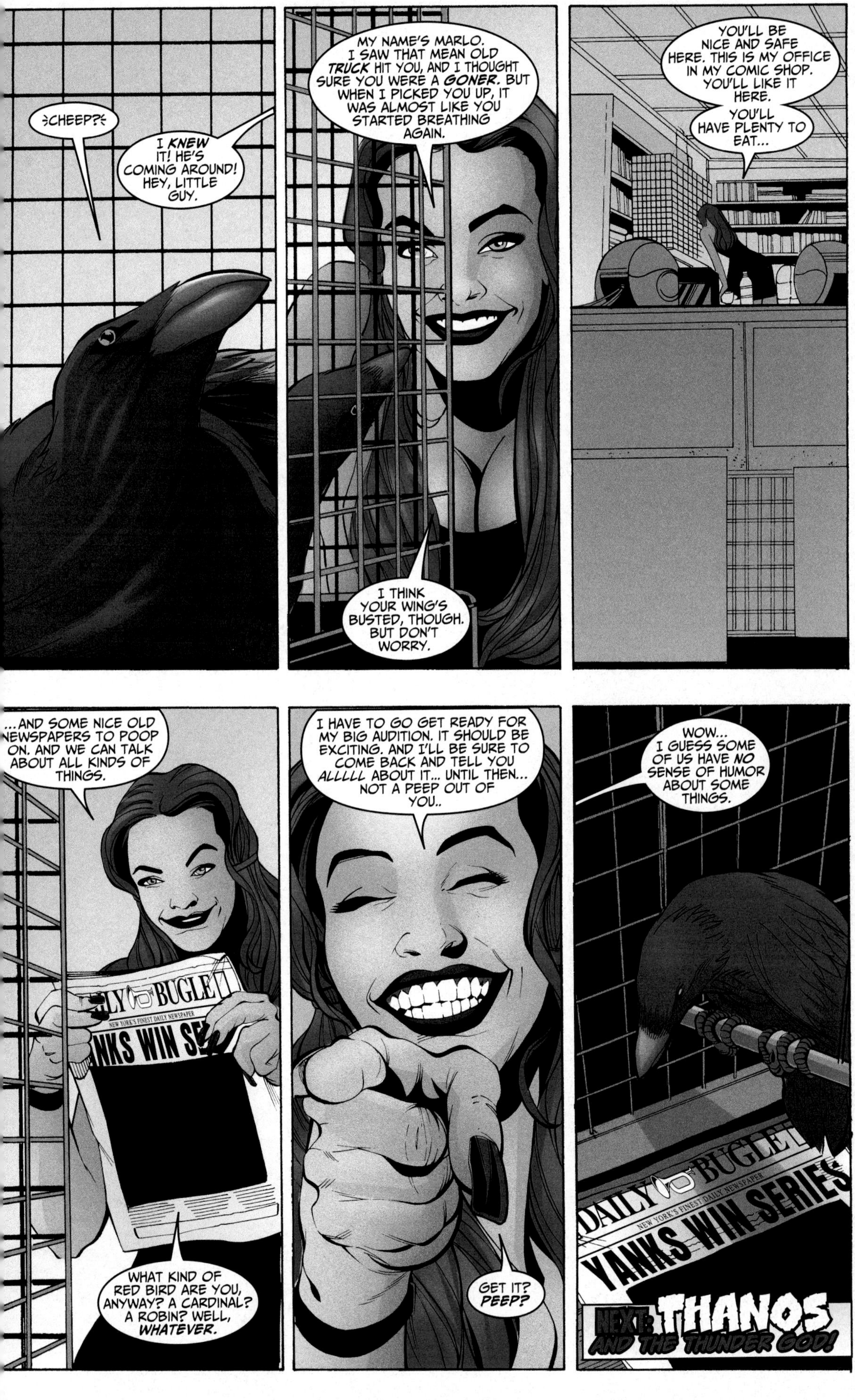

CHEEP?
I KNEW IT! HE'S COMING AROUND! HEY, LITTLE GUY.
MY NAME'S MARLO. I SAW THAT MEAN OLD TRUCK HIT YOU, AND I THOUGHT SURE YOU WERE A GONER. BUT WHEN I PICKED YOU UP, IT WAS ALMOST LIKE YOU STARTED BREATHING AGAIN.
I THINK YOUR WING'S BUSTED, THOUGH. BUT DON'T WORRY.
YOU'LL BE NICE AND SAFE HERE. THIS IS MY OFFICE IN MY COMIC SHOP. YOU'LL LIKE IT HERE.
YOU'LL HAVE PLENTY TO EAT...
...AND SOME NICE OLD NEWSPAPERS TO POOP ON. AND WE CAN TALK ABOUT ALL KINDS OF THINGS.
DAILY BUGLE
NEW YORK'S FINEST DAILY NEWSPAPER
YANKS WIN SE
WHAT KIND OF RED BIRD ARE YOU, ANYWAY? A CARDINAL? A ROBIN? WELL, WHATEVER.
I HAVE TO GO GET READY FOR MY BIG AUDITION. IT SHOULD BE EXCITING. AND I'LL BE SURE TO COME BACK AND TELL YOU ALLLLL ABOUT IT... UNTIL THEN... NOT A PEEP OUT OF YOU..
GET IT? PEEP?
WOW... I GUESS SOME OF US HAVE NO SENSE OF HUMOR ABOUT SOME THINGS.
DAILY BUGLE
NEW YORK'S FINEST DAILY NEWSPAPER
YANKS WIN SERIES
NEXT: THANOS AND THE THUNDER GOD!

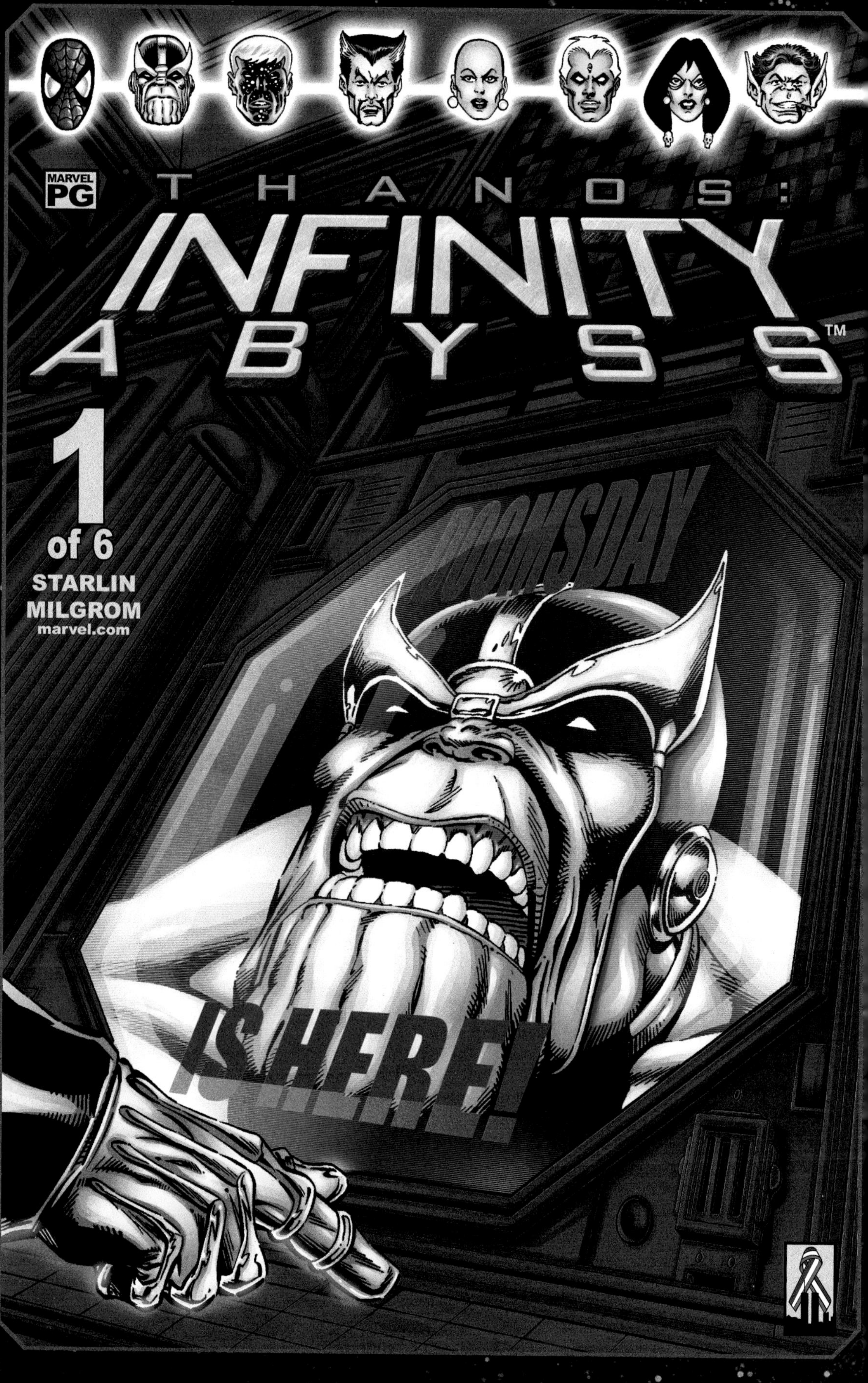
MARVEL PG
THANOS:
INFINITY
ABYSS™
1
of 6
STARLIN
MILGROM
marvel.com
DOOMSDAY
IS HERE!

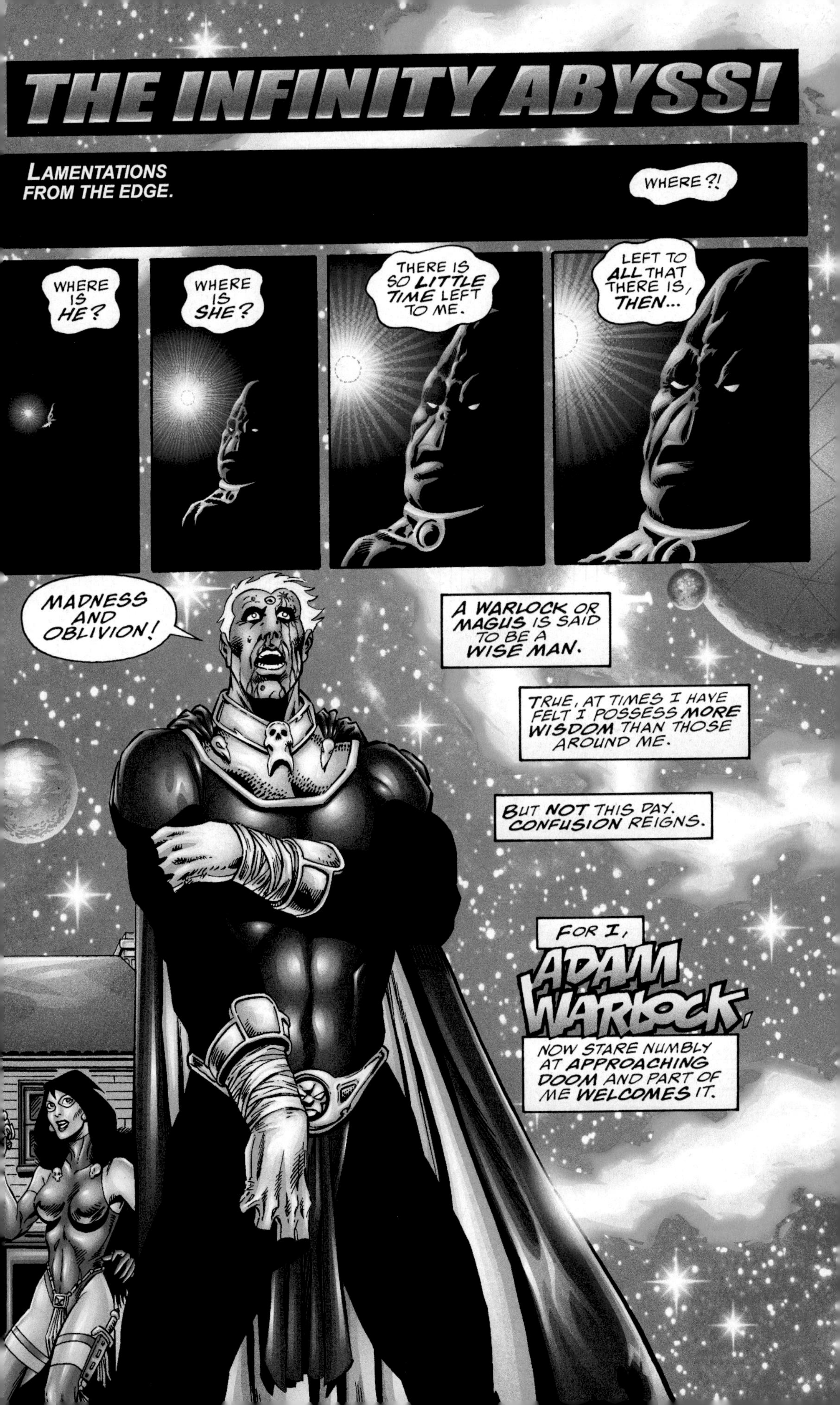
THE INFINITY ABYSS!
LAMENTATIONS FROM THE EDGE.
WHERE ?!
WHERE IS HE?
WHERE IS SHE?
THERE IS SO LITTLE TIME LEFT TO ME.
LEFT TO ALL THAT THERE IS, THEN...
MADNESS AND OBLIVION!
A WARLOCK OR MAGUS IS SAID TO BE A WISE MAN.
TRUE, AT TIMES I HAVE FELT I POSSESS MORE WISDOM THAN THOSE AROUND ME.
BUT NOT THIS DAY. CONFUSION REIGNS.
FOR I,
ADAM WARLOCK,
NOW STARE NUMBLY AT APPROACHING DOOM AND PART OF ME WELCOMES IT.

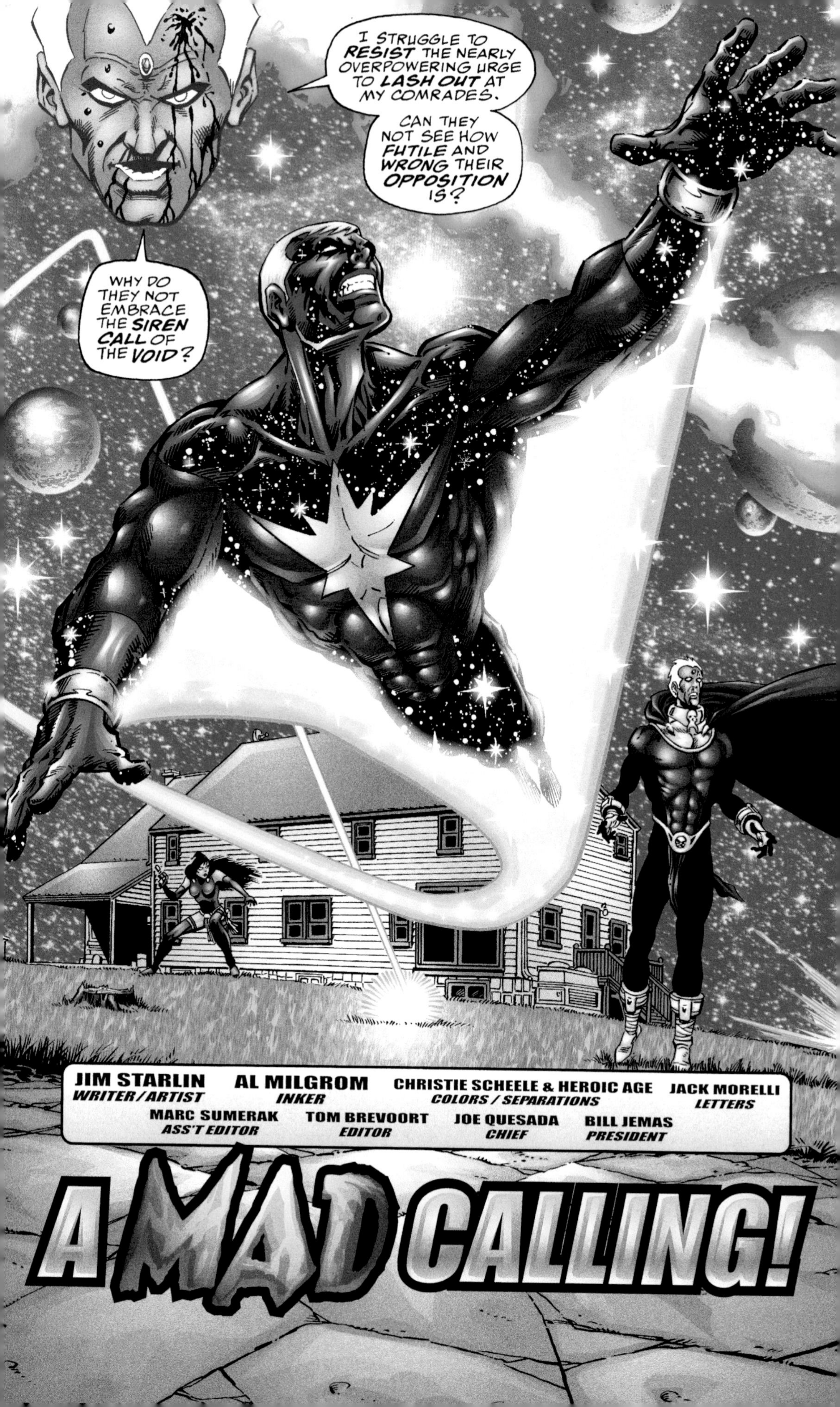

I STRUGGLE TO RESIST THE NEARLY OVERPOWERING URGE TO LASH OUT AT MY COMRADES.
CAN THEY NOT SEE HOW FUTILE AND WRONG THEIR OPPOSITION IS?
WHY DO THEY NOT EMBRACE THE SIREN CALL OF THE VOID?
JIM STARLIN WRITER/ARTIST
AL MILGROM INKER
CHRISTIE SCHEELE & HEROIC AGE COLORS / SEPARATIONS
JACK MORELLI LETTERS
MARC SUMERAK ASS'T EDITOR
TOM BREVOORT EDITOR
JOE QUESADA CHIEF
BILL JEMAS PRESIDENT
A MAD CALLING!

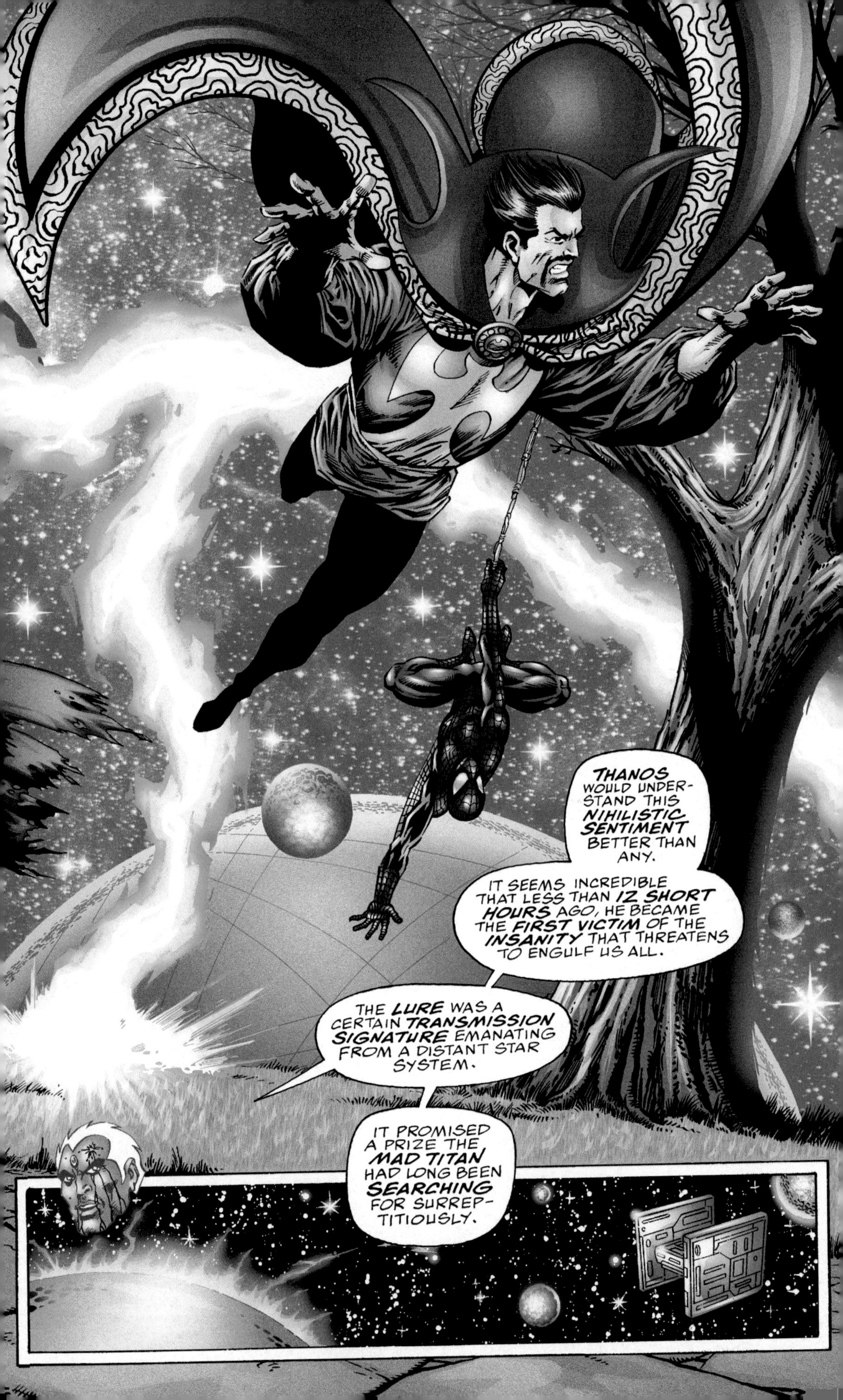
THANOS WOULD UNDERSTAND THIS NIHILISTIC SENTIMENT BETTER THAN ANY.
IT SEEMS INCREDIBLE THAT LESS THAN 12 SHORT HOURS AGO, HE BECAME THE FIRST VICTIM OF THE INSANITY THAT THREATENS TO ENGULF US ALL.
THE LURE WAS A CERTAIN TRANSMISSION SIGNATURE EMANATING FROM A DISTANT STAR SYSTEM.
IT PROMISED A PRIZE THE MAD TITAN HAD LONG BEEN SEARCHING FOR SURREPTITIOUSLY.

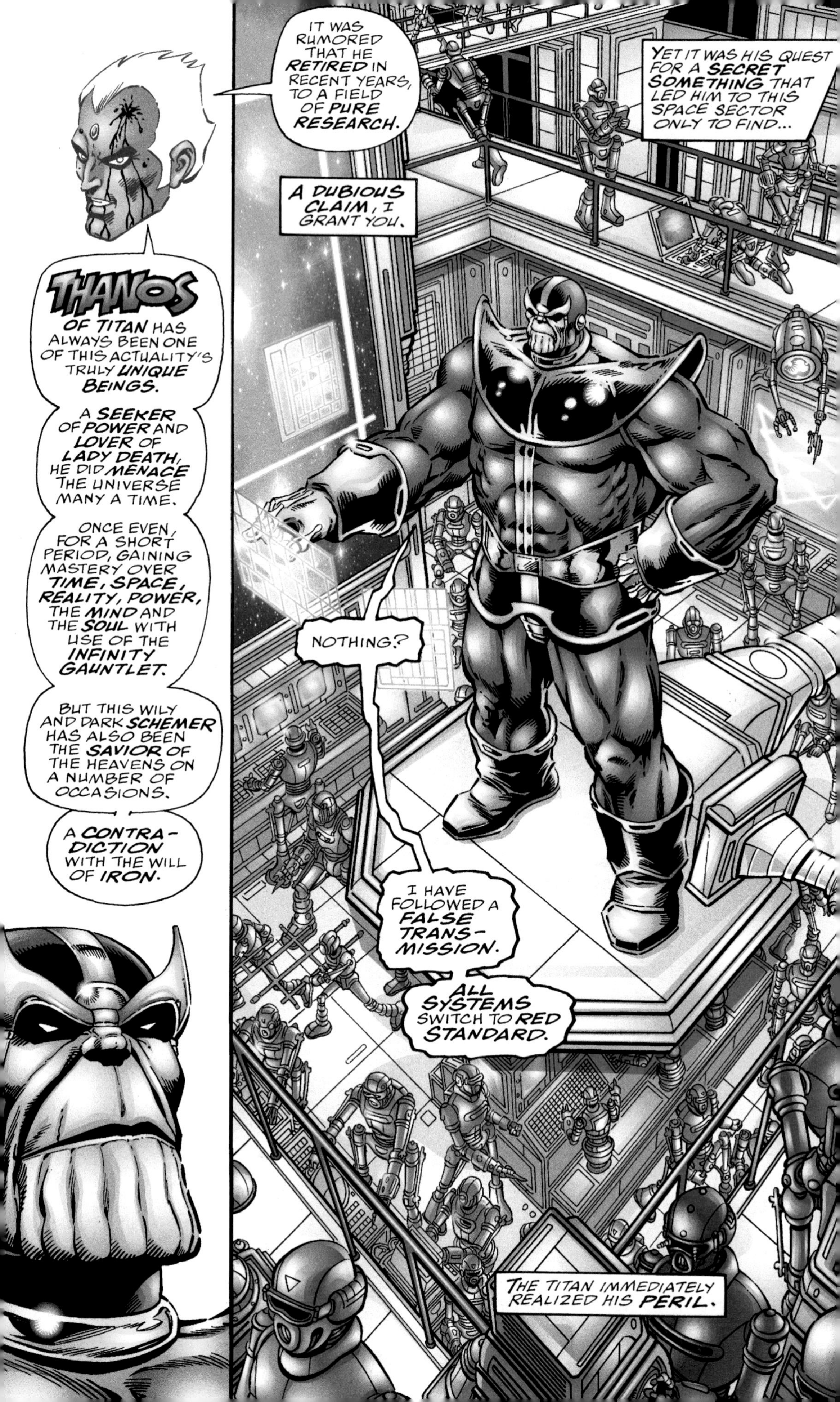

THANOS OF TITAN HAS ALWAYS BEEN ONE OF THIS ACTUALITY'S TRULY UNIQUE BEINGS.
A SEEKER OF POWER AND LOVER OF LADY DEATH, HE DID MENACE THE UNIVERSE MANY A TIME.
ONCE EVEN, FOR A SHORT PERIOD, GAINING MASTERY OVER TIME, SPACE, REALITY, POWER, THE MIND AND THE SOUL WITH USE OF THE INFINITY GAUNTLET.
BUT THIS WILY AND DARK SCHEMER HAS ALSO BEEN THE SAVIOR OF THE HEAVENS ON A NUMBER OF OCCASIONS.
A CONTRA-DICTION WITH THE WILL OF IRON.
IT WAS RUMORED THAT HE RETIRED IN RECENT YEARS, TO A FIELD OF PURE RESEARCH.
A DUBIOUS CLAIM, I GRANT YOU.
YET IT WAS HIS QUEST FOR A SECRET SOMETHING THAT LED HIM TO THIS SPACE SECTOR ONLY TO FIND...
NOTHING?
I HAVE FOLLOWED A FALSE TRANS-MISSION.
ALL SYSTEMS SWITCH TO RED STANDARD.
THE TITAN IMMEDIATELY REALIZED HIS PERIL.

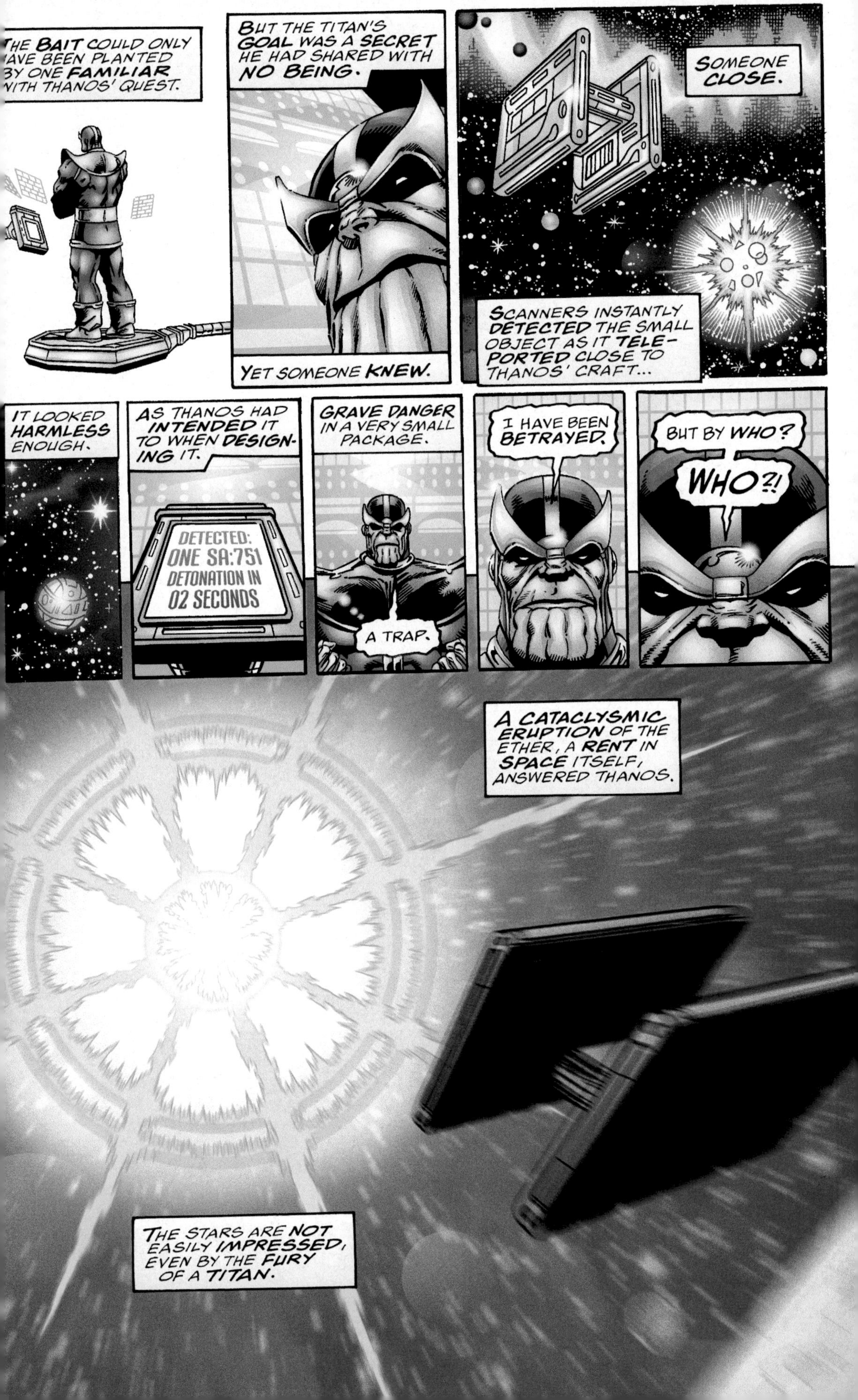
THE BAIT COULD ONLY HAVE BEEN PLANTED BY ONE FAMILIAR WITH THANOS' QUEST.
BUT THE TITAN'S GOAL WAS A SECRET HE HAD SHARED WITH NO BEING.
YET SOMEONE KNEW.
SOMEONE CLOSE.
SCANNERS INSTANTLY DETECTED THE SMALL OBJECT AS IT TELE-PORTED CLOSE TO THANOS' CRAFT...
IT LOOKED HARMLESS ENOUGH.
AS THANOS HAD INTENDED IT TO WHEN DESIGN-ING IT.
DETECTED: ONE SA:751 DETONATION IN 02 SECONDS
GRAVE DANGER IN A VERY SMALL PACKAGE.
A TRAP.
I HAVE BEEN BETRAYED.
BUT BY WHO?
WHO?!
A CATACLYSMIC ERUPTION OF THE ETHER, A RENT IN SPACE ITSELF, ANSWERED THANOS.
THE STARS ARE NOT EASILY IMPRESSED, EVEN BY THE FURY OF A TITAN.

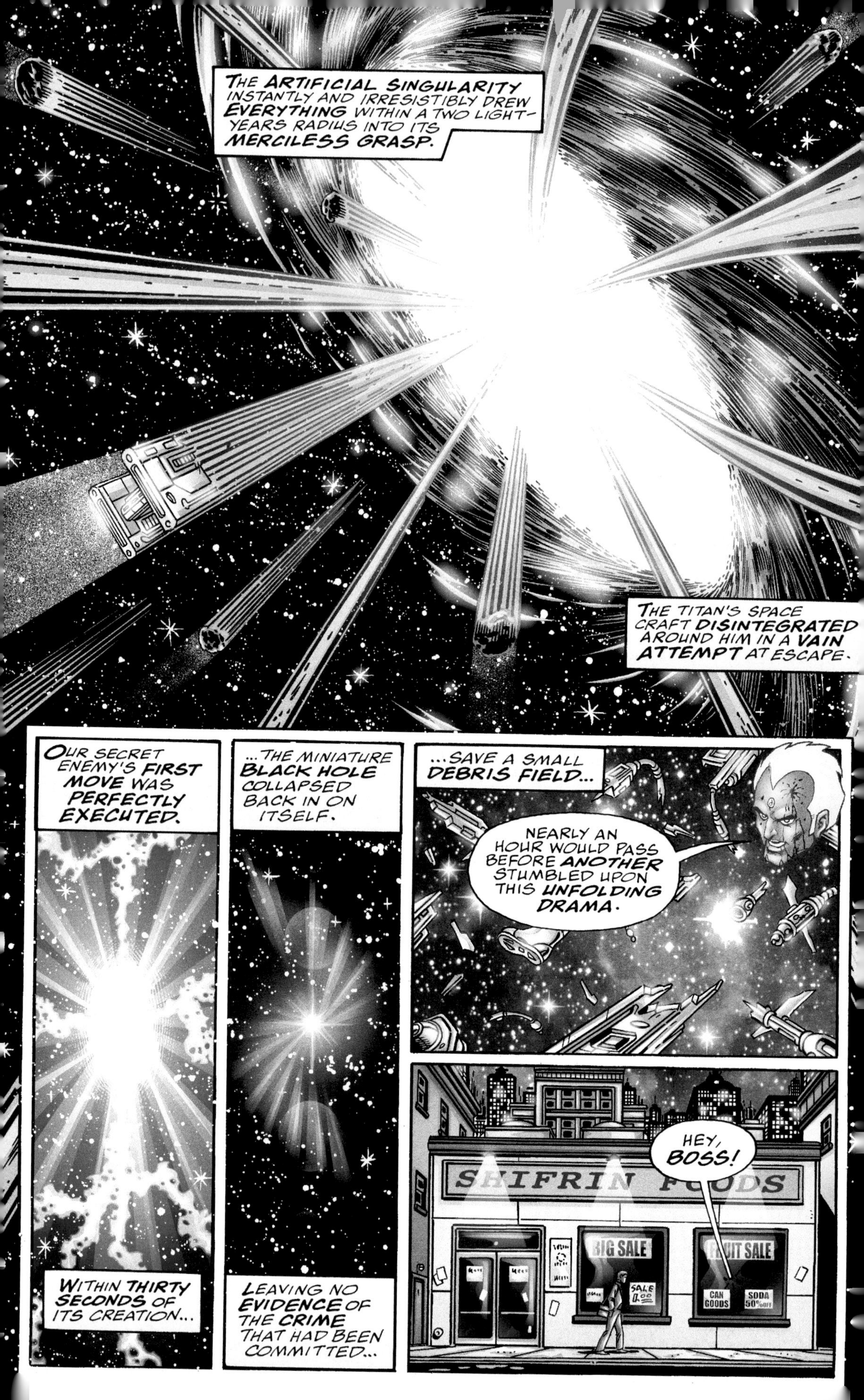
THE ARTIFICIAL SINGULARITY INSTANTLY AND IRRESISTIBLY DREW EVERYTHING WITHIN A TWO LIGHT-YEARS RADIUS INTO ITS MERCILESS GRASP.
THE TITAN'S SPACE CRAFT DISINTEGRATED AROUND HIM IN A VAIN ATTEMPT AT ESCAPE.
OUR SECRET ENEMY'S FIRST MOVE WAS PERFECTLY EXECUTED.
WITHIN THIRTY SECONDS OF ITS CREATION...
...THE MINIATURE BLACK HOLE COLLAPSED BACK IN ON ITSELF.
LEAVING NO EVIDENCE OF THE CRIME THAT HAD BEEN COMMITTED...
...SAVE A SMALL DEBRIS FIELD...
NEARLY AN HOUR WOULD PASS BEFORE ANOTHER STUMBLED UPON THIS UNFOLDING DRAMA.
SHIFRIN FOODS
BIG SALE
FRUIT SALE
SALE
CAN GOODS
SODA 50% OFF
HEY, BOSS!

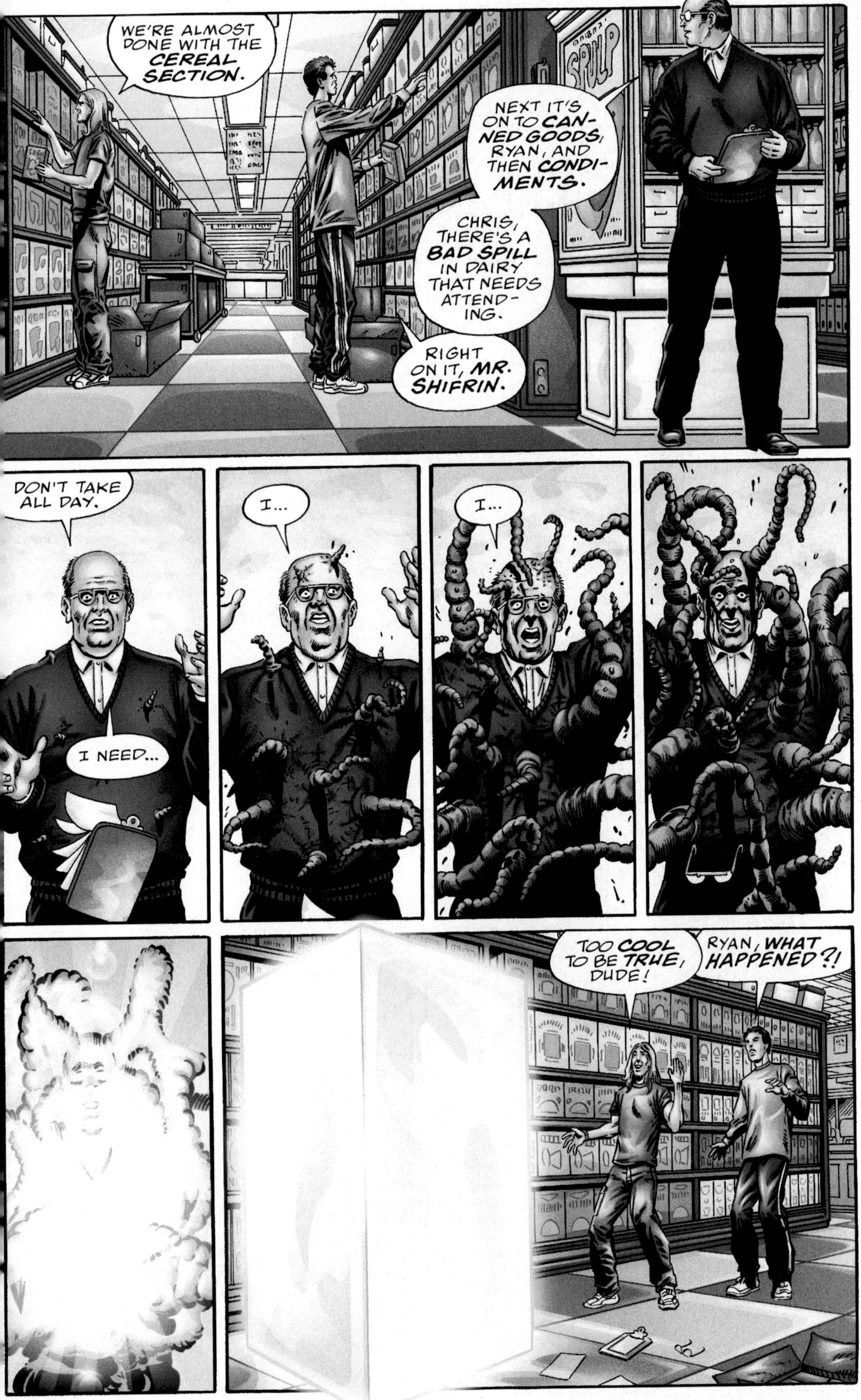
WE'RE ALMOST DONE WITH THE CEREAL SECTION.
NEXT IT'S ON TO CANNED GOODS, RYAN, AND THEN CONDIMENTS.
CHRIS, THERE'S A BAD SPILL IN DAIRY THAT NEEDS ATTENDING.
RIGHT ON IT, MR. SHIFRIN.
DON'T TAKE ALL DAY.
I NEED...
I...
I...
TOO COOL TO BE TRUE, DUDE!
RYAN, WHAT HAPPENED?!

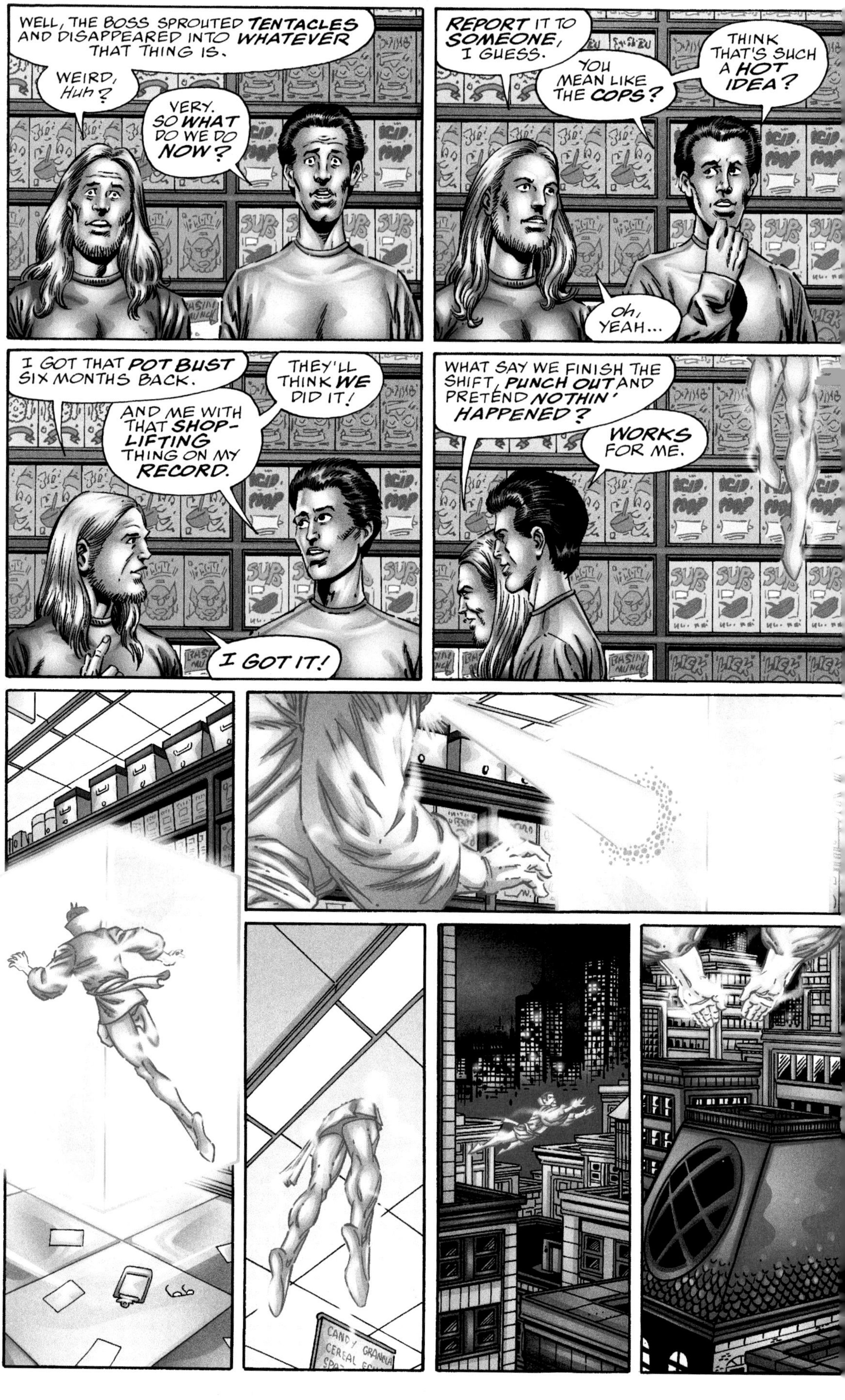

WELL, THE BOSS SPROUTED TENTACLES AND DISAPPEARED INTO WHATEVER THAT THING IS.
WEIRD, Huh?
VERY. SO WHAT DO WE DO NOW?
REPORT IT TO SOMEONE, I GUESS.
YOU MEAN LIKE THE COPS?
THINK THAT'S SUCH A HOT IDEA?
Oh, YEAH...
I GOT THAT POT BUST SIX MONTHS BACK.
AND ME WITH THAT SHOP-LIFTING THING ON MY RECORD.
THEY'LL THINK WE DID IT!
I GOT IT!
WHAT SAY WE FINISH THE SHIFT, PUNCH OUT AND PRETEND NOTHIN' HAPPENED?
WORKS FOR ME.

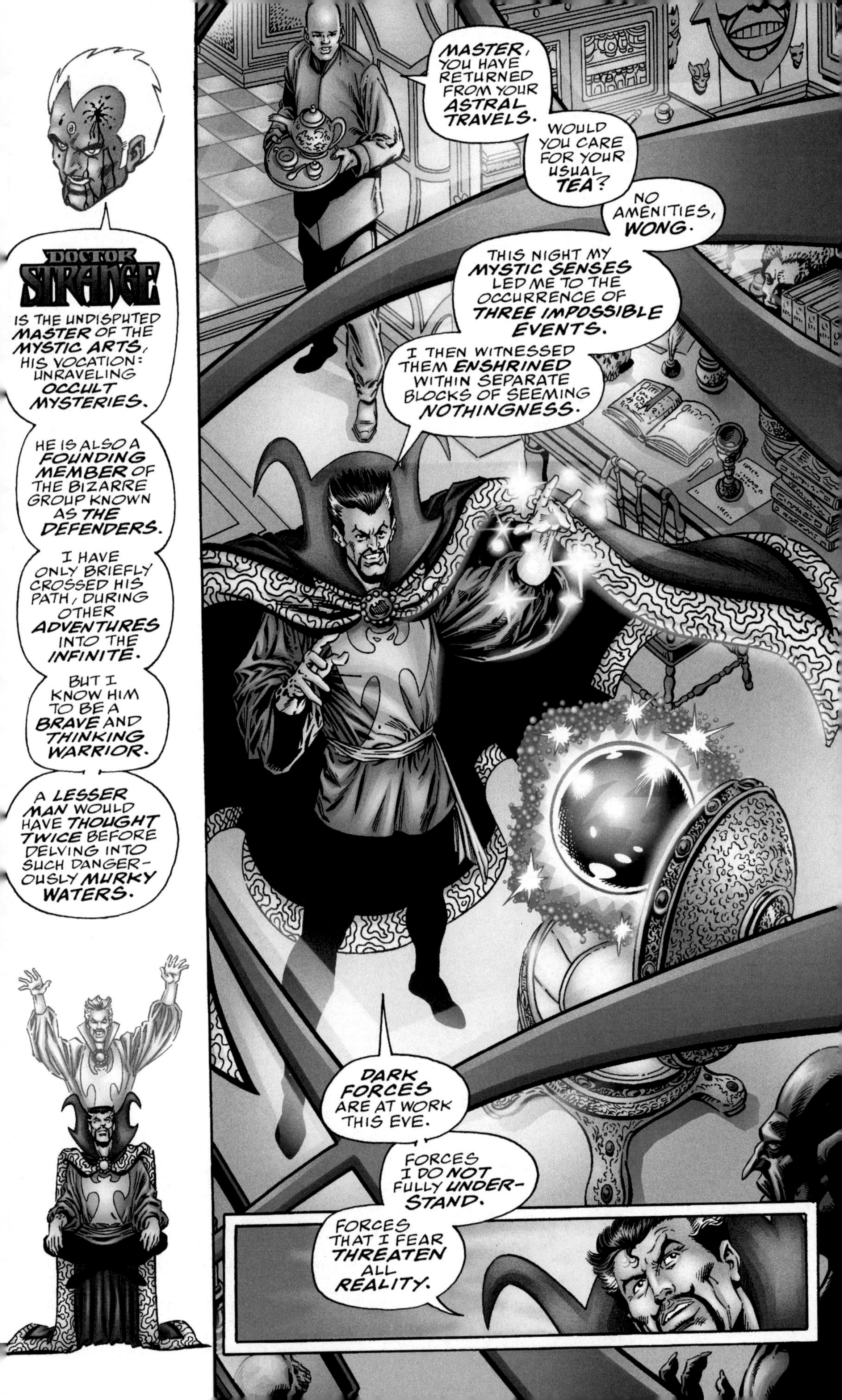
MASTER, YOU HAVE RETURNED FROM YOUR ASTRAL TRAVELS.
WOULD YOU CARE FOR YOUR USUAL TEA?
NO AMENITIES, WONG.
THIS NIGHT MY MYSTIC SENSES LED ME TO THE OCCURRENCE OF THREE IMPOSSIBLE EVENTS.
I THEN WITNESSED THEM ENSHRINED WITHIN SEPARATE BLOCKS OF SEEMING NOTHINGNESS.
DARK FORCES ARE AT WORK THIS EVE.
FORCES I DO NOT FULLY UNDER-STAND.
FORCES THAT I FEAR THREATEN ALL REALITY.
DOCTOR STRANGE IS THE UNDISPUTED MASTER OF THE MYSTIC ARTS, HIS VOCATION: UNRAVELING OCCULT MYSTERIES.
HE IS ALSO A FOUNDING MEMBER OF THE BIZARRE GROUP KNOWN AS THE DEFENDERS.
I HAVE ONLY BRIEFLY CROSSED HIS PATH, DURING OTHER ADVENTURES INTO THE INFINITE.
BUT I KNOW HIM TO BE A BRAVE AND THINKING WARRIOR.
A LESSER MAN WOULD HAVE THOUGHT TWICE BEFORE DELVING INTO SUCH DANGER-OUSLY MURKY WATERS.

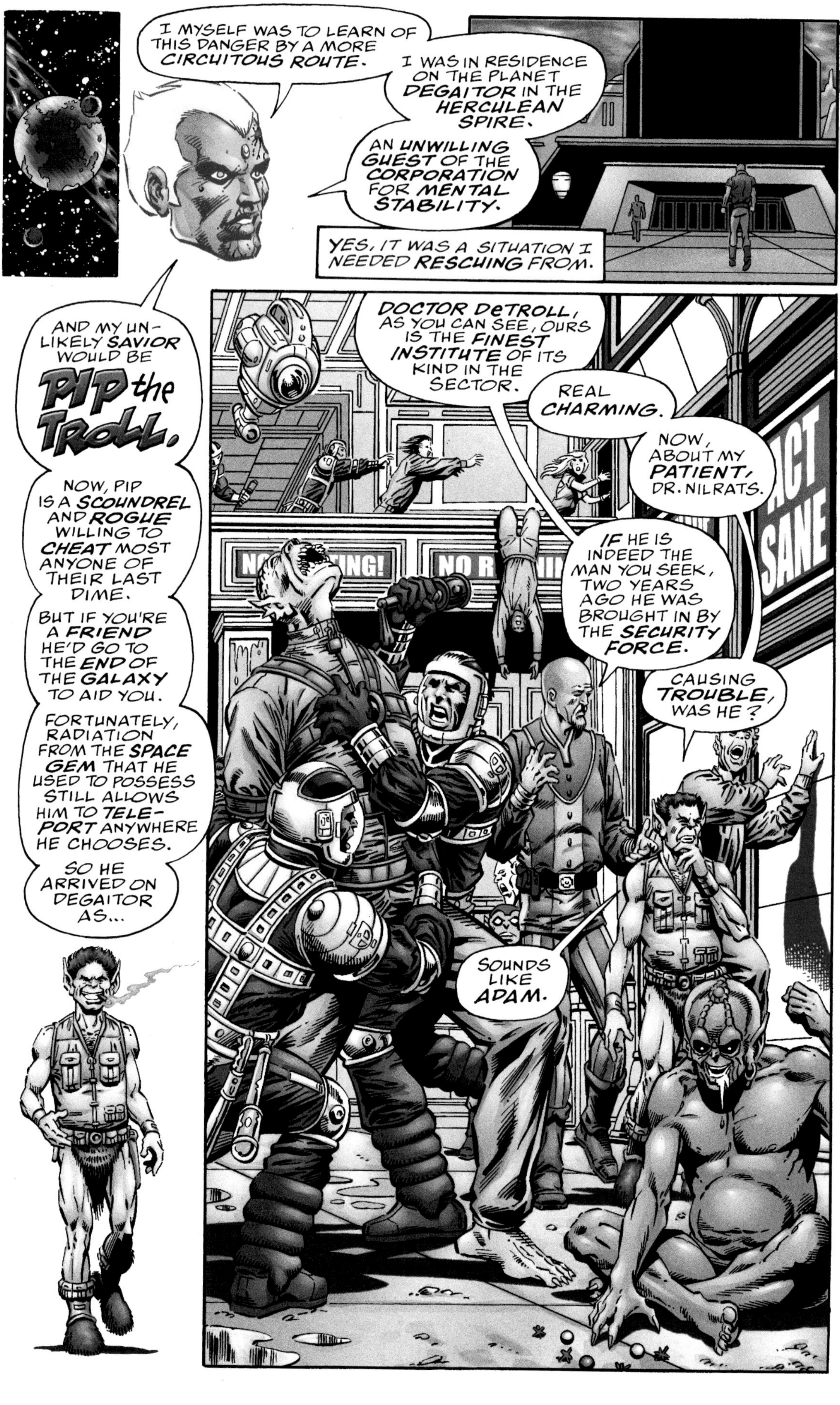
I MYSELF WAS TO LEARN OF THIS DANGER BY A MORE CIRCUITOUS ROUTE.
I WAS IN RESIDENCE ON THE PLANET DEGAITOR IN THE HERCULEAN SPIRE.
AN UNWILLING GUEST OF THE CORPORATION FOR MENTAL STABILITY.
YES, IT WAS A SITUATION I NEEDED RESCUING FROM.
AND MY UNLIKELY SAVIOR WOULD BE
PIP the TROLL.
NOW, PIP IS A SCOUNDREL AND ROGUE WILLING TO CHEAT MOST ANYONE OF THEIR LAST DIME.
BUT IF YOU'RE A FRIEND HE'D GO TO THE END OF THE GALAXY TO AID YOU.
FORTUNATELY, RADIATION FROM THE SPACE GEM THAT HE USED TO POSSESS STILL ALLOWS HIM TO TELEPORT ANYWHERE HE CHOOSES.
SO HE ARRIVED ON DEGAITOR AS...
DOCTOR DeTROLL, AS YOU CAN SEE, OURS IS THE FINEST INSTITUTE OF ITS KIND IN THE SECTOR.
REAL CHARMING.
NOW, ABOUT MY PATIENT, DR. NILRATS.
IF HE IS INDEED THE MAN YOU SEEK, TWO YEARS AGO HE WAS BROUGHT IN BY THE SECURITY FORCE.
CAUSING TROUBLE, WAS HE?
SOUNDS LIKE ADAM.
ACT SANE

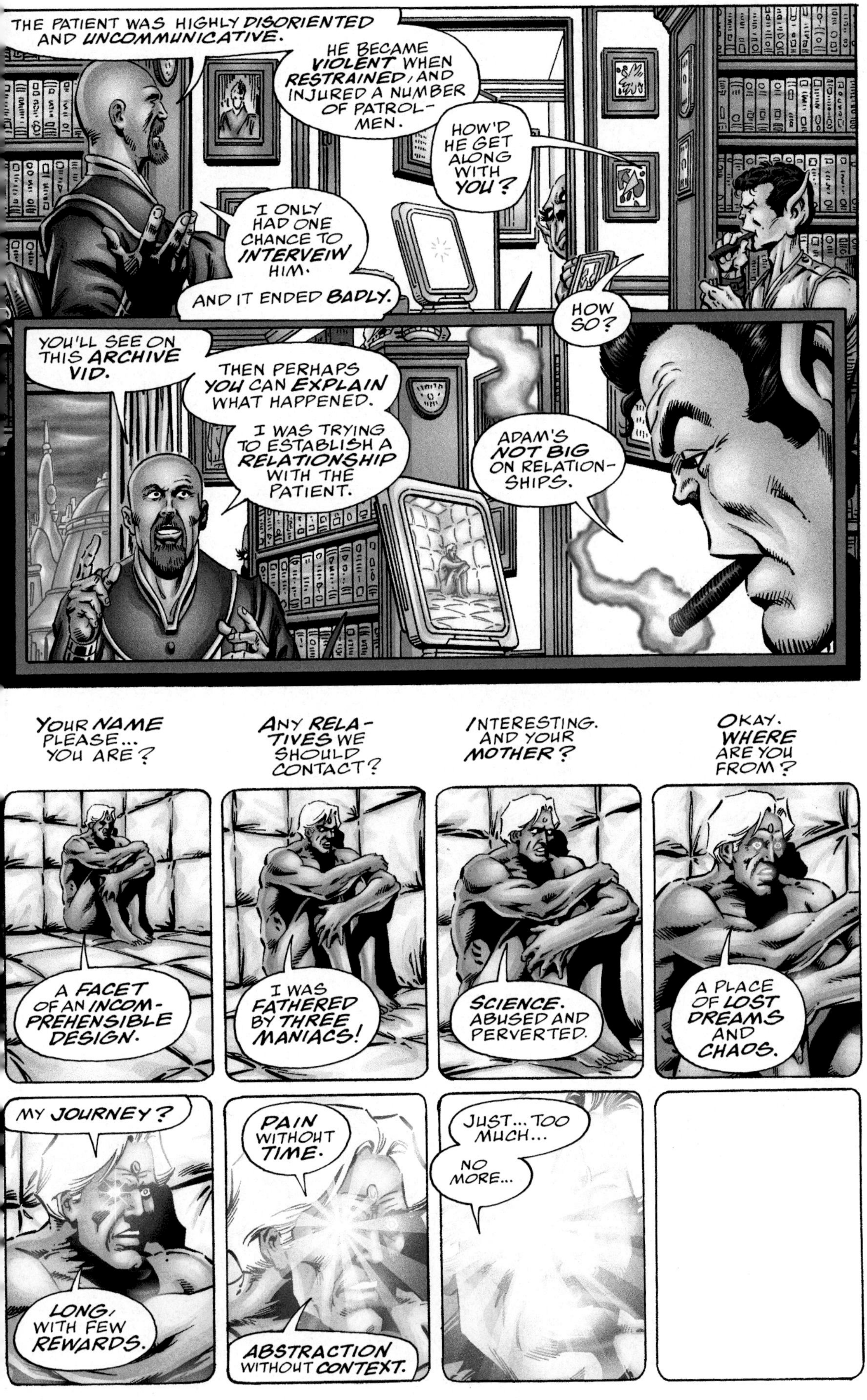
THE PATIENT WAS HIGHLY DISORIENTED AND UNCOMMUNICATIVE.
HE BECAME VIOLENT WHEN RESTRAINED, AND INJURED A NUMBER OF PATROL-MEN.
HOW'D HE GET ALONG WITH YOU?
I ONLY HAD ONE CHANCE TO INTERVEIW HIM.
AND IT ENDED BADLY.
HOW SO?
YOU'LL SEE ON THIS ARCHIVE VID.
THEN PERHAPS YOU CAN EXPLAIN WHAT HAPPENED.
I WAS TRYING TO ESTABLISH A RELATIONSHIP WITH THE PATIENT.
ADAM'S NOT BIG ON RELATION-SHIPS.
YOUR NAME PLEASE... YOU ARE?
A FACET OF AN INCOM-PREHENSIBLE DESIGN.
ANY RELA-TIVES WE SHOULD CONTACT?
I WAS FATHERED BY THREE MANIACS!
INTERESTING. AND YOUR MOTHER?
SCIENCE. ABUSED AND PERVERTED.
OKAY. WHERE ARE YOU FROM?
A PLACE OF LOST DREAMS AND CHAOS.
MY JOURNEY?
LONG, WITH FEW REWARDS.
PAIN WITHOUT TIME.
ABSTRACTION WITHOUT CONTEXT.
JUST... TOO MUCH...
NO MORE...

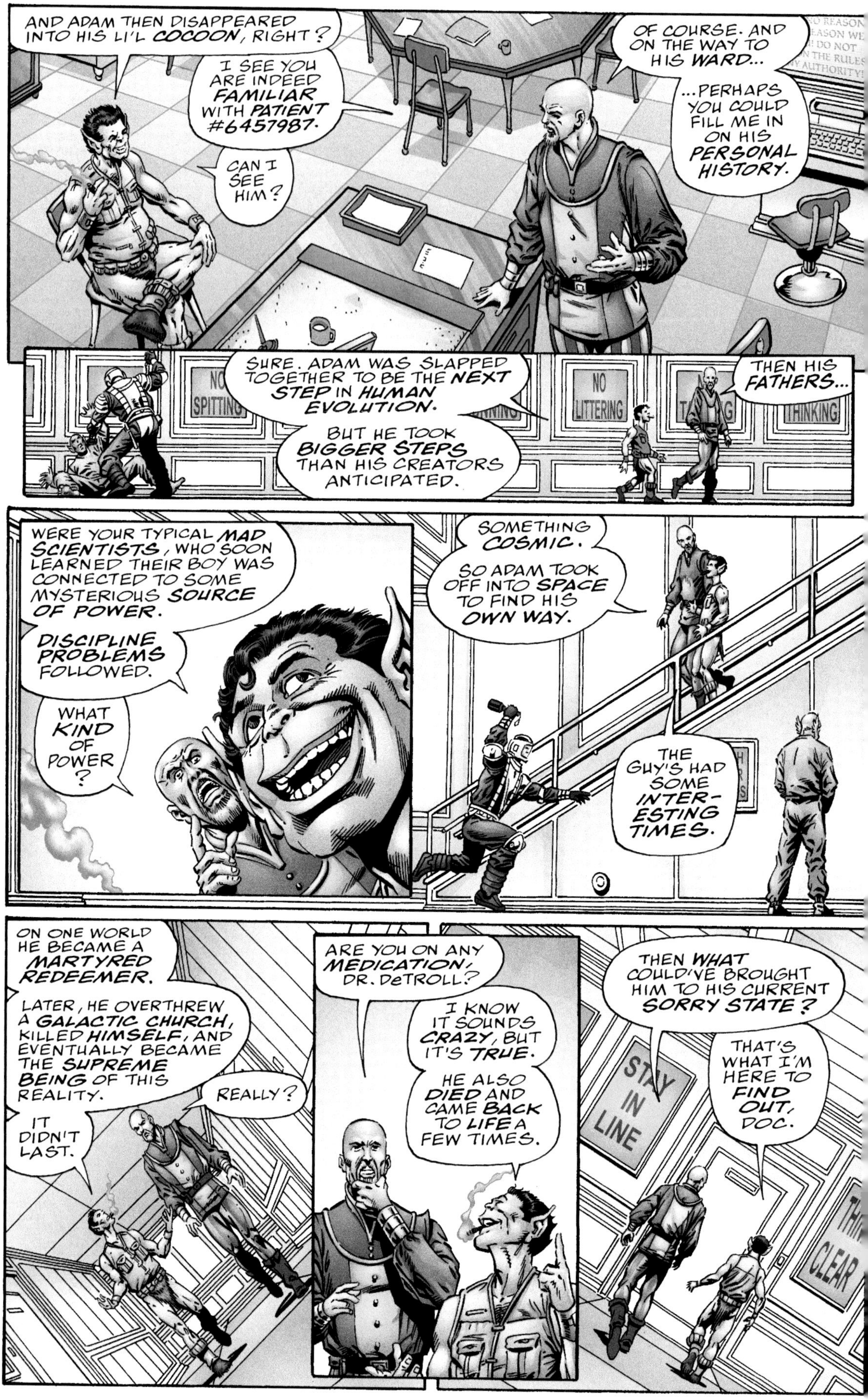

AND ADAM THEN DISAPPEARED INTO HIS LI'L COCOON, RIGHT?
I SEE YOU ARE INDEED FAMILIAR WITH PATIENT #6457987.
CAN I SEE HIM?
OF COURSE. AND ON THE WAY TO HIS WARD...
...PERHAPS YOU COULD FILL ME IN ON HIS PERSONAL HISTORY.
NO SPITTING
SURE. ADAM WAS SLAPPED TOGETHER TO BE THE NEXT STEP IN HUMAN EVOLUTION.
BUT HE TOOK BIGGER STEPS THAN HIS CREATORS ANTICIPATED.
NO LITTERING
THINKING
THEN HIS FATHERS...
WERE YOUR TYPICAL MAD SCIENTISTS, WHO SOON LEARNED THEIR BOY WAS CONNECTED TO SOME MYSTERIOUS SOURCE OF POWER.
DISCIPLINE PROBLEMS FOLLOWED.
WHAT KIND OF POWER?
SOMETHING COSMIC.
SO ADAM TOOK OFF INTO SPACE TO FIND HIS OWN WAY.
THE GUY'S HAD SOME INTER-ESTING TIMES.
ON ONE WORLD HE BECAME A MARTYRED REDEEMER.
LATER, HE OVERTHREW A GALACTIC CHURCH, KILLED HIMSELF, AND EVENTUALLY BECAME THE SUPREME BEING OF THIS REALITY.
REALLY?
IT DIDN'T LAST.
ARE YOU ON ANY MEDICATION, DR. DeTROLL?
I KNOW IT SOUNDS CRAZY, BUT IT'S TRUE.
HE ALSO DIED AND CAME BACK TO LIFE A FEW TIMES.
THEN WHAT COULD'VE BROUGHT HIM TO HIS CURRENT SORRY STATE?
STAY IN LINE
THAT'S WHAT I'M HERE TO FIND OUT, DOC.

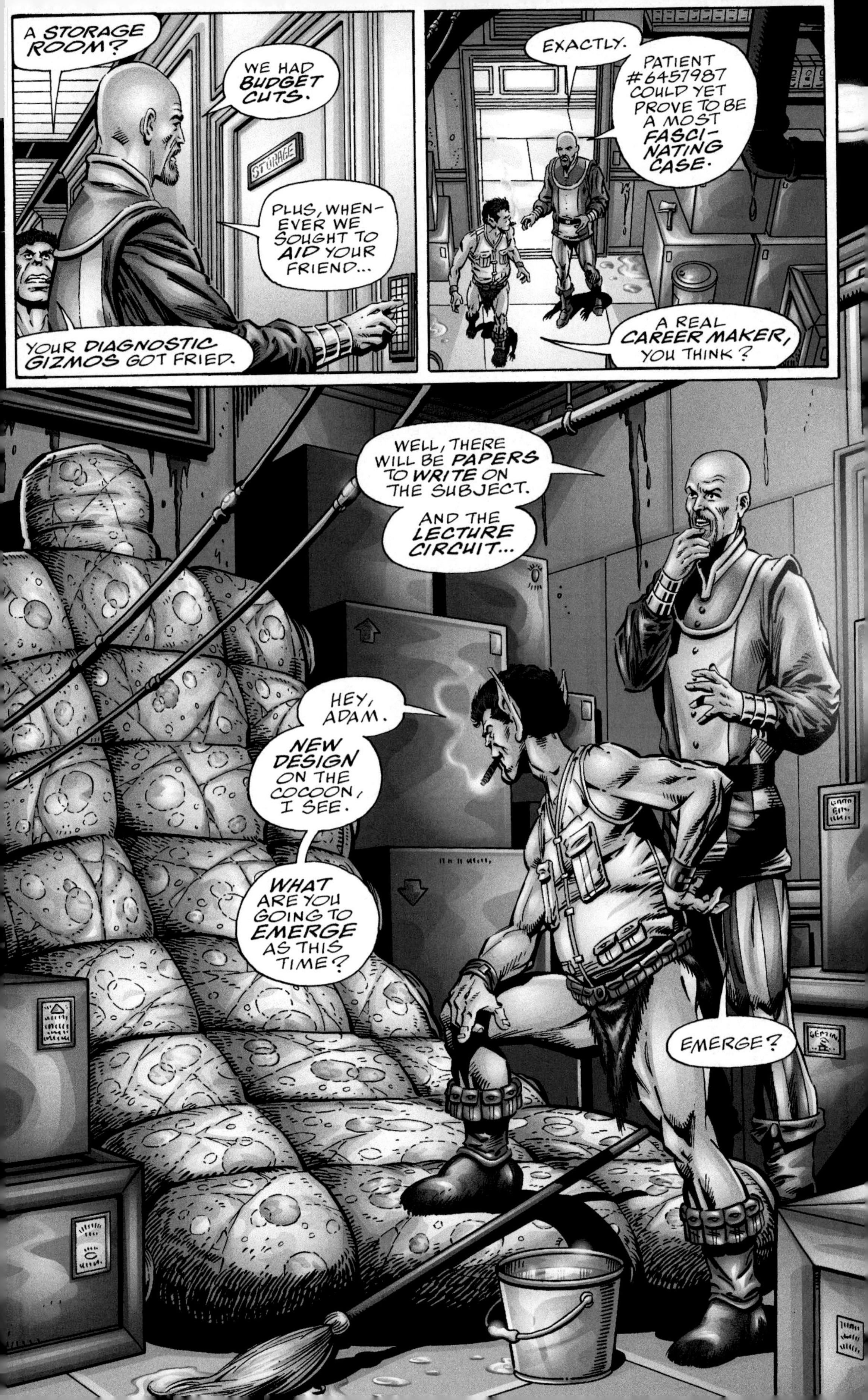

A STORAGE ROOM?
WE HAD BUDGET CUTS.
STORAGE
PLUS, WHENEVER WE SOUGHT TO AID YOUR FRIEND...
YOUR DIAGNOSTIC GIZMOS GOT FRIED.
EXACTLY.
PATIENT #6457987 COULD YET PROVE TO BE A MOST FASCINATING CASE.
A REAL CAREER MAKER, YOU THINK?
WELL, THERE WILL BE PAPERS TO WRITE ON THE SUBJECT.
AND THE LECTURE CIRCUIT...
HEY, ADAM.
NEW DESIGN ON THE COCOON, I SEE.
WHAT ARE YOU GOING TO EMERGE AS THIS TIME?
EMERGE?

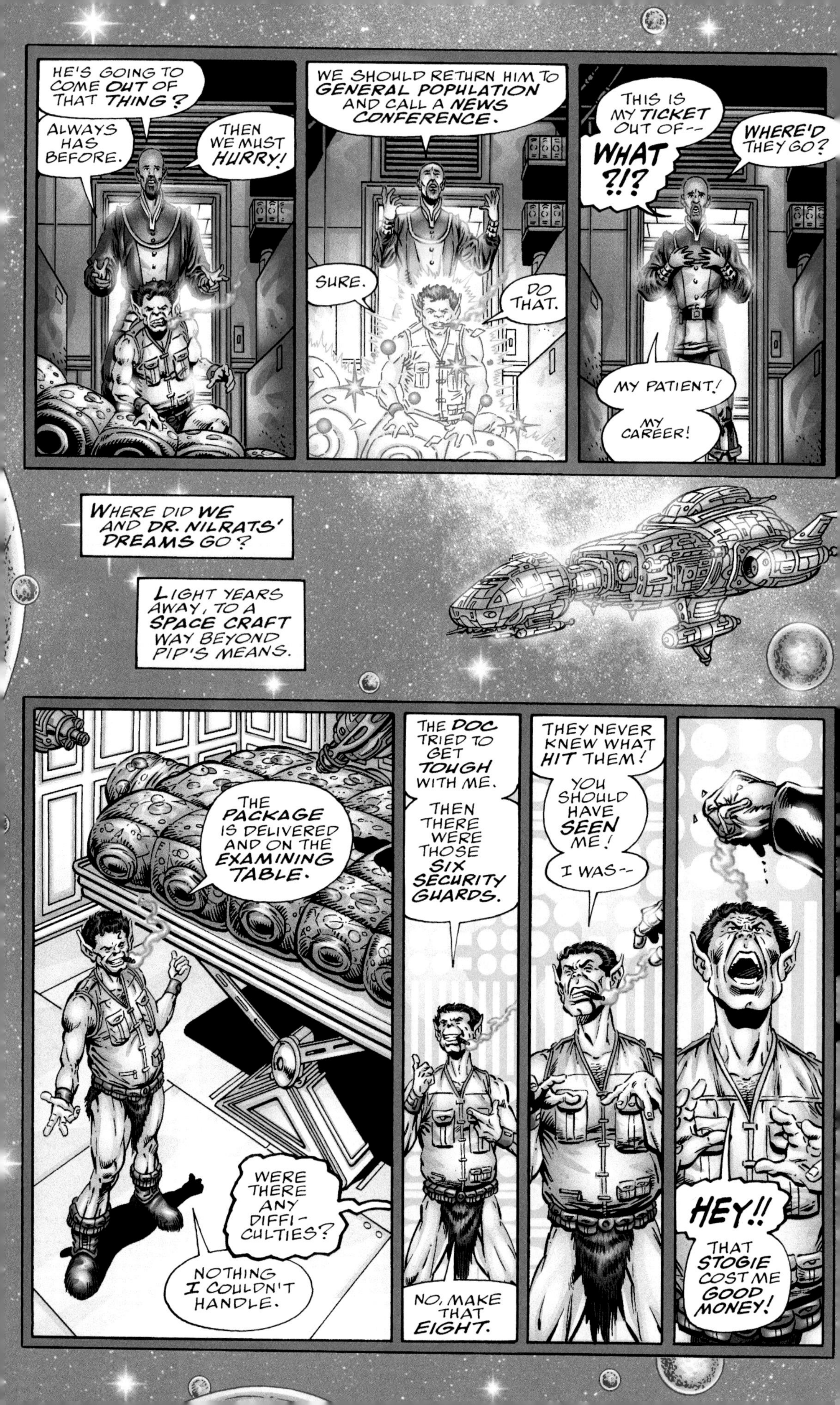
HE'S GOING TO COME OUT OF THAT THING?
ALWAYS HAS BEFORE.
THEN WE MUST HURRY!
WE SHOULD RETURN HIM TO GENERAL POPULATION AND CALL A NEWS CONFERENCE.
SURE.
DO THAT.
THIS IS MY TICKET OUT OF--
WHAT?!?
WHERE'D THEY GO?
MY PATIENT!
MY CAREER!
WHERE DID WE AND DR. NILRATS' DREAMS GO?
LIGHT YEARS AWAY, TO A SPACE CRAFT WAY BEYOND PIP'S MEANS.
THE PACKAGE IS DELIVERED AND ON THE EXAMINING TABLE.
WERE THERE ANY DIFFI-CULTIES?
NOTHING I COULDN'T HANDLE.
THE DOC TRIED TO GET TOUGH WITH ME.
THEN THERE WERE THOSE SIX SECURITY GUARDS.
NO, MAKE THAT EIGHT.
THEY NEVER KNEW WHAT HIT THEM!
YOU SHOULD HAVE SEEN ME!
I WAS--
HEY!!
THAT STOGIE COST ME GOOD MONEY!

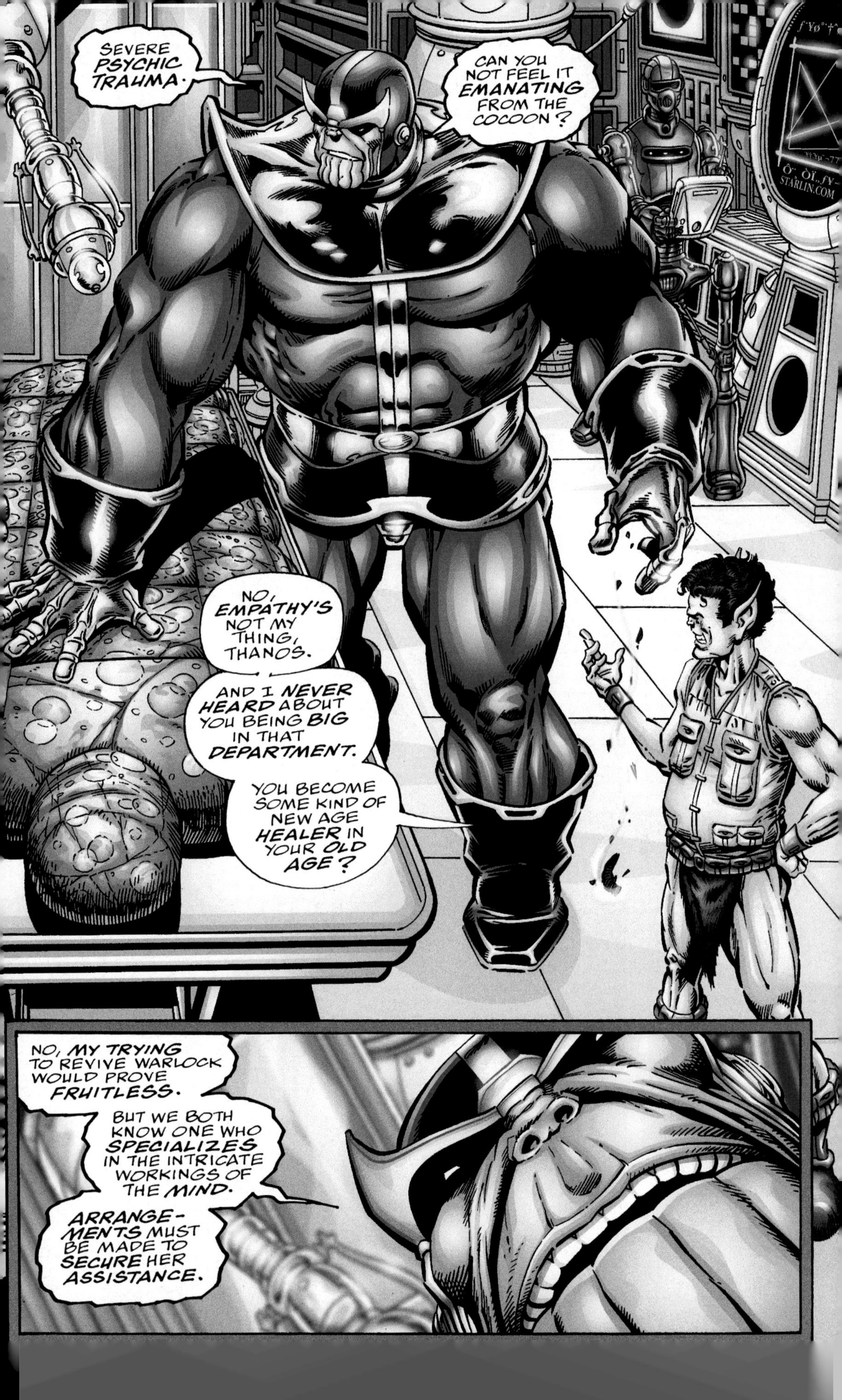

SEVERE PSYCHIC TRAUMA.
CAN YOU NOT FEEL IT EMANATING FROM THE COCOON?
NO, EMPATHY'S NOT MY THING, THANOS.
AND I NEVER HEARD ABOUT YOU BEING BIG IN THAT DEPARTMENT.
YOU BECOME SOME KIND OF NEW AGE HEALER IN YOUR OLD AGE?
STARLIN.COM
NO, MY TRYING TO REVIVE WARLOCK WOULD PROVE FRUITLESS.
BUT WE BOTH KNOW ONE WHO SPECIALIZES IN THE INTRICATE WORKINGS OF THE MIND.
ARRANGEMENTS MUST BE MADE TO SECURE HER ASSISTANCE.

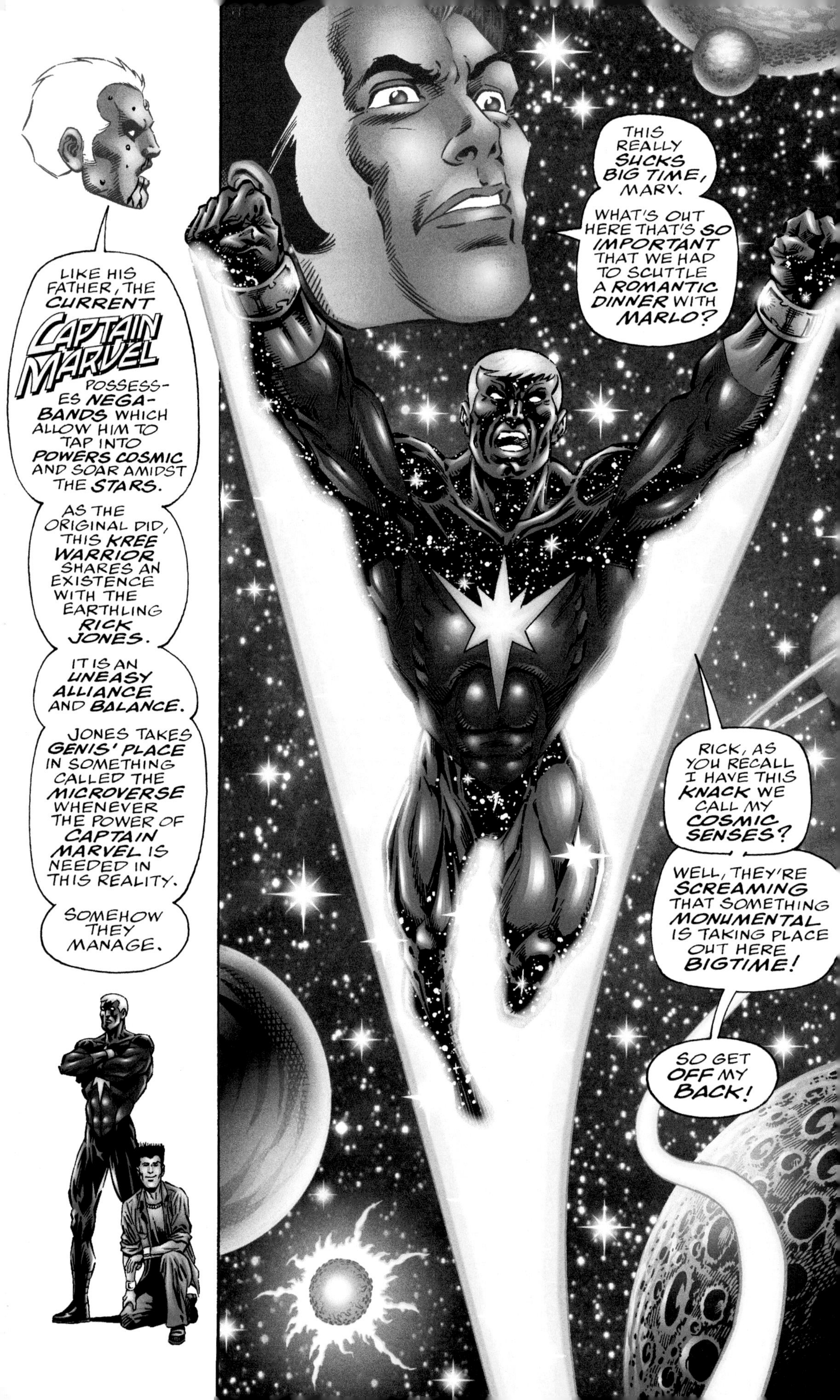
LIKE HIS FATHER, THE CURRENT CAPTAIN MARVEL POSSESS-ES NEGA-BANDS WHICH ALLOW HIM TO TAP INTO POWERS COSMIC AND SOAR AMIDST THE STARS.
AS THE ORIGINAL DID, THIS KREE WARRIOR SHARES AN EXISTENCE WITH THE EARTHLING RICK JONES.
IT IS AN UNEASY ALLIANCE AND BALANCE.
JONES TAKES GENIS' PLACE IN SOMETHING CALLED THE MICROVERSE WHENEVER THE POWER OF CAPTAIN MARVEL IS NEEDED IN THIS REALITY.
SOMEHOW THEY MANAGE.
THIS REALLY SUCKS BIG TIME, MARV.
WHAT'S OUT HERE THAT'S SO IMPORTANT THAT WE HAD TO SCUTTLE A ROMANTIC DINNER WITH MARLO?
RICK, AS YOU RECALL I HAVE THIS KNACK WE CALL MY COSMIC SENSES?
WELL, THEY'RE SCREAMING THAT SOMETHING MONUMENTAL IS TAKING PLACE OUT HERE BIGTIME!
SO GET OFF MY BACK!

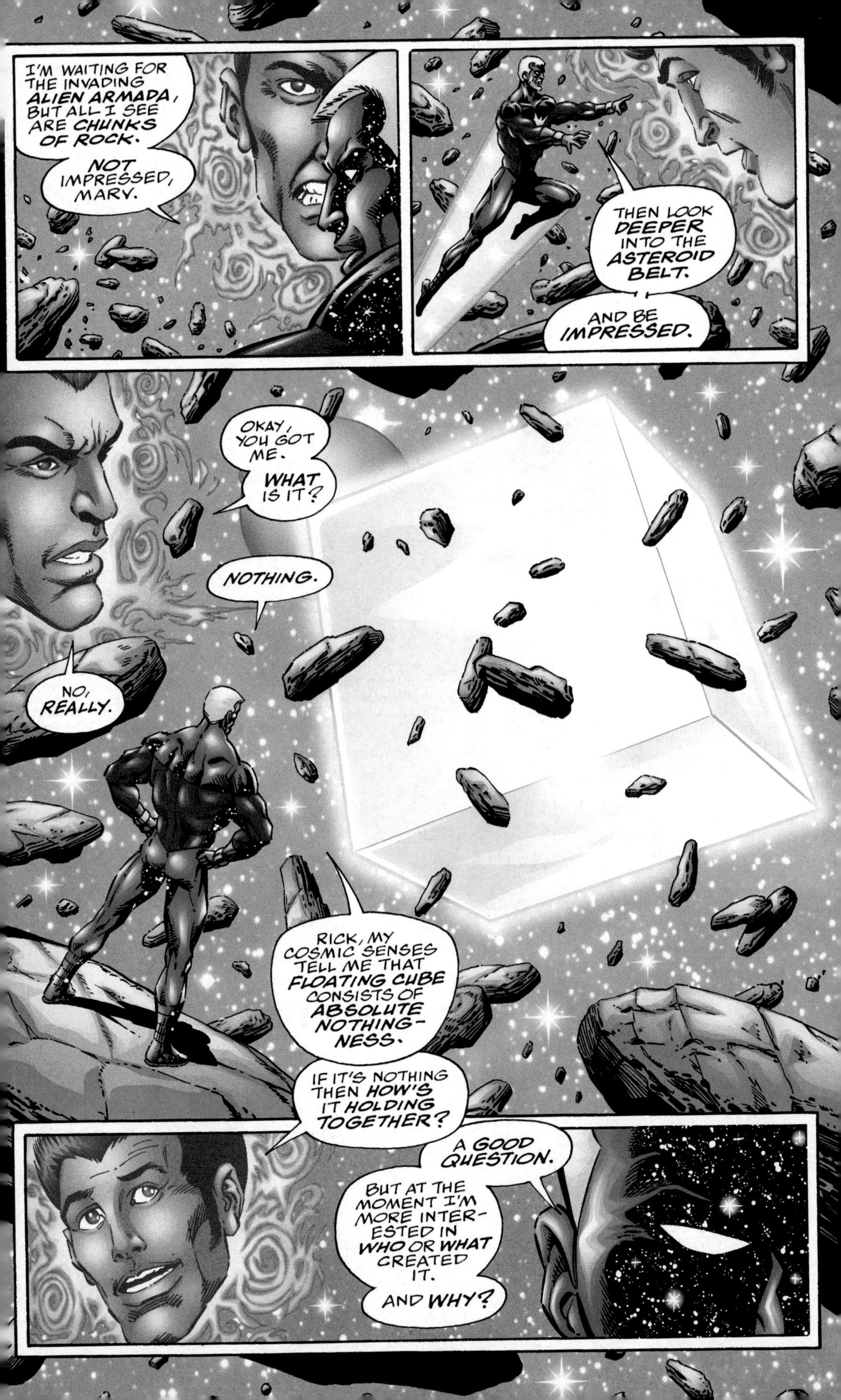

I'M WAITING FOR THE INVADING ALIEN ARMADA, BUT ALL I SEE ARE CHUNKS OF ROCK.
NOT IMPRESSED, MARY.
THEN LOOK DEEPER INTO THE ASTEROID BELT.
AND BE IMPRESSED.
OKAY, YOU GOT ME. WHAT IS IT?
NOTHING.
NO, REALLY.
RICK, MY COSMIC SENSES TELL ME THAT FLOATING CUBE CONSISTS OF ABSOLUTE NOTHING-NESS.
IF IT'S NOTHING THEN HOW'S IT HOLDING TOGETHER?
A GOOD QUESTION.
BUT AT THE MOMENT I'M MORE INTER-ESTED IN WHO OR WHAT CREATED IT.
AND WHY?

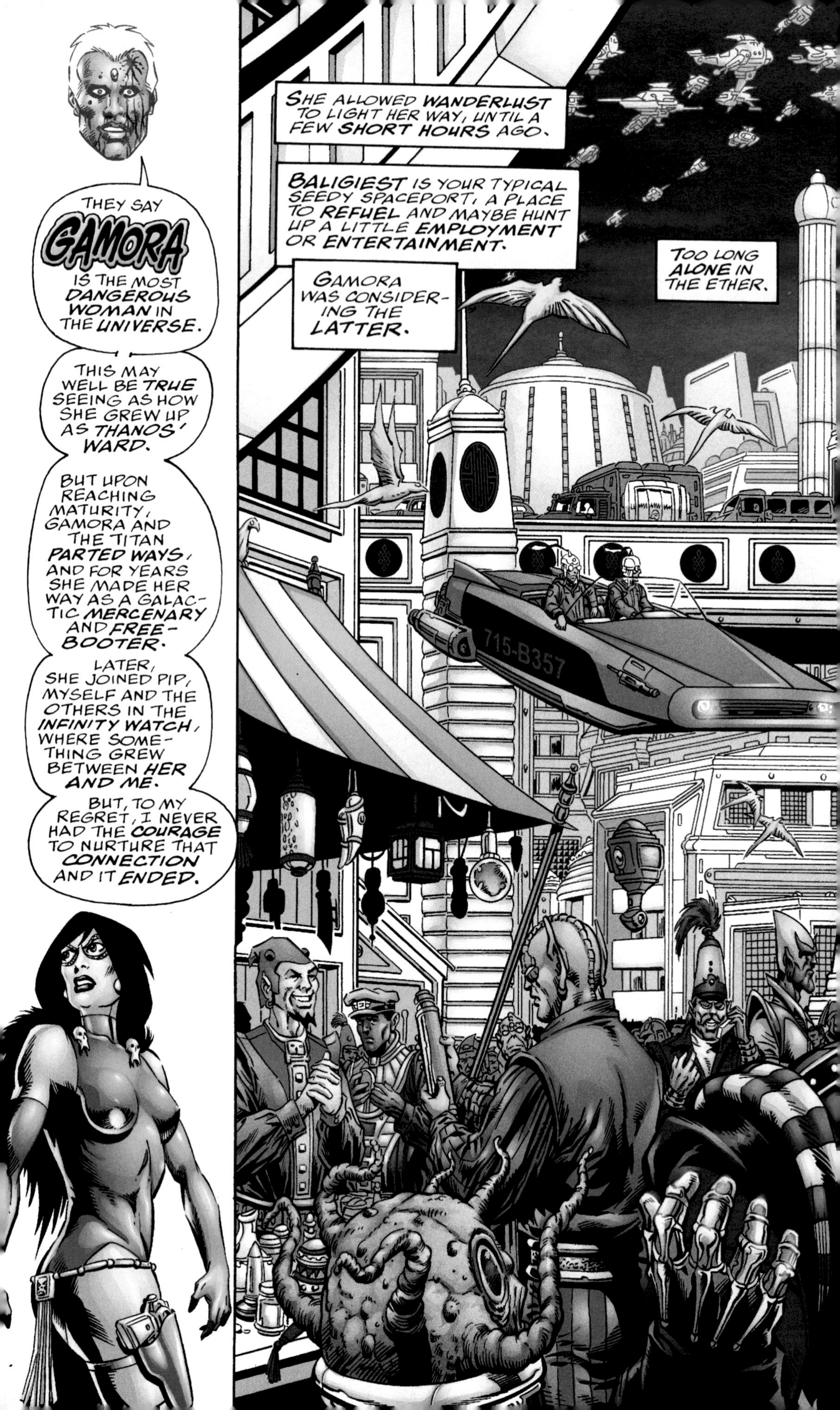

THEY SAY GAMORA IS THE MOST DANGEROUS WOMAN IN THE UNIVERSE.
THIS MAY WELL BE TRUE SEEING AS HOW SHE GREW UP AS THANOS' WARD.
BUT UPON REACHING MATURITY, GAMORA AND THE TITAN PARTED WAYS, AND FOR YEARS SHE MADE HER WAY AS A GALACTIC MERCENARY AND FREE-BOOTER.
LATER, SHE JOINED PIP, MYSELF AND THE OTHERS IN THE INFINITY WATCH, WHERE SOMETHING GREW BETWEEN HER AND ME.
BUT, TO MY REGRET, I NEVER HAD THE COURAGE TO NURTURE THAT CONNECTION AND IT ENDED.
SHE ALLOWED WANDERLUST TO LIGHT HER WAY, UNTIL A FEW SHORT HOURS AGO.
BALIGIEST IS YOUR TYPICAL SEEDY SPACEPORT, A PLACE TO REFUEL AND MAYBE HUNT UP A LITTLE EMPLOYMENT OR ENTERTAINMENT.
GAMORA WAS CONSIDERING THE LATTER.
TOO LONG ALONE IN THE ETHER.
715-B357

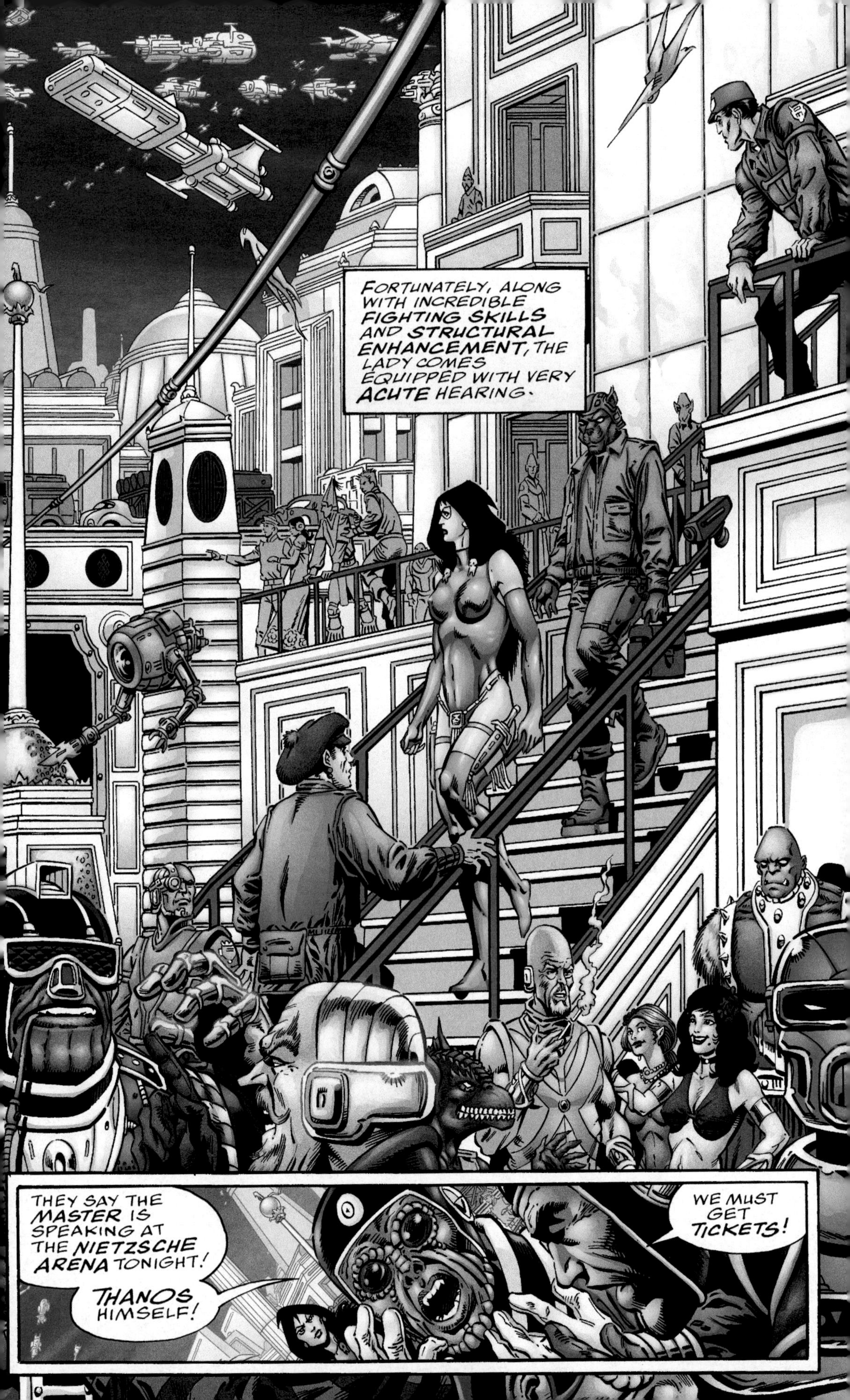

FORTUNATELY, ALONG WITH INCREDIBLE FIGHTING SKILLS AND STRUCTURAL ENHANCEMENT, THE LADY COMES EQUIPPED WITH VERY ACUTE HEARING.
THEY SAY THE MASTER IS SPEAKING AT THE NIETZSCHE ARENA TONIGHT!
THANOS HIMSELF!
WE MUST GET TICKETS!

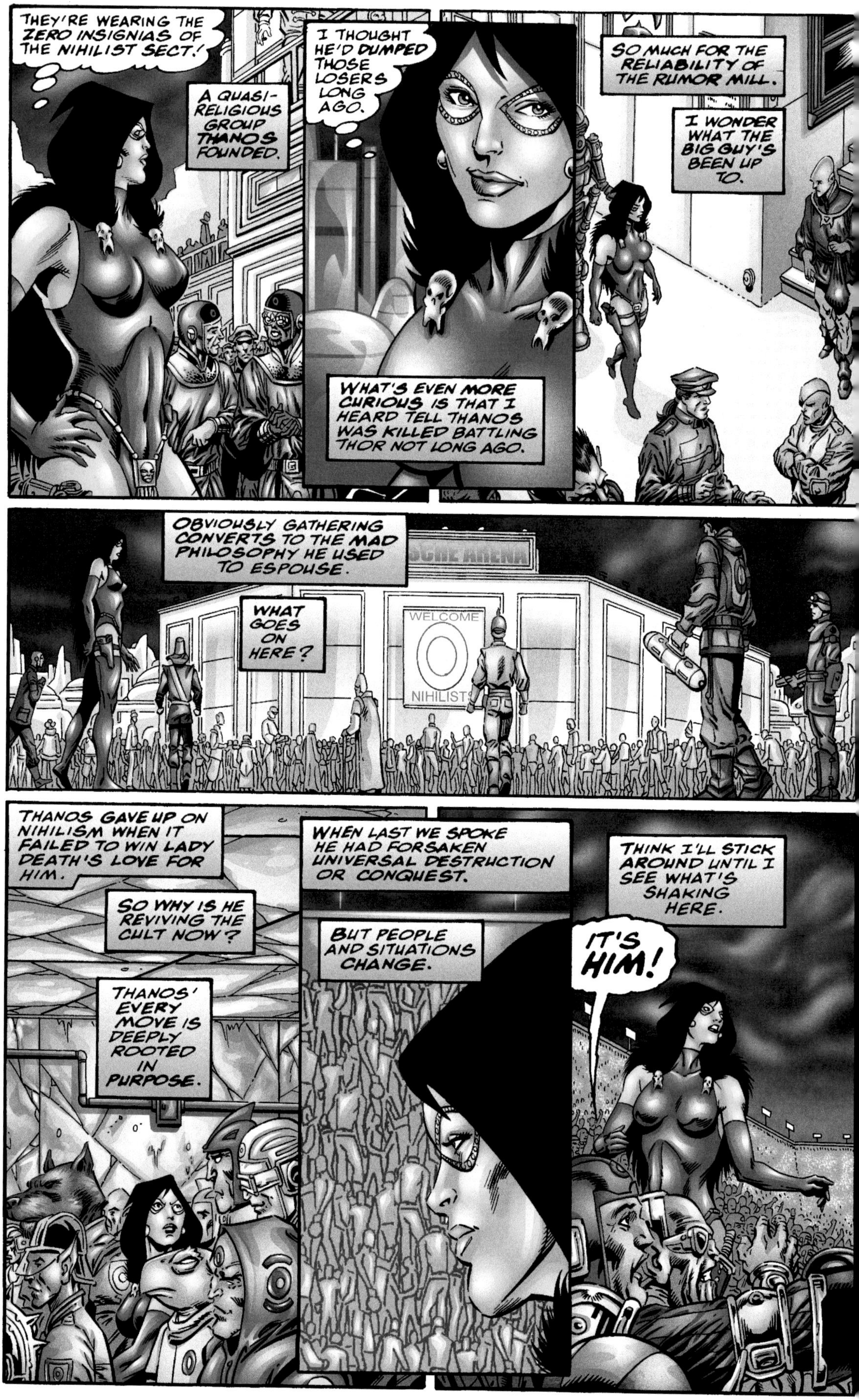
THEY'RE WEARING THE ZERO INSIGNIAS OF THE NIHILIST SECT!
A QUASI-RELIGIOUS GROUP THANOS FOUNDED.
I THOUGHT HE'D DUMPED THOSE LOSERS LONG AGO.
WHAT'S EVEN MORE CURIOUS IS THAT I HEARD TELL THANOS WAS KILLED BATTLING THOR NOT LONG AGO.
SO MUCH FOR THE RELIABILITY OF THE RUMOR MILL.
I WONDER WHAT THE BIG GUY'S BEEN UP TO.
OBVIOUSLY GATHERING CONVERTS TO THE MAD PHILOSOPHY HE USED TO ESPOUSE.
WHAT GOES ON HERE?
WELCOME
NIHILISTS
THANOS GAVE UP ON NIHILISM WHEN IT FAILED TO WIN LADY DEATH'S LOVE FOR HIM.
SO WHY IS HE REVIVING THE CULT NOW?
THANOS' EVERY MOVE IS DEEPLY ROOTED IN PURPOSE.
WHEN LAST WE SPOKE HE HAD FORSAKEN UNIVERSAL DESTRUCTION OR CONQUEST.
BUT PEOPLE AND SITUATIONS CHANGE.
THINK I'LL STICK AROUND UNTIL I SEE WHAT'S SHAKING HERE.
IT'S HIM!

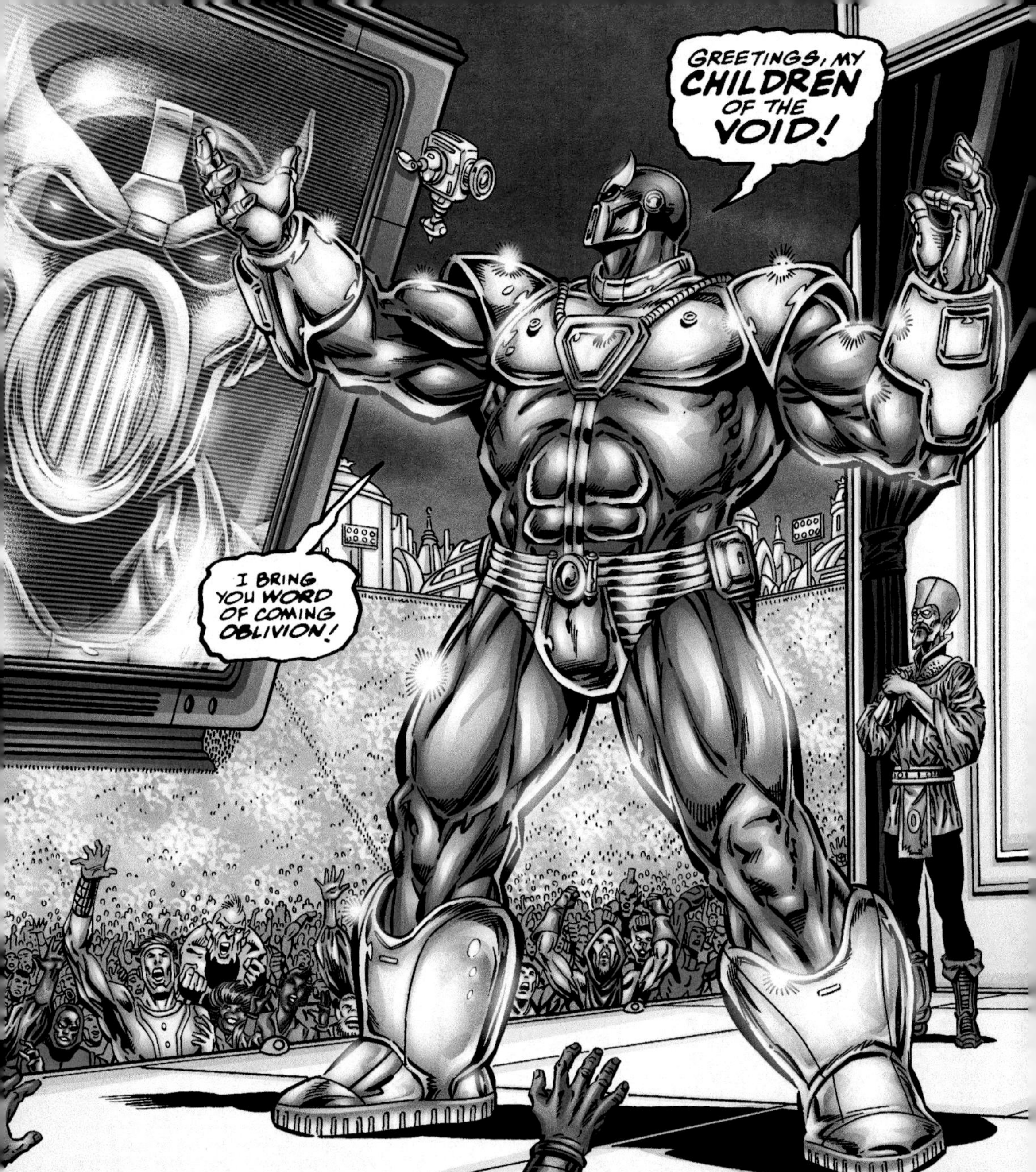
GREETINGS, MY CHILDREN OF THE VOID!
I BRING YOU WORD OF COMING OBLIVION!

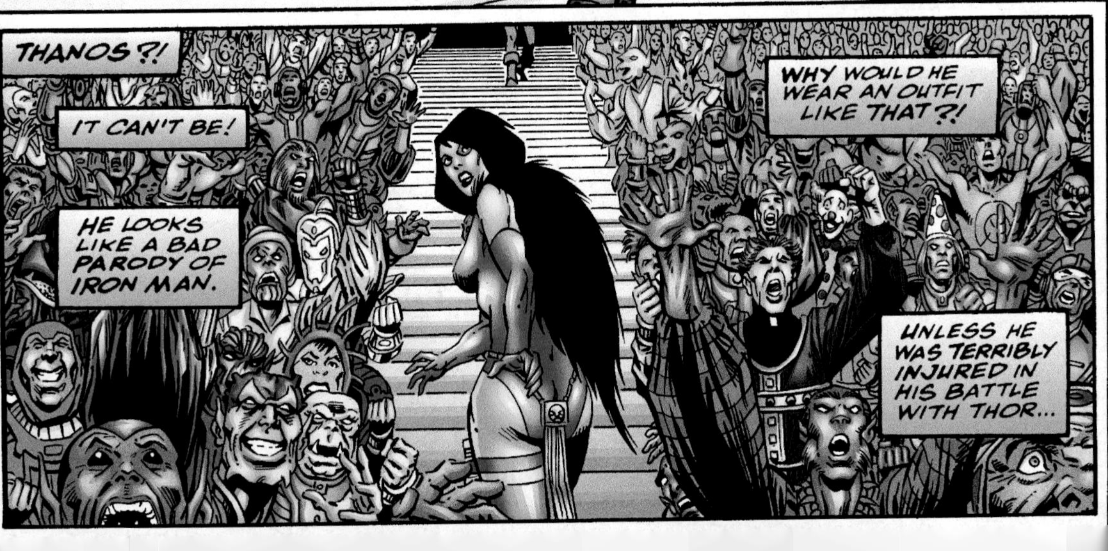
THANOS?!
IT CAN'T BE!
HE LOOKS LIKE A BAD PARODY OF IRON MAN.
WHY WOULD HE WEAR AN OUTFIT LIKE THAT?!
UNLESS HE WAS TERRIBLY INJURED IN HIS BATTLE WITH THOR...

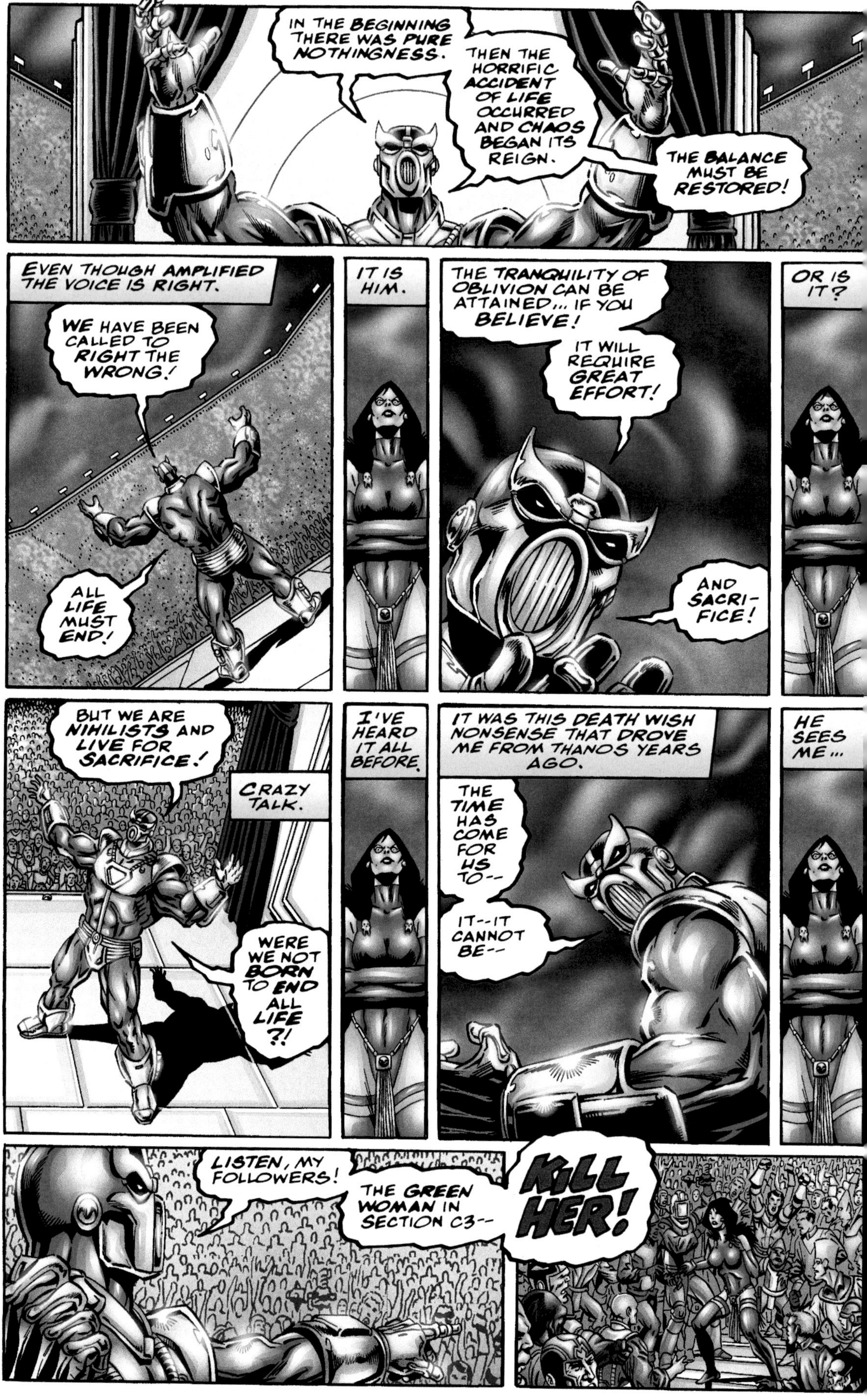

IN THE BEGINNING THERE WAS PURE NOTHINGNESS.
THEN THE HORRIFIC ACCIDENT OF LIFE OCCURRED AND CHAOS BEGAN ITS REIGN.
THE BALANCE MUST BE RESTORED!
EVEN THOUGH AMPLIFIED THE VOICE IS RIGHT.
WE HAVE BEEN CALLED TO RIGHT THE WRONG!
ALL LIFE MUST END!
IT IS HIM.
THE TRANQUILITY OF OBLIVION CAN BE ATTAINED... IF YOU BELIEVE!
IT WILL REQUIRE GREAT EFFORT!
AND SACRI- FICE!
OR IS IT?
BUT WE ARE NIHILISTS AND LIVE FOR SACRIFICE!
CRAZY TALK.
WERE WE NOT BORN TO END ALL LIFE?!
I'VE HEARD IT ALL BEFORE.
IT WAS THIS DEATH WISH NONSENSE THAT DROVE ME FROM THANOS YEARS AGO.
THE TIME HAS COME FOR US TO--
IT--IT CANNOT BE--
HE SEES ME...
LISTEN, MY FOLLOWERS!
THE GREEN WOMAN IN SECTION C3--
KILL HER!

SUDDENLY IT DOESN'T MATTER WHETHER IT IS REALLY THANOS OR NOT.
I SWITCH OVER TO SURVIVAL MODE.
IN A SITUATION LIKE THIS YOU ALWAYS TAKE OUT THE BIG ONES FIRST.
THAT WAY THE OTHERS TRIP OVER THEM, TRYING TO REACH YOU.
DESTROY HER!
THEN QUICKLY GET YOUR WEAPONS INTO PLAY.
BEDLAM AND MOVEMENT KEEP YOU FROM BEING AN EASY TARGET.

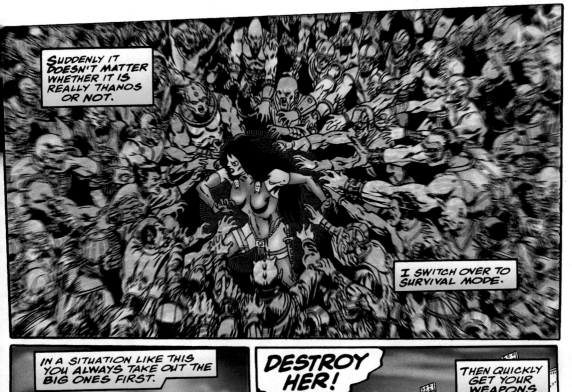

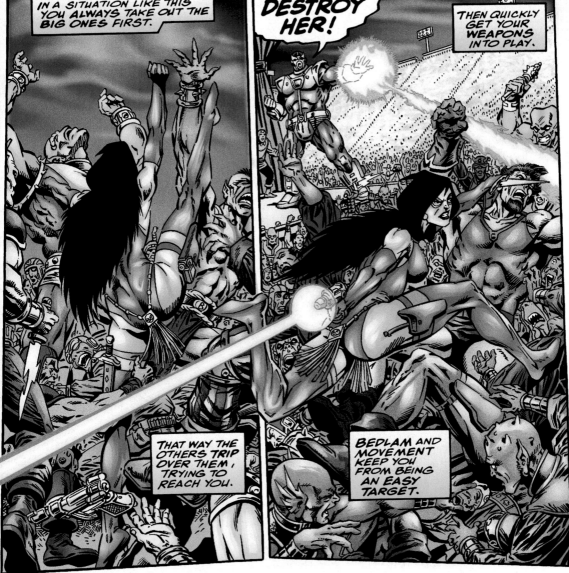

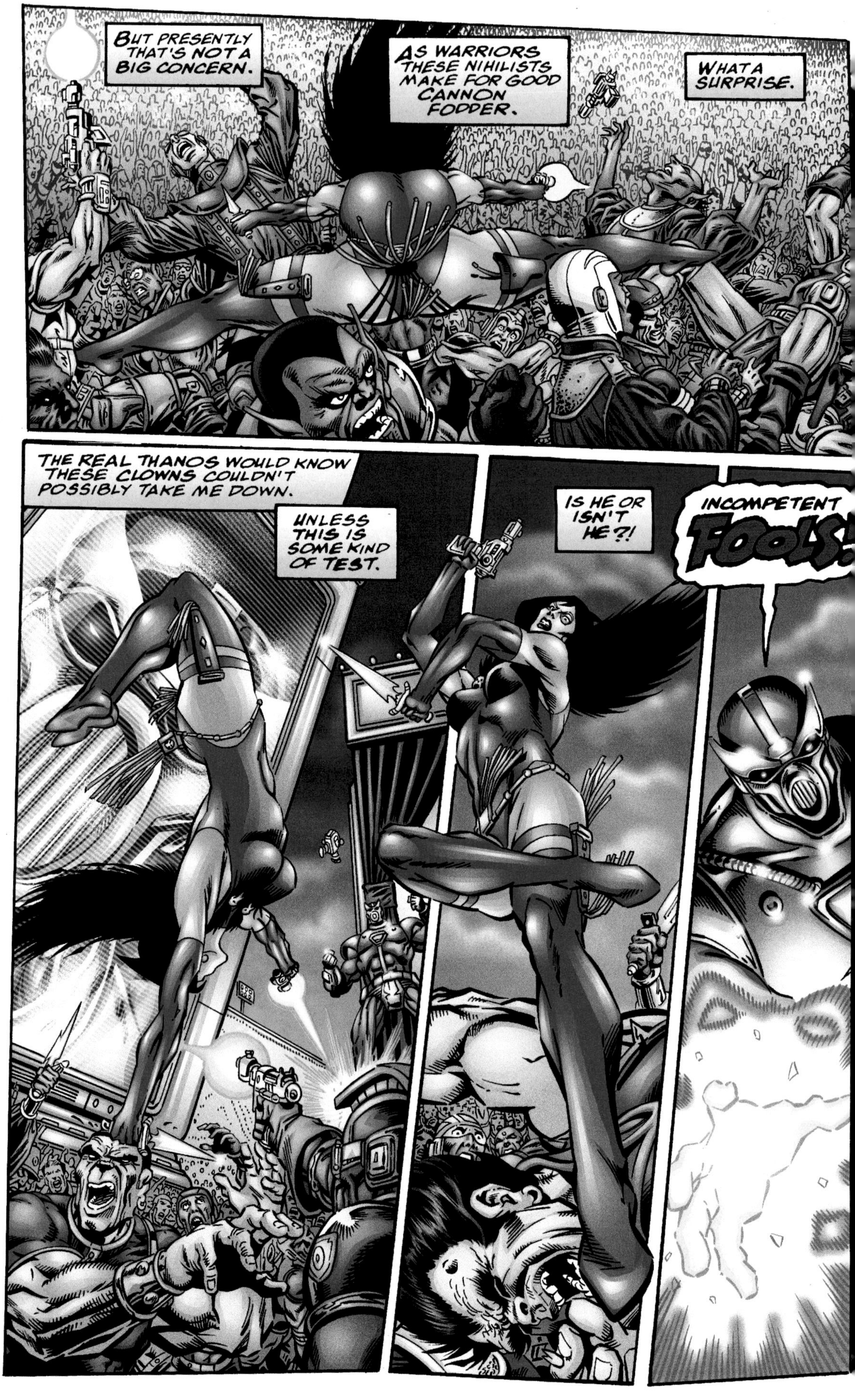
BUT PRESENTLY THAT'S NOT A BIG CONCERN.
AS WARRIORS THESE NIHILISTS MAKE FOR GOOD CANNON FODDER.
WHAT A SURPRISE.
THE REAL THANOS WOULD KNOW THESE CLOWNS COULDN'T POSSIBLY TAKE ME DOWN.
UNLESS THIS IS SOME KIND OF TEST.
IS HE OR ISN'T HE?!
INCOMPETENT FOOLS!

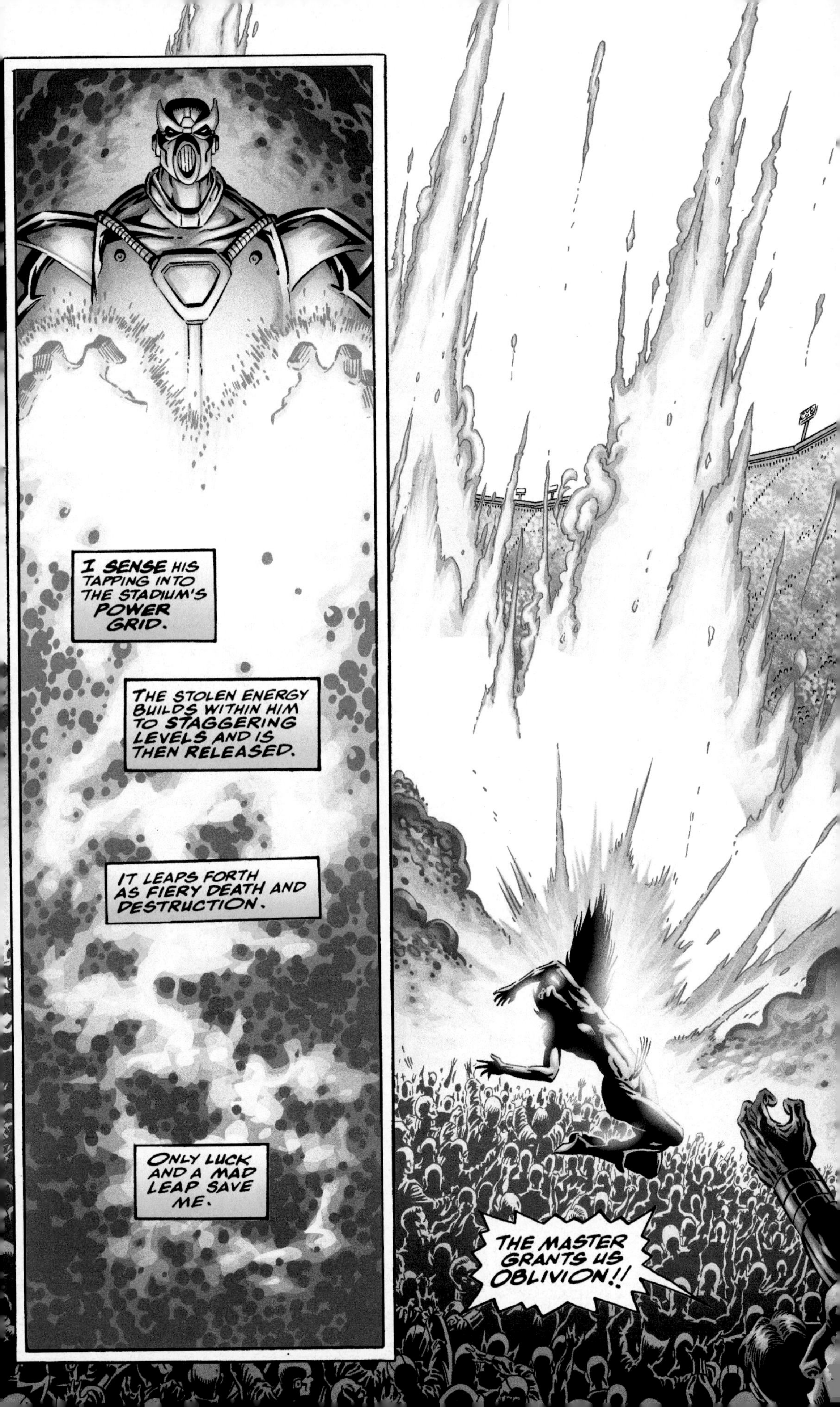

I SENSE HIS TAPPING INTO THE STADIUM'S POWER GRID.
THE STOLEN ENERGY BUILDS WITHIN HIM TO STAGGERING LEVELS AND IS THEN RELEASED.
IT LEAPS FORTH AS FIERY DEATH AND DESTRUCTION.
ONLY LUCK AND A MAD LEAP SAVE ME.
THE MASTER GRANTS US OBLIVION!!

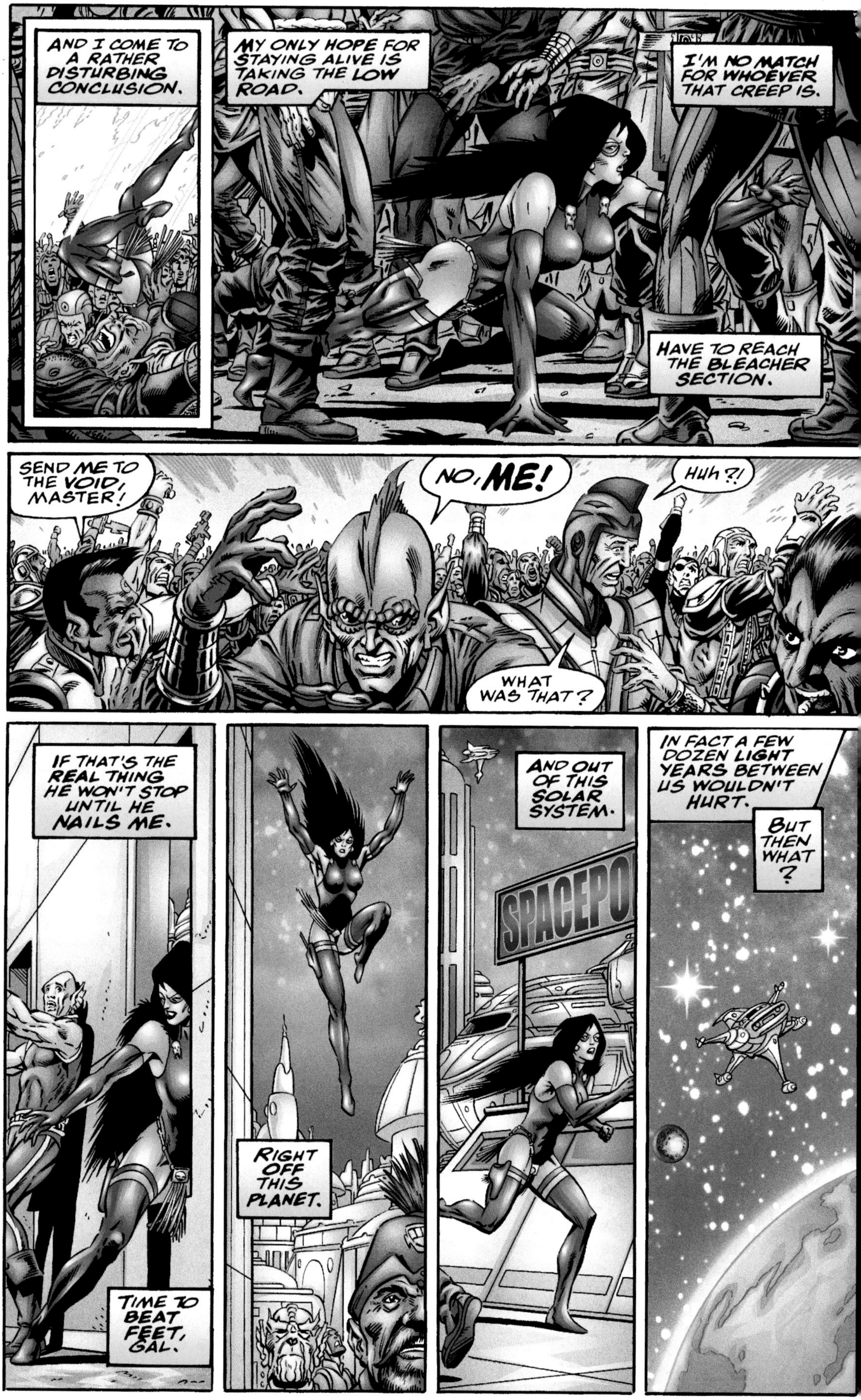
AND I COME TO A RATHER DISTURBING CONCLUSION.
MY ONLY HOPE FOR STAYING ALIVE IS TAKING THE LOW ROAD.
I'M NO MATCH FOR WHOEVER THAT CREEP IS.
HAVE TO REACH THE BLEACHER SECTION.
SEND ME TO THE VOID, MASTER!
NO, ME!
HUH ?!
WHAT WAS THAT?
IF THAT'S THE REAL THING HE WON'T STOP UNTIL HE NAILS ME.
TIME TO BEAT FEET, GAL.
RIGHT OFF THIS PLANET.
AND OUT OF THIS SOLAR SYSTEM.
SPACEPO
IN FACT A FEW DOZEN LIGHT YEARS BETWEEN US WOULDN'T HURT.
BUT THEN WHAT?

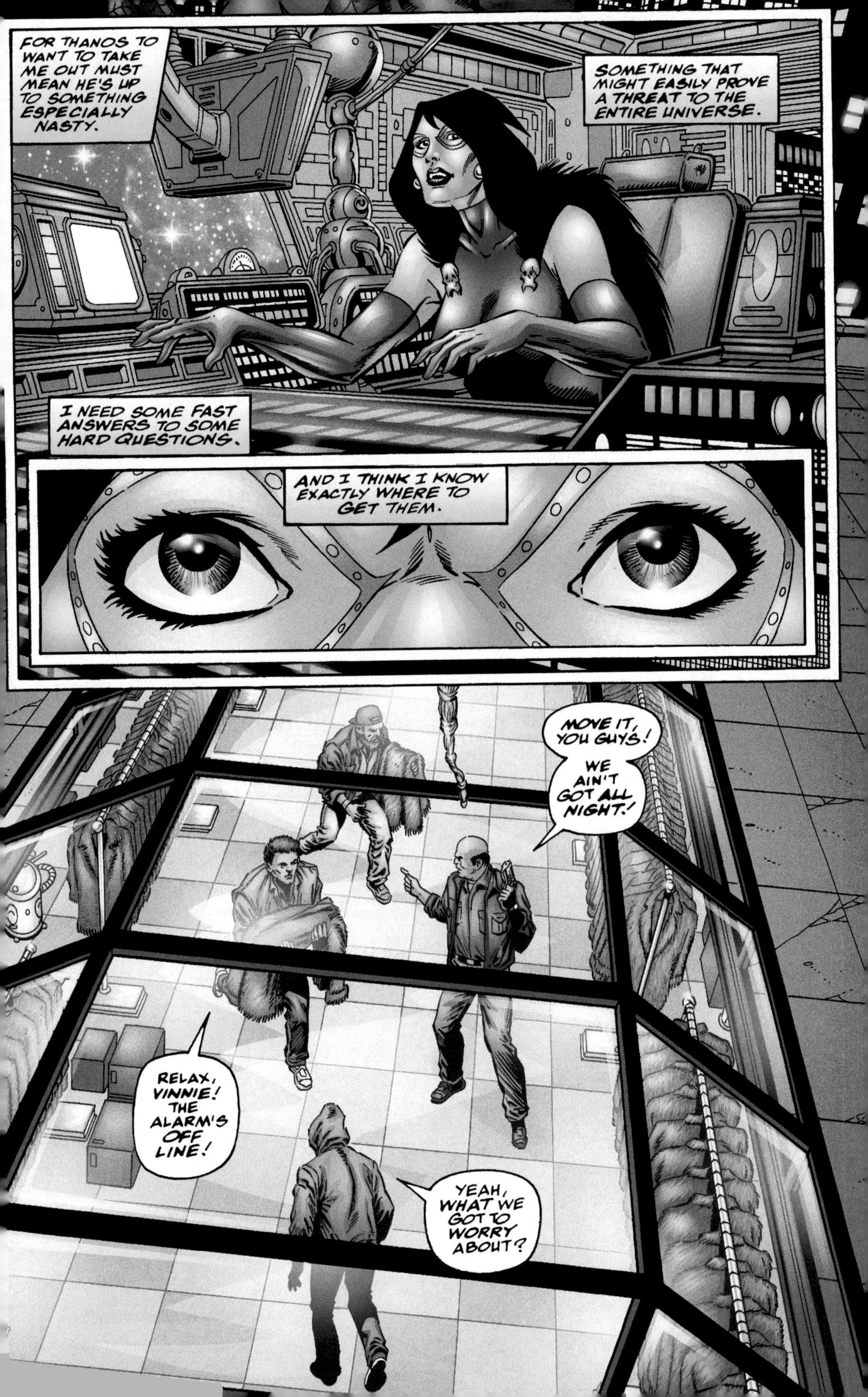
FOR THANOS TO WANT TO TAKE ME OUT MUST MEAN HE'S UP TO SOMETHING ESPECIALLY NASTY.
SOMETHING THAT MIGHT EASILY PROVE A THREAT TO THE ENTIRE UNIVERSE.
I NEED SOME FAST ANSWERS TO SOME HARD QUESTIONS.
AND I THINK I KNOW EXACTLY WHERE TO GET THEM.
MOVE IT, YOU GUYS!
WE AIN'T GOT ALL NIGHT!
RELAX, VINNIE! THE ALARM'S OFF LINE!
YEAH, WHAT WE GOT TO WORRY ABOUT?

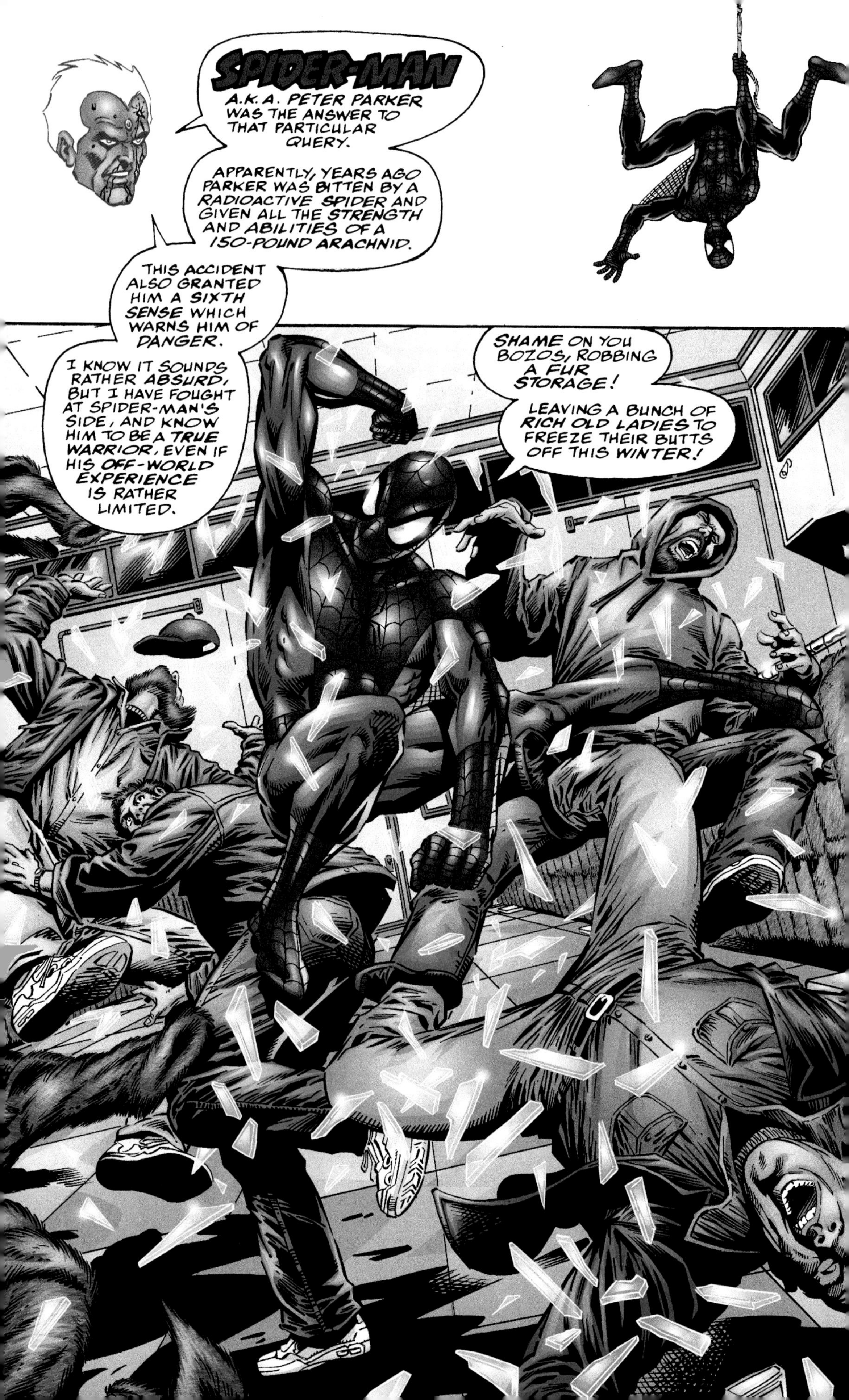
SPIDER-MAN
A.K.A. PETER PARKER WAS THE ANSWER TO THAT PARTICULAR QUERY.
APPARENTLY, YEARS AGO PARKER WAS BITTEN BY A RADIOACTIVE SPIDER AND GIVEN ALL THE STRENGTH AND ABILITIES OF A 150-POUND ARACHNID.
THIS ACCIDENT ALSO GRANTED HIM A SIXTH SENSE WHICH WARNS HIM OF DANGER.
I KNOW IT SOUNDS RATHER ABSURD, BUT I HAVE FOUGHT AT SPIDER-MAN'S SIDE, AND KNOW HIM TO BE A TRUE WARRIOR, EVEN IF HIS OFF-WORLD EXPERIENCE IS RATHER LIMITED.
SHAME ON YOU BOZOS, ROBBING A FUR STORAGE!
LEAVING A BUNCH OF RICH OLD LADIES TO FREEZE THEIR BUTTS OFF THIS WINTER!

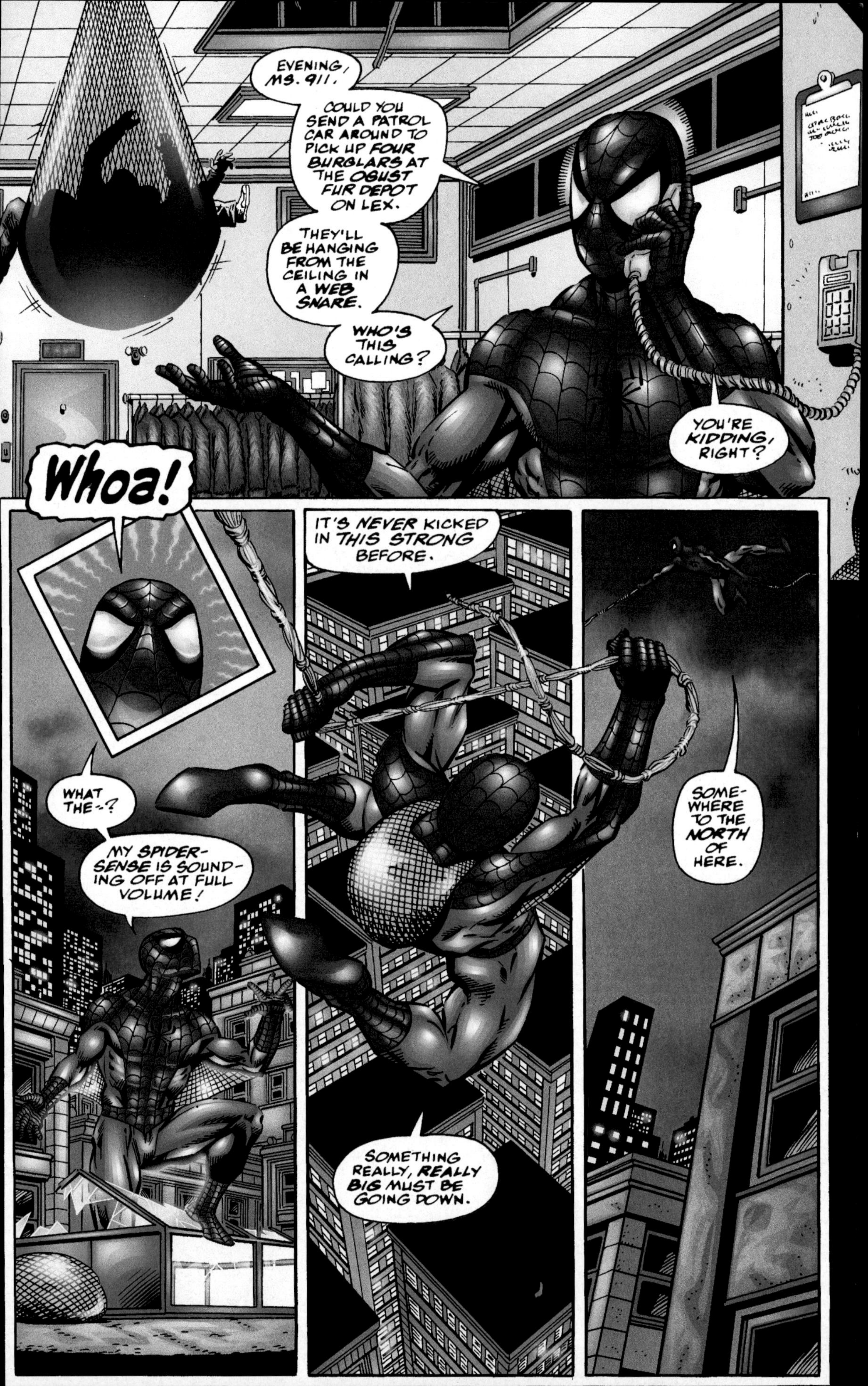
EVENING, MS. 911.
COULD YOU SEND A PATROL CAR AROUND TO PICK UP FOUR BURGLARS AT THE OGUST FUR DEPOT ON LEX.
THEY'LL BE HANGING FROM THE CEILING IN A WEB SNARE.
WHO'S THIS CALLING?
YOU'RE KIDDING, RIGHT?
Whoa!
WHAT THE--?
MY SPIDER-SENSE IS SOUNDING OFF AT FULL VOLUME!
IT'S NEVER KICKED IN THIS STRONG BEFORE.
SOMETHING REALLY, REALLY BIG MUST BE GOING DOWN.
SOME-WHERE TO THE NORTH OF HERE.

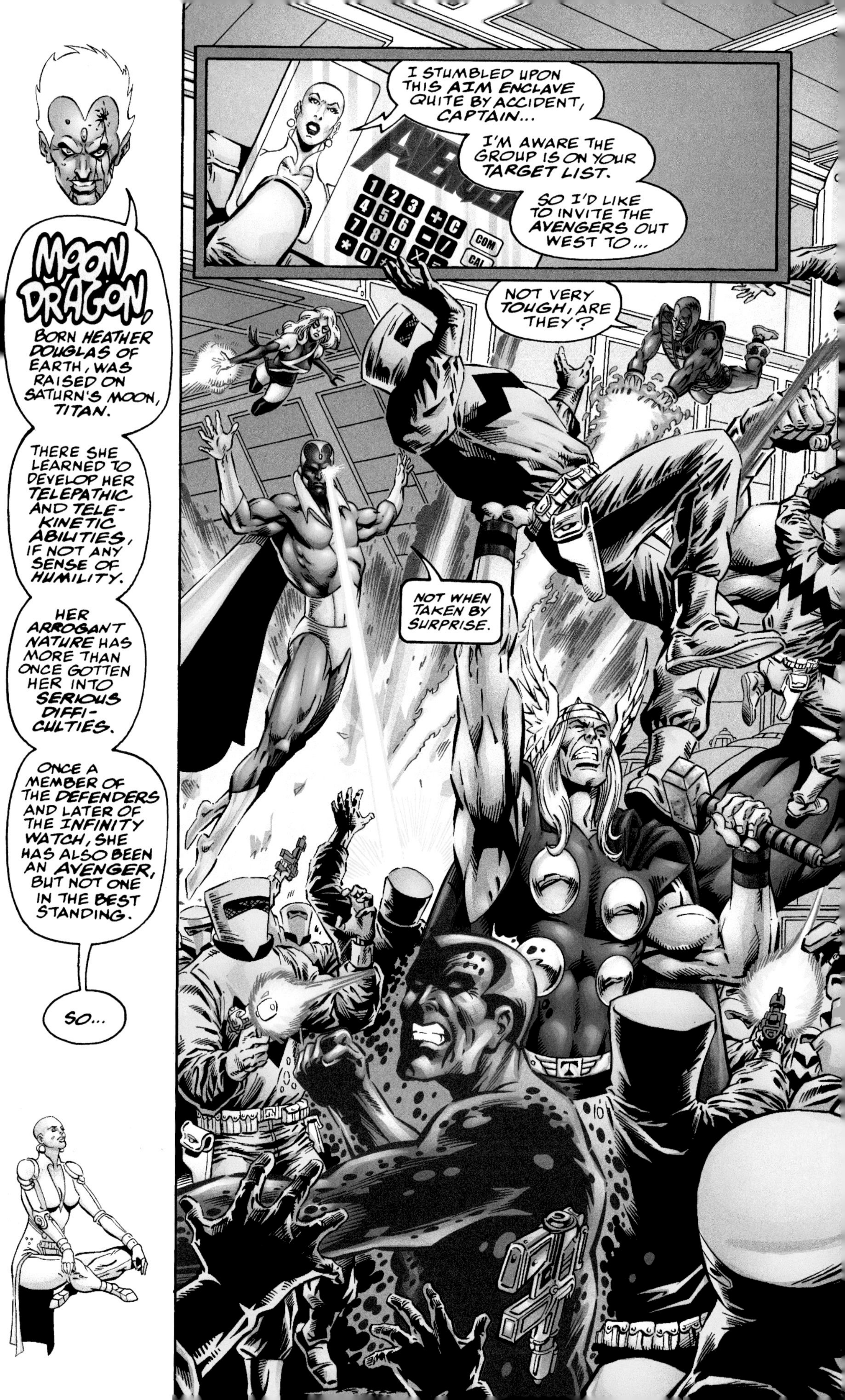
MOONDRAGON,
BORN HEATHER DOUGLAS OF EARTH, WAS RAISED ON SATURN'S MOON, TITAN.
THERE SHE LEARNED TO DEVELOP HER TELEPATHIC AND TELEKINETIC ABILITIES, IF NOT ANY SENSE OF HUMILITY.
HER ARROGANT NATURE HAS MORE THAN ONCE GOTTEN HER INTO SERIOUS DIFFICULTIES.
ONCE A MEMBER OF THE DEFENDERS AND LATER OF THE INFINITY WATCH, SHE HAS ALSO BEEN AN AVENGER, BUT NOT ONE IN THE BEST STANDING.
SO...
I STUMBLED UPON THIS AIM ENCLAVE QUITE BY ACCIDENT, CAPTAIN...
I'M AWARE THE GROUP IS ON YOUR TARGET LIST.
SO I'D LIKE TO INVITE THE AVENGERS OUT WEST TO...
NOT VERY TOUGH, ARE THEY?
NOT WHEN TAKEN BY SURPRISE.

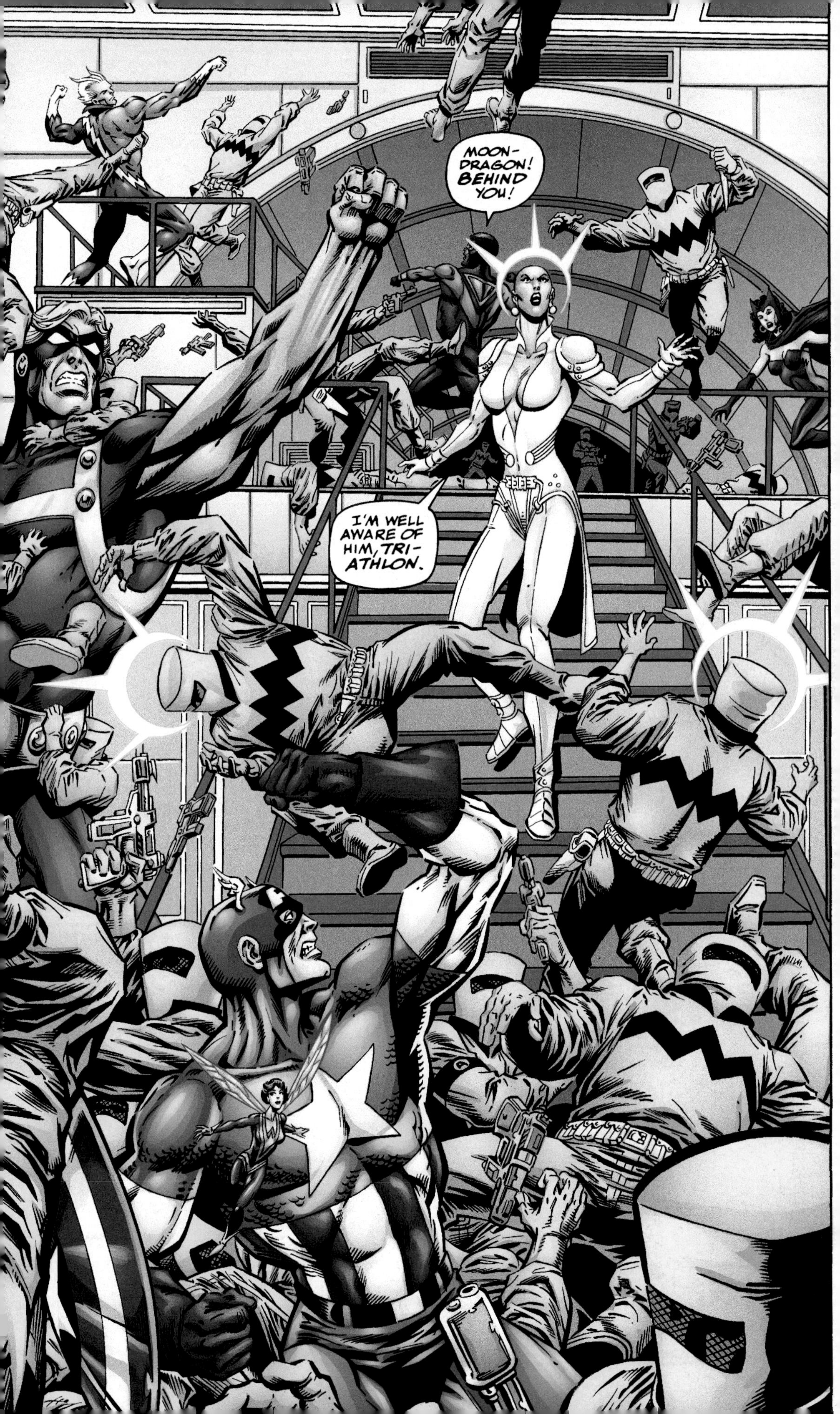
MOON-DRAGON! BEHIND YOU!
I'M WELL AWARE OF HIM, TRI-ATHLON.

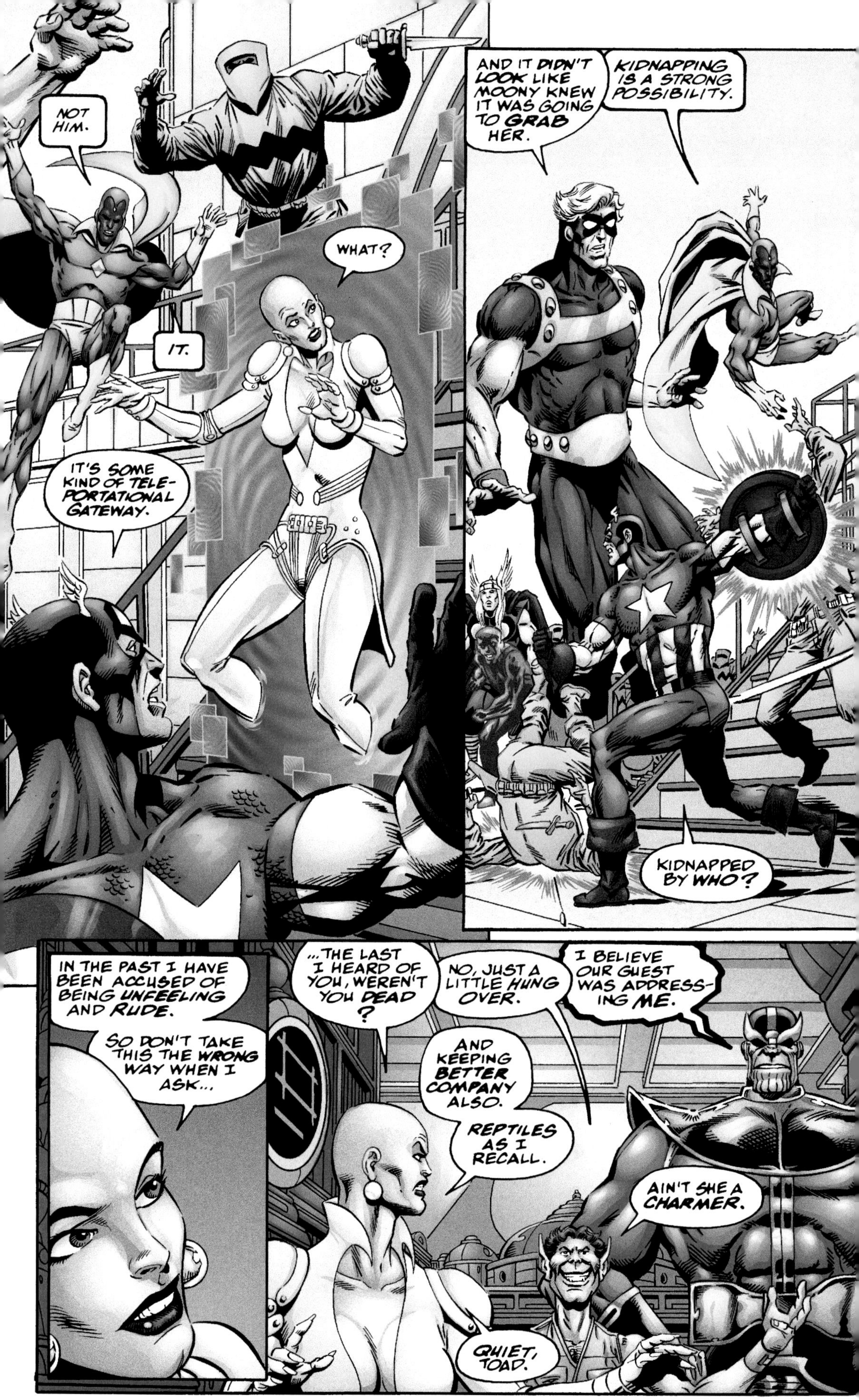
NOT HIM.
WHAT?
IT.
IT'S SOME KIND OF TELE-PORTATIONAL GATEWAY.
AND IT DIDN'T LOOK LIKE MOONY KNEW IT WAS GOING TO GRAB HER.
KIDNAPPING IS A STRONG POSSIBILITY.
KIDNAPPED BY WHO?
IN THE PAST I HAVE BEEN ACCUSED OF BEING UNFEELING AND RUDE.
SO DON'T TAKE THIS THE WRONG WAY WHEN I ASK...
...THE LAST I HEARD OF YOU, WEREN'T YOU DEAD?
NO, JUST A LITTLE HUNG OVER.
AND KEEPING BETTER COMPANY ALSO.
REPTILES AS I RECALL.
I BELIEVE OUR GUEST WAS ADDRESS-ING ME.
AIN'T SHE A CHARMER.
QUIET, TOAD.

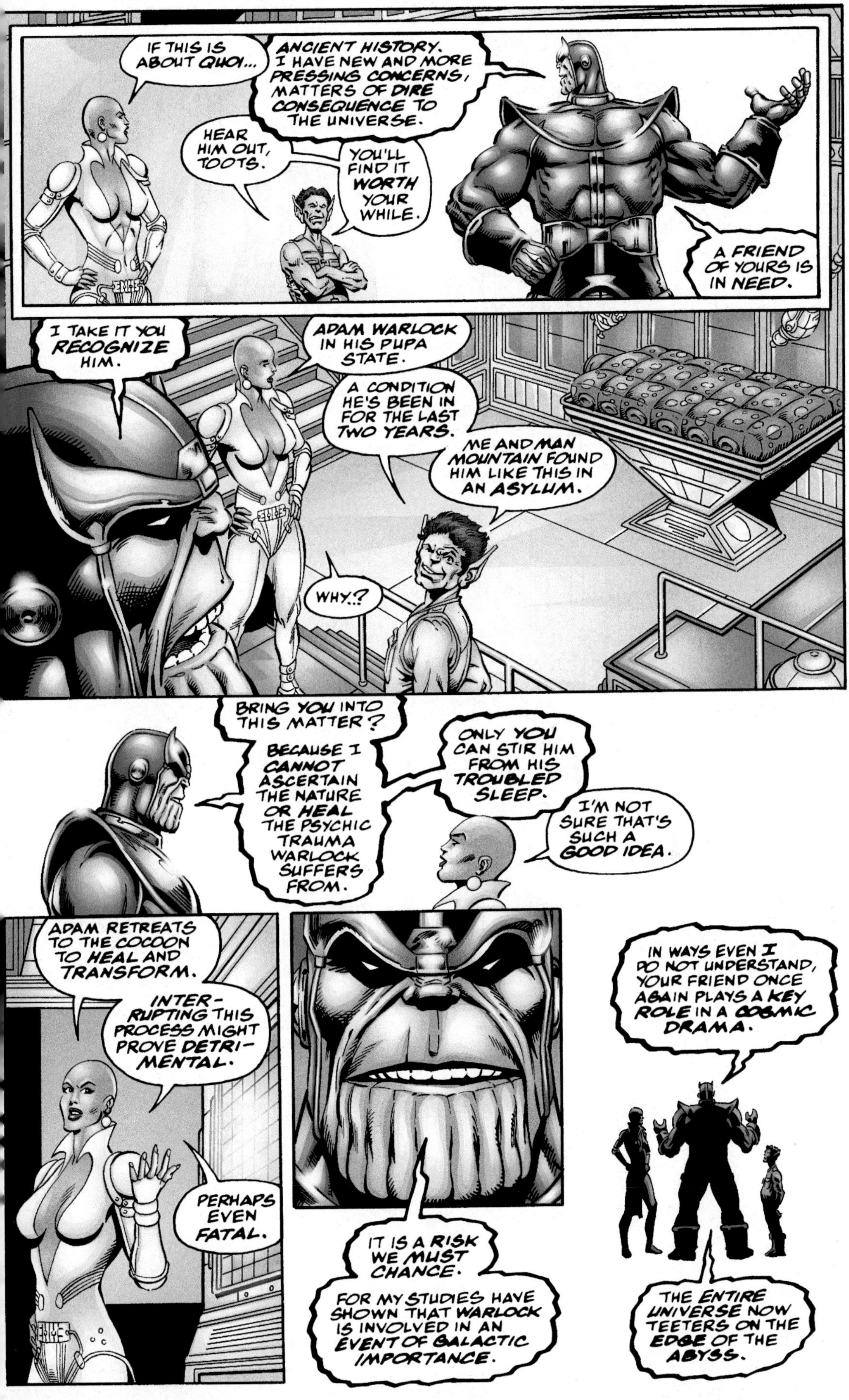

IF THIS IS ABOUT QUOI...
ANCIENT HISTORY. I HAVE NEW AND MORE PRESSING CONCERNS, MATTERS OF DIRE CONSEQUENCE TO THE UNIVERSE.
HEAR HIM OUT, TOOTS.
YOU'LL FIND IT WORTH YOUR WHILE.
A FRIEND OF YOURS IS IN NEED.
I TAKE IT YOU RECOGNIZE HIM.
ADAM WARLOCK IN HIS PUPA STATE.
A CONDITION HE'S BEEN IN FOR THE LAST TWO YEARS.
ME AND MAN MOUNTAIN FOUND HIM LIKE THIS IN AN ASYLUM.
WHY..?
BRING YOU INTO THIS MATTER?
BECAUSE I CANNOT ASCERTAIN THE NATURE OR HEAL THE PSYCHIC TRAUMA WARLOCK SUFFERS FROM.
ONLY YOU CAN STIR HIM FROM HIS TROUBLED SLEEP.
I'M NOT SURE THAT'S SUCH A GOOD IDEA.
ADAM RETREATS TO THE COCOON TO HEAL AND TRANSFORM.
INTER-RUPTING THIS PROCESS MIGHT PROVE DETRI-MENTAL.
PERHAPS EVEN FATAL.
IT IS A RISK WE MUST CHANCE.
FOR MY STUDIES HAVE SHOWN THAT WARLOCK IS INVOLVED IN AN EVENT OF GALACTIC IMPORTANCE.
IN WAYS EVEN I DO NOT UNDERSTAND, YOUR FRIEND ONCE AGAIN PLAYS A KEY ROLE IN A COSMIC DRAMA.
THE ENTIRE UNIVERSE NOW TEETERS ON THE EDGE OF THE ABYSS.

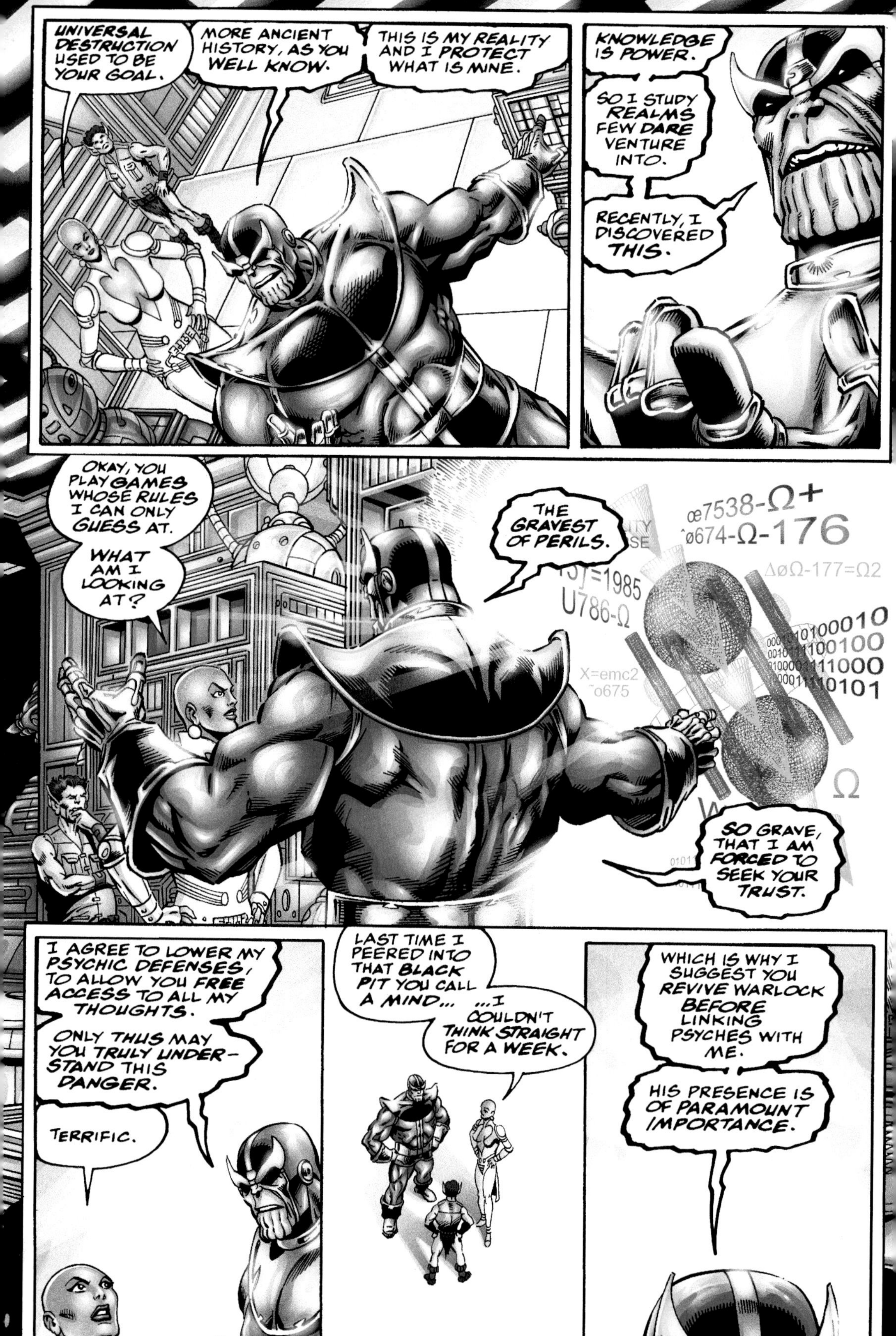
UNIVERSAL DESTRUCTION USED TO BE YOUR GOAL.
MORE ANCIENT HISTORY, AS YOU WELL KNOW.
THIS IS MY REALITY AND I PROTECT WHAT IS MINE.
KNOWLEDGE IS POWER.
SO I STUDY REALMS FEW DARE VENTURE INTO.
RECENTLY, I DISCOVERED THIS.
OKAY, YOU PLAY GAMES WHOSE RULES I CAN ONLY GUESS AT.
WHAT AM I LOOKING AT?
THE GRAVEST OF PERILS.
œ7538-Ω+
ˆø674-Ω-176
ΔøΩ-177=Ω2
U786-Ω
X=emc2
SO GRAVE, THAT I AM FORCED TO SEEK YOUR TRUST.
I AGREE TO LOWER MY PSYCHIC DEFENSES, TO ALLOW YOU FREE ACCESS TO ALL MY THOUGHTS.
ONLY THUS MAY YOU TRULY UNDERSTAND THIS DANGER.
TERRIFIC.
LAST TIME I PEERED INTO THAT BLACK PIT YOU CALL A MIND...
...I COULDN'T THINK STRAIGHT FOR A WEEK.
WHICH IS WHY I SUGGEST YOU REVIVE WARLOCK BEFORE LINKING PSYCHES WITH ME.
HIS PRESENCE IS OF PARAMOUNT IMPORTANCE.

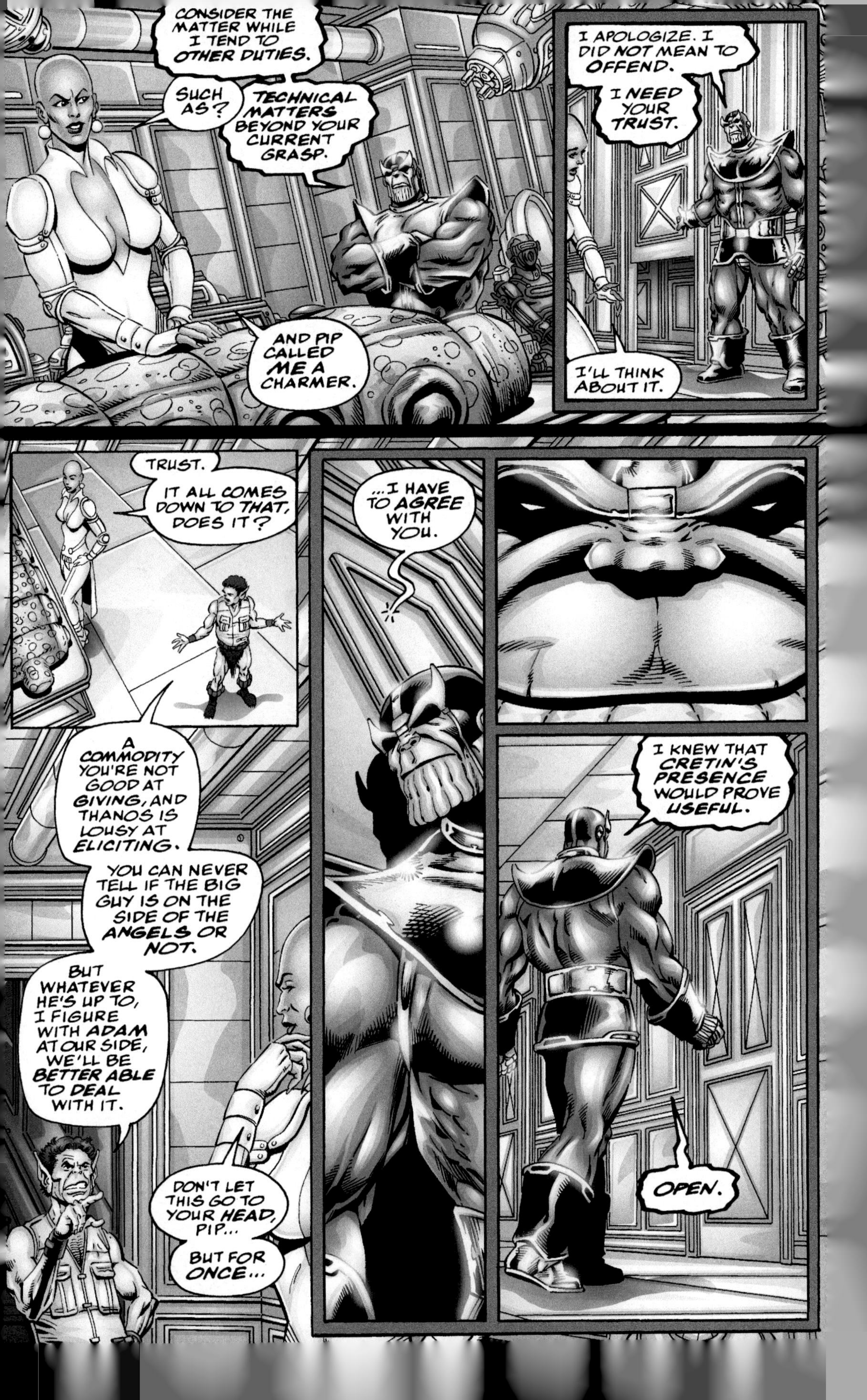
CONSIDER THE MATTER WHILE I TEND TO OTHER DUTIES.
SUCH AS?
TECHNICAL MATTERS BEYOND YOUR CURRENT GRASP.
AND PIP CALLED ME A CHARMER.
I APOLOGIZE. I DID NOT MEAN TO OFFEND.
I NEED YOUR TRUST.
I'LL THINK ABOUT IT.
TRUST.
IT ALL COMES DOWN TO THAT, DOES IT?
A COMMODITY YOU'RE NOT GOOD AT GIVING, AND THANOS IS LOUSY AT ELICITING.
YOU CAN NEVER TELL IF THE BIG GUY IS ON THE SIDE OF THE ANGELS OR NOT.
BUT WHATEVER HE'S UP TO, I FIGURE WITH ADAM AT OUR SIDE, WE'LL BE BETTER ABLE TO DEAL WITH IT.
DON'T LET THIS GO TO YOUR HEAD, PIP...
BUT FOR ONCE...
...I HAVE TO AGREE WITH YOU.
I KNEW THAT CRETIN'S PRESENCE WOULD PROVE USEFUL.
OPEN.

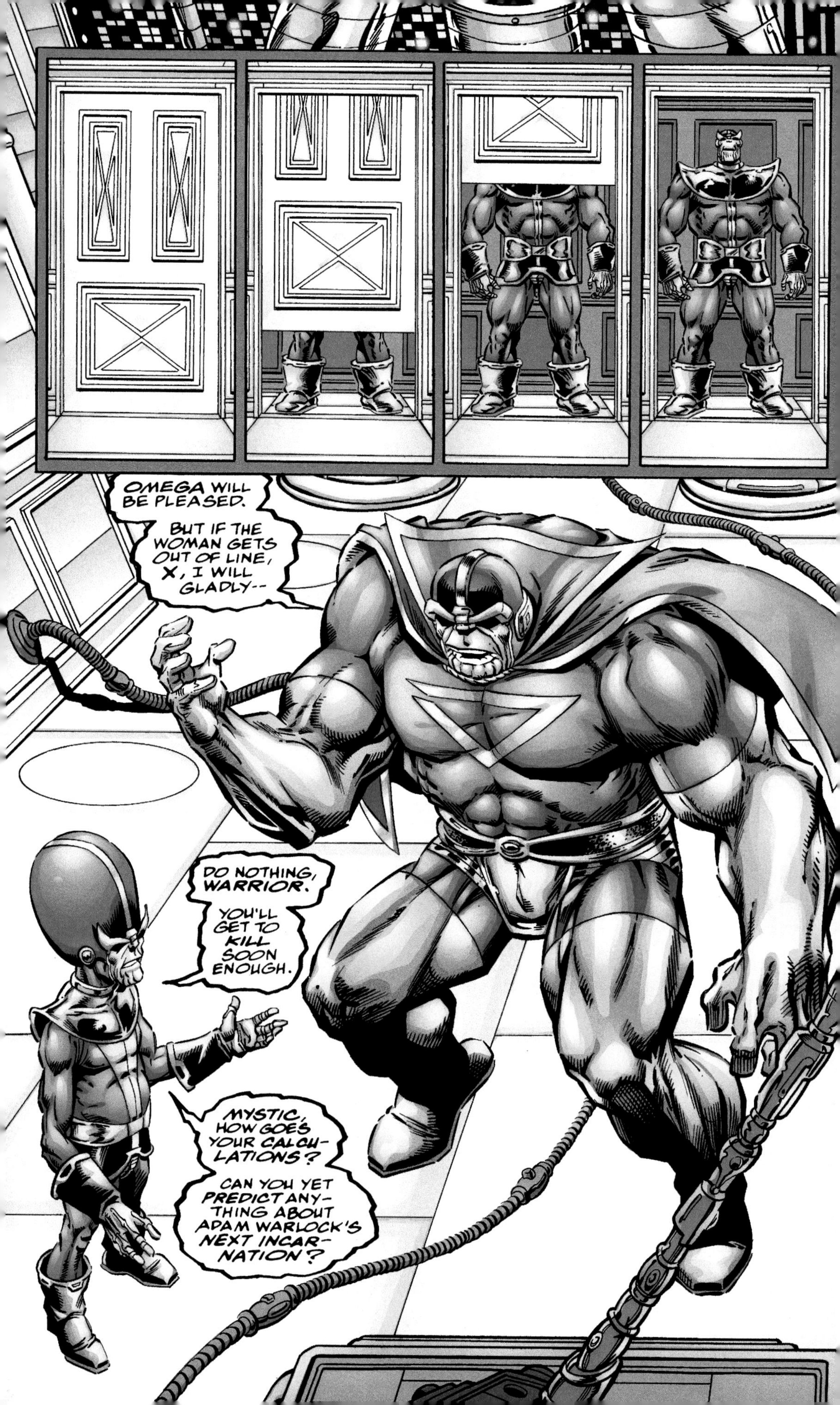

OMEGA WILL BE PLEASED.
BUT IF THE WOMAN GETS OUT OF LINE, X, I WILL GLADLY--
DO NOTHING, WARRIOR.
YOU'LL GET TO KILL SOON ENOUGH.
MYSTIC, HOW GOES YOUR CALCULATIONS?
CAN YOU YET PREDICT ANYTHING ABOUT ADAM WARLOCK'S NEXT INCARNATION?

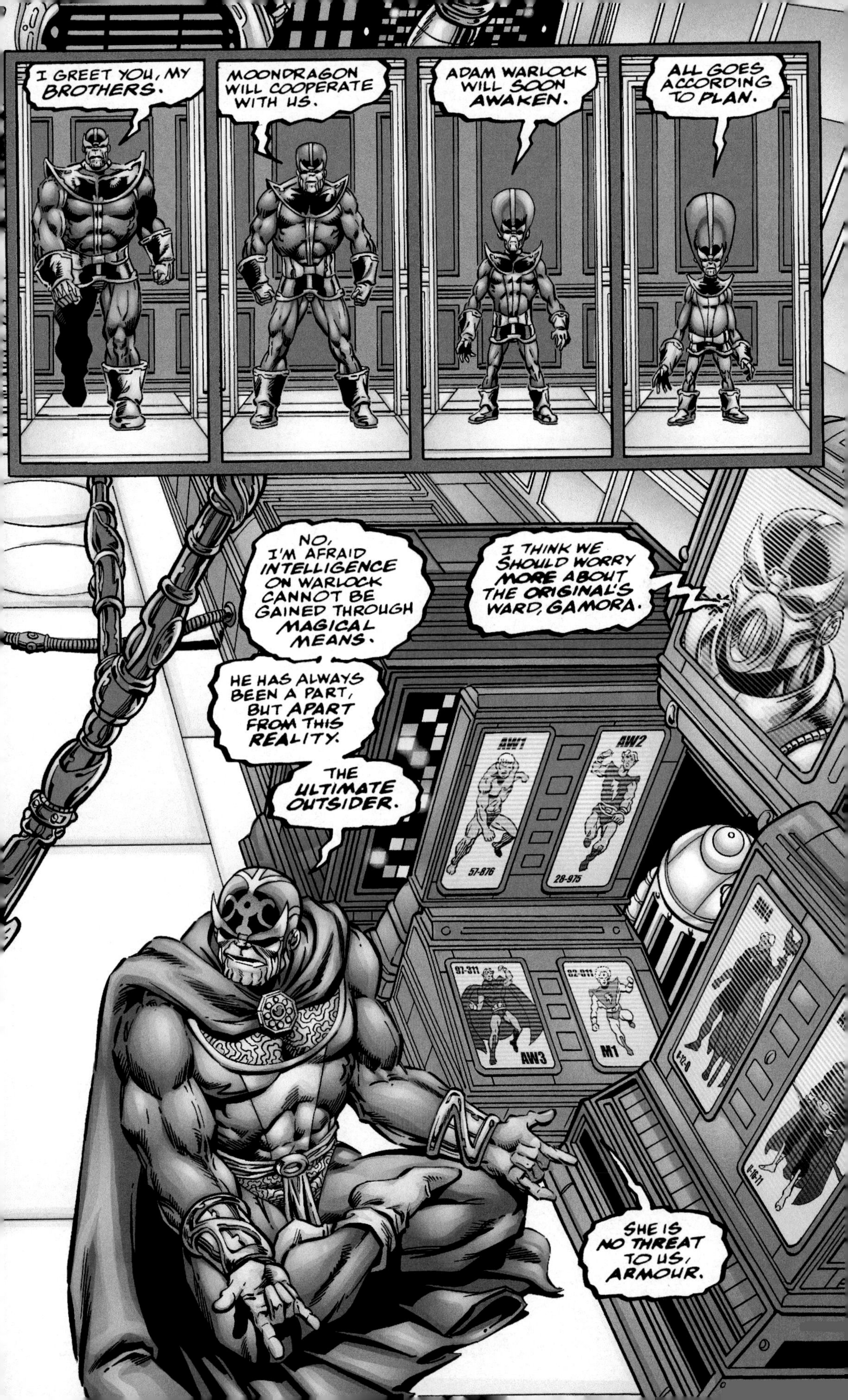
I GREET YOU, MY BROTHERS.
MOONDRAGON WILL COOPERATE WITH US.
ADAM WARLOCK WILL SOON AWAKEN.
ALL GOES ACCORDING TO PLAN.
NO, I'M AFRAID INTELLIGENCE ON WARLOCK CANNOT BE GAINED THROUGH MAGICAL MEANS.
HE HAS ALWAYS BEEN A PART, BUT APART FROM THIS REALITY.
THE ULTIMATE OUTSIDER.
I THINK WE SHOULD WORRY MORE ABOUT THE ORIGINAL'S WARD, GAMORA.
AW1
57-876
AW2
28-975
97-311
AW3
02-011
M1
SHE IS NO THREAT TO US, ARMOUR.

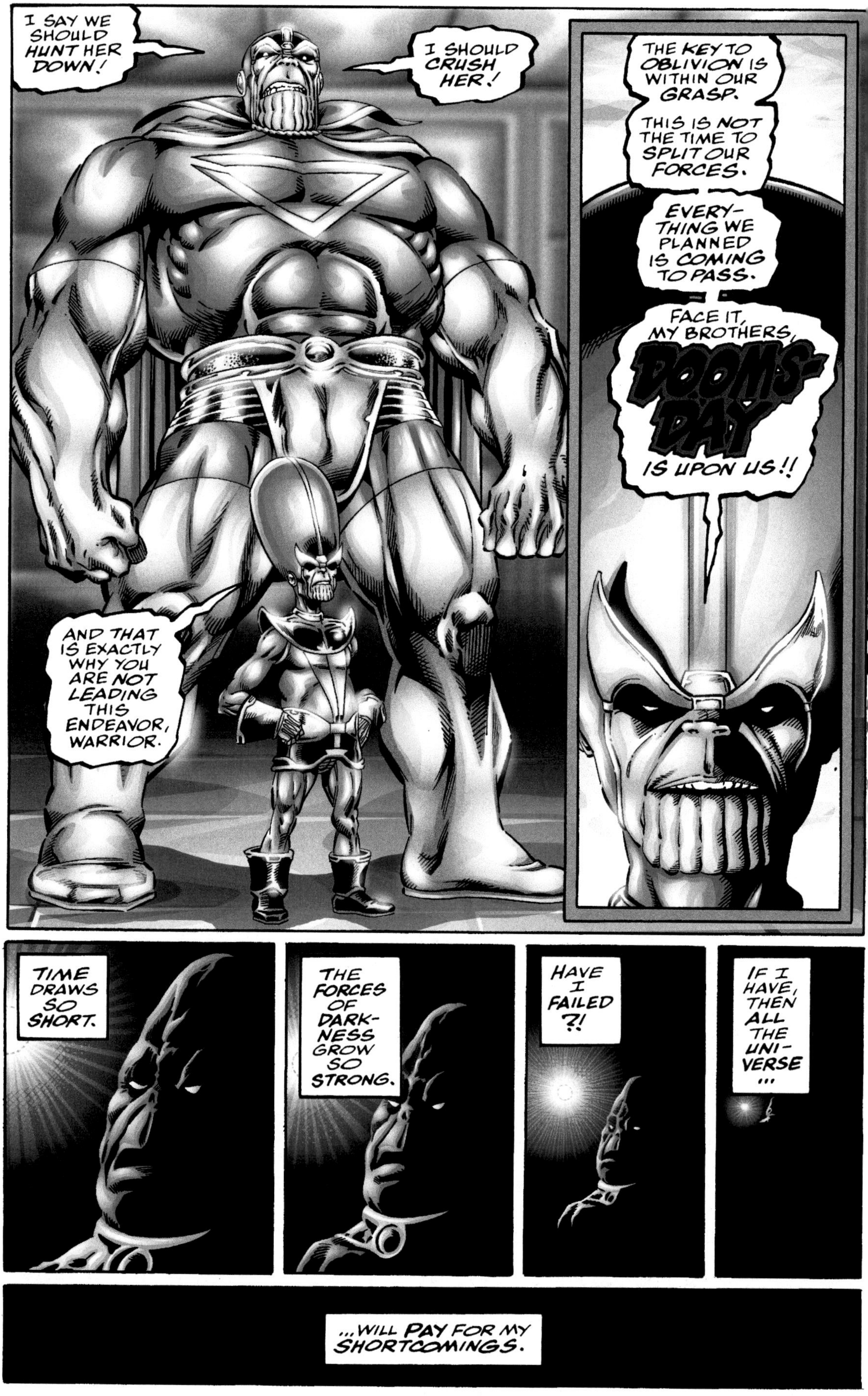
I SAY WE SHOULD HUNT HER DOWN!
I SHOULD CRUSH HER!
THE KEY TO OBLIVION IS WITHIN OUR GRASP.
THIS IS NOT THE TIME TO SPLIT OUR FORCES.
EVERY-THING WE PLANNED IS COMING TO PASS.
FACE IT, MY BROTHERS, DOOMS-DAY IS UPON US!!
AND THAT IS EXACTLY WHY YOU ARE NOT LEADING THIS ENDEAVOR, WARRIOR.
TIME DRAWS SO SHORT.
THE FORCES OF DARK-NESS GROW SO STRONG.
HAVE I FAILED ?!
IF I HAVE, THEN ALL THE UNI-VERSE ...
...WILL PAY FOR MY SHORTCOMINGS.

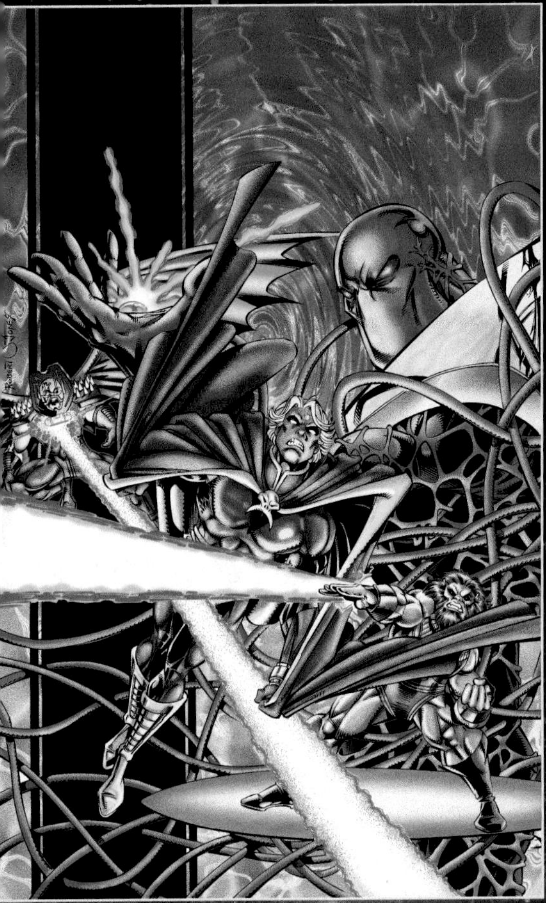

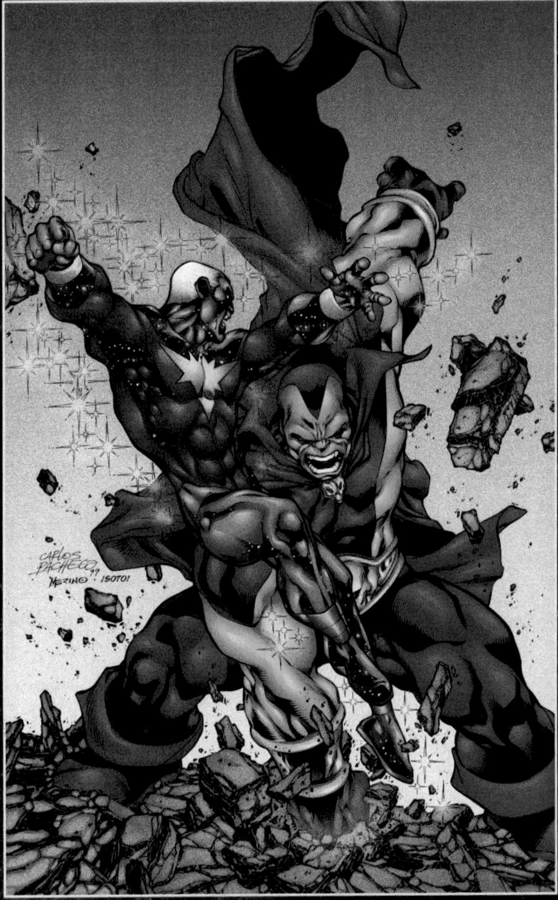

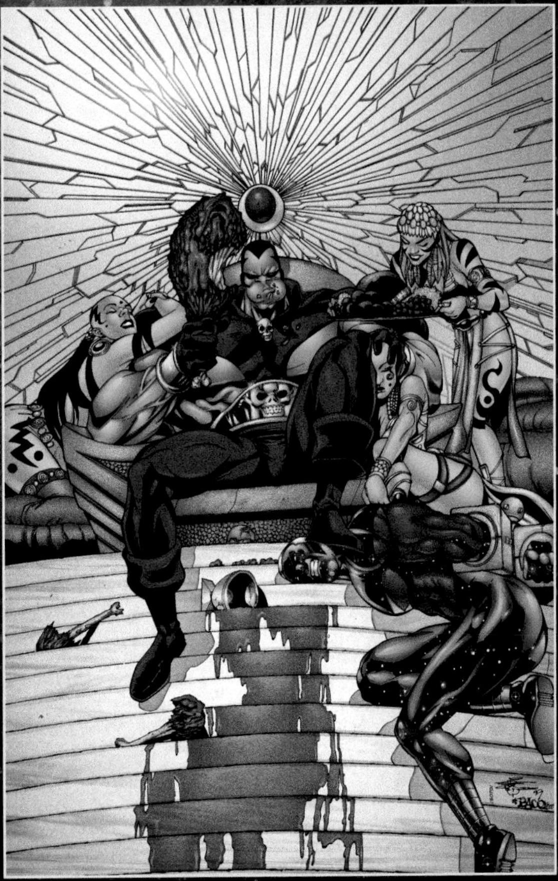

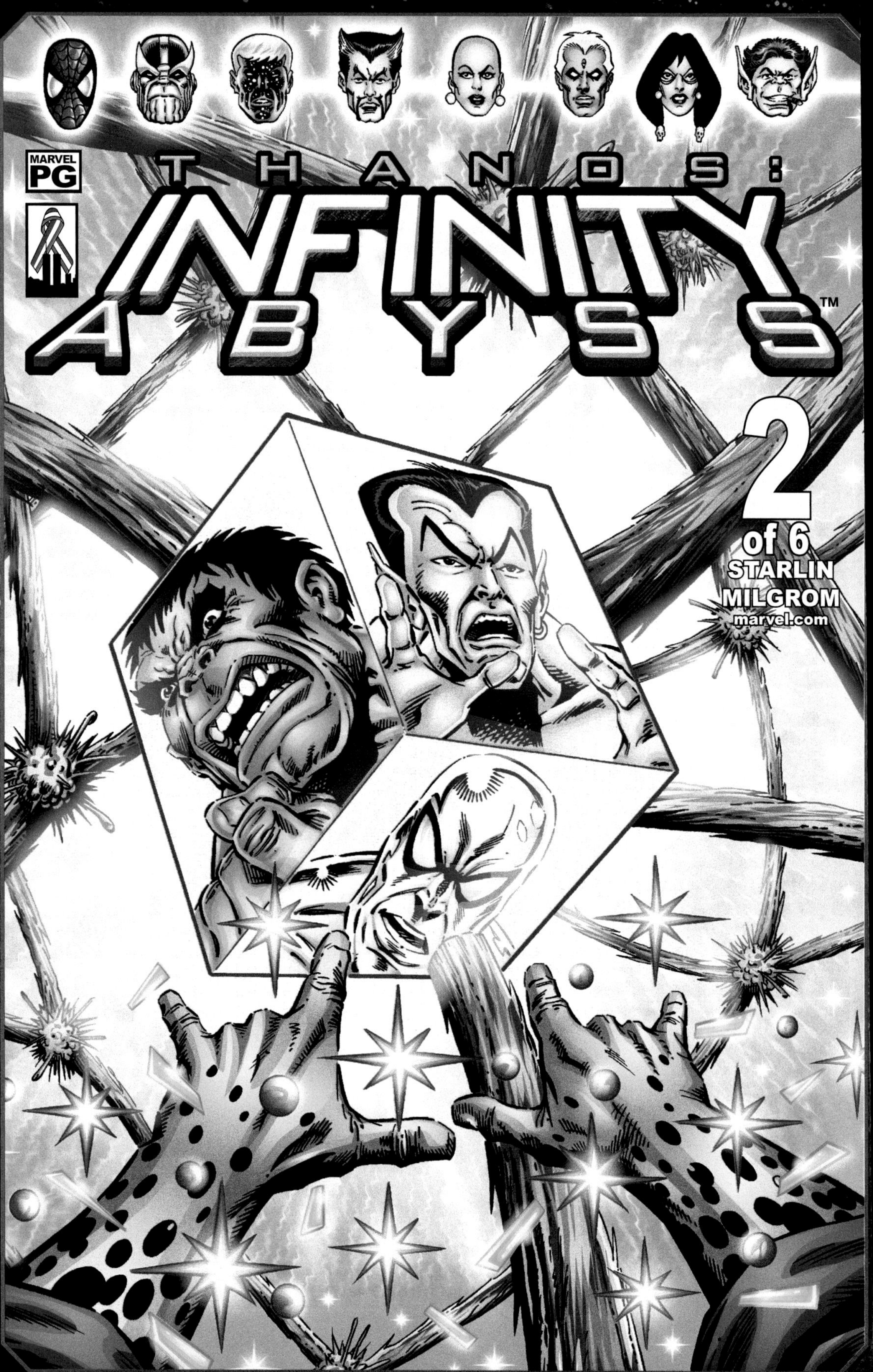

MARVEL PG
THANOS:
INFINITY ABYSS™
2 of 6
STARLIN
MILGROM
marvel.com

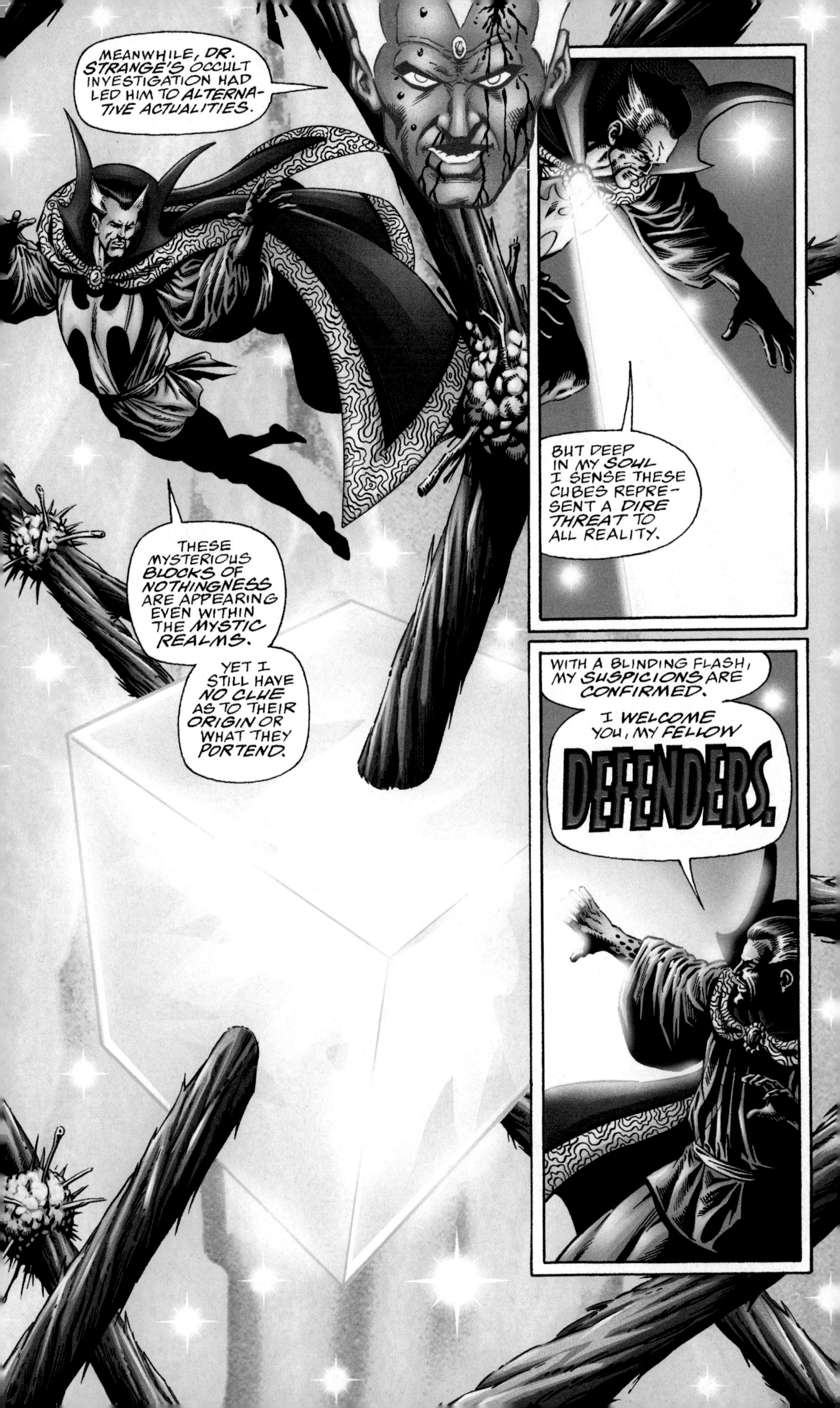

MEANWHILE, DR. STRANGE'S OCCULT INVESTIGATION HAD LED HIM TO ALTERNATIVE ACTUALITIES.
THESE MYSTERIOUS BLOCKS OF NOTHINGNESS ARE APPEARING EVEN WITHIN THE MYSTIC REALMS.
YET I STILL HAVE NO CLUE AS TO THEIR ORIGIN OR WHAT THEY PORTEND.
BUT DEEP IN MY SOUL I SENSE THESE CUBES REPRESENT A DIRE THREAT TO ALL REALITY.
WITH A BLINDING FLASH, MY SUSPICIONS ARE CONFIRMED.
I WELCOME YOU, MY FELLOW
DEFENDERS.

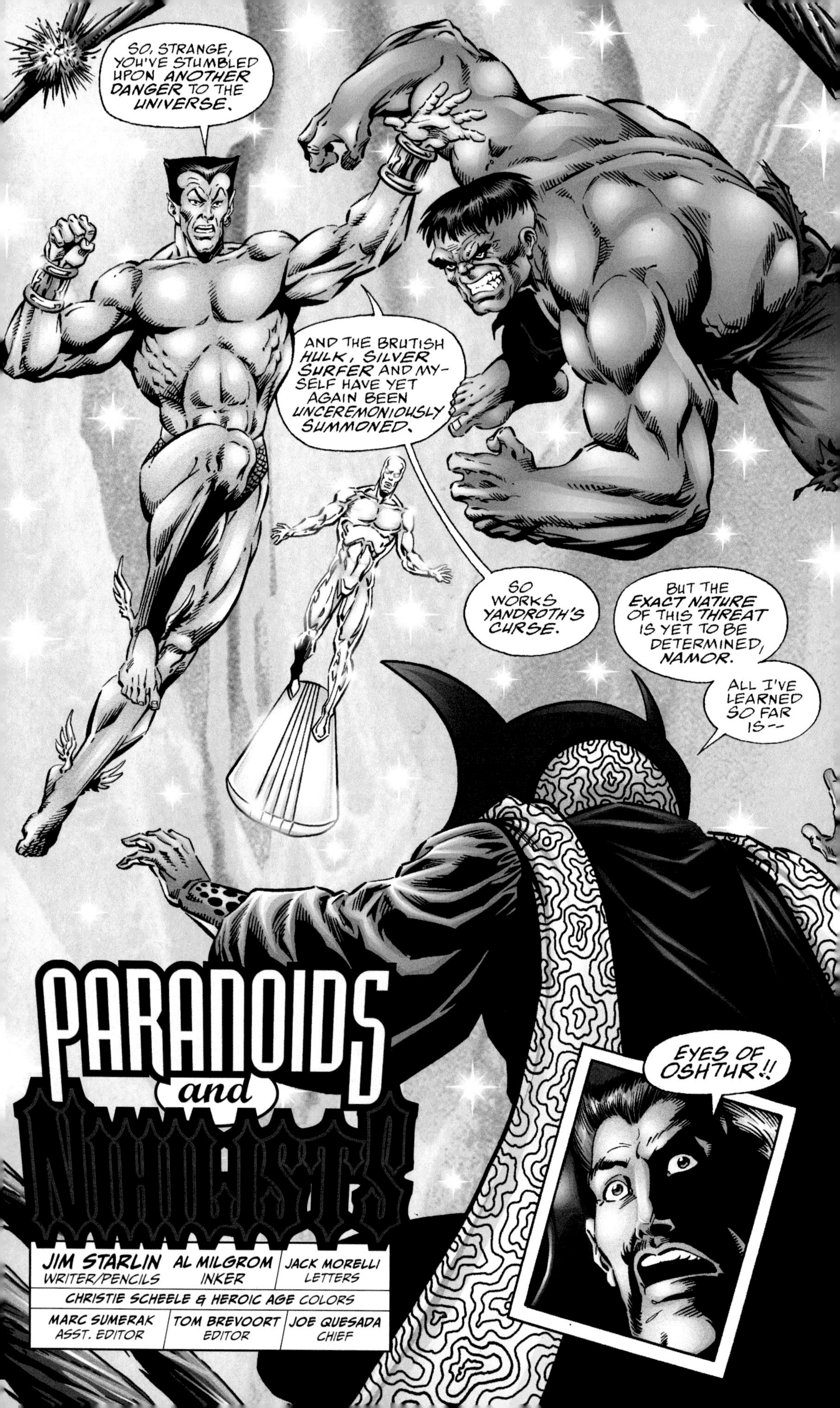
SO, STRANGE, YOU'VE STUMBLED UPON ANOTHER DANGER TO THE UNIVERSE.
AND THE BRUTISH HULK, SILVER SURFER AND MY-SELF HAVE YET AGAIN BEEN UNCEREMONIOUSLY SUMMONED.
SO WORKS YANDROTH'S CURSE.
BUT THE EXACT NATURE OF THIS THREAT IS YET TO BE DETERMINED, NAMOR.
ALL I'VE LEARNED SO FAR IS--
PARANOIDS and NIHILISTS
JIM STARLIN WRITER/PENCILS
AL MILGROM INKER
JACK MORELLI LETTERS
CHRISTIE SCHEELE & HEROIC AGE COLORS
MARC SUMERAK ASST. EDITOR
TOM BREVOORT EDITOR
JOE QUESADA CHIEF
EYES OF OSHTUR!!

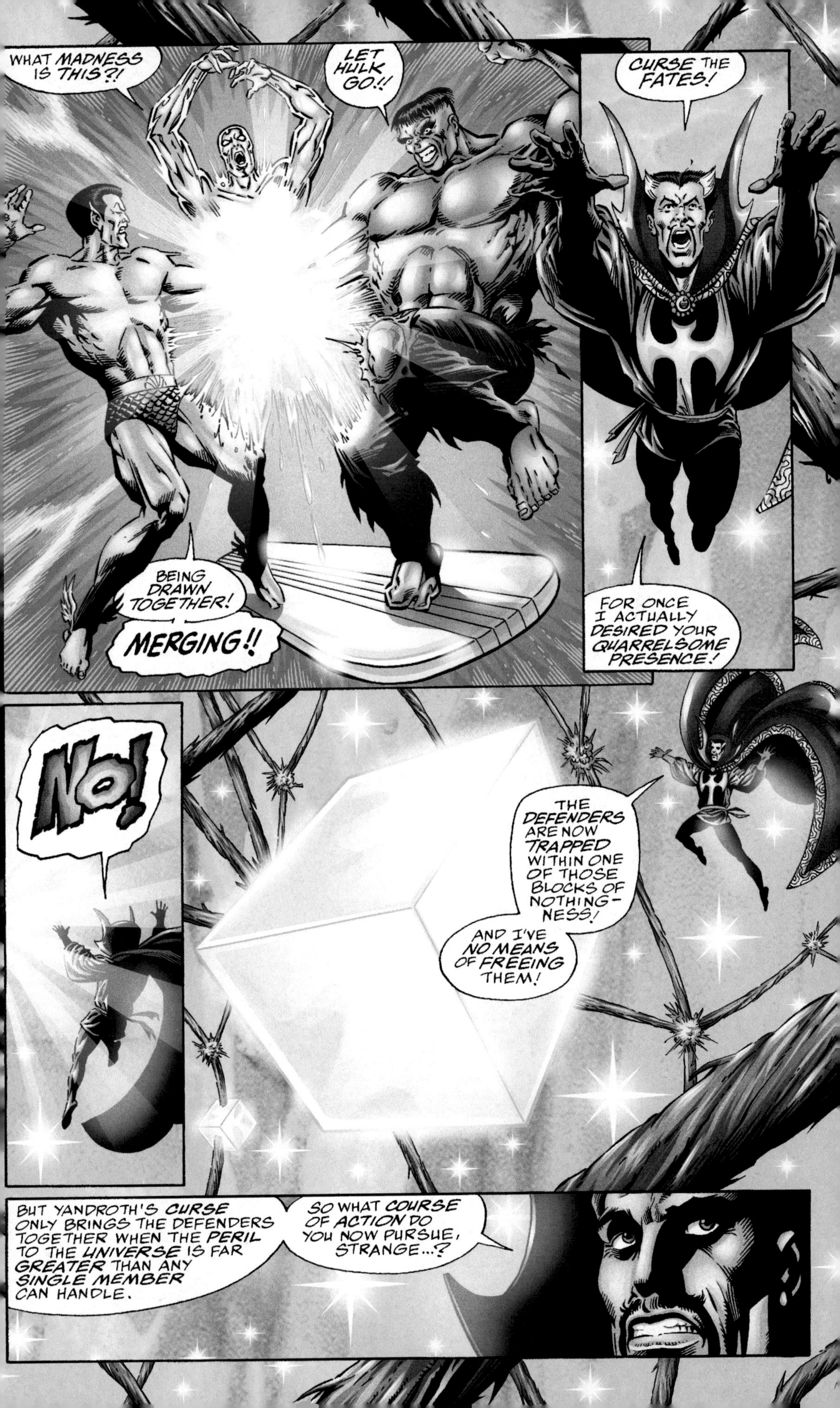

WHAT MADNESS IS THIS?!
LET HULK GO!!
CURSE THE FATES!
BEING DRAWN TOGETHER!
MERGING!!
FOR ONCE I ACTUALLY DESIRED YOUR QUARRELSOME PRESENCE!
NO!
THE DEFENDERS ARE NOW TRAPPED WITHIN ONE OF THOSE BLOCKS OF NOTHING-NESS!
AND I'VE NO MEANS OF FREEING THEM!
BUT YANDROTH'S CURSE ONLY BRINGS THE DEFENDERS TOGETHER WHEN THE PERIL TO THE UNIVERSE IS FAR GREATER THAN ANY SINGLE MEMBER CAN HANDLE.
SO WHAT COURSE OF ACTION DO YOU NOW PURSUE, STRANGE...?

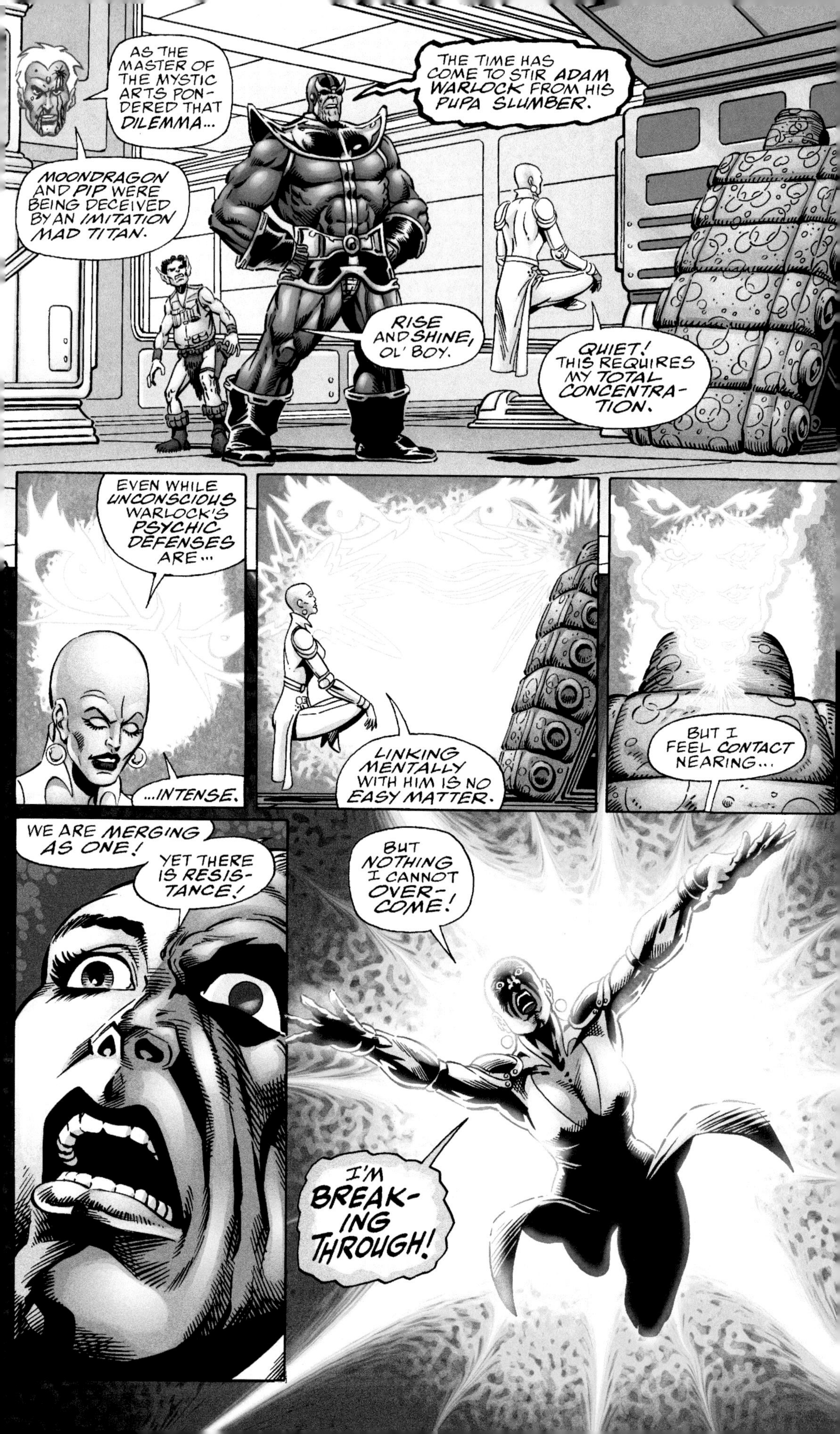

AS THE MASTER OF THE MYSTIC ARTS PON-DERED THAT DILEMMA...
MOONDRAGON AND PIP WERE BEING DECEIVED BY AN IMITATION MAD TITAN.
THE TIME HAS COME TO STIR ADAM WARLOCK FROM HIS PUPA SLUMBER.
RISE AND SHINE, OL' BOY.
QUIET! THIS REQUIRES MY TOTAL CONCENTRA-TION.
EVEN WHILE UNCONSCIOUS WARLOCK'S PSYCHIC DEFENSES ARE...
...INTENSE.
LINKING MENTALLY WITH HIM IS NO EASY MATTER.
BUT I FEEL CONTACT NEARING...
WE ARE MERGING AS ONE!
YET THERE IS RESIS-TANCE!
BUT NOTHING I CANNOT OVER-COME!
I'M BREAK-ING THROUGH!

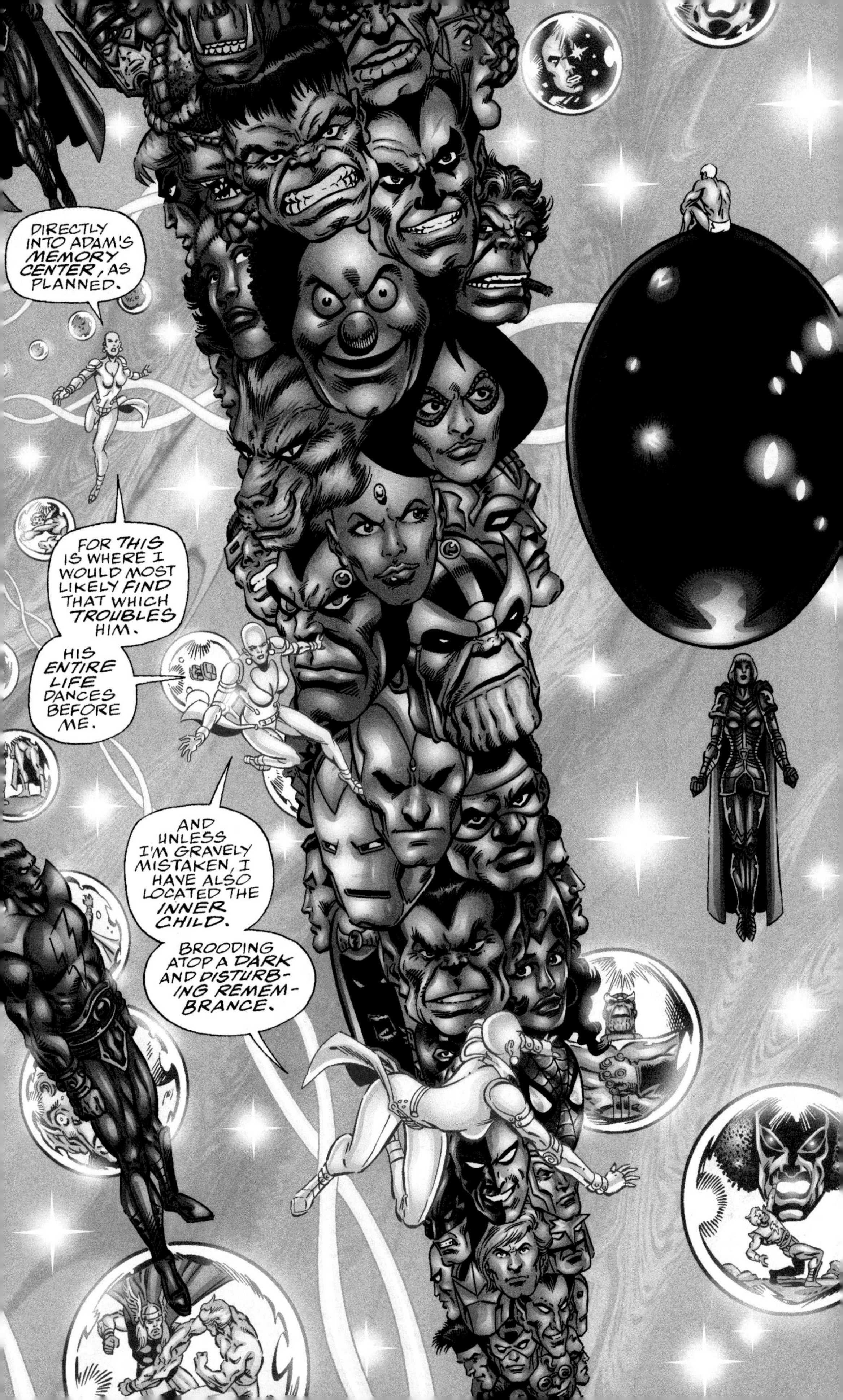

DIRECTLY INTO ADAM'S MEMORY CENTER, AS PLANNED.
FOR THIS IS WHERE I WOULD MOST LIKELY FIND THAT WHICH TROUBLES HIM.
HIS ENTIRE LIFE DANCES BEFORE ME.
AND UNLESS I'M GRAVELY MISTAKEN, I HAVE ALSO LOCATED THE INNER CHILD.
BROODING ATOP A DARK AND DISTURBING REMEMBRANCE.

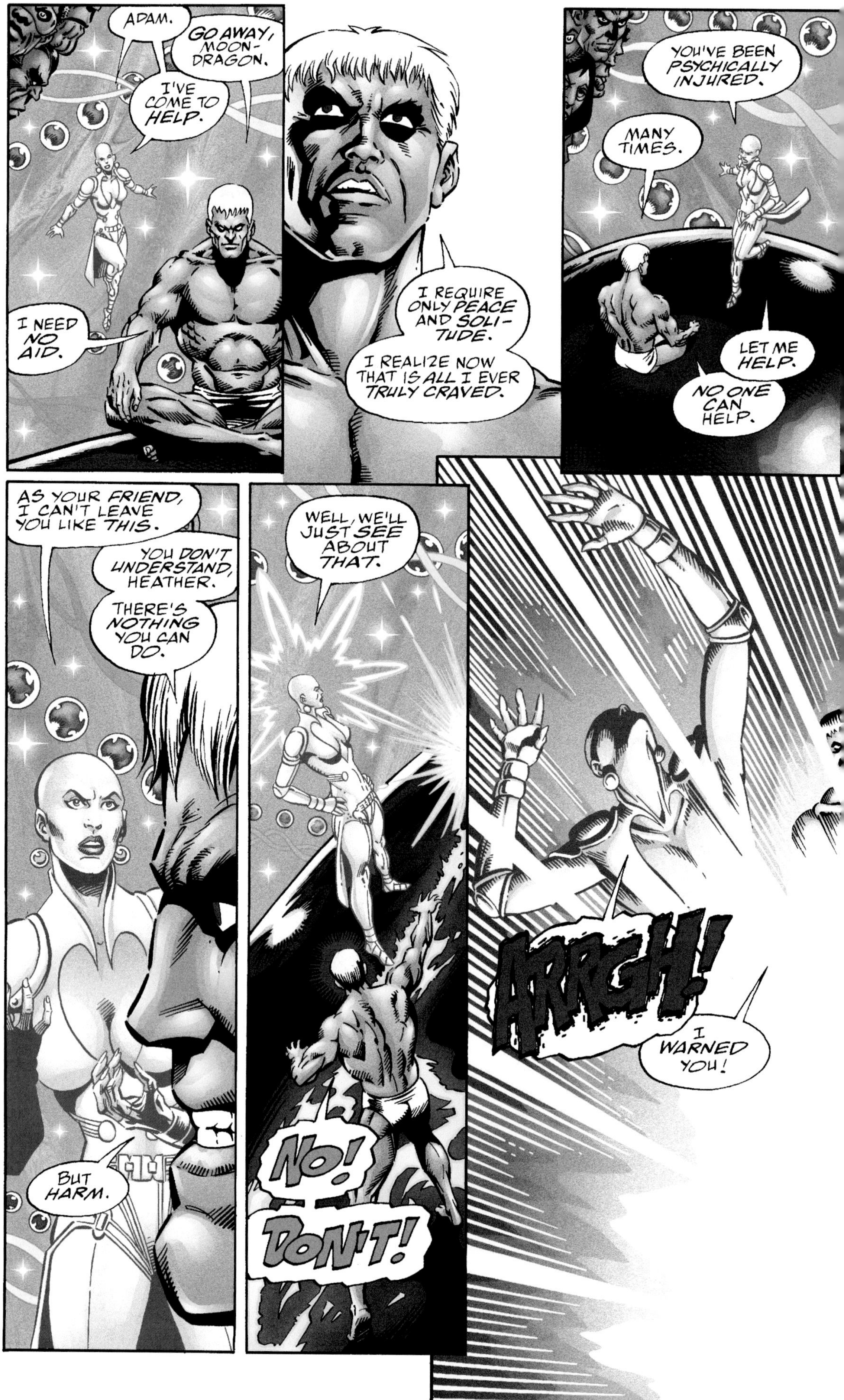
ADAM.
GO AWAY, MOON-DRAGON.
I'VE COME TO HELP.
I NEED NO AID.
I REQUIRE ONLY PEACE AND SOLI-TUDE.
I REALIZE NOW THAT IS ALL I EVER TRULY CRAVED.
YOU'VE BEEN PSYCHICALLY INJURED.
MANY TIMES.
LET ME HELP.
NO ONE CAN HELP.
AS YOUR FRIEND, I CAN'T LEAVE YOU LIKE THIS.
YOU DON'T UNDERSTAND, HEATHER.
THERE'S NOTHING YOU CAN DO.
BUT HARM.
WELL, WE'LL JUST SEE ABOUT THAT.
NO!
DON'T!
ARRGH!
I WARNED YOU!

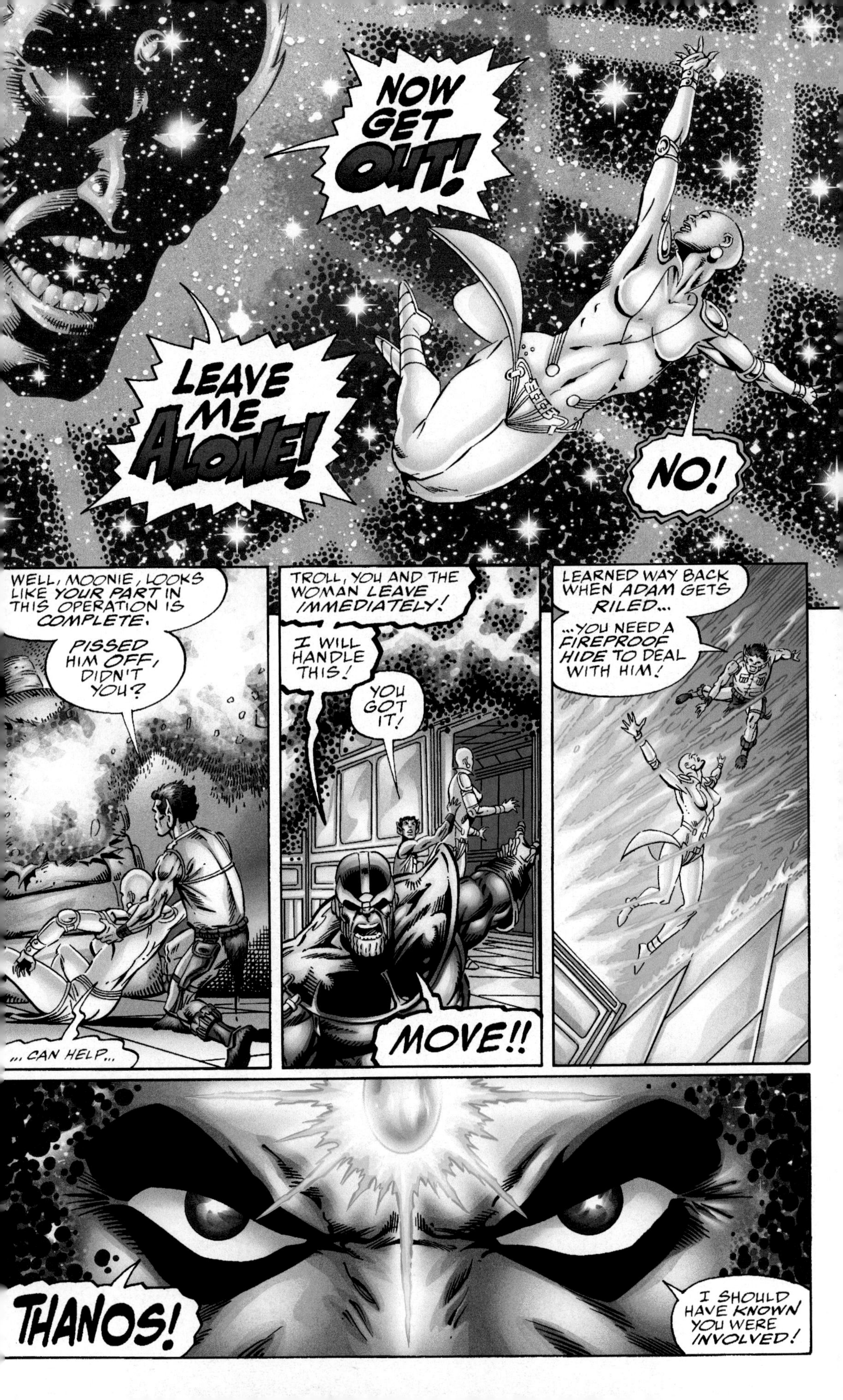

NOW GET OUT!
LEAVE ME ALONE!
NO!
WELL, MOONIE, LOOKS LIKE YOUR PART IN THIS OPERATION IS COMPLETE.
PISSED HIM OFF, DIDN'T YOU?
...CAN HELP...
TROLL, YOU AND THE WOMAN LEAVE IMMEDIATELY!
I WILL HANDLE THIS!
YOU GOT IT!
MOVE!!
LEARNED WAY BACK WHEN ADAM GETS RILED...
...YOU NEED A FIREPROOF HIDE TO DEAL WITH HIM!
THANOS!
I SHOULD HAVE KNOWN YOU WERE INVOLVED!

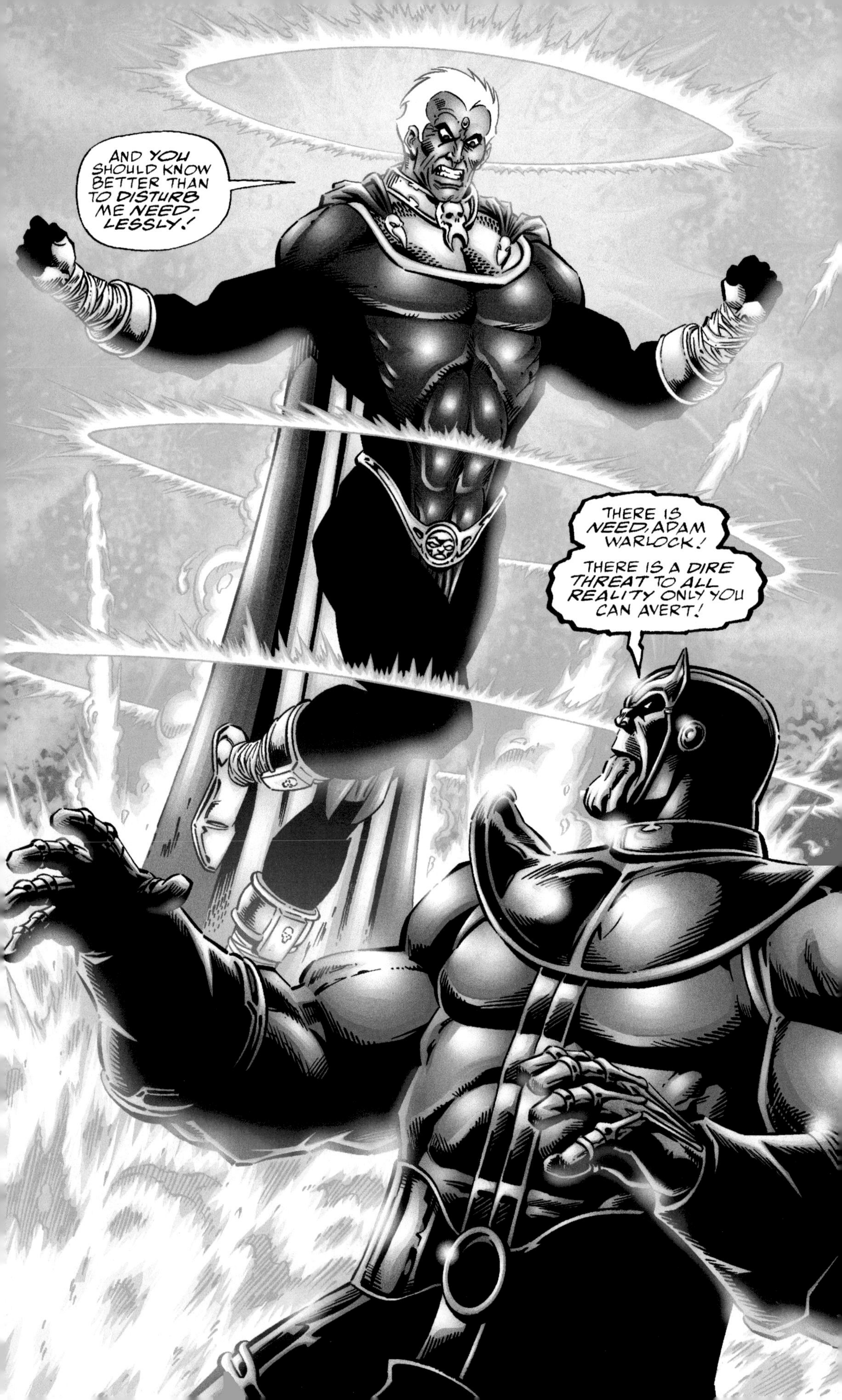
AND YOU SHOULD KNOW BETTER THAN TO DISTURB ME NEED-LESSLY!
THERE IS NEED, ADAM WARLOCK!
THERE IS A DIRE THREAT TO ALL REALITY ONLY YOU CAN AVERT!

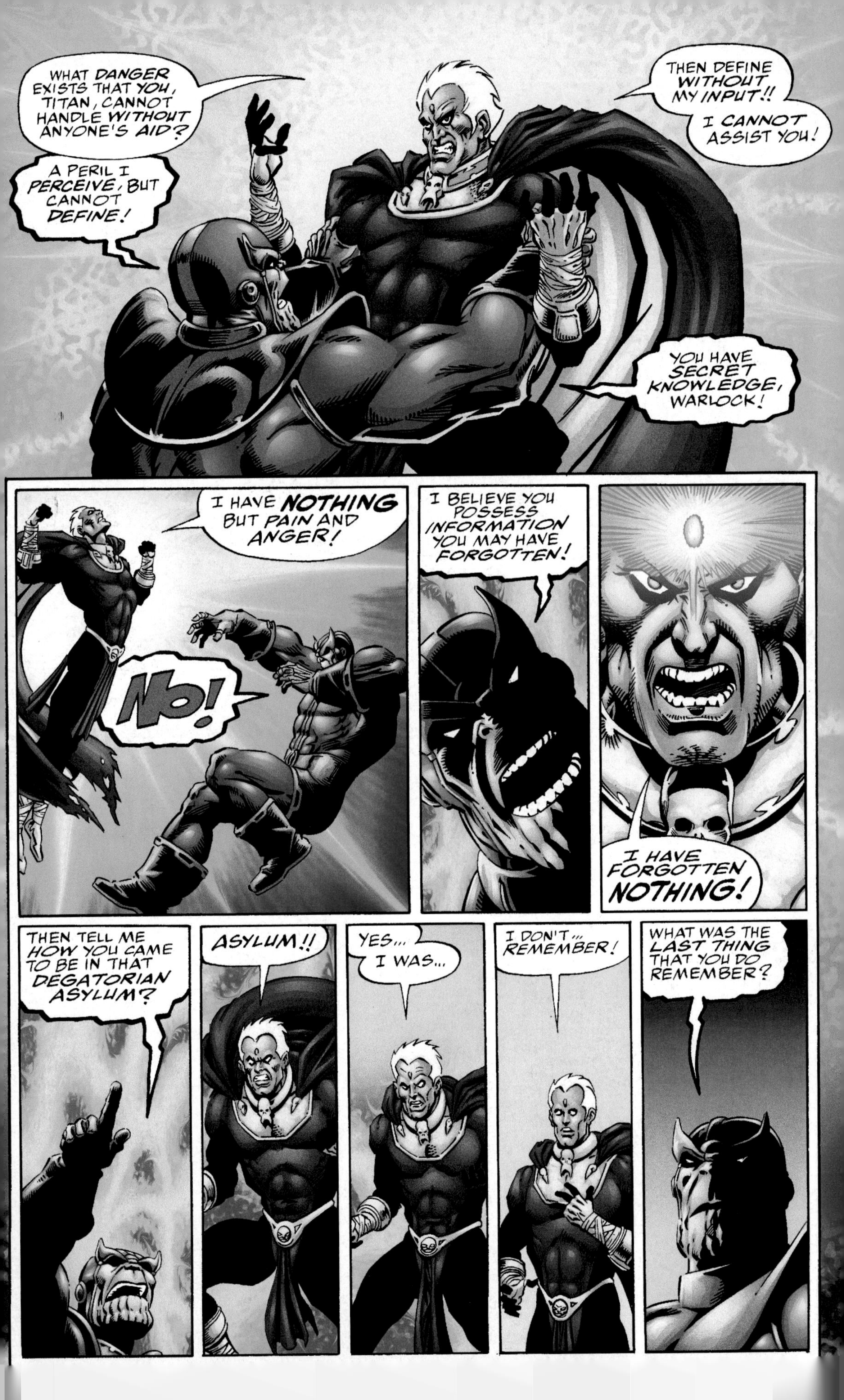
WHAT DANGER EXISTS THAT YOU, TITAN, CANNOT HANDLE WITHOUT ANYONE'S AID?
A PERIL I PERCEIVE, BUT CANNOT DEFINE!
THEN DEFINE WITHOUT MY INPUT!!
I CANNOT ASSIST YOU!
YOU HAVE SECRET KNOWLEDGE, WARLOCK!
I HAVE NOTHING BUT PAIN AND ANGER!
NO!
I BELIEVE YOU POSSESS INFORMATION YOU MAY HAVE FORGOTTEN!
I HAVE FORGOTTEN NOTHING!
THEN TELL ME HOW YOU CAME TO BE IN THAT DEGATORIAN ASYLUM?
ASYLUM!!
YES... I WAS...
I DON'T... REMEMBER!
WHAT WAS THE LAST THING THAT YOU DO REMEMBER?

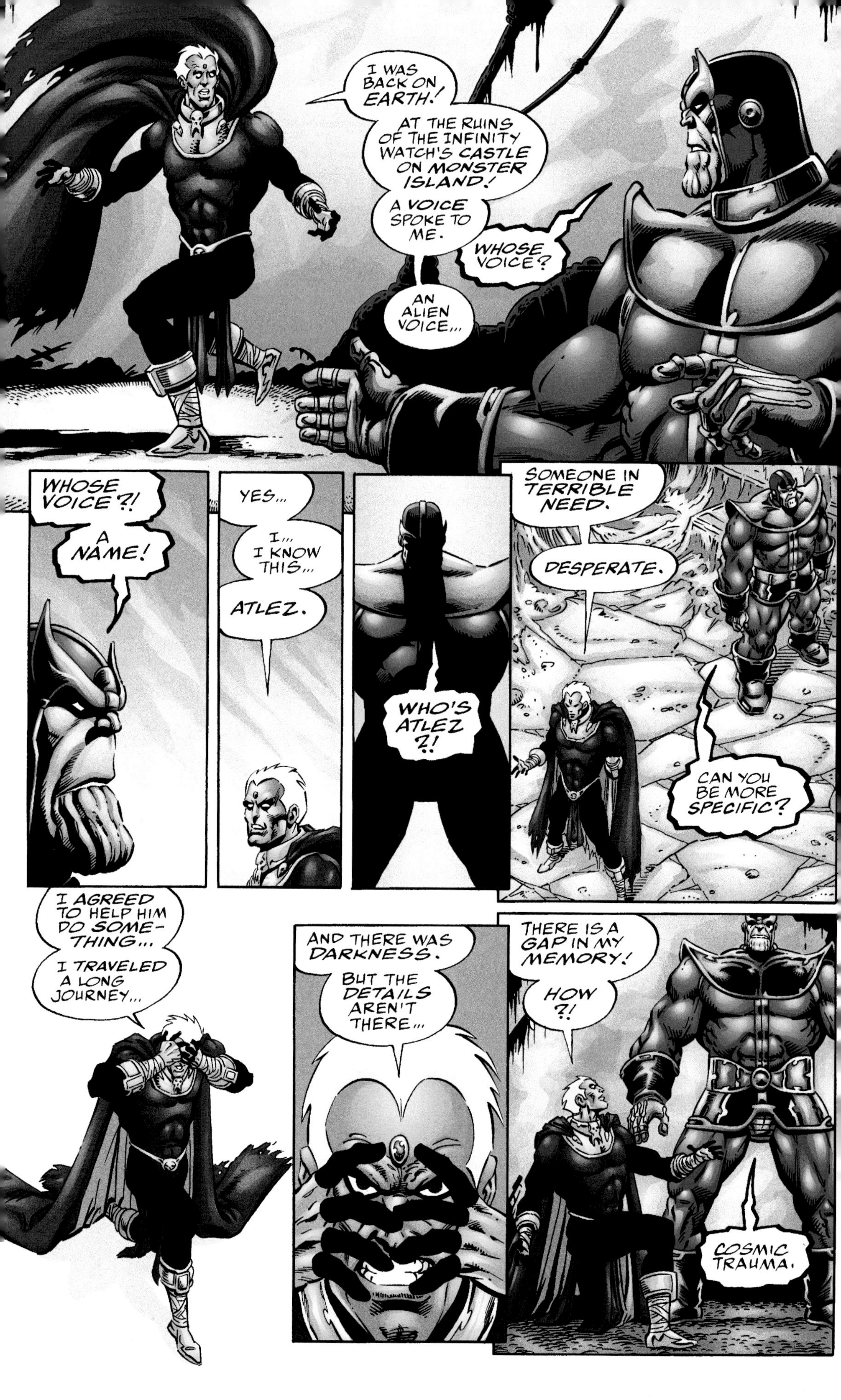

I WAS BACK ON EARTH!
AT THE RUINS OF THE INFINITY WATCH'S CASTLE ON MONSTER ISLAND!
A VOICE SPOKE TO ME.
WHOSE VOICE?
AN ALIEN VOICE...
WHOSE VOICE?!
A NAME!
YES...
I... I KNOW THIS...
ATLEZ.
WHO'S ATLEZ ?!
SOMEONE IN TERRIBLE NEED.
DESPERATE.
CAN YOU BE MORE SPECIFIC?
I AGREED TO HELP HIM DO SOME-THING...
I TRAVELED A LONG JOURNEY...
AND THERE WAS DARKNESS.
BUT THE DETAILS AREN'T THERE...
THERE IS A GAP IN MY MEMORY!
HOW ?!
COSMIC TRAUMA.

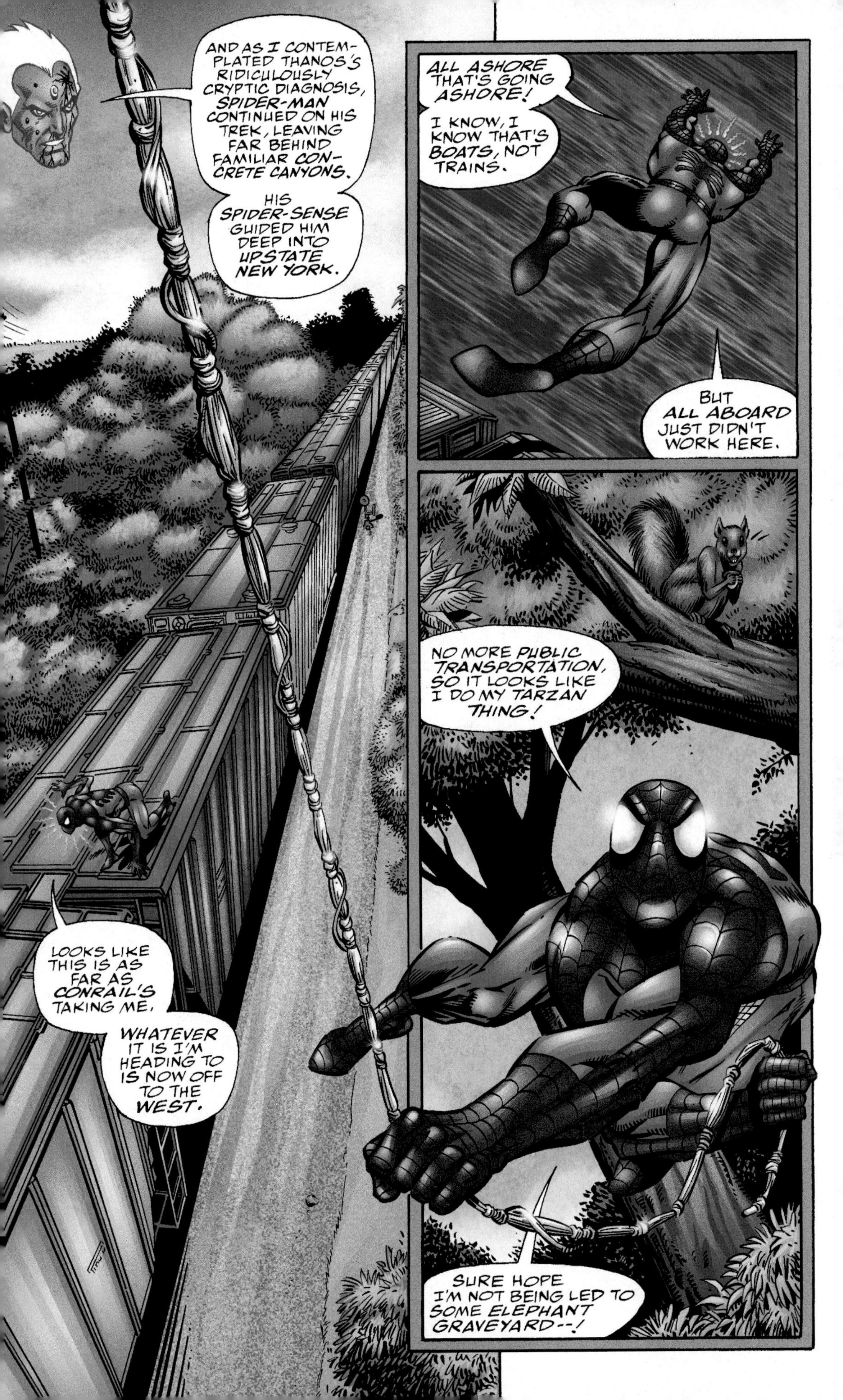
AND AS I CONTEMPLATED THANOS'S RIDICULOUSLY CRYPTIC DIAGNOSIS, SPIDER-MAN CONTINUED ON HIS TREK, LEAVING FAR BEHIND FAMILIAR CONCRETE CANYONS.
HIS SPIDER-SENSE GUIDED HIM DEEP INTO UPSTATE NEW YORK.
LOOKS LIKE THIS IS AS FAR AS CONRAIL'S TAKING ME.
WHATEVER IT IS I'M HEADING TO IS NOW OFF TO THE WEST.
ALL ASHORE THAT'S GOING ASHORE!
I KNOW, I KNOW THAT'S BOATS, NOT TRAINS.
BUT ALL ABOARD JUST DIDN'T WORK HERE.
NO MORE PUBLIC TRANSPORTATION, SO IT LOOKS LIKE I DO MY TARZAN THING!
SURE HOPE I'M NOT BEING LED TO SOME ELEPHANT GRAVEYARD--!

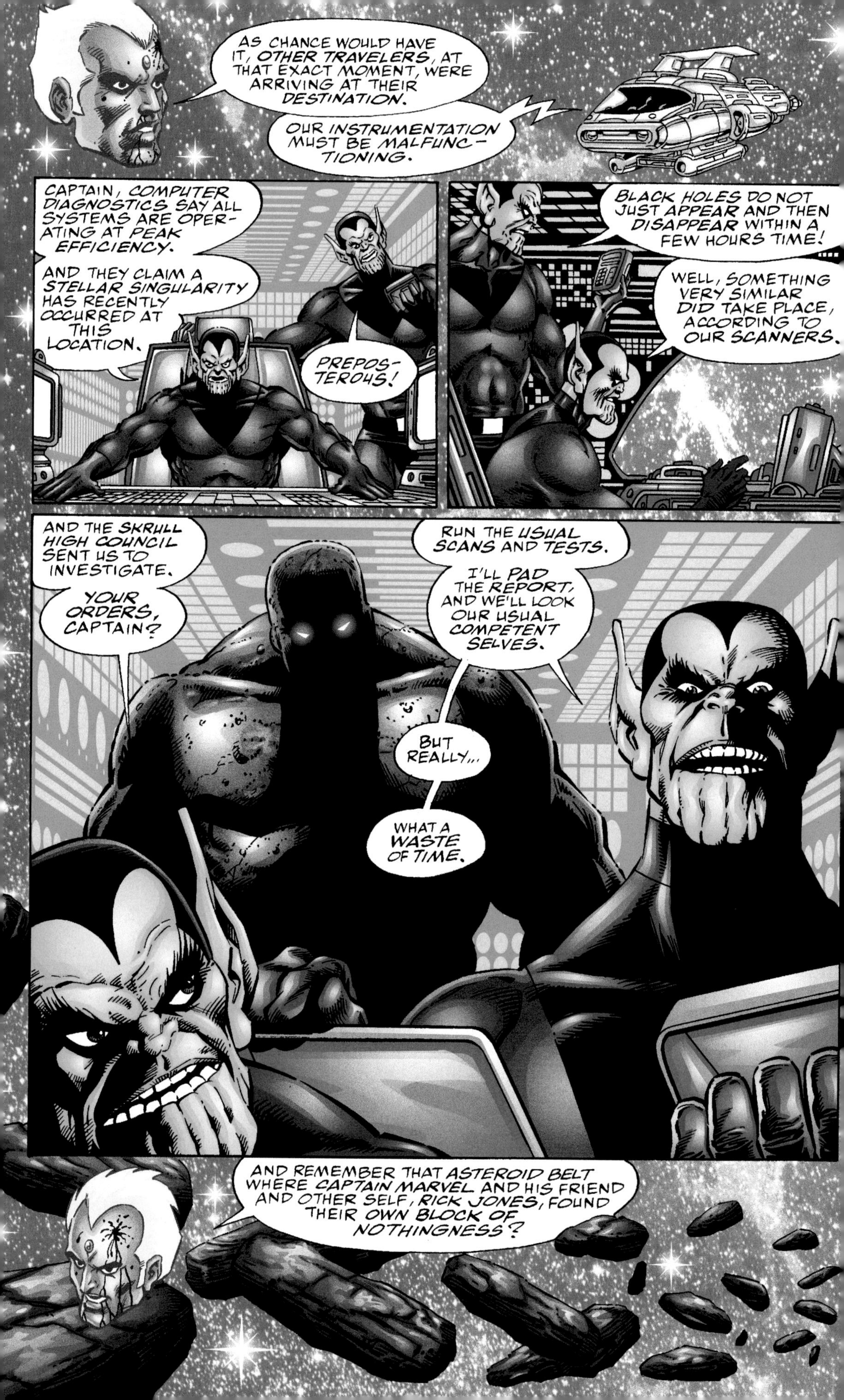
AS CHANCE WOULD HAVE IT, OTHER TRAVELERS, AT THAT EXACT MOMENT, WERE ARRIVING AT THEIR DESTINATION.
OUR INSTRUMENTATION MUST BE MALFUNCTIONING.
CAPTAIN, COMPUTER DIAGNOSTICS SAY ALL SYSTEMS ARE OPERATING AT PEAK EFFICIENCY.
AND THEY CLAIM A STELLAR SINGULARITY HAS RECENTLY OCCURRED AT THIS LOCATION.
PREPOSTEROUS!
BLACK HOLES DO NOT JUST APPEAR AND THEN DISAPPEAR WITHIN A FEW HOURS TIME!
WELL, SOMETHING VERY SIMILAR DID TAKE PLACE, ACCORDING TO OUR SCANNERS.
AND THE SKRULL HIGH COUNCIL SENT US TO INVESTIGATE.
YOUR ORDERS, CAPTAIN?
RUN THE USUAL SCANS AND TESTS.
I'LL PAD THE REPORT, AND WE'LL LOOK OUR USUAL COMPETENT SELVES.
BUT REALLY...
WHAT A WASTE OF TIME.
AND REMEMBER THAT ASTEROID BELT WHERE CAPTAIN MARVEL AND HIS FRIEND AND OTHER SELF, RICK JONES, FOUND THEIR OWN BLOCK OF NOTHINGNESS?

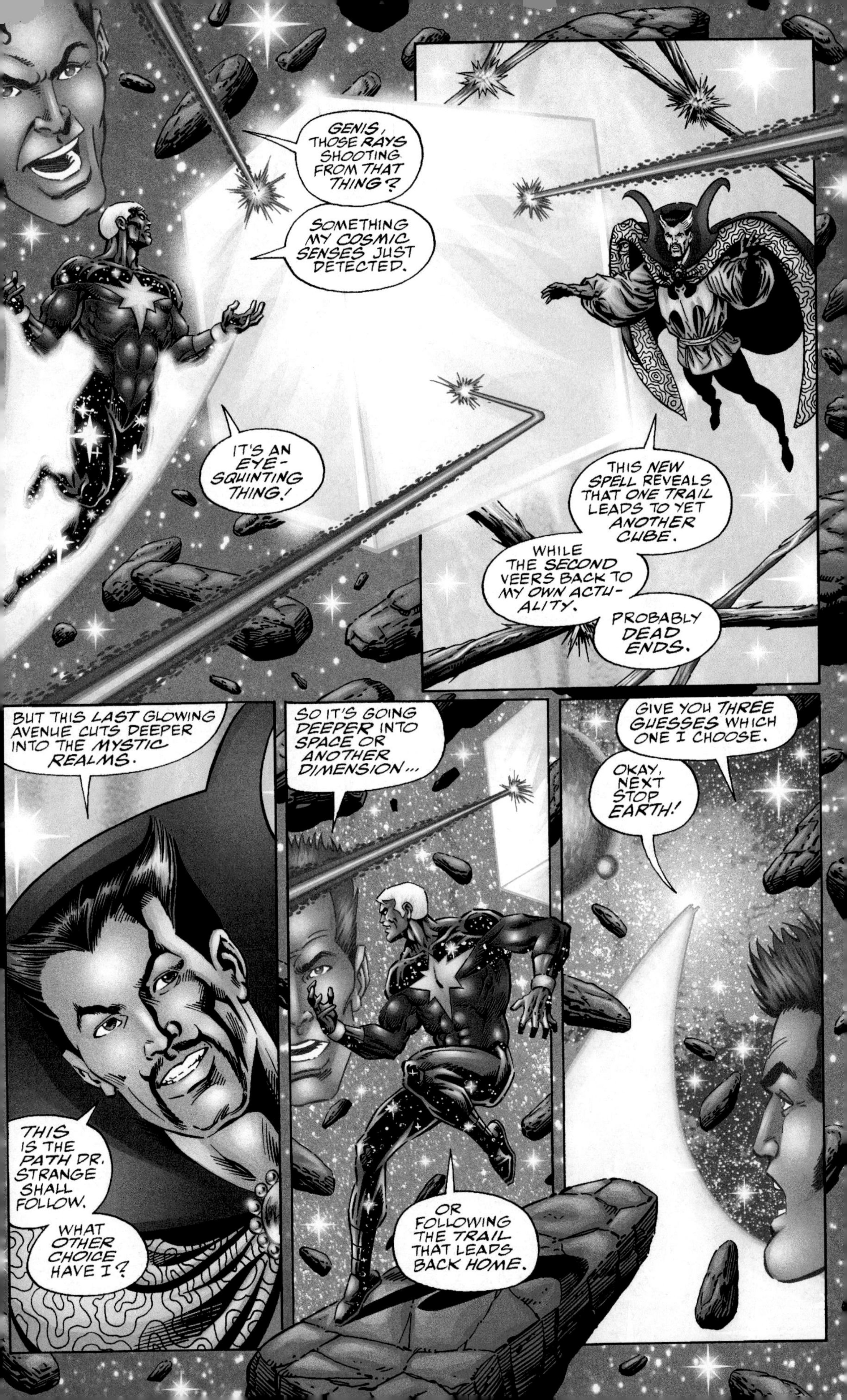
GENIS, THOSE RAYS SHOOTING FROM THAT THING?
SOMETHING MY COSMIC SENSES JUST DETECTED.
IT'S AN EYE-SQUINTING THING!
THIS NEW SPELL REVEALS THAT ONE TRAIL LEADS TO YET ANOTHER CUBE.
WHILE THE SECOND VEERS BACK TO MY OWN ACTUALITY.
PROBABLY DEAD ENDS.
BUT THIS LAST GLOWING AVENUE CUTS DEEPER INTO THE MYSTIC REALMS.
THIS IS THE PATH DR. STRANGE SHALL FOLLOW.
WHAT OTHER CHOICE HAVE I?
SO IT'S GOING DEEPER INTO SPACE OR ANOTHER DIMENSION...
OR FOLLOWING THE TRAIL THAT LEADS BACK HOME.
GIVE YOU THREE GUESSES WHICH ONE I CHOOSE.
OKAY, NEXT STOP EARTH!

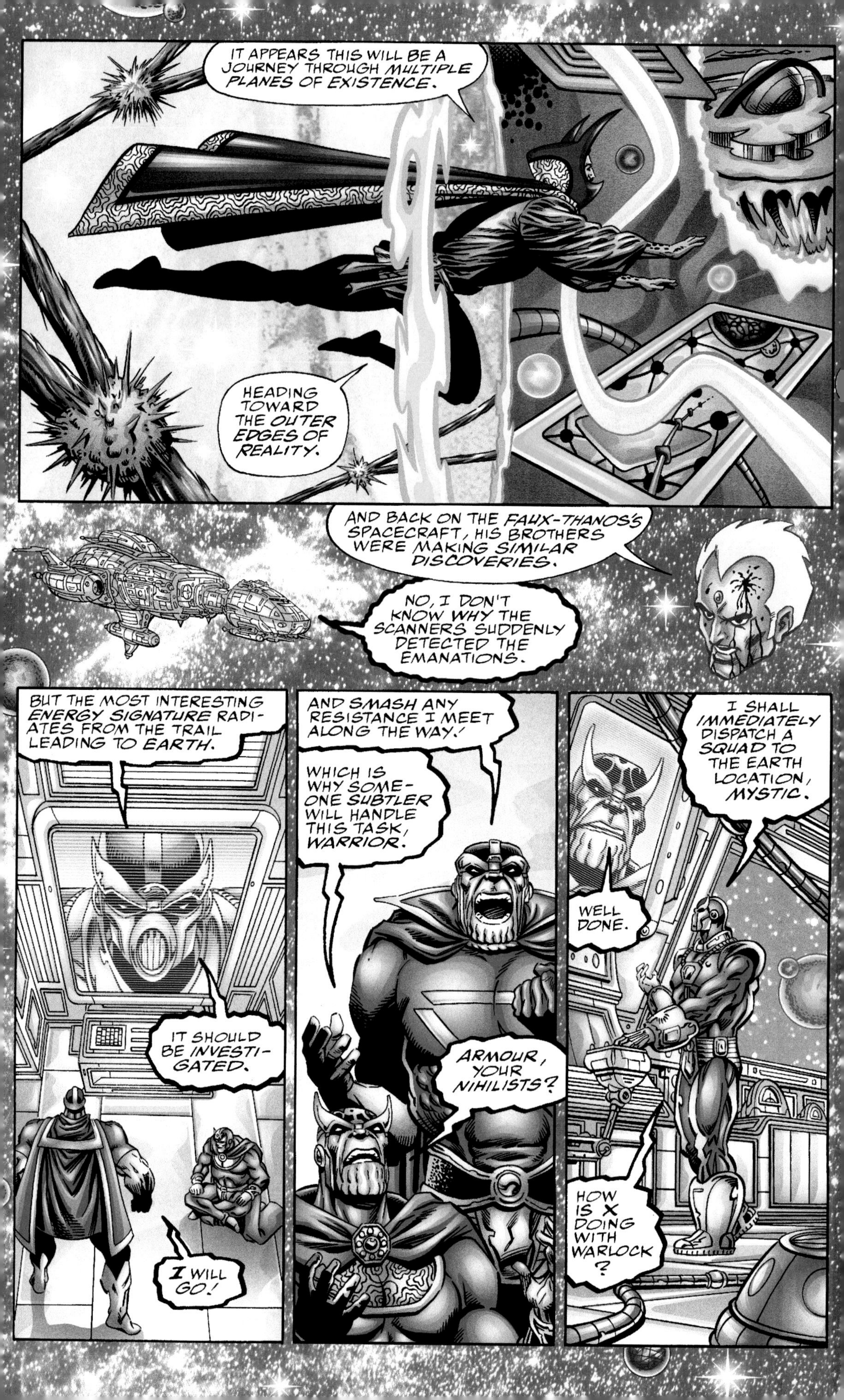
IT APPEARS THIS WILL BE A JOURNEY THROUGH MULTIPLE PLANES OF EXISTENCE.
HEADING TOWARD THE OUTER EDGES OF REALITY.
AND BACK ON THE FAUX-THANOS'S SPACECRAFT, HIS BROTHERS WERE MAKING SIMILAR DISCOVERIES.
NO, I DON'T KNOW WHY THE SCANNERS SUDDENLY DETECTED THE EMANATIONS.
BUT THE MOST INTERESTING ENERGY SIGNATURE RADIATES FROM THE TRAIL LEADING TO EARTH.
IT SHOULD BE INVESTIGATED.
I WILL GO!
AND SMASH ANY RESISTANCE I MEET ALONG THE WAY!
WHICH IS WHY SOMEONE SUBTLER WILL HANDLE THIS TASK, WARRIOR.
ARMOUR, YOUR NIHILISTS?
I SHALL IMMEDIATELY DISPATCH A SQUAD TO THE EARTH LOCATION, MYSTIC.
WELL DONE.
HOW IS X DOING WITH WARLOCK?

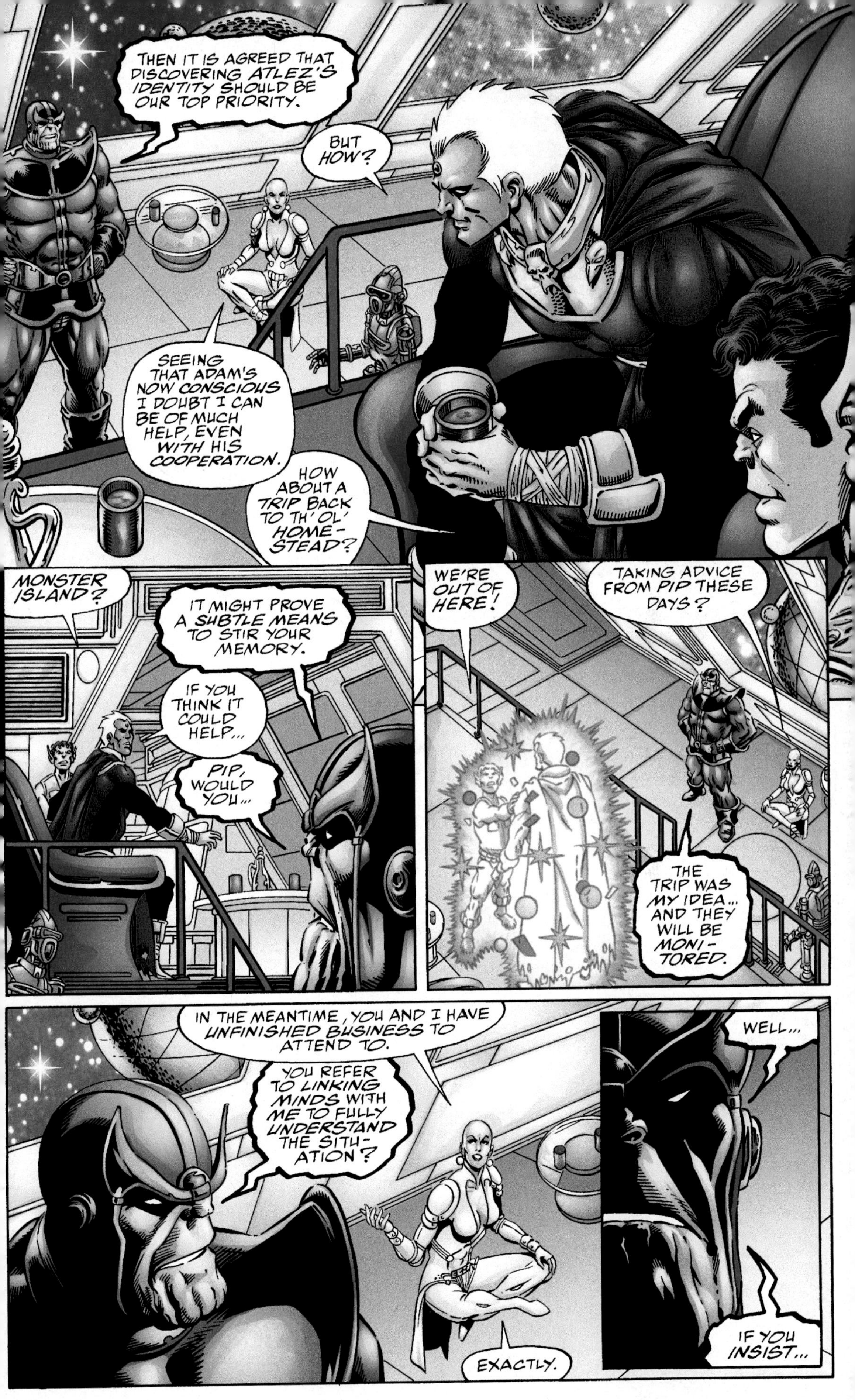
THEN IT IS AGREED THAT DISCOVERING ATLEZ'S IDENTITY SHOULD BE OUR TOP PRIORITY.
BUT HOW?
SEEING THAT ADAM'S NOW CONSCIOUS I DOUBT I CAN BE OF MUCH HELP, EVEN WITH HIS COOPERATION.
HOW ABOUT A TRIP BACK TO TH' OL' HOME-STEAD?
MONSTER ISLAND?
IT MIGHT PROVE A SUBTLE MEANS TO STIR YOUR MEMORY.
IF YOU THINK IT COULD HELP...
PIP, WOULD YOU...
WE'RE OUT OF HERE!
TAKING ADVICE FROM PIP THESE DAYS?
THE TRIP WAS MY IDEA... AND THEY WILL BE MONI-TORED.
IN THE MEANTIME, YOU AND I HAVE UNFINISHED BUSINESS TO ATTEND TO.
YOU REFER TO LINKING MINDS WITH ME TO FULLY UNDERSTAND THE SITU-ATION?
EXACTLY.
WELL...
IF YOU INSIST...

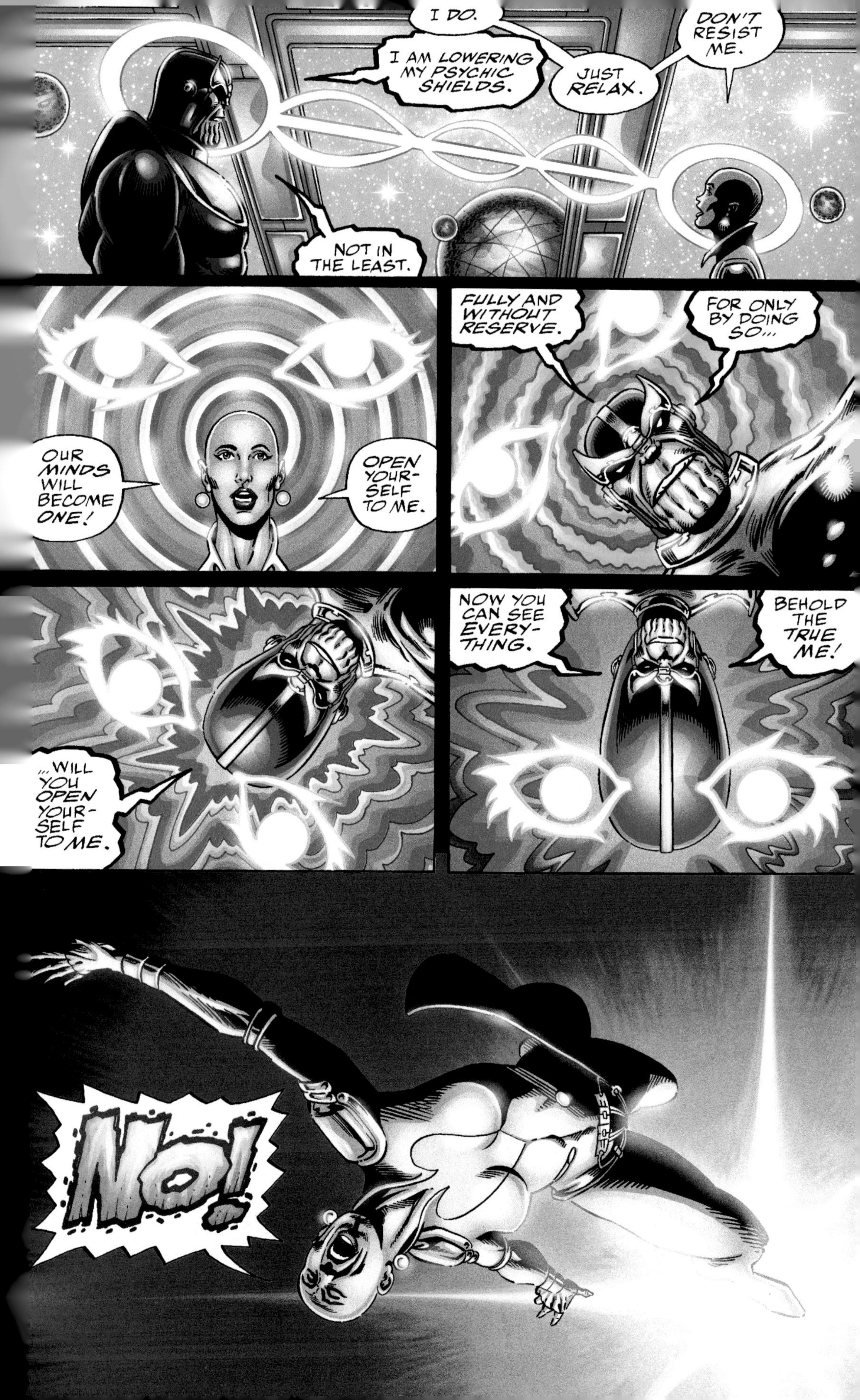

I DO.
I AM LOWERING MY PSYCHIC SHIELDS.
JUST RELAX.
DON'T RESIST ME.
NOT IN THE LEAST.
OUR MINDS WILL BECOME ONE!
OPEN YOURSELF TO ME.
FULLY AND WITHOUT RESERVE.
FOR ONLY BY DOING SO...
...WILL YOU OPEN YOURSELF TO ME.
NOW YOU CAN SEE EVERYTHING.
BEHOLD THE TRUE ME!
NO!

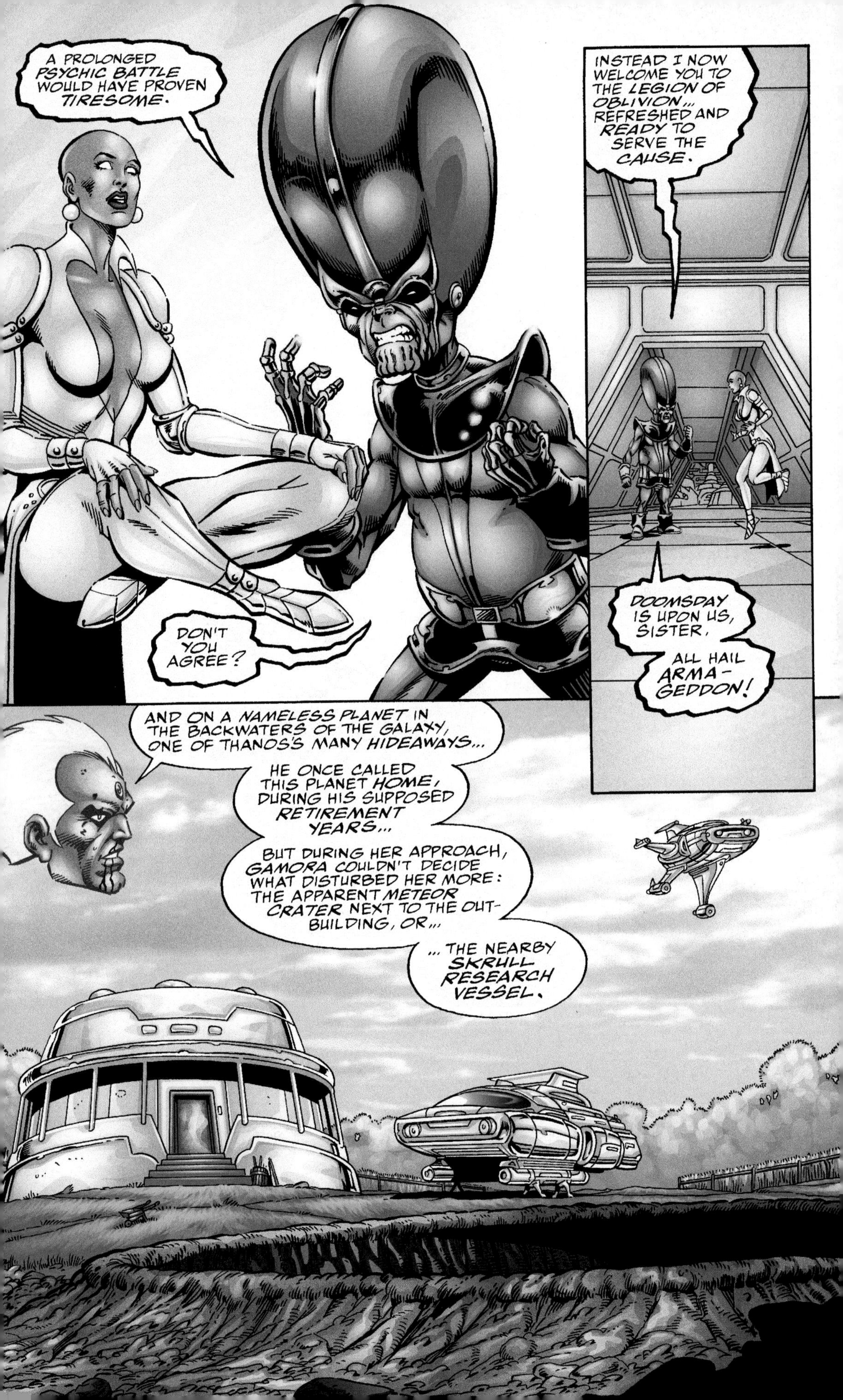
A PROLONGED PSYCHIC BATTLE WOULD HAVE PROVEN TIRESOME.
DON'T YOU AGREE?
INSTEAD I NOW WELCOME YOU TO THE LEGION OF OBLIVION... REFRESHED AND READY TO SERVE THE CAUSE.
DOOMSDAY IS UPON US, SISTER.
ALL HAIL ARMA-GEDDON!
AND ON A NAMELESS PLANET IN THE BACKWATERS OF THE GALAXY, ONE OF THANOS'S MANY HIDEAWAYS...
HE ONCE CALLED THIS PLANET HOME, DURING HIS SUPPOSED RETIREMENT YEARS...
BUT DURING HER APPROACH, GAMORA COULDN'T DECIDE WHAT DISTURBED HER MORE: THE APPARENT METEOR CRATER NEXT TO THE OUT-BUILDING, OR...
...THE NEARBY SKRULL RESEARCH VESSEL.

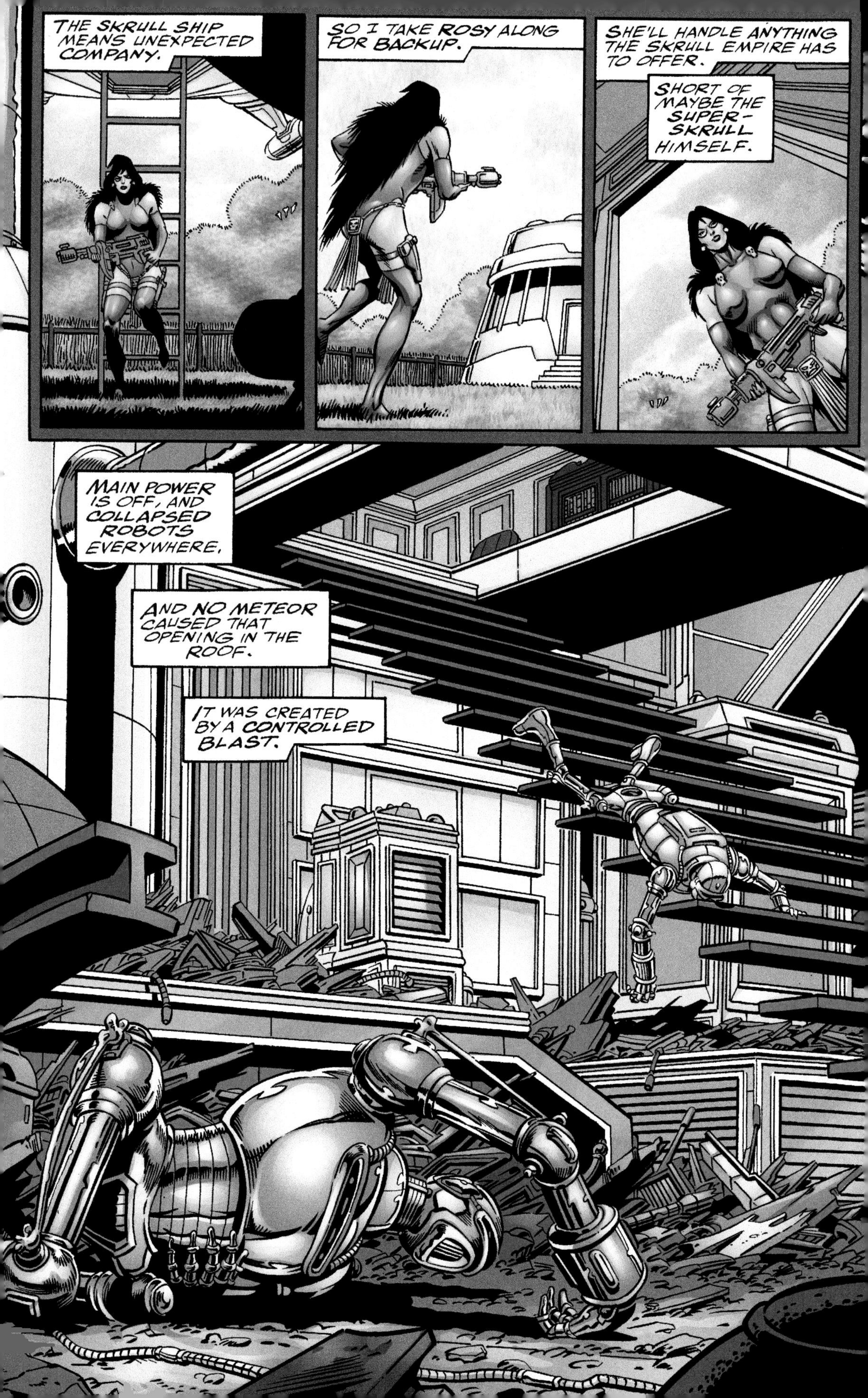

THE SKRULL SHIP MEANS UNEXPECTED COMPANY.
SO I TAKE ROSY ALONG FOR BACKUP.
SHE'LL HANDLE ANYTHING THE SKRULL EMPIRE HAS TO OFFER.
SHORT OF MAYBE THE SUPER-SKRULL HIMSELF.
MAIN POWER IS OFF, AND COLLAPSED ROBOTS EVERYWHERE.
AND NO METEOR CAUSED THAT OPENING IN THE ROOF.
IT WAS CREATED BY A CONTROLLED BLAST.

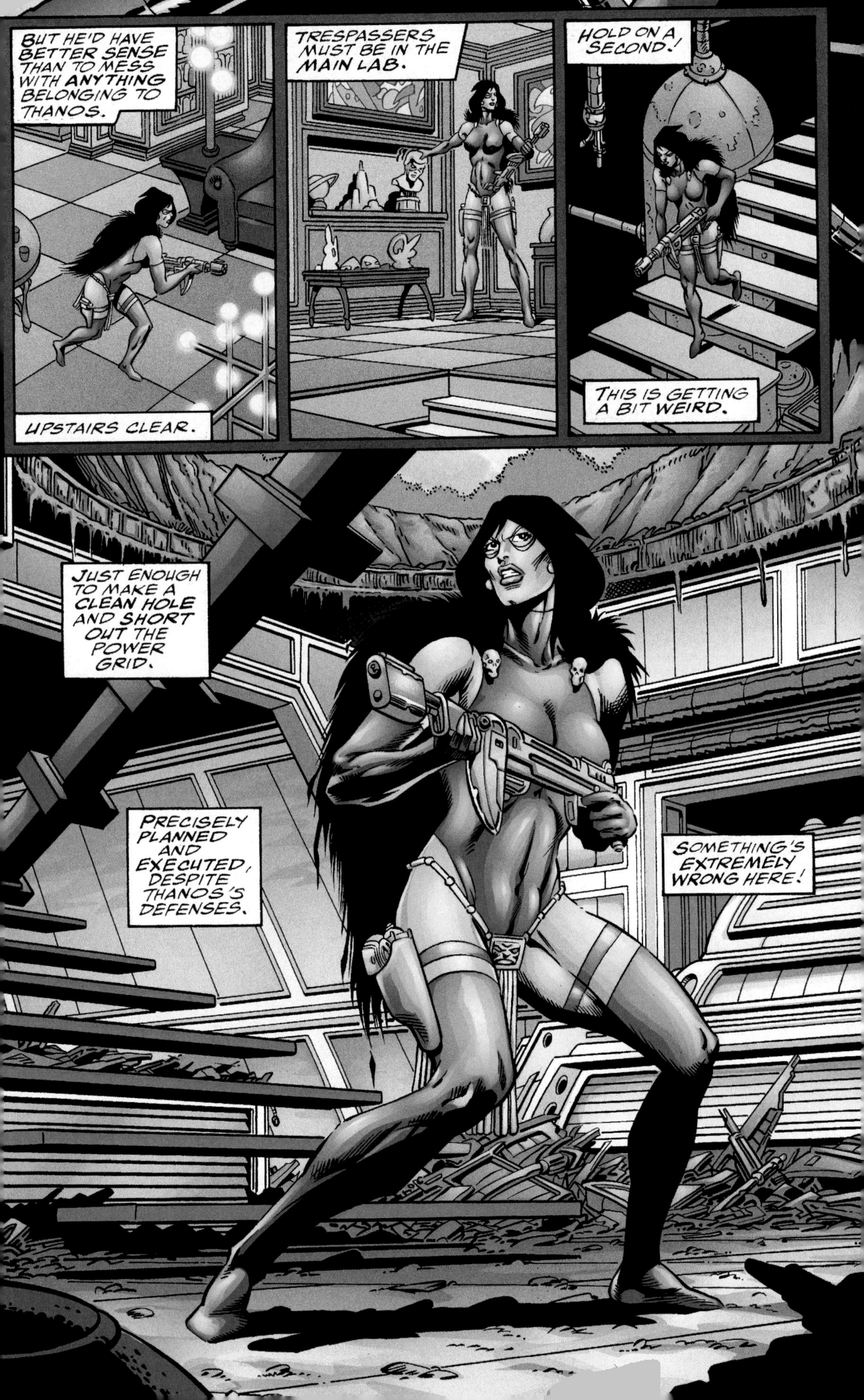
BUT HE'D HAVE BETTER SENSE THAN TO MESS WITH ANYTHING BELONGING TO THANOS.
UPSTAIRS CLEAR.
TRESPASSERS MUST BE IN THE MAIN LAB.
HOLD ON A SECOND!
THIS IS GETTING A BIT WEIRD.
JUST ENOUGH TO MAKE A CLEAN HOLE AND SHORT OUT THE POWER GRID.
PRECISELY PLANNED AND EXECUTED, DESPITE THANOS'S DEFENSES.
SOMETHING'S EXTREMELY WRONG HERE!

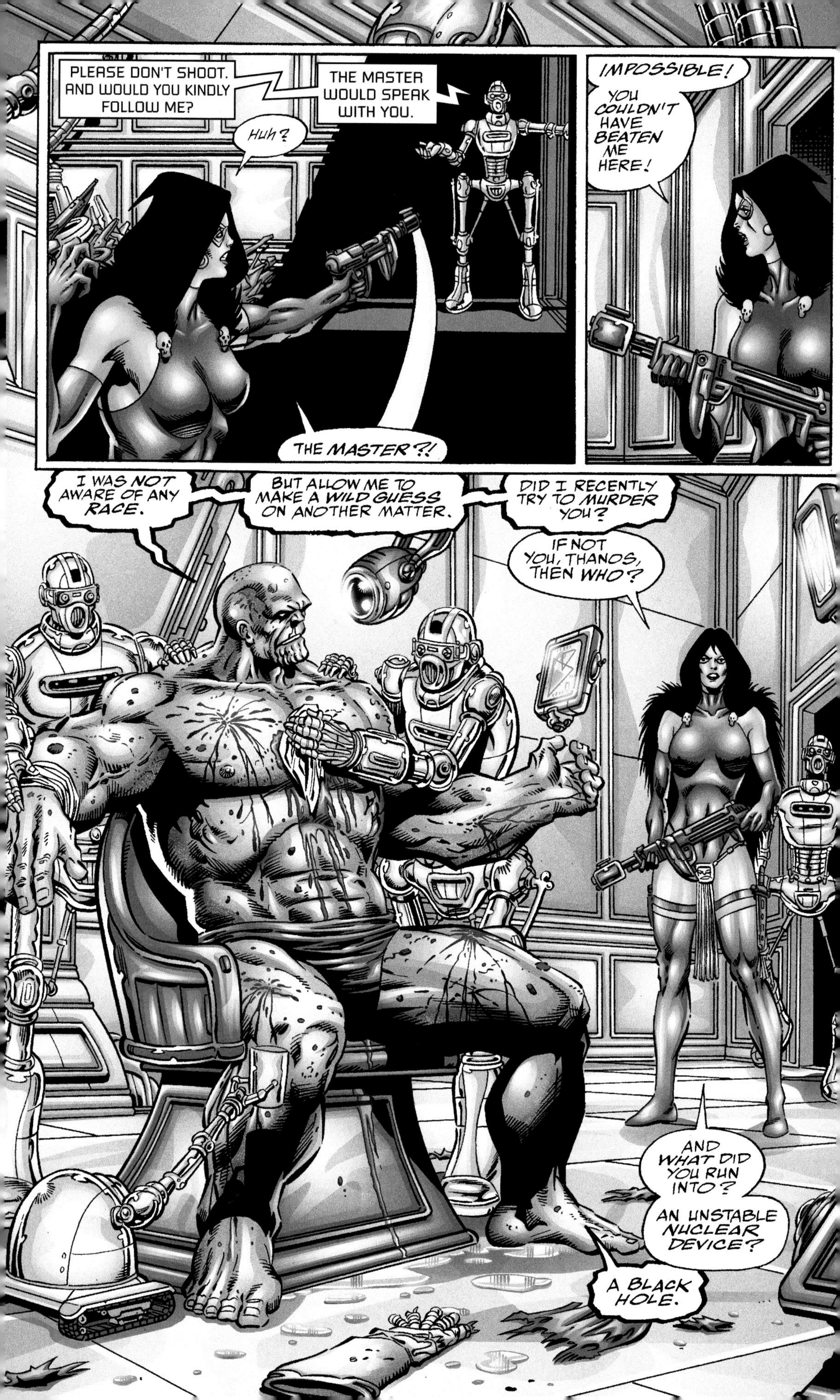
PLEASE DON'T SHOOT. AND WOULD YOU KINDLY FOLLOW ME?
THE MASTER WOULD SPEAK WITH YOU.
Huh?
THE MASTER?!
IMPOSSIBLE!
YOU COULDN'T HAVE BEATEN ME HERE!
I WAS NOT AWARE OF ANY RACE.
BUT ALLOW ME TO MAKE A WILD GUESS ON ANOTHER MATTER.
DID I RECENTLY TRY TO MURDER YOU?
IF NOT YOU, THANOS, THEN WHO?
AND WHAT DID YOU RUN INTO?
AN UNSTABLE NUCLEAR DEVICE?
A BLACK HOLE.

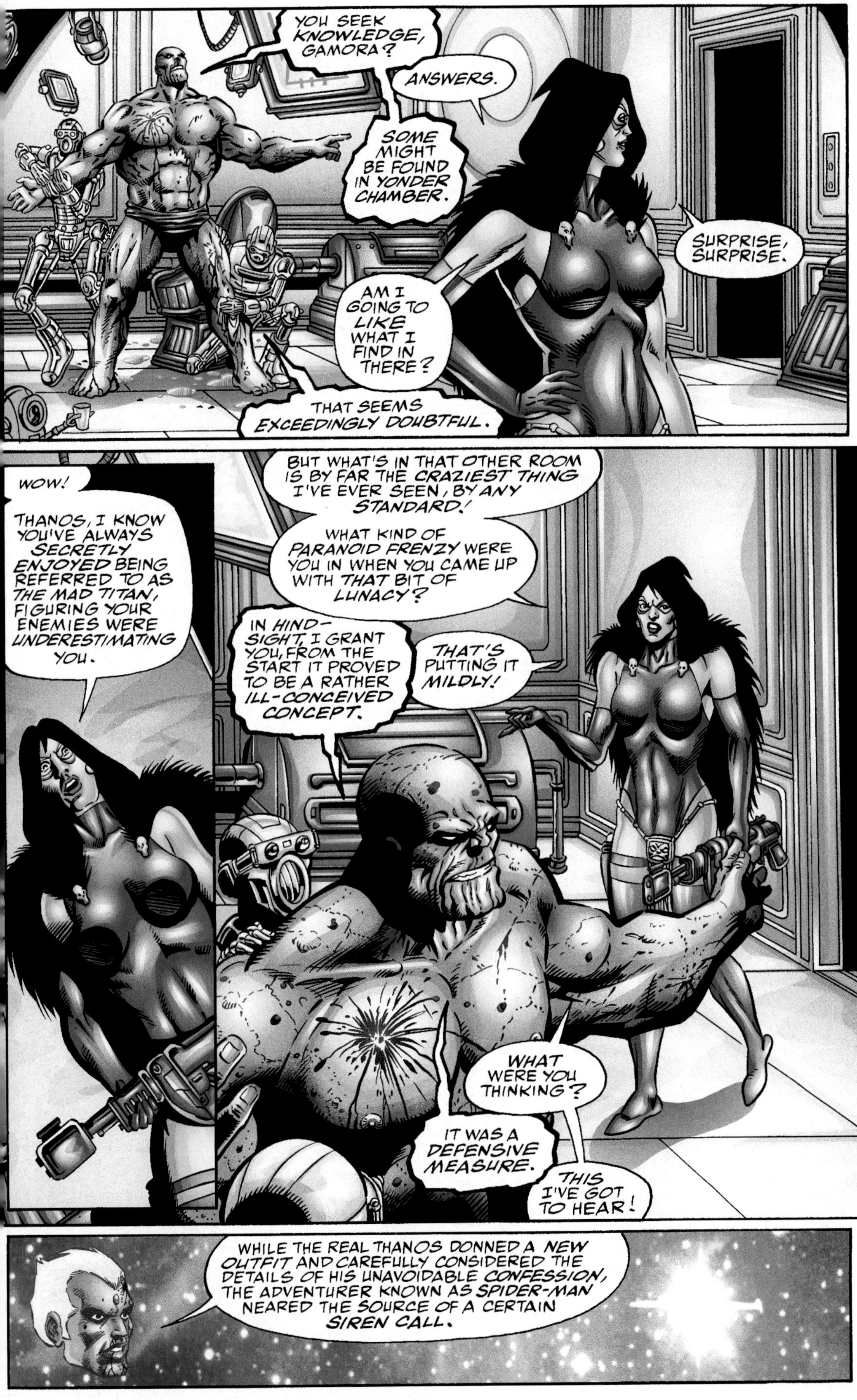

YOU SEEK KNOWLEDGE, GAMORA?
ANSWERS.
SOME MIGHT BE FOUND IN YONDER CHAMBER.
SURPRISE, SURPRISE.
AM I GOING TO LIKE WHAT I FIND IN THERE?
THAT SEEMS EXCEEDINGLY DOUBTFUL.
WOW!
THANOS, I KNOW YOU'VE ALWAYS SECRETLY ENJOYED BEING REFERRED TO AS THE MAD TITAN, FIGURING YOUR ENEMIES WERE UNDERESTIMATING YOU.
BUT WHAT'S IN THAT OTHER ROOM IS BY FAR THE CRAZIEST THING I'VE EVER SEEN, BY ANY STANDARD!
WHAT KIND OF PARANOID FRENZY WERE YOU IN WHEN YOU CAME UP WITH THAT BIT OF LUNACY?
IN HINDSIGHT, I GRANT YOU, FROM THE START IT PROVED TO BE A RATHER ILL-CONCEIVED CONCEPT.
THAT'S PUTTING IT MILDLY!
WHAT WERE YOU THINKING?
IT WAS A DEFENSIVE MEASURE.
THIS I'VE GOT TO HEAR!
WHILE THE REAL THANOS DONNED A NEW OUTFIT AND CAREFULLY CONSIDERED THE DETAILS OF HIS UNAVOIDABLE CONFESSION, THE ADVENTURER KNOWN AS SPIDER-MAN NEARED THE SOURCE OF A CERTAIN SIREN CALL.

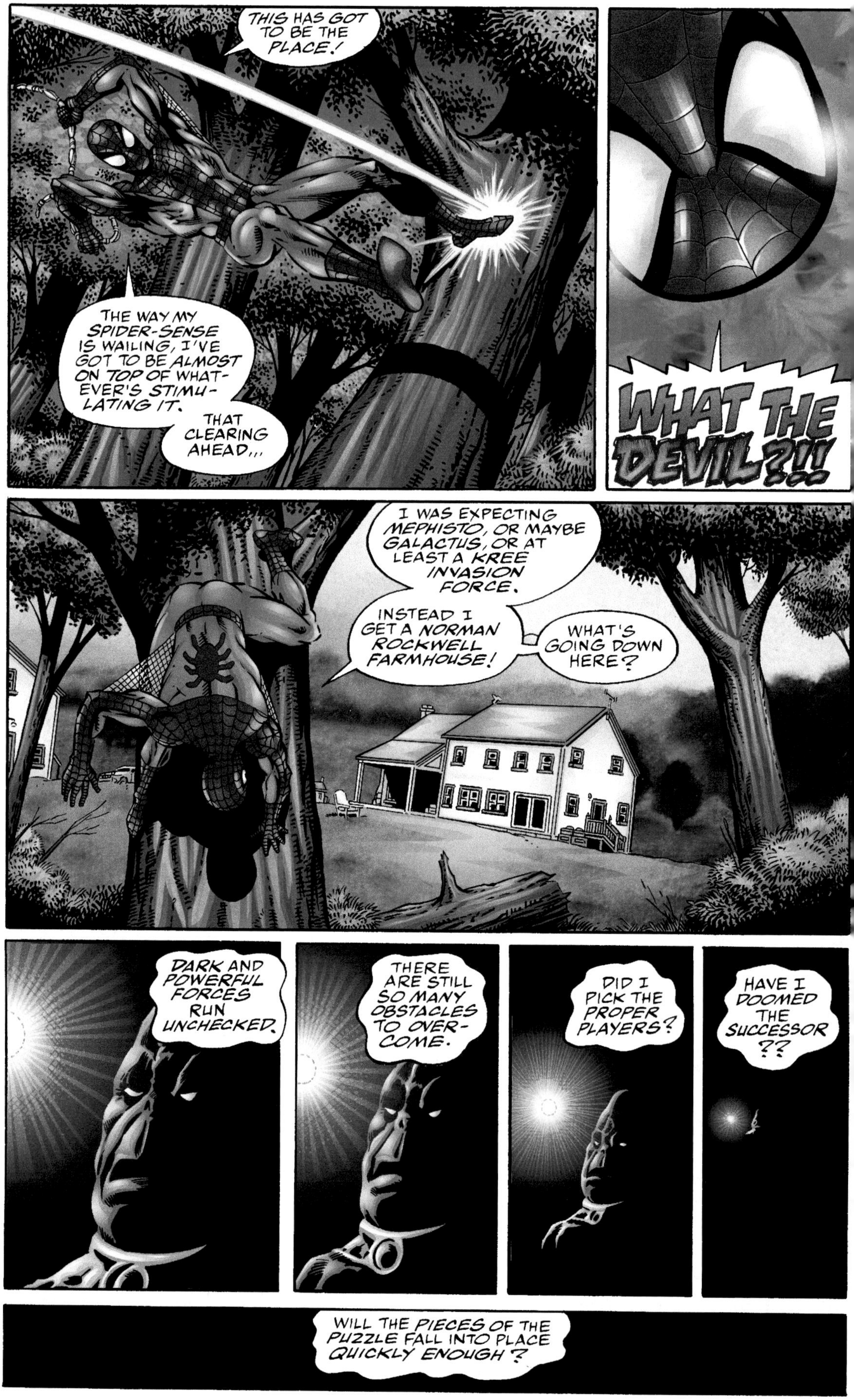
THIS HAS GOT TO BE THE PLACE!
THE WAY MY SPIDER-SENSE IS WAILING, I'VE GOT TO BE ALMOST ON TOP OF WHAT-EVER'S STIMU-LATING IT.
THAT CLEARING AHEAD...
WHAT THE DEVIL?!!
I WAS EXPECTING MEPHISTO, OR MAYBE GALACTUS, OR AT LEAST A KREE INVASION FORCE.
INSTEAD I GET A NORMAN ROCKWELL FARMHOUSE!
WHAT'S GOING DOWN HERE?
DARK AND POWERFUL FORCES RUN UNCHECKED.
THERE ARE STILL SO MANY OBSTACLES TO OVER-COME.
DID I PICK THE PROPER PLAYERS?
HAVE I DOOMED THE SUCCESSOR??
WILL THE PIECES OF THE PUZZLE FALL INTO PLACE QUICKLY ENOUGH?

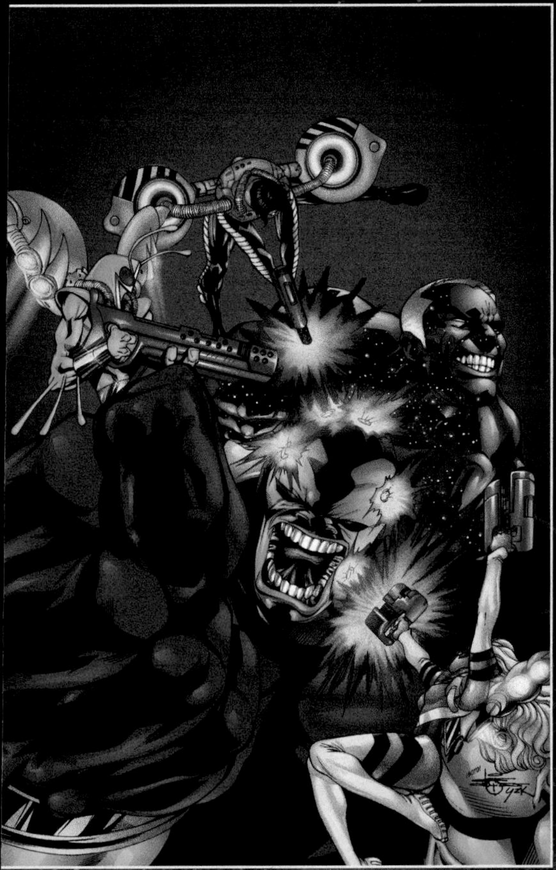

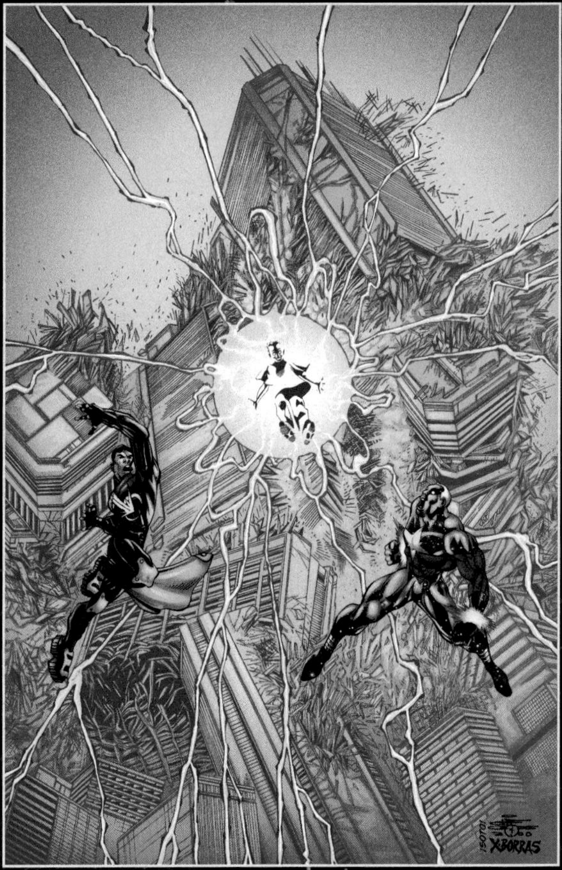

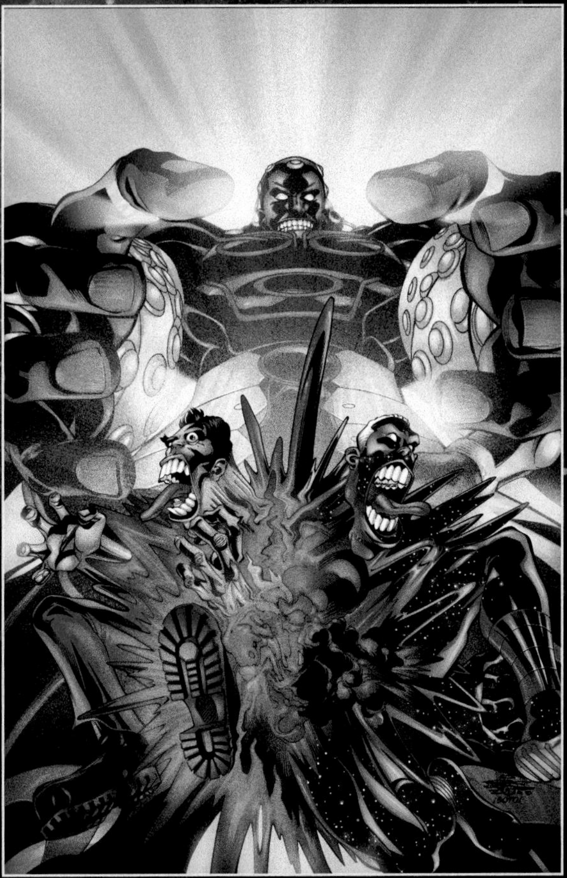

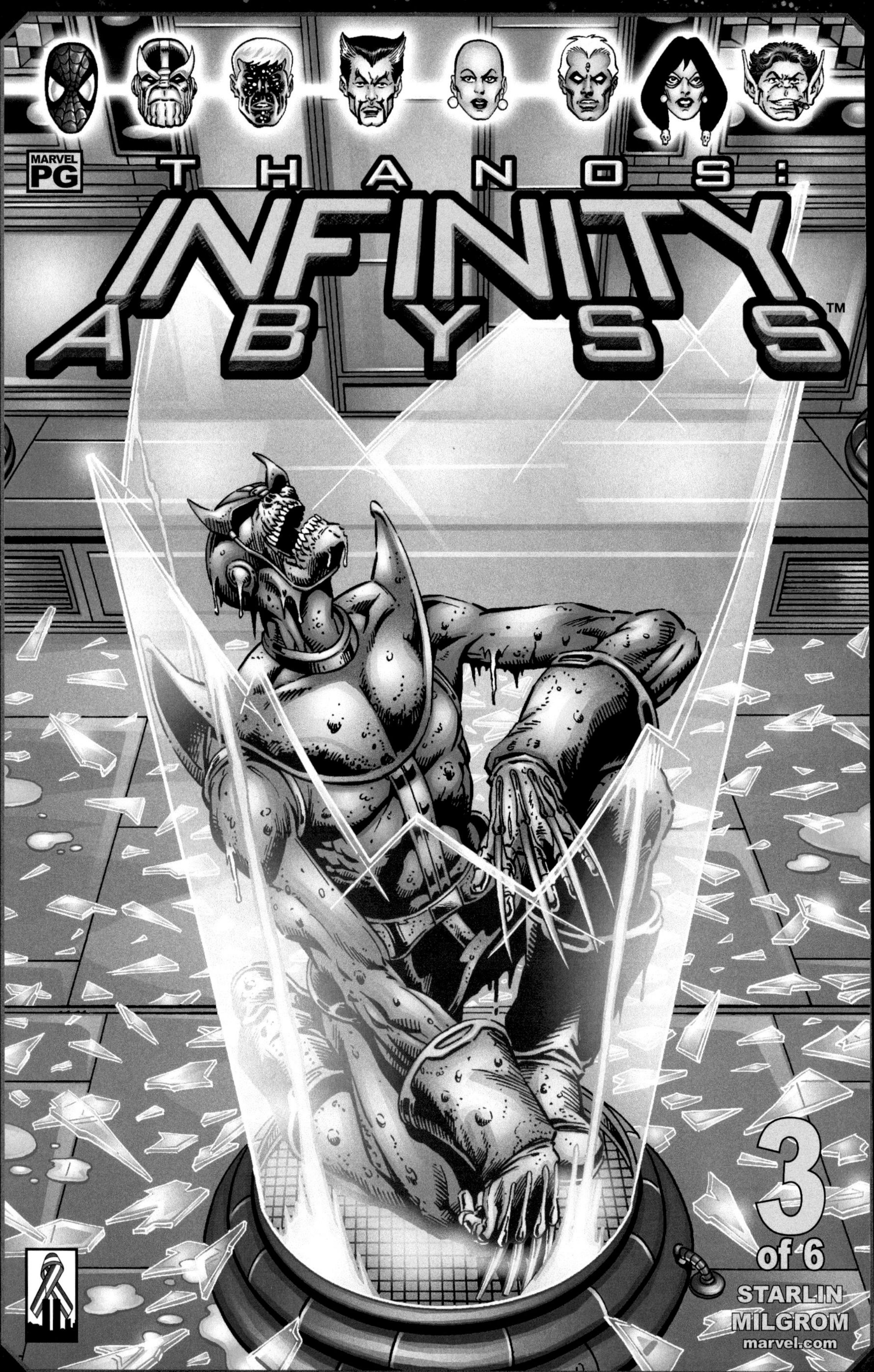

MARVEL PG
THANOS:
INFINITY
ABYSS™
3
of 6
STARLIN
MILGROM
marvel.com

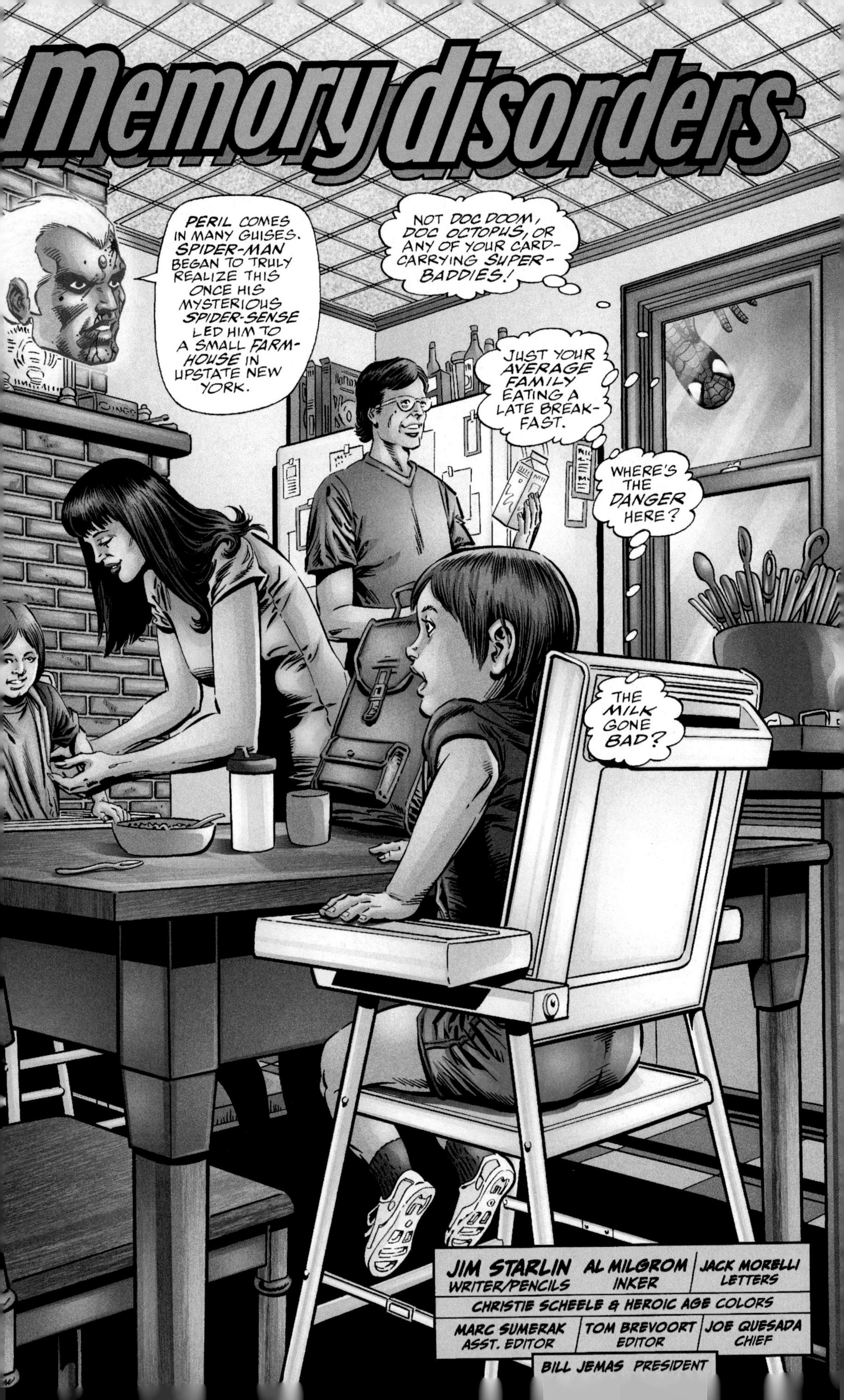
Memory disorders
PERIL COMES IN MANY GUISES. SPIDER-MAN BEGAN TO TRULY REALIZE THIS ONCE HIS MYSTERIOUS SPIDER-SENSE LED HIM TO A SMALL FARM-HOUSE IN UPSTATE NEW YORK.
NOT DOC DOOM, DOC OCTOPUS, OR ANY OF YOUR CARD-CARRYING SUPER-BADDIES!
JUST YOUR AVERAGE FAMILY EATING A LATE BREAK-FAST.
WHERE'S THE DANGER HERE?
THE MILK GONE BAD?
JIM STARLIN WRITER/PENCILS
AL MILGROM INKER
JACK MORELLI LETTERS
CHRISTIE SCHEELE & HEROIC AGE COLORS
MARC SUMERAK ASST. EDITOR
TOM BREVOORT EDITOR
JOE QUESADA CHIEF
BILL JEMAS PRESIDENT

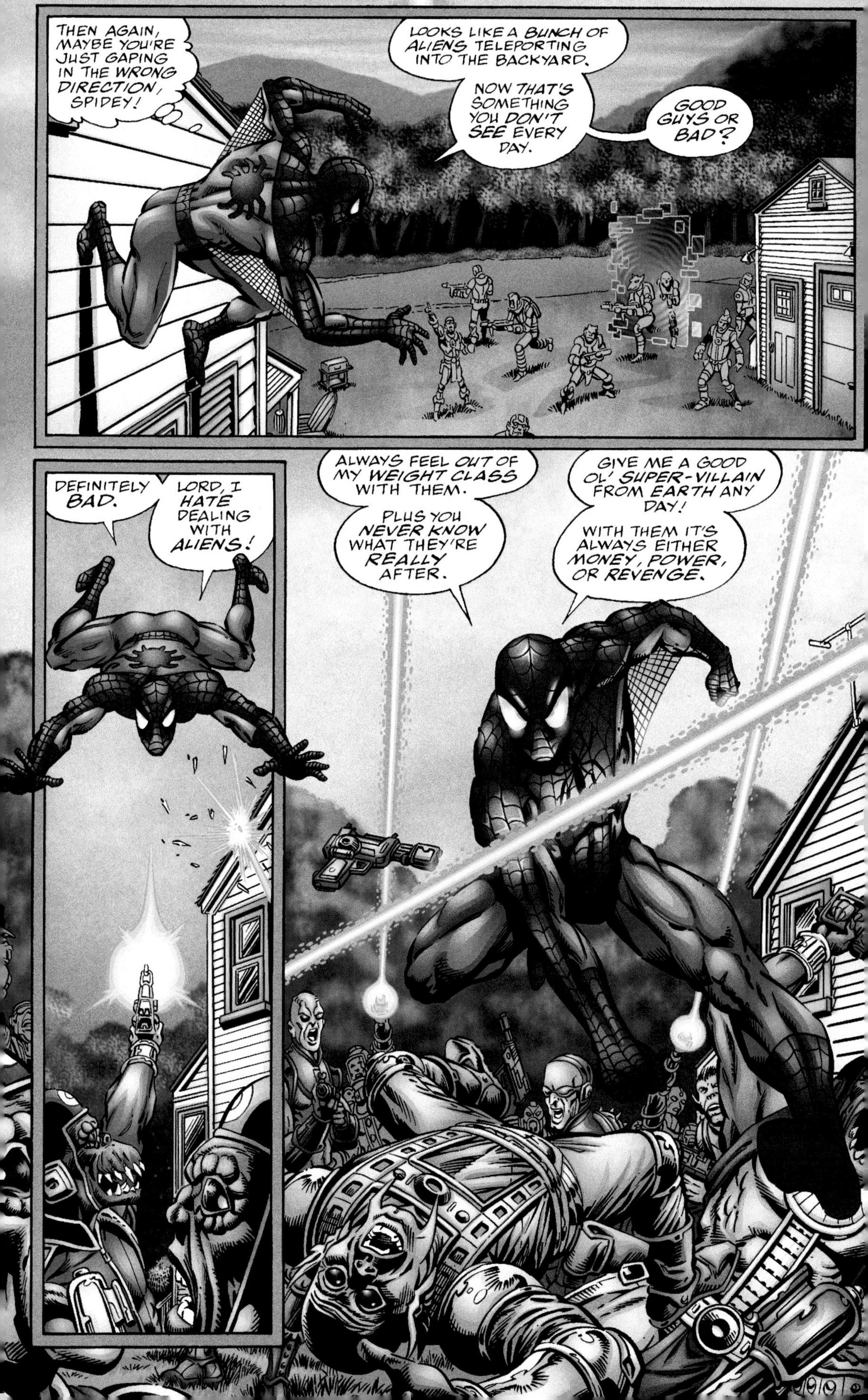
THEN AGAIN, MAYBE YOU'RE JUST GAPING IN THE WRONG DIRECTION, SPIDEY!
LOOKS LIKE A BUNCH OF ALIENS TELEPORTING INTO THE BACKYARD.
NOW THAT'S SOMETHING YOU DON'T SEE EVERY DAY.
GOOD GUYS OR BAD?
DEFINITELY BAD.
LORD, I HATE DEALING WITH ALIENS!
ALWAYS FEEL OUT OF MY WEIGHT CLASS WITH THEM.
PLUS YOU NEVER KNOW WHAT THEY'RE REALLY AFTER.
GIVE ME A GOOD OL' SUPER-VILLAIN FROM EARTH ANY DAY!
WITH THEM IT'S ALWAYS EITHER MONEY, POWER, OR REVENGE.

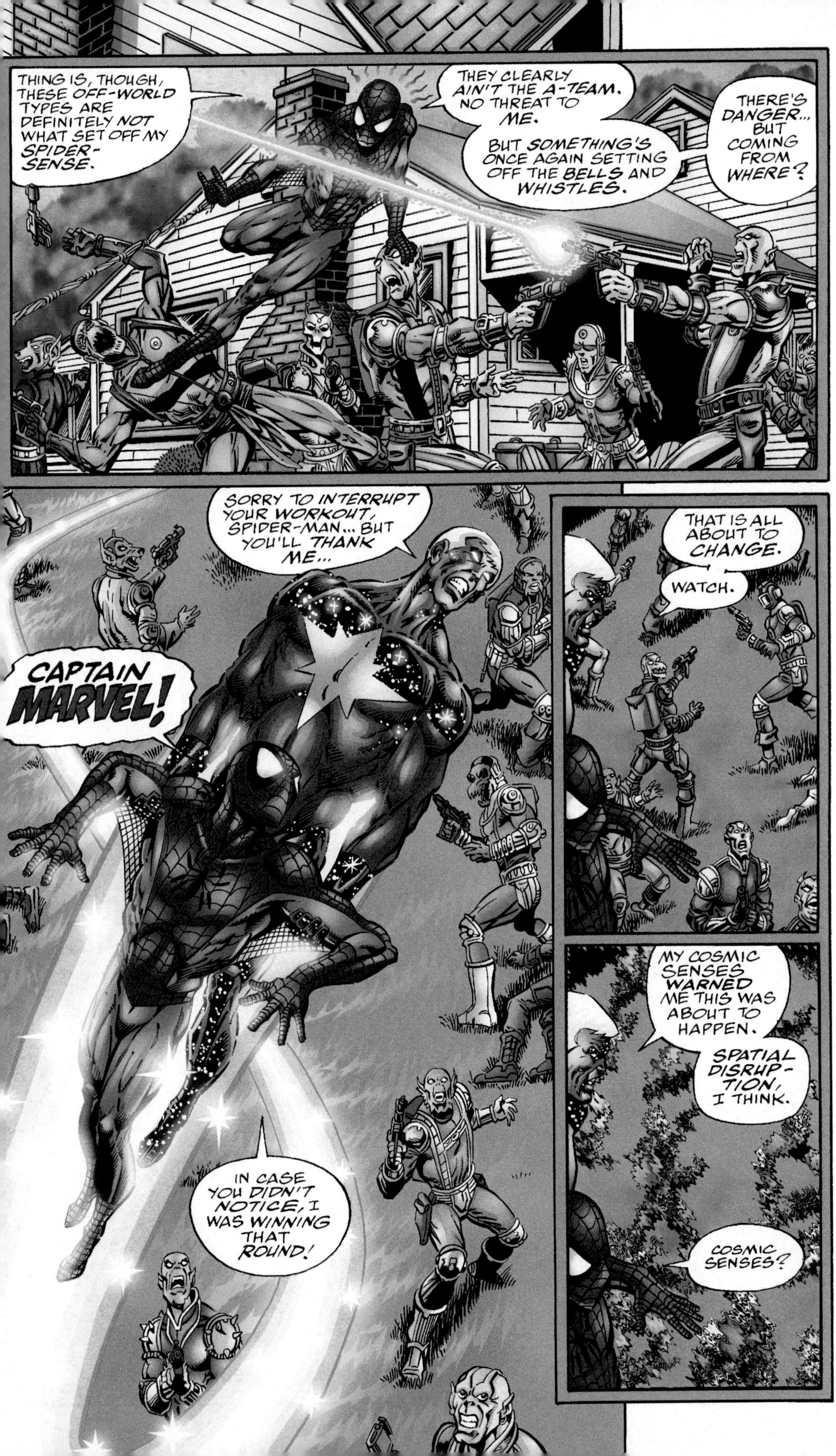
THING IS, THOUGH, THESE OFF-WORLD TYPES ARE DEFINITELY NOT WHAT SET OFF MY SPIDER-SENSE.
THEY CLEARLY AIN'T THE A-TEAM. NO THREAT TO ME.
BUT SOMETHING'S ONCE AGAIN SETTING OFF THE BELLS AND WHISTLES.
THERE'S DANGER... BUT COMING FROM WHERE?
SORRY TO INTERRUPT YOUR WORKOUT, SPIDER-MAN... BUT YOU'LL THANK ME...
CAPTAIN MARVEL!
IN CASE YOU DIDN'T NOTICE, I WAS WINNING THAT ROUND!
THAT IS ALL ABOUT TO CHANGE.
WATCH.
MY COSMIC SENSES WARNED ME THIS WAS ABOUT TO HAPPEN.
SPATIAL DISRUPTION, I THINK.
COSMIC SENSES?

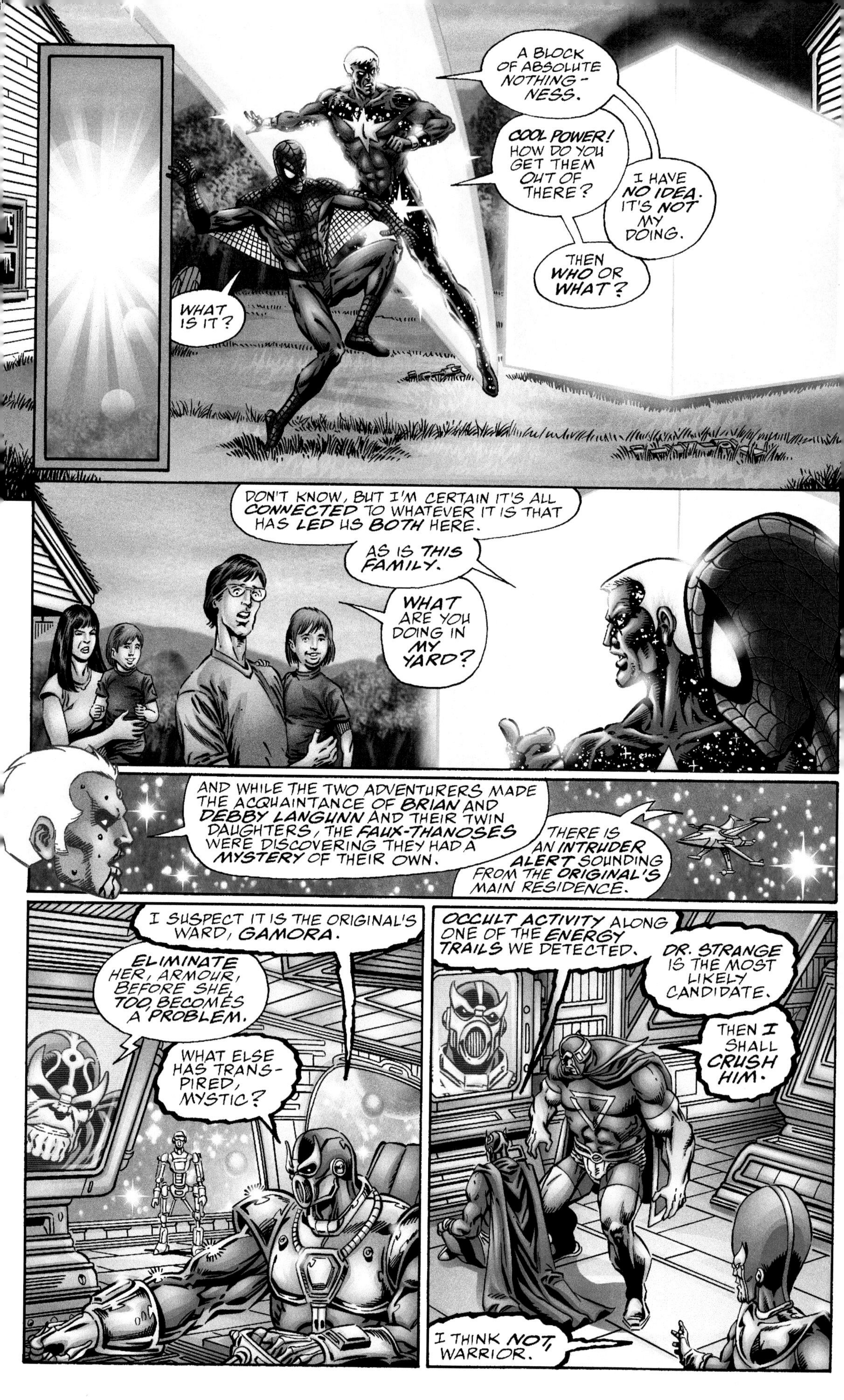
A BLOCK OF ABSOLUTE NOTHING-NESS.
COOL POWER! HOW DO YOU GET THEM OUT OF THERE?
I HAVE NO IDEA. IT'S NOT MY DOING.
THEN WHO OR WHAT?
WHAT IS IT?
DON'T KNOW, BUT I'M CERTAIN IT'S ALL CONNECTED TO WHATEVER IT IS THAT HAS LED US BOTH HERE.
AS IS THIS FAMILY.
WHAT ARE YOU DOING IN MY YARD?
AND WHILE THE TWO ADVENTURERS MADE THE ACQUAINTANCE OF BRIAN AND DEBBY LANGUNN AND THEIR TWIN DAUGHTERS, THE FAUX-THANOSES WERE DISCOVERING THEY HAD A MYSTERY OF THEIR OWN.
THERE IS AN INTRUDER ALERT SOUNDING FROM THE ORIGINAL'S MAIN RESIDENCE.
I SUSPECT IT IS THE ORIGINAL'S WARD, GAMORA.
ELIMINATE HER, ARMOUR, BEFORE SHE, TOO, BECOMES A PROBLEM.
WHAT ELSE HAS TRANS-PIRED, MYSTIC?
OCCULT ACTIVITY ALONG ONE OF THE ENERGY TRAILS WE DETECTED.
DR. STRANGE IS THE MOST LIKELY CANDIDATE.
THEN I SHALL CRUSH HIM.
I THINK NOT, WARRIOR.

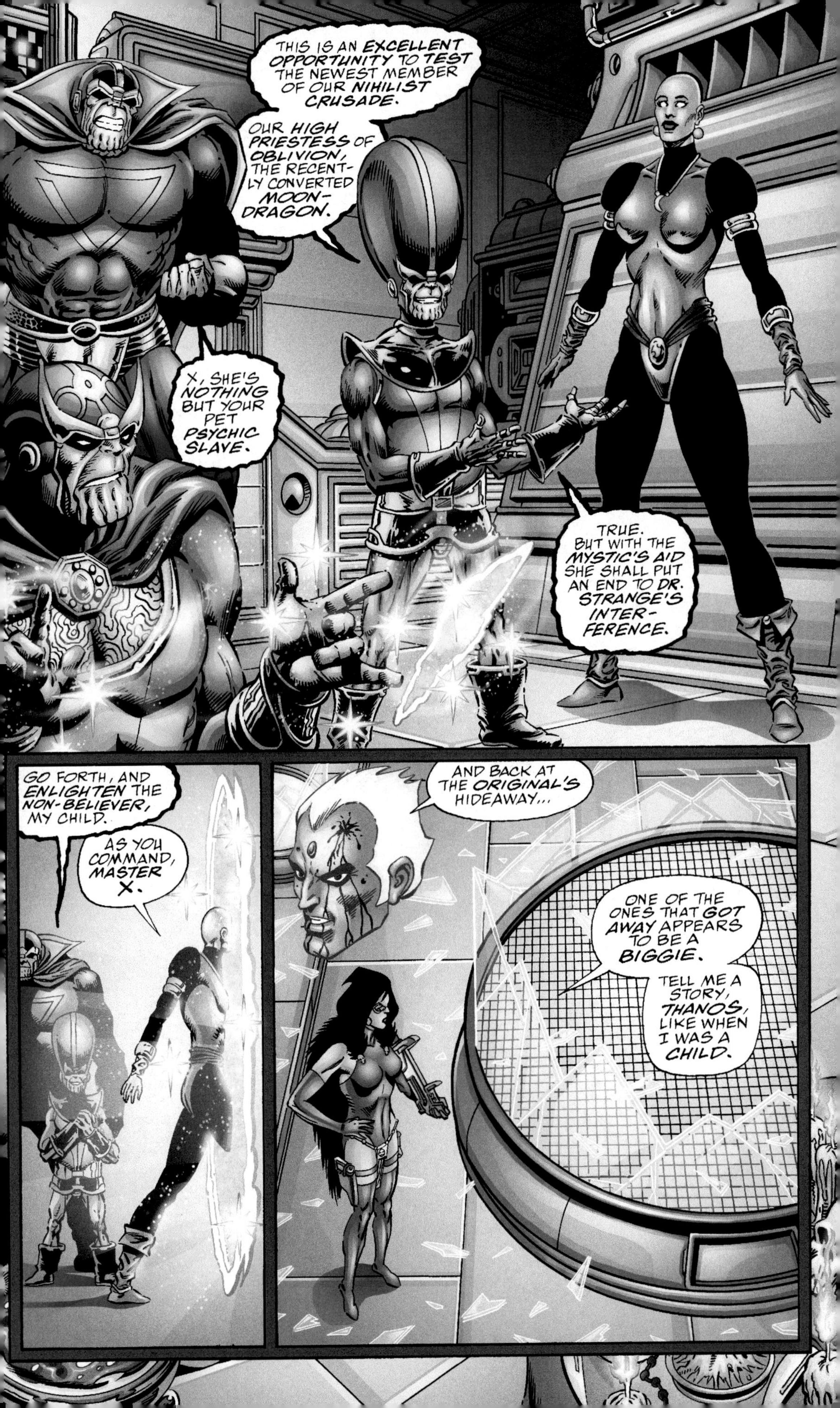
THIS IS AN EXCELLENT OPPORTUNITY TO TEST THE NEWEST MEMBER OF OUR NIHILIST CRUSADE.
OUR HIGH PRIESTESS OF OBLIVION, THE RECENTLY CONVERTED MOON-DRAGON.
X, SHE'S NOTHING BUT YOUR PET PSYCHIC SLAVE.
TRUE. BUT WITH THE MYSTIC'S AID SHE SHALL PUT AN END TO DR. STRANGE'S INTER-FERENCE.
GO FORTH, AND ENLIGHTEN THE NON-BELIEVER, MY CHILD.
AS YOU COMMAND, MASTER X.
AND BACK AT THE ORIGINAL'S HIDEAWAY...
ONE OF THE ONES THAT GOT AWAY APPEARS TO BE A BIGGIE.
TELL ME A STORY, THANOS, LIKE WHEN I WAS A CHILD.

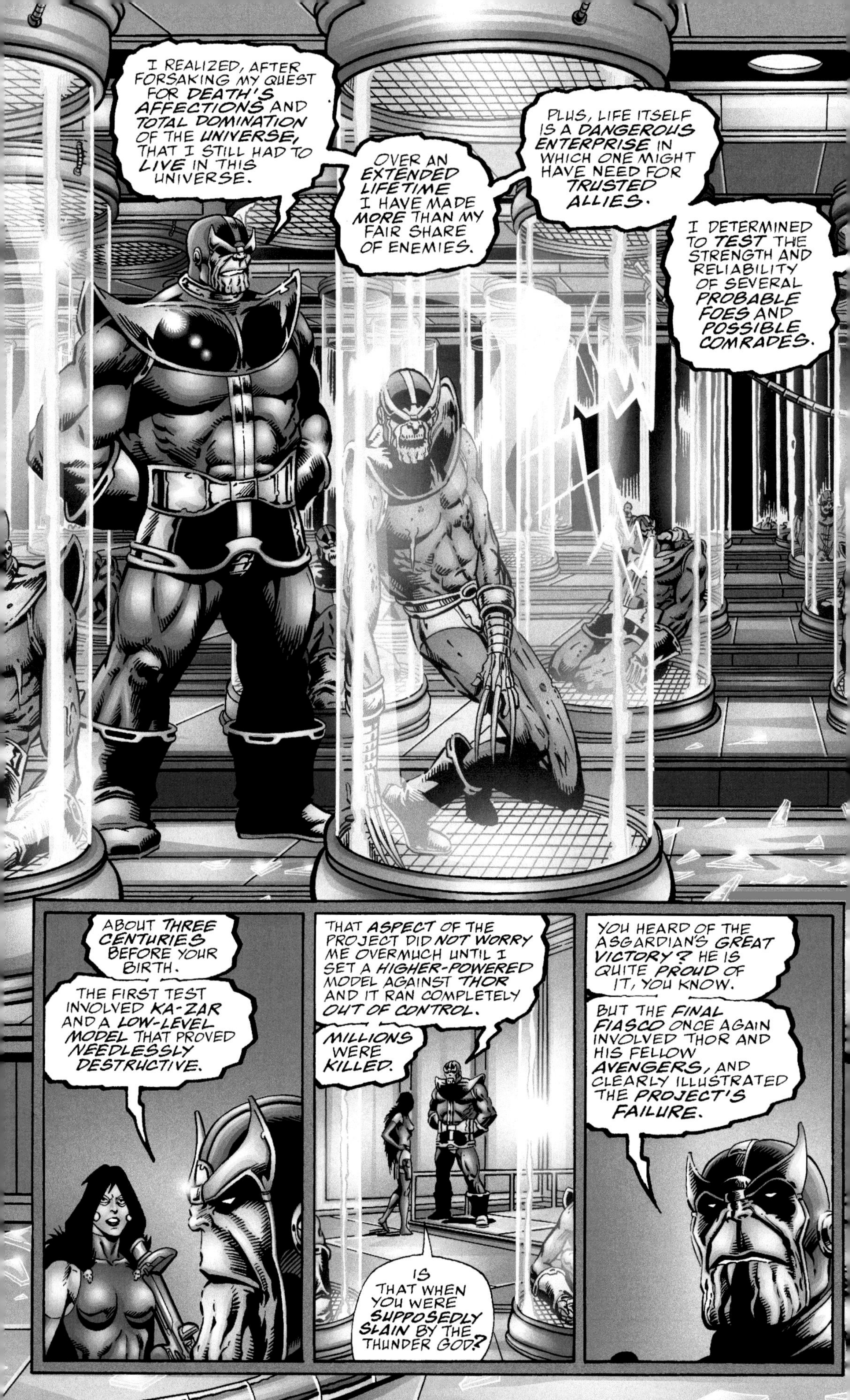
I REALIZED, AFTER FORSAKING MY QUEST FOR DEATH'S AFFECTIONS AND TOTAL DOMINATION OF THE UNIVERSE, THAT I STILL HAD TO LIVE IN THIS UNIVERSE.
OVER AN EXTENDED LIFETIME I HAVE MADE MORE THAN MY FAIR SHARE OF ENEMIES.
PLUS, LIFE ITSELF IS A DANGEROUS ENTERPRISE IN WHICH ONE MIGHT HAVE NEED FOR TRUSTED ALLIES.
I DETERMINED TO TEST THE STRENGTH AND RELIABILITY OF SEVERAL PROBABLE FOES AND POSSIBLE COMRADES.
ABOUT THREE CENTURIES BEFORE YOUR BIRTH.
THE FIRST TEST INVOLVED KA-ZAR AND A LOW-LEVEL MODEL THAT PROVED NEEDLESSLY DESTRUCTIVE.
THAT ASPECT OF THE PROJECT DID NOT WORRY ME OVERMUCH UNTIL I SET A HIGHER-POWERED MODEL AGAINST THOR AND IT RAN COMPLETELY OUT OF CONTROL.
MILLIONS WERE KILLED.
IS THAT WHEN YOU WERE SUPPOSEDLY SLAIN BY THE THUNDER GOD?
YOU HEARD OF THE ASGARDIAN'S GREAT VICTORY? HE IS QUITE PROUD OF IT, YOU KNOW.
BUT THE FINAL FIASCO ONCE AGAIN INVOLVED THOR AND HIS FELLOW AVENGERS, AND CLEARLY ILLUSTRATED THE PROJECT'S FAILURE.

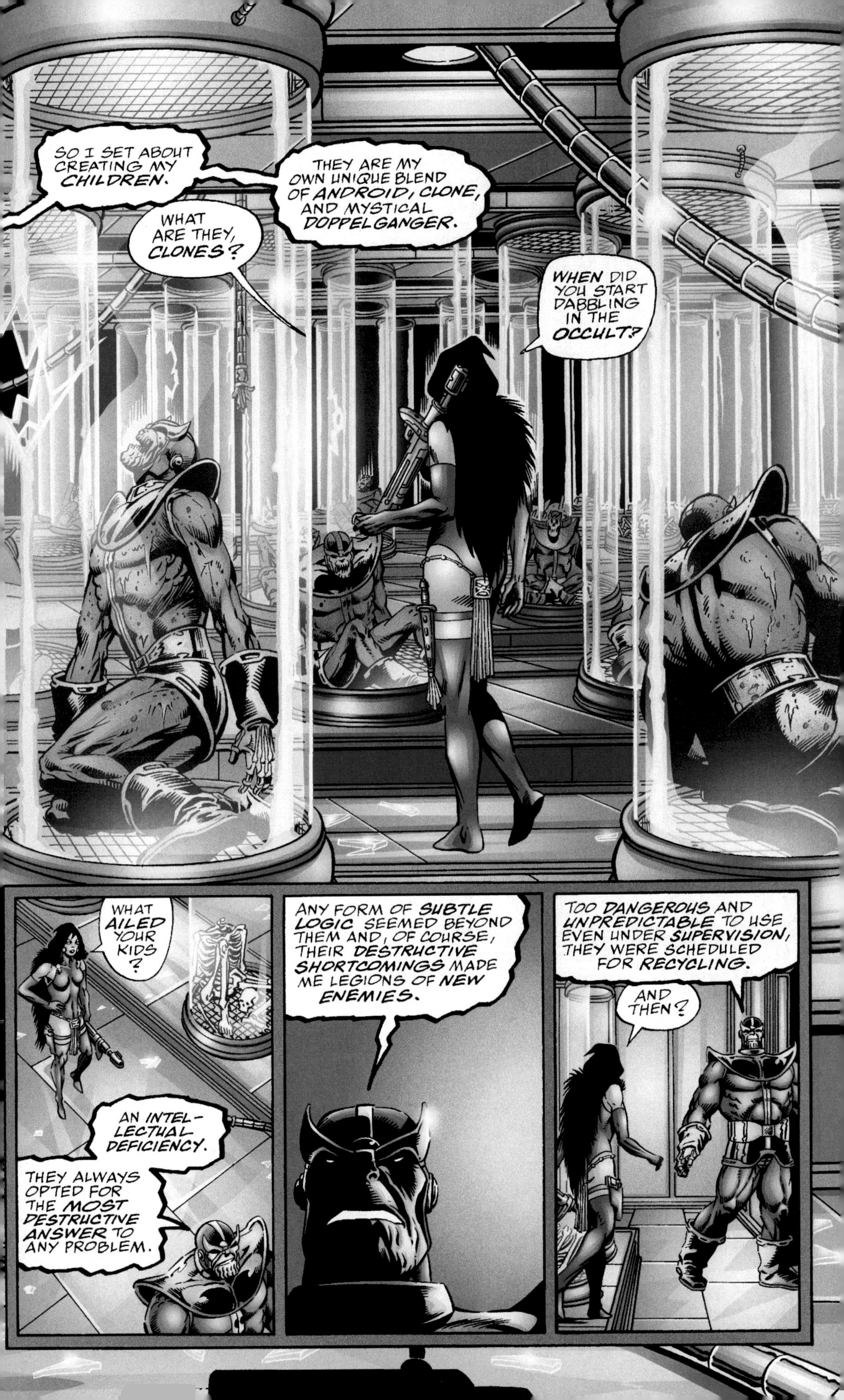
SO I SET ABOUT CREATING MY CHILDREN.
WHAT ARE THEY, CLONES?
THEY ARE MY OWN UNIQUE BLEND OF ANDROID, CLONE, AND MYSTICAL DOPPELGANGER.
WHEN DID YOU START DABBLING IN THE OCCULT?
WHAT AILED YOUR KIDS?
AN INTEL-LECTUAL DEFICIENCY.
THEY ALWAYS OPTED FOR THE MOST DESTRUCTIVE ANSWER TO ANY PROBLEM.
ANY FORM OF SUBTLE LOGIC SEEMED BEYOND THEM AND, OF COURSE, THEIR DESTRUCTIVE SHORTCOMINGS MADE ME LEGIONS OF NEW ENEMIES.
TOO DANGEROUS AND UNPREDICTABLE TO USE EVEN UNDER SUPERVISION, THEY WERE SCHEDULED FOR RECYCLING.
AND THEN?

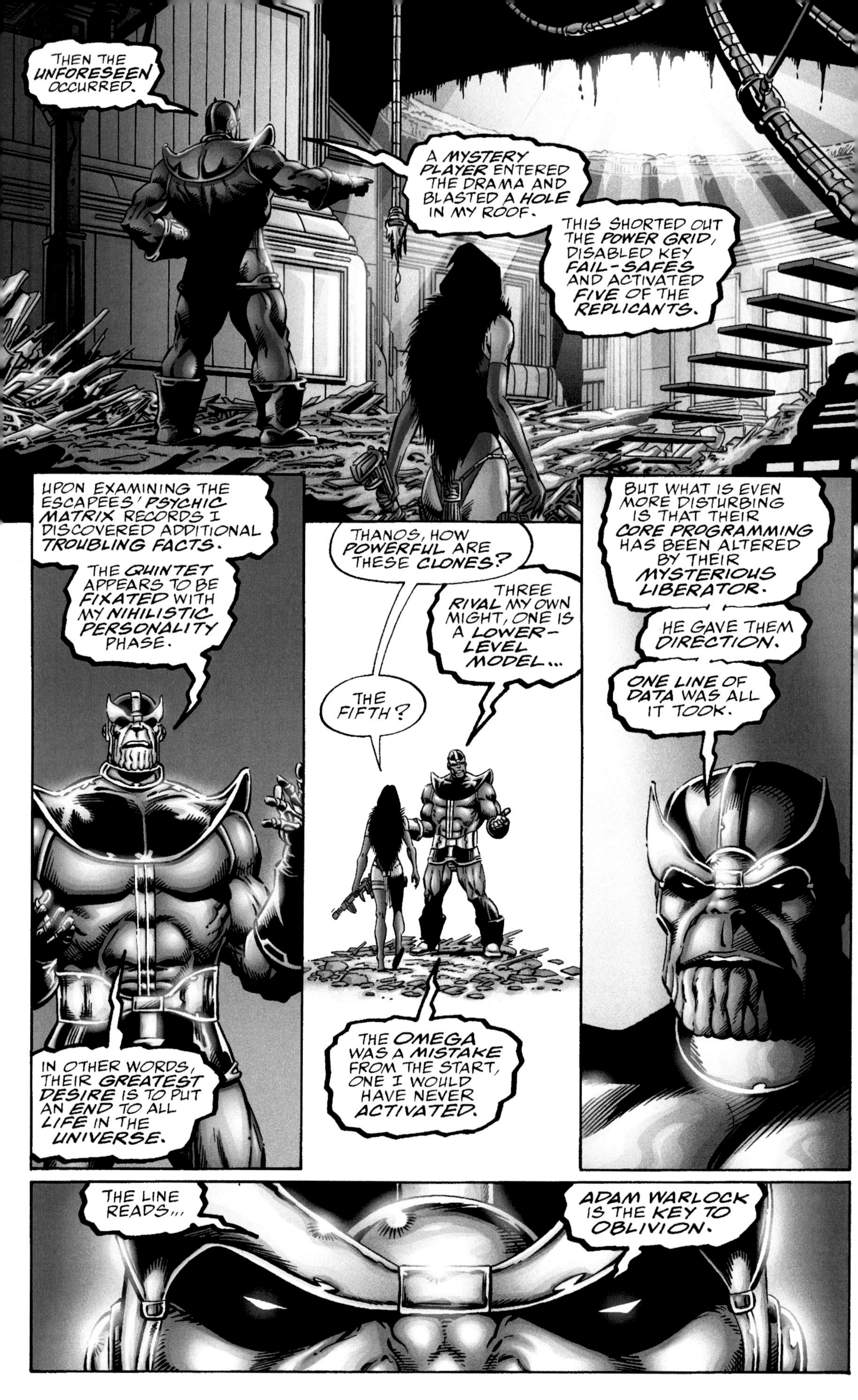
THEN THE UNFORESEEN OCCURRED.
A MYSTERY PLAYER ENTERED THE DRAMA AND BLASTED A HOLE IN MY ROOF.
THIS SHORTED OUT THE POWER GRID, DISABLED KEY FAIL-SAFES AND ACTIVATED FIVE OF THE REPLICANTS.
UPON EXAMINING THE ESCAPEES' PSYCHIC MATRIX RECORDS I DISCOVERED ADDITIONAL TROUBLING FACTS.
THE QUINTET APPEARS TO BE FIXATED WITH MY NIHILISTIC PERSONALITY PHASE.
IN OTHER WORDS, THEIR GREATEST DESIRE IS TO PUT AN END TO ALL LIFE IN THE UNIVERSE.
THANOS, HOW POWERFUL ARE THESE CLONES?
THREE RIVAL MY OWN MIGHT, ONE IS A LOWER-LEVEL MODEL...
THE FIFTH?
THE OMEGA WAS A MISTAKE FROM THE START, ONE I WOULD HAVE NEVER ACTIVATED.
BUT WHAT IS EVEN MORE DISTURBING IS THAT THEIR CORE PROGRAMMING HAS BEEN ALTERED BY THEIR MYSTERIOUS LIBERATOR.
HE GAVE THEM DIRECTION.
ONE LINE OF DATA WAS ALL IT TOOK.
THE LINE READS...
ADAM WARLOCK IS THE KEY TO OBLIVION.

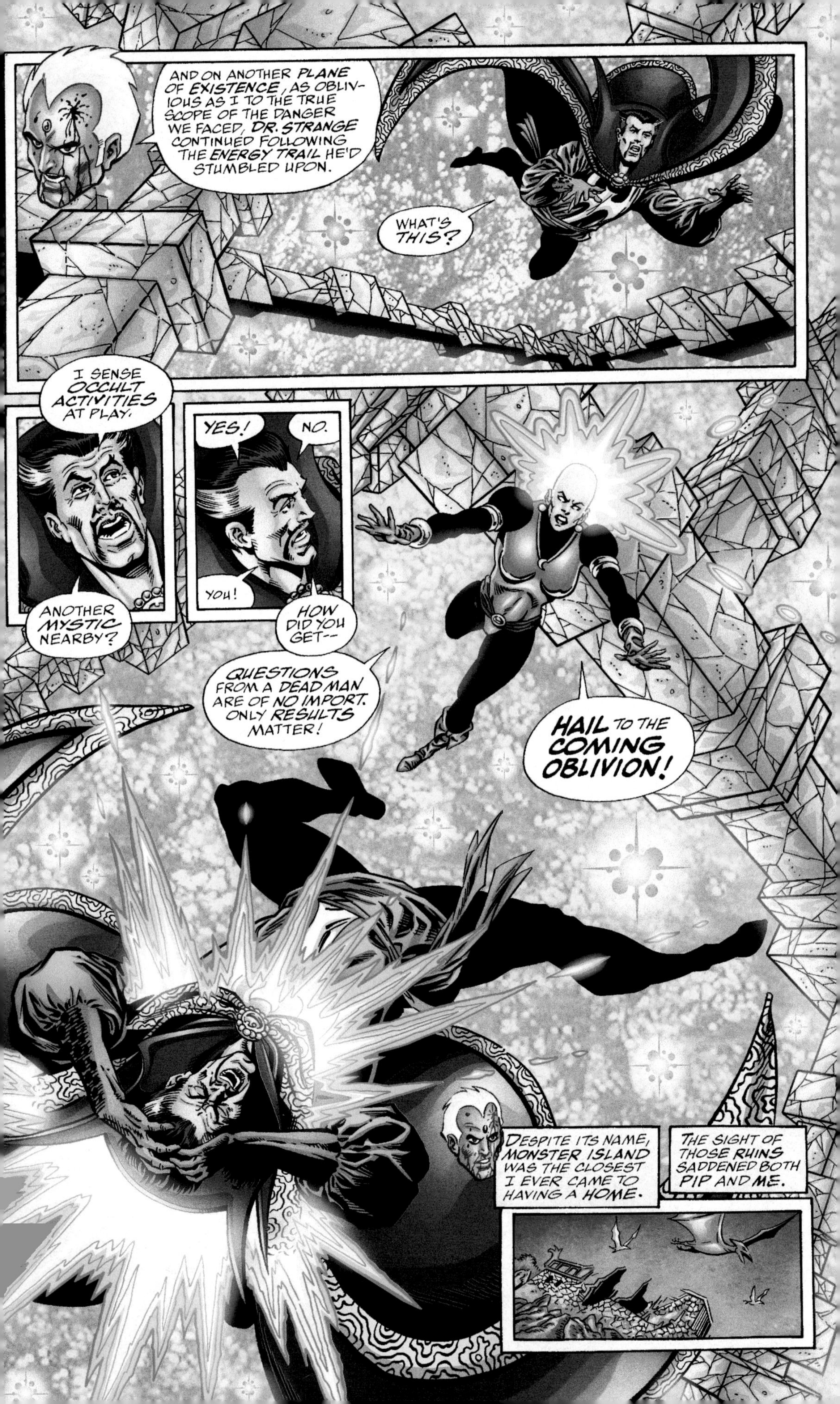

AND ON ANOTHER PLANE OF EXISTENCE, AS OBLIVIOUS AS I TO THE TRUE SCOPE OF THE DANGER WE FACED, DR. STRANGE CONTINUED FOLLOWING THE ENERGY TRAIL HE'D STUMBLED UPON.
WHAT'S THIS?
I SENSE OCCULT ACTIVITIES AT PLAY.
ANOTHER MYSTIC NEARBY?
YES!
NO.
YOU!
HOW DID YOU GET--
QUESTIONS FROM A DEAD MAN ARE OF NO IMPORT. ONLY RESULTS MATTER!
HAIL TO THE COMING OBLIVION!
DESPITE ITS NAME, MONSTER ISLAND WAS THE CLOSEST I EVER CAME TO HAVING A HOME.
THE SIGHT OF THOSE RUINS SADDENED BOTH PIP AND ME.

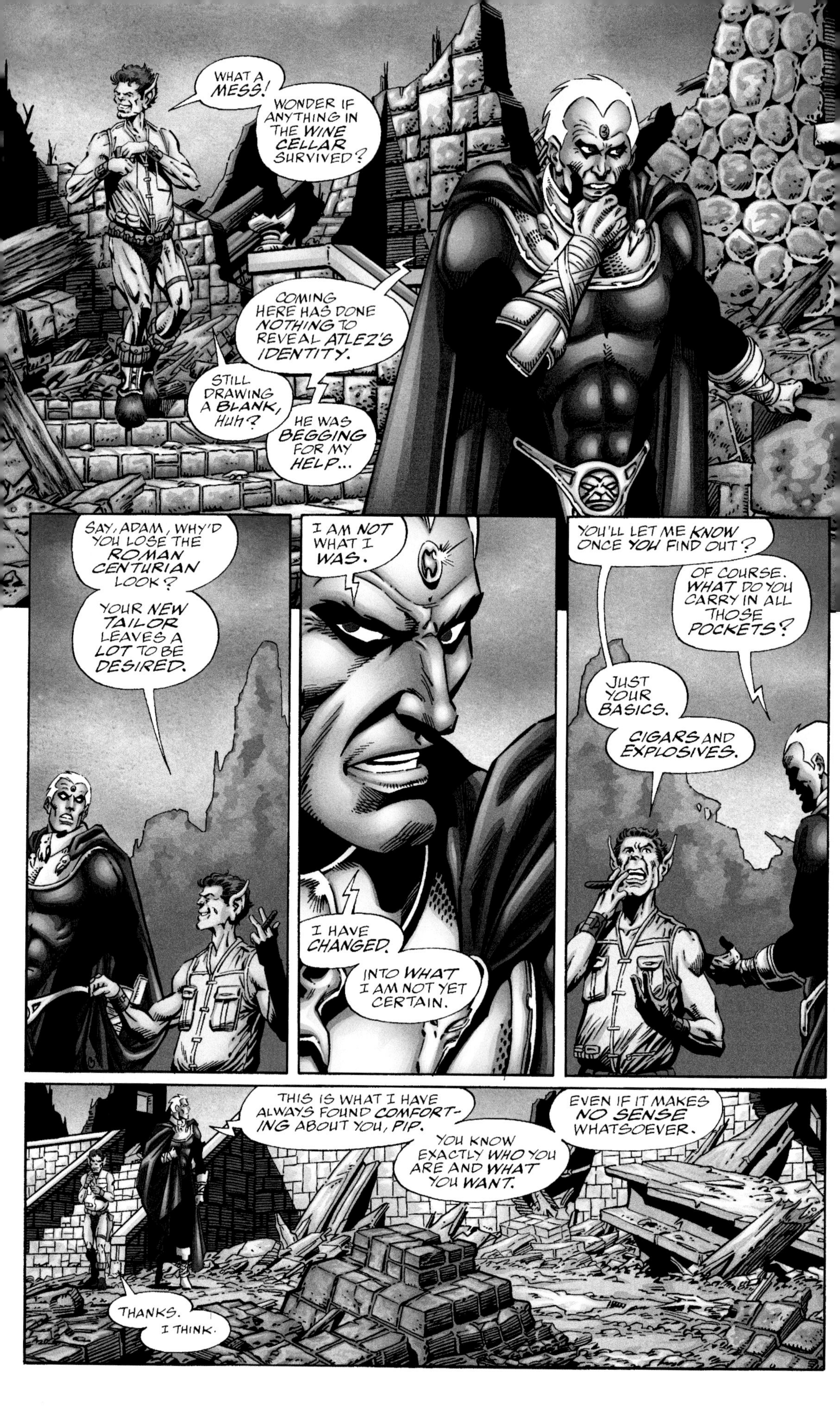

WHAT A MESS!
WONDER IF ANYTHING IN THE WINE CELLAR SURVIVED?
COMING HERE HAS DONE NOTHING TO REVEAL ATLEZ'S IDENTITY.
STILL DRAWING A BLANK, HUH?
HE WAS BEGGING FOR MY HELP...
SAY, ADAM, WHY'D YOU LOSE THE ROMAN CENTURIAN LOOK?
YOUR NEW TAILOR LEAVES A LOT TO BE DESIRED.
I AM NOT WHAT I WAS.
I HAVE CHANGED.
INTO WHAT I AM NOT YET CERTAIN.
YOU'LL LET ME KNOW ONCE YOU FIND OUT?
OF COURSE. WHAT DO YOU CARRY IN ALL THOSE POCKETS?
JUST YOUR BASICS.
CIGARS AND EXPLOSIVES.
THIS IS WHAT I HAVE ALWAYS FOUND COMFORT-ING ABOUT YOU, PIP.
YOU KNOW EXACTLY WHO YOU ARE AND WHAT YOU WANT.
EVEN IF IT MAKES NO SENSE WHATSOEVER.
THANKS. I THINK.

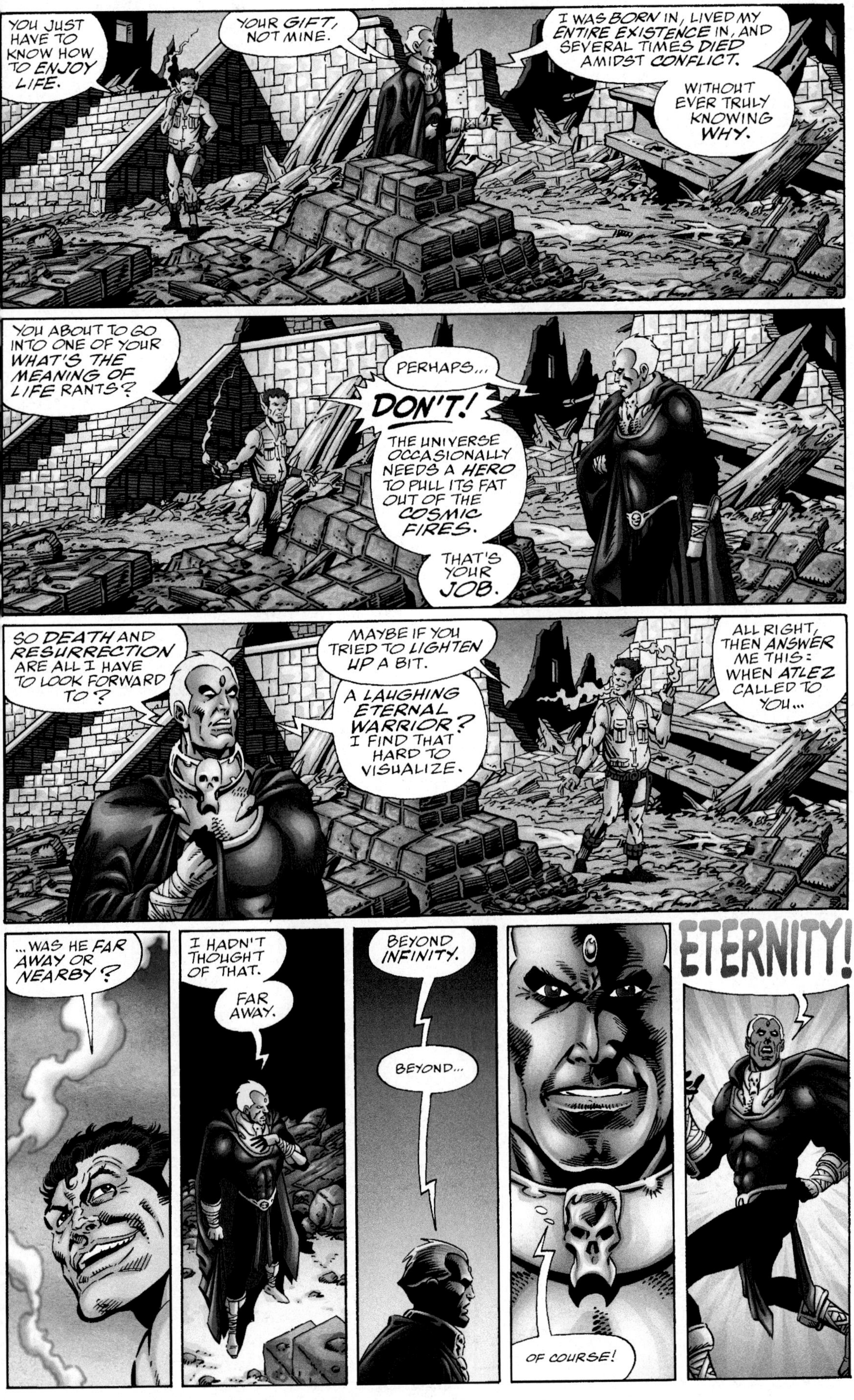

YOU JUST HAVE TO KNOW HOW TO *ENJOY* LIFE.
YOUR *GIFT*, NOT MINE.
I WAS *BORN* IN, LIVED MY *ENTIRE EXISTENCE* IN, AND SEVERAL TIMES *DIED* AMIDST *CONFLICT*.
WITHOUT EVER TRULY KNOWING *WHY*.
YOU ABOUT TO GO INTO ONE OF YOUR *WHAT'S THE MEANING OF LIFE* RANTS?
PERHAPS...
DON'T!
THE UNIVERSE OCCASIONALLY NEEDS A *HERO* TO PULL ITS FAT OUT OF THE *COSMIC FIRES*.
THAT'S *YOUR JOB*.
SO *DEATH* AND *RESURRECTION* ARE ALL I HAVE TO LOOK FORWARD TO?
MAYBE IF YOU TRIED TO *LIGHTEN UP* A BIT.
A *LAUGHING ETERNAL WARRIOR?* I FIND THAT HARD TO VISUALIZE.
ALL RIGHT, THEN *ANSWER* ME THIS: WHEN *ATLEZ* CALLED TO YOU...
...WAS HE *FAR AWAY* OR *NEARBY*?
I HADN'T THOUGHT OF THAT.
FAR AWAY.
BEYOND *INFINITY*.
BEYOND...
OF COURSE!
ETERNITY!

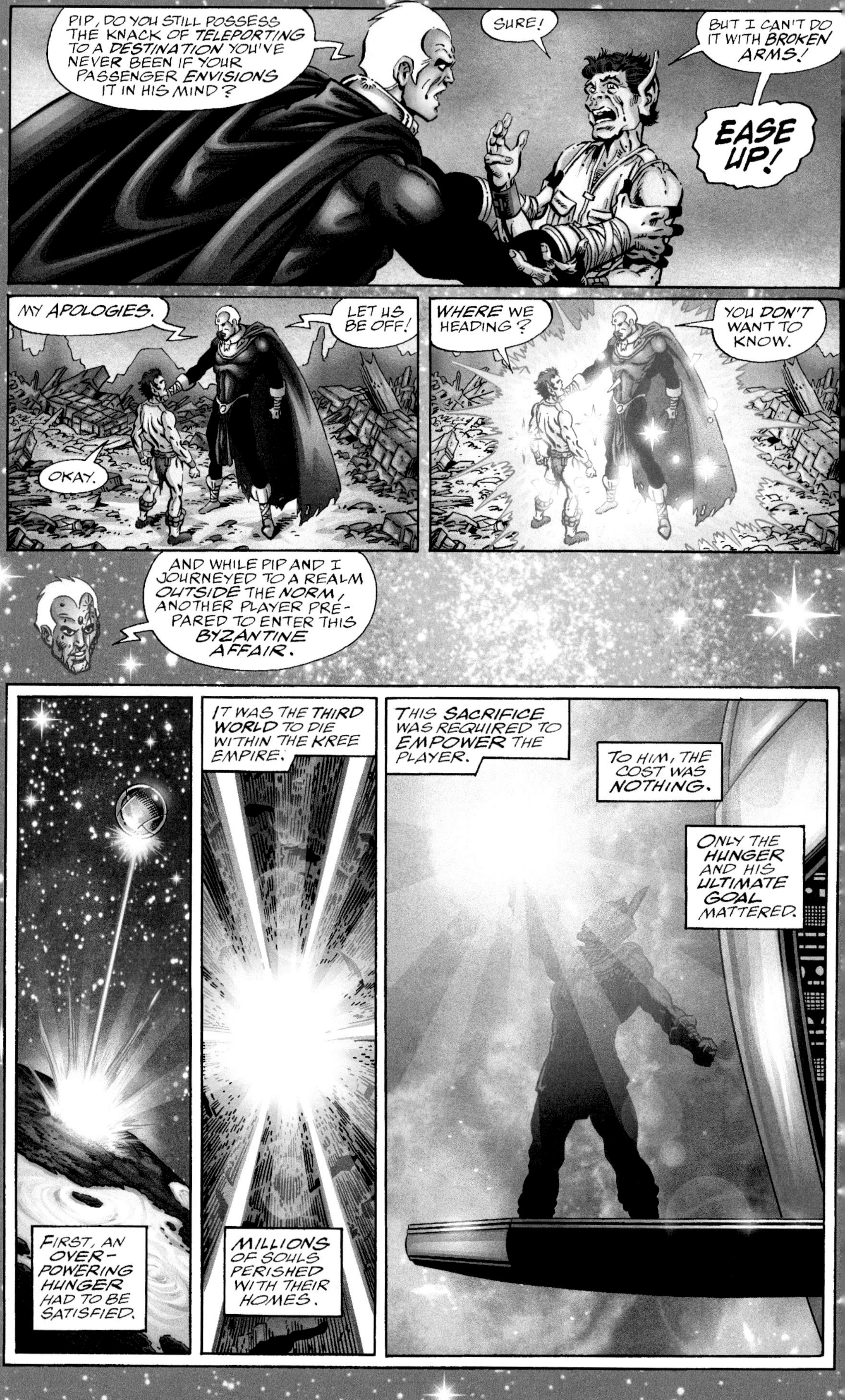
PIP, DO YOU STILL POSSESS THE KNACK OF TELEPORTING TO A DESTINATION YOU'VE NEVER BEEN IF YOUR PASSENGER ENVISIONS IT IN HIS MIND?
SURE!
BUT I CAN'T DO IT WITH BROKEN ARMS!
EASE UP!
MY APOLOGIES.
LET US BE OFF!
OKAY.
WHERE WE HEADING?
YOU DON'T WANT TO KNOW.
AND WHILE PIP AND I JOURNEYED TO A REALM OUTSIDE THE NORM, ANOTHER PLAYER PREPARED TO ENTER THIS BYZANTINE AFFAIR.
FIRST, AN OVER-POWERING HUNGER HAD TO BE SATISFIED.
IT WAS THE THIRD WORLD TO DIE WITHIN THE KREE EMPIRE.
MILLIONS OF SOULS PERISHED WITH THEIR HOMES.
THIS SACRIFICE WAS REQUIRED TO EMPOWER THE PLAYER.
TO HIM, THE COST WAS NOTHING.
ONLY THE HUNGER AND HIS ULTIMATE GOAL MATTERED.

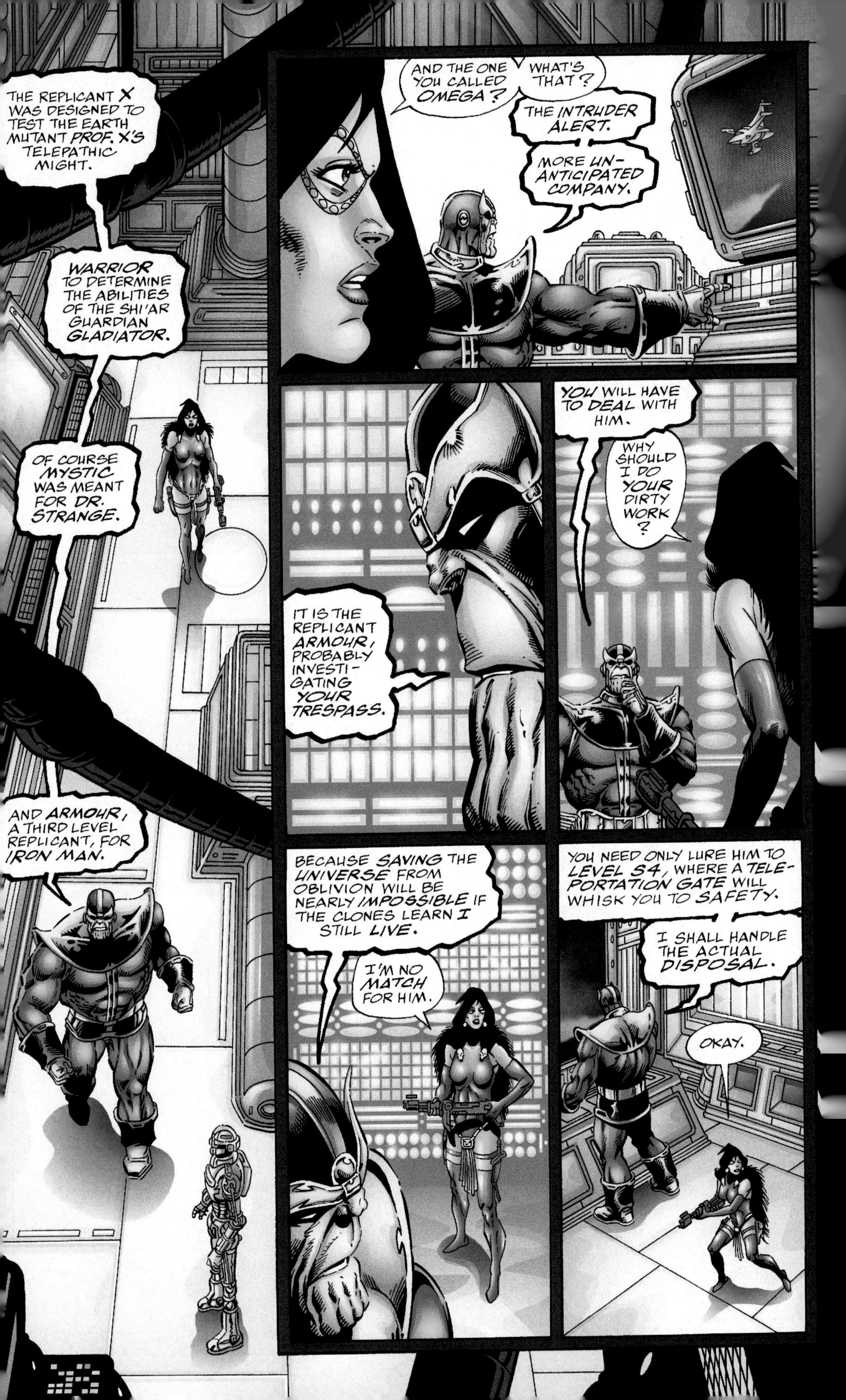
THE REPLICANT X WAS DESIGNED TO TEST THE EARTH MUTANT PROF. X'S TELEPATHIC MIGHT.
WARRIOR TO DETERMINE THE ABILITIES OF THE SHI'AR GUARDIAN GLADIATOR.
OF COURSE MYSTIC WAS MEANT FOR DR. STRANGE.
AND ARMOUR, A THIRD LEVEL REPLICANT, FOR IRON MAN.
AND THE ONE YOU CALLED OMEGA?
WHAT'S THAT?
THE INTRUDER ALERT.
MORE UN-ANTICIPATED COMPANY.
IT IS THE REPLICANT ARMOUR, PROBABLY INVESTI-GATING YOUR TRESPASS.
YOU WILL HAVE TO DEAL WITH HIM.
WHY SHOULD I DO YOUR DIRTY WORK?
BECAUSE SAVING THE UNIVERSE FROM OBLIVION WILL BE NEARLY IMPOSSIBLE IF THE CLONES LEARN I STILL LIVE.
I'M NO MATCH FOR HIM.
YOU NEED ONLY LURE HIM TO LEVEL S4, WHERE A TELE-PORTATION GATE WILL WHISK YOU TO SAFETY.
I SHALL HANDLE THE ACTUAL DISPOSAL.
OKAY.

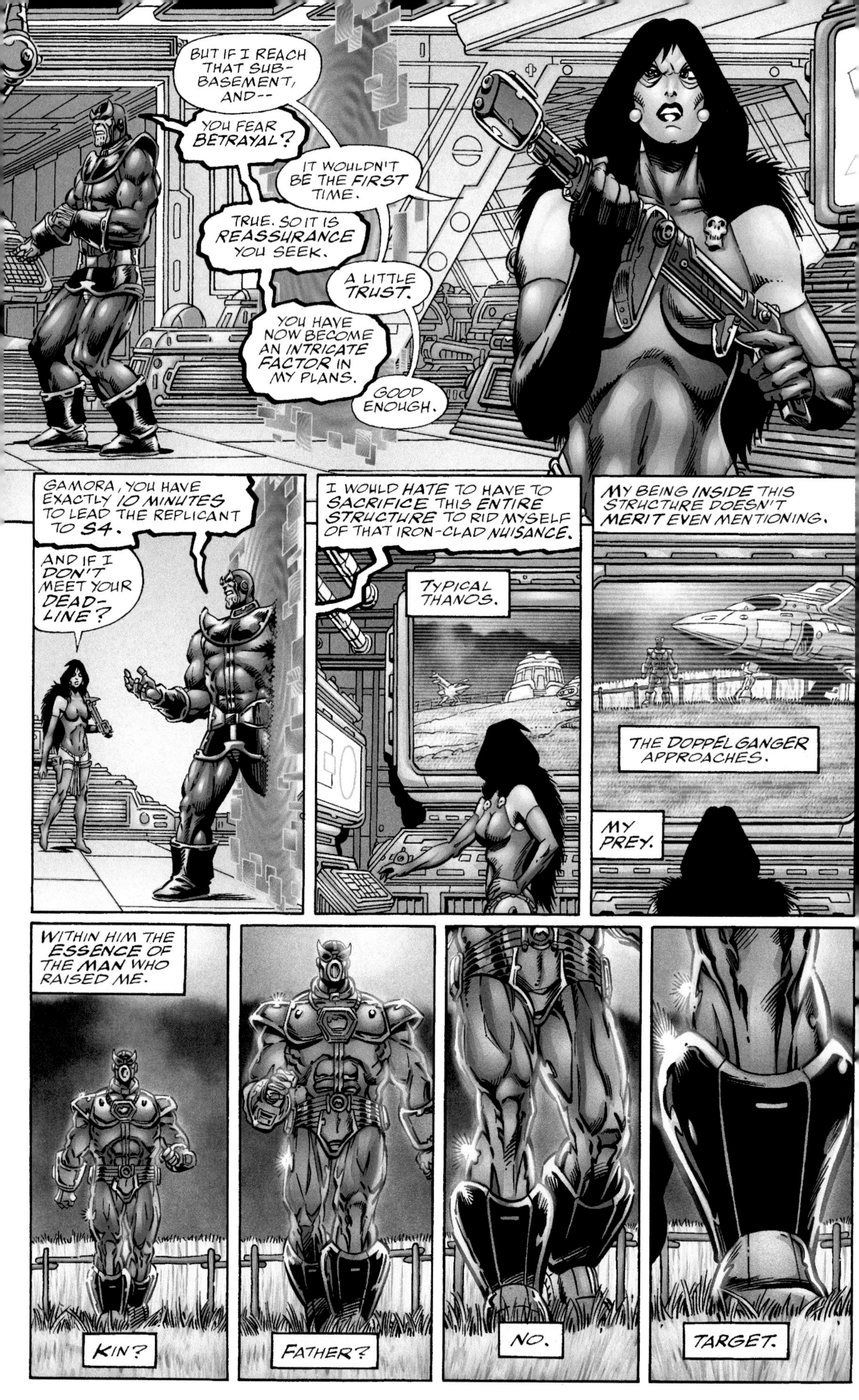

BUT IF I REACH THAT SUB-BASEMENT, AND--
YOU FEAR BETRAYAL?
IT WOULDN'T BE THE FIRST TIME.
TRUE. SO IT IS REASSURANCE YOU SEEK.
A LITTLE TRUST.
YOU HAVE NOW BECOME AN INTRICATE FACTOR IN MY PLANS.
GOOD ENOUGH.
GAMORA, YOU HAVE EXACTLY 10 MINUTES TO LEAD THE REPLICANT TO S4.
AND IF I DON'T MEET YOUR DEAD-LINE?
I WOULD HATE TO HAVE TO SACRIFICE THIS ENTIRE STRUCTURE TO RID MYSELF OF THAT IRON-CLAD NUISANCE.
TYPICAL THANOS.
MY BEING INSIDE THIS STRUCTURE DOESN'T MERIT EVEN MENTIONING.
THE DOPPELGANGER APPROACHES.
MY PREY.
WITHIN HIM THE ESSENCE OF THE MAN WHO RAISED ME.
KIN?
FATHER?
NO.
TARGET.

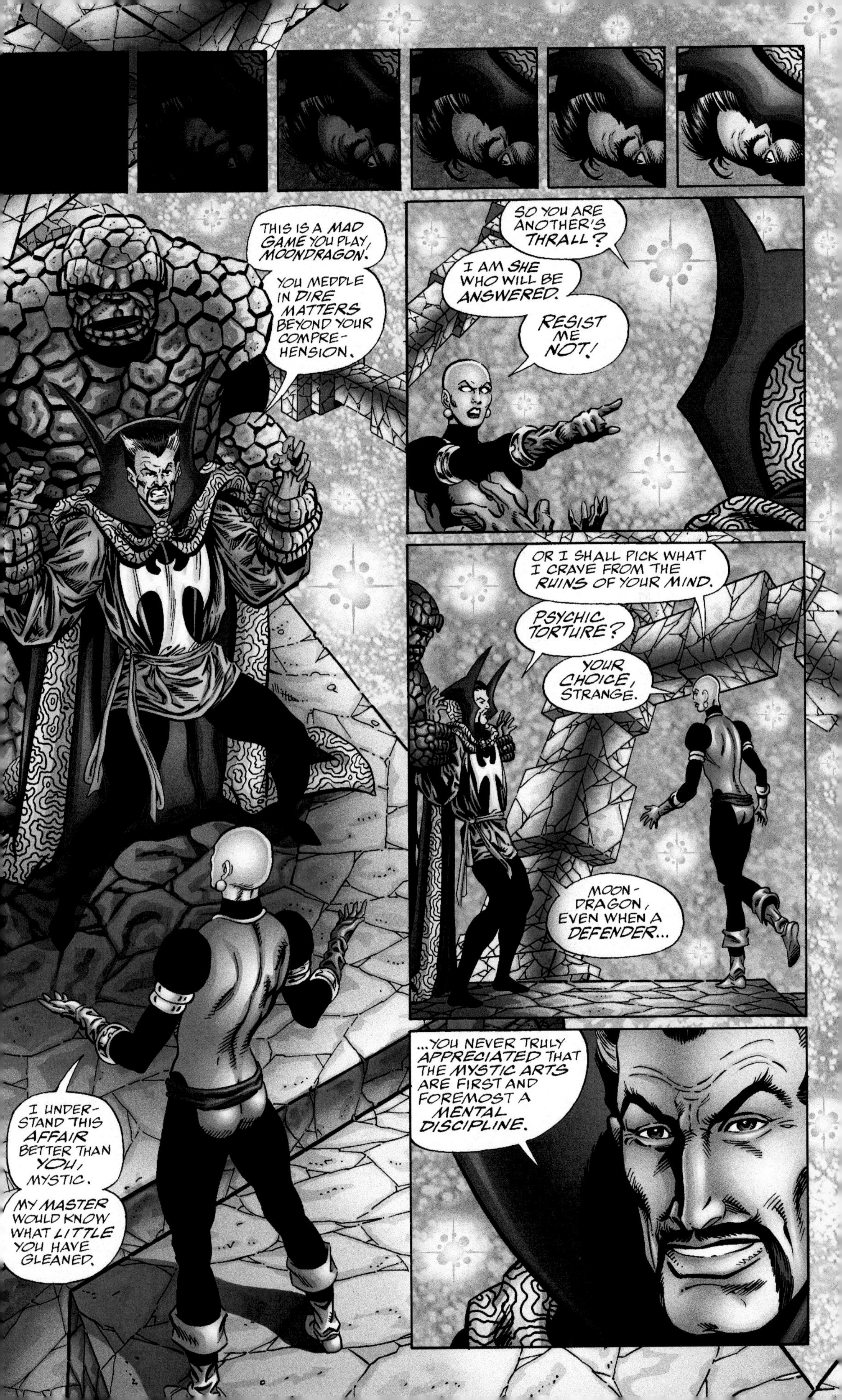

THIS IS A MAD GAME YOU PLAY, MOONDRAGON.
YOU MEDDLE IN DIRE MATTERS BEYOND YOUR COMPRE-HENSION.
SO YOU ARE ANOTHER'S THRALL?
I AM SHE WHO WILL BE ANSWERED.
RESIST ME NOT!
OR I SHALL PICK WHAT I CRAVE FROM THE RUINS OF YOUR MIND.
PSYCHIC TORTURE?
YOUR CHOICE, STRANGE.
MOON-DRAGON, EVEN WHEN A DEFENDER...
...YOU NEVER TRULY APPRECIATED THAT THE MYSTIC ARTS ARE FIRST AND FOREMOST A MENTAL DISCIPLINE.
I UNDER-STAND THIS AFFAIR BETTER THAN YOU, MYSTIC.
MY MASTER WOULD KNOW WHAT LITTLE YOU HAVE GLEANED.

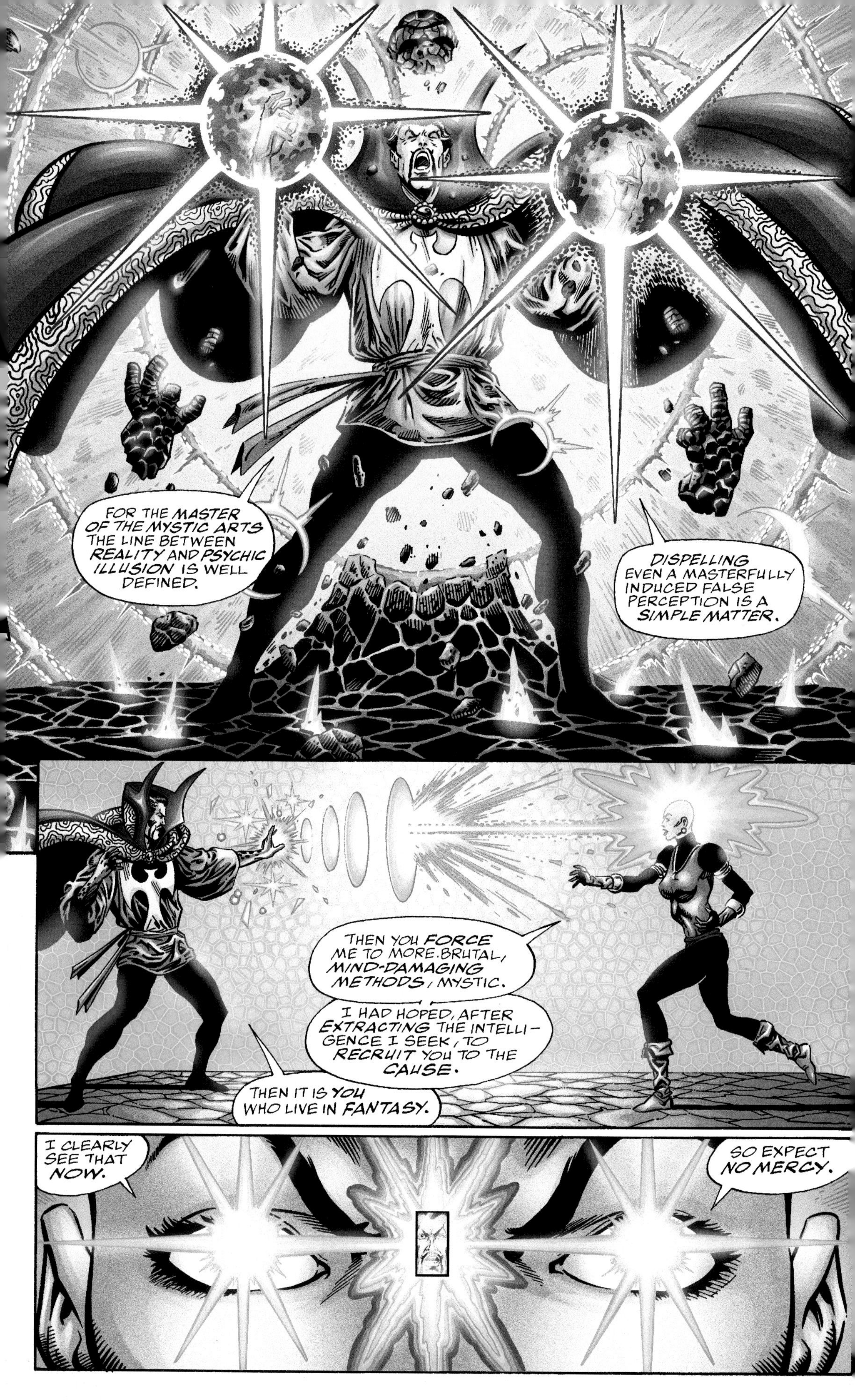
FOR THE MASTER OF THE MYSTIC ARTS THE LINE BETWEEN REALITY AND PSYCHIC ILLUSION IS WELL DEFINED.
DISPELLING EVEN A MASTERFULLY INDUCED FALSE PERCEPTION IS A SIMPLE MATTER.
THEN YOU FORCE ME TO MORE BRUTAL, MIND-DAMAGING METHODS, MYSTIC.
I HAD HOPED, AFTER EXTRACTING THE INTELLIGENCE I SEEK, TO RECRUIT YOU TO THE CAUSE.
THEN IT IS YOU WHO LIVE IN FANTASY.
I CLEARLY SEE THAT NOW.
SO EXPECT NO MERCY.

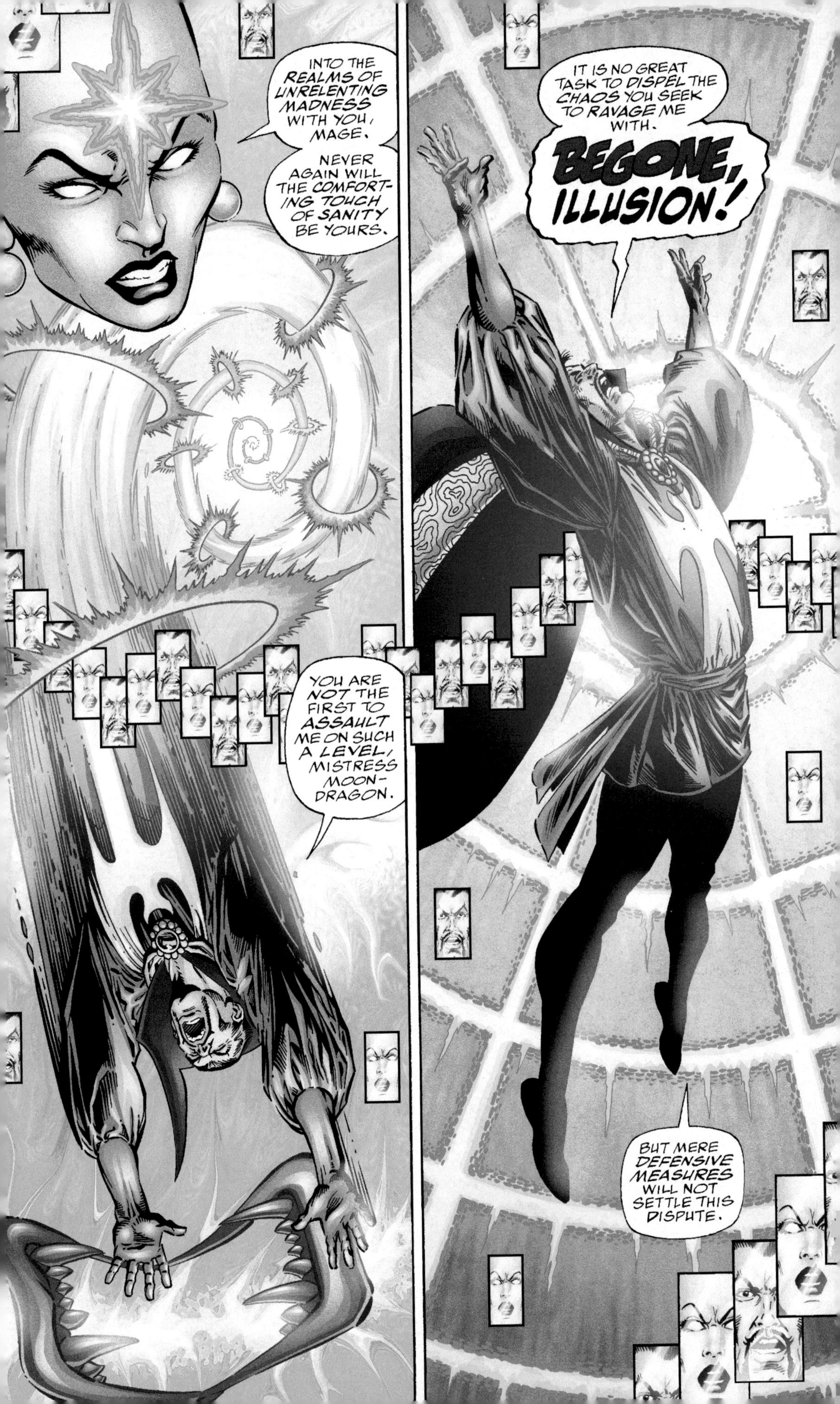
INTO THE REALMS OF UNRELENTING MADNESS WITH YOU, MAGE.
NEVER AGAIN WILL THE COMFORTING TOUCH OF SANITY BE YOURS.
YOU ARE NOT THE FIRST TO ASSAULT ME ON SUCH A LEVEL, MISTRESS MOONDRAGON.
IT IS NO GREAT TASK TO DISPEL THE CHAOS YOU SEEK TO RAVAGE ME WITH.
BEGONE, ILLUSION!
BUT MERE DEFENSIVE MEASURES WILL NOT SETTLE THIS DISPUTE.

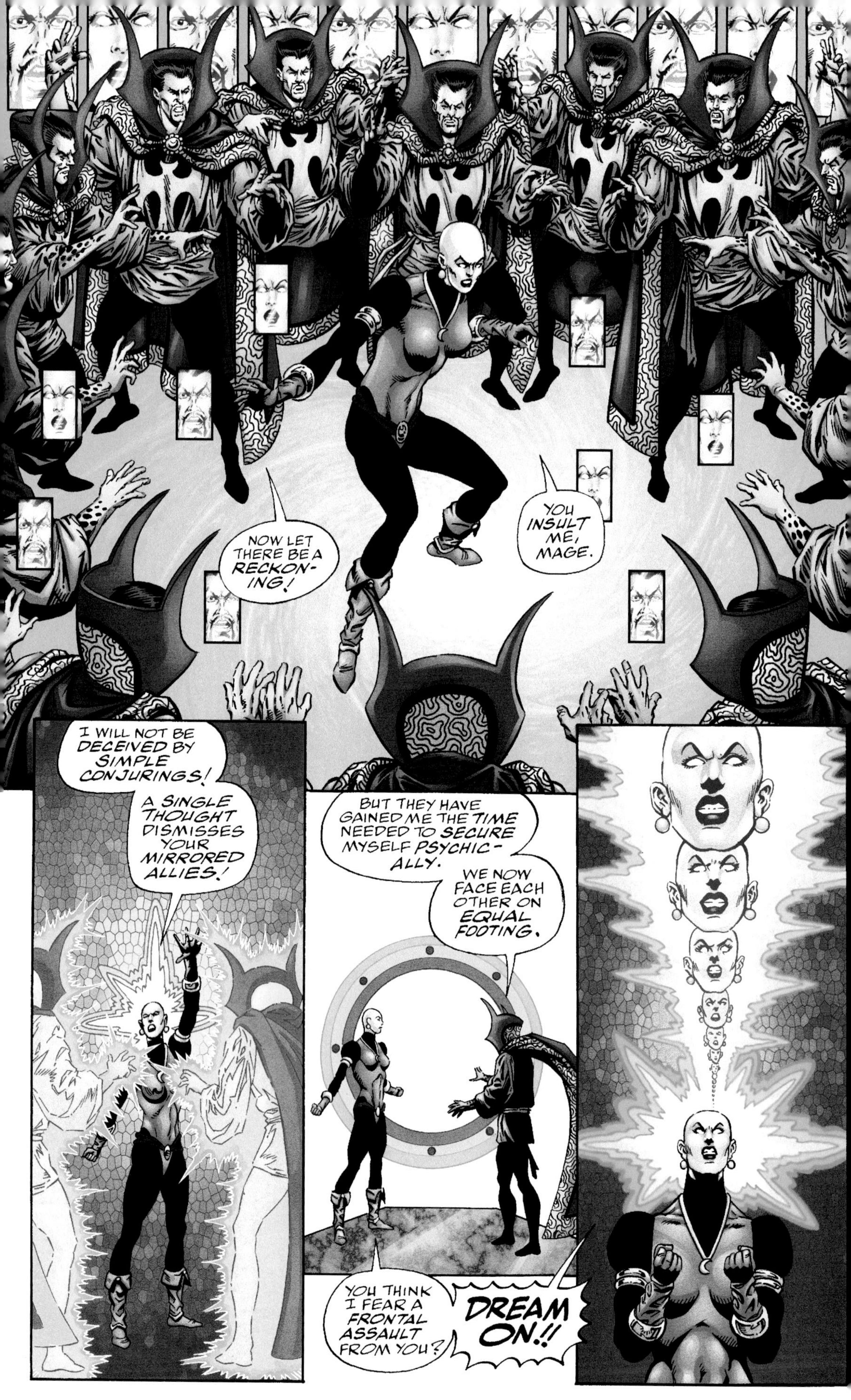
NOW LET THERE BE A RECKONING!
YOU INSULT ME, MAGE.
I WILL NOT BE DECEIVED BY SIMPLE CONJURINGS!
A SINGLE THOUGHT DISMISSES YOUR MIRRORED ALLIES!
BUT THEY HAVE GAINED ME THE TIME NEEDED TO SECURE MYSELF PSYCHIC-ALLY.
WE NOW FACE EACH OTHER ON EQUAL FOOTING.
YOU THINK I FEAR A FRONTAL ASSAULT FROM YOU?
DREAM ON!!

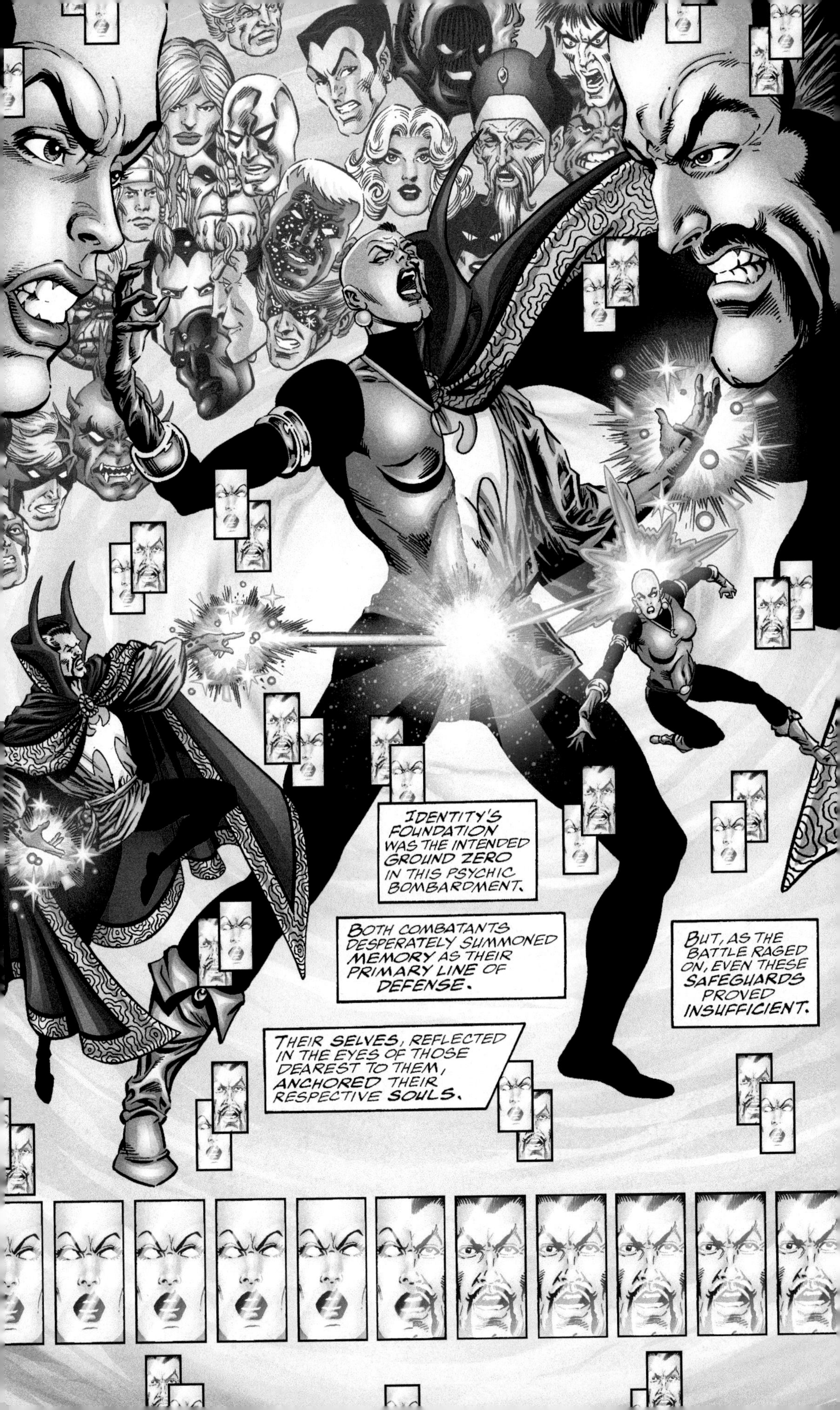
IDENTITY'S FOUNDATION WAS THE INTENDED GROUND ZERO IN THIS PSYCHIC BOMBARDMENT.
BOTH COMBATANTS DESPERATELY SUMMONED MEMORY AS THEIR PRIMARY LINE OF DEFENSE.
THEIR SELVES, REFLECTED IN THE EYES OF THOSE DEAREST TO THEM, ANCHORED THEIR RESPECTIVE SOULS.
BUT, AS THE BATTLE RAGED ON, EVEN THESE SAFEGUARDS PROVED INSUFFICIENT.

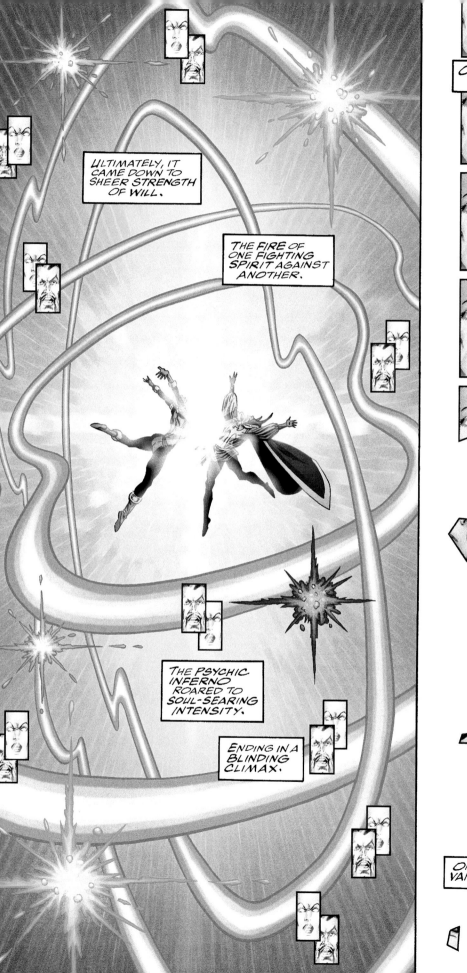

ULTIMATELY, IT CAME DOWN TO SHEER STRENGTH OF WILL.

THE FIRE OF ONE FIGHTING SPIRIT AGAINST ANOTHER.

THE PSYCHIC INFERNO ROARED TO SOUL-SEARING INTENSITY.

ENDING IN A BLINDING CLIMAX.

ONE THE VICTOR.

ONE THE VANQUISHED.

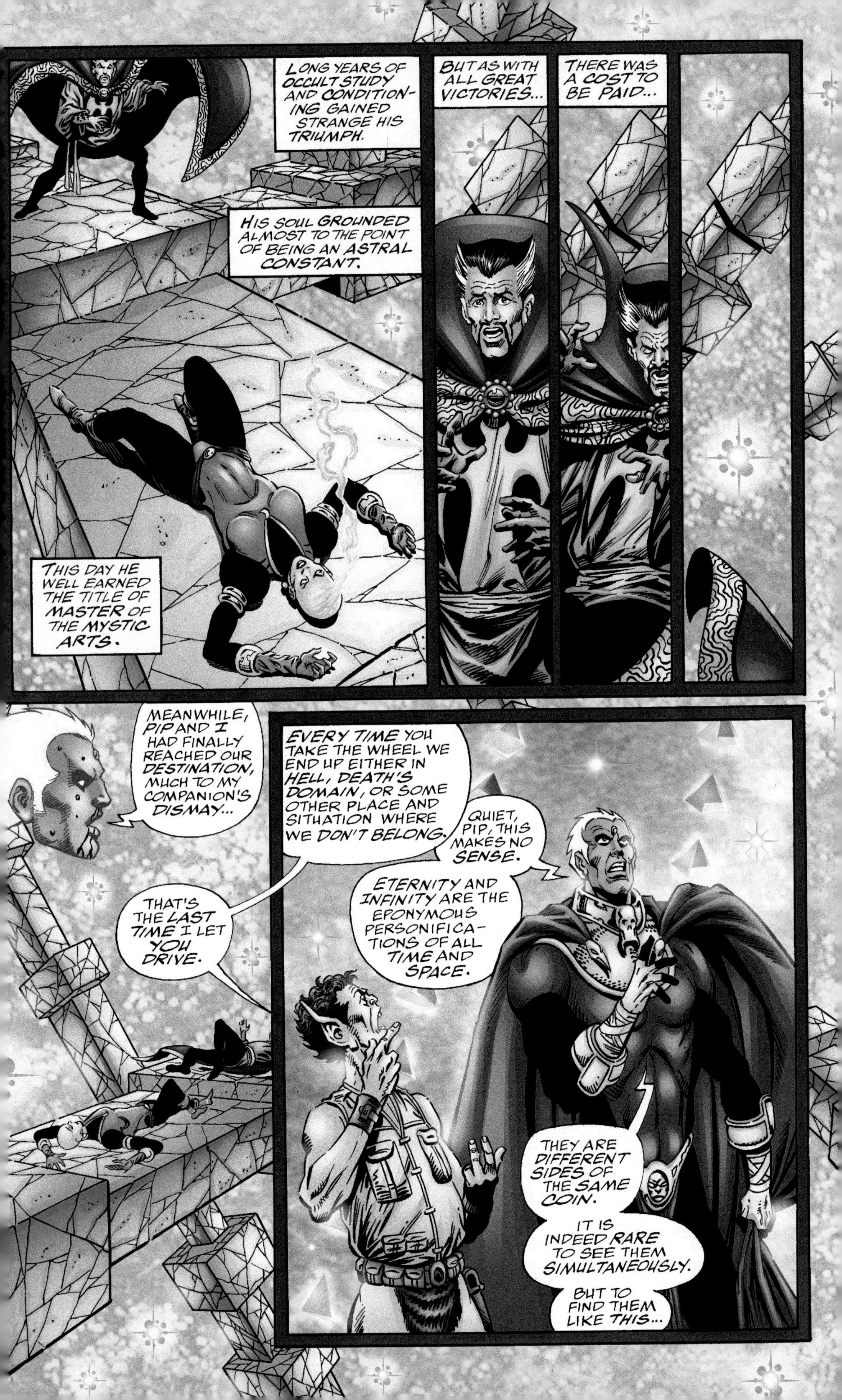

LONG YEARS OF OCCULT STUDY AND CONDITIONING GAINED STRANGE HIS TRIUMPH.
HIS SOUL GROUNDED ALMOST TO THE POINT OF BEING AN ASTRAL CONSTANT.
THIS DAY HE WELL EARNED THE TITLE OF MASTER OF THE MYSTIC ARTS.
BUT AS WITH ALL GREAT VICTORIES...
THERE WAS A COST TO BE PAID...
MEANWHILE, PIP AND I HAD FINALLY REACHED OUR DESTINATION, MUCH TO MY COMPANION'S DISMAY...
EVERY TIME YOU TAKE THE WHEEL WE END UP EITHER IN HELL, DEATH'S DOMAIN, OR SOME OTHER PLACE AND SITUATION WHERE WE DON'T BELONG.
THAT'S THE LAST TIME I LET YOU DRIVE.
QUIET, PIP, THIS MAKES NO SENSE.
ETERNITY AND INFINITY ARE THE EPONYMOUS PERSONIFICATIONS OF ALL TIME AND SPACE.
THEY ARE DIFFERENT SIDES OF THE SAME COIN.
IT IS INDEED RARE TO SEE THEM SIMULTANEOUSLY.
BUT TO FIND THEM LIKE THIS...

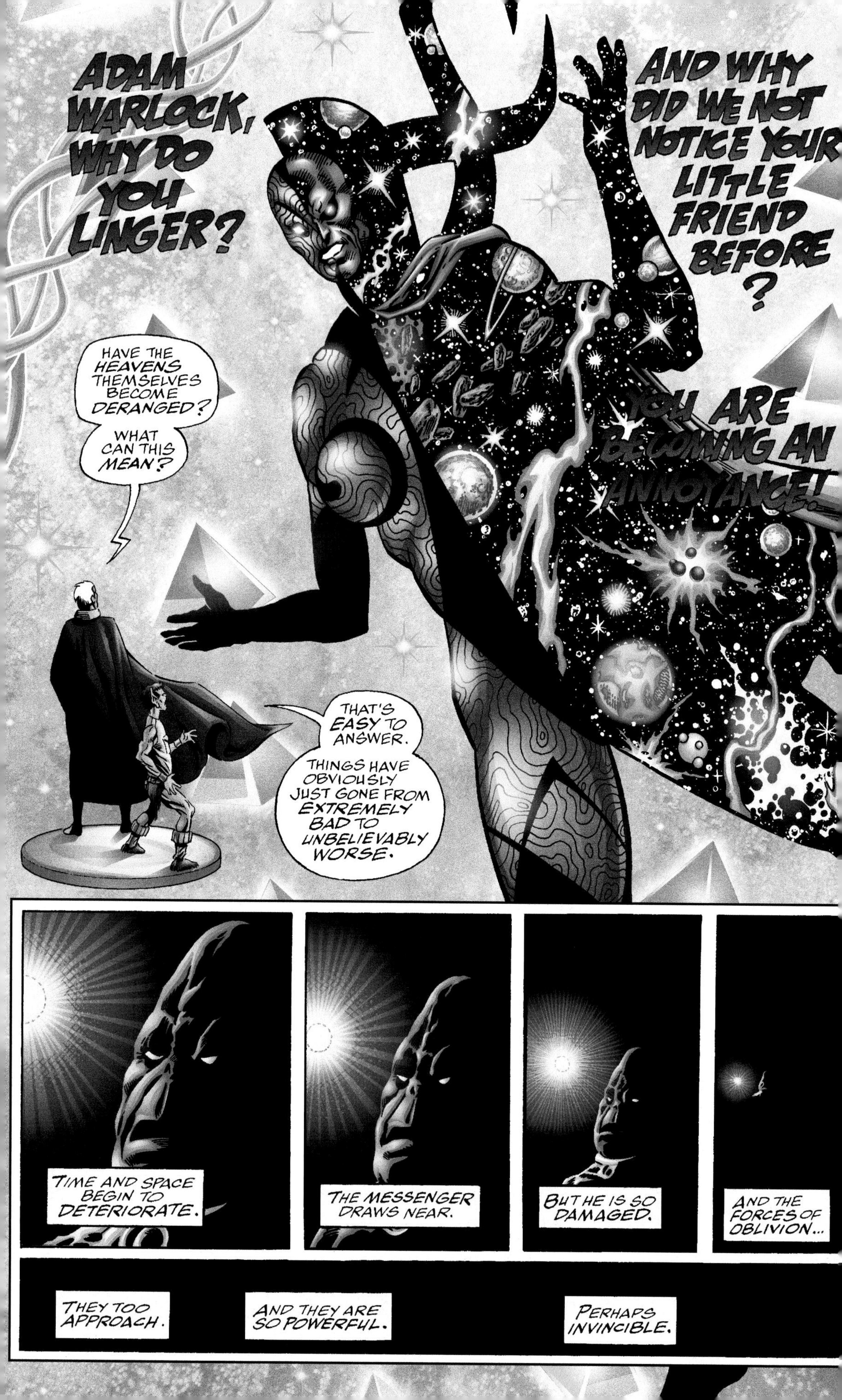
ADAM WARLOCK, WHY DO YOU LINGER?
AND WHY DID WE NOT NOTICE YOUR LITTLE FRIEND BEFORE?
YOU ARE BECOMING AN ANNOYANCE!
HAVE THE HEAVENS THEMSELVES BECOME DERANGED?
WHAT CAN THIS MEAN?
THAT'S EASY TO ANSWER.
THINGS HAVE OBVIOUSLY JUST GONE FROM EXTREMELY BAD TO UNBELIEVABLY WORSE.
TIME AND SPACE BEGIN TO DETERIORATE.
THE MESSENGER DRAWS NEAR.
BUT HE IS SO DAMAGED.
AND THE FORCES OF OBLIVION...
THEY TOO APPROACH.
AND THEY ARE SO POWERFUL.
PERHAPS INVINCIBLE.

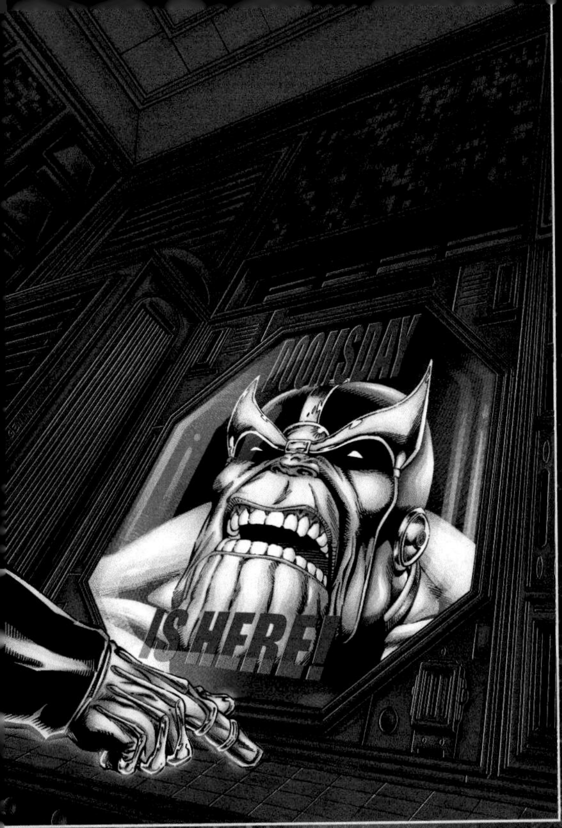
DOOMSDAY
IS HERE!
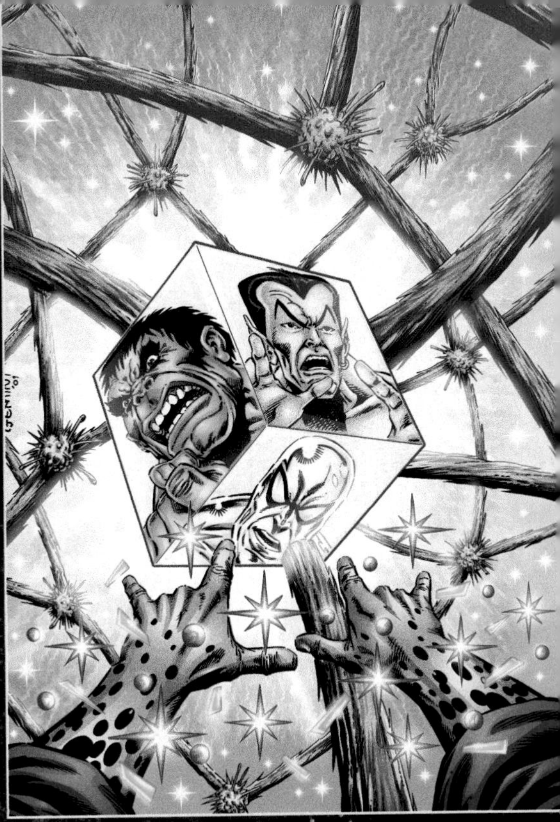
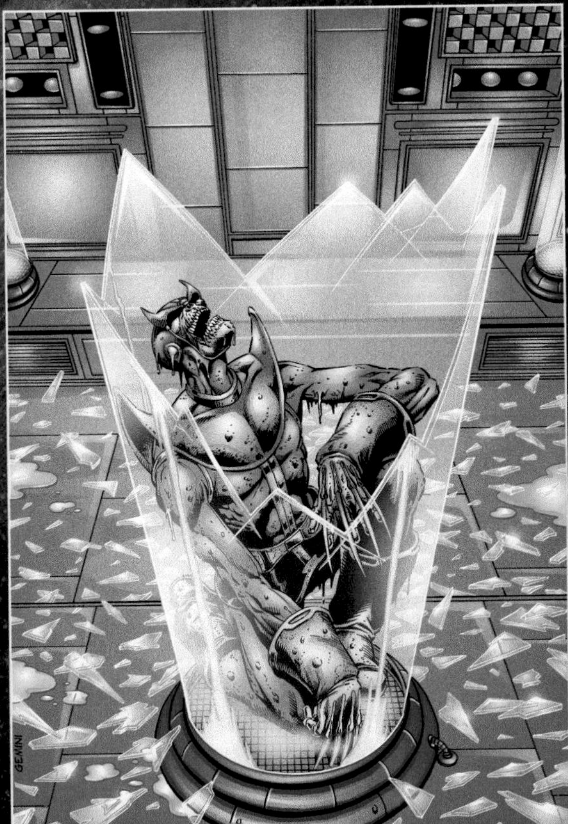

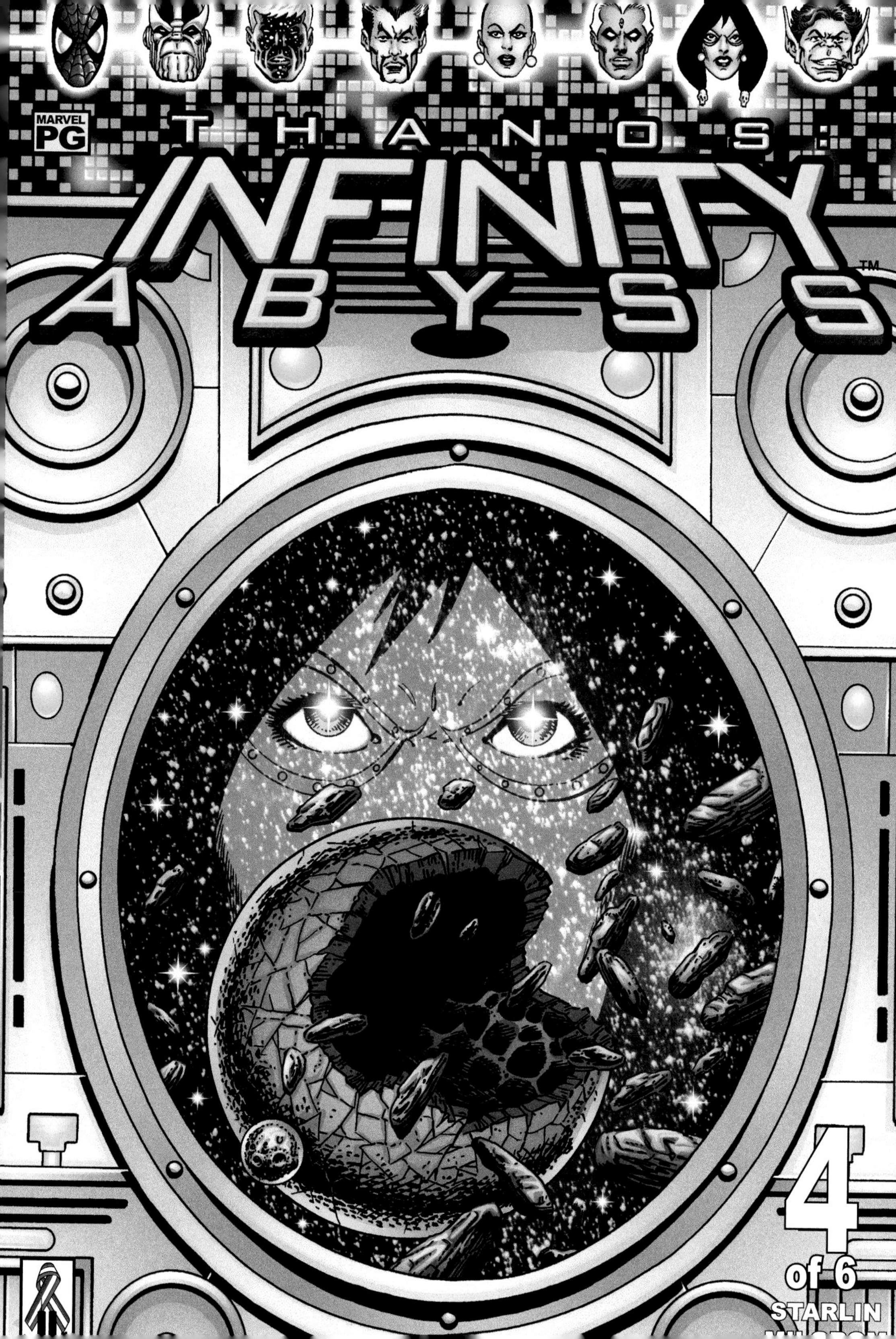
MARVEL PG
THANOS:
INFINITY ABYSS™
4 of 6
STARLIN

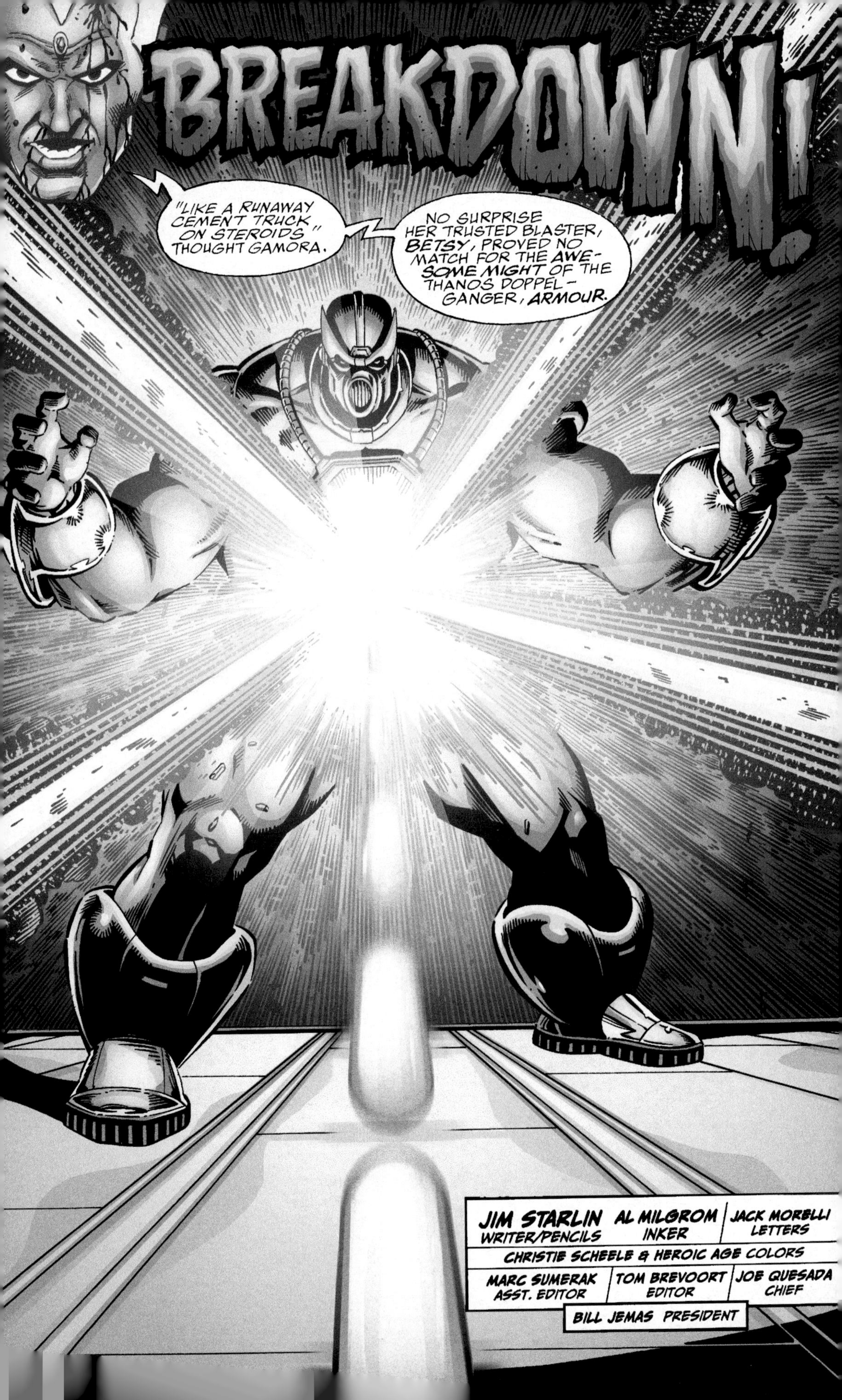
BREAKDOWN!
"LIKE A RUNAWAY CEMENT TRUCK ON STEROIDS" THOUGHT GAMORA.
NO SURPRISE HER TRUSTED BLASTER, BETSY, PROVED NO MATCH FOR THE AWESOME MIGHT OF THE THANOS DOPPELGANGER, ARMOUR.
JIM STARLIN WRITER/PENCILS
AL MILGROM INKER
JACK MORELLI LETTERS
CHRISTIE SCHEELE & HEROIC AGE COLORS
MARC SUMERAK ASST. EDITOR
TOM BREVOORT EDITOR
JOE QUESADA CHIEF
BILL JEMAS PRESIDENT

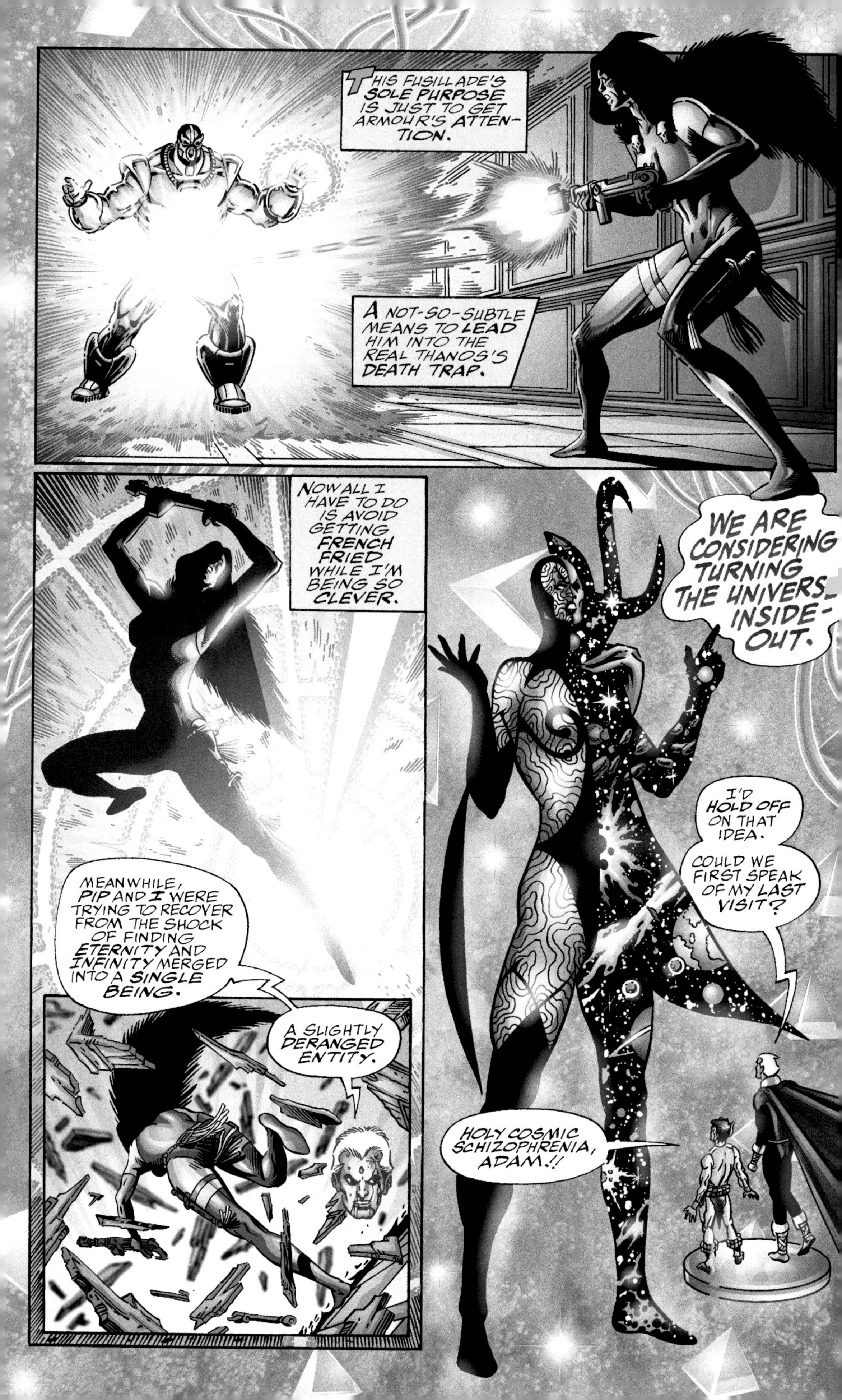

THIS FUSILLADE'S SOLE PURPOSE IS JUST TO GET ARMOUR'S ATTENTION.
A NOT-SO-SUBTLE MEANS TO LEAD HIM INTO THE REAL THANOS'S DEATH TRAP.
NOW ALL I HAVE TO DO IS AVOID GETTING FRENCH FRIED WHILE I'M BEING SO CLEVER.
MEANWHILE, PIP AND I WERE TRYING TO RECOVER FROM THE SHOCK OF FINDING ETERNITY AND INFINITY MERGED INTO A SINGLE BEING.
A SLIGHTLY DERANGED ENTITY.
WE ARE CONSIDERING TURNING THE UNIVERSE INSIDE-OUT.
I'D HOLD OFF ON THAT IDEA.
COULD WE FIRST SPEAK OF MY LAST VISIT?
HOLY COSMIC SCHIZOPHRENIA, ADAM!!

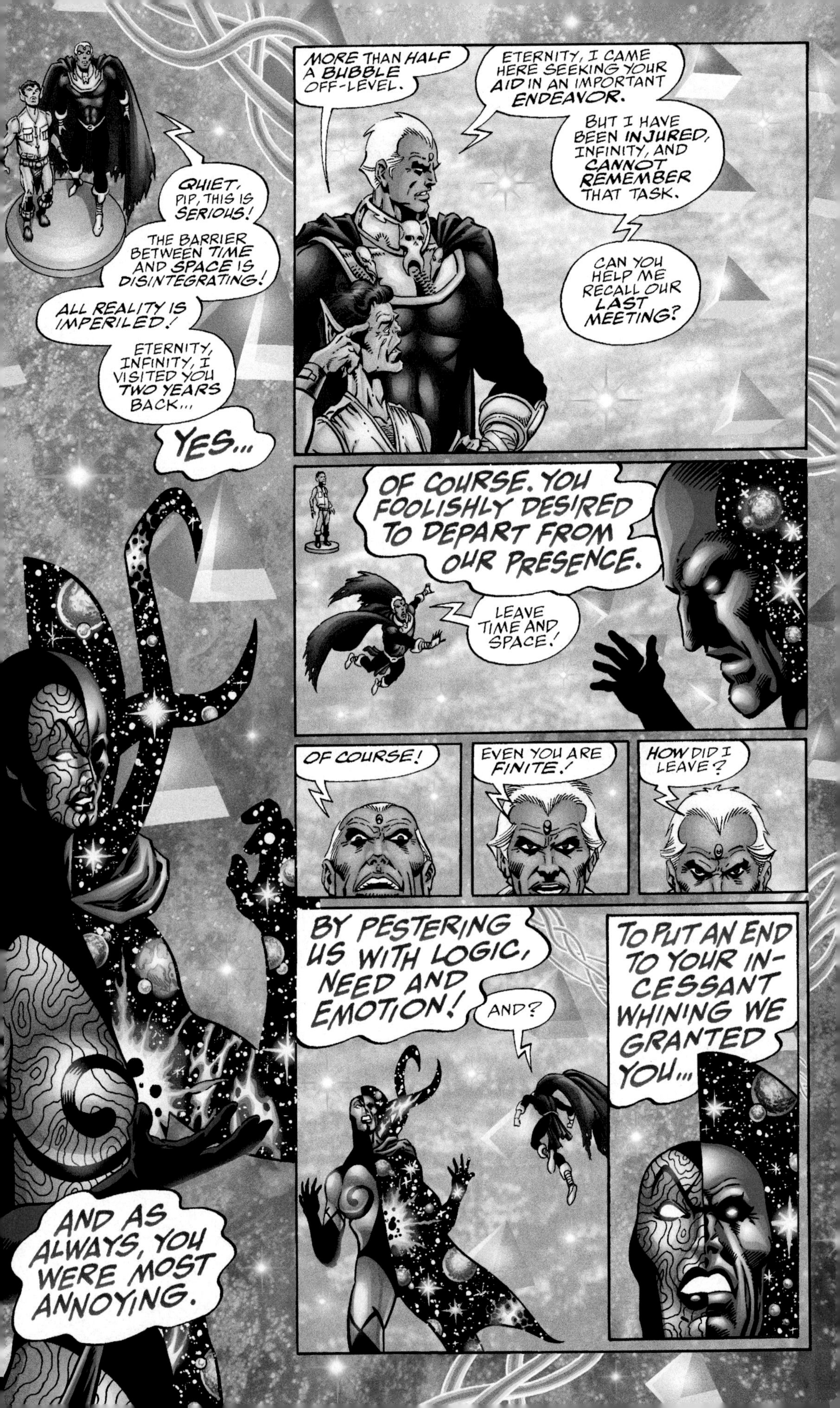

QUIET, PIP, THIS IS SERIOUS!
THE BARRIER BETWEEN TIME AND SPACE IS DISINTEGRATING!
ALL REALITY IS IMPERILED!
ETERNITY, INFINITY, I VISITED YOU TWO YEARS BACK...
YES...
MORE THAN HALF A BUBBLE OFF-LEVEL.
ETERNITY, I CAME HERE SEEKING YOUR AID IN AN IMPORTANT ENDEAVOR.
BUT I HAVE BEEN INJURED, INFINITY, AND CANNOT REMEMBER THAT TASK.
CAN YOU HELP ME RECALL OUR LAST MEETING?
OF COURSE. YOU FOOLISHLY DESIRED TO DEPART FROM OUR PRESENCE.
LEAVE TIME AND SPACE!
OF COURSE!
EVEN YOU ARE FINITE!
HOW DID I LEAVE?
AND AS ALWAYS, YOU WERE MOST ANNOYING.
BY PESTERING US WITH LOGIC, NEED AND EMOTION!
AND?
TO PUT AN END TO YOUR INCESSANT WHINING WE GRANTED YOU...

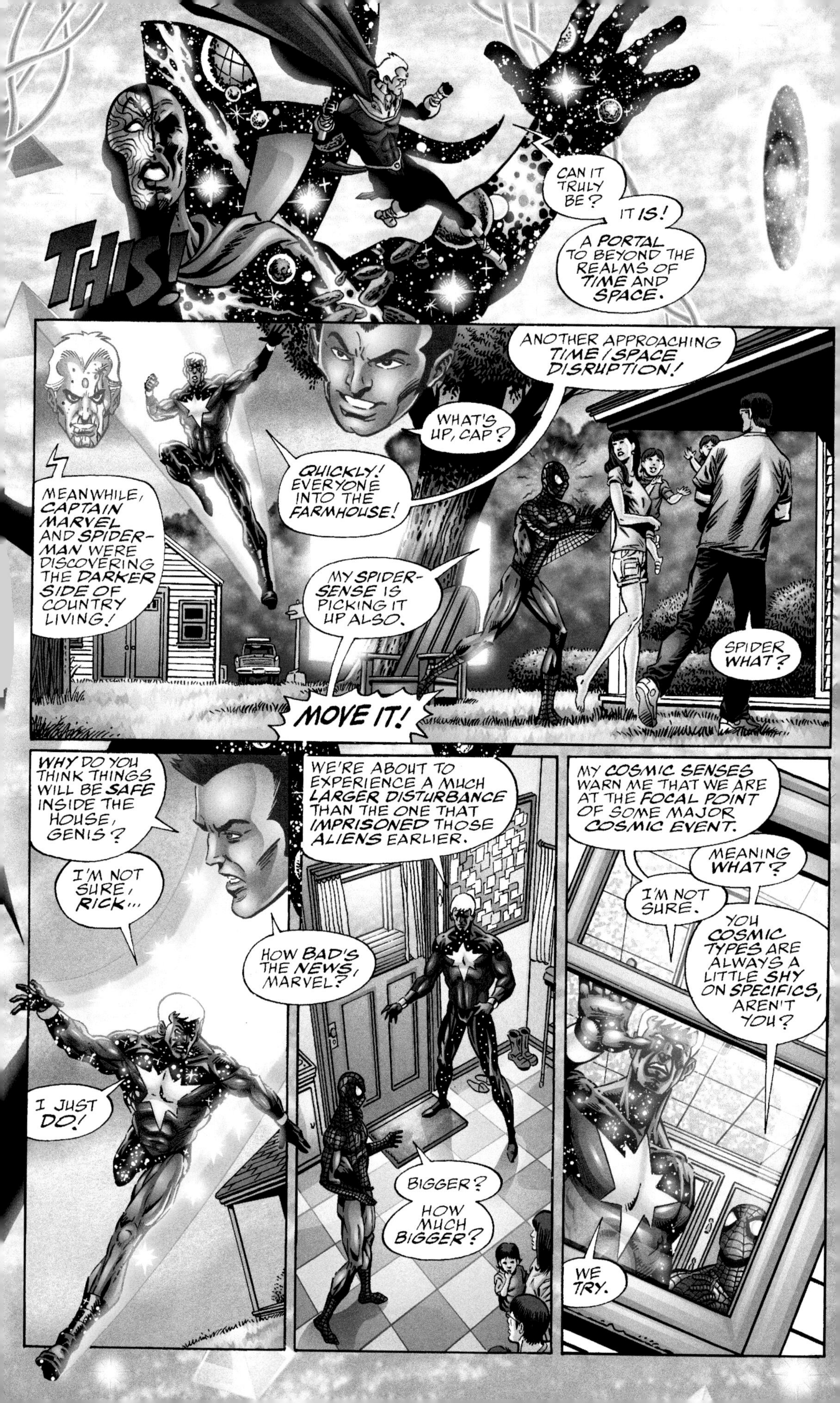

THIS!
CAN IT TRULY BE?
IT IS!
A PORTAL TO BEYOND THE REALMS OF TIME AND SPACE.
MEANWHILE, CAPTAIN MARVEL AND SPIDER-MAN WERE DISCOVERING THE DARKER SIDE OF COUNTRY LIVING!
ANOTHER APPROACHING TIME/SPACE DISRUPTION!
WHAT'S UP, CAP?
QUICKLY! EVERYONE INTO THE FARMHOUSE!
MY SPIDER-SENSE IS PICKING IT UP ALSO.
SPIDER WHAT?
MOVE IT!
WHY DO YOU THINK THINGS WILL BE SAFE INSIDE THE HOUSE, GENIS?
I'M NOT SURE, RICK...
I JUST DO!
WE'RE ABOUT TO EXPERIENCE A MUCH LARGER DISTURBANCE THAN THE ONE THAT IMPRISONED THOSE ALIENS EARLIER.
HOW BAD'S THE NEWS, MARVEL?
BIGGER?
HOW MUCH BIGGER?
MY COSMIC SENSES WARN ME THAT WE ARE AT THE FOCAL POINT OF SOME MAJOR COSMIC EVENT.
MEANING WHAT?
I'M NOT SURE.
YOU COSMIC TYPES ARE ALWAYS A LITTLE SHY ON SPECIFICS, AREN'T YOU?
WE TRY.

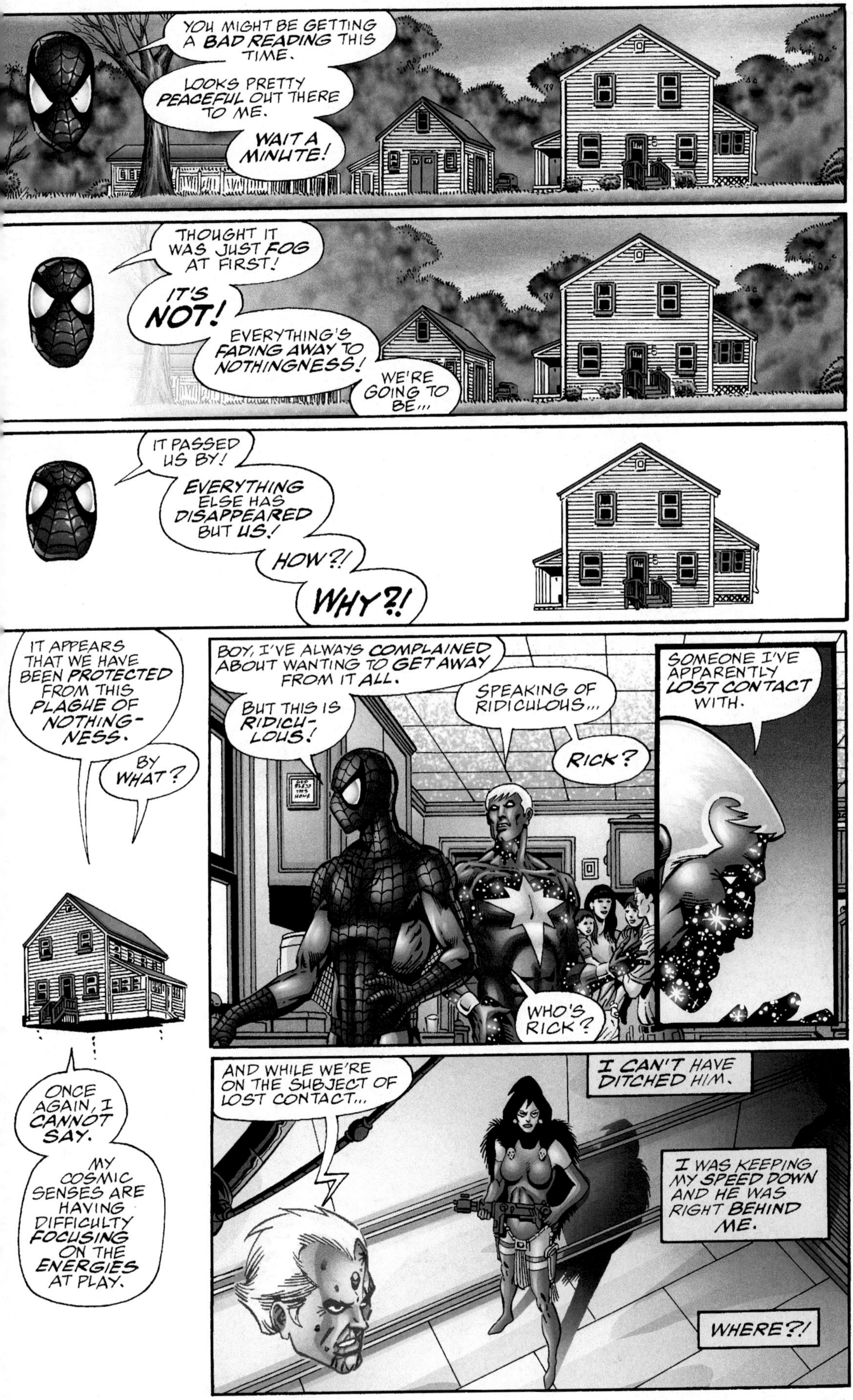

YOU MIGHT BE GETTING A BAD READING THIS TIME.
LOOKS PRETTY PEACEFUL OUT THERE TO ME.
WAIT A MINUTE!
THOUGHT IT WAS JUST FOG AT FIRST!
IT'S NOT!
EVERYTHING'S FADING AWAY TO NOTHINGNESS!
WE'RE GOING TO BE...
IT PASSED US BY!
EVERYTHING ELSE HAS DISAPPEARED BUT US!
HOW?!
WHY?!
IT APPEARS THAT WE HAVE BEEN PROTECTED FROM THIS PLAGUE OF NOTHING-NESS.
BY WHAT?
ONCE AGAIN, I CANNOT SAY.
MY COSMIC SENSES ARE HAVING DIFFICULTY FOCUSING ON THE ENERGIES AT PLAY.
BOY, I'VE ALWAYS COMPLAINED ABOUT WANTING TO GET AWAY FROM IT ALL.
BUT THIS IS RIDICU-LOUS!
SPEAKING OF RIDICULOUS...
RICK?
WHO'S RICK?
SOMEONE I'VE APPARENTLY LOST CONTACT WITH.
AND WHILE WE'RE ON THE SUBJECT OF LOST CONTACT...
I CAN'T HAVE DITCHED HIM.
I WAS KEEPING MY SPEED DOWN AND HE WAS RIGHT BEHIND ME.
WHERE?!

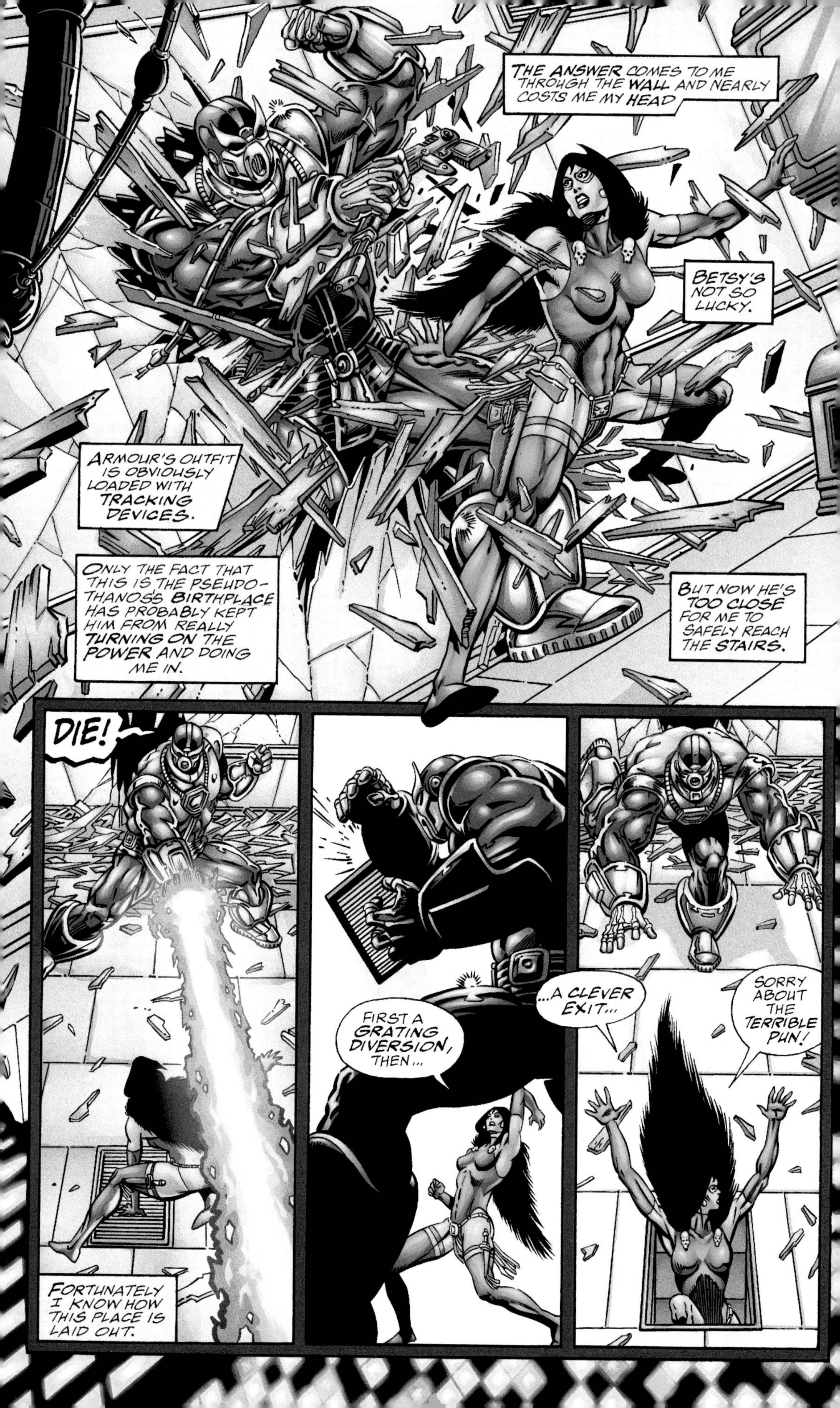

THE ANSWER COMES TO ME THROUGH THE WALL AND NEARLY COSTS ME MY HEAD
BETSY'S NOT SO LUCKY.
ARMOUR'S OUTFIT IS OBVIOUSLY LOADED WITH TRACKING DEVICES.
ONLY THE FACT THAT THIS IS THE PSEUDO-THANOS'S BIRTHPLACE HAS PROBABLY KEPT HIM FROM REALLY TURNING ON THE POWER AND DOING ME IN.
BUT NOW HE'S TOO CLOSE FOR ME TO SAFELY REACH THE STAIRS.
DIE!
FORTUNATELY I KNOW HOW THIS PLACE IS LAID OUT.
FIRST A GRATING DIVERSION, THEN...
...A CLEVER EXIT...
SORRY ABOUT THE TERRIBLE PUN!

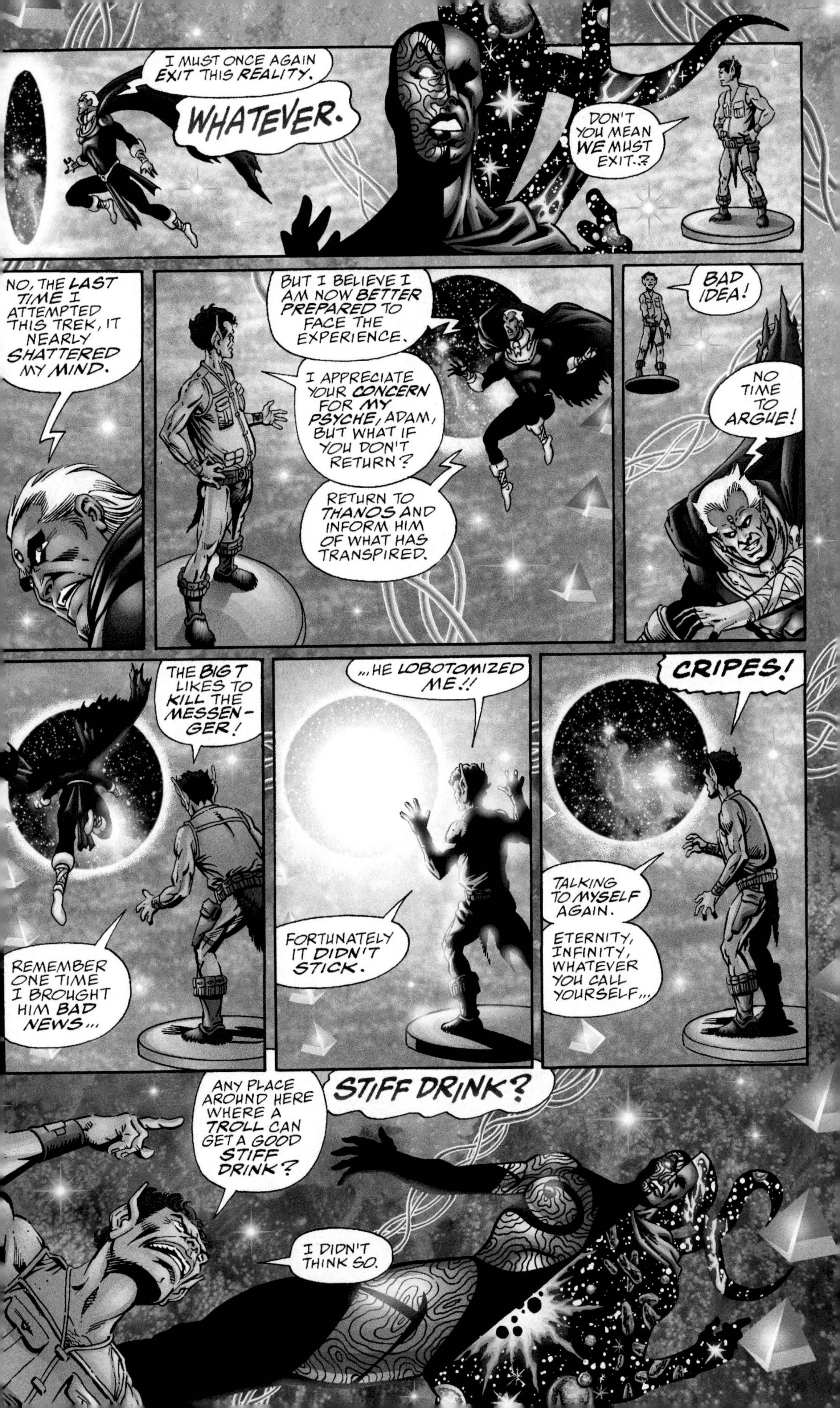
I MUST ONCE AGAIN EXIT THIS REALITY.
WHATEVER.
DON'T YOU MEAN WE MUST EXIT..?
NO, THE LAST TIME I ATTEMPTED THIS TREK, IT NEARLY SHATTERED MY MIND.
BUT I BELIEVE I AM NOW BETTER PREPARED TO FACE THE EXPERIENCE.
I APPRECIATE YOUR CONCERN FOR MY PSYCHE, ADAM, BUT WHAT IF YOU DON'T RETURN?
RETURN TO THANOS AND INFORM HIM OF WHAT HAS TRANSPIRED.
BAD IDEA!
NO TIME TO ARGUE!
THE BIG T LIKES TO KILL THE MESSENGER!
REMEMBER ONE TIME I BROUGHT HIM BAD NEWS...
...HE LOBOTOMIZED ME!!
FORTUNATELY IT DIDN'T STICK.
CRIPES!
TALKING TO MYSELF AGAIN.
ETERNITY, INFINITY, WHATEVER YOU CALL YOURSELF...
ANY PLACE AROUND HERE WHERE A TROLL CAN GET A GOOD STIFF DRINK?
STIFF DRINK?
I DIDN'T THINK SO.

ESCAPING THEIR *CURRENT* SITUATION SEEMED THE MOST APPROPRIATE *NEXT STEP* TO SPIDER-MAN AND CAPTAIN MARVEL.

AND SEEING HOW THE WEB-SLINGER WAS *INCAPABLE* OF FLIGHT...

...AND I'LL RETURN ONCE I'VE CONTACTED THE *AVENGERS*.

THE *FANTASTIC FOUR* MIGHT BE A BETTER BET.

RICHARDS HAS TONS OF EXPERIENCE WITH *INTER-DIMENSIONAL WEIRDNESS.*

MEANWHILE I'LL MAKE MYSELF *USEFUL* BY ENTERTAINING THE KIDS WITH SOME *WEB TRICKS.*

SPIDER-MAN, BETTER THAN A FOR-HIRE *PARTY CLOWN.*

MAYBE I CAN--

HUH?!

THAT CLEARLY *DIDN'T* WORK OUT SO WELL.

THE OL' *MOBIUS STRIP* DILEMMA?

OR MAYBE OUR PRISON IS *SPHERICAL.*

OR PERHAPS SOME VERY BASIC *LAWS OF PHYSICS* DON'T APPLY IN THIS VOID.

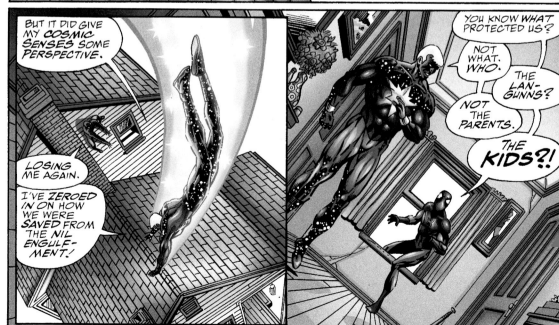

BUT IT DID GIVE MY *COSMIC SENSES* SOME PERSPECTIVE.

LOSING ME AGAIN.

I'VE ZEROED IN ON HOW WE WERE *SAVED* FROM THE NIL ENGULF-MENT!

YOU KNOW *WHAT* PROTECTED US?

NOT WHAT. *WHO.*

THE *LAN-GUNNS?*

NOT THE PARENTS.

THE KIDS?!

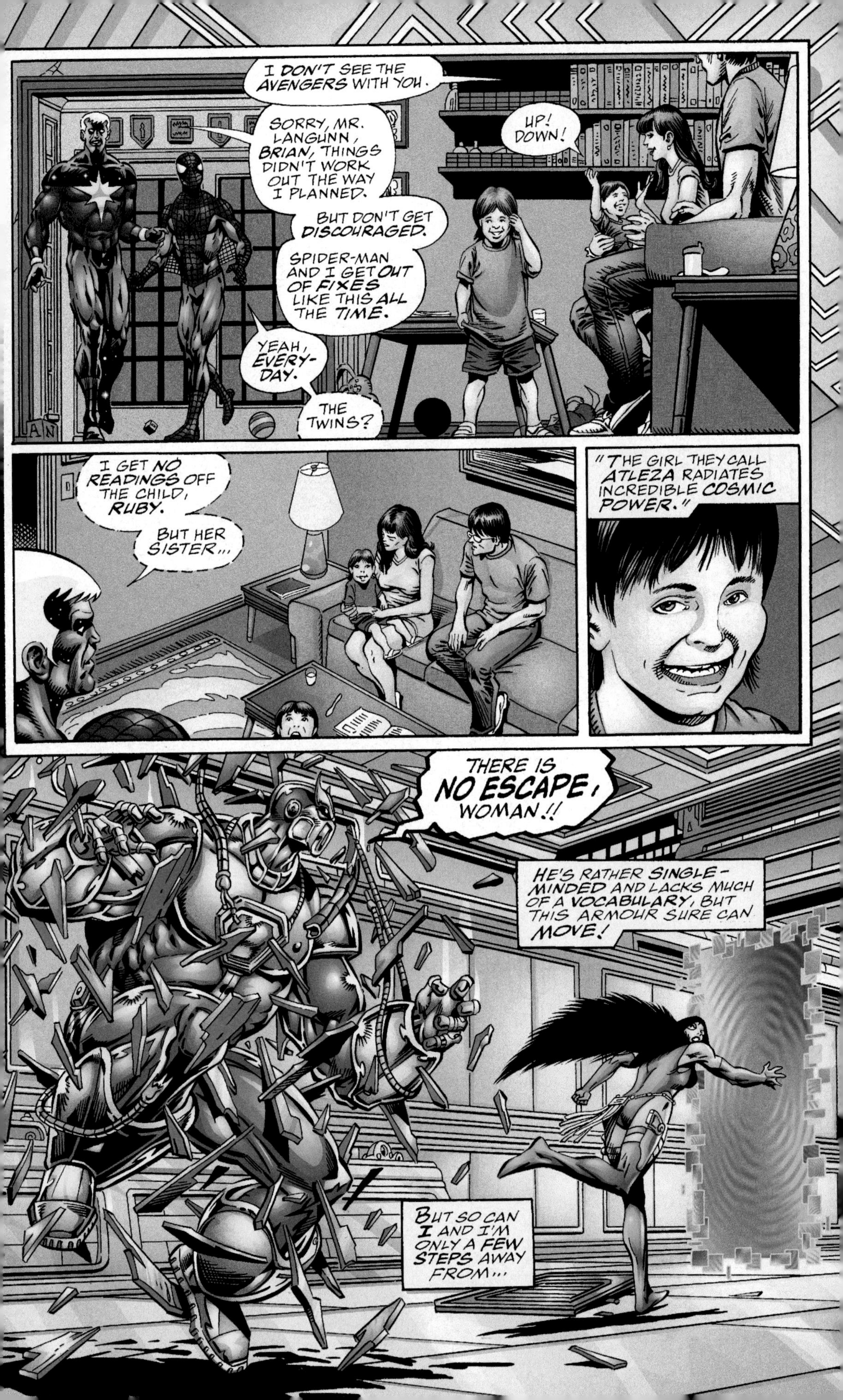

I DON'T SEE THE AVENGERS WITH YOU.
SORRY, MR. LANGUNN, BRIAN, THINGS DIDN'T WORK OUT THE WAY I PLANNED.
UP! DOWN!
BUT DON'T GET DISCOURAGED.
SPIDER-MAN AND I GET OUT OF FIXES LIKE THIS ALL THE TIME.
YEAH, EVERY-DAY.
THE TWINS?
I GET NO READINGS OFF THE CHILD, RUBY.
BUT HER SISTER...
"THE GIRL THEY CALL ATLEZA RADIATES INCREDIBLE COSMIC POWER."
THERE IS NO ESCAPE, WOMAN!!
HE'S RATHER SINGLE-MINDED AND LACKS MUCH OF A VOCABULARY, BUT THIS ARMOUR SURE CAN MOVE!
BUT SO CAN I AND I'M ONLY A FEW STEPS AWAY FROM...

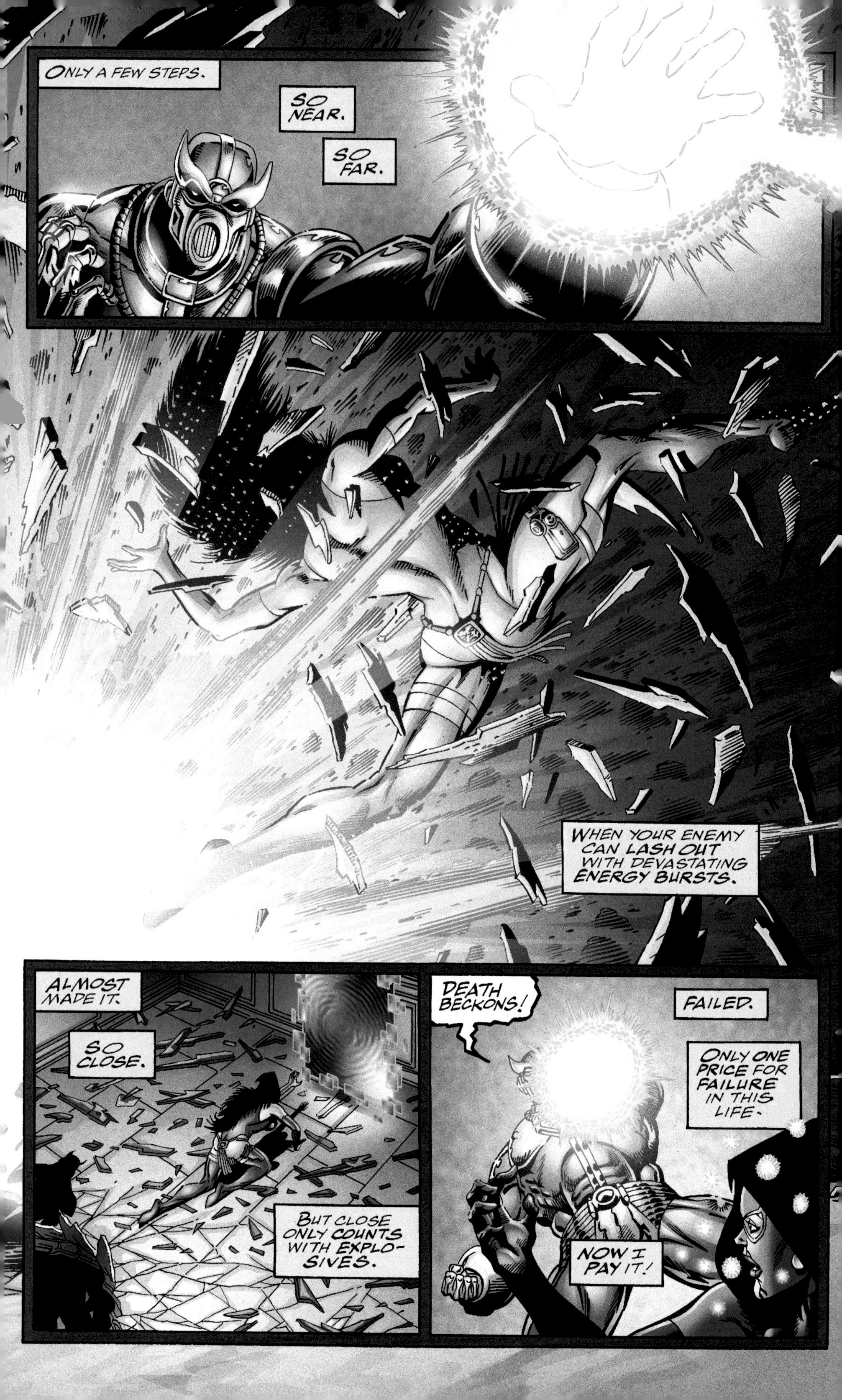
ONLY A FEW STEPS.
SO NEAR.
SO FAR.
WHEN YOUR ENEMY CAN LASH OUT WITH DEVASTATING ENERGY BURSTS.
ALMOST MADE IT.
SO CLOSE.
BUT CLOSE ONLY COUNTS WITH EXPLOSIVES.
DEATH BECKONS!
FAILED.
ONLY ONE PRICE FOR FAILURE IN THIS LIFE.
NOW I PAY IT!

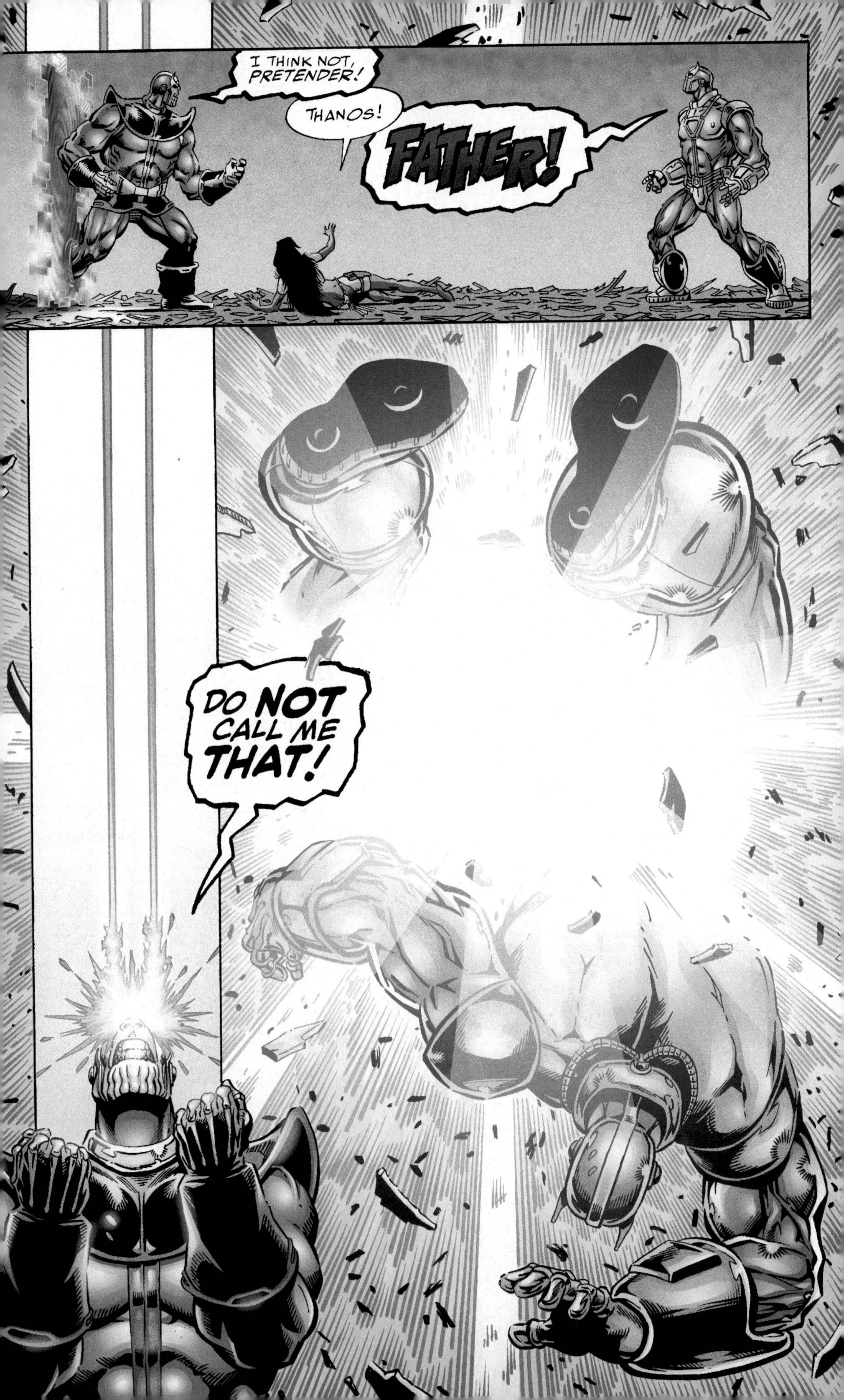
I THINK NOT, PRETENDER!
THANOS!
FATHER!
DO NOT CALL ME THAT!

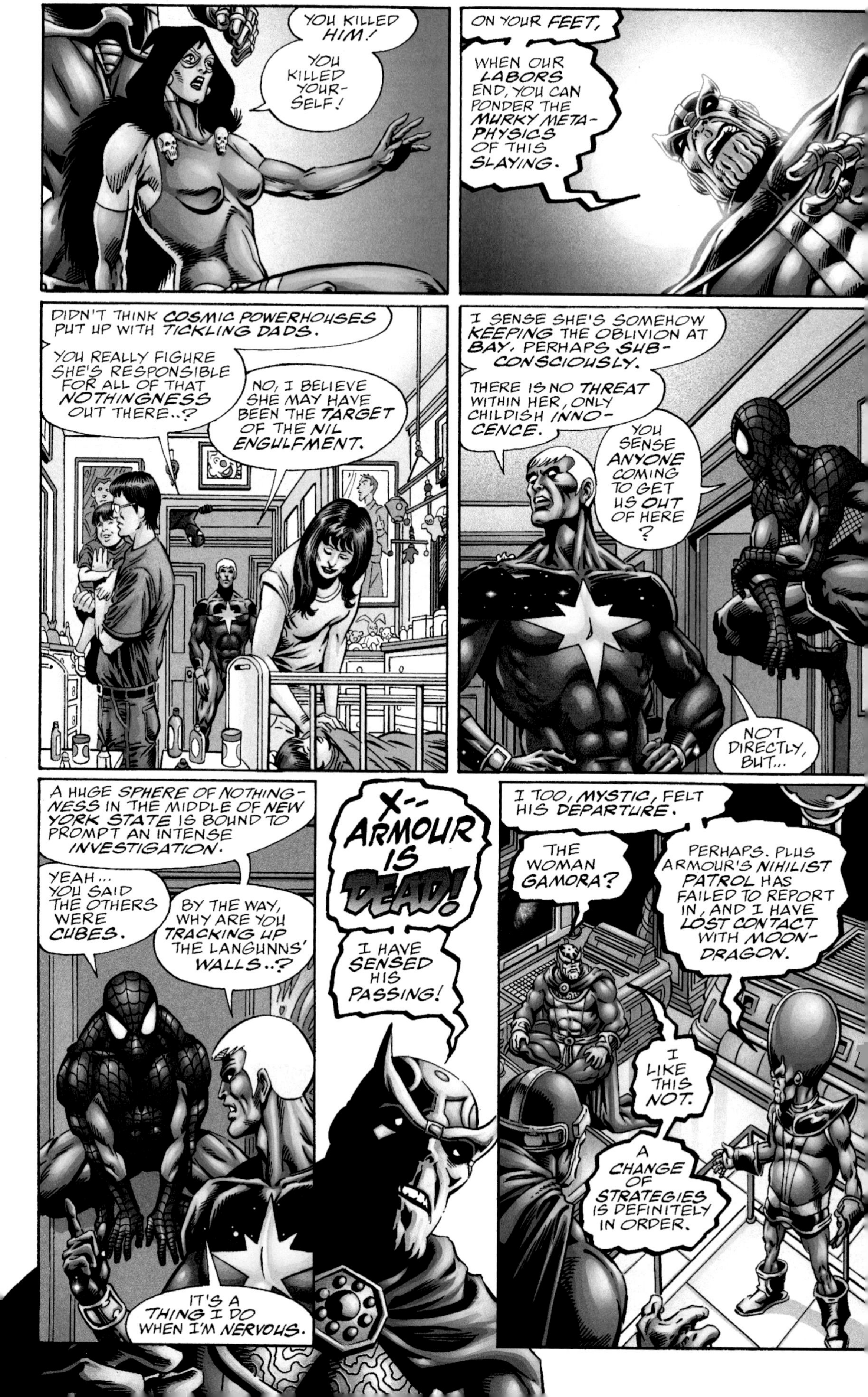

YOU KILLED HIM!
YOU KILLED YOURSELF!
ON YOUR FEET,
WHEN OUR LABORS END, YOU CAN PONDER THE MURKY METAPHYSICS OF THIS SLAYING.
DIDN'T THINK COSMIC POWERHOUSES PUT UP WITH TICKLING DADS.
YOU REALLY FIGURE SHE'S RESPONSIBLE FOR ALL OF THAT NOTHINGNESS OUT THERE..?
NO, I BELIEVE SHE MAY HAVE BEEN THE TARGET OF THE NIL ENGULFMENT.
I SENSE SHE'S SOMEHOW KEEPING THE OBLIVION AT BAY. PERHAPS SUBCONSCIOUSLY.
THERE IS NO THREAT WITHIN HER, ONLY CHILDISH INNOCENCE.
YOU SENSE ANYONE COMING TO GET US OUT OF HERE?
NOT DIRECTLY, BUT...
A HUGE SPHERE OF NOTHINGNESS IN THE MIDDLE OF NEW YORK STATE IS BOUND TO PROMPT AN INTENSE INVESTIGATION.
YEAH... YOU SAID THE OTHERS WERE CUBES.
BY THE WAY, WHY ARE YOU TRACKING UP THE LANGUNNS' WALLS..?
IT'S A THING I DO WHEN I'M NERVOUS.
X-- ARMOUR IS DEAD!
I HAVE SENSED HIS PASSING!
I TOO, MYSTIC, FELT HIS DEPARTURE.
THE WOMAN GAMORA?
PERHAPS. PLUS ARMOUR'S NIHILIST PATROL HAS FAILED TO REPORT IN, AND I HAVE LOST CONTACT WITH MOONDRAGON.
I LIKE THIS NOT.
A CHANGE OF STRATEGIES IS DEFINITELY IN ORDER.

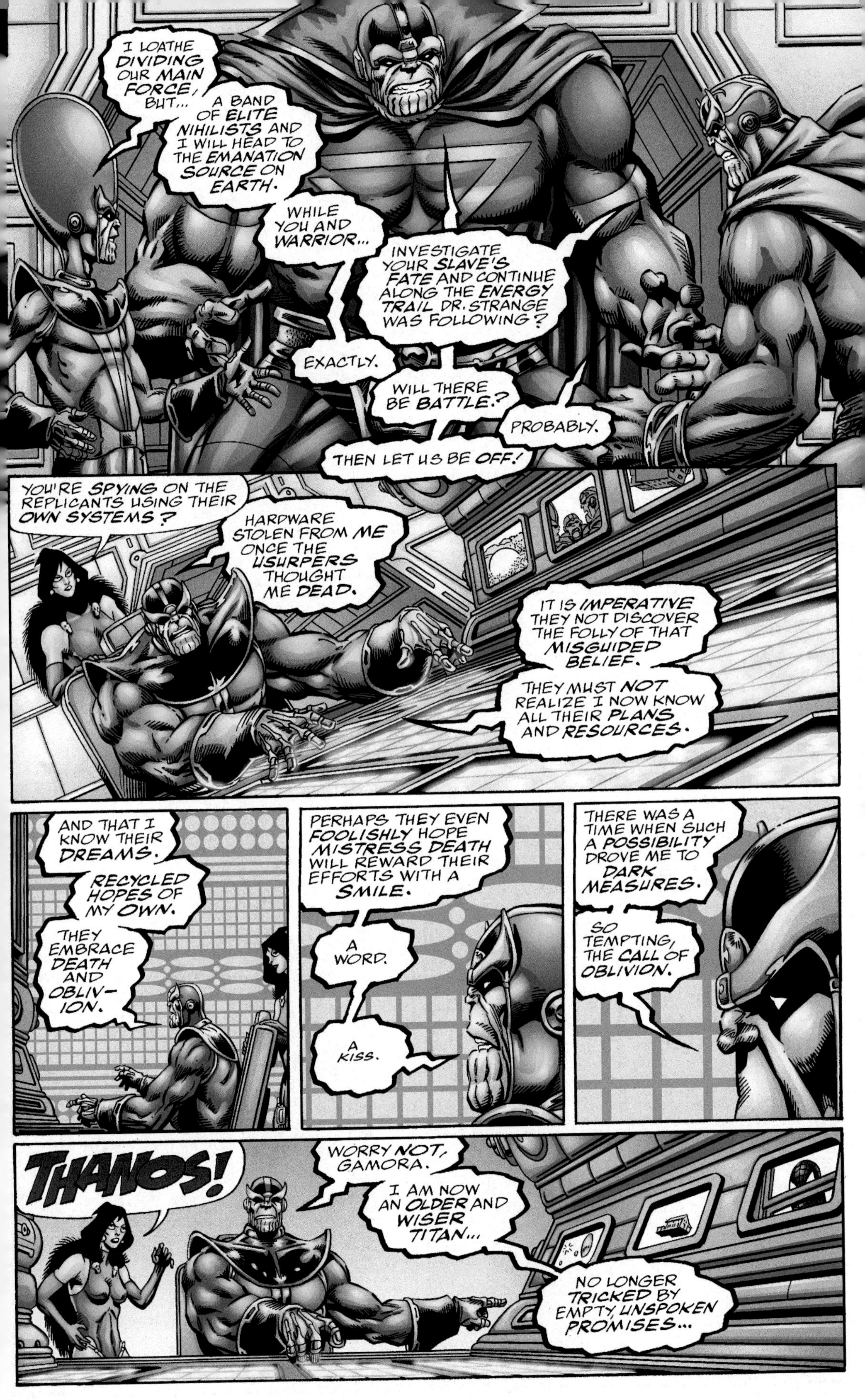
I LOATHE DIVIDING OUR MAIN FORCE, BUT...
A BAND OF ELITE NIHILISTS AND I WILL HEAD TO THE EMANATION SOURCE ON EARTH.
WHILE YOU AND WARRIOR...
INVESTIGATE YOUR SLAVE'S FATE AND CONTINUE ALONG THE ENERGY TRAIL DR. STRANGE WAS FOLLOWING?
EXACTLY.
WILL THERE BE BATTLE?
PROBABLY.
THEN LET US BE OFF!
YOU'RE SPYING ON THE REPLICANTS USING THEIR OWN SYSTEMS?
HARDWARE STOLEN FROM ME ONCE THE USURPERS THOUGHT ME DEAD.
IT IS IMPERATIVE THEY NOT DISCOVER THE FOLLY OF THAT MISGUIDED BELIEF.
THEY MUST NOT REALIZE I NOW KNOW ALL THEIR PLANS AND RESOURCES.
AND THAT I KNOW THEIR DREAMS.
RECYCLED HOPES OF MY OWN.
THEY EMBRACE DEATH AND OBLIV-ION.
PERHAPS THEY EVEN FOOLISHLY HOPE MISTRESS DEATH WILL REWARD THEIR EFFORTS WITH A SMILE.
A WORD.
A KISS.
THERE WAS A TIME WHEN SUCH A POSSIBILITY DROVE ME TO DARK MEASURES.
SO TEMPTING, THE CALL OF OBLIVION.
THANOS!
WORRY NOT, GAMORA.
I AM NOW AN OLDER AND WISER TITAN...
NO LONGER TRICKED BY EMPTY, UNSPOKEN PROMISES...

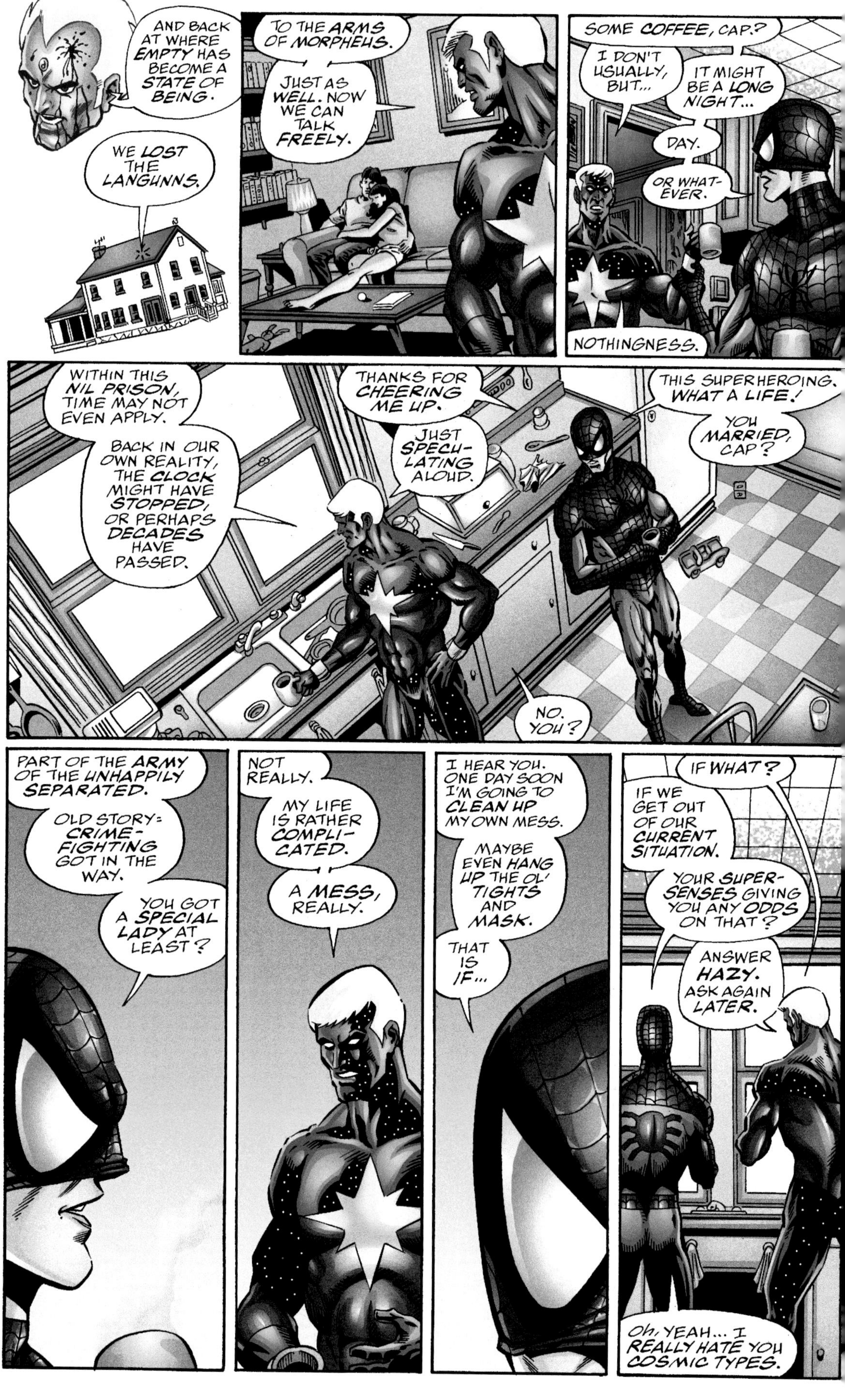
AND BACK AT WHERE EMPTY HAS BECOME A STATE OF BEING.
WE LOST THE LANGUNNS.
TO THE ARMS OF MORPHEUS.
JUST AS WELL. NOW WE CAN TALK FREELY.
SOME COFFEE, CAP?
I DON'T USUALLY, BUT...
IT MIGHT BE A LONG NIGHT...
DAY.
OR WHAT-EVER.
NOTHINGNESS.
WITHIN THIS NIL PRISON, TIME MAY NOT EVEN APPLY.
BACK IN OUR OWN REALITY, THE CLOCK MIGHT HAVE STOPPED, OR PERHAPS DECADES HAVE PASSED.
THANKS FOR CHEERING ME UP.
JUST SPECU-LATING ALOUD.
THIS SUPERHEROING. WHAT A LIFE!
YOU MARRIED, CAP?
NO. YOU?
PART OF THE ARMY OF THE UNHAPPILY SEPARATED.
OLD STORY: CRIME-FIGHTING GOT IN THE WAY.
YOU GOT A SPECIAL LADY AT LEAST?
NOT REALLY.
MY LIFE IS RATHER COMPLI-CATED.
A MESS, REALLY.
I HEAR YOU. ONE DAY SOON I'M GOING TO CLEAN UP MY OWN MESS.
MAYBE EVEN HANG UP THE OL' TIGHTS AND MASK.
THAT IS IF...
IF WHAT?
IF WE GET OUT OF OUR CURRENT SITUATION.
YOUR SUPER-SENSES GIVING YOU ANY ODDS ON THAT?
ANSWER HAZY. ASK AGAIN LATER.
Oh, YEAH... I REALLY HATE YOU COSMIC TYPES.

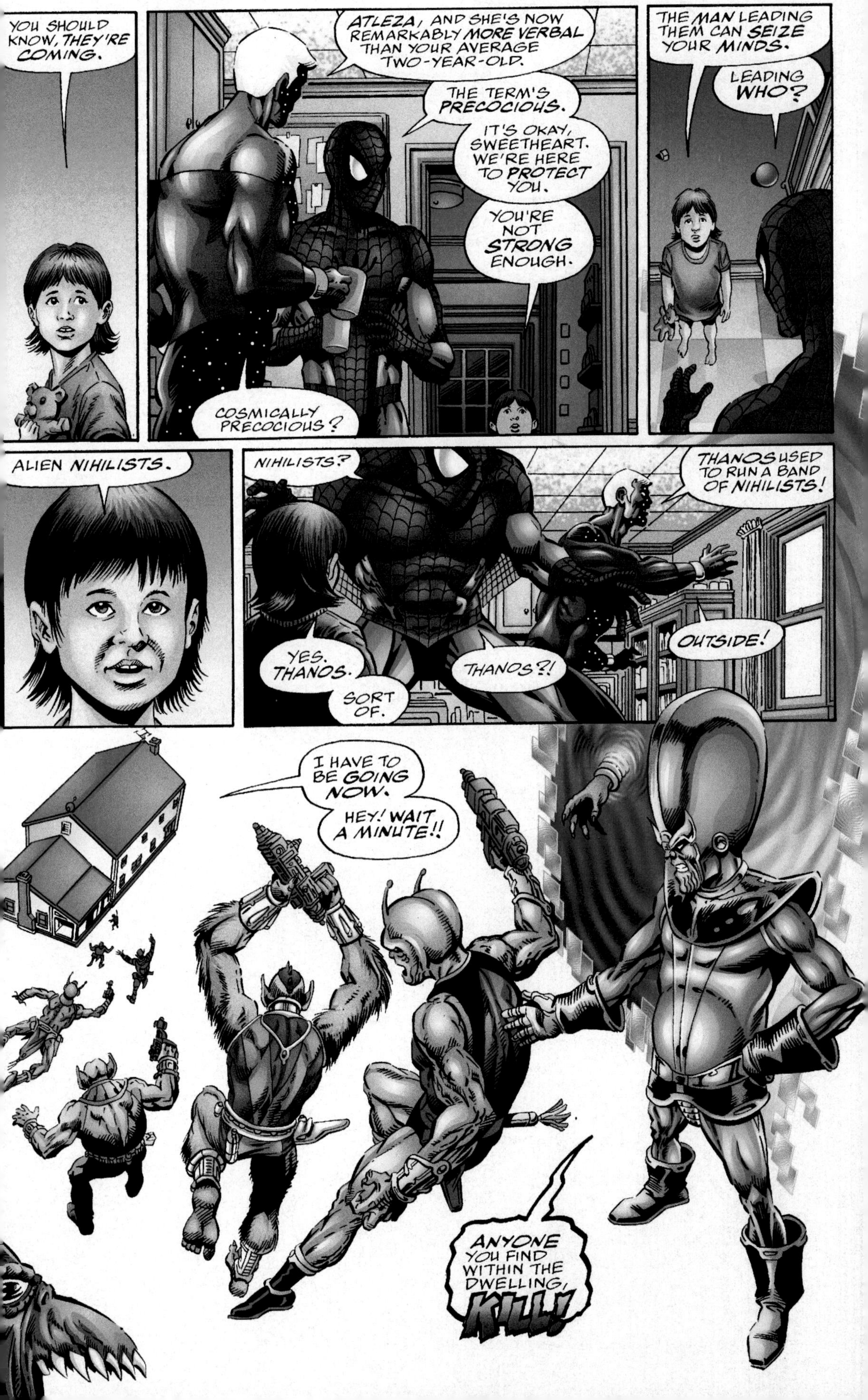
YOU SHOULD KNOW, THEY'RE COMING.
ATLEZA, AND SHE'S NOW REMARKABLY MORE VERBAL THAN YOUR AVERAGE TWO-YEAR-OLD.
THE TERM'S PRECOCIOUS.
IT'S OKAY, SWEETHEART. WE'RE HERE TO PROTECT YOU.
YOU'RE NOT STRONG ENOUGH.
COSMICALLY PRECOCIOUS?
THE MAN LEADING THEM CAN SEIZE YOUR MINDS.
LEADING WHO?
ALIEN NIHILISTS.
NIHILISTS?
THANOS USED TO RUN A BAND OF NIHILISTS!
YES. THANOS.
SORT OF.
THANOS?!
OUTSIDE!
I HAVE TO BE GOING NOW.
HEY! WAIT A MINUTE!!
ANYONE YOU FIND WITHIN THE DWELLING, KILL!

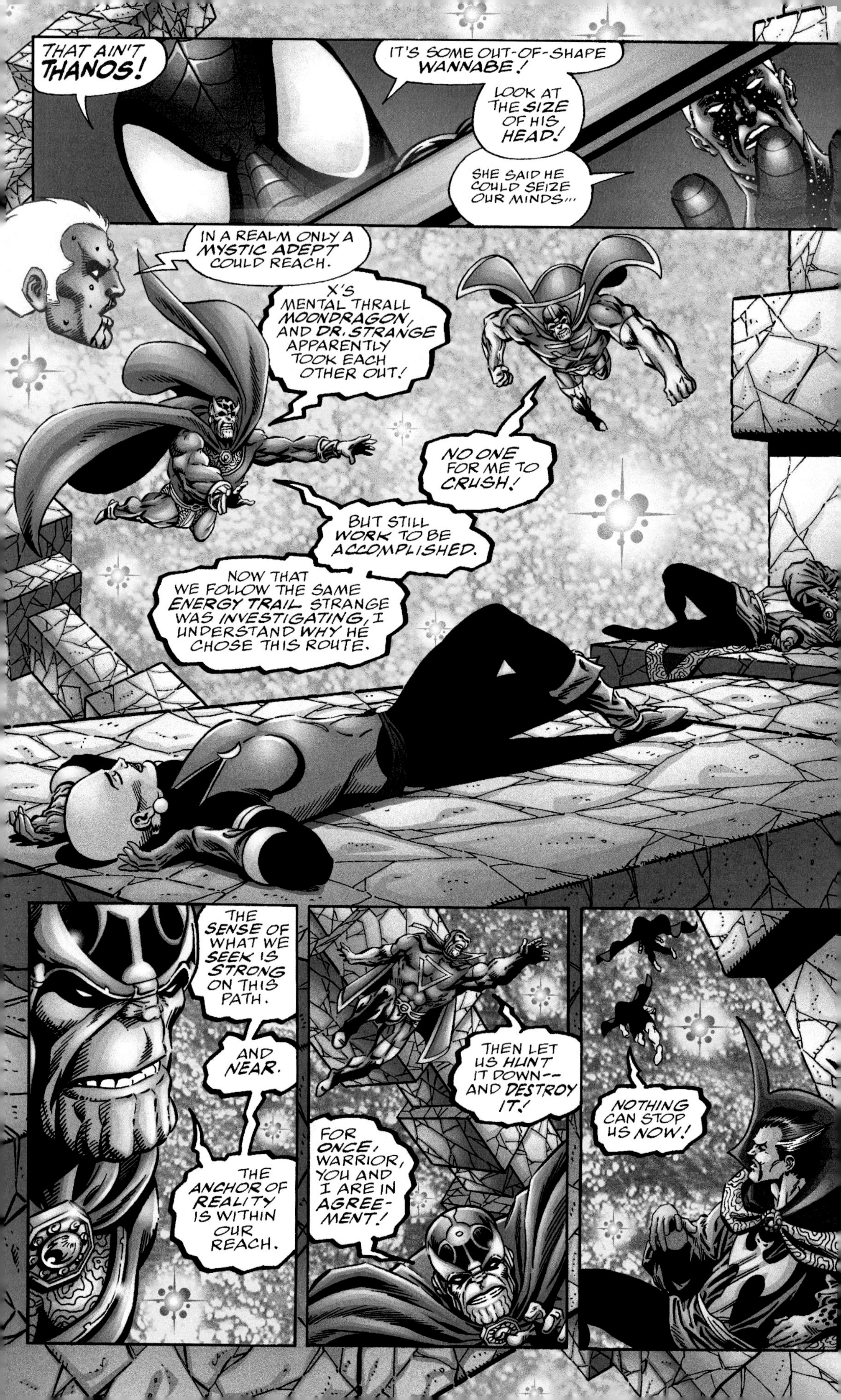
THAT AIN'T THANOS!
IT'S SOME OUT-OF-SHAPE WANNABE!
LOOK AT THE SIZE OF HIS HEAD!
SHE SAID HE COULD SEIZE OUR MINDS...
IN A REALM ONLY A MYSTIC ADEPT COULD REACH.
X'S MENTAL THRALL MOONDRAGON, AND DR. STRANGE APPARENTLY TOOK EACH OTHER OUT!
NO ONE FOR ME TO CRUSH!
BUT STILL WORK TO BE ACCOMPLISHED.
NOW THAT WE FOLLOW THE SAME ENERGY TRAIL STRANGE WAS INVESTIGATING, I UNDERSTAND WHY HE CHOSE THIS ROUTE.
THE SENSE OF WHAT WE SEEK IS STRONG ON THIS PATH.
AND NEAR.
THE ANCHOR OF REALITY IS WITHIN OUR REACH.
THEN LET US HUNT IT DOWN-- AND DESTROY IT!
FOR ONCE, WARRIOR, YOU AND I ARE IN AGREE-MENT!
NOTHING CAN STOP US NOW!

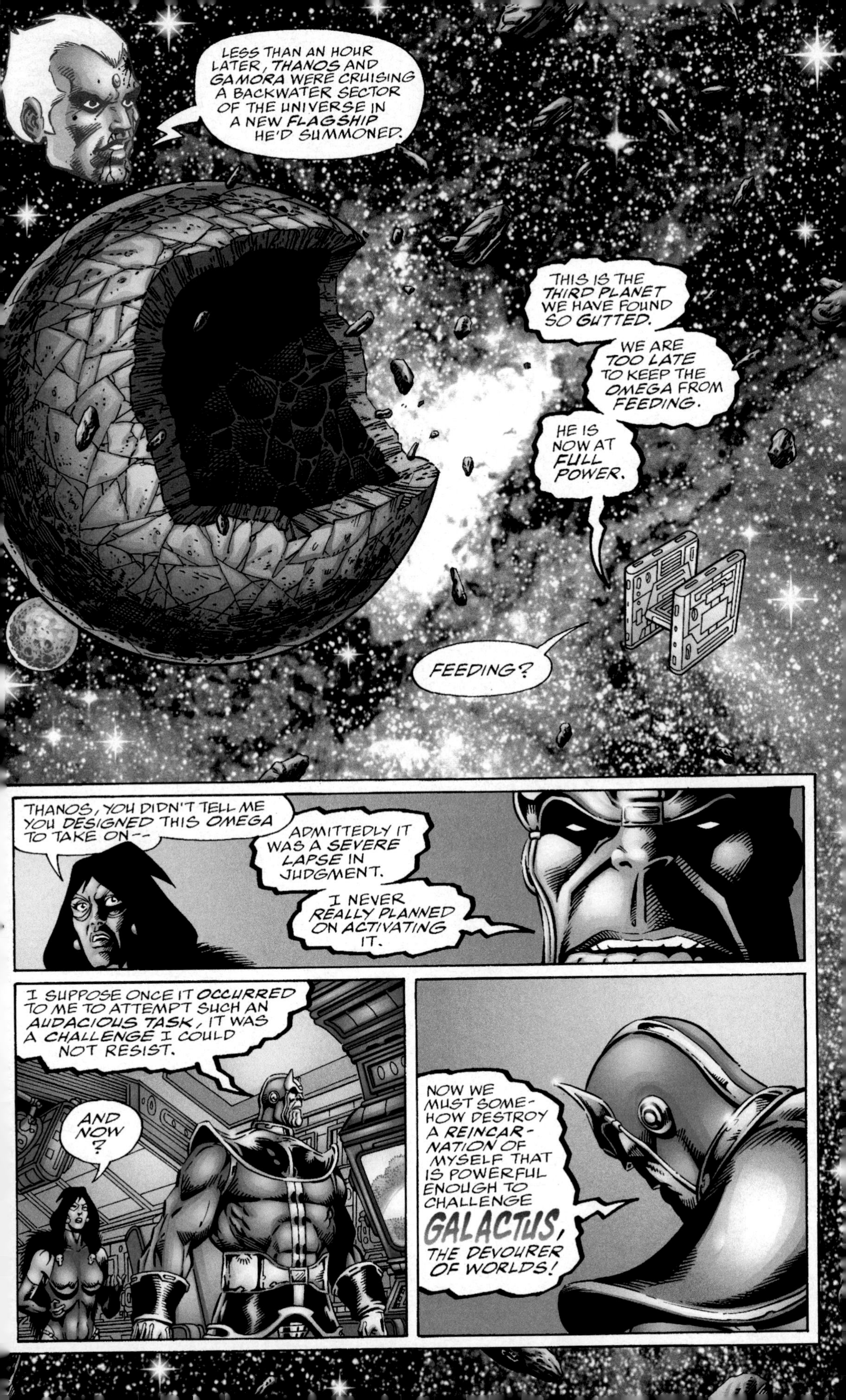
LESS THAN AN HOUR LATER, THANOS AND GAMORA WERE CRUISING A BACKWATER SECTOR OF THE UNIVERSE IN A NEW FLAGSHIP HE'D SUMMONED.
THIS IS THE THIRD PLANET WE HAVE FOUND SO GUTTED.
WE ARE TOO LATE TO KEEP THE OMEGA FROM FEEDING.
HE IS NOW AT FULL POWER.
FEEDING?
THANOS, YOU DIDN'T TELL ME YOU DESIGNED THIS OMEGA TO TAKE ON--
ADMITTEDLY IT WAS A SEVERE LAPSE IN JUDGMENT.
I NEVER REALLY PLANNED ON ACTIVATING IT.
I SUPPOSE ONCE IT OCCURRED TO ME TO ATTEMPT SUCH AN AUDACIOUS TASK, IT WAS A CHALLENGE I COULD NOT RESIST.
AND NOW?
NOW WE MUST SOMEHOW DESTROY A REINCARNATION OF MYSELF THAT IS POWERFUL ENOUGH TO CHALLENGE GALACTUS, THE DEVOURER OF WORLDS!

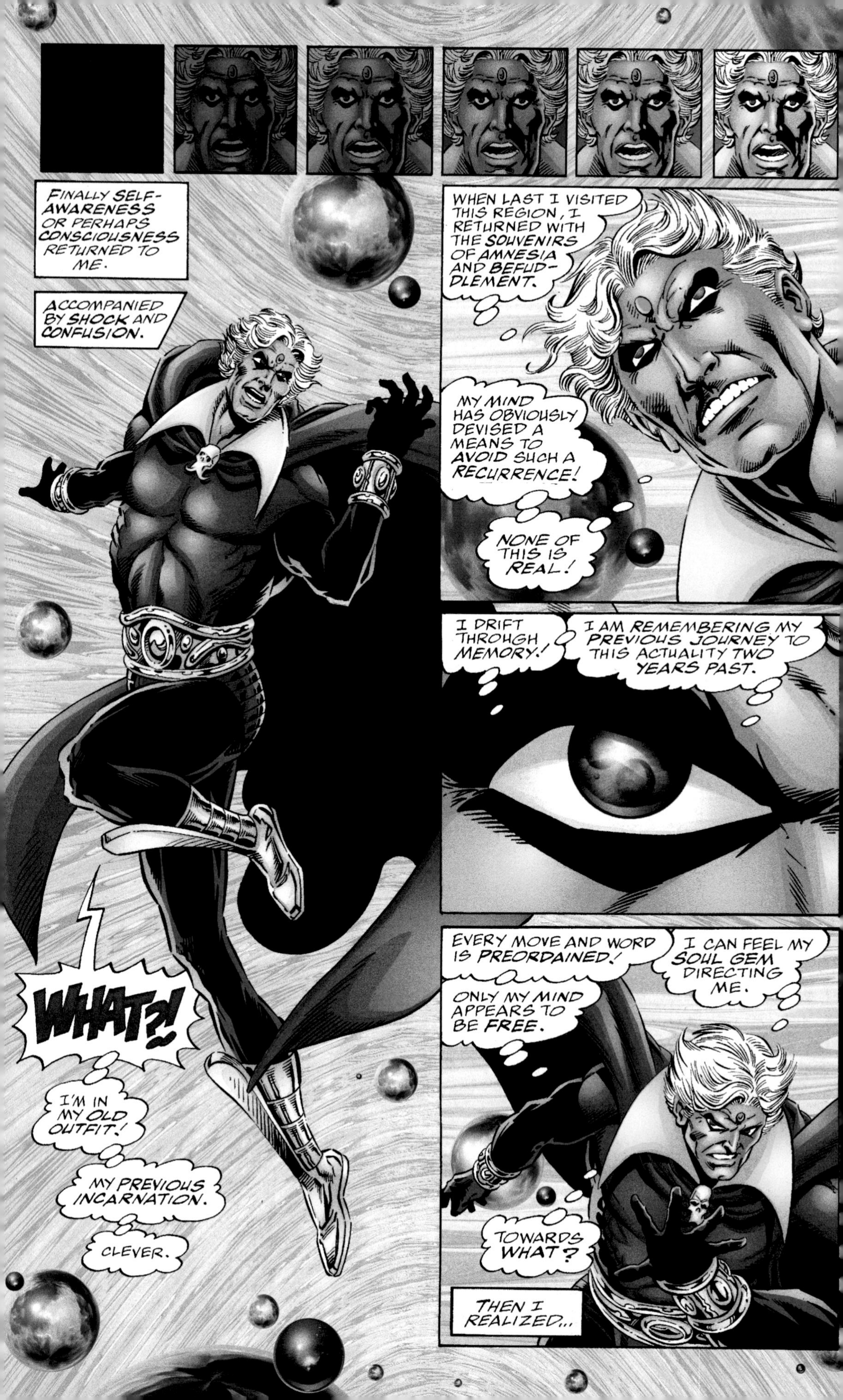
FINALLY SELF-AWARENESS OR PERHAPS CONSCIOUSNESS RETURNED TO ME.
ACCOMPANIED BY SHOCK AND CONFUSION.
WHAT?!
I'M IN MY OLD OUTFIT!
MY PREVIOUS INCARNATION.
CLEVER.
WHEN LAST I VISITED THIS REGION, I RETURNED WITH THE SOUVENIRS OF AMNESIA AND BEFUDDLEMENT.
MY MIND HAS OBVIOUSLY DEVISED A MEANS TO AVOID SUCH A RECURRENCE!
NONE OF THIS IS REAL!
I DRIFT THROUGH MEMORY!
I AM REMEMBERING MY PREVIOUS JOURNEY TO THIS ACTUALITY TWO YEARS PAST.
EVERY MOVE AND WORD IS PREORDAINED!
ONLY MY MIND APPEARS TO BE FREE.
I CAN FEEL MY SOUL GEM DIRECTING ME.
TOWARDS WHAT?
THEN I REALIZED...

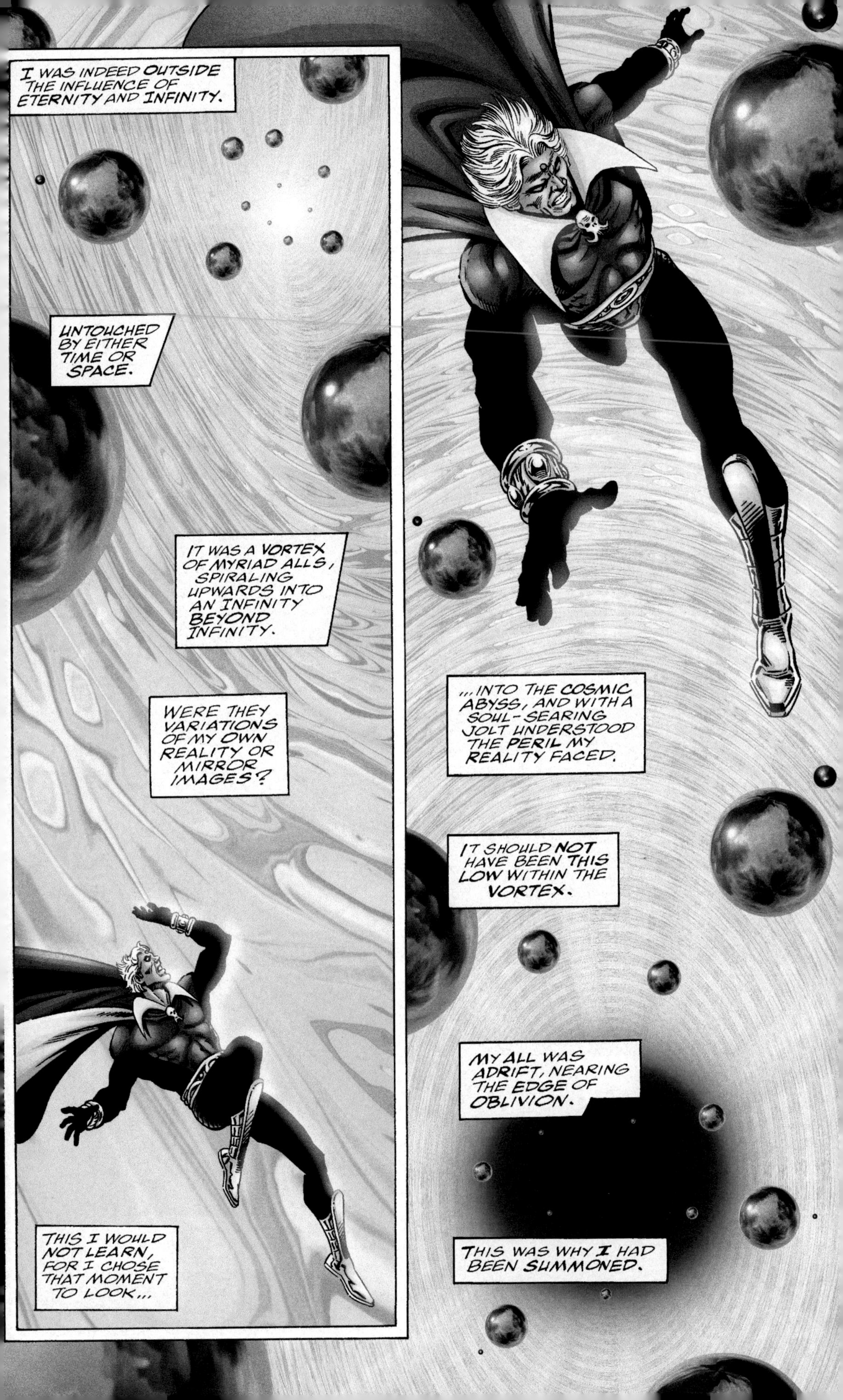
I WAS INDEED OUTSIDE THE INFLUENCE OF ETERNITY AND INFINITY.
UNTOUCHED BY EITHER TIME OR SPACE.
IT WAS A VORTEX OF MYRIAD ALLS, SPIRALING UPWARDS INTO AN INFINITY BEYOND INFINITY.
WERE THEY VARIATIONS OF MY OWN REALITY OR MIRROR IMAGES?
THIS I WOULD NOT LEARN, FOR I CHOSE THAT MOMENT TO LOOK...
...INTO THE COSMIC ABYSS, AND WITH A SOUL-SEARING JOLT UNDERSTOOD THE PERIL MY REALITY FACED.
IT SHOULD NOT HAVE BEEN THIS LOW WITHIN THE VORTEX.
MY ALL WAS ADRIFT, NEARING THE EDGE OF OBLIVION.
THIS WAS WHY I HAD BEEN SUMMONED.

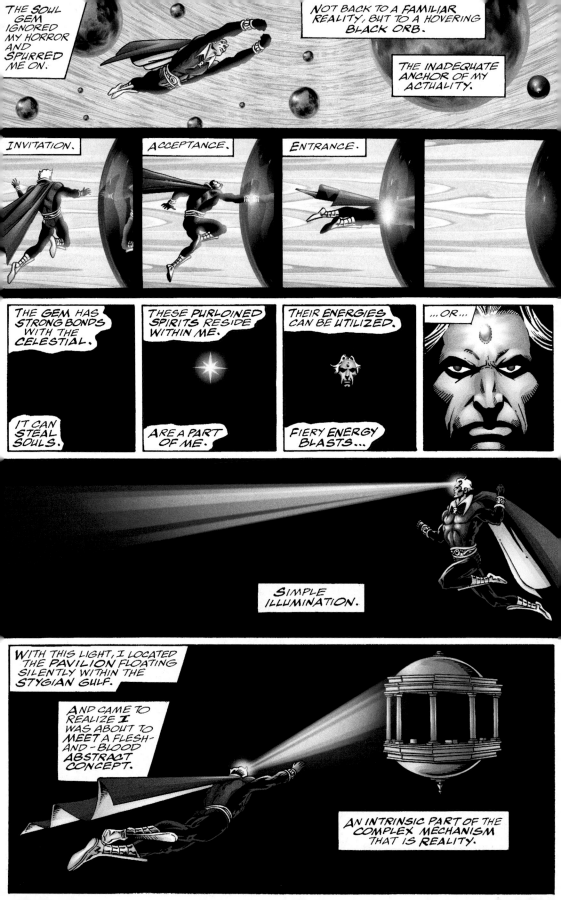

THE SOUL GEM IGNORED MY HORROR AND SPURRED ME ON.

NOT BACK TO A FAMILIAR REALITY, BUT TO A HOVERING BLACK ORB.

THE INADEQUATE ANCHOR OF MY ACTUALITY.

INVITATION.

ACCEPTANCE.

ENTRANCE.

THE GEM HAS STRONG BONDS WITH THE CELESTIAL.

IT CAN STEAL SOULS.

THESE PURLOINED SPIRITS RESIDE WITHIN ME.

ARE A PART OF ME.

THEIR ENERGIES CAN BE UTILIZED.

FIERY ENERGY BLASTS...

...OR...

SIMPLE ILLUMINATION.

WITH THIS LIGHT, I LOCATED THE PAVILION FLOATING SILENTLY WITHIN THE STYGIAN GULF.

AND CAME TO REALIZE I WAS ABOUT TO MEET A FLESH-AND-BLOOD ABSTRACT CONCEPT.

AN INTRINSIC PART OF THE COMPLEX MECHANISM THAT IS REALITY.

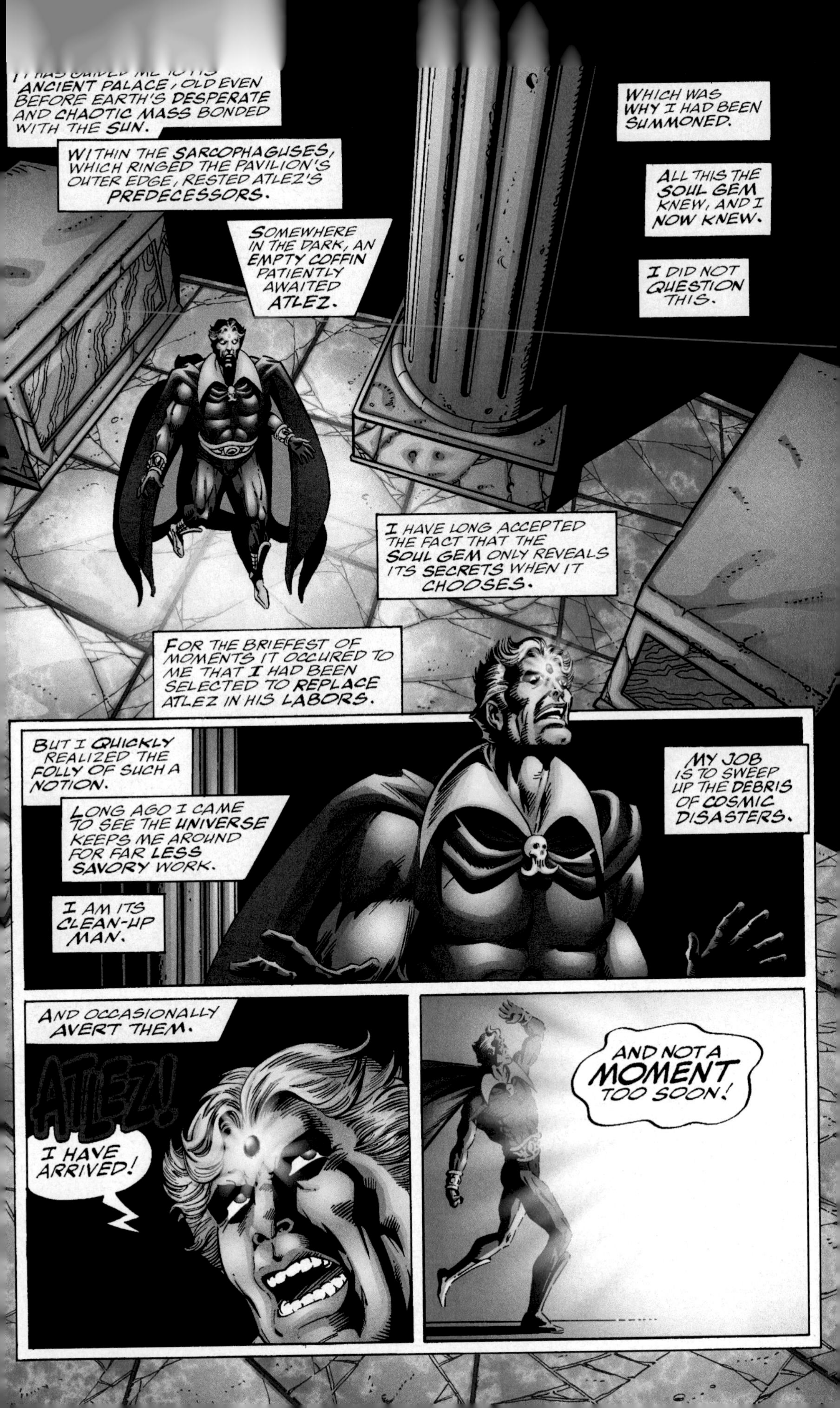

ANCIENT PALACE, OLD EVEN BEFORE EARTH'S DESPERATE AND CHAOTIC MASS BONDED WITH THE SUN.
WITHIN THE SARCOPHAGUSES, WHICH RINGED THE PAVILION'S OUTER EDGE, RESTED ATLEZ'S PREDECESSORS.
SOMEWHERE IN THE DARK, AN EMPTY COFFIN PATIENTLY AWAITED ATLEZ.
WHICH WAS WHY I HAD BEEN SUMMONED.
ALL THIS THE SOUL GEM KNEW, AND I NOW KNEW.
I DID NOT QUESTION THIS.
I HAVE LONG ACCEPTED THE FACT THAT THE SOUL GEM ONLY REVEALS ITS SECRETS WHEN IT CHOOSES.
FOR THE BRIEFEST OF MOMENTS IT OCCURED TO ME THAT I HAD BEEN SELECTED TO REPLACE ATLEZ IN HIS LABORS.
BUT I QUICKLY REALIZED THE FOLLY OF SUCH A NOTION.
LONG AGO I CAME TO SEE THE UNIVERSE KEEPS ME AROUND FOR FAR LESS SAVORY WORK.
I AM ITS CLEAN-UP MAN.
MY JOB IS TO SWEEP UP THE DEBRIS OF COSMIC DISASTERS.
AND OCCASIONALLY AVERT THEM.
ATLEZ!
I HAVE ARRIVED!
AND NOT A MOMENT TOO SOON!

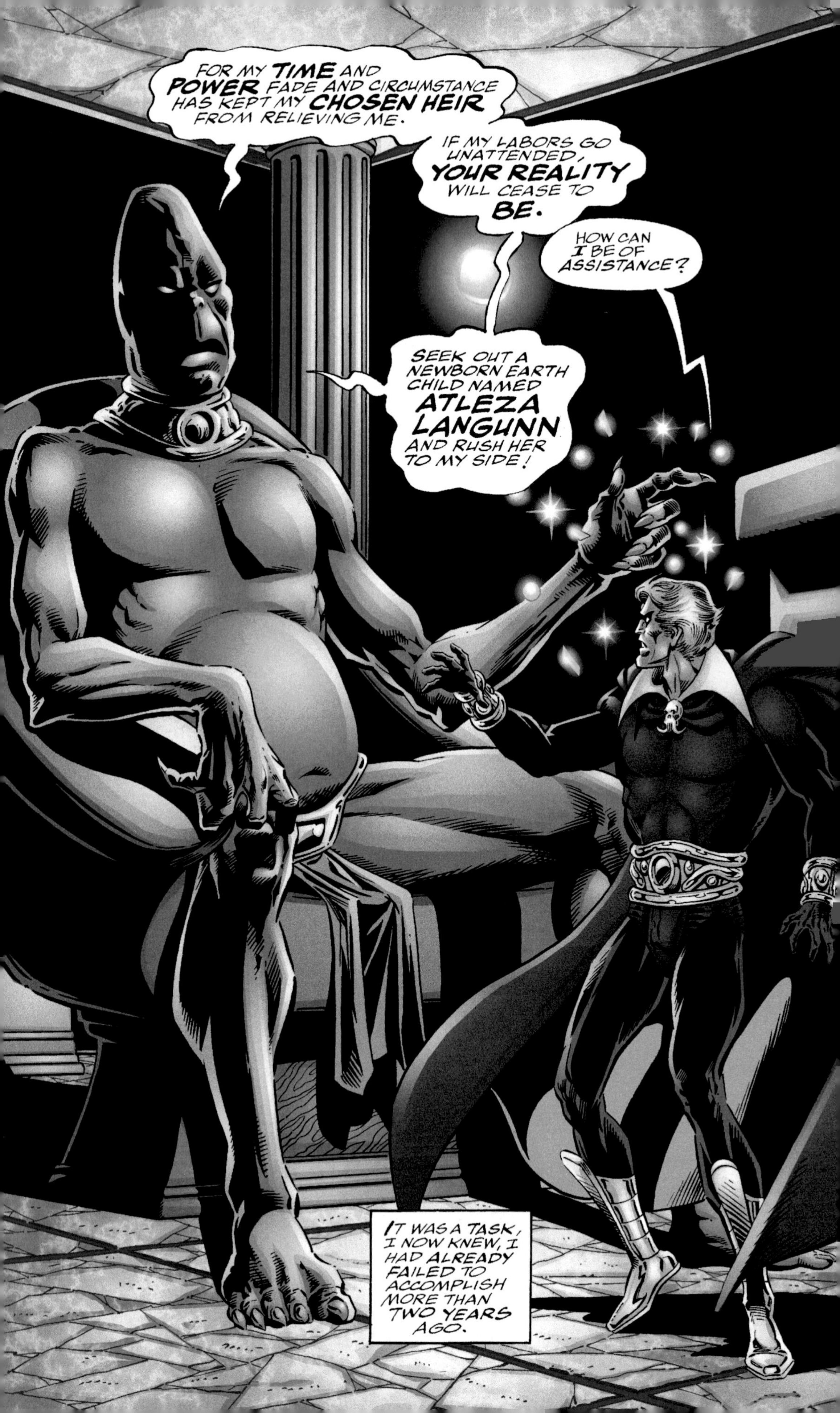
FOR MY TIME AND POWER FADE AND CIRCUMSTANCE HAS KEPT MY CHOSEN HEIR FROM RELIEVING ME.
IF MY LABORS GO UNATTENDED, YOUR REALITY WILL CEASE TO BE.
HOW CAN I BE OF ASSISTANCE?
SEEK OUT A NEWBORN EARTH CHILD NAMED ATLEZA LANGUNN AND RUSH HER TO MY SIDE!
IT WAS A TASK, I NOW KNEW, I HAD ALREADY FAILED TO ACCOMPLISH MORE THAN TWO YEARS AGO.

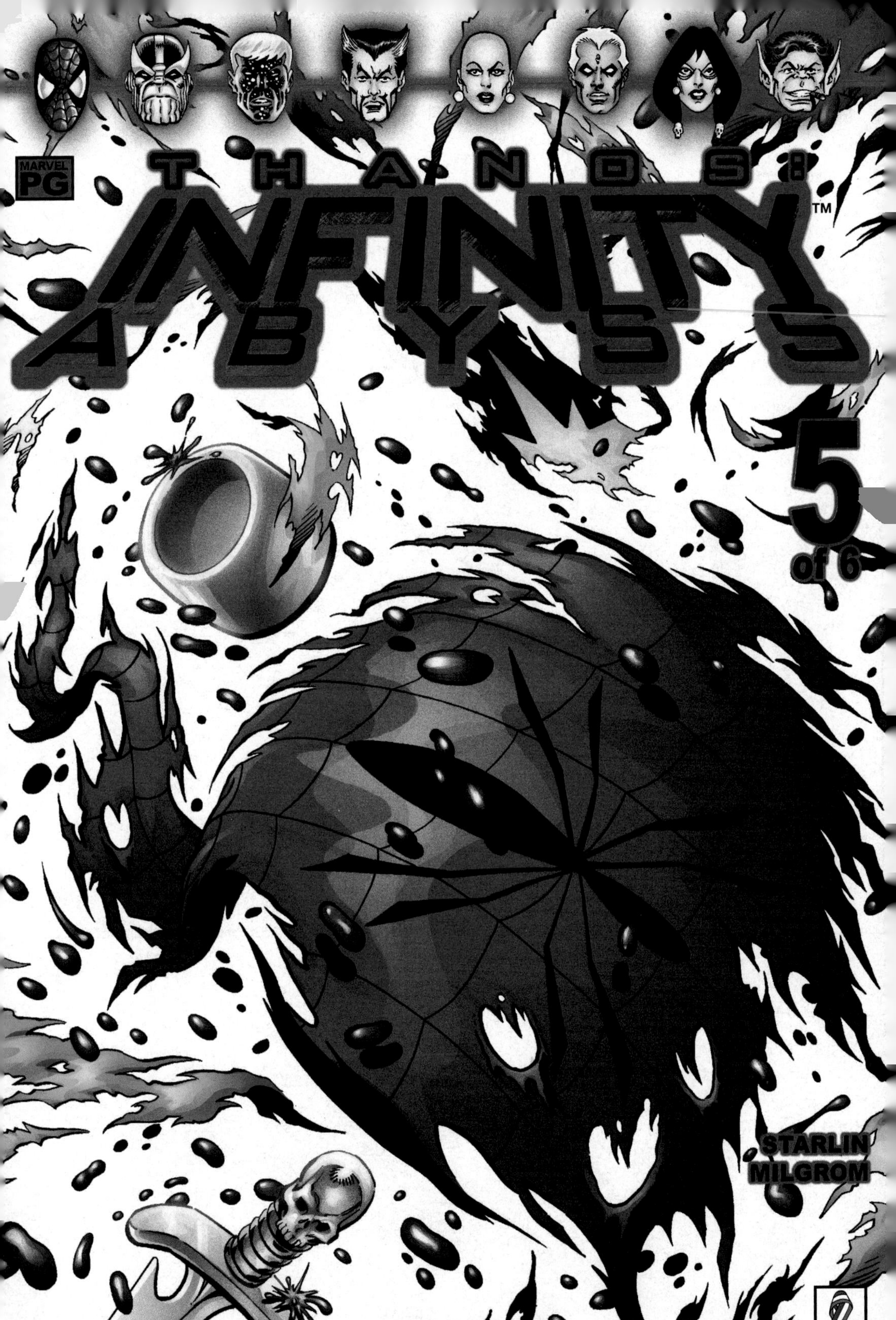
MARVEL PG
THANOS: INFINITY ABYSS™
5 of 6
STARLIN
MILGROM

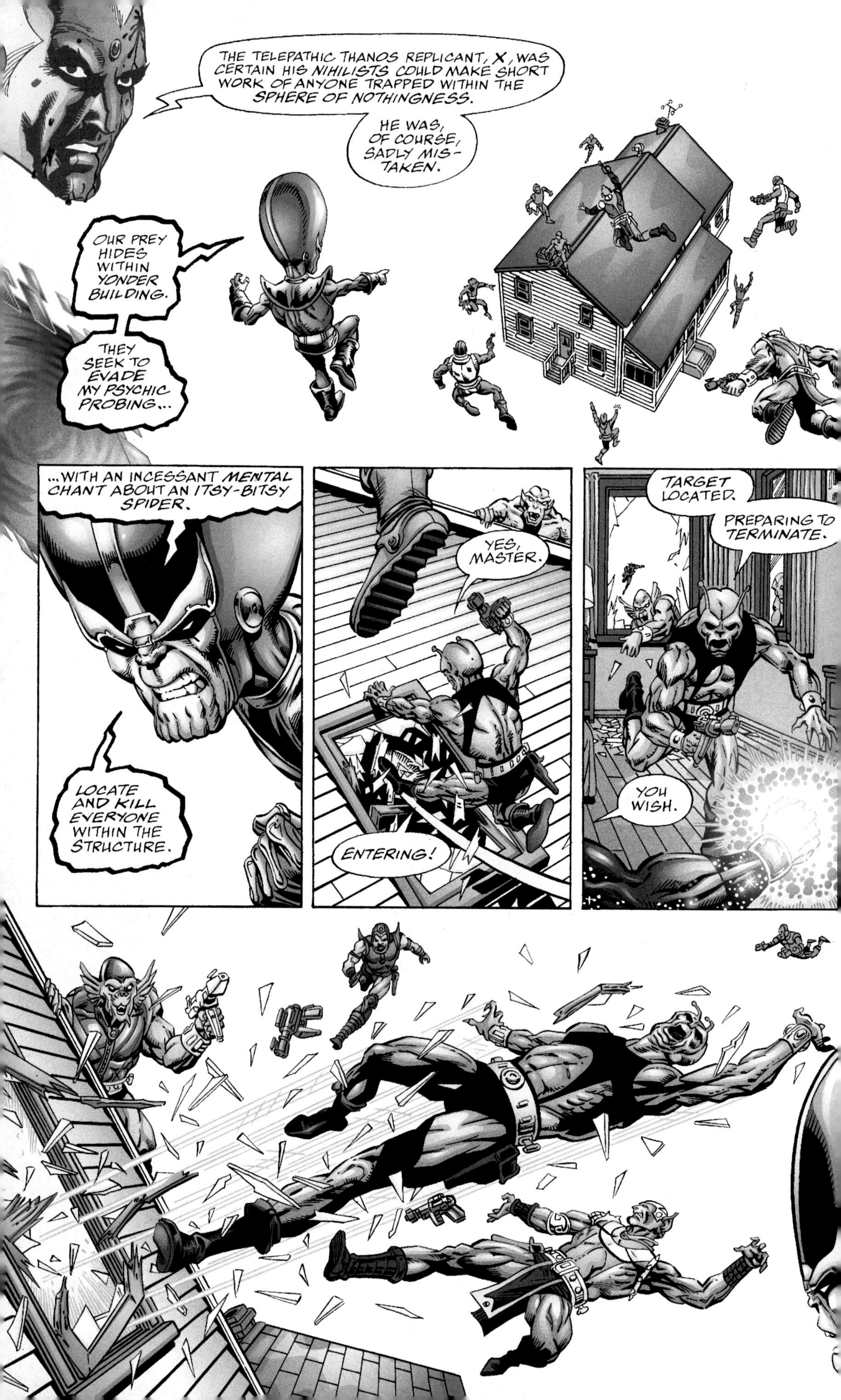

THE TELEPATHIC THANOS REPLICANT, X, WAS CERTAIN HIS NIHILISTS COULD MAKE SHORT WORK OF ANYONE TRAPPED WITHIN THE SPHERE OF NOTHINGNESS.
HE WAS, OF COURSE, SADLY MIS-TAKEN.
OUR PREY HIDES WITHIN YONDER BUILDING.
THEY SEEK TO EVADE MY PSYCHIC PROBING...
...WITH AN INCESSANT MENTAL CHANT ABOUT AN ITSY-BITSY SPIDER.
LOCATE AND KILL EVERYONE WITHIN THE STRUCTURE.
YES, MASTER.
ENTERING!
TARGET LOCATED.
PREPARING TO TERMINATE.
YOU WISH.

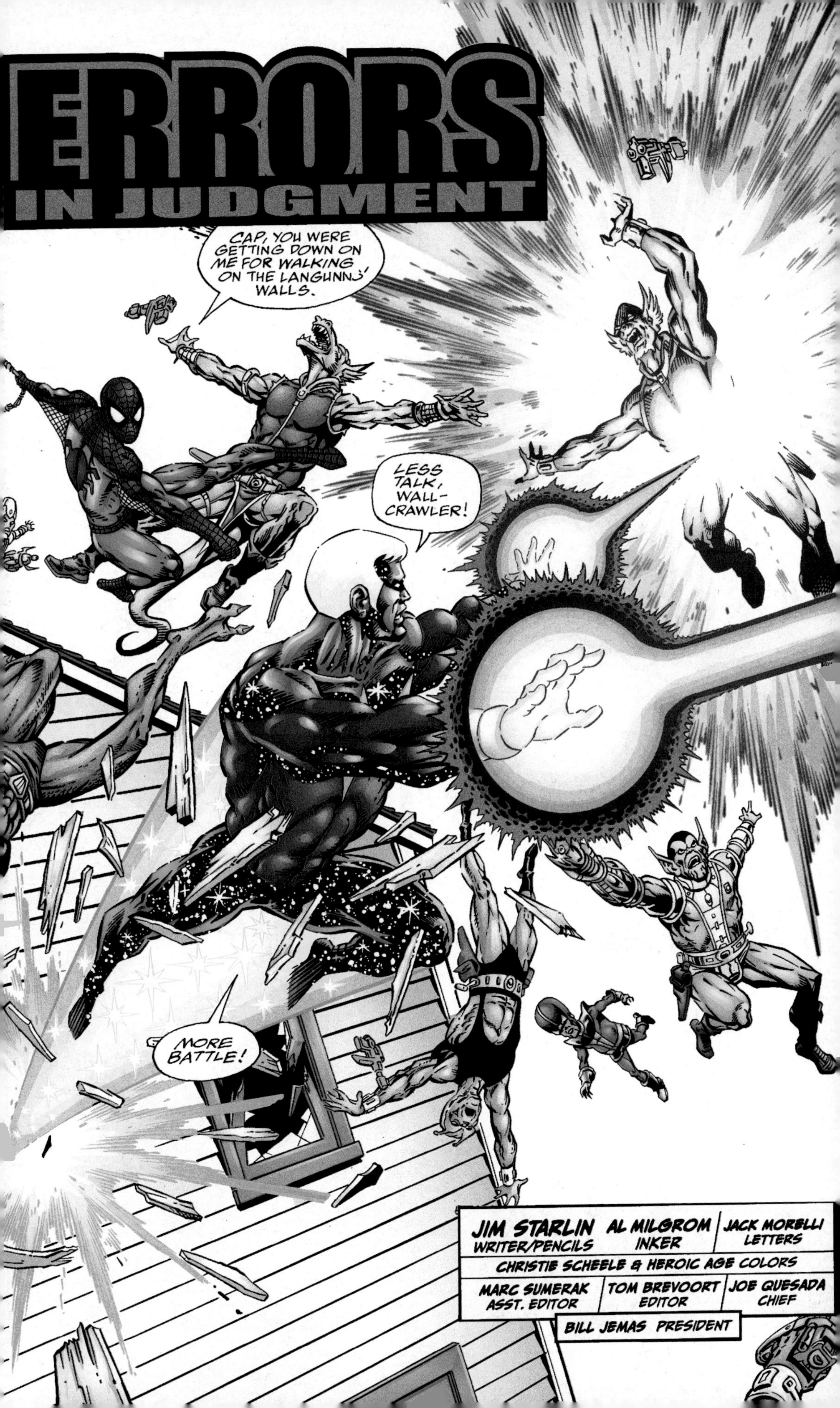
ERRORS
IN JUDGMENT
CAP, YOU WERE GETTING DOWN ON ME FOR WALKING ON THE LANGUNNS' WALLS.
LESS TALK, WALL-CRAWLER!
MORE BATTLE!
JIM STARLIN WRITER/PENCILS
AL MILGROM INKER
JACK MORELLI LETTERS
CHRISTIE SCHEELE & HEROIC AGE COLORS
MARC SUMERAK ASST. EDITOR
TOM BREVOORT EDITOR
JOE QUESADA CHIEF
BILL JEMAS PRESIDENT

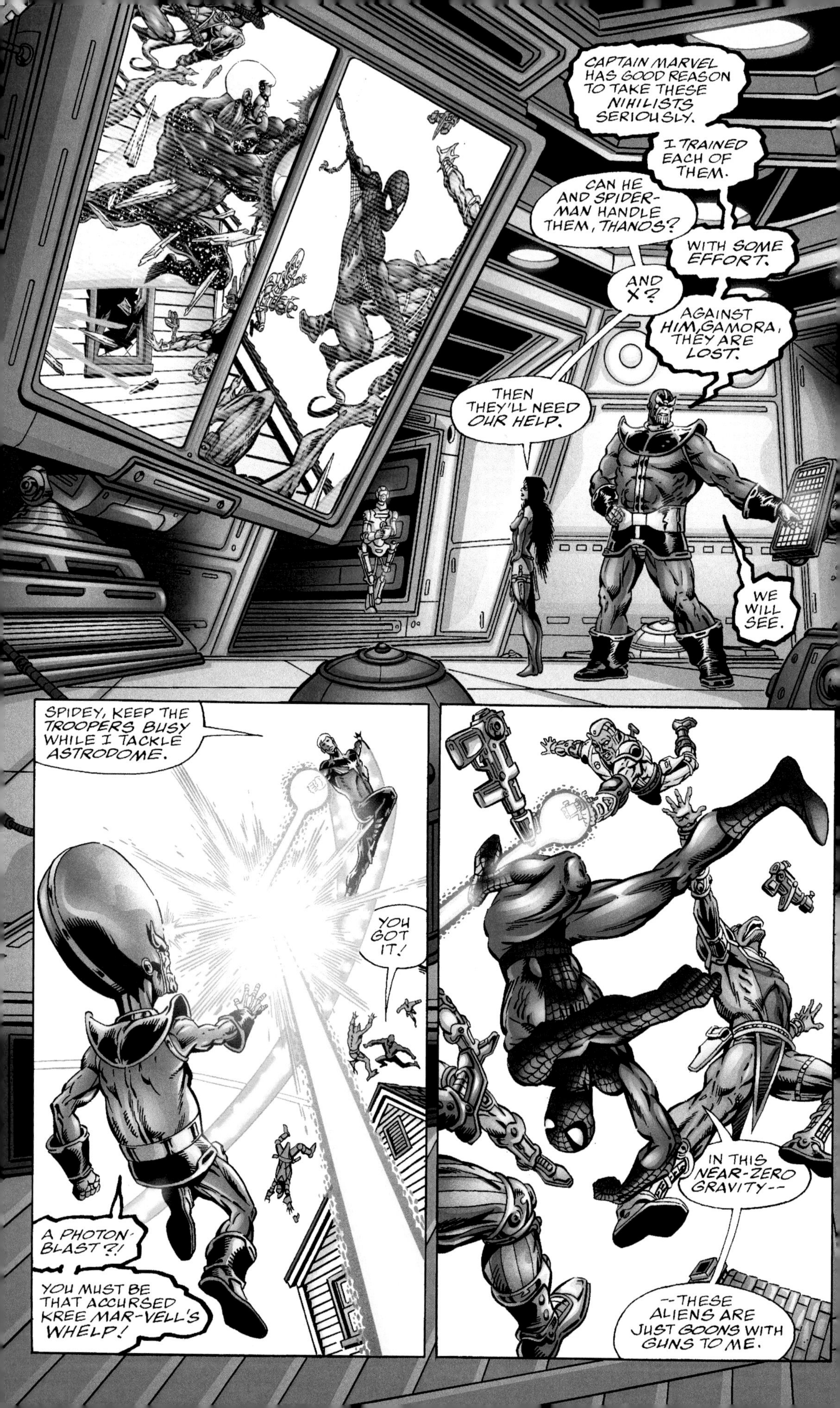
CAPTAIN MARVEL HAS GOOD REASON TO TAKE THESE NIHILISTS SERIOUSLY.
I TRAINED EACH OF THEM.
CAN HE AND SPIDER-MAN HANDLE THEM, THANOS?
WITH SOME EFFORT.
AND X?
AGAINST HIM, GAMORA, THEY ARE LOST.
THEN THEY'LL NEED OUR HELP.
WE WILL SEE.
SPIDEY, KEEP THE TROOPERS BUSY WHILE I TACKLE ASTRODOME.
YOU GOT IT!
A PHOTON-BLAST?!
YOU MUST BE THAT ACCURSED KREE MAR-VELL'S WHELP!
IN THIS NEAR-ZERO GRAVITY--
--THESE ALIENS ARE JUST GOONS WITH GUNS TO ME.

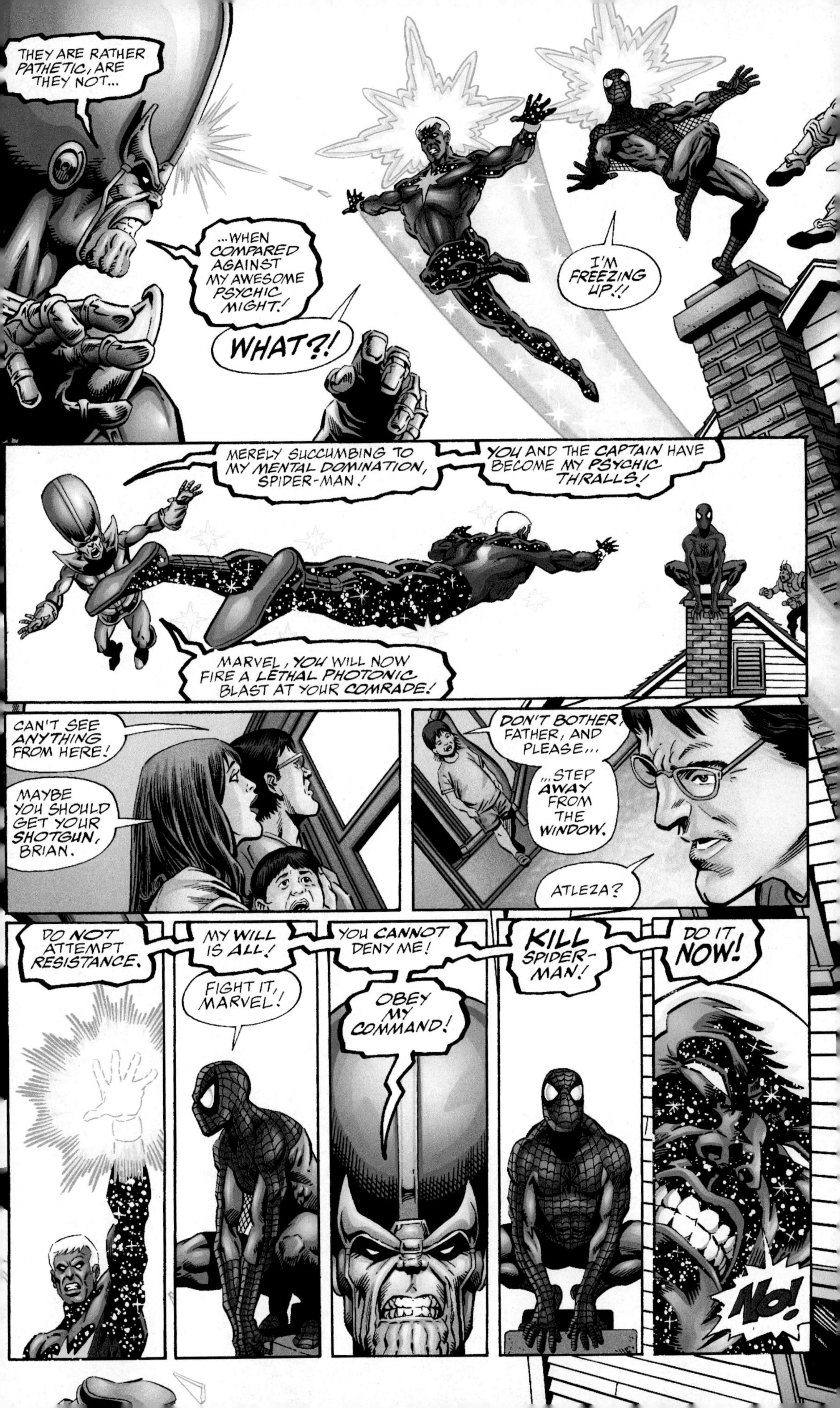
THEY ARE RATHER PATHETIC, ARE THEY NOT...
...WHEN COMPARED AGAINST MY AWESOME PSYCHIC MIGHT!
WHAT?!
I'M FREEZING UP!!
MERELY SUCCUMBING TO MY MENTAL DOMINATION, SPIDER-MAN!
YOU AND THE CAPTAIN HAVE BECOME MY PSYCHIC THRALLS!
MARVEL, YOU WILL NOW FIRE A LETHAL PHOTONIC BLAST AT YOUR COMRADE!
CAN'T SEE ANYTHING FROM HERE!
MAYBE YOU SHOULD GET YOUR SHOTGUN, BRIAN.
DON'T BOTHER, FATHER, AND PLEASE...
...STEP AWAY FROM THE WINDOW.
ATLEZA?
DO NOT ATTEMPT RESISTANCE.
MY WILL IS ALL!
FIGHT IT, MARVEL!
YOU CANNOT DENY ME!
OBEY MY COMMAND!
KILL SPIDER-MAN!
DO IT NOW!
NO!

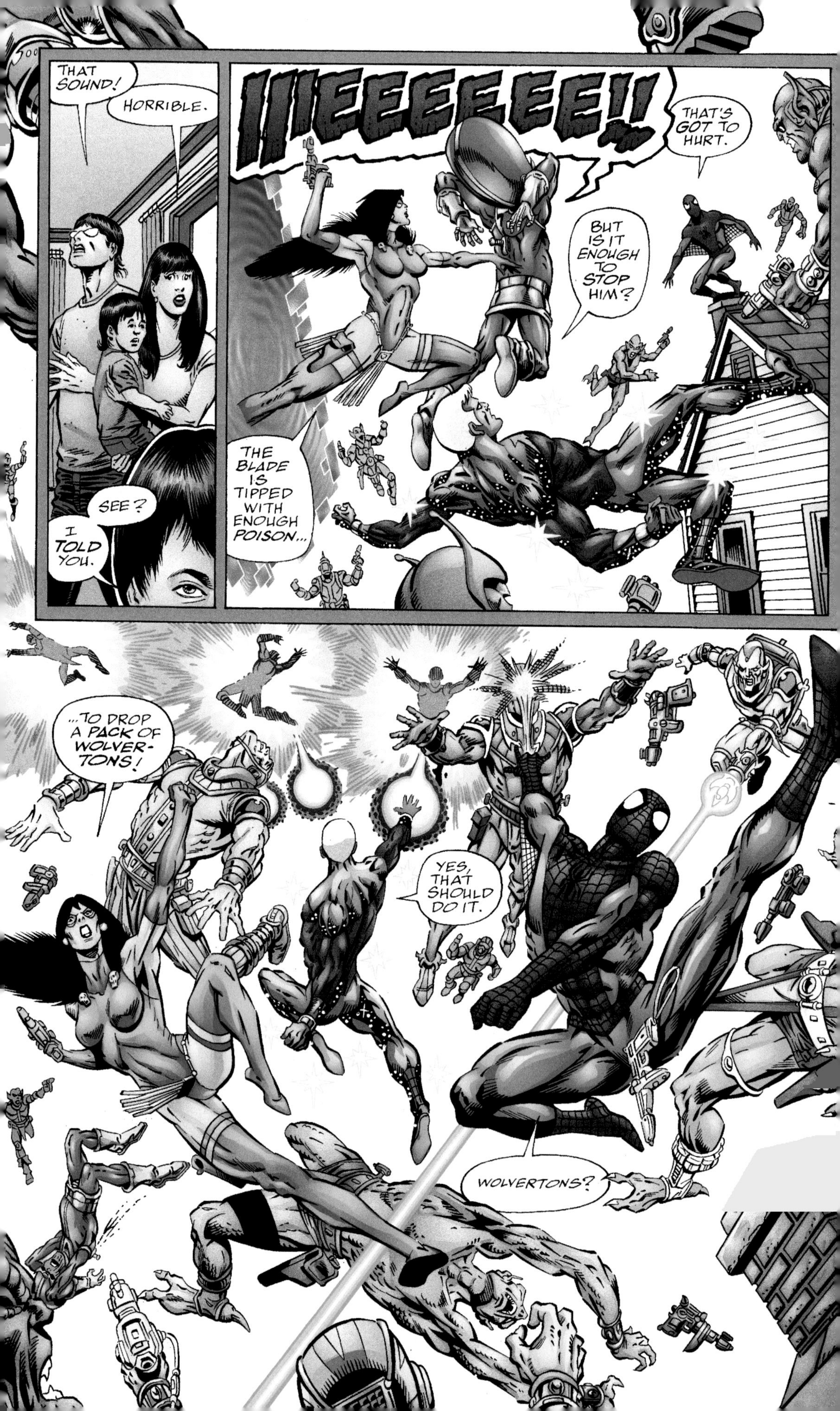
THAT SOUND!
HORRIBLE.
SEE?
I TOLD YOU.
IIIEEEEEEE!!
THAT'S GOT TO HURT.
BUT IS IT ENOUGH TO STOP HIM?
THE BLADE IS TIPPED WITH ENOUGH POISON...
...TO DROP A PACK OF WOLVERTONS!
YES, THAT SHOULD DO IT.
WOLVERTONS?

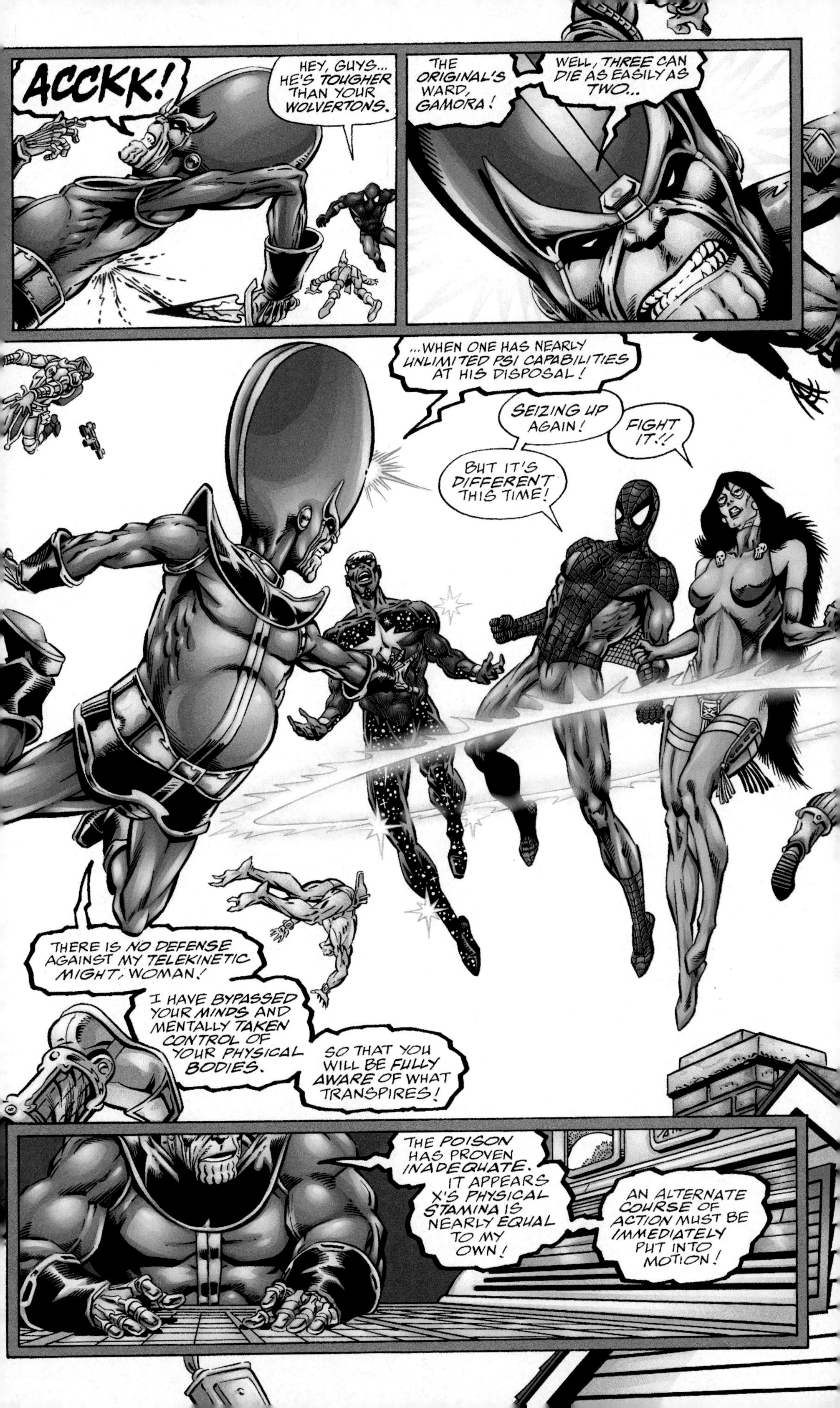
ACCKK!
HEY, GUYS... HE'S TOUGHER THAN YOUR WOLVERTONS.
THE ORIGINAL'S WARD, GAMORA!
WELL, THREE CAN DIE AS EASILY AS TWO...
...WHEN ONE HAS NEARLY UNLIMITED PSI CAPABILITIES AT HIS DISPOSAL!
SEIZING UP AGAIN!
FIGHT IT!!
BUT IT'S DIFFERENT THIS TIME!
THERE IS NO DEFENSE AGAINST MY TELEKINETIC MIGHT, WOMAN!
I HAVE BYPASSED YOUR MINDS AND MENTALLY TAKEN CONTROL OF YOUR PHYSICAL BODIES.
SO THAT YOU WILL BE FULLY AWARE OF WHAT TRANSPIRES!
THE POISON HAS PROVEN INADEQUATE. IT APPEARS X'S PHYSICAL STAMINA IS NEARLY EQUAL TO MY OWN!
AN ALTERNATE COURSE OF ACTION MUST BE IMMEDIATELY PUT INTO MOTION!

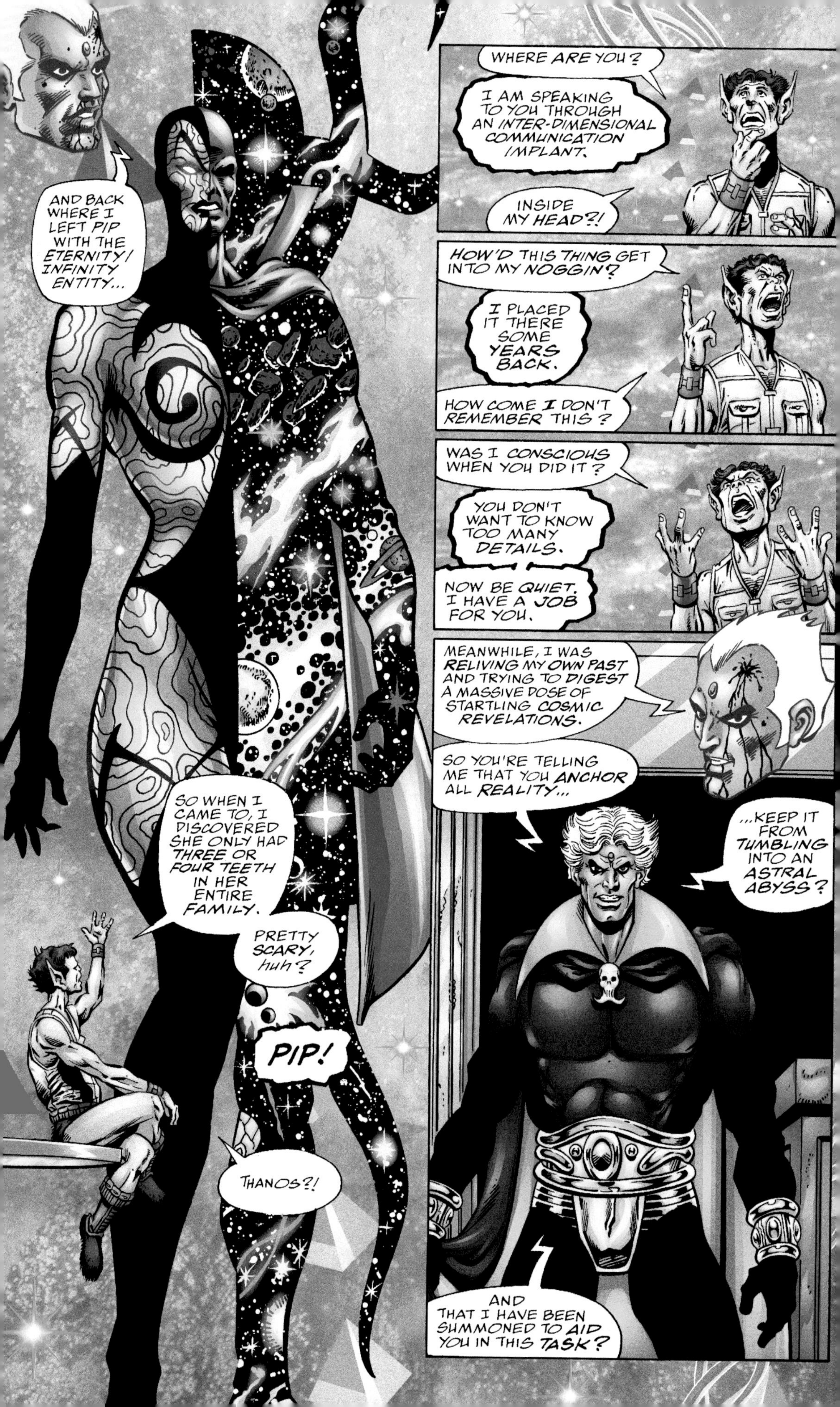
AND BACK WHERE I LEFT PIP WITH THE ETERNITY/INFINITY ENTITY...
WHERE ARE YOU?
I AM SPEAKING TO YOU THROUGH AN INTER-DIMENSIONAL COMMUNICATION IMPLANT.
INSIDE MY HEAD?!
HOW'D THIS THING GET INTO MY NOGGIN?
I PLACED IT THERE SOME YEARS BACK.
HOW COME I DON'T REMEMBER THIS?
WAS I CONSCIOUS WHEN YOU DID IT?
YOU DON'T WANT TO KNOW TOO MANY DETAILS.
NOW BE QUIET. I HAVE A JOB FOR YOU.
SO WHEN I CAME TO, I DISCOVERED SHE ONLY HAD THREE OR FOUR TEETH IN HER ENTIRE FAMILY.
PRETTY SCARY, huh?
PIP!
THANOS?!
MEANWHILE, I WAS RELIVING MY OWN PAST AND TRYING TO DIGEST A MASSIVE DOSE OF STARTLING COSMIC REVELATIONS.
SO YOU'RE TELLING ME THAT YOU ANCHOR ALL REALITY...
...KEEP IT FROM TUMBLING INTO AN ASTRAL ABYSS?
AND THAT I HAVE BEEN SUMMONED TO AID YOU IN THIS TASK?

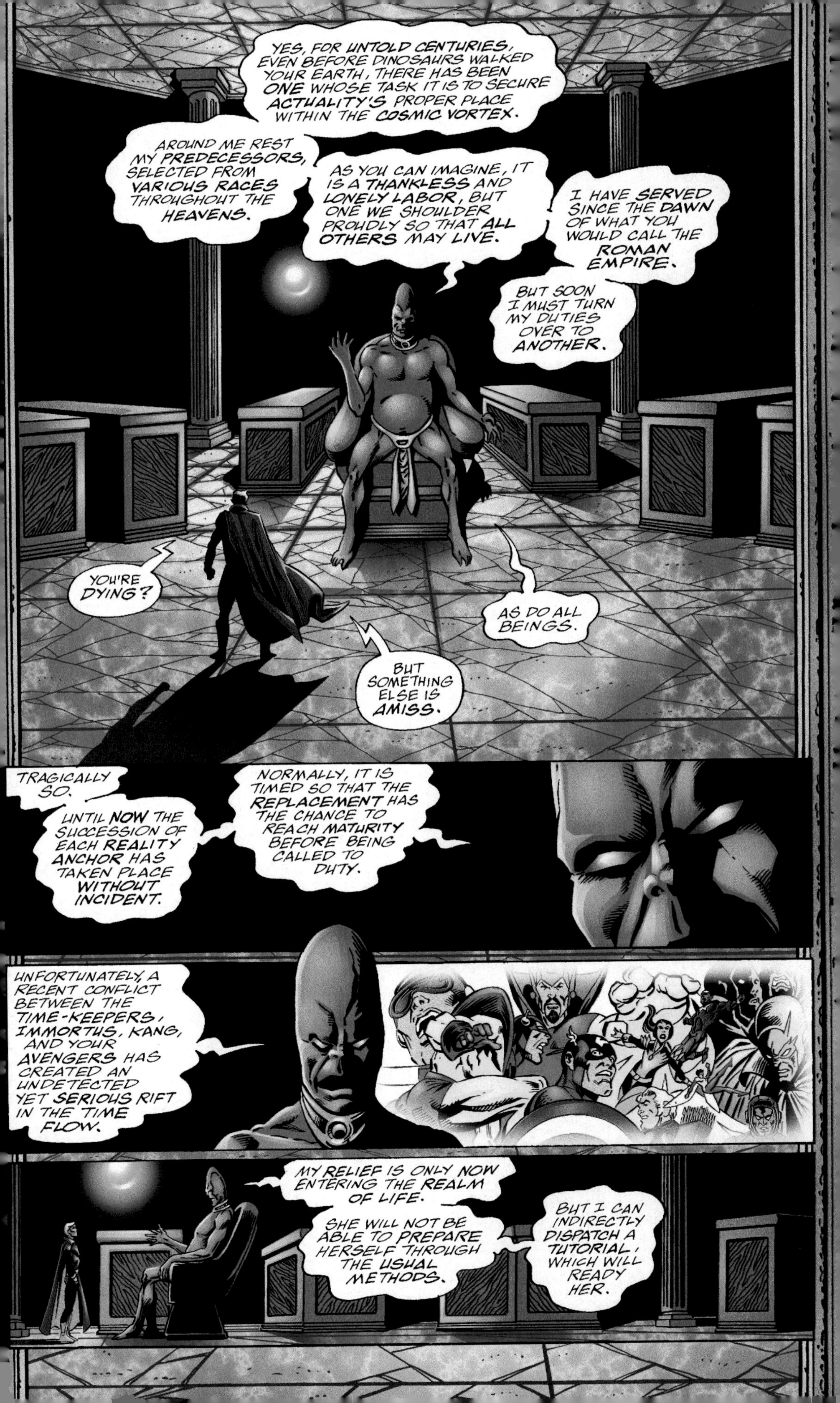

YES, FOR UNTOLD CENTURIES, EVEN BEFORE DINOSAURS WALKED YOUR EARTH, THERE HAS BEEN ONE WHOSE TASK IT IS TO SECURE ACTUALITY'S PROPER PLACE WITHIN THE COSMIC VORTEX.
AROUND ME REST MY PREDECESSORS, SELECTED FROM VARIOUS RACES THROUGHOUT THE HEAVENS.
AS YOU CAN IMAGINE, IT IS A THANKLESS AND LONELY LABOR, BUT ONE WE SHOULDER PROUDLY SO THAT ALL OTHERS MAY LIVE.
I HAVE SERVED SINCE THE DAWN OF WHAT YOU WOULD CALL THE ROMAN EMPIRE.
BUT SOON I MUST TURN MY DUTIES OVER TO ANOTHER.
YOU'RE DYING?
AS DO ALL BEINGS.
BUT SOMETHING ELSE IS AMISS.
TRAGICALLY SO.
UNTIL NOW THE SUCCESSION OF EACH REALITY ANCHOR HAS TAKEN PLACE WITHOUT INCIDENT.
NORMALLY, IT IS TIMED SO THAT THE REPLACEMENT HAS THE CHANCE TO REACH MATURITY BEFORE BEING CALLED TO DUTY.
UNFORTUNATELY, A RECENT CONFLICT BETWEEN THE TIME-KEEPERS, IMMORTUS, KANG, AND YOUR AVENGERS HAS CREATED AN UNDETECTED YET SERIOUS RIFT IN THE TIME FLOW.
MY RELIEF IS ONLY NOW ENTERING THE REALM OF LIFE.
SHE WILL NOT BE ABLE TO PREPARE HERSELF THROUGH THE USUAL METHODS.
BUT I CAN INDIRECTLY DISPATCH A TUTORIAL, WHICH WILL READY HER.

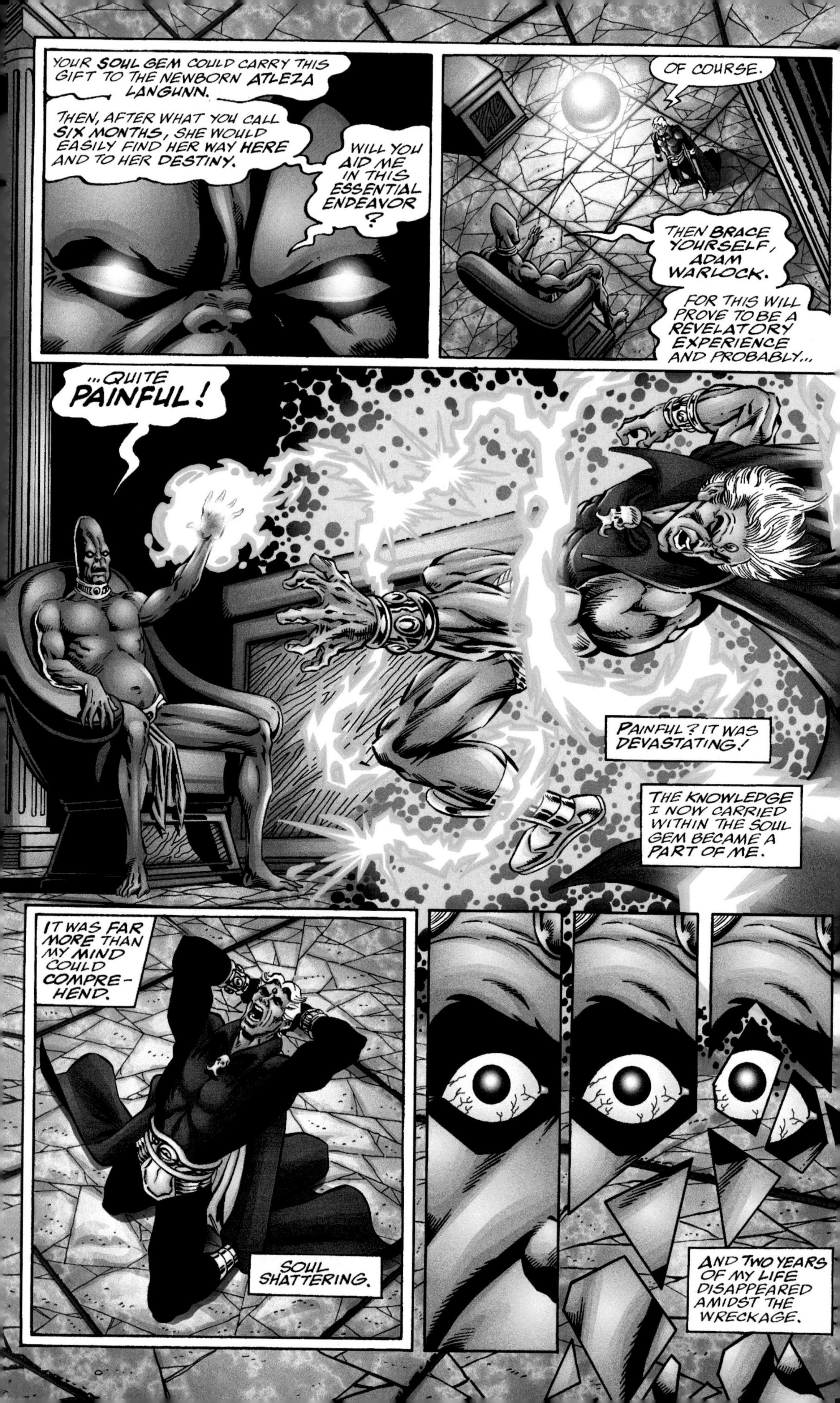

YOUR SOUL GEM COULD CARRY THIS GIFT TO THE NEWBORN ATLEZA LANGUNN.
THEN, AFTER WHAT YOU CALL SIX MONTHS, SHE WOULD EASILY FIND HER WAY HERE AND TO HER DESTINY.
WILL YOU AID ME IN THIS ESSENTIAL ENDEAVOR?
OF COURSE.
THEN BRACE YOURSELF, ADAM WARLOCK.
FOR THIS WILL PROVE TO BE A REVELATORY EXPERIENCE AND PROBABLY...
...QUITE PAINFUL!
PAINFUL? IT WAS DEVASTATING!
THE KNOWLEDGE I NOW CARRIED WITHIN THE SOUL GEM BECAME A PART OF ME.
IT WAS FAR MORE THAN MY MIND COULD COMPRE-HEND.
SOUL SHATTERING.
AND TWO YEARS OF MY LIFE DISAPPEARED AMIDST THE WRECKAGE.

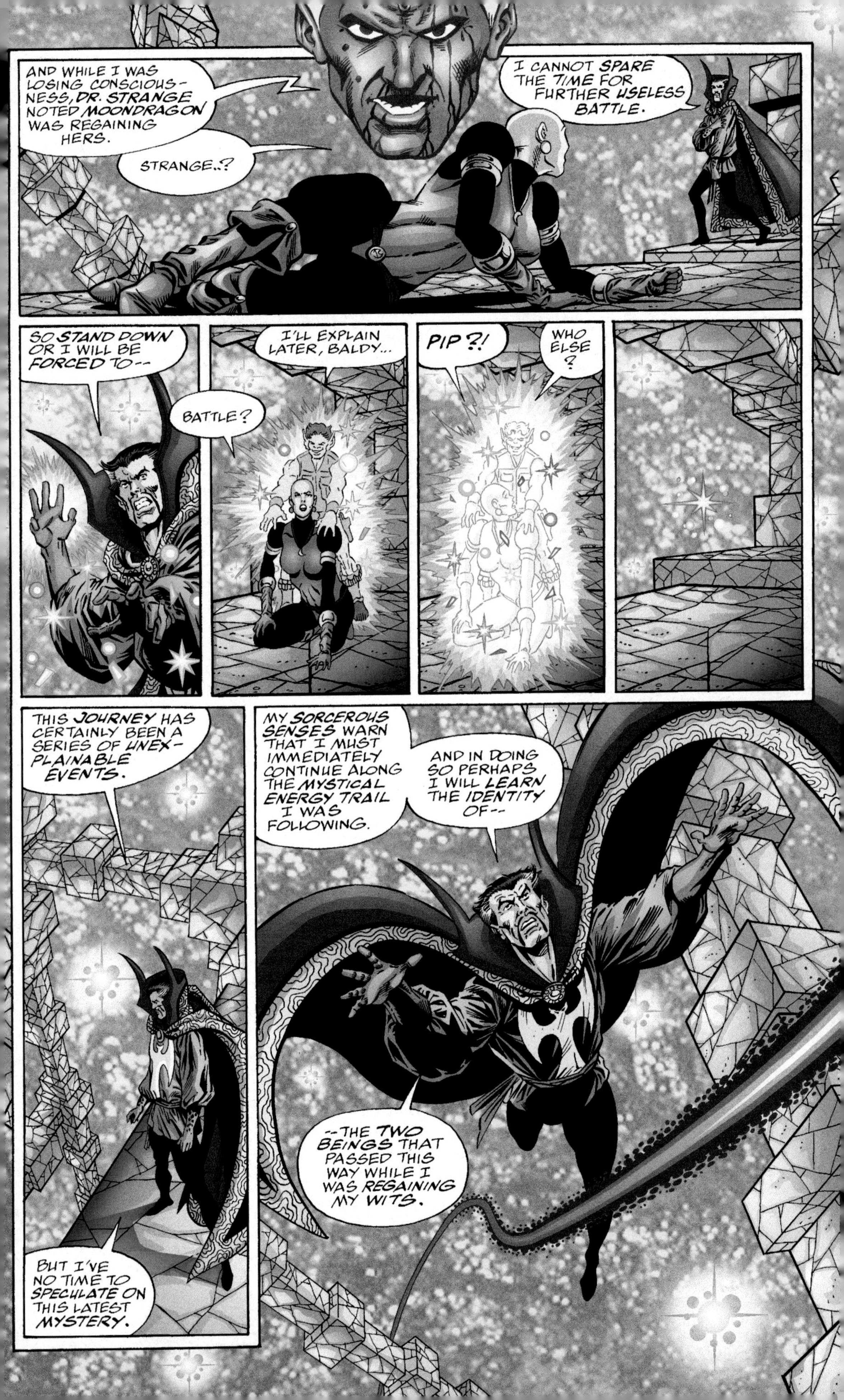
AND WHILE I WAS LOSING CONSCIOUSNESS, DR. STRANGE NOTED MOONDRAGON WAS REGAINING HERS.
STRANGE..?
I CANNOT SPARE THE TIME FOR FURTHER USELESS BATTLE.
SO STAND DOWN OR I WILL BE FORCED TO--
BATTLE?
I'LL EXPLAIN LATER, BALDY...
PIP?!
WHO ELSE?
THIS JOURNEY HAS CERTAINLY BEEN A SERIES OF UNEXPLAINABLE EVENTS.
BUT I'VE NO TIME TO SPECULATE ON THIS LATEST MYSTERY.
MY SORCEROUS SENSES WARN THAT I MUST IMMEDIATELY CONTINUE ALONG THE MYSTICAL ENERGY TRAIL I WAS FOLLOWING.
AND IN DOING SO PERHAPS I WILL LEARN THE IDENTITY OF--
--THE TWO BEINGS THAT PASSED THIS WAY WHILE I WAS REGAINING MY WITS.

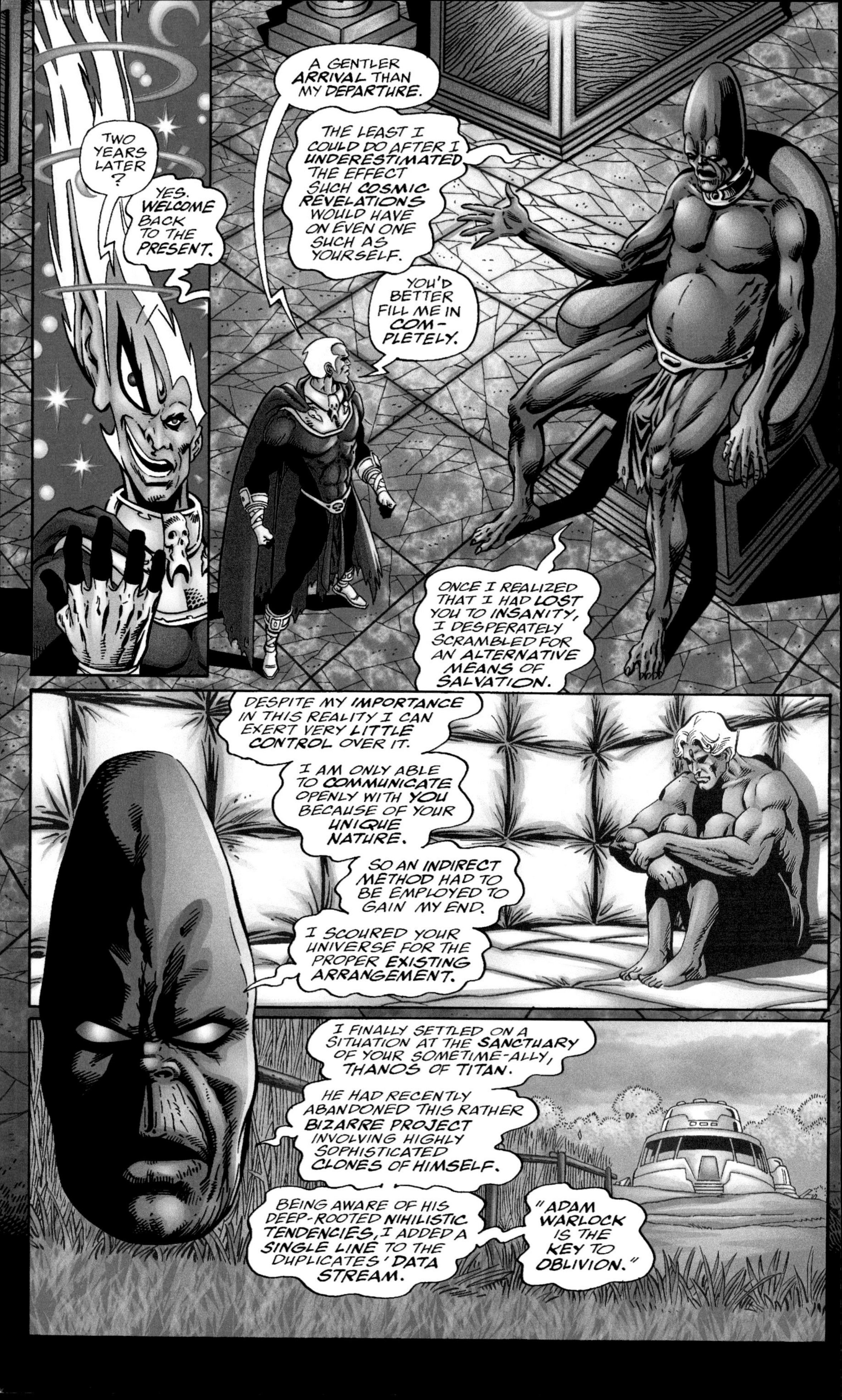
TWO YEARS LATER?
YES. WELCOME BACK TO THE PRESENT.
A GENTLER ARRIVAL THAN MY DEPARTURE.
THE LEAST I COULD DO AFTER I UNDERESTIMATED THE EFFECT SUCH COSMIC REVELATIONS WOULD HAVE ON EVEN ONE SUCH AS YOURSELF.
YOU'D BETTER FILL ME IN COM-PLETELY.
ONCE I REALIZED THAT I HAD LOST YOU TO INSANITY, I DESPERATELY SCRAMBLED FOR AN ALTERNATIVE MEANS OF SALVATION.
DESPITE MY IMPORTANCE IN THIS REALITY I CAN EXERT VERY LITTLE CONTROL OVER IT.
I AM ONLY ABLE TO COMMUNICATE OPENLY WITH YOU BECAUSE OF YOUR UNIQUE NATURE.
SO AN INDIRECT METHOD HAD TO BE EMPLOYED TO GAIN MY END.
I SCOURED YOUR UNIVERSE FOR THE PROPER EXISTING ARRANGEMENT.
I FINALLY SETTLED ON A SITUATION AT THE SANCTUARY OF YOUR SOMETIME-ALLY, THANOS OF TITAN.
HE HAD RECENTLY ABANDONED THIS RATHER BIZARRE PROJECT INVOLVING HIGHLY SOPHISTICATED CLONES OF HIMSELF.
BEING AWARE OF HIS DEEP-ROOTED NIHILISTIC TENDENCIES, I ADDED A SINGLE LINE TO THE DUPLICATES' DATA STREAM.
"ADAM WARLOCK IS THE KEY TO OBLIVION."

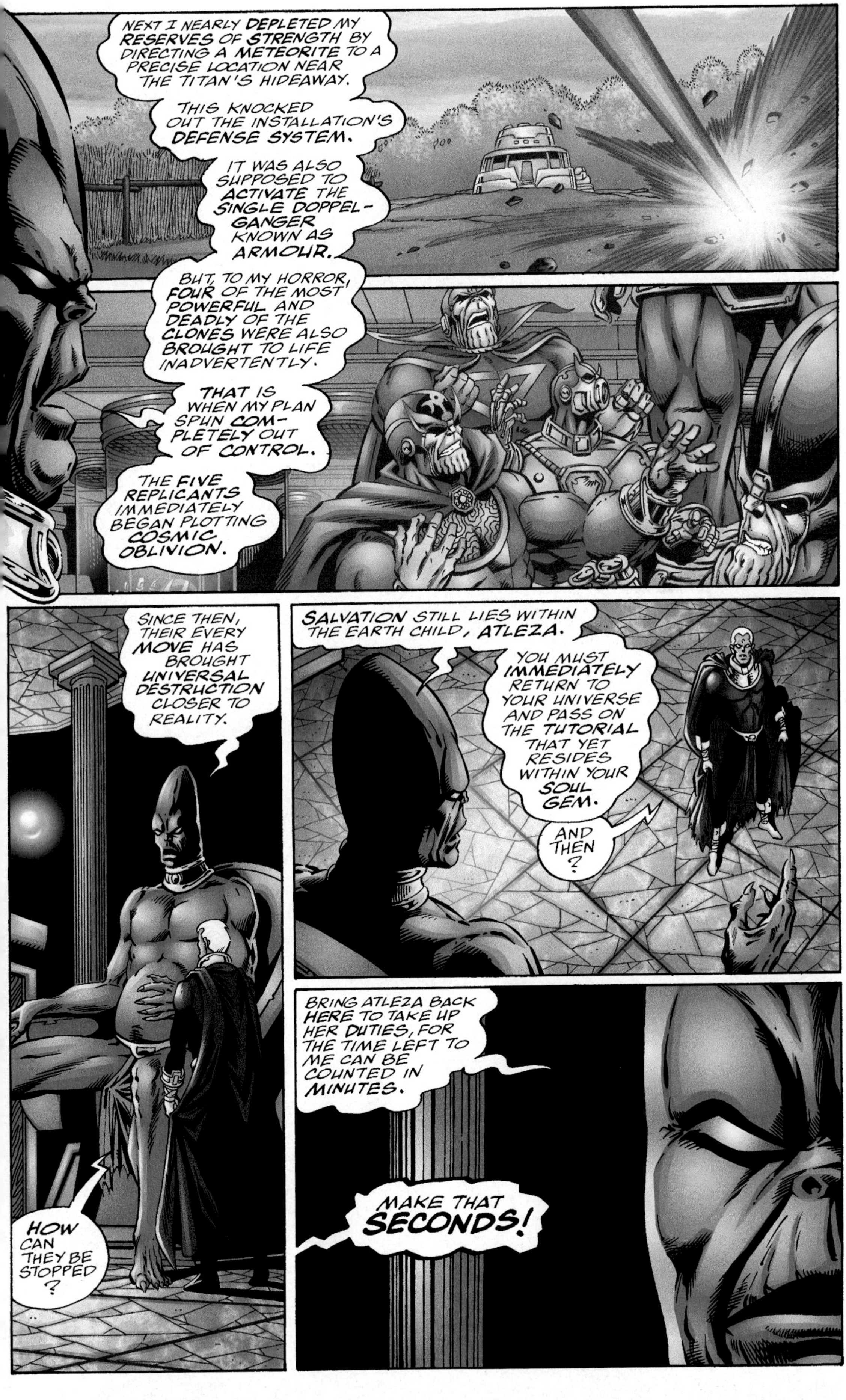
NEXT I NEARLY DEPLETED MY RESERVES OF STRENGTH BY DIRECTING A METEORITE TO A PRECISE LOCATION NEAR THE TITAN'S HIDEAWAY.
THIS KNOCKED OUT THE INSTALLATION'S DEFENSE SYSTEM.
IT WAS ALSO SUPPOSED TO ACTIVATE THE SINGLE DOPPEL-GANGER KNOWN AS ARMOUR.
BUT, TO MY HORROR, FOUR OF THE MOST POWERFUL AND DEADLY OF THE CLONES WERE ALSO BROUGHT TO LIFE INADVERTENTLY.
THAT IS WHEN MY PLAN SPUN COM-PLETELY OUT OF CONTROL.
THE FIVE REPLICANTS IMMEDIATELY BEGAN PLOTTING COSMIC OBLIVION.
SINCE THEN, THEIR EVERY MOVE HAS BROUGHT UNIVERSAL DESTRUCTION CLOSER TO REALITY.
HOW CAN THEY BE STOPPED?
SALVATION STILL LIES WITHIN THE EARTH CHILD, ATLEZA.
YOU MUST IMMEDIATELY RETURN TO YOUR UNIVERSE AND PASS ON THE TUTORIAL THAT YET RESIDES WITHIN YOUR SOUL GEM.
AND THEN?
BRING ATLEZA BACK HERE TO TAKE UP HER DUTIES, FOR THE TIME LEFT TO ME CAN BE COUNTED IN MINUTES.
MAKE THAT SECONDS!

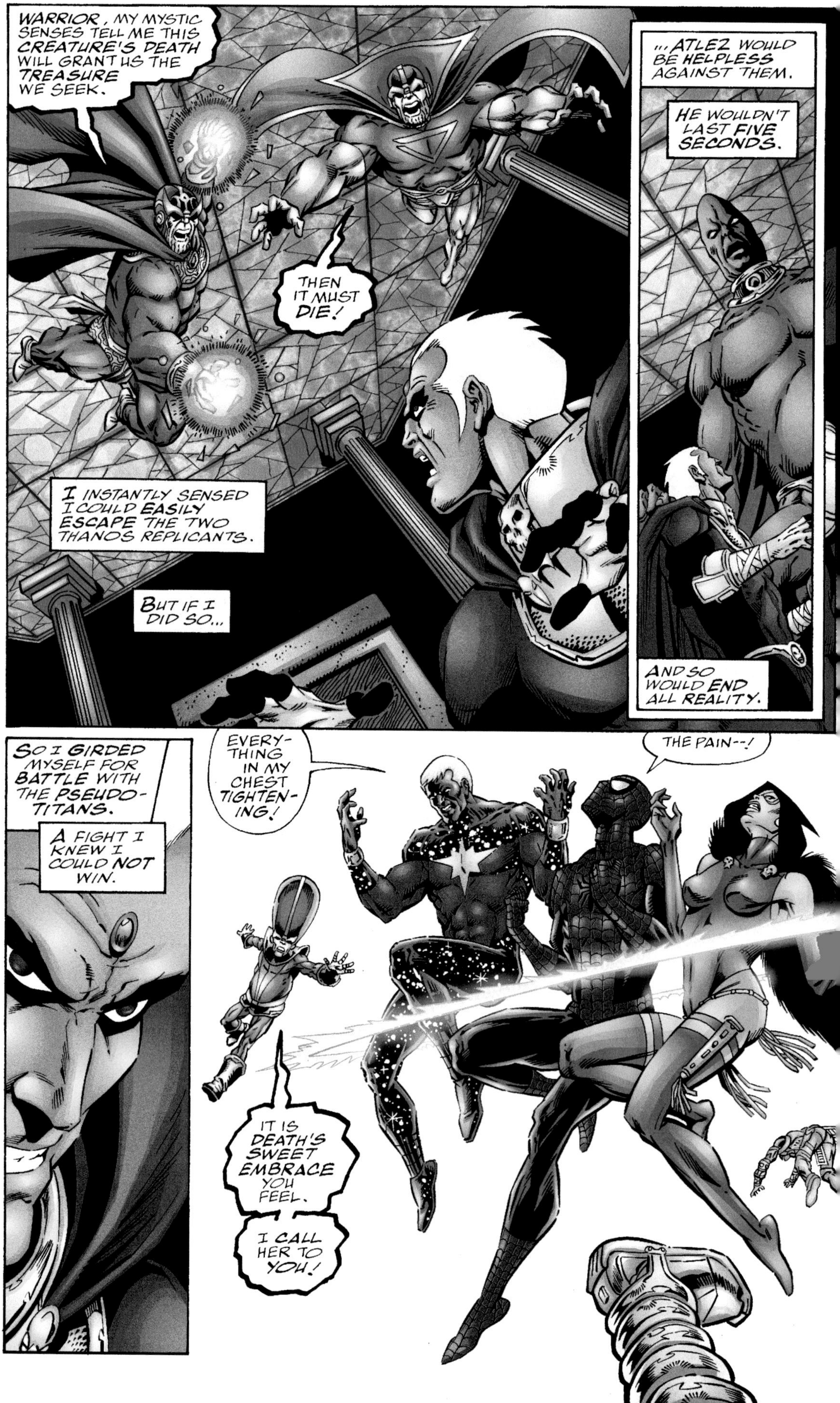
WARRIOR, MY MYSTIC SENSES TELL ME THIS CREATURE'S DEATH WILL GRANT US THE TREASURE WE SEEK.
THEN IT MUST DIE!
I INSTANTLY SENSED I COULD EASILY ESCAPE THE TWO THANOS REPLICANTS.
BUT IF I DID SO...
...ATLEZ WOULD BE HELPLESS AGAINST THEM.
HE WOULDN'T LAST FIVE SECONDS.
AND SO WOULD END ALL REALITY.
SO I GIRDED MYSELF FOR BATTLE WITH THE PSEUDO-TITANS.
A FIGHT I KNEW I COULD NOT WIN.
EVERY-THING IN MY CHEST TIGHTEN-ING!
THE PAIN--!
IT IS DEATH'S SWEET EMBRACE YOU FEEL.
I CALL HER TO YOU!

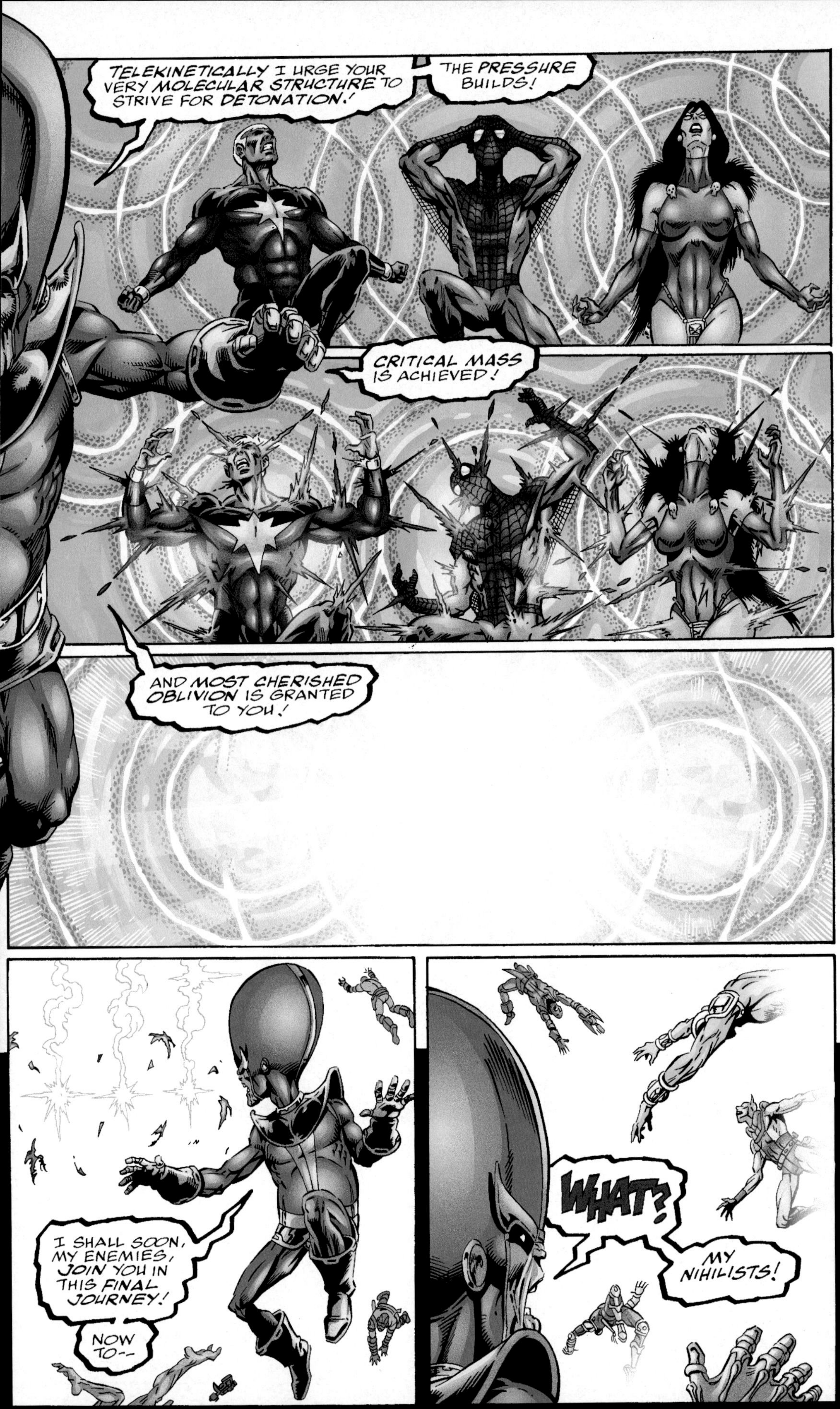
TELEKINETICALLY I URGE YOUR VERY MOLECULAR STRUCTURE TO STRIVE FOR DETONATION!
THE PRESSURE BUILDS!
CRITICAL MASS IS ACHIEVED!
AND MOST CHERISHED OBLIVION IS GRANTED TO YOU!
I SHALL SOON, MY ENEMIES, JOIN YOU IN THIS FINAL JOURNEY!
NOW TO--
WHAT?
MY NIHILISTS!

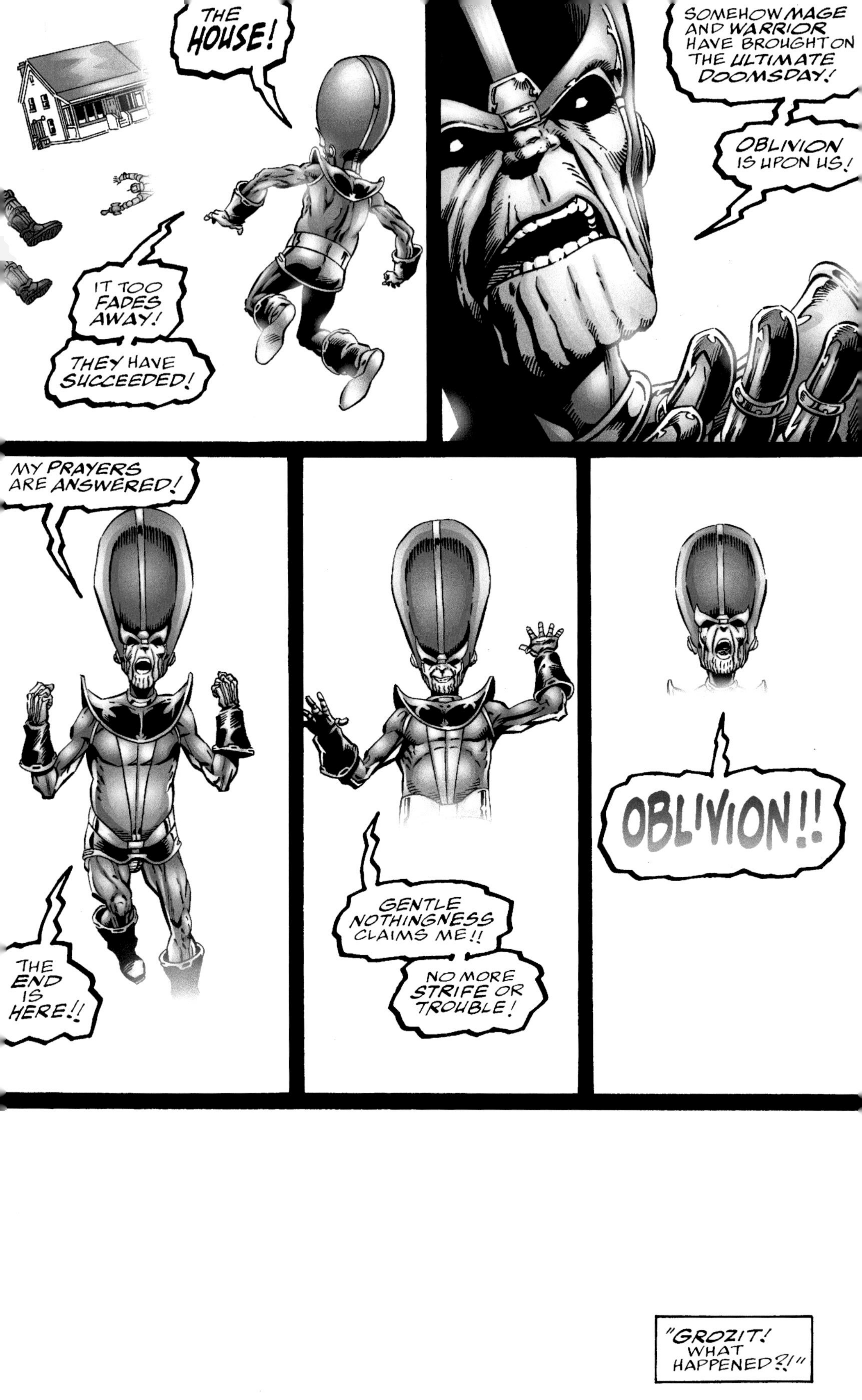
THE HOUSE!
IT TOO FADES AWAY!
THEY HAVE SUCCEEDED!
SOMEHOW MAGE AND WARRIOR HAVE BROUGHT ON THE ULTIMATE DOOMSDAY!
OBLIVION IS UPON US!
MY PRAYERS ARE ANSWERED!
THE END IS HERE!!
GENTLE NOTHINGNESS CLAIMS ME!!
NO MORE STRIFE OR TROUBLE!
OBLIVION!!
"GROZIT! WHAT HAPPENED?!"

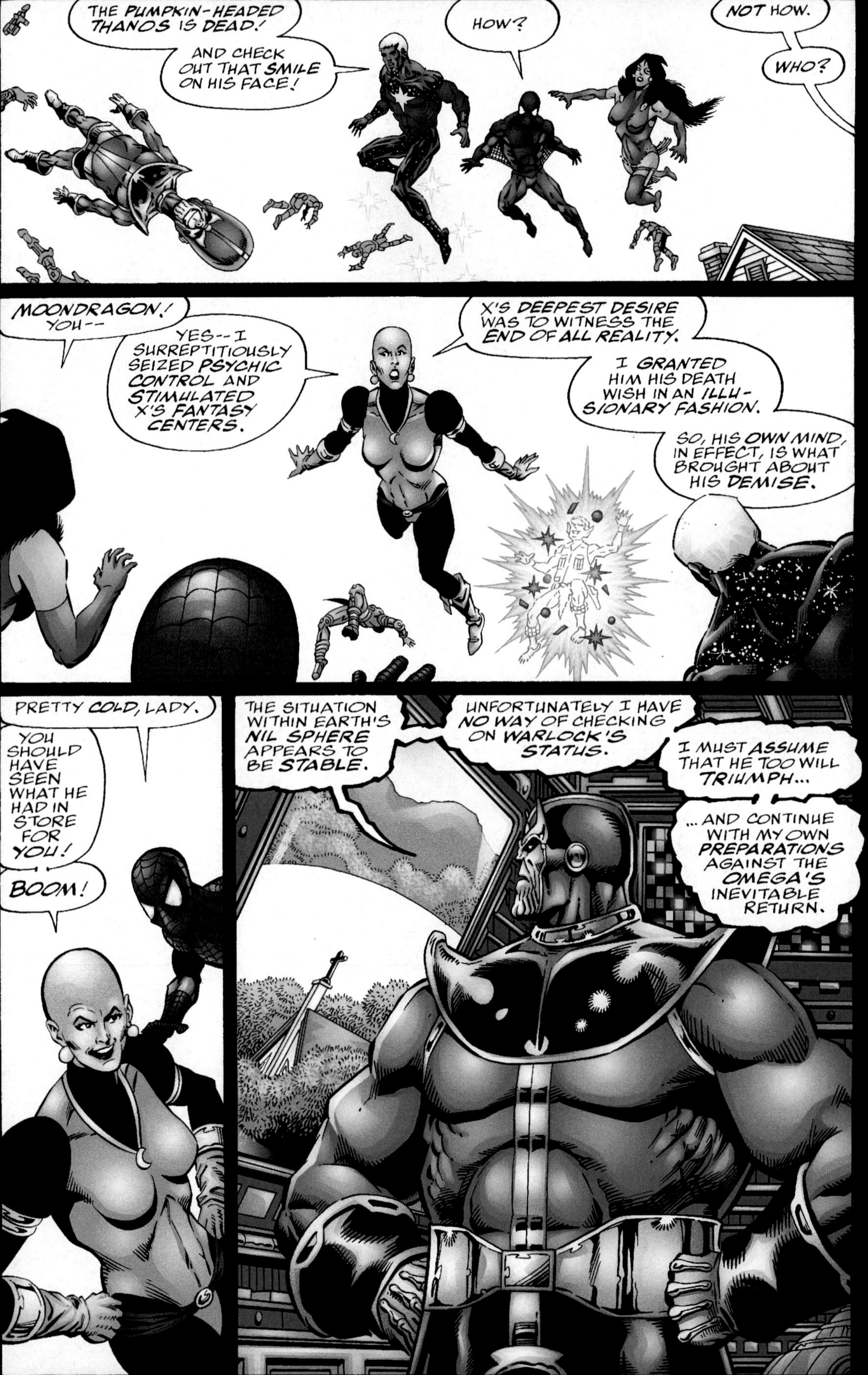

THE PUMPKIN-HEADED THANOS IS DEAD!
AND CHECK OUT THAT SMILE ON HIS FACE!
HOW?
NOT HOW.
WHO?
MOONDRAGON! YOU--
YES--I SURREPTITIOUSLY SEIZED PSYCHIC CONTROL AND STIMULATED X'S FANTASY CENTERS.
X'S DEEPEST DESIRE WAS TO WITNESS THE END OF ALL REALITY.
I GRANTED HIM HIS DEATH WISH IN AN ILLUSIONARY FASHION.
SO, HIS OWN MIND, IN EFFECT, IS WHAT BROUGHT ABOUT HIS DEMISE.
PRETTY COLD, LADY.
YOU SHOULD HAVE SEEN WHAT HE HAD IN STORE FOR YOU!
BOOM!
THE SITUATION WITHIN EARTH'S NIL SPHERE APPEARS TO BE STABLE.
UNFORTUNATELY I HAVE NO WAY OF CHECKING ON WARLOCK'S STATUS.
I MUST ASSUME THAT HE TOO WILL TRIUMPH...
...AND CONTINUE WITH MY OWN PREPARATIONS AGAINST THE OMEGA'S INEVITABLE RETURN.

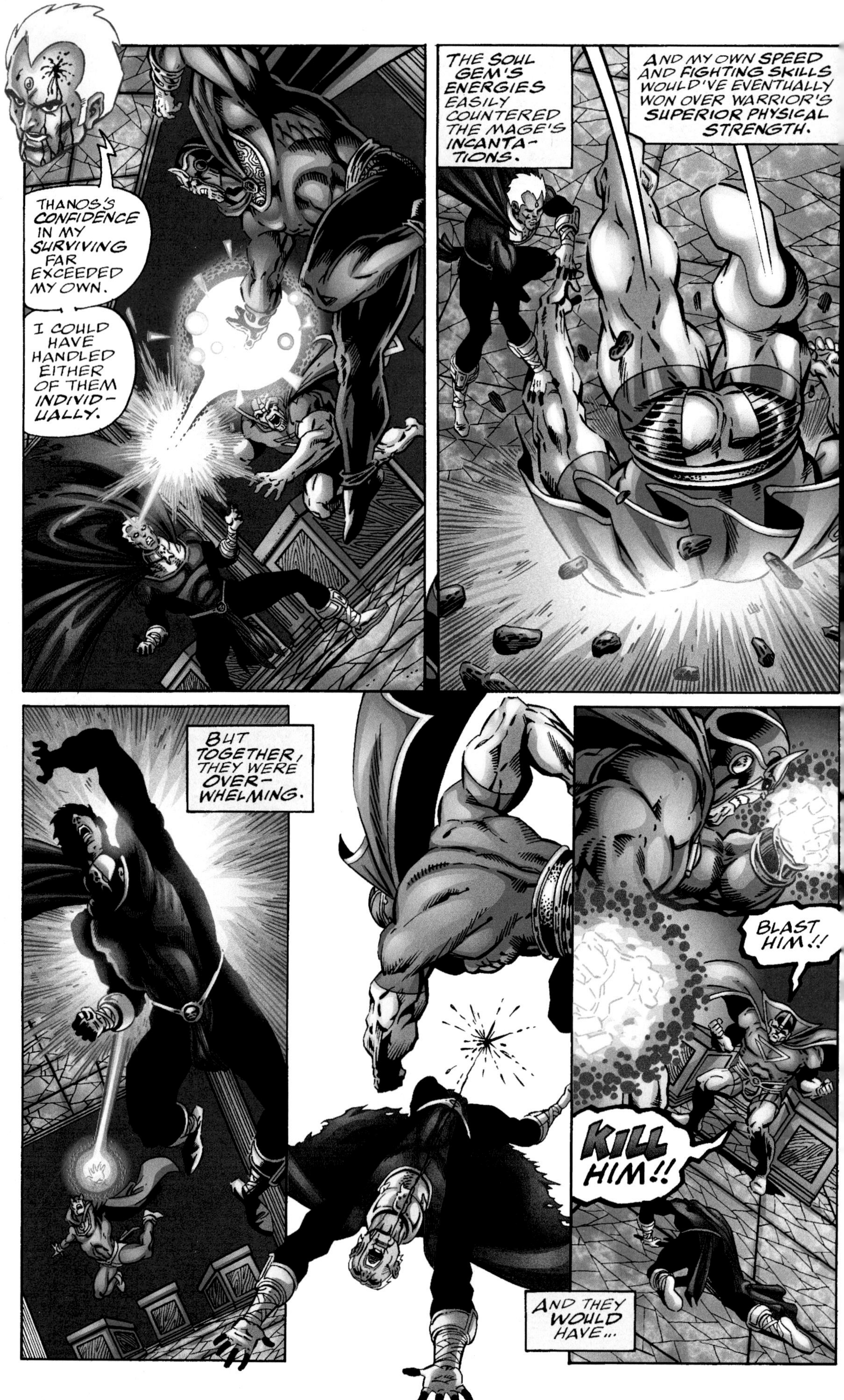
THANOS'S CONFIDENCE IN MY SURVIVING FAR EXCEEDED MY OWN.
I COULD HAVE HANDLED EITHER OF THEM INDIVID-UALLY.
THE SOUL GEM'S ENERGIES EASILY COUNTERED THE MAGE'S INCANTA-TIONS.
AND MY OWN SPEED AND FIGHTING SKILLS WOULD'VE EVENTUALLY WON OVER WARRIOR'S SUPERIOR PHYSICAL STRENGTH.
BUT TOGETHER, THEY WERE OVER-WHELMING.
BLAST HIM!!
KILL HIM!!
AND THEY WOULD HAVE...

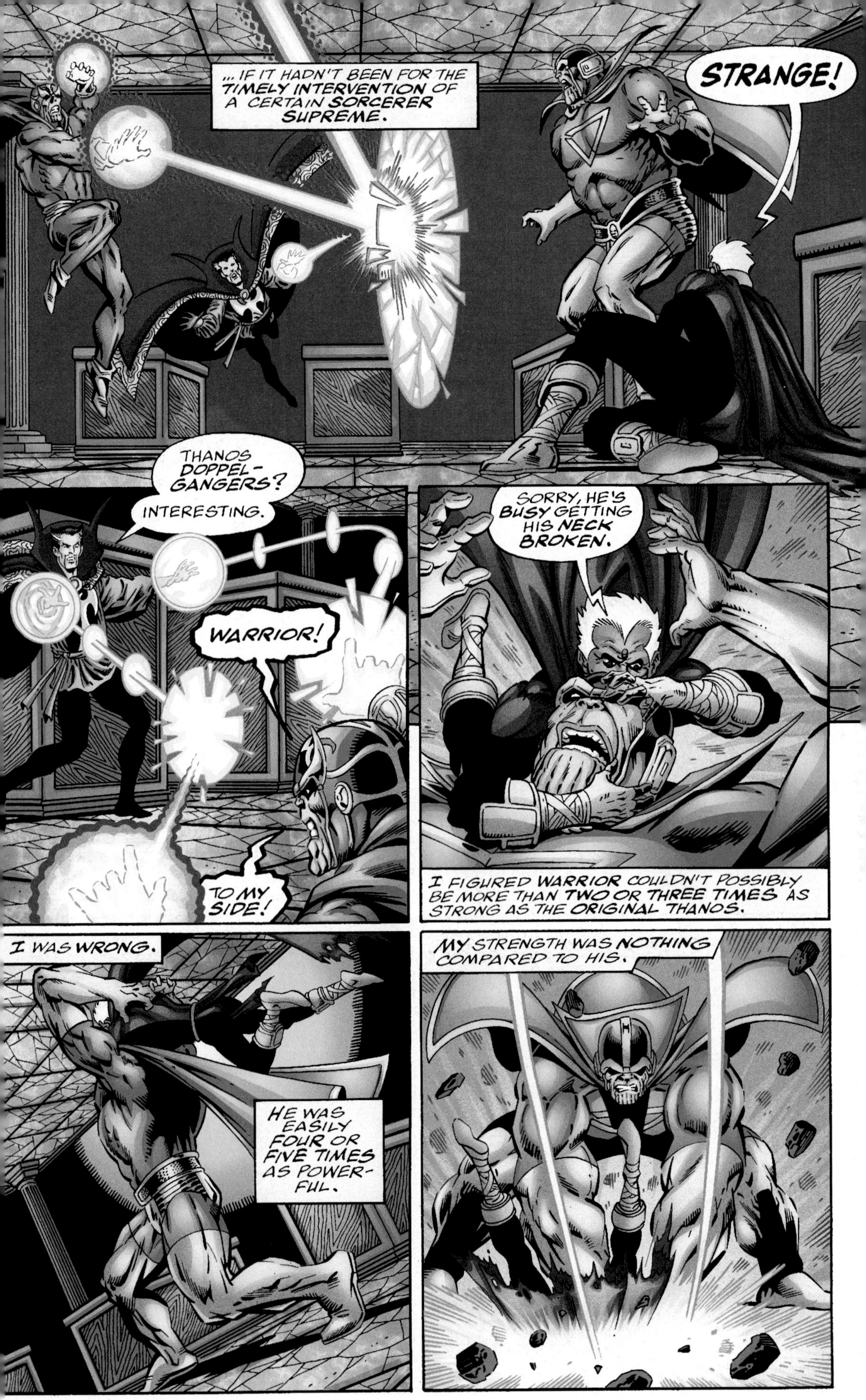
...IF IT HADN'T BEEN FOR THE TIMELY INTERVENTION OF A CERTAIN SORCERER SUPREME.
STRANGE!
THANOS DOPPEL-GANGERS? INTERESTING.
WARRIOR!
TO MY SIDE!
SORRY, HE'S BUSY GETTING HIS NECK BROKEN.
I FIGURED WARRIOR COULDN'T POSSIBLY BE MORE THAN TWO OR THREE TIMES AS STRONG AS THE ORIGINAL THANOS.
I WAS WRONG.
HE WAS EASILY FOUR OR FIVE TIMES AS POWER-FUL.
MY STRENGTH WAS NOTHING COMPARED TO HIS.

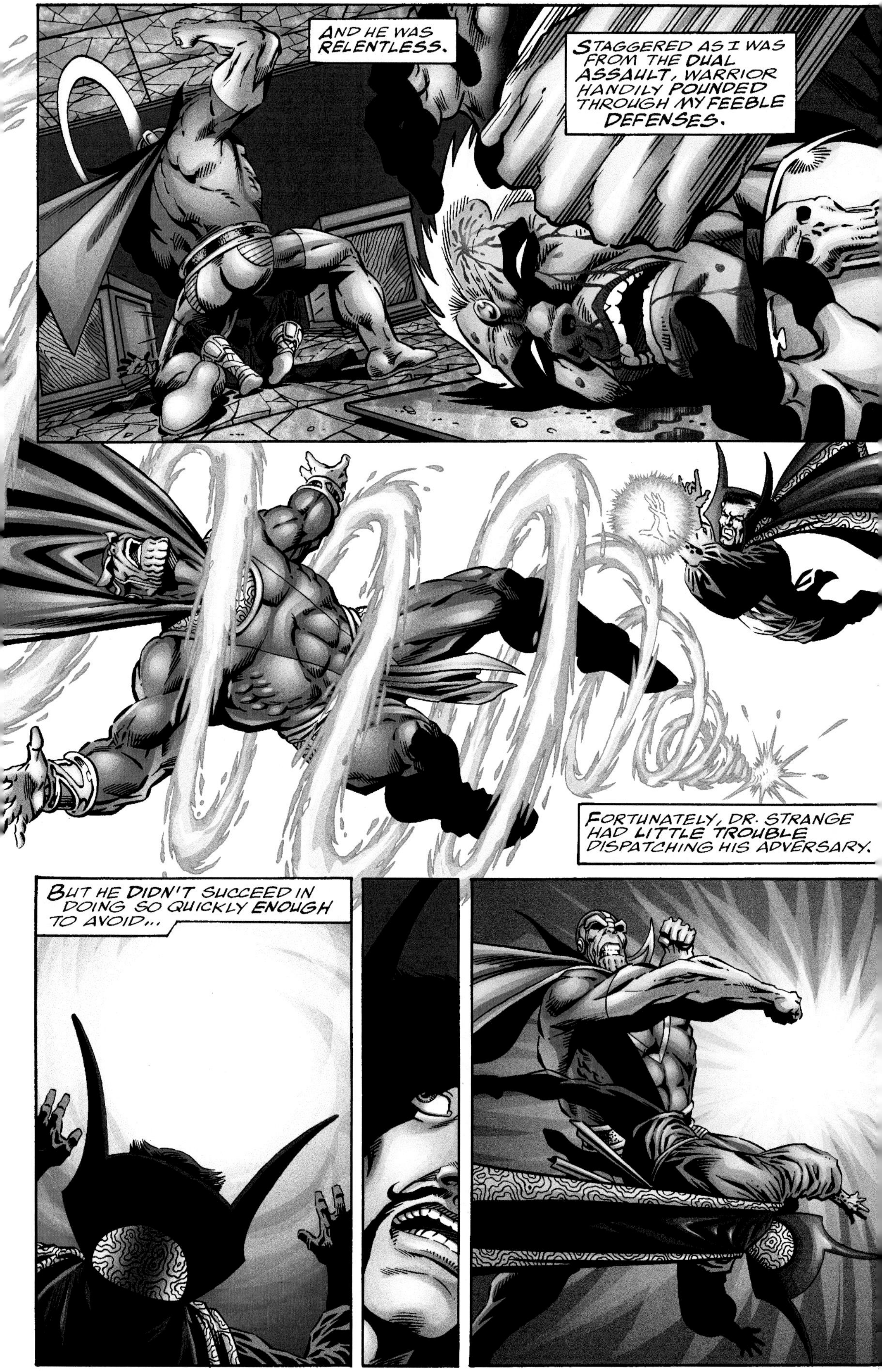

AND HE WAS RELENTLESS.
STAGGERED AS I WAS FROM THE DUAL ASSAULT, WARRIOR HANDILY POUNDED THROUGH MY FEEBLE DEFENSES.
FORTUNATELY, DR. STRANGE HAD LITTLE TROUBLE DISPATCHING HIS ADVERSARY.
BUT HE DIDN'T SUCCEED IN DOING SO QUICKLY ENOUGH TO AVOID...

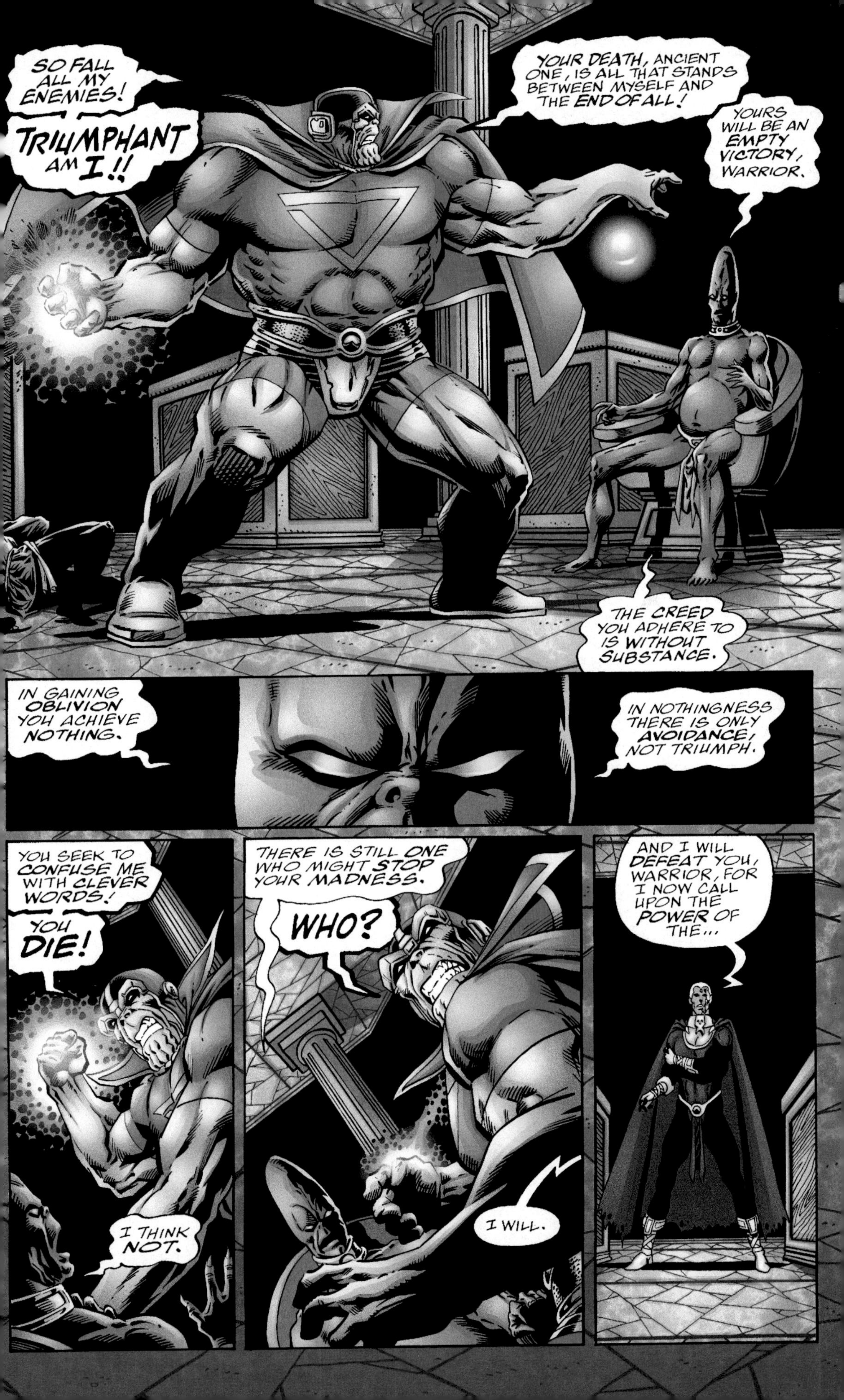
SO FALL ALL MY ENEMIES!
TRIUMPHANT AM I!!
YOUR DEATH, ANCIENT ONE, IS ALL THAT STANDS BETWEEN MYSELF AND THE END OF ALL!
YOURS WILL BE AN EMPTY VICTORY, WARRIOR.
THE CREED YOU ADHERE TO IS WITHOUT SUBSTANCE.
IN GAINING OBLIVION YOU ACHIEVE NOTHING.
IN NOTHINGNESS THERE IS ONLY AVOIDANCE, NOT TRIUMPH.
YOU SEEK TO CONFUSE ME WITH CLEVER WORDS!
YOU DIE!
I THINK NOT.
THERE IS STILL ONE WHO MIGHT STOP YOUR MADNESS.
WHO?
I WILL.
AND I WILL DEFEAT YOU, WARRIOR, FOR I NOW CALL UPON THE POWER OF THE...

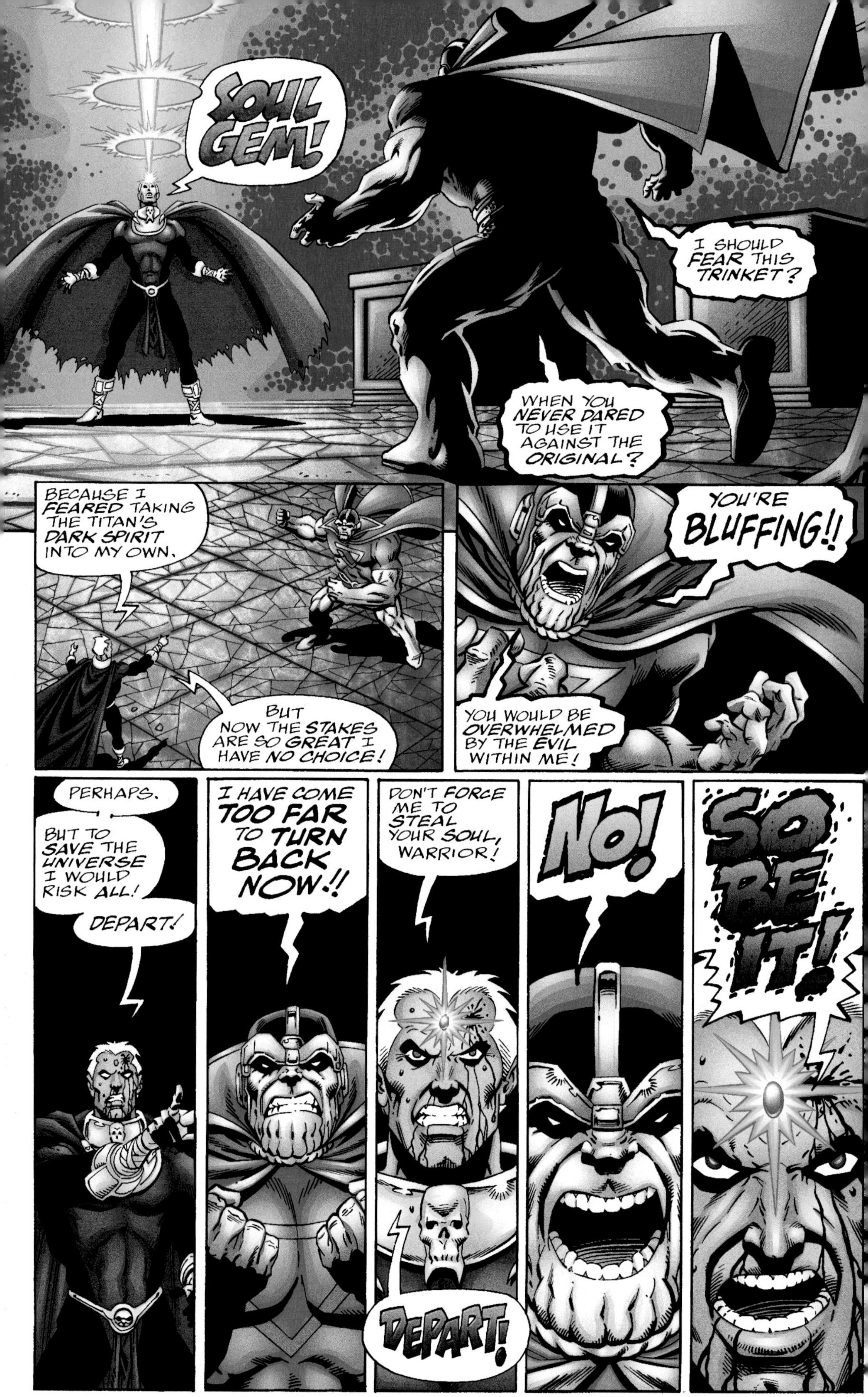
SOUL GEM!
I SHOULD FEAR THIS TRINKET?
WHEN YOU NEVER DARED TO USE IT AGAINST THE ORIGINAL?
BECAUSE I FEARED TAKING THE TITAN'S DARK SPIRIT INTO MY OWN.
BUT NOW THE STAKES ARE SO GREAT I HAVE NO CHOICE!
YOU'RE BLUFFING!!
YOU WOULD BE OVERWHELMED BY THE EVIL WITHIN ME!
PERHAPS.
BUT TO SAVE THE UNIVERSE I WOULD RISK ALL!
DEPART!
I HAVE COME TOO FAR TO TURN BACK NOW!!
DON'T FORCE ME TO STEAL YOUR SOUL, WARRIOR!
DEPART!
NO!
SO BE IT!

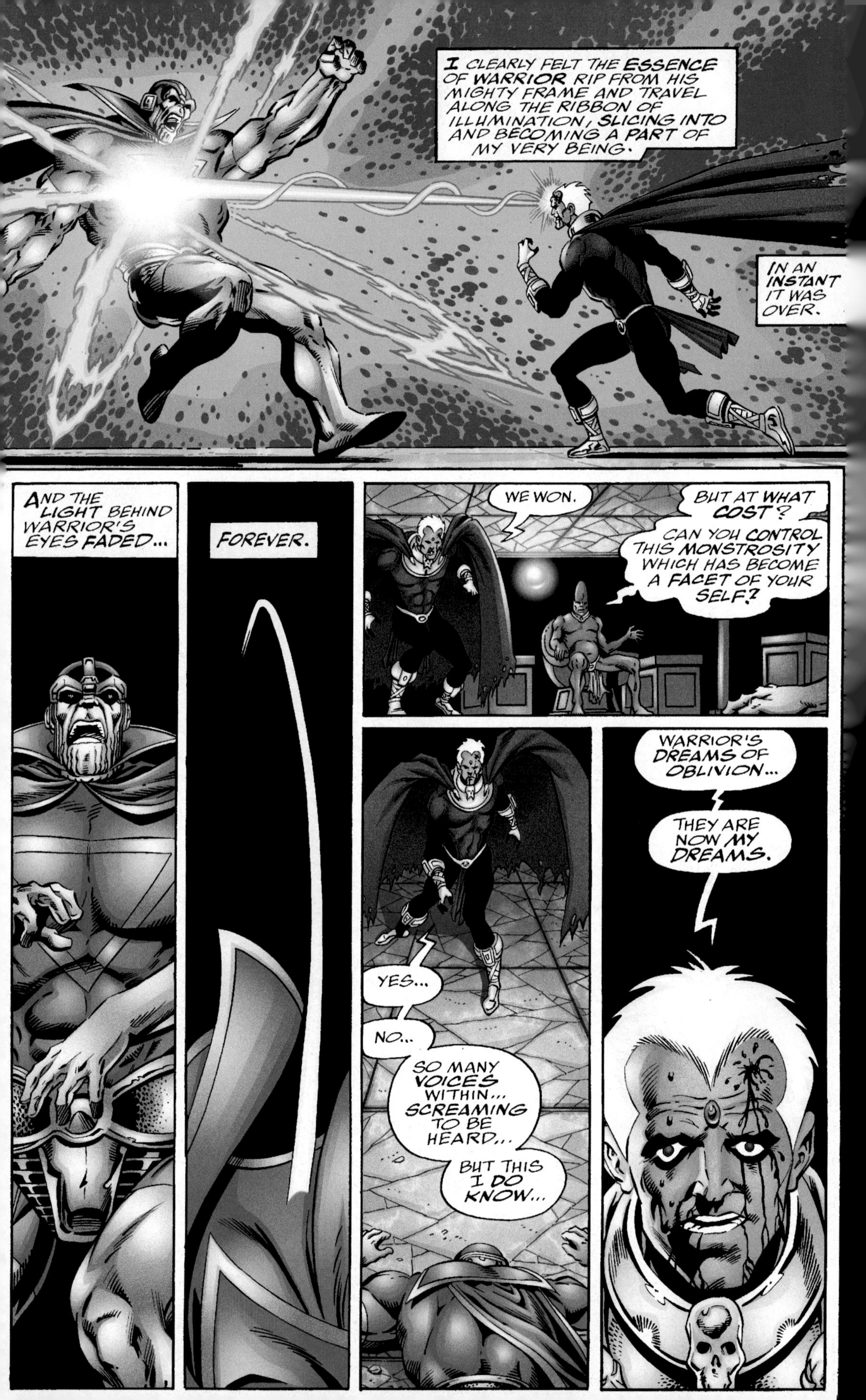

I CLEARLY FELT THE ESSENCE OF WARRIOR RIP FROM HIS MIGHTY FRAME AND TRAVEL ALONG THE RIBBON OF ILLUMINATION, SLICING INTO AND BECOMING A PART OF MY VERY BEING.
IN AN INSTANT IT WAS OVER.
AND THE LIGHT BEHIND WARRIOR'S EYES FADED...
FOREVER.
WE WON.
BUT AT WHAT COST?
CAN YOU CONTROL THIS MONSTROSITY WHICH HAS BECOME A FACET OF YOUR SELF?
YES...
NO...
SO MANY VOICES WITHIN... SCREAMING TO BE HEARD...
BUT THIS I DO KNOW...
WARRIOR'S DREAMS OF OBLIVION...
THEY ARE NOW MY DREAMS.

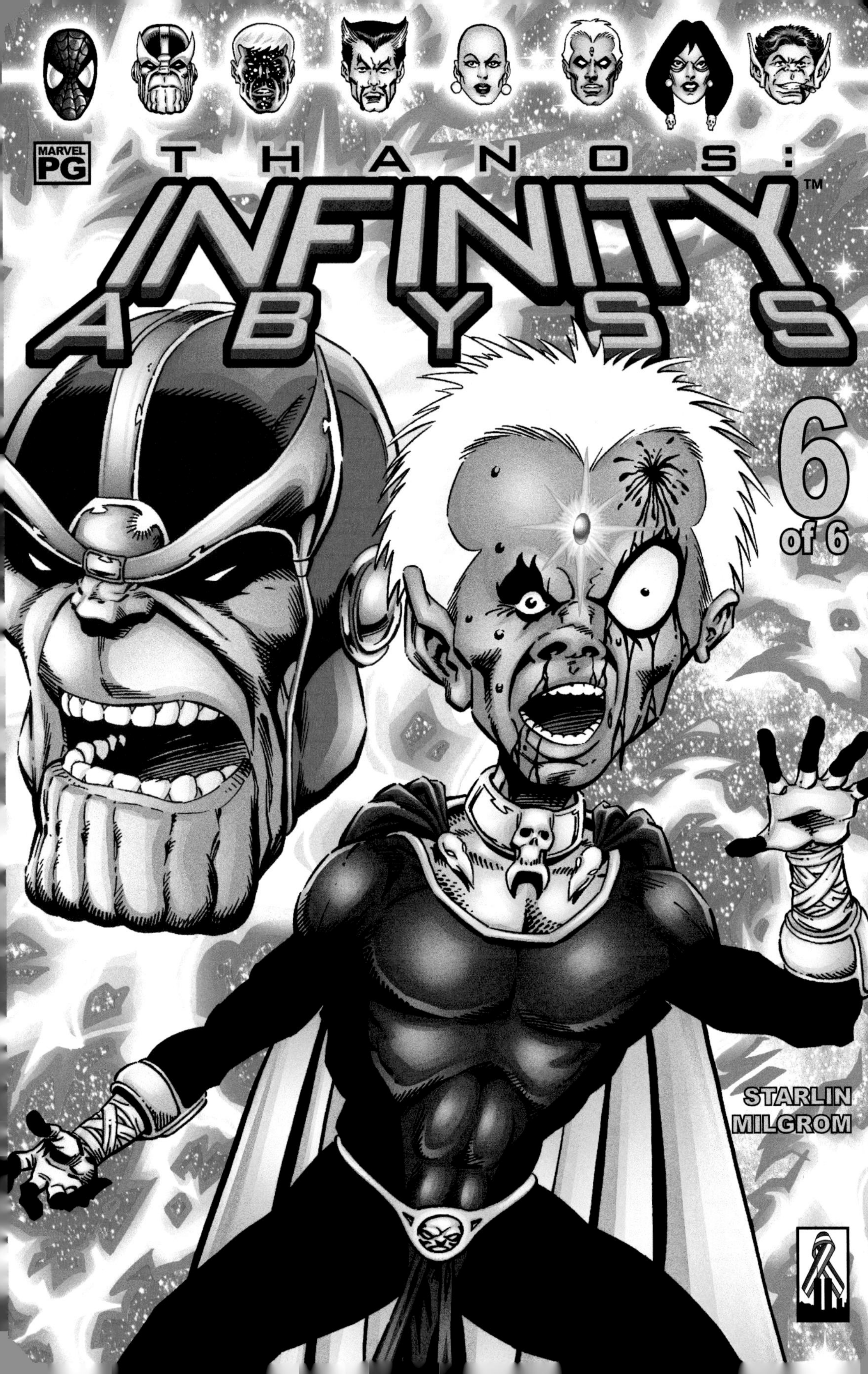
MARVEL PG
THANOS:
INFINITY ABYSS™
6 of 6
STARLIN
MILGROM

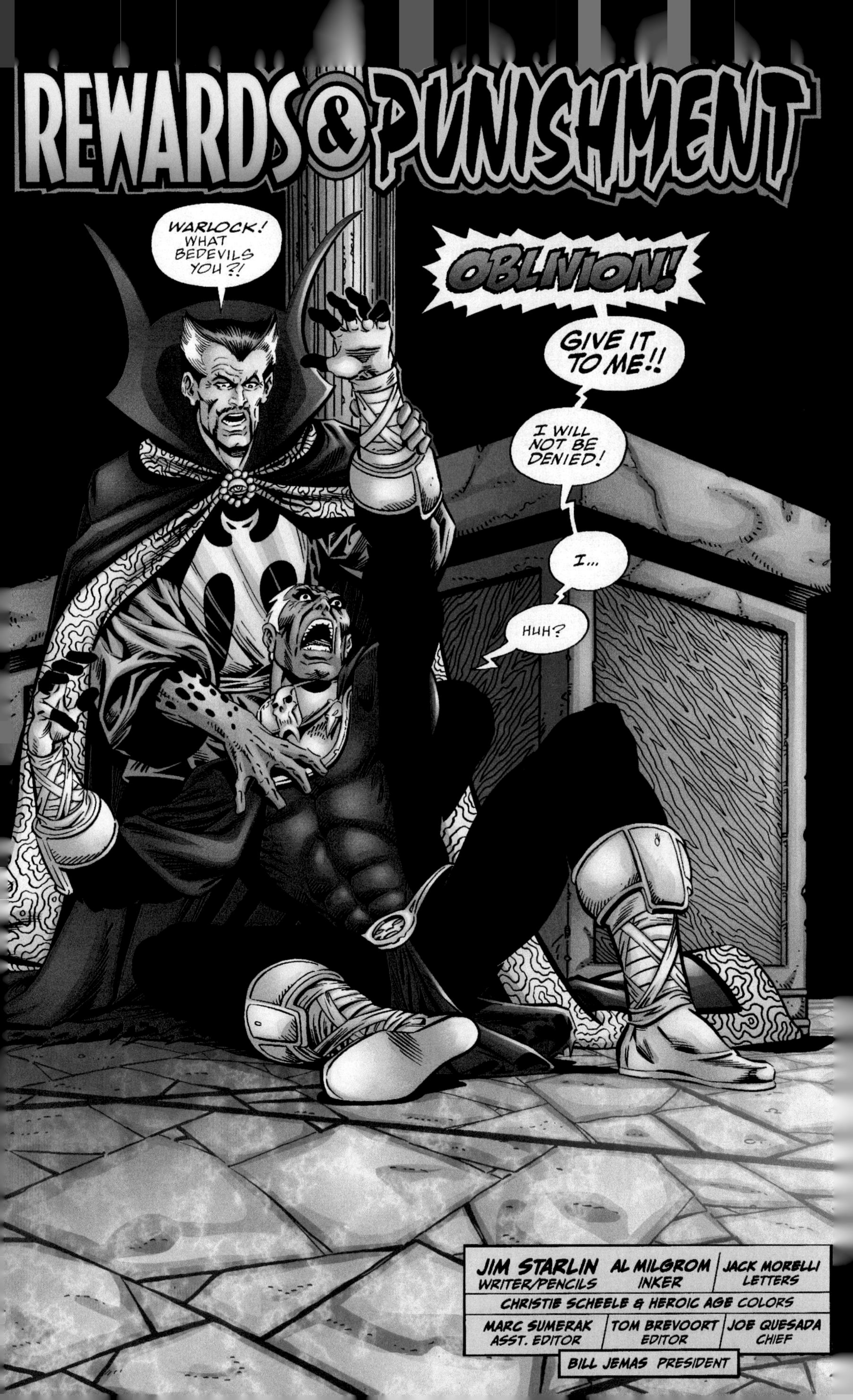

REWARDS & PUNISHMENT
WARLOCK! WHAT BEDEVILS YOU?!
OBLIVION!
GIVE IT TO ME!!
I WILL NOT BE DENIED!
I...
HUH?
JIM STARLIN WRITER/PENCILS
AL MILGROM INKER
JACK MORELLI LETTERS
CHRISTIE SCHEELE & HEROIC AGE COLORS
MARC SUMERAK ASST. EDITOR
TOM BREVOORT EDITOR
JOE QUESADA CHIEF
BILL JEMAS PRESIDENT

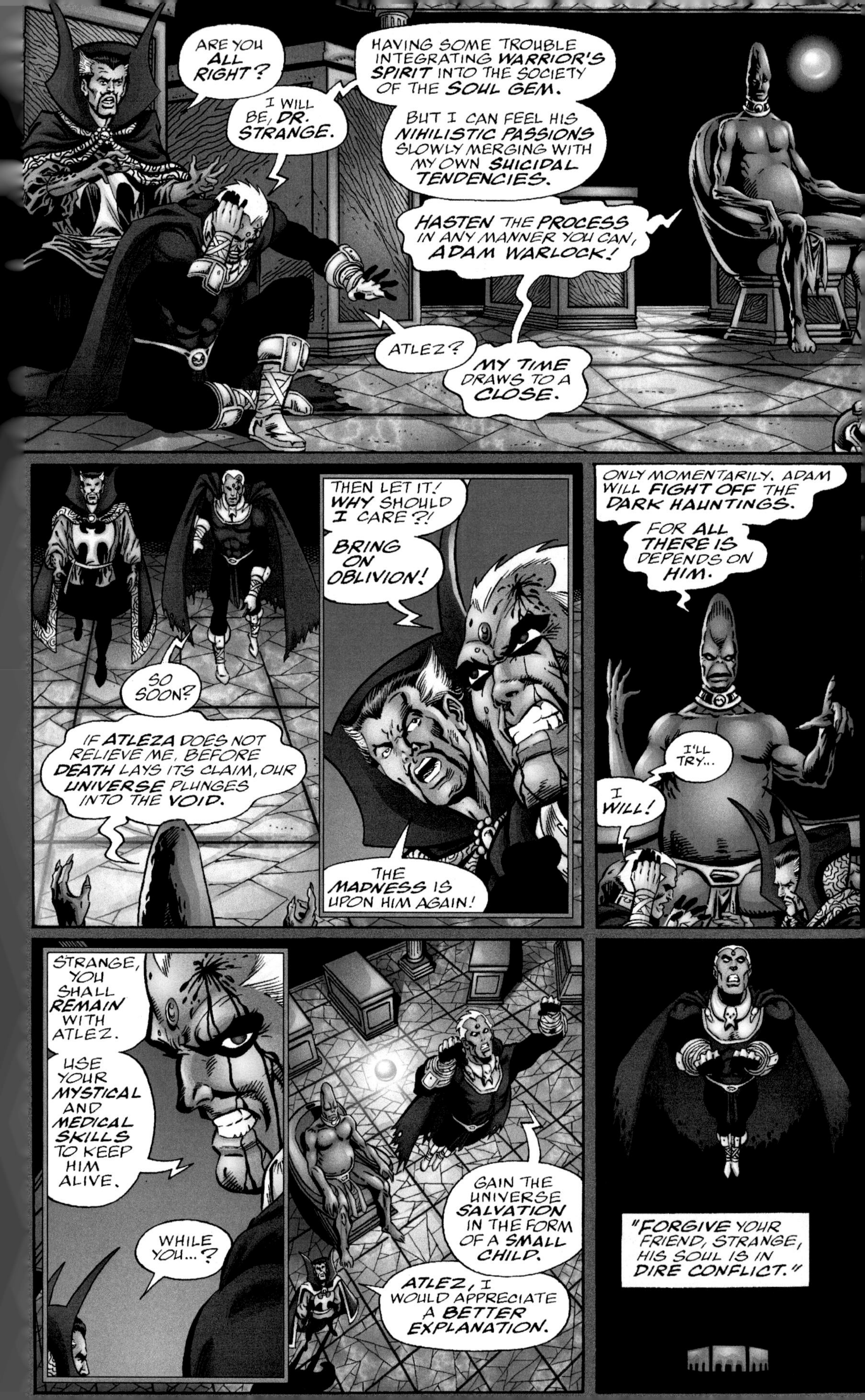
ARE YOU ALL RIGHT?
I WILL BE, DR. STRANGE.
HAVING SOME TROUBLE INTEGRATING WARRIOR'S SPIRIT INTO THE SOCIETY OF THE SOUL GEM.
BUT I CAN FEEL HIS NIHILISTIC PASSIONS SLOWLY MERGING WITH MY OWN SUICIDAL TENDENCIES.
HASTEN THE PROCESS IN ANY MANNER YOU CAN, ADAM WARLOCK!
ATLEZ?
MY TIME DRAWS TO A CLOSE.
SO SOON?
IF ATLEZA DOES NOT RELIEVE ME, BEFORE DEATH LAYS ITS CLAIM, OUR UNIVERSE PLUNGES INTO THE VOID.
THEN LET IT! WHY SHOULD I CARE?!
BRING ON OBLIVION!
THE MADNESS IS UPON HIM AGAIN!
ONLY MOMENTARILY. ADAM WILL FIGHT OFF THE DARK HAUNTINGS.
FOR ALL THERE IS DEPENDS ON HIM.
I'LL TRY...
I WILL!
STRANGE, YOU SHALL REMAIN WITH ATLEZ.
USE YOUR MYSTICAL AND MEDICAL SKILLS TO KEEP HIM ALIVE.
WHILE YOU...?
GAIN THE UNIVERSE SALVATION IN THE FORM OF A SMALL CHILD.
ATLEZ, I WOULD APPRECIATE A BETTER EXPLANATION.
"FORGIVE YOUR FRIEND, STRANGE, HIS SOUL IS IN DIRE CONFLICT."

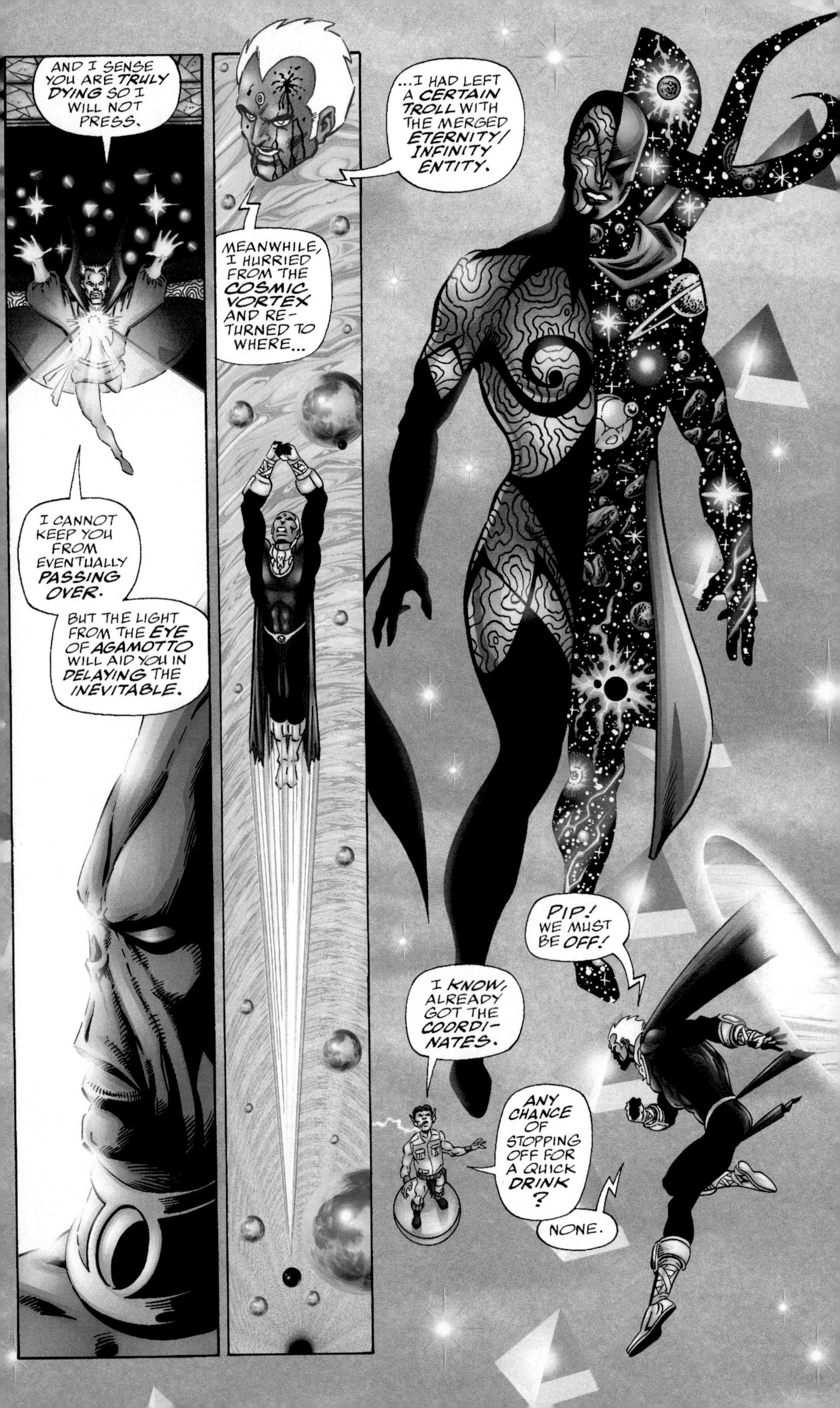
AND I SENSE YOU ARE TRULY DYING SO I WILL NOT PRESS.
I CANNOT KEEP YOU FROM EVENTUALLY PASSING OVER.
BUT THE LIGHT FROM THE EYE OF AGAMOTTO WILL AID YOU IN DELAYING THE INEVITABLE.
...I HAD LEFT A CERTAIN TROLL WITH THE MERGED ETERNITY/INFINITY ENTITY.
MEANWHILE, I HURRIED FROM THE COSMIC VORTEX AND RE-TURNED TO WHERE...
PIP! WE MUST BE OFF!
I KNOW, ALREADY GOT THE COORDI-NATES.
ANY CHANCE OF STOPPING OFF FOR A QUICK DRINK?
NONE.

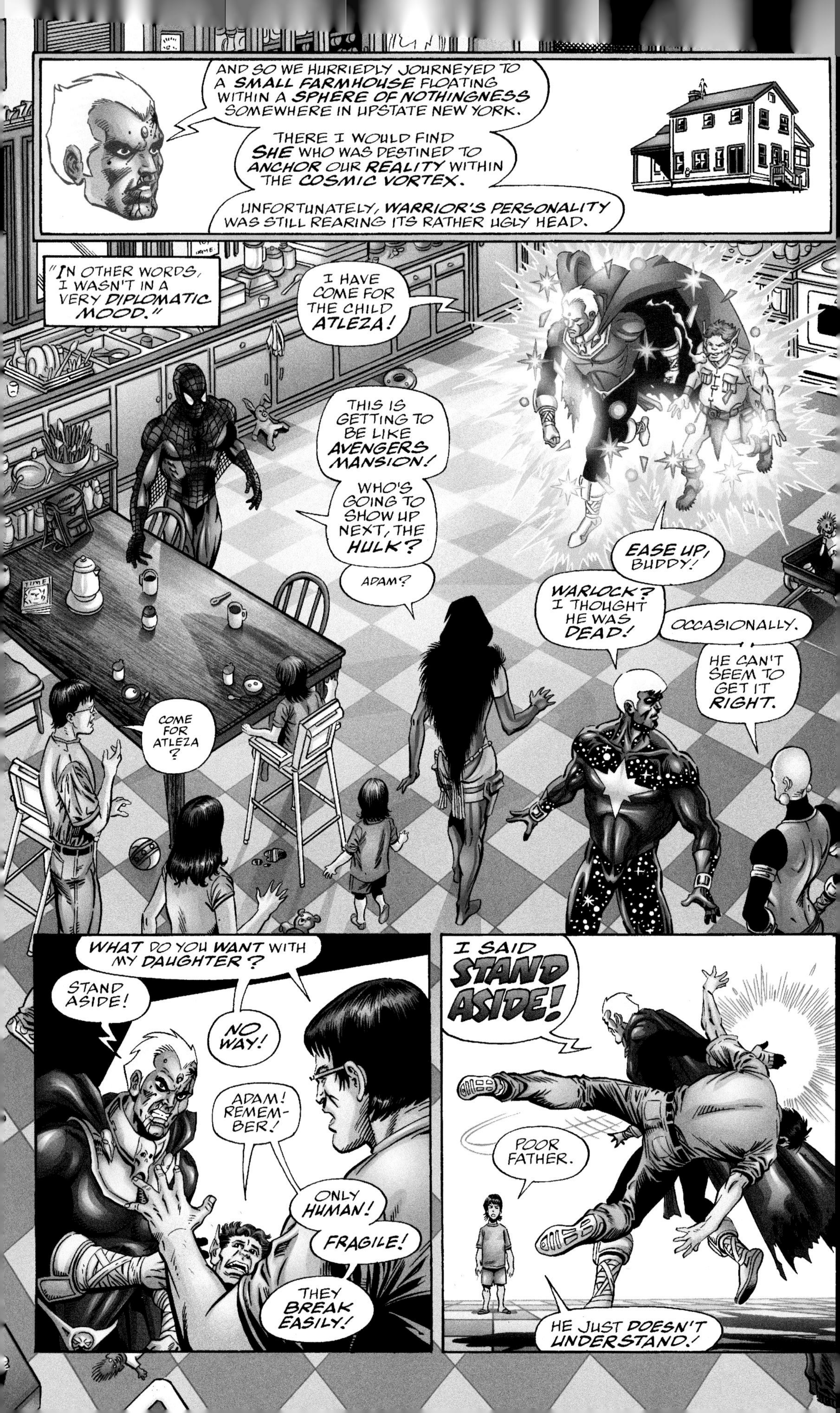

AND SO WE HURRIEDLY JOURNEYED TO A SMALL FARMHOUSE FLOATING WITHIN A SPHERE OF NOTHINGNESS SOMEWHERE IN UPSTATE NEW YORK.
THERE I WOULD FIND SHE WHO WAS DESTINED TO ANCHOR OUR REALITY WITHIN THE COSMIC VORTEX.
UNFORTUNATELY, WARRIOR'S PERSONALITY WAS STILL REARING ITS RATHER UGLY HEAD.
"IN OTHER WORDS, I WASN'T IN A VERY DIPLOMATIC MOOD."
I HAVE COME FOR THE CHILD ATLEZA!
THIS IS GETTING TO BE LIKE AVENGERS MANSION!
WHO'S GOING TO SHOW UP NEXT, THE HULK?
ADAM?
EASE UP, BUDDY!
WARLOCK? I THOUGHT HE WAS DEAD!
OCCASIONALLY.
HE CAN'T SEEM TO GET IT RIGHT.
COME FOR ATLEZA?
WHAT DO YOU WANT WITH MY DAUGHTER?
STAND ASIDE!
NO WAY!
ADAM! REMEMBER!
ONLY HUMAN!
FRAGILE!
THEY BREAK EASILY!
I SAID STAND ASIDE!
POOR FATHER.
HE JUST DOESN'T UNDERSTAND.

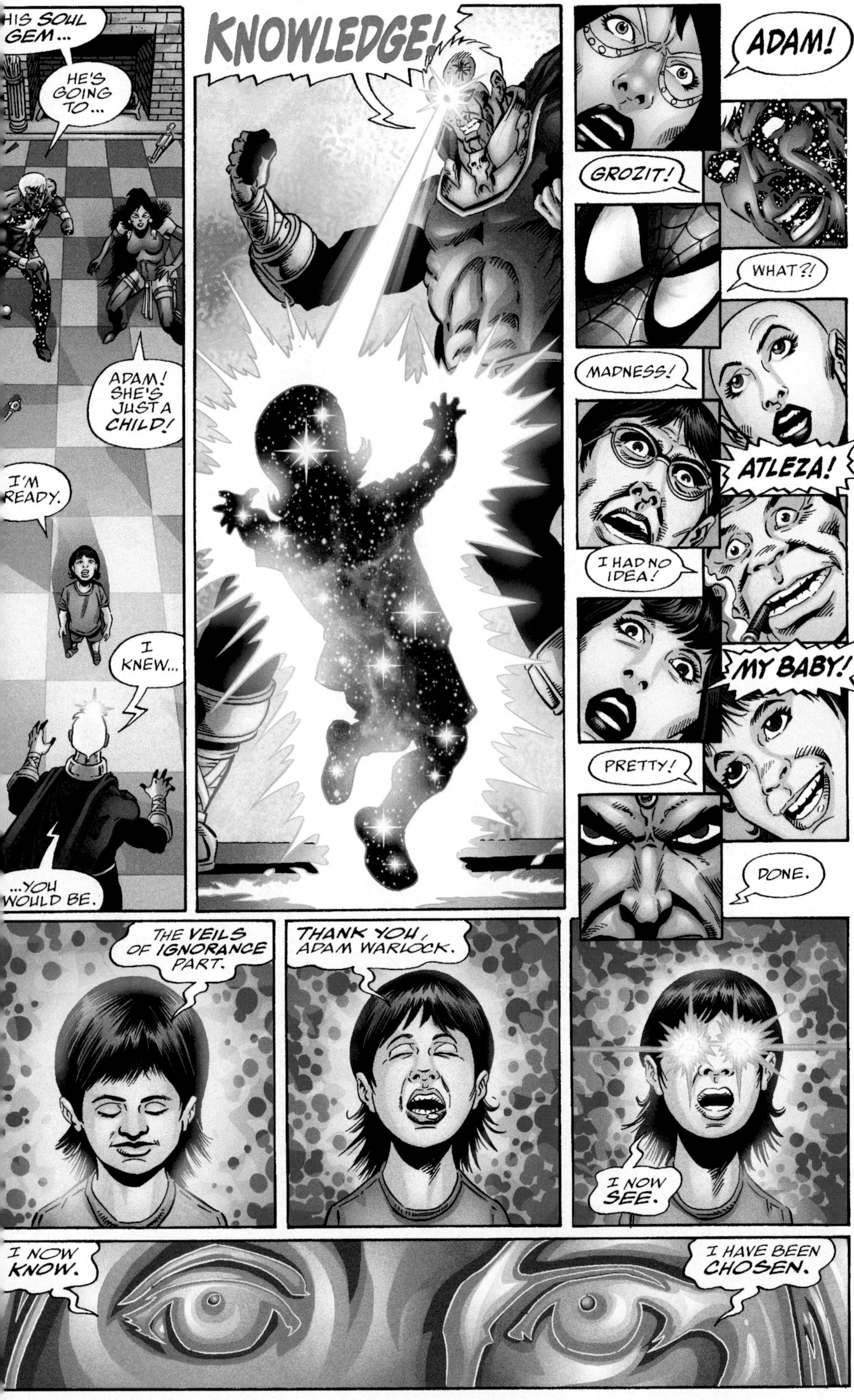

HIS SOUL GEM...
HE'S GOING TO...
ADAM! SHE'S JUST A CHILD!
I'M READY.
I KNEW...
...YOU WOULD BE.
KNOWLEDGE!
ADAM!
GROZIT!
WHAT?!
MADNESS!
ATLEZA!
I HAD NO IDEA!
MY BABY!
PRETTY!
DONE.
THE VEILS OF IGNORANCE PART.
THANK YOU, ADAM WARLOCK.
I NOW SEE.
I NOW KNOW.
I HAVE BEEN CHOSEN.

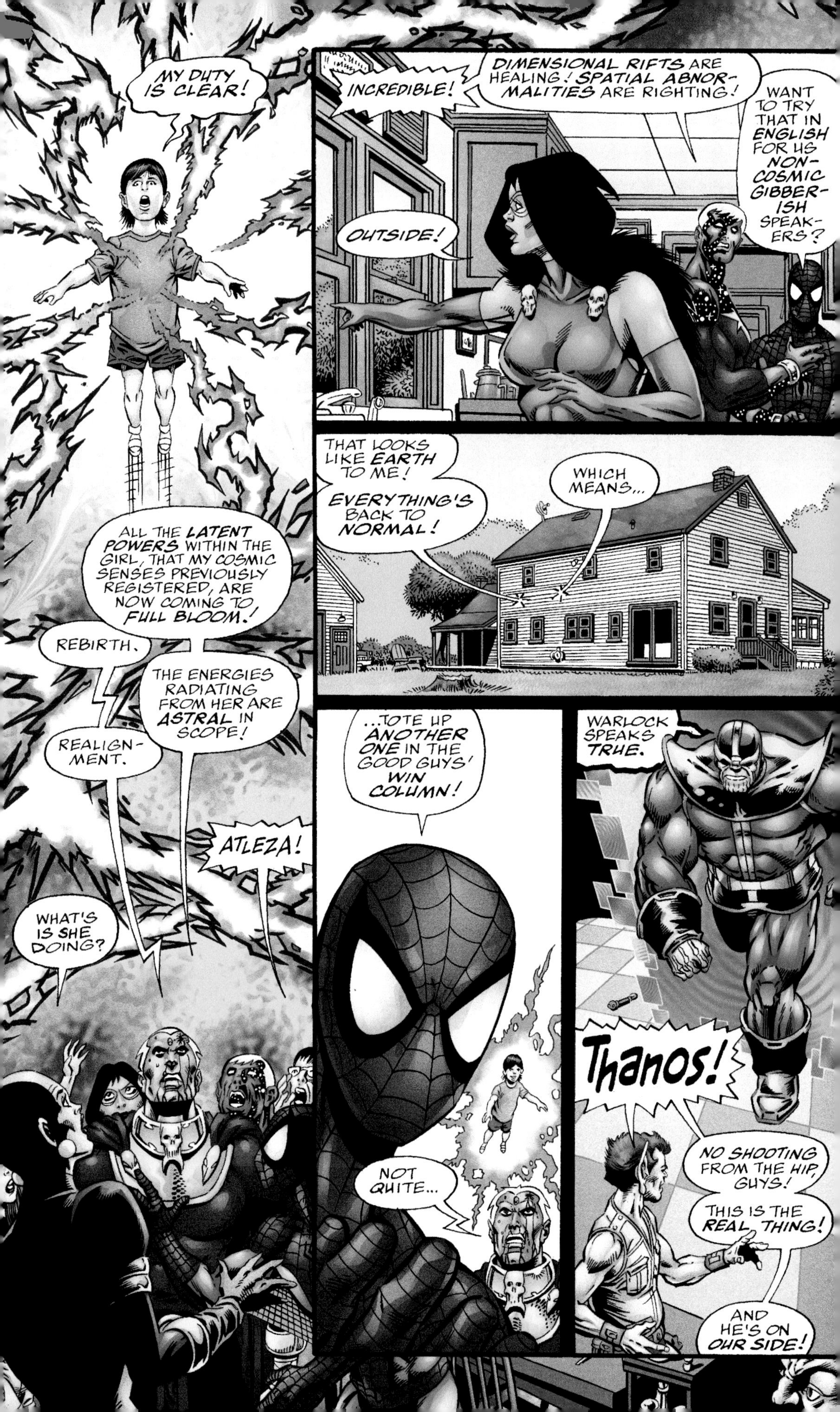
MY DUTY IS CLEAR!
ALL THE LATENT POWERS WITHIN THE GIRL, THAT MY COSMIC SENSES PREVIOUSLY REGISTERED, ARE NOW COMING TO FULL BLOOM.!
REBIRTH.
THE ENERGIES RADIATING FROM HER ARE ASTRAL IN SCOPE!
REALIGNMENT.
ATLEZA!
WHAT'S IS SHE DOING?
INCREDIBLE!
DIMENSIONAL RIFTS ARE HEALING! SPATIAL ABNORMALITIES ARE RIGHTING!
WANT TO TRY THAT IN ENGLISH FOR US NON-COSMIC GIBBERISH SPEAKERS?
OUTSIDE!
THAT LOOKS LIKE EARTH TO ME!
EVERYTHING'S BACK TO NORMAL!
WHICH MEANS...
...TOTE UP ANOTHER ONE IN THE GOOD GUYS' WIN COLUMN!
NOT QUITE...
WARLOCK SPEAKS TRUE.
Thanos!
NO SHOOTING FROM THE HIP, GUYS!
THIS IS THE REAL THING!
AND HE'S ON OUR SIDE!

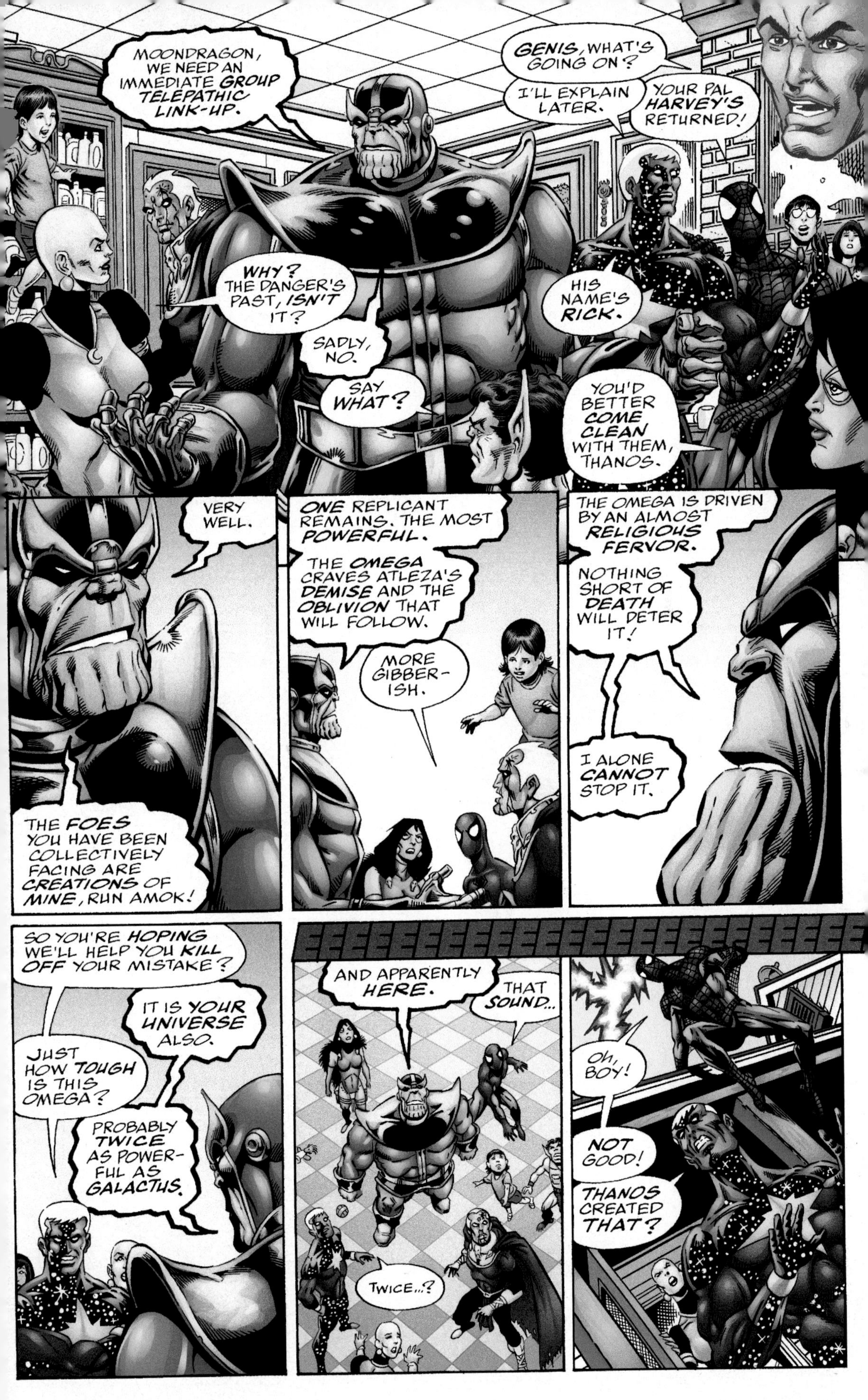
MOONDRAGON, WE NEED AN IMMEDIATE GROUP TELEPATHIC LINK-UP.
GENIS, WHAT'S GOING ON?
I'LL EXPLAIN LATER.
YOUR PAL HARVEY'S RETURNED!
WHY? THE DANGER'S PAST, ISN'T IT?
HIS NAME'S RICK.
SADLY, NO.
SAY WHAT?
YOU'D BETTER COME CLEAN WITH THEM, THANOS.
VERY WELL.
THE FOES YOU HAVE BEEN COLLECTIVELY FACING ARE CREATIONS OF MINE, RUN AMOK!
ONE REPLICANT REMAINS. THE MOST POWERFUL.
THE OMEGA CRAVES ATLEZA'S DEMISE AND THE OBLIVION THAT WILL FOLLOW.
MORE GIBBER-ISH.
THE OMEGA IS DRIVEN BY AN ALMOST RELIGIOUS FERVOR.
NOTHING SHORT OF DEATH WILL DETER IT!
I ALONE CANNOT STOP IT.
SO YOU'RE HOPING WE'LL HELP YOU KILL OFF YOUR MISTAKE?
IT IS YOUR UNIVERSE ALSO.
JUST HOW TOUGH IS THIS OMEGA?
PROBABLY TWICE AS POWER-FUL AS GALACTUS.
EEEEEEEEEEEEEEEEEEEEEEE
AND APPARENTLY HERE.
THAT SOUND...
TWICE...?
OH, BOY!
NOT GOOD!
THANOS CREATED THAT?

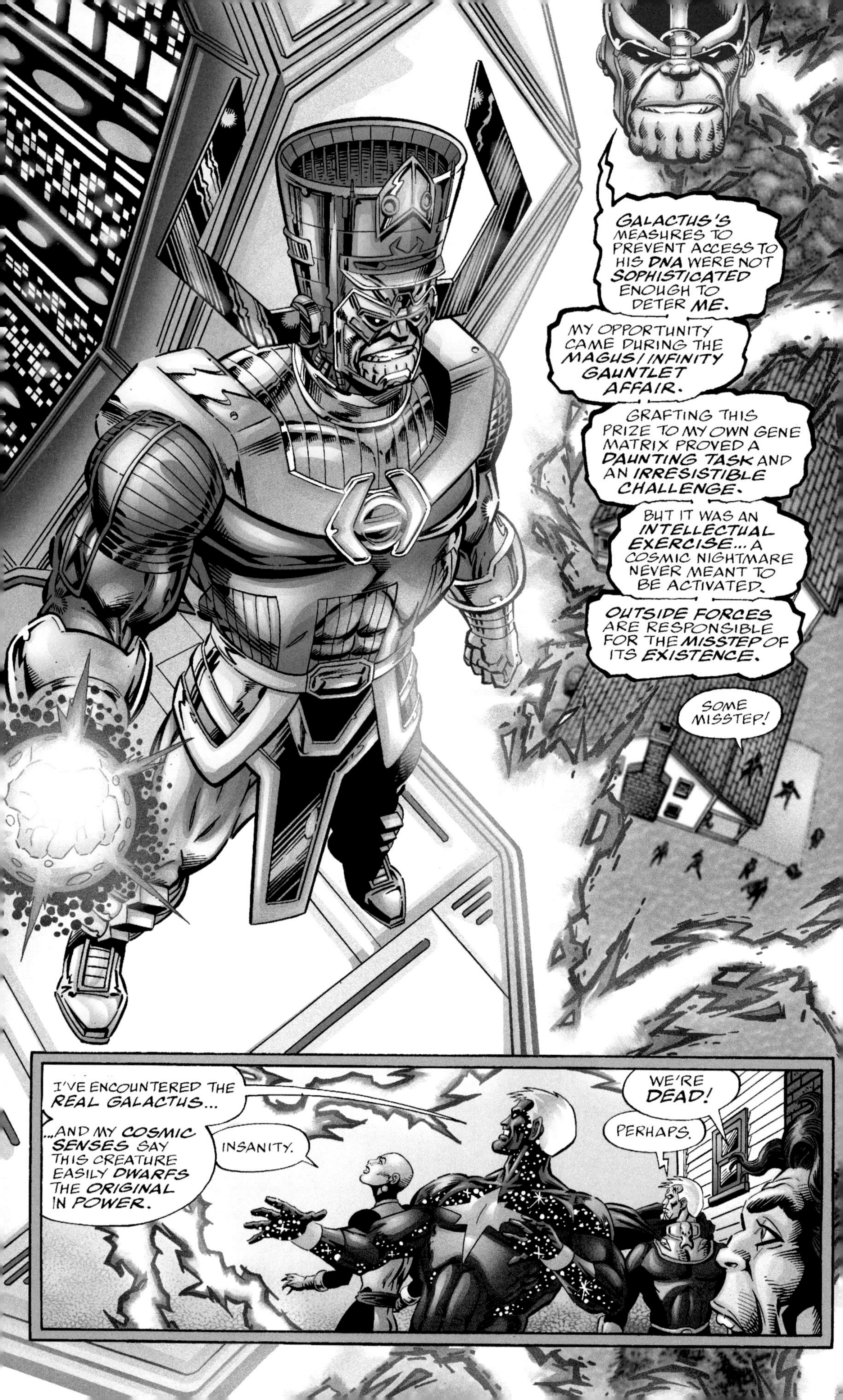

GALACTUS'S MEASURES TO PREVENT ACCESS TO HIS DNA WERE NOT SOPHISTICATED ENOUGH TO DETER ME.
MY OPPORTUNITY CAME DURING THE MAGUS/INFINITY GAUNTLET AFFAIR.
GRAFTING THIS PRIZE TO MY OWN GENE MATRIX PROVED A DAUNTING TASK AND AN IRRESISTIBLE CHALLENGE.
BUT IT WAS AN INTELLECTUAL EXERCISE... A COSMIC NIGHTMARE NEVER MEANT TO BE ACTIVATED.
OUTSIDE FORCES ARE RESPONSIBLE FOR THE MISSTEP OF ITS EXISTENCE.
SOME MISSTEP!
I'VE ENCOUNTERED THE REAL GALACTUS...
...AND MY COSMIC SENSES SAY THIS CREATURE EASILY DWARFS THE ORIGINAL IN POWER.
INSANITY.
WE'RE DEAD!
PERHAPS.

SURPRISE #1.

THERE WAS **NO PREAMBLE** TO THE OMEGA'S ASSAULT.

THANOS HADN'T BURDENED HIS FRANKENSTEIN WITH THE **GIFT OF SPEECH.**

WHY COMMUNICATE **VERBALLY** WHEN YOU WIELD SUCH **MIGHT?**

BUT WHEN DEALING WITH THE **MAD TITAN** ONE SHOULD **ALWAYS** EXPECT THE **UNEXPECTED.**

A **FORCE-FIELD!** PROTECTING THE **HOUSE** AND **US!**

THIS HAS TO BE **THANOS'S** DOING!

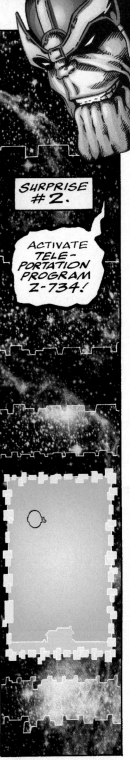

SURPRISE #2.

ACTIVATE **TELE-PORTATION** PROGRAM Z-734!

WHAT HAS THAT MANIAC DONE NOW?

WE'VE BEEN TRANSPORTED OFF **EARTH!**

MANIAC?

HEY! I DIDN'T DO THIS!

VERY CLEVER.

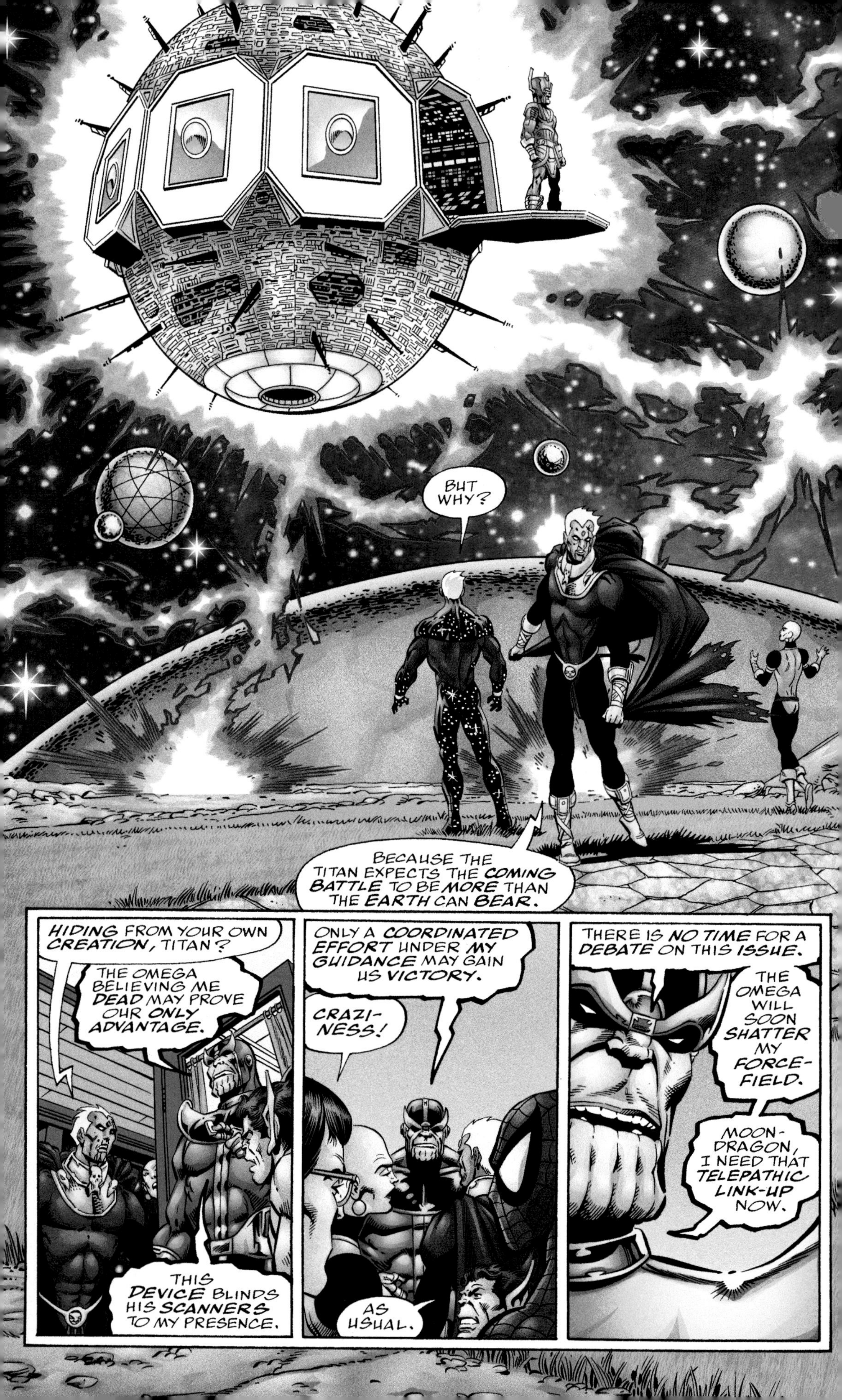
BUT WHY?
BECAUSE THE TITAN EXPECTS THE COMING BATTLE TO BE MORE THAN THE EARTH CAN BEAR.
HIDING FROM YOUR OWN CREATION, TITAN?
THE OMEGA BELIEVING ME DEAD MAY PROVE OUR ONLY ADVANTAGE.
THIS DEVICE BLINDS HIS SCANNERS TO MY PRESENCE.
ONLY A COORDINATED EFFORT UNDER MY GUIDANCE MAY GAIN US VICTORY.
CRAZI- NESS!
AS USUAL.
THERE IS NO TIME FOR A DEBATE ON THIS ISSUE.
THE OMEGA WILL SOON SHATTER MY FORCE- FIELD.
MOON- DRAGON, I NEED THAT TELEPATHIC LINK-UP NOW.

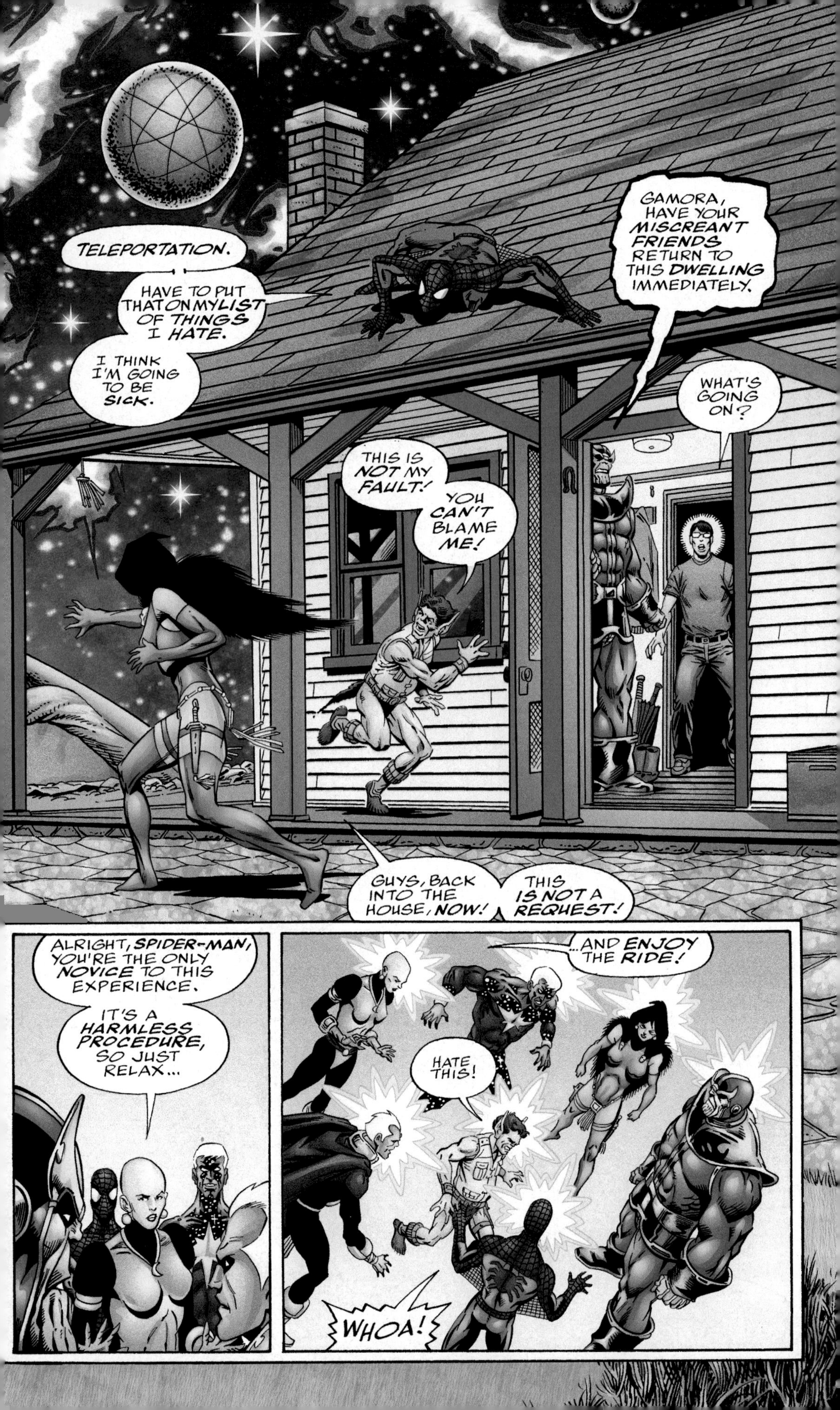
TELEPORTATION.
HAVE TO PUT THAT ON MY LIST OF THINGS I HATE.
I THINK I'M GOING TO BE SICK.
GAMORA, HAVE YOUR MISCREANT FRIENDS RETURN TO THIS DWELLING IMMEDIATELY.
WHAT'S GOING ON?
THIS IS NOT MY FAULT!
YOU CAN'T BLAME ME!
GUYS, BACK INTO THE HOUSE, NOW!
THIS IS NOT A REQUEST!
ALRIGHT, SPIDER-MAN, YOU'RE THE ONLY NOVICE TO THIS EXPERIENCE.
IT'S A HARMLESS PROCEDURE, SO JUST RELAX...
...AND ENJOY THE RIDE!
HATE THIS!
WHOA!

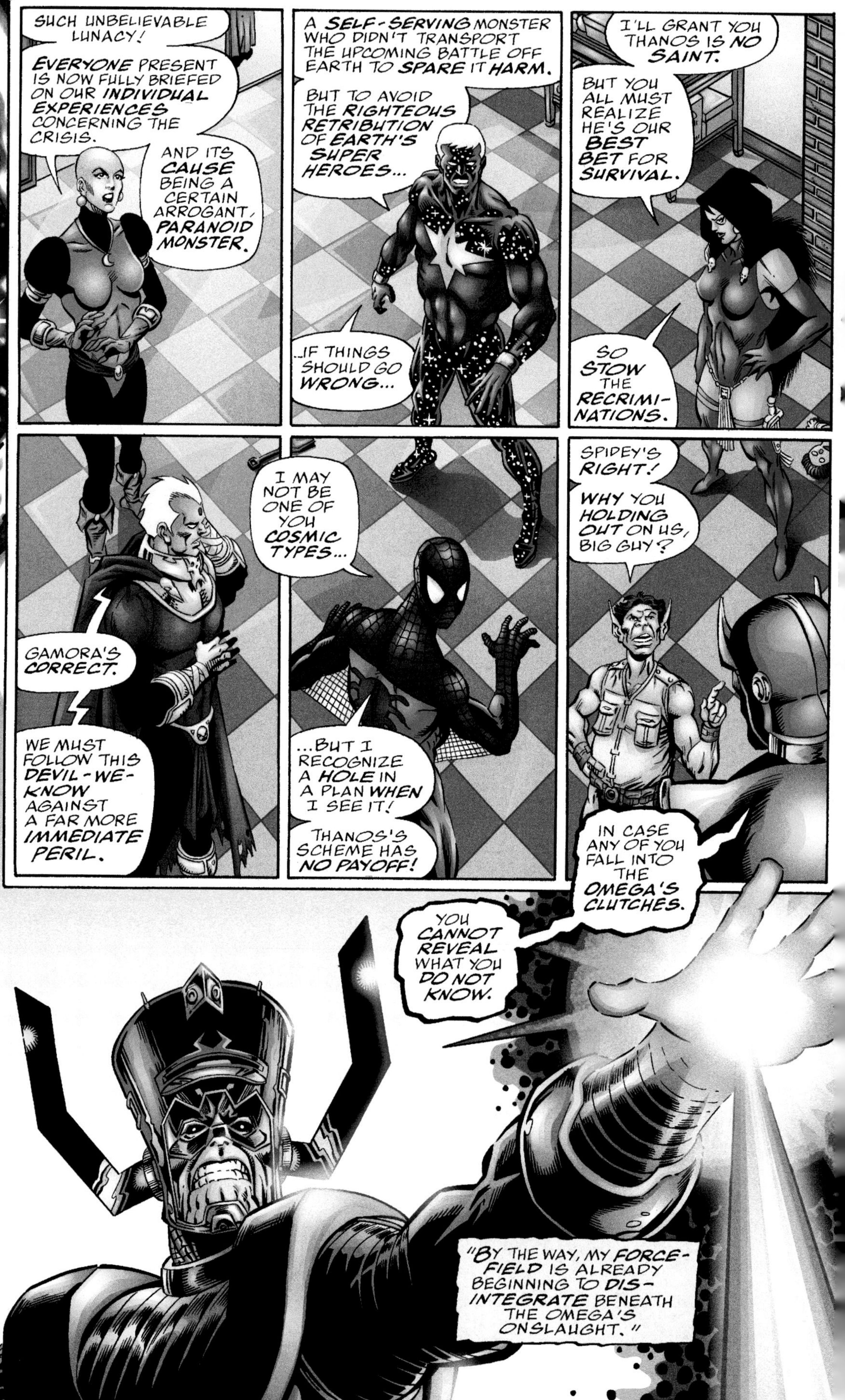

SUCH UNBELIEVABLE LUNACY!
EVERYONE PRESENT IS NOW FULLY BRIEFED ON OUR INDIVIDUAL EXPERIENCES CONCERNING THE CRISIS.
AND ITS CAUSE BEING A CERTAIN ARROGANT, PARANOID MONSTER.
A SELF-SERVING MONSTER WHO DIDN'T TRANSPORT THE UPCOMING BATTLE OFF EARTH TO SPARE IT HARM.
BUT TO AVOID THE RIGHTEOUS RETRIBUTION OF EARTH'S SUPER HEROES...
...IF THINGS SHOULD GO WRONG...
I'LL GRANT YOU THANOS IS NO SAINT.
BUT YOU ALL MUST REALIZE HE'S OUR BEST BET FOR SURVIVAL.
SO STOW THE RECRIMI-NATIONS.
GAMORA'S CORRECT.
WE MUST FOLLOW THIS DEVIL-WE-KNOW AGAINST A FAR MORE IMMEDIATE PERIL.
I MAY NOT BE ONE OF YOU COSMIC TYPES...
...BUT I RECOGNIZE A HOLE IN A PLAN WHEN I SEE IT!
THANOS'S SCHEME HAS NO PAYOFF!
SPIDEY'S RIGHT!
WHY YOU HOLDING OUT ON US, BIG GUY?
IN CASE ANY OF YOU FALL INTO THE OMEGA'S CLUTCHES.
YOU CANNOT REVEAL WHAT YOU DO NOT KNOW.
"BY THE WAY, MY FORCE-FIELD IS ALREADY BEGINNING TO DIS-INTEGRATE BENEATH THE OMEGA'S ONSLAUGHT."

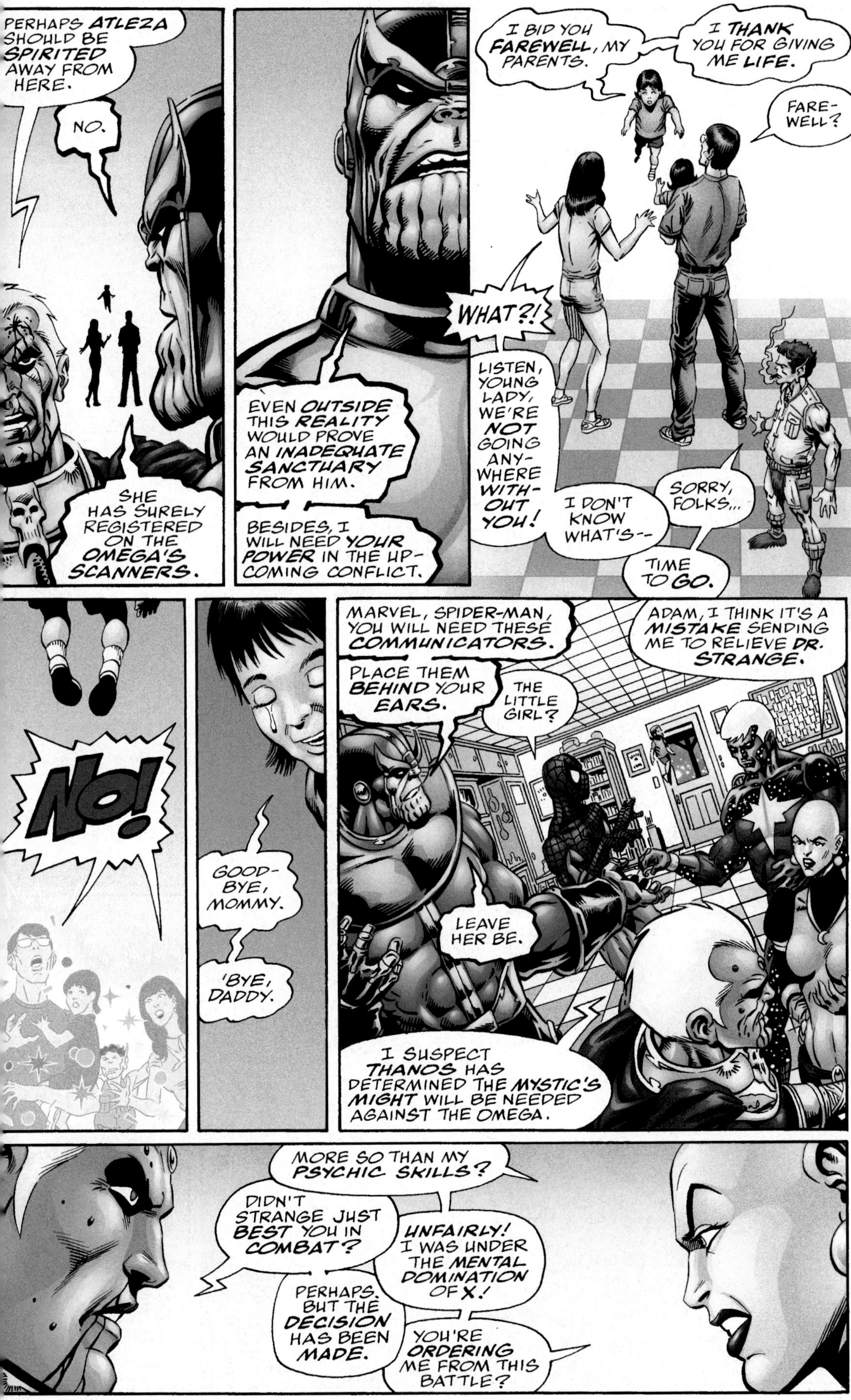

PERHAPS ATLEZA SHOULD BE SPIRITED AWAY FROM HERE.
NO.
SHE HAS SURELY REGISTERED ON THE OMEGA'S SCANNERS.
EVEN OUTSIDE THIS REALITY WOULD PROVE AN INADEQUATE SANCTUARY FROM HIM.
BESIDES, I WILL NEED YOUR POWER IN THE UP-COMING CONFLICT.
I BID YOU FAREWELL, MY PARENTS.
I THANK YOU FOR GIVING ME LIFE.
FARE-WELL?
WHAT?!
LISTEN, YOUNG LADY, WE'RE NOT GOING ANY-WHERE WITH-OUT YOU!
I DON'T KNOW WHAT'S--
SORRY, FOLKS...
TIME TO GO.
NO!
GOOD-BYE, MOMMY.
'BYE, DADDY.
MARVEL, SPIDER-MAN, YOU WILL NEED THESE COMMUNICATORS.
PLACE THEM BEHIND YOUR EARS.
THE LITTLE GIRL?
LEAVE HER BE.
ADAM, I THINK IT'S A MISTAKE SENDING ME TO RELIEVE DR. STRANGE.
I SUSPECT THANOS HAS DETERMINED THE MYSTIC'S MIGHT WILL BE NEEDED AGAINST THE OMEGA.
MORE SO THAN MY PSYCHIC SKILLS?
DIDN'T STRANGE JUST BEST YOU IN COMBAT?
UNFAIRLY! I WAS UNDER THE MENTAL DOMINATION OF X!
PERHAPS. BUT THE DECISION HAS BEEN MADE.
YOU'RE ORDERING ME FROM THIS BATTLE?

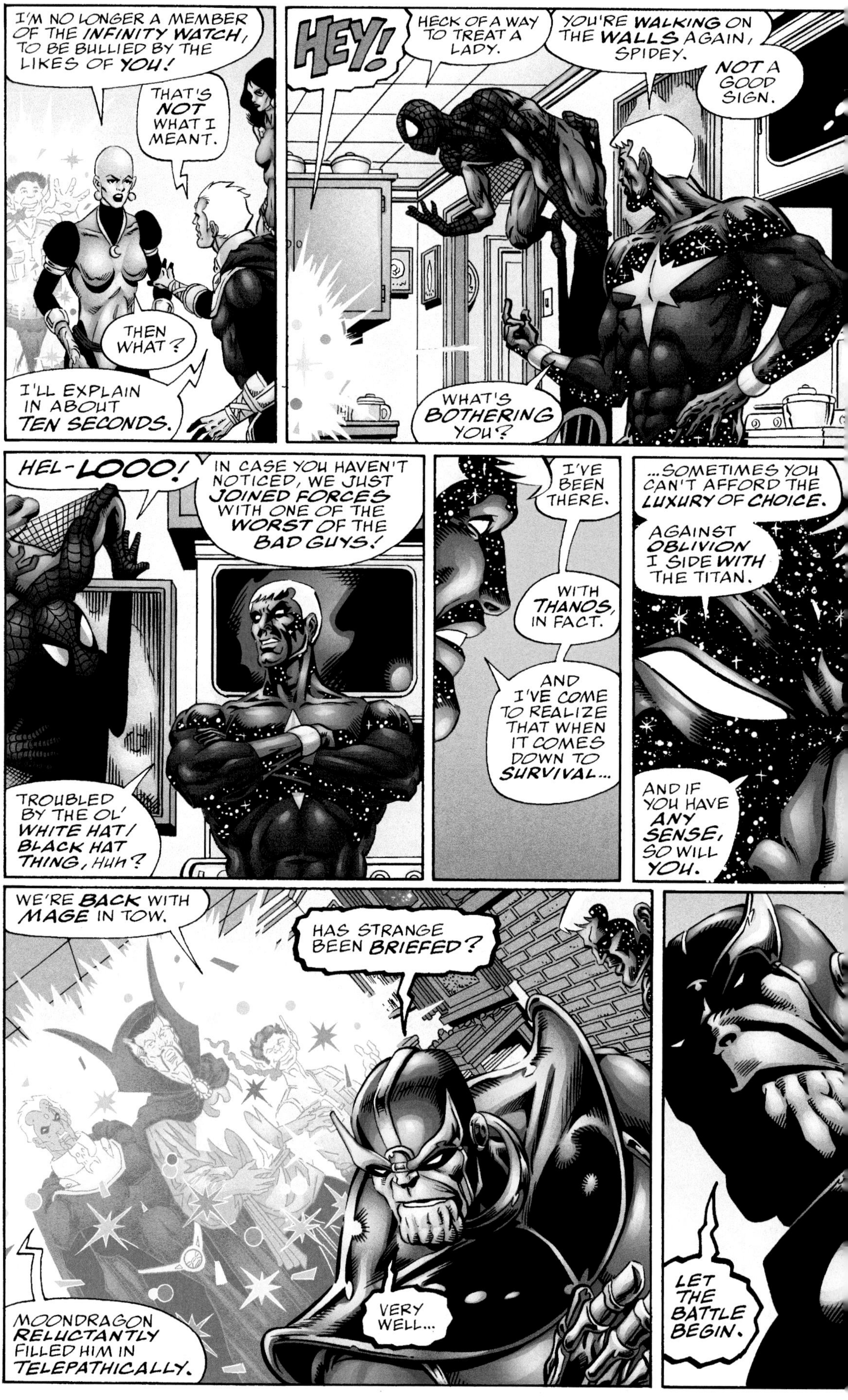

I'M NO LONGER A MEMBER OF THE INFINITY WATCH, TO BE BULLIED BY THE LIKES OF YOU!
THAT'S NOT WHAT I MEANT.
THEN WHAT?
I'LL EXPLAIN IN ABOUT TEN SECONDS.
HEY!
HECK OF A WAY TO TREAT A LADY.
YOU'RE WALKING ON THE WALLS AGAIN, SPIDEY.
NOT A GOOD SIGN.
WHAT'S BOTHERING YOU?
HEL-LOOO!
IN CASE YOU HAVEN'T NOTICED, WE JUST JOINED FORCES WITH ONE OF THE WORST OF THE BAD GUYS!
TROUBLED BY THE OL' WHITE HAT/ BLACK HAT THING, HUH?
I'VE BEEN THERE.
WITH THANOS, IN FACT.
AND I'VE COME TO REALIZE THAT WHEN IT COMES DOWN TO SURVIVAL...
...SOMETIMES YOU CAN'T AFFORD THE LUXURY OF CHOICE.
AGAINST OBLIVION I SIDE WITH THE TITAN.
AND IF YOU HAVE ANY SENSE, SO WILL YOU.
WE'RE BACK WITH MAGE IN TOW.
HAS STRANGE BEEN BRIEFED?
MOONDRAGON RELUCTANTLY FILLED HIM IN TELEPATHICALLY.
VERY WELL...
LET THE BATTLE BEGIN.

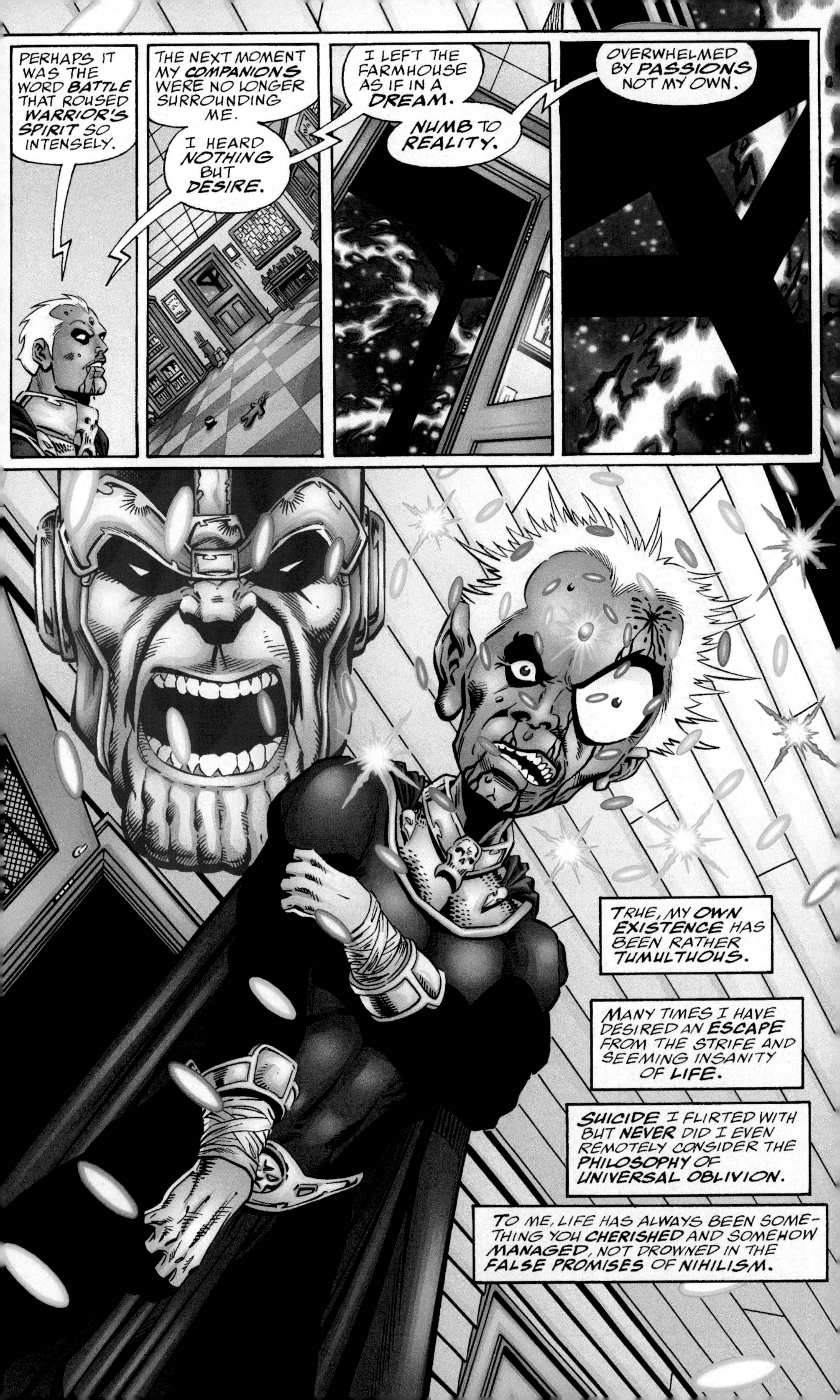
PERHAPS IT WAS THE WORD BATTLE THAT ROUSED WARRIOR'S SPIRIT SO INTENSELY.
THE NEXT MOMENT MY COMPANIONS WERE NO LONGER SURROUNDING ME.
I HEARD NOTHING BUT DESIRE.
I LEFT THE FARMHOUSE AS IF IN A DREAM.
NUMB TO REALITY.
OVERWHELMED BY PASSIONS NOT MY OWN.
TRUE, MY OWN EXISTENCE HAS BEEN RATHER TUMULTUOUS.
MANY TIMES I HAVE DESIRED AN ESCAPE FROM THE STRIFE AND SEEMING INSANITY OF LIFE.
SUICIDE I FLIRTED WITH BUT NEVER DID I EVEN REMOTELY CONSIDER THE PHILOSOPHY OF UNIVERSAL OBLIVION.
TO ME, LIFE HAS ALWAYS BEEN SOME-THING YOU CHERISHED AND SOMEHOW MANAGED, NOT DROWNED IN THE FALSE PROMISES OF NIHILISM.

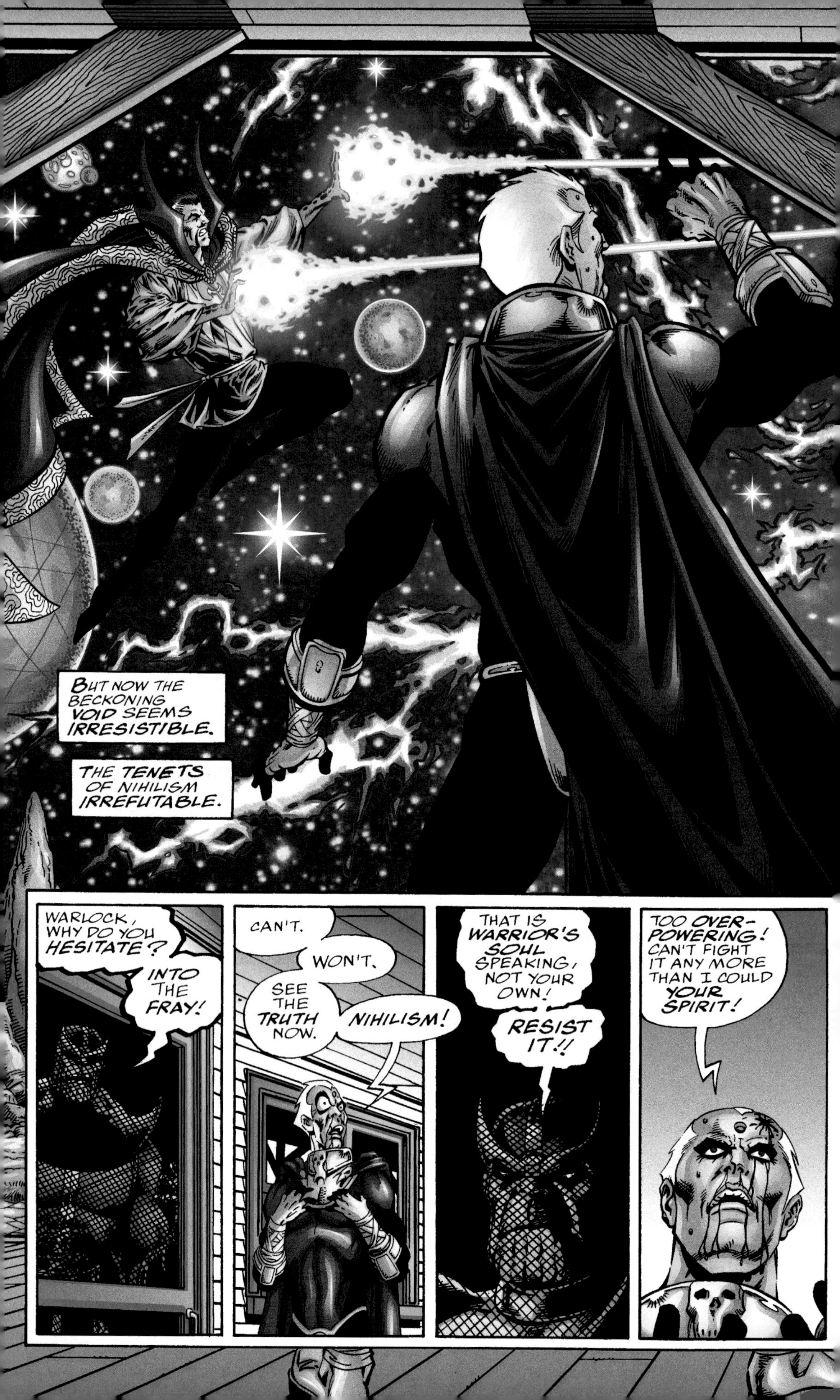

BUT NOW THE BECKONING VOID SEEMS IRRESISTIBLE.
THE TENETS OF NIHILISM IRREFUTABLE.
WARLOCK, WHY DO YOU HESITATE?
INTO THE FRAY!
CAN'T.
WON'T.
SEE THE TRUTH NOW.
NIHILISM!
THAT IS WARRIOR'S SOUL SPEAKING, NOT YOUR OWN!
RESIST IT!!
TOO OVER-POWERING! CAN'T FIGHT IT ANY MORE THAN I COULD YOUR SPIRIT!

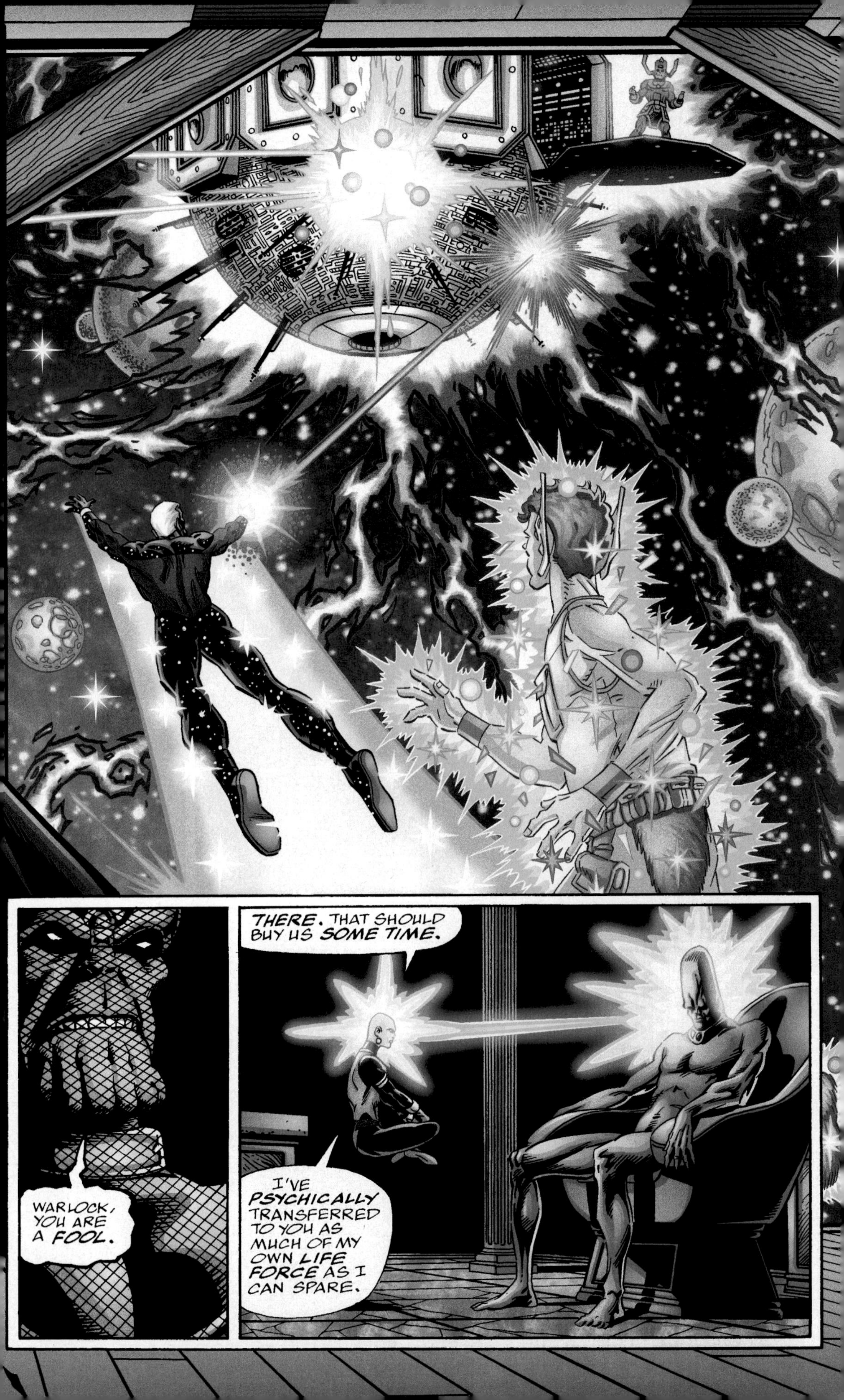
THERE. THAT SHOULD BUY US SOME TIME.
WARLOCK, YOU ARE A FOOL.
I'VE PSYCHICALLY TRANSFERRED TO YOU AS MUCH OF MY OWN LIFE FORCE AS I CAN SPARE.

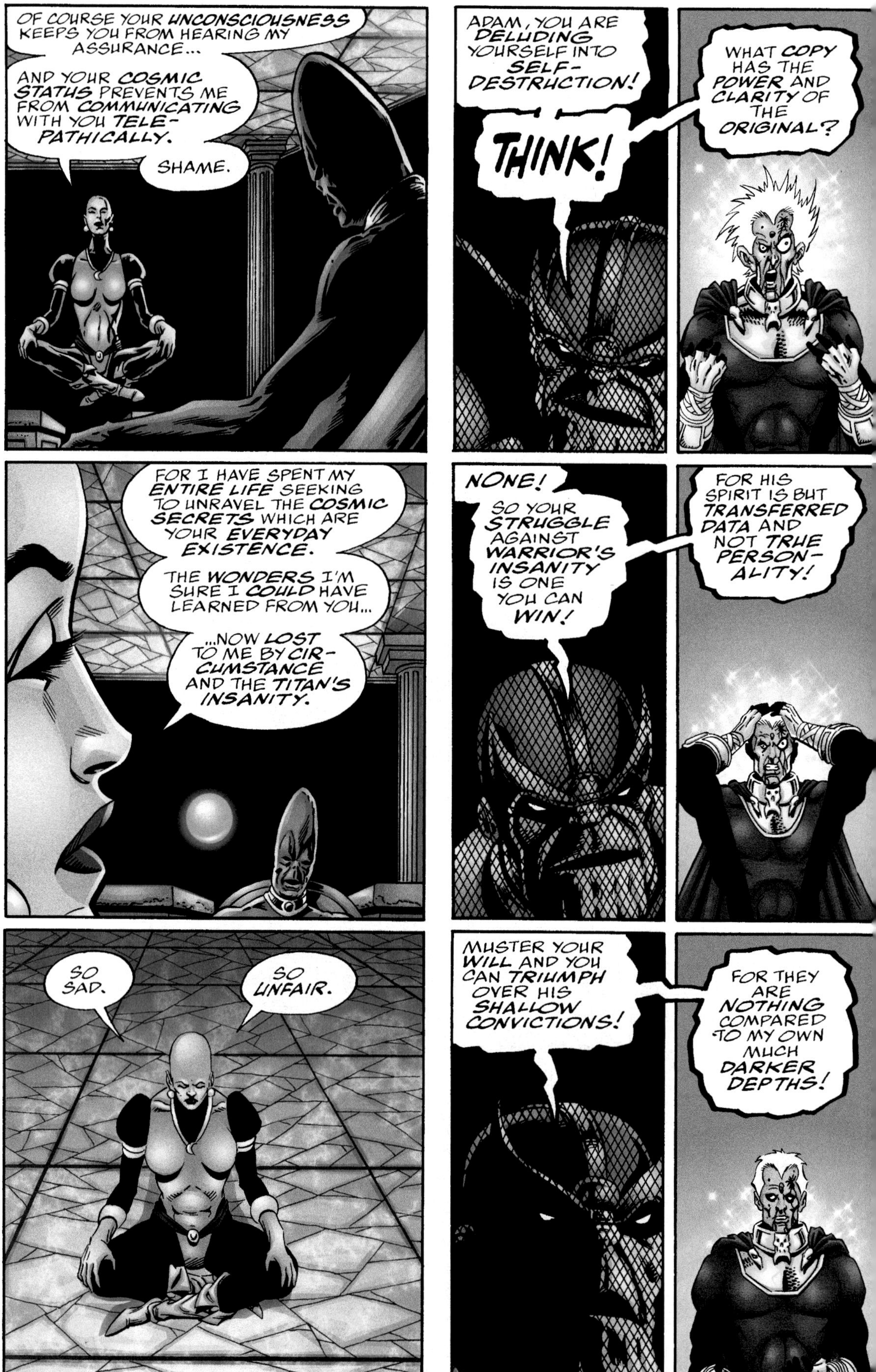

OF COURSE YOUR UNCONSCIOUSNESS KEEPS YOU FROM HEARING MY ASSURANCE...
AND YOUR COSMIC STATUS PREVENTS ME FROM COMMUNICATING WITH YOU TELE-PATHICALLY.
SHAME.
ADAM, YOU ARE DELUDING YOURSELF INTO SELF-DESTRUCTION!
THINK!
WHAT COPY HAS THE POWER AND CLARITY OF THE ORIGINAL?
FOR I HAVE SPENT MY ENTIRE LIFE SEEKING TO UNRAVEL THE COSMIC SECRETS WHICH ARE YOUR EVERYDAY EXISTENCE.
THE WONDERS I'M SURE I COULD HAVE LEARNED FROM YOU...
...NOW LOST TO ME BY CIR-CUMSTANCE AND THE TITAN'S INSANITY.
NONE!
SO YOUR STRUGGLE AGAINST WARRIOR'S INSANITY IS ONE YOU CAN WIN!
FOR HIS SPIRIT IS BUT TRANSFERRED DATA AND NOT TRUE PERSON-ALITY!
SO SAD.
SO UNFAIR.
MUSTER YOUR WILL AND YOU CAN TRIUMPH OVER HIS SHALLOW CONVICTIONS!
FOR THEY ARE NOTHING COMPARED TO MY OWN MUCH DARKER DEPTHS!

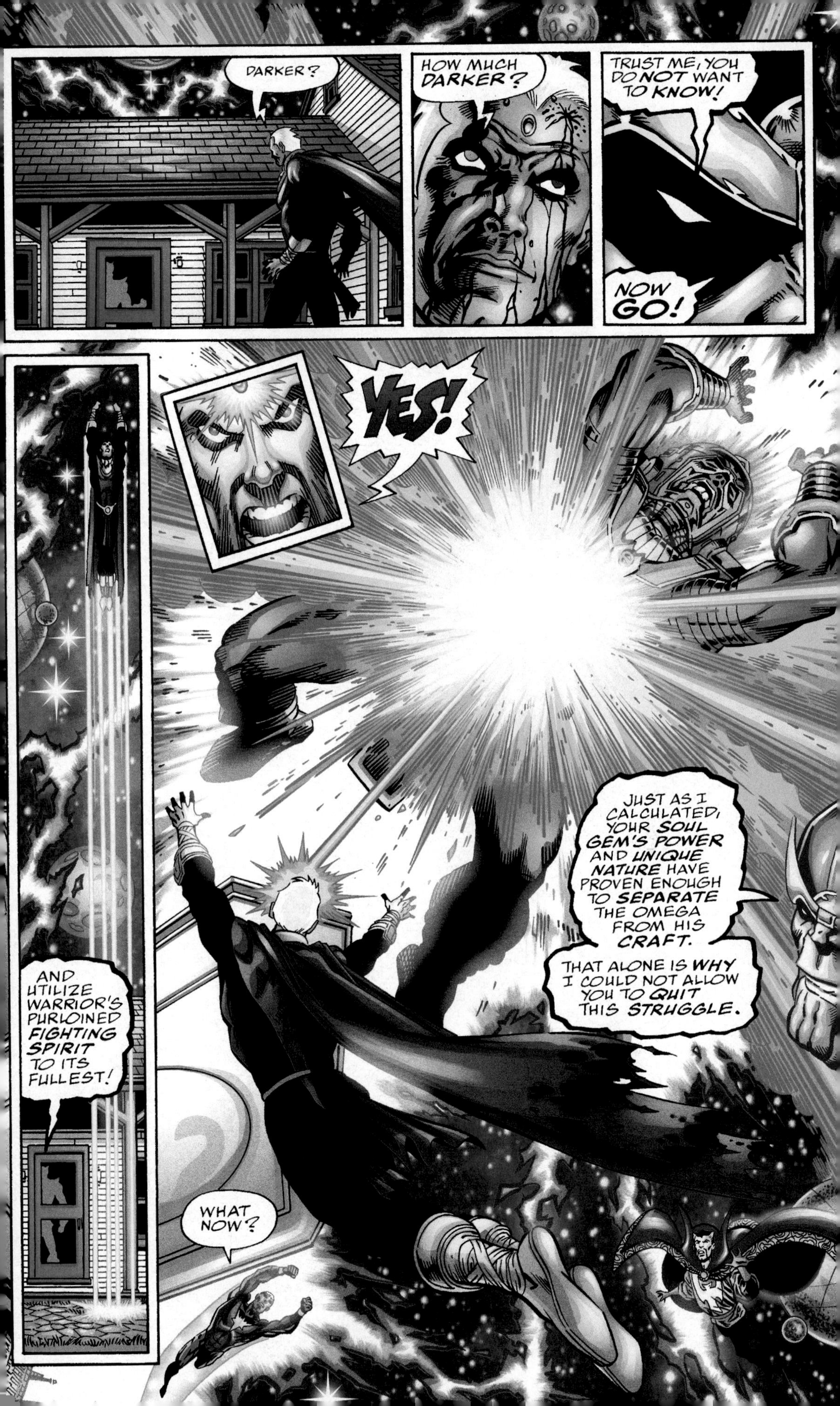
DARKER?
HOW MUCH DARKER?
TRUST ME, YOU DO NOT WANT TO KNOW!
NOW GO!
YES!
JUST AS I CALCULATED, YOUR SOUL GEM'S POWER AND UNIQUE NATURE HAVE PROVEN ENOUGH TO SEPARATE THE OMEGA FROM HIS CRAFT.
THAT ALONE IS WHY I COULD NOT ALLOW YOU TO QUIT THIS STRUGGLE.
AND UTILIZE WARRIOR'S PURLOINED FIGHTING SPIRIT TO ITS FULLEST!
WHAT NOW?

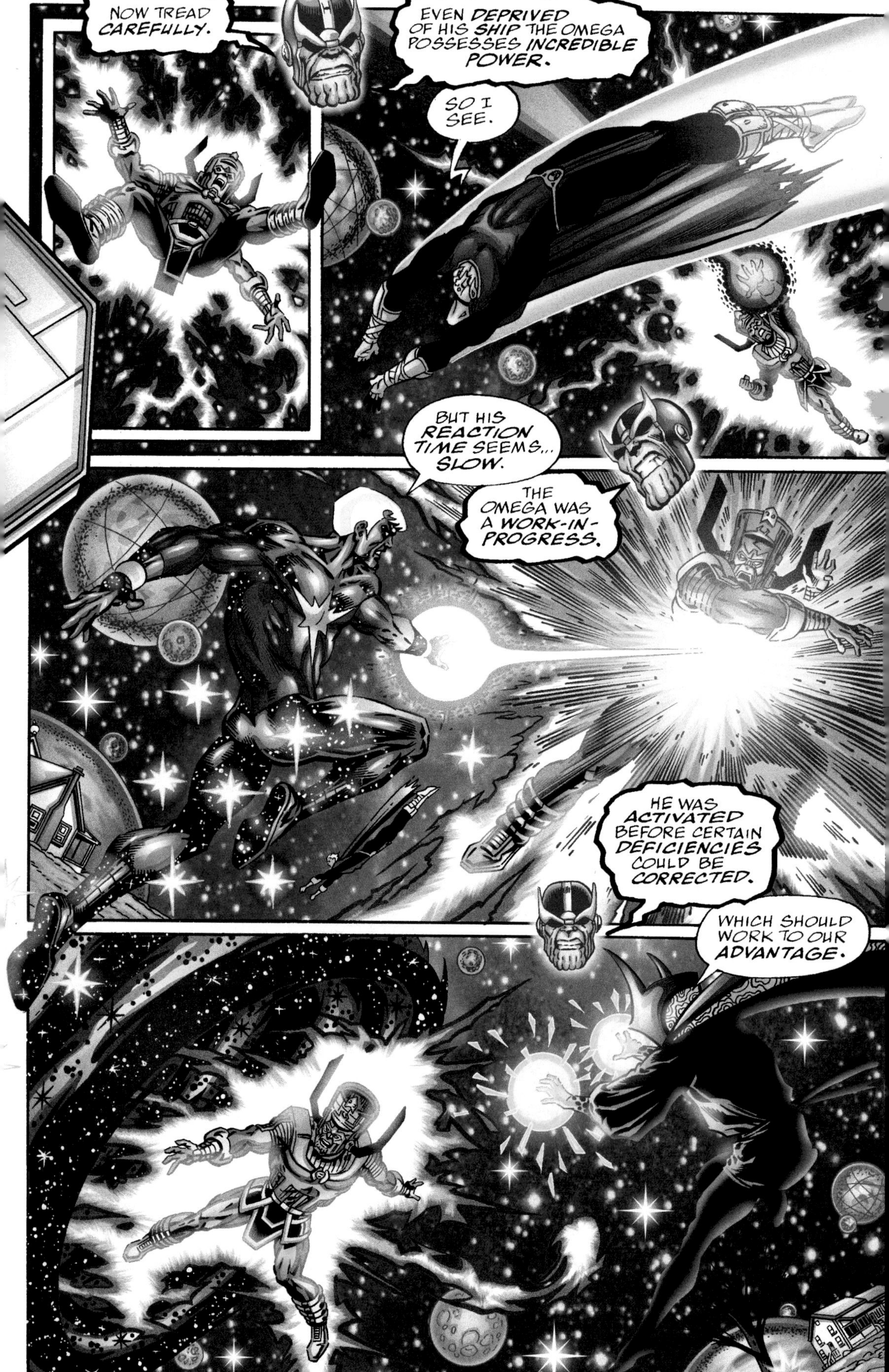
NOW TREAD CAREFULLY.
EVEN DEPRIVED OF HIS SHIP THE OMEGA POSSESSES INCREDIBLE POWER.
SO I SEE.
BUT HIS REACTION TIME SEEMS... SLOW.
THE OMEGA WAS A WORK-IN-PROGRESS.
HE WAS ACTIVATED BEFORE CERTAIN DEFICIENCIES COULD BE CORRECTED.
WHICH SHOULD WORK TO OUR ADVANTAGE.

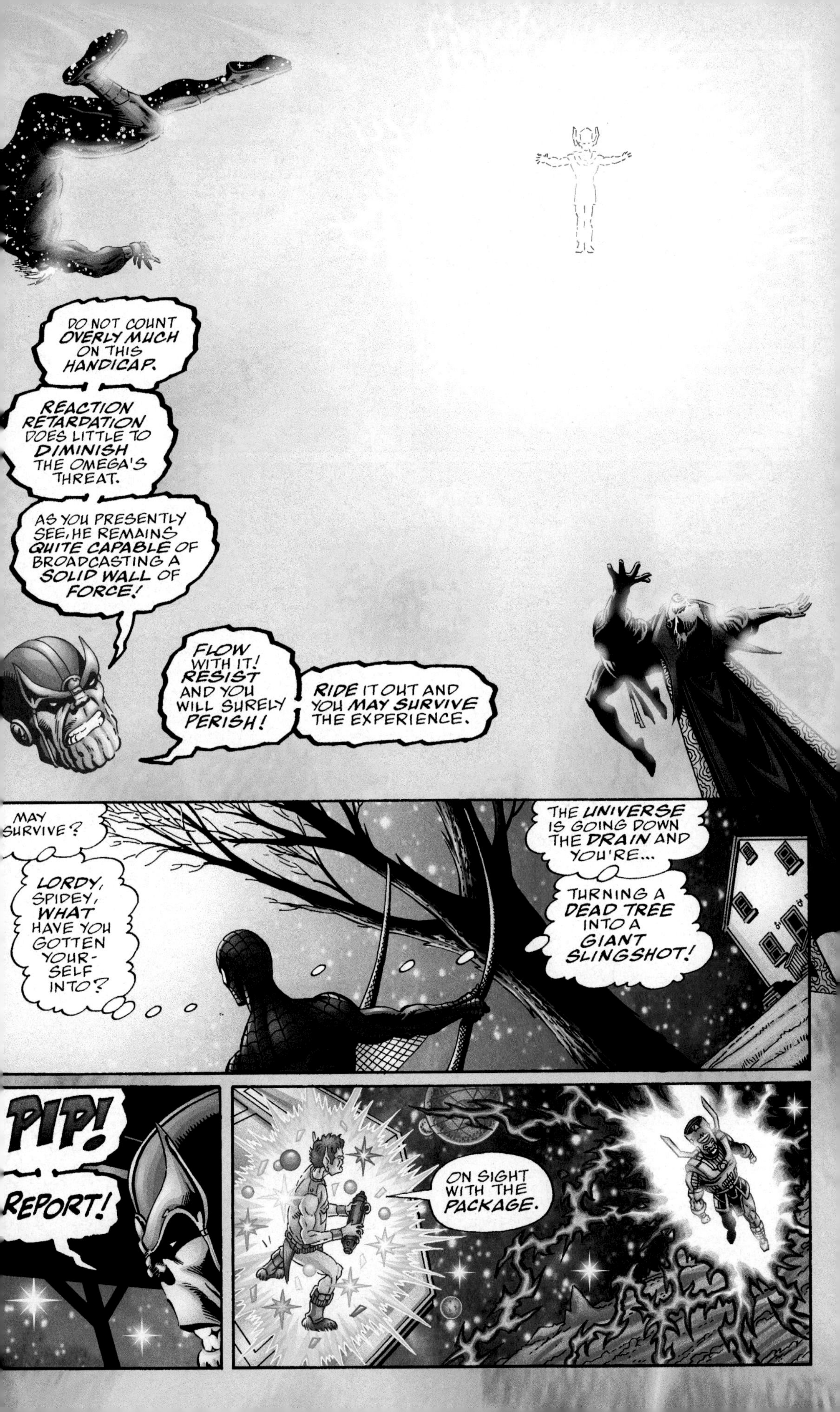
DO NOT COUNT OVERLY MUCH ON THIS HANDICAP.
REACTION RETARDATION DOES LITTLE TO DIMINISH THE OMEGA'S THREAT.
AS YOU PRESENTLY SEE, HE REMAINS QUITE CAPABLE OF BROADCASTING A SOLID WALL OF FORCE!
FLOW WITH IT! RESIST AND YOU WILL SURELY PERISH!
RIDE IT OUT AND YOU MAY SURVIVE THE EXPERIENCE.
MAY SURVIVE?
LORDY, SPIDEY, WHAT HAVE YOU GOTTEN YOURSELF INTO?
THE UNIVERSE IS GOING DOWN THE DRAIN AND YOU'RE...
TURNING A DEAD TREE INTO A GIANT SLINGSHOT!
PIP!
REPORT!
ON SIGHT WITH THE PACKAGE.

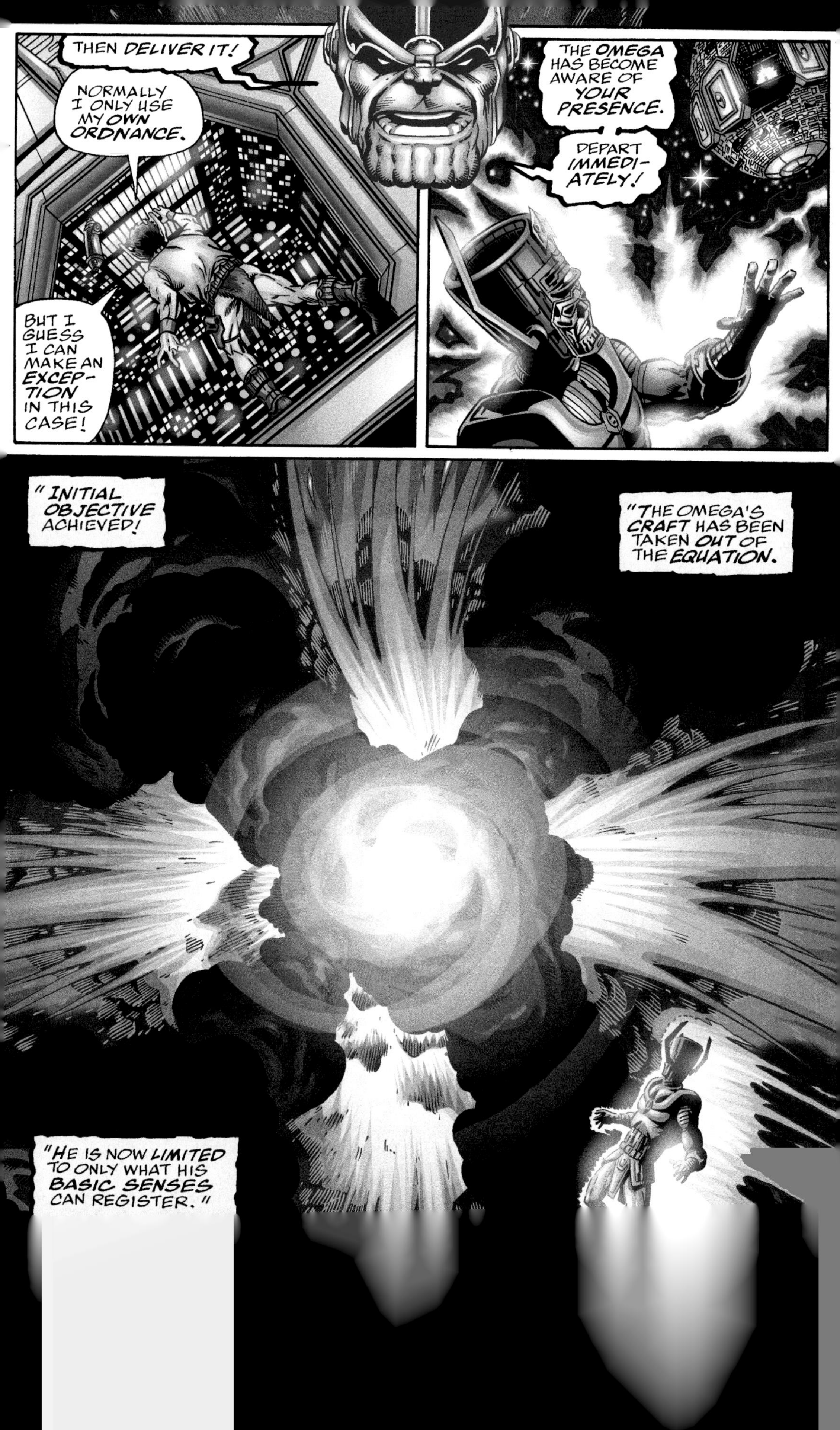
THEN DELIVER IT!
NORMALLY I ONLY USE MY OWN ORDNANCE.
BUT I GUESS I CAN MAKE AN EXCEPTION IN THIS CASE!
THE OMEGA HAS BECOME AWARE OF YOUR PRESENCE.
DEPART IMMEDIATELY!
"INITIAL OBJECTIVE ACHIEVED!
"THE OMEGA'S CRAFT HAS BEEN TAKEN OUT OF THE EQUATION.
"HE IS NOW LIMITED TO ONLY WHAT HIS BASIC SENSES CAN REGISTER."

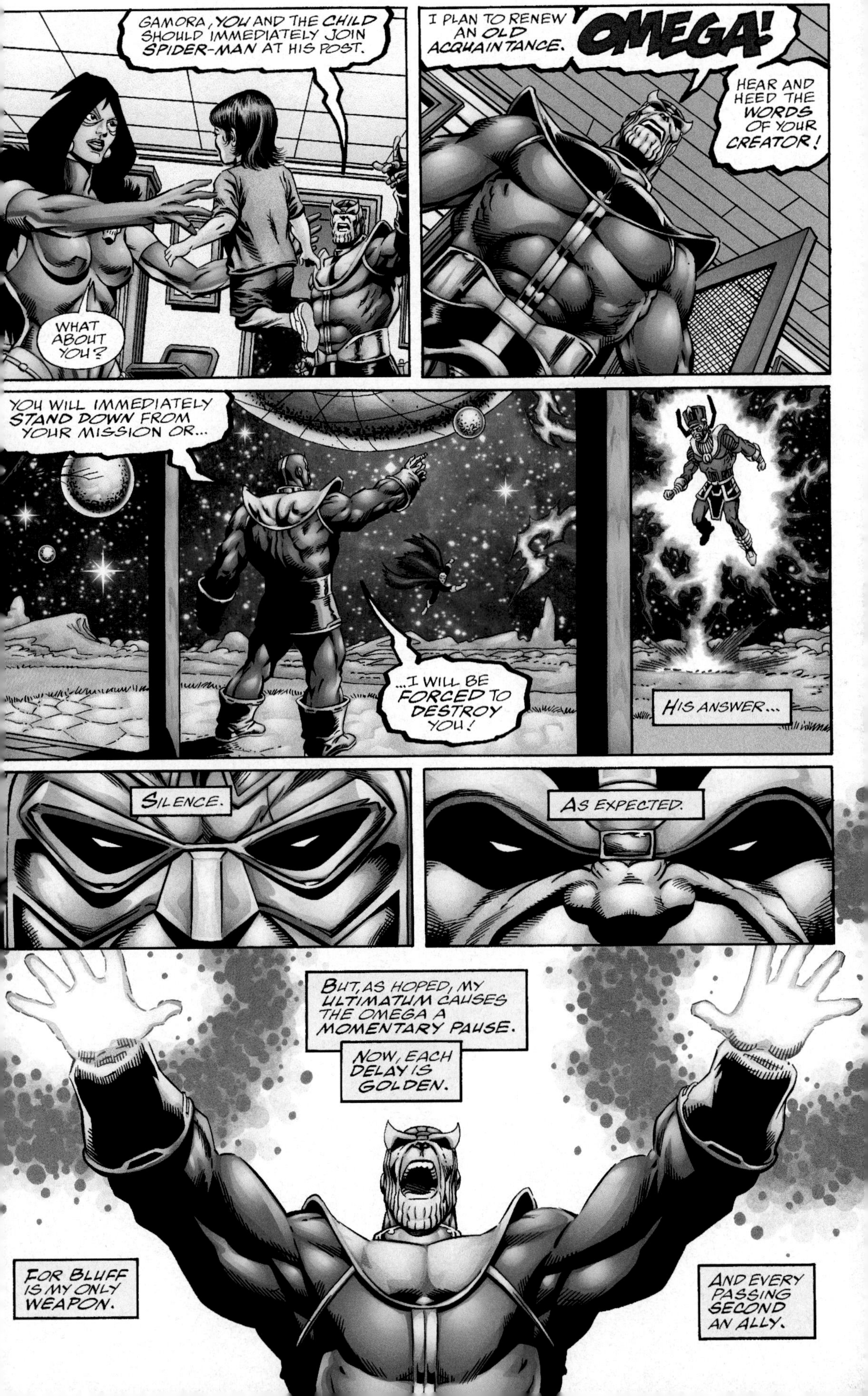
GAMORA, YOU AND THE CHILD SHOULD IMMEDIATELY JOIN SPIDER-MAN AT HIS POST.
WHAT ABOUT YOU?
I PLAN TO RENEW AN OLD ACQUAINTANCE.
OMEGA!
HEAR AND HEED THE WORDS OF YOUR CREATOR!
YOU WILL IMMEDIATELY STAND DOWN FROM YOUR MISSION OR...
...I WILL BE FORCED TO DESTROY YOU!
HIS ANSWER...
SILENCE.
AS EXPECTED.
BUT, AS HOPED, MY ULTIMATUM CAUSES THE OMEGA A MOMENTARY PAUSE.
NOW, EACH DELAY IS GOLDEN.
FOR BLUFF IS MY ONLY WEAPON.
AND EVERY PASSING SECOND AN ALLY.

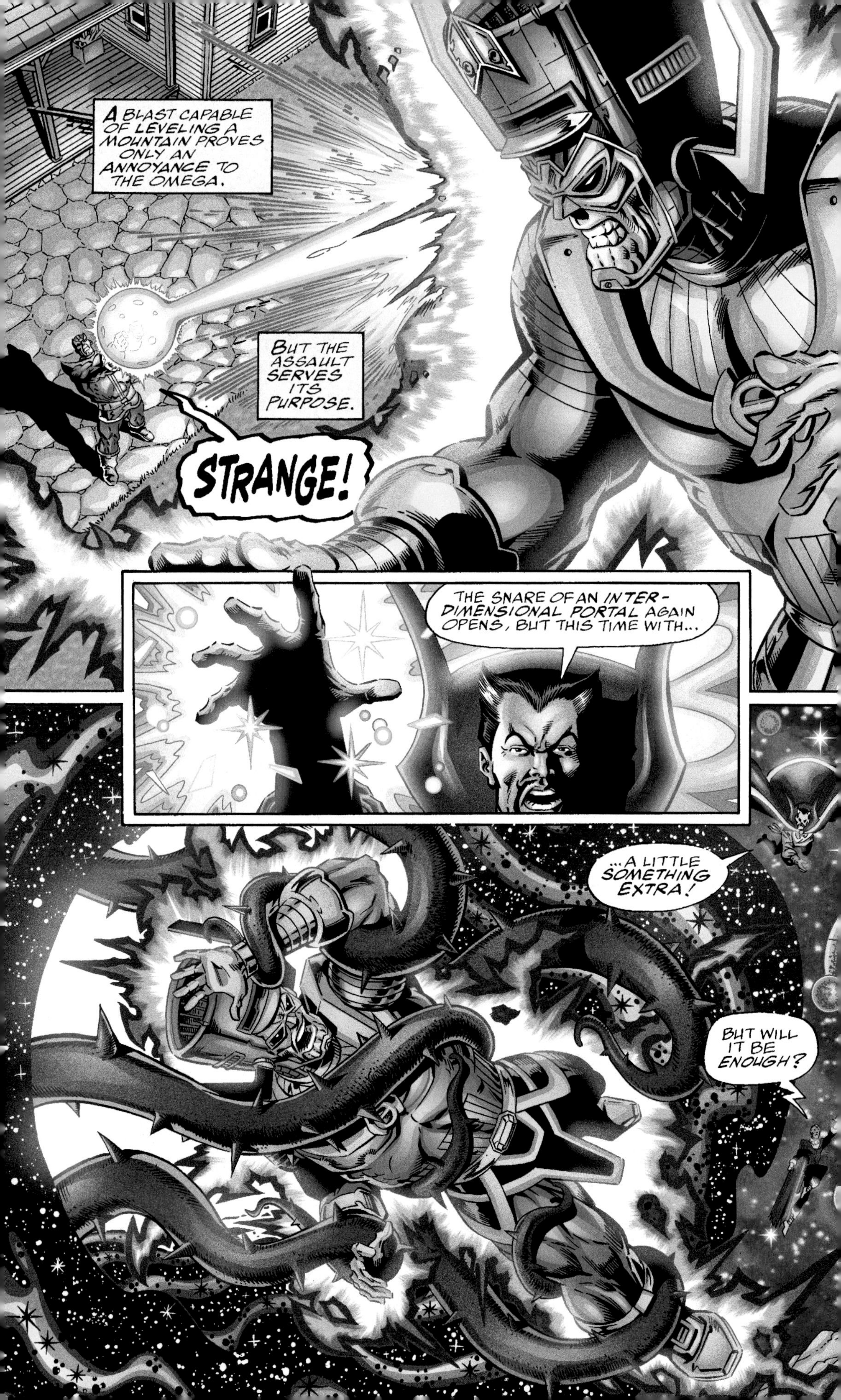
A BLAST CAPABLE OF LEVELING A MOUNTAIN PROVES ONLY AN ANNOYANCE TO THE OMEGA.
BUT THE ASSAULT SERVES ITS PURPOSE.
STRANGE!
THE SNARE OF AN INTER-DIMENSIONAL PORTAL AGAIN OPENS, BUT THIS TIME WITH...
...A LITTLE SOMETHING EXTRA!
BUT WILL IT BE ENOUGH?

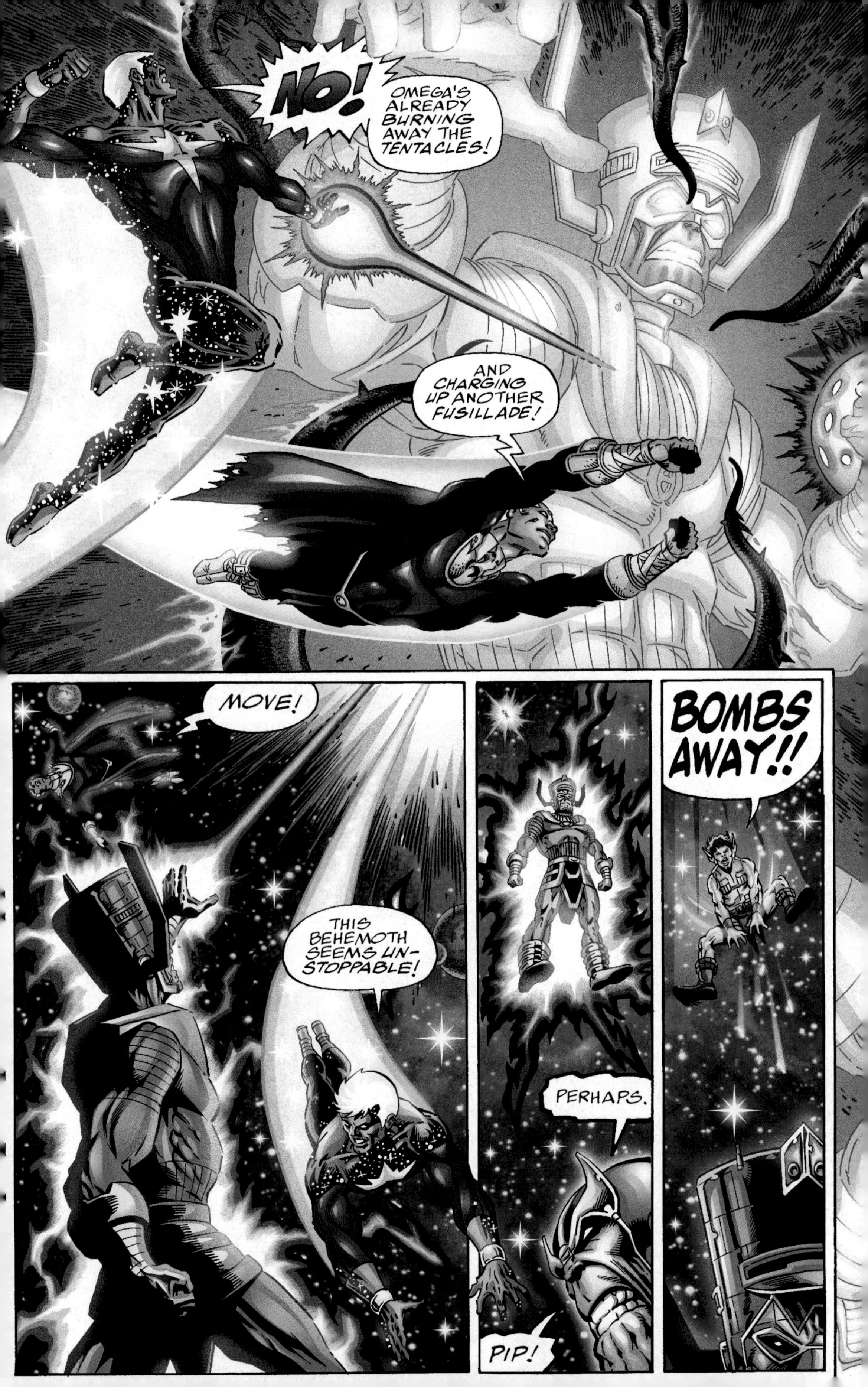
NO!
OMEGA'S ALREADY BURNING AWAY THE TENTACLES!
AND CHARGING UP ANOTHER FUSILLADE!
MOVE!
THIS BEHEMOTH SEEMS UN-STOPPABLE!
PERHAPS.
PIP!
BOMBS AWAY!!

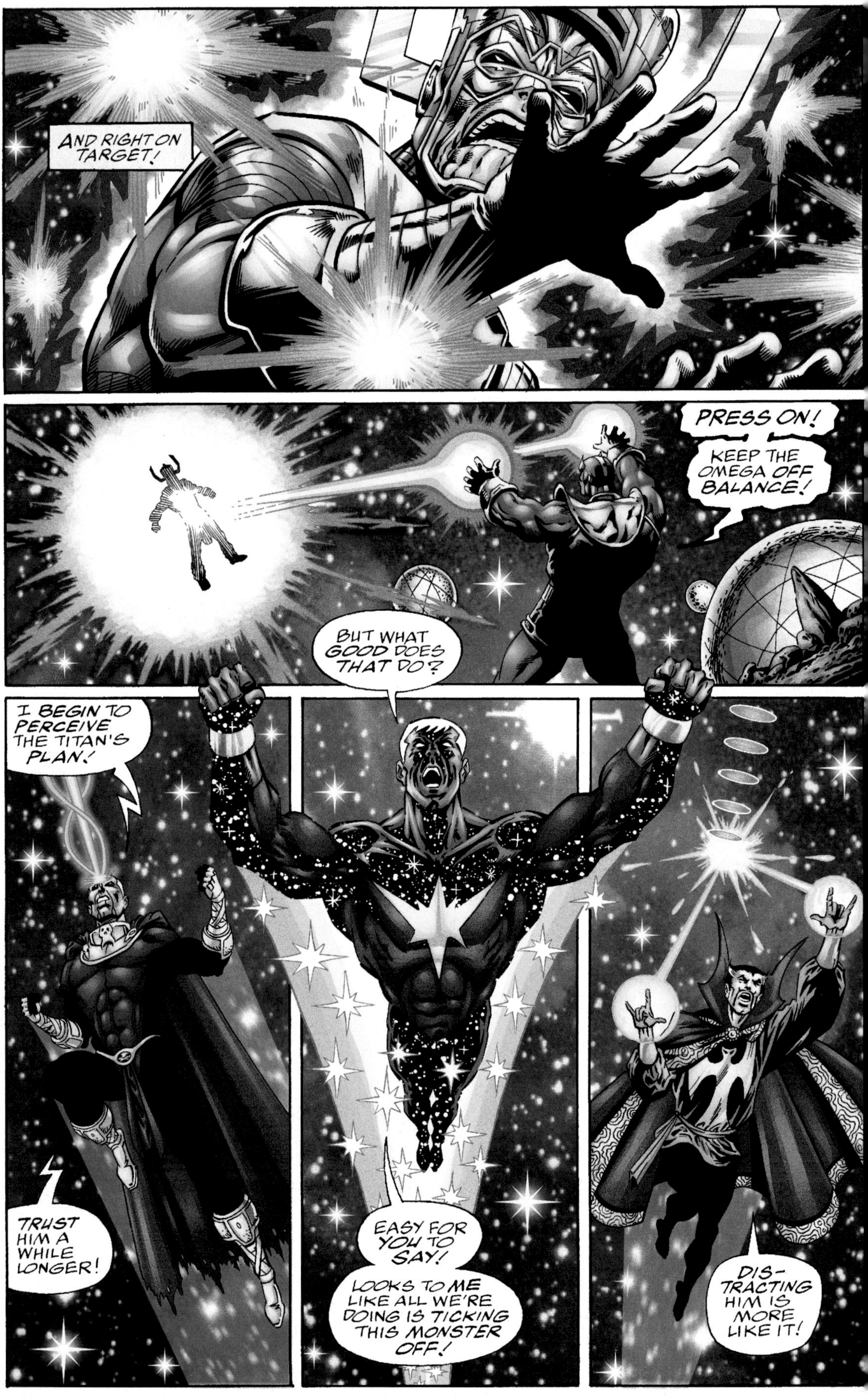
AND RIGHT ON TARGET!
PRESS ON!
KEEP THE OMEGA OFF BALANCE!
BUT WHAT GOOD DOES THAT DO?
I BEGIN TO PERCEIVE THE TITAN'S PLAN!
TRUST HIM A WHILE LONGER!
EASY FOR YOU TO SAY!
LOOKS TO ME LIKE ALL WE'RE DOING IS TICKING THIS MONSTER OFF!
DIS-TRACTING HIM IS MORE LIKE IT!

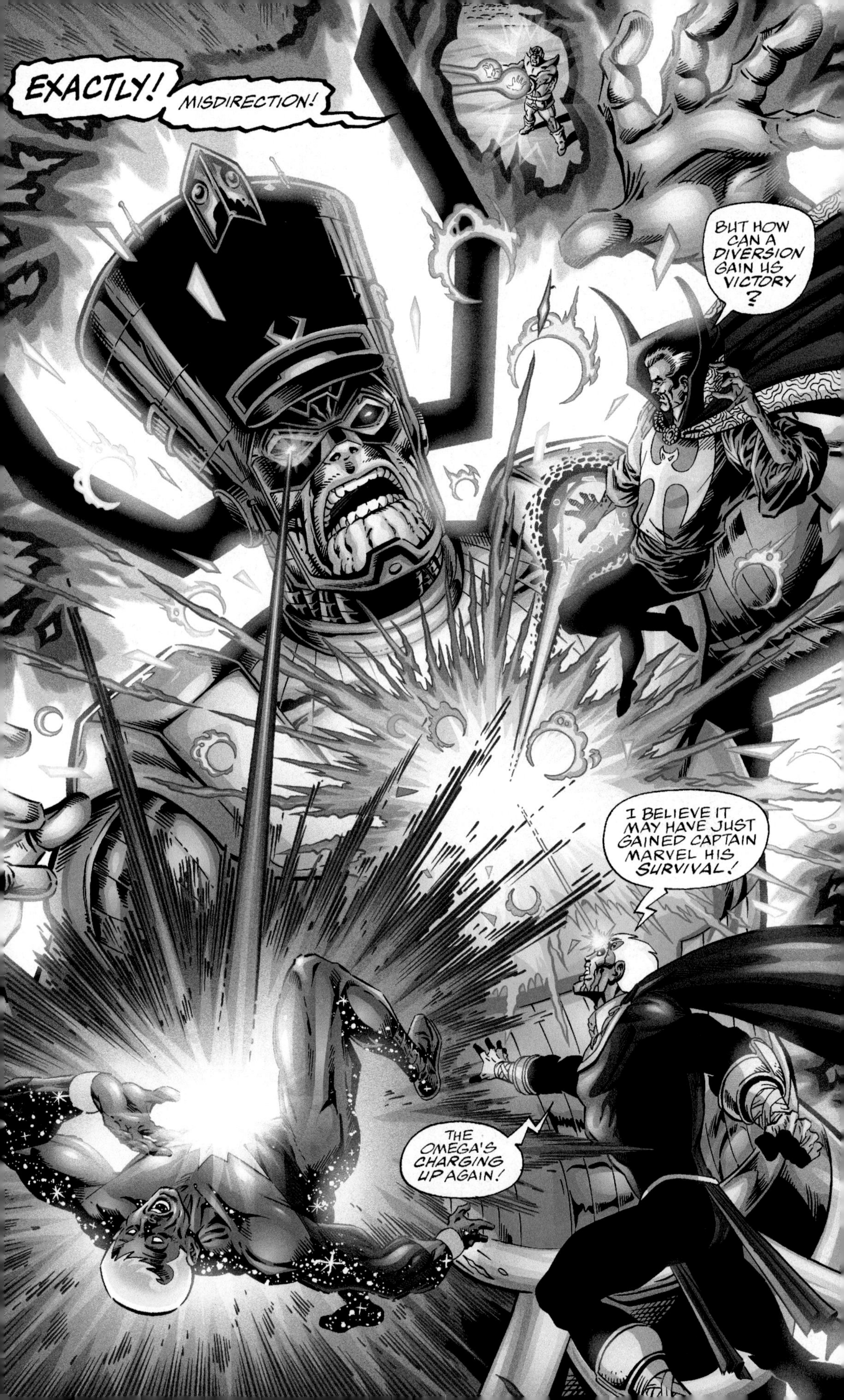
EXACTLY!
MISDIRECTION!
BUT HOW CAN A DIVERSION GAIN HIS VICTORY?
I BELIEVE IT MAY HAVE JUST GAINED CAPTAIN MARVEL HIS SURVIVAL!
THE OMEGA'S CHARGING UP AGAIN!

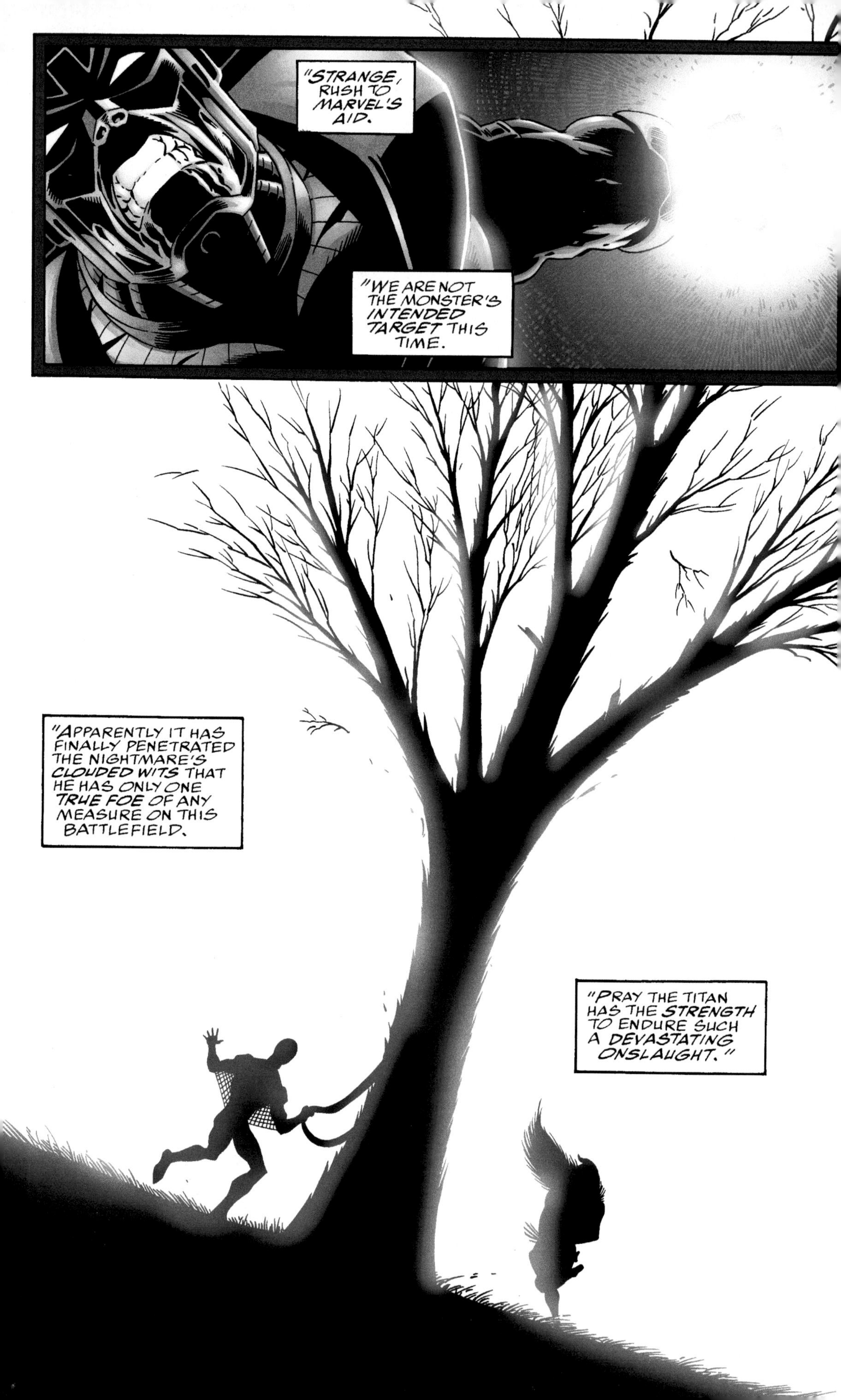
"STRANGE, RUSH TO MARVEL'S AID.
"WE ARE NOT THE MONSTER'S INTENDED TARGET THIS TIME.
"APPARENTLY IT HAS FINALLY PENETRATED THE NIGHTMARE'S CLOUDED WITS THAT HE HAS ONLY ONE TRUE FOE OF ANY MEASURE ON THIS BATTLEFIELD.
"PRAY THE TITAN HAS THE STRENGTH TO ENDURE SUCH A DEVASTATING ONSLAUGHT."

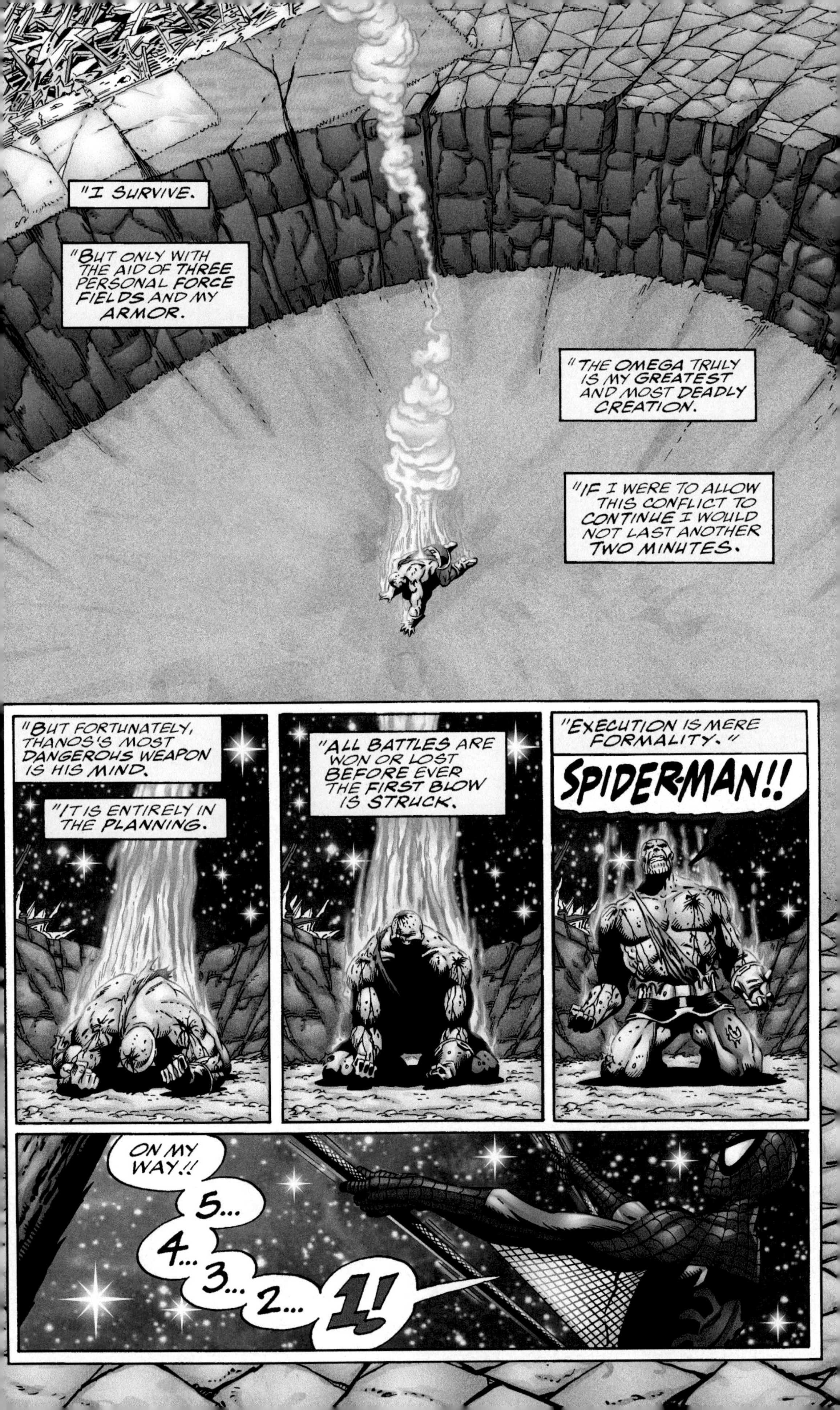
"I SURVIVE.
"BUT ONLY WITH THE AID OF THREE PERSONAL FORCE FIELDS AND MY ARMOR.
"THE OMEGA TRULY IS MY GREATEST AND MOST DEADLY CREATION.
"IF I WERE TO ALLOW THIS CONFLICT TO CONTINUE I WOULD NOT LAST ANOTHER TWO MINUTES.
"BUT FORTUNATELY, THANOS'S MOST DANGEROUS WEAPON IS HIS MIND.
"IT IS ENTIRELY IN THE PLANNING.
"ALL BATTLES ARE WON OR LOST BEFORE EVER THE FIRST BLOW IS STRUCK.
"EXECUTION IS MERE FORMALITY."
SPIDER-MAN!!
ON MY WAY!!
5...
4...
3...
2...
1!

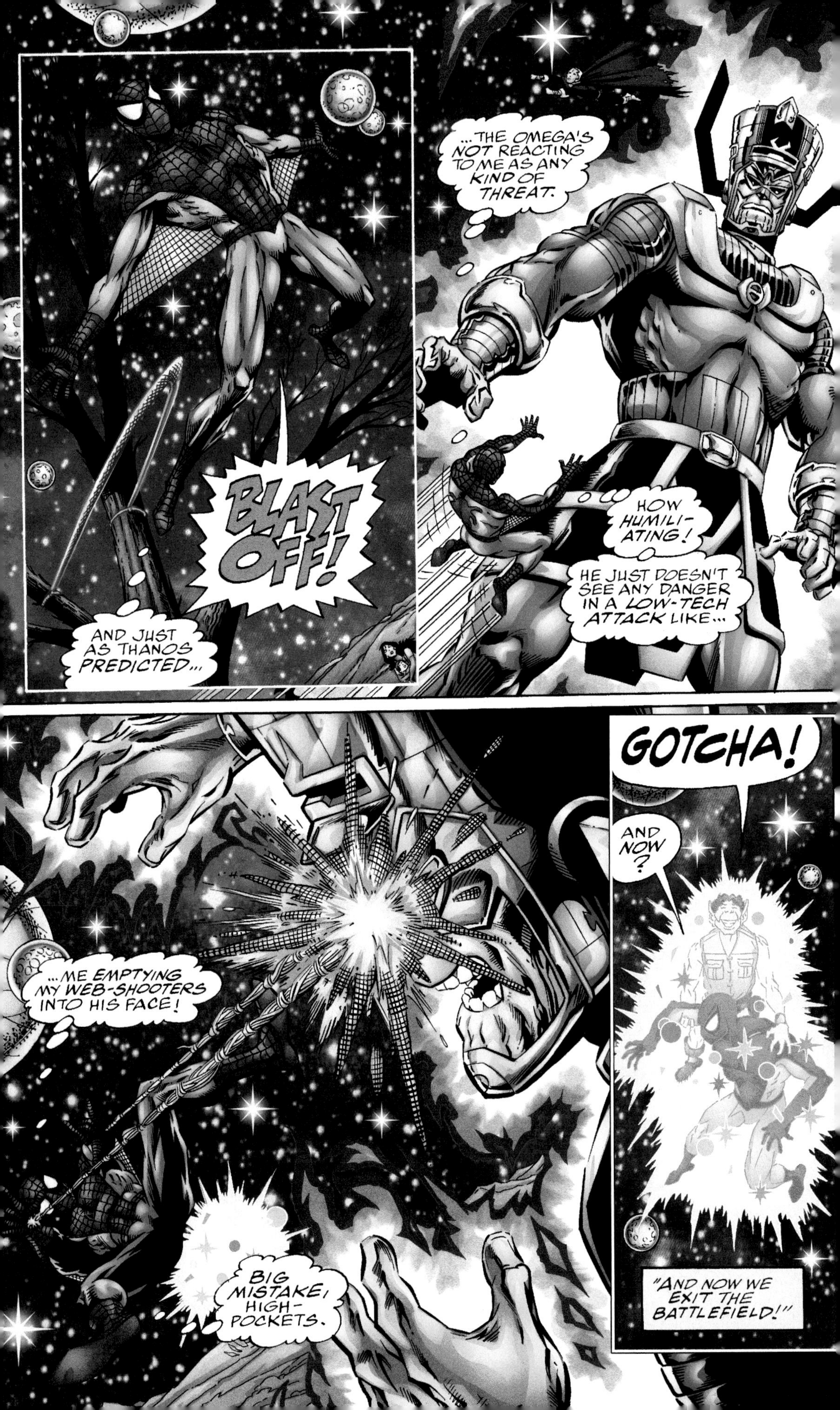

AND JUST AS THANOS PREDICTED...
BLAST OFF!
...THE OMEGA'S NOT REACTING TO ME AS ANY KIND OF THREAT.
HOW HUMILI-ATING!
HE JUST DOESN'T SEE ANY DANGER IN A LOW-TECH ATTACK LIKE...
...ME EMPTYING MY WEB-SHOOTERS INTO HIS FACE!
BIG MISTAKE, HIGH-POCKETS.
GOTCHA!
AND NOW?
"AND NOW WE EXIT THE BATTLEFIELD!"

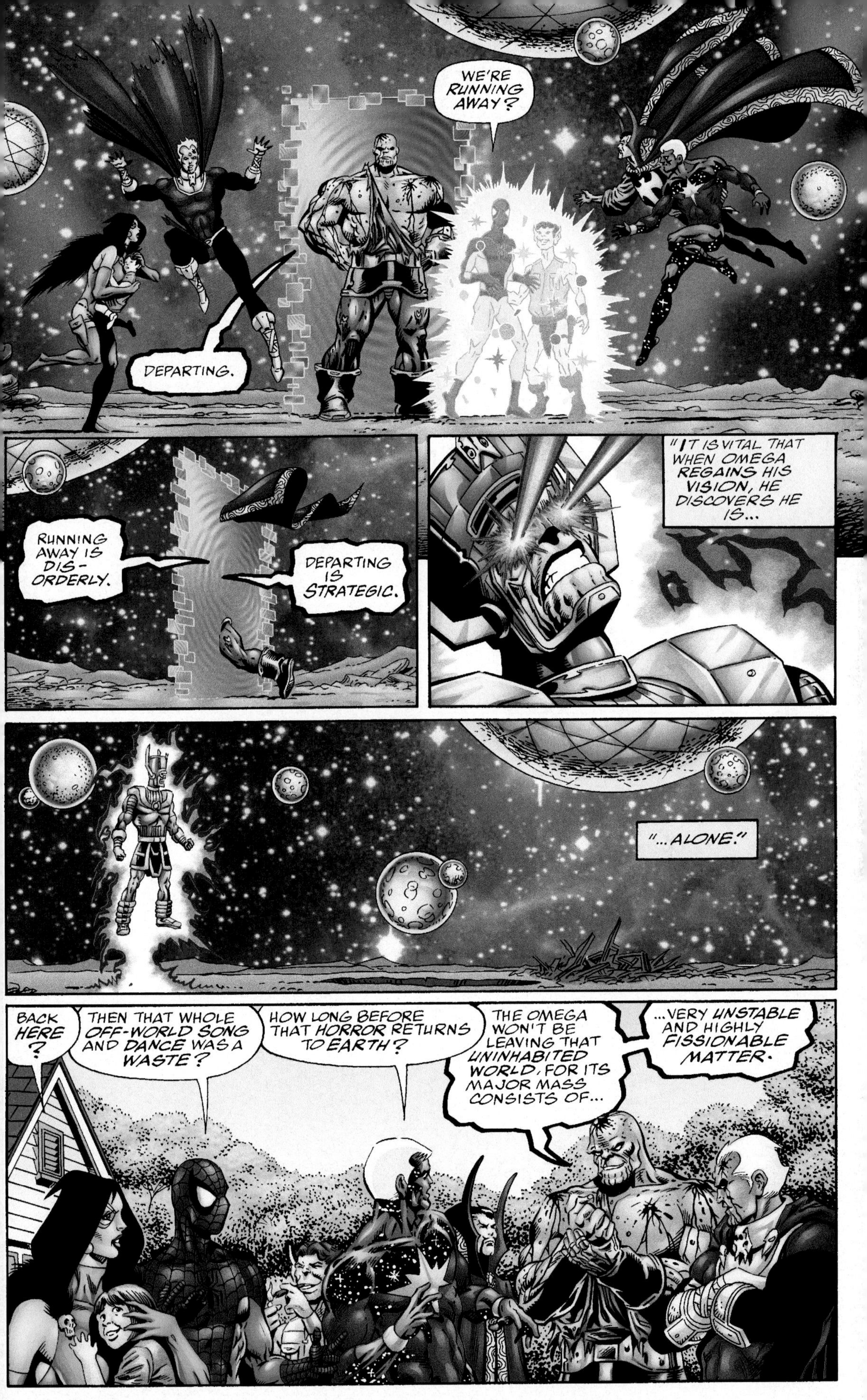
WE'RE RUNNING AWAY?
DEPARTING.
RUNNING AWAY IS DIS-ORDERLY.
DEPARTING IS STRATEGIC.
"IT IS VITAL THAT WHEN OMEGA REGAINS HIS VISION, HE DISCOVERS HE IS...
"...ALONE."
BACK HERE?
THEN THAT WHOLE OFF-WORLD SONG AND DANCE WAS A WASTE?
HOW LONG BEFORE THAT HORROR RETURNS TO EARTH?
THE OMEGA WON'T BE LEAVING THAT UNINHABITED WORLD, FOR ITS MAJOR MASS CONSISTS OF...
...VERY UNSTABLE AND HIGHLY FISSIONABLE MATTER.

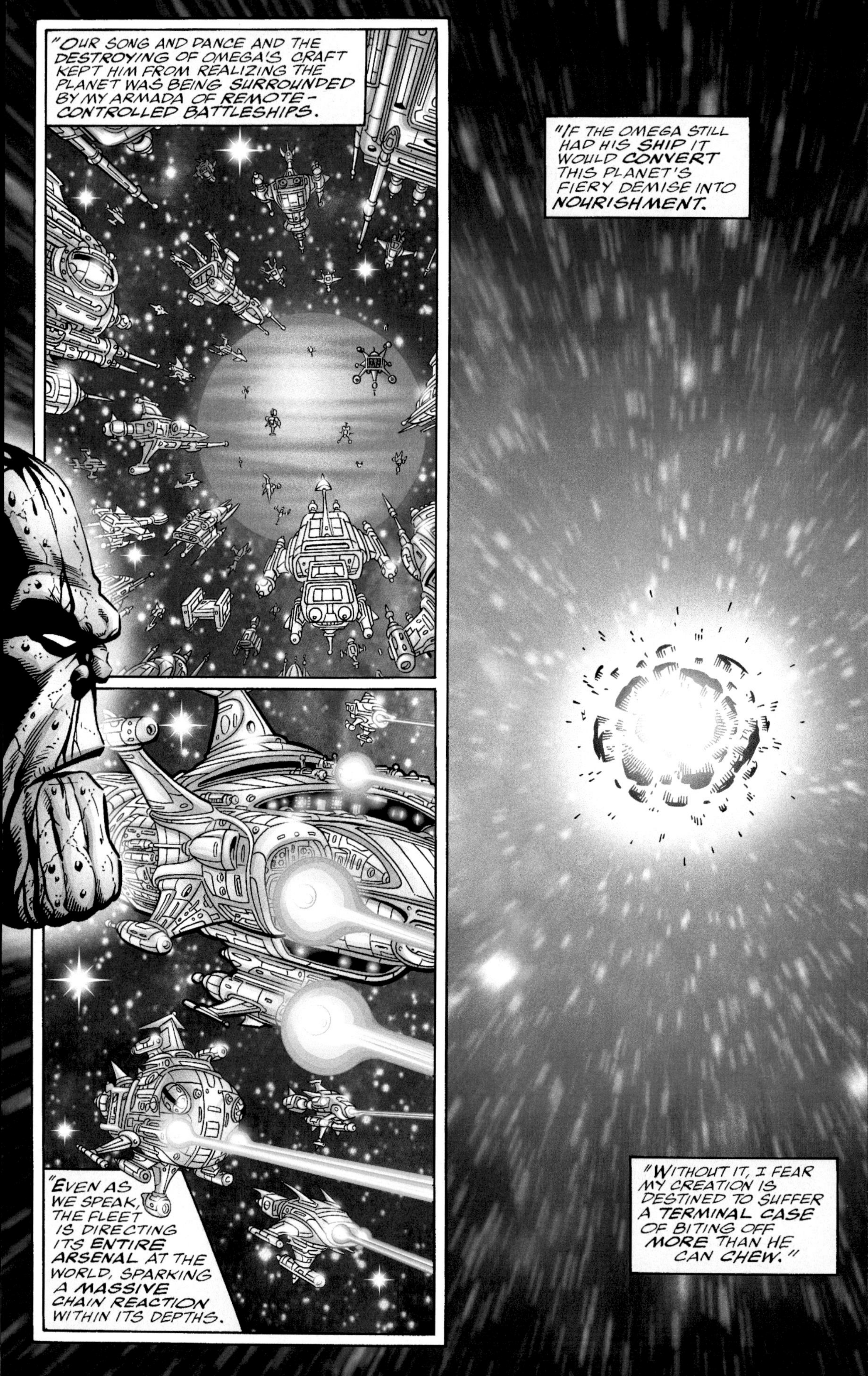
"OUR SONG AND DANCE AND THE DESTROYING OF OMEGA'S CRAFT KEPT HIM FROM REALIZING THE PLANET WAS BEING SURROUNDED BY MY ARMADA OF REMOTE-CONTROLLED BATTLESHIPS.
"EVEN AS WE SPEAK, THE FLEET IS DIRECTING ITS ENTIRE ARSENAL AT THE WORLD, SPARKING A MASSIVE CHAIN REACTION WITHIN ITS DEPTHS.
"IF THE OMEGA STILL HAD HIS SHIP IT WOULD CONVERT THIS PLANET'S FIERY DEMISE INTO NOURISHMENT.
"WITHOUT IT, I FEAR MY CREATION IS DESTINED TO SUFFER A TERMINAL CASE OF BITING OFF MORE THAN HE CAN CHEW."

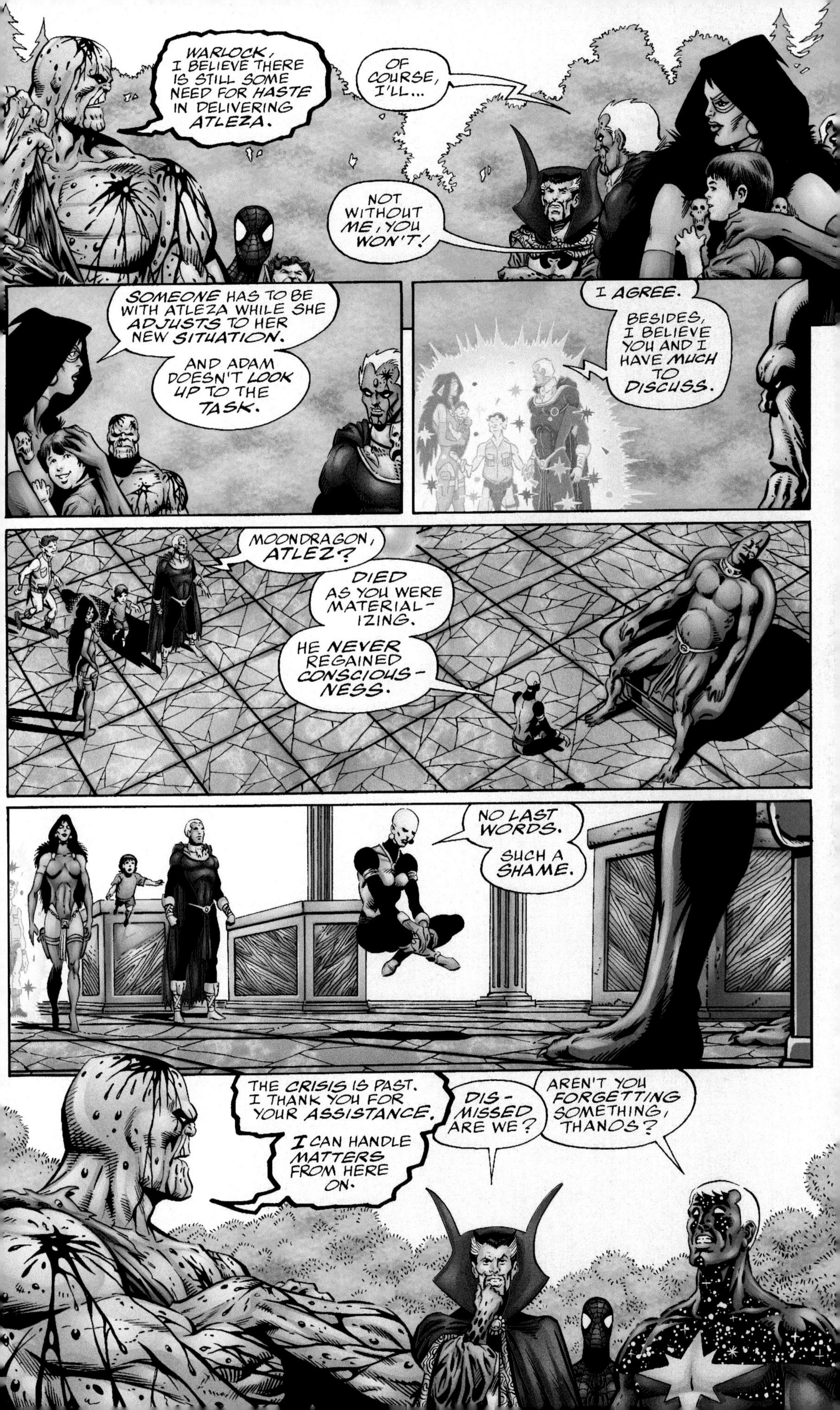
WARLOCK, I BELIEVE THERE IS STILL SOME NEED FOR HASTE IN DELIVERING ATLEZA.
OF COURSE, I'LL...
NOT WITHOUT ME, YOU WON'T!
SOMEONE HAS TO BE WITH ATLEZA WHILE SHE ADJUSTS TO HER NEW SITUATION.
AND ADAM DOESN'T LOOK UP TO THE TASK.
I AGREE.
BESIDES, I BELIEVE YOU AND I HAVE MUCH TO DISCUSS.
MOONDRAGON, ATLEZ?
DIED AS YOU WERE MATERIAL-IZING.
HE NEVER REGAINED CONSCIOUS-NESS.
NO LAST WORDS.
SUCH A SHAME.
THE CRISIS IS PAST. I THANK YOU FOR YOUR ASSISTANCE.
I CAN HANDLE MATTERS FROM HERE ON.
DIS-MISSED ARE WE?
AREN'T YOU FORGETTING SOMETHING, THANOS?

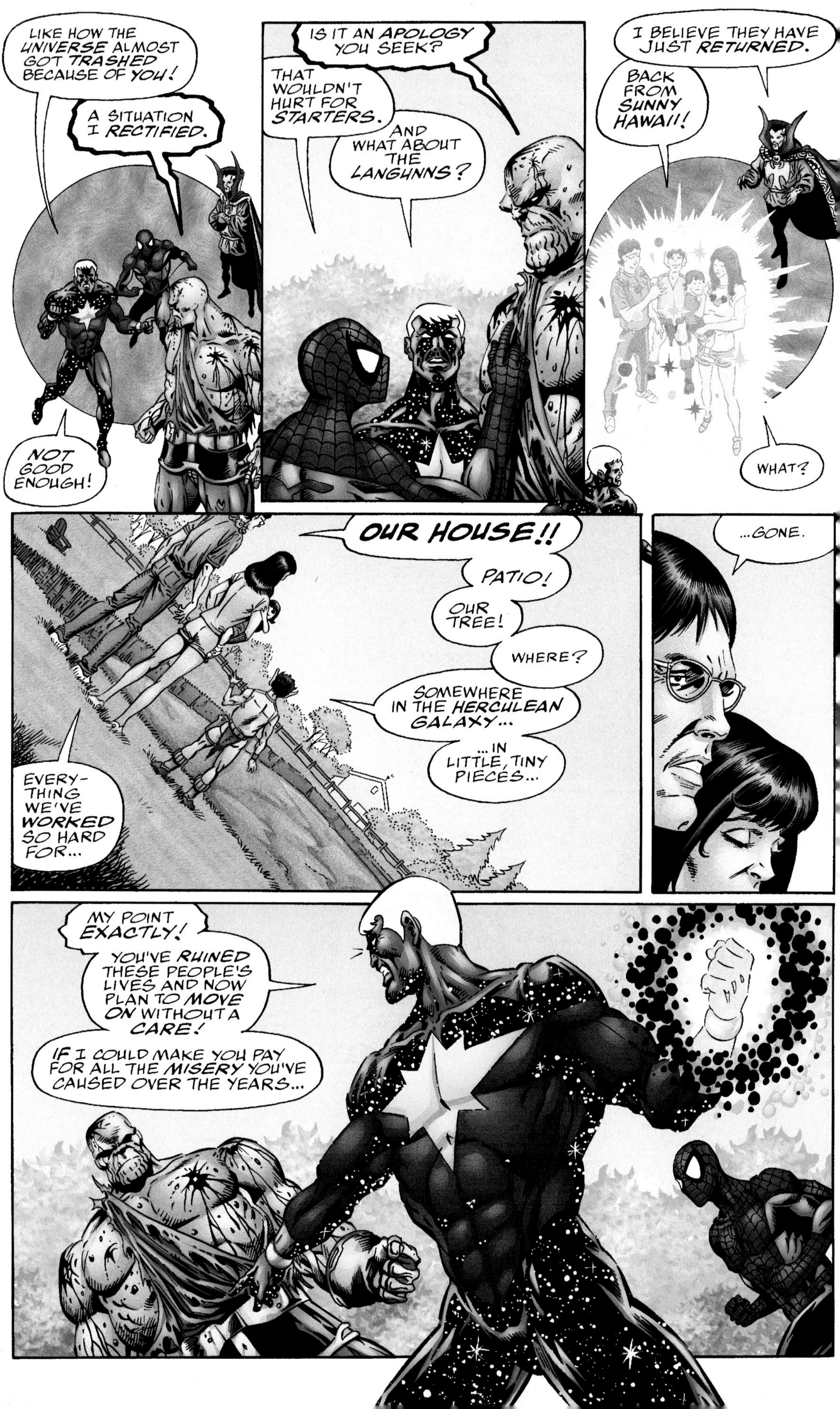
LIKE HOW THE UNIVERSE ALMOST GOT TRASHED BECAUSE OF YOU!
A SITUATION I RECTIFIED.
NOT GOOD ENOUGH!
IS IT AN APOLOGY YOU SEEK?
THAT WOULDN'T HURT FOR STARTERS.
AND WHAT ABOUT THE LANGUNNS?
I BELIEVE THEY HAVE JUST RETURNED.
BACK FROM SUNNY HAWAII!
WHAT?
OUR HOUSE!!
PATIO!
OUR TREE!
WHERE?
SOMEWHERE IN THE HERCULEAN GALAXY...
...IN LITTLE, TINY PIECES...
EVERY-THING WE'VE WORKED SO HARD FOR...
...GONE.
MY POINT EXACTLY!
YOU'VE RUINED THESE PEOPLE'S LIVES AND NOW PLAN TO MOVE ON WITHOUT A CARE!
IF I COULD MAKE YOU PAY FOR ALL THE MISERY YOU'VE CAUSED OVER THE YEARS...

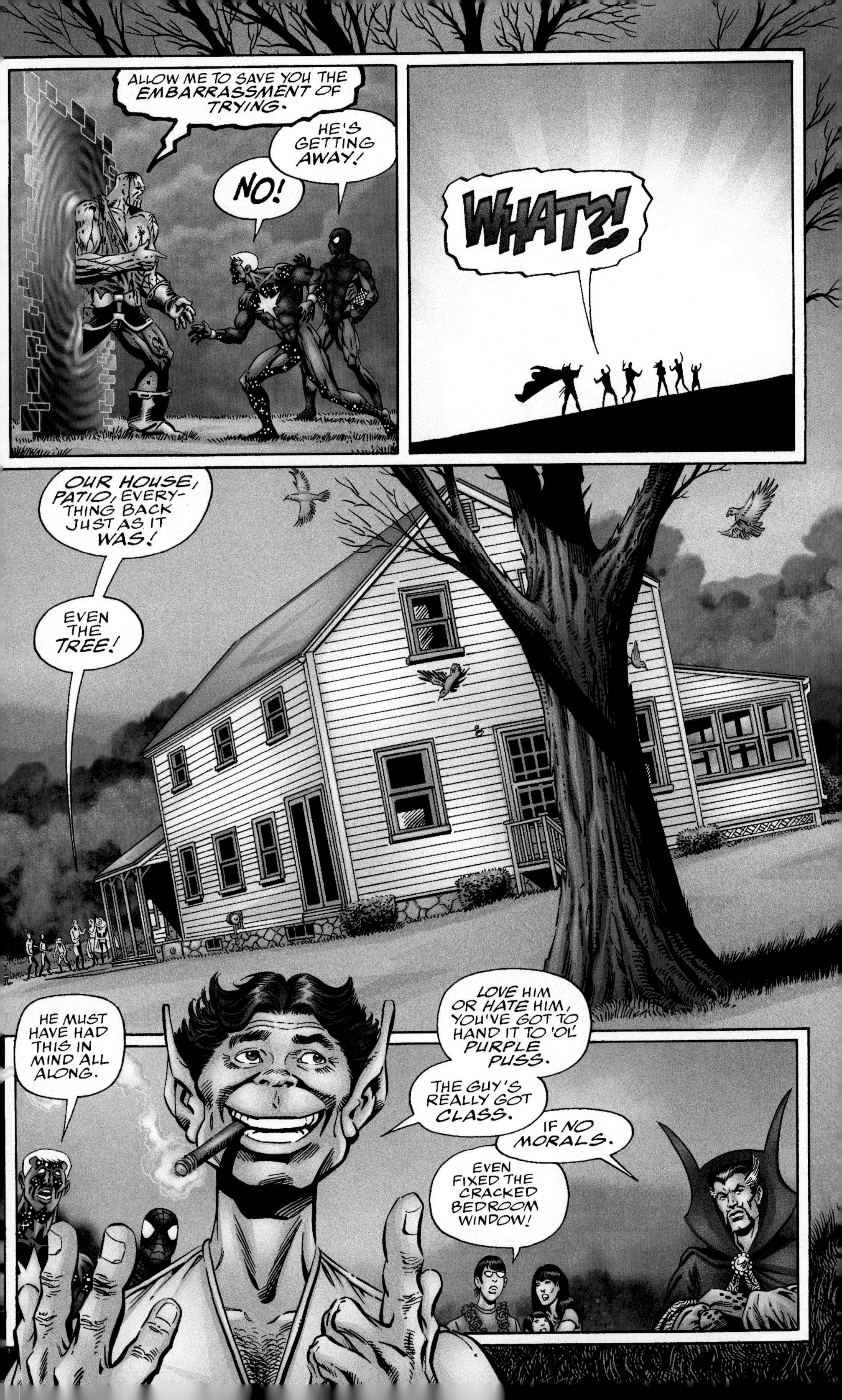

ALLOW ME TO SAVE YOU THE EMBARRASSMENT OF TRYING.
HE'S GETTING AWAY!
NO!
WHAT?!
OUR HOUSE, PATIO, EVERYTHING BACK JUST AS IT WAS!
EVEN THE TREE!
HE MUST HAVE HAD THIS IN MIND ALL ALONG.
LOVE HIM OR HATE HIM, YOU'VE GOT TO HAND IT TO 'OL' PURPLE PUSS.
THE GUY'S REALLY GOT CLASS.
IF NO MORALS.
EVEN FIXED THE CRACKED BEDROOM WINDOW!

AND SO, WITH *DISASTER* AT LEAST PRESENTLY *AVERTED,* THE UNIVERSE *RETURNS* TO ITS *NORMAL* RHYTHM.

ALL INVOLVED *RESUME* THEIR *LIVES,* DIGESTING AND ADJUSTING TO *SURVIVAL.*

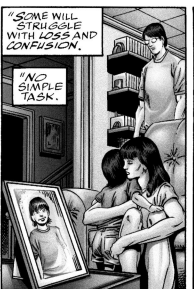

"SOME WILL STRUGGLE WITH *LOSS* AND *CONFUSION.*

"*NO* SIMPLE *TASK.*

"*WHILE* OTHERS CARRY *LESS* WEIGHT.

"*THERE* WILL BE CHERISHED *REUNIONS.*

"*ONE* TENDER...

"ANOTHER A BIT MORE *ACRIMONIOUS.*

"*EXPLANATIONS* WILL NOT BE *EASY.*

"BUT THEY WILL BE *MADE,* AND *EVENTUALLY ACCEPTED.*

"*ONE* WILL RETURN TO HER *SEARCH* FOR *UNDERSTAND-ING* AND *TRUTH.*

"*WHILE* ANOTHER...

... *SEEING* THANOS WAS SO *HELPFUL,* I HAD TO *LET* HIM *ESCAPE...*

AND THAT'S HOW *I* SAVED THE UNIVERSE!

"AND..."

GONE *EIGHTEEN* HOURS AND HE DOESN'T HAVE A *CLUE* WHAT HAPPENED.

MAYBE WE OUGHT TO *TELL* HIM.

THAT'LL ONLY GET HIM PULLING OUT HIS LI'L *DRUG-TESTING* CUPS AGAIN.

FORGET IT.

AND GAMORA AND I? WELL, WE HAVE SORT OF SET UP HOUSE IN THE HEART OF DARKNESS WHILE ATLEZA LEARNS AND GROWS.

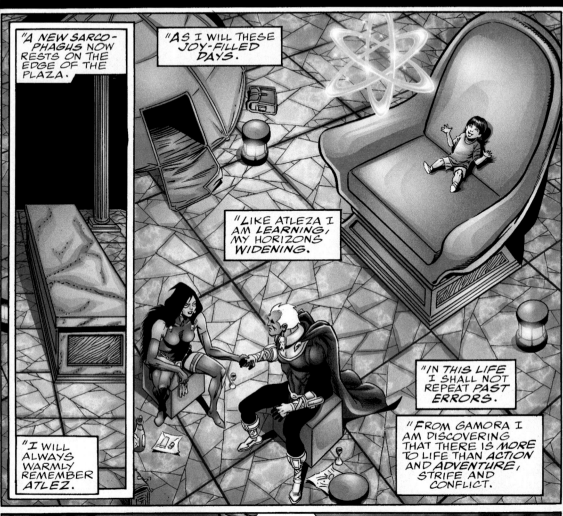

"A NEW SARCO-PHAGUS NOW RESTS ON THE EDGE OF THE PLAZA.

"AS I WILL THESE JOY-FILLED DAYS.

"LIKE ATLEZA I AM LEARNING, MY HORIZONS WIDENING.

"IN THIS LIFE I SHALL NOT REPEAT PAST ERRORS.

"FROM GAMORA I AM DISCOVERING THAT THERE IS MORE TO LIFE THAN ACTION AND ADVENTURE, STRIFE AND CONFLICT.

"I WILL ALWAYS WARMLY REMEMBER ATLEZ.

"I NEVER REALIZED THAT MERE WORDS OR A TOUCH COULD PROVE TO BE SUCH SUBTLE TREASURES.

"KEYS TO UNIMAGINED HAPPINESS.

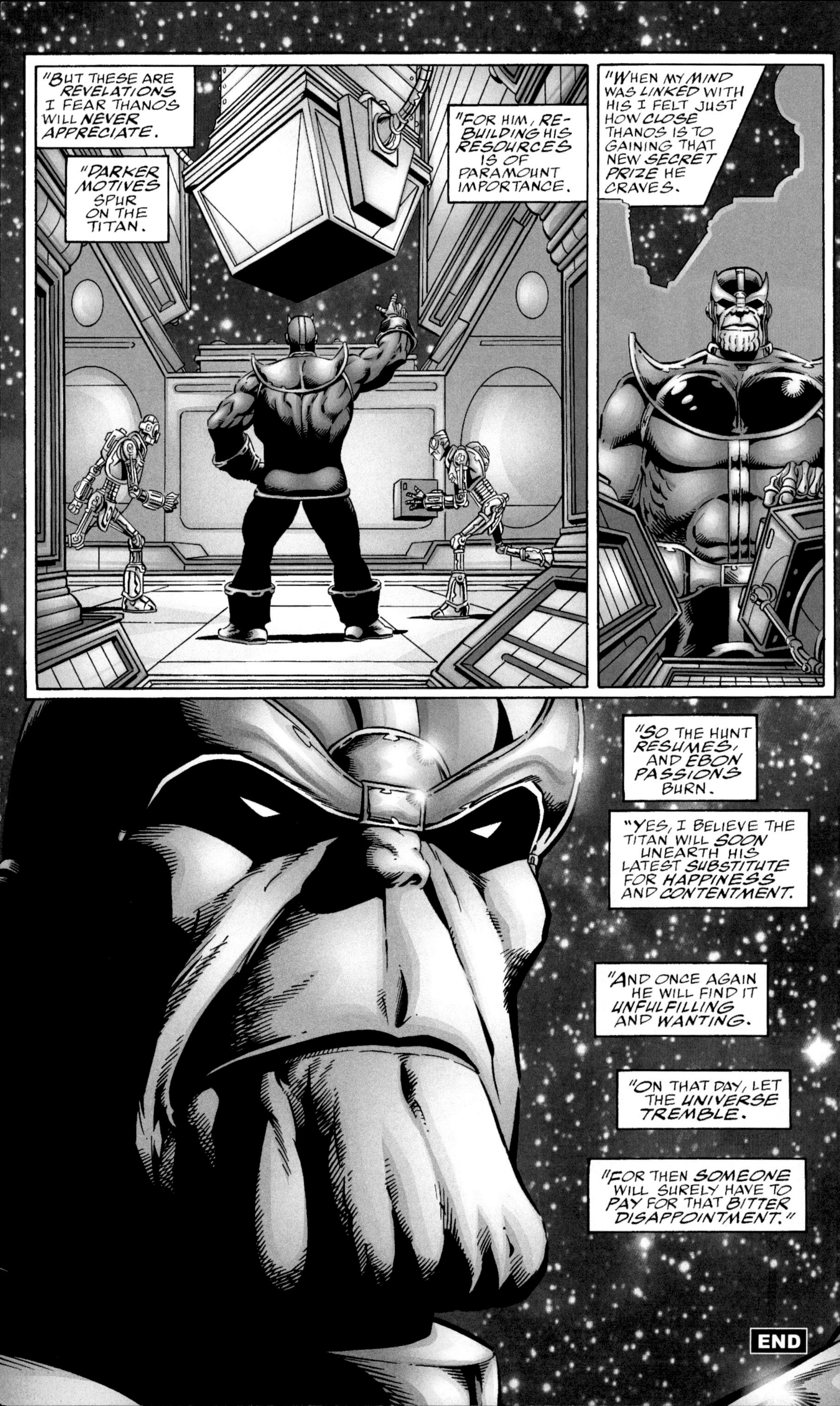
"BUT THESE ARE REVELATIONS I FEAR THANOS WILL NEVER APPRECIATE.
"DARKER MOTIVES SPUR ON THE TITAN.
"FOR HIM, RE-BUILDING HIS RESOURCES IS OF PARAMOUNT IMPORTANCE.
"WHEN MY MIND WAS LINKED WITH HIS I FELT JUST HOW CLOSE THANOS IS TO GAINING THAT NEW SECRET PRIZE HE CRAVES.
"SO THE HUNT RESUMES, AND EBON PASSIONS BURN.
"YES, I BELIEVE THE TITAN WILL SOON UNEARTH HIS LATEST SUBSTITUTE FOR HAPPINESS AND CONTENTMENT.
"AND ONCE AGAIN HE WILL FIND IT UNFULFILLING AND WANTING.
"ON THAT DAY, LET THE UNIVERSE TREMBLE.
"FOR THEN SOMEONE WILL SURELY HAVE TO PAY FOR THAT BITTER DISAPPOINTMENT."
END

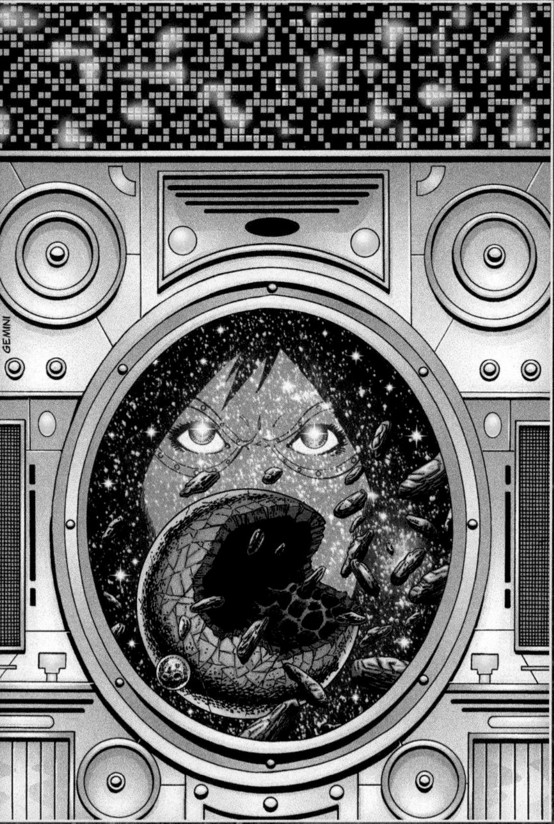
GEMINI

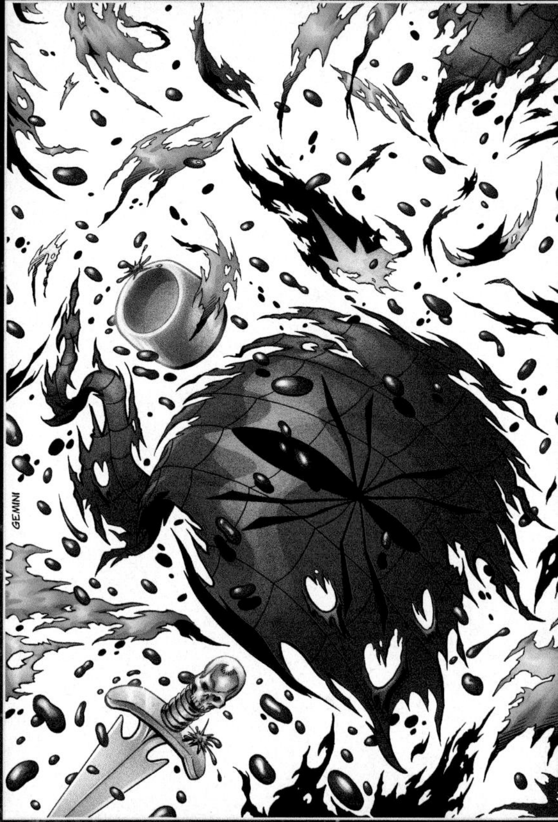
GEMINI

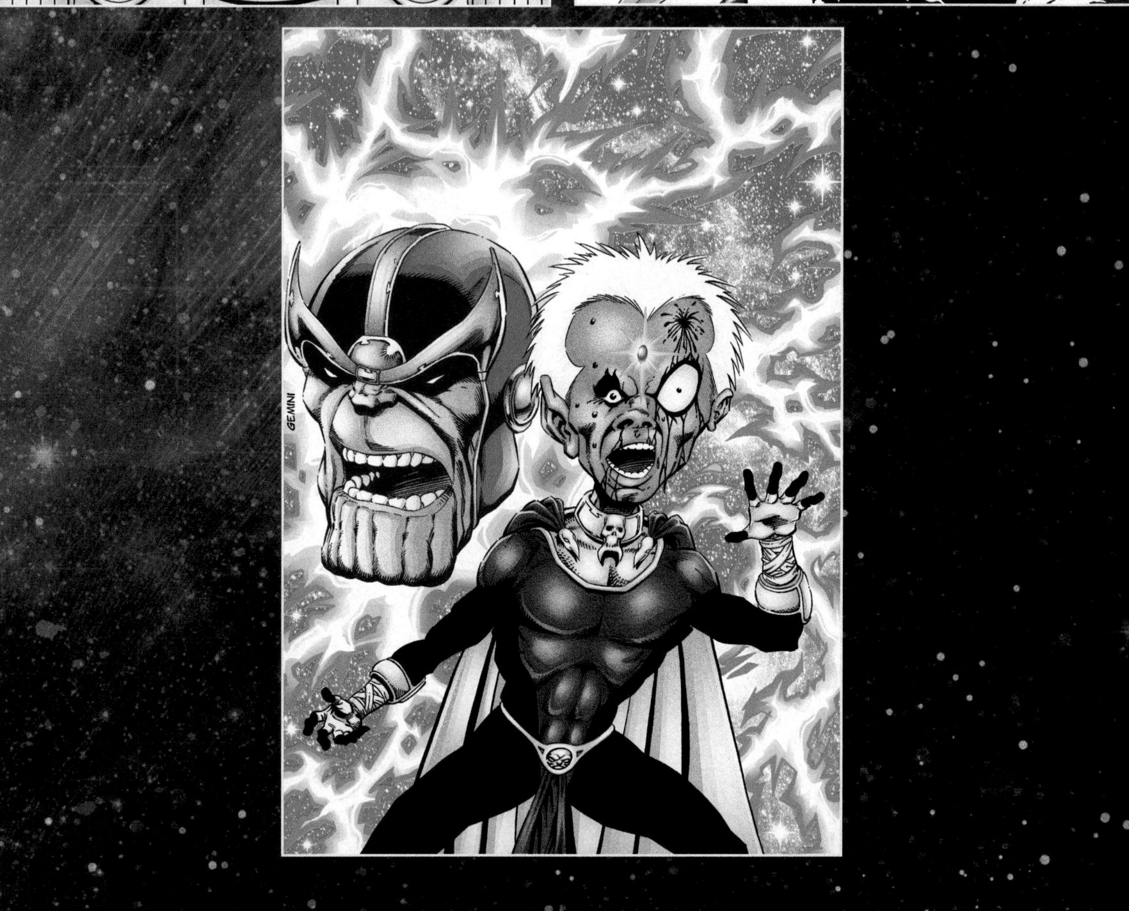
GEMINI

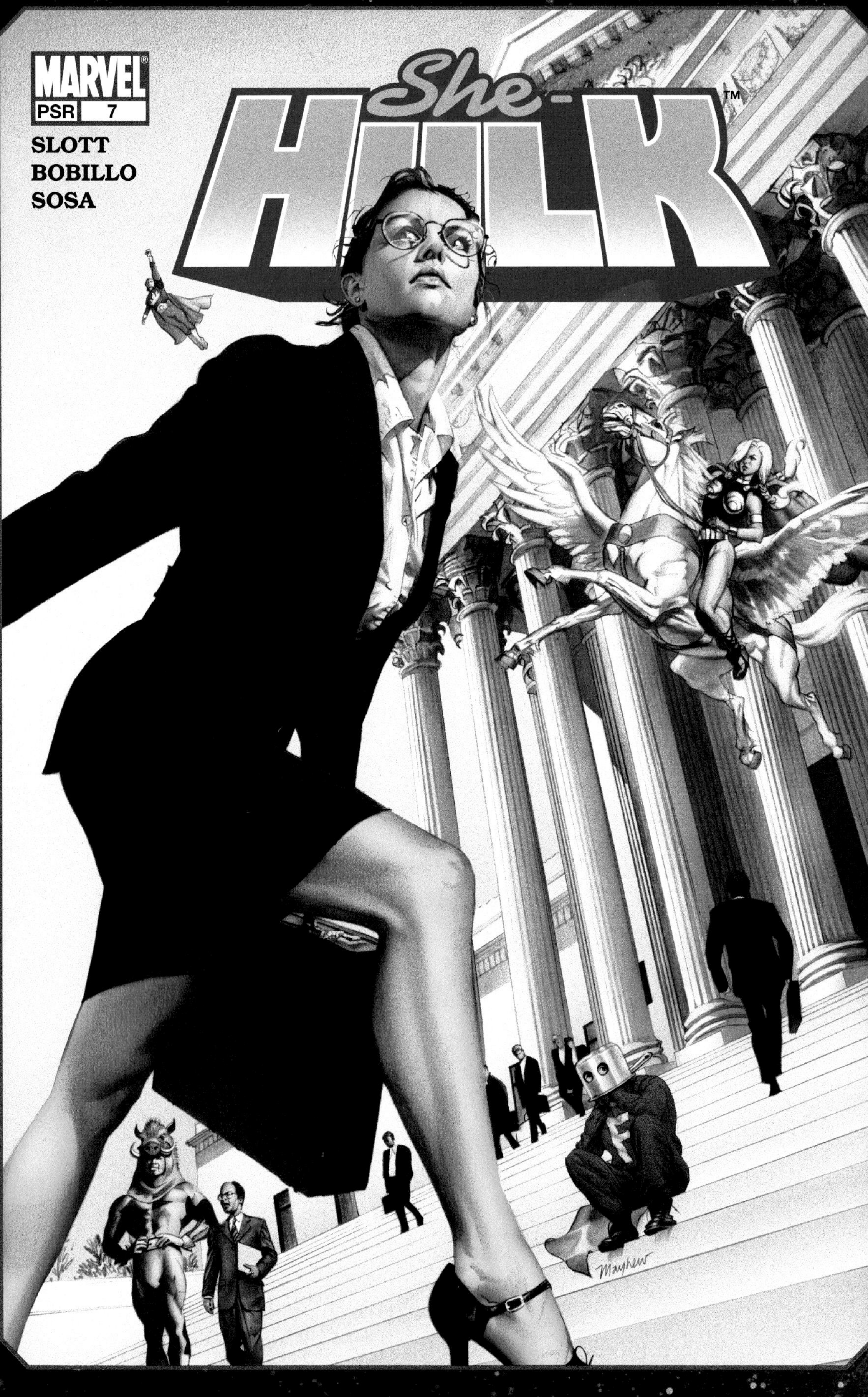
MARVEL
PSR 7
She-HULK™
SLOTT
BOBILLO
SOSA
Mayhew

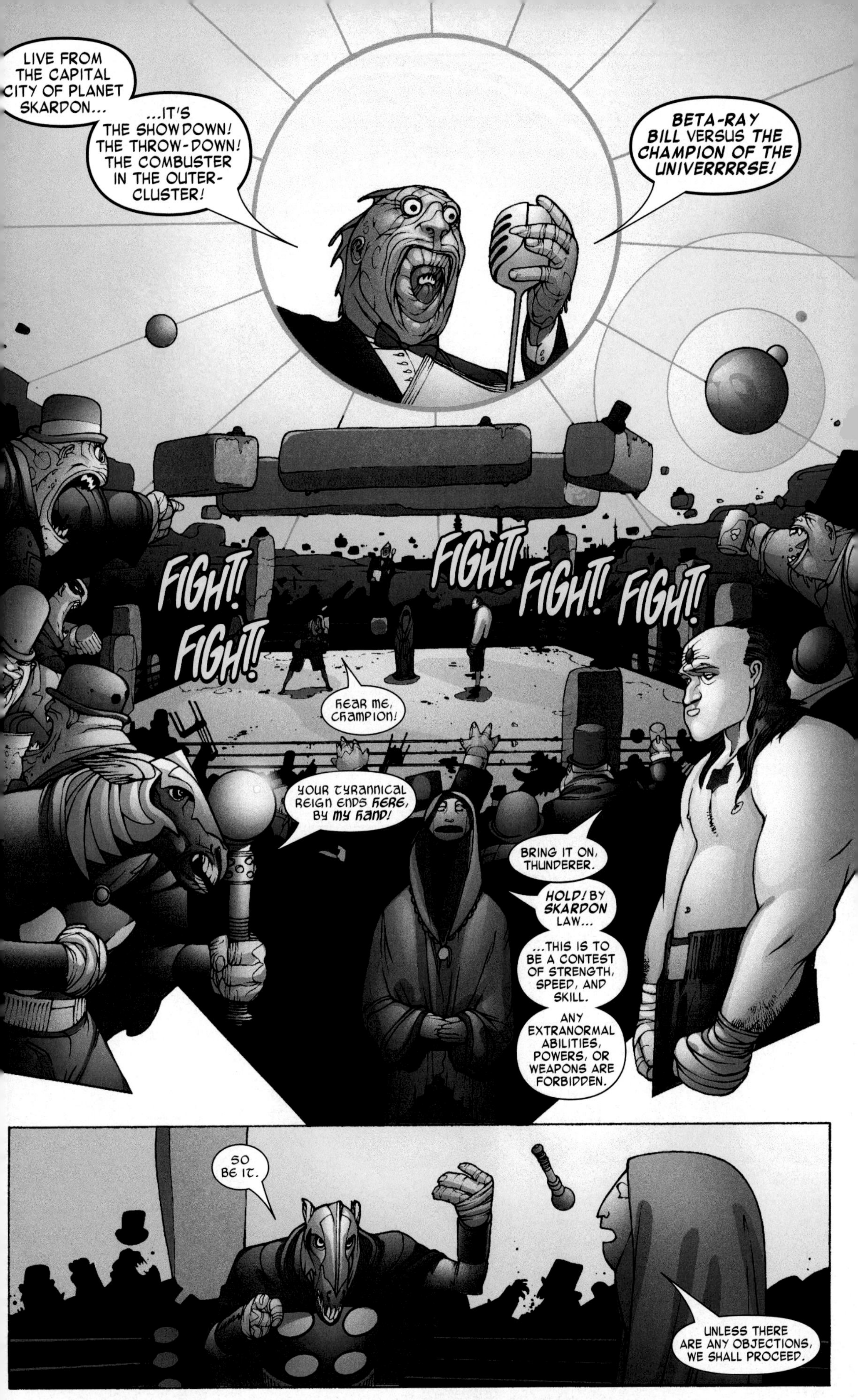

LIVE FROM THE CAPITAL CITY OF PLANET SKARDON...
...IT'S THE SHOWDOWN! THE THROW-DOWN! THE COMBUSTER IN THE OUTER-CLUSTER!
BETA-RAY BILL VERSUS THE CHAMPION OF THE UNIVERRRRSE!
FIGHT! FIGHT!
FIGHT! FIGHT! FIGHT!
HEAR ME, CHAMPION!
YOUR TYRANNICAL REIGN ENDS HERE, BY MY HAND!
BRING IT ON, THUNDERER.
HOLD! BY SKARDON LAW...
...THIS IS TO BE A CONTEST OF STRENGTH, SPEED, AND SKILL.
ANY EXTRANORMAL ABILITIES, POWERS, OR WEAPONS ARE FORBIDDEN.
SO BE IT.
UNLESS THERE ARE ANY OBJECTIONS, WE SHALL PROCEED.

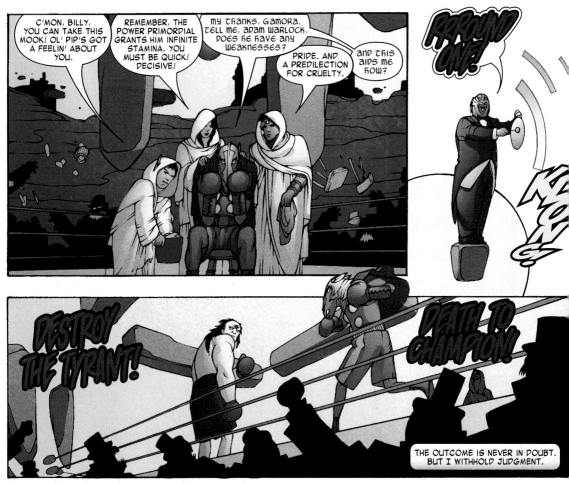

C'MON, BILLY, YOU CAN TAKE THIS MOOK! OL' PIP'S GOT A FEELIN' ABOUT YOU.

REMEMBER, THE POWER PRIMORDIAL GRANTS HIM INFINITE STAMINA. YOU MUST BE QUICK! DECISIVE!

MY THANKS, GAMORA. TELL ME, ADAM WARLOCK, DOES HE HAVE ANY WEAKNESSES?

PRIDE. AND A PREDILECTION FOR CRUELTY.

AND THIS AIDS ME HOW?

RRROUND ONE!

DESTROY THE TYRANT!

DEATH TO CHAMPION!

THE OUTCOME IS NEVER IN DOUBT. BUT I WITHHOLD JUDGMENT.

TRYCO SLATTERUS, THE CHAMPION, IS AN ELDER OF THE UNIVERSE. HE LIVES ONLY FOR SPORT SUCH AS THIS.

SINCE THE BEGINNING OF TIME, HE'S NEVER LOST A MATCH INSIDE THE RING.

EVEN THOUGH THIS CHALLENGER IS THE FIERCEST WARRIOR FROM THE BURNING GALAXY--

--AND EMPOWERED BY THE GODS OF ASGARD THEMSELVES--

--IN THE END, I'M CERTAIN HE'LL FALL.

FWAKK

WUMF

PTAM

STILL, UNTIL THAT TIME, I MUST WITHHOLD JUDGMENT.

FOR I AM A MEMBER OF THE MAGISTRATI, AND THAT IS OUR WAY.

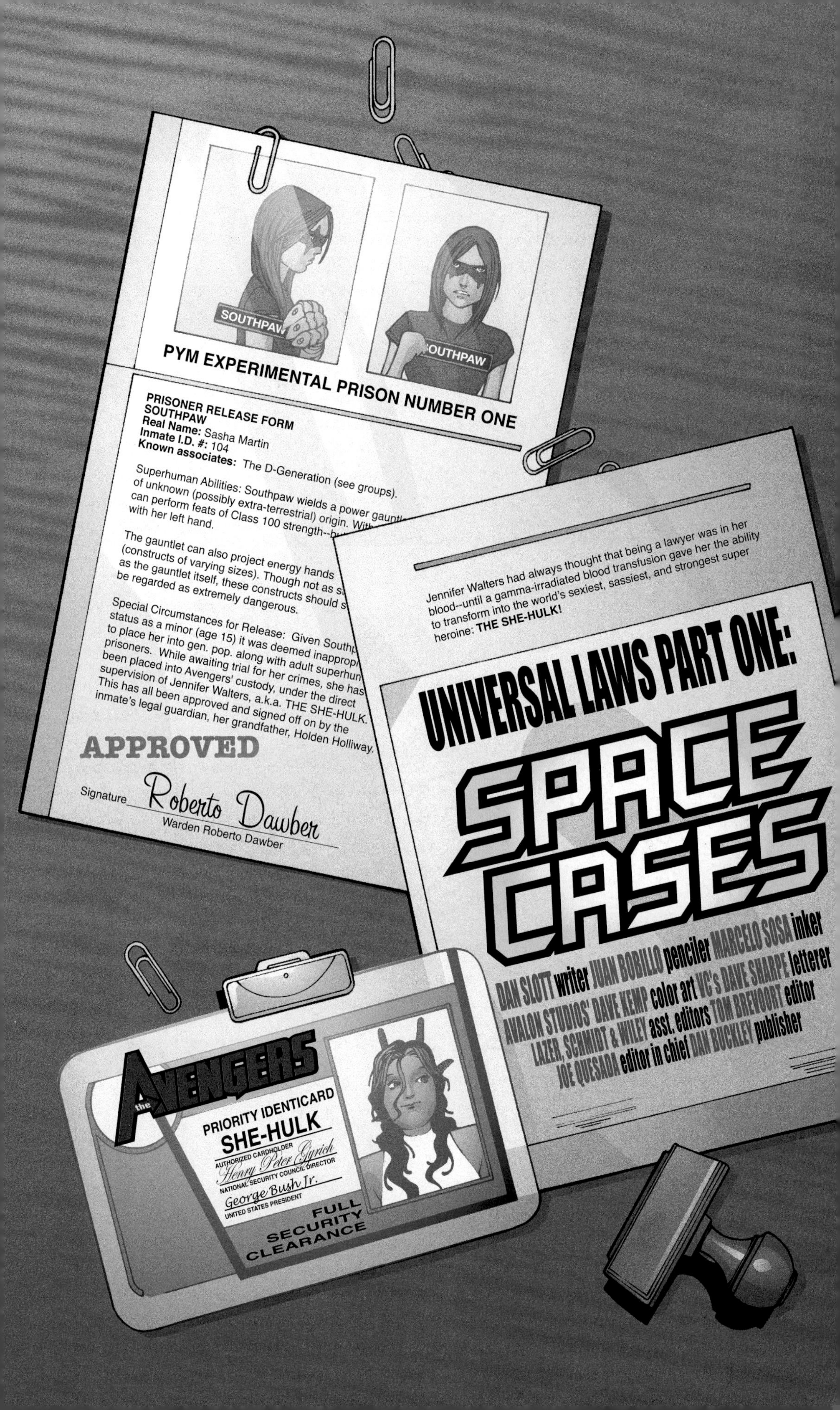

SOUTHPAW
SOUTHPAW
PYM EXPERIMENTAL PRISON NUMBER ONE
PRISONER RELEASE FORM
SOUTHPAW
Real Name: Sasha Martin
Inmate I.D. #: 104
Known associates: The D-Generation (see groups).
Superhuman Abilities: Southpaw wields a power gauntl of unknown (possibly extra-terrestrial) origin. With can perform feats of Class 100 strength--bu with her left hand.
The gauntlet can also project energy hands (constructs of varying sizes). Though not as s as the gauntlet itself, these constructs should s be regarded as extremely dangerous.
Special Circumstances for Release: Given Southp status as a minor (age 15) it was deemed inapprop to place her into gen. pop. along with adult superhun prisoners. While awaiting trial for her crimes, she has been placed into Avengers' custody, under the direct supervision of Jennifer Walters, a.k.a. THE SHE-HULK. This has all been approved and signed off on by the inmate's legal guardian, her grandfather, Holden Holliway.
APPROVED
Signature Roberto Dawber
Warden Roberto Dawber
Jennifer Walters had always thought that being a lawyer was in her blood--until a gamma-irradiated blood transfusion gave her the ability to transform into the world's sexiest, sassiest, and strongest super heroine: THE SHE-HULK!
UNIVERSAL LAWS PART ONE:
SPACE CASES
DAN SLOTT writer JUAN BOBILLO penciler MARCELO SOSA inker
AVALON STUDIOS' DAVE KEMP color art VC's DAVE SHARPE letterer
LAZER, SCHMIDT & WILEY asst. editors TOM BREVOORT editor
JOE QUESADA editor in chief DAN BUCKLEY publisher
the AVENGERS
PRIORITY IDENTICARD
SHE-HULK
AUTHORIZED CARDHOLDER
Henry Peter Gyrich
NATIONAL SECURITY COUNCIL DIRECTOR
George Bush Jr.
UNITED STATES PRESIDENT
FULL SECURITY CLEARANCE

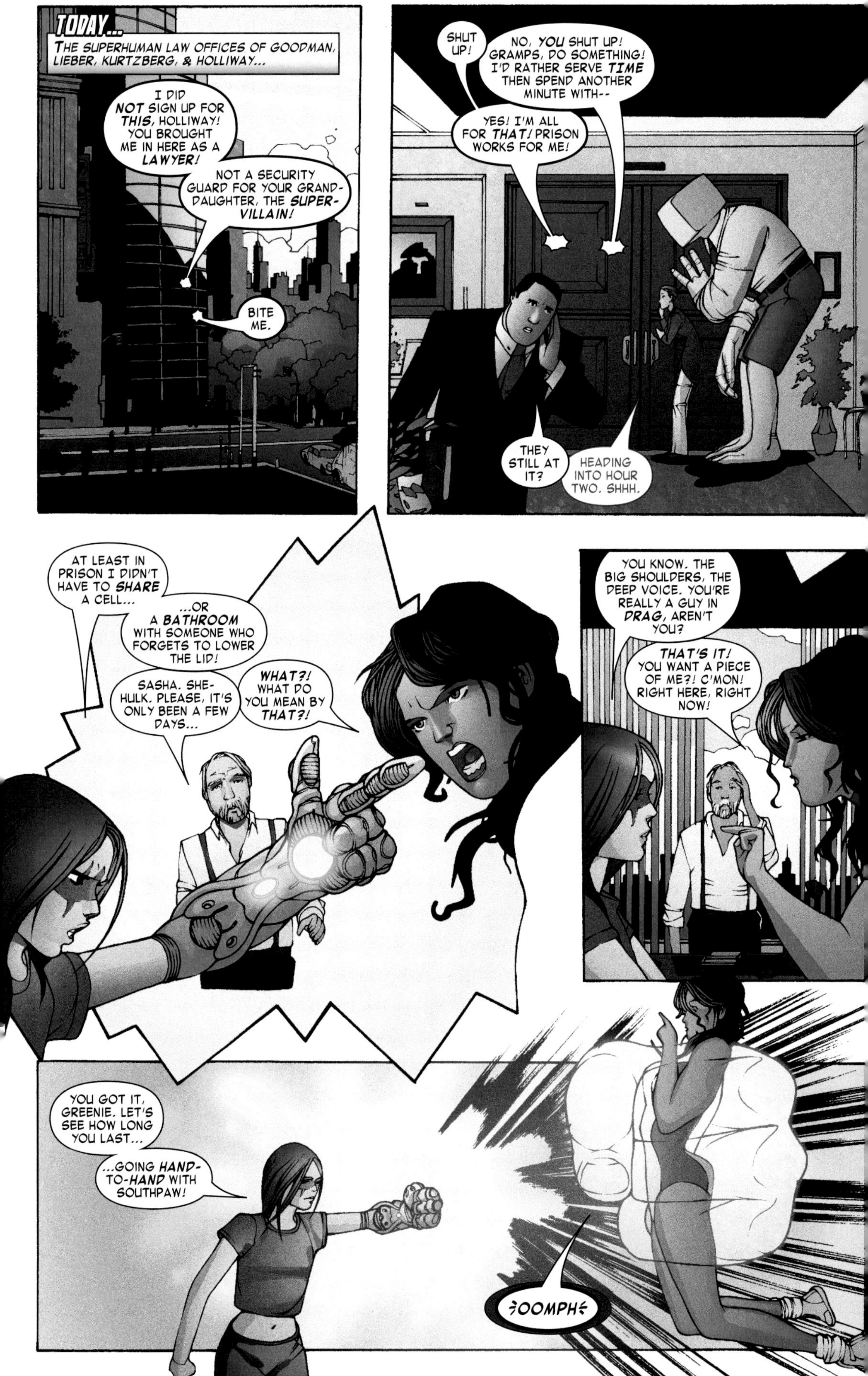
TODAY...
THE SUPERHUMAN LAW OFFICES OF GOODMAN, LIEBER, KURTZBERG, & HOLLIWAY...
I DID NOT SIGN UP FOR THIS, HOLLIWAY! YOU BROUGHT ME IN HERE AS A LAWYER!
NOT A SECURITY GUARD FOR YOUR GRAND-DAUGHTER, THE SUPER-VILLAIN!
BITE ME.
SHUT UP!
NO, YOU SHUT UP! GRAMPS, DO SOMETHING! I'D RATHER SERVE TIME THEN SPEND ANOTHER MINUTE WITH--
YES! I'M ALL FOR THAT! PRISON WORKS FOR ME!
THEY STILL AT IT?
HEADING INTO HOUR TWO. SHHH.
AT LEAST IN PRISON I DIDN'T HAVE TO SHARE A CELL...
...OR A BATHROOM WITH SOMEONE WHO FORGETS TO LOWER THE LID!
SASHA. SHE-HULK. PLEASE, IT'S ONLY BEEN A FEW DAYS...
WHAT?! WHAT DO YOU MEAN BY THAT?!
YOU KNOW. THE BIG SHOULDERS, THE DEEP VOICE. YOU'RE REALLY A GUY IN DRAG, AREN'T YOU?
THAT'S IT! YOU WANT A PIECE OF ME?! C'MON! RIGHT HERE, RIGHT NOW!
YOU GOT IT, GREENIE. LET'S SEE HOW LONG YOU LAST...
...GOING HAND-TO-HAND WITH SOUTHPAW!
OOMPH

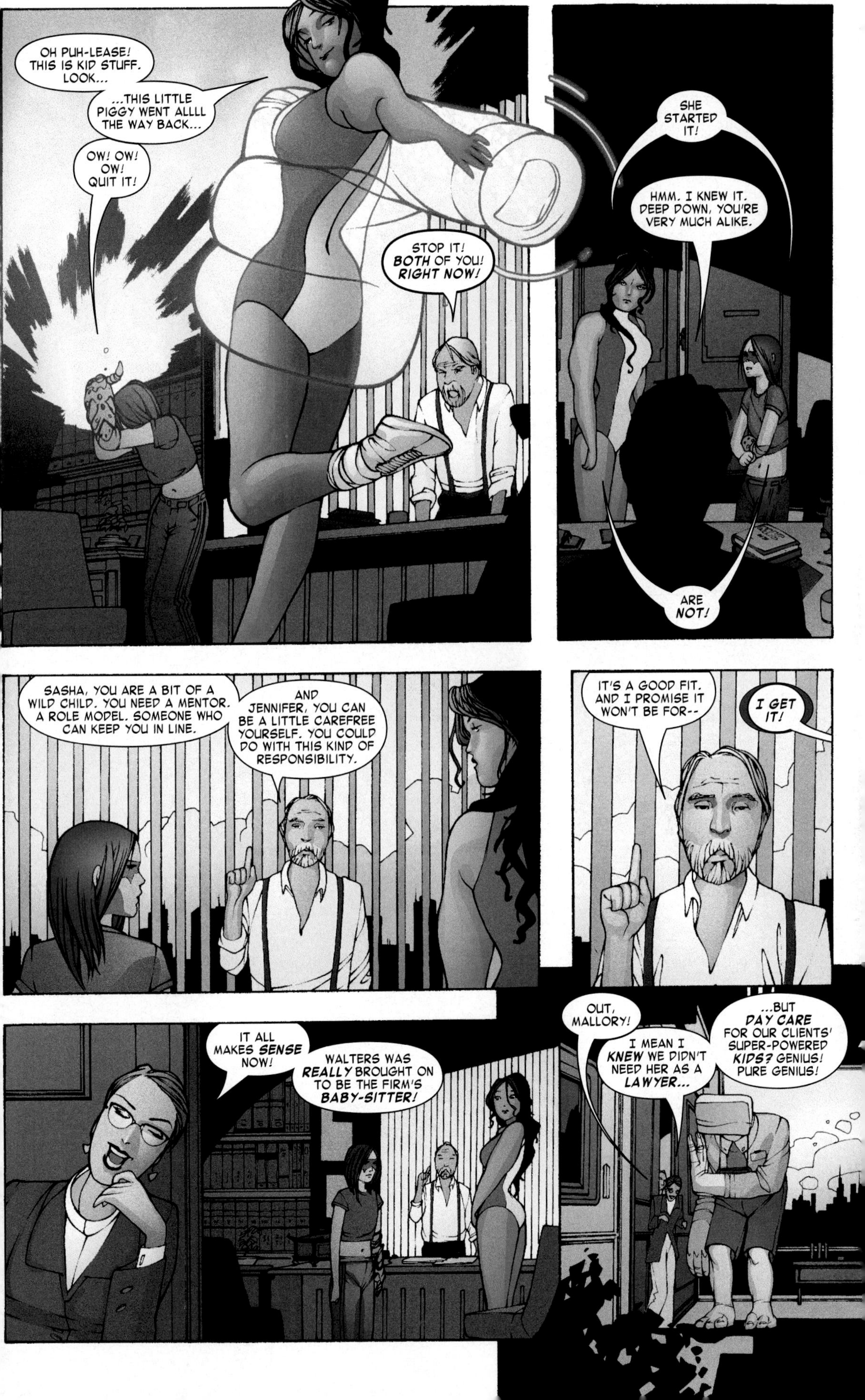

OH PUH-LEASE! THIS IS KID STUFF. LOOK...
...THIS LITTLE PIGGY WENT ALLLL THE WAY BACK...
OW! OW! OW! QUIT IT!
STOP IT! BOTH OF YOU! RIGHT NOW!
SHE STARTED IT!
HMM. I KNEW IT. DEEP DOWN, YOU'RE VERY MUCH ALIKE.
ARE NOT!
SASHA, YOU ARE A BIT OF A WILD CHILD. YOU NEED A MENTOR. A ROLE MODEL. SOMEONE WHO CAN KEEP YOU IN LINE.
AND JENNIFER, YOU CAN BE A LITTLE CAREFREE YOURSELF. YOU COULD DO WITH THIS KIND OF RESPONSIBILITY.
IT'S A GOOD FIT. AND I PROMISE IT WON'T BE FOR--
I GET IT!
IT ALL MAKES SENSE NOW!
WALTERS WAS REALLY BROUGHT ON TO BE THE FIRM'S BABY-SITTER!
OUT, MALLORY!
I MEAN I KNEW WE DIDN'T NEED HER AS A LAWYER...
...BUT DAY CARE FOR OUR CLIENTS' SUPER-POWERED KIDS? GENIUS! PURE GENIUS!

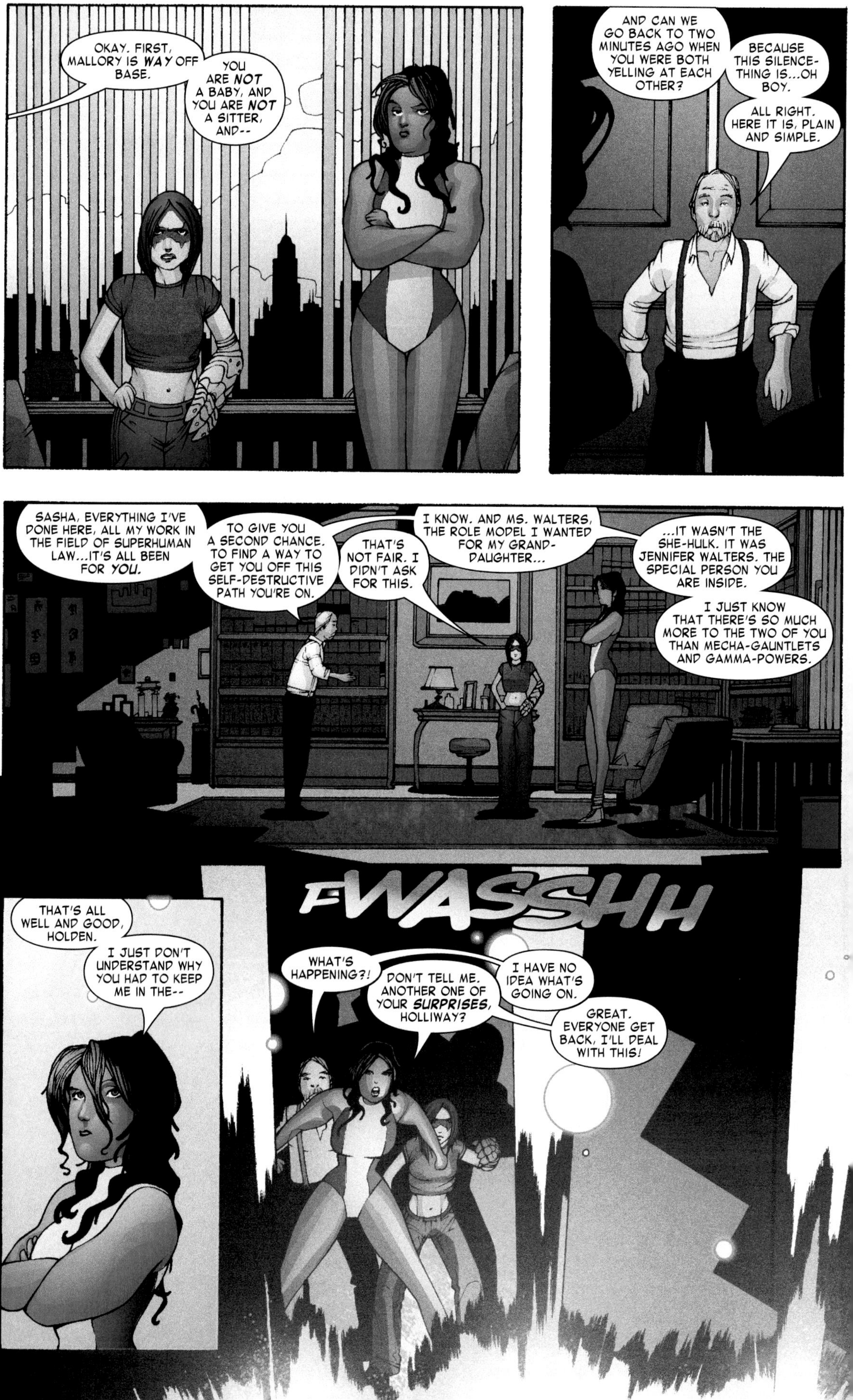

OKAY. FIRST, MALLORY IS **WAY** OFF BASE.
YOU ARE **NOT** A BABY, AND YOU ARE **NOT** A SITTER, AND--
AND CAN WE GO BACK TO TWO MINUTES AGO WHEN YOU WERE BOTH YELLING AT EACH OTHER?
BECAUSE THIS SILENCE-THING IS...OH BOY.
ALL RIGHT. HERE IT IS, PLAIN AND SIMPLE.
SASHA, EVERYTHING I'VE DONE HERE, ALL MY WORK IN THE FIELD OF SUPERHUMAN LAW...IT'S ALL BEEN FOR **YOU.**
TO GIVE YOU A SECOND CHANCE. TO FIND A WAY TO GET YOU OFF THIS SELF-DESTRUCTIVE PATH YOU'RE ON.
THAT'S NOT FAIR. I DIDN'T ASK FOR THIS.
I KNOW. AND MS. WALTERS, THE ROLE MODEL I WANTED FOR MY GRAND-DAUGHTER...
...IT WASN'T THE SHE-HULK. IT WAS JENNIFER WALTERS. THE SPECIAL PERSON YOU ARE INSIDE.
I JUST KNOW THAT THERE'S SO MUCH MORE TO THE TWO OF YOU THAN MECHA-GAUNTLETS AND GAMMA-POWERS.
THAT'S ALL WELL AND GOOD, HOLDEN.
I JUST DON'T UNDERSTAND WHY YOU HAD TO KEEP ME IN THE--
FWASSHH
WHAT'S HAPPENING?!
DON'T TELL ME. ANOTHER ONE OF YOUR **SURPRISES,** HOLLIWAY?
I HAVE NO IDEA WHAT'S GOING ON.
GREAT. EVERYONE GET BACK, I'LL DEAL WITH THIS!

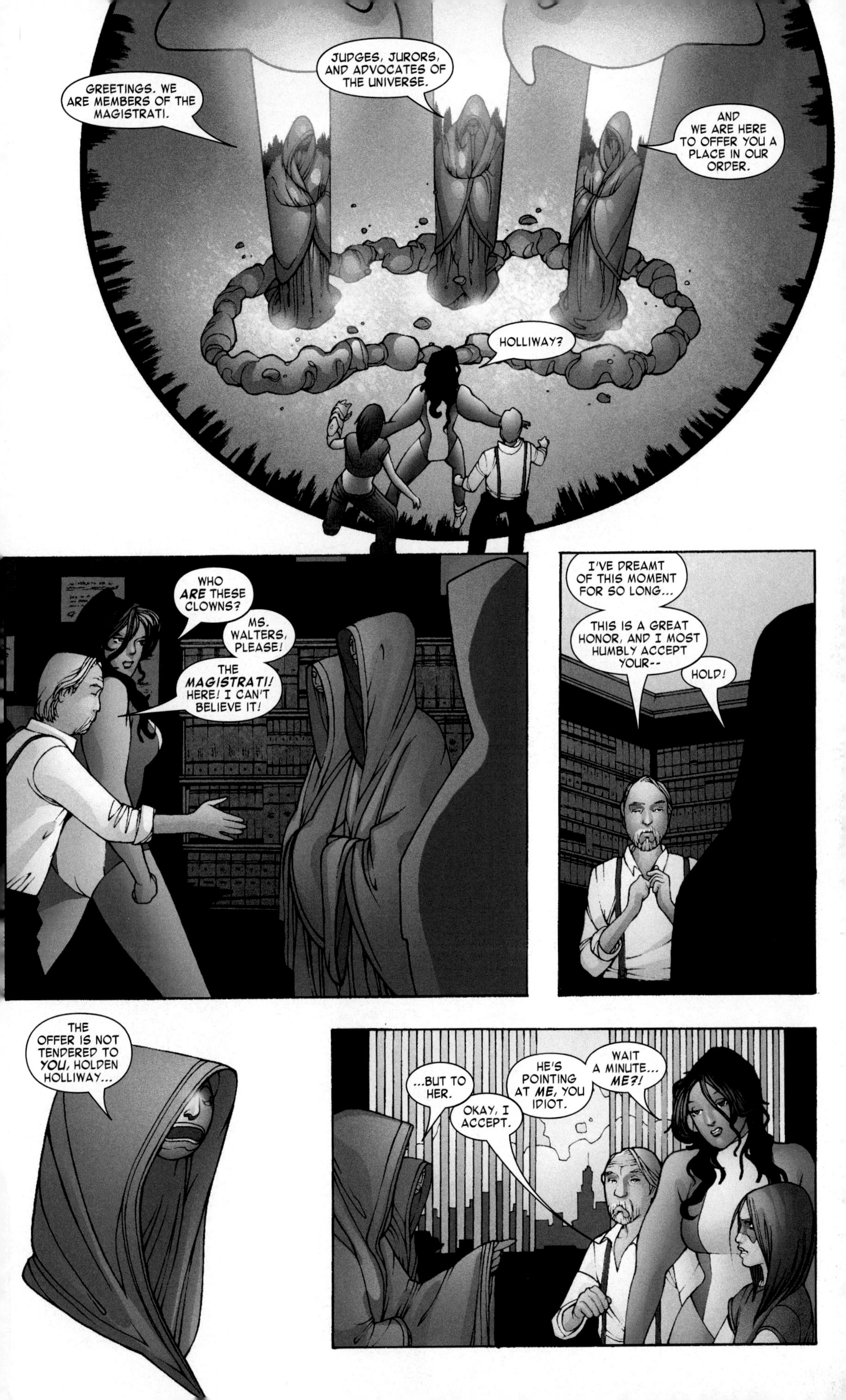
GREETINGS. WE ARE MEMBERS OF THE MAGISTRATI.
JUDGES, JURORS, AND ADVOCATES OF THE UNIVERSE.
AND WE ARE HERE TO OFFER YOU A PLACE IN OUR ORDER.
HOLLIWAY?
WHO ARE THESE CLOWNS?
MS. WALTERS, PLEASE!
THE MAGISTRATI! HERE! I CAN'T BELIEVE IT!
I'VE DREAMT OF THIS MOMENT FOR SO LONG...
THIS IS A GREAT HONOR, AND I MOST HUMBLY ACCEPT YOUR--
HOLD!
THE OFFER IS NOT TENDERED TO YOU, HOLDEN HOLLIWAY...
...BUT TO HER.
OKAY, I ACCEPT.
HE'S POINTING AT ME, YOU IDIOT.
WAIT A MINUTE... ME?!

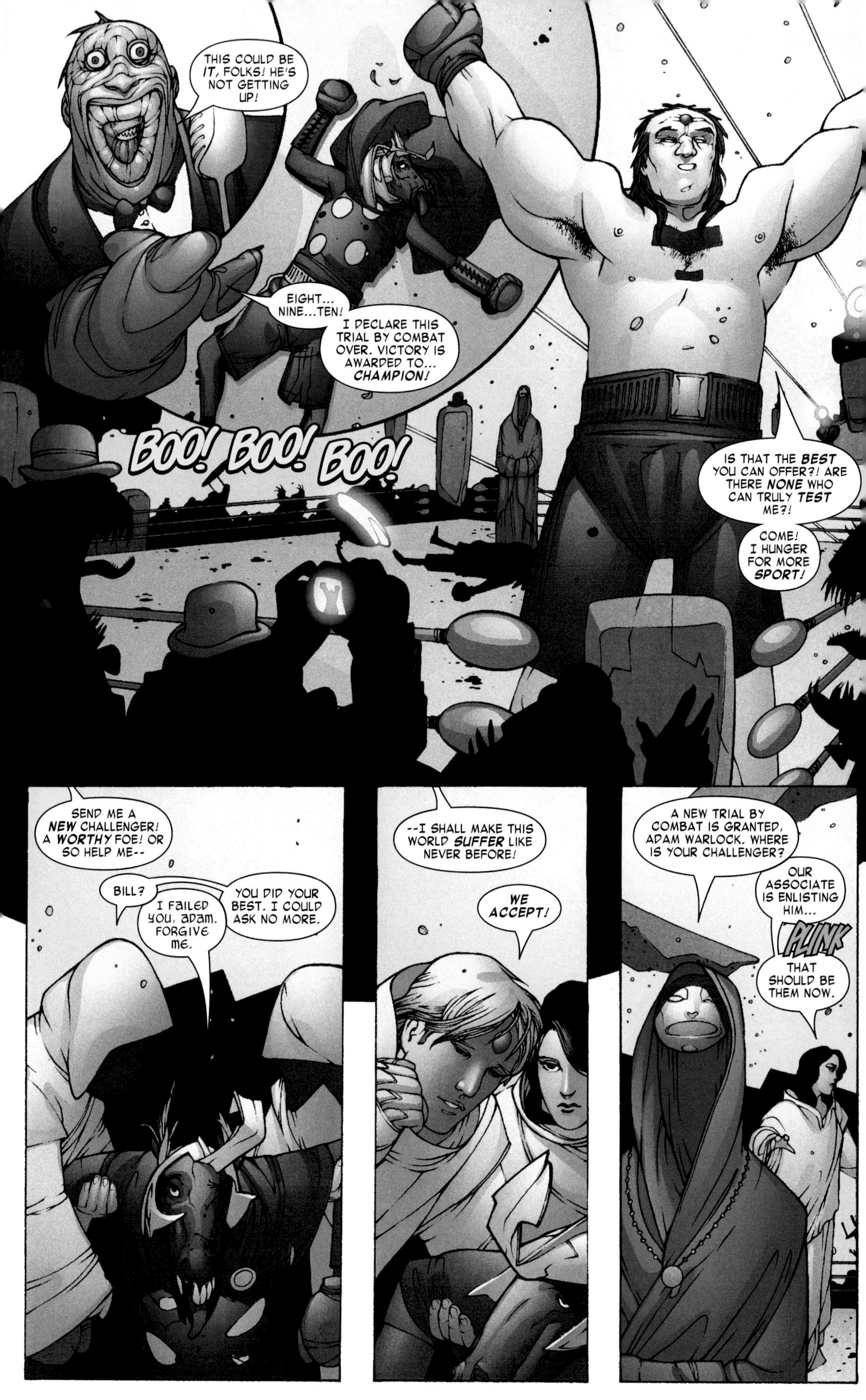
THIS COULD BE *IT*, FOLKS! HE'S NOT GETTING UP!
EIGHT... NINE...TEN!
I DECLARE THIS TRIAL BY COMBAT OVER. VICTORY IS AWARDED TO... *CHAMPION!*
BOO! BOO! BOO!
IS THAT THE *BEST* YOU CAN OFFER?! ARE THERE *NONE* WHO CAN TRULY *TEST* ME?!
COME! I HUNGER FOR MORE *SPORT!*
SEND ME A *NEW* CHALLENGER! A *WORTHY* FOE! OR SO HELP ME--
BILL?
I FAILED YOU, ADAM. FORGIVE ME.
YOU DID YOUR BEST. I COULD ASK NO MORE.
--I SHALL MAKE THIS WORLD *SUFFER* LIKE NEVER BEFORE!
WE ACCEPT!
A NEW TRIAL BY COMBAT IS GRANTED, ADAM WARLOCK. WHERE IS YOUR CHALLENGER?
OUR ASSOCIATE IS ENLISTING HIM...
PLINK
THAT SHOULD BE THEM NOW.

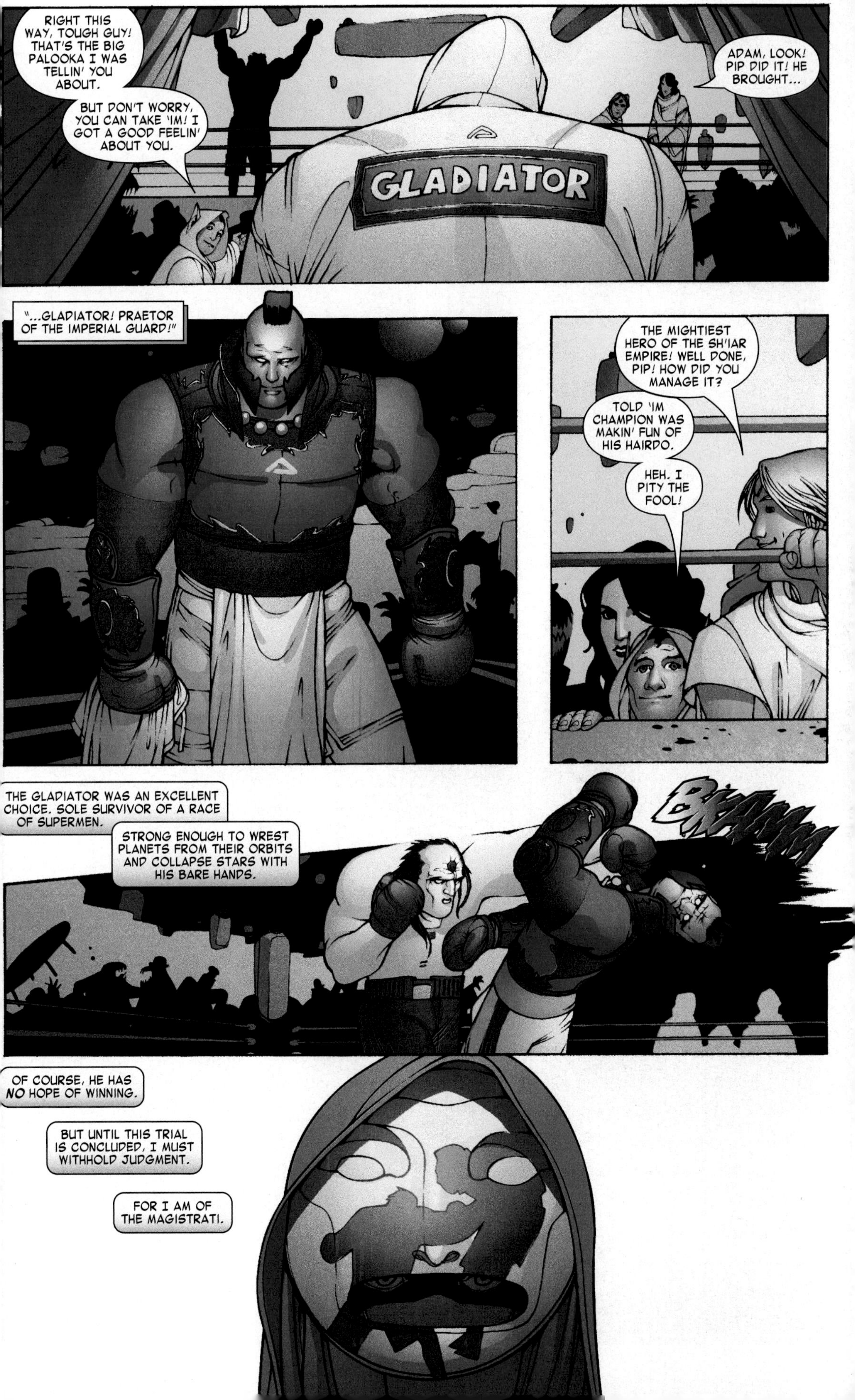

RIGHT THIS WAY, TOUGH GUY! THAT'S THE BIG PALOOKA I WAS TELLIN' YOU ABOUT.
BUT DON'T WORRY, YOU CAN TAKE 'IM! I GOT A GOOD FEELIN' ABOUT YOU.
ADAM, LOOK! PIP DID IT! HE BROUGHT...
GLADIATOR
"...GLADIATOR! PRAETOR OF THE IMPERIAL GUARD!"
THE MIGHTIEST HERO OF THE SH'IAR EMPIRE! WELL DONE, PIP! HOW DID YOU MANAGE IT?
TOLD 'IM CHAMPION WAS MAKIN' FUN OF HIS HAIRDO.
HEH. I PITY THE FOOL!
THE GLADIATOR WAS AN EXCELLENT CHOICE. SOLE SURVIVOR OF A RACE OF SUPERMEN.
STRONG ENOUGH TO WREST PLANETS FROM THEIR ORBITS AND COLLAPSE STARS WITH HIS BARE HANDS.
BKRAMM
OF COURSE, HE HAS NO HOPE OF WINNING.
BUT UNTIL THIS TRIAL IS CONCLUDED, I MUST WITHHOLD JUDGMENT.
FOR I AM OF THE MAGISTRATI.

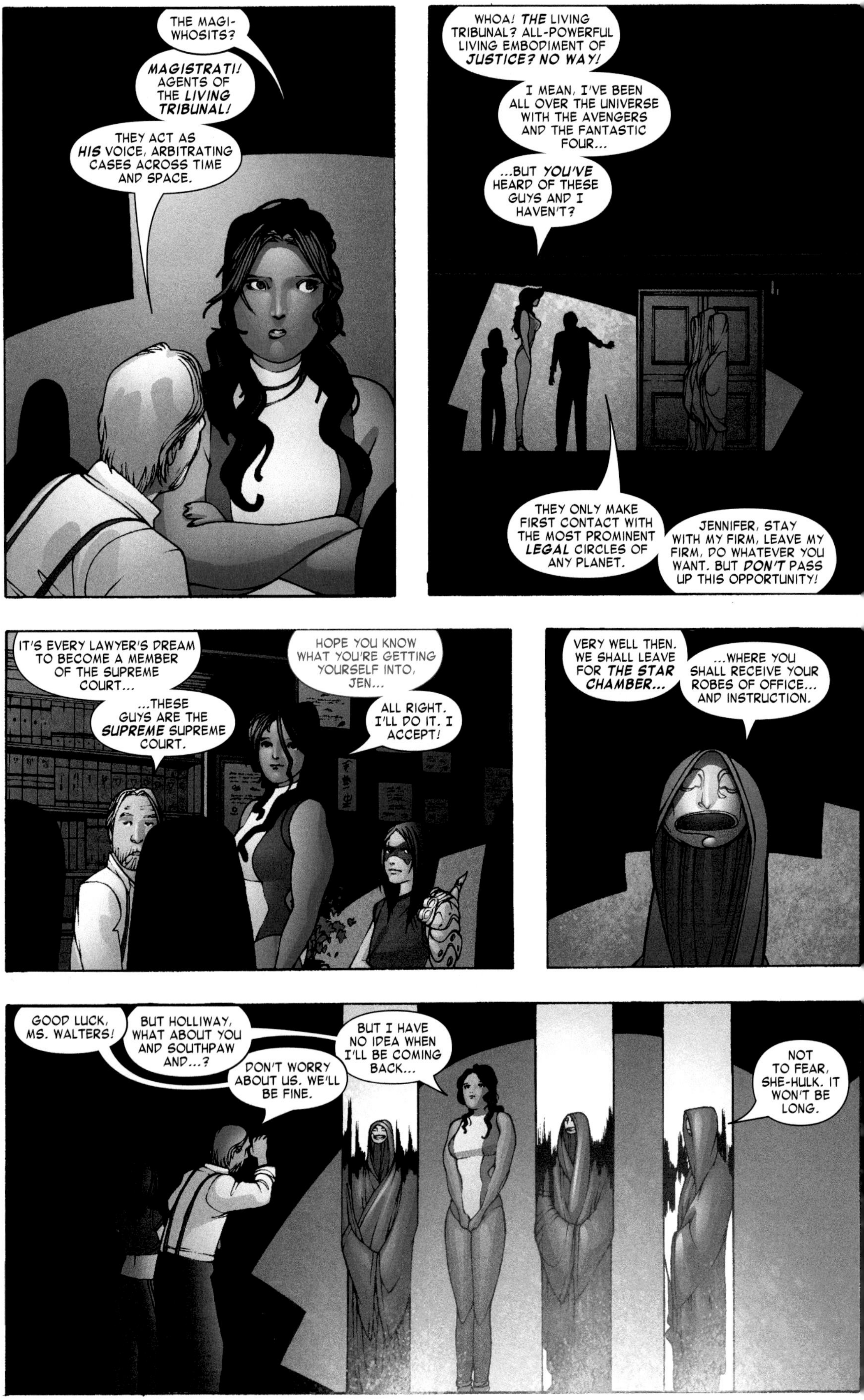

THE MAGI-WHOSITS?
MAGISTRATI! AGENTS OF THE LIVING TRIBUNAL!
THEY ACT AS HIS VOICE, ARBITRATING CASES ACROSS TIME AND SPACE.
WHOA! THE LIVING TRIBUNAL? ALL-POWERFUL LIVING EMBODIMENT OF JUSTICE? NO WAY!
I MEAN, I'VE BEEN ALL OVER THE UNIVERSE WITH THE AVENGERS AND THE FANTASTIC FOUR...
...BUT YOU'VE HEARD OF THESE GUYS AND I HAVEN'T?
THEY ONLY MAKE FIRST CONTACT WITH THE MOST PROMINENT LEGAL CIRCLES OF ANY PLANET.
JENNIFER, STAY WITH MY FIRM, LEAVE MY FIRM, DO WHATEVER YOU WANT. BUT DON'T PASS UP THIS OPPORTUNITY!
IT'S EVERY LAWYER'S DREAM TO BECOME A MEMBER OF THE SUPREME COURT...
...THESE GUYS ARE THE SUPREME SUPREME COURT.
HOPE YOU KNOW WHAT YOU'RE GETTING YOURSELF INTO, JEN...
ALL RIGHT. I'LL DO IT. I ACCEPT!
VERY WELL THEN. WE SHALL LEAVE FOR THE STAR CHAMBER...
...WHERE YOU SHALL RECEIVE YOUR ROBES OF OFFICE... AND INSTRUCTION.
GOOD LUCK, MS. WALTERS!
BUT HOLLIWAY, WHAT ABOUT YOU AND SOUTHPAW AND...?
DON'T WORRY ABOUT US. WE'LL BE FINE.
BUT I HAVE NO IDEA WHEN I'LL BE COMING BACK...
NOT TO FEAR, SHE-HULK. IT WON'T BE LONG.

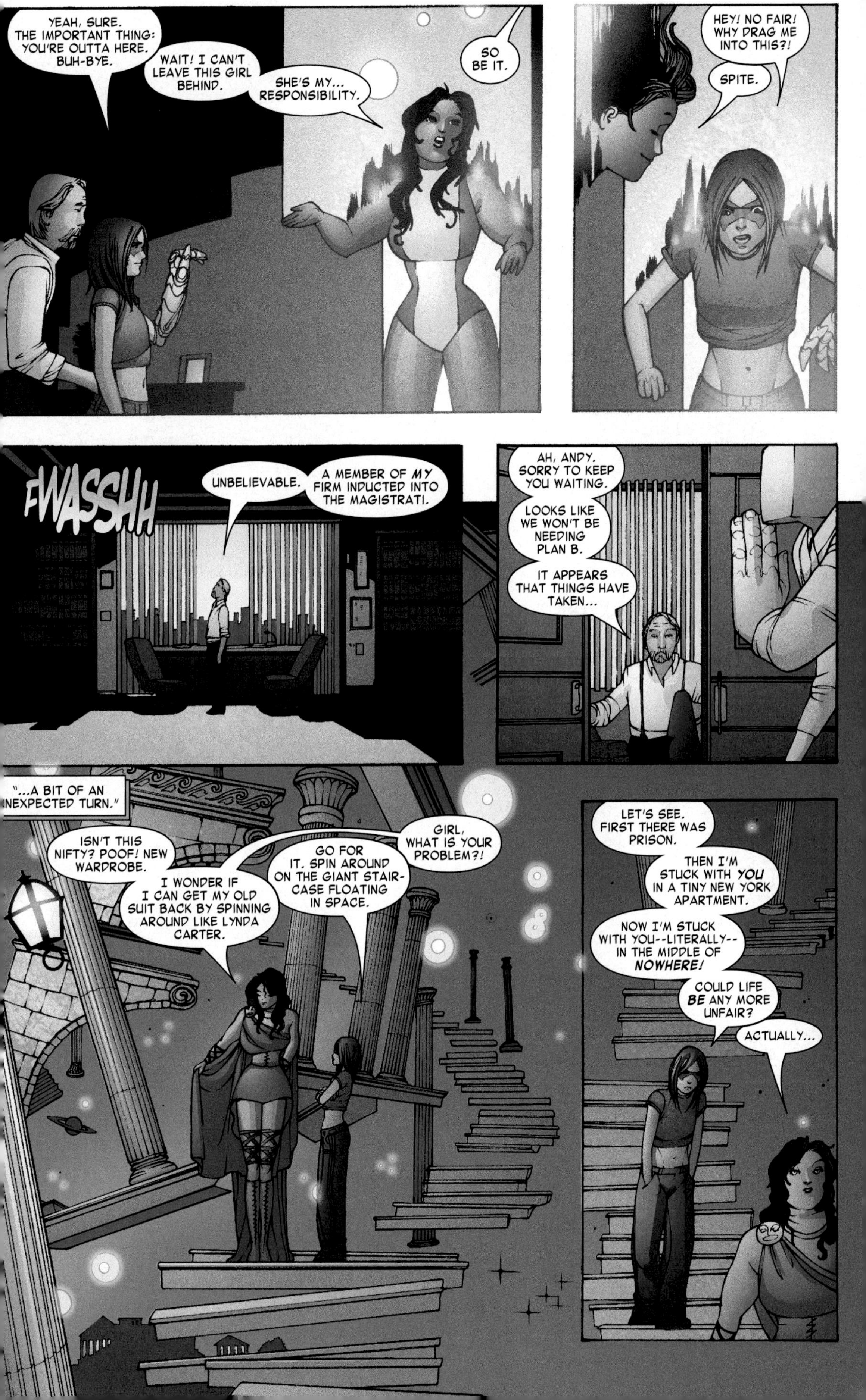

YEAH, SURE. THE IMPORTANT THING: YOU'RE OUTTA HERE. BUH-BYE.
WAIT! I CAN'T LEAVE THIS GIRL BEHIND.
SHE'S MY... RESPONSIBILITY.
SO BE IT.
HEY! NO FAIR! WHY DRAG ME INTO THIS?!
SPITE.
FWASSHH
UNBELIEVABLE.
A MEMBER OF MY FIRM INDUCTED INTO THE MAGISTRATI.
AH, ANDY. SORRY TO KEEP YOU WAITING.
LOOKS LIKE WE WON'T BE NEEDING PLAN B.
IT APPEARS THAT THINGS HAVE TAKEN...
"...A BIT OF AN UNEXPECTED TURN."
ISN'T THIS NIFTY? POOF! NEW WARDROBE.
I WONDER IF I CAN GET MY OLD SUIT BACK BY SPINNING AROUND LIKE LYNDA CARTER.
GO FOR IT. SPIN AROUND ON THE GIANT STAIRCASE FLOATING IN SPACE.
GIRL, WHAT IS YOUR PROBLEM?!
LET'S SEE. FIRST THERE WAS PRISON.
THEN I'M STUCK WITH YOU IN A TINY NEW YORK APARTMENT.
NOW I'M STUCK WITH YOU--LITERALLY-- IN THE MIDDLE OF NOWHERE!
COULD LIFE BE ANY MORE UNFAIR?
ACTUALLY...

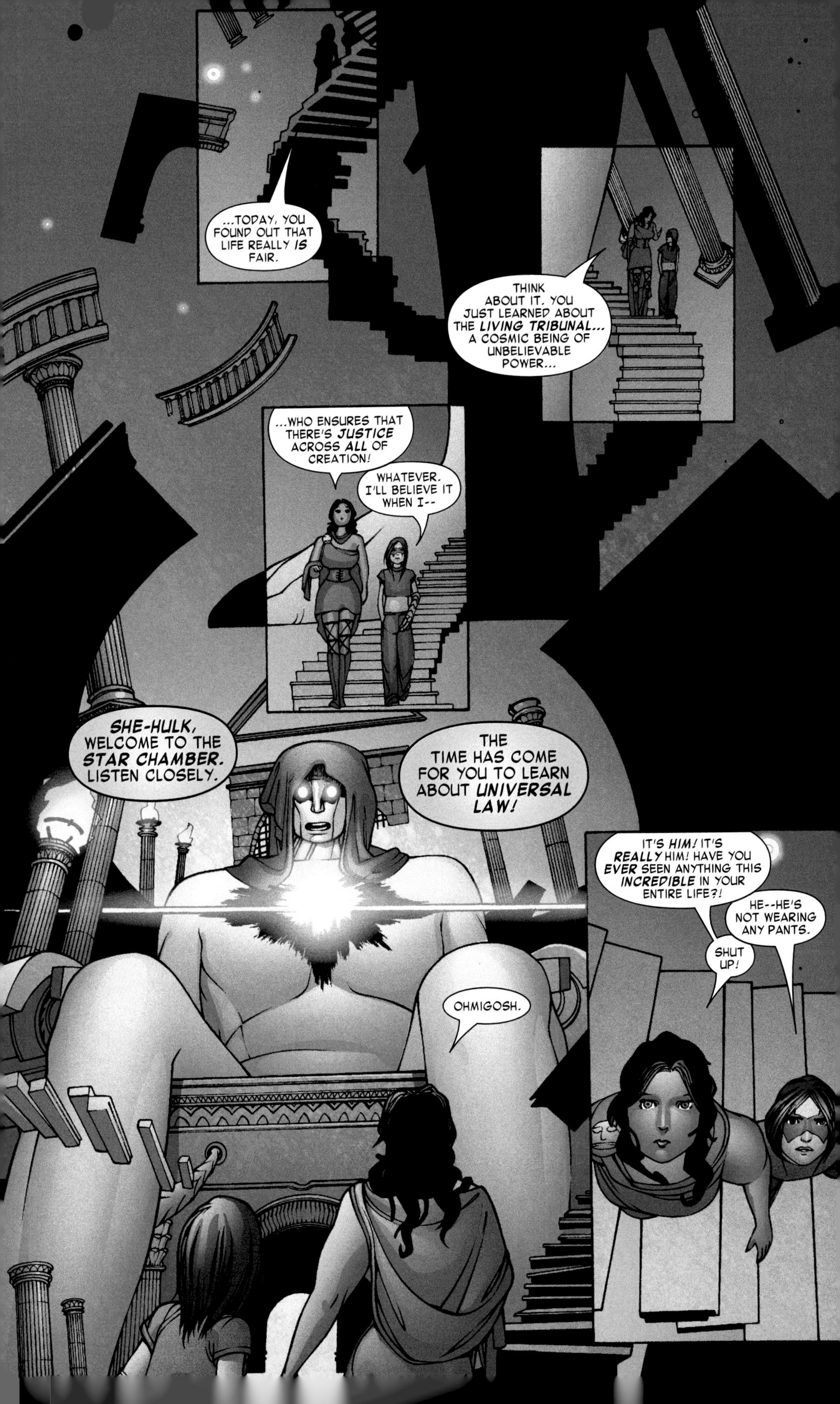
...TODAY, YOU FOUND OUT THAT LIFE REALLY *IS* FAIR.
THINK ABOUT IT. YOU JUST LEARNED ABOUT THE *LIVING TRIBUNAL...* A COSMIC BEING OF UNBELIEVABLE POWER...
...WHO ENSURES THAT THERE'S *JUSTICE* ACROSS *ALL* OF CREATION!
WHATEVER. I'LL BELIEVE IT WHEN I--
SHE-HULK, WELCOME TO THE *STAR CHAMBER.* LISTEN CLOSELY.
THE TIME HAS COME FOR YOU TO LEARN ABOUT *UNIVERSAL LAW!*
OHMIGOSH.
IT'S *HIM!* IT'S *REALLY* HIM! HAVE YOU *EVER* SEEN ANYTHING THIS *INCREDIBLE* IN YOUR ENTIRE LIFE?!
HE--HE'S NOT WEARING ANY PANTS.
SHUT UP!

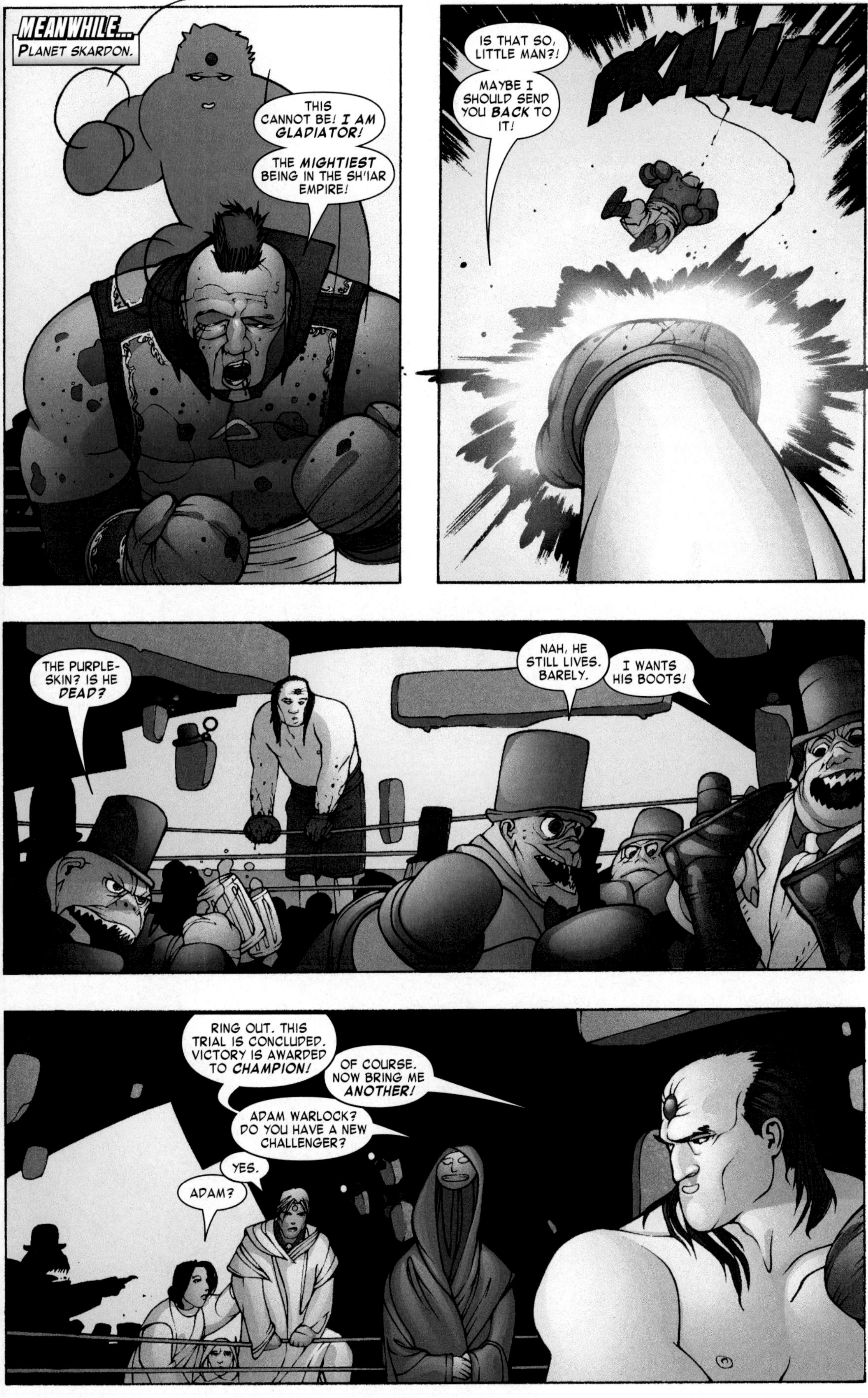
MEANWHILE...
PLANET SKARDON.
THIS CANNOT BE! I AM GLADIATOR!
THE MIGHTIEST BEING IN THE SH'IAR EMPIRE!
IS THAT SO, LITTLE MAN?!
MAYBE I SHOULD SEND YOU BACK TO IT!
PKAWWM
THE PURPLE-SKIN? IS HE DEAD?
NAH, HE STILL LIVES. BARELY.
I WANTS HIS BOOTS!
RING OUT. THIS TRIAL IS CONCLUDED. VICTORY IS AWARDED TO CHAMPION!
OF COURSE. NOW BRING ME ANOTHER!
ADAM WARLOCK? DO YOU HAVE A NEW CHALLENGER?
YES.
ADAM?

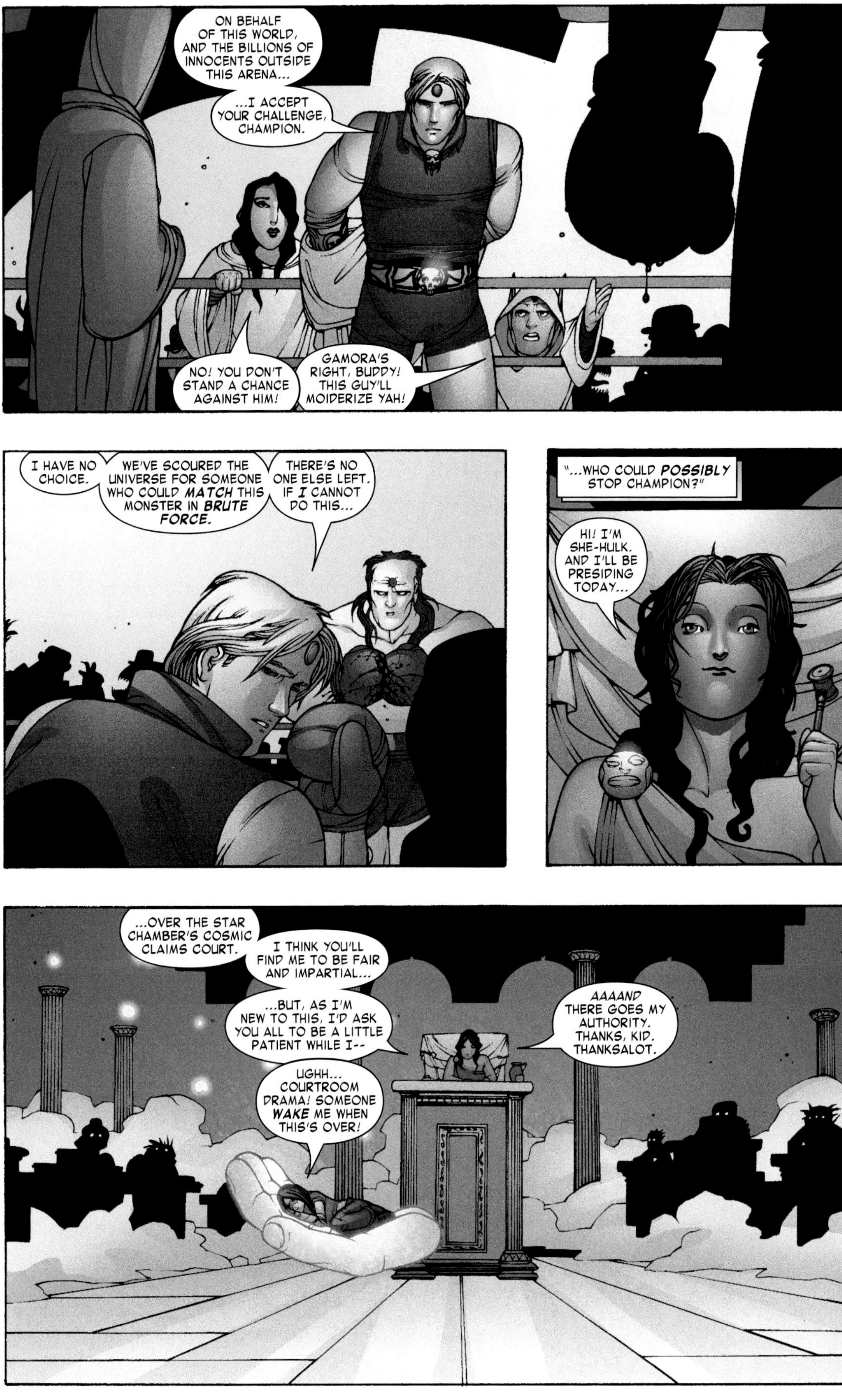
ON BEHALF OF THIS WORLD, AND THE BILLIONS OF INNOCENTS OUTSIDE THIS ARENA...
...I ACCEPT YOUR CHALLENGE, CHAMPION.
NO! YOU DON'T STAND A CHANCE AGAINST HIM!
GAMORA'S RIGHT, BUDDY! THIS GUY'LL MOIDERIZE YAH!
I HAVE NO CHOICE.
WE'VE SCOURED THE UNIVERSE FOR SOMEONE WHO COULD *MATCH* THIS MONSTER IN *BRUTE FORCE.*
THERE'S NO ONE ELSE LEFT. IF *I* CANNOT DO THIS...
"...WHO COULD *POSSIBLY* STOP CHAMPION?"
HI! I'M SHE-HULK. AND I'LL BE PRESIDING TODAY...
...OVER THE STAR CHAMBER'S COSMIC CLAIMS COURT.
I THINK YOU'LL FIND ME TO BE FAIR AND IMPARTIAL...
...BUT, AS I'M NEW TO THIS, I'D ASK YOU ALL TO BE A LITTLE PATIENT WHILE I--
UGHH... COURTROOM DRAMA! SOMEONE *WAKE* ME WHEN THIS'S OVER!
AAAAND THERE GOES MY AUTHORITY. THANKS, KID. THANKSALOT.

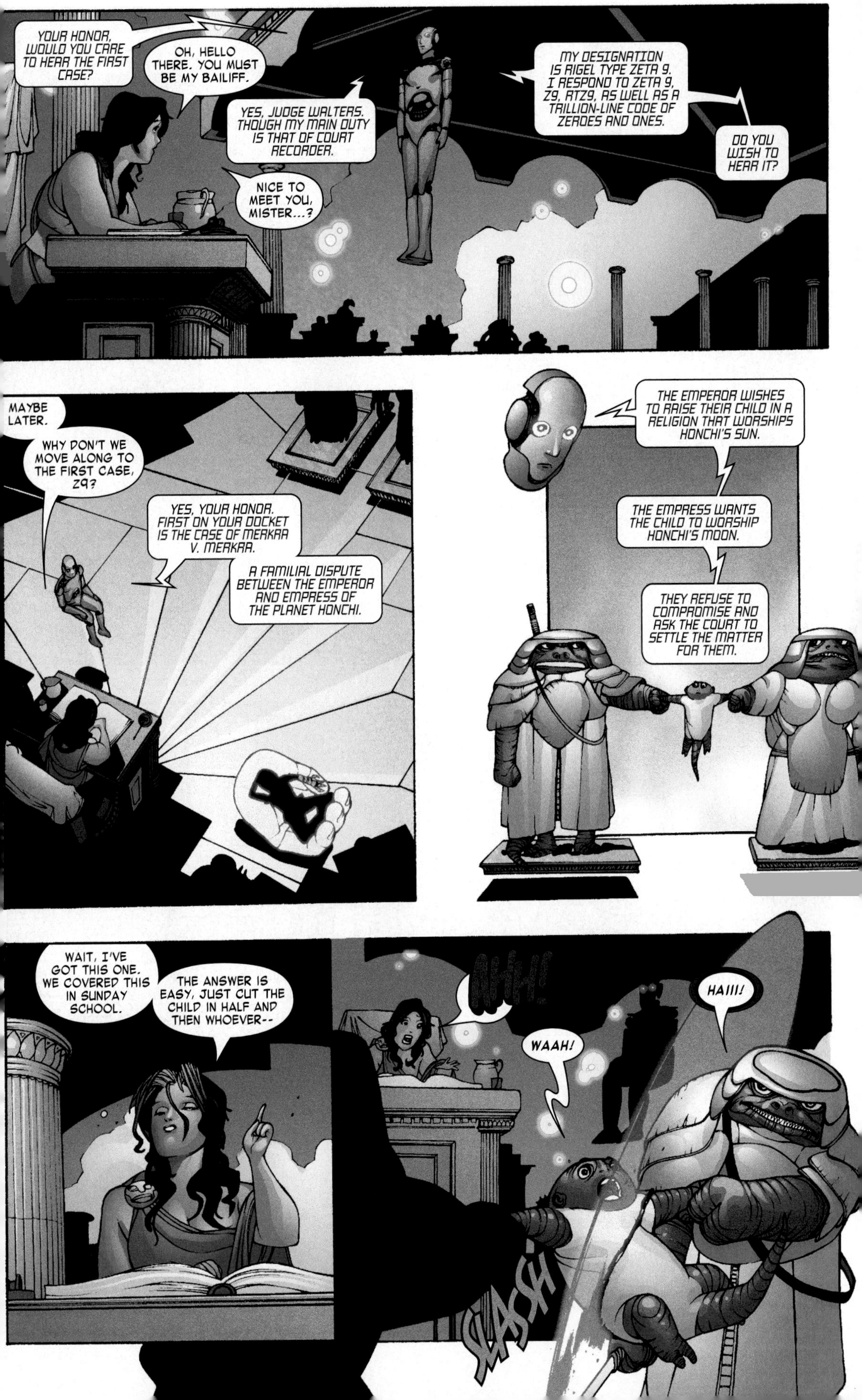

YOUR HONOR, WOULD YOU CARE TO HEAR THE FIRST CASE?
OH, HELLO THERE. YOU MUST BE MY BAILIFF.
YES, JUDGE WALTERS. THOUGH MY MAIN DUTY IS THAT OF COURT RECORDER.
NICE TO MEET YOU, MISTER...?
MY DESIGNATION IS RIGEL TYPE ZETA 9. I RESPOND TO ZETA 9, Z9, RTZ9, AS WELL AS A TRILLION-LINE CODE OF ZEROES AND ONES.
DO YOU WISH TO HEAR IT?
MAYBE LATER.
WHY DON'T WE MOVE ALONG TO THE FIRST CASE, Z9?
YES, YOUR HONOR. FIRST ON YOUR DOCKET IS THE CASE OF MERKRA V. MERKRA.
A FAMILIAL DISPUTE BETWEEN THE EMPEROR AND EMPRESS OF THE PLANET HONCHI.
THE EMPEROR WISHES TO RAISE THEIR CHILD IN A RELIGION THAT WORSHIPS HONCHI'S SUN.
THE EMPRESS WANTS THE CHILD TO WORSHIP HONCHI'S MOON.
THEY REFUSE TO COMPROMISE AND ASK THE COURT TO SETTLE THE MATTER FOR THEM.
WAIT, I'VE GOT THIS ONE. WE COVERED THIS IN SUNDAY SCHOOL.
THE ANSWER IS EASY, JUST CUT THE CHILD IN HALF AND THEN WHOEVER--
AHH!
HAIII!
WAAH!
SLASH

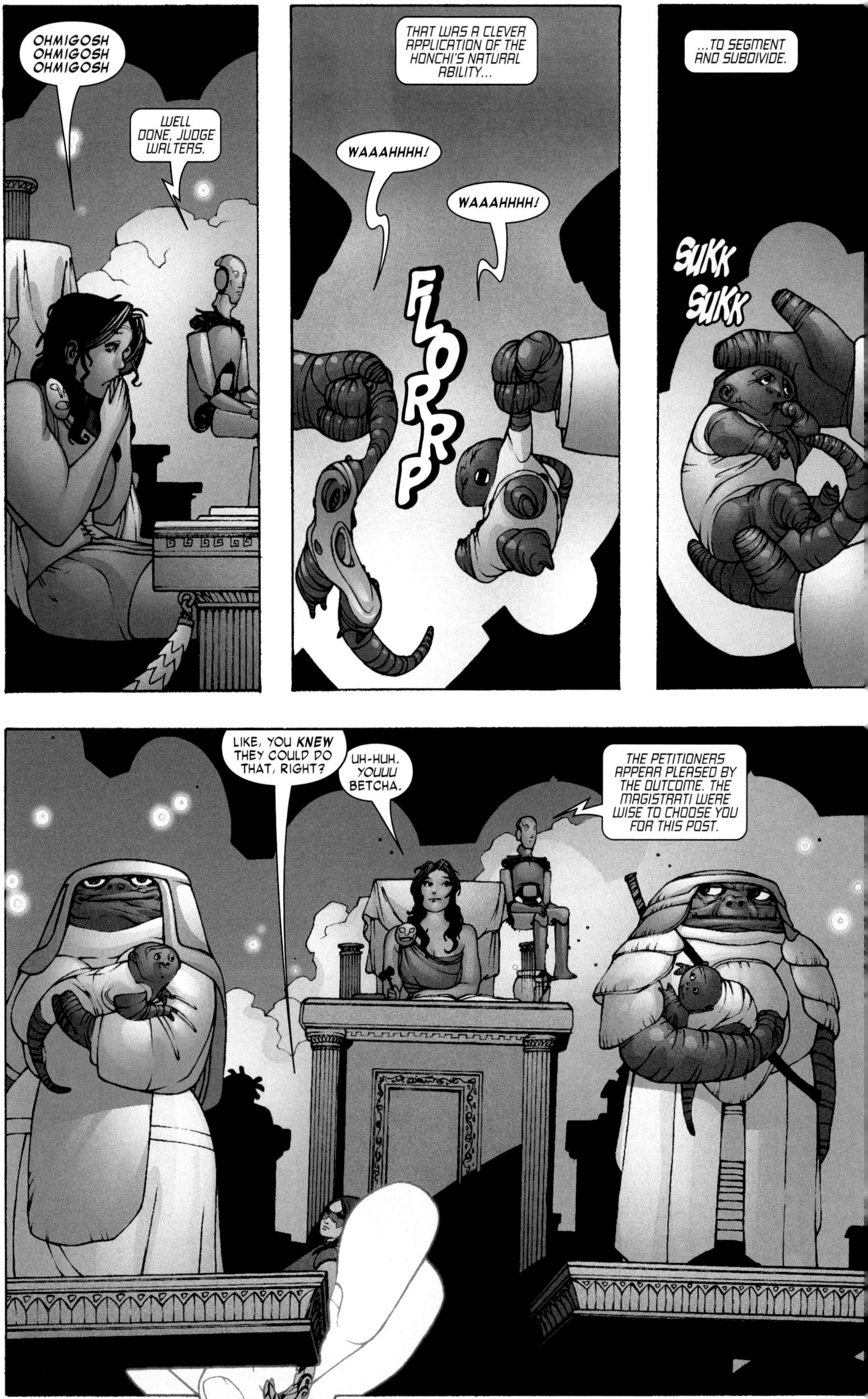
OHMIGOSH OHMIGOSH OHMIGOSH
WELL DONE, JUDGE WALTERS.
THAT WAS A CLEVER APPLICATION OF THE HONCHI'S NATURAL ABILITY...
WAAAHHHH!
WAAAHHHH!
FLORRP
...TO SEGMENT AND SUBDIVIDE.
SUKK SUKK
LIKE, YOU KNEW THEY COULD DO THAT, RIGHT?
UH-HUH. YOUUU BETCHA.
THE PETITIONERS APPEAR PLEASED BY THE OUTCOME. THE MAGISTRATI WERE WISE TO CHOOSE YOU FOR THIS POST.

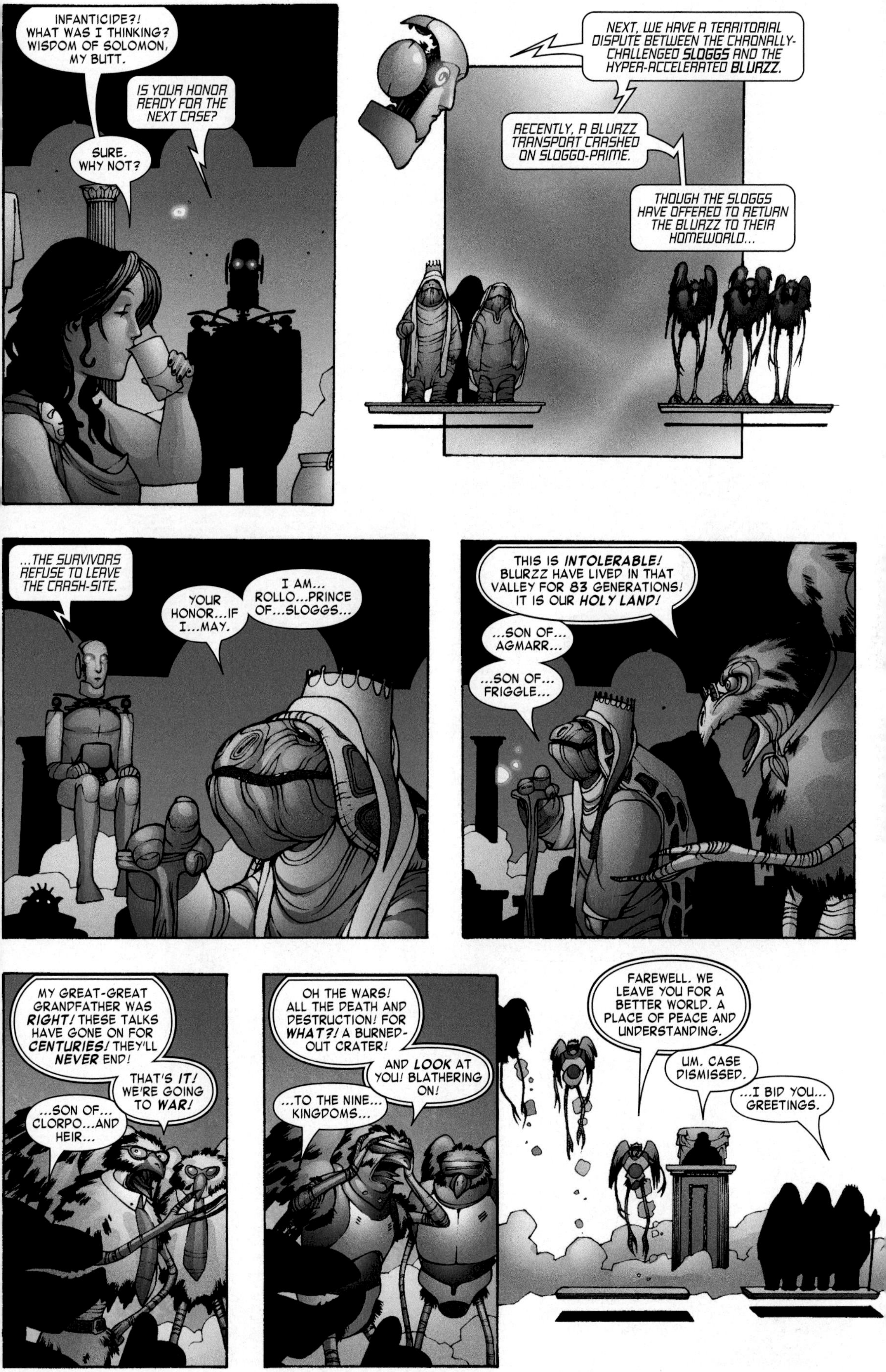
INFANTICIDE?! WHAT WAS I THINKING? WISDOM OF SOLOMON, MY BUTT.
IS YOUR HONOR READY FOR THE NEXT CASE?
SURE. WHY NOT?
NEXT, WE HAVE A TERRITORIAL DISPUTE BETWEEN THE CHRONALLY-CHALLENGED SLOGGS AND THE HYPER-ACCELERATED BLURZZ.
RECENTLY, A BLURZZ TRANSPORT CRASHED ON SLOGGO-PRIME.
THOUGH THE SLOGGS HAVE OFFERED TO RETURN THE BLURZZ TO THEIR HOMEWORLD...
...THE SURVIVORS REFUSE TO LEAVE THE CRASH-SITE.
YOUR HONOR...IF I...MAY.
I AM... ROLLO...PRINCE OF...SLOGGS...
THIS IS INTOLERABLE! BLURZZ HAVE LIVED IN THAT VALLEY FOR 83 GENERATIONS! IT IS OUR HOLY LAND!
...SON OF... AGMARR...
...SON OF... FRIGGLE...
MY GREAT-GREAT GRANDFATHER WAS RIGHT! THESE TALKS HAVE GONE ON FOR CENTURIES! THEY'LL NEVER END!
THAT'S IT! WE'RE GOING TO WAR!
...SON OF... CLORPO...AND HEIR...
OH THE WARS! ALL THE DEATH AND DESTRUCTION! FOR WHAT?! A BURNED-OUT CRATER!
AND LOOK AT YOU! BLATHERING ON!
...TO THE NINE... KINGDOMS...
FAREWELL. WE LEAVE YOU FOR A BETTER WORLD. A PLACE OF PEACE AND UNDERSTANDING.
UM. CASE DISMISSED.
...I BID YOU... GREETINGS.

YOUR HONOR, NEXT UP IS A SUIT BEING BROUGHT AGAINST *THE WATCHERS.*

STANDING BEFORE YOU, REPRESENTING THEIR RACE, ARE *ZOMA*, *UATU*, AND *QYRE.*

JENNIFER.

UATU. IT'S GOOD TO SEE YOU AGAIN.

PSST! HEY, WHAT'S UP WITH THE BIG BALD GUYS?

EXCUSE ME FOR A MOMENT.

SOUTHPAW, PLEASE! THESE ARE THE WATCHERS! THE OLDEST AND MOST REVERED BEINGS IN THE UNIVERSE!

THEY SEE *EVERYTHING* AND RECORD THE TOTAL HISTORY OF THE COSMOS.

OH YEAH? POP QUIZ, CUEBALL. WHAT WAS I DOING AT TWELVE NOON?

MAKING FALSE ACCUSATIONS AGAINST SHE-HULK.

SHE IS FEMALE, AND SHE ALWAYS KEEPS THE LID DOWN.

EWW! THAT'S NOT JUST CREEPY, IT'S WRONG ON SO MANY LEVELS!

AGREED! IT IS AN OFFENSE OF THE *HIGHEST* ORDER!

RECORDER?

THOSE ARE THE COMPLAINANTS, YOUR HONOR, SPEAKING *THROUGH* ME.

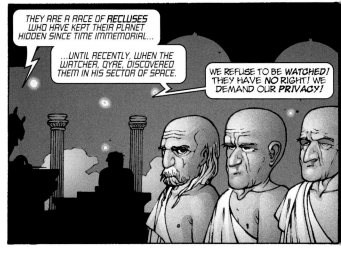

THEY ARE A RACE OF *RECLUSES* WHO HAVE KEPT THEIR PLANET HIDDEN SINCE TIME IMMEMORIAL...

...UNTIL RECENTLY, WHEN THE WATCHER, QYRE, DISCOVERED THEM IN HIS SECTOR OF SPACE.

WE REFUSE TO BE *WATCHED!* THEY HAVE *NO RIGHT!* WE DEMAND OUR *PRIVACY!*

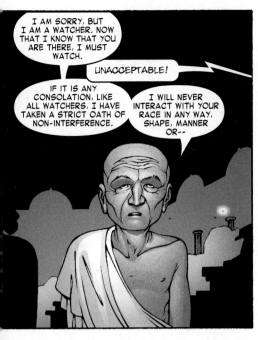

I AM SORRY, BUT I AM A WATCHER. NOW THAT I KNOW THAT YOU ARE THERE, I MUST WATCH.

UNACCEPTABLE!

IF IT IS ANY CONSOLATION, LIKE ALL WATCHERS, I HAVE TAKEN A STRICT OATH OF NON-INTERFERENCE.

I WILL NEVER INTERACT WITH YOUR RACE IN ANY WAY, SHAPE, MANNER OR--

IRRELEVANT! WE BOTHER NO ONE! WE KEEP TO OURSELVES!

BUT NOW YOU HAVE SEEN US! YOUR ENTIRE RACE HAS SEEN US!

IF THAT'S THE CASE, THEN IT SOUNDS LIKE THE GENIE'S OUT OF THE BOTTLE.

WHAT DO YOU EXPECT THIS COURT TO DO?

YOUR HONOR, THE COMPLAINANT MISSPOKE. ONLY MY COUSIN, QYRE, HAS "SEEN" THESE CREATURES' TRUE FORMS.

TRUE, WATCHERS SEE ALL AND KNOW ALL, BUT ONLY FOR OUR ASSIGNED SECTORS OF SPACE.

AT TIMES WE MEET FOR A GATHERING.

IT IS THERE THAT WE POOL OUR ACCUMULATED KNOWLEDGE AND SHARE WHAT WE HAVE SEEN--IN A WAY NO OTHER RACE CAN COMPREHEND.

SO...IF QYRE DIDN'T TAKE PART IN THIS "GATHERING"...

...IF HE REMAINED SILENT AND DIDN'T SHARE WHAT HE KNEW WITH ANYONE?

HIS VISIONS, HIS KNOWLEDGE, WOULD BE HIS AND HIS ALONE.

A DARK SECTOR, UNWATCHED BY ALL BUT ONE.

WOULD THIS MAKE AMENDS?

WE FIND THIS DECISION...

...ACCEPTABLE.

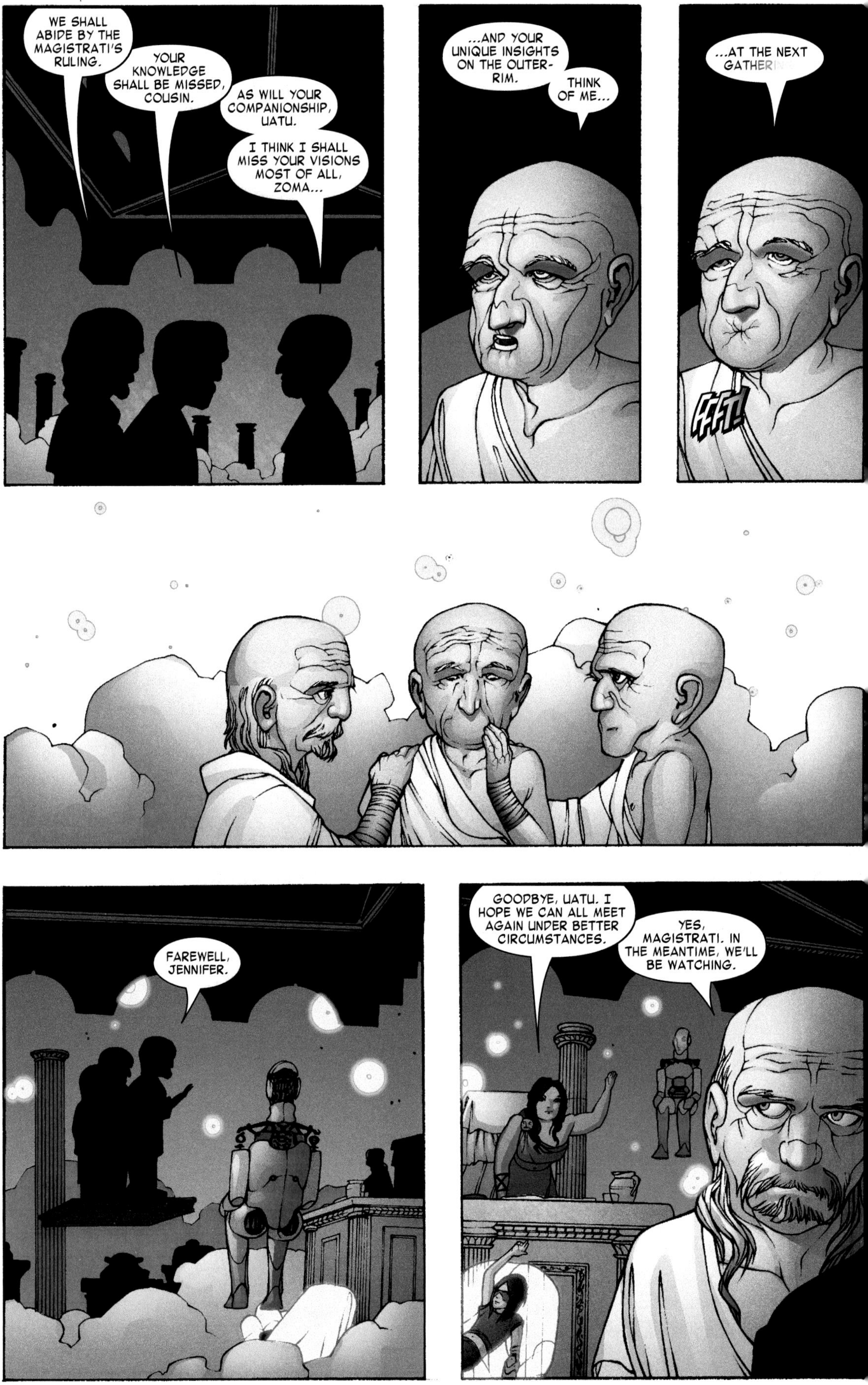

WE SHALL ABIDE BY THE MAGISTRATI'S RULING.
YOUR KNOWLEDGE SHALL BE MISSED, COUSIN.
AS WILL YOUR COMPANIONSHIP, UATU.
I THINK I SHALL MISS YOUR VISIONS MOST OF ALL, ZOMA...
...AND YOUR UNIQUE INSIGHTS ON THE OUTER-RIM.
THINK OF ME...
...AT THE NEXT GATHER
FFFT!
FAREWELL, JENNIFER.
GOODBYE, UATU. I HOPE WE CAN ALL MEET AGAIN UNDER BETTER CIRCUMSTANCES.
YES, MAGISTRATI. IN THE MEANTIME, WE'LL BE WATCHING.

BREATHE, JEN! C'MON, DEEP BREATH.

WHEW! THAT WAS PRETTY *COSMIC* BACK THERE! THIS IS ALL JUST A LITTLE TOO MUCH!

OH, PLEASE! GET OVER YOURSELF! I MEAN, WHAT HAVE YOU DONE HERE, REALLY?

YOU GOOFED UP THE FIRST THING, DID NOTHING FOR THE SECOND...

...AND ON THE THIRD ONE, YOU TOLD A GUY TO STOP STARING AND--

SHUT UP!

EXACTLY.

SO, ZETA-9? ANY MORE CASES OR IS THAT IT?

ONE MOMENT, JUDGE WALTERS.

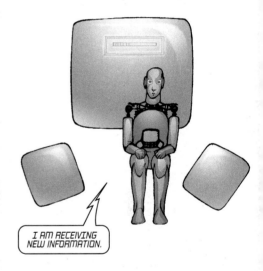

I AM RECEIVING NEW INFORMATION.

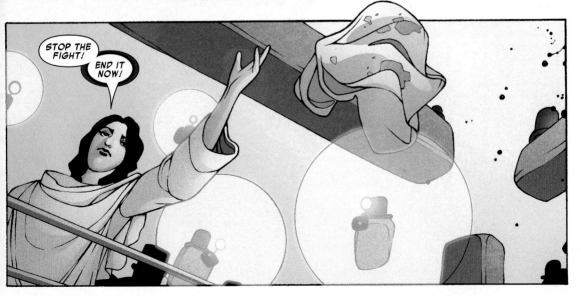

STOP THE FIGHT!

END IT NOW!

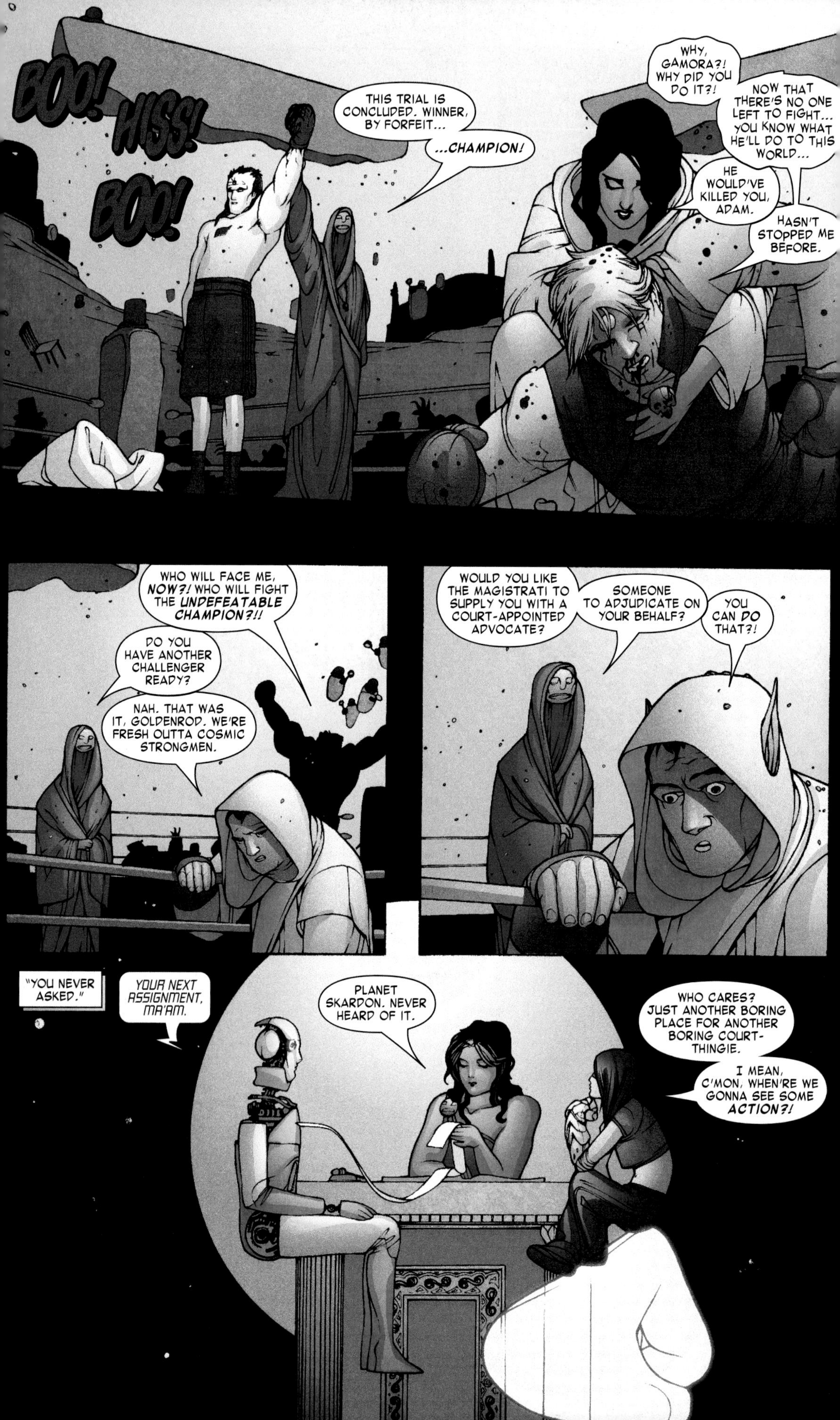
BOO! HISS! BOO!
THIS TRIAL IS CONCLUDED. WINNER, BY FORFEIT...
...CHAMPION!
WHY, GAMORA?! WHY DID YOU DO IT?!
NOW THAT THERE'S NO ONE LEFT TO FIGHT... YOU KNOW WHAT HE'LL DO TO THIS WORLD...
HE WOULD'VE KILLED YOU, ADAM.
HASN'T STOPPED ME BEFORE.
WHO WILL FACE ME, NOW?! WHO WILL FIGHT THE UNDEFEATABLE CHAMPION?!!
DO YOU HAVE ANOTHER CHALLENGER READY?
NAH. THAT WAS IT, GOLDENROD. WE'RE FRESH OUTTA COSMIC STRONGMEN.
WOULD YOU LIKE THE MAGISTRATI TO SUPPLY YOU WITH A COURT-APPOINTED ADVOCATE?
SOMEONE TO ADJUDICATE ON YOUR BEHALF?
YOU CAN DO THAT?!
"YOU NEVER ASKED."
YOUR NEXT ASSIGNMENT, MA'AM.
PLANET SKARDON. NEVER HEARD OF IT.
WHO CARES? JUST ANOTHER BORING PLACE FOR ANOTHER BORING COURT-THINGIE.
I MEAN, C'MON, WHEN'RE WE GONNA SEE SOME ACTION?!

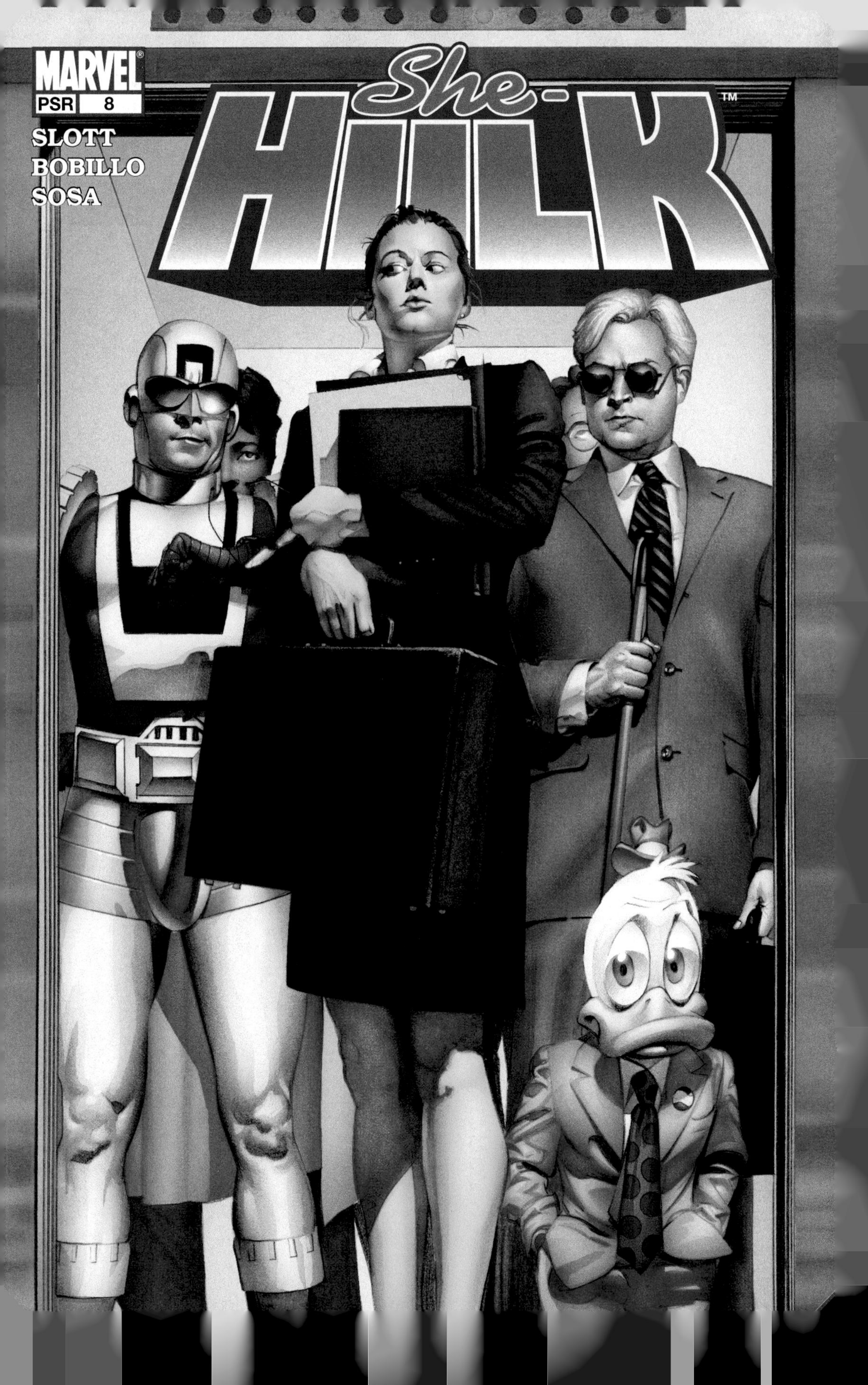
MARVEL
PSR 8
SLOTT
BOBILLO
SOSA
She-Hulk™

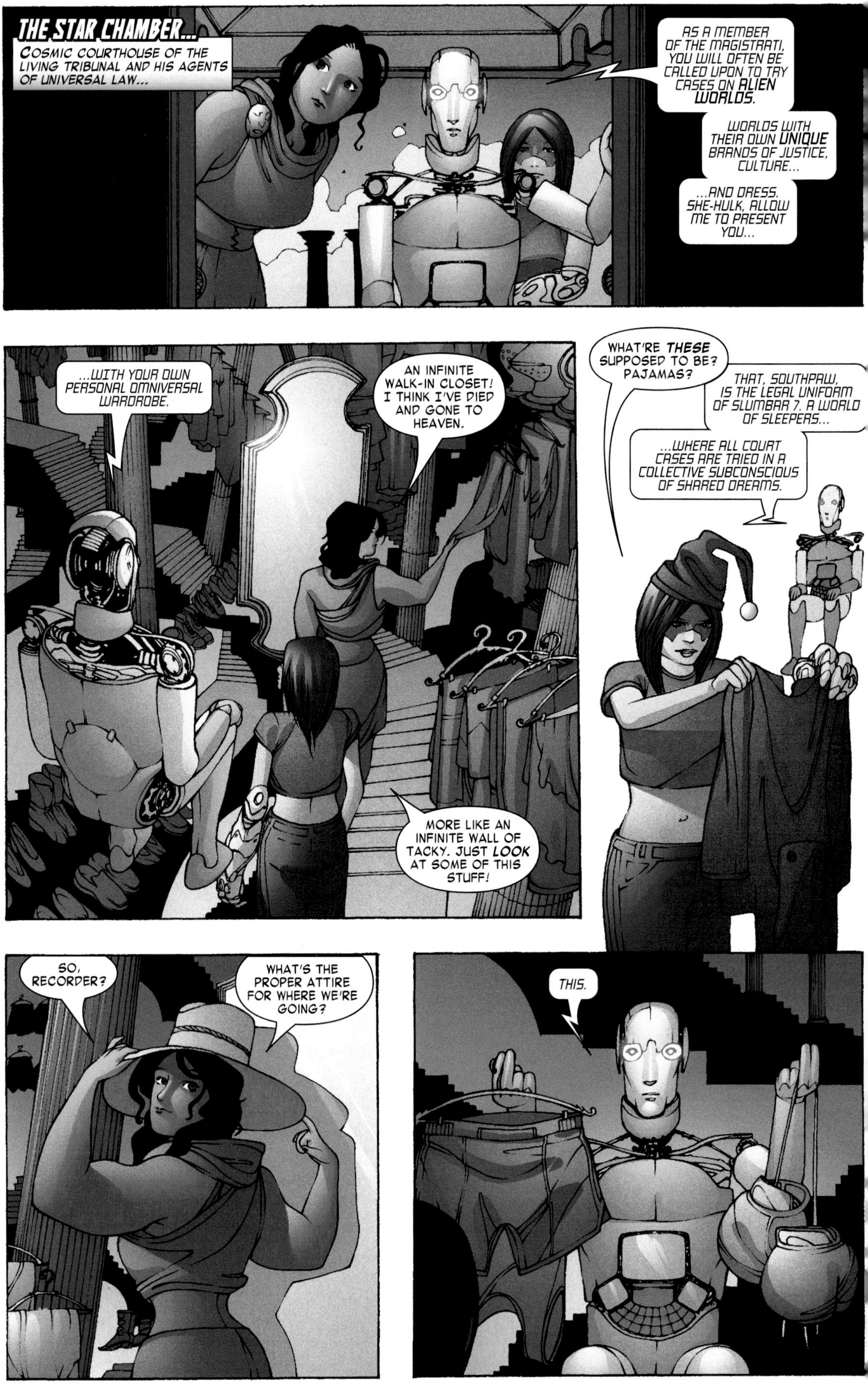
THE STAR CHAMBER...
COSMIC COURTHOUSE OF THE LIVING TRIBUNAL AND HIS AGENTS OF UNIVERSAL LAW...
AS A MEMBER OF THE MAGISTRATI, YOU WILL OFTEN BE CALLED UPON TO TRY CASES ON ALIEN WORLDS.
WORLDS WITH THEIR OWN UNIQUE BRANDS OF JUSTICE, CULTURE...
...AND DRESS. SHE-HULK, ALLOW ME TO PRESENT YOU...
...WITH YOUR OWN PERSONAL OMNIVERSAL WARDROBE.
AN INFINITE WALK-IN CLOSET! I THINK I'VE DIED AND GONE TO HEAVEN.
MORE LIKE AN INFINITE WALL OF TACKY. JUST LOOK AT SOME OF THIS STUFF!
WHAT'RE THESE SUPPOSED TO BE? PAJAMAS?
THAT, SOUTHPAW, IS THE LEGAL UNIFORM OF SLUMBAR 7. A WORLD OF SLEEPERS...
...WHERE ALL COURT CASES ARE TRIED IN A COLLECTIVE SUBCONSCIOUS OF SHARED DREAMS.
SO, RECORDER?
WHAT'S THE PROPER ATTIRE FOR WHERE WE'RE GOING?
THIS.

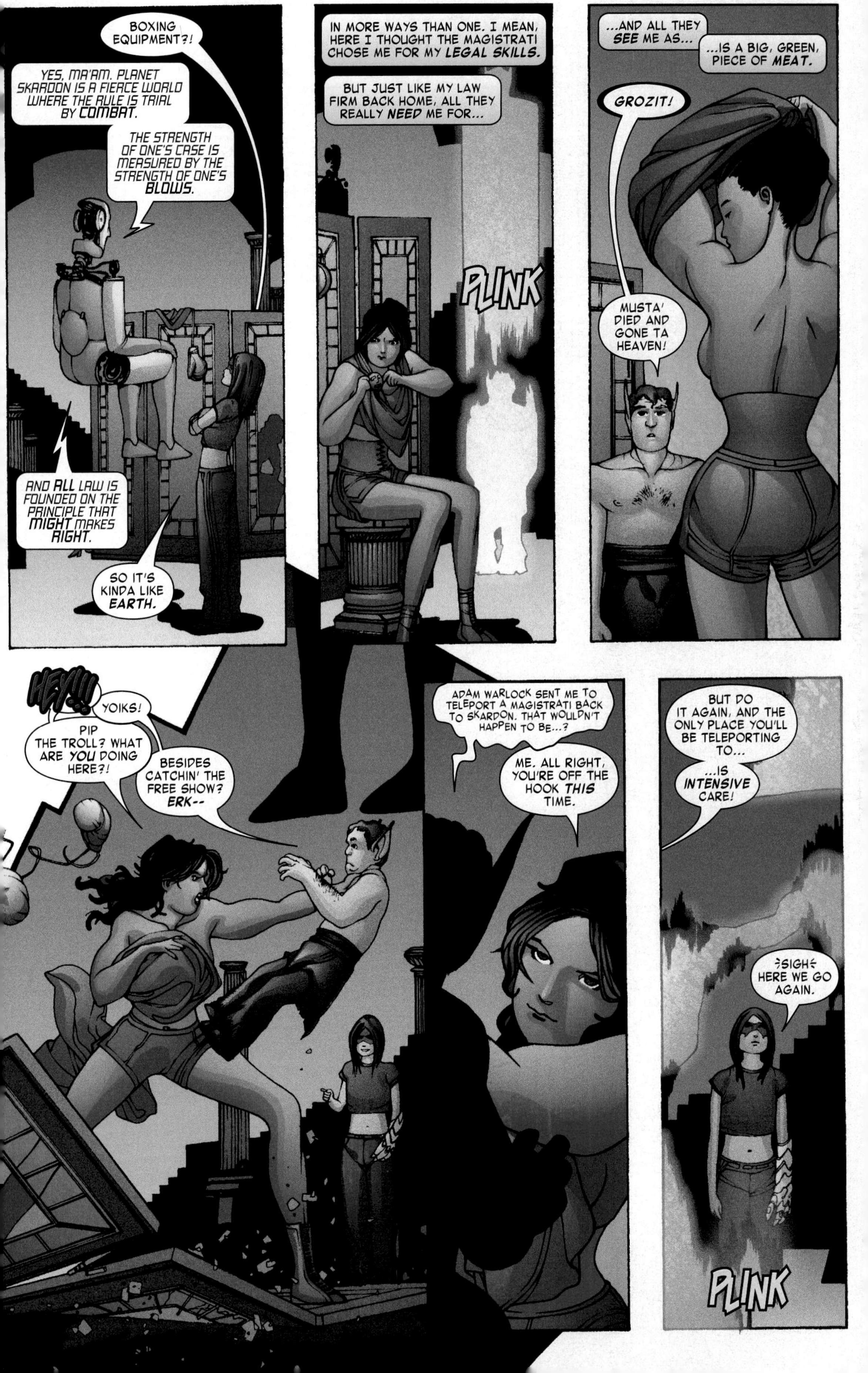

BOXING EQUIPMENT?!
YES, MA'AM. PLANET SKARDON IS A FIERCE WORLD WHERE THE RULE IS TRIAL BY COMBAT.
THE STRENGTH OF ONE'S CASE IS MEASURED BY THE STRENGTH OF ONE'S BLOWS.
AND ALL LAW IS FOUNDED ON THE PRINCIPLE THAT MIGHT MAKES RIGHT.
SO IT'S KINDA LIKE EARTH.
IN MORE WAYS THAN ONE. I MEAN, HERE I THOUGHT THE MAGISTRATI CHOSE ME FOR MY LEGAL SKILLS.
BUT JUST LIKE MY LAW FIRM BACK HOME, ALL THEY REALLY NEED ME FOR...
PLINK
...AND ALL THEY SEE ME AS...
...IS A BIG, GREEN, PIECE OF MEAT.
GROZIT!
MUSTA' DIED AND GONE TA HEAVEN!
HEY!!!
YOIKS!
PIP THE TROLL? WHAT ARE YOU DOING HERE?!
BESIDES CATCHIN' THE FREE SHOW? ERK--
ADAM WARLOCK SENT ME TO TELEPORT A MAGISTRATI BACK TO SKARDON. THAT WOULDN'T HAPPEN TO BE...?
ME. ALL RIGHT, YOU'RE OFF THE HOOK THIS TIME.
BUT DO IT AGAIN, AND THE ONLY PLACE YOU'LL BE TELEPORTING TO...
...IS INTENSIVE CARE!
SIGH HERE WE GO AGAIN.
PLINK

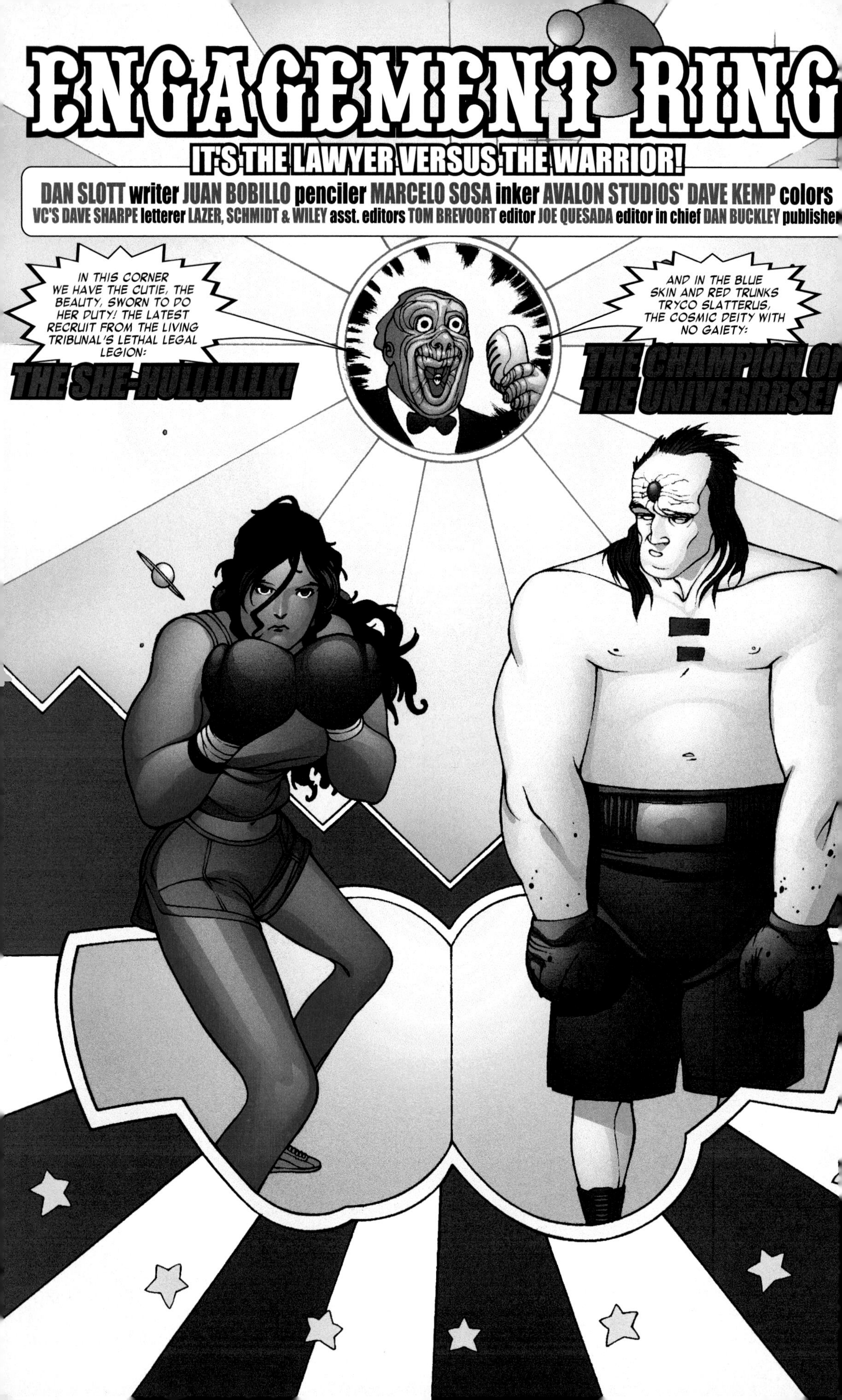
ENGAGEMENT RING
IT'S THE LAWYER VERSUS THE WARRIOR!
DAN SLOTT writer JUAN BOBILLO penciler MARCELO SOSA inker AVALON STUDIOS' DAVE KEMP colors
VC'S DAVE SHARPE letterer LAZER, SCHMIDT & WILEY asst. editors TOM BREVOORT editor JOE QUESADA editor in chief DAN BUCKLEY publisher
IN THIS CORNER WE HAVE THE CUTIE, THE BEAUTY, SWORN TO DO HER DUTY! THE LATEST RECRUIT FROM THE LIVING TRIBUNAL'S LETHAL LEGAL LEGION:
THE SHE-HULLLLLLK!
AND IN THE BLUE SKIN AND RED TRUNKS TRYCO SLATTERUS, THE COSMIC DEITY WITH NO GAIETY:
THE CHAMPION OF THE UNIVERRRSE!

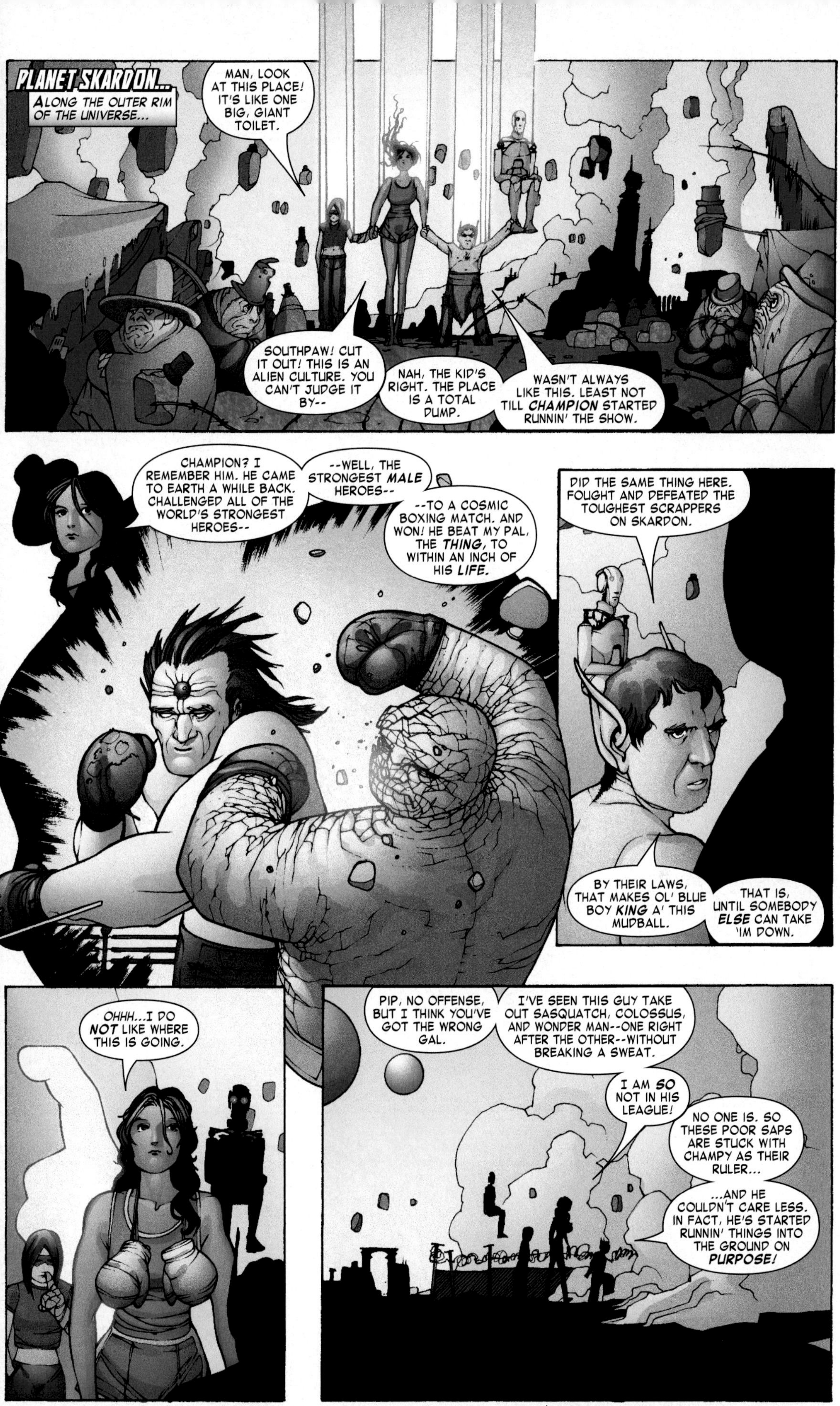
PLANET SKARDON...
ALONG THE OUTER RIM OF THE UNIVERSE...
MAN, LOOK AT THIS PLACE! IT'S LIKE ONE BIG, GIANT TOILET.
SOUTHPAW! CUT IT OUT! THIS IS AN ALIEN CULTURE. YOU CAN'T JUDGE IT BY--
NAH, THE KID'S RIGHT. THE PLACE IS A TOTAL DUMP.
WASN'T ALWAYS LIKE THIS. LEAST NOT TILL CHAMPION STARTED RUNNIN' THE SHOW.
CHAMPION? I REMEMBER HIM. HE CAME TO EARTH A WHILE BACK. CHALLENGED ALL OF THE WORLD'S STRONGEST HEROES--
--WELL, THE STRONGEST MALE HEROES--
--TO A COSMIC BOXING MATCH. AND WON! HE BEAT MY PAL, THE THING, TO WITHIN AN INCH OF HIS LIFE.
DID THE SAME THING HERE. FOUGHT AND DEFEATED THE TOUGHEST SCRAPPERS ON SKARDON.
BY THEIR LAWS, THAT MAKES OL' BLUE BOY KING A' THIS MUDBALL.
THAT IS, UNTIL SOMEBODY ELSE CAN TAKE 'IM DOWN.
OHHH...I DO NOT LIKE WHERE THIS IS GOING.
PIP, NO OFFENSE, BUT I THINK YOU'VE GOT THE WRONG GAL.
I'VE SEEN THIS GUY TAKE OUT SASQUATCH, COLOSSUS, AND WONDER MAN--ONE RIGHT AFTER THE OTHER--WITHOUT BREAKING A SWEAT.
I AM SO NOT IN HIS LEAGUE!
NO ONE IS. SO THESE POOR SAPS ARE STUCK WITH CHAMPY AS THEIR RULER...
...AND HE COULDN'T CARE LESS. IN FACT, HE'S STARTED RUNNIN' THINGS INTO THE GROUND ON PURPOSE!

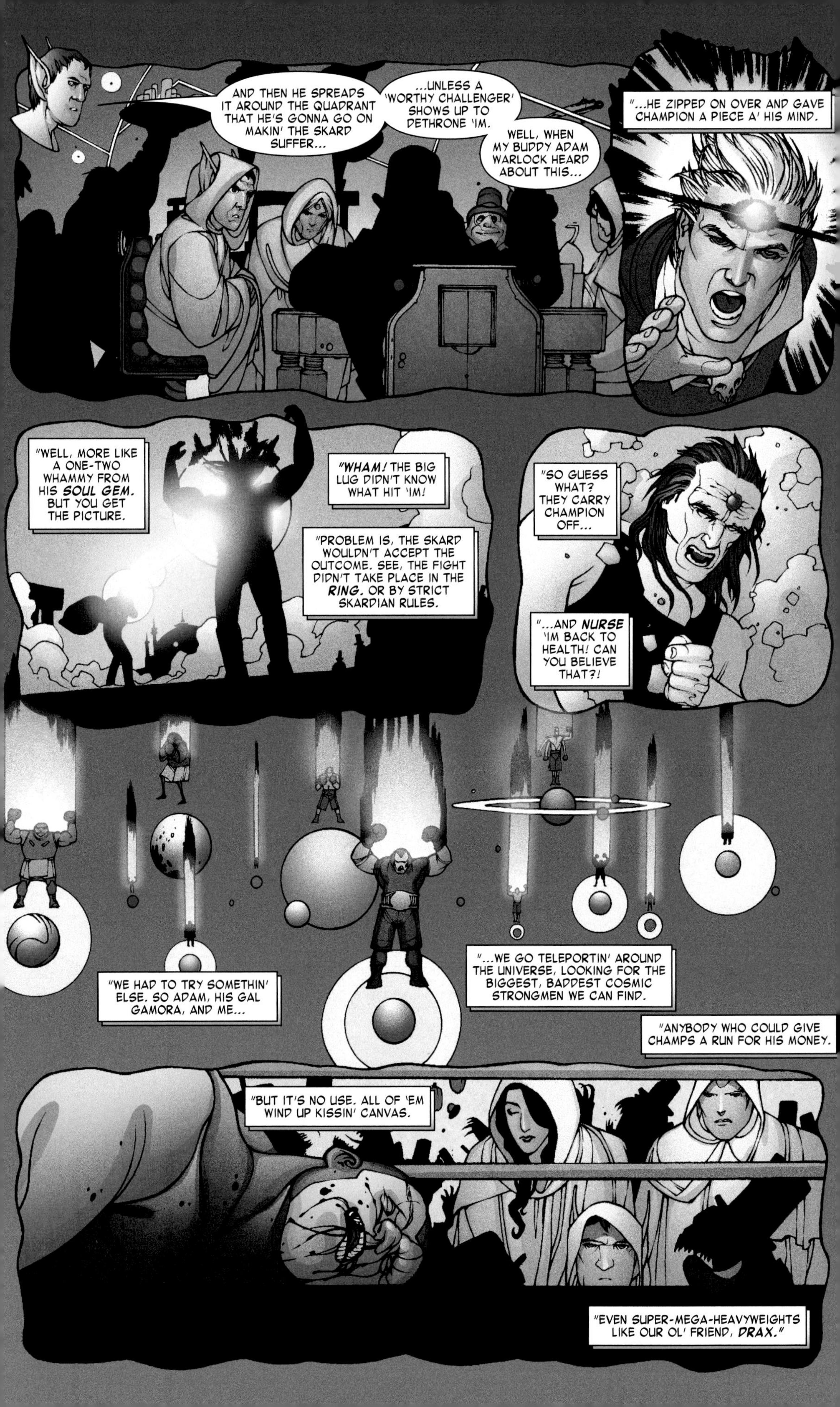
AND THEN HE SPREADS IT AROUND THE QUADRANT THAT HE'S GONNA GO ON MAKIN' THE SKARD SUFFER...
...UNLESS A 'WORTHY CHALLENGER' SHOWS UP TO DETHRONE 'IM.
WELL, WHEN MY BUDDY ADAM WARLOCK HEARD ABOUT THIS...
"...HE ZIPPED ON OVER AND GAVE CHAMPION A PIECE A' HIS MIND.
"WELL, MORE LIKE A ONE-TWO WHAMMY FROM HIS SOUL GEM. BUT YOU GET THE PICTURE.
"WHAM! THE BIG LUG DIDN'T KNOW WHAT HIT 'IM!
"PROBLEM IS, THE SKARD WOULDN'T ACCEPT THE OUTCOME. SEE, THE FIGHT DIDN'T TAKE PLACE IN THE RING. OR BY STRICT SKARDIAN RULES.
"SO GUESS WHAT? THEY CARRY CHAMPION OFF...
"...AND NURSE 'IM BACK TO HEALTH! CAN YOU BELIEVE THAT?!
"WE HAD TO TRY SOMETHIN' ELSE. SO ADAM, HIS GAL GAMORA, AND ME...
"...WE GO TELEPORTIN' AROUND THE UNIVERSE, LOOKING FOR THE BIGGEST, BADDEST COSMIC STRONGMEN WE CAN FIND.
"ANYBODY WHO COULD GIVE CHAMPS A RUN FOR HIS MONEY.
"BUT IT'S NO USE. ALL OF 'EM WIND UP KISSIN' CANVAS.
"EVEN SUPER-MEGA-HEAVYWEIGHTS LIKE OUR OL' FRIEND, DRAX."

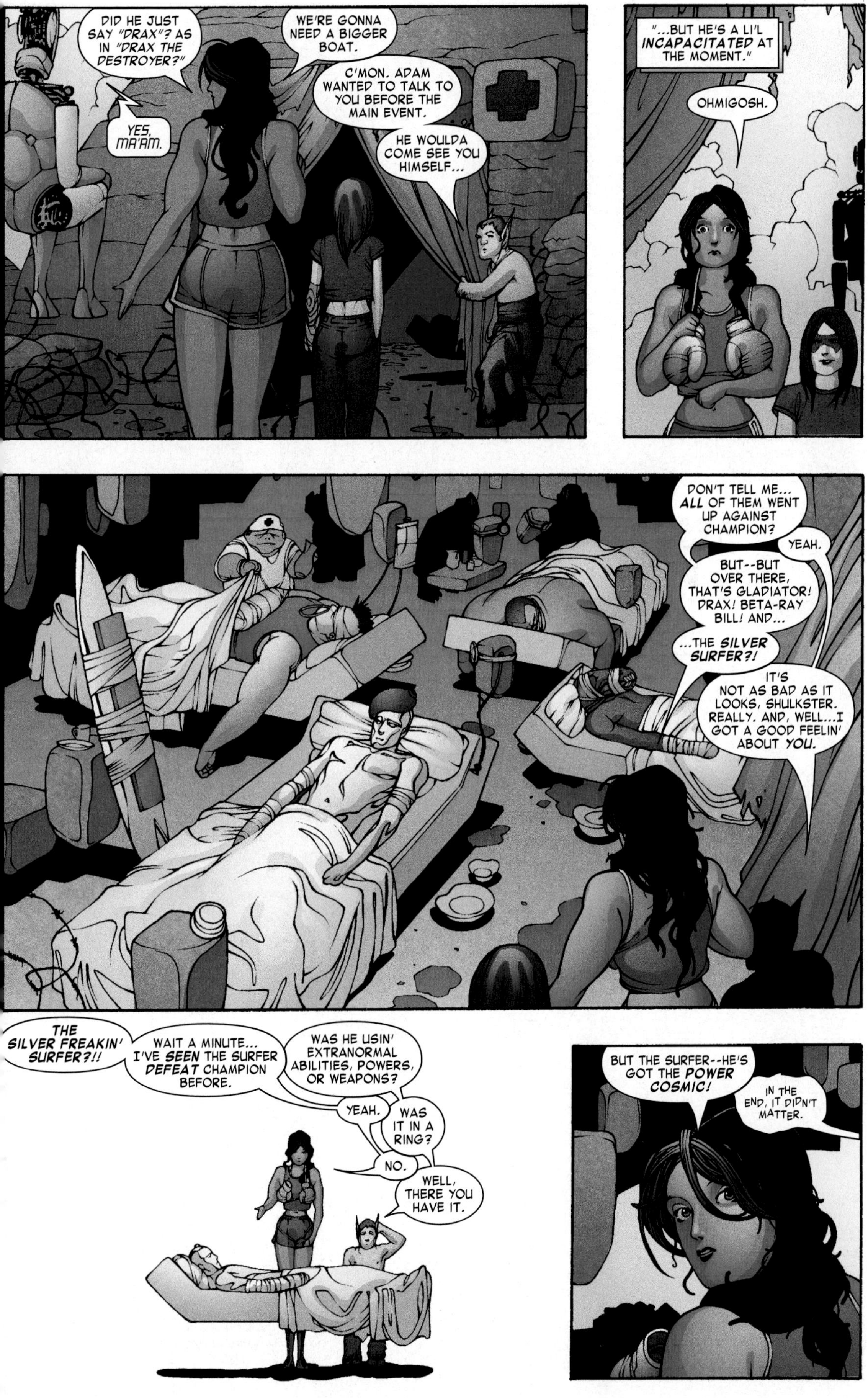
DID HE JUST SAY "DRAX"? AS IN "DRAX THE DESTROYER?"
YES, MA'AM.
WE'RE GONNA NEED A BIGGER BOAT.
C'MON. ADAM WANTED TO TALK TO YOU BEFORE THE MAIN EVENT.
HE WOULDA COME SEE YOU HIMSELF...
"...BUT HE'S A LI'L INCAPACITATED AT THE MOMENT."
OHMIGOSH.
DON'T TELL ME... ALL OF THEM WENT UP AGAINST CHAMPION?
YEAH.
BUT--BUT OVER THERE, THAT'S GLADIATOR! DRAX! BETA-RAY BILL! AND...
...THE SILVER SURFER?!
IT'S NOT AS BAD AS IT LOOKS, SHULKSTER. REALLY. AND, WELL...I GOT A GOOD FEELIN' ABOUT YOU.
THE SILVER FREAKIN' SURFER?!!
WAIT A MINUTE... I'VE SEEN THE SURFER DEFEAT CHAMPION BEFORE.
WAS HE USIN' EXTRANORMAL ABILITIES, POWERS, OR WEAPONS?
YEAH.
WAS IT IN A RING?
NO.
WELL, THERE YOU HAVE IT.
BUT THE SURFER--HE'S GOT THE POWER COSMIC!
IN THE END, IT DIDN'T MATTER.

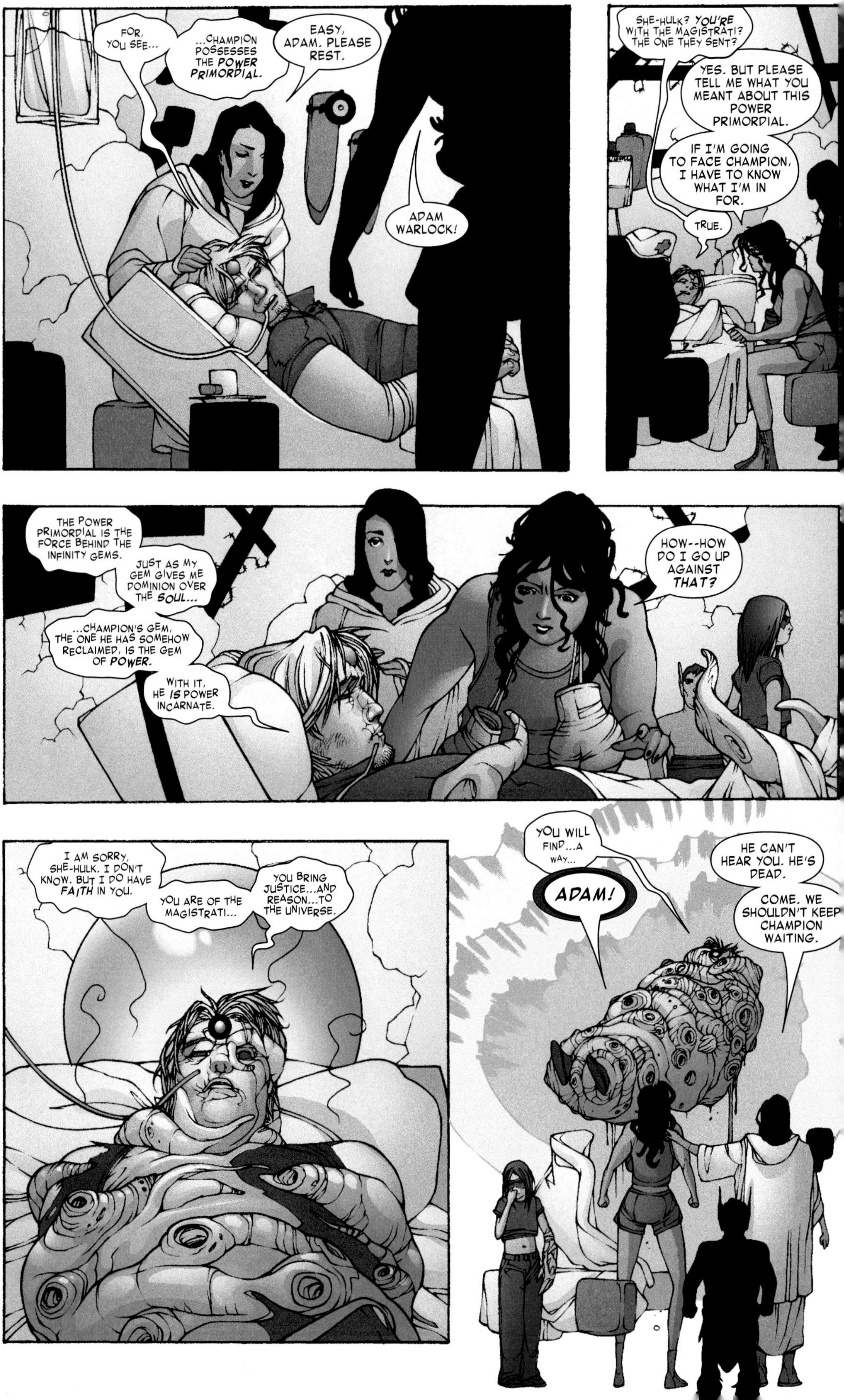
FOR, YOU SEE...
...CHAMPION POSSESSES THE POWER PRIMORDIAL.
EASY, ADAM. PLEASE REST.
ADAM WARLOCK!
SHE-HULK? YOU'RE WITH THE MAGISTRATI? THE ONE THEY SENT?
YES. BUT PLEASE TELL ME WHAT YOU MEANT ABOUT THIS POWER PRIMORDIAL.
IF I'M GOING TO FACE CHAMPION, I HAVE TO KNOW WHAT I'M IN FOR.
TRUE.
THE POWER PRIMORDIAL IS THE FORCE BEHIND THE INFINITY GEMS.
JUST AS MY GEM GIVES ME DOMINION OVER THE SOUL...
...CHAMPION'S GEM, THE ONE HE HAS SOMEHOW RECLAIMED, IS THE GEM OF POWER.
WITH IT, HE IS POWER INCARNATE.
HOW--HOW DO I GO UP AGAINST THAT?
I AM SORRY, SHE-HULK. I DON'T KNOW. BUT I DO HAVE FAITH IN YOU.
YOU ARE OF THE MAGISTRATI...
YOU BRING JUSTICE...AND REASON...TO THE UNIVERSE.
YOU WILL FIND...A WAY...
ADAM!
HE CAN'T HEAR YOU. HE'S DEAD.
COME. WE SHOULDN'T KEEP CHAMPION WAITING.

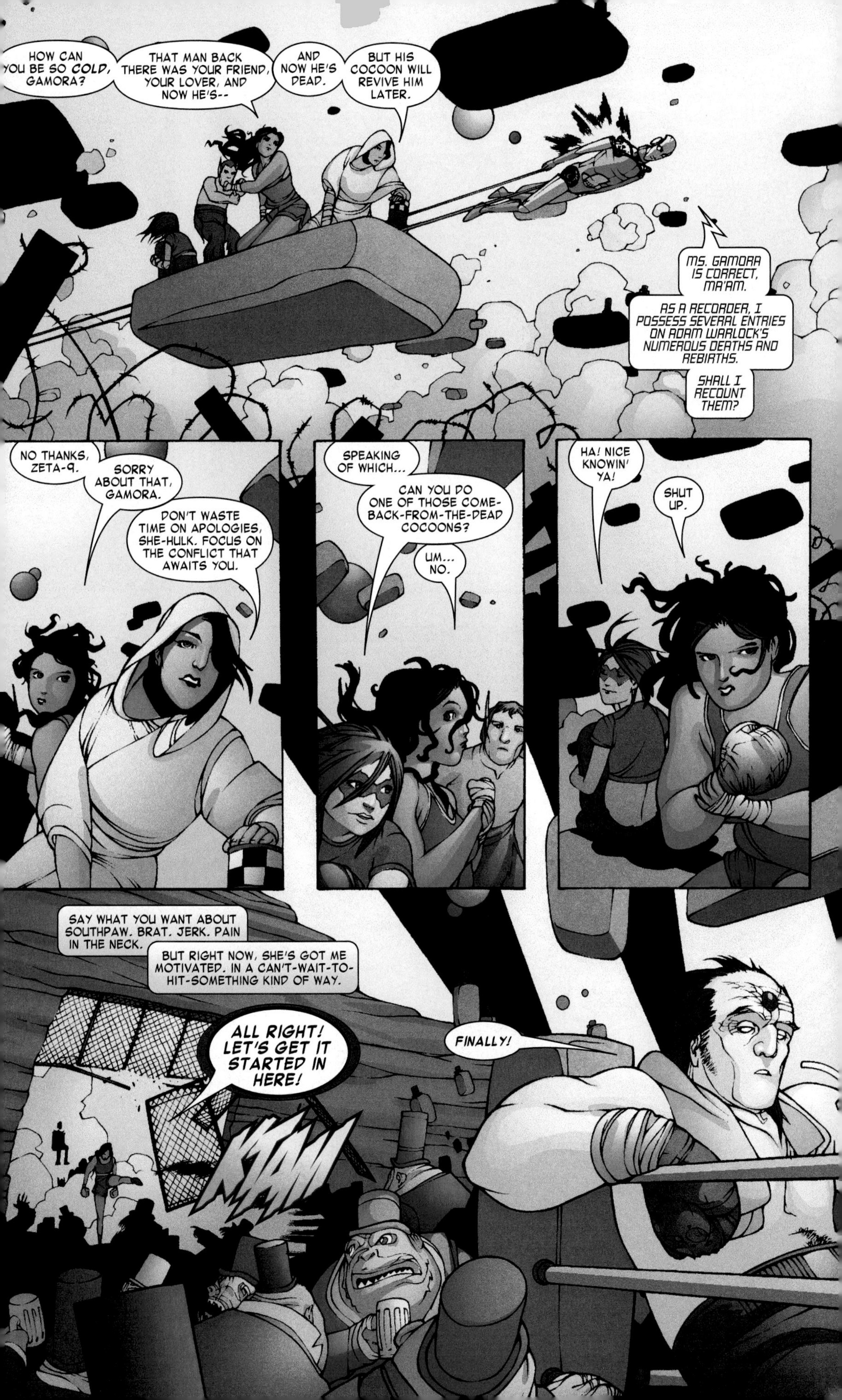
HOW CAN YOU BE SO COLD, GAMORA?
THAT MAN BACK THERE WAS YOUR FRIEND, YOUR LOVER, AND NOW HE'S--
AND NOW HE'S DEAD.
BUT HIS COCOON WILL REVIVE HIM LATER.
MS. GAMORA IS CORRECT, MA'AM.
AS A RECORDER, I POSSESS SEVERAL ENTRIES ON ADAM WARLOCK'S NUMEROUS DEATHS AND REBIRTHS.
SHALL I RECOUNT THEM?
NO THANKS, ZETA-9.
SORRY ABOUT THAT, GAMORA.
DON'T WASTE TIME ON APOLOGIES, SHE-HULK. FOCUS ON THE CONFLICT THAT AWAITS YOU.
SPEAKING OF WHICH...
CAN YOU DO ONE OF THOSE COME-BACK-FROM-THE-DEAD COCOONS?
UM... NO.
HA! NICE KNOWIN' YA!
SHUT UP.
SAY WHAT YOU WANT ABOUT SOUTHPAW. BRAT. JERK. PAIN IN THE NECK.
BUT RIGHT NOW, SHE'S GOT ME MOTIVATED. IN A CAN'T-WAIT-TO-HIT-SOMETHING KIND OF WAY.
ALL RIGHT! LET'S GET IT STARTED IN HERE!
FINALLY!

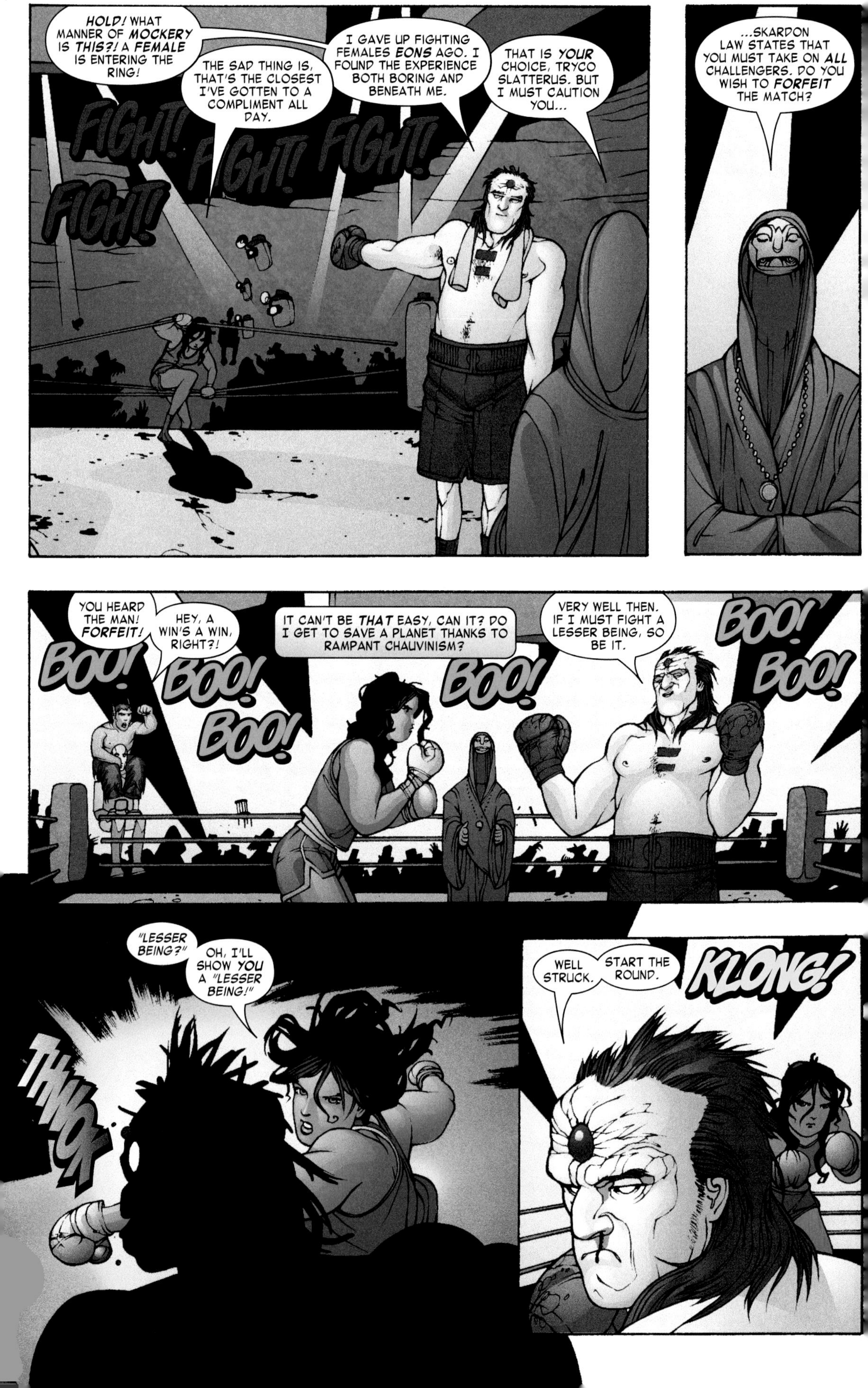
HOLD! WHAT MANNER OF MOCKERY IS THIS?! A FEMALE IS ENTERING THE RING!
THE SAD THING IS, THAT'S THE CLOSEST I'VE GOTTEN TO A COMPLIMENT ALL DAY.
FIGHT! FIGHT! FIGHT! FIGHT!
I GAVE UP FIGHTING FEMALES EONS AGO. I FOUND THE EXPERIENCE BOTH BORING AND BENEATH ME.
THAT IS YOUR CHOICE, TRYCO SLATTERUS. BUT I MUST CAUTION YOU...
...SKARDON LAW STATES THAT YOU MUST TAKE ON ALL CHALLENGERS. DO YOU WISH TO FORFEIT THE MATCH?
YOU HEARD THE MAN! FORFEIT!
HEY, A WIN'S A WIN, RIGHT?!
BOO! BOO! BOO! BOO!
IT CAN'T BE THAT EASY, CAN IT? DO I GET TO SAVE A PLANET THANKS TO RAMPANT CHAUVINISM?
VERY WELL THEN. IF I MUST FIGHT A LESSER BEING, SO BE IT.
BOO! BOO!
"LESSER BEING?"
OH, I'LL SHOW YOU A "LESSER BEING!"
THWOK
WELL STRUCK.
START THE ROUND.
KLONG!

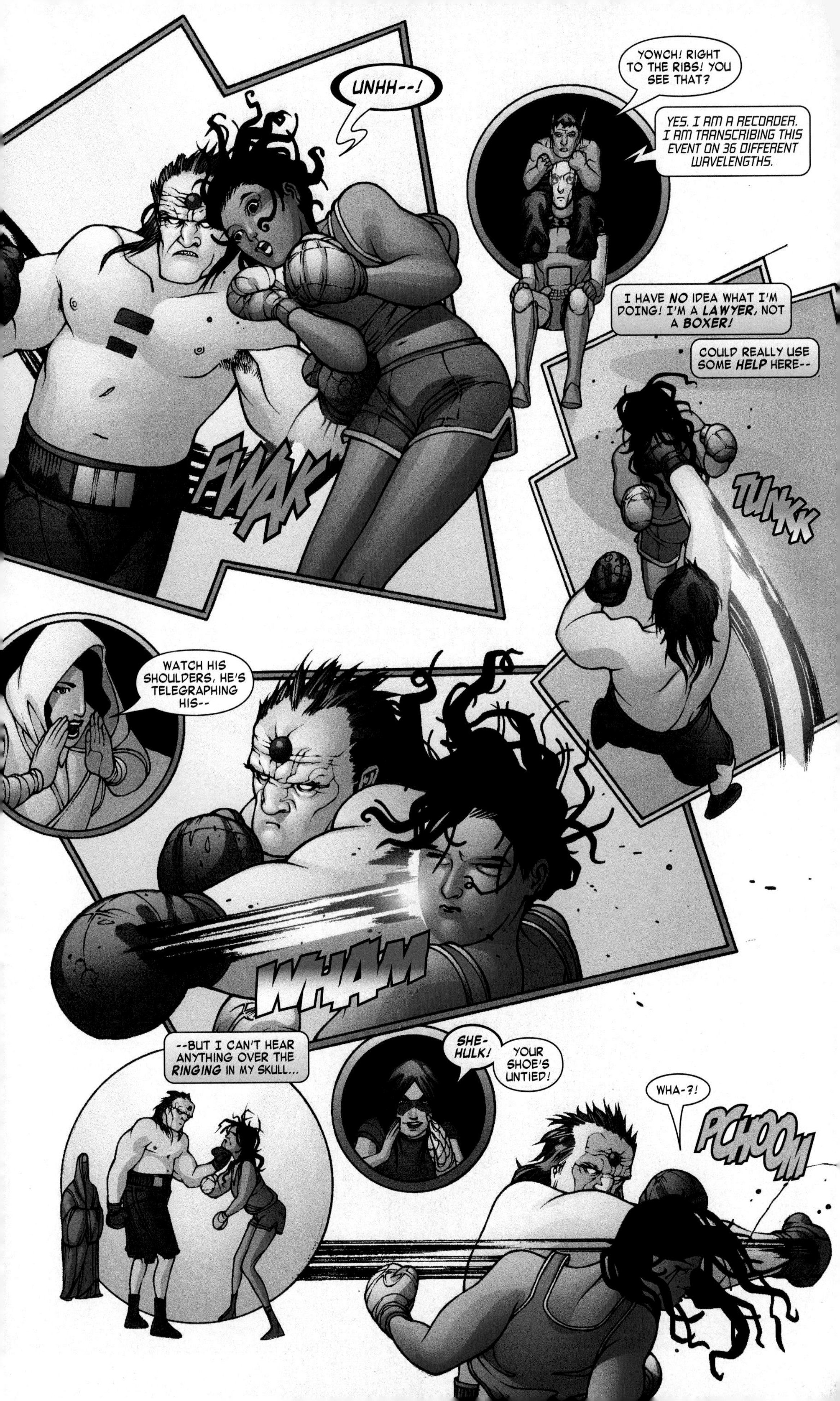
UNHH--!
FWAK
YOWCH! RIGHT TO THE RIBS! YOU SEE THAT?
YES. I AM A RECORDER. I AM TRANSCRIBING THIS EVENT ON 36 DIFFERENT WAVELENGTHS.
I HAVE NO IDEA WHAT I'M DOING! I'M A LAWYER, NOT A BOXER!
COULD REALLY USE SOME HELP HERE--
TUNKK
WATCH HIS SHOULDERS, HE'S TELEGRAPHING HIS--
WHAM
--BUT I CAN'T HEAR ANYTHING OVER THE RINGING IN MY SKULL...
SHE-HULK!
YOUR SHOE'S UNTIED!
WHA-?!
PCHOOM

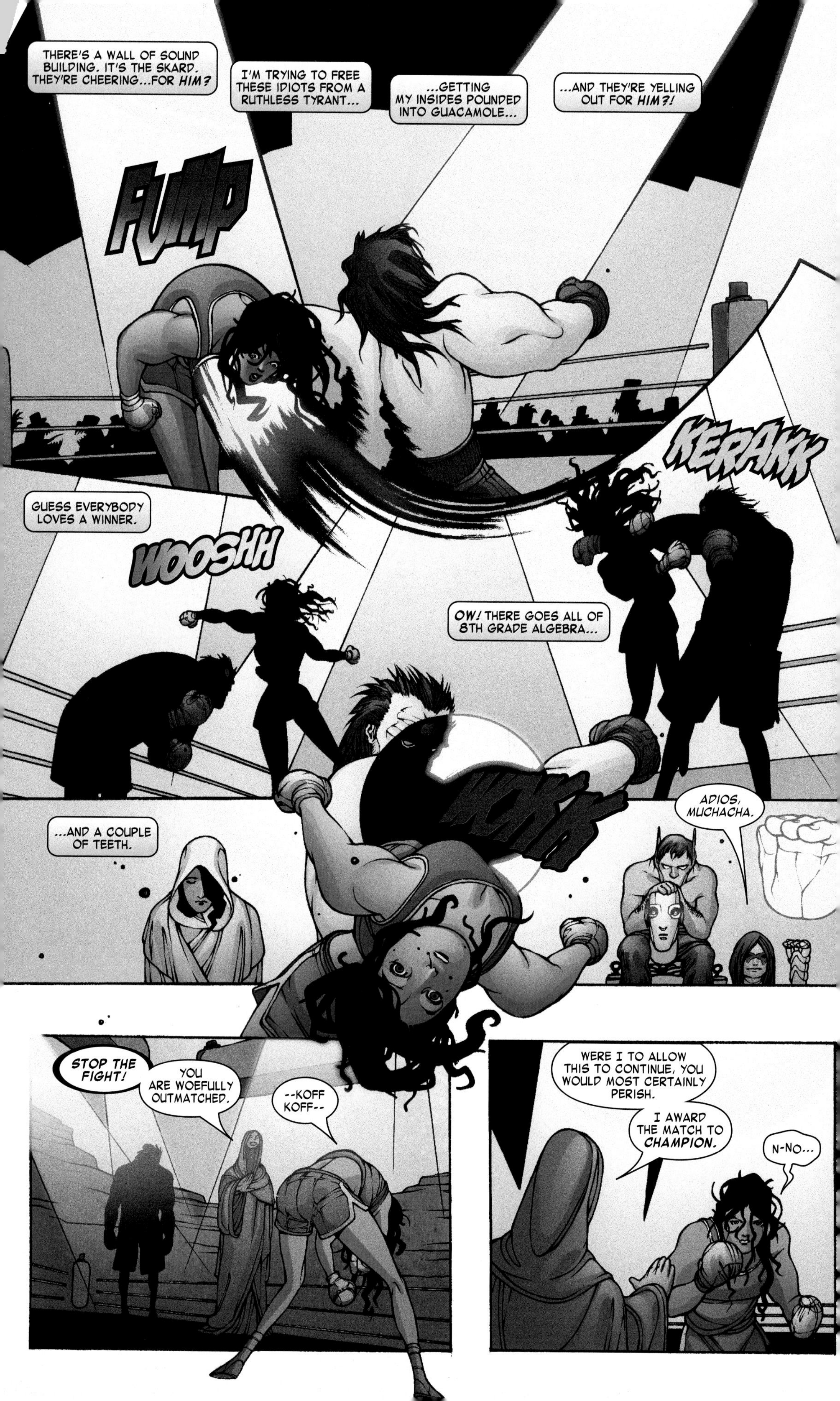
THERE'S A WALL OF SOUND BUILDING. IT'S THE SKARD. THEY'RE CHEERING...FOR HIM?
I'M TRYING TO FREE THESE IDIOTS FROM A RUTHLESS TYRANT...
...GETTING MY INSIDES POUNDED INTO GUACAMOLE...
...AND THEY'RE YELLING OUT FOR HIM?!
FUMP
KERAKK
GUESS EVERYBODY LOVES A WINNER.
WOOSHH
OW! THERE GOES ALL OF 8TH GRADE ALGEBRA...
...AND A COUPLE OF TEETH.
ADIOS, MUCHACHA.
STOP THE FIGHT!
YOU ARE WOEFULLY OUTMATCHED.
--KOFF KOFF--
WERE I TO ALLOW THIS TO CONTINUE, YOU WOULD MOST CERTAINLY PERISH.
I AWARD THE MATCH TO CHAMPION.
N-NO...

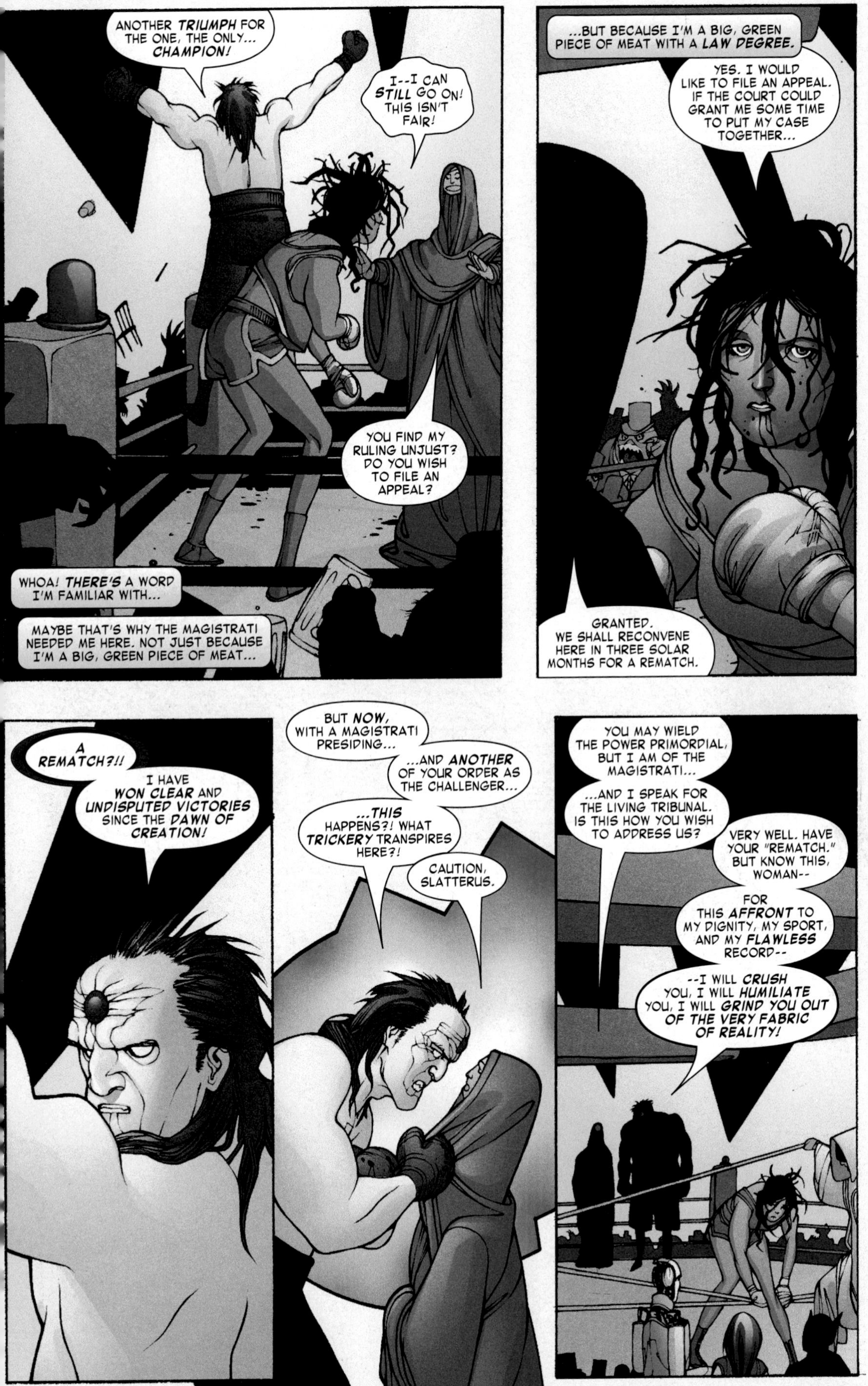
ANOTHER TRIUMPH FOR THE ONE, THE ONLY... CHAMPION!
I--I CAN STILL GO ON! THIS ISN'T FAIR!
YOU FIND MY RULING UNJUST? DO YOU WISH TO FILE AN APPEAL?
WHOA! THERE'S A WORD I'M FAMILIAR WITH...
MAYBE THAT'S WHY THE MAGISTRATI NEEDED ME HERE. NOT JUST BECAUSE I'M A BIG, GREEN PIECE OF MEAT...
...BUT BECAUSE I'M A BIG, GREEN PIECE OF MEAT WITH A LAW DEGREE.
YES. I WOULD LIKE TO FILE AN APPEAL. IF THE COURT COULD GRANT ME SOME TIME TO PUT MY CASE TOGETHER...
GRANTED. WE SHALL RECONVENE HERE IN THREE SOLAR MONTHS FOR A REMATCH.
A REMATCH?!!
I HAVE WON CLEAR AND UNDISPUTED VICTORIES SINCE THE DAWN OF CREATION!
BUT NOW, WITH A MAGISTRATI PRESIDING...
...AND ANOTHER OF YOUR ORDER AS THE CHALLENGER...
...THIS HAPPENS?! WHAT TRICKERY TRANSPIRES HERE?!
CAUTION, SLATTERUS.
YOU MAY WIELD THE POWER PRIMORDIAL, BUT I AM OF THE MAGISTRATI...
...AND I SPEAK FOR THE LIVING TRIBUNAL. IS THIS HOW YOU WISH TO ADDRESS US?
VERY WELL. HAVE YOUR "REMATCH." BUT KNOW THIS, WOMAN--
FOR THIS AFFRONT TO MY DIGNITY, MY SPORT, AND MY FLAWLESS RECORD--
--I WILL CRUSH YOU, I WILL HUMILIATE YOU, I WILL GRIND YOU OUT OF THE VERY FABRIC OF REALITY!

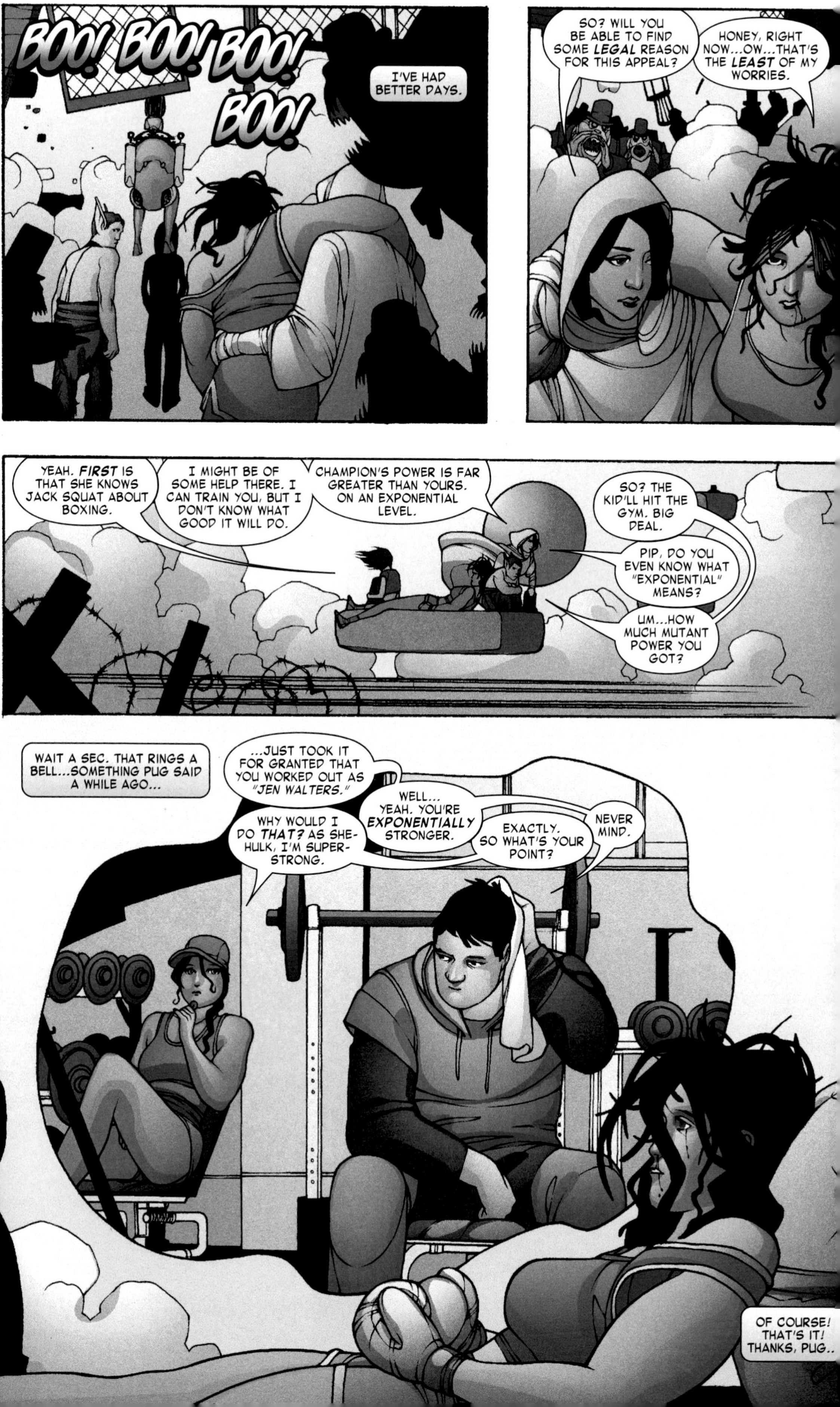
BOO! BOO! BOO! BOO!
I'VE HAD BETTER DAYS.
SO? WILL YOU BE ABLE TO FIND SOME LEGAL REASON FOR THIS APPEAL?
HONEY, RIGHT NOW...OW...THAT'S THE LEAST OF MY WORRIES.
YEAH. FIRST IS THAT SHE KNOWS JACK SQUAT ABOUT BOXING.
I MIGHT BE OF SOME HELP THERE. I CAN TRAIN YOU, BUT I DON'T KNOW WHAT GOOD IT WILL DO.
CHAMPION'S POWER IS FAR GREATER THAN YOURS. ON AN EXPONENTIAL LEVEL.
SO? THE KID'LL HIT THE GYM. BIG DEAL.
PIP, DO YOU EVEN KNOW WHAT "EXPONENTIAL" MEANS?
UM...HOW MUCH MUTANT POWER YOU GOT?
WAIT A SEC. THAT RINGS A BELL...SOMETHING PUG SAID A WHILE AGO...
...JUST TOOK IT FOR GRANTED THAT YOU WORKED OUT AS "JEN WALTERS."
WHY WOULD I DO THAT? AS SHE-HULK, I'M SUPER-STRONG.
WELL... YEAH. YOU'RE EXPONENTIALLY STRONGER.
EXACTLY. SO WHAT'S YOUR POINT?
NEVER MIND.
OF COURSE! THAT'S IT! THANKS, PUG..

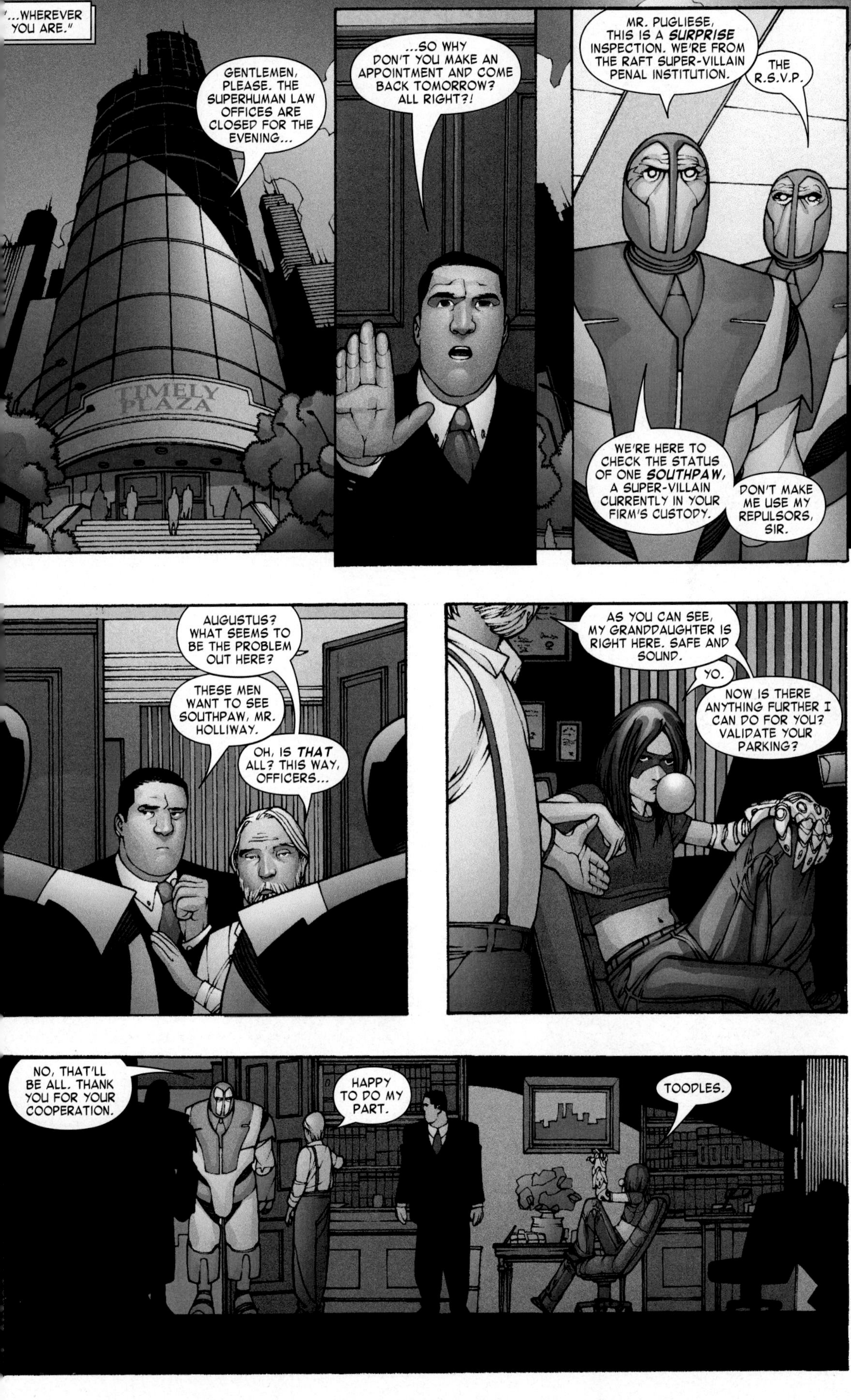
"...WHEREVER YOU ARE."
GENTLEMEN, PLEASE. THE SUPERHUMAN LAW OFFICES ARE CLOSED FOR THE EVENING...
TIMELY PLAZA
...SO WHY DON'T YOU MAKE AN APPOINTMENT AND COME BACK TOMORROW? ALL RIGHT?!
MR. PUGLIESE, THIS IS A SURPRISE INSPECTION. WE'RE FROM THE RAFT SUPER-VILLAIN PENAL INSTITUTION.
THE R.S.V.P.
WE'RE HERE TO CHECK THE STATUS OF ONE SOUTHPAW, A SUPER-VILLAIN CURRENTLY IN YOUR FIRM'S CUSTODY.
DON'T MAKE ME USE MY REPULSORS, SIR.
AUGUSTUS? WHAT SEEMS TO BE THE PROBLEM OUT HERE?
THESE MEN WANT TO SEE SOUTHPAW, MR. HOLLIWAY.
OH, IS THAT ALL? THIS WAY, OFFICERS...
AS YOU CAN SEE, MY GRANDDAUGHTER IS RIGHT HERE. SAFE AND SOUND.
YO.
NOW IS THERE ANYTHING FURTHER I CAN DO FOR YOU? VALIDATE YOUR PARKING?
NO, THAT'LL BE ALL. THANK YOU FOR YOUR COOPERATION.
HAPPY TO DO MY PART.
TOODLES.

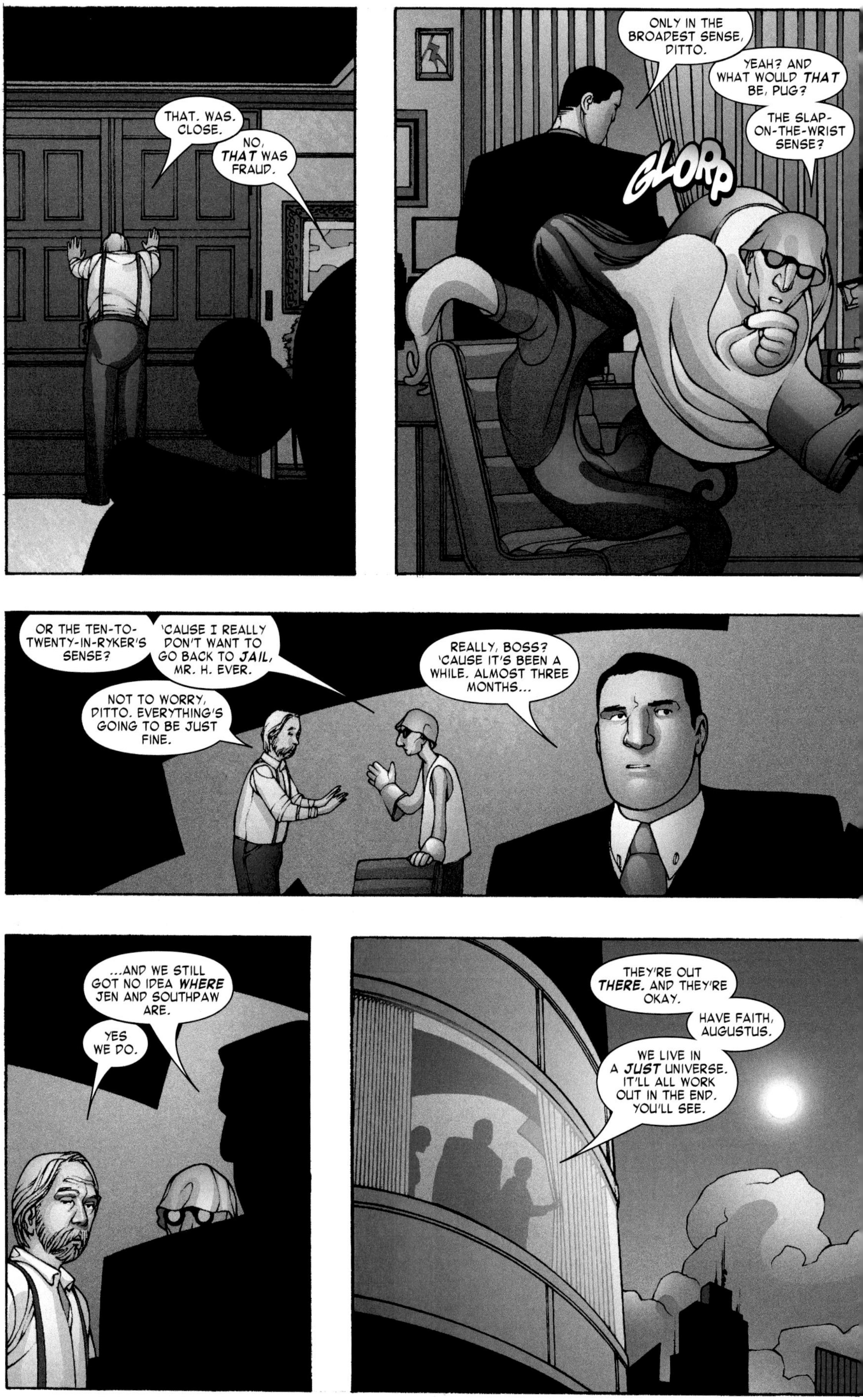
THAT. WAS. CLOSE.
NO, THAT WAS FRAUD.
ONLY IN THE BROADEST SENSE, DITTO.
YEAH? AND WHAT WOULD THAT BE, PUG?
THE SLAP-ON-THE-WRIST SENSE?
GLORP
OR THE TEN-TO-TWENTY-IN-RYKER'S SENSE?
'CAUSE I REALLY DON'T WANT TO GO BACK TO JAIL, MR. H. EVER.
NOT TO WORRY, DITTO. EVERYTHING'S GOING TO BE JUST FINE.
REALLY, BOSS? 'CAUSE IT'S BEEN A WHILE. ALMOST THREE MONTHS...
...AND WE STILL GOT NO IDEA WHERE JEN AND SOUTHPAW ARE.
YES WE DO.
THEY'RE OUT THERE. AND THEY'RE OKAY.
HAVE FAITH, AUGUSTUS.
WE LIVE IN A JUST UNIVERSE. IT'LL ALL WORK OUT IN THE END. YOU'LL SEE.

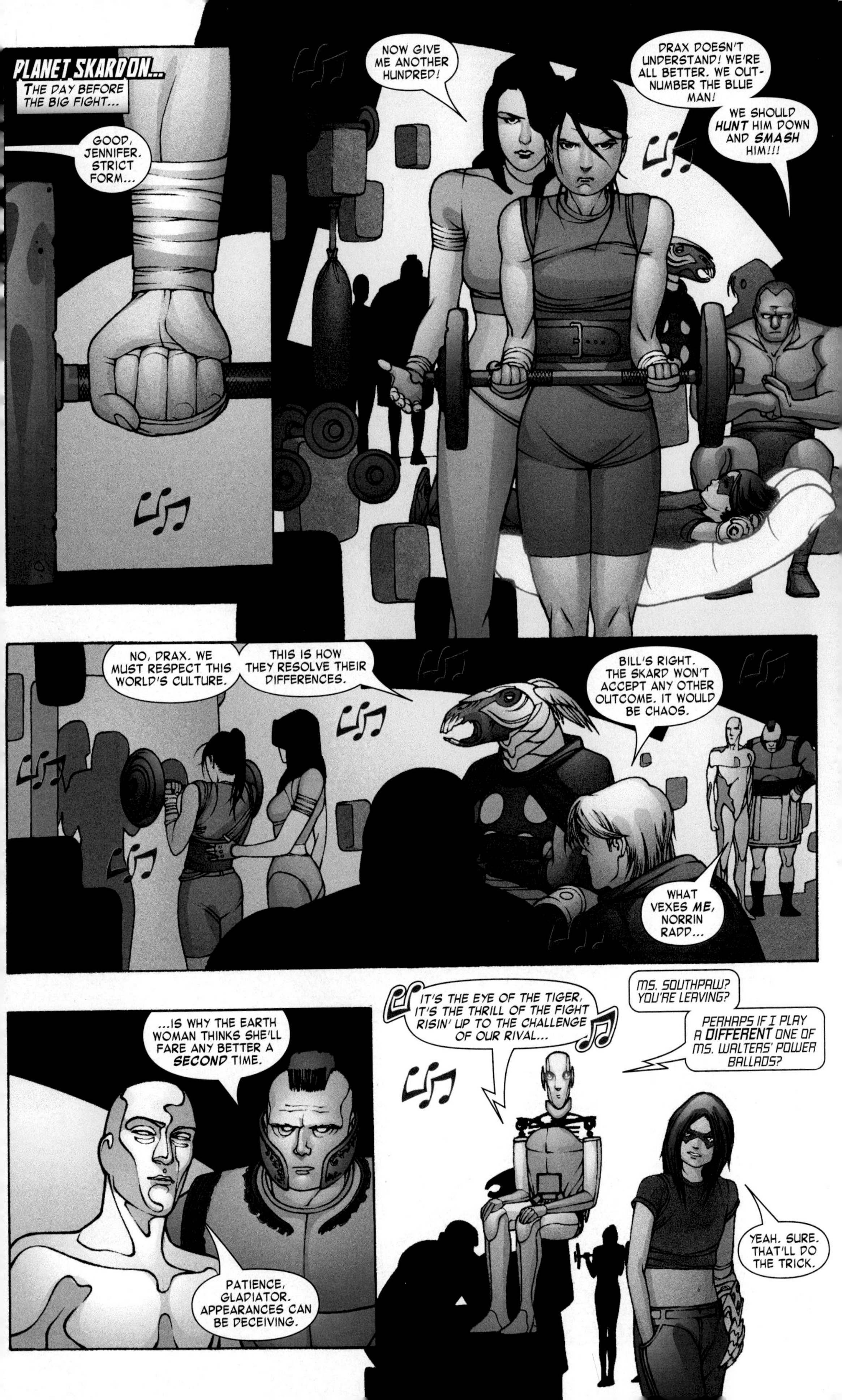

PLANET SKARDON...
THE DAY BEFORE THE BIG FIGHT...
GOOD, JENNIFER. STRICT FORM...
NOW GIVE ME ANOTHER HUNDRED!
DRAX DOESN'T UNDERSTAND! WE'RE ALL BETTER. WE OUT-NUMBER THE BLUE MAN!
WE SHOULD HUNT HIM DOWN AND SMASH HIM!!!
NO, DRAX. WE MUST RESPECT THIS WORLD'S CULTURE.
THIS IS HOW THEY RESOLVE THEIR DIFFERENCES.
BILL'S RIGHT. THE SKARD WON'T ACCEPT ANY OTHER OUTCOME. IT WOULD BE CHAOS.
WHAT VEXES ME, NORRIN RADD...
...IS WHY THE EARTH WOMAN THINKS SHE'LL FARE ANY BETTER A SECOND TIME.
PATIENCE, GLADIATOR. APPEARANCES CAN BE DECEIVING.
IT'S THE EYE OF THE TIGER, IT'S THE THRILL OF THE FIGHT RISIN' UP TO THE CHALLENGE OF OUR RIVAL...
MS. SOUTHPAW? YOU'RE LEAVING?
PERHAPS IF I PLAY A DIFFERENT ONE OF MS. WALTERS' POWER BALLADS?
YEAH. SURE. THAT'LL DO THE TRICK.

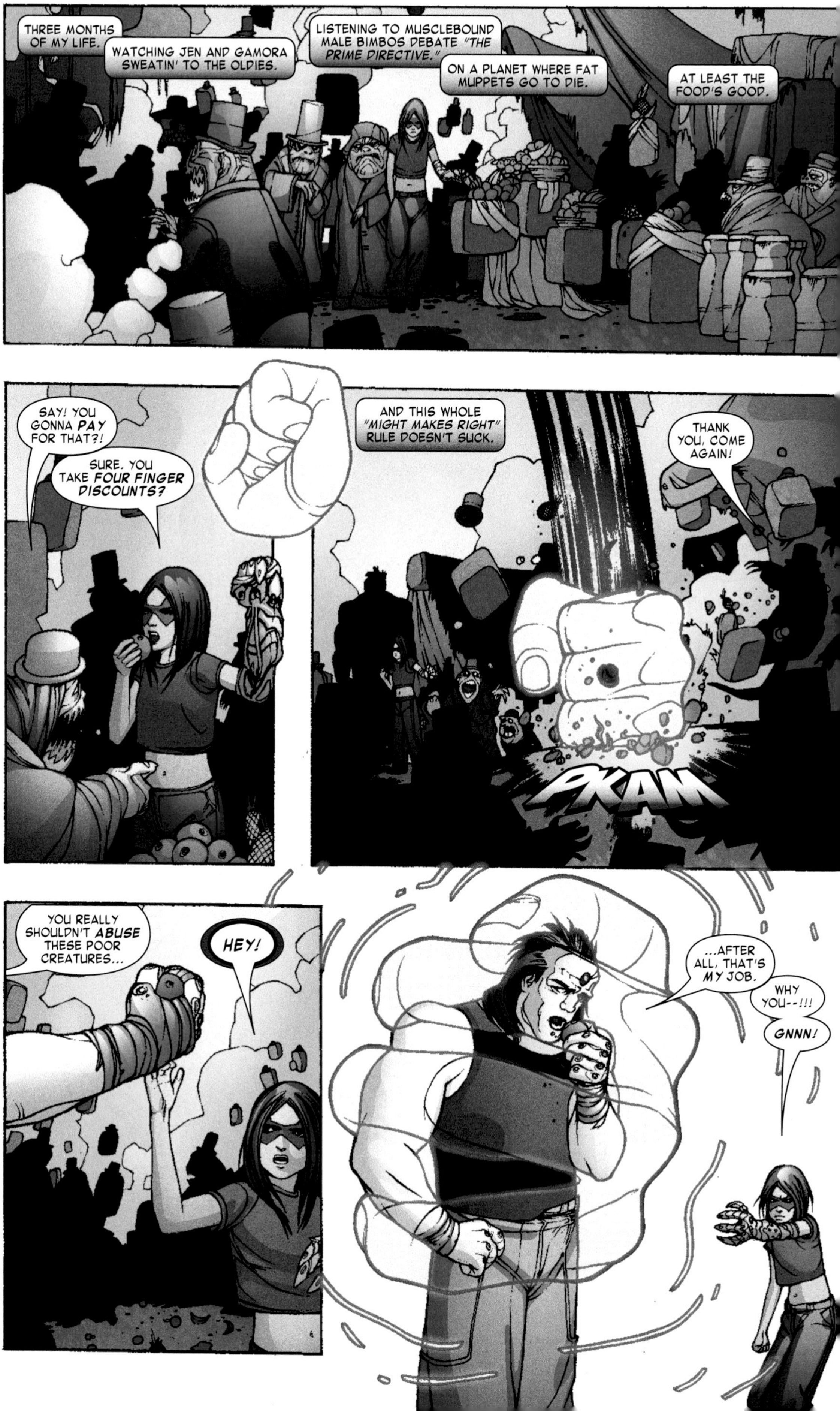

THREE MONTHS OF MY LIFE.
WATCHING JEN AND GAMORA SWEATIN' TO THE OLDIES.
LISTENING TO MUSCLEBOUND MALE BIMBOS DEBATE "THE PRIME DIRECTIVE."
ON A PLANET WHERE FAT MUPPETS GO TO DIE.
AT LEAST THE FOOD'S GOOD.
SAY! YOU GONNA PAY FOR THAT?!
SURE. YOU TAKE FOUR FINGER DISCOUNTS?
AND THIS WHOLE "MIGHT MAKES RIGHT" RULE DOESN'T SUCK.
THANK YOU, COME AGAIN!
PKAM
YOU REALLY SHOULDN'T ABUSE THESE POOR CREATURES...
HEY!
...AFTER ALL, THAT'S MY JOB.
WHY YOU--!!!
GNNN!

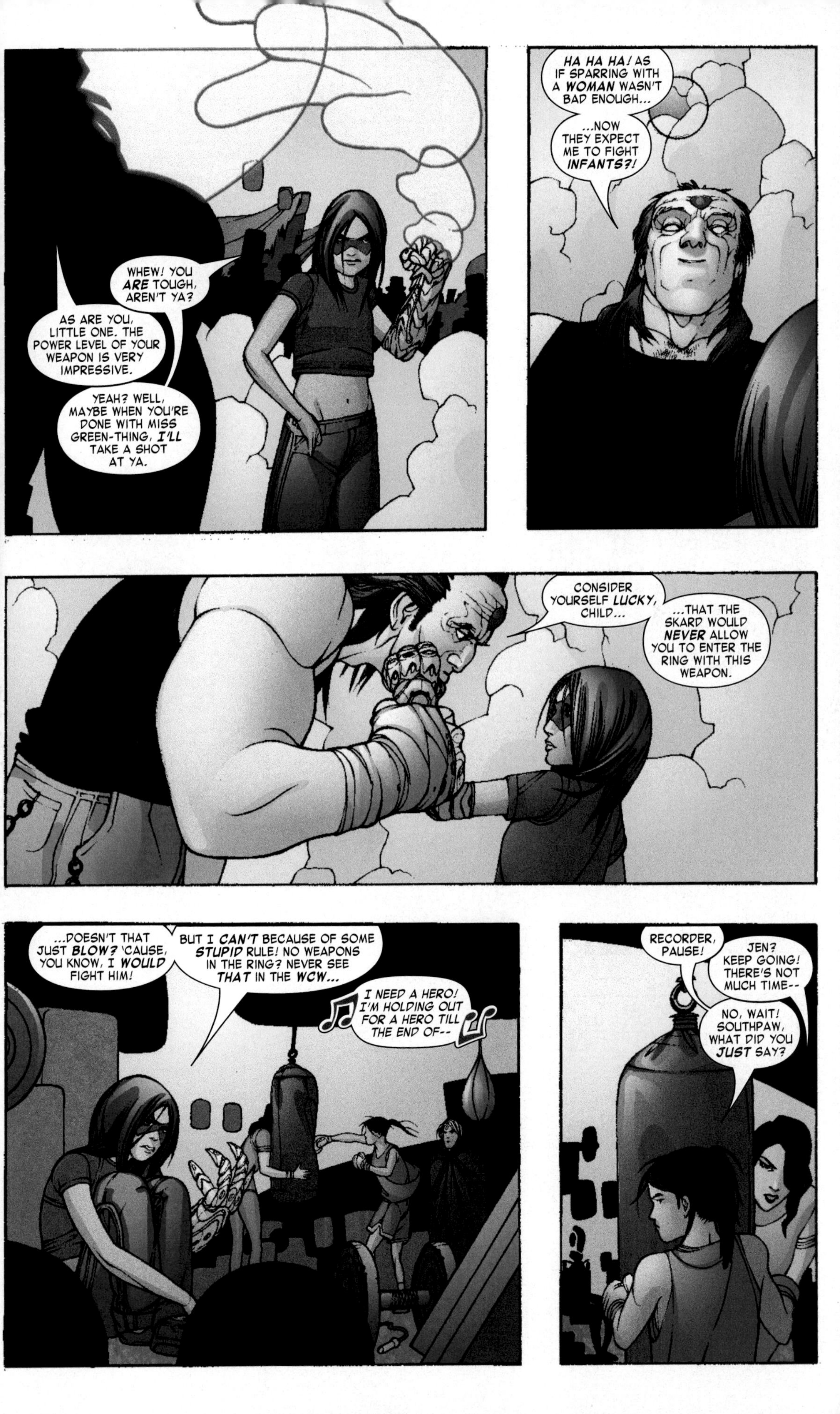

WHEW! YOU ARE TOUGH, AREN'T YA?
AS ARE YOU, LITTLE ONE. THE POWER LEVEL OF YOUR WEAPON IS VERY IMPRESSIVE.
YEAH? WELL, MAYBE WHEN YOU'RE DONE WITH MISS GREEN-THING, I'LL TAKE A SHOT AT YA.
HA HA HA! AS IF SPARRING WITH A WOMAN WASN'T BAD ENOUGH...
...NOW THEY EXPECT ME TO FIGHT INFANTS?!
CONSIDER YOURSELF LUCKY, CHILD...
...THAT THE SKARD WOULD NEVER ALLOW YOU TO ENTER THE RING WITH THIS WEAPON.
...DOESN'T THAT JUST BLOW? 'CAUSE, YOU KNOW, I WOULD FIGHT HIM!
BUT I CAN'T BECAUSE OF SOME STUPID RULE! NO WEAPONS IN THE RING? NEVER SEE THAT IN THE WCW...
I NEED A HERO! I'M HOLDING OUT FOR A HERO TILL THE END OF--
RECORDER, PAUSE!
JEN? KEEP GOING! THERE'S NOT MUCH TIME--
NO, WAIT! SOUTHPAW, WHAT DID YOU JUST SAY?

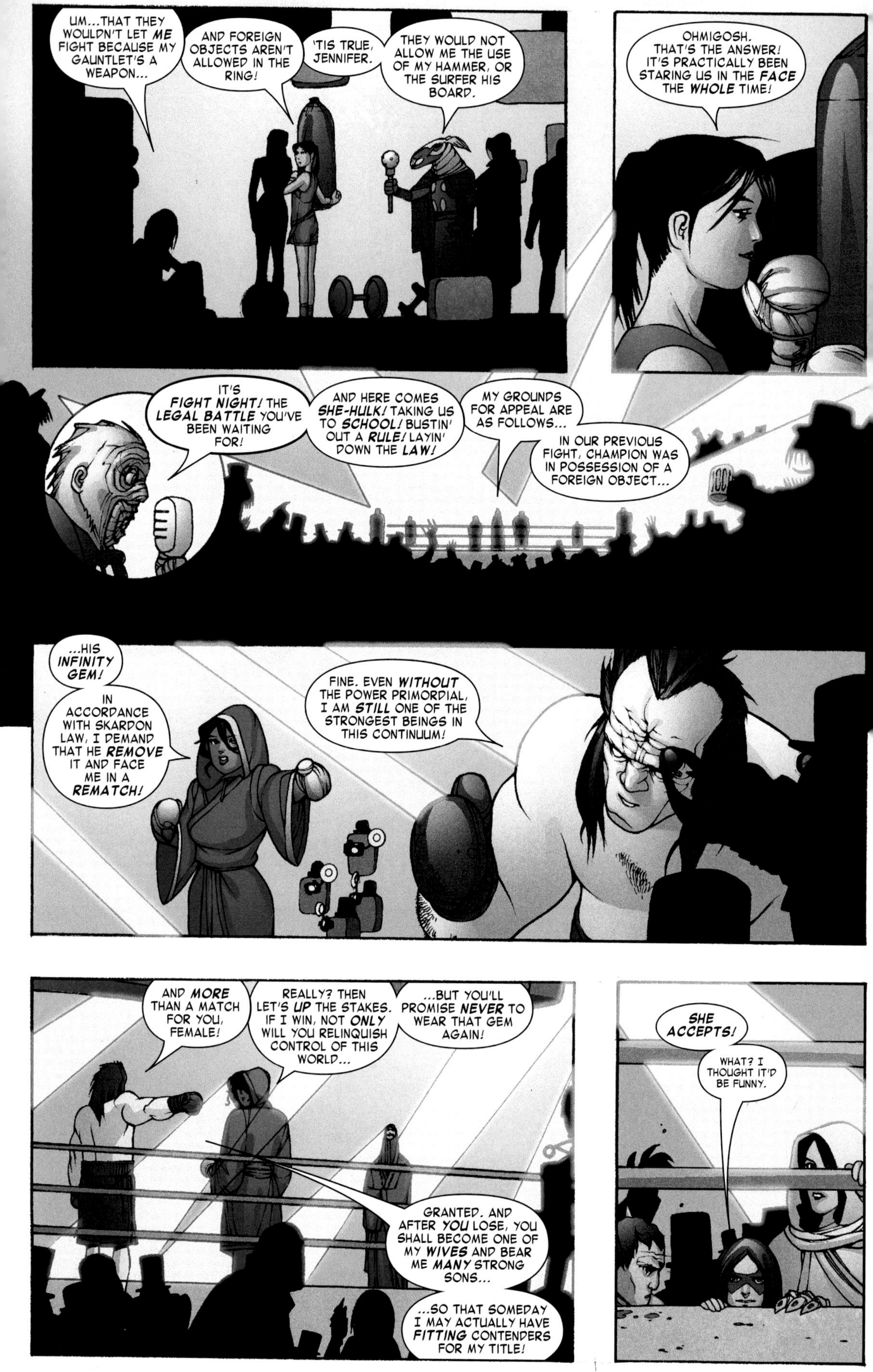
UM...THAT THEY WOULDN'T LET ME FIGHT BECAUSE MY GAUNTLET'S A WEAPON...
AND FOREIGN OBJECTS AREN'T ALLOWED IN THE RING!
'TIS TRUE, JENNIFER.
THEY WOULD NOT ALLOW ME THE USE OF MY HAMMER, OR THE SURFER HIS BOARD.
OHMIGOSH. THAT'S THE ANSWER! IT'S PRACTICALLY BEEN STARING US IN THE FACE THE WHOLE TIME!
IT'S FIGHT NIGHT! THE LEGAL BATTLE YOU'VE BEEN WAITING FOR!
AND HERE COMES SHE-HULK! TAKING US TO SCHOOL! BUSTIN' OUT A RULE! LAYIN' DOWN THE LAW!
MY GROUNDS FOR APPEAL ARE AS FOLLOWS...
IN OUR PREVIOUS FIGHT, CHAMPION WAS IN POSSESSION OF A FOREIGN OBJECT...
...HIS INFINITY GEM!
IN ACCORDANCE WITH SKARDON LAW, I DEMAND THAT HE REMOVE IT AND FACE ME IN A REMATCH!
FINE. EVEN WITHOUT THE POWER PRIMORDIAL, I AM STILL ONE OF THE STRONGEST BEINGS IN THIS CONTINUUM!
AND MORE THAN A MATCH FOR YOU, FEMALE!
REALLY? THEN LET'S UP THE STAKES. IF I WIN, NOT ONLY WILL YOU RELINQUISH CONTROL OF THIS WORLD...
...BUT YOU'LL PROMISE NEVER TO WEAR THAT GEM AGAIN!
GRANTED. AND AFTER YOU LOSE, YOU SHALL BECOME ONE OF MY WIVES AND BEAR ME MANY STRONG SONS...
...SO THAT SOMEDAY I MAY ACTUALLY HAVE FITTING CONTENDERS FOR MY TITLE!
SHE ACCEPTS!
WHAT? I THOUGHT IT'D BE FUNNY.

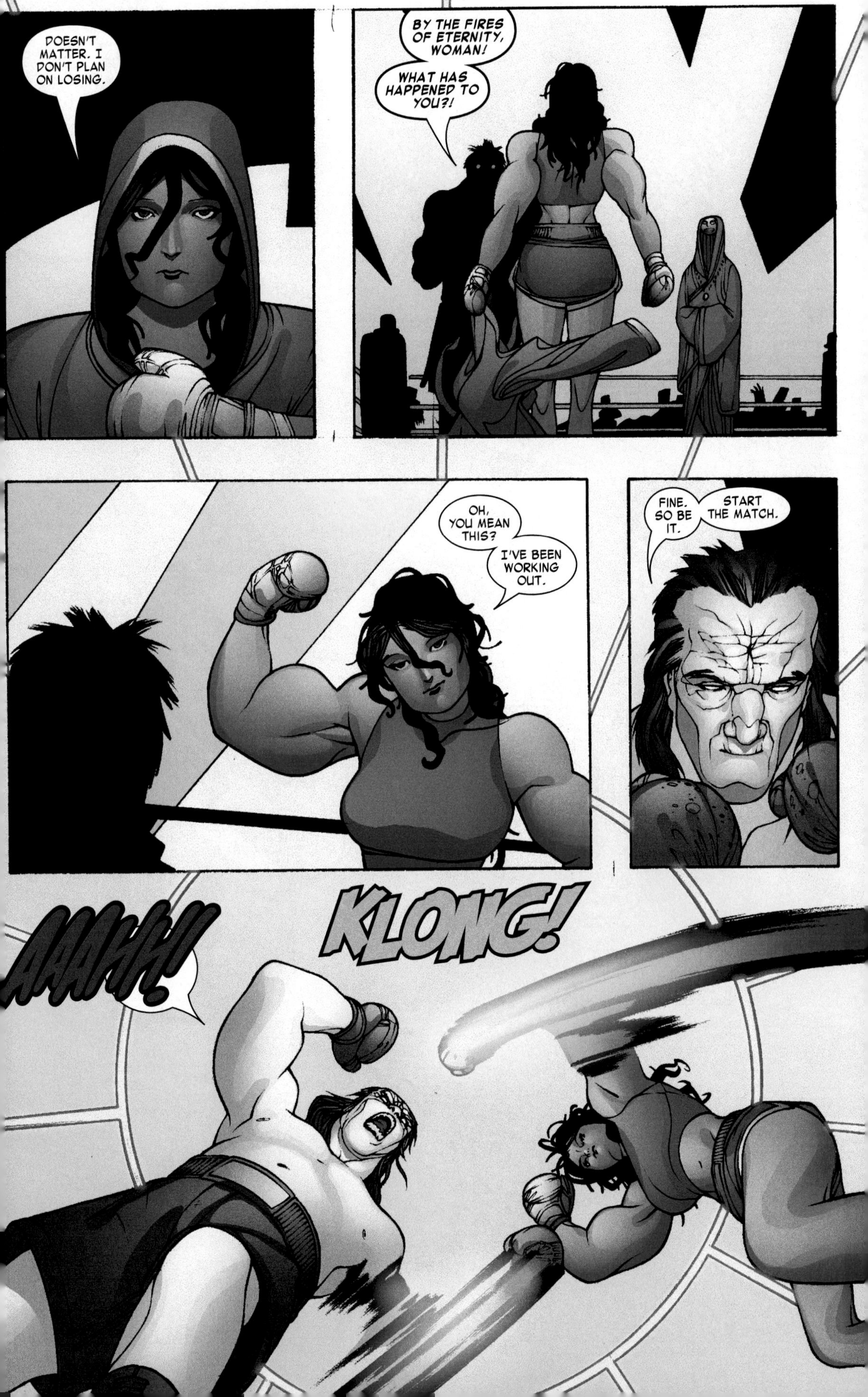
DOESN'T MATTER. I DON'T PLAN ON LOSING.
BY THE FIRES OF ETERNITY, WOMAN!
WHAT HAS HAPPENED TO YOU?!
OH, YOU MEAN THIS?
I'VE BEEN WORKING OUT.
FINE. SO BE IT.
START THE MATCH.
AAAHH!
KLONG!

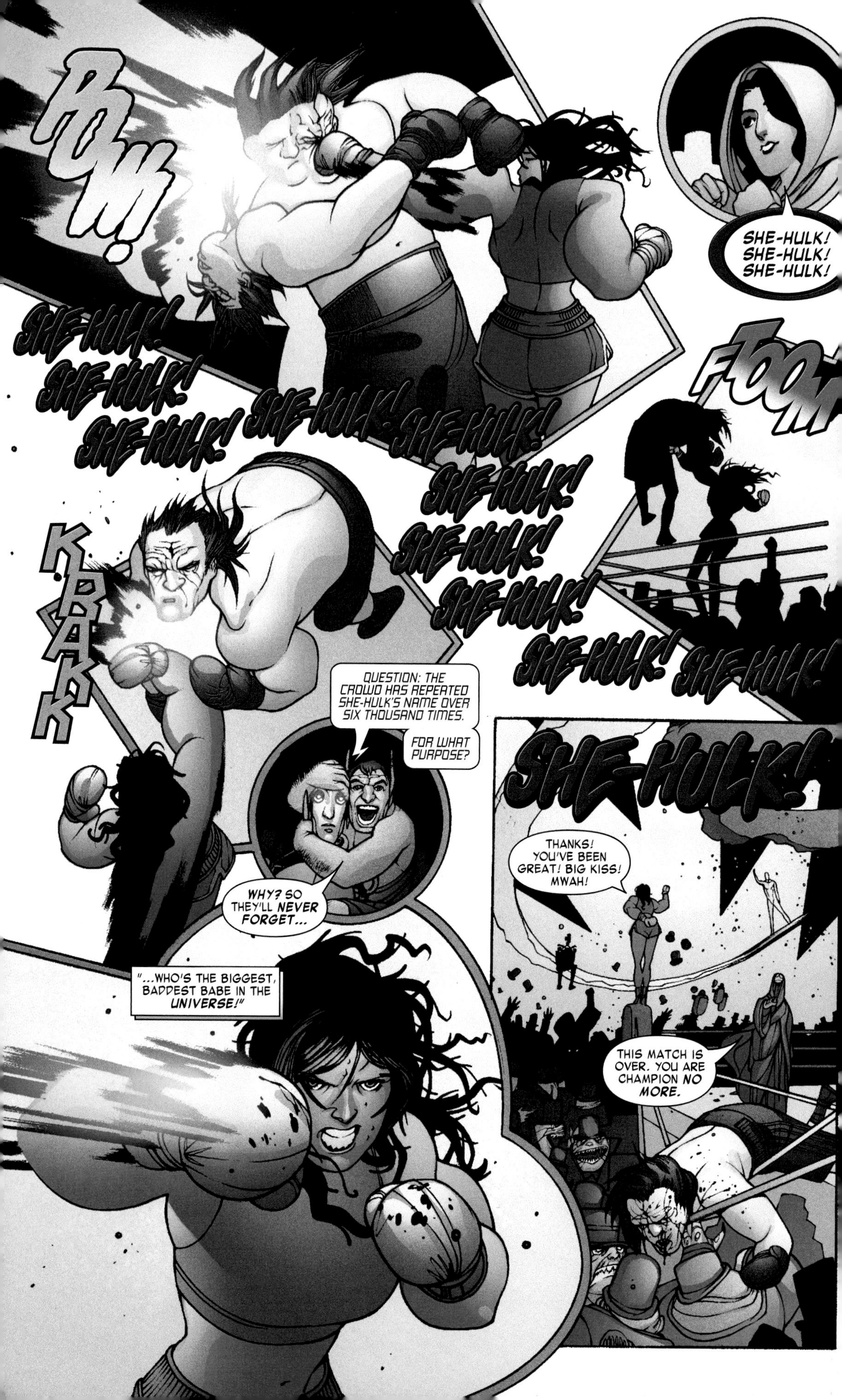
POW!
SHE-HULK! SHE-HULK! SHE-HULK!
SHE-HULK!
SHE-HULK!
SHE-HULK!
SHE-HULK!
SHE-HULK!
FOOM
SHE-HULK!
SHE-HULK!
SHE-HULK!
SHE-HULK!
SHE-HULK!
KRAKK
QUESTION: THE CROWD HAS REPEATED SHE-HULK'S NAME OVER SIX THOUSAND TIMES.
FOR WHAT PURPOSE?
WHY? SO THEY'LL NEVER FORGET...
SHE-HULK!
THANKS! YOU'VE BEEN GREAT! BIG KISS! MWAH!
"...WHO'S THE BIGGEST, BADDEST BABE IN THE UNIVERSE!"
THIS MATCH IS OVER. YOU ARE CHAMPION NO MORE.

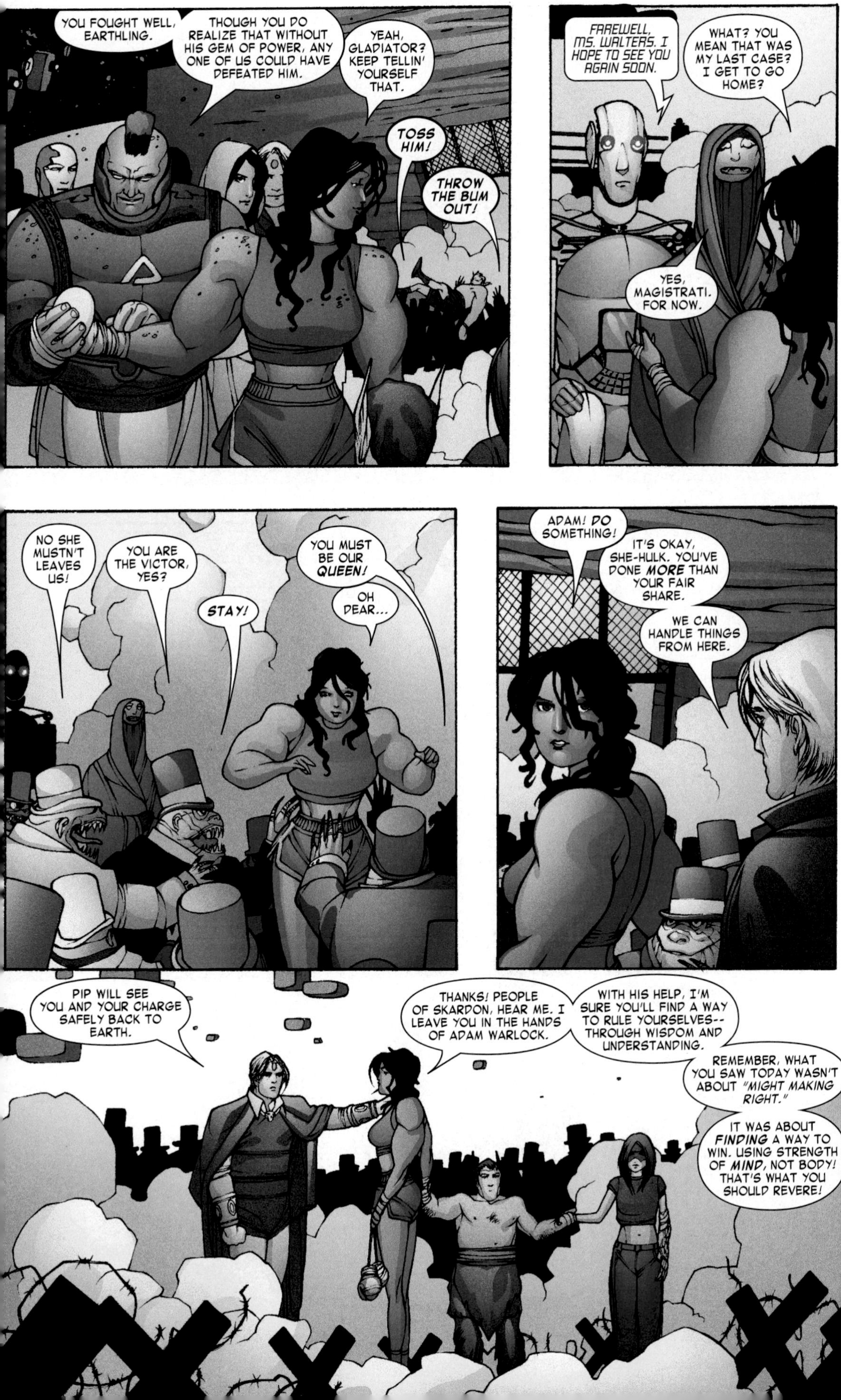

YOU FOUGHT WELL, EARTHLING.
THOUGH YOU DO REALIZE THAT WITHOUT HIS GEM OF POWER, ANY ONE OF US COULD HAVE DEFEATED HIM.
YEAH, GLADIATOR? KEEP TELLIN' YOURSELF THAT.
TOSS HIM!
THROW THE BUM OUT!
FAREWELL, MS. WALTERS. I HOPE TO SEE YOU AGAIN SOON.
WHAT? YOU MEAN THAT WAS MY LAST CASE? I GET TO GO HOME?
YES, MAGISTRATI. FOR NOW.
NO SHE MUSTN'T LEAVES US!
YOU ARE THE VICTOR, YES?
STAY!
YOU MUST BE OUR QUEEN!
OH DEAR...
ADAM! DO SOMETHING!
IT'S OKAY, SHE-HULK. YOU'VE DONE MORE THAN YOUR FAIR SHARE.
WE CAN HANDLE THINGS FROM HERE.
PIP WILL SEE YOU AND YOUR CHARGE SAFELY BACK TO EARTH.
THANKS! PEOPLE OF SKARDON, HEAR ME. I LEAVE YOU IN THE HANDS OF ADAM WARLOCK.
WITH HIS HELP, I'M SURE YOU'LL FIND A WAY TO RULE YOURSELVES-- THROUGH WISDOM AND UNDERSTANDING.
REMEMBER, WHAT YOU SAW TODAY WASN'T ABOUT "MIGHT MAKING RIGHT."
IT WAS ABOUT FINDING A WAY TO WIN. USING STRENGTH OF MIND, NOT BODY! THAT'S WHAT YOU SHOULD REVERE!

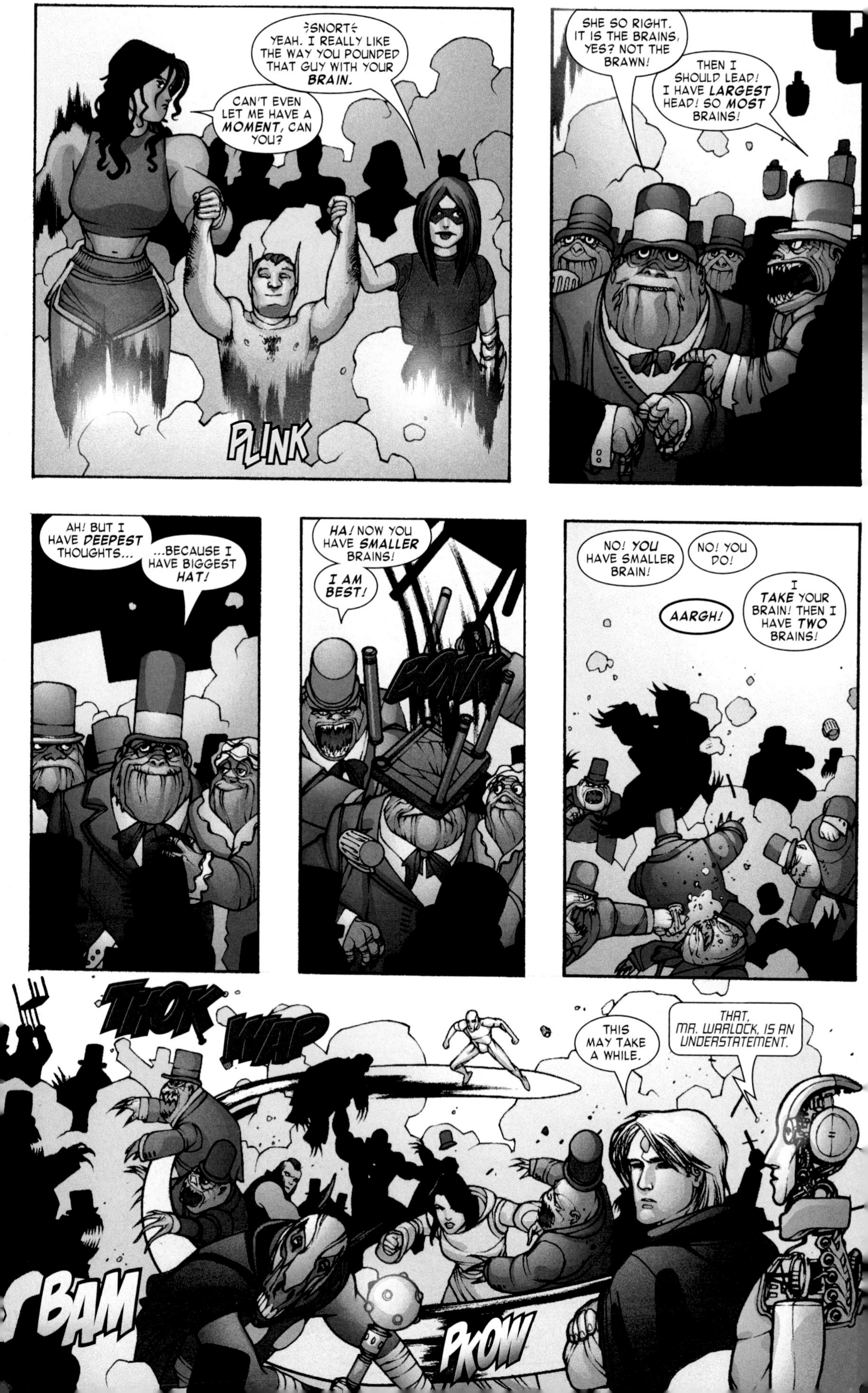

CAN'T EVEN LET ME HAVE A MOMENT, CAN YOU?
≑SNORT≑ YEAH. I REALLY LIKE THE WAY YOU POUNDED THAT GUY WITH YOUR BRAIN.
PLINK
SHE SO RIGHT. IT IS THE BRAINS, YES? NOT THE BRAWN!
THEN I SHOULD LEAD! I HAVE LARGEST HEAD! SO MOST BRAINS!
AH! BUT I HAVE DEEPEST THOUGHTS...
...BECAUSE I HAVE BIGGEST HAT!
HA! NOW YOU HAVE SMALLER BRAINS!
I AM BEST!
BONK
NO! YOU HAVE SMALLER BRAIN!
NO! YOU DO!
AARGH!
I TAKE YOUR BRAIN! THEN I HAVE TWO BRAINS!
THOK
WAP
THIS MAY TAKE A WHILE.
THAT, MR. WARLOCK, IS AN UNDERSTATEMENT.
BAM
PKOW

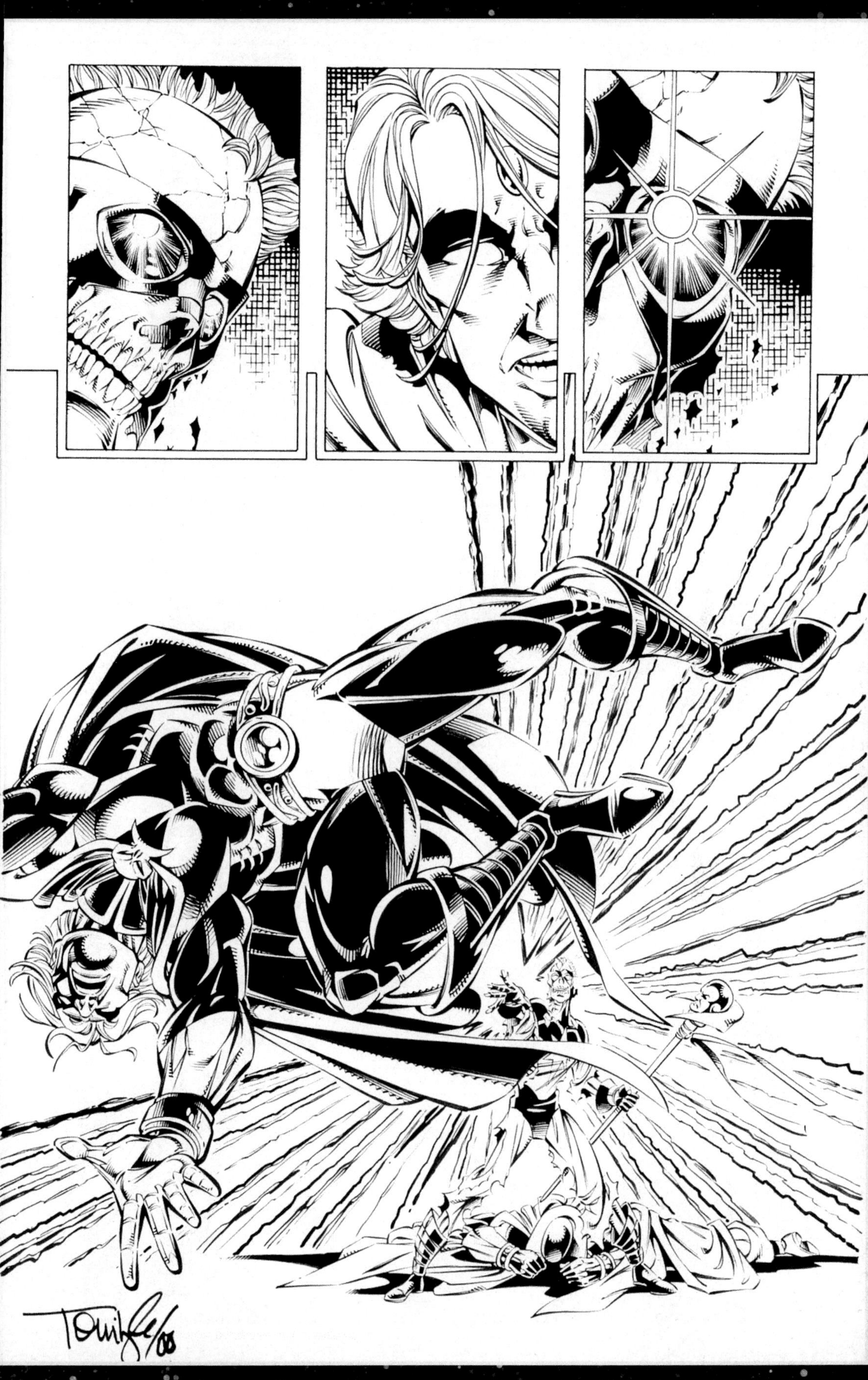

WARLOCK #2, page 3 art by TOM LYLE & ROBERT JONES

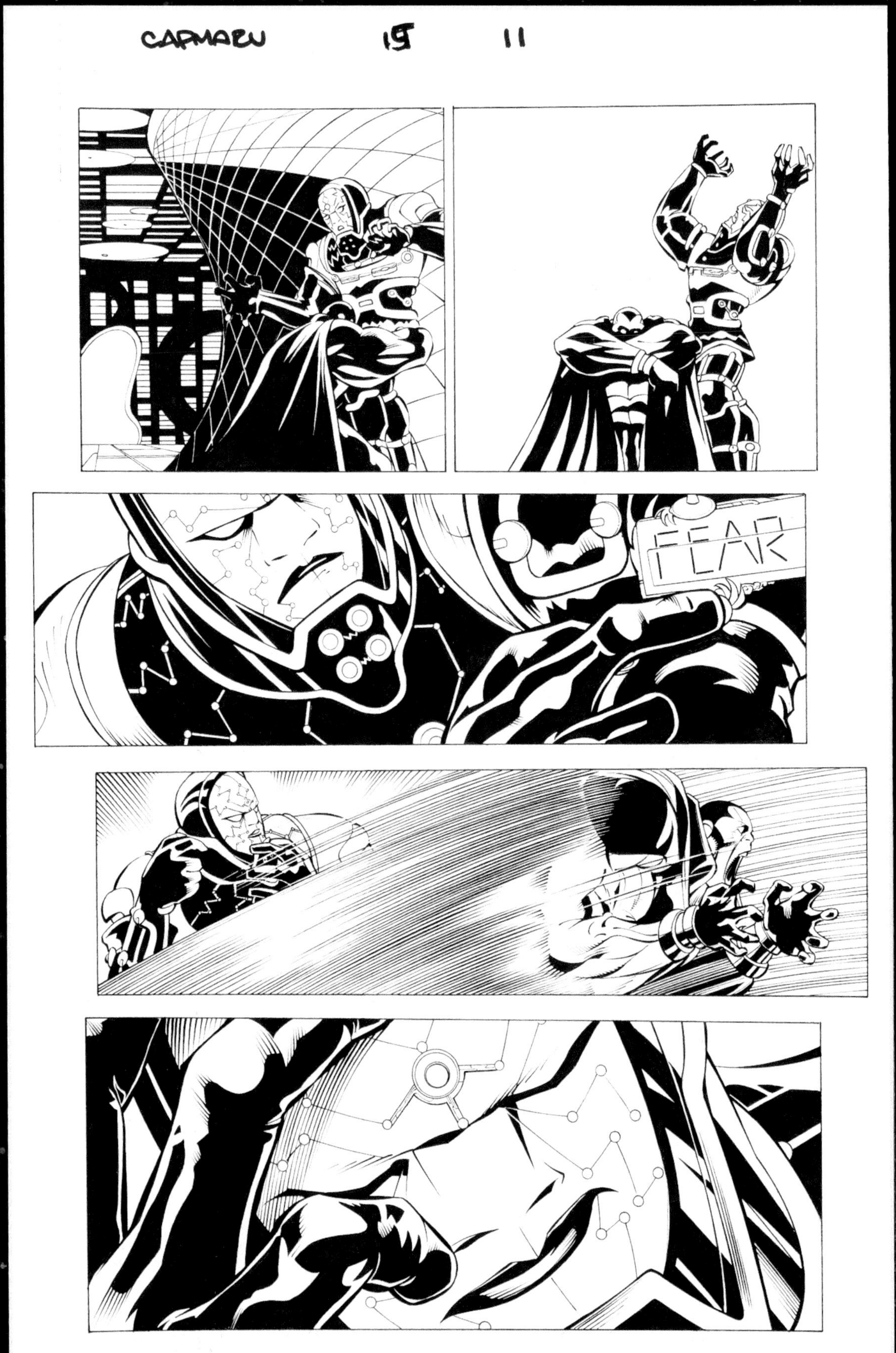
FEAR

CAPTAIN MARVEL #15, page 11 art by CHRISCROSS

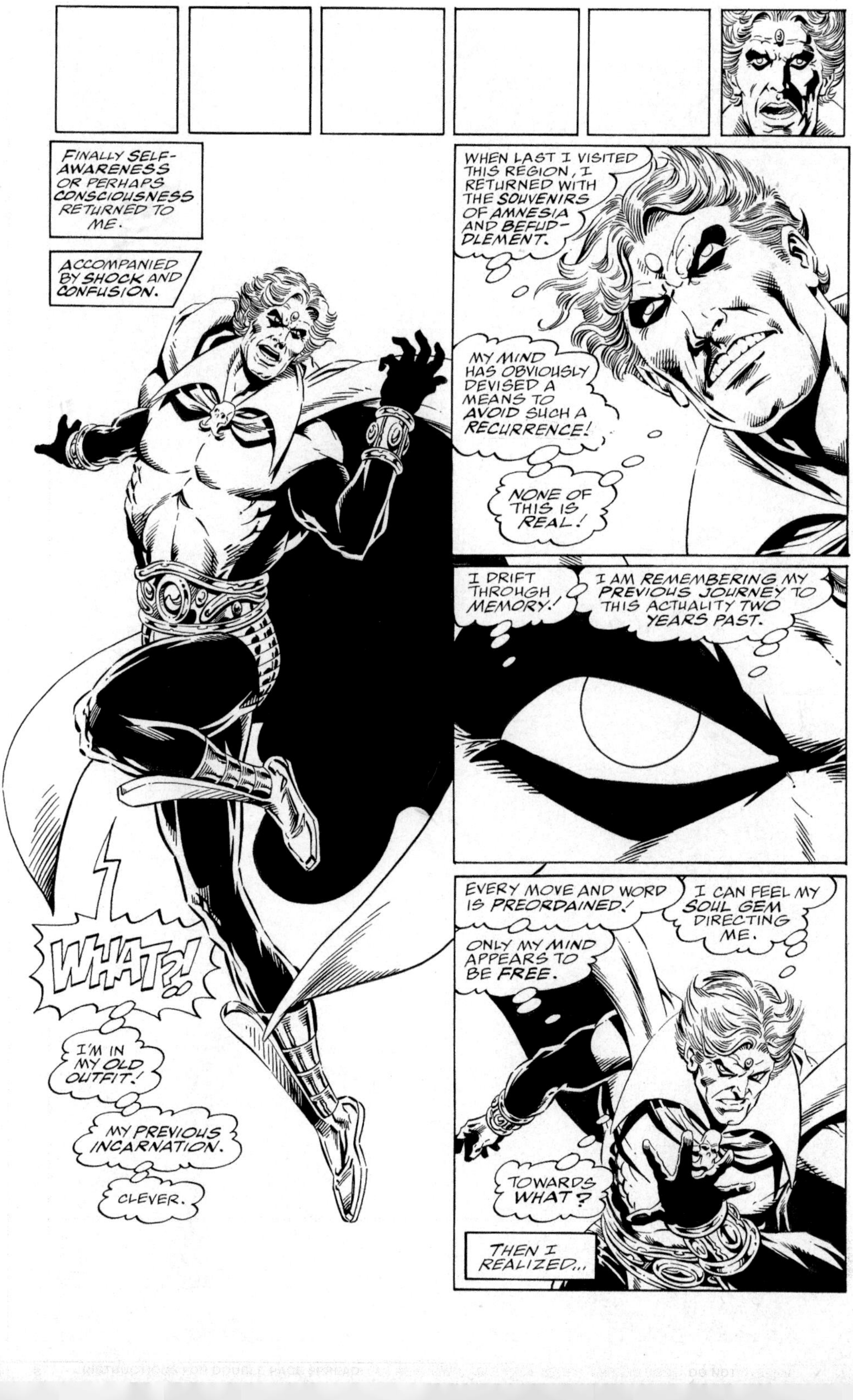
FINALLY SELF-AWARENESS OR PERHAPS CONSCIOUSNESS RETURNED TO ME.
ACCOMPANIED BY SHOCK AND CONFUSION.
WHAT?!
I'M IN MY OLD OUTFIT!
MY PREVIOUS INCARNATION.
CLEVER.
WHEN LAST I VISITED THIS REGION, I RETURNED WITH THE SOUVENIRS OF AMNESIA AND BEFUDDLEMENT.
MY MIND HAS OBVIOUSLY DEVISED A MEANS TO AVOID SUCH A RECURRENCE!
NONE OF THIS IS REAL!
I DRIFT THROUGH MEMORY!
I AM REMEMBERING MY PREVIOUS JOURNEY TO THIS ACTUALITY TWO YEARS PAST.
EVERY MOVE AND WORD IS PREORDAINED!
I CAN FEEL MY SOUL GEM DIRECTING ME.
ONLY MY MIND APPEARS TO BE FREE.
TOWARDS WHAT?
THEN I REALIZED...